WEBSTER'S POCKET DICTIONARY

OF THE ENGLISH LANGUAGE

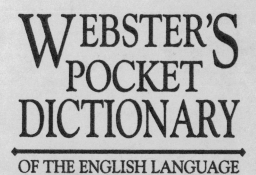

Five-Star rating

A Gift For

_____

From

_____

SCHOLASTIC

N NICHOLS

Publishing Group

Copyright © 2000 V. Nichols
Imprint of Allied Publishing Group, Inc.
Printed in U.S.A.

A, a (ā) *n*. The first letter of the English alphabet; the highest grade, meaning excellent or best.

aah (ä) *v*. To exclaim in joy.

aard-vark (ärd´värk´) *n*. A burrowing African animal, which resembles the anteater and feeds on ants and termites.

a-ba (*a* bä´) *n*. A striped fabric, woven of goat's or camel's hair; an outer garment made from this fabric or silk, worn by Arabs.

a-ba-ca (ä´bä kä´) *n*. A plant from the Philippines whose leafstalks are the source of Manila hemp.

a-back (*a* bak´) *adv*. Unexpectedly; by surprise; startled; confused.

a-bac-te-ri-al (ā bak tir´ ē al) *adj*. Not caused by bacteria.

ab-a-cus (ab´ *a* kəs) *n*. A frame holding parallel rods with beads, used for manual computation, especially by the Chinese.

a-baft (*a* baft´) *adv*. On or toward the stern, aft, or hind part of a ship.

ab-a-lo-ne (ab´*a* lō´nē) *n*. A member of the genus of gastropod mollusks that will cling to rocks and have a shell which is flat and lined with mother of pearl.

a-ban-don (*a* ban´dən) *v*. To yield utterly; to desert; to forsake; to withdraw protection, support, or help, to give up all rights or interest. **abandonment** *n*.

a-ban-doned (*a* ban´dənd) *adj*. To be deserted; to be forsaken.

a-ban-don-ee (*a* ban´don ē´) *n*. The person to whom a thing is abandoned.

a-ban-don-ment (*a* ban´don ment) *n*. The state of being abandoned; or the act of abandoning; to surrender, relinquishment; free from constraint.

a-base (*a* bās´) *v*. To lower in rank, prestige, position, or estimation; to cast down, to humble. **abaser** *n*. **abatable** *adj*.

a-base-ment (*a* bās´ment) *n*. A state of depression, degradation, or humiliation.

a-bash (*a* bash´) *v*. To embarrass; to disconcert; to make ashamed or uneasy.

a-bash-ment (*a* bash´ment) *n*. The state of something being abashed.

a-bate (a bāt´) *v*. To deduct; to make less; to reduce in quantity, value, force, or intensity. **abater** *n*. **abatable** *adj*.

a-bate-ment (*a* bāt´ment) *n*. The process of abating something; the amount which is abated.

ab-a-tis (ab´*a* tē´) *n*. The collection of felled trees of which the smaller branches have already been cut off.

ab-at-toir (ab´*a* twär´) *n*. The public slaughterhouse.

ab-ax-i-al (ab ak´sēal) *adj*. To be positioned or situated out of the axis of something.

abb (ab) *n*. A type of low grade wool that is from the inferior parts of a fleece.

ab-bre-vi-ate (*a* brē´vē āt´) *v*. To make briefer; to abridge; to shorten; to reduce to a briefer form, as a word or phrase.

ab-bre-vi-a-tion (*a* brē´vē ā´shən) *n*. A shortened form of a word or phrase, used to represent the full form. **abbreviator** *n*. **abbreviatory** *adj*.

ab-di-cate (ab´di kāt´) *v*. To relinquish power or responsibility formally; to renounce. **abdication** *n*.

ab-do-men (ab´do men) *n*. That part of the human body that lies between the thorax and the pelvis; it contains the stomach, spleen, liver, kidneys, bladder, pancreas, and the intestines.

ab-dom-i-nal (ab dom´i nal) *adj*. Having to do with the abdomen; in, on, or for the abdomen.

ab-dom-i-nous (ab dom´i nus) *adj*. Abdominal; having a large belly.

ab-du-cens nerve *n*. The 6th cranial motor nerves that supply the eye muscles.

ab-du-cent (ab dū´sent) *adj*. Pulling back, or drawing away.

abducent muscles *n*. Muscles that pull back certain parts of the body from the mesial line.

ab-duct (ab dukt´) *v*. To carry away wrongfully, as by force or fraud; to kidnap; to draw aside or away.

ab-duc-tion (ab duk´shən) *n*. An action of abducting. *Med*. Descriptive of the movement of a limb or part of a limb away from the midline of the body.

ab-duc-tor (ab duk´tér) *n*. A person who or that which abducts; *Med*. muscle that moves certain body parts from the axis of the body.

a-beam (*a* bēm´) *adv*. At right angles to the keel of a ship.

a-be-ce-dar-i-an (ā´bē sē dâr´ē an) *n*. A person who teaches the letters of the alphabet, or a person learning the letters. A beginner in any area of learning.

a-be-ce-da-ry (ā´bē sē´da rē) *adj*. Formed by or pertaining to the letters of the alphabet.

a-bed (*a* bed´) *adv*. In bed; on a bed; to bed; restricted to bed.

a-bel-mosk (ā´bel mosk´) *n*. A type of herb which is found in Asia and the East Indies and the musky seeds are used to flavor coffee and for perfumes.

abend In computer science, the termination of processing due to program or system fault; abnormal ending.

ab-er-rant (ab er´ent) *adj*. Straying from the right way or usual course; not being proper or truthful; abnormal or exceptional. **aberrantly** *adv*.

ab-er-ra-tion (ab´er ā´shan) *n*. The disorder of the mind; deviation from a type or standard. **aberrational** *adj.*

a-bet (*a* bet´) *v.* To incite, encourage, or assist by countenance, aid, or approval. **abetment** *n.* **abetter** *n.*

a-bey-ance (*a* bā´ans) *n.* State of expectation, for an occupant or holder; a feeling or state of temporary suspension.

a-bey-ant (*a* bā´ant) *adj.* Temporarily inactive.

ab-hor (ab hor´) *v.* To dislike intensely; to loathe. **abhorrer** *n.* **abhorrence** *n.*

ab-hor-rence (ab hor´rens) *n.* The state of abhorring.

ab-hor-rent (ab hor´ent) *adj.* To be feeling abhorrence; hating; detesting.

a-bid-ance (*a* bĭd´ans) *n.* The state of abiding; compliance.

a-bide (*a* bĭd´) *v.* To tolerate; to bear; to remain; to last; to conform to; to comply with. **abider** *n.*

a-bid-ing (*a* bī´ding) *adj.* To be enduring.

ab-i-gail (ab´e gāl) *n.* A personal maid of a lady.

-a-bil-i-ty (*e* bil´et ē) *n.* *suffix* Tendency to act in a specified manner or way.

a-bil-i-ty (*a* bil´i tē) *n.* State of being able; possession of qualities necessary; competence; skill; a particular talent.

ab-i-o-gen-i-sis (ab´ē ō jen´i sis) *n.* An origination of something living from something that is not living.

abi-o-log-i-cal (ā bī *e* läj´i kel) *adj.* Not being made or produced by organisms.

a-bi-otic (ā bī ˝ät ik) *adj.* Not being biotic.

ab-ir-ri-tant (ab ir´i tant) *n.* A lotion used to reduce irritation.

ab-ject (ab´jekt) *adj.* Sunk to a low condition; mean; despicable; worthless. **abject** *n.* A person who is an outcast. **abjection** (ab jek´shan) *n.* A state which is downcast. **abjectness** *n.*

ab-ju-ra-tion (ab˝ jū rā´shan) *n.* The process of abjuring.

ab-jure (ab jūr´) *v.* To renounce solemnly or on oath; to repudiate; to forswear, to abstain or reject. **-er** *n.*

abl *abbr.* Ablative.

ab-lac-tate (ab lak´tāt) *v.* The act of weaning small infants from the breast.

ab-lac-ta-tion (ab˝lak tā´shan) *n.* The weaning from the breast.

ab-late (*a* blāt´) *v.* To remove something by cutting or erosion.

ab-la-tion (ab lā´shan) *n.* A removal of a part; a process of ablating. *Med.* Removal of a part of the body by surgery

a-blaze (*a* blāz´) *adv.* On fire; brilliantly lighted up; very excited; angry.

a-ble (ā´bl) *adj.* Having sufficient ability; capable or talented. **able** *adj.* *suffix* To be worthy of. **ably** *adv.*

a-ble–bod-ied (ā´bl bod´ēd) *adj.* Having a sound, strong body; competent for physical service.

a-bloom (*a* blöm´) *adj.* To be abounding with blooms such as a plant.

ab-lu-ent (ab´lö ent) *adj.* Cleansing by water or liquids. *n.* Something that washes off impurities; detergent or soap.

ab-lut-ed (ab´löt ed) *adj.* Being washed and clean.

ab-lu-tion (ab lö´shan) *n.* The act of washing, cleansing, or purification by a liquid, usually water; specifically, a washing of the body as a part of religious rites. **ablutionary** *adj.*

a-bly (ā´blē) *adv.* To do something in an able manner.

ab-ne-gate (ab´na gāt) *v.* To deny; to refuse or renounce; to relinquish or surrender.

ab-ne-ga-tion (ab˝ne gā´shan) *n.* The act of relinquishing rights; denial.

ab-ne-ga-tor (ab´na gāt´er) *n.* A person who denies or renounces.

ab-nor-mal (ab nor´mel) *adj.* Descriptive of that which is unusual, not normal; irregular; unnatural. **abnormally** *adv.* **abnormality** *n.*

abnormal psychology *n.* A type of psychology that deals with the behaviors of people.

a-board (*a* bōrd´) *adv.* On board a ship or other vehicle.

a-bode (*a* bōd´) *n.* A dwelling place; home; place of residence; habitation.

a-bol-ish (*a* bol´ish) *v.* To put an end to; to annul, to do away with; nullify; destroy; to put out of existence.

a-bol-ish-a-ble (*a* bol´ish *a* bl) *adj.* Capable of being abolished.

a-bol-ish-er (*a* bol´ish ėr) *n.* A person who abolishes.

ab-o-li-tion (ab´o lish´an) *n.* The state of being abolished. **abolitionary** *adj.*

ab-o-li-tion-ism (ab´o lish´a niz˝um) *n.* The measures that will foster abolition.

ab-o-ma-sum (ab´o mā´sum) *n.* The fourth digestive stomach of the ruminant, lying next to the third stomach or omasum.

a-bom-i-na-ble (*a* bom´i na bal) *adj.* Detestable; repugnant; loathsome. **abominably** *adv.* **abominableness** *n.*

a-bom-i-nate (*a* bom´i nāt) *v.* To loathe intensely; to detest; to hate extremely.

ab-o-ral (ab ōr´al) *adj.* To be situated away from the mouth.

ab-o-rig-i-nal (ab´o rij´i nal) *adj.* To be the first in a region; primitive when compared with a more advanced type.

ab-o-rig-i-ne (ab´o rij´i nē) *n.* The first inhabitants of a country; *pl.* original animals and flowers of an area or region.

a-bort (*a* bort´) *v.* To terminate or cause to terminate an operation or procedure before completion; to miscarry in giving birth. In computer science, to terminate a process before completion.

a-bound (*a* bound´) *v.* To have plenty; to exist in large numbers.

a-bout (*a* bout´) *adv.* Approximately; on every side, here and there.

a-bove (*a* buv´) *adv.* Higher or greater than; in or at a higher place.

a-bove–all *adv.* To be before all other considerations.

ab-ra-ca-dab-ra (ab´ra ka dab´ra) *n.* A word believed by some to have magical powers, used in casting spells; nonsense, foolish talk.

a-bra-dant (*a* brād´ant) *n.* A material used for polishing and grinding, as sand, or glass. **abradant** *adj.* Having an abrasive surface and quality.

a-brade (*a* brād´) *v.* To wear or rub off; to grate off; abrasive, scouring.

a-bra-sion (*a* brā´zhan) *n.* The injury to the skin by scraping the outer layer; any scraped surface; the grinding of a surface using friction.

a-bra-sive (*a* brā´siv) *n.* A substance employed in grinding or abrading. *adj.* to tend to abrade.

ab-re-act (ab´rē akt´) *v.* To release an emotion that is forgotten in psychoanalysis.

ab-re-ac-tion (ab´rē ak´shan) *n.* To eliminate a bad experience by reliving it.

a-breast (*a* brest´) *adv.* Side by side.

a-bri (*a* brē´) *n.* Place of refuge; shelter.

a-bridge (*a* brij´) *v.* To make smaller, fewer, or shorter while keeping essential contents. **abridger** *n.*

a-bridg-ment (ā brij´ment) *n.* The state of being abridged.

a-broach (*a* brōch´) *adv.* In agitation or action.

a-broad (*a* brod´) *adv.* Widely; in many places; outside one's country; at large.

ab-ro-gate (ab´ro gāt´) *v.* To cancel; to put an end to; to repeal. **abrogation** *n.* **abrogable** *adj.* **abrogative** *adj.*

ab-rupt (*a* brupt´) *adj.* Happening or coming suddenly with no warning; very gruff; steep, craggy of rocks, precipices, etc.; sudden; brusque, without notice to prepare the mind for the event.

ab-rup-tion (*a* brup´shan) *n.* The sudden breaking away of something.

ab-rupt-ly (*a* brupt´lē) *adv.* In an abrupt manner, sudden and without any notice.

ab-rupt-ness (*a* brupt´nis) *n.* The state or quality of being abrupt; precipitousness; suddenness; unceremonious haste or vehemence.

ab-scess (ab´ses) *n.* An infected place in the body which is sore and swollen, tender or painful, and contains pus, the body's natural response to bacterial infection or an infection. **-ed** *adj.*

ab-scind (ab sind´) *v.* To cut off; to sever; to pare away; to separate.

ab-scise (ab sīz´) *v.* To part or separate with abscission.

abscisic acid *n.* A type of plant hormone that will promote leaf abscission and dormancy.

ab-scis-sa (ab sis´a) *n.* Any part of the diameter or transverse axis of a conic section, as an ellipse.

ab-scis-sion (ab sizh´an) *n.* A natural separation of fruit, flowers, or the leaves of a plant.

ab-scond (ab skond´) *v.* To run away; to flee from justice. **absconder** *n.*

ab-seil (äp´zil) *n.* A means of descending from a cliff by securing a line at the peak.

ab-sence (ab´sens) *n.* Being absent, not present; inattention.

ab-sent (ab´sent) *adj.* Not present; away; lacking; nonexistent. **absently** *adv.*

ab-so-lute (ab´so löt´) *adj.* Unconditional; without restraint; perfect; complete. **absoluteness** *n.* **absolutely** *adv.*

ab-so-lu-tion (ab´sa lö´shan) *n.* The state or act of being absolved; forgiven, discharged.

ab-so-lut-ism (ab´so lö˝tiz˝um) *n.* The exercise or principle of absolute power in government.

ab-so-lut-ize (ab solöt iz´) *v.* To make something absolute.

ab-sol-u-to-ry (ab sol´ü tör´ē) *adj.* In an absolving manner; having the capacity to absolve.

ab-solve (ab zolv´) *v.* To set free or release from duties, guilt, debt, or penalty.

ab-so-nant (ab´so nant) *adj.* Contrary, discordant; dissonant; incongruous, abhorrent.

ab-sorb (ab sorb´) *v.* To take in; to take up the full attention; to engage one's whole attention. **absorbable** *adj.*

ab-sorp-tion (ab sorp´shan) *n.* The act of giving full attention or having great interest. *Med.* The process of assimilating food or other substances into the body, which may take place through the gastrointestinal tract, the skin, or the mucous membranes of the eyes, nose, etc.

ab-stain (ab stān´) *v.* To refrain from doing something. **abstainer** *n.*

ab-ste-mi-ous (ab stē´mē us) *adj.* Showing moderation in the use of drink and food. **abstemiousness** *n.* **abstemiously** *adv.*

ab-sten-tion (ab sten´shan) *n.* The act of holding off from using or doing something.

ab-sterge (ab stürj´) *v.* To make clean by wiping; to wash away.

ab-ster-gent (ab stür´jent) *adj.* Having purgative or cleaning properties. *n.* a detergent or anything that aids in cleaning.

ab-stract (ab strakt´) v. To remove material from, to reduce or summarize. **abstractedness** n.

ab-stract-ed (ab strak´tid) adj. Absorbed in thought; absent in mind; inattentive.

ab-strac-tion (ab strak´shan) n. The act of separating, withdrawing; something abstract.

ab-strac-tion-ism (ab strak she´nizem) n. Practice of making abstract art.

ab-strac-tive (ab strak´tiv) adj. Having the power or quality of abstracting.

ab-strict (ab strikt) v. To cause an abstraction.

ab-stric-tion (ab strik´shan) adj. A forming of spores with the cutting off of parts of the sporophore.

ab-struse (ab strös´) adj. Difficult or hard to understand or comprehend. **abstruseness** n. **abstrusely** adv.

ab-surd (ab sürd´) adj. Contrary to reason; clearly untrue or unreasonable. **absurdity** n. **absurdness** n.

ab-surd-ism (ab sürd iz em) n. The philosophy which is based on the idea and belief that man lives in a meaningless universe and the search for order will bring him and the universe into conflict. **absurdist** n.

a-bub-ble (a ´beb el) adj. To be in the process of bubbling.

a-build-ing (a ´bil din) adj. To be in the process of constructing or building.

a-bu-li-a (a bū´lē a) n., Psychol. Form of mental derangement where volition is lost or impaired.

a-bun-dance (a bun´dans) n. Ample supply; plenty; amount more than enough.

a-bun-dant (a bun´dant) adj. Plentiful; sufficient; overflowing, abounding.

a-bun-dant-ly (a bun´dant lē) adv. In sufficient degree; amply; plentifully.

a-buse (a būz´) v. To use in an improper or wrong way. **abuse** n. Improper treatment or employment; improper use or application; misuse. **abuser** n.

a-bu-sive (a bū´siv) adj. Practicing abuse; bad treatment of another. **-ness** n.

a-but (a but´) v. To border; to touch at one end; to be contiguous to; to join at a boundary; to form a point or line of contact, used with on, upon, against.

a-bu-ti-lon (a būt´i lon˝) n. A member of the genus of mallow family that has lobed leaves and bell-shaped flowers.

a-but-ment (a but´ment) n. Support at the end of an arch or bridge.

a-but-tal (a but´al) n. The bordering part of a piece of land.

a-but-ting (a but´ing) adj. To abut or to serve as an abutment of something.

a-buzz (a buz) adj. To be filled with a buzzing.

a-bys-mal (a biz´mal) adj. Immeasurably deep or low; profound.

a-byss (a bis´) n. A deep crack or gap in the earth. **abyssal** adj.

ac-a-deme (ak´a dēm´) n. The place where instruction is given to pupils.

ac-a-dem-ic (ak´a dem´ik) adj. Higher education; relating to classical or liberal studies, rather than vocational.

a-cad-e-my (a kad´e mē) n., pl. **academies** A private school for special training, as in music, art, or military. A school holding a rank between a college and an elementary school.

a-can-tha (a kan´tha) n. The prickle of a plant; an animal spine; one of the acute processes of the vertebrae of animals.

ac-an-tha-ceous (ak an thā´shus) adj. Armed with prickles.

a-can-thine (a kan´thin) adj. Pertaining to or resembling the plant acanthus.

a-can-tho-ceph-a-la (a kan´tha sef´a la) n. One of the intestinal worms that have a hooked proboscis and will absorb food out of the digestive tract.

a-can-tho-ceph-a-lan (a kan´tha sef´a lan) adj. Having spines or hooks on the head, as certain intestinal worms (the Acanthocephala), which are attached within the bodies of animals.

a cap-pel-la (ä´ka pel´a) adj. Singing without instrumental accompaniment.

ac-a-ri-a-sis (ak´a rī´a sis) n. An infestation that is caused by mites.

ac-a-rid (ak´a rid) n. A member of the order of arachnids that includes ticks and mites.

ac-a-roid (ak´a roid˝) adj. Having the resemblance of a mite.

acaroid resin n. A type of resin that is alcohol soluble and is obtained from the Australian grass trees.

a-car-pel-ous (ā kär´pe lus) adj. To be without carpels.

a-car-pous (ā kär´pus) adj. Barren; not producing fruit.

a-cat-a-lec-tic (ā kat´a lek´tik) adj. Not stopping short; having the complete number of syllables in a line of verse.

a-cau-date (ä kä´dāt) adj. Having no tail.

ac-au-les-cent (ak´a les´ent) adj. Bot. Stemless.

ac-cede (ak sēd´) v. To consent; to agree; to arrive at a certain condition or state.

ac-cel-er-ate (ak sel´a rāt´) v. To make work or run faster; to increase speed; to hasten or quicken; cause to advance faster, to take extra courses. **acceleration** n.

ac-cel-er-a-tion (ak sel´a rā´shan) n. The process of accelerating something.

ac-cel-er-a-tive (ak sel´e rā´tiv) adj. To be pertaining to acceleration.

ac-cel-er-a-tor (ak sel´e rā´tor) n. Something that accelerates something else.

ac-cel-er-om-e-ter (ak sel´e rom´i tẽr) *n*. An instrument used to measure and record the acceleration of aircraft speed.

ac-cent (ak´sent) *n*. An effort to make one syllable more prominent than the others.

ac-cen-tu-al (ak sen´chŏ al) *adj*. To be pertaining to or having an accent.

accentual verse *n*. A verse where the accentuation is the basis of the rhythm.

ac-cen-tu-ate (ak sen´chŏ āt´) *v*. To make a part more pronounced; to emphasize.

ac-cept (ak sept´) *v*. To take what is given; to believe to be true; to agree, to receive. **accepter** *n*. **acceptor** *n*.

ac-cept-able (ak sep´ta bl) *adj*. Satisfactory; proper; good enough. **acceptableness** *n*. **acceptability** *n*.

ac-cep-tance (ak sep´tans) *n*. Approval or belief; an accepting or being accepted.

ac-cep-tant (ak sep´tant) *adj*. To be willing to accept something.

ac-cep-ta-tion (ak´sep tā´shan) *n*. The act of receiving; favorable reception.

ac-cept-ed (ak sep´tid) *adj*. Commonly approved; generally thought of as right or normal; conventional.

ac-cep-tive (ak sep´tiv) *adj*. Willing to accept or receive.

ac-cess (ak´ses) *n*. Entrance, admission; near approach; admittance; the state of being approachable; passage that allows communication. In computer science, to call up a program or data.

ac-ces-si-bil-i-ty (ak ses´i bil´i tē) *n*. The quality of being accessible.

ac-ces-si-ble (ak ses´i bl) *adj*. Able to be attained or approached; easy of access.

ac-ces-sion (ak sesh´an) *n*. In Computer Science, the act of obtaining data from storage; the ability to store data.

ac-ces-so-ri-al (ak´si sōr´ē al) *adj*. To be pertaining to an accessory.

ac-ces-so-ri-ly (ak ses´sa ri lē) *adv*. An accessory; supplementary; not as principal but as a subordinate.

ac-ces-so-ri-ness (ak ses´sa rē nes) *n*. The state of being accessory, or of being or acting in a secondary character.

ac-ces-so-rize (ak ses´sō riz) *v*. To wear with accessories.

ac-ces-so-ry (ak ses´o rē) *adj*. Aiding in producing some effect; acting in subordination to the principal agent; contributing to a general effect.

accessory nerves *n*. The pair of 11th cranial nerves activating the muscles of the chest, shoulders, back, and pharynx.

access code In computer science, the user name or security code required to use a computer, program or certain files.

ac-ciac-ca-tu-ra (ä chä´ka tür´a) *n*. Music note, a half step below, and struck at the same time as, the main note.

ac-ci-dence (ak´si dens) *n*. A book that contains the rudiments of grammar; the elementary parts of a subject.

ac-ci-dent (ak´si dent) *n*. A happening that is not planned or expected.

ac-ci-den-tal (ak´si den´tal) *adj*. Happening by chance; unexpected.

ac-cip-i-ter (ak sip´i tẽr) *n*. A short-winged hawk that has a flight pattern that is darting and low. **accipitrine** *adj*.

ac-claim (*a* klām´) *v*. To greet with strong approval loud applause; to hail or cheer.

ac-cla-ma-tion (ak´la mā´shan) *n*. An expression of approval, usually loud.

ac-cli-mate (*a* klī´mit) *v*. To get used to a different climate or new surroundings.

ac-cli-ma-ti-za-tion (*a* klī´ma tī zā´shan) *n*. The result of acclimatizing.

ac-cli-ma-tize (*a* klī´ma tīz´) *v*. To change to or to adapt to a change in altitude, climate, or temperature.

ac-cliv-i-ty (*a* kliv´i tē) *n*. An ascending slope.

ac-co-lade (ak´a lād´) *n*. Award; ceremony used in conferring knighthood. *Arch*. A curved molding above an arched opening.

ac-com-mo-date (*a* kom´a dāt´) *v*. To give room or lodging; to make fit; to adjust.

ac-com-pa-ni-ment (*a* kum´pa ni ment) *n*. Something that goes well with another.

ac-com-pa-ny (*a* kum´pa nē) *v*. To be together with; to go along with; to go with or attend as a companion or associate; to go together; to be associated or connected with.

ac-com-plice (*a* kom´plis) *n*. Companion who helps another break the law; a partner or partaker in guilt, usually a subordinate.

ac-com-plish (*a* kom´plish) *v*. To perform; to carry out; to complete; to do. **accomplisher** *n*.

ac-cord (*a* kord´) *n*. Harmony; agreement. **accord** *v*. To grant or award.

ac-cost (a kost´) *v*. To come close to and to speak first in an unfriendly manner.

ac-couche-ment (*a* kösh´mänt) *n*. Childbirth; confinement.

ac-cou-cheur (ä kö shoer´) *n*. A surgeon who attends women in childbirth.

ac-cou-cheuse (ä kö shoez´) *n*. Midwife.

ac-count (*a* kount´) *n*. A description; a statement of debts and credits in money transactions; a record; a report.

ac-count-a-ble (*a* kount´ta bl) *adj*. Liable to be held responsible; able to be explained. **accountably** *adv*.

ac-count-ant (*a* koun´taut) *n*. A person who keeps or examines accounts; a profession.

account executive *n*. Administrator of a client's account; a business service.

ac-count-ing (*a* koun´ting) *n*. A report on how accounts have been balanced; the system of keeping business records or accounts.

ac-cou-tre (*a* kō´tėr) *v*. To give or to provide with furnishings.

ac-cred-it (*a* kred´it) *v*. To authorize someone; to give official power.

ac-cres-cent (*a* kres´ent) *adj*. Increasing; growing.

ac-crete (*a* krēt´) *v*. To grow together or join.

ac-cre-tion (*a* krē´shan) *n*. The process of enlarging something. **-ary** *adj*.

ac-cru-al (*a* krō´al) *n*. Process or act of accruing; something accrued.

ac-crue(*a* krō´) *v*. To result naturally; to increase at certain times.

acct *abbr*. Account.

ac-cul-tur-a-tion (*a* kul´cha rā´ shan) *n*. The modification of one's culture with a prolonged interaction involving another culture.

ac-cum-ben-cy (*a* kum´ben sē) *n*. State of being accumbent.

ac-cum-bent(*a* kum´bent) *adj*. Leaning or reclining; lying against anything.

ac-cu-mu-late (*a* kū´mya lāt´) *v*. To collect or gather over a period of time; pile up.

ac-cu-ra-cy (ak´yur *a* sē) *n., pl.* **accuracies** Exactness; precision; the fact of being accurate or without mistakes.

ac-cu-rate (ak´yur it) *adj*. Without mistakes or errors; careful and exact; correct. **accurately** *adv*.

ac-curse (*a* kürs´) *v*. To curse.

ac-curs-ed (*a* kür´sid) *adj*. Sure to end badly; under a curse; unpleasant or annoy-ing; very bad. **accursedness** *n*.

ac-cu-sa-tive (*a* kū´za tiv) *adj*. Relating to the direct object of a preposition or of a verb.

ac-cuse (*a* kūz´) *v*. To find fault with; to blame; to charge someone with doing wrong or breaking the law. **-er** *n*.

ac-cused (*a* kūzd´) *n*. One charged with a crime; a defendant in a court of law.

ac-cus-tom (*a* kus´tom) *v*. To familiarize by habit.

ac-cus-tomed (*a* kus´tomd) *adj*. Often practiced; familiar; usual.

ace (ās) *n*. The face of a die or a playing card marked with one spot; in tennis and some other sports, a score made by a serve that is not returned.

a-ce-di-a (*a* sē´dē *a*) *n*. Loss of interest for living.

a-cel-lu-lar (ā sel´ū lar) *adj*. Having no cells.

a-cen-tric (ā sen´trik) *adj*. To be missing a centromere.

a-ceph-a-lous (ā sef´*a* lus) *adj*. To be without a head.

a-ce-quia (*a* sā´kya) *n*. A type of ditch which can be used for irrigation.

ac-er-ate (as´*e* rāt´) *adj*. Pointed; sharp.

a-cerb (*a* sürb´) *adj*. To be acid in one's mood; critical; bitter, sour, harsh to the taste.

a-cer-bi-ty (*a* sür´bi tē) *n*. Sourness, with roughness of taste.

a-ce-rous (ā sēr´us) *adj*. Without horns.

a-cer-vate (*a* sür´vit) *adj*. To be living or growing in heaps. **acervately** *adv*.

a-ces-cent (*a* ses´ent) *adj*. Slightly sour, turning sour.

ac-e-tab-u-lar-ia (as´i tab´yu lar´ē a) *n*. A type of single-celled alga found in the warm seas which look like mushrooms in shape.

ac-e-tab-u-lum (as´i tab´yu lum) *n*. The socket of the hipbone. **acetabular** *adj*.

ac-e-tal (as´i tal´) *n., Chem*. The liquid formed by imperfect oxidation of alcohol.

ac-et-a-min-o-phen (as *et e* min *e* fen) *n*. A compound which is used for the purpose of relieving pain and fever.

ac-e-tate (as´i tāt´) *n*. Salt formed by union of acetic acid with a base, used in making rayon and plastics.

a-cet-ic (*a* sē´tik) *adj*. To be pertaining to or related to vinegar or acetic acid.

acetic acid (*a* sē´tik as´id) *n*. The main ingredient of vinegar; a sour, colorless liquid that has a sharp smell.

a-ce-ti-fy (*a* set´i fī´) *v*. To change or to turn into acetic acid. **acetification** *n*.

ac-e-tom-e-ter (as´i tom´i tėr) *n*. Instrument for determining the purity or strength of acetic acid in a solution.

ac-e-to-phe-net-i-din (as´i tō fe net´i din) *n*. A type of compound which is used for relief of pain and fever.

a-cet-y-lene (*a* set´e len´) *n*. A highly inflammable, poisonous, colorless gas that burns brightly with a hot flame, used in blowtorches for metal working.

ache (āk) *v*. To give or have a dull, steady pain; to want very much; to long for.

a-chene (ā kēn´) *n*. A type of indehiscent one-seeded fruit that has developed from an ovary. **achenial** *adj*.

a-chiev-a-ble (*a* chēv´a bl) *adj*. Being capable to be achieved or performed; attainable.

a-chieve (*a* chēv´) *v*. To reach by trying hard; to do; to succeed in doing; to accomplish. **achiever** *n*.

a-chieve-ment (*a* chēv´ ment) *n*. Something achieved by work or skill.

Achilles tendon (*a* kil´ēz ten´ don) *n*. The tendon that connects the heel bone and calf muscles.

a-chlor-hy-dri-a (ā̆ klŏr hī´ drē a) *n.* Absence of hydrochloric acid from gastric juices.

a-chon-drite (ā kon drīt) *n.* A type of stony meteorite that does not have rounded grains.

a-chon-dro-pla-sia (ā kon˝dro plā´zha) *n.* The failure of the cartilage to develop in a normal manner which results in dwarfism. **-plastic** *adj.*

ach-ro-mat-ic (ak´ro mat´ik) *adj.* The transmitting of light without decomposing it into primary colors.

a-chro-ma-tin (ā krō´ma tin) *n.* Biol. The portion in the nucleus of a cell that is unstainable.

a-chro-ma-tism (ā krō´m a tiz´um) *n.* A quality of giving of images practically free from extraneous colors.

a-chro-ma-tous (ā krō´ma tus) *adj.* Having no color; of a lighter color than is usual or normal.

achy (āk´ē) *adj.* To have aches.

a-cic-u-la (a sik´yu la) *n.* Spine of an animal or plant.

ac-id (as´id) *n.* A chemical compound containing hydrogen that forms a salt when combined with a base, dissolves in water, has a very sour taste, makes litmus paper turn red.

ac-id-fast (as´id fast´) *adj.* Not easily decolorized by acid.

acid head *n.* A user of the drug LSD.

a-cid-ic (a sid´ik) *adj.* Chem. Pertaining to acid; to contain a large amount of an acid constituent.

a-cid-i-fi-er (a sid´i fī´ĕr) *n.* Any chemical that produces an acid effect.

a-cid-i-fy (a sid´ifī´) *v.* To make some substance acid.

ac-i-dim-e-ter (as˝i dim´itĕr) *n.*, Chem. Instrument used for measuring the amount of acid in a particular volume or weight of a solution.

a-cid-i-ty (a sid´i tē) *n.* Condition or quality of being acid.

ac-i-do-phile (as´i dō fil´) *n.*, Biol. Tissue, cell, organism, or substance that shows an affinity towards an acidic environment.

ac-i-do-phil-ic (as˝i dō fil´ik) *adj.* Having the quality to be easily stained with acid; thriving in acid.

ac-i-do-sis (as˝i dō´sis) *n.* The abnormally high concentration of acid in body tissues and blood.

acid rain *n.* Acid precipitation that falls as rain.

acid rock *n.* Lyrics from Rock music that suggest drug-related experiences.

a-cid-u-late (a sij´u lāt´) *v.* To become or make somewhat acid.

a-cid-u-lous (a sij´u lus) *adj.* To be slightly acid in taste.

ac-i-na-ceous (as˝i nā´shus) *adj.* Full of seeds or kernels.

ac-i-nac-i-form (as´i nas´i form´) *adj.* Formed like or resembling a scimitar sword.

ac-i-nar (as e ner) *adj.* To be pertaining to an acinus.

ac-i-nus (as´i nus) *n.* A sac of a racemose gland which is lined with secreting cells.

ac-know-ledge (ak nol´ij) *v.* To admit the truth, existence or reality.

ac-knowl-edg-ment (ak nol´ij ment) *n.* To acknowledge or own up to something; recognition; confession; something that is given or done in return for a favor.

a-clin-ic (ā klin´ik) *adj.* Applied to an imaginary line that is near the earth's equator where a magnetic needle has no dip. **aclinic line** *n.*

ac-me (ak´mē) *n.* The highest point of attainment; peak.

ac-ne (ak´nē) *n.* An inflammation of the sebaceous or oil-secreting glands of the skin, manifested by eruptions of hard, inflamed pimples. Increased production of androgens, hormones, in both male and female during puberty causes the sebaceous glands to become active and secrete large amounts of sebum, which block the glands and hair follicles.

ac-o-nite (ak´a nit´) *n.* A poisonous plant with flowers resembling hoods; sometimes called monkshood.

a-corn (ā´kon) *n.* The nut of the oak tree, seated in a woody cup.

a-cot-y-le-don (ā˝kot e lēd´on) *n.* A plant as a fern or moss, which does not have seed leaves.

a-cous-tic (a kö´stik) *adj.* Having to do with sound or the sense of hearing; the sense of sound; absorbing sound. **acoustical** *n.* **acoustically** *adv.*

acoustic nerve *n.* The nerve that serves the ear.

a-cous-tics (a kö´stiks) *n.* The scientific study of sound; total effect of sound, especially in an enclosed space.

ac-quaint (a kwänt´) *v.* To make familiar; to let know, to make aware; to inform.

ac-quaint-ance (a kwän´tans) *n.* A person whom one knows but not as a close friend. **acquaintanceship** *n.*

ac-qui-esce (ak˝wē es´) *v.* To agree without arguing; to comply without protest, to comply. **acquiescent** *adj.*

ac-qui-es-cence (ak´wē es´ens) *n.* The act of giving or acquiescing a quiet; a yielding.

ac-quir-a-ble (a kwī er´ a bl) *adj.* Capable of being acquired.

ac-quire (a kwier´) *v.* To secure control or possession; to become the owner.

acquired immunity *n.* Immunity against disease one develops during a lifetime.

ac-quire-ment (a kwī er´ ment) *n.* The

act of acquiring something, as a skill gained by learning.

ac-qui-si-tion (ak´wĭ zish´ɑn) n. Something that is acquired; the act of acquiring.

ac-quis-i-tive (a kwiz´ĭ tiv) adj. Eager to gain and possess things; greedy.

ac-quis-i-tive-ly (a kwiz´ĭ tiv lē) adv. An acquisitive manner.

ac-quis-i-tive-ness (a kwiz´ĭ tiv nis) n. The quality of being acquisitive.

ac-quit (a kwĭt´) v. To rule that a person accused of something is not guilty; to conduct oneself; to behave.

a-cre (ā´kėr) n. A measurement of land that equals 43,560 square feet.

a-cre-age (ā´kėr ij) n. The total number of acres in a section of land.

ac-rid (ak´rid) adj. Having a sharp, bitter, or irritating taste or smell. **acridity** n. **acridness** n. **acridly** adv.

ac-ri-mo-ni-ous (ak´ri mō´nē us) adj. Sharp or bitter in speech or manner.

ac-ri-mo-ny (ak´ri mō´nē) n. Sharpness or severity of temper; bitterness of expression.

a-crit-i-cal (ā krit´ĭ kɑl) adj., Med. Not critical.

ac-ro-bat (ak´ro bat´) n. One who is skilled in gymnastic feats. **-ic** adj.

ac-ro-bat-ics (ak´ro bat´iks) n. The performance of an acrobat.

ac-ro-car-pous (ak´ro kär´pus) adj., Bot. Applied to mosses whose fruit terminates the growth of a primary root.

ac-ro-cen-tric (ak rō sen trik) adj. To have a centromere that is located so one chromosomal arm is longer than the other arm.

ac-ro-dont (ak´ro dont) adj. Having rootless teeth that are joined to the ridges of the upper and lower jaws. n. Animals possessing such teeth.

a-crop-e-tal (a krop´ĭ tal) adj., Bot. Starting at the base and going toward the highest or narrowest point.

ac-ro-pho-bi-a (ak´ro fō´bē a) n. Unusual fear of heights.

ac-ro-spire (ak´ro spiėr´) n. The first leaf that rises above the ground as grain starts to germinate.

a-cross (a kros´) adv. & prep. From side to side; to one side from the other.

a-cros-tic (a kro´stik) n. A series of lines or a poem in which certain letters in each line form a name or motto.

ac-ro-tism (ak´ro tiz´um) n. The weakness or absence of the pulse.

a-cryl-ic (a kril´ik) n. Relating to or of acrylic acid or its derivatives.

acrylic fiber n. A fiber which is made of chemicals, used in making fabrics.

ac-ry-lo-ni-trile (ak´re lō nī´tril) n. A liquid organic compound used to make acrylic fibers and rubber.

act (akt) n. Doing something; a thing

done; deed; an action; a showing of emotion which is not real or true; a law; decree; one of the main parts of a play, opera, etc.

act (akt) v. To exert power; to produce effects; to be in action or motion; to behave, demean, or conduct oneself; to perform, as an actor; to substitute for; as, to act as captain; to transact; to do or perform; to represent as real; to feign or counterfeit. **act as** To serve as; perform the function or duties of. **act on** To act or obey in accordance with; to affect. **act out** To demonstrate or perform. **act out** Psychol. To express openly subconscious emotions. **act up** To behave in a manner that is unruly or capricious.

act-a-ble (akt´abl) adj. Capable of being acted or performed. **actability** n.

ac-tin (ak´tĭn) n. A type of protein that is in the muscle and becomes active in muscle contractions.

act-ing (ak´tĭng) adj. Temporarily performing the duties, services, or functions of another person.

ac-tin-i-a (ak tĭn´ē a) n. A sea anemone; having a mouth surrounded by tentacles in circle.

ac-tin-ic (ak tĭn´ik) adj. Pertaining to rays, esp. the chemical rays of the sun.

ac-tin-i-form (ak tĭn´iform´) adj. Bearing a resemblance to an actinia.

ac-tin-ism (ak´tĭ nĭz´um) n. The radiation of heat or light.

ac-tin-o-gen (ak tĭn´o jen´) n. An element which is radioactive.

ac-tin-o-graph (ak tĭn´o graf´) n. Instrument used to measure and register variations of actinic or chemical influence in the solar rays.

ac-ti-nom-e-ter (ak´ti nom´itėr) n. An instrument for measuring the intensity of the sun's actinic rays.

ac-ti-no-my-cin (ak´ti nōmīs´in) n. One of the yellow-red or red polypeptide antibiotics that is separated from soil bacteria.

ac-ti-non (ak´ti non´) n. A radioactive, gaseous element, existing for only a few seconds, which is isotopic with radon.

ac-tion (ak´shɑn) n. The process of doing or acting; an effect produced by something; a lawsuit.

ac-tion-able (ak´sha na bl) adj. To be affording ground for a suit at law.

ac-tion-less (ak shen les) adj. To be characterized by inaction and lack of movement.

action painting n. A style of painting where paint is often smeared or dribbled to give a thickly textured surface.

ac-ti-vate (ak´ti vāt´) v. To put into action. **activation** n.

ac-tive (ak´tiv) *adj.* Working; full of action; busy; lively; quick, constant. **activeness** *n.* **actively** *adv.*

ac-tiv-ism (ak´ti viz˝um) *n.* A practice based on direct action to affect changes in government and social conditions.

ac-tiv-i-ty (ak tiv´i tē) *n.* Being active, in motion; normal power of body or mind.

act of God *n.* An unforeseeable, uncontrollable happening caused by nature.

ac-tor (ak´tor) *n.* A person who acts in movies, plays, television shows, etc.

ac-tress (ak´tris) *n.* A female actor.

ac-tu-al (ak´chŏ al) *adj.* Acting or existing in fact or reality; as it really is; true. **actualness** *n.*

ac-tu-ar-y (ak´chŏ er´ē) *n.* A person who will figure or calculate insurance.

ac-tu-ate (ak´chŏ āt˝) *v.* To put into motion or action. **actuation** *n.*

ac-tu-a-tor (ak´chŏ ā˝tôr) *n.* Something that will control something else indirectly.

a-cu-i-ty (a kū´i tē) *n.* A sharp perception of something.

a-cu-le-ate (a kū´lē it) *adj.* To have a sting.

a-cu-men (a kū´men) *n.* The quickness of perception; mental acuteness, the keenness of insight.

a-cu-mi-nate (a kū´mi nat˝) *adj.* To taper to a point which is slender in shape.

ac-u-punc-ture (ak´ū pungk˝chur) *n.* A traditional Chinese means of treating some illnesses or of lessening pain by putting thin needles into certain parts of the body.

a-cute (a kūt´) *adj.* Extremely sensitive; sharp and quick, as pain; shrewd. **acuteness** *n.* **acutely** *adv.*

acute accent *n.* A mark to indicate heavy stress on a syllable.

ADC In computer science, Analog to Digital Converter; a device that converts analog signals to digital data.

ad-age (ad´ij) *n.* A proverb; a wise or true saying.

ad-a-mant (ad´a mant) *adj.* Standing firm; not giving in easily; unyielding.

Adams, John *n.* (1735-1826) The second president of the United States from 1797-1801.

Adams, John Quincy *n.* (1767-1848) The sixth president of the United States from 1825-1829.

a-dapt (a dapt´) *v.* To fit or suit; to change oneself so as to adjust to new conditions.

a-dapt-a-ble (adap´ta bl) *adj.* Being capable of adapting; able to adjust oneself without difficulty to new, unfamiliar, or unexpected conditions. **adaptability** *n.*

ad-ax-i-al (ad ak´sē al) *adj.* To be

positioned on one side of the axis.

ADP In computer science, Automatic Data Processing; the manipulation of data with with the use of a computer.

add (ad) *v.* To join or put something with another so that there will be more; to cause an increase. **add up** To make sense; to be reasonable; to arrive or to come to the expected total of a group of numbers. **addable, addible** *adj.*

ad-dend (ad´end) *n.* The number that is added to another number.

ad-den-dum (a den´dum) *n. pl.* **addenda** An addition; an appendix to a book or literacy work; something which is added.

ad-dict (ad´ikt) *n.* A person with a habit so strong that he cannot easily give it up. **addiction** *n.* **addicted** *adj.*

ad-di-tion (adish´an) *n.* An adding of numbers to find their total; the act of joining one thing to another. **-ally** *adv.*

ad-di-tive (ad´i tiv) *n.* A substance added to another in small amounts to alter it.

ad-dress (ad dres´) *v.* To direct or aim; to speak to; to give attention to. **address** *n.* The location to which mail or goods can be sent to a person, business, or organization. In *computer science* the location, in the memory of a computer, where data is kept, to which data is sent, or from where data is drawn.

ad-duce (ad dōs´) *v.* To offer as proof or give as a reason. **adducer** *n.*

ad-du-cent (ad dō´sent) *adj.* Bringing together or forward.

ad-duct (ad dukt´) *v.* To move or draw, such as a limb, toward the median axis of the body.

a-demp-tion (a demp´shn) *n., Law* Act of revoking a legacy.

ad-e-ni-tis (ad´e nī tes) *n.* The swelling or inflammation of lymph nodes.

ad-e-noi-dal (ad e noid l) *adj.* To be pertaining to or related to the adenoids.

ad-e-noids (ad´e noid˝) *n.* Lymphoid tissue growths in the upper part of the throat behind the nose, that may need to be removed surgically.

ad-e-no-ma (ad´e nō´ma) *n., Pathol.* Benign tumor that originates in a gland.

a-den-o-sine tri-phos-phate (a den´o sēn˝ trī fos´fat) *n.* A nucleotide occurring in all cells, representing the reserve energy of muscle that is important to many biochemical processes that produce or require energy.

adenosis *n.* A disease of a gland, particularly the abnormal development of glandular tissue.

a-dept (ad´ept) *adj.* Highly skilled; expert. **adeptly** *adv.* **adeptness** *n.*

ad-e-qua-cy (ad´e kwa sē) *n.* The state

ad-e-quate (ad´e kwit) *adj.* Sufficient; good enough for what is needed. **adequateness** *n.* **adequately** *adv.*

ad eun-dem (ad´ē an´dem) *adj.* To, in, or of the same rank.

ad-here (ad hēr´) *v.* To stay attached; to stick and not come loose; to stay firm in support.

ad-her-ence (ad hēr´ens) *n.* The quality of adhering.

ad-her-end (ad hēr´end) *n.* A surface to which an adhesive is able to adhere.

ad-her-ent (ad hēr´ent) *n.* A person who follows a leader, party, or belief; a believer or supporter.

ad-he-sion (ad hē´zhan) *n.* The act or state of sticking to something or of being stuck together.

ad-he-sive (ad hē´siv) *adj.* Tending to stick and not come loose; having a sticky surface. **adhesiveness** *n.*

adhesive tape *n.* A type of tape that has an adhesive on one side or two sides.

ad hoc (ad hok´) *adv.* For this particular purpose, without larger applications.

ad ho-mi-nem (ad hō´mi nem´) *adj.* Appealing to one's personal feelings and prejudices rather than to intellect and reason.

ad-i-a-bat-ic (ad´ēa bat´ik) *adj.* Referring to physical changes without gain or loss of heat.

ad-i-aph-o-ra (ad ē af´o ra) *n.* Things morally indifferent; matters that have no moral merit or demerit.

a-dieu (a dö´) *interj.* & *n.* French word for goodby.

ad interim *adj.* & *adv.* In the meantime.

a-di-os (ä´dē ōs´) *interj.* Spanish word for goodby.

ad-i-pose (ad´i pōs´) *n.* Fat; animal fat stored in the cells of adipose tissue.

adipose tissue *n.* A type of connective tissue where fat is stored in the body, mainly directly under the skin acting as an insulation and a source of energy.

ad-i-po-si-ty (ad´i po´si tē) *n.* Obesity.

ad-ja-cen-cy (a jā sen sē) *n.* The state of being adjacent.

ad-ja-cent (a jā´sent) *adj.* Nearby; bordering upon; adjoining; neighboring.

ad-jec-ti-val (aj´ik ti´val) *adj.* Belonging to or similar to an adjective.

ad-jec-tive (aj´ik tiv) *n.* A word used to describe a noun or pronoun, indicating which, what kind of, how many, or whose.

ad-join (a join´) *v.* To be next to; to be in or nearly in contact with.

ad-journ (a jern´) *v.* To close a meeting or session for a time; to move from one location to another.

ad-journ-ment (a jern´ment) *n.* The act of adjourning; the period when a legislature or other public body adjourns its meetings.

ad-judge (a juj´) *v.* To decide by judicial procedure. To pronounce or declare formally by law; to sentence or condemn; to adjudicate upon; to rule upon; to settle.

ad-ju-di-cate (a jö´di kāt´) *v.* To settle a dispute judicially. **adjudicator** *n.*

ad-ju-di-ca-tion (a jö´di kā´shan) *n.* Judicial decision. **adjudicatory** *adj.*

ad-junct (aj´ungkt) *n.* Something less important added to something with more importance. **adjunctive** *adj.*

ad-junc-tion (a jungk´shan) *n.* Act of adjoining.

ad-jure (ajer´) *v.* To ask urgently; to command solemnly. **adjuration** *n.*

ad-just (ajust´) *v.* To arrange or change; to make work correctly; to regulate.

ad-just-ment (a just´ment) *n.* The act or process of changing; a settlement of a suit or claim.

ad-ju-tan-cy (aj´u tan sē) *n.* The rank of an adjutant.

ad-ju-tant (aj´u tant) *n.* Administrative staff officer who serves as an assistant to the commanding officer.

ad-ju-vant (aj´u vant) *n.* Assistant. *Med.* The substance added to a prescription to aid in the operation of the principal ingredient.

ad-meas-ure (ad mezh´ér) *v.* To judge the dimensions, size, or capacity of something; to measure.

ad-meas-ure-ment (ad mezh´ur ment) *n.* The measure of something, or dimensions ascertained.

ad-min-is-ter (ad min´i stèr) *v.* To direct or manage; to give or carry out instructions. **administrable** *adj.*

ad-min-is-tra-tion (ad min´i strä´shan) *n.* The people who manage a school, company, or organization; the act of administering.

ad-mire (ad mīer´) *v.* To hold a high opinion; to regard with wonder, delight, and pleased approval; to regard with admiration. **admiringly** *adv.* **-er** *n.*

ad-mis-si-ble (ad mis´i bl) *adj.* Capable of being admitted, accepted or allowed.

ad-mis-sion (ad mish´an) *n.* The right or act of being admitted; an admitting of the truth of something; a confession.

ad-mit (ad mit´) *v.* To take or accept as being the truth; to permit or give the right to enter.

ad-mit-tance (ad mit´ans) *n.* Permission to enter.

ad-mit-ted-ly (ad mit´id lē) *adv.* By one's own admission or confession.

ad-mix-ture (ad miks´cher) *n.* Blend; mingling.

ad-mon-ish (ad mon´ish) *v.* To warn a person to correct a fault; to criticize in a gentle way. **admonisher** *n.*

ad-mo-ni-tion (ad´mo nish´an) *n.* A mild criticism or warning.

a-do (a dö´) *n.* Fuss or trouble.

a-do-be (a dö´bē) *n.* A brick or building material made from clay and straw and then dried in the sun.

ad-o-les-cence (ad´o les´ans) *n.* Period of physical and psychological development between childhood and adulthood; also known as youth.

ad-o-les-cent (ad´oles´ent) *n.* A person in the transitional period between childhood and adulthood.

a-dopt (adopt´) *v.* To legally take into one's family and raise as one's own.

a-dop-tion (a dop´shan) *n.* Act of adopting, or the state of being adopted.

a-dore (a dör´) *v.* To love greatly; to worship or honor; to like very much; to regard with admiration. **adorer** *n.*

a-dorn (a dorn´) *v.* To add splendor or beauty.

ad rem *adj.* Relevant to a point at issue.

ad-re-nal (a drē´nal) *adj.* Pertaining to the product of the adrenal gland, that is located on or near the kidney.

adrenal gland *n.* A small endocrine gland that consists of a medulla and cortex, located near the kidney.

ad-ren-er-gic (ad´re nėr´jik) *adj. Med.* Liberated or activated by epinephrine or a similar substance.

a-drift (adrift´) *adv.* Drifting; floating freely without being steered; having no clear purpose or aim.

a-droit (a droit´) *adj.* Skillful and clever in difficult circumstances. **adroitly** *adv.*

ad-sci-ti-tious (ad´si tish´us) *adj.* Derived from without; adventitious.

ad-script (ad´skript) *adj.* Written to the right of and in line with another letter or symbol.

ad-sorb (ad sorb´) *v.* To collect and hold as molecules of gases, liquids; to become adsorbed. **adsorbable** *adj.*

ad-sorb-ate (ad sor´bāt) *n.* The adsorbed substance in the process of adsorption.

a-du-late (aj´u lāt´) *v.* To give greater praise or flattery than is proper or deserved.

a-du-la-tion (aj´u lā´shan) *n.* Praise in excess, or beyond what is merited; high compliment.

a-dult (a dult´) *n.* A man or woman who is fully grown; a mature person. **adult** *adj.* Having reached full size and strength. **adulthood** *n.*

a-dul-ter-ate (a dul´te rāt´) *v.* To make impure or of less quality by adding improper ingredients.

ad-um-brate (ad um´brāt) *v.* To give a faint shadow or brief outline of; to over-shadow.

a-dust (a dust´) *adj.* Scorched; parched; looking as if burned or scorched.

ad va-lo-rem (ad va lōr´um) *adj.* According to value.

ad-vance (ad vans´) *v.* To move ahead; to make or become higher; to increase in value or price. *adj.* Something made or given ahead of time.

ad-vanced (ad vanst´) *adj.* Ahead in time; beyond beginning status.

ad-vance-ment (ad vans´ment) *n.* A promotion in position; progression; money ahead of time.

ad-van-tage (ad van´taj) *n.* A better chance or more forcible position; a condition, thing or event that can help or benefit; the first point, after deuce scored in the game of tennis.

ad-vene (ad vēn´) *v.* To accede or become added to.

ad-vent (ad´vent) *n.* A coming or arrival; the four Sundays before Christmas.

ad-ven-ti-ti-a (ad´ven tish´ē a) *n.* An external connective tissue which covers an organ.

ad-ven-ture (ad ven´chur) *n.* An exciting and dangerous experience; a risky undertaking; an unusual experience; uncertain outcome. **adventure** *v.*

ad-verb (ad´verb) *n.* A word used with a verb, adjective, or another adverb to tell when, where, how, what kind, or how much.

ad ver-bum (ad ver´bum) *adv.* Exactly word for word.

ad-ver-sar-y (ad´ver ser´ē) *n.* An enemy, or a person having hostility toward another person or group of people.

ad-ver-sa-tive (ad ver´sa tiv) *adj.* Expressing difference, or opposition.

ad-verse (ad´vers) *adj.* Opposed; not helpful; against someone or something. **adverseness** *n.* **adversely** *adv.*

ad-ver-si-ty (ad ver´si tē) *n.* Bad luck or misfortune; calamity; bad experience.

ad-vert (ad vert´) *v.* To turn the attention or mind; to regard, notice or observe.

ad-ver-tise (ad´ver tīz´) *v.* To draw public attention to a product you wish to sell, often by printed or broadcast media.

ad-ver-tise-ment (ad´ver tīz´ment) *n.* A public notice designed to advertise something.

ad-vice (ad vīs´) *n.* Suggestion or recommendation regarding a decision or course of action.

ad-vis-a-bil-i-ty (ad vī´za bil´i tē) *n.* Quality of being advisable.

ad-vise (ad vīz´) *v.* To counsel; to inform; to give information to; to give notice.

ad-vised (ad vīzd´) *adj.* Prudent; cautious; informed; thoughtfully considered.

ad-vis-ed-ness (ad vīz´id nis) *n.* The state of being advised; caution.

ad-vise-ment (ad vīz´ment) *n.* Careful

thought and consideration.

ad-vis-er (ad vī´zėr) *n.* A person who gives an opinion or advises.

ad-vi-so-ry (ad vī´z o rē) *adj.* Exercising or having the power to advise; giving or containing advice.

ad-vo-ca-cy (ad´vo ka sē) *n.* Act of advocating.

ad-vo-cate (ad´vo kit) *v.* To write or speak in favor of or support.

ad-y-na-mi-a (ad´e nă mē´ a) *n.* Deficiency of vital power; weakness.

ad-y-tum (ad´i tum) *n.* The innermost shrine or sanctuary; in ancient temples, the sanctuary where only priests were permitted to enter.

adz (adz) *n.* An instrument, similar to the ax type, used for chipping timber.

ad-zu-ki bean (ad zö´kē bēn) *n.* An annual, bushy bean, cultivated in Japan.

a-e-des (ā ē´ dēz) *n.* A mosquito that transmits yellow fever.

ae-gis (ē´jis) *n.* Protection; support or sponsorship.

ae-on (ē´on) *n.* A period of time of indefinite length.

aer-ate (âr´āt) *v.* To purify by exposing to the open air.

aer-a-tor (âr´ā tor) *n.* An apparatus for making carbonated beverages.

aer-i-al (âr´ē al) *adj.* Of or in the air; pertaining to aircraft. *n.* An antenna for television or radio. **aerially** *adv.*

aer-ie (âr´ē) *n.* The nest of a predatory bird, built on a cliff or other high places.

aer-i-form (âr´i form´) *adj.* Having the form or nature of air.

aer-i-fy (âr´i fī´) *v.* To blow air into; to fill with air; to combine with air.

aer-o (âr´ō) *adj.* Having to do with air, aircraft, or the flying of aircraft.

aer-o-bal-lis-tics (âr´ō ba lis´iks) *n.* The ballistics of projectiles dropped, fired, or launched from aircraft.

aer-o-bics (â rō´ biks) *n.* Strenuous exercise that increases oxygen to the heart and lungs, therefore strengthening them.

aer-o-bi-o-sis (âr´ō bī ō´sis) *n.* Life in an atmosphere of oxygen or air.

aer-o-em-bo-lism (âr´ō em´bo lizm) *n.* Occlusion of blood vessels by nitrogen gas bubbles that form when the body undergoes rapid decrease in air pressure.

aer-og-ra-phy (â rog´rafē) *n.* Description of the air or atmosphere; meteorology.

aer-ol-o-gist (âr ol´o jist) *n.* One who is versed in aerology.

aer-o-nau-tics (âr´o no´tiks) *n.* The science of designing, constructing and operating aircraft. **aeronautic** *adj.*

ae-ron-o-my (â ron´o mē) *n.* Study of chemical and physical phenomena located in the upper regions of the atmosphere.

aer-o-pause (âr´ o poz´) *n.* The region in the upper atmosphere where aircraft cannot fly.

aer-o-phore (âr´o fōr´´) *n.* Portable equipment for purifying air.

aer-o-plane (âr´o plān´) *n.* British word for airplane.

aer-o-sol (âr´o sōl) *n.* A liquid substance under pressure within a metal container.

aer-o-sphere (âr´o sfēr´) *n.* Body of air above the earth's atmosphere.

aer-o-train (âr´a trān) *n.* A train which runs at high speed.

Ae-sop (ē´săp) *n.* Greek writer of fables from the sixth century B.C.

aes-thet-ic (es thet´ik) *adj.* Having a love for beauty; pertaining to the sense or study of beauty or taste. **aesthete** *n.*

aes-thet-ics (es thet´iks) *n.* The study of the nature of beauty. **aesthetically** *adv.* **aesthetician** *n.*

a-far (a fär´) *adv.* Far off; far away.

af-fa-ble (af´a bl) *adj.* Good-natured, easy to talk to; friendly. **affably** *adv.*

af-fa-bil-i-ty (af a bil´i tē) *n.* Quality of being sociable.

af-fair (a fär´) *n.* An event or happening; matters of business or public concern.

af-fect (a fekt´) *v.* To move emotionally; to influence; to bring about a change in. **affected** *adj.*

af-fec-ta-tion (af ek tā´shan) *n.* Artificial behavior that is meant to impress others. False pretense, artificial show or appearance.

af-fec-tion-ate (a fek´sha nit) *adj.* Loving and gentle. Warmly attached; kind; fond; loving. **affectionately** *adv.* In an affectionate manner; fondly; tenderly; kindly.

af-fen-pin-scher (af en pin´sher) *n.* A small dog breed with stiff red, black, or gray coat, pointed ears, and shaggy hairs about the eyes, nose, and chin.

af-fi-ance (a fī ans) *v.* To bind by promise of marriage; to betroth.

af-fi-da-vit (af i dā´vit) *n.* A written statement by a person swearing that something is the truth.

af-fil-i-ate (a fil´ē āt´) *v.* To join in, connect, or associate with. **-ion** *n.*

af-fine (a fin´) *n.* Relative by marriage.

af-fin-i-ty (a fin´i tē) *n.* A special attraction with kinship; a natural attraction or liking.

af-firm (a ferm´) *v.* To declare positively and be willing to stand by the truth.

af-fir-ma-tion (af ir mā´shan) *n.* Act of asserting or affirming something as being true; that which is asserted; confirmation; ratification.

af-fix (af´iks) *v.* To attach; to fasten; to add at the end. **affix** *n.* A prefix or suffix added to a word.

af-fla-tus (a flā´tus) *n.* Creative

inspiration.

af-flict (*aflikt´*) *v.* To cause suffering or pain; to cause mental suffering.

af-flic-tion (*aflik´shən*) *n.* A state of distress or acute pain of the body or mind.

af-flu-ence (*af´löens*) *n.* Riches, wealth; abundance; plentiful supply of worldly goods.

af-flu-ent (*af´lö ent*) *adj.* Prosperous; rich; having all the wealth or money needed. **affluently** *adv.*

af-ford (*a förd´*) *v.* To be able to provide; to have enough money to spare.

af-for-est (*a for´ist*) *v.* To turn open land into forest. **afforestation** *n.*

af-fran-chise (*afran´chīz*) *v.* To make free; to grant full citizenship.

af-fray (*a frā´*) *n.* Brawl or noisy fight.

af-freight (*a frāt´*) *v.* To hire, for the transportation of freight or goods.

af-fright (*a frīt´*) *v.* To impress with sudden terror or fear of; to frighten unexpectedly or suddenly.

af-front (*afrunt´*) *v.* To insult one to his face; to confront.

af-fuse (*a füz´*) *adj.* Pour upon; to sprinkle with a liquid.

af-ghan (*af´gan*) *n.* A crocheted or knitted cover in colorful designs.

a-field (*afēld´*) *adv.* Away from home or the usual path.

a-fire (*afīr´*) *adj. & adv.* Burning.

a-flame (*a flām´*) *adj. & adv.* Burning; in flames; glowing.

a-float (*a flōt´*) *adv.* Floating on the surface of water; circulating.

a-flut-ter (*e ´flet er*) *adj.* Nervously excited.

a-foot (*a fet´*) *adj.* In the progress of happening; walking; on foot.

a-fore (*afōr´*) *adv.* Before as in place or time.

a-fore-men-tioned (*a för´men˜shand*) *adj.* Mentioned before.

a-fore-said (*a för´sed˜*) *adj.* Having spoken of something before; mentioned previously in the same discourse.

a-fore-thought (*a för´thot*) *adj.* Premeditated; planned beforehand; thought of previously.

a-foul (*a foul´*) *adv.* Tangled; entangled in a collision.

a-fraid (*a frād´*) *adj.* Hesitant; filled with fear; reluctant.

a-fresh (*a fresh´*) *adv.* Once more; again; after a pause.

aft (*aft*) *adv.* At, close to, near, or toward the rear of an aircraft or stern of a ship.

af-ter (*af´tēr*) *adv.* In the rear. **after** *prep.* Following; later in time.

af-ter-ef-fect (*af´tēr i fekt´*) *n.* An effect coming after; a delayed effect.

af-ter-thought (*af´tēr thot´*) *n.* An idea occurring later.

af-ter-ward *or* **af-ter-wards** (*af´tēr*

ward) *adv.* In later time.

a-gain (*a gen´*) *adv.* Moreover; another time; once more.

a-gainst (*agenst´*) *prep.* In opposition to; in preparation for; in contact with.

a-gape (*a gāp´*) *adv.* With expectation; in wonder; open-mouthed.

ag-ate (*ag´it*) *n.* The type of quartz that has bands of colors.

agate line *n.* Unit of measurement used in classified advertising.

a-ga-ve (*a gä´vē*) *n.* Fleshy-leaved tropical American plant.

age (*āj*) *n.* The length of time from beginning to a certain date; the time of life when a person has full legal rights; the age of 21. **age** *v.* To grow or become old; to mature.

aged (*ā´jid*) *adj.* Grown or become old. **agedness** *n.* **agedly** *adv.*

a-gen-cy (*ā´jen sē*) *n.* A business or service that acts for others; action; active influence; power.

a-gen-da (*a jen´da*) *n.* Program or list of things to be done.

a-gen-e-sis (*ā jen´i sis*) *n.* *Med.* The lack of, or an imperfect, development.

a-gent (*ā´jent*) *n.* One who acts as the representative of another; one who acts or exerts power.

ag-gior-na-men-to (*e jór ne ´men tō*) *n.* Bringing up to date.

ag-glom-er-ate (*a glom´e rāt´*) *v.* To collect; to form into a mass.

ag-glu-ti-nate (*a glöt´i nāt´*) *v.* To join by adhesion; to cause red blood cells to clump together.

ag-glu-ti-nin (*e ´glü n en*) *n.* A substance that causes agglutination; a group or mass formed by the union of separate elements.

ag-grade (*agrād´*) *v.* To raise the level or grade of a river valley.

ag-gran-dize (*ag´ran dīz´*) *n.* To enlarge, to extend; to increase.

ag-gra-vate (*ag´ravāt´*) *v.* To annoy; to make worse.

ag-gra-va-tion (*ag´ra vä´shan*) *n.* Act of making worse or aggravating; irritation; annoyance.

ag-gre-gate (*ag´re git*) *adj.* To gather together into a mass or whole.

ag-gress (*a gres´*) *v.* To commit the first act of offense or hostility.

ag-gres-sion (*a gresh´an*) *n.* Hostile action or behavior; an unprovoked assault.

ag-gres-sive (*a gres´iv*) *adj.* Offensive; distressing; pushy; afflicting.

ag-gres-sor (*agres´ēr*) *n.* An invader.

ag-grieved (*agrēvd´*) *adj.* Wronged or injured.

a-ghast (*agast´*) *adj.* Appalled; struck with amazement.

ag-ile (*aj´il*) *adj.* Marked by the ability to move quickly and easily; nimble.

ag-i-o (ag´ē ō´) *n.* The difference in value between one kind of money or another.

ag-i-o-tage (aj´ē ə tij) *n.* Business of a person who deals in foreign exchange.

ag-i-tate (aj´i tāt´) *v.* To disturb; to upset; to stir or move with violence; to try to arouse the public interest. **-ion** *n.*

ag-i-ta-tor (aj´i tā´tor) *n.* One who or that which stirs up public discontent, agitates, or arouses; a mixing device.

a-gleam (a glēm´) *adj.* Gleaming.

ag-let (ag´lit) *n.* A metal tag at the end of a shoelace.

a-gley (aglā´) *adv.* Wrong; awry.

a-glim-mer (a glim´ér) *adj.* Glimmering.

a-glit-ter (a glit´ér) *adj.* Glittering.

a-glow (a glō´) *adj.* Glowing.

ag-nail (ag´nāl) *n.* Inflammation of a fingernail or toenail; hangnail.

ag-nate (ag´nāt) *n.* Any male relation on the father's side.

ag-no-men (ag nō´men) *n.* An additional word, phrase or nickname, often used to designate a person in place of their real name.

ag-nos-tic (ag nos´tik) *n.* One who doubts that there is a God or life hereafter. **agnosticism** *n.*

a-go (a gō´) *adj.* In the past; gone by.

a-gog (a gog´) *adj.* Excited; eagerly expectant.

ag-o-nal (ag´o nal) *adj.* Relating to or having the characteristic of agony.

agonic line (ā gä´ik lin) *n.* The imaginary line on the earth's surface that joins places having no magnetic declination and where the magnetic needle points to the true north as well as magnetic north.

ag-o-nize (ag´oniz´) *v.* To afflict with great anguish or to suffer agony. **agonized** *adj.* **agonizing** *adj.*

ag-o-ny (ag´o nē) *n., pl.* **agonies** Intense mental distress or physical pain.

ag-o-ra-pho-bi-a (ag´or afo´bē a) *n.* Fear of open spaces.

a-graffe (a graf´) *n.* The ornamental clasp used for hooking parts of clothing together.

a-gran-u-lo-cy-to-sis (a gran´yu lo si tō´ sis) *n.* Destructive blood disease that is distinguished by a decrease of the leukocytes.

a-graph-i-a (a graf´ə) *n.* The cerebral disorder in which a patient cannot express ideas by written signs.

a-grar-i-an (agrär´ē ən) *adj.* Pertaining to or of land and its ownership; pertaining to farming; agricultural.

a-grar-i-an-ism (a grär´ē ə nizm) *n.* The movement and doctrine advocating equal divisions of lands and property.

a-gree (a grē´) *v.* To give assent; to consent; to share an understanding or opinion; to be beneficial or suitable; to correspond.

a-gree-a-ble (a grē´ə bl) *adj.* Pleasant; pleasing; willing; ready to consent. **agreeableness** *n.* **agreeably** *adv.*

a-gree-ment (a grē´ment) *n.* Harmony; concord; state or act of agreeing.

ag-ri-cul-ture (ag´ri kul˝chur) *n.* Raising of livestock; farming and cultivating the crops. **agriculturalist** *n.*

ag-ri-ol-o-gy (ag´rē ol´o jē) *n.* The study of human customs, especially those customs of man in a civilization of lesser development.

ag-ro-bi-ol-o-gy (ag´rō biäl´o jē) *n.* The science of plant nutrition and life in relation to the production of crops.

a-ground (a ground´) *adv.* Stranded; on the ground; to run ashore; beached. **aground** *adj.* Stranded; on the ground; to run ashore; beached.

a-gue (ā´gū) *n.* Fever accompanied by chills or shivering and sweating.

a-head (a hed´) *adv.* Before; in advance; to or at the front of something.

a-hoy (a hoi´) *interj.* A nautical call or greeting.

aid (ād) *v.* To give help or assistance.

AIDS *n.* Disease that destroys the body's immunological system; Acquired Immune Deficiency Syndrome.

ai-guille (ā gwēl´) *n.* The needle-like tops of rocks and mountain masses.

ail (āl) *v.* To feel sick; to make ill or uneasy.

ail-ment (āl´ment) *n.* A mild illness.

aim (ām) *v.* To direct a weapon; to direct purpose. **aim** *n.* Intention.

aim-less (ām´lis) *adj.* Lacking of purpose.

ain't (ānt) *contr.* Am not, are not, is not, has not, or have not.

air (âr) *n.* An odorless, tasteless, colorless, gaseous mixture; primarily composed of nitrogen (78%) and oxygen (21%); the sky; a breeze. **on the air** Broadcasting.

air-lift (âr´lift´) *n.* System of transporting supplies or troops by air when ground routes are blocked.

air-plane (âr´plān´) *n.* A vehicle capable of flight, heavier than air, and propelled by jet engines or propellers.

air-wave (âr´wāv´) *n.* The medium of television and radio transmission and communication.

aisle (īl) *n.* Passageway between rows of seats, as in a church, auditorium, or airplane, or meeting place.

a-jar (a jär´) *adv. & adj.* Partially opened.

a-kim-bo (akim´bō) *adj. & adv.* Bent; with a crook; arms bent with elbows out, hands on hips.

a-kin (akin´) *adj.* Related, as in family; similar in quality or character.

Alabama *n.* A state located in the southeastern part of the United States, statehood December 14, 1819, state capital Montgomery.

al-a-bas-ter (al´*a* bas˘tẽr) *n*. A dense, translucent, tinted or white, fine-grained gypsum. **alabastrine** *adj*.

a la carte (ä˘la kärt´) *adj*. Separate price for each item on the menu.

a-lack (*a* lak´) *interj*. An exclamation expressive of sorrow.

a-lac-ri-ty (*a* lak´ri tē) *n*. Readiness; cheerfulness; eagerness; briskness.

a la mode (al´*a* mōd´) *adj*. Served with ice cream, as pie; fashionable.

a-larm (a lärm´) *n*. A warning of danger; sudden feeling of fear; the bell or buzzer of a clock. **alarm** *v*. To frighten or warn by an alarm. **alarming** *adj*.

a-las (*a* las´) *interj*. Expressive of anxiety or regret.

Alaska *n*. A state located in the northwestern part of the United States, statehood January 3, 1959, capital Juneau.

a-late *or* **a-lat-ed** (ä´lāt, ä´lā ted) *adj*. Winged; having wings. **alation** *n*.

alb (alb) *n*. White linen robe worn by clergy during Mass.

al-ba-core (al´*ba* kōr˘) *n*. Large marine fish; major source of canned tuna.

al-ba-ta (al bā´*ta*) *n*. Alloy that consists of a combination of tin, nickel, zinc, and copper.

al-be-do (al bē´dō) *n., Astron*. Measurement of light rays upon a satellite or planet.

al-be-it (ol bē´it) *conj*. Although; even though.

al-bi-no (al bī´nō) *n*. An animal or person with an abnormal whiteness of the skin and hair and pink-colored eyes.

al-bum (al´*bum*) *n*. A book for photographs, autographs, stamps; a book of collections.

al-bu-men (al bū´*men*) *n*. White of an egg.

al-bu-min (al bū´men) *n*. Several proteins found in the white of eggs, blood serum, milk, and plant and animal tissue.

al-bu-mi-nu-ri-a (al bū˘mi ne´rē a) *n. Pathol*. The condition where the urine contains albumen, that often indicates diseased kidneys.

al-co-hol (al´*ko* hol´) *n*. Intoxicating liquor containing alcohol; ethanol; a series of related organic compounds.

al-cove (al´kōv) *n*. Recess or partly enclosed extension of a room.

al-de-hyde (al´*de* hīd´) *n*. Any of a class of highly reactive compounds obtained by oxidation of alcohols.

al-der-man (ol´dẽr m*a*n) *n*. Member of a municipal legislative body.

ale (āl) *n*. Beverage similar to, but more bitter than beer, made from malt by fermentation.

a-lee (*a* lē´) *adv. Naut*. On the sheltered side; opposite of a weather.

a-lem-bic (*a* lem´bik) *n*. A glass or metal vessel formerly used in distillation.

a-leph-null (ä´lef´nul´) *n. Math*. Smallest infinite non-ordinal number.

a-lert (*a* lert´) *adj*. Vigilant; brisk; watchful; active. **alert** *n*. A danger signal. **alertly** *adv*. **alertness** *n*.

a-lex-in (a lek´sin) *n*. Any of certain substances found in normal bloodserum, capable of destroying bacteria.

a-lex-i-phar-mic (alek´si fär´mik) *adj*. Acting as a means of warding off disease or the effects of poison.

al-fa (al´fa) *n*. A code word in communications to represent the letter A.

al-for-ja (al for´j*a*) *n*. Leather pouch or saddlebag.

al-fres-co (al fres´kō) *adj. & adv*. In the fresh air; outside.

al-gae (al´jē) *n*. Various primitive, chiefly aquatic, one-celled or multi-cellular plants, as the seaweed.

al-ge-bra (al´je bra) *n*. Generalization of math in which symbols represent members of a specified set of numbers and are related by operations that hold for all numbers in the set. **algebraic** *adj*. **algebraical, algebraically** *adv*.

al-go-pho-bi-a (al˘go fō˘bē a) *n*. The extreme fear of pain.

algorithm In computer science, precise instructions for performing a specific task.

a-li-as (ä´lē as) *n., pl.* **aliases** Assumed name. **alias** *adv*. Otherwise known as. In computer science, a name assigned to a file or a block of data to address it for processing.

al-i-bi (al´*i* bī´) *n*. A form of defense, an attempt by a defendant to prove he was elsewhere when a crime was committed; an excuse.

a-li-en (āl´yen) *adj*. Owing allegiance to a government or country, not one's own; unfamiliar; repugnant; from another region or country. **alien** *n*. A stranger; a foreigner.

al-ien-a-ble (āl´ye na bl) *adj*. Able to be transferred to the ownership of another. **alienability** *n*.

al-ien-ate (āl´ye nāt´) *v*. To cause to become indifferent or unfriendly.

al-ien-ist (āl´ye nist) *n*. A psychiatrist accepted by a court as an expert on mental stability.

a-light (*a* līt´) *v*. To settle; to come down; to dismount. **alight** *adj. & adv*. Burning, lighted.

a-lign *or* **a-line** (*a* līn´) *v*. To arrange in a line; to take one side of an argument or cause. **aligner** *n*.

a-lign-ment *or* **a-line-ment** (*a* līn´m ent) *n*. Arrange or position in a straight line.

a-like (*a* līk´) *adj*. Similar, having close resemblance. **alike** *adv*. In the same manner, way, or degree.

al-i-ment (al′i ment) *n.* Nourishment; food. **alimentation** *n.* **alimental** *adj.*

al-i-men-ta-ry (al′i men′ta rē) *adj.* Pertaining to nutrition or food.

alimentary canal *n.* The tube of the digestive system from the mouth to the anus, including the pharynx, esophagus, stomach, and intestines.

al-i-mo-ny (al′i mō′nē) *n.* Court ordered allowance for support, usually given by a man to his former wife following a divorce or legal separation.

al-i-phat-ic (al′i fat′ik) *adj.* Having to do with organic chemical compounds where the carbon atoms are linked in open chains.

al-i-quant (al′i kwant) *adj.* Applied to a number which will not divide into another number equally.

a-li-un-de (ā′lē un′dē) *adv.* From another source or means .

a-live (a līv′) *adj.* Living; having life; in existence or effect; full of life.

a-li-yah (ä′lē yä) *n.* Immigration of Jews to Israel.

a-liz-a-rin (a liz′ér in) *n.* A red-orange compound used in dyes.

al-ka-li (al′ka lī′) *n. pl.* **alkalies** *or* **alkalis** A hydroxide or carbonate of an alkali metal, whose aqueous solution is slippery, bitter, caustic, and basic in reactions.

al-ka-lin-ize (al′ka li nīz) *adj.* To make alkaline.

al-ka-loid (al′ka loid) *n.* Any of various nitrogen-containing organic bases obtained from plants. **alkaloidal** *adj.*

al-ka-lo-sis (al′ka lō′sis) *n.* Unusually high alkali content in the blood and tissues.

al-ka-net (al′ka net′) *n.* A plant whose root yields a red dye.

al-kyd res-in (al′kid rez′en) *n.* Group of sticky resins coming from phthalic acid and glycerol, that are used primarily in paints and adhesives.

all (awl) *adj.* Total extent or total entity; being a whole number, amount, or quantity; every.

al-lan-to-is (a lan′tō is) *n.* A sac that is developed from the posterior end of the abdominal cavity in reptiles, birds, and some mammals.

all–a-round (ol′a round′) *n.* Variance of all–round.

al-lay (a lā′) *v.* To relieve; to lessen; to calm; to pacify. **allayer** *n.*

al-le-ga-tion (al′e gā′shan) *n.* The act or result of alleging.

al-lege (a lej′) *v.* To affirm; to assert to be true; to declare without proof.

al-le-giance (a lē′jans) *n.* Loyalty to one's nation, cause, or sovereign; obligations of a vassal to an overlord.

al-le-giant (a lē′ja′nt) *n.* A person who owes allegiance.

al-le-go-ry (al′e gōr′ē) *n. pl.* **allegories** A dramatic, literary, or pictorial device in which each object, character, and event symbolically illustrates a religious or moral principle. **allegoric, allegorical** *adj.* **allegorist** *n.*

al-lele (a lēl′) *n.* Any of a group of possible mutational forms of a gene. **allelism** *n.* **allelic** *adj.*

al-le-lu-ia (al′e lō′ya) *interj.* Expressing praise to God or of thanksgiving.

al-ler-gen (al′ér jen′) *n.* Substance which causes an allergy. **allergenic** *adj.*

al-ler-gy (al′ér jē) *n., pl.* **allergies** Pathological or abnormal reaction to environmental substances, as foods, dust, pollens, or microorganisms.

al-le-vi-ate (a lē′vē āt′) *v.* To make more bearable. **alleviation** *n.* **alleviator** *n.*

al-ley (al′ē) *n., pl.* **alleys** A narrow passageway for access between or behind buildings.

al-li-a-ceous (al′ē ā′shus) *adj.* Having the properties of an onion or garlic.

al-li-ance (a lī′ans) *n.* A union, relationship, or connection by kinship, marriage, or common interest; a confederation of nations by a formal treaty; an affinity.

al-lied (a līd′) *adj.* United by agreement, or other means.

al-li-ga-tor (al′i gā′tor) *n.* Large amphibious reptile with very sharp teeth, powerful jaws, and a shorter snout than the related crocodile.

al-lit-er-ate (a lit′e rāt′) *v.* To arrange or form words beginning with the same sound, compose or arrange.

al-lit-er-a-tion (a lit′e rā′shan) *n.* Occurrence of two or more words having the same initial sound. .

al-li-um (al′ē um) *n.* Any bulb plant, such as garlic or onion.

al-lo-cate (al′o kāt′) *v.* To assign; to allot.

al-lo-cu-tion (al′o kū′shan) *n.* A formal speech.

al-log-a-mous (a log′amus) *adj.* Having the property of reproduction by cross-fertilization.

al-lo-graph (al′o graf′) *n.* Something written by someone on behalf of another.

al-lo-nym (al′o nim) *n.* The name of another person assumed by an author.

al-lot (a lot′) *v.* To distribute or set aside as a share of something, to divide, assign, or parcel out in parts or portions.

al-lot-ment (a lot′ment) *n.* A shared part, or portion granted or distributed.

al-lo-tropy (al′o trōp ē) *n.* One of two or more existing forms of a chemical element. **allotropic, allotropical** *adj.*

all out (ol′out′) *adv.* With every possible effort or resource.

all-o-ver (ol′ō′vér) *n.* A design or pattern

that covers the entire surface.

al-low (a lou´) v. To make a provision for, to permit; to permit to have; to admit; to concede. **allowable** adj.

al-low-ance (a lou´ans) n. The act of allowing something, such as a regular amount of money or food; a price discount.

al-loy (aloi´) n. Something that has been added to or reduced in purity or value.

all right adj. Acceptable; meets satisfaction; correct; safe. Slang Good; of sound character; dependable. **all right** adv. Satisfactorily; correctly; unhurt.

all-round (ol´round´) adj. Versatile, including all aspects.

al-lude (a lōd´) n. To refer to something indirectly, to hint at.

al-lure (a lür´) v. To entice; to tempt. **allure** n. Attraction; charm; enticement; prospect of attracting. **allurement** n. **allurer** n. **alluringly** adv.

al-lu-sion (a lö´zhan) n. The act of referring to something indirectly; a hint.

al-lu-sive (a lö´siv) adj. Reference to something that is not fully expressed. **allusively** adv. **allusiveness** n.

al-lu-vi-um (a lö´vē um) n. Sediment deposited by flowing water as in a river bed. **alluvial** adj.

al-ly (a li´) v. To connect or unite in a formal or close relationship or bond. **ally** n. One united with another in a formal or personal relationship.

alma mater n. College, school, or university one has attended; the anthem of that college, school, or university.

al-ma-nac (ol´ma nak´) n. Annual publication having calendars with weather forecasts, astronomical information, and other useful facts.

al-man-dine (al´man dēn´) n. A name given to the violet variety of the ruby spinel or sapphire; purple Indian garnet.

al-might-y (ol mi´tē) adj. Having absolute power. n. The Almighty God.

al-most (ol´mōst) adv. Not quite; slightly short of.

alms (ämz) n. Goods or money given to the poor in charity.

alms-house (ämz´hous´) n. A poorhouse.

al-ni-co (al´ni kō´) n. A powerful permanent magnet alloy of aluminum, iron, nickel, and other elements.

al-oe (al´ō) n. Any of various mostly African plants having fleshy, spiny-toothed leaves; a cathartic drug made from the juice of the leaves of this plant.

a-loft (a loft´) adv. Toward the upper rigging of a ship; in or into a high place; in the air.

a-lone (a lōn´) adj. Away from other people; single; solitary; excluding anyone or anything else; with nothing

further; sole; only; unaccompanied by others. **alone** adv. **aloneness** n.

a-long (a long´) adv. In a line with; following the length or path; in association; together; as a companion.

a-long-shore (along´shōr) adv. Being near, along, or by the shore, either on land or in the water.

a-long-side (a long´sīd´) adv. Along, at, near, or to the side of; side by side with.

a-loof (alöf´) adj. Indifferent; distant. **aloofness** n. **aloofly** adv.

a-loud (a loud´) adv. Orally; audibly.

a-low (a lō´) adv. In a low place, as in the ship's hold.

al-pen-horn (al´pen horn) n. Long curved horn used to send signals.

al-pen-stock (al´pen stok´) n. Long staff with an iron point used by mountain climbers.

al-pes-trine (al pes´trin) adj. Pertaining to mountain regions; growing at very high elevations but not above the timberline.

alpha and omega n. The beginning and the end; the first and last letters of the Greek alphabet.

al-pha-bet (al´fa bet´) n. The letters of a language, arranged in an order fixed by custom.

alpha decay n. Decay of an atomic nucleus as it emits an alpha particle.

alpha ray n. A stream of alpha particles.

al-read-y (ol red´ē) adv. By this or a specified time.

al-sike (al´sik) n. A European perennial clover with white or light pink flowers.

al-so (ol´sō) adv. Likewise; besides; in addition.

al-tar (ol´tēr) n. An elevated structure before which religious ceremonies may be held or sacrifices offered.

al-ter (ol´tēr) v. To make change or become different; to modify; to castrate or spay, as an animal. **alteration** n.

al-ter-a-tive (ol´te rā´tiv) adj. Tending to alter or produce alterations.

al-ter-ca-tion (ol´tēr kā´shan) n. Noisy and heated quarrel.

al-ter-nate (ol´tēr nāt´) v. To happen or follow in turn; to occur in successive turns. **alternate** n. Substitute.

alternate key (ALT) In computer science, an alternate shift key used in conjunction with other keys to execute commands.

alternating current n. Electric current that reverses direction at regular intervals.

al-ter-na-tive (ol´tēr´n ativ) n. A choice between two or more possibilities; one of the possibilities to be chosen. **alternative** adj. Allowing a choice.

al-ter-na-tor (ol´tēr nā´tēr) n. Electric generator producing alternating current.

alt-horn (alt´horn´) n. A tenor saxhorn,

often substituted for the French horn in bands.

al-though (ol thō´) *conj.* Even though.

al-tim-e-ter (al tim´i tèr) *n.* Instrument for measuring and indicating altitude.

al-ti-tude (al´ti tūd´) *n.* The height of a thing above a reference level; above the earth's surface; above sea level.

al-to (al´tō) *n.* Low female singing voice; the range between soprano and tenor.

al-to-geth-er (ol´to geth´ér) *adv.* Entirely; with all included or counted.

al-tru-ism (al´trō iz´um) *n.* Selfless concern for the welfare of others. **altruist** *n.* **altruistic** *adj.*

ALU In computer science, Arithmetic and Logic Unit; the part of the CPU that performs arithmetic and logic functions.

al-um (al´um) *n.* Any one of several similar double sulfates.

a-lu-mi-na (a lŏ´mi na) *n.* Any of several forms of aluminum oxide.

a-lu-mi-num (a lŏ´mi num) *n.* A silvery-white, ductile metallic element used to form many hard, light, corrosion-resistant alloys.

a-lum-na (a lum´na) *n., pl.* **alumnae** Female graduate or former student of a school, college, or university.

a-lum-nus (a lum´nus) *n. pl.* **alumni** A graduate or former student of a school, college, or university.

al-ve-o-lar (al vē´o lèr) *adj.* Containing or pertaining to sockets, specifically the part of the jaws where the teeth arise.

al-ways (ol´wāz) *adv.* Continuously; forever; on every occasion; at all times.

a-lys-sum (a lis´um) *n.* Herbs of the mustard family bearing small yellow or white racemose flowers with hairy leaves.

am (am) *v.* First person, singular, present tense of the verb to *be*.

AM *abbr.* Ante meridian, Latin for "before noon."

a-mal-gam (a mal´gam) *n.* An alloy of mercury with other metals, as with tin or silver; a blend of diverse elements.

a-mal-ga-mate (a mal´ga māt´) *v.* To mix so as to make a unified whole; to blend. **amalgamation** *n.*

a-man-dine (a man dēn´) *adj.* Made with or garnished with almonds.

am-a-ranth (am´aranth´) *n.* Various weedy plants that have greenish or purplish flowers; an imaginary flower that never fades.

a-mass (a mas´) *v.* To gather a great mass or number of; to accumulate.

am-a-teur (am´a cher´) *n.* One who engages in an activity as a pastime rather than as a profession; one who lacks expertise. **amateurish** *adj.*

am-a-tive (am´a tiv) *adj.* Disposed or

disposing of love; full of love; inclined to love.

am-a-tol (am´a tol´) *n.* An explosive consisting of ammonium nitrate and trinitrotoluene (TNT).

am-a-to-ry (am´a tōr´ē) *adj.* Of or expressive of sexual love.

am-au-ro-sis (am´o rō´sis) *n.* A partial or complete loss of sight due to the loss of power in the optic nerve or retina.

a-maze (amāz´) *v.* To astound; to affect with surprise or wonder. **amazingly** *adv.* **amazedness** *n.* **amazing** *adj.*

a-maze-ment (a māz´ment) *n.* The quality or state of being amazed or astounded.

am-a-zon-ite (am´a zo nīt´) *n.* A semiprecious green variety of microcline found near the Amazon River.

am-bass-a-dor (am bas´a dor) *n.* High ranking official, accredited by one government to another. **ambassadorial** *adj.* **ambassadorship** *n.*

am-ber (am´bèr) *n.* A hard, translucent, yellow, brownish-yellow, or orange fossil resin, used for jewelry and ornaments; medium to dark orange yellow color.

am-ber-gris (am´bèr grēs´) *n.* A waxy, grayish substance produced by sperm whales, and used in making perfumes.

am-bi-dex-trous (am´bi dek´strus) *adj.* Capable of using both the right and left hands with equal facility.

am-bi-ence (am´bēens) *n.* Environment; surrounding atmosphere.

am-bi-ent (am´bē ent) *adj.* Surrounding; on all sides.

am-bi-gu-i-ty (am´bi gū´i tē) *n.* The quality of being obscure or ambiguous.

am-big-u-ous (am big´ū us) *adj.* Doubtful; uncertain, open to interpretation. In computer science, imprecise; of a program command or formula that is stated in such a way that it may yield an undesirable result. **ambiguousness** *n.* **ambiguously** *adv.*

am-bi-tion (am bish´an) *n.* Strong desire to achieve; will to succeed; the goal or object desired.

am-bi-tious (am bish´us) *adj.* Challenging. **ambitiousness** *n.* **ambitiously** *adv.*

am-biv-a-lence (am biv´a lens) *n.* Existence of mutually different feelings about a person or thing.

am-bi-vert (am´bivürt´) *n.* A person having the characteristics of both introvert and extrovert.

am-ble (am´bl) *v.* To move at a leisurely pace. **ambler** *n.*

am-bly-o-pi-a (am´blē ō´pē a) *n.* Dullness or dimness of eyesight without apparent change or defect in the organs.

am-boi-na wood (am boi´na wod) *n.* A curled and mottled wood used in cabinet making.

am-bro-sia (am´brō´zha) n. Food of the Greek Gods and immortals; food having exquisite flavor or fragrance.

am-bu-lance (am´bū lans) n. Vehicle equipped to transport the injured or sick.

am-bu-lant (am´bū lant) adj. To move from one place to another.

am-bu-la-to-ry (am´bū la tōr´ē) n. Any sheltered part of a building intended as a passageway for walking. adj. Moving about; movable; able to walk.

am-bush (am´bush) n. Surprise attack made from a hidden position. **ambush** v. **ambusher** n. **ambushment** n.

ameba or **amoeba** (a mē´ba) n. A minute single-celled, semi-fluid organism of indefinite, changeable form.

a-mel-io-rate (a mēl´yu rāt´) v. To make better or more tolerable; to improve. **ameliorator** n. **ameliorative** adj.

a-men (ā´men´) interj. Used at the end of a prayer to express solemn approval.

a-me-na-bil-i-ty (a mē´na bil´i tē) n. State of being amenable.

a-me-na-ble (a mē´na bl) adj. Responsive; tractable; accountable.

a-mend (a mend´) v. To correct; to improve; to rectify. **amendable** adj.

a-mend-ment (a mend´ment) n. Correction, reformation or improvement; a legislative bill change or the parliamentary procedure where such alteration is made.

a-mends (a mendz´) n. Compensation for insult or injury.

a-men-i-ty (a men´i tē) n. pl. **amenities** Agreeableness; means of comfort or convenience.

a-merce (a murs´) v. To punish by a fine decided by the court.

a-merce-ment (a murs´ment) n. Fine imposed on an offender at the discretion of the court.

am-e-thyst (am´i thist) n. Violet or purple form of transparent corundum or quartz, used as a gemstone.

am-e-tro-pi-a (am´i trō´pē a) n. An abnormal condition of the eye where images fail to focus upon the retina.

a-mi-a-ble (ā´mē abl) adj. Friendly and pleasant. **amiableness** n. **amiability** n. **amiably** adv.

am-i-ca-ble (am´i ka bl) adj. Harmonious; friendly; peaceable. **amicability** n. **amicableness** n. **amicably** adv.

a-mi-cus cu-ri-ae (a mī´kus kūr´ē ē´) n. A professional who is asked for or volunteers information on some matter of law that directly affects a particular case.

a-mid (a mid´) prep. In the middle of; surrounded by, among.

a-mid-ships (a mid´ships) adv. Halfway between the bow and the stern.

a-midst (a midst´) prep. In the middle of; surrounded by; during.

a-mi-go (a mē´gō) n. A friend.

a-miss (a mis´) adj. Out of order or place; in an improper or wrong way.

am-i-ty (am´i tē) n. Relationships that are friendly, as between two states.

am-me-ter (am´mē´tèr) n. A tool measuring electric current.

am-mo (am´ō) n. Ammunition.

am-mo-nia (a mōn´ya) n. Colorless, pungent gas.

ammonium hydroxide n. A colorless, basic aqueous solution of ammonia.

am-ne-sia (am nē´zha) n. The partial or complete loss of memory.

am-nes-ty (am´ni stē) n. pl. **amnesties** Pardon for political offenders.

am-ni-on (am´nē on) n. The innermost membrane that surrounds the fetus of birds, mammals, and reptiles.

a-moe-ba Variant of *ameba*.

a-mong (a mung´) prep. In or through the midst of; between one another.

a-mon-til-la-do (a mon´ti lä´dō) n. A pale, dry, sweet sherry.

a-mor-al (ā mor´al) adj. Neither moral nor immoral. **amorality** n.

am-o-rous (am´ér us) adj. Inclined to or indicative of sexual love.

a-mor-phous (a mor´fus) adj. Lacking definite form; shapeless; general; vague.

am-or-tize (am´ér tīz´) v. To liquidate a loan by installment payments; to repay a loan. **amortization** n.

a-mount (a mount´) n. Aggregate, sum or total quantity. **amount** v. To be equivalent.

a-mour (a mur´) n. A forbidden love affair.

amour–propre n. Self-respect.

am-pe-lop-sis (am´pe lop´sis) n. Any plant having climbing woody vines or shrubs.

am-per-age (am´pér ij) n. Strength of an electric current, expressed in amperes.

am-pere (am´pēr) n. Unit of electric current equal to a flow of one amp per second.

am-pere-turn (am´pēr türn´) n. One complete turn or convolution of a conducting coil, through which one ampere of electric current passes.

am-per-sand (am´pér sand´) n. The character or sign that represents and (&).

am-phet-a-mine (am fet´a mēn´) n. Colorless volatile compound used as a drug.

amphi prefix Around, on both sides, all around on all sides.

am-phib-i-an (am fīb´ē an) n. An organism, as a frog or toad, developing from an aquatic state into an air-breathing state; aircraft that can take off and land on land or water; a vehicle that can move on land or water.

am-phi-bole (am´fi bōl´) *n.* A silicate mineral of varying composition, that usually consists of a magnesium, silicate of calcium, and one or more other metals.

am-phi-pod (am´fi pod´) *n.* One of an order of small crustaceous animals having a laterally compressed body and commonly found in fresh and salt water.

am-phi-the-a-ter (am´fi thē´a tèr) *n.* A round or oval building having tiers of seats rising around an arena.

am-pho-ter-ic (am´fo ter´ik) *adj.* Able to react chemically either as an acid or base.

am-ple (am´pel) *adj.* Sufficient; abundant; large. **ampleness** *n.*

am-pli-dyne (am´pli dīn´) *n.* Direct current generator.

am-pli-fi-ca-tion (am´pli fi kā´shan) *n.* An enlargement; an example or product of amplifying.

am-pli-fi-er (am´pli fī´ér) *n.* That which amplifies or enlarges.

am-pli-fy (am´pli fī´) *v.* To make larger, more extended; to explain in greater detail.

am-pli-tude (am´pli tōd) *n.* Maximum value of a periodically varying quantity; greatness of size; fullness.

am-ply (am´plē) *adv.* In sufficient manner.

am-pul *or* **am-pule** (am´pūl) *n.* A small, sealed vial containing a hypodermic injection solution.

am-pu-tate (am´pū tāt´) *v.* To cut off; to remove, as a limb from one's body.

a-muck (*a* muk´) *adv.* In an uncontrolled manner; a murderous frenzy; out of control.

am-u-let (am´ū lit) *n.* A charm worn as protection against evil or injury.

a-muse (*a* mūz´) *v.* To entertain in an agreeable, pleasing way. **-ment** *n.*

am-yl-ase (am´elās´) *n.* Any of the enzymes that change starch into sugar.

am-y-lol-y-sis (am´e lol´i sis) *n.* The conversion of starch into soluble products.

a-my-o-to-ni-a (ā´mī o tō´nē) *adj.* Deficiency of muscle tone.

an (*an*) *adj.* One; one sort of; each; form of "a" used before words beginning with a vowel or with an unpronounced "h" as in elephant or honor.

a-na (ā´na) *n.* A collection of memorable sayings, information, or anecdotes about a person or place.

a-nach-ro-nism (*a* nak´ro niz˝um) *n.* An error in chronology; connecting of a thing, person or happening with another that came later in history;

anything that is out of place in history; any error which implies the misplacing, usually earlier, of person or events in time.

an-a-co-lu-thic (an´a ko lō´ thik) *adj.* Lacking grammatical sequence; inconsistency within a sentence.

an-a-con-da (an´a kon´ da) *n.* A large tropical South American snake which kills its prey by crushing it to death in its coils.

an-a-dem (an´a dem´) *n.* A wreath for the head.

a-nad-ro-mous (a nad´ro mus) *adj.* Migrating up river from the sea to breed in fresh water, as a salmon.

anaemia *n.* Variant of anemia.

an-aes-the-sia (an´is thē´zha) *n.* Variant of anesthesia.

an-a-gram (an´agram´) *n.* Word formed by transposing the letters of another word. **anagrammatical** *adj.*

a-nal (ān´al) *adj.* Of or relating to the anus.

a-nal-cime (*a* nal´sim) *n.* A white or slightly colored mineral with frequent occurrence in igneous rock masses.

an-a-lects (an´a lekts´) *n.* Selected miscellaneous extracts or small pieces selected from different authors and combined.

an-al-ge-sia (an´al jē´zē a) *n.* Inability to feel pain while awake.

an-al-get-ic (an´al jed´ik) *n.* A remedy or treatment that removes pain.

analog In computer science, description of data represented as a continuous variable, such as sound.

analog computer *n.* A computer which calculates by using physical analogs, where numerical data is represented by measurable quantities as lengths, electrical signals, or voltage.

analog to digital converter In computer science, a device that converts analog data to digital data.

a-nal-o-gous (*a* nal´o gus) *adj.* Similar; corresponding in certain ways.

an-a-logue (an´a log´) *n.* Something that bears resemblance to something else.

a-nal-o-gy (a nal´o jē) *n. pl.* **analogies** Connection between things that are other-wise dissimilar; a conclusion or opinion that if two things are alike in some respects they must be alike in others.

an-al-pha-bet (an al´fa bet) *n.* A person who is totally illiterate; one who cannot read.

a-nal-y-sis (*a* nal´i sis) *n.* Breaking up or separation of something into its parts so as to examine them and see how they fit together; result.

an-a-lyst (an´a list) *n.* A person who analyzes or who is skilled in analysis.

analytic geometry *n.* The study of

geometry properties where procedures of algebraic reasoning are applied.

an-a-lyze (an´a līz´) v. To make an analysis of.

an-am-ne-sis (an´am nē´sis) n. The recalling to mind of things past; recollection; reminiscence.

an-a-pest (an´a pest´) n. Metrical foot make up of two short syllables followed by one long one. **anapestic** adj.

a-naph-o-ra (a naf´or a) n. The repetition of the same word or words at the beginning of two or more successive clauses or verses.

an-a-plas-ty (an´a plas´tē) n. Plastic surgery.

an-arch (an´ärk) n. A leader who excites disorder or revolt.

an-ar-chic (an är´kik) adj. Of, like, or promoting confusion or disorder.

an-ar-chism (an´ar kiz´um) n. Belief that all forms of government act in an unnecessary and unfair way against the liberty of a person and should be done away with.

an-ar-chist (an´ar kist) n. One who rebels with violent revolution against the established order.

an-ar-chy (an´ar kē) n. Lack of political authority, disorder and confusion; the absence of any purpose or standard.

an-as-tig-mat (a nas´tig mat´) n. System of lenses where astigmatic defects are overcome.

a-nas-to-mo-sis (a nas´to mō´sis) n. Connection or union of branches, as of rivers, leaf veins, or blood vessels.

a-nas-tro-phe (a nas´tro fē) n. Changing the normal syntactic order of words.

a-nath-e-ma (a nath´a ma) n. Curse; ban; or excommunication.

a-nath-e-ma-tize (a nath´e ma tīz) v. To curse; to ban.

a-nat-o-mist (a nat´o mist) n. A person who is skilled in dissection; one who analyzes critically.

a-nat-o-mize (a nat´o miz´) v. To examine in great detail; to analyze; in biology, to cut in pieces for the purpose of displaying or examining the structure.

a-nat-o-my (a nat´o mē) n. pl. anatomies The branch of morphology dealing with the structure of an organ or organism; a detailed analysis; the art of dissecting or artificially separating the different parts of an organized body, to discover their situation, structure, and function. **anatomical** adj. **anatomic** adj.

an-ces-tor (an´ses tèr) n. A person who comes before one in a family line; someone earlier than a grandparent; forefather. **ancestral** adj.

an-cho-ret (ang´kèr it) or **an-cho-rite** (ang´kè rīt´) n. A hermit; a recluse; one living in seclusion for religious

reasons.

anchor man n. The managing newscaster who coordinates the reports of other participants in a newscast or in live coverage of a news event.

an-cien ré-gime (on sē´an rā jēm´) n. Ancient or old system of government; system no longer prevailing.

an-cient (ān´shent) adj. Anything belonging to the early history of people; very old. **ancientness** n.

an-con (ang´kon) n. The upper end of the ulna or elbow; an architectural support, as a bracket or projection.

and (and) conj. Together with; along with; as well as; added to; as a result; plus; also.

an-dan-te (an dan´tē) adv. Mus. Rather slow in tempo. **andante** adj.

an-dan-ti-no (an´dan tē´nō) adj. Mus. Slightly faster in tempo than andante.

an-des-ite (an´di zīt´) n. A dark grayish rock consisting mostly of feldspar.

and-i-ron (and´ī èrn) n. Heavy metal support for logs or wood in a fireplace.

andr n. The male sex; masculine.

an-dro-gen (an´dro jen) n. Hormone that develops and maintains masculine characteristics. **androgenic** adj.

an-droid (an´droyd) n. In science fiction, a synthetic man made to look like a human.

an-ec-dote (an´ik dōt´) n. Short account of a story of some happening or about some person. **anecdotal** adj. **anecdotic** adj. **anecdotist** n.

an-e-cho-ic (an´e kō´ik) adj. Neither having nor producing echoes.

a-ne-mi-a (a nē´mē a) n. The condition in which a person's blood does not have enough red corpuscles or hemoglobin and, therefore, does not carry a normal amount of oxygen.

a-ne-mic (a nē´mik) adj. Of or having anemia.

an-e-mom-e-ter (an´e mom´i tèr) n. Instrument for measuring wind force and speed.

an-e-moph-i-lous (an´emof´i lus) adj. Wind-pollinated.

a-nem-o-scope (a nem´o skōp´) n. A device that indicates the direction of the wind.

a-nent (a nent´) prep. Regarding; concerning.

an-er-oid (an´e roid) adj. Capability to function without fluid.

an-es-the-sia (an´is thē´zha) n. Condition in which one has no feeling of heat, touch, or pain in all or part of the body.

an-es-the-si-ol-o-gy (an´is thē´zē ol o´ jē) n. The medical study and use of anesthetics. **anesthesiologist** n.

an-es-thet-ic (an´is thet´ik) adj. Taking away the feeling of pain. **anesthetic** n. Drug, gas, or substance used to bring on anesthesia before surgery.

an-es-the-tize (*a* nes´thi tīz´) *v.* To bring on unconsciousness by giving anesthetics; to remove the capacity to feel pain in a localized area.

an-eu-rysm (an´yu riz´um) *n.* A dilation of a blood vessel or artery, that is due to the pressure of blood acting on a part weakened by disease or injury.

a-new (*a* nō´) *adv.* Again; once more; in a new way.

an-gel (ān´jel) *n.* An immortal being attendant upon God; a very kind and lovable person; a helping or guiding spirit.

an-ger (ang´gėr) *n.* Feeling of extreme hostility; rage; wanting to fight back.

an-gi-na (an jī´na) *n.* A disease marked by painful choking spasms and attacks of suffocation pain. **anginous** *adj.* **anginose** *adj.* **anginal** *adj.*

an-gi-na pec-to-ris (an jī´na pek´to ris) *n.* Severe pain in the chest, associated with feelings of apprehension and suffocation.

an-gi-ol-o-gy (an´jē ol´o jē) *n.* The study of blood vessels and lymphatics.

an-gle (ang´gl) *n.* A shape made from two straight lines meeting in a point or two surfaces meeting along a line.

an-gli-cize (ang´gli sīz´) *v.* To make English in form, idiom, or character.

an-gling (ang´gling) *n.* The act of fishing with a hook and line.

an-go-ra (an gōr´a) *n.* The long silky hair of the Angora rabbit or Angora goat; yarn or fabric made from the hair of an Angora goat or rabbit.

an-gri-ly (aŋ´gri lē) *adv.* To threaten in an angry manner.

an-gry (aŋ´grē) *adj.* Feeling or showing anger; having a menacing aspect; inflamed.

an-gu-lar (aŋ´gū lėr) *adj.* Having angles or sharp corners; measured by an angle or degrees of an arc; forming an angle; gaunt, bony, lean. **angularity** *n.*

an-hy-dride (an hī´drid) *n.* Chemical compound formed from another by removing the water.

an-hy-drous (an hī´drus) *adj.* Does not contain any water.

an-i-line (an´i lin) *n.* Colorless, oily, poisonous liquid, used to make rubber, dyes, resins, pharmaceuticals, and varnishes.

an-i-mad-vert (an´i mad vürt´) *v.* To make an ill-natured or unfair criticism. **animadversion** *n.* A critical remark.

an-i-mal (an´i mal) *n.* Any being other than a human being; any four-footed creature; beast. **animalize** *v.*

an-i-mate (an´i māt´) *v.* To give liveliness, life or spirit to; to cause to act; to inspire. **animation** *n.*

a-ni-ma-to (ä´ni mä´tō) *adv. Mus.* In a

lively or animated manner; used as a direction.

an-i-ma-tor (an *e* māter) *n.* One who animates, such as an artist or technician who produces an animation, as a cartoon or movie film.

an-i-mé (an´i mā´) *n.* Resin that is exuded from a large tropical tree from which varnish, lacquers, and flavorings are produced.

an-i-mism (an´i miz´um) *n.* A belief in primitive tribes that natural objects and forces have souls. **animist** *n.*

an-i-mos-i-ty (an´i mos´i tē) *n. pl.* **animosities** Hostility; bitterness; hatred.

an-i-mus (an´o mus) *n.* Feeling of animosity.

an-i-on (an´ī´on) *n.* An ion with a negative charge that is attracted to an anode; electrolysis.

an-ise (an´is) *n.* A plant with yellowish-white flower clusters and licorice-flavored seeds.

an-i-seed (an´i sēd´) *n.* Seed used for flavoring and in medicine.

an-i-sette (an´i set´) *n.* Anise-flavored liqueur.

an-kle (ang´kl) *n.* Joint that connects the foot with the leg; slender section of the leg immediately above this joint.

an-ky-lo-sis (ang´ki lo´sis) *n.* Stiffness, fixation or immovability of a joint, due to a disease or as a result of surgery.

an-la-ge (än´lä ge) *n.* The first recognizable accumulation of cells in a developing organ or part.

an-nals (an´alz) *n. pl.* Descriptive record; history. **annalist** *n.*

an-nat-to (*a* nat´ō) *n.* The red dye made from the pulp from around the seeds of a small tropical American tree.

an-neal (*a* nēl´) *v.* To heat and then cool glass slowly to make it less brittle.

an-nex (*a* neks´) *v.* To add or join a small thing to a larger one. **annexation** *n.*

an-ni-hi-late (*a* nī´i lāt´) *v.* To destroy completely; totally. **annihilator** *n.*

an-ni-ver-sa-ry (an *i* vür´sa rē) *n., pl.* **anniversaries** The date on which something happened at an earlier time; this event celebrated on this date each year.

an-no-tate (an´ō tāt´) *v.* To use notes to give one's opinions. **annotator** *n.*

an-no-ta-tion (an´ō tā´shan) *n.* Critical note on some passage of a book.

an-nounce (*a* nouns´) *v.* To proclaim; to give notice.

an-noy (*a* noi´) *v.* To bother; to irritate; to make slightly angry.

an-nu-al (an´ū al) *adj.* Recurring or done at the same time each year; a yearly publication, as a yearbook.

an-nu-i-ty (*a* nō´i tē) *n. pl.* **annuities** Annual payment of an income or allowance.

an-nul (*a* nul´) *v.* To cancel a marriage or a law; to do away with; to put an end to. **annullable** *adj.* **annulment** *n.*

an-nu-lar (an´yu lẽr) *adj.* Shaped like or forming a ring. **annularly** *adv.*

an-nun-ci-ate (*a* nun´sē āt´) *v.* To proclaim; to announce.

an-nun-ci-a-tion (*a* nun´sē ā´shan) *n.* The act of announcing or being announced; an announcement.

an-ode (an´ōd) *n.* Positively charged electrode. **anodic** *adj.* **anodically** *adv.*

an-o-dize (an´o dīz´) *v.* To coat a metallic surface by electrolysis with a protective oxide.

a-noint (*a* noint´) *v.* To apply oil in a religious ceremony. **anointment** *n.*

a-nom-a-ly (*a* nom´a lē) *n., pl.* **anomalies** Anything irregular or abnormal.

a-non (*a* non´) *adv.* Soon; in a short period of time.

a-non-y-mous (*a* non´i mus) *adj.* An unknown or withheld name, agency, lacking a name. **anonymity** *n.*

a-no-rak (ä´no räk) *n.* Parka; a hooded jacket.

an-o-rex-i-a (an´o rek´sē a) *n.* The loss of appetite that is accompanied by psychotic symptoms.

an-os-mi-a (an oz´mē a) *adj.* The loss or deficiency of the sense of smell.

an-oth-er (*a* nuth´ẽr) *adj.* Additional; one more different, but of the same character.

an-ox-i-a (an ok´sē a) *n.* Lack of oxygen supply in the body tissue and the complications that result from this lack of oxygen.

an-swer (an´sẽr) *n.* A written or spoken reply, as to a question; a result or solution, as to a problem. **answer** *v.* To respond; to be responsible for.

an-tag-o-nism (an tag´o niz´um) *n.* Hostility; condition of being against; the feeling of unfriendliness toward.

an-tag-o-nize (an tag´o nīz´) *v.* To arouse hostility; to make an enemy of someone.

ant-arc-tic (ant ärk´tik) *n.* Large area of land completely covered with ice; the South Pole. **antarctic** *adj.*

antarctic circle *n.* An imaginary line parallel to the equator that encircles the antarctic area.

an-te-cede (an´ti sēd´) *v.* To go before; to precede in time.

an-te-ce-dent (an´ti sēd´ent) *adj.* One event that precedes another; previous.

an-te-date (an´ti dāt´) *v.* To precede in time; to give an earlier date than the actual date.

ante meridiem *n.* Time before noon, abbreviated as *a.m.*

an-ten-na (an ten´a) *n.* Feelers on the head of an insect, lobster, crab, etc.;

wire or set of wires used in radio and television to send and receive signals.

an-te-ri-or (an tēr´ē or) *adj.* Toward or at the front; coming before; earlier.

an-them (an´them) *n.* Hymn of praise or loyalty; an official song of a country, school, etc.

an-ther (an´thẽr) *n.* The part of the flower where the pollen is located at the end of a stamen.

an-thol-o-gy (an thol´o jē) *n.* A collection of stories, poems, or other writings.

an-thra-cite (an´thra sīt´) *n.* Coal with a high carbon content; hard coal.

an-thrax (an´thraks) *n.* The infectious, usually fatal disease found in animals such as cattle and sheep; disease that can be transmitted to man.

an-throp-ic (an throp´ik) *adj.* Relating to man, or to the period of mankind's existence on earth.

an-thro-po-cen-tric (an´thro pō sen´trik) *adj.* To interpret reality in terms of human experience and values.

an-ti (an´tī) *n.* One who opposes a group, policy, practice, or proposal.

an-ti-anx-i-ety (an´tī an̗´zī et ē) *adj.* Preventing or relieving anxiety.

an-ti-bi-ot-ic (an´tī bī ot´ik) *n.* A substance, as streptomycin or penicillin, effective in the destruction of microorganisms and used widely to prevent or treat diseases.

an-ti-bod-y (an´tī bod´ē) *n.* Substances generated in the blood that react to foreign proteins or carbohydrates, producing immunity against certain microorganisms or their toxins.

an-tic (an´tik) *n.* Mischievous caper or act.

an-tic-i-pate (an tis´i pāt) *v.* To look forward; to act in advance of; to foresee. **anticipatory** *adj.*

an-tic-i-pa-tion (an tis´i pā´shan) *n.* The act of looking forward; expectation of a future event.

an-ti-cli-max (an´tī klī´maks) *n.* A letdown or decline; a commonplace conclusion; a series of significant events followed by a trivial event.

an-ti-co-ag-u-lant (an´tē kō ag´ū lant) *n.* Any agent which hinders the coagulation of the blood.

an-ti-dote (an´ti dōt´) *n.* A substance that counteracts an injury or poison.

an-ti-gen (an´ti jen) *n.* Substance, when introduced into the body, stimulates the production of antibodies.

an-ti-his-ta-mine (an´tī his´ta mēn´) *n.* A drug used to relieve the symptoms of allergies and colds by interfering with the production of histamines.

an-ti-ox-i-dant (an´tē ok´si dant) *n.* A substance that inhibits oxidation.

an-ti-par-ti-cle (an´tē pär´ti kal) *n.*

Identically matched atomic particles, but with exactly opposite electrically charged magnetic properties and spin.

an-tip-a-thy (an tĭp´a thē) *n., pl.* **antipathies** Feeling of repugnance or opposition. **antipathetic** *adj.*

an-ti-per-spi-rant (an tĭ per´spe rent) *n.* Substance applied to the underarm to reduce excessive perspiration.

an-ti-phlo-gis-tic (an´tē flŏ jĭs´tĭk) *n.* A medicine which counteracts inflammation.

an-ti-pode (an´tĭ pŏd´) *n.* A direct opposite. **antipodal** *adj.*

an-ti-pro-ton (an´tē prō´ton) *n.* The antiparticle of a proton.

an-ti-quar-y (an´tĭ kwer´ē) *n.* A person devoted to the study of rare relics.

an-ti-quate (an´tĭ kwāt´) *v.* To make old, obsolete or outdated by substituting something new or more practical.

an-ti-quat-ed (an´tĭ kwā´tĭd) *adj.* Obsolete; out of style; behind the times.

an-tique (an tēk´) *adj.* Belonging to or of ancient times. *n.* An object that is over 100 years old. **antique** *v.*

an-ti-sep-sis (an´tĭ sep´sĭs) *n.* Condition of being free from pathogenic bacteria.

an-ti-sep-tic (an´tĭ sep´tĭk) *adj.* Pertaining or capable of producing antisepsis; thoroughly clean.

an-tith-e-sis (an tĭth´i sĭs) *n., pl.* **antitheses** Direct opposition or contrast. **antithetical** *adj.*

an-ti-tox-ic (an´tĭ tok´sĭk) *adj.* Counteracting poisons or toxic influences.

an-ti-tox-in (an´tĭ tok´sĭn) *n.* An antibody formed in the body, capable of neutralizing a specific toxin or infective agent used to produce immunity against infectious diseases.

an-ti-trust (an´tē trust´) *adj.* Having to do with the regulation of trusts, monopolies, and cartels.

an-ti-tus-sive (an´tĭ tus´ĭv) *adj.* Capable of controlling or preventing a cough.

an-ti-ven-in (an´tē ven´ĭn) *n.* An antitoxin to a venom, produced by repeated injections of such venom.

anti-virus *n.* In *computer science*, a program designed to detect unauthorized alteration of a computer program.

an-ti-viv-i-sec-tion-ist (an´tē vĭv ĭ sek´shan ist) *n.* A person opposed to experiments on living animals.

an-to-nym (an´to nĭm) *n.* A word opposite in meaning to another word.

a-nus (ā´nus) *n.* The lower opening of the alimentary canal.

an-vil (an´vĭl) *n.* A heavy block of steel or iron on which metal is formed.

anx-i-e-ty (ang zī´i tē) *n.* A state of uncertainty; disturbance of the mind regarding uncertain events.

anx-ious (angk´shus) *adj.* Troubled in mind or worried about some uncertain

matter or event. **anxiousness** *n.*

an-y (en´ē) *adj.* One; no matter which; some; every; any quantity or part.

an-y-bo-dy (en´ē bod´ē) *pron.* Anyone; any person.

an-y-how (en´ē hou´) *adv.* By any means; in any way; whatever.

an-y-more (en´ē mōr´) *adv.* At present and from now on.

an-y-one (en´ē wun´) *pron.* Any person; anybody.

an-y-place (en´ē plās´) *adv.* Anywhere.

an-y-thing (en´ē thĭng´) *pron.* Any occurrence, object or matter.

an-y-time (en ē tĭm) *adv.* At any time whatever.

an-y-way (en´ē wā´) *adv.* Nevertheless; anyhow; in any manner; carelessly.

an-y-where (en´ē hwâr´) *adv.* In, at, or to any place; to any degree or extent.

a-or-ta (ā or´ta) *n.* Main artery that carries blood away from the heart and distributes blood to all of the body except the lungs. **aortal** *adj.* **aortic** *adj.*

a-pace (a pās´) *adv.* At a rapid or quick pace.

a-part (a pärt´) *adv.* Separate; at a distance; in pieces; to pieces.

a-part-heid (a pärt´hāt) *n.* In the Republic of South Africa, an obsolete policy of discrimination and segregation against non-whites.

a-part-ment (a pärt´ment) *n.* A suite or room in a building equipped for individual living.

ap-a-thy (ap´a thē) *n.* The lack of emotions or feelings. **apathetic** *adj.*

ap-er-ture (ap´ér chér) *n.* An opening or open space; a mouth, hole, a passage.

a-pex (ā´peks) *n. pl.* **apexes** *or* **apices** The highest point; tip; top.

a-pha-sia (a fā´zha) *n.* Any partial or total loss of the ability to express ideas, resulting from brain damage. **aphasiac** *n.* **aphasic** *adj.* **aphasic** *n.*

a-phe-li-on (a fē´lē on) *n.* The point in an orbit farthest from the sun.

a-pho-ni-a (ā fō´nē a) *n.* A loss of voice to a whisper.

aph-o-rism (af´o rĭz˝um) *n.* Brief statement of truth or principal.

a-pho-tic (ā fō´tĭk) *adj.* Without light.

aph-ro-dis-i-ac (af´ro dĭz´ē ak´) *adj.* Increasing or arousing the sexual desire or potency.

a-pi-ar-y (ā´pēer´ē) *n.* Place where bees are kept and raised for their honey.

ap-i-cal (ap´i kal) *adj.* Relating to or formed with the tip of a tongue; belonging to the pointed end of a cone-shaped body.

a-pi-cul-ture (ā´pi kul´chér) *n.* The keeping of bees; beekeeping.

a-piece (a pēs´) *adv.* For or to each one.

a-pla-sia (a plā´zha) *n.* Defective development of a tissue or organ.

a-plomb (*a* plom´) *n.* Assurance; poise; self-confidence.

a-poc-o-pe (*a* pok´*o* pē) *n.* The loss of the last of one or more sounds, letters, or syllables at the end of a word.

a-poc-ry-phal (*a* pok´ri fal) *adj.* False; of questionable authenticity.

ap-o-gee (ap´*o* jē) *n.* The point most distant from earth in the moon's orbit.

ap-o-graph (ap´*o* graf) *n.* A transcript or copy, as a manuscript.

a-pol-it-i-cal (ā po lit´i kal) *adj.* Having no interest in or involvement in politics.

a-pol-o-get-ic (*a* pol´*o* jet´ik) *adj.* Making an expression of apology. **apologetical** *adj.* **apologetically** *adv.*

a-pol-o-gist (*a* pol´*o* jist) *n.* A person who speaks in defense of a cause, faith or an institution.

a-pol-o-gize (*a* pol´*o* jīz´) *v.* To make an apology.

a-pol-o-gy (*a* pol´*o* jē) *n., pl.* **apologies** A statement expressing regret for an action or fault; a formal justification or defense.

a-poph-y-sis (*a* pof´i sis) *n.* An expanded or projecting part of a bone.

ap-o-plex-y (ap´*o* plek´sē) *n.* Sudden loss of muscular control, consciousness, and sensation resulting from a blockage of the blood vessel in the brain.

a-port (*a* pōrt´) *adv. Naut.* To the left side of a ship.

ap-o-si-o-pe-sis (ap´*o* sī´*o* pē´sis) *n.* Sudden stopping short and leaving a thought or statement unfinished for the sake of effect.

a-pos-tate (*a* pos´tāt) *n.* One who forsakes his faith or principles.

a-pos-ta-tize (*a* pos´ta tīz´) *v.* To abandon religious faith, principles, or party. **apostasy** *n.*

a-pos-te-ri-o-ri (ā´po stēr´ē ōr´ī) *adj.* Inductive; reasoning from facts to principles or from effect to cause.

a-pos-tro-phe (*a* pos´tro fē) *n.* The mark (´) used to indicate the removal of letters or figures, the plural of letters or figures, and the possessive case; the act of turning away; addressing the usually absent person or a usually personified thing rhetorically.

a-pos-tro-phize (*e*´päs tre fīz) *v.* To make use of apostrophe.

a-poth-e-car-y (*a* poth´e ker´ē) *n., pl.* **apothecaries** A person who prepares and sells drugs for medical uses; a druggist; pharmacist; drugstore.

a-po-the-ci-um (*a*´ po *e* thē´ shē em) *n.* A single-celled structure in many lichens and fungi that consists of a cupped body bearing asci on the exposed flat or concave surface.

ap-o-thegm (ap´*o* them´) *n.* A short, essential, and instructive formulation or saying. **apothegmatic** *adj.*

a-po-the-o-sis (*a* poth´ē ō´sis) *n.* The perfect example; the glorification of a person. **apotheosize** *v.*

ap-pall (*a* pol´) *v.* To overcome by shock or dismay; to overpower with fear; to become pale.

ap-pall-ing (*a* pol´ing) *adj.* Disgusting; dismay or disgust caused by an event or a circumstance. **appallingly** *adv.*

ap-pa-ra-tus (ap´*a* rat´us) *n., pl.* **apparatuses** Appliance or an instrument designed and used for a specific operation.

ap-par-el (*a* par´el) *v.* To dress or put on clothing; to adorn or embellish. **apparel** *n.* Clothing. *Naut.* The sails and rigging of a ship.

ap-par-ent (*a* par´ent) *adj.* Clear and opened to the eye and mind; open to view, visible. **apparently** *adv.*

ap-pa-ri-tion (ap´*a* rish´an) *n.* An unusual or unexpected appearance; the act of being visible; a ghostly figure.

ap-par-i-tor (*a* par´i tor) *n.* An official person sent to carry out the order of a judge, court, or magistrate.

ap-peal (*a* pēl´) *n.* Power to arouse a sympathetic response; an earnest plea; a legal proceeding where a case is brought from a lower court to a higher court for a rehearing. **appeal** *v.* To make a request; to ask another person for corroboration, vindication, or decision on a matter of importance.

ap-pear (*a* pēr´) *v.* To come into existence; to come into public view; to come formally before an authorized person.

ap-pear-ance (*a* pēr´ans) *n.* The action or process of appearing; an outward indication or showing.

ap-pease (apēz´) *v.* To give peace; to cause to stop or subside; to calm; to pacify. **appeasement** *n.*

ap-pel-late (*a* pel´it) *adj.* Having the power to hear and review the decisions of the lower courts.

ap-pel-la-tion (ap´*e* lā´shan) *n.* Identifying by a name or title.

ap-pend (*a* pend´) *v.* To add an appendix or supplement, as to a book; to attach.

ap-pend-age (*a* pen´dij) *n.* Something added to something more important or larger; a subordinate or a dependent person.

ap-pen-di-ci-tis (*a* pen´di sī´tis) *n.* Inflammation of the vermiform appendix.

ap-pen-dix (*a* pen´diks) *n., pl.* **appendixes** Supplementary material usually found at the end of something that has been written; *Med.* A small hollow blind process; the vermiform appendix.

ap-per-ceive (ap´ẽr sēv) *v.* To be conscious of perceiving; to have apperception of something.

ap-per-cep-tion (ap´ér sep´shan) *n*. The mental understanding of something perceived in terms of previous experience. **apperceptively** *adv*. **apperceptive** *adj*.

ap-per-tain (ap´ér tān´) *v*. To belong to or connect with, as a rightful part.

ap-pe-tence (ap´i tens) *n*. Appetite; a strong natural craving.

ap-pe-tite (ap´i tīt´) *n*. The craving or desire for food. **appetitive** *adj*.

ap-plaud (*a* plod´) *v*. To express or show approval by clapping the hands.

ap-plause (*a* ploz´) *n*. The expression of public approval. **applausive** *adj*.

ap-ple (ap´l) *n*. The round, red, yellow, or green edible fruit of a tree.

ap-pli-ance (*a* plī ans) *n*. A piece of equipment or device designed for a particular use.

ap-pli-ca-ble (ap´li ka bl) *adj*. Appropriate; suitable; capable of being applied.

ap-pli-cant (ap´li kant) *n*. A person who applies for a job or position.

ap-pli-ca-tion (ap li kā´shan) *n*. The act of putting something to use; the act of superimposing or administering; request or petition; in *computer science*, a program designed for a particular use, as a word processor or spreadsheet.

application generator *n*. In *computer science*, a program feature to assist in creating custom designed applications.

ap-pli-ca-tive (ap´li kā tiv) *adj*. Practical; applied; having an application.

ap-pli-ca-tor (ap´li kā tor) *n*. A device used to apply a substance.

ap-plied *adj*. Putting something to practical use to solve definite problems.

ap-ply (*a* plī´) *v*. To make a request using a written application; to put into use for a practical purpose or reason; to put into operation or to bring into action; to employ with close attention.

ap-point (*a* point´) *v*. To arrange something; to fix or set officially; designate. **appointed** *adj*.

ap-point-ment (*a* point´ment) *n*. The act of appointing; arrangement for a meeting; a nonelective position or office; an engagement or meeting.

ap-por-tion (*a* pōr´han) *v*. To divide and share according to a plan or agreement.

ap-pose (*a* pōz´) *v*. To place next to another; to put before. **apposable** *adj*.

ap-po-site (ap´o zit) *adj*. Highly appropriate or pertinent; applicable.

ap-po-si-tion (ap´o zish´an) *n*. A grammatical construction where a noun or noun phrase is followed by another; the explanatory equivalent.

ap-pos-i-tive (*a* poz´i tiv) *adj*. Relating to or standing in apposition.

ap-prais-al (*a* prā´z al) *n*. The evaluation of property by an authorized person.

ap-praise (*a* prāz´) *v*. To estimate the value, worth, or status of an item.

ap-prais-er (*a* prāz´ér) *n*. One who gives an expert judgment of the value of something.

ap-pre-ci-ate (*a* prē´shē āt´) *v*. To recognize the worth, quality, or significance; to value very highly; to be aware of; to realize; to increase in price or value. **appreciatory** *adj*.

ap-pre-ci-a-tion (*a* prē´shē ā´shan) *n*. The expression of admiration, gratitude, or approval; increase in value.

ap-pre-cia-tive (*a* prē´sha tiv) *adj*. Having or showing appreciation.

ap-pre-hend (ap´ri hend´) *v*. To anticipate with anxiety, dread or fear; to recognize the meaning of; to grasp; to understand.

ap-pren-tice (*a* pren´tis) *n*. One who is learning a trade, art, or occupation under a skilled worker for a prescribed period of time. **apprentice** *v*. To work under supervision of a skilled worker.

ap-pressed (*a* prest´) *adj*. Pressed close to or lying flat against.

ap-prise (*a* prīz´) *v*. To give notice, to inform in verbal or written form.

ap-proach (*a* prōch´) *v*. To come near to or draw closer; to be close in appearance. **approach** *n*. Access to or reaching something.

ap-pro-bate (ap´robāt´) *v*. To express approval, or satisfaction of; to approve.

ap-pro-ba-tion (ap´ro bā´shan) *n*. A formal approval.

ap-pro-pri-ate (*a* prō´prēāt´) *v*. To take possession of; to take without permission. **appropriate** *adj*. Suitable for a use or occasion; fitting. **appropriately** *adv*. **appropriator** *n*.

ap-pro-pri-a-tion (*a* prō´prē ā´shan) *n*. Money set apart for a particular use; the act or instance of appropriating.

ap-prov-able (*a* prōv´a bl) *adj*. Something or someone that is capable of being approved. **approvably** *adv*.

ap-prove (*a* prōv´) *v*. To regard or express a favorable opinion; to give formal or official approval.

ap-prox-i-mate (*a* prok´si māt´) *adj*. Located close together; almost accurate or exact. **approximate** *v*. To bring close or near to; approach; estimate; be nearly the same. **approximately** *adv*.

ap-prox-i-ma-tion (*a* prok´si mā´sh an) *n*. An approximate amount or estimate.

ap-pur-te-nance (*a* pür´te nans) *n*. Something that belongs with another more important thing.

ap-pur-te-nant (*a* per´te nant) *adj*. Constituting a legal attachment; belonging.

a-prax-ia (*a* prak´sē a) *n*. Inability to execute complex coordinated movement. **apraxic** *adj*. **apraxic** *adj*.

a-pri-cot (ap´ri kot´) *n*. An oval,

orange-colored fruit resembling the peach and plum in flavor, varying in color, normally a medium orange.

A-pril (ā´pril) *n*. The fourth month of the calendar year.

a-pri-o-ri (ā´prī ōr´ī) *adj*. Based on theory rather than personal experience; deductive.

a-pron (ā´prŏn) *n*. A garment used to protect clothing; paved area around an airport terminal building or hangar; waterfront edge of a wharf or pier.

ap-ro-pos (ap´ro pō´) *adv*. At a good time; by the way; pertinent.

apse (aps) *n*. A semicircular or polygonal projection of a building or church.

apt (apt) *adj*. Unusually qualified or fitting; appropriate; having a tendency; suitable; quick to understand. **-ly** *adv*.

ap-ti-tude (ap´ti tŏd´) *n*. A natural talent or ability; quickness in learning or understanding.

aq-ua (ak´wa) *n*., *pl*. **aquae** *or* **aquas** Water; aquamarine.

aq-ua-ma-rine (ak´wa ma rēn´) *n*. A color of pale blue to light green; a mineral that is blue, blue-green, or green in color.

aq-ua pu-ra (ak´wa pū´ro) *n*. Pure water; distilled water.

aqua regia (ak´wa rē´jē a) *n*. Mixture of hydrochloric and nitric acids that dissolves platinum or gold.

a-quar-i-um (a kwâr´ē um) *n*. An artificial pond where living plants and aquatic animals are maintained.

a-quat-ic (a kwat´ik) *adj*. Anything occurring on or in the water.

aq-ua vi-tae (ak´wa vī´tē) *n*. A very strong liquor; alcohol.

aq-ue-duct (ak´wi dukt´) *n*. A conduit for carrying a large quantity of flowing water; a bridge-like structure supporting a canal over a river.

aq-ue-ous (ā´kwē us) *adj*. Resembling water; dissolved in water; watery.

aqueous humor *n*. The clear fluid in the chamber of the eye between the cornea and lens.

aq-ui-cul-ture *or* **aq-ua-cul-ture** (ak´wi kul´chĕr) *n*. Breeding fish or produce in natural water; hydroponics.

aq-ui-fer (ak´wi fĕr) *n*. The layer of underground gravel, sand, or rocks where water collects.

aq-ui-line (ak´wi lĭn´) *adj*. Resembling or related to an eagle; hooked or curved like the beak on an eagle.

a-quiv-er (a kwiv er) *adj*. Trembling.

ar-a-besque (ar´a besk´) *n*. An intricate style or design of interwoven leaves, flowers, and geometric forms.

ar-a-ble (ar´a bl) *adj*. Land that is suitable for cultivation by plowing.

a-rach-nid (a rak´nid) *n*. Arthropod that is usually air-breathing, having four

pairs of legs but no antennae; a mite, a spider or scorpions. **arachnid** *adj*.

a-rach-noid (arak´noid) *adj*. Having a covering of loose hair or fibers resembling a spider web.

a-ra-ne-id (a rā´nē id) *n*. A breed of spider.

ar-bi-ter (är´bi tĕr) *n*. A person chosen to decide a dispute, having absolute power of determining and judging.

ar-bi-tra-ble (är´bi tra bl) *adj*. Subject to arbitration.

ar-bi-trar-y (är´bi trer´ē) *adj*. Something based on whim or impulse. **arbitrarily** *adv*. **arbitrariness** *n*.

ar-bi-tra-tion (är´bi trā´shan) *n*. The hearing and determination of a case in controversy, by a person or persons chosen by the parties.

ar-bi-tra-tor (är´bi trā´tor) *n*. A person chosen to settle a dispute or controversy between parties.

ar-bor (är´bor) *n*. A garden shelter that is shady and covered with or made of climbing plants.

Arbor Day *n*. A day assigned as a day for planting trees.

ar-bo-re-al (är bōr´ē al) *adj*. Resembling or related to a tree; living in trees or among trees. **arboreally** *adv*.

ar-bo-re-ous (är bōr´ē us) *adj*. Living in a wooded area; an area surrounded by trees.

ar-bo-re-tum (är´bo rē´tum) *n*. A place for studying and exhibiting trees, shrubs, and plants cultivated for educational and for scientific purposes.

ar-bor-ist (är bo rest) *n*. A specialist in the maintenance and care of trees.

ar-bo-rize (är bo rīz) *v*. To branch repeatedly and freely.

ar-bo-vi-rus (är bo ´vi res) *n*. Various viruses transmitted by arthropods, including the causative agents for yellow fever and encephalitis.

arc (ärk) *n*. Something that is curved or arched; the luminous discharge of electric current across a gap between two electrodes.

ar-cade (är kād´) *n*. An arched covered passageway supported by columns; a long arched gallery or building.

ar-cad-ed (är kād´ed) *adj*. Furnished with arcades or arches.

ar-ca-dia (är kā´dē a) *n*. The ancient Greek area usually chosen as background for poetry; region of simple quiet and pleasure.

ar-cane (är kān´) *adj*. Secret; hidden; obscure.

arch (ärch) *n*. A structure that spans over an open area and gives support. **archly** *adv*. **archness** *n*.

ar-chae-ol-o-gy (är´kē ol´o jē) *n*. Scientific study of ancient times and ancient peoples. **archaeological** *adj*.

ar-cha-ic (är kā´ik) *adj.* Something that belongs to an earlier time; any word characteristic of an earlier language, now used only in special cases.

ar-cha-ism (är´kē iz´um) *n.* Something that is outdated or old-fashioned, as an expression or word. **archaistic** *adj.*

arch-er (är´chér) *n.* A person who is trained in the uses or skill of the bow and arrow.

ar-cher-y (är´che rē) *n.* The practice or art of shooting with a bow and arrow; the equipment used by an archer.

ar-che-spore (är´ki spōer) *n.* A single cell or group of cells from which a mother spore is formed.

ar-che-type (är´ki tīp´) *n.* An original from which other things are patterned.

arch-fiend (ärch´fēnd´) *n.* A chief or principal fiend; a person of great wickedness, especially Satan.

ar-chi-pel-a-go (är´ki pel´a gō´) *n.* Any water space scattered with many islands; a group of islands.

ar-chi-tect (är´ki tekt´) *n.* A person who may plan, design, and supervise the construction of large structures.

ar-chi-tec-ture (är´ki tek´chér) *n.* The science of designing and building structures; a method or style of construction or building; in *computer science*, the design of a computer that defines such things as type of processor, speed, bus size, etc.

ar-chives (är´kīv) *n.* Public documents or records; the place where archives are kept. **archival** *adj.* **archivist** *n.*

arch-way (ärch´wā´) *n.* A passage or way under an arch; an arch over a passage.

arc lamp *n.* Electric lamp which produces light when a current passes between two incandescent electrodes.

arc-tic (ärk´tik) *adj.* Extremely cold or frigid; relating to the territory north of the arctic circle. **arctic** *n.* A waterproof, ankle-length boot.

arctic circle *n.* Parallel of the latitude that is approximately 66.5 degrees north of the equator.

ar-dor (är´dér) *n.* Extreme warmth or passion; emotion; intense heat.

ar-du-ous (är´jū us) *adj.* Taking much effort to bring forth; difficult.

are (är) *v.* First, second, and third person plural and second person singular of the verb "to be."

ar-e-a (âr´ē a) *n.* A flat or level piece of ground. **areal** *adj.*

ar-e-a code (â´ē a) *n.* The three digit number assigned to each telephone area in the United States, used to call.

ar-e-a-way (âr´ē a wā´) *n.* A sunken space that offers access, light and air to a basement; a sunken area forming a passageway to a basement.

a-re-na (a rē´na) *n.* Enclosed area for public entertainment such as football.

ar-e-na-ceous (ar´e nā´shus) *adj.* Having the properties of sand.

aren't (ärnt) *contr.* Are not.

ar-gon (är´gon) *n.* A colorless, odorless, gaseous element found in the air and in volcanic gases and is used in electric bulbs and electron tubes.

ar-go-sy (är´go sē) *n., pl.* **argosies** A fleet of ships; a large merchant ship.

ar-got (är´gō) *n.* An often secret, specialized vocabulary.

ar-gu-a-ble (är´gū a bl) *adj.* Open to argument; questionable. **arguably** *adv.*

ar-gue (är´gū) *v.* To debate, to offer reason for or against a subject; to dispute, argue, or quarrel; to persuade or influence, to debate over an opinion. **argument** *n.* **arguer** *n.*

ar-gu-men-ta-tive (är´gya men´ta tiv) *adj.* Given to argument; debating or disputing.

a-ri-a (är´ē a) *n.* A vocal piece with accompaniment sung in solo; part of an opera.

a-ri-bo-fla-vin-o-sis (ā´rī bo flā´vi nō´sis) *n. Med.* A vitamin deficiency, in which the mucous membrane of the mouth becomes irritated and some discoloration of the tongue may occur.

ar-id (ar´id) *adj.* Insufficient rain; dry; lacking in interest or feeling; dull.

ar-il (ar´il) *n.* The extra covering of the seed of some plants, such as the nutmeg.

a-rise (a rīz´) *v.* To come from a source; to come to attention; to come into view; to mount; to move to a higher place; to get out of bed.

a-ris-ta (a ris´ta) *n, pl.* **aristae** or **aristas** Bristle-like appendage or structure.

ar-is-toc-ra-cy (ar´i stok´ra sē) *n.* A government by select individuals or by a small privileged class; class or group viewed as superior; the hereditary privileged ruling nobility.

a-rith-me-tic (a rith´me tik) *adj.* Branch of math that deals with addition, subtraction, multiplication, division. **arithmetic** *adj.* **arithmetically** *adv.*

arithmetic mean *n.* The number received by dividing the sum of a set of quantities by the number of quantities in the set.

arithmetic progression *n.* A progression in which the difference between any term and the one before or after is constant, as 2,4,6,8, etc.

Arizona *n.* A state located in the southwestern part of the United States, statehood February 14, 1912, capital Phoenix.

Arkansas *n.* A state located in the south-central part of the United States, statehood June 15, 1836, capital Little Rock.

arm (ärm) *n.* The part between the shoulder and the wrist; upper limb of the human body. **arm** *v.* To furnish with protection against danger.

ar-ma-da (är mä´da) *n.* A fleet of warships; a large force of moving things.

Ar-ma-ged-don (är´ma ged´on) *n.* A final battle between the forces of good and evil.

ar-ma-ment (är´ma ment) *n.* Military supplies and weapons; the process of preparing for battle.

ar-ma-ture (är´ma chĕr) *n.* The main moving part of an electric device or machine; a piece of soft iron that connects the poles of a magnet.

arm-ful (ärm´fel´) *n. pl.* **armfuls** *or* **arms-ful** As much as the arm can hold.

arm-hole (ärm´hōl´) *n.* The opening in a garment for the arm.

ar-mi-stice (är´mi stis) *n.* The temporary suspension of combat by mutual agreement; truce.

Armistice Day *n.* November 11, 1918 ending of World War I; name of day changed to Veterans Day in 1954.

ar-moire (ärm wär) *n.* A large wardrobe.

ar-mor (är´mor) *n.* Covering used in combat to protect the body, made from a heavy metal. **armor** *v.* **armored** *adj.*

ar-mor-er (är´mor ĕr) *n.* A person who makes armor; one who assembles, repairs, and tests firearms.

ar-mor-y (är´mo rē) *n, pl.* **armories** The supply of arms for attack or defense; the place where military equipment is stored.

ar-o-mat-ic (ar´o mat´ik) *adj.* Fragrant; giving out an aroma; sweet-scented; pleasant scent.

arm-pit (ärm´pit´) *n.* Hollow area under the arm where it joins the shoulder.

ar-my (är´mē) *n. pl.* **armies** A group of persons organized for a country's protection; the land forces of a country.

a-ro-ma (a rō´ma) *n.* A distinctive fragrance or pleasant odor, fragrance. **aromatical** *adj.* **aromatic** *adj.*

a-round (a round´) *adv. & prep.* To or on all sides; in succession or rotation; from one place to another; in a circle or circular movement.

a-rouse (a rouz´) *v.* To wake up from a sleep; to stir; to excite. **arousal** *n.*

ar-raign (a rān´) *v.* To call before a court to answer a charge or indictment; to accuse of imperfection, inadequacy, or of wrongdoing. **arraignment** *n.*

ar-range (a rānj´) *v.* To put in correct sequence; to prepare for something; to take steps to organize something; to bring about an agreement; to change a musical composition for different instruments or voices.

ar-range-ment (a rānj´ment) *n.* The state

or being arranged; something made by arranging things or parts together.

ar-rant (ar´ant) *adj.* Extreme; being notoriously without moderation.

ar-ras (ar´as) *n.* A screen or wall hanging of tapestry.

ar-ray (a rā´) *v.* To place or set in order; to draw up; to decorate or dress in an impressive attire. **arrayer** *n.*

ar-rears (a rēr´) *n.* The state of being behind something, as an obligation, payment, etc.; an unfinished duty.

ar-rest (a rest´) *n.* To stop or to bring an end to; to capture; to seize; to hold in custody by the authority of law.

ar-rest-ing (a res´ting) *adj.* Very impressive or striking; catching the attention. **arrestingly** *adv.*

ar-rhyth-mi-a (a rith´mē a) *n.* The alteration in rhythm of the heartbeat, either in force or time.

ar-rhyth-mic (a rith´mik) *adj.* Lacking regularity or rhythm.

ar-ris (ar´is) *n.* The line where two meeting surfaces of a body form an angle, as in moldings.

ar-riv-al (a rī´val) *n.* The act of arriving.

ar-rive (a rīv´) *v.* To reach or get to a destination.

ar-ro-gance (ar´o gans) *n.* An overbearing manner, intolerable presumption; an insolent pride.

ar-ro-gant (ar´o gant) *adj.* Overbearing manner; proud and assuming, self-important. **arrogantly** *adv.*

ar-ro-gate (ar´o gāt´) *v.* To demand unduly or presumptuously.

ar-row (ar´ō) *n.* A weapon shot from a bow; a sign or mark to show direction.

ar-row-head (ar´ō hed´) *n.* The striking end of an arrow, shaped like a wedge.

ar-row-root (ar´ō rōt´) *n.* A starch-yielding plant of tropical America.

ar-roy-o (a roi´ō) *n.* The dry bed of a stream or creek; a gully or channel.

ar-se-nal (är´se nal) *n.* A collection of weapons; a place where arms and military equipment are manufactured or stored.

ar-se-nic (är´se nik) *n.* A solid, poisonous element, steel-gray in color, used to make insecticide or weed killer. **arsenic** *adj.* **arsenical** *adj.*

ar-son (är´son) *n.* The fraudulent burning of property. **arsonist** *n.* **arsonous** *adj.*

art (ärt) *n.* A human skill of expression of other objects by painting, drawing, sculpture, etc.; a branch of learning.

ar-te-ri-al (är tēr´ē al) *adj.* Having to do with an artery or the oxygenated blood contained in the arteries.

ar-te-ri-og-ra-phy (är tēr´ē äg´ra fē) *n.* The visualization of an artery or arterial system after the injection of a radiopaque substance.

ar-te-ri-ole (är tēr´ē ōl´) *n.* One of the

small terminal twigs of an artery that ends in capillaries.

ar-te-ri-o-scle-ro-sis (är tēr″ē ō sklē rō′sis) *n.* A disease that causes the thickening of arterial walls and impedes circulation of the blood.

ar-ter-y (är′te rē) *n. pl.* **arteries** A blood vessel that carries blood from the heart to the other parts of the body; a major means for transportation. **arterial** *adj.*

ar-te-sian (är tē′zhun) *adj.* Referring to a well dug by perpendicular boring into the ground, at great depths, which allows water to rise to the surface of the soil by subterranean pressure.

art-ful (ärt′fel) *adj.* Showing or performed with skill or art; devious; cunning. **artfully** *adv.* **artfulness** *n.*

ar-thral-gia (är thral′je) *n.* Pain that occurs in one or more joints.

ar-thrit-ic (är thrit′ik) *n.* A person who has arthritis. **arthritic** *adj.*

ar-thri-tis (är thrī′tis) *n.* Inflammation of body joints.

ar-thro-pod (är′thro pod″) *n.* An animal with jointed limbs and a segmented body, as a spider. **arthropodal** *adj.* **arthropodan** *adj.* **arthropodous** *adj.*

Arthur, Chester A. *n.* (1829-1886) The twenty-first president of the United States from 1881-1885.

ar-ti-ad (är′tē ad″) *n.* An element with an even atomic number.

ar-ti-cle (är′ti kəl) *n.* A term or clause in a contract; a paragraph or section; a condition or rule; an object or item.

ar-tic-u-lar (är tik′yu lĕr) *adj.* Related to or of a joint.

ar-tic-u-late (är tik′yu lit) *adj.* Able to express oneself clearly, effectively, or readily; speaking in distinct words, or syllables. **articulate** *v.*

ar-ti-fact (är′ti fakt″) *n.* Something made by man showing human modification or workmanship.

ar-ti-fice (är′ti fis) *n.* An artful or clever skill; ingenuity.

ar-ti-fi-cial (är″ti fish′al) *adj.* Not genuine; made by man; not found in nature. **artificially** *adv.*

artificial horizon *n.* The aeronautical indicator of an airplane designed to give a surface that is constantly perpendicular to the vertical and therefore is parallel to the horizon.

artificial language In *computer science,* a programming language with a distinct set of rules and vocabulary.

artificial respiration *n.* A method by which air is rhythmically forced into and out of the lungs of a person whose breathing has ceased.

ar-ti-san (är′ti zan) *n.* A person skilled in any art or trade.

art-ist (är′tist) *n.* A person who practices the fine arts of painting, sculpture, etc.

ar-tis-tic (är tis′ik) *adj.* Relating to the characteristic of an artist or art.

art-ist-ry (är′ti strē) *n.* The artistic ability or quality of workmanship.

art-less (ärt′lis) *adj.* Lacking knowledge, art, or skill; crude; natural; simple.

as (az) *adv.* In the manner like; of the same degree or amount; similar to.

as-bes-tos (as bes′tus) *n.* A noncombustible, fibrous, mineral form of magnesium silicate that is used in insulating and fireproofing.

as-cend (*a* send′) *v.* To rise up from a lower level; to climb; to mount; to walk up. **ascendible** *adj.* **ascendable** *adj.*

as-cen-dant or **as-cen-dent** (*a* sen′dant) *adj.* Rising; moving up.

as-cent (*a* sent′) *n.* A way up; a slope; the act of rising.

as-cer-tain (as″ĕr tān′) *v.* To find out for certain; to make sure, confirm. **ascertainment** *n.* **ascertainable** *adj.*

as-cet-ic (*a* set′ik) *n.* One who retires from the world and practices strict self-denial as spiritual discipline; hermit.

as-cet-i-cism (*a* set′i siz″um) *n.* The practice of strict self-denial through personal and spiritual discipline.

ASCII *abbr.* American Standard Code for Information Interchange; in *computer science,* a standard code for representing characters in the computer.

ascorbic acid *n.* The anti-scurvy vitamin present in citrus fruits, tomatoes, and green vegetables; vitamin C.

as-cot (as′kot) *n.* A scarf or broad tie that is placed under the chin.

as-cribe (*a* skrīb′) *v.* To assign or attribute to something. **ascribable** *adj.*

a-sep-tic (*a* sep′tik) *adj.* Free or freed from septic material.

a-sex-u-al (ā sek′shō al) *adj.* Lacking sexual reproductive organs; without sex. **asexuality** *n.*

ash (ash) *n.* A type of tree with a hard, tough elastic wood; the grayish dust remaining after something has burned.

a-shamed (*a* shāmd′) *adj.* Feeling guilt, disgrace, or shame; feeling unworthy or inferior. **ashamedly** *adv.*

a-shore (*a* shōr′) *adv.* On or to the shore.

a-side (*a* sīd′) *adv.* Out of the way; to a side; to one side; something that is said in an undertone and not meant to be heard by someone.

ask (ask) *v.* To request; to require or seek information. **asker** *n.*

a-skance (*a* skans′) *adv.* With a side glance; with suspicion or distrust.

a-skew (*a* skū′) *adv. & adj.* Out of line, not straight.

a-slant (*a* slänt′) *adv.* In a slanting direction.

a-sleep (*a* slēp′) *adj. & adv.* In a state of sleep; lacking sensation; not alert.

a-so-cial (ā sō′shal) *adj.* Selfish, not

social; withdrawn.

as-par-a-gus (*a* spar´*a* gus) *n*. A vegetable with tender shoots, very succulent when cooked.

as-pect (as´pekt) *n*. The situation, position, view, or appearance of something.

aspect ratio *n*. The ratio of one dimension to another.

as-per-i-ty (*a* sper´i tē) *n*., *pl*. **asperities** Roughness in manner.

as-per-sion (*a* sper´zhan) *v*. False charges or slander; defamation; maligning.

as-phalt (as folt) *n*. A sticky, thick, blackish mixture of petroleum tar used in paving roads and roofing buildings.

as-phyx-ia (as fik´sē *a*) *n*. Lack of oxygen or an excess of carbon dioxide in the system.

as-phyx-i-ate (as fik´sē at´) *v*. To suffocate, to prevent from breathing; choking. **asphyxiation** *n*.

as-pi-rate (as´pi rāt´) *v*. To give pronunciation with a full breathing sound; to draw out using suction.

as-pire (*a* spīr´) *v*. To desire with ambition; to strive towards something higher. **aspiringly** *adv*. **aspirer** *n*.

as-pi-rin (as´pi rin) *n*. Medication used for the relief of pain and fever.

ass (as) *n*. A hoofed animal; a donkey; a stupid or foolish person.

as-sail (*a* sāl´) *v*. To attack violently with words or blows. **assailant** *n*.

as-sas-sin (*a* sas´in) *n*. Murderer, especially one that murders a politically important person either for fanatical motives or for hire.

as-sas-si-nate (*a* sas´i nāt´) *v*. To murder a prominent person by secret or sudden attack. **assassination** *n*.

as-sault (*a* solt´) *n*. A very violent physical or verbal attack on a person.

as-say (*a* sā´) *n*. To evaluate or to assess; to try; to attempt. **assayer** *n*.

as-sem-blage (*a* sem´blij) *n*. A collection of things or people; artistic composition made from junk and scraps.

as-sem-ble (*a* sem´bl) *v*. To put together the parts of something; to come together as a group. **assembly** n.

assembler In *computer science*, a program that translates a programming language into instructions that are understood directly by the computer.

assembly line *n*. The arrangement of workers, machines, and equipment which allows work to pass from operation to operation in the correct order until the product is assembled.

as-sent (*a* sent´) *v*. To agree on something. **assenter** *n*.

as-sert (*a* sert´) *v*. To declare or state positively, to maintain; to defend.

as-ser-tion (*a* ser´shan) *n*. Maintaining claim; the act of affirming.

as-sess (*a* ses´) *v*. To fix or assign a value to something. **assessor** *n*.

as-set (as´et) *n*. A valuable quality or possession; all of the property of a business or a person that can be used to cover liabilities.

as-sid-u-ous (*a* sij´ō us) *adj*. Devoted; constant in application; attentive.

as-sign (*a* sīn´) *v*. To designate as to duty; to give or allot; to attribute; to transfer.

as-sign-ee (*a* sī nē´) *n*. The person appointed to act for another; the person to whom property or the right to something is legally transferred.

as-sign-ment (*a* sīn´ment) *n*. A given amount of work or task to undertake; a post, position, or office to which one is assigned.

as-sim-i-late (*a* sim´i lāt´) *v*. To take in, to understand; to make similar; to digest or to absorb into the system.

as-sist (*a* sist´) *v*. To give support, to aid, to give help. **assistant**, **assistance** *n*.

as-size (*a* sīz´) *n*. A fixed or customary standard.

as-so-ci-ate (*a* sō´shē it) *v*. To connect or join together. *n*. A partner, colleague, or companion.

as-so-ci-a-tion (*a* sō´sē ā´shan) *n*. An organized body of people having a common interest; a society.

as-so-nance (as´*o* nans) *n*. The repetition of sound in words or syllables; using the same vowel sound with different consonants. **assonant** *adj*.

as-sort (*a* sort´) *v*. To distribute into groups of a classification or kind.

as-sort-ed (*a* sort´id) *adj*. Made up of different or various kinds.

as-sort-ment (*a* sort´ment) *n*. The act or state of being assorted; a collection of different things.

as-suage (*a* swāj´) *v*. To quiet, pacify; to put an end to by satisfying.

as-sume (*a* sōm´) *v*. To take upon oneself to complete a job or duty; to take responsibility for; to take for granted.

as-sum-ing (*a* sōm´ing) *adj*. Putting on airs of superiority; overbearing.

as-sump-tion (*a* sump´shan) *n*. An idea believed to be true without proof.

as-sur-ance (*a* sher´ans) *n*. A statement made to inspire confidence of mind or manner; freedom from uncertainty or self-doubt; self-reliance.

as-sure (*a* sher´) *v*. To give the feeling of confidence; to make sure or certain.

as-sured (*a* sherd´) *adj*. Satisfied as to the truth or certainty. **assuredly** *adv*.

as-sur-er (*a* sher´ér) *n*. A person who gives assurance.

as-sur-gent (*a* ser´jent) *adj*. Moving or directed upward.

as-ter-isk (as´te risk) *n*. The character (*) used to indicate letters omitted or as a reference to a footnote.

a-stern (*a stern´*) *adv. & adj.* Toward the rear or back of an aircraft or ship.

as-ter-oid (*as´te roid*) *n.* One of thousands of small planets that orbit the sun.

asth-ma (*az´ma*) *n.* A respiratory disease marked by labored breathing, wheezing, and coughing. **asthmatic** *adj.*

as though *conj.* As if.

a-stig-ma-tism (*a stig´ma tiz˝um*) *n.* A defect of the lens of an eye resulting in blurred or imperfect images.

as to *prep.* With reference to or regard to; concerning; according to.

as-ton-ish (*a ston´ish*) *v.* To strike with sudden fear, wonder, or surprise.

as-ton-ish-ment (*a ston´ish ment*) *n.* The state of being amazed or astonished.

as-tound (*a stound´*) *v.* To fill with wonder and bewilderment, amazement. **astounding** *adj.* **astoundingly** *adv.*

as-tral (*as´tral*) *adj.* Resembling or related to the stars.

a-stray (*a strā´*) *adv.* Away from a proper path or development.

a-stride (*a strīd´*) *prep.* One leg on either side of something; placed or lying on both sides of; extending across or over.

as-trin-gent (*a strin´jent*) *adj.* Able to draw together or to constrict tissues.

as-tro-dome (*as´tro dōm˝*) *n.* A large stadium covered by a dome.

as-trol-o-gy (*a strol´o jē*) *n.* The study of the supposed influences of the planets and stars and their movements and positions on human affairs.

as-tro-naut (*as´tro not˝*) *n.* A person who travels in a spacecraft beyond the earth's atmosphere.

as-tute (*a stōt´*) *adj.* Sharp in discernment; very shrewd; cunning; keen.

a-sun-der (*a sun´dėr*) *adv.* Separate into parts or positions apart from each other.

a-sy-lum (*a sī´lum*) *n.* A refuge or institution for the care of the needy or sick; a place of security and retreat.

a-sym-met-ric (*ā´si me´trik*) *adj.* Something that is not symmetrical.

a-syn-de-ton (*a sin´di ton˝*) *n.* A figure of speech with conjunctions omitted.

at (*at*) *prep.* To indicate presence, occurrence, or condition; used to indicate time, action, etc.

a-the-ism (*ā´thē iz˝um*) *n.* The disbelief that God exists. **atheist** *n.*

ath-lete (*ath´lēt*) *n.* A person who participates in exercise or in sports.

a-thwart (*a thwort´*) *adv.* Opposition to the expected or right; from one side to another.

a-tilt (*a tilt´*) *adj. & adv.* Inclined upward or tilted in some way.

at-las (*at´las*) *n.* A collection or book of maps.

ATM *abbr.* Automatic Teller Machine; a banking terminal that allows a customer to deposit or withdraw money by inserting a card and entering a private number code.

at-mos-phere (*at´mos fēr´*) *n.* A gaseous mass that surrounds a celestial body, as the earth; a predominant mood.

at-om (*at´om*) *n.* A tiny particle, the smallest unit of an element.

a-tone (*a tōn´*) *v.* To give satisfaction; to make amends.

a-tone-ment (*a tōn´ment*) *n.* Amends for an injury or a wrong doing; the reconciliation between God and man for sins.

a-tri-um (*ā´trē um*) *n.* One of the heart chambers; the main hall of a hotel or large house. **atrial** *adj.*

a-tro-cious (*a trō´shus*) *adj.* Extremely cruel or evil, horrible. **atrociously** *adv.*

a-troc-i-ty (*a tros´i tē*) *n. pl.* atrocities The condition of being atrocious; horrible; an inhuman, atrocious act.

a-tro-phy (*a´trō fē*) *v.* To decrease in size; to waste away.

at-tach (*a tach´*) *v.* To bring together; to fasten or become fastened; to bind by personal attachments; to tie together.

at-tack (*a tak´*) *v.* To threaten with force, to assault; to work on with vigor.

at-tain (*a tān´*) *v.* To arrive at or reach a goal, to accomplish; to achieve or obtain by effort. **attainable** *adj.*

at-taint (*a tānt´*) *v.* To disgrace or stain; to find guilty of a crime.

at-tar (*at´ar*) *n.* The fragrant oil from flowers.

at-tempt (*a tempt´*) *v.* To make an effort to do something. **attempt** *n.*

at-tend (*a tend´*) *v.* To be present; to take charge of or to look after.

at-ten-tion (*a ten´shan*) *n.* Observation, notice, or mental concentration.

at-ten-tive (*a ten´tiv*) *adj.* Observant; paying or giving attention. **attentively** *adv.* **attentiveness** *n.*

at-ten-u-ate (*a ten´ū āt˝*) *v.* To lessen the force, amount or value; to make fine or thin. **attenuation** *n.*

at-test (*a test´*) *v.* To give testimony or to sign one's name as a witness; to declare as truth. **attestation** *n.*

at-ti-tude (*at´tōd˝*) *n.* Mental position; the feeling one has for oneself.

at-tor-ney (*a ter´nē*) *n.* A person with legal training who is appointed by another to transact business for him.

at-tract (*a trakt´*) *v.* To draw by appeal; to cause to draw near by appealing qualities.

at-trac-tion (*a trak´shan*) *n.* The capability of attracting; something that attracts or is meant to attract.

at-trac-tive (*a trak´tiv*) *adj.* Having the power of charming, or quality of attracting. **attractively** *adv.*

at-trib-ute (*a trib´yŏt*) *v.* To explain by

showing a cause.

at-trib-ute (*á* trib yūt) *n.* A characteristic of a thing or person. In *computer science,* a characteristic, as of a file that is read-only, archived or hidden.

at-tri-tion (*a* trish´*a*n) *n.* Wearing down by friction; a rubbing against.

at-tune (*a* tūn´) *v.* To bring something into harmony; to put in tune; to adjust.

a-typ-i-cal (ā tip´i k*a*l) *adj.* Not conforming to the typical type; different than the usual. **atypically** *adv.*

auc-tion (ok´sh*a*n) *n.* A public sale of merchandise to the highest bidder.

au-da-cious (aw dā´shus) *adj.* Bold, daring, or fearless; insolent.

au-di-ble (aw´di bl) *adj.* Capable of being heard.

au-di-ence (aw´dē ens) *n.* A group of spectators or listeners; the opportunity to express views; a formal hearing.

au-di-o (aw´dē ō´) *adj.* Of or relating to sound or its high-fidelity reproduction.

au-dit (aw´dit) *n.* Verification or examination of financial accounts or records.

au-di-to-ri-um (aw´di tōr´ē um) *n.* A large room that holds many people.

au-di-to-ry (aw´di tōr´ē) *adj.* Related to the organs or sense of hearing.

aught (awt) *n.* Zero (0).

aug-ment (awg ment´) *v.* To add to or increase; to enlarge; in *computer science,* to expand capabilities, as by increasing speed or memory size.

au jus (ō zhōs´) *adj.* Served in the juices obtained from roasting.

au-ra (or´*a*) *n.* An emanation said to come from a person's body.

au-ral (or´*a*l) *adj.* Relating to the ear or the sense of hearing. **aurally** *adv.*

au-re-ole (or´ē ōl´) *n.* A halo.

au re-voir (ō´ re vwär´) *interj.* Farewell; goodbye until we meet again.

au-ri-cle (or´i k*a*l) *n.* One of the two upper chambers of the heart; the internal ear.

au-ric-u-lar (o rik´yu lèr) *adj.* Relating to the sense of hearing or of being in the shape of the ear.

au-ric-ul-ate (o rik´yu lit) *adj.* Shaped like the ear; having ears or some kind of extentions resembling ears.

aus-cul-ta-tion (o´skul tā´sh*a*n) *n.* The act of listening to sounds of the internal parts of the body, particularly the chest.

aus-pi-cious (*a* spish´us) *adj.* Indicating success or a favorable outcome.

aus-tere (o stēr´) *adj.* Stern in manner and appearance. **austerity** *n.*

aus-tral (o´str*a*l) *adj.* Southern.

au-then-tic (o then´tik) *adj.* Real; genuine; worthy of acceptance.

au-then-ti-cate (o then´ti kāt´) *v.* To prove something is true or genuine; real; not an imitation. **authenticity** *n.*

au-thor (a´thor) *n.* A person who writes an original literary work. **author** *v.*

au-thor-i-tar-i-an (*a* thor´i târ´ē *a*n) *adj.* Demanding blind submission and unquestioned obedience to authority.

au-thor-i-ty (*a* thor´i tē) *n. pl.* **authorities** A group or person with power; a government; an expert.

au-thor-i-za-tion (o´thor i zā´shan) *n.* The act of authorizing something.

au-thor-ize (o´thо rīz´) *v.* To give authority, to approve, to justify.

au-tism (o´tiz´um) *n.* Absorption in a self-centered mental state, such as fantasies, daydreams or hallucinations in order to escape from reality.

au-to-bi-og-ra-phy (o´to bī og´ra fē) *n., pl.* **autobiographies** The life story of a person, written by that person.

au-toc-ra-cy (o tok´ra sē) *n.* Government by one person who has unlimited power. **autocrat** *n.* **autocratic** *adj.*

au-to-graph (o´to graf) *n.* A handwritten signature.

au-to-mate (o´to māt´) *v.* To operate by automation; to convert something to automation, to automatize.

au-to-mat-ic (o´to mat´ik) *adj.* Operating with very little control; self-regulating.

automatic backup *n.* In *computer science,* a program that creates a backup copy of files at a set time.

automatic link *n.* in *computer science,* a connection between objects so that the update of one instances will change all occurrences.

automatic load *n.* In *computer science,* a program that is brought on line by a predetermined signal, as of a timer.

au-to-ma-tion (o´to mā´sh*a*n) *n.* The equipment and techniques used to make a process or system automatic.

autonomic nervous system *n.* The part of the body's nervous system which is regulated involuntarily.

au-ton-o-mous (o ton´o mus) *adj.* Self-governing; subject to its own laws.

au-ton-o-my (o ton´o mē) *n.* Independence; self-government.

au-top-sy (o´top sē) *n., pl.* **autopsies** Postmortem examination; the examination of a body after death to find the cause of death. **autopsic** *adj.*

au-tumn (o´tum) *n.* The season between summer and winter. **autumnal** *adj.*

aux-il-ia-ry (og zil´ya rē) *adj.* Providing help or assistance to someone; giving support.

auxiliary verb *n.* A verb that accompanies a main verb and expresses the mood, voice, or tense.

a-vail (a vāl´) *v.* To be of advantage or use; to use. **avail** *n.* The advantage toward attaining a purpose or goal.

a-vail-a-bil-i-ty (*a* vā´la bil´i tē) *n.* The state of being available.

a-vail-a-ble (*a* vā´la bl) *adj.* Ready or present for immediate use; accessible. **availably** *adv.* **availableness** *adj.*

available resources *n.* In *computer science,* all of the processing capacity, memory, storage and peripherals that remains for use after discounting those occupied by primary processing.

a-vant–garde (*a* vänt gärd´) *n.* The people who apply and invent new ideas and styles in a certain field.

av-a-rice (av´ar is) *n.* One's desire to have wealth and riches.

a-va-ri-cious (av´a rish´us) *adj.* Miserly.

a-vast (*a* vast´) *interj. Naut.* A command to stop or cease.

a-ve (ä´vā) *interj.* Farewell; hail.

a-venge (*a* venj´) *v.* To take revenge for something; to vindicate by inflicting pain. **avenger** *n.*

a-ver (*a* ver´) *v.* To be firm and to state positively.

av-er-age (av´ér ij) *n.* Something that is typical or usual, not being exceptional; common.

a-verse (*a* vers´) *adj.* Having a feeling of distaste or repugnance.

a-vert (*a* vert´) *v.* To prevent or keep from happening; to turn aside or away from; to direct away.

a-vi-a-tion (ä´vēä´shan) *n.* The operation of planes and other aircraft; design and manufacture of planes. **aviator** *n.*

a-vi-cul-ture (ä´vi kul´chur) *n.* Raising and breeding of birds.

av-id (av´id) *adj.* Greedy; eager; enthusiastic. **avidly** *adv.*

a-vi-fau-na (ä´vi fo na) *n.* A name for the birds of a certain period or region.

av-o-ca-tion (av´o kā´ shan) *n.* A pleasurable activity that is in addition to regular work a person must do.

a-void (*a* void´) *v.* To stay away from; to shun; to prevent or keep from happening; to elude. **avoidably** *adv.*

a-void-a-ble (*a* void´a bl) *adj.* That which can be avoided; able to get away.

a-void-ance (*a* void´ans) *n.* The act of making something void.

a-vouch (*a* vouch´) *v.* To assert; to guarantee; to vouch for; to admit.

a-vow (*a* vou´) *v.* To state openly on a subject; to confess; to own up to.

a-vow-al (*a* vou´al) *n.* Open declaration; acknowledge frankly.

a-vowed (*a* voud´) *adj.* Acknowledged.

a-wait (*a* wāt´) *v.* To wait for something; to expect; to be ready.

a-wake (*a* wāk´) *v.* To wake up; to be alert or watchful.

a-wak-en (*a* wā´ken) *v.* To awake or rouse from sleep.

a-ward (*a* word´) *v.* To give or confer as being deserved, needed, or merited. *n.* A judgment or decision; a prize.

a-ware (*a* wâr´) *adj.* Being conscious or mindful of something; informed.

a-way (*a* wā´) *adv.* At a distance; to another place; apart from.

awe (o) *n.* A feeling of wonder mixed with reverence. **awe** *v.*

a-wea-ry (*a* wē´rē) *adj.* Tired; weary.

a-weigh (*a* wā´) *adj.* To hang just clear of the ground, said of a ship's anchor.

awe-some (o´sum) *adj.* Expressive of awe. **awesomeness** *n.* **awesomely** *adv.*

awe-strick-en (o´strik´en) *adj.* Impressed with awe.

aw-ful (o´ful) *adj.* Very unpleasant or dreadful. **awfully** *adv.*

aw-ful-ness (o´ful nis) *n.* The state or quality of being awful.

a-while (*a* hwīl´) *adv.* For a short time.

a-whirl (*a* hwerl´) *adj.* To spin around.

awk-ward (ok´ward) *adj.* Not graceful; clumsy; to cause embarrassment.

awl (ol) *n.* Tool used to make holes in leather.

awn (on) *n.* The part of a piece a grass which resembles a bristle. **awned** *adj.*

awn-ing (o´ning) *n.* Structure that serves as a shelter over a window.

a-wry (*a* rī´) *adj. & adv.* In a twisted or turned position.

ax *or* **axe** (aks) *n.* A tool with a steel head attached to a wooden handle.

ax-il-la (ak sil´a) *n.* The armpit; the area under a bird's wing.

ax-il-lar (ak´si lar) *n.* The underwing, weaker feathers of a bird.

ax-il-lar-y (ak´si ler´ē) *adj.* Growing from the axil of something as a plant.

ax-i-om (ak´sē um) *n.* Statement recognized as being true; something assumed to be true without proof.

ax-i-o-mat-ic *adj.* Obvious; self-evident.

ax-is (ak´sis) *n., pl.* **axes** The line around which an object rotates or may be thought to rotate.

ax-le (ak´sel) *n.* A spindle or shaft around which a wheel or pair of wheels revolve.

ax-le-tree (ak´sel trē´) *n.* A bar which a wheel turns upon.

ax-on (ak´son) *n.* A single, long, nerve cell that carries transmitted nerve impulses away from the body of a cell.

aye (ī) *interj.* Yes, a sound of affirmation; indeed. **aye** *n.* An affirmative vote.

az-i-muth (az´i muth) *n.* Usually recognized as an angle, in air navigation is measured clockwise from the magnetic or true north.

a-zo-ic (*a* zō´ik) *adj.* Time period which occurred before life first appeared on the earth.

az-oth (az´oth) *n.* Mercury, the assumed first principle of all known metals.

AZT *abbr.* Azidothymidine; a drug that relieves the symptoms of AIDS.

az-ure (azh´ur) *n.* The blue color of the sky.

B, b (bē) *n.* The second letter of the English alphabet; a student's grade rating of good, but not excellent.

ba-ba (bä bä) *n.* A rich cake soaked in infant.

ba-bel (bā´bel) *n.* Babbling noise of many people talking at the same time.

ba-biche (bạ bēsh´) *n.* A thong or lacing made from animal skin; rawhide.

ba-boon (bạ bön´) *n.* A species of the monkey family with a large body and big canine teeth.

ba-bu (bä´bö) *n.* A Hindu gentleman.

ba-bul (be´bül) *n.* An acacia tree in northern Africa and Asia which yields gum arabic as well as fodder and timber.

ba-bush-ka (bạ besh´ka) *n.* A kerchief folded into a triangle and worn as a covering on the head.

ba-by (bā´bē) *n., pl.* **babies** A young child; infant. **babyish** *adj.*

baby's breath *n.* A tall herb bearing numerous small, fragrant, white or pink flowers.

baby–sit (bā bē sit) *v.* To assume the responsibility and care for a child or children during the absence of the parents.

bac-ca-lau-re-ate (bak˝a lor´ē it) *n.* A degree given by universities and colleges; an address given to a graduating class.

bac-ca-rat (bäk e ´rä bak) *n.* A game of cards played by any number of players betting against a banker.

bac-cha-nal (bak e nal) *adj.* Reveling in or characterized by intemperate drinking; riotous; noisy.

bac-cha-na-lia (bak˝a nā´lē a) *n.* A Roman festival celebrated with dancing and song.

bach (bach) *v. Slang* To live by oneself as does a bachelor.

bach-e-lor (bach´e lor) *n.* An unmarried male; the first degree one can receive from a four year university.

ba-cil-lus (bạ sil´us) *n., pl.* **bacilli** A rod-like microscopic organism which can cause certain diseases.

bac-i-tra-cin (bas´i trā´sin) *n.* An antibiotic used topically against cocci.

back (bak) *n.* The rear part of the human body from the neck to the end of the spine, also the rear part of an animal; a position in the game of football, in which the player lines up behind the front line of players; the final nine holes of an 18-hole golf course.

back-ward (bak´ward) *adv.* Toward the back; to or at the back; in a reverse order. **backwards** *adv.*

bac-te-ri-cide (bak tēr´i sīd[˝) *n.* A substance that kills bacteria.

bac-te-ri-ol-o-gy (bak tēr˝ē ol´ o jē) *n.* Scientific study of bacteria and its

relationship to medicine, etc.

bac-te-ri-o-phage (bak tēr˝ē o fāj´) *n.* Any of a group of viruses commonly found in sewage or body products.

bac-te-ri-ol-y-sis (bak tēr˝ē o stā´sis) *n.* The process of dissolution or destruction of bacteria.

bac-te-ri-um (bak tēr´ē um) *n., pl.* **bacteria** Any of various forms of numerous unicellular microorganisms that cause disease, some of which are used in industrial work. **bacterial** *adj.*

bad (bad) *adj.* Naughty or disobedient; unfavorable; inferior; poor; spoiled; invalid. **badly** *adv.* **badness** *n.*

badge (baj) *n.* An emblem worn for identification.

badg-er (baj´ér) *n.* A sturdy burrowing mammal. **badger** *v.* To trouble persistently.

bad-lands (bad´landz˝) *n. pl.* Area with sparse life, peaks, and eroded ridges.

bad-min-ton (bad´min tọn) *n.* A court game played with long-handled rackets and a shuttlecock.

baf-fle (baf´fl) *v.* To puzzle; to perplex. **baffle** *n.* A device that checks or regulates the flow of gas, sound, or liquids.

bag (bag) *n.* A flexible container used for holding, storing, or carrying something; a square white canvas container used to mark bases in baseball. **bagful** *n.*

ba-gasse (bạ gas´) *n.* Plant residue.

bag-a-telle (bag´a tel´) *n.* A game played with a cue and balls on an oblong table.

ba-gel (bā´gel) *n.* A hard, glazed, round roll with a chewy texture and a hole in the middle.

bag-gage (bag´ij) *n.* The personal belongings of a traveler.

bag-gy (bag´ē) *adj.* Loose. **baggily** *adv.*

bail-iff (bā´lif) *n.* The officer who guards prisoners and keeps order in a courtroom

bait (bāt) *v.* To lure; to entice. **bait** *n.* Food that is used to catch or trap an animal.

baize (bāz) *n.* A coarse woolen or cotton cloth.

bake (bāk) *v.* To cook in an oven; to harden or dry. **baker** *n.* **baked** *adj.*

bak-sheesh (bak´shēsh) *n.* A tip or gratuity.

bal-a-lai-ka (bal´a lī kạ) *n.* A three-stringed musical instrument.

bal-ance (bal´ạns) *n.* Device for determining the weight of something; the agreement of totals in the debit and credit records of an account

bal-co-ny (bal´kọ nē) *n., pl.* **balconies** Gallery or platform projecting from the wall of a building.

bald (bold) *adj.* Lacking hair on the head. **baldish** *adj.* **baldness** *n.*

bal-da-chin (bal′*da* kin) *n.* An embroidered fabric of silk and gold used to carry over an important person or sacred object.

bald eagle *n.* The eagle of North America that is dark when young, but has a white head and neck feathers when mature.

bal-der-dash (bol′*dĕr* dash˘) *n.* Nonsense.

bal-dric (bol drik) *n.* A broad belt, stretching from the right or left shoulder diagonally across the body, either as an ornament or to suspend a sword or horn.

bale (bāl) *n.* A large, bound package or bundle.

ba-leen (*ba* lēn′) *n.* A whalebone.

bale-fire (bāel fier)*n.* A signal fire; an alarm fire.

bale-ful (bāel fel) *adj.* Destructive; deadly; foreboding.

balk (bok) *v.* To refuse to go on; to stop short of something. *n.* A rafter or crossbeam extending from wall to wall. **balky** *adj.*

bal-kan-ize (bol k*e* nīz) *v.* To partition, as an area, into various small, politically ineffective divisions.

ball (bol) *n.* A round body or mass; a pitched baseball that is delivered outside of the strike zone.

bal-lad (bal′*ad*) *n.* A narrative story or poem of folk origin; a romantic song.

bal-lade (bol lād˘) *n.* A verse form consisting of three stanzas with recurrent rhymes and a refrain for each part.

bal-lad-eer (bal *e* di er) *n.* A person who sings ballads.

bal-last (bal′*ast*) *n.* Heavy material placed in a vehicle to give stability and weight.

ball bearing *n.* A bearing that reduces friction by separating the stationary parts from the moving ones.

bal-le-ri-na (bal′*e* rē′na) *n.* A female ballet dancer in a company.

bal-let (ba lā˘) *n.* An artistic expression of dance by choreographic design.

ballistic missile *n.* A projectile that is self-powered, is guided during ascent, and has a free-fall trajectory at descent.

bal-lis-tics (b*a* lis′tiks) *n.* The science of motion in flight; the firing character-istics of a firearm.

bal-lo-net (bal′*o* net′) *n.* A compartment within the interior of a balloon or airship to control ascent and descent.

bal-loon (ba lŏn′) *n.* A bag inflated with gas lighter than air which allows it to float in the atmosphere, often having a basket or compartment for carrying passengers; a bag made of rubber that is used as a child's toy.

bal-lot (bal′*ot*) *n.* A slip of paper used in secret voting. *v.* To vote by ballot.

bal-lotte-ment (be lät ment) *n.* A method of diagnosing pregnancy, in which a sudden shock is imparted to the fetus, as through the uterine wall, causing it to move suddenly.

ball-park (bol pärk) *n.* A stadium where ball games are played.

ball-point (bol′point˘) *n.* A pen that has a small self-inking writing point.

bal-ly-hoo (bal′ē hŏ˘) *n.* Exaggerated advertising.

balm (bäm) *n.* A fragrant ointment that soothes, comforts, and heals.

bal-ne-ol-o-gy (bal nē äl *e* jē) *n.* The study of the effects of baths employed in therapy.

ba-lo-ney (b*a* lō′nē) *n.*, *Slang* Nonsense.

bal-sa (bol′sa) *n.* American tree whose wood is very light in weight.

bal-sam (bol′sam)*n.* A fragrant ointment from different trees; a plant cultivated for its colorful flowers.

bal-us-ter (bal′*u* stĕr) *n.* The upright post that supports a handrail.

bal-us-trade (bal *e* strād) *n.* A row of small columns or balusters, joined by a rail, serving as an enclosure for altars, balconies, staircases, and terraces.

bam-boo (bam bŏ˘) *n.* Tropical, tall grass with hollow, pointed stems.

bam-boo-zle (bam bŏ˘zl) *v.* To trick or deceive.

ban (ban) *v.* To prohibit; to forbid.

ba-nal (bān′al) *adj.* Trite; lacking freshness.

ba-nan-a (b*a* nan′a) *n.* The crescent-shaped usually yellow, edible fruit of a tropical plant.

band (band) *n.* A strip used to trim, finish, encircle, or bind; the range of a radio wave length; a group of musicians who join together to play their instruments.

band-age (ban′dij) *n.* A strip of cloth used to protect an injury. **bandage** *v.*

ban-dan-na (ban dan′*a*) *n.* A brightly colored cotton or silk handkerchief.

ban-deau (ban dō˘) *n.* A narrow band worn in the hair; a narrow brassiere.

ban-dit (ban′dit) *n. pl.* bandits, banditti A gangster or robber. **banditry** *n.*

band-mas-ter (band mast*er*) *n.* The conductor and trainer of a band or musicians.

ban-do-leer (ban˘do lēr′) *n.* A belt worn over the shoulder with pockets for cartridges.

ban-dore (ban dōr′) *n.* A three-stringed instrument resembling a guitar.

band-stand (band′stand˘) *n.* A raised platform on which an orchestra or band perform.

ban-dy (ban′dē) *adj.* Bent; crooked; curved outward. **bandy** *v.*

bane (bān) *n.* A cause of destruction or

ruin. **baneful** *adj.* **banefully** *adv.*

bang (bang) *n.* A sudden loud noise; short hair cut across the forehead. **bang** *v.* To move or hit with a loud noise

ban-gle (bang´gel) *n.* A bracelet worn around the wrist or ankle.

ban-ish (ban´ish) *v.* To leave; to drive away; to remove from the mind; to condemn to exile. **banishment** *n.*

ban-is-ter (ban´i ster) *n.* The upright supports of a handrail on a staircase; a handrail.

ban-jo (ban´jō) *n.* A stringed instrument similar to a guitar. **banjoist** *n.*

bank (bangk) *n.* A slope of land adjoining water; an establishment that performs financial transactions.

bank-rupt (bangk´rupt) *n.* A person who is legally insolvent and whose remaining property is divided among creditors. **bankrupt** *v.*

ban-ner (ban´ér) *n.* A piece of cloth, such as a flag, that is used as a standard by a commander or monarch. *adj.* Outstanding.

ban-nock (ban´ak) *n.* Unleavened or flat cake made from barley or oatmeal.

banns (banz) *n.* The announcement of a forthcoming marriage.

ban-quet (bang´kwit) *n.* An elaborate dinner or feast.

ban-shee (ban´shē) *n.* A spirit in folklore whose appearance warns a family of approaching death of a member.

ban-ter (bant er) *v.* To attack with jokes or jests; to make fun of.

ban-yan (ban´yan) *n.* A tree from the tropics whose aerial roots grow downward to form additional roots.

bap-tism (bap tizem) *n.* A Christian sacrament of spiritual rebirth through the application of water.

bap-tize (bap tīz´) *v.* To immerse or sprinkle with water during baptism. **baptizer** *n.*

bar (bär) *n.* A rigid piece of material used as a support; a barrier or obstacle; a counter where a person can receive drinks. **bar** *v.* To prohibit or exclude.

barb (bärb) *n.* A sharp projection that extends backward making it difficult to remove; a breed of horses from Africa noted for their speed and endurance. **barbed** *adj.*

bar-bar-i-an (bär bâr´ē an) *n.* A person or culture thought to be primitive and therefore inferior. **barbarous** *adj.*

bar-be-cue (bär´be kū´) *n.* An outdoor

bar-bel (bär bel) *n.* A freshwater fish having four beardlike appendages on its upper jaw.

bar-bell (bär´bel) *n.* A bar with weights at both ends, used for exercise.

bar-ber (bär´bér) *n.* A person whose business is cutting and dressing hair and also shaving and trimming beards.

bar-bette (bär bet´) *n.* A cylinder protecting a gun turret on a warship.

bar-bi-tal (bär´bi tal´) *n.* A white hypnotic administered in the form of sodium salt.

bar-bi-tu-rate (bär bich´e ret) *n.* A derivative of barbituric acid.

bar-ca-role (bär´ka rōl´) *n.* A Venetian boat song with a strong and weak beat which suggests a rowing rhythm.

bard (bärd) *n.* A poet; a piece of armor for a horse's neck. **bardic** *adj.*

bare (bär) *adj.* Exposed to view; without coloring. **bare** *v.* **bareness** *n.*

bare-back (bär´bak´) *adv. & adj.* Riding a horse without a saddle.

bare-foot (bär fut) *adj.* With the feet bare; without shoes or stockings.

ba-rege (be´rezh) *n.* A sheer fabric for women's clothing.

bare-ly (bär´lē) *adv.* Sparsely; by a very little amount.

barf (bärf) *v. Slang* To vomit.

bar-gain (bär´gin) *n.* A contract or agreement on the purchase or sale of an item; a purchase made at a favorable or good price. **bargain** *v.* To negotiate over a price of something that is being sold or bought. **bargainer** *n.*

barge (bärj) *n.* A flat-bottomed boat. **barge** *v.* To intrude abruptly.

barge-board (bärj´bōrd´) *n.* A board which conceals roof timbers that project over gables.

barg-ee (bär ´jē) *n.* One of the crew of a barge or canal boat.

barge-man (bärj´man) *n.* A deckhand of a barge.

bar graph *n.* A graphic representation of statistics by means of bars of various, proportionate lengths.

bar-i-tone (bar´i tōn´) *n.* A male voice in the range between tenor and bass.

bark (bärk) *n.* The outer protective covering of a tree; the abrupt, harsh sound made by a dog. **bark** *v.*

bar-ken-tine (bär´ken tēn´) *n.* A three-masted ship with fore-and-aft rigging.

bar-ker (bär´kér) *n.* A person in the circus who stands at the entrance and advertises the show.

bar-ley (bär´lē) *n.* A type of grain used for food and for making whiskey and beer.

bar-low (bär lō) *n.* A sturdy jackknife.

barm (bärm) *n.* A yeast which forms on fermenting malt liquors.

bar mitzvah *n.* A Jewish boy who, having reached the age of 13, assumes the moral and religious duties of an adult; the ceremony that recognizes a boy as a bar mitzvah.

barn (bärn) *n.* A farm building used to shelter animals and to store farm equipment and products.

bar-na-cle (bär´na kl) *n.* A fish with a

hard shell that remains attached to an underwater surface.

ba-rom-et-er (*ba* rom´i tèr) *n*. An instrument that records the weight and pressure of the atmosphere.

bar-on (bar´*on*) *n*. The lowest rank of nobility in Great Britain. **baroness** *n*.

ba-rong (*ba* rong´) *n*. A thin-edged knife or sword.

ba-roque (*ba* rōk´) *adj*. An artistic style characterized by elaborate and ornate forms.

bar-o-tal-gi-a *n*. An ailment of the middle ear resulting from high altitude flying without a pressurized cabin.

ba-rouche (*ba* rōsh´) *n*. A four-wheeled carriage.

bar-rack (bar´ak) *n*. A building for housing soldiers.

bar-ra-cu-da (bar´*a* kö´da) *n*. *pl*. **barracuda, barracudas** A fish with a large, narrow body, found in the Atlantic Ocean.

bar-rage (bär´ij) *n*. A concentrated out-pouring or discharge of missiles from small arms; an artificial dam to increase the depth of water for use in irrigation or navigation.

bar-ra-tor (bar *et* er) *n*. One who frequently incites suits at law; an encourager of litigation.

bar-ra-try (bar´*a* trē) *n*. The unlawful breach of duty by a ship's crew that results in injury to the ship's owner.

barre (bär) *n*. A waist-high bar attached to the walls of a ballet school, used for body support while practicing.

bar-rel (bar´el) *n*. Wooden container with round, flat ends of equal size and sides that bulge.

bar-ren (bar´en) *adj*. Lacking vegetation; sterile.

bar-rette (*ba* ret´) *n*. A clasp or small bar used to hold hair in place.

bar-ri-cade (bar´i kād´) *n*. Barrier; to stop up, or block off, by a barricade.

bar-ri-er (bar´ē ér) *n*. A structure that restricts or bars entrance.

barrier reef *n*. A coral reef parallel to shore separated by a lagoon.

bar-room (bär´rōm´) *n*. A building or room where a person can purchase alcoholic beverages sold at a counter.

bar-row (bar´ō) *n*. A rectangular, flat frame with handles; a wheelbarrow.

bar-tend-er (bär´ten´dèr) *n*. A person who serves alcoholic drinks and other refreshments at a bar.

bar-ter (bär´tèr) *v*. To trade something for something else without the exchange of money; one commodity for another. **bartering, bartered** *v*.

bar-ti-zan (bär´ti zan) *n*. A small structure serving as a lookout.

bar-y-on (bar ē än) *n*. Any of the heavier subatomic particles having

masses greater than a neutron.

basal metabolism *n*. The amount of energy required by a person to maintain minimum vital functions.

ba-salt (bo solt´) *n*. A greenish-black volcanic rock.

base (bās) *n*. The fundamental part; the point from which something begins; headquarters; the lowest part; the bottom. **base** *v*. **basely** *adv*.

base-ball (bās´bol´) *n*. A game played with a ball and bat; the ball used in a baseball game.

base-ment (bās´ment) *n*. The foundation of a building or home.

base pay *n*. Wages as determined by the amount earned during a given work period exclusive of bonuses, overtime, or other compensation.

base rate *n*. The rate of pay for a stated output or period of labor.

bash (bash) *v*. To smash with a heavy blow; *Slang* A party. **bash** *v*.

bash-ful (bash´ful) *adj*. Socially shy. self-conscious. **bashfully** *adv*.

ba-sic (bā´sik) *adj*. Forming the basis; fundamental. **basically** *adv*.

BASIC *n*., *Computer Science* A common computer programming language. (Beginner's All-purpose Symbolic Instruction Code.)

ba-sic-i-ty (bā ´sis et ē) *n*. The power of an acid to unite with one or more atoms of a base.

basic skills *n*. A term used in education to denote those skills in any given field which must be acquired as fundamental to further learning.

ba-si-fy (bā se fī) *v*. To cause to become alkaline.

bas-il (baz´il) *n*. An herb used as seasoning in cooking.

bas-i-lisk (bas´i lisk) *n*. A tropical American lizard.

ba-sin (bā´sin) *n*. A sink; a washbowl; a round open container used for washing; an area that has been drained by a river system.

ba-sis (bā´sis) *n*., *pl*. **bases** The main part; foundation.

bask (bask) *v*. To relax in the warmth of the sun.

bas-ket (bas´kit) *n*. An object made of woven material, as straw, cane, or other flexible items.

bas-ket-ball (bas´kit bol) *n*. A game played on a court with two teams; each team trying to throw the ball through the basketball hoop at the opponents' end of the court.

bas mitzvah *n*. A Jewish girl who, having reached the age of 13, assumes the moral and religious duties of an adult.

ba-so-phil (bā se fil) *n*. A tissue or cell having a natural inclination for basic stains.

bas–re·lief (bä ri lēf) n. A mode of sculpturing figures on a flat surface, the figures being raised above the surface.

bass (bas) n., pl. **basses** A freshwater fish, one of the perch family.

bass drum n. A large drum with a low booming sound.

bass fiddle n. The largest, lowest-pitched of the stringed musical instruments.

bass horn n. A tuba.

bas·si·net (bas´a net´) n. A basket on legs used as an infant's crib; a basket made of wicker with a covering or hood over one end, used as an infant's bed.

bas·soon (ba sön´) n. A woodwind instrument with a low-pitched sound.

bast (bast) n. The inner bark of exogenous trees, consisting of several layers of fibers.

baste (bāst) v. To run a loose stitch to hold a piece of material in place for a short time; to moisten meat while cooking it by pouring on liquids.

bas·tille (ba stēl´) n. A tower in France used as a jail.

bas·ti·na·do (bas te nā ō) n. A beating with a stick or cudgel; a mode of punishment in oriental countries.

bast·ing (bā sting) n. The long stitches by which pieces of garments are temporarily sewn to each other.

bat (bat) n. A wooden stick made from strong wood; a nocturnal flying mammal. **batter** n.

batch (bach) n. A group of work entered on a computer at one time; a quantity (as of cook-ies, etc.) baked at one time.

bate (bāt) v. To abate, lessen, or reduce; to diminish.

ba·teau (ba tō) n. A light, broad, and flat-bottomed boat.

batement light n. A section of a window having vertical sides and a curved or inclined bottom.

bat·fowl·ing (bat faul-ing) n. A mode of catching birds at night by means of a light and nets.

bath (bath) n., pl. **baths** The act of washing the body.

bathe (bāth) v. To take a bath.

bath·house (bath haus) n. A house or building fitted up for bathing; a structure, as at the seaside, serving as a dressing room for bathers; a building for bathing equipped with medical facilities.

ba·thom·e·ter (ba thom´i tèr) n. An instrument which is used to measure the depth of water.

bath·y·scaphe (bath´i skāf) n. A submersible ship for deep sea exploration.

bath·y·sphere (bath´i sfier) n. A diving sphere used for observation of deep sea life.

ba·tik (ba tēk´) n. A method of dying fabric, in which parts not to be dyed are coated with wax.

ba·tiste (ba tēst´) n. A sheer, soft fabric.

bat·on (be ´tän) n. The wand used by a conductor for beating time; the stick used by a band's drum major.

bat·tal·ion (be´tal¯yon) n. A body of troops; a large group of any kind.

bat·tery (bat´e rē) n. A group of heavy guns.

bat·ting (bat´ing) n. Cotton wool in rolls or sheets, used as stuffing or lining.

bat·tle (bat´l) n. A struggle; combat between opposing forces. **battle** v. To engage in a war or battle.

baux·ite (bok sīt) n. A mineral consisting essentially of a hydrated aluminum oxide, used as a source of alum and aluminum.

bawd (bod) n. A prostitute. **bawdy** adj.

bawl (bol) v. To cry very loudly.

bay (bā) n. The inlet of a body of water; a main division or compartment; an animal that is reddish brown in color.

ba·ya·dere (bī e dif er) adj. Stripes on fabrics, running crosswise.

bay antler n. The second branch from the base of a stag's horn.

bay·ber·ry (bā´ber ē) n. Evergreen shrub used for decorations and making candles.

bay leaf n. The leaf of the bay tree, dried for use as a flavoring in cooking.

bay·o·net (bā´o nit) n. A spear–like weapon.

bay·ou (bī ō) n. An arm or outlet of a lake, river.

bay rum n. A fragrant liquid from the leaves of the bayberry used in cosmetics and medicine.

bay salt n. Coarse-grained salt, especially that obtained by evaporation of seawater.

ba·zaar (ba zär´) n. A fair where a variety of items are sold as a money making project for charity, clubs, churches, or other such organizations.

be (bē) v. To occupy a position; to exist; used with the present participle of a verb to show action; used as a prefix to construct compound words, as behind, before, because, etc.

beach (bēch) n. Pebbly or sandy shore of a lake, ocean, sea, or river.

beach-comb-er (bēch kōmer) n. One who earns a living by collecting redeemable wreckage along ocean beaches; a beach-front vagrant.

bea·con (bē´kan) n. A coastal guiding or signaling device.

bead (bēd) n. A small round piece of material with a hole for threading. **bead** v. To adorn with beads. **beading** n.

bead-roll (bēd rōl) n. A list of persons for whom prayers are to be said.

bead-work (bĕd werk) *n.* Ornamental work made with beads.

bea-gle (bē´gl) *n.* A small breed of hunting dog with short legs.

beak (bēk) *n.* The bill of a bird; resembling a beak. **beaked** *adj.*

beak-er (bē´ker) *n.* Large, wide-mouthed cup for drinking; a cylindrical, glass laboratory vessel with a lip for pouring.

beak-i-ron (bēk îern) *n.* The horn or tapering end of an anvil.

beam (bēm) *n.* Large, oblong piece of wood or metal used in construction. **beam** *v.* To shine.

bean (bēn) *n.* An edible seed or seed pod.

bean caper *n.* A small tree growing in warm climates, the flower buds of which are used as capers.

bean curd *n.* A soft vegetable cheese usually found in the Orient.

bear (bâr) *n.* A shaggy, carnivorous mammal. *Slang* A rough or gruff person. **bear** *v.* To endure; to carry; to support. **bearable** *adj.* **bearer** *n.*

bear-cat (bâr´kat) *n.* A panda.

beard (bērd) *n.* Hair growing on the chin and cheeks. **bearded** *adj.*

beast (bēst) *n.* A four–legged animal. *Slang* A brutal person. **beastly** *adj.*

beast of burden *n.* An animal used to perform heavy work and transport heavy materials.

beat (bēt) *v.* To strike repeatedly; to defeat. *adj.* Exhausted, very tired; fatigue. **beat, beater** *n.*

beat-en (bēt´n) *adj.* Made smooth by beating or treading; worn by use; conquered; vanquished.

be-a-tif-ic (bē´a tif´ik) *adj.* Giving or showing extreme bliss or joy.

be-at-i-tude (bē at´i tŏd´) *n.* The highest form of happiness; heavenly bliss.

beat-nik (bēt´nik) *n.* A person who lives a nonconformist life; a member of the beat generation.

beau (bō) *n.* Sweetheart; dandy.

beau monde *n.* People of distinguished family, wealth, fame and fashion.

beau-ti-cian (bū tish´an) *n.* One whose business is to improve the appearance of a person's hair, nails, and complexion.

beau-ti-fi-ca-tion (bū´ti fi kā´shon) *n.* The act of beautifying or rendering beautiful; decoration; adornment; embellishment.

beau-ti-ful (būti ful) *adj.* Having the qualities that constitute beauty; highly pleasing to the eye, the ear, or the mind.

beau-ty (bū´tē) *n.* Quality that is pleasing to the eye. **beautifully** *adv.*

beaux arts *n.* The fine arts, as painting and sculpture.

bea-ver (bē´vér) *n.* A large semiaquatic rodent with webbed feet and flat tail which yields valuable fur for coats, hats, etc.

be-bop (bē´bop´) *n. Slang* Jazz music.

be-calm (bē kăm´) *v.* To make quiet or calm. **becalming** *v.*

be-cause (bē koz´) *conj.* For a reason; since.

because of *prep.* On account of; as a result of.

bech-a-mel (bā´sha mel´) *n.* A white sauce, seasoned occasionally with onion and nutmet.

beck (bek) *n.* A summons; a call.

beck-et (bek´it) *n.* A loop for holding something in place.

beck-on (bek´n) *v.* To summon someone with a nod or wave.

be-cloud (bē koud´) *v.* To darken; to obscure; to cause confusion about.

be-come (bē kum´) *v.* To come to be, or to grow. **becoming** *adj.*

be-com-ing (bē kuming) *adj.* Suitable; proper; appropriate; befitting.

bed (bed) *n.* Furniture for sleeping; a piece of planted or cultivated ground. **bedding** *n.* **bed** *v.*

be-daub (bē daub´) *v.* To daub over; to soil with anything thick, slimy, and dirty.

bed-fast (bed´fast´) *adj.* Confined to a bed; bed-ridden.

bed-lam (bed´lam) *n.* A state or situation of confusion.

bee (bē) *n.* A hairy-bodied insect characterized by structures for gathering pollen and nectar from flowers.

beech (bēch) *n.* A tree of light-colored bark, with edible nuts.

beef (bēf) *n., pl.* **beefs** *or* **beeves** A cow, steer, or bull that has been fattened for consumption of its meat. **beefy** *adj.*

beef cattle *n.* Cattle raised for food.

beep (bēp) *n.* A warning sound coming from a horn.

beer (bēr) *n.* An alcoholic beverage.

bees-wax (bēz´waks) *n.* The wax from bees that is used for their honeycombs.

beet (bēt) *n.* The root from a cultivated plant that can be used as a vegetable or a source of sugar.

bee-tle (bēt´l) *n.* An insect with modified, horny front wings, which cover the membranous back wings when it is at rest.

be-fall (bi fol´) *v.* To happen or occur to.

be-fit (bi fit´) *v.* To be suitable; appropriate. **befitting** *adj.*

be-fool (bi fōl´) *v.* To make a fool of; to deceive.

be-fore (bi fōr´) *adv.* Earlier; previously. **before** *prep.* In front of.

be-fore-hand (bi fōr´hand´) *adv.* At a time prior to; in advance.

be-foul (bi foul´) *v.* To soil.

be-friend (bi frend´) *v.* To be a friend to someone.

beg (beg) *v.* To make a living by asking for charity. **beggar** *n.* **beggarly** *adj.*

be-gan (bi gan)*v.* The past tense of begin.

be-get (bi get´) *v.* To cause or produce; to cause to exist.

be-gin (bi gin´) *v.* To start; to come into being; to commence. **beginner** *n.* **beginning** *n.*

be-gone (bi gon´) *interj.* Command to go away.

be-go-nia (bi gōn´ya) *n.* A tropical plant with waxy flowers and showy leaves.

be-grime (bi grīm´) *v.* To make dirty; to soil with grime.

be-grudge (bi gruj´) *v.* To envy someone's possessions or enjoyment.

be-guile (bi gīl´) *v.* To deceive; to delight; to charm.

be-guine (bi gēn´) *n.* A popular dance of the Caribbean which resembles the rumba.

be-gum (bē´gum) *n.* A Muslim woman.

be-gun (bi gun) *v.* The past participle of begin.

be-half (bi haf´) *n.* The support or interest of another person.

be-have (bi hāv´) *v.* To function in a certain manner; to conduct oneself in a proper manner.

be-hav-ior (bi hāv´yè) *n.* Manner of behaving or acting; conduct. **behavior-ism** *n.*

be-head (bi hed´) *v.* To remove the head from the body; to decapitate.

be-held *v.* Past participle of behold.

be-hind (bi hīnd´) *adv.* To or at the back; late or slow in arriving.

be-hold (bi hōld´) *v.* To look at; to see.

be-hoove (bi höv´) *v.* To benefit or give advantage.

beige (bāzh) *n. & adj.* A light brownish, grey color.

being (bē´ing) *n.* One's existence.

be-jew-el (bi jō´el) *v.* To adorn with jewels.

be-la-bor (bi lā´bèr) *v.* To work on or to discuss beyond the point where it is necessary; to carry to absurd lengths.

be-lat-ed (bi lā´ted) *adj.* Tardy; late, delayed. **belatedly** *adv.*

bel canto (bel´ kan´tō) *n.* Operatic singing with rich lyricism and brilliant vocal means.

belch (belch) *v.* To expel stomach gas through the mouth.

be-lea-guer (bi lē´gèr) *v.* To surround with an army as to preclude escape; to blockade; to harass.

bel-fry (bel´frē) *n., pl.* **belfries** The tower that contains the bell of a church.

be-lief (bi lēf´) *n.* Something that is trusted or believed.

be-lieve (bi lēv´) *v.* To accept as true or real; to hold onto religious beliefs. **believable** *adj.* **believer** *n.*

be-lit-tle (bi lit´l) *v.* To think or speak in a slighting manner of someone or something.

bell (bel) *n.* A metal instrument that gives a ringing sound when struck.

bel-lig-er-ent (be lij´ér ent) *adj.* Hostile and inclined to be aggressive. **belligerence, belligerent** *n.*

bel-low (bel´ō) *v.* To make a deep, powerful roar like a bull. **bellow** *n.* **bellowing** *adj.*

bel-lows (bel´ōz) *n.* An instrument that produces air in a chamber and expels it through a short tube.

be-long (bi long´) *v.* To be a part of. **belonging** *n.*

be-loved (bi luv´id) *adj.* To be dearly loved.

be-low (bi lō´) *adv.* At a lower level or place below. *prep.* To be inferior to.

belt (belt) *n.* A band worn around the waist; a zone or region that is distinctive in a special way.

belt-way (belt´wā) *n.* A highway that encircles an urban area.

be-lu-ga (be lö´ga) *n.* A large white sturgeon whose roe is used to make caviar.

be-moan (bi mōn´) *v.* To moan or mourn for.

be-muse (bi mūz´) *v.* To bewilder or confuse; to be lost in thought. -ed *adj.*

bench (bench) *n.* A long seat for more than two people; the seat of the judge in a court of law.

bench-er (ben´chèr) *n.* A person who sits on a bench as a judge or a member of Parliament.

bend (bend) *v.* To arch; to change the direct course; to deflect. **bending** *v.*

bends (bendz) *n. pl.* Stomach and chest pains caused by the reduction of air pressure in the lungs, the result of rising too quickly from deep ocean levels.

beneath (bi nēth´) *adv.* To be in a lower position; below; underneath.

ben-e-dict (ben´i dikt) *n.* A previously confirmed bachelor who was recently married.

ben-e-dic-tion (ben´i dik´shan) *n.* A blessing given at the end of a religious service.

ben-e-fac-tion (ben´e fak´shan) *n.* A charitable donation; a gift.

ben-e-fice (ben´e fis) *n.* Fixed capital assets of a church that provide a living.

be-nef-i-cence (be nef´i sens) *n.* The quality of being kind or charitable.

be-nef-i-cent (be nef´sent)*adj.* Performing acts of charity and kindness; doing good.

ben-e-fi-cial (ben´e fish´al) *adj.* Advantageous; helpful; contributing to a valuable end. **beneficially** *adv.*

ben-e-fi-ci-ar-y (ben´e fish´ē er´ē) *n.*

The person named to the estate of another in case of death.

ben-e-fit (ben´e fĭt) *n.* Aid; help; an act of kindness; a social event or entertainment to raise money for a person or cause. **benefit** *v.*

be-nev-o-lence (be nev´o lens) *n.* The inclination to be charitable.

be-nev-o-lent (be nev´o lent) *adj.* Doing good; organized for good works.

ben-ga-line (beng´ga lēn˘) *n.* A fabric with narrow transverse cords, usually made of rayon, cotton, or silk and similar to poplin.

be-night-ed (bi nī´tid) *adj.* Overtaken by night.

be-nign (bi nīn´) *adj.* Having a gentle and kind disposition; gracious; not malignant. **benignly** *adv.*

be-nig-nan-cy (bi nig´nan sē) *n.* The condition of being benevolent, gentle, mild.

be-nig-nant (bi nig´nant) *adj.* Kind; gracious; favorable; beneficial.

ben-i-son (ben´i zen) *n.* A blessing; benediction.

ben-ne (ben´ē) *n.* An East Indian plant known as Sesame, from which edible oil is extracted.

bent (bent) *adj.* Curved, not straight. **bent** *n.* A fixed determination; purpose.

ben-thos (ben´thos) *n.* The whole amount of all organisms that live under water either near the shore or at great depths.

be-numb (bi num´) *v.* To dull; to make numb.

ben-zal-de-hyde (ben zal´de hīd˘) *n.* An aromatic liquid used in flavoring and perfumery.

ben-zene (ben´zēn) *n.* A flammable toxic liquid used as a motor fuel.

be-queath (bi kwēth´) *v.* To give or leave to someone by will; to hand down, legacy. **bequeathal** *n.*

be-quest (bi kwest´) *n.* Something that is bequeathed.

be-rate (bi rāt´) *v.* To scold severely.

ber-ceuse (ber suz´) *n.* A lullaby.

bere (bēr) *n.* A barley species.

be-reave (bi rēv´) *v.* To deprive; to suffer the loss of a loved one. **bereft** *adj.* **bereavement** *n.*

be-ret (be rā´) *n.* A round, brimless woolen cap.

berg (berg) *n.* A large mass of ice; iceberg.

ber-ga-mot (bür´ga mot˘) *n.* A pear-shaped orange, the rind of which has a fragrant oil used in perfumery.

ber-i-ber-i (ber´ē ber´ē) *n.* Nervous disorder from the deficiency of vitamin B producing partial paralysis of the extremities.

ber-ry (ber´ē) *n., pl.* **berries** An edible fruit, such as a strawberry or black-berry.

ber-serk (ber serk´) *adj.* Destructively violent.

berth (berth) *n.* Space at a wharf for a ship or boat to dock; a built-in bunk or bed on a train or ship.

ber-yl (ber´il) *n.* A mineral composed of silicon, oxygen, and beryllium that is the major source of beryllium; a precious stone which is exceptionally hard.

be-ryl-li-um (bi ril´ē um) *n.* A corrosion-resistant, rigid, lightweight metallic element.

be-seech (bi sēch´) *v.* To ask or request earnestly.

be-set (bi set´) *v.* To set, stud, or surround with something.

be-set-ting (bi set´ing) *adj.* Habitually attacking.

be-show (bi shō´) *n.* An edible fish of the western coast of North America.

be-side (bi sīd´) *prep.* At the side of; next to.

be-sides (bi sīdz´) *adv.* Along the side of; over and above.

be-siege (bi sēj´) *v.* To surround with troops; to harass with requests.

be-smear (bi smir´) *v.* To soil; to smear.

be-smirch (bi smürch´) *v.* To tarnish.

be-som (bē´zum) *n.* A broom made of twigs that are attached to a handle, used to sweep floors.

be-sot (bi sot´) *v.* To make mentally dull, as with drink.

be-spat-ter (bi spat´ér) *v.* To splash; to soil.

be-speak (bi spēk´) *v.* To indicate; to speak; to foretell. **bespoken** *adj.*

be-sprin-kle (bi spring´kl) *v.* To sprinkle over; to cover by scattering.

best (best) *adj.* Exceeding all others in quality or excellence; most suitable, desirable, or useful. **best** *v.*

bes-tial (bĕs´chal) *adj.* Of or relating to an animal; brutish, having the qualities of a beast. **bestially** *adv.* **bestiality** *adv.*

bes-tial-i-ty (bes´chē al´i tē) *n.* The quality of a beast; beastliness.

bes-ti-ar-y (bes´chē er´ē) *n.* A medieval collection of fables about imaginary and real animals, each with a moral.

be-stir (bi stér´) *v.* To rouse into action; to stir; to put into brisk or vigorous action.

best man *n.* The attendant of a bride-groom at a wedding.

be-stow (bi stō´) *v.* To present or to give honor.

be-strew (bi strō´) *v.* To scatter over.

be-stride (bi strīd´) *v.* To step over or to straddle.

best seller *n.* A book or an article which has a high volume of sale.

bet (bet) *n.* An amount rised on a stake or wager. **bet** *abbr.* Between.

be-ta (bā´ta) *n.* The second letter of the

Greek alphabet.

be-take (bi tāk´) v. To cause oneself to make one's way; move or to go.

beta particle n. High–speed positron or electron coming from an atomic nucleus that is undergoing radioactive decay.

be-ta-tron (bā´ta tron´) n. Accelerator in which electrons are propelled by the inductive action of a rapidly varying magnetic field.

Bethlehem n. The birthplace of Jesus.

be-tide (bi tīd´) v. To happen to; to take place.

be-to-ken (bi tō´ken) v. To show by a visible sign.

be-tray (bi trā´) v. To be disloyal or unfaithful; to indicate; to deceive; treachery. **betrayal** n.

be-troth (bi trōth´) v. To promise to take or give in marriage. **betrothal** n.

be-trothed (bi trōthd´) n. A person to whom one is engaged to marry.

bet-ta (bä´t a) n. A brightly colored freshwater fish of southeastern Asia.

bet-ter (bet´ėr) adj. More suitable, useful, desirable, or higher in quality. **better** v. To improve oneself.

bet-tor, bet-ter (bet´ėr) n. A person who makes bets or wagers.

be-tween (bi twēn´) prep. The position or time that separates; in the middle or shared by two.

be-twixt (bi twikst´) prep. Not knowing which way one should go; between.

bev-el (bev´el) n. The angle at which one surface meets another when they are not at right angles.

bev-er-age (bev´er ij) n. A refreshing liquid for drinking other than water.

bev-y (bev´ē) n., pl. **bevies** A collection or group; a flock of birds.

be-wail (bi wāl´) v. To express regret or sorrow.

be-ware (bi wâr´) v. To be cautious; to be on guard.

be-wilder (bi wil´dėr) v. To confuse; to perplex or puzzle. **bewilderment** n.

be-witch (bi wich´) v. To fascinate or captivate completely; to cast a spell over. **bewitchery** n. **bewitchment** v.

bey (bā) n. The Turkish title of respect and honor.

be-yond (bē ond´) prep. Outside the reach or scope; something past or to the far side.

bez-el (bez´el) n. A flange or groove that holds the beveled edge of an object such as a gem in a ring mounting.

be-zique (be zēk´) n. A card game that uses a deck of 64 cards, similar to pinochle.

bhang (bang) n. An intoxicant or narcotic obtained from the leaves and flowering tops of hemp used in India for swallowing or smoking.

bi- pref. Two; occurring two times; used when constructing nouns.

bi-a-ly (bē ´al ē) n. A baked roll with onions on the top.

bi-an-nu-al (bī an ´ū al) adj. Taking place twice a year; semiannual.

bi-as (bī´as) n. A line cut diagonally across the grain of fabric; prejudice. **bias** v. To be or to show prejudice.

bi-au-ral (bī or´al) adj. Hearing with both ears.

bib (bib) n. A cloth that is tied under the chin of small children to protect their clothing; the section of overalls or aprons that is above the waist..

bibb (bib) n. A piece of timber bolted to the ship's mast for support.

Bi-ble (bī´bl) n. the holy book of Christianity, containing the Old and New Testaments. **Biblically** adv.

bib-li-og-ra-phy (bib lē og´ra fē) n., pl. **bibliographies** A list of work by a publisher or writer; a list of sources of information. **bibliographer** n.

bib-lio-phile (bib´lē o fīl´) n. A person who collects books.

bib-li-ot-ics (bib´lē ot´iks) n. The study of handwriting, often used to determine authorship.

bib-u-lous (bib´ya les) adj. Inclined to drink; of or related to drinking.

bi-cen-ten-ni-al (bī´sen ten´ē al) adj. Happening once every 200 years. **bicentennial** n. Anniversary or celebration of 200 years.

bi-ceps (bī´seps) n. Large muscle in the front of the upper arm and at the back of the thigh. **bicipital** adj.

bick-er (bik´er) v. To quarrel or argue. **bicker** n.

bi-con-cave (bī kon´kāv) adj. Bowing in on two sides.

bi-cul-tur-al (bī kul´chur al) adj. Having or containing two distinct cultures.

bi-cus-pid (bī kus´pid) n. A tooth with two roots.

bi-cy-cle (bī´si kl) n. A two-wheeled vehicle propelled by pedals. **-ist** n.

bid (bid) v. To request something; to offer to pay a certain price. n. One's intention in a card game. **bidder** n.

bid-dy (bid´ē) n. A young chicken; hen. Slang A fussy woman.

bide (bīd) v. To remain; to wait.

bi-det (bī´dā) n. A basin for bathing the genital and anal areas.

bi-en-ni-al (bī en´ē el) adj. Occurring every two years; lasting or living for only two years.. **biennial** n.

bi-en-ni-um (bī en´ē um) n. Period of two years.

bier (bēr) n. A stand on which a coffin is placed before burial.

bi-fo-cal (bī fō´kal) adj. Having two different focal lengths.

bi-fo-cals (bī´fō´kal) n. Lenses used to

correct both close and distant vision.

bi-fur-cate (bī´fer kāt) v. To divide into two parts. **bifurcation** n. **bifurcate** adj.

bight (bīt) n. The slack in a rope; a bend in the shoreline.

big league n. Major league.

big-ot (big´ot) n. A person who is fanatically devoted to one group, religion, politics, or race. **bigotry** n.

bike (bīk) n. A bicycle. **biker** n. **bike** v.

bi-ki-ni (bi kē´nē) n. A scanty, two-piece bathing suit. **bikinied** adj.

bi-lan-der (bil´an dèr) n. A small merchant vessel having two masts.

bi-lat-er-al (bī lat´er al) adj. Having or relating to two sides. **bilaterally** adv.

bil-bo (bil´bō´) n. An iron bar with sliding shackles to confine prisoners on shipboard.

bile (bīl) n. A brownish-yellow alkaline liquid that is secreted by the liver to help digest fats. **biliary** adj.

bi-lev-el (bī lev el) adj. Divided into two floor levels.

bilge (bilj) n. Lowest inside part of the hull of a ship.

bilge keel n. A projection like a fin along a ship on either side to check rolling.

bi-lin-gual (bī ling´gwal) adj. Able to speak two languages with equal ability.

bil-ious (bil´yus) adj. Suffering gastric distress from a sluggish gallbladder or liver.

bilk (bilk) v. To cheat or swindle.

bill (bil) n. Itemized list of fees for services rendered; a document presented containing a formal statement of a case complaint or petition; the beak of a bird. **biller** n.

bil-la-bong (bil´a bong´) n. A blind channel coming from a river; a dry stream bed which fills up after seasonal rains.

bill-board (bil´bōrd´) n. A place for displaying advertisements.

billed (bild) adj. Having a bill or beak.

bil-let (bil´it) n. An official document which provides a member of the military with board and lodging.

bil-liards (bil´yardz) n. Game played on a table with cushioned edges.

bil-lion (bil´yon) n. A thousand million.

bil-lion-aire (n. A person whose wealth equals at least one billion dollars.

bill of lading n. A form issued by the carrier for promise of delivery of merchandise listed.

Bill of Rights n. The first ten amendments to the United States Constitution.

bill of sale n. A formal instrument for the transfer of personal property.

bil-low (bil´ō) n. Large swell of water or smoke; wave. **billowy** adj.

billy goat n. A male goat.

bi-man-u-al (bīman´ūal) adj. Involving the use of both hands.

bi-met-al-ism (bī met´al iz´um) n. The use of two metals, gold and silver, as legal tenders.

bi-month-ly (bī munth´lē) adj. Occurring every two months.

bin (bin) n. An enclosed place for storage.

bi-na-ry (bī´na rē) adj. Made of two different components or parts.

bind (bīnd) v. To hold with a belt or rope; to bandage; to fasten and enclose pages of a book between covers. **binding** n.

bind-er (bīnd´ér) n. A notebook for holding paper; payment or written statement legally binding an agreement.

bind-er-y (bīn´da rē) n. pl. **binderies** The place where books are taken to be bound.

binge (binj) n. Uncontrollable self-indulgence; a spree.

bin-na-cle (bin´a kal) n. A place where a ship's compass is contained.

bi-noc-u-lar (bi nok´ū lér) n. A device designed for both eyes to bring objects that are far away into focus. Also **binoculars**. **binocularity** n.

bi-o-chem-is-try (bī´ō kem´i strē) n. Chemistry of substances and biological processes.

bi-o-de-grad-a-ble (bī di grā e bel) adj. Decomposable by natural processes.

bi-o-feed-back (bio fēd bak) n. The technique of controlling involuntary bodily functions, such as blood pressure and heartbeat.

bi-o-geo-chem-is-try (bī´o jē ō´kem e strē) n. Science dealing with the relation of earth chemicals to plant and animal life.

bi-og-ra-pher (bī og´ra fer) n. The person who writes a biography.

bi-o-haz-ard (bī ō haz erd) n. Biological material that threatens humans, other living beings, or their environment.

biological warfare n. Warfare that uses disease-producing microorganisms to destroy crops, livestock, or human life.

bi-ol-o-gist (bī ol´o jist) n. A person skilled in or who studies biology.

bi-ol-o-gy (bī ol´o jē) n. Science of living organisms and the study of their structure, reproduction, and growth. **biological** adj.

bi-o-med-i-cine (bī´ō med´i sin) n. Medicine that has to do with human response to environmental stress.

bi-on-ics (bī´än iks) n. Application of biological principles to the study and design of engineering systems, as electronic systems.

bi-o-phys-ics (bī´ō fiz´iks) n. The physics of living organisms. **biophysical** adj.

bi-op-sy (bī´op sē) n., pl. **biopsies** The examination for the detection of a disease in tissues, cells, or fluids removed from a living organism.

bi-ot-ic (bī ŏt´ĭk) *adj.* Related to specific life conditions or to life itself.

bi-o-tin (bī´o tĭn) *n.* Part of the vitamin B complex found in liver, milk, yeast, and egg yolk.

bi-par-ti-san (bī pär´ti zan) *adj.* Supported by two political parties; working together. **bipartisanship** *n.*

bi-ped (bī´ped) *n.* An animal having two feet.

bi-plane (bī´plān´) *n.* A glider or airplane with wings on two levels.

bi-pod (bī´pod) *n.* Stand supported by two legs.

bi-po-lar (bī pō´lar) *adj.* Having or related to two poles; concerning the earth's North and South Poles.

bi-ra-cial (bī rā´shal) *adj.* Composed of or for members of two races.

bi-ra-mose (bī rā´mōs) *adj.* Having, or consisting of, two branches.

birch (berch) *n.* A tree providing hard, close-grained wood.

bird (berd) *n.* A warm-blooded, egg-laying animal whose body is covered by feathers.

birth (berth) *n.* The beginning of existence.

birth certificate *n.* An official record of a person's date and place of birth.

birth-wort (berth´wert) *n.* An herb with aromatic roots used in medicine to aid in childbirth.

bis (bis) *adv. Mus.* Direction to repeat.

bis-cuit (bis´kit) *n.* Small piece of bread made with baking soda or baking powder; a cookie, or cracker.

bi-sect (bī sekt´) *v.* To divide or cut into two equal parts. **bisection** *n.*

bi-sex-u-al (bī sek´shō al) *adj.* Sexually relating to both sexes. **bisexuality** *n.* **bisexually** *adv.*

bis-muth (biz´muth) *n.* A white, crystalline metallic element.

bi-son (bī´son) *n.* A large buffalo of northwestern America, with a dark brown coat and short, curved horns.

bisque (bisk) *n.* A creamy soup made from fish or vegetables; unglazed clay.

bis-sex-tile (bī seks´til) *adj.* Related to the extra day occurring in a leap year.

bis-tort (bis´tort) *n.* An American herb with twisted roots used as astringents.

bis-tou-ry (bis´to rē) *n.* A small, narrow surgical knife.

bis-tro (bis´trō) *n., pl.* **bistros** A bar or small nightclub. **bistroic** *adj.*

bit (bit) *n.* A tiny piece or amount of something; a tool designed for boring or drilling, such as drilling for oil; metal mouthpiece of a horse bridle; in *computer science*, either of two characters, as the binary digits zero and one, of a language that has only two characters; a unit of information or storage capacity, as a computer memory.

bite (bīt) *v.* To cut, tear, or crush with the teeth. **bite** *n.* **bitingly** *adv.*

bit-stock (bit´stok´) *n.* A brace that secures a drilling bit.

bit-ter (bit´er) *adj.* Having a sharp, unpleasant taste. **bitterness** *n.*

bit-tern (bit´ern) *n.* A small to medium-sized heron with a booming cry.

bit-ter-sweet (bit´er swēt´) *n.* A woody vine whose root, when chewed, has first a bitter, then a sweet taste.

bituminous coal *n.* Coal that contains a high ratio of bituminous material and burns with a smoky flame.

bi-valve (bī´valv´) *n.* A mollusk that has a hinged two-part shell; a clam or oyster.

biv-ou-ac (biv´ō ak´) *n.* A temporary military camp in the open air. **bivouac** *v.* To camp overnight in the open air.

bi-week-ly (bī wēk´lē) *n.* Occurring every two weeks.

bi-year-ly (bī yēr´lē) *n.* Occurring every two years.

bi-zarre (bi zär´) *adj.* Extremely strange or odd. **bizarrely** *adv.* **bizarreness** *n.*

bi-zon-al (bī´zōn´al) *adj.* Pertaining to two combined zones.

blab (blab) *v.* To reveal a secret by indiscreetly talking; to gossip.

blab-ber (blab´er) *v.* To chatter; to blab. **blabber** *n.*

black (blak) *adj.* Very dark in color; depressing; cheerless. **black** *n.* Darkness; the absence of light. **blackly** *adv.*

black-ball (blak´bol) *n.* A vote that prevents a person's admission to an organization or club.

black market (blak´mär´kit) *n.* The illegal buying or selling of merchandise or items.

blad-der (blad´er) *n.* The expandable sac in the pelvis that holds urine.

blade (blād) *n.* The cutting part of a knife; the leaf of a plant or a piece of grass.

blah (blä) *n.* A feeling of general dissatisfaction.

blame (blām) *v.* To hold someone guilty for something; to find fault. **blameless** *n.* **blamelessly** *adv.* **blamelessness** *n.*

blame-wor-thy (blām´wur´the) *adj.* Deserving blame.

blanch (blanch) *v.* To remove the color from something, as to bleach; to pour scalding hot water over fresh vegetables.

bland (bland) *adj.* Lacking taste or style. **blandly** *adv.* **blandness** *n.*

blan-dish (blan´dish) *v.* To coax by flattery.

blank (blangk) *adj.* Having no markings or writing; empty; confused, having no interest or emotion on one's face or look. **blankly** *adv.* **blankness** *n.*

blank check n. Carte blanche; freedom of action.

blan-ket (blang´kit) n. A woven covering used on a bed.

blank verse n. A poem of lines that have rhythm but do not rhyme.

blan-quette (blän ket´) n. A stew with a white sauce, usually served with onions or mushrooms.

blare (blâr) v. To make or cause a loud sound.

blar-ney (blär´nē) n. Talk that is deceptive or nonsense; charming or smooth flattery. **blarney** v.

bla-sé (bla zā´) adj. Indifferent to pleasure or excitement; world-weary.

blas-pheme (blas fēm´) v. To speak with irreverence. **blasphemously** adv. **blasphemousness** n.

blas-phem-ous (blas´ fa mus) adj. Containing or exhibiting blasphemy.

blast (blast) n. A strong gust of air; the sound produced when a horn is blown. **blasted** adj.

blast–off (blast´of´) n. The launching of a space ship.

blat (blat) v. To cry, as a calf; to bleat, as a sheep.

bla-tan-cy (blä´tan sē) n. The quality or state of being offensively loud or clamorous.

bla-tant (blät´ant) adj. Unpleasant; offensively loud; shameless.

blath-er (blath´ér) v. To talk without making sense. **blatherer** n.

blath-er-skite (blath´ér skīt´) n. One given to voluble, empty talk.

blaze (blāz) n. A bright burst of fire; a sudden outburst of anger; a trail marker; a white mark on an animal's face. **blaze** v.

bla-zer (blā´zér) n. A jacket with notched collar and patch pockets.

bla-zon (blā´z n) v. To make known; to announce. **blazoner** n.

bldg abbr. Building.

bleach (blēch) v. To remove the color from a fabric; to become white.

bleach-ers (blē´chérz) n. Seating for spectators in a stadium.

bleak (blēk) adj. Discouraging and depressing; barren; cold; harsh. **bleakness** n. **bleakly** adv.

blear-y (blēr´ē) adj. Unclearly defined; blurred vision from fatigue or lack of sleep.

bleat (blēt) n. The cry of a sheep or goat.

bleed (blēd) v. To lose blood, as from an injury; to extort money; to mix or allow dyes to run together.

bleep (blēp) n. A signal with a quick, loud sound.

blem-ish (blem´ish) n. A flaw or defect.

blench (blench) v. To turn aside from lack of courage.

blend (blend) v. To mix together smoothly, to obtain a new substance; to combine together. **blender** n.

bless (bles) v. To honor or praise; to confer prosperity or well-being.

bless-ed (bles´id) adj. Holy; enjoying happiness. **blessedly** adv.

bless-ing (bles´ing) n. A short prayer before a meal.

blight (blīt) n. A disease of plants that can cause complete destruction.

blimp (blimp) n. A large aircraft with a non–rigid gas filled hull.

blind (blīnd) adj. Not having eyesight; something that is not based on facts **blind.** n. A shelter that conceals hunters; a window shade.

blink (blingk) v. To squint; to open and close the eyes quickly; to take a quick glance.

blintz (blints) n. A very thin pancake rolled and stuffed with cottage cheese or other fillings.

blip (blip) v. To remove; erase sounds from a recording. **blip** n. The brief interruption as the result of blipping.

bliss (blis) n. To have great happiness or joy. **blissful** adj. **blissfully** adv.

blis-ter (blis´tér) n. The swelling of a thin layer of skin that contains a watery liquid. **blister** v. **blisteringly** adj.

blithe (blīth) adj. Carefree or casual. **blithely** adv. **blitheness** n.

blitz (blits) n. A sudden attack; an intensive and forceful campaign.

bliz-zard (bliz´ard) n. A severe winter storm characterized by wind and snow.

blk abbr. Black, block.

bloat (blōt) v. To swell or puff out. **bloat** n. **bloated** adj.

blob (blob) n. A small shapeless mass.

bloc (blok) n. A united group formed for a common action or purpose.

block (blok) n. A solid piece of matter; the act of obstructing or hindering something. **blockage** n.

block-ade (blo käd´) n. The closure of an area. **blockader** n. **blockade** v

block-y (blok´ē) adj. Similar to a block in form; stocky; chunky.

blond (blond) adj. Of a golden or flaxen color; a man with blond hair.

blonde (blond) adj. A woman or girl with blond hair.

blood (blud) n. The red fluid circulated by the heart that carries oxygen and nutrients to all parts of the body.

blood pressure n. A pressure exerted by the blood against the walls of the blood vessels; a measure of heart efficiency.

blood type n. Blood group.

blood vessel n. Any canal in which blood circulates, such as a vein, artery, or capillary.

bloom (blöm) v. To bear flowers; to flourish; to have a healthy look; radiance. **bloom** n. **blooming** adj.

bloom-ers (blö´mērz) n. Loose pants or trousers that are gathered at the knee or just below.

bloop-er (blö´pér) n. An embarrassing blunder made in public; in baseball, a high pitch lobbed to the batter.

blos-som (blos´om) n. A flower or a group of flowers of a plant that bears seeds. **blossom** v. To flourish; to grow; to develop. **blossomy** adj.

blot (blot) n. A spot or stain. **blot** v. To dry with an absorbent material.

blotch (bloch) n. An area of a person's skin that is discolored; a blemish. **blotchy** adj. **blotchily** adv.

blot out v. To obliterate or obscure; to make unimportant.

blot-ter (blot´ér) n. A piece of paper used to blot ink; a book for temporary entries.

blotting paper n. A porous paper used to absorb excess ink.

blouse (blous) n. A loosely fitting shirt or top.

blow (blö) v. To move or be in motion because of a current of air. **blow** n. A sudden hit with a hand or fist. **-er** n.

blow up v. Inflate the truth.

blub-ber (blub´ér) n. The fat removed from whales and other marine mammals from which oil comes.

blub-ber-y (blub´a rē) adj. Abounding in or resembling blubber.

bludg-eon (bluj´an) n. A stick with a loaded end used as a weapon.

blue (blö) n. A color the same as the color of a clear sky; the hue that is between violet and green.

bluff (bluf) v. To deceive or mislead; to intimidate by showing more confidence than the facts can support. **bluff** n. A steep and ridged cliff. **bluffly** adv. **bluffness** n.

blun-der (blun´dér) n. An error or mistake caused by ignorance. **blunder** v. To move clumsily. **blunderer** n.

blunt (blunt) adj. Frank and abrupt; a dull end or edge. **blunt** n. **bluntly** adv.

blur (bler) v. To smudge or smear; to become hazy. **blur** n.

blurt (blert) v. To speak impulsively.

blush (blush) v. To be embarrassed from modesty or humiliation and to turn red in the face; to feel ashamed. **blush** n. Make-up used to give color to the cheekbones. **blushing** adj.

blus-ter (blus´tér) n. A violent and noisy wind in a storm. **bluster** v. **-erer** n.

bo-a (bö´a) n. A large nonvenomous snake which coils around prey and crushes it; a long fluffy scarf.

boar (bör) n. A male pig; wild pig.

board (börd) n. A flat piece of sawed lumber; a flat area on which games are played; a group of people with managerial powers. **board** v. To receive lodging, meals or both, usually for pay; to enter a club, train, or plane.

board-er (börd er) n. A person who lives in someone's house and is provided food as well as lodging.

board game n. A game played by moving pieces or objects on a board.

board-ing-house (börding haus) n. A house in which meals and lodging are provided.

board-walk (börd´wok˜) n. A wooden walkway along a beach.

boast (bost) v. To brag about one's own accomplishments. **boaster, boastful-ness** n. **boastful** adj. **boastfully** adv.

boat (bot) n. A small open craft or ship.

bob (bob) v. To cause to move up and down in a quick, jerky movement.

bob-bin (bob´in) n. A spool that holds thread in a sewing machine.

bob-by (bob´ē) n. An English police officer.

bobby socks n. Girls' ankle socks.

bob-cat (bob´kat˜) n. A wildcat of North America, with reddish-brown fur, small ears, and a short tail.

bo-beche (bö besh´) n. A glass collar on a candlestick to catch the wax drippings from the candle.

bob-o-link (bob´a lingk˜) n. An American song bird, the male having black, yellowish, and white feathers.

bob-sled (bob´sled˜) n. Racing sled which has steering controls on the front runners. **bobsled** v. **bobsledder** n.

bob-white (bob´hwīt˜) n. A game bird of the eastern United States; the common North American quail.

bo-cac-cio (bö kä´chö) n. A large rockfish found primarily off the Pacific coast.

bode (böd) v. To foretell by omen or sign.

bo-de-ga (bö dā´ga) n. A wine shop and grocery store.

bod-ice (bod´is) n. The piece of a dress that extends from the shoulder to the waist.

bod-ied (bod´ēd) adj. Having a body.

bod-i-less (bod´ē lis) adj. Having no body or material form.

bod-kin (bod´kin) n. A small instrument with a sharp point for making holes in fabric or leather goods.

bod-y (bod´ē) n. The main part of something; the physical part of a person; a human being. **bodily** adv.

bodybuilding n. The development and toning of the body through diet and exercise. **bodybuilder** n.

bog (bog) n. A poorly drained, spongy area.

bo-gey (bö´gē) n. In golf, one stroke over par for a hole. **bogey** v.

bog-gle (bog´l) v. To pull away from with astonishment. **boggler** n.

bo-gus (bö´gas) adj. Not genuine;

counterfeit; worthless in value.

bo-hea (bŏ hē´) n. A black China tea.

boil (boil) v. To raise the temperature of water or other liquid until it bubbles; to evaporate; reduce in size by boiling. **boil** n. A very painful pus-filled swollen area of the skin caused by bacteria in the skin.

boil-er (boil´ẽr) n. A vessel that contains water and is heated for power.

bois-ter-ous (boi´stẽr us) adj. Violent, rough and stormy; undisciplined. **boisterously** adv. **boisterousness** n.

bold (bōld) adj. Courageous; showing courage; distinct and clear; conspicuous; confident. **boldly** adv. **-ness** n.

bold-face (bōld´fās´) n. A style of printing type with heavy thick lines.

bole (bōl) n. A tree trunk.

bo-le-ro (ba lâr´o) n. A short jacket without sleeves, worn open in the front.

boll (bōl) n. A rounded capsule that contains seeds, as from the cotton plant.

bol-lard (bōl´ẽrd) n. A post of wood on a wharf to fasten mooring lines.

boll weevil n. A small beetle whose larvae damage cotton bolls.

bo-lo-gna (ba lō´nē) n. A seasoned, smoked sausage.

bolo tie n. A tie made of cord and fastened with an ornamental clasp.

bol-ster (bōl´stẽr) n. A long, round pillow.

bolt (bōlt) n. A threaded metal pin designed with a head at one end and a removable nut at the other; a thunderbolt; a quick flash of lightning; a large roll of material. **bolt** v. To run or move suddenly.

bolt-er n. One who bolts.

bomb (bom) n. A weapon that is detonated upon impact releasing destructive material as gas or smoke. *Slang* A complete and total failure.

bom-bard (bom bärd´) v. To attack repeatedly with missiles or bombs. **bombarder** n. **bombardment** n.

bom-bar-dier (bom´bẽr dēr´) n. A crew member who releases the bombs from a military aircraft.

bom-ba-zine (bom´ba zēn´) n. Silk or cotton fabric woven with diagonal ribbing.

bombed adj. *Slang* Drunk.

bomb-er (bom´ẽr) n. A military aircraft that carries and drops bombs.

bona fide adj. Performed in good faith; genuine; authentic.

bo-nan-za (ba nan´za) n. A profitable pocket or vein of ore; great prosperity.

bon-bon (bon´bon˝) n. Chocolate or fondant candy with a creamy, fruity, or nutty center.

bond (bond) n. Something that fastens or binds together; a duty or binding agreement; an insurance agreement in which the agency guarantees to pay the employer in the event an employee is accused of causing financial loss.

bond-age (bon´dij) n. Slavery; servitude; restraint of a person's freedom.

bond-ed adj. Secured by a bond to insure the safety of money or goods.

bond paper n. A superior grade of paper used for stationery goods.

bond servant n. One who agrees to work without pay.

bonds-man (bondz´man) n. One who agrees to provide bond for someone else.

bone (bōn) n. The calcified connecting tissue of the skeleton. **bone** v.

bone-dry (bōn dīr) adj. Completely without water.

bone-head (bōn´hed˝) n. *Slang* A stupid person. **boneheaded** adj.

bon-er (bō´nẽr) n. *Slang* A mistake or blunder.

bon-fire (bon´fīẽr) n. An open outdoor fire.

bon-go (bong´gō) n. A pair of small drums played with the hands.

bon-i-face (bon´a fās˝) n. The proprietor of a hotel, inn, etc.

bo-ni-to (ba nē´tō) n. A game fish related to the tuna.

bon-kers (bän kerz) adj. *Slang* Acting in a crazy fashion.

bon-net (bon´it) n. A woman's hat that ties under the chin.

bon-ny (bon´ē) adj. Attractive or pleasing; pretty.

bon-sai (bōn´si) n. A small ornamental shrub grown in a shallow pot.

bon ton n. High style or fashion.

bo-nus (bō´nas) n., pl. **bonuses** Something that is given over and above what is expected.

bon vivant n. One who lives well or luxuriously.

bon voyage n. A farewell wish for a traveler to have a pleasant and safe journey.

bon-y (bō´nē) adj. Pertaining to, consisting of, or resembling bone.

boo (bö) n. Verbal expression showing disapproval or contempt.

book (bük) n. A group of pages fastened along the left side and bound between protective covers; literary work that is written or printed. **Book** The Bible.

book-bind-ing (bük´bīn˝ding) n. The act or trade of binding books.

book-case (bük´kās˝) n. A piece of furniture with shelving for storing books.

book-ing (bük´ing) n. A scheduled engagement.

book-keep-er (bük´kē˝pẽr) n. A person who keeps accounts and records business.

book-keep-ing (bük´kē˝ping) n. The

business of recording the accounts and transactions of a business.-**keeper** n.

book-let (bŭk´lĭt) n. A small book.

book-man (bŭk´măn) n. A person interested or versed in books.

book-mark (bŭk´märk´) n. Something inserted in a book to mark a place.

book-match (bŭk´măch´) v. To match patterns on separate sheets so that they appear to be mirror images of one another.

book of account n. A book or records used for recording business transactions.

book re-port (bŭk´rē pōrt´) n. A written or oral review of a book, given after reading the book

book review n. A critical, usually written, review of a book..

book seller n. A person who specializes in selling books.

book shelf n. An open shelf area used to display and store books.

book-stall (bŭk´sal´) n. A counter or stand where secondhand books are sold.

book-store (bŭk´stōr´) n. A place of business that sells reading material, especially books.

book value n. The value of something as shown in books about similar businesses.

boom (bōm) n. A deep, resonant sound; a long pole extending to the top of a derrick giving support to guide lifted objects. **boom** v. To flourish or grow swiftly.

boo-me-rang (bōō´ma rang´) n. A curved, flat missile that can be thrown so that it returns to the thrower.

boom town n. Slang A town with sudden prosperity or growth.

boon (bōn) n. Something that is pleasant or beneficial; a blessing; favor.

boon-docks n. Slang Backcountry; an out-of-the-way place.

boon-dog-gle (bōn´dog´al) n. A useless activity; a waste of time; a useless article produced with little skill.

boor (ber) n. A person with clumsy manners and little refinement; rude person. **boorishly** adv. -**ness** n.

boost (bōst) v. To increase; to raise or lift by pushing up from below. **boost** n. An increase in something.

booster cable n. Electric cables used to jump start a battery from another battery or power source.

boot (bōt) n. A protective covering for the foot; any protective sheath or covering. Computer Science To load a computer with an operating system or other software.

boot camp n. A military training camp for new recruits.

booth (bōth) n. A small enclosed compartment or area; an area at trade shows for displaying merchandise for sale; an area in a restaurant with a table and benches.

boot-leg (bōt´lĕg´) v. Slang To sell, make, or transport liquor illegally.

boot-less (bōt´lĕs) adj. Without profit or advantage; useless.

booze (bōz) n. Slang An alcoholic drink.

bor abbr. Borough.

bo-ra (bōr´a) n. A cold wind of the Adriatic.

bo-rac-ic (bō rasʹĭk) adj. Pertaining to or produced from borax.

bo-rax (bōr´aks) n. A crystalline compound used in manufacturing detergents and pharmaceuticals.

bor-der (bor´dĕr) n. A surrounding margin or edge; a political or geographic boundary. **border** v. To have the edge or boundary adjoining.

bore (bōr) v. To make a hole through or in something using a drill; to become tired, repetitious, or dull. **boredom** n.

bo-re-al (bōr´ē al) adj. Located in or of the north.

bore-dom (bōr´dam) n. State of being bored.

bor-er (bōr´ĕr) n. A tool used to bore holes.

boric acid n. A colorless or white mixture that is used as a preservative and as a weak antiseptic.

bor-ing (bōr´ ĭng) adj. That which is tiresome, causes boredom.

born (born) adj. Brought into life or being.

bo-ron (bōr´on) n. A soft, brown nonmetallic element used in nuclear reactor control elements, abrasives, and flares.

bor-ough (ber´ō) n. A self-governing incorporated town, found in some United States cities; an incorporated British town that sends one or more representatives to Parliament.

bor-row (bor´ō) v. To receive money with the intentions of returning it; to use another's idea as one's own.

borscht (borsh) n. Hot or cold beet soup.

bor-stal (bor´stal) n. An institution for delinquent boys and girls.

bort (bort) n. Imperfect diamond fragments used as an abrasive.

bor-zoi (bor´zoi) n. A breed of long-haired dogs of the greyhound family.

bosh (bosh) n. Foolish talk.

bos-ky (bosk´ē) adj. Thickly covered with trees or shrubs; related to a wooded area.

bos-om (bez´am) n. The female's breasts; the human chest; the heart or center of something. **bosomy** adj.

boss (bos) n. An employer or supervisor for whom one works. **boss** v. To command or supervise.

bot-a-nist (bot´a nist) n. A person skilled

in botany.

bot-a-nize (bŏt´a nīz) v. To collect and study plants while on a field trip.

bot-a-ny (bŏt´a nē) n. The science of plants.

botch (bŏch) v. To ruin something by clumsiness; to repair clumsily. **botch** n. A sore; patchwork. **botcher** n.

both (bōth) adj. & pron. Two in conjunction with one another.

both-er (bŏth´ĕr) v. To pester, harass, or irritate; to be concerned about something. **bothersome** adj.

bot-o-pho-bi-a n. Fear of underground places.

bot-tle (bŏt´al) n. A receptacle, usually made of glass, with a narrow neck and a top that can be capped or corked; formula or milk that is fed to a baby.

bottle-fed (bŏt´al fed) adj. Fed from a bottle.

bottle gourd n. A type of gourd.

bot-tle-neck (bŏt´al nek´) n. A narrow, obstructed passage, highway, road, etc.; a hindrance to progress or production.

bot-tle-nosed dolphin n. A stout-bodied whale having a prominent beak and dorsal fin.

bot-tom (bŏt´am) n. The lowest or deepest part of anything; the base; underside; the last; the land below a body of water. *Informal* The buttocks. **bottom** adj. **bottomer** n.

bot-tom-less (bŏt´am lis) adj. Extremely deep; seemingly without a bottom. **bottomlessness** n. **bottomlessly** adv.

bottom line n. The end result; lowest line of a financial statement, showing net loss or gain.

bot-tom-most (bŏt´om mīst´) adj. Being at the very bottom.

bottom round n. A cut of beef taken above the upper leg and below the rump.

bot-u-lism (bŏch´a liz´am) n. Food poisoning, often fatal, caused by bacteria that grows in improperly prepared food.

bou-clé (bō klā) n. An uneven yarn which forms loops at different intervals.

bouf-fant (bō fänt´) adj. Full; puffed out.

bou-gain-vil-lae-a (bō´gan vil´ē a) n. A flower of the 4 o'clock family with purple or red floral flowers.

bough (bou) n. The large branch of a tree.

bou-gie (bō´jē) n. A candle.

bouil-la-baisse (böl´ya bās´) n. A fish stew using at least two kinds of fish which is highly seasoned.

bouil-lon (bel´yon) n. A clear broth made from meat.

bouillon cube n. A compressed cube of seasoned meat extract.

boul-der (bōl´dĕr) n. A large round rock. **bouldered, bouldery** adj.

boul-e-vard (bül´a värd) n. A broad city street lined with trees.

bou-le-ver-se-ment (bü laver semänt) n. Violent disorder.

bounce (bouns) v. To rebound or cause to rebound; to leap or spring suddenly; to be returned by a bank as being worthless or having no value.

bounce-a-ble (bouns´abl) adj. Capable of bouncing

bounce back v. To recover rapidly from shock, illness or defeat.

bounc-er (boun´sĕr) n. A person who removes disorderly people from a public place.

bounc-ing (boun´sing) adj. Healthy; vigorous; robust; lively and spirited.

bound (bound) n. Legal or physical restraint. **bound** v. To limit; to be tied.

bound-a-ry (boun´da rē) n., pl. **boundaries** A limit or border.

bound-er (boun´dĕr) n. A vulgar person.

bound-less (bound´lis) adj. Without limits. **boundlessly** adv. **-lessness** n.

boun-te-ous (boun´tē as) adj. Plentiful or generous; giving freely. **bounteously** adv. **bounteousness** n.

boun-ti-ful (boun´ti fal) adj. Abundant; plentiful. **bountifully** adv

bounty (boun´tē) n. Generosity; an inducement or reward given for the return of something; a good harvest.

bou-quet (bō kā´) n. A group of cut flowers; the aroma of wine; a distinctive fragrance.

bour-bon (bẽr´bon) n. Whiskey distilled from fermented corn mash.

bour-geois (ber´zhwä) n., pl. **bourgeois** A member of the middle class. **bourgeois** adj.

bout (bout) n. A contest or match; the length of time spent in a certain way.

bou-tique (bō tēk´) n. A small retail shop that sells specialized gifts, accessories, and fashionable clothes.

bou-ton-niere (bŏt´o nēr´) n. A flower worn in the buttonhole of a man's jacket.

bou-zou-ki (bō zü kē) n. A long-necked stringed instrument resembling a mandolin.

bo-vine (bō´vīn) adj. Of or relating to an ox or cow. **bovinely** adv.

bowd-ler-ize (bōd´la rīz´) v. To expurgate. **bowdlerization** n.

bow-el (bou´al) n. The digestive tract located below the stomach; the intestines.

box (boks) n. A small container or chest, usually with a lid; a special area in a theater that holds a small group of people; a shrub or evergreen with leaves and hard wood that is yellow in color. v. To fight with the fists.

boy (boi) n. A male youth or child. **boyhood** n. **boyish** adj. **boyishly** adv.

boy-cott (boi´kot) v. To abstain from

dealing with, buying, or using as a means of protest. **boycott** *n*.

boy friend *n*. A male companion.

boy scout *n*. A boy who belongs to a worldwide organization that emphasizes citizenship training and character development; one who gives assistance.

boy-sen-ber-ry (boi´zan ber´ē) *n*. A trailing hybrid which bears fruit developed by crossing blackberries and raspberries.

bra (brä) *n*. Brassiere.

brace (brās) *n*. A device that supports or steadies something. **brace** *v*.

brace-let (brās´lit) *n*. An ornamental band for the wrist.

brac-er (brā´sér) *n*. A person who or that which braces; a tonic or stimulating drink.

bra-ce-ro (brä´serō) *n*. A Mexican laborer.

brack-en (brak´an) *n*. A large species of fern with tough stems and finely divided fronds.

brack-et (brak´it) *n*. A support attached to a vertical surface that projects in order to hold a shelf or other weight. **bracket** *v*. To enclose a word in brackets [ ].

brack-ish (brak´ish) *adj*. Containing salt; distasteful. **brackishness** *n*.

bract (brakt) *n*. A leaf-like plant below a flower cluster or flower. **bracteate, bracteal, bracted** *adj*.

brad (brad) *n*. A nail that tapers to a small head. **brad** *v*.

brad-awl (brad´ol) *n*. A tool used to make holes for brads or screws.

brag (brag) *v*. To assert or talk boastfully. **bragger** *n*. **braggy** *adj*.

brag-ga-do-ci-o (brag´ a dō´shēō) *n*. A cockiness or arrogant manner; empty bragging.

brag-gart (brag´art) *n*. A person who brags.

braid (brād) *v*. To interweave three or more strands of something; to plait. **braider, braiding** *n*. **braided** *adj*.

braille (brāl) *n*. A system of printing for the blind, consisting of six dots, two across and four directly under the first two. Numbers and letters are represented by raising certain dots in each group of six.

brain (brān) *n*. The large mass of nerve tissue enclosed in the cranium, responsible for the interpretation of sensory impulses, control of the body, and coordination; the center of thought and emotion in the body. **brain** *v*. *Slang* To hit someone on the head.

brain case *n*. The bony cranium or skull that surrounds the brain.

braise (brāz) *v*. To cook by first browning in a small amount of fat, adding a liquid such as water, and then simmering in a covered container.

brake (brāk) *n*. A device designed to stop or slow the motion of a vehicle or machine. **brake** *v*.

brake fluid *n*. The liquid contained in hydraulic brake cylinders.

brake-man (brāk´man) *n*. A train crew member who assists the conductor; the man who operates the brake on a bobsled.

bram-ble (bram´bl) *n*. A prickly shrub or plant such as the raspberry or blackberry bush.

bran (bran) *n*. The husk of cereal grains that is separated from the flour.

branch (branch) *n*. An extension from the main trunk of a tree. **branch** *v*. To grow out from a main stem in different directions. *Computer Science* To execute a different routine due to a decision statement in the program.

branch office *n*. An office located away from the central location of a business.

brand (brand) *n*. A trademark or label that names a product; a mark of disgrace or shame; a piece of charred or burning wood; a mark made by a hot iron to show ownership. **branch** *v*. **brander** *n*.

bran-dish (bran´dish) *v*. To wave or flourish a weapon.

brand-ling (brand´ling) *n*. A small earthworm.

brand name *n*. A company's trademark.

brand–new (brand´nō´) *adj*. New and unused.

brant (brant) *n*. A wild goose which breeds in the Arctic but migrates southward.

brash (brash) *adj*. Hasty, rash, and unthinking; insolent; impudent.

brass (bras) *n*. An alloy of zinc, copper and other metals in lesser amounts. *Slang* A high-ranking officer in the military.

bras-sard (bras´ärd) *n*. A piece of armor to protect the arm.

brass band *n*. A band with brass and percussion instruments only.

brass-bound (bras´bound´) *adj*. Having a border made of brass or a similar metal.

bras-siere (bra zēr´) *n*. A woman's undergarment with cups to support the breasts.

brass tacks *n*. The details of immediate, practical importance.

brass-y (bras´ē) *adj*. Of or like brass; brazen or impudent.

brat (brat) *n*. An ill-mannered child.

brat-wurst (brat werst) *n*. A fresh pork sausage.

bra-va-do (bra vä´dō) *n*. A false showing of bravery.

brave (brāv) *adj*. Having or displaying courage. **brave** *v*. To face with courage.

brav-er-y (brā´va rē) n. The quality of or state of being brave.

bra-vo (brä´vō) interj. Expressing approval.

bra-vu-ra (brä vö´ra) n. A musical passage which requires exceptional technical skill.

brawl (brol) n. A noisy argument or fight. **brawl** v. **brawler** n.

brawn (brän) n. Well-developed and solid muscles. **brawniness** n.

brawn-y (brän´ē) adj. Having large strong muscles; strong.

bray (brā) v. To make a loud cry like a donkey.

braze (brāz) v. To solder using a nonferrous alloy that melts at a lower temperature than that of the metals being joined together.

bra-zen (brā´zan) adj. Made of brass; shameless or impudent.

bra-zier (brā´zhèr) n. A person who works with brass; a metal pan that holds burning charcoal or coals.

breach (brēch) n. Ruptured, broken, or torn condition or area; a break in friendly relations. **breach** v. To break the law or an obligation.

breach of promise n. The violation of a promise.

bread (bred) n. A leavened food made from a flour or meal mixture and baked. Slang Money. **bread** v. To cover with bread crumbs before cooking.

break (brāk) v. To separate into parts with violence or suddenness; to collapse or give way; to change suddenly. Informal A stroke of good luck.

break-age (brā´kij) n. Things that are broken.

break-a-way (brāk´a wā´) n. A breaking away; a start, as of competitors in a contest.

break-fast (brek´fost) n. The first meal of the day.

break-up n. A disruption; a dissolution of connection.

breast (brest) n. The milk producing glandular organs on a woman's chest; the area of the body from the neck to the abdomen.

breast-bone (brest´bōn´) n. The sternum.

breast wall n. A retaining wall.

breath (breth) n. The air inhaled and exhaled in breathing; a very slight whisper, fragrance or breeze.

breathe (brēth) v. To draw air into and then expel it from the lungs; to take a short rest

breech (brēch) n. The buttocks; the hind end of the body; the part of a gun or firearm located at the rear of the bore. **breeches** Trousers that fit tightly around the knees.

breed (brēd) v. The genetic strain of

domestic animals, developed and maintained by mankind. **breeding** n.

breeze (brēz) n. A slight gentle wind; something that is accomplished with very little effort.

breez-i-ness (brē´zē nes) n. The state of experiencing breezes.

breezy adj. Brisk, cool.

breve (brēv) n. The curved mark over a vowel to indicate a short or unstressed syllable

bre-vet (bra vet´) n. A commission giving a military officer a higher rank than the one for which he is being paid.

bre-vi-ar-y (brē´vē er´ē) n. A book that contains prayers and psalms for the canonical hours.

brev-i-pen-nate (brev´e pen´āt) adj. Having short wings.

brev-i-ros-trate (bre´e ros´trāt) adj. Having a short bill or beak.

brev-i-ty (brev´i tē) n., pl. **brevities** Of brief duration; concise in expression.

brew (brö) v. To make beer from malt and hops by boiling, infusion, and fermentation. **brew** n.

brew-age (brö´ij) n. Fermented beverage.

brew-er n. A person whose occupation is to brew malt liquors.

brew-er-y (brö´a rē) n. A building or plant where beer or ale is brewed.

bri-ard (brē är´) n. A breed of large strong black dogs of France.

brib-a-ble (brīb´a bl) adj. Capable of being bribed.

bribe (brīb) v. To influence or induce by giving a token or anything of value for a service. **bribe** n.

brib-er-y (brī´ba rē) n. The practice of giving or receiving a bribe.

bric-a-brac (brik´a brak´) n. A collection of small objects.

brick (brik) n. A molded block of baked clay, usually rectangular in shape.

brick-bat (brik´bat´) n. A piece of a brick used as a weapon when thrown as a missile.

brick-kiln (brik´kil´) n. A furnace in which bricks are baked at a high temperature.

brick-lay-er (brik´lā´ėr) n. A person who lays bricks as a profession.

bri-dal (brīd´al) adj. Relating to a bride or a nuptial ceremony.

bride (brīd) n. A woman just married or about to be married.

bride-groom (brīd´gröm´) n. A man just married or about to be married.

brides-maid (brīdz´mād´) n. A woman who attends a bride at her wedding.

bridge (brij) n. A structure that provides passage over a depression or obstacle; a card game for four players; the platform on a ship from which it is steered.

bri-dle (brīd´al) n. A harness used to

restrain or guide a horse. **bridle** v. To restrain or control. **bridler** n.

bridle path n. A path or road used only for riding horseback.

brief (brēf) n. A concise, formal statement of a client's case. **brief** adj. Short in duration. **brief** v. To summarize or inform in a short statement. n.

brief-ing (brē'fing) n. The act of giving essential information.

brief-less (brēf'lis) adj. Having no legal clients.

brief-ly (brēf'lē) adv. In a brief way or short span of time.

bri-er (brī'ér) n. A woody, thorny, or prickly plant. **briery** adj.

brig (brig) n. A prison on a ship; a twinmasted, square-rigged sailing ship.

bri-gade (bri gād') n. A military unit organized for a specific purpose.

brig-a-dier (brig'a dēr') n. An officer in the British army.

brigadier general n. A commissioned officer in the armed forces who ranks above a colonel; insignia is one star.

brig-and (brig'and) n. A person who lives as a robber; bandit.

brig-an-dine (brig'an dēn') n. A medieval body armor.

brig-an-tine (brig'an tēn') n. A square-rigged two-masted ship.

bright (brīt) adj. Brilliant in color; vivid; shining and emitting or reflecting light; happy; cheerful; lovely. **-ness** n.

bright-en (brīt'n) v. To make things brighter. **brightener** n.

bril-liant (bril'yant) adj. Very bright and shiny; sparkling; radiant; extraordinarily intelligent; showing cleverness. **brilliantly** adv.

bril-lian-tine (bril'yan tēn') n. A light woven fabric similar to alpaca.

brim (brim) n. The edge or rim of a cup. **brim** v. **brimmed** adj.

brim-ful (brim'fel) adj. Completely full.

brim-mer (brim'ér) n. A cup or other container that is full to the top.

brim-stone (brim'stōn') n. Sulfur.

brin-dle (brin'dl) adj. Having dark streaks or flecks on a gray or tawny background.

brine (brīn) n. Water saturated with salt; the water contained in the oceans and seas.

bring (bring) v. To carry with oneself to a certain place; to cause, act, or move in a special direction.

brink (bringk) n. The upper edge or margin of a very steep slope.

bri-oche (brē'ōsh) n. A roll made from flour, eggs, butter, and yeast.

bri-o-lette (brē'a let') n. A pear-shaped diamond cut into facets.

bri-quette (bri ket') n. A small brick-shaped piece of charcoal.

brisk (brisk) adj. Moving or acting

quickly; being sharp in tone or manner; energetic, invigorating or fresh, pertaining to weather. **briskly** adv.

bris-ket (bris'kit) n. The meat from the lower chest or breast of an animal.

bris-ling (bris'ling) n. A small fish that is processed like a sardine.

bris-tle (bris'al) n. Short, stiff, coarse hair. **bristle** v. To react in angry defiance and manner. **bristly** adv.

britch-es (brich'iz) n. Trousers.

brit-tle (brit'l) adj. Very easy to break; fragile. **brittleness** n.

bro abbr. Brother.

broach (brōch) n. A tapered and serrated tool used for enlarging and shaping a hole. **broach** v.

broad (brod) adj. Covering a wide area; from side to side; clear; bright. **broadly** adv. **broadness** n.

bro-cade (brō kād') n. A silk fabric with raised patterns in silver and gold.

broc-co-li (brok'a lē) n. A green vegetable from the cauliflower family, eaten before the small buds open.

bro-chette (brō shet') n. A skewer used in cooking.

bro-chure (brō sher') n. A booklet or pamphlet.

brock-et (brok'it) n. A small deer of South America.

bro-gan (brō'gan) n. A sturdy oxford shoe.

brogue (brōg) n. A strong regional accent; a heavy shoe with a hobnail sole.

broil (broil) v. To cook by exposure to direct radiant heat.

broil-er (broi'lér) n. A device, usually a part of a stove, that is used for broiling meat; a young chicken.

broke (brōk) adj. Penniless; completely without money.

bro-ken (brō'ken) adj. Separated violently into parts. **brokenly** adv.

bro-ker (brō'kér) n. A person who acts as a negotiating agent for contracts, sales, or purchases in return for payment.

bro-ker-age (brō'kér ij) n. The establishment of a broker.

brome-grass (brōm'gras') n. A type of tall grasses having sagging spikelets.

bro-me-li-ad (brō'mē lē ad) n. The family of tropical American plants including the pineapple.

bro-mide (brō'mīd) n. A compound of bromine with other elements; a sedative; a commonplace idea or notion; one who is tiresome.

bro-mine (brō'mēn) n. A nonmetallic element of a deep red, toxic liquid that gives off a disagreeable odor.

bro-mo (brō mō) n. An effervescent mixture used as a sedative or a headache remedy.

headache remedy.

bron-chi-al (brong kē´el)) *adj.* Pertaining to the bronchi or their extensions, through which air flows to reach the lungs. **bronchially** *adv.*

bron-chi-tis (brong kī´tis) *n.* An acute inflammation of the bronchial tubes.

bron-cho-scope (brong´ka sköp´) *n.* A tubular instrument which is illuminated for inspecting the bronchi.

bron-chus (brong´kus) *n., pl.* **bronchi** Either of two main branches of the trachea that lead directly to the lungs.

bron-co (brong´kō) *n.* A wild horse of western North America.

bron-co-bust-er (brong´kō bus´ter) *n.* The man who breaks wild horses.

bron-to-saur (bron´ta sor´) *n.* A very large dinosaur which grew to a height of 12 feet and a length of over 70 feet.

bronze (bronz) *n.* An alloy of tin, copper, and zinc; moderate olive brown to yellow in color. **bronze** *v.* **bronze** *adj.*

Bronze Age *n.* Human culture between the Iron Age and the Stone Age.

brooch (brōch) *n.* A large decorative pin.

brood (brōd) *n.* The young of an animal; a family of young. **brood** *v.* To produce by incubation; to hatch; to think about at length.

brood-er (brōd er) *n.* An enclosed heated area for raising young chickens.

brook (brek) *n.* A small freshwater stream that contains many rocks.

brook trout *n.* A cold–water fish of eastern North America.

broom (brōm) *n.* A long-handled implement used for sweeping; a shrub with small leaves and yellow flowers.

broth (broth) *n.* The liquid in which fish, meat, or vegetables have been cooked; also called stock.

broth-er (bruth´ér) *n.* A male who shares the same parents as another person.

brough-am (brō´am) *n.* A vehicle without a cover over the driver's seat.

brought *v.* The past tense of bring.

brow (brou) *n.* The ridge above the eye where the eyebrow grows.

brown (broun) *n.* A color between yellow and red; a dark or tanned complexion.

brown-out (broun´out´) *n.* An interruption of electrical power.

browse (brouz) *v.* To look over something in a leisurely and casual way. **browser** *n.*

bruise (brōz) *n.* An injury that ruptures small blood vessels and discolors the skin without breaking it.

brum-by (brem bē) *n.* An unbroken horse.

brum-ma-gem (brum´a jam) *n.* Something inferior.

brunch (brunch) *n.* A combination of a late breakfast and an early lunch.

bru-net *or* **bru-nette** (brö net´) *n.* A person with dark brown hair.

bru-ni-zem (brö´na zem´) *n.* A dark-colored soil found in some of the areas in the Mississippi Valley.

brunt (brunt) *n.* The principal shock, or force.

brush (brush) *n.* A tool with bristles set into a handle for sweeping, painting, or grooming; a brief encounter.

brush discharge *n.* A discharge of low-intensity electric current with dimly luminous circuit ends.

brusque (brusk) *adj.* Being blunt or short in manner or speech; harsh. **brusquely** *adv.* **brusqueness** *n.*

bru-tal (brŏt al) *adj.* Very harsh or cruel treatment. **brutally** *adv.*

bru-tal-i-ty (brö tal´ī tē) *n.* A brutal course of action; ruthless or inhuman behavior.

bru-tal-ize (brö tal īz) *v.* To make inhuman, insensitive.

brute (brōt) *n.* A person characterized by physical power rather than intelligence; a person who behaves like an animal, crude. **brutish** *adj.*

brux-ism (brek´siz em) *n.* The unconscious grinding of the teeth during sleep.

bry-o-ny (brī´a nē) *n.* A vine of the gourd family having large leaves and fruit.

bry-o-phyte (brī´a fīt´) *n.* A division of nonflowering plant which includes the liverworts and mosses.

bub-ble (bub´l) *n.* A small round object, usually hollow; a small body of gas contained in a liquid. **bubble** *v.* To produce bubbles.

bub-bler (bub´lér) *n.* A drinking fountain where water bubbles upward.

bub-bly (bub blē) *adj.* Something containing or full of bubbles. *Slang* Champagne.

bu-bo (bū´bō) *n.* Inflammatory swelling of the lymphatic glands, especially in the area of the groin or armpits.

bubonic plague *n.* The contagious and normally fatal disease that is transmitted by fleas from infected rats, characterized by fever, diarrhea, chills, and vomiting.

Buchanan, James *n.* (1791-1868) The fifteenth president of the United States from 1857-1861.

buck (buk) *n.* The adult male deer; a male animal; the lowest grade in the military category. *Slang* A dollar. **buck** *v.* To arch the back and move so as to throw a rider; to oppose the system.

buck-et (buk´it) *n.* A vessel used to carry liquids or solids; a pail.

bucket brigade *n.* A line of people who pass buckets of water from hand to hand in order to extinguish a fire.

buck-eye (buk´ī) *n.* A tree with flower clusters and glossy brown nuts.

buck-hound (buk´hound˝) *n.* A small dog used in hunting deer and other animals.

buckle (buk´l) *v.* To warp, crumple, or bend under pressure. **buckle** *n.* Metal clasp for fastening one end to another..

buckle down *v.* To apply oneself.

bu-col-ic (bū kol´ik) *n.* A pastoral poem; someone that is rural or countrified.

bud (bud) *n.* Something that has not developed completely; a small structure that contains flowers or leaves that have not developed.

bud-dy (bud´ē) *n.* A good companion, partner, or friend.

budge (buj) *v.* To give way to; to cause to move slightly.

bud-ger-i-gar (buj´a rē gär´) *n.* A small Australian parrot.

bud-get (buj´it) *n.* The total amount of money allocated for a certain purpose. **budget** *v.*

budg-et-eer (buj´i tēr´) *n.* A person who prepares a budget for someone.

buff (buf) *n.* A leather made mostly from skins of buffalo, elk, or oxen, having the color of light to moderate yellow.

buf-fa-lo (buf´a lō) *n.* A wild ox with heavy forequarters, short horns, and a large muscular hump. **buffalo** *v.* To bewilder, to intimidate.

buf-fet (ba fā´) *n.* A meal placed on a side table so that people may serve themselves; a side table for serving food.

buffet (buf´et) *v.* To strike with the hand; to hit repeatedly.

buffing wheel *n.* The round surface of a wheel covered with cloth used to polish or shine something.

bug (bug) *n.* Any small insect; a concealed listening device. **bug** *v.* To bother or annoy. **buggy** *adj.*

bug-bane (bug´bān) *n.* An herb of the buttercup family with white flowers.

bug-eye (beg ī) *n.* A small boat with a flat bottom.

bug-gy (bug´ē) *n.* A small carriage pulled behind a horse.

bu-gle (bū´gal) *n.* A brass instrument without keys or valves. **bugler** *n.*

buhr-stone (ber´stōn˝) *n.* A rock used to make a grinding stone.

build (bild) *v.* To erect by uniting materials into a composite whole; to fashion or create; to develop or add to. **build** *n.* The form or structure of a person.

build-er (bil´dėr) *n.* A person who supervises the construction of a building project.

build-ing (bil´ding) *n.* A roofed and walled structure for permanent use.

build-up (bild´up˝) *n.* A collection of materials for a future need.

bulb (bulb) *n.* A rounded underground plant such as a tulip that lies dormant in the winter and blooms in the spring; an incandescent light for electric lamps. **bulbed, bulbaceous** *adj.*

bul-bous (bul´bus) *adj.* Resembling a bulb in shape.

bul-bul (bel´bel) *n.* A songbird often mentioned in poetry.

bulge (bulj) *n.* A swelling of the surface caused by pressure from within.

bul-gur (bul´ger) *n.* Wheat prepared for human consumption.

bu-lim-i-a (bū lim´ēa) *n.* An eating disorder in which a person overeats and then throws up in order to remain thin.

bulk (bulk) *n.* A large mass; anything that has great size, volume, or units.

bulk-age (bulk´āg) *n.* A substance that increases the bulk of material in the intestine, thus stimulating peristalsis.

bulk-head (bulk´hed˝) *n.* The partition that divides a ship into compartments; a retaining wall along a waterfront.

bulk-y (bül´kē) *adj.* **bulkiness** *n.*

bul-la (bül´a) *n.* A blister or vesicle.

bull-doz-er (bül´dō´zėr) *n.* A tractor-like machine with a large metal blade in front for moving earth and rocks.

bul-let (bül´it) *n.* A cylindrical projectile that is fired from a gun.

bul-le-tin (bül´i tan) *n.* A broadcasted statement of public interest; a public notice.

bulletin board *n.* A board on which messages and notices are posted.

bul-rush (bül´rush˝) *n.* Tall grass as found in a marsh.

bul-wark (bül´wėrk) *n.* A strong protection or support.

bum (bum) *n.* One who begs from others; one who spends time unemployed; one who devotes all his time to fun and recreation. **bum** *v.* To loaf.

bum-ble-bee (bum´bl bē´) *n.* A large hairy bee.

bun (bun) *n.* Any of a variety of plain or sweet small breads; tightly rolled hair that resembles a bun.

bunch (bunch) *n.* A cluster or group of items that are the same.

bun-dle (bun´dl) *n.* Anything wrapped or held together. *Slang* A large amount of money. **bundle** *v.* **bundler** *n.*

bundle up *v.* To dress warmly, usually using many layers of clothing.

bung (bung) *n.* The cork used to plug the bunghole in a cork cask.

bun-ga-low (bung´ga lō˝) *n.* A small one story cottage.

bung-hole (bung´hōl) *n.* A filling hole in a barrel through which it is filled, which is then closed by a plug.

bun-gle (bung´gl) *v.* To work or act

bun-ion (bun´yɑn) *n.* An inflamed, painful swelling of the small sac on the first joint of the big toe.

bun-ker (bung´kèr) *n.* A tank for storing fuel on a ship; an embankment or a sand trap creating a hazard on a golf course.

bun-kum (bung´kam) *n.* Meaningless talk.

bunt (bunt) *v.* To tap a pitched ball with a half swing. **bunt** *n.* The center of a square sail.

bunt-ing (bun´ting) *n.* A hooded blanket for a baby; a type of stout-billed bird.

buoy (bŏ´ē) *n.* A floating object to mark a channel or danger. **buoy** *v.* To stay afloat.

buoy-an-cy (boi´an sē) *n.* The tendency of an object or body to remain afloat in liquid or to rise in gas or air.

buoy-ant (boi ent) *adj.* Having the quality of floating or rising in a fluid.

bur-ble (bûr´bl) *n.* A gentle, bubbling flow; a bubbling speech pattern.

bur-bot (ber´bat) *n.* A freshwater fish of the cod family.

bur-den (ber´dan) *n.* Something that is hard to bear; a duty or responsibility; a ship's capacity for carrying cargo. **burden** *v.* **burdensome** *adj.*

bur-dock (ber´dok) *n.* A coarse plant with purplish flowers.

bu-reau (bûr´ō) *n., pl.* **bureaus** A low chest for storing clothes; a branch of the government or a subdivision of a department.

bu-reauc-ra-cy (bū rok´ra sē) *n., pl.* **bureaucracies** A body of non-elected officials in a government; the administration of a government through bureaus.

bu-reau-crat (bū´ra krat´) *n.* A government official who has great authority in his own department.

bu-reau-crat-ic (bū´ra krat ic) *adj.*

bu-rette (bū ret´) *n.* A glass tube for measuring quantities of liquid or gas that are discharged or taken in.

burg (berg) *n.* A town or city.

burg-age (ber´gij) *n.* A tenure held under the king for a yearly rent.

bur-geon (ber´jan) *v.* To put forth new life as in leaves, buds, etc.

burg-er (ber´gèr) *n. Slang* A hamburger.

bur-gess (ber´jis) *n.* A representative of the legislature of colonial Maryland and Vir-ginia.

burgh (bürg) *n.* A borough or chartered towns in Scotland.

burgh-er (bür´gèr) *n.* The inhabitant of a borough; a citizen.

bur-glar (ber´glèr) *n.* A person who steals personal items from another person's home.

bur-i-al (ber´ē al) *n.* The process or act of burying, especially the act of burying a deceased person.

bu-rin (bûr´in) *n.* An engraver's cutting tool; a flint tool with a beveled point.

burl (berl) *n.* A woody, often flat and hard, hemispherical growth on a tree.

bur-la-der-o (ber le der´ō) *n.* A wooden barrier to protect the bullfighter from the charge of the bull.

bur-lap (ber´lap) *n.* A coarse cloth woven from hemp or jute.

bur-lesque (bèr lesk´) *n.* Theatrical entertainment with comedy and mocking imitations. **burlesque** *adj.*

bur-ly (ber´lē) *adj.* Very heavy and strong. **burlily** *adv.* **burliness** *n.*

burn (bern) *v.* To be destroyed by fire; to consume fuel and give off heat, char or scorch. **burn** *n.* An injury produced by fire, heat, or steam; the firing of a rocket engine in space. **burning** *adj.*

bur-nish (ber´nish) *v.* To make shiny by rubbing; to polish.

burnt (bernt) *adj.* Scorched or darkened as if by burning.

burp (berp) *n.* A belch. **burp** *v.* To expel gas from the stomach.

burp gun *n.* Small submachine gun.

bur-ro (ber´ō) *n.* A small donkey.

bur-row (ber´ō) *n.* A tunnel dug in the ground by an animal. **burrow** *v.* To construct by tunneling through the earth.

bur-sa (ber´sa) *n.* A sac between the bone and the tendon.

bur-sar (ber´sèr) *n.* The person or official in charge of monies at a college.

bur-sa-ry (ber´sa rē) *n.* The treasury of a college; a grant to a needy student.

burse (bers) *n.* A square cloth used in a Communion service.

bur-si-tis (ber sī´tis) *n.* An inflammation of the small sac between a tendon of the knee, elbow, or shoulder joints.

burst (berst) *v.* To explode or experience a sudden outbreak; to suddenly become visible or audible. **burst** *n.* A sudden explosion or outburst.

bur-ton (ber´ton) *n.* A single or double blocking tackle used for hoisting.

bur-y (ber´ē) *v.* To hide by covering with earth; to inter a body at a funeral service.

bus (bus) *n., pl.* **busses** A large passenger vehicle; a small hand truck; a conductor for collecting electric currents.

bus-by (buz´bē) *n.* A fur hat that is worn in certain regiments of the British Army.

bush (bush) *n.* A low plant with branches near the ground; a dense tuft or growth; land that is covered thickly with undergrowth.

bush basil *n.* A small annual herb.

bush bean *n.* A variety of green beans grown on bushes.

bushed (busht) *adj. Slang* Extremely exhausted; tired.

bush-el (bush´l) *n.* A unit of dry measurement which equals four pecks or 2,150.42 cubic inches; a container that holds a bushel.

bush-fire *n.* A fire burning out of control in the bush.

Bush, George *n.* (1924-) The forty-first president of the United States from 1989-1993.

bush league *n.* An inferior class or team.

bush-y (besh´ē) *adj.* Overgrown with a dense growth of bushes.

bus-i-ly (biz´e lē) *adv.* In a busy manner.

busi-ness (biz´nes) *n.* One's professional dealings or occupation; an industrial or commercial establishment.

busk-er (bes ker) *n.* A person who entertains on the street corner.

bus-kin (bus´kin) *n.* A boot that reaches halfway to the knee; tragedy as that of an ancient Greek drama.

buss (bus) *n.* A kiss.

bust (bust) *n.* A sculpture that resembles the upper part of a human body; the breasts of a woman. **bust** *v.* To break or burst; to become short of money. *Slang* To place a person under arrest.

bus-tle (bus´al) *n.* A padding that gives extra bulk to the back of a woman's skirt. **bustle** *v.* To move energetically; to make a show of being busy.

bus-y (biz´ē) *adj.* Full of activity; engaged in some form of work.

but (but) *conj.* On the contrary to; other than; if not; except for the fact.

bu-tane (bū´tān) *n.* A gas produced from petroleum, used as a fuel refrigerant and aerosol propellant.

butch-er (bech´er) *n.* One who slaughters animals and dresses them for food.

bu-te-o (bū´tē o´) *n.* Hawks with broad wings and soaring flight.

but-ler (but´lėr) *n.* A male servant of a household.

butt (but) *n.* The object of ridicule; the thick large or blunt end of something. **butt** *v.* To hit with horns or the head; to be joined at the end.

butte (būt) *n.* A small mountain with steep precipitous sides with a smaller summit area than a mesa.

but-ter (but´ér) *n.* A fatty substance churned from milk.

but-ter-fly (but´ėr flī) *n., pl.* **butterflies** A narrow-bodied insect with four broad, colorful wings; a person occupied with the pursuit of pleasure; a swimming stroke.

but-tocks (but´akz) *n.* The two round fleshy parts of the rump.

but-tress (bu´tris) *n.* A support made of either brick or stone and built against or projecting from a building or wall used for the purpose of giving stability;

a support or prop. **buttress** *v.*

butyl alcohol *n.* Chemically related form of alcohol that contains the butyl radical, used in manufacturing perfumes, lacquers and other organic compounds.

bu-tyr-a-ceous (bū´ta rā´shus) *adj.* Having the qualities of butter.

bu-ty-rin (bū´tėr in) *n.* A yellowish liquid fat that is present in butter, and is formed from butyric acid.

bux-om (buk´som) *adj.* Lively; full of life; happy; pleasantly plump, cheerful.

bux-om-ly (buk´som lē) *adv.* Vigorously; briskly.

buy (bī) *v.* To purchase in exchange for money; to acquire possession of something.. *n.* Anything that is bought.

buy-er (bī´ér) *v.* A person who buys from a store or an individual; a person employed to make purchases for a company.

buy out *v.* To obtain release from a responsibility, by making a payment; to purchase shares in a business concern or investment.

buy up *v.* To buy extensively or freely.

buzz (buz) *v.* To make a low vibrating sound, as a bee; the continuous humming sound of a bee.

buzz-er (buz´ér) *n.* An electrical signaling device that makes a buzzing sound; one that buzzes.

buzz-word (buz´werd) *n.* An important sounding technical word or phrase, which might have little meaning .

by (bī) *prep.* Up to and beyond; to go past; not later than; next to; according to; beside or near; according to; in relation to.

by and large *adv.* In general.

bye (bī) *n.* A position in which a contestant has no opponent after pairs are drawn for a tournament, and, therefore, advances to the next round; something that is aside from the main consideration or course.

bye-bye (bī bī) *Slang* Farewell.

by-gone (bī´gon´) *adj.* Gone by; past; former; departed; out of date..

by-law (bī´lo) *n.* A rule or law governing internal affairs of a group or organization.

by-pass *n.* A secondary route to avoid congested areas; a replacement artery to carry blood past an obstruction.

by-street *n.* A side or secondary street.

byte (bīt) *n.* In *computer science,* a sequence of adjacent binary digits operated on as a unit.

by-way (bī wā) *n.* A secondary or little traveled road; a little known aspect.

by-word (bī werd) *n.* A frequent or commonly used phrase or word; a proverbial saying.

C, c (sē) The third letter of the English

C, c (sē) The third letter of the English alphabet; the Roman numeral for 100; *Mus.* The keynote of the C major scale.

cab (kab) *n.* A taxicab; the compartment where a person sits to drive a large truck or machinery.

ca-bal (ka bal´) *n.* A group that conspires against a government or other public institution.

cab-by (kab´ē) *n.* Cab driver.

cab-in (kab´ in) *n.* A small, roughly-built house, especially one made from logs.

ca-ble (kā´bl) *n.* A heavy rope made from fiber or steel; a bound group of insulated conductors; a cablegram.

ca-boo-dle (ka böd´l) *n. Slang* The entire unit, amount, or collection.

ca-boose (ka bös´) *n.* The last car of a train that contains the eating and sleeping quarters for the crew.

cab-o-tage (kab´ a tij) *n.* Coastal navigation; the carrying of cargo or passengers within the borders of a nation.

ca-bret-ta (ka bret´a) *n.* Sheepskin used in the making of shoes and gloves.

cab-ri-o-let (kab´rē o lā) *n.* A lightweight one horse carriage with a single seat and two wheels; a type of automobile similar to a convertible.

ca-ca-o (ka kā´ō) *n.* Any tree of the chocolate family; the dried seed of the cacao tree from which chocolate and cocoa are made.

cach-a-lot (kash´a lot´) *n.* A sperm whale.

cache (kash) *n.* A safe place to hide and conceal goods. **cache** *v.*

ca-chet (ka shā´) *n.* A mark of distinction or authenticity; a seal on a letter or an important document showing that it is official.

cack-le (kak´l) *v.* To laugh with the characteristic shrill noise a hen makes after laying an egg; to talk or laugh with a similar sound. **cackler** *n.*

cac-o-e-thes (kak´ō ē´thēz) *n.* A strong compulsion; a bad habit.

ca-coph-o-ny (ka kof´a nē) *n.* A harsh and disagreeable sound. **cacophonous** *adj.* **cacophonously** *adv.*

cad (kad) *n.* An ungentlemanly man. **caddish** *adj.*

ca-das-tre *or* **ca-das-ter** (ka das´tér) *n.* An official survey of the value, or worth, and ownership of an area's real estate which is used in assessing taxes.

ca-dav-er (ka dav´ér) *n.* The body of a person who has died; a corpse.

cad-dis (kad´is) *n.* A woolen fabric; worsted ribbon, yarn or binding.

cad-dish (kad´is) *adj.* Unprincipled; like a cad; ungentlemanly.

cade (kād) *adj.* Of an animal's offspring, abandoned by the mother and brought up by human beings.

ca-delle (ka del´) *n.* A black beetle, that eats stored grain.

ca-dence (kād´ens) *n.* A rhythmic movement or flow.

ca-den-za (ka den´za) *n.* An elaborate ornamental section for a soloist near the end of a concerto.

ca-det (ka det´) *n.* A student in training at a naval or military academy.

cadge (kaj) *v.* To beg or to receive by begging; to mooch. **cadger** *n.*

ca-du-ce-us (ka dö´sē us) *n.* The symbol of the medical profession, a winged staff with two serpents entwined around it.

ca-du-ci-ty (ka dö´si tē) *n.* The tendency to fall; senility; the infirmity of old age.

cae-su-ra (si zher´a) *n.* A pause or break in a line of verse or poetry; a pause or division in a verse; a separation, by the ending of a word or by a pause in the sense, of syllables rhythmically connected.

caf-feine (ka fēn´) *n.* A stimulant found in coffee, tea, and dark colas; a slightly bitter alkaloid used as a stimulant and diuretic.

caf-tan (kaf´tan) *n.* A loose-fitting, full-length garment worn in the Near East.

ca-gey (kā´jē) *adj.* Shrewd, wary, or cautious.

ca-hier (kä yā´) *n.* A number of sheets of paper or leaves of a book placed together, as for binding; a report of the proceedings of any body, as a legislature.

cais-son (kā´san) *n.* A waterproof structure that is used for construction work underwater.

cai-tiff (kā´tif) *n.* A miserable person; a vile person.

ca-jole (ka jōl´) *v.* To wheedle or coax someone into doing something.

cal-a-boose (kal´a bös´) *n.*, *Slang* A jail.

ca-la-di-um (ka lā´dē um) *n.* Tropical plant having large, beautiful leaves of variegated colors, cultivated as a pot plant for its foliage.

cal-a-man-der (kal´a man´dér) *n.* A variety of extremely hard wood from an East India tree.

cal-a-mine (kal´a mīn´) *n.* A pink powder of zinc oxide and ferric oxide mixed with mineral oils to form a lotion for skin irritations such as poison ivy.

ca-lam-i-ty (ka lam´i tē) *n.*, *pl.* **calamities** Misfortune or great distress, adversity or mishap; great misery. **calamitous** *adj.* **calamitously** *adv.*

cal-a-mus (kal´amus) *n.* A cane or reed; any palm that yields rattan or canes; the quill of a feather.

ca-lan-do (kä län´dō) *adv. Mus.* Becoming gradually slower and softer in sound; diminishing.

cal-ca-ne-us (kăl kā´nē us) *n.* The largest bone of the tarsus; the heel bone in man.

cal-car (kal´kär) *n.* A spur-like node on the leg of a bird; an oven or reverberating furnace, used in glassworks.

cal-cic (kal´ sik) *adj.* Pertaining to lime; containing calcium.

cal-cif-ic (kal sif´ik) *adj.* Forming salts of calcium.

cal-ci-fi-ca-tion (kal´si fi kā´shan) *n.* Process of changing a substance through the deposition of lime.

cal-ci-fuge (kal´si füj´) *n.* A plant that cannot thrive in limestone or in soil saturated with lime.

cal-ci-fy (kal´si´fi´) *v.* To become or make chalky or stony.

cal-ci-mine (kal´si mīn´) *n.* A tinted or white liquid that contains water, glue, coloring matter, and whiting, used to paint walls or ceilings, but which cannot withstand washing.

cal-cine (kal´sīn) *v.* To heat to a high temperature without melting, but causing loss of moisture and reduction.

cal-cite (kal´sīt) *n.* Calcium carbonate mineral, that is found in crystal forms including limestone, chalk and marble.

cal-ci-um (kal´sē um) *n.* The alkaline element that is found in teeth and bones; symbol Ca.

cal-cu-late (kal´kū lāt) *v.* To figure by a mathematical process, to evaluate; to estimate. **calculable** *adj.* **calculably** *adv.* **calculative** *adj.*

cal-cu-lat-ed (kal´kū lā´tid) *adj.* Worked out beforehand with careful estimation, mathematical computation.

cal-cu-lat-ing (kal´kū lā´ting) *adj.* Shrewd consideration of self-interest.

cal-cu-la-tion (kal´kū lā´shan) *n.* The act or the result of mathematical computation.

cal-cu-la-tor (kal´kū lā´tĕr) *n.* A machine with a keyboard for automatic mathematical operation.

cal-cu-lus (kal´kū lus) *n.* A stone in the gallbladder or kidneys; the mathematics of integral and differential calculus.

cal-de-ra (kal der´a) *n.* A large crater formed by the collapse of the main part of a volcano, caused by violent volcanic action.

cal-dron (kol´drən) *n.* A large boiler or kettle.

cal-e-fac-to-ry (kal e´fak terē) *n.* A room in a monastery that is heated and used as a sitting room.

cal-en-dar (kal´an dĕr) *n.* A system for showing time divisions by years, months, weeks, and days; the twelve months in a year.

cal-ends (kal´endz) *n.* The first day of the month on the Roman calendar.

ca-len-du-la (ka len´ja la) *n.* A marigold; the dried flowers of this plant, used to promote healing.

cal-en-ture (kal´an chĕr) *n.* A delirium caused in the tropics by exposure to excessive heat.

ca-les-cence (ka les´ans) *n.* Growing warmth; growing heat.

cal-i-ber (kal´i bĕr) *n.* The inner diameter of a tube or gun; the quality or worth of something.

cal-i-brate (kal´ibrāt) *v.* To determine the caliber of; to check or correct the scale of a measuring instrument. **calibration** *n.*

cal-i-co (kal´i kō) *n.* Cotton fabric with figured patterns.

ca-lic-u-lus (ka lik´ya lus) *n.* A small cup-like object.

California *n.* A state located on the western coast of the United States, statehood September 9, 1850, state capital Sacramento.

cal-i-for-nite (kal a for´nīt) *n.* Mineral that resembles jade.

cal-i-per (kal´i pĕr) *n.* An instrument with two curved, hinged legs, used to measure inner and outer dimensions.

ca-liph (kā´lif) *n.* A religious and secular head in Islam. **caliphate** *n.*

cal-is-then-ics (kal´is then´iks) *n.* Exercises that develop muscular tone and promote good physical condition.

calk (kok) *n.* A projection tilted downward on the shoe of a horse to prevent slipping; a similar device on the sole of a shoe or boot.

call (kol) *v.* To speak to attract attention; to name or designate; to telephone; to pay a short visit; to demand payment; in card games, to demand the opponent show his cards; to stop officially.

cal-la *or* **cal-la lily (kal´a)** *n.* A family of white and yellow flowers enclosing a club-like flower stalk.

cal-lig-ra-pher (ka lig´ra fĕr) *n.* A person who writes beautiful handwriting.

cal-lig-ra-phy (ka lig´ra fē) *n.* The art of writing with a pen using different slants and positions; fine penmanship.

call-ing (ko´ling) *n.* The occupation or profession of a person.

cal-li-o-pe (ka lī´ə pē´) *n.* A keyboard musical instrument that is fitted with steam whistles.

Cal-lis-to (ka lis´tō) *n.* The largest of Jupiter's moons.

call money *n.* Money loaned on call or available for call loans.

call off *v.* To cancel, as that which has been planned; to speak or read out loud.

cal-lose (kal´us) *n.* An occasional carbohydrate or periodic component of plant cell walls, which forms the callus at an injury site.

cal-los-i-ty (ka los´i tē) *n.* The condition

of being callous or hardened; abnormal thickness and hardness of the skin and other tissues.

cal-lous (kal´us) *adj.* Having calluses; to be without emotional feelings; unfeeling. **callously** *adv.* **-ness** *n.*

call rate *n.* The interest which is charged on a loan repayable on demand.

cal-lus (kal´us) *n., pl.* **calluses** A thickening of the horny layer of the skin.

calm (kom) *adj.* Absence of motion; having little or no wind, storms, or rough water.

cal-ma-tive (kal´ma tiv) *n.* A tranquilizer.

cal-o-mel (kal´e mel´) *n.* A white, tasteless compound used as a purgative.

cal-o-rie (kal´a rē) *n.* A measurement of the amount of heat or energy produced by food. **caloric** *adj.*

cal-o-rif-ic (kal a rif´ik) *adj.* Capable of producing heat or causing heat.

cal-o-rim-e-ter (kal e rim´i tėr) *n.* An instrument for measuring heat; any of several apparatuses for measuring quantities of heat absorbed or produced by a body.

ca-lotte (ka lot´) *n.* A small domed cap for the skull.

cal-trops (kal´trops) *n.* Plants having spiny heads or fruit.

cal-u-met (kal´ya met´) *n.* A pipe used by the North American Indians during ceremonies; also known as a peace pipe.

ca-lum-ni-ate (ka lum´nē āt´) *v.* To slander; to malign.

cal-um-ny (kal´am nē) *n., pl.* **calumnies** A statement that is malicious, false, and damaging to someone's reputation.

cal-va-dos (kal´va dōs´) *n.* An applejack; brandy, distilled from hard apple cider.

Cal-va-ry (kal´va rē) *n.* The location where Jesus Christ was crucified.

calve (kav) *v.* To give birth to a calf.

calx (kalks) *n.* The oxide or ashy residue that remains after metals or minerals have been subjected to combustion.

ca-lyp-so (ka lip´sō) *n. pl.* **calypsos** Improvised ballad of the West Indies with lyrics on topical or humorous subjects.

ca-lyp-tra (ka lip´tra) *n.* A hood-like part connected with the organs of fructification in flowering plants.

ca-lyx (kā´liks) *n., pl.* **calyxes** The outer cover of a flower.

cam (kam) *n.* A curved wheel used to produce a reciprocating motion.

ca-ma-ra-de-rie (kä´ma rä´de rē) *n.* Good will among friends.

cam-a-ril-la (kam´a ril´a) *n.* A group of private unofficial secret counselors or advisers.

cam-ber (kam´bėr) *n.* A slight curve upward in the middle.

cam-bist (kam´bist) *n.* A person who is well versed in the science of monetary exchange; a dealer in bills of exchange.

cam-bi-um (kam´bē um) *n.* The layer of soft cellular tissue between the bark and wood in trees and shrubs responsible for secondary growth.

cam-bric (kām´brik) *n.* A cotton fabric or white linen.

cambric tea *n.* A mixture of hot water and milk, with sugar and a little tea.

came (kām) *n.* A grooved lead bar that is used to hold together the panes of glass in lattice work or stained-glass windows. *v.* Past tense of to come.

cam-el (kam´el) *n.* An animal used as a beast of burden in desert regions, having either one or two humps on its back.

ca-mel-lia (ka mēl´ya) *n.* A greenhouse shrub with shiny green leaves and various colored flowers, used in corsages.

ca-mel-o-pard (ka mel´e pärd) *n.* A giraffe.

camel's hair *n.* The cloth made of camel's hair.

cam-e-o (kam´ē ō´) *n.* A gem usually cut with one layer contrasting with another serving as a background; a brief appearance by a famous performer in a single scene on a television show or in a movie.

cam-er-a (kam´er a) *n.* An apparatus for taking photographs in a lightproof enclosure with an aperture and shuttered lens through which the image is focused and recorded on photosensitive film.

cam-er-al (kam´ėr al) *adj.* Pertaining to public revenues or finances.

camino real *n.* Highway; main road.

cam-i-on (kam´ē an) *n.* A sturdy cart for transporting heavy loads.

ca-mise (ka mēz´) *n.* A loose smock or shirt.

cam-i-sole (kam´i sōl´) *n.* A woman's short, sleeveless undergarment.

cam-let (kam´lit) *n.* A rich fabric made from goat's hair, a durable waterproof cloth.

cam-o-mile (kam´a mīl) *n.* Herb with strongly scented flowers that are used medicinally.

cam-ou-flage (kam´a fläzh´) *v.* To disguise by creating the effect of being part of the natural surroundings.

camp (kamp) *n.* A temporary lodging or makeshift shelter.

cam-paign (kam pān´) *n.* An organized operation designed to bring about a particular political, commercial, or social goal. **campaigner** *n.*

cam-pa-ni-le (kam pa nē´lē) *n.* A free standing bell tower.

cam-pan-u-late (kam pan´ya lit) *adj.*
Shaped like a bell, usually as a
description for flower petals.

cam-pes-tral (kam pes´tral) *adj.*
Relating to the fields or country
settings.

camp-ground (kamp graund) *n.* A
specially prepared area for camping.

cam-phor (kam´fer) *n.* A crystalline
compound used as an insect repellent.

cam-pim-e-ter (kam pim´i tèr) *n.* An
apparatus used to measure color range
of sensitivity of the retina.

campo santo *n.* A burial ground; a
cemetery.

camp-site (kamp sīt) *n.* The area used
for camping.

cam-pus (kam´pus) *n.* The buildings and
grounds of a college, school, or
university.

cam-shaft (kam´shaft´) *n.* The shaft of
an engine that is fitted with cams.

can (kan) *v.* To know how to do
something; to be physically or mentally
able; to have the ability to do
something; to preserve fruit or
vegetables by sealing in an airtight
container. **can** *n.* An airtight container.

ca-nal (ka nal´) *n.* A man-made water
channel for irrigating land.

can-a-lic-u-lus *n.* A tubular or canal-like
passage or channel, as in a bone.

ca-nal-ize (ka nal´īz) *v.* To convert into
canals; to make new canals.

ca-nard (ka närd´) *n.* An untrue story
circulated as true; a hoax.

ca-nar-y (ka nâr´ē) *n. pl.* **-ies** A green
or yellow songbird which is popular
as a caged bird.

can-cel (kan´sel) *v.* To invalidate or
annul; to cross out; to neutralize; in
mathematics, to remove a common
factor from the numerator and the
denominator of a fraction; in computer
science, to abort or stop a procedure
or program. **cancellation** *n.*

can-cel-la-tion (kan´sa lā´shan) *n.* The
act of making void, or invalid; a mark
used to cancel something.

can-cer (kan´ser) *n.* A malignant tumor
that invades healthy tissue and spreads
to other areas; the disease marked by
such tumors. **cancerous** *adj.*

can-cri-zans *adj.* Going or moving
backward.

can-de-la-bra (kan´de lä´bra) *n. pl.*
candelabrum A decorative candlestick with several branching arms for
candles.

can-did (kan´did) *adj.* Free from bias,
malice, or prejudice; honest and
sincere.

can-di-date (kan´di dāt´) *n. pl.* A
person who aspires to or is nominated
or qualified for a membership, award,
or office. **candidacy** *n.*

can-died (kan´dēd) *adj.* Preserved;
encrusted with sugar.

can-dle (kan´dl) *n.* A slender, cylindrical
mass of wax or tallow containing a
linen or cotton wick which is burned
to produce light. *v.* To hold something
between the eye and a light, as to test
eggs for blood clots, growths, or
fertility. **candler** *n.*

can-dor (kan´dér) *n.* Straightforwardness; frankness of expression.

cane (kān) *n.* A pithy or hollow, flexible,
jointed stem of bamboo or rattan that
is split for basketry or wicker work;
a walking stick. **cane** *v.*

cane-brake (kān´brāk) *n.* A thick growth
of cane.

ca-nel-la (ka nel´a) *n.* The cinnamon-
like bark from a tree of a West Indian,
used as medicine and a condiment.

can-er (kā´nėr) *n.* A person who weaves
cane, especially for chair seats and
backs.

cane sugar *n.* Sugar obtained from the
sugar cane, sucrose.

ca-nine (kā´nīn) *adj.* Relating to or
resembling a dog; of the dog family.

Canis Major (kā´nis mā´jèr) *n.* A
constellation in the Southern Hemisphere that contains the Dog Star.

can-ker (kang´kèr) *n.* An ulcerated sore
in the mouth.

can-na (kan´a) *n.* Tropical plant with
large leaves and showy flowers.

can-na-bin (kan´a bin) *n.* A poisonous
resin that comes from Indian hemp.

can-ni-kin (kan´i kin) *n.* A small can;
a cup.

can-nu-la (kan´ya la) *n.* A small tube
of metal or the like which draws off
fluid or injects medicine into the body.

can-ny (kan´ē) *adj.* Thrifty; careful;
cautious; shrewd. **cannily** *adv.*,

can-not (kan´ot) *v.* Can not.

ca-noe (ka nö´) *n.* A lightweight, slender
boat with pointed ends which moves
by paddling. **canoe** *v.* **canoeist** *n.*

can-on (kan´en) *n.* The laws established
by a church council; a priest serving
in a collegiate church or cathedral;
clergyman. **canonical** *adj.*

can-on-i-cal (ka non´i kal) *n.* The most
convenient and simplest form of an
equation.

can-on-i-za-tion (kan´a ni zā´shan) *n.*
Process of being named to sainthood.

can-on-ize (kan´a nīz´) *v.* To officially
declare a deceased person a saint; to
place in the catalogue of the saints; to
glorify.

can-o-py (kan´o pē) *n., pl.* **canopies**
A cloth covering used as an ornamental
structure over a bed; the supporting
surface of a parachute; the transparent
cover over the cockpit of an airplane.

cant (kant) *n.* The external angle of a

building. *v.* To throw off by tilting.

can't (kant) *contr.* Can not.

can-ta-bi-le (kän tä´bi lā´) *n.* A lyrical, flowing style of music.

can-ta-loupe (kan´ta lōp´) *n.* A sweet-tasting, orange-colored muskmelon.

can-tan-ker-ous (kan tang´kèr us) *adj.* Bad-tempered and argumentative. **cantankerously** *adv.*

can-ta-ta (kan tä´ta) *n.* A drama that is sung but not acted.

can-ta-trice (kän´tä trē´che) *n.* A professional female singer.

can-thar-is (kan thar´is) *n.* A preparation obtained from dried, crushed blister beetles, used in medicine.

can-thus (kan´thus) *n.* The angle formed by the junction of the upper and lower eyelids.

can-ti-cle (kan´ti kl) *n.* A hymn or chant sung in church.

can-ti-lev-er (kan´ti lev´èr) *n.* A long structure, such as a beam, supported only at one end.

can-ton (kan´ton) *n.* A small area of a country divided into parts.

can-ton-ment (kan ton´ment) *n.* One or more temporary billets for troops.

can-tor (kan´tèr) *n.* The chief singer in a synagogue.

can-tus (kan´tus) *n.* A church song or melody.

can-vas (kan´vas) *n.* A heavy fabric used in making tents and sails for boats; a piece of canvas used for oil paintings.

can-vass (kan´vas) *v.* To travel through a region to solicit opinions or votes; to take a poll or survey. **canvasser** *n.*

can-yon (kan´yun) *n.* A deep and narrow gorge with steep sides.

cap (kap) *n.* A covering for the head, usually brimless and made of a soft material; the final or finishing touch to something; a small explosive charge that is used in cap guns.

ca-pa-ble (kā´pa bl) *adj.* Having the ability to perform in an efficient way; qualified. **capability** *n.* **capably** *adv.*

ca-pa-cious (ka pā´shus) *adj.* Having a lot of room or space.

ca-pac-i-tance (ka pas´i tans) *n.* The property of a body or circuit which allows it to store an electrical charge.

ca-pac-i-tate (ka pas´i tāt´) *v.* To make capable; to qualify.

ca-pa-ci-tive (ka pas´i tiv) *adj.* Coupling or connector that joins circuits by means of a condenser.

ca-pac-i-tor (ka pas´i tèr) *n.* The circuit element composed of metallic plates that are separated by a dielectric and are used to store a charge temporarily.

ca-pac-i-ty (ka pas´i tē) *n., pl.* **capacities** The ability to contain, receive, or absorb; having the aptitude or ability to do something; the maximum

production or output; in *computer science*, the total amount of data or information that can be processed, stored, or generated.

cap-e-lin (kap´a lin) *n.* A small edible fish, allied to the smelt; codfish.

ca-per (kā´pèr) *n.* A prank; antic.

cap-er-cail-lie (kap´èr kāl´yē) *n.* The largest wood grouse of the Old World.

cape-skin (kāp skin) *n.* A light flexible leather made from the skins of goats from which gloves are frequently made.

ca-pi-as (kā pē as) *n.* An arrest warrant authorizing the act of taking a person or possessions into custody.

cap-il-lar-i-ty (kap´i lar´i tē) *n.* The action of molecules on the surface of a liquid in contact with a solid.

cap-il-lary (kap´i ler´ē) *n. pl.* **-ies** Any of the small vessels that connect the veins and arteries. *adj.* Having a hair-like bore; very fine or small in size.

cap-il-lar-y at-trac-tion *n.* The apparent attraction between a liquid and a solid in capillarity.

cap-i-tal (kap´i tal) *n.* The town or city that is designated as the seat of government for a nation or state; material wealth in the form of money or property that is used to produce more wealth; funds that are contributed to a business by the stockholders or owners; net worth of a company or business.

capital account *n.* An account that shows an individual person or shareholder's financial interest in a business.

capital assets *n.* Business assets that are of a fixed, or permanent nature and not commonly bought and sold.

capital gain *n.* The gains from the sale of capital assets.

cap-i-tal-ism (kap´i ta liz´um) *n.* The economic system in which the means of distribution and production are privately own-ed and operated for private profit.

capital levy *n.* Levy put on capital assets apart from the income tax.

capital punishment *n.* The death penalty.

cap-i-ta-tion (kap´i tā´shan) *n.* A census or tax of equal amount for each person.

cap-i-tol (kap´i tol) *n.* The building used for meetings of the state legislative body; the building in Washington DC where the United States congress meets.

ca-pit-u-late (ka pich´u lāt´) *v.* To surrender under terms of an agreement. **capitulator** *n.* **capitulatory** *adj.*

ca-pit-u-lum (ka pich´u lum) *n.* The rounded part of a bone; a rounded or flattened cluster of flowers.

ca-pote (ka pōt´) *n.* A long hooded cloak with a close-fitting cap-like bonnet worn by women and children.

capric acid *n.* A fatty acid, found in coconut oil, used for synthetic dyes, perfumes and flavorings.

ca-price (ka prēs´) *n.* A sudden change of action or mind without adequate reason; a whim; an impulse **capricious** *adj.* **capriciousness** *n.*

ca-pri-cious (ka prish´us) *adj.* Apt to change opinions unpredictably; subject to change.

cap-ri-fig (kap´ri fig´) *n.* Uncultivated form of the common fig.

cap-ri-ole (kap´rē ōl´) *n.* A spring or standing still leap given by a horse in exhibitions; a playful leap.

cap-size (kap´sīz) *v.* To overturn in a boat.

cap-stan (kap´stan) *n., Naut.* A drumlike apparatus rotated to hoist weights by winding in a cable on a ship or boat.

cap-su-late (kap´sa lāt´) *adj.* Formed into a capsule.

cap-su-lated (kap´sa lā´tid) *adj.* Formed or in a capsule-like state.

cap-sule (kap´sul) *n.* A small gelatinous case for a dose of oral medicine; a fatty sac that surrounds an organ of the body, as the kidney, and protects it; a summary in a brief form. **sular** *adj.*

cap-tion (kap´shan) *n.* A subtitle; a description of an illustration or picture.

cap-tious (kap´shus) *adj.* Deceptive; critical.

cap-ti-vate (kap´ti vāt´) *v.* To hold the attention, fascinate, or charm a person or group of people. **captivation** *n.*

cap-tive (kap´tiv) *n.* A person being held as a prisoner.

cap-tiv-i-ty (kap tiv´i tē) *n.* The period of being captive.

cap-ture (kap´cher) *v.* To take something or someone by force. **capturer** *n.*

ca-puche (ka pōsh) *n.* A hood or cowl.

cap-y-ba-ra (kap´i bär´a) *n.* A rodent that lives in rivers of South America, and feeds on vegetables and fish.

car (kär) *n.* An automobile; an enclosed vehicle, as a railroad car.

ca-ra-ca-ra (kär´a kär´a) *n.* Various vulture-like birds of the falcon family.

car-ack (kar´ak) *n.* A large, merchant vessel, of the 15th and 16th centuries.

ca-ra-cole (kar´a kōl´) *n.* A half turn to the right or left executed by a trained saddle horse.

ca-rafe (ka raf´) *n.* A glass bottle for serving wine or water.

car-a-mel (kar´a mel) *n.* A chewy substance primarily composed of sugar, butter, and milk.

car-a-mel-ize (kar´a ma līz) *v.* To make into caramel.

car-a-pace (kar´a pās´) *n.* The hard, bony shield covering an animal's back, as a turtle's shell.

car-at (kar´at) *n.* The unit of weight for gems that equals 200 milligrams.

car-a-way (kar´a wā´) *n.* An aromatic seed used in cooking.

car-ba-mate (kär´ba māt´) *n.* A salt of carbamic acid.

car-ba-zole (kär´ba zōl´) *n.* A white, basic cyclic compound, found in coal tar, used in making dyes, explosives, insecticides and lubricants.

car-bide (kär´bīd) *n.* A carbon compound with a more electropositive element.

car-bi-nol *n.* Methyl alcohol, or similar alcohol, such as isopropyl alcohol.

carbocyclic compound *n.* Organic compounds having a ring formation made up of carbon atoms, as benzene.

car-bo-hy-drate (kär´bō hī´drāt) *n.* A group of compounds, including starches, celluloses, and sugars that contain carbon, hydrogen, and oxygen.

car-bo-late (kär´bo lāt) *n.* A carbolic acid salt.

car-bo-lat-ed (kär´bo lā´tid) *adj.* Containing carbolic acid.

car-bon (kär´ben) *n.* A nonmetallic element that occurs as a powdery noncrystalline solid; the element symbolized by C. **carbonization** *n.* **carbonize** *v.* **carbonous** *n.*

car-bo-na-do (kär´bo nä´dō) *n.* A piece of meat that has been scored before cooking or grilling.

carbon dating *n.* Process that determines the age of old materials such as archeological and geological specimens.

carbonic acid *n.* A weak dibasic acid, that reacts with bases to form carbonates, and decomposes into water plus carbon dioxide.

carbonium ion *n.* An organic ion having a positive charge at a carbon position.

car-bon-ize (kär´bo nīz´) *v.* To change into carbon or a carbonic residue, as by partial combustion.

carbon monoxide *n.* An odorless, colorless very toxic gas, formed by the incomplete combustion of carbon, burns with a blue flame; highly poisonous when inhaled.

car-cass (kär´kas) *n.* The dead body of an animal; something that no longer has life.

car-cin-o-gen (kär sin´ o jen) *n.* A substance or agent that produces cancer.

car-ci-no-ma (kär´si nō´ma) *n.* A malignant tumor; cancer.

car-ci-no-ma-to-sis *n.* A state in which multiple carcinomas develop at the exact same time.

car-di-ac (kär´dē ak´) *adj.* Relating to the heart.

car-di-o-gram (kär´dē o gram´) *n.* The curve or tracing made by a cardiograph and used in the diagnosis of heart defects; the record of a heart's action made by a cardiograph.

cardiopulmonary resuscitation *n.* A procedure used to restore normal breathing after cardiac arrest by using mouth-to-mouth resuscitation, clearing the air passages to the lungs, heart massage by chest compressions and if necessary the use of drugs.

car-di-tis (kär dī´tis) *n.* Inflammation of the heart muscles.

care (kâr) *n.* A feeling of concern, anxiety, or worry; guardianship or custody. *v.* To show interest or regard.

ca-reen (ka rēn´) *v.* To lurch or twist from one side to another while moving rapidly.

ca-reer (ka rēr´) *n.* The profession or occupation a person takes in life.

care-ful (kâr´ful) *adj.* Exercising care; cautious; watchful.

care-less (kâr´lis) *adj.* Not showing or receiving care; being heartless; lacking in consideration.

ca-ress (ka res´) *v.* To gently show affection by touching or stroking. **caress** *n.*

care-tak-er (kâr´tā˝kèr) *n.* One who takes care of land or maintains a building in the owner's absence.

care-worn (kâr´wōrn´) *adj.* Showing the effects of anxiety; drained due to prolonged overwork.

car-fare (kär´fâr´) *n.* Passenger fare on a public vehicle, such as a bus.

car-go (kär´gō) *n.* Freight; the goods and merchandise carried on a ship, plane, or other vehicle.

car-hop (kär´hop´) *n.* A person who waits on customers at a drive-in restaurant.

Caribbean Sea *n.* An arm of the Atlantic Ocean bounded by the coasts of South and Central America and the West Indies.

car-i-bou (kar´i bö˝) *n.* A large antlered deer of northern North America.

car-i-ca-ture (kar´a ka chèr) *n.* An exaggerated representation, picture or description, in which peculiarities or defects of person or thing are ridiculously exaggerated. **caricature** *v.* To make a caricature of; to represent in a ridiculous and exaggerated fashion.

car-ies (kâr´ēz) *n.* The decay of a bone or tooth.

car-il-lon (kar´i lon) *n.* A set of tuned bells in a tower, that are usually played by a keyboard.

car-i-o-ca (kar˝ē ō´ka) *n.* A South American dance and its accompanying music, variation of the samba.

car-min-a-tive (kär min´a tiv) *adj.* Expelling gas from the body.

car-mine (kär min) *n.* A vivid red color;

crimson; deep purplish red.

car-nage (kär´nij) *n.* A bloody slaughter; war; massacre.

car-nal (kär´nal) *adj.* Relating to sensual desires. **carnality** *n.* **carnally** *adv.*

car-nall-ite (kär´na līt˝) *n.* A mineral consisting of a hydrous potassium-magnesium chloride which provides a valuable source of potassium.

car-nas-si-al (kär nas´ē al) *adj.* Of or pertaining to teeth of a carnivore adapted for cutting rather than tearing flesh.

car-na-tion (kär nā´shan) *n.* A fragrant perennial flower in a variety of colors.

carnauba wax *n.* Wax obtained from the Brazilian wax palm, and used as a base in polishes.

car-nel-ian (kär nēl´yan) *n.* A clear red chalcedony that is used as a gem.

car-ni-val (kär´ni val) *n.* A traveling amusement show with side shows, a Ferris wheel, and merry-go-rounds; any kind of a happy celebration; the period of festivity preceding Lent.

car-ni-vore (kär´ni vōr˝) *n.* A flesh-eating animal. **carnivorous** *adj.*

car-ob (kar´ob) *n.* A Mediterranean tree, the pods of which, are known as locust beans, contains a sweet pulp.

car-ol (kar´ol) *n.* A song to celebrate joy or praise. **caroler** *n.* **carol** *v.*

car-o-tene (kar´o tēn˝) *n.* Pigment of orange or red found in some vegetable and animal fats, can be turned into vitamin A.

ca-rot-i-noid (ka rot´e noid˝) *n.* Red and yellow pigments found in plants, and animals.

ca-rouse (ka rouz´) *v.* To be rowdy and to be in a drunken state. **carouser** *n.*

carp (kärp) *v.* To find unreasonable fault with something or someone; to complain unduly. **carp** *n.* A freshwater fish that contains many small bones but can be eaten with caution.

car-pal (kär´pal) *adj.* Pertaining to the wrist and the bones in the wrist.

car-pel (kär´pel) *n.* Bot. A seed vessel or pistil.

car-pen-ter (kär´pen tèr) *n.* A person who builds and repairs wooden structures. **carpentry** *n.*

car-pet (kär´pit) *n.* A thick, woven or felt floor covering that helps to insulate the floors. **carpet** *n.*

car-pet-ing (kär´pit ing) *n.* Material for carpets; carpets in general.

car-pol-o-gy *n.* The division of botany relating to the structure of seeds and seed vessels.

car-port (kär´port) *n.* A roof attached to the side of a building to give shelter for a vehicle.

car-pus (kär´pus) *n.* The bones of the wrist or the wrist itself.

car-riage (kar´ij) *n.* A horse-drawn cart for passengers.

carron oil *n.* Ointment composed of equal parts of limewater and olive oil, used as a treatment for burns and scalds.

car-rot (kar´ot) *n.* An orange vegetable that is an edible root.

car-rou-sel (kar´a sel´) *n.* A merry-go-round.

car-ry (kar´e) *v.* To transport from one place to another; to bear the burden, weight, or responsibility of; to keep or have available for sale; to maintain on business books for future settlement.

car-ry-all (kar´e ol´) *n.* A capacious bag or suitcase for carrying items.

carrying charge *n.* The amount charged over the regular price a merchandise sold on installments.

carry on *n.* Luggage carried on an airplane by passengers.

car sickness *n.* Nausea caused by motion.

cart (kärt) *n.* A two-wheeled vehicle for moving heavy goods; a small lightweight vehicle that can be moved around by hand. **carter** *n.*

carte blanche *n.* Unrestricted authority to make decisions.

car-tel (kär tel´) *n.* A group of independent companies that have organized to control prices, production, etc.

Carter, James Earl Jr. (Jimmy) *n.* (1924-) The thirty-ninth president of the United States from 1977-1981.

car-ti-lage (kär´ti lij) *n.* A tough, elastic substance of connective tissue attached to the surface of bones near the joints. **cartilaginous** *adj.*

car-ti-lag-i-nous (kär´ti laj´i nus) *adj.* Having or resembling cartilage.

car-to-gram (kär´to gram´) *n.* A map giving simplified statistical information by using shading.

car-tog-ra-pher (kär tog´ra fèr) *n.* One who makes and or publishes maps.

car-tog-ra-phy (kär tog´ra fē) *n.* The art of developing charts and maps. **cartographer** *n.* **cartographic** *adj.*

car-ton (kär´ ton) *n.* A container made from cardboard.

car-tridge (kär´trij) *n.* A case made of metal, pasteboard, etc., that contains a charge of powder; the primer and shot or projectile for a firearm.

cartridge paper *n.* A durable, strong paper used for making cartridges.

car-tu-lar-y *n.* A record or register of title deeds and other documents; the keeper of such a records or archives.

car-va-crol *n.* A thick, colorless oil.

carve (kärv) *v.* To slice meat or poultry; to cut into something; to create, as sculpture. **carver** *n.*

cary-at-id (kar´e at´id) *n.* A supporting column sculptured in the form of a female figure.

car-y-op-sis (kar´e op´ss) *n.* A small, one-seeded, dry, indehiscent fruit in which the seed and fruit fuse in a single grain.

ca-sa-ba (ka sä´ba) *n.* A sweet, edible winter melon having a yellow skin.

cas-cade (kas käd´) *n.* A waterfall that flows over steep rocks.

cas-ca-ril-la (kas ka ril´a) *n.* The bitter aromatic bark of a West Indian shrub used for making incense and as a tonic.

case (kās) *n.* A particular occurrence or in- stance; an injury or disease; an argument, supporting facts, or reasons that justify a situation; a box or housing to carry things in, as a briefcase; in the law, a suit of action brought against a person.

ca-se-a-tion (kā´sē ā´shan) *n.* The separation of casein from coagulating milk, to form a soft cheesy substance or curd.

case-book (kās´buk´) *n.* A book containing detailed records of cases, that is used for reference and instruction in law, psychology, sociology, and medicine.

case history *n.* A factual information about an individual's personal history.

ca-sein (kā´sēn) *n.* A dairy protein that is used in foods and in manufacturing adhesives and plastics.

case law *n.* Law made by decided cases that serve as precedents.

case system *n.* A method of teaching law based primarily on reported cases instead of textbooks.

case-work *n.* Social work with direct contact and consideration of a patient, his family, and their problems.

cash *n.* Money, or an equivalent, as a check, paid at the time of making a purchase.

cash flow *n.* Reported net income after taxes; the liquidity of a corporation plus amounts charged off plus noncash charges.

cash-ier (ka shēr´) *n.* An employee who handles cash as part of his job description; an officer in a bank in charge of receiving or distributing money.

cashier's check *n.* A check drawn by a bank upon its own funds and signed by its cashier.

cash items *n.* Items such as, government bonds, bank deposits, securities, and the like that are considered equivalent to cash in a corporate statement.

cash-mere (kazh´mēr) *n.* The wool from the Kashmir goat; the yarn made from this wool.

cas-ing (kās ing) *n.* A protective covering; a supporting frame as used around a door or window.

ca-si-no (ka sē´nō) *n.,k pl.* **casinos** A

public establishment open especially for gambling.

cask (kask) *n.* A large wooden vessel or barrel; the quantity that a cask will hold.

cas-ket (kas'kit) *n.* A coffin; a small chest or box.

cas-que (kask) *n.* A helmet. **casqued** *adj.*

cas-sa-va (ka sä'va) *n.* A slender erect shrub grown in the tropics.

cas-se-role (kas'e rōl) *n.* A dish in which the food is baked and also served; food cooked and served in this manner.

cas-sette (ka set') *n.* A cartridge of magnetic tape used in tape recorders to play and record.

cas-sit-er-ite (ka sit'a rīt') *n.* A brown or black mineral that consists of tin dioxide, the chief source of metallic tin.

cas-sock (kas'ok) *n.* A close-fitting garment worn by members of the clergy.

cas-so-war-y (kas'o wer'ē) *n.* A large, three-toed, flightless ratite bird; closely related to emu.

cast (kast) *v.* To hurl or throw with force.

cast-a-way (kast'a wā') *adj.* Throw away. **castaway** *n.* One who is shipwrecked or discarded.

caste (kast) *n.* A social separation based on a profession, hereditary, or financial hierarchy.

cas-tel-lat-ed (kas'te lā'tid) *adj.* Adorned by battlements and turrets.

cast-er (kas'tèr) *n.* A small set of swiveling rollers that are fastened under pieces of furniture and the like.

cas-ti-gate (kas'ti gāt') *v.* To punish or criticize severely. **castigation** *n.*

cast-ing (kas'ting) *n.* The act of one that casts.

casting vote *n.* A deciding vote cast by a president or chairman to break a tie.

cast iron *n.* A hard, brittle, commercial alloy of iron, carbon, and silicon that is cast into a mold.

cas-tle (kas'el) *n.* A fort or fortified dwelling for nobility; any large house or place of refuge; a stronghold.

cast-off (kas tof) *adj.* Discarded; thrown away; thrown to the side.

cas-tor (kas ter) *n.* A beaver; a beaver hat, or a hat that resembles one.

cas-trate (kas'trāt) *v.* To remove the testicles; to remove the ovaries; to spay, to remove something from. **-tion** *n.*

ca-su-al (kazh'ö al) *adj.* Informal; occurring by chance; uncertain. **casually** *adv.* **casualness** *n.*

cas-u-al-ism (kazh'ö a liz'um) *n.* The state of things where chance prevails; the belief that all things exist or are governed by chance or accident.

ca-su-al-ty (kazh'ö al tē) *n., pl.* **casualties** One who is injured or killed in an accident. *Milit.* One who is killed, wounded, taken prisoner by the enemy, or missing in action.

cas-u-ist (kazh'ö ist) *n.* A person who studies and resolves cases of conscience or conduct.

ca-tab-o-lism (ka tab'o liz'um) *n.* In living organisms, a breaking down of more complex molecules into simpler ones, involving the release of energy.

cat-a-chre-sis (kat'a krē'sis) *n.* Misuse of a word context.

cat-a-clysm (kat'a kliz um) *n.* A sudden and violent event; an extensive flood; a deluge. **cataclysmic** *adj.*

cat-a-comb (kat'a kōm') *n.* An underground passage with small rooms for coffins.

ca-tad-ro-mous (ka tad'ro mus) *adj.* Of fish living in freshwater and going down to the sea to spawn.

cat-a-falque (kat'a falk') *n.* The structure that supports a coffin during a state funeral.

cat-a-lep-sy (kat'a lep'sē) *n.* A condition in which there is a rigidity of the muscles, causing the patient to remain in a fixed position or posture.

cat-a-log (kat'a log) *n.* A publication containing a list of names, objects, etc.

ca-tal-pa (katal'pa) *n.* A hardy, small ornamental tree found in Asia and America and noted for its heart-shaped leaves and pale showy flowers.

cat-a-lyst (kat'a list) *n., Chem.* Any substance that alters and decreases the time it takes a chemical reaction to occur.

cat-a-ma-ran (kat'a ma ran') *n.* A boat with twin hulls.

cat-am-ne-sis (kat'am nē'sis) *n.* The medical history of a patient taken during, or after recovering from, an illness.

cat-a-mount (kat'amount') *n.* A wild cat; as the cougar or lynx.

cat-a-pla-sia (kat'a plā'zha) *n.* The reverting of cells or tissues to an earlier or more primitive stage.

cat-a-plex-y (kat'a plek'sē) *n.* A sudden loss of muscle power caused by a strong emotional shock.

cat-a-pult (kat'a pult') *n.* An ancient military device for throwing arrows or stones; a device for launching aircraft from the deck of a ship, such as a aircraft carrier.

cat-a-ract (kat'a rakt') *n.* A large waterfall or downpour. *Pathol.* A disease of the lens of the eye, causing total or partial blindness.

ca-tarrh (ka tär') *n., Pathol.* Inflammation of the nose and throat. **-al** *adj.*

ca-tas-ta-sis (ka tas'ta sis) *n.* The climax of a play.

ca-tas-tro-phe (ka tas'tro fē) *n.* A

terrible and sudden disaster; a calamity.

catastophic adj. **catastrophically** adv.

cat-a-to-ni-a (kat´a tō´nē a) n. The state of suspended animation and the loss of voluntary motion.

ca-taw-ba (ka to´ba) n. A pale red native American grape that is cultivated into a wine of the same name.

catch (kach) v. To take; to seize or capture; to reach in time; to intercept; to become entangled or fastened.

catch-all (kach´ol´) n. A container or bag for odds and ends.

catch-ment (kach´ment) n. The act of catching water; a drainage system that catches water, as a reservoir.

catch on v. To understand, learn; to become popular.

catch-word n. A word or phrase often repeated; an expression repeated until it represents an idea, party, school, or product.

cat-e-chize (kat´a kiz´) v. To teach or instruct orally by means of questions and answers.

cat-e-chu n. Any of several dry, earthy, or resinous astringent substances obtained from the wood of tropical plants of Asia and used for medicine, dyeing, or tanning.

cat-e-gor-i-cal (kat´a gor´i kal) adj. Absolute; certain; related to or included in a category without qualification.

cat-e-go-rize (kat´a go riz´) v. To place in categories.

cat-e-go-ry (kat´a gōr´ē) n. pl. **-ries** A general group to which something belongs.

cat-e-nate (kat´e nāt´) v. To connect in a series; links; to concatenate.

ca-ter (kā´tèr) v. To provide a food service; to act deferentially toward.

cat-er-pil-lar (kat´a pil´er) n. The very fuzzy, worm-like, brightly-colored spiny larva of a moth or butterfly.

cat-gut (kat´gut´) n. A thin, tough cord made from the fried intestines of sheep.

ca-the-dral (ka thē´dral) n. A large and important church, containing the seat of a bishop.

cath-e-ter (kath´i tèr) n., Med. A thin, flexible tube that is inserted into the body cavity for drainage and to draw urine from the bladder. **catheterize** v.

ca-thex-is n. The channeling of psychic energy in an object.

cath-ode (kath´ōd) n. The negatively charged electrode which receives positively charged ions during electrolysis.

cathode ray n. A stream of electrons projected from the heated cathode of a vacuum tube under the propulsion of a very strong electric field.

cathode ray tube n. The vacuum tube on which images are found, used in

a computer screen.

ca-thol-i-con (ka thol´ kon) n. A remedy for all diseases; cure-all.

cat-i-on (kat´ī´on) n. A positively charged ion that is attracted to electrolytes to a negative electrode.

cat-kin (kat´kin) n. The spike-like blossom of the willow, birch trees that resemble a cat's tail.

cat-nap (kat´nap´) n. A short nap.

cat-o'-nine-tails (kat´o nīn´tālz´) n. A hand-made whip with nine knotted cords fastened to a handle.

ca-top-tric (ka top´trik) adj. Pertaining or relating to a reflected light or a mirror.

ca-top-trics (ka top´trik) n. The branch of optics that relates to a mirror or reflected light.

cat rig n. A rig consisting of a single mast set well forward and carrying one large sail extended by a long boom and gaff.

CAT scan n. A cross-sectional picture produced by a scanner, used to x-ray the body by using computerized axial tomography.

CAT scanner n. The machine used to produce a cross-sectional picture of the body.

cat-sup (kat´sup) n. Variation of ketchup. A condiment made from tomatoes, water, sugar, and other spices.

cat-tle (kat´al) n. pl. Farm animals raised for meat and dairy products.

cat-tle-man (kat´al man) n. A person in the business of raising or tending cattle.

cat-ty (kat´ē) adj. Malicious or spiteful. **cattily** adv. **cattiness** n.

cat-ty-cor-nered (kat´ē kor´nèrd) adj. Not straight; sitting at an angle.

cat-walk (kat´wok´) n. Any very narrow path, as along-side a bridge.

Cau-ca-sian (ko kā´zhan) n. An inhabitant of Caucasus. **Caucasian** adj. Relating to a major ethnic division of the human race; of or relating to the white race.

cau-cus (ko´kus) n. A meeting of a political party to make policy decisions and to select candidates. **caucus** v.

cau-dal (kod´al) adj. Toward the tail or posterior end of the body.

caudal anesthesia n. Insensibility to pain in the lower portion of the body, due to the injection of an anesthetic drug into the caudal part of the spinal canal.

cau-dex (ko´deks) n. The woody base of a perennial plant, including roots and stem.

cau-dle (kod´al) n. A warm drink usually made of spices, ale, bread, eggs, and sugar.

caught v. Past tense of catch.

caul-dron (kol´dron) n. A large metal kettle or boiler.

caulk (kok) v. To seal seams and edges against leakage of water and air with some substance. **caulker** n.

caus-al (ko´zal) adj. Relating to or constituting a cause or causes; implying, involving, or expressing a cause or causes.

cau-sa-tion (ko zā´shan) n. The act or process of causing or producing an effect.

cause (koz) v. To produce a result, consequence, or effect. n. A goal, principle; a reason; motive. **causer** n.

cau-se-rie (kō´za rē´) n. A short informal conversation or chat.

cause-way (koz´wā´) n. A paved highway through a marsh tract; raised road over water.

caus-tic (ko´stik) n. A curve to which all light rays originating from a point and reflected by a curved surface are tangent.

cau-ter-ize (ko´ta rīz´) v. To sear or burn with a hot blade or instrument or fire, as in dead tissue, a hot iron.

cau-ter-y (ko´ta rē) n. A very hot instrument used to destroy tissue that does not seem normal.

cau-tion (ko´shan) n. A warning; careful planning. **cautionary** adj.

cau-tious (ko´shus) adj. Very careful.

cav-al-cade (kav´al kād´) n. A group of horse-drawn carriages or riders, forming a procession.

cav-a-lier (kav´a lēr´) n. A very gallant gentleman; a knight.

cav-al-ry (kav´al rē) n., pl. cavalries Army troops trained to fight on horseback or in armored vehicles. **cavalryman** n.

ca-vate (kā´vāt) adj. Hollowed or dug out; giving the appearance of a cave.

cav-a-ti-na (kav´a tē´na) n. A simple operatic song or solo.

cave (kāv) n. An underground tomb or chamber with an opening at the ground surface.

ca-ve-at (kā´vē at´) n. A formal legal notice to stop the proceedings until both sides have a hearing; a warning or caution.

cave dweller n. A person, as a prehistoric man, who lives in caves.

cave–in n. The action of collapsing or caving in; a place where the ground has fallen in.

cave-man (kāv man) n. A person who lives in caves; especially of the Stone Age; a person who acts in a very rough primitive manner.

ca-vern (kav´ern) n. A very large underground cave. **cavernous** adj.

cav-i-ar or **cav-i-are (kav´ē är´)** n. The eggs of large fish, eaten as an appetizer.

cav-il (kav´il) v. To raise captious and trivial objections; to find fault without good reason.

cav-i-ty (kav´i tē) n., pl. cavities A decayed place in a tooth; a hollow or hole.

cay (kā) n. A range or reef of sand or coral a lying near the surface of the water.

cay-man (kā´mam) n. A tropical American crocodile which is fundamentally similar to the alligator.

cay-use (kī ūs´) n. A small native range horse of the western United States.

CD abbr. Compact disk; civil defense; certificate of deposit.

cease (sēs) v. To come to an end or put an end to; to stop.

cease-fire (sēs´fī´er) v. To stop fighting, usually as a result of a truce.

cease-less (sēs´lis) adj. Endless; without a stop or pause; continual; without intermission. **ceaselessly** adv.

ce-cum (se´kum) n. The pouch where the large intestine begins.

ce-dar (se´dėr) n. An evergreen tree with fragrant, red wood.

cede (sēd) v. To formally resign and surrender to another, usually by treaty.

ce-dil-la (si dil´a) n. A diacritical mark placed under the letter c (ç) in the French vocabulary to indicate a modification or alteration of the usual phonetic sound.

ceil-ing (sē´ling) n. The overhead covering of a room; the maximum limit to some-thing; the maximum height for visibility under specified conditions for aircraft.

ceiling unlimited n. A cloudless or almost cloudless sky.

ceiling zero n. A cloud ceiling at a height of 50 feet or lower.

ceil-om-e-ter (sē lom´i tėr) n. Meteor. A photoelectric instrument for measuring and recording the height of a cloud ceiling.

cel-a-don (sel´a don´) n. A pale green ceramic glaze, used in Chinese porcelains and stonewares.

cel-an-dine (sel´an dīn´) n. A biennial herb of the poppy family which emits a bright orange-colored juice when its leaves or stems are crushed. The juice from this plant is used in medicine as a diuretic, purgative and fungicide.

cel-e-brate (sel´e brāt´) v. To observe with ceremonies, rejoicing, or festivity. **celebration** n.

cel-e-brat-ed (sel´e brā´tid) adj. Famous, well-known.

cel-e-bra-tion (sel e´brā shen) n. The act of celebrating; to demonstrate satisfaction in a festive way.

cel-leb-ri-ty (se leb´ri tē) n. pl. -ies A famous person.

ce-ler-i-ac (se ler´ē ak´) n. A variety of celery, grown for its knobby edible turnip-like root.

ce-ler-i-ty (se ler´i tē) *n.* Swiftness; speed; rapid motion.

cel-er-y (sel´e rē) *n.* A green vegetable with an edible stalk.

ce-les-ta (se les´ta) *n.* A musical instrument which produces bell-like tones when the keyboard and metal plates are struck by hammers.

ce-les-tial (se les´chel) *adj.* Heavenly; spiritual.

celestial body *n.* Any body of matter in the universe, such as a planet, star, or comet.

celestial equator *n.* The great circle of the celestial sphere, midway between the celestial poles, assumed to be the extension of the plane of the earth's equator.

celestial navigation *n.* Navigation by which a geographical location is determined by the position of celestial bodies.

celestial pole *n.* The two points on the celestial sphere around which the stars appear to revolve.

ce-li-ac (sē´lē ak´)*adj.* Relating or pertaining to the cavity of the abdomen.

celiac disease *n.* A chronic nutritional disease of young children, common in the tropics, characterized by anemia, sore tongue, and diarrhea.

cel-i-bate (sel´a bit) *n.* A person who remains unmarried because of religious vows; one who is sexually abstinent. **celibacy** *n.* **celibate** *adj.*

cell (sel) *n.* A prison; a small room; the smallest unit of any organism that is cap-able of independent function, is composed of a small mass of cyto-plasm, usually encloses a central nucleus, and is surrounded by a membrane or a rigid cell wall; a cavity of an ovary or pericarp that is seed-bearing. *Electr.* The part of a battery that generates the electricity; in computer science, the location in memory that holds a single unit of information; a byte.

cel-lar (sel´er) *n.* An underground area, beneath a building, used for storage.

cel-lar-ette (sel´a ret´) *n.* A cabinet or case for holding bottles of liquors or wines.

cell division *n.* The process of dividing both the cytoplasm and nucleus of a cell into two, in the process of reproduction.

cel-list (chel´ist) *n.* A person who plays the cello.

cell membrane *n.* The thin membrane enclosing the protoplasmic material of the cell; the cell wall.

cel-lo (chel´ō) *n.* A base instrument of the violin family. **list** *n.*

cel-lo-phane (sel´e fān´) *n.* A transparent paper–like material made from treated cellulose that has been processed in thin, clear strips.

cel-lu-lar (sel´ya lèr) *adj.* Consisting of cells.

cel-lu-lase (sel´ya lās´) *n.* An enzyme that hydrolyzes cellulosic; obtained from a fungus, and used in medicine, septic systems, and brewing.

cel-lu-lite (sel ye līt) *n.* A fatty deposit or area under the skin found in the hips, thighs, and buttocks.

cel-lu-lose (sel´ya lōs´) *n.* A carbohydrate that is insoluble in ordinary solvents and forms the fundamental material for the structure of plants.

cell wall *n.* The definite boundary, formed by the protoplasm, that surrounds a biological cell.

ce-men-tum (si men´tum) *n.* The external layer of bony tissue that forms the outer surface of a tooth within the gum.

cem-e-ter-y (sem´i ter´ē) *n. pl.* **-ies** The place for burying the dead.

ce-no-bite (sē´no bīt´) *n.* One of the religious groups that live in a convent or community.

ce-nog-a-my (sē nog´amē) *n.* The practice of having spouses in common, as primitive tribes.

cen-ser (sen´sèr) *n.* A vessel or container for burning incense.

cen-sor (sen´sèr) *n.* A person who examines films and printed materials to determine what might be objection-able and offensive. **censorship** *n.*

cen-sor-ship (sen´sèr ship´) *n.* The practice of censoring; the authority of a censor.

cen-sure (sen´shur) *n.* An expression of criticism and disapproval.

cen-sus (sen´sus) *n.* An official count of the population.

cent (sent) *n.* One; one hundredth of a dollar.

cen-tare (sen´târ) *n.* A square meter.

cen-taur (sen´tor) *n.* In Greek mythol-ogy, a monster that has a man's arms, head, and trunk, but a horse's body and legs.

cen-te-nar-i-an (sen´te nâr´ē an) *n.* A person who has reached the age of 100 or more.

cen-te-na-ry (sen´te ner´ē) *n.* A period or age of 100 years; a century.

cen-ter (sen´tèr) *n.* The place of equal distance from all sides; the heart; in sports, a person who holds the middle position, as in the forward line.

cen-tile (sen´til) *n.* A scale of comparison from lowest to highest, derived at by dividing into 100 ranks with the lowest as the first.

centile rank *n.* A score that shows percent of a total distribution is below a certain score.

cen-ti-me-ter (sen´ti mē´tèr) n. A metric system of measurement; hundredth part of a meter; slightly more than 0.39 of an inch.

cen-ti-pede (sen´ti pēd´) n. A flat arthropod with numerous body segments and legs.

cen-to (sen´tō) n. A literary or musical composition made up of parts from other sources.

cen-tral (sen´tral) adj. In, near, or at the center; of primary importance. **centrally** adv. **centralize** v.

cen-tral-i-za-tion (sen´tra li zā´shan) n. The concentration of authority within any groups or organizations.

central nervous system n. The nervous system that consists of the spinal cord and the brain.

cen-trif-u-gal (sen trif´ū gal) adj. Moving or directing away from a center location.

cen-tri-fuge (sen´tri fūj´) n. A machine for inducing artificial gravity, used to test the ability of flying personnel, animal subjects, and equipment to withstand the above normal gravitational forces.

cen-tro-bar-ic (sen´tro bar´ik) adj. Having to do with the center of gravity; possessing a center of gravity.

cen-tro-sphere (sen´tro sfēr´) n. The thick material in the central part of the earth.

cen-tu-ry (sen´cha rē) n., pl. **centuries** A period consisting of 100 years.

ceph-a-lal-gia (sef´a lal´ja) n. Headache.

ceph-a-li-za-tion (sef´a li zā´shan) n. An evolutionary tendency in the development of animals to localization of sensory and neural organs or parts in or near the head.

ceph-a-lo-pod (sef´a lo pod´) n. Any class of mollusks, including the octopus, cuttlefish, and squids, having a tubular siphon under the head.

ceph-a-lo-tho-rax (sef´a lō thōr´aks) n. The outer division of the body in crustaceans, spiders, etc. which consists of the united head and thorax.

ce-ram-ic (se ram´ik) adj. Of or relating to a brittle material made by firing a nonmetallic mineral, such as clay.

ceramics (se ram´iks) n. The art of making a ceramic piece.

cer-a-mist (ser´a mist) n. A person who works with ceramics.

ce-rar-gy-rite (se rär´jē rīt´) n. Native chloride of silver, having the appearance of horn, and forms an important ore of silver.

ce-rate (sēr´āt) n. A thick ointment made by mixing oils with wax, resin, and medicinal ingredients.

cer-car-i-a (sèr kâr´ē a) n. A larval stage of worms, characterized by an oval or tadpole shape.

cere (sēr) n. A protuberance or wax-like skin growth that contains the nostrils, located at the base of the bill of a bird.

ce-re-al (sēr´ē al) n. An edible grain eaten as a breakfast food.

cer-e-bel-lum (ser´e bel´um) n. pl.-bellums The part of the brain responsible for the coordination of voluntary muscular movements.

cerebral (ser´e bral) adj. Pertaining to the cerebrum or brain; relating to intellect.

cerebral hemisphere n. The two convoluted lateral halves into which the cerebrum is divided.

cerebral hemorrhage n. The rupture of a blood vessel or artery in the brain, therefore allowing blood to escape.

cerebral palsy n. A disability that usually occurred at birth and impairs motor function and speech; paralysis, due to brain damage prior to birth or during delivery.

cer-e-brate (ser´e brāt´) v. To have or exhibit brain action; to think; to use the mind.

cer-e-brum (ser´e brum) n. pl. -brums or -bra The brain structure that is divided into two cerebral hemispheres and occupies most of the cranial cavity.

cere-ment (sēr´ment) n. A shroud for wrapping a corpse; any burial cloth.

cer-e-mo-ni-al (ser´e mō´nē al) adj. Mark by or relating to a ceremony for a particular occasion.

cer-e-mo-ny (ser´e mō´nē) n. pl. -ies A ritual or formal act performed in a certain manner. **ceremonious** adj.

ce-rise (se rēs´) n. The color of deep purplish red.

ce-rite (sēr´īt) n. A rare mineral, of a pale rose-red color.

cer-met (sür´met) n. A strong heat-resistant compound, made by bonding a metal and a ceramic substance.

ce-ro (sēr´ō) n. Either of two large sport and food fishes of the mackerel family, found in the warmer parts of the western Atlantic ocean.

ce-ro-plas-tic (sēr´o plas´tik) adj. Pertaining to art modeling in wax.

cer-tain (sèr´tan) adj. pl. -ties Being very sure of something; without any doubt; inevitable; not mentioned but assumed. **tainly** adv. **certainty** n.

cer-tif-i-cate (sèr tif´i kāt´) n. A document stating the truth or accuracy of something; a document that certifies fulfillment of duties or requirements, as of a course of study.

cer-tif-i-ca-tion (ser´ti fi kā´shan) n. A certified statement.

certified check n. A check certified as good for payment by the bank upon which it is drawn.

certified mail *n.* First-class mail accompanied by a receipt to be signed by the addressee and returned to the sender.

certified public accountant *n.* A public accountant who has met the requirements of state government and has been granted a certificate from the state in which he/she works or practices.

cer-ti-fy (sẽr´ti fī´) *v.* To testify in writing that something is true or a fact.

cer-ti-o-ra-ri (sẽr´shē o rãr´ē) *n.* A writ from a superior court to call up the records of an inferior court for trial or review.

cer-ti-tude (sẽr´ti tōd´) *n.* Certainty; state of being or feeling certain.

ce-ruse (sẽr´ōs) *n.* White lead as a pigment, used in painting and cosmetics.

cer-ve-lat (sẽr´ve lat´) *n.* A kind of highly seasoned, dry sausage, usually of young pork salted.

cer-vi-cal (sẽr´vi kal) *adj.* Relating to the neck of the cervix.

cer-vi-ci-tis (sẽr´vi sī´tis) *n.* Inflammation of the uterine cervix.

cer-vix *n.* The neck, esp. the back of the neck; the narrow outer end of the uterus.

ce-sar-ean (si zâr´ē an) *n.* A surgical operation which involves cutting through the abdomen and the uterus to remove a baby when normal delivery is not advisable.

ce-si-um (sē´zē um) *n.* An electro-metal, white in color, from the alkali group, used in photoelectric cells.

ces-sa-tion (se sā´shan) *n.* The act of stopping or ceasing.

ces-sion (sesh´on) *n.* The act of giving up territory or rights to another.

cess-pool (ses´pōl´) *n.* A pit or hole for the collection of drainage from toilets, and sinks and other waste water.

ces-tode (ses´tōd) *adj.* Belonging to the class or group of internally parasitic flatworms, including the tapeworm.

ces-tus (ses´tus) *n.* A leather hand covering, often loaded with lead or iron, worn by gladiators.

ce-ta-cean (si tā´shan) *n.* Marine mammals that include whales, dolphins, and porpoises.

ce-tane (sē´tān) *n.* A colorless, oily hydrocarbon liquid, used an additive to improve diesel fuel.

cetane number *n.* The measure of diesel fuel ignition; rating similar to the octane number rating for gasoline.

chafe (chāf) *v.* To become sore by rubbing; to irritate.

chaff (chaf) *n.* The husks of corn and other debris separated from the corn by thrashing, sifting; straw or hay cut up as for food for cattle.

chaf-fer (chā´fẽr) *v.* To bargain; to haggle.

cha-grin (sha grin´) *n.* A feeling of distress caused by disappointment, failure, or humiliation. **chagrin** *v.*

chain (chān) *n.* A connection of several links; anything that confines or restrains. **chain gang** Prisoners that are chained together.

chain reaction *n.* Series of events each of which is initiated by the preceding one.

chair-person (châr´per´san) *n.* The person presiding over a committee, board, or other meeting.

chaise (shāz) *n.* A one horse vehicle for two people.

chaise lounge (shāz´loung´) *n.* A chair that reclines and gives support for a person's legs and feet; a kind of reclining-chair with an elongated seat.

chal-ced-o-ny (kal sed´o nē) *n.* A translucent quartz, often pale blue or grayish with a waxlike shine.

chal-co-cite (kal´ko sīt´) *n.* Native sulfide of copper, a mineral having a dark-gray to black color and a metallic shine, occurring in crystals, and forms an important ore of copper.

cha-let (sha lā´) *n.* A cottage that has a gently sloping and overhanging roof.

chal-ice (chal´is) *n.* A drinking goblet or cup.

chalk (chok) *n.* A soft mineral made from fossil seashells, used for marking on a sur- face, such as a slate board.

chalk-board (chok bōerd) *n.* A blackboard made from slate.

chalk-stone (chok ´stōn´) *n.* A chalk-like mass in the small joints of person affected with gout.

chalk up *v.* To credit or attribute to.

chal-lah *or* **cha-lah (käl e)** *n.* A loaf of leavened white bread that is usually braided and eaten by Jews on holidays and the Sabbath.

chal-lenge (chal´inj) *n.* A demand for a contest; a protest. **challenge** *v.* To call into question. **challenger** *n.*

chal-lis (shal´ē) *n.* A lightweight printed cloth in rayon, cotton, or wool.

chal-one (kā´lōn) *n.* A secretion of endocrine origin which inhibits bodily activity.

cha-lu-meau (shal´ū mō) *n.* Woodwind instrument having the lowest register of the clarinet.

cha-lyb-e-ate (ka lib´ē it) *n.* Water or medicine that contains iron.

cham-ber (chām´bẽr) *n.* A bedroom in a large private home; a judge's office; a meeting place or hall for a legislative body; the compartment of a gun that holds the charge.

cham-ber-lain (chām´bẽr lin) *n.* The high ranking official of a royal court; an officer charged with the direction and management of the private apartments of a monarch or nobleman..

chamber of commerce *n.* Organization of business people and merchants who meet in an effort to promote and regulate commercial and industrial interests in their area.

cham-fer (cham´fẽr) *n.* A small gutter cut in wood or other hard materials; a beveled edge.

champ (chămp) *v.* To crush with the teeth; to chew vigorously or noisily; to show impatience in waiting.

cham-pagne (sham pān´) *n.* A white sparkling wine.

cham-per-ty (cham pert ē) *n.* An illegal proceeding whereby a person not concerned in a lawsuit bargains to aid a plaintiff or defendant in consideration of a share of any proceeds gained from the suit.

cham-pi-gnon (sham´pin yen) *n.* The common edible meadow mushroom.

cham-pi-on (cham´pē ɑn) *n.* The holder of first place in a contest; one who defends another person.

cham-pi-on-ship (cham´pē ɑn ship´) *n.* The competition that determines a winner.

chance (chăns) *n.* The random existence of something happening; a gamble or a risk, unexpected. **chance** *v.*

chance-ful (chăns´ful) *adj.* Eventful; full of chances or accidents; hazardous.

chan-cel (chan´sel) *n.* The area of a church that contains the altar and choir.

chance–med-ley (chăns´med¯lē) *n.* A sudden, accidental homicide; a violent altercation; haphazard action.

chan-cer-y (chan´se rē) *n.* The office for the safekeeping of official records.

chan-cre (shang´kẽr) *n.* A lesion that is the first indication of syphilis.

chan-croid (shang´kroid) *n.* A sore or lesion in the genital area that is similar to a chancre, but does not involve syphilis.

chanc-y (chan´sē) *adj.* Risky; dangerous.

chan-de-lier (shan´de lēr´) *n.* A light fixture with many branches for lights that is suspended from the ceiling.

chan-dler (chănd´lẽr) *n.* A person who makes and sells candles.

change (chānj) *v.* To become or make different; to alter; to put with another; to use to take the place of another; to freshen a bed by putting clean coverings on. **change** *n.* Coins; money given back when the payment exceeds the bill. **changer** *n.*

change-a-ble (chān je bel) *adj.* Liable or capable to change; subject to alteration; unstable. **changeably** *adv.* **changeability** *n.*

change of life *n.* The process of menopause for women, when they stop

having regular monthly periods.

chan-nel (chan´el) *n.* The deepest part of a stream, river, or harbor; the course that anything moves through or past; a groove. **channel** *v.*

chant (chănt) *n.* A melody in which all words are sung on the same note. **chant** *v.* To celebrate with a song.

chan-teuse (shan tŏs´) *n.* A professional female singer and entertainer, one who performs in cabarets or nightclubs.

chan-ti-cleer (chan´ti klẽr´) *n.* A rooster.

Cha-nu-kah (chä´ne kä´) *n.* Variation of *Hanukkah.*

cha-os (kā´os) *n.* Total disorder. **chaotic** *adj.* **chaotically** *adv.*

chap (chap) *n., Slang* A fellow; a man. *v.* To dry and split open from the cold and wind.

chap-ar-ral (chap´a ral´) *n.* A thicket of low growing evergreen oaks.

chap-book (chap´bŭk¯) *n.* A small book which contains poems, popular stories, fairy tales, ballads, or songs.

chap-el (chap´el) *n.* A place to worship, usually contained in a church.

chap-er-on *or* **chap-er-one (shap´e rŏn´)** *n.* An older person who supervises younger people.

chap-fall-en (chap´fo¯len) *adj.* Having the lower jaw depressed and hanging loosely from exhaustion or humiliation.

chap-i-ter (chap´i tẽr) *n.* The upper part or capital of a column.

chap-lain (chap´lin) *n.* A clergyman who conducts religious services for a group.

chap-let (chap´lit) *n.* A garland for the head; a string of beads.

chap-ter (chap´tẽr) *n.* One division of a book; a branch of a fraternity, religious order, or society.

cha-que-ta (chä ke´tä) *n.* A leather jacket worn by cowboys of western United States.

char *or* **charr (chär)** *n.* Name given to a species of scaled trouts.

char-a-cin (kar´a sin) *n.* A member of the family of freshwater fishes, brightly colored for use in aquariums.

char-ac-ter (kar´ik tẽr) *n.* A quality or trait that distinguishes an individual or group; a person that is portrayed in a play; a distinctive quality or trait. *adj.* Distinctive; peculiar.

char-ac-ter-i-za-tion (kar´ik tẽ i zā´shan) *n.* The act of characterizing; portrayal; description; artistic representation.

char-ac-ter-ize (kar´ik te rīz´) *v.* To describe the character or quality of; to be characteristic of.

cha-rade (sha räd´) *n.* A game in which words are represented or acted out by pantomime, and the other players must guess the word or phrase.

char-coal (chär´kōl´) *n.* A carbonaceous

material resulting from the imperfect combustion of organic matter, such as wood; material used to draw pictures.

chard (chärd) *n.* On edible white beet with large, succulent leaves.

charge (chärj) *v.* To give responsibility; to ask a price; to accuse; to impute something to; to command; to record a debt owed. *n.* Management; custody; supervision; an expense or price. *Slang* A thrill; excited. **chargeable** *adj.*

charge account *n.* A credit arrangement account where a customer may make im-mediate purchases and delay payment.

charge d'affaires *n.* A subordinate official who is in charge of diplomatic business during the temporary absence of an ambassador or minister.

charg-er (chär´jẽr) *n.* An apparatus for recharging a battery.

char-i-ot (char´ē ot) *n.* An ancient horse-drawn vehicle used to fight battles. **charioteer** *n.*

char-i-ot-eer (char´ē o tẽr) *n.* One who drives a chariot.

char-i-ta-ble (char´i ta bl) *adj.* Pertaining to or characterized by good will or tenderness toward others; benevolent and kind to the poor.

char-i-ty (char´i tē) *n.* Money or help given to aid the needy; an organization, fund, or institution whose purpose is to aid those in need.

cha-ri-va-ri (sha riv´a rē´) *n.* A mock serenade to newlyweds, performed with horns, tin pans, etc.

char-kha (char´ka) *n.* A spinning wheel used in India for spinning cotton.

char-la-tan (shär´la tan) *n.* One who falsely claims to possess knowledge or a skill he does not have; impostor.

char-lock (char lok) *n.* The wild mustard, often troublesome in grainfields.

char-lotte (shär´lot) *n.* A dessert consisting of fruit, custard, or whipped cream and cake or ladyfingers.

charm (chärm) *n.* The ability to delight or please; a small ornament that has a special meaning, usually worn on a bracelet.

char-meuse (shär mõz´) *n.* A soft, variety of satin.

char-nel (chär´nel) *n.* A special room or building that contains the bones or bodies of the dead.

char-qui (chär´kē) *n.* Jerked beef; beef dried by exposure to the sun.

chart (chärt) *n.* A map, graph, or table that gives information in a form that is easy to read. **chart** *v.*

char-ta-ceous *adj.* Resembling paper: applied to the paper-like texture of leaves or bark.

char-ter (chär´tẽr) *n.* An official

document that grants certain privileges and rights. *v.* To lease or hire a vehicle or aircraft.

char-tist (chär´tist) *n.* An analyst of stock market prices, whose predictions are based on charts and graphics of past performance and information.

char-treuse (shär tröz´) *n.* A light yellowish green.

char-y (chär´ē) *adj.* Wary; cautious; not wasting time, resources, or money. **charily** *adv.* **chariness** *n.*

chase (chās) *v.* To follow quickly; to pursue; to run after. **chaser** *n.*

chasm (kaz´um) *n.* A very deep crack in the earth's surface.

chas-sis (shas´ē) *n.* The rectangular framework that supports the body and engine of a motor vehicle.

chaste (chāst) *adj.* Morally pure; modest; not guilty of participating in sexual intercourse.

chas-ten *v.* To inflict suffering upon for purposes of moral improvement; discipline or subdue, as by adversity.

chas-tise (chas tīz´) *v.* To severely reprimand; to punish by beating; as flogging. **chastisement** *n.*

chas-u-ble (chaz´ū bl) *n.* The vestment without sleeves worn over the alb by a priest when celebrating mass.

chat (chat) *v.* To converse in a friendly manner.

cha-toy-ant (sha toi´ant) *adj.* Having a changeable undulating luster or color. **chatoyant** *n.* Any gem, as a cat's-eye, which is cut in a cabochon and reflects a single band of light.

chat-tel (chatel) *n.* An item of tangible movable personal property.

chauf-feur (shō´fẽr) *n.* A person who is hired to drive an automobile for another person.

chaus-sure (shō syr´) *n.* A boot, shoe, slipper; a foot covering.

chau-vin (shō´vin) *n.* Anyone possessed by an absurdly enthusiasm for a cause.

chau-vin-ism (shō ve nizem) *n.* Unreasonable belief in the superiority of one's own group or organization. **chauvinist** *n.* **chauvinistic** *adj.*

chaw (cho) *v.* To chew; to chew tobacco.

cheap (chēp) *adj.* Inexpensive; low in cost; of poor quality. **cheap** *adv.* **cheaply** *adv.* **cheapness** *n.*

cheapen (chē´pen) *v.* To lessen the value; to make cheap.

cheap-skate (chēp´skāt´) *n.* A person who is very cheap and refuses to spend money.

cheat (chēt) *v.* To deprive of by deceit; to break the rules. **cheater** *n.*

check (chek) *v.* To control or restrain; to examine for correctness or condition. **check** *n.* The act of verifying, comparing, or testing; a bill one receives at a restaurant; a written order on one's bank to pay money from funds on deposit; the act of comparing item to item; a move in chess which threatens a king and which forces the opponent to move the king to safety.

check-book (chek´bek´) *n.* A book containing blank checks for a checking account.

checking account *n.* A bank account by which the depositor can draw checks.

check list *n.* An alphabetical or systematic list of names of persons or things, intended for purposes of reference.

check-point (chek´point) *n.* A point where inspections are made.

check-up (chek´up´) *n.* A complete physical examination.

ched-dar (ched´ẽr) *n.* A firm, smooth cheese which ranges in flavor from mild to sharp.

cheek (chēk) *n.* The fleshy part of the face just below the eye and above and to the side of the mouth.

cheek-bone (chēk´bōn´) *n.* The facial bone below the eyes.

cheeky (chē´kē) *adj.* Insolent; impudent.

cheep (chēp) *n.* To utter high-pitched sounds.

cheer (chẽr) *v.* To give courage to; to instill with courage or hope.

cheese (chēz) *n.* A food made from the curd of milk that is seasoned and aged.

cheese-par-ing (chēz´pâr´ing) *n.* Something worthless and insignificant.

chee-tah (chē´ta) *n.* A swift-running, long-legged African wildcat.

chef (shef) *n.* A male cook who manages a kitchen; the head cook.

che-la (kē´la) *n.* The pincer-like claw of an arachnid.

che-lo-ni-an (ki lō´nē an) *n.* Tortoise; the tortoise family.

chem-i-cal (kem´i kal) *adj.* Of or related to chemistry. **chemically** *adv.*

chemical engineering *n.* A branch of chemistry that deals with the industrial application of chemistry.

chem-i-lum-i-nes-cence (kem´i lö´mi nes´ans) *n.* Light produced due to chemical reactions at low temperatures.

chemin de fer *n.* A card game similar to baccarat.

che-mise (she mēz´) *n.* A woman's loose undergarment which resembles a slip; a loose-fitting dress that hangs straight down from the shoulders.

chem-i-sorp-tion (kem´ē sorp´shan) *n.* Adsorption during a reaction between two or more chemicals.

chem-ist (kem´ist) *n.* A person who is versed in chemistry.

chem-is-try (kem´i strē) *n.* The scientific study of the composition, structure, and properties of substances and their react-ions.

chem-o-pro-phy-lax-is (kem´ō prö´fa lak´sis) *n.* The prevention of infectious disease by the use of chemical drugs or agents.

chem-os-mo-sis (kem´oz mō´sis) *n.* The chemical action between substances that occurs through an intervening membrane.

chem-o-syn-the-sis (kem´o sin´thi sis) *n.* The process by which organic compounds are formed from chemical components by energy derived from chemical reactions.

chem-o-tax-is (kem´o tak´sis) *n.* The orientation or movement of a cell or organism toward or away from a chemical stimulus.

che-mo-ther-a-py (kem´o ther´a pē) *n.* The treatment of a disease, such as cancer, with chemicals.

che-mot-ro-pism (ki mo´tro piz´um) *n.* The turning or bending of a plant or other organism in relation to chemical stimuli.

chem-ur-gy (kem´ü jē) *n.* A branch of applied chemistry dealing with industrial utilization of organic raw materials, especially from farm products.

cher-ish (cher´ish) *v.* To treat with love; to hold dear.

che-root (she röt´) *n.* A cigar that is cut off square at both ends.

cher-ry (cher´ē) *n., pl.* **cherries** A fruit tree bearing a small, round, red, or purplish red fruit with a small, hard stone.

cher-so-nese (kür´so nēz´) *n.* A peninsula.

chert (chürt) *n.* A compact siliceous rock resembling flint and composed essentially of chalcedonic or opaline silica, either alone or in combination.

cher-ub (cher´ub) *n.* A beautiful young child; a representation of an angel resembling a child with a rosy face and wings.

cher-vil (chür´vil) *n.* An aromatic herb of the carrot family, leaves of which are used in soups and salads.

chest (chest) *n.* The part of the upper body that is enclosed by the thorax; the ribs; a box usually having a hinged lid, used for storage.

cheval glass *n.* A full-length mirror that may be tilted.

chew (chö) *v.* To crush or grind with the teeth; to masticate. **chew** *n.* The act of chewing. **chewer** *n.* **chewy** *adj.*

chi-an-ti (kē än´tē) *n.* A dry red or white wine from Italy.

chi-a-ro-scu-ro (kē är´o sker´ō) *n.* The distribution of shade and light in a picture.

chi-cane (shi kān´) *v.* To quibble over.

chick (chik) *n.* A young chicken or bird. *Slang* A young woman.

chick-en (chik'en) *n.* A domestic fowl; the edible meat of a chicken. *Slang* Cowardly; afraid; losing one's nerve.

chicken pox *n.* A contagious childhood disease, characterized by skin eruptions and fever.

chic-o-ry (chik'o rē) *n. pl.* **-ies** An herb with blue flowers used in salads, the dried, roasted roots of which are used as a coffee substitute.

chide (chīd) *v.* To scold or find fault, rebuke. **chider** *n.*

chief (chēf) *n.* The person of highest rank. *Slang* Boss. **chiefly** *adj.*

chief-ly (chēf'lē) *adv.* For the most part; mostly; most importantly.

chief-tain (chēf'tan) *n.* The head of a group, clan, or tribe.

chif-fon (shi fon') *n.* A sheer fabric made from rayon or silk. *adj.* In cooking, having a fluffy texture.

chif-fo-nier (shif'o nēr') *n.* A tall chest of drawers with a mirror at the top.

chig-ger (chig'ér) *n.* A mite that attaches itself to the skin and causes intense itching.

chi-gnon (shēn'yon) *n.* A roll of hair worn at the back of the neck; a large roll, knot, or twist of hair worn at the back of the head.

chig-oe (chig'ō) *n.* A tropical flee that closely resembles the common flea.

chil-blain (chil'blān') *n.* An inflammation of the hands and feet caused by exposure to cold.

child (chīld) *n. pl.* **children** A young person of either sex; adolescent; a person between infancy and youth.

child abuse *n.* Sexual or physical mistreatment of a child by a parent, guardian, or other adult.

child-birth (chīld'berth') *n.* The act of giving birth.

child-hood (chīld'hed) *n.* The time or period of being a child.

child-like (chīld'līk') *adj.* Characteristic of a child.

chil-i (chilē) *n.* A hot pepper; a thick sauce made of meat and chili powder.

chil-i-ad (kil'ē ad') *n.* A group of one thousand; a period of 1000 years.

chill (chil) *v.* To be cold, often with shivering; to reduce to a lower temperature. *n.* A feeling of cold.

chime (chīm) *n.* A group or set of bells tuned to a scale. *v.* To announce on the hour, by sounding a chime.

chi-me-ra (ki mēr'a) *n.* An absurd fantasy; an imaginary monster with a goat's body, a lion's head, and a serpent's tail.

chi-mer-ic (ki mer'ik) *adj.* Pertaining to or being chimera; unreal; imaginary.

chin (chin) *n.* The lower part of the face.

v. To lift oneself up while grasping an overhead bar until the chin is level with the bar.

chi-na (chī'na) *n.* An earthenware or porcelain made in China.

chi-na-ware (chī'na wâr') *n.* Tableware made of china or porcelain.

chine (chīn) *n.* The spine or backbone of animals.

chink (chingk) *n.* A narrow crack.

chi-no (chē'nō) *n.* A heavy cotton twill used for military uniforms.

chi-noi-se-rie (shēn woz'e rē) *n.* A style of Chinese art and ornamentation that reflects Chinese qualities, characterized by intricate patterns and motifs.

chintz (chints) *n.* A printed cotton fabric which is glazed.

chintz-y (chint'sē) *adj.* Cheap.

chip (chip) *n.* A small piece that has been broken or cut from another source; a disk used in the game of poker; in *computer science*, an integrated circuit engraved on a silicone substrate.

chip-per (chip'ér) *adj.* Cheerful; happy.

chi-rog-ra-phy (kī rog'ra fē) *n.* Penmanship; handwriting.

chi-ro-man-cy (kī'ro man sē) *n.* The ability of foretelling one's fortune by reading the lines of his hand.

chi-rop-o-dist (kī rop'o dist) *n.* One who treats ailments and irregularities of both the hands and feet.

chi-ro-prac-tic (kī'ro prak'tik) *n.* A method of therapy in which the body is manipulated to adjust the spine. **chiropract** *n.*

chirp (cherp) *n.* The high-pitched sound made by a cricket or certain small birds.

chirr (chûr) *v.* To make a short vibrant or trilling sound, as a grasshopper.

chis-el (chiz'el) *n.* A tool with a sharp edge which is used to shape and cut metal, wood, or stone.

chis-eled (chiz'eld) *adj.* Formed or shaped with a chisel.

chit (chit) *n.* A voucher indicating the amount owed for food or drink; a lively girl.

chi-tin (kī'tin) *n.* The substance that forms the hard outer cover of insects.

chit-ter-lings (chit'ér ling) *n. pl.* The small intestines of a pig, used as food.

chiv-al-ry (shiv'al rē) *n. pl.* **-ies** The brave and courteous qualities of an ideal knight.

chive (chīv) *n.* An herb used as flavoring in cooking.

chlo-ral (klōral) *n.* A pungent colorless oily liquid first prepared from chlorine and alcohol; used in making DDT.

chlo-ral-ose (klōr'a lōs') *n.* A crystalline compound of combining chloral dextrose, used in medicine as a hypnotic.

chlo-rate (klōr'āt) *n.* A chloric acid salt.

chlo-ride (klōr´īd) n. A compound of chlorine with a double positive element.

chlo-rin-ate (klō´i nāt´) v. To combine or treat with chlorine or a chlorine compound; to disinfect.

chlo-rine (klōr´ēn) n. A greenish-yellow compound used to purify water, bleach, and disinfectant.

chlo-rite (klōr´īt) n. A name for a group of usually green minerals, hydrous silicates of aluminum, ferrous iron, and magnesium.

chlo-ro-form (klōr´i form´) n. A colorless, volatile liquid of an agreeable smell and taste; used as a veterinary anesthetic.

chlo-ro-phyll (klōr´a fil) n. The green pigment that is found in photosynthetic organisms.

chlo-ro-pic-rin (klō´o pik´rin) n. A slightly oily, colorless, poisonous liquid that causes vomiting and tears used as a soil fumigant.

chlo-ro-sis (kla rō´sis) n. Iron-deficiency in a plant, from lack of iron in the soil or other causes.

chlor-prop-amide(klōr prōp´ amīd) n. An oral drug used to lower blood sugar, used to treat mild diabetes.

chock (chok) n. A wedge or block placed under a wheel to prevent motion.

choc-o-late (cho´ko lit) n. A preparation of ground and roasted cacao nuts that is usually sweetened; a candy or beverage made from chocolate. **chocolaty** adj.

choice (chois) n. To select or choose; the opportunity, right, or power to choose.

choir (kwīr) n. An organized group of singers that usually perform in a church.

choir-mas-ter (kwī´mas´tēr) n. The director of a choir, a conductor.

choke (chōk) v. To stop normal breathing by an obstruction in the windpipe; to strangle.

chok-er (chō´kēr) n. A necklace that fits tightly around the neck.

chol-e-cys-tec-to-my (kol´i si stek´to mē) n. The surgical removal of the gall bladder.

chol-er (kol´ēr) n. Anger, wrath; the state of easily provoked anger.

chol-er-a (kol´ēr a) n. Any of several infectious diseases of man and domestic animals usually showing signs of severe gastrointestinal symptoms.

chol-er-ic (kol´ēr ik) adj. Easily irritated; hot tempered; inclined to excessive anger.

cho-les-ter-ol (ka les´te rōl´) n. A fatty crystalline substance that is derived from bile and is present in most gallstones, the brain, and blood cells.

cho-line (kō´lēn) n. A basic substance that occurs in many animal and plant products and is a member of the vitamin-B complex essential to the function of the liver.

chol-la (chōl´yä) n. A very spiny, treelike cacti of southwestern United States and Mexico.

choose (chōz) v. To select or pick out; to prefer; to make a choice. **choosy** or **chosen** adj. **choosey** adj.

choos-y (chō´zē) adj. Hard to please; particular, selective.

chop (chop) v. To cut by making a sharp downward stroke; to cut into bits or small pieces.

cho-ral (kōr´al) adj. Pertaining to, written for, or sung by a choir or chorus, adapted. **chorally** adv.

cho-rale (ko ral´) n. A Protestant hymn with a simple melody, sung in unison.

chord (kord) n. The sounding of three or more musical notes simultaneously.

chord-al (kor´dial) adj. Relating to music characterized by harmony rather than by counterpoint.

chore (chōr) n. A daily task; a task that becomes unpleasant or burdensome.

cho-re-a (ko rē´a) n. An acute nervous dis ease especially of children, marked by irregular and uncontrollable movement of muscles.

cho-re-og-ra-phy (kōr´ē og´ra fē) n. The creation of a dance routine for entertainment. **choreographic** adj.

cho-ri-o-al-lan-to-is (kōr´ē ō a lan´tō is) n. Vascular fetal membrane formed in the fetal tissue of birds, reptiles, and some mammals.

chor-is-ter (kor´i stēr) n. A choirboy or a member of a choir; a singer in a choir.

cho-rog-ra-phy (ko rog´ra fē) n. The art of mapping, or of describing particular regions, countries, or districts.

cho-rus (kōr´us) n. pl. **-ses** A group of people who sing together; the repeated verses of a song.

chose (shōz) v. The past tense of choose.

cho-sen (chō´zen) adj. Selected or preferred above all.

chow-der (chou´dēr) n. A soup dish made with fish or clams, often having a milk base.

Christ (krīst) n. Jesus; The Messiah; God's son who died to save Christians from sin.

chris-ten (kris´n) v. To baptize; to give a Christian name at baptism; to use for the first time. **christening** n.

Chris-tian (kris´chan) n. A believer and follower of the teachings of Jesus. **Christianly** adv. **Christianity** n.

Christ-mas(kris´mas) n. December 25th, the anniversary of the birth of Jesus Christ, observed as a holiday or holy day.

chro-ma (krō'ma) *n*. The purity or quality of a color, that combines hue and saturation.

chro-mat-ic (krō mat'ik) *adj*. Relating to color.

chrome alum *n*. A dark-violet salt in dyeing, tanning, and photography.

chro-mo-lith-o-graph (krō'mōli thog'ra fē) *n*. A picture printed in colors by means of the lithographic process.

chro-mo-plast (krō'mo plast') *n*. A plastid, or mass of protoplasm, containing red or yellow pigment.

chro-mo-pro-tein (kro'mo prō'tēn) *n*. A protein compound, as hemoglobin, with a metal-containing pigment or a carotenoid.

chro-mo-some (kro'mə sōm') *n*. One of several small bodies in the nucleus of a cell, containing genes responsible for the determination and transmission of hereditary characteristics.

chro-mo-sphere (krō'mo sfēr') *n*. A gaseous layer surrounding the sun above the photosphere, consisting primarily of hydrogen.

chron-ic (kron'ik) *adj*. Long duration; frequently recurring; continuing for long periods of time; suffering from a disease for a long time.

chron-i-cle (kron'i kəl) *n*. A record of events written in the order in which they occurred. **chronicle** *v*. **-er** *n*.

chron-o-graph (kron'o graf') *n*. An astronomical instrument for recording the exact instant of occurrences.

chro-nol-o-gy (kro nol'o jē) *n*. The science of measuring times, periods or years when past events or transactions took place, and arranging them in order of occurrence.

chron-o-scope (kron'o skōp') *n*. An instrument for precise measuring of extremely short-lived phenomena.

chrys-a-lis (kris'a lis) *n*. *pl*.- *ses* The enclosed pupa from which a moth or butterfly develops.

chry-san-the-mum (kri san'the mum) *n*. A cultivated plant having large, showy flowers.

chrys-o-ber-yl (kris'o ber'il) *n*. A mineral, usually of a yellow or greenish color, sometimes used as a gem.

chrys-o-lite (kris'o lit') *n*. A native silicate that varies from yellow to green in color, and in some forms used as a gem.

chtho-ni-an (thō'nē an) *adj*. Dwelling beneath the surface of the earth.

chub (chub) *n*. A freshwater fish related to the carp.

chub-by (chub'ē) *adj*. Plumb; rounded. **chubbiness** *n*.

chuck (chuk) *v*. To tap or pat affectionately under the chin. *Slang* To throw out or to throw away; to quit; to give

up. **chuck** *n*. A cut of beef extending from the neck to the ribs.

chuck-hole (chuk'hōl') *n*. A hole in the street or the pavement.

chuck-le (chuk'ul) *v*. To laugh quietly with satisfaction. **chuckler** *n*.

chug (chug) *n*. A short, dull, explosive noise, as from a malfunctioning engine.

chuk-ka (chuk'a) *n*. An ankle-length of boot often made of leather, and laced through pairs of eyelets or a buckle.

chum (chum) *n*. A close friend or pal.

chunk (chungk) *n*. A thick piece of anything; a large quantity of something; a lump.

church (cherch) *n*. A building for Christian worship; a congregation of public Christian worship.

churl (cherl) *n*. A rude or rustic person. **churlish** *adj*. **churlishness** *n*.

churr (chür) *n*. The vibrant or whirring noise made by insects and some birds, such as a partridge.

chute (shōt) *n*. An incline passage through which water, coal, etc., may travel to a destination. *Slang* A parachute.

chut-ney (chut'nē) *n*. An agreeable condiment of fruit, spices, and herbs.

chyme (kīm) *n*. The semi-liquid mass into which food is expelled and converted by gastric secretion during digestion.

ci-ca-da (si kā da) *n*. The popular and generic name of insects with a stout body, large transparent wings and a wide blunt head.

ci-der (sī'dèr) *n*. The juice from apples.

ci-gar (si gär') *n*. Rolled tobacco leaves used for smoking.

cig-a-rette (sig'a ret') *n*. A small amount of tobacco rolled in thin paper for smoking.

cil-i-a (sil'ē a) *n*. The hairs that grow from the edge of the eyelids; eyelashes.

cil-i-ar-y (sil'ē er'ē) *adj*. Pertaining to the eyelids or eyelashes.

cil-ice (sil'is) *n*. A stiff undergarment made of horse or camel hair, formally worn by monks.

cinch (sinch) *n*. The strap for holding a saddle. *v*. To assure. *Slang* Something easy to do.

cin-cho-na (sin kō'na) *n*. A tree in South America whose bark yields quinine.

cin-chon-ism (sin'ko niz'um) *n*. A disorder of the body characterized by dizziness, ear ringing, temporary deafness, and headache, the result of overdoses of cinchona or its alkaloids.

cinc-ture (singk'chèr) *n*. A belt or cord to put around the waist. *v*. To encircle or sur-round with a cincture.

cin-der (sin'dèr) *n*. A piece of something that is partially burned. **cindery** *adj*.

cin-e-ma (sin'a ma) *n*. A motion picture;

a motion picture theater; the business of making a motion picture.

cin-e-mat-o-graph (sin´e mat´o graf´) *n.* A movie projector or camera.

cin-e-ma-tog-ra-phy (sin´e ma tog´ra fē) *n.* The art of photographing a motion picture. **cinematographer** *n.*

cin-e-rar-i-um (sin´a rã´e um) *n.* A place for receiving the ashes of the dead after cremation.

ci-ne-re-ous (si nēr´ē us) *adj.* Resembling the color of wood ashes.

cin-na-bar (sin´a bär´) *n.* A mineral which is the principal source of mercury.

cin-na-mon (sin´a mon) *n.* The aromatic inner bark of a tropical Asian tree, used as a spice, reddish brown in color.

ci-pher (sī´fėr) *n.* The symbol for the absence of quantity; O; secret writing that has a prearranged key or scheme.

cir-cle (sėr´kl) *n.* A process that ends at its starting point; a group of people having a common interest or activity.

cir-cuit (sėr´kit) *n.* The closed path through which an electric current flows.

circuit breaker *n.* A switch that automatic-ally interrupts the flow of an electric current in an overloaded circuit.

circuit court *n.* The lowest court of record, located in two or more locations within one jurisdiction.

cir-cuit-ry (sėr´ki trē) *n.* The arrangement or detailed plan of an electric circuit.

cir-cu-lar (sėr´kū lėr) *adj.* Moving in a circle or round-like fashion; relating to something in a circle; having free motion, as the air. **circularity** *n.*

cir-cu-late (sėr´kū lāt´) *v.* To pass from place to place or person to person; to distribute in a wide area. **circulation** *n.* **culator** *n.* **circulatory** *adj.*

cir-cu-la-tion (sėr´kū lā´shan) *n.* The movement, or flow of blood through the vessels by the pumping action of the heart; the passing or transmission from one person to another.

cir-cum-cise (sėr´kum sīz´) *v.* To remove the foreskin on the male penis, sometimes as a religious rite. **circumcision** *n.*

cir-cum-fer-ence (ser kum´fėr ens) *n.* The perimeter or boundary of a circle. **circumferential** *adj.*

cir-cum-flex (sėr´kum fleks´) *n.* A mark indicating the quality or sound of vowels as they appear in words.

cir-cum-gy-ra-tion (sėr´kym jī rā´shan) *n.* A movement in a circular course.

cir-cum-ja-cent (sėr´kum jā´sent) *adj.* Bordering on all sides; surrounding.

cir-cum-lo-cu-tion (sėr´kum lō kū´shan) *n.* The use of more or unnecessarily large words to express an idea.

cir-cum-lu-nar (sür´cum lö´nėr) *adj.* Revolving about or surrounding the moon.

cir-cum-scribe (ser´kum skrīb´) *v.* To confine something within drawn boundaries; to surround.

cir-cum-spect (sür´kum spekt´) *adj.* Examining carefully all circumstances and possible consequences.

cir-cum-stance (ser´kum stans´) *n.* A fact or condition that must be considered when making a decision.

cir-cum-stan-tial (ser´kum stan´shal) *adj.* Incidental; not essential; dependent on circumstances.

cir-cum-stan-ti-ate (ser´kum stan´shē āt) *adj.* Providing support or circumstantial evidence.

cir-cum-vent (ser´kum vent´) *v.* To outwit or gain advantage; to avoid or go around. **circumvention** *n.*

cir-cum-vo-lu-tion (sür´kum vo lö´shan) *n.* The act or rolling or turning around an axis; a single complete turn.

cir-cum-volve (sür´kum volv´) *v.* To revolve about.

cir-cus (ser´kus) *n. pl.* **-cuses** Entertainment featuring clowns, acrobats, and trained animals.

cirque (sürk) *n.* A deep steep-walled circular space, a natural amphitheater.

cir-rho-sis (si rō´sis) *n.* A liver disease that is ultimately fatal. **cirrhotic** *adj.*

cir-ro-cu-mu-lus (sir´ō kū´mū lus) *n.* A cloud of high altitude, consisting of small white rounded masses.

cir-ro-stra-tus (sir´ō strā´tus) *n.* A whitish fairly uniformed layer of cloud or haze.

cir-rus (sir´us) *n. pl.* **cirri** A high altitude, white, wispy cloud.

cis-co (sis´kō) *n.* Any of various species of whitefish found in the Great Lakes area.

cis-tern (sis´tėrn) *n.* A man-made tank or artificial reservoir for holding rain water.

cis-tron (sis´tron) *n.* The segment of DNA; the smallest single functional unit of genetic substance, considered equivalent to a gene in molecular biology.

cit-a-del (sit´a del) *n.* A fortress commanding a city; a stronghold.

ci-ta-tion (sī tā´shan) *n.* An official summons from a court; a quotation used in literary or legal material; an honor.

cite (sīt) *v.* To bring forward as proof; to summon to action; to rouse; to summon to appear in court.

cit-i-zen (sit´i zen) *n.* A resident of a town or city; a native or naturalized person entitled to protection from a government; a native or naturalized, as opposed to alien, member of a state or nation. **citizenry, citizenship** n.

cit·i·zen's band n. A two-way radio frequency band for private use.

cit·ral (si´tral) n. A liquid aldehyde with a strong lemon odor, obtained from oils of lemons or oranges, or synthetically manufactured, and used in perfumery and flavoring.

cit·ric a·cid (si´trik) n. A colorless acid found in lime, lemon, and other juices; the acid derived from lemons and similar fruits or obtained by the fermentation of carbohydrates, and used to flavor foods, beverages, and pharmaceuticals.

cit·ri·cul·ture (si´tri kul˝chèr) n. The cultivation of citrus fruits.

cit·ron·el·la (si˝tra nel´a) n. A fragrant grass of southern Asia, found in many oils and used in making insect repellant, liniment, perfume, and soap.

cit·rus (sit´rus) n. pl. **citrus, citruses** Any of a variety of trees bearing fruit with thick skins, as limes, oranges, lemons, and grapefruits.

cit·tern (sit´ern) n. An ancient stringed instrument, somewhat resembling a guitar but with a more flat pear-shaped body.

cit·y (sit´ē) n. A place larger than a town.

city council n. The legislative body of a municipality or city with administrative and legislative power.

civ·et (siv´it) n. A cat-like mammal that secretes a musky fluid from the genital glands, which is used in perfumery.

civ·ic (siv´ik) adj. Relating to or of a citizen, city, or citizenship.

civ·ics (siv´iks) n. The social or political science of the rights and duties of citizens.

civ·il (siv´il) adj. Relating to citizens; relating to the legal proceedings concerned with the rights of private individuals.

civil aviation n. Aviation by commercial or private concerns as separated from military aviation.

civil defense n. A civilian program of volunteers ready to provide protection in case of a natural disaster, invasion, or enemy attack.

ci·vil·ian (si vil´yen) n. A person not serving in the military, as a firefighter, or as a policeman.

civ·i·li·za·tion (siv´i li zā´shan) n. A high level of social, cultural, and political development.

civ·i·lize (siv´i liz´) v. To bring out of a state of savagery into one of education and refinement.

civil rights n. pl. The nonpolitical rights guaranteed to citizens; the rights provided by the 13th and 14th amendments of the United States Constitution.

civil service n. The administrative or executive service of a government or international agency separate from the armed forces.

clack (klak) n. A sharp, abrupt sound, continuous talk; chatter.

clack valve n. A hinged valve in pumps with a single flap, that permits the flow of fluid in one direction only.

claim (klām) v. To ask for one's due; to hold something to be true; to make a statement that something is true; to demand. **claim** n. **claimant** n.

clair·voy·ance (klâr voi´ans) n. The ability to visualize in the mind distant objects or objects hidden from the senses; a mesmeric state.

clam (klam) n. Any of various marine and freshwater bivalve mollusks. Slang To become silent; to clam up.

clam·my (klam´ē) adj. Damp, cold, and sticky. **clammily** adv. **clamminess** n.

clam·or (klam´ér) n. A loud noise or outcry; a vehement protest or demand. **clamourous** adj. **clamorously** adv.

clamp (klamp) n. A device designed for holding or fastening things together.

clamp down v. The action of making or increasing restrictions or regulations.

clam·shell (klam´shel˝) n. The shell of a clam; a dredging bucket having two hinged jaws.

clan (klan) n. A large group of people who are related to one another by a common ancestor. **clannish** adj.

clan·des·tine (klan des´tin) adj. Kept or done in secrecy for a purpose.

clang (klang) v. To cause or make a loud, ringing, metallic sound.

clan·gor (klang´ér) n. A loud series of clangs.

clank (klangk) n. A sharp, quick, metallic sound.

clap (klap) v. To applaud; to strike the hands together with an explosive sound.

clap·board (klab´ord) n. A narrow board with one end thicker than the other, used to cover the outside of buildings so as to weatherproof the inside.

claque (klak) n. A group hired to attend and applaud at a performance.

clar·en·don (klar´en don) n. A condensed style of printing type, similar to roman but with thicker lines.

clar·et (klar´it) n. A red Bordeaux table wine; similar red wines produced elsewhere.

clar·i·fy (klar´i fī´) v. To become or make clearer. **clarification** n.

clar·i·net (klar´i net´) n. A woodwind instrument with a single reed. **clarinetist** n.

clar·i·ty (klar´i tē) n. The state or quality of being clear.

clark·i·a (klär´kē a) n. A flowering annual herb of the evening primrose family.

cla-ro (klä´ō) *n.* A light-colored and typically mild cigar.

clar-y (klâr´ē) *n.* An aromatic mint herb used as a potherb and for medicinally.

clash (klash) *v.* To bring or strike together; to collide; to conflict.

clasp (klasp) *n.* A hook to hold parts of objects together; a grasp or grip of the hands. **clasp** *v.*

class (klas) *n.* A group or set that has certain social or other interests in common; a group of students who graduate at the same time.

clas-sic (klas´ik) *adj.* Belonging in a certain category of excellence; having a lasting artistic worth.

clas-si-cal (klas´i kal) *adj.* Relating to the style of the ancient Roman or Greek classics; standard and authoritative, not experimental or new.

clas-si-cism (klas´i siz´um) *n.* A belief in the esthetic principles of ancient Rome and Greece.

clas-si-cist (klas´i sist) *n.* A classical scholar; a follower of classicism.

clas-si-fi-ca-tion (klas´i fi ka´shan) *n.* The act of classifying; to systematically bring together those things which most resemble each other; arrange in categories.

clas-si-fied (klas´i fid) *adj.* Arranged or divided into classes; withheld from the general public; confidential; secret.

clas-si-fy (klas´i fi´) *v.* To arrange or assign items, people, etc., into the same class or category. **classification** *n.*

class-mate (klas´māt) *n.* A member of the same class in a school or college.

class-room (klas´rōm) *n.* A room where students meet for classes and to study.

clas-tic (klas´tik) *adj.* Breaking up or made of fragments or parts.

clat-ter (klat´er) *v.* To make or to cause a rattling sound. **clatter** *n.*

clause (klos) *n.* A group of words which are part of a simple compound, or complex sentence, containing a subject and predicate.

claus-tro-pho-bia (klo´stro fō´bē a) *n.* A fear of small or enclosed places.

cla-ve (klä´vä) *n.* One of a pair of cylindrical hardwood sticks or blocks of wood, held in the hands and clicked together to the rhythm of music.

clav-i-chord (klav´i kord´) *n.* A keyboard instrument which is one step down from the piano.

clav-i-cle (klav´i kl) *n.* The bone that connects the breastbone and the shoulder blade.

cla-vier (kla vēr´) *n.* An instrument with a keyboard, such as the harpsichord.

claw (klo) *n.* A sharp, curved nail on the foot of an animal; the pincer of certain crustaceans, such as crab, lobster, etc.

clay (klā) *n.* A fine-grained, pliable earth that hardens when fired, used to make pottery, bricks, and tiles.

clean (klēn) *adj.* Free from impurities, dirt, or contamination; neat in habits.

clean-cut *adj.* Distinctly outlined or defined; cut so the surface or edge is smooth and clean; a wholesome and neat appearance.

clean out *v., Slang* To empty, as a store; to deprive of resources.

cleanse (klenz) *v.* To make pure or clean. **cleanser** *n.*

clean-up (klēn´up´) *n.* An act or instance of cleaning; *Slang* A large profit on a bet or investment.

clear (klēr) *adj.* Free from precipitation and clouds; able to hear, see, or think easily; distinctly, free from doubt or confusion; free from a burden, obligation, or guilt. **clearly** *adv.*

clearance (klēr´ans) *n.* The distance that one object clears another by; a permission to proceed.

clear-head-ed (klēr´hed´id) *adj.* Having a clear understanding of something.

clearing house *n.* Stock Exchange and the Board of Trade, similar clearing houses exist for the facilitation of trading in stocks, grain, or other commodities.

cleat (klēt) *n.* A metal projection that provides support, grips, or prevents slipping.

cleav-a-ble (klē´va bl) *adj.* Capable of being separated or divided.

cleav-age (klē´vij) *n.* The process, act, or result of splitting; the cleft a woman displays in low-cut clothes.

cleave (klēv) *v.* To divide or split by a cutting blow, along a natural division line, as the grain of wood; split; to penetrate or pass through.

cleav-er (klē´vér) *n.* A knife used by butchers.

cleek (klēk) *n.* A large iron hook, used to suspend a pot over a fire.

clef (klef) *n.* A symbol indicating which pitch each line and space represents on a musical staff.

cleft (kleft) *n.* A space or opening made by partially splitting; a crevice.

clem-ent (klem´ent) *adj.* Merciful; mild.

clench (klench) *v.* To clinch; to hold firmly, as with the hands or teeth, close tightly.

clep-sy-dra (klep´si dra) *n.* A name for common devices used for measuring time by the regulated discharge of water; a water clock.

clep-to-ma-ni-a *n.* Compulsive stealing.

cler-gy (klér´jē) *n.* The group of men and women who are ordained as religious leaders and servants of God.

cler-ic (kler´ik) *adj.* Pertaining to the clergy; clerical.

cler-i-cal (kler′i kal) *adj.* Trained to handle office duties.

clerk (klork) *n.* A worker in an office who keeps accounts, records, and correspondence up to date; a person who works in the sales department of a store.

Cleveland, Stephen Grover *n.* (1837-1908) The twenty-second and twenty-fourth president of the United States, from 1885-1889 and 1893-1897.

clev-er (klev′ér) *adj.* Mentally quick; showing dexterity and skill. **cleverly** *adv.* **cleverness** *n.*

clev-is (klev′is) *n.* A piece of metal, usually U-shaped, having a pin or bolt that connects the two sides; shackle.

clew (klö) *n.* A ball of thread, cord, or yarn; a lower corner or loop of a sail.

click (klik) *v.* To make a small sharp sound; to move, strike or produce with a click.

cli-ent (klī′ent) *n.* A person who secures the professional services of another.

cli-en-tele (klī′en tel′) *n.* A collection of patients, customers, or clients.

cliff (klif) *n.* A high, steep edge or face of a rock.

cliff-hanger (klif′hang′ér) *n.* Anything which causes suspense and anticipation until the final outcome is known.

cli-mate (klī′mit) *n.* The weather conditions of a certain region generalized or averaged over a period of years; the prevailing atmosphere. **climatic** *adj.* **climatically** *adv.*

cli-ma-tol-o-gy (klī′ma tol′o jē) *n.* The science that deals with climates, an investigation of their phenomena.

cli-max (klī′maks) *n.* The point of greatest intensity and fullest suspense; the culmination.

climb (klīm) *v.* To move to a higher or lower location; to advance in rank or status. **climbable** *adj.* **climber** *n.*

clinch (klinch) *v.* To secure; to fasten; to settle definitively. **clinch** *n.*

cling (kling) *v.* To hold fast to; to grasp or stick; to hold on and resist emotional separation. **clinger** *n.*

clin-ic (klin′ik) *n.* A medical establishment connected with a hospital; a center that offers instruction or counseling.

clinical thermometer *n.* An instrument used in medical practice to measure the body temperature.

cli-ni-cian (kli nish′an) *n.* A physician or one qualified in clinical method skills.

clink (klingk) *v.* To cause a light ringing sound.

clink-er (kling′ker) *n.* An over baked, hard yellowish Dutch brick used for paving. *n., Slang* A blunder; a flop.

clink-er–built *adj.* Having external plates

overlapping one another; as the clapboards of a house.

clin-quant (kling′kant) *adj.* Glittering with tinsel or gold.

Clinton, William *n.* (1946-) The forty-second president of the United States from 1993-.

clip (klip) *v.* To cut off; to curtail; to cut short. *n.* Something that grips, holds, or clasps articles together.

clip artist *n., Slang* A person who makes a profession of robbing or swindling.

clip-board (klip′bōrd′) *n.* A small writing board, having a spring clip, usually at the top, to hold sheets of paper.

clip-per (klip′ér) *n.* A sailing vessel that travels at a high rate of speed.

clip-per (klip′ér) *n.* A tool used for cutting.

clique (klēk) *n.* A small and exclusive group of people.

cloak (klōk) *n.* A loose outer garment that conceals or covers.

clob-ber (klob′ér) *v., Slang* To hit repeatedly and violently.

cloche (klōsh) *n.* A bell-shaped, close-fitting hat.

clock (klok) *n.* An instrument that measures time. **clock** *v.* To time with a watch, clock, stopwatch, etc.

clock-wise (klok′wiz′) *adv.* In the direction the hands of a clock rotate.

clod (klod) *n.* A large piece or lump of earth; a stupid, ignorant person.

clog (klog) *v.* To choke up. *n.* A shoe with a wooden sole.

clois-ter (kloi′stér) *v.* To confine or seclude in a cloister or convent.

clone (klōn) *n.* An identical reproduction grown from a single cell of the original.

clop (kläp) *v.* To produce a hollow sound, as if done by a horse's hoof or wooden shoe.

close (klōs) *adj.* Near, as in time, space, or relationship; nearly even, as in competition; fitting tightly. *v.* To shut.

closed (klōzd) *adj.* Forming a self-contained barrier; limited as to season for hunting or fishing.

closed circuit *n.* An unbroken circuit permitting a signal to be transmitted by wire to a limited number of receivers.

close–out (klōz′out′) *n.* A clearance sale of merchandise usually at a reduced price.

close shave *n., Slang* A narrow escape.

clos-et (kloz′it) *n.* A small cabinet, compartment, or room for storage.

close-up (klōs′up′) *n.* A picture taken at close range; a close view or examination of something.

clo-sure (klō′zhér) *n.* The act or condition of being closed; an end or conclusion.

clot (klot) *n.* A thick or solid mass, as of blood. **clot** *v.*

cloth (kloth) *n. pl.* **cloths** A knitted, woven, or matted piece of fabric, used to cover a table; the professional clothing of the clergy.

clothe (klōth) *v.* To provide clothes; to cover with clothes; to wrap.

clothes (klōz) *n.* Cloth items of a person that can be worn and are washable; dress.

cloth-ing (klō thing) *n.* Garments in general; clothes.

clo-ture (klō´shér) *n.* A parliamentary action that calls for an immediate vote.

cloud (kloud) *n.* A visible body of water or ice particles floating in the atmosphere; something that obscures; a cloud of dust or smoke. **cloudy** *adj.*

cloud-i-ly (kloud´i lē) *adv.* In an obscure or cloudy manner.

clout (klout) *n.* A heavy blow with the hand. *Slang* The amount of influence or pull a person may have. **clout** *v.*

clove (klōv) *n.* A spice from an evergreen tree; a small bud that is part of a larger group, as a clove of garlic.

clo-ver (klō´vér) *n.* A plant that has a dense flower and trifoliolate leaves.

cloy (kloi) *v.* To make one sick or disgusted with too much sweetness.

club (klub) *n.* A heavy wooden stick, used as a weapon; a group of people who have organized themselves with or for a com-mon purpose.

clue (klö) *n.* Reliable information that leads to the solution of a problem, crime or mystery.

clump (klump) *n.* A group of things in a cluster or group; a shapeless mass. *v.* To plant or place in a clump.

clum-sy (klum´zē) *adj.* Lacking coordination, grace, or dexterity; not tactful or skillful. **clumsily** *adv.*

clus-ter (klus´tér) *n.* A bunch; a group.

clutch (kluch) *v.* To seize or attempt to seize and hold tightly. *n.* A tight grasp; a device for connecting and disconnecting the engine and the drive shaft in an automobile or other mechanism.

clut-ter (klut´ér) *n.* A confused mass of disorder.

coach (kōch) *n.* An automobile that is closed and usually has four doors and four wheels; a trainer or director of athletics, drama, etc.

coach-man (kōch´mam) *n.* A man employed to drive a carriage or coach.

co-ad-ju-tor (kō aj u tér) *n.* An assistant.

co-ag-u-la-bil-i-ty (kō ag´ū la bil´i tē) *n.* The capacity of being coagulated.

co-ag-u-lant (kō ag´ū lant) *n.* A substance that causes coagulation.

co-ag-u-late (kō ag´ū lāt´) *v.* To clot or congeal. **coagulation** *n.*

coal (kōl) *n.* A mineral widely used as a natural fuel; an ember.

coal-er (kō´lér) *n.* A person who sells or provides coal; something used to haul or transport coal.

co-a-lesce (kō´a les´) *v.* To come together or to grow as one.

co-ali-tion (kō´a lish´an) *n.* A temporary alliance.

co-apt (kō apt´) *v.* To fit together and make fast, as in the setting of broken bones.

co-arc-tate (kō ärk´tāt) *adj.* Pressed together; compressed; enclosed in a rigid case.

coarse (kōrs) *adj.* Lacks refinement; of inferior or low quality; having large particles; harsh. **coarseness** *v.*

coast (kōst) *v.* To move without propelling oneself; to use the force of gravity alone; to slide or glide along. *n.* The land bordering the sea.

coat (kōt) *n.* An outer garment with sleeves, worn over other clothing; a layer that covers a surface.

co-au-thor (kō o´thér) *n.* A person who writes with the assistance of one or more other authors.

coax (kōks) *v.* To persuade by tact, gentleness, or flattery. **coaxingly** *adv.*

co-ax-i-al (kō ak´sē al) *adj.* Having common coincident axes.

coaxial cable *n.* A transmission cable consisting of two or more insulated conductors capable of transmitting television, telegraph, signals of high frequency.

cob (kob) *n.* A male swan; a corncob; a thick-set horse that has short legs.

co-balt (kō´bolt) *n.* A hard, lustrous metallic element that resembles iron and nickel.

cob-ble (kob´l) *v.* To make or repair shoes; to make or put together roughly. **cobbler, cobble** *n.*

CO-BOL (kō´böl) *n.* In Computer Science, computer programming that is simple and based on English.

cob-web (kob´web´) *n.* The fine thread from a spider which is spun into a web and used to catch prey.

co-caine (kō kān´) *n.* An alkaloid used as an anesthetic and narcotic.

co-cain-ism (kō kā´niz um) *n., Pathol.* The addiction to the use of cocaine.

coc-cyx (kok´siks) *n.* The small bone at the bottom of the spinal column.

coch-i-neal (koch´i nēl´) *n.* A brilliant scarlet dye prepared from the dried, pulverized bodies of certain female insects of tropical America.

coch-le-a (kok´lē a) *n.* The spiral tube of the inner ear, forming an essential part for hearing.

cock (kok) *n.* The adult male in the domestic fowl family; the rooster; the hammer of a firearm and the readiness for firing. *v.* To raise in preparation for hitting; to ready a firearm for firing.

cock-ade (ko kād´) *n.* A knot of ribbon or something similar worn on a hat as a badge.

cock-eyed (kok´īd) *adj., Slang* Absurdly wrong; slightly crazy; foolishly twisted to one side.

cock-i-ly (kok´i lē) *adv.* In a cocky manner.

cock-loft (kok´loft) *n.* A small loft in the top of a house; a small garret.

cock-pit (kok´pit´) *n.* The compartment of an airplane where the pilot and the crew sit.

cock-roach (kok´rōch´) *n.* A flat-bodied, fast running, chiefly nocturnal insect, many of which are household pests.

cock-sure (kok´shŭr´) *adj.* Perfectly sure or certain; sometimes on inadequate grounds.

co-co (kō´kō) *n.* The fruit obtained from the coconut palm.

co-coa (kō´kō) *n.* The powder from the roasted husked seed kernels of the cacao.

cocoa butter *n.* A pale fatty substance obtained from cacao beans, used in cosmetics and lotions.

co-co-nut (kō´ko nut) *n.* The nut of the coconut palm, having a hard-shell, with a white edible meat, and contains a milky liquid.

co-coon (ko kōn´) *n.* The protective fiber or silk pupal case that is spun by insect larvae.

cod (kod) *n.* A large fish of the North Atlantic that is important as food.

cod-dle (kod´el) *v.* To cook just below the boiling point; to simmer.

code (kōd) *n.* A system of set rules; a set of secret words, numbers, or letters used as a means of communication; in *Computer Science*, the method of representing information or data by using a set sequence of characters, symbols, or words. **code** *v.*

code conversion *n., Computer* The conversion of information from one code to another.

co-de-fend-ant (kō´di fen´dant)) *n.* One or more defendants in a legal action; a joint defendant.

co-dex (kō´deks) *n.* An ancient manuscript of the classics or Scriptures.

codg-er (koj´ér) *n.* An odd or eccentric old man.

cod-i-fy (kod´i fī) *v.* To reduce to a code.

co-ed (kō´ed´) *adj.* For, open to or including both men and women; to include both sexes.

co-ed-u-ca-tion (kō´ej e kā´shan) *n.* An educational system for both men and women at the same institution. **coeducational** *adj.*

co-e-qual (kō ē´kwal) *adj.* Equal with

one another, person or thing.

co-erce (kō ers´) *v.* To restrain or dominate with force; to compel by law, authority, fear, or force.

co-e-ta-ne-ous (kō´i tā´nē us) *adj.* Beginning to grow or exist at the same time.

co-e-ter-nal (kō´i tür´nal) *adj.* Equally or jointly eternal with another.

co-e-val (kō ē´val) *adj.* Of the same time period. **coeval** *n.*

co-ex-ec-u-tor (kō´ig zek´ū tér) *n.* A joint executor of a will.

co-ex-ist (kō´ig zist´) *v.* To exist at the same time or together; the ability to live peaceably with others in spite of differences. **coexistence** *n.*

co-ex-ten-sive (kō´ik sten´siv) *adj.* Having the same boundaries.

cof-fee (ko´fē) *n.* A beverage prepared from ground beans of the coffee tree.

cof-fer (ko´fér) *n.* A strongbox or chest made for valuables.

cof-fin (ko´fin) *n.* A box in which a corpse is buried.

cog (kog) *n.* A tooth or one of a series of teeth on the rim of a wheel in a machine or a mechanical device.

co-gent (kō´jent) *adj.* Compelling; forceful; convincing.

cog-i-tate (koj´i tāt´) *v.* To think carefully about or to ponder; give thought to. **cogitation** *n.* **cogitative** *adj.*

co-gnac (kōn´yak) *n.* A fine brandy made in France.

cog-nate (kog´nāt) *adj.* From a common ancestor; identical or similar in nature; related.

cog-na-tion (kog nā´shan) *n.* Relationship by blood.

cog-ni-za-ble (kog´ni za bl) *adj.* Capable of being noticed or observed.

cog-ni-zance (kog´ni zans) *n.* Perception of fact; awareness; recognition; observation.

cog-ni-zant (kog´ni zant) *adj.* Obtained knowledge through personal experiences.

cog-nize (kog nīz´) *v.* To recognize as an object of thought; to perceive; understand.

cog-no-men (kog nō´men) *n.* *pl.* **cognomens** A person's surname; nickname.

cog-nos-ci-ble (kog nos´ībl) *adj.* Capable of being known; knowable.

cog-wheel (kog´hwēl´) *n.* A wheel with cogs or teeth; a gear wheel.

co-hab-it (kō hab´it) *v.* To live together as husband and wife.

co-heir (kō âr´) *n.* A joint heir; a person who shares an inheritance with another.

co-here (kō hēr´) *v.* To stick or hold together.

co-her-ent (kō hēr´ent) *adj.* Sticking together; consistent; to remain united.

co-he-sion (kō hē´zhan) *n.* The act or

state of sticking together.

co-he-sive (kō hē'siv) *adj.* Sticking together.

co-hort (kō'hort) *n.* A group of people who are united in one effort; an accomplice.

coif (koif) *n.* A close-fitting hat that is worn under a nun's veil.

coif-feur (kwä fyür') *n.* A male hairdresser.

coil (koil) *n.* A series of connecting rings. *v.* To wind in spirals.

coin (koin) *n.* A flat, rounded piece of metal used as money. *v.* To invent or make a new phrase or word.

co-in-cide (kō'in sīd') *v.* To happen at the same time; to agree exactly.

co-in-ci-dence (kō in'si dens) *n.* Two events happening at the same time by accident but appearing to have some connection.

co-in-ci-dent (kō in'si dent) *adj.* Occupying the same place, position or time simultaneously.

co-in-ci-den-tal (kō in'si den'tal) *adj.* Involving or resulting from a coincidence; happening or existing at the same time.

co-in-her-it-ance (kō'in her'i tans) *n.* Joint inheritance.

co-in-stan-ta-ne-ous (kō'in stan tā'nē us) *adj.* Happening at the same time or instant.

co-in-sur-ance (kō'in shür'ans) *n.* Insurance jointly assumed by another or others.

co-in-sure (kō'in shür') *v.* To insure jointly with another.

co-i-tus (kō'i tus) *n.* Physical union of male and female sexual organs; sexual intercourse.

coke (kōk) *n.* A solid, carbonaceous fuel made by heating soft coal until some of its gases have been removed. *Slang* Cocaine.

co-l-an-der (kul'an dér) *n.* A utensil with a perforated bottom, used for washing or draining food and straining liquids.

cold (kōld) *adj.* Having a low temperature; feeling uncomfortable; without sufficient warmth; lacking in affection or sexual desire; frigid. *n.* An infection of the upper respiratory tract resulting in coughing, sneezing, etc. -ness *n.*

cold boot *n., Computer Science* The boot performed when power is turned on for the first time each day.

cole (kōl) *n.* A plant such as the cabbage or a vegetable of the same family.

co-lec-to-my (ko lek'to mē) *n., Surg.* Complete or partial removal of the colon or large intestine.

col-ic (kol'ik) *n.* A sharp pain in the abdomen caused by muscular cramps or spasms, occurring most often in very young babies.

col-i-se-um (kol'i sē'um) *n.* A large amphitheater used for sporting games.

col-lit-is (ko lī'tis) *n., Pathol.* Inflammation of the colon.

col-lab-o-rate (ko lab'o rāt') *v.* To cooperate or work with another person. **collaboration** *n.* **collaborator** *n.*

col-lapse (ko laps') *v.* To fall; to give way; to fold and assume a smaller size; to lose all or part of the air in a lung.

col-lar (kol'ér) *n.* The upper part of a garment that encircles the neck and is often folded over.

col-lar-bone (kol'ér bōn') *n., Anat.* The clavicle, located near the neck.

col-lard (kol'ard) *n.* A smooth-leaved vegetable of the kale family.

col-late (ko lāt') *v.* To compare in a critical fashion; to assemble in correct sequence or order.

col-lat-er-al (ko lat'ér al) *adj.* Serving to support; guaranteed by stocks, property, bonds, etc.

col-league (kol'ēg) *n.* Someone who works in the same profession or official body.

col-lect (ko lekt') *v.* To gather or assemble; to gather donations or payments. **collectible** *n.* **collection** *n.*

col-lec-tion (ko lek'shan) *n.* The act or process of collecting or gathering.

col-lec-tive (ko lek'tiv) *adj.* Formed by a number of things or persons.

col-lec-tiv-i-ty (kol'ek tiv'i tē) *n.* Collective character; the state of being collective.

col-lege (kol'ij) *n.* An institution of higher education which grants a bachelor's degree; a school of special instruction or special fields.

col-le-gian (ko lē'jan) *n.* A student or graduate of a college.

col-lide (ko līd') *v.* To come together with a direct impact; to clash; to come into conflict.

col-li-mate (kol'i māt) *v.* To adjust or to bring into line; make parallel.

col-lin-e-ar (ko lin'ē ar) *adj.* Lying in or passing through the same straight line.

col-li-sion (ko lizh'on) *n.* The act of striking or colliding together.

col-lo-cate (kol'o kāt') *v.* To compare facts and arrange in correct order; to set or place with, or in relation to.

col-lo-di-on (ko lō'dē on) *n.* A highly flammable spray solution used to protect wounds and used for photographic plates.

col-loid (kol'oid) *n.* A glue-like substance, such as gelatin, that cannot pass through animal membranes.

col-lo-quy (kol'o kwē) *n. pl.* -quies A formal conversation or conference.

col-lude (ko lōd') *v.* To act together through a secret understanding.

col-lusion (ko lö´zhan) *n.* A secret agreement between two or more people for an illegal purpose.

co-logne (ko lōn´) *n.* A perfumed substance of fragrant oils and alcohol.

co-lon (kō´lon) *n.* A punctuation mark (:) used to introduce an example or series; used to separate words and numbers; the section of the large intestine that extends from the cecum to the rectum. **colonic** *adj.*

colo-nel (ker´nel) *n.* An officer in the armed forces that ranks above a lieutenant colonel and below a brigadier general.

co-lo-ni-al (ko lō´nē al) *adj.* Pertaining to a colony or colonies.

co-lo-ni-al-ism (ko lō´nē a liz´um) *n.* The colonial system; the control over an area of people; a policy based on such control.

col-o-ny (kol´o nē) *n.* *pl* **-ies** A group of emigrants living in a new land away from, but under the control of, the parent country; a group of insects, as ants.

col-o-phon (kol´o fon´) *n.* The inscription at the end of a book that gives the publication facts.

col-or (kul´ėr) *n.* The aspect of things apart from the shape, size, and solidity; a hue or tint that is caused by the different degrees of light that are reflected or emitted by them. **colored** *adj.* **colorful** *adj.* **coloring** *n.*

Col-o-ra-do *n.* A state located in the western central part of the United States, statehood August 1, 1876, state capital Denver.

col-or-a-tion (kul´o rā´shan) *n.* The arrangement of different colors or shades.

col-or-bear-er (kul´é bâr˜ėr) *n.* The person in charge of carrying the colors, as of a military formation.

col-or-blind (kul´ėr blīnd´) *adj.* Unable to distinguish colors, either totally or partially.

col-or-cast (kul´ėr käst´) *n.* A television broadcast or program presented in color.

col-or-fast (kul´ėr fast´) *adj.* Color that will not run or fade with washing or wearing. **colorfastness** *n.*

color guard *n.* A person in charge of the colors, the flag, as of a military unit.

col-or-ist (kul´ėr ist) *n.* A person who colors or works with colors.

col-or-less (kul´ėr lis) *adj.* Destitute or lacking color; washed-out.

co-los-sal (ko los´al) *adj.* Very large or gigantic in degree or size.

co-los-sus (ko los´us) *n.* Something that is very large, as a huge state, thing, or person.

col-por-teur (kol´pōr˜tėr) *n.* A person

who travels from place to place distributing or peddling religious materials and Bibles.

colt (költ) *n.* A very young male horse.

col-umn (kol´um) *n.* A decorative and or supporting pillar used in construction; a vertical division of typed or printed lines on paper.

co-lum-nar (ko lum´nėr) *adj.* Of, pertaining to, or relating to columns.

col-lum-ni-a-tion (ko lum˜nē ā´shan) *n.* The arrangement of columns in a structure.

col-um-nist (kol´um nist) *n.* A person who writes a newspaper or magazine column.

co-ma (kō´ma) *n.* A deep sleep or unconsciousness caused by an illness or injury.

co-ma-tose (kom´a tōs´) *adj.* Unconscious.

comb (kōm) *n.* A toothed instrument made from a material such as plastic used for smoothing and arranging the hair; the fleshy crest on the head of a fowl.

com-bat (kom bat´) *v.* To fight against; to oppose; to contend. *n.* A struggle; a fight or contest especially with armed conflict, as a battle, war with others.

com-ba-tive (kom bat´iv) *adj.* Marked by eagerness to fight.

comb-er (kō´mėr) *n.* A machine or person that combs wool or cotton.

com-bin-a-ble (kom bī´na bl) *adj.* That which may be combined.

com-bi-na-tion (kom´bi nā´shan) *n.* The process of combining or the state of being combined; a series of numbers or letters needed to open certain locks.

com-bine (kom bīn´) *v.* To unite; to merge. *n.* A farm machine that harvests by cutting, threshing, and cleaning the grain.

com-bo (kom´bō) *n.* A small jazz group of three or four musicians who dances.

com-bust (kom bust´) *adj.* To burn up.

com-bus-ti-bil-i-ty (kom bus´ti bil´i tē) *n.* The state of being combustible.

com-bus-ti-ble (kom bus´ti bl) *adj.* Having the capability of burning. *n.* A combustible material as paper or wood.

com-bus-tion (kom bus´chan) *n.* The chemical change that occurs rapidly and pro-duces heat and light; a burning; fire **combustive** *adj.*

come (kum) *v.* To arrive; to approach; to reach a certain position, state, or result; to appear; to come into view.

come about *v.* To come to pass.

come across *v.* To find by chance; to produce an impression

come along *v.* To improve.

come back *v.* To return to health or to a former position or success.

co-me-di-an (ko mē'dē an) *n.* An actor of comedy.

come down *v.* To be humbled; to lose rank or position.

com-e-dy (kom'i dē) *n. pl.* -ies A humorous, entertaining performance with a happy ending; a real-life comical situation. **comedic** *adj.*

come in *v.* To enter; to become fashionable; to be brought into use.

co-mes-ti-ble (ko mes'ti bl) *n.* Something that is fit to eat. *adj.* Fit to eat.

com-et (kom'it) *n.* A celestial body that moves in an orbit around the sun, consisting of a solid head that is surrounded by a bright cloud with a long, vaporous tail.

com-fort (kum'fért) *v.* To console in time of grief or fear; to make someone feel better; to help; to assist, to have relief or satisfaction; solace. *n.*

com-fort-a-ble (kumf'ta bl) *adj.* In a state of comfort; financially secure, content and happy. **comfortably** *adv.*

com-ic (kom'ik) *adj.* Characteristic of comedy. *n.* A comedian; comic book. Comics Comic strips.

com-i-cal (kom'i kal) *adj.* Amusing; humorous.

comic strip *n.* Narrative cartoons appearing in sequence, usually found in newspapers.

com-ing (kum'ing) *n.* Approach; instance of arriving.

com-ma (kom'a) *n.* The punctuation mark (,) used to indicate separation of ideas or a series in a sentence.

com-mand (ko mand') *v.* To rule; to give orders; to dominate. *n., Computer Science* The instruction given that specifies an operation to be performed.

com-man-deer (kom'an dēr') *v.* To force into active military service; to seize.

com-mand-er (kom'an dėr') *n.* The person authorized to command; a leader or chief officer.

com-mand-ment (ko mand'ment) *n.* The act, or power of commanding; a command or mandate.

com-mem-o-rate (ko mem'o rāt') *v.* To honor the memory of; to create a memorial to. **commemorative** *n.* **commemoration** *n.* **commemorator** *n.*

com-mence (ko mens') *v.* To begin; to start.

com-mence-ment (ko mens'ment) *n.* A graduation ceremony.

com-mend (ko mend') *v.* To give praise; to applaud. **commendable** *adj.* **commendably** *adv.* **commendation** *n.*

com-men-da-tion (kom'en dā'shan) *n.* The act of commending; praise; a favorable representation in words that commends.

com-men-su-rate (ko men'sėr it) *adj.* Equal in duration, extent, or size. **commensuration** *n.*

com-ment (kom'ent) *n.* A statement of criticism, analysis, or observation.

com-men-tar-y (kom'en ter'ē) *n.* A series of comments.

com-mer-cial (ko mer'shal) *adj.* Of or relating to a product; supported by advertising. *n.* An advertisement on radio or television.

com-mer-cial-ize (ko mür'sha līz') *v.* To render commercial in character, methods, or spirit; to exploit for profit.

com-min-gle (ko ming'gel) *v.* To mix together; to mingle in one mass; to blend thoroughly.

com-mi-nute (kom'i nöt') *v.* To make small or fine; to reduce to minute particles; to pulverize.

com-mis-er-ate (ko miz'e rat') *v.* To display or feel sympathy for someone.

com-mis-sar (kom'i sär') *n.* An official of the Communist Party whose duties include the enforcement of party loyalty and political indoctrination.

com-mis-sar-i-at (kom'i sär'ē at) *n.* The department of an army which supplies food for the troops.

com-mis-sar-y (kom'i ser'ē) *n. pl.* -ies A store that sells food and supplies on a military base.

com-mis-sion (ko mish'on) *n.* The percentage of the money received from a total, that is paid to a person for his service in the area of sales.

com-mis-sure *n.* A joint, or line of union; the junction between two anatomical parts.

com-mit (ko mit) *v.* To put in trust or charge; consign for safe-keeping or preservation.

com-mit-ment (ko mit'ment) *n.* The act of committing; the agreement to do something in the future.

com-mit-tal (ko mit'al) *n.* Commitment.

com-mit-tee (k o mit'ē) *n.* A group of persons appointed or elected to perform a particular task or function. **committeeman** *n.* **committeewoman** *n.*

com-mode (ko mōd') *n.* A movable washstand with storage underneath; a toilet; a low chest of drawers or bureau.

com-mo-di-ous (ko mō'dē us) *adj.* Roomy; spacious. **modiously** *adv.*

com-mod-i-ty (ko mod'i tē) *n.* Something valuable or useful.

com-mon (kom'on) *adj.* Having to do with, belonging to, or used by an entire community or public; vulgar; unrefined.

com-mon-age (kom'o nij) *n.* Community property; anything in common.

com-mon-al-ty (kom'o nal tē) *n.* The common people; general group.

common denominator *n.* The number

that can be divided evenly by all denominators of a number of fractions.

com-mon-er (kom´o ně) *n.* Common people.

common fraction *n.* A fraction where both the denominator and numerator are whole numbers.

common law *n.* Unwritten law based on judicial decisions, customs, and usages.

common multiple *n., Math.* A multiple of each of two or more numbers, quantities, or expressions.

com-mon-place (kom´on plās´) *n.* A trite or obvious observation; something easily taken for granted.

common sense *n.* Sound practical judgment; but often unsophisticated.

common touch *n.* The personal quality of appealing to common people.

com-mon-weal-th (kom´on welth´) *n.* The common good of the whole group of people.

com-mo-tion (ko mō´shan) *n.* Disturbance; mental excitement; total confusion.

com-move (ko mōv´) *v.* To move violently; to excite.

com-mu-nal (ko mūn´al) *adj.* Relating to a community; characterized by common sharing or collective ownership by members of a community.

com-mu-nal-i-ty (kom´ū nal´it ē) *n.* Group solidarity; communal character; similar opinions of a group.

com-mune (ko mūn´) *v.* To converse; to talk together; discuss; to exchange ideas. *n.* A small rural community.

com-mu-ni-ca-ble (ko mū´ni ka bl) *adj.* Capable of being transmitted, as with a disease. **communicability** *n.*

com-mu-ni-cate (ko mū´ni kāt´) *v.* To make known; to cause others to partake or share something.

com-mu-ni-ca-tion (ko mū´ni kā´shan) *n.* The act of transmitting ideas through writing or speech; the means to transmit messages between person or places.

com-mu-ni-ca-tive (ko mū´ ni kā´tiv) *adj.* Inclined to communicate; talkative.

com-mun-ion (ko mūn´yan) *n.* The mutual sharing of feelings and thoughts; a religious fellowship between members of a church.

com-mun-ion (ko mūn´yan) *n.* A sacrament in which bread and wine are consumed to commemorate the death of Christ.

com-mu-nism (kom´ū niz´um) *n.* A system of government in which goods and production are commonly owned; the theory of social change and struggle toward communism through revolution.

com-mu-ni-ty (ko mū´ni tē) *n. pl.* -ies A group of people living in the same area and under the same government; a class or group having common interests and likes; the state of being held in common; common possession, enjoyment, liability, etc.; common character; agreement; identity.

community property *n.* Jointly held property by both husband and wife.

com-mu-nize (kom´ū nīz´) *v.* To transfer individual ownership to community or state owned.

com-mut-a-ble (ko mū´ta bl) *adj.* Exchangeable.

com-mu-ta-tive (ko mū´ ta tiv) *adj.* Of or pertaining to commutation.

com-mute (ko mūt´) *v.* To travel a long distance to one's job each day; to exchange or to substitute.

com-muter (ko mū´tėr) *n.* One who travels a long distance on a regular basis.

com-pact (kom pakt´) *adj.* Packed together or solidly united; firmly and closely united.

com-pact-i-ble (kom pakt´i bl) *adj.* Having the qualities for being compacted.

com-pac-tor (kom pak tōr) *n.* A device for compressing trash into a small mass for disposal.

com-pan-ion (kom pan´yon) *n.* An associate; a person employed to accompany or assist another; one hired to travel or live with another.

com-pan-ion-a-ble (kom pan´yo na bl) *adj.* Friendly; sociable. **-ly** *adv.*

com-pan-ion-ate (kom pan´yo nit) *adj.* Of or relating to companions.

com-pan-ion-way (kom pan´yon wā´) *n., Naut.* A stairway leading from a ship's deck to the cabin below.

com-pa-ny (kum´pa nē) *n. pl.* -ies The gathering of persons for a social purpose; a number of persons who are associated for a common purpose, as in business; a business.

com-pa-ra-ble (kom´par a bl) *adj.* Capable of comparison; worthy of comparison; similar. **comparability** *n.* **comparably** *adv.* **comparative** *adj.*

com-pare (kom pâr´) *v.* To speak of or represent as similar or equal to; to note the similarities or likenesses of.

com-par-i-son (kom par´i son) *n.* Likeness; similarity. *Gram.* Modification of a verb or adjective that indicates the positive, comparative, or superlative degree.

com-part (kom pärt´) *v.* To divide into parts according to a plan.

com-part-ment (kom pärt´ment) *n.* One of the sections into which an enclosed area is divided.

com-pass (kum´pas) *n.* An instrument used to determine geographic direction; an enclosed area or space; the extent of reach of something; range or area; scope; a device shaped like a V that is used for drawing circles.

com-pas-sion (kom pash´on) *n.* Sympathy for a person who is suffering or distressed in someway.

com-pa-thy (kom´pa thē) *n.* Feelings of grief or joy shared with another.

com-pat-i-ble (kom pat´i bl) *adj.* Able to function, exist, or live together harmoniously. **compatibility** *n.*

com-pa-tri-ot (kom pā´trēot) *n.* A person of the same country.

com-peer (kom pēr´) *n.* A person that is a peer or equal.

com-pel (kom pel´) *v.* To urge or force action.

com-pel-la-tion (kom´pe lā´shan) *n.* The act of addressing someone.

com-pen-di-ous (kom pen´dē us) *adj.* Containing the substance of a comprehensive subject in a brief form.

com-pen-dium (kom pen´dēum) *n. pl.* **-diums** A short summary.

com-pen-sa-ble (kom pen´sa bl) *adj.* That is or is entitled to compensation.

com-pen-sate (kom´pen sāt´) *v.* To make up for; to make amends; to pay; to neutralize or counter balance. **compensation** *n.* **compensatory** *adj.*

com-pete (kom pēt´) *v.* To contend with others; to engage in a contest or competition.

com-pe-tent (kom´pi tent) *adj.* Having sufficient ability; being capable. **competence** *n.* **competency** *n.*

com-pe-ti-tion (kom´pi tish´an) *n.* The act of rivalry or competing; a trial of skill or ability; a contest between teams or individuals. **competitive** *adj.*

com-pet-i-tor (kom pet´i tēr) *n.* One who competes against another.

com-pi-la-tion (kom´pi lā´shan) *n.* The act or process of collecting or compiling.

com-pile (kom pīl´) *v.* To put together material gathered from a number of sources; in Computer Science, to convert our language into machine language. **compilation** *n.*

com-pla-cence (kom plā´sens) *n.* A feeling of secure self-satisfaction.

com-pla-cent (kom plā´sent) *adj.* Pleased with one's merits or advantages; self-satisfied.

com-plain (kom plān´) *v.* To express grief, pain, uneasiness, or discontent.

com-plain-ant (kom plā´nant) *n.* A person filing a formal charge.

com-plaint (kom plānt´) *n.* An expression of pain, dissatisfaction, or resentment; a cause or reason for complaining; a grievances.

com-plai-sance (kom plā´sans) *n.* The willingness to please, to oblige, to help. **complaisant** *adj.*

com-plai-sant (kom plā´sant) *adj.* Marked by a need to please; obliging; gracious.

com-ple-ment (kom´ple ment) *n.* Something that perfects, completes, or adds to. **complementary** *adj.*

com-ple-men-tal (kom´ple men´tal) *adj.* Relating to or forming a complement.

complementary colors *n. pl.* Primary or secondary colors in the spectrum, when combined produce a neutral color.

com-plete (kom plēt´) *adj.* Having all the necessary parts; whole; concluded. **completion** *n.*

com-ple-tion (kom plē´shan) *n.* The process or act of completing.

com-plex (kom pleks´) *adj.* Consisting of various intricate parts. **complexity** *n.* **complexly** *adv.*

com-plex-ion (kom plek´shan) *n.* The natural color and texture of the skin, also the disposition of the mind and body. **complexioned** *adj.*

com-plex-i-ty *n.* The state or quality of being complex; intricacy; something complex.

com-pli-ance (kom plī´ans) *n.* The act of agreeing passively to a request, rule, or demand; the tendency to yield to others. **compliant** *adj.* **compliancy** *n.*

com-pli-ant (kom plī´ant) *adj.* Ready to comply; yielding; obliging.

com-pli-cate (kom´pli kāt´) *v.* To make or become involved or complex.

com-pli-ca-tion (kom´pli kā´shan) *n.* The situation of complicating or the state of being complicated; entanglement; complexity; something complicated.

com-plic-i-ty (kom plis´i tē) *n.* An involvement or association with a crime.

com-pli-er (kom plī´ēr) *n.* One who complies.

com-pli-ment (kom´pli ment) *n.* An expression of praise or admiration.

com-pli-men-ta-ry (kom´pli men´ta rē) *adj.* Conveying a compliment.

com-ply (kom plī´) *v.* To agree, to consent to, or obey a command or wish; requirements. **complier** *n.*

com-po-nent (kom pō´nent) *n.* A constituent part.

com-port (kom pōrt´) *v.* To behave or conduct oneself in a certain way.

com-port-ment (kom pōrt´ment) *n.* Behavior; demeanor; deportment.

com-pose (kom pōz´) *v.* To make up from elements or parts; to produce or create a song; to arrange, as to typeset; artistic composition. **composer** *n.*

com-posed (kom pōzd´) *adj.* Calm.

com-pos-er (kom pō´zēr) *n.* One who composes; a person who writes an original work.

com-pos-ite (kom poz´it) *adj.* Made up

from separate elements or parts; combined or compounded. Characteristic of a plant with densely clustered flowers.

com-po-si-tion (kom´po zish´on) n. The act of putting together artistic or literary work; a short essay written for an assignment in school.

com-post (kom´pōst) n. A fertilizing mixture that consists of decomposed vegetable matter.

com-po-sure (kom pō´zhẽr) n. Tranquility; calm self-possession.

com-pote (kom´pōt) n. Fruit that is preserved or stewed in syrup; a dish used for holding fruit, candy, etc.

com-pound (kom´pound) n. The combination of two or more parts, elements, or ingredients; In grammar, a new word that is composed of two or more words joined with a hyphen or written as a solid word. *Chem.* A definite substance that results from combining specific radica n. Elements in certain or fixed proportions. v. To combine; to increase.

compound fracture n. A broken bone that breaks and protrudes through the skin.

compound interest n. Interest computed on the original principal plus accrued interest.

compound sentence n. A sentence compiled of two or more independent clauses.

compound word n. A word made up of two or more words that retain their separate form and signification.

com-pre-hend (kom´pri hend´) v. To perceive, to grasp mentally, or to understand fully; to comprise; to include. **comprehension** n.

com-pre-hen-si-ble (kom´pri hen´si bl) adj. Capable of being understood. **comprehensibility** n. **-hensibly** adv.

com-pre-hen-sion (kom´pri hen shan) n. The act of understanding or comprehending; the knowledge gained.

com-pre-hen-sive (kom´pri hen´siv) adj. Large in content or scope.

com-press (kom´pres) v. To press together into a smaller space; to condense. n. A soft pad sometimes medicated, for applying cold, heat, moisture, or pressure to a part of the body. **compression, compressibility** adj. **compressible** adj.

compressed air n. Air that is under greater pressure than the atmosphere.

com-pres-sive (kom pres´iv) adj. Having the power to compress; tending to compress.

com-pres-sor (kom pres´ẽr) n. Something that compresses; a machine that is used for compressing air to utilize its expansion.

com-prise (kom prīz´) v. To consist of; to be made up of. **comprisable** adj.

com-pro-mise (kom´pro miz´) n. The process of settling or the settlement of differences between opposing sides, with each side making concessions. **compromiser** n. **compromise** v.

comp-trol-ler (kon trō´lẽr) n. A person appointed to examine and verify accounts.

com-pul-sion (kom pul´shan) n. The act or state of being compelled; an irresistible urge or impulse to act irrationally.

compulsive (kom pul´siv) adj. An act or state of being compelled.

com-pul-so-ry (kom pul´so rē) adj. Enforced, mandatory.

com-punc-tion (kom pungk´shan) n. Anxiety arising from guilt or awareness.

com-pur-ga-tion (kom´pẽr gā´shan) n. The clearing of an accused person by the oaths of persons who swear his innocence.

com-put-a-ble (kom pūt´a bl) adj. Capable of being computed.

com-pu-ta-tion (kom´pū tā´shan) n. The action or act of computing. The operation of a computer.

com-pute (kom pūt´) v. To ascertain or determine by the use of mathematics; to determine something by the use of a computer. **computability** n. **computation** n. **computable** adj.

com-put-er (kom pū´tẽr) n. A person who computes; a high speed, electronic machine which performs logical calculations, processes, stores, and retrieves programmed information.

com-put-er-ese (kom pū´trēz) n. The jargon used by computer technologists.

com-put-er-i-za-tion (kom pū´te rī zā´shan) n. The operation or procedure of computerizing.

com-puter-ize (kom pū´te rīz´) v. To process or store information on a computer; to switch from manual operations to computers.

computer language n. The various codes and information that are used to give data and instructions to computers.

computer program n. A system used to find and correct a problem on a computer.

com-rade (kom´rad) n. An associate, friend, or companion who shares one's interest or occupation. **-ship** n.

con (kon) v. To study carefully. *Slang* To swindle or trick.

co-na-tus (kō nā´tus) n. A natural impulse, tendency or striving.

con brio (kon brē´ō) adv. In a brisk or vigorous manner.

conc abbr. Concentrated; concentration or concentrate.

con-cat-e-nate (kon kat´e nāt´) v. To
join, connect, or link together.
concatenate adj. **con-catenation** n.

con-cave (kon´kāv) adj. Hollowed and
curved inward. **concavely** adv.

con-cav-i-ty (kon kav´i tē) n. A concave
surface; quality of being concave.

con-ceal (kon sēl´) v. To keep from
disclosure, sight, or knowledge; to hide
or withhold. **concealable** adj.
concealer n. **concealment** n.

con-cede (kon sēd´) v. To grant or yield
to a right or privilege; to acknowledge
as true. **conceder** n. **conceded** adj.

con-ceit (kon sēt´) n. An exaggerated
personal opinion of one's own
importance.

con-ceit-ed (kon sē´tid) adj. Having an
exaggerated or excessively high
opinion of oneself.

con-ceive (kon sēv´) v. To become
pregnant; to create a mental image.
conceivability n. **conceivable** adj.

con-cen-ter (kon sen´tèr) v. To converge
or draw to a common center.

con-cen-trate (kon´sen trāt´) v. To give
intense thought to; to draw to a
common point; to intensify by
removing certain elements; to become
compact. **concentrative** adj.

con-cen-tra-tion (kon´sen trā´shan) n.
The state of being concentrated or the
act of concentrating; the process or act
of giving complete attention to a certain
problem or task.

concentration camp n. An enclosed camp
or prison where political prisoners,
aliens, or prisoners of war are confined.

con-cen-tric (kon sen´trik) adj. Having
a common center, as circles or spheres.

con-cept (kon´sept) n. A generalized idea
formed from particular occurrences
or instances; an opinion.

con-cep-tion (kon sep´shon) n. The
union of sperm and egg; a mental
thought or plan.

con-cern (kon sèrn´) n. Something to
consider; sincere interest; something
that affects one's business or affairs.
v. To be interested in; to be involved
with. **concerned** adj.

con-cern-ing (kon sür´ning) prep.
Relating to; regarding.

con-cern-ment (kon sürn´ment) n.
Relation or bearing; something in
which one is interested or concerned.

con-cert (kon´sèrt) n. A musical
performance for a group of people;
agreement in purpose, action, or
feeling. v. To act or plan together.
concerted adj.

con-cer-ti-no (kon´cher tē´nō) n. A short
concerto.

con-cer-to (kon cher´tō) n. pl. -tos, -ti
A composition that features one or
more solo instruments.

con-ces-sion (kon sesh´an) n. The act
of conceding; something that has been
conceded; a tract of land that is granted
by a government for a particular use.

con-ces-sion-aire (kon sesh´o nâr´) n.
The operator or holder of a concession.

con-ces-sive (kon ses´iv) adj. Tending
or serving to concede; making for a
concession.

conch (kongk) n. A tropical marine
mollusk having a large spiral shell and
flesh that is edible.

con-chol-o-gy (kong kol´o jē) n. The
study of mollusks and shells.
conchological adj. **conchologist** n.

con-cil-i-ar (kon sil´ēér) adj. Pertaining
to, or issued by a council.

con-cil-i-ate (k on sil´ē āt´) v. To win
over or to gain a friendship. **concilia-
tion** n. **conciliator** n. **conciliatory** adj.

con-cin-ni-ty (kon sin´i tē) n. Harmonious adaptation of parts to a whole.

con-cise (kon sīs´) adj. Short and to the
point.

con-ci-sion (kon sizh´on) n. Concise
quality or state.

con-clave (kon´klāv) n. A private or
secret meeting; the private meeting of
the Roman Catholic cardinals to elect
a new pope.

con-clude (kon klōd´) v. To close or
bring to an end; to bring about an
agreement; to arrive at a decision; to
resolve.

con-clu-sion (kon klō´zham) n. The
close or end; the final decision, the last
main division of a discourse.

con-clu-sive (kon klō´siv) adj. Putting
an end to any questions or doubt.

con-coct (kon kokt´) v. To make by
combining ingredients; to devise or
to plan. **concoction** n.

con-com-i-tant (kon kom´i tant) adj.
Accompanying. **concomitance** n. .

con-cord (kon´kord) n. Accord; harmony; friendly and peaceful relationships.

con-cor-dance (kon kor´dans) n. A
condition of concord or agreement; the
alphabetical index of major words used
by an author, listed in the order of use
in a book.

con-cor-dant (kon kor´dant) adj. Exist
in agreement; harmonious.

con-cor-dat (kon kor´dat) n. An
agreement between a pope and a
government; a compact.

con-course (kon´kōrs) n. A large, open
space for the assembling or passage
of crowds.

con-cres-cence (kon kres´ens) n. Increase
by the addition of particles; growing
together.

con-crete (kon´krēt) adj. Pertaining to
a specific instance or thing; naming
a specific class of things. n. A

construction material made from sand, gravel, and cement. v. To bring together in one body or mass. **concretely** adv.

con-cre-tion (kon krē'shen) n. The act or process of concreting; the state of being concreted; something concreted.

con-cu-bine (kong'kū bīn') n. A woman living with a man and not being legally married to him. **concubinage** n.

con-cu-pis-cence (kon kū'pi sens) n. A strong sexual desire; lust.

con-cur (kon kėr') v. To agree or express approval; to cooperate; to happen at the same time; to coincide.

con-cur-rence (kon kėr'ans) n. The act of concurring; a agreement in opinion simultaneous happening in time and place.

con-cur-rent (kon kėr'ant) adj. Referring to an event that happens at the same time as another; acting together.

con-cuss (kon kus') v. To affect with a concussion.

con-cus-sion (kon kush'on) n. A sudden and violent jolt; a violent injury to an organ, especially the brain.

con-demn (kon dem') v. To find to be wrong; to show the guilt; to announce judgment upon; to officially declare unfit for use. **condemnable** adj. **condemnatory** adj. **condemnation** n.

con-den-sate (kon den'sāt) n. A product of condensation, water from steam.

con-den-sa-tion (kon'den sā'shan) n. The act of condensing.

con-dense (kon dens') v. To make more dense, concentrated or compact. **condensability** n. **condensation** n. **condenser** n. **condensable** adj.

con-de-scen-sion (kon'di sen'shan) n. The act of condescending; a patronizing behavior.

con-dign (kon dīn') adj. Well deserved; appropriate.

con-di-ment (kon'di ment) n. A relish, spice, or sauce used to season food.

con-dis-ci-ple (kon'di sī'pl) n. A fellow student.

con-di-tion (kon dish'on) n. The mode or state of existence of a thing or person; a circumstance that is found to be necessary to the occurrence of another; a provision in a contract or will that leaves room for modification or changes at a future date. Slang A sickness or ailment.

con-di-tion-al (kon dish'a nal) adj. Tentative; depending on a condition; implying or expressing a condition. Gram. A mood, clause, tense, or condition. **conditionality** n.

con-di-tion-ed (kon dish'ond) adj. Prepared for a certain process or action by past experience.

con-do (kon dō) n. Slang Condominium.

con-dole (kon dōl') v. To express sympathetic sorrow at the loss or misfortune of another.

con-dom (kon'dom) n. A thin rubber sheath used to cover the penis, serving as an anti-venereal or contraceptive purpose during sexual intercourse.

con-do-min-i-um (kon'do min'ē um) n. A joint ownership; an apartment in which all units are owned separately; a building in which the units are owned by each tenant.

con-do-na-tion (kon'dōnā'shan) n. The pardoning of a wrong act.

con-done (kon dōn') v. To overlook; to forgive; to disregard. **condoner** n.

con-dor (kon'dor) v. One of the largest flying birds, with a bare head and a white downy neck. A very large American vulture with a bare neck and head with dull black plumage and white patches on the wings and neck.

con-du-cive (kon dō'siv) adj. Contributing towards or promotion; helpful.

con-duct (kon dukt') v. To lead and direct a performance of a band or orchestra; to guide or show the way; to lead; to direct or control the course of; to transmit heat, electricity, or sound. n. Behavior. **conductibility** n.

con-duc-tiv-i-ty (kon'duk tiv'i tē) n. The quality of conducting heat, sound or electricity.

con-duit (kon'dwit) n. A pipe used to pass electric wires or cable through; a channel or pipe that water passes through.

con-du-pli-cate (kon dō'pli kit) adj. Doubled or folded lengthwise.

cone (kōn) n. A solid body that is tapered evenly to a point from a base that is circular; a wafer that is cone-shaped and used for holding ice cream.

cone-nose (kōn'nōz') n. A large blood-sucking insect, a species of assassin bug infesting houses in the southern and western United States.

con-fab (kon'fab) n. Discussion.

con-fab-u-late (kon fab'ū lāt') v. To chat or speak informally. **confabulation** n. **confabulator** n. **confabulatory** adj.

con-fec-tion-er-y (kon fek'sha ner'ē) n. Candy and sweets as a whole; a store that sells candy and sweets.

con-fec-tion-a-ry (kon fek'sha ner'ē) adj. Of or pertaining to confections or their making; sweets.

con-fec-tion-er (kon fek'sha nėr) n. A person who manufacturers or sells candies and other sweets.

con-fed-er-a-cy (kon fed'ėr a sē) n. pl. **-ies** The union of eleven southern states that seceded from the United States during the Civil War of 1861-1865 and established the Confederate State of America.

con-fed-er-ate (kon fed´ér it) *n*. An ally or friend; a person who supports the Confederacy. **confederate** *v*.

con-fed-er-a-tion (kon fed´e rā´shan) *n*. An act of confederating; the state of being confederated.

con-fer (kon fer´) *v*. To consult with another; to hold a conference; to give or grant. **conferment** *n*. **conferral** *n*. **conferrer** *n*. **conferrable** *adj*.

con-fer-ence (kon´fér ens) *n*. A formal meeting for discussion; a league of churches, schools, or athletic teams.

con-fess (kon fes´) *v*. To disclose or admit to a crime, fault, sin, or guilt; to tell a priest or God of one's sins.

con-fes-sion (kon fesh´on) *n*. The act of confessing.

con-fes-sion-al (kon fesh´o nal) *n*. The small enclosure where a priest hears confessions.

con-fes-sor (kon fes´ér) *n*. A person who confesses; one who acknowledges a fault.

con-fet-ti (kon fet´ē) *n*. Small pieces of paper thrown during a celebration.

con-fide (kon fīd´) *v*. To entrust a secret to another. **confider** *n*. **confiding** *adj*.

con-fi-dence (kon´fi dens) *n*. A feeling of self-assurance; a feeling of trust in a person; reliance; good faith.

con-fi-den-tial (kon´fi den´shal) *adj*. Hold as a secret; having another's entrusted confidence on spoken or written matters. **confidentiality** *n*. **confidentially** *adv*.

con-fid-ing (kon fīd´ing) *adj*. Trusting; reposing confidence; trustful.

con-fig-u-ra-tion (kon fig´ü rā´shan) *n*. An arrangement of parts or things; the arrangement of elements.

con-fig-ure (kon fig´ür) *v*. To make or arrange for operation in a certain form or particular way.

con-fine (kon fīn´) *v*. To keep within a certain boundary or limits. **confines** *n*. **confinement** *n*. **confiner** *n*.

con-firm (kon férm´) *v*. To establish or support the truth of something; to make stronger; to ratify and bind by a formal approval. **confirmable** *adj*.

con-fir-ma-tion (kon´fér mā´shan) *n*. The act of confirming to show proof; a religious rite that admits a person to full membership in a church.

con-fir-ma-to-ry (kon fér´ma tōr´ē) *adj*. Giving additional strength; serving to confirm.

con-firm-ed (kon férmd´) *adj*. Fixed.

con-fis-cate (kon´fi skāt´) *v*. To seize for public use; to officially seize. **confiscation** *n*. **confiscator** *n*.

con-fla-gra-tion (kon´fla grā´shan) *n*. A large fire, or the burning of a large mass of combustibles.

con-flate (kon´flāt) *v*. To combine two different ideas into a whole.

con-fla-tion (kon flā´shan) *n*. The result of merging various elements; blend.

con-flict (kon flikt´) *n*. A battle; clash; a disagreement of ideas, or interests, opposition. **conflict** *v*. **conflictive** *adj*.

conflict of interest *n*. The conflict when the private financial interests of a public officer stand to benefit by the influence from this position.

con-flu-ence (kon´flō ens) *n*. The flowing together of two streams or rivers; the point where the two join. **confluent** *n*. **confluently** *adv*.

con-flu-ent (kon´flō eny) *adj*. Flowing or coming together; run together.

con-flux (kon´fluks) *n*. A flowing together; a meeting or joining; a crowd.

con-fo-cal (kon fō´kal) *adj*. Of the same focus.

con-form (kon form´) *v*. To be similar in form or character; to adhere to prevailing customs or modes. **conformable** *adj*. **conformably** *adv*.

con-form-a-ble (kor´ma bl) *adj*. Corresponding in form, manners, or opinions.

con-for-ma-tion (kon´for mā´shan) *n*. The manner in which something is shaped, structured, or arranged.

con-form-i-ty (kon for´mi tē) *n*. Likeness; harmony; accordance.

con-found (kon found´) *v*. To amaze, confuse, or perplex; to confuse one thing for another.

con-found-ed (kon foun´ded) *adj*. Annoying bothersome.

con-fra-ter-ni-ty (kon´fra tér´ni tē) *n*. A brotherhood society devoted to a purpose.

con-frere (kon´frâr) *n*. A fellow colleague; a fraternity or profession.

con-front (kon frunt´) *v*. To put or stand face to face with defiance; to face; to stand or be in front of, providing resistance, as an obstacle; to meet in hostility; to oppose. **confrontation** *n*.

con-fuse (kon fūz´) *v*. To mislead or bewilder; to jumble or mix up. **confusedness** *n*. **confusingly** *adv*.

con-fu-sion (kon fū´zhan) *n*. The state of being confused.

con-fu-ta-tion (kon´fū tā´shan) *n*. The disproving, or proving to be false or invalid.

con-fute (kon fūt´) *v*. To prove to be invalid or false. **confutable** *adj*. **confutation** *n*. **confutative** *adj*.

con-geal (kon jēl´) *v*. To jell; to solidify; to change from a liquid to a solid form.

con-ge-la-tion (kon´je lā´shan) *n*. That which is congealed or solidified or the state of being congealed.

con-ge-ner (kon´je nér) *n*. A member of the same genus as another plant or animal.

con-gen-ial (kon jēn´yal) *adj.* Having similar character habits, or tastes; sociable; friendly. **congeniality** *n.*

con-gen-i-tal (kon jen´i tal) *adj.* Existing from the time of birth, but not from heredity.

conger eel *n.* A large scaleless eel used for food along the coasts of Europe.

con-gest (kon jest´) *v.* To enlarge with an excessive accumulation of blood; to clog. **congestion** *n.* **congestive** *adj.*

con-glo-bate (kon glō´bāt) *v.* To form or gather into a ball or small spherical body.

con-glo-ba-tion (kon´glō bā´shan) *n.* The act of or gathering into a ball; a round body.

con-glom-er-ate (kon glom´ér it) *n.* A business consisting of many different companies; gravel that is embedded in cement material.

con-gou (kong´gō) *n.* A black tea from China.

con-grat-u-late (kon grach´u lāt) *v.* To acknowledge an achievement with praise. **congratulator** *n.*

con-grat-u-la-tions (kon grach´lā shans) *n. pl.* The expression of or the act of congratulating.

con-grat-u-la-to-ry (kon grach´u la tōr´ē)*adj.* Expressing congratulations.

con-gre-gate (kong´gre gāt´) *v.* To assemble together in a crowd.

con-gre-ga-tion (kong´gre gā´shan) *n.* A group of people meeting together for worship.

con-gre-ga-tion-al (kong´gre gā´shal) *adj.* Of or pertaining to a congregation; recognizing the importance and governing power of the congregation.

Con-gress (kong´gris) *n.* The United States legislative body, consisting of the Senate and the House of Representatives. **Congressional** *adj.*

con-gru-ent (kong´grō ent) *adj.* Agreeing to conform; in mathematics, having exactly the same size and shape.

con-gru-ous (kong´grō us) *adj.* Being in agreement; appropriate or fitting.

con-ic *or* **con-i-cal** (kon´ik) *adj.* Related to and shaped like a cone.

co-nid-i-um (kō nid´ē um) *n.* A propagative body or cell, asexual in its origin and functions.

co-ni-fer (kōni´fér) *n.* Evergreen trees and shrubs, that include the pine, fir, spruce, and other conebearing trees.

co-ni-ine (kō´nē ēn´) *n.* A highly poisonous alkaloid found in hemlock.

conj *abbr.* Conjunction.

con-jec-ture (kon jek´chér) *n.* A guess or conclusion based on incomplete evidence. **conjecturable, conjectural** *adj.* **conjecture** *v.*

con-join (kon join´) *v.* To unite; join together.

con-ju-gal (kon´ju gal) *adj.* Pertaining to the relationship or marriage of husband and wife.

con-ju-gate (kon´ju git) *adj.* To change the form of a verb; to join in pairs. **conjugately** *adv.* **conjugative** *adj.* **conjuga-tor** *n.*

con-junct (kon jungkt´) *adj.* Combined; joined together.

con-junc-tion (kon jungk´shan) *n.* The act of joining; the state of being joined. *Gram.* A word used to join or connect other words, phrases, sentences, or clauses.

con-junc-ti-va (kon´jungk tī´va) *n. pl.* **-vas, -vae** The membrane lining of the eyelids.

con-junc-tive (kon jungk´tiv) *adj.* Connective; joining. *Gram.* Serving as a conjunction.

con-junc-ti-vi-tis (kon jungk´ti vī´tis) *n., Pathol.* Inflammation of the membrane that lines the eyelids.

con-jur-a-tion (kon´ju rā´shan) *n.* The act of binding by an oath; a solemn appeal.

con-jure (kon´jér) *v.* To bring into the mind; to appeal or call on solemnly; to practice magic.

con man *n., Slang.* A confidence man; a swindler.

con-nate (kon´āt) *adj.* Existing from birth; born or originating together.

con-nect (ko nekt´) *v.* To join; to unite; to associate, as to relate. **connectedly** *adv.* **connector** *n.* **connecter** *n.*

con-nect-ed (ko nek´tid) *adj.* Linked, bound or fastened together; joined in order or sequence.

Con-nect-i-cut *n.* A state located in the north eastern part of the United States; statehood January 9, 1788; state capital Hartford.

con-nec-tion (ko nek´shan) *n.* An association of one person or thing to another; a union, link, or bond; an influential group of friends or associates.

con-nec-tive (ko nek´tiv) *adj.* Capable of connecting; tending to connect. *n.* something that connects as a word.

connective tissue *n.* Tissue which connects, supports, or surrounds other tissues or organs.

con-nip-tion (ko nip´shan) *n.* A fit of alarm or hysterical excitement.

con-nive (kon nīv´) *v.* To ignore a known wrong, therefore implying sanction; to conspire; to cooperate in secret.

con-nois-seur (kon´o ser´) *n.* A person whose expertise in an area of art or taste allows him to be a judge; an expert. **connoisseurship** *n.*

con-no-ta-tion (kon´o tā´shan) *n.* The associative meaning of a word in addition to the literal meaning.

con-no-ta-tive *adj.*

con-note (ko nōt´) *v.* To imply along with the literal meaning.

con-nu-bi-al (ko nö´bē al) *adj.* Having to do with marriage or the state of marriage. **connubiality** *n.* **-ly** *adv.*

con-quer (kong´kẽr) *v.* To subdue; to win; to overcome by physical force.

con-quest (kon´kwest) *n.* The process or act of conquering; acquisition by force.

con-qui-an *n.* A card game for two players with 40 cards; the game from which all rummy games originate.

con-quis-ta-dor (kon kwis´ta dor´) *n.* *pl.* **-dors** A Spanish conqueror of the sixteenth century.

con-san-guin-e-ous (kon´sang gwin´ē us) *adj.* Having the same blood; descended from the same ancestor. **consanguineously** *adv.*

con-science (kon´shens) *n.* The ability to recognize right and wrong regarding one's own behavior.

conscience clause *n.* A clause inserted in a law, that relieves persons whose religious beliefs forbid their compliance.

con-sci-en-tious (kon´shē en´shus) *adj.* Honest; scrupulous; careful.

con-scious (kon´shus) *adj.* Aware of one's own existence and environment; aware of facts or objects.

con-script (kon´skript) *n.* One who is drafted or forced to enroll for a service or a job.

con-se-crate (kon´se krāt´) *v.* To declare something to be holy; to dedicate to sacred uses.

con-se-cra-tion (kon´se krā´shan) *n.* The act or state of consecrating.

con-se-cu-tion (kon´se kū´shan) *n.* Sequence; succession; logical sequence.

con-sec-u-tive (kon sek´ū tiv) *adj.* Following in uninterrupted succession. **consecutively** *adv.* **-tiveness** *n.*

con-sen-sus (kon sen´sus) *n.* A general agreement; a collective opinion.

con-sent (kon sent´) *v.* To agree; an acceptance. **consenter** *n.*

con-se-quence (kon´se kwens´) *n.* The natural result from a preceding condition or action; the effect.

con-se-quent (kon´se kwent´) *adj.* Following as a natural result or effect; logical conclusion. **consequently** *adv.*

con-se-quen-tial (kon´se kwen´shal) *adj.* Having or showing self-importance. **consequentially** *adv.*

con-serv-a-tive (kon sẽr´va tiv) *adj.* Opposed to change; desiring the preservation of the existing order of things; moderate; cautious; wanting to conserve. **conservatively** *adv.* .

con-ser-va-tor (kon´sẽr vā tor) *n.* A person who preserves; a person or institution responsible for protecting another's interests.

con-ser-va-to-ry (kon sẽr´va tōr´ē) *n.* *pl.* **-ries** A school of dramatic art or music; a greenhouse.

con-serve (kon sẽrv´) *v.* To save something from decay, loss, or depletion; to maintain; to preserve fruits with sugar. *n.* A mixture of several fruits cooked together with sugar and sometimes raisins or nuts. **conservable** *adj.* **conserver** *n.*

con-sid-er (kon sid´ẽr) *v.* To seriously think about; to examine mentally; to believe or hold as an opinion; to deliberate.

con-sid-er-a-ble (kon sid´ẽr a bl) *adj.* Large in amount or extent; important; worthy of consideration. **-ly** *adv.*

con-sid-er-a-tion (kon sid´e rā´shan) *n.* The taking into account of circumstance before forming an opinion; care and thought; a kind or thoughtful treatment or feeling. **considering** *prep.*

con-sign (kon sīn´) *v.* To commit to the care of another; to deliver or forward, as merchandise; to put aside, as for specific use. **consignee** *n.* **consignable** *adj.* **consignor** *n.* **consignment** *n.*

con-sign-ee (kon´sī nē´) *n.* The person to whom goods are consigned.

con-sign-ment *n.* The act of consigning; goods sent or delivered to an agent for sale.

con-sist (kon sist´) *v.* To be made up of.

con-sis-ten-cy (kon sis´ten sē) *n.* *pl.* **-cies** Agreement or compatibility among ideas, events, or successive acts; the degree of texture, viscosity, or density; coherence. **consistent** *adj.*

con-so-ci-ate (kon sō´shē āt´) *v.* To bring together or into association.

con-so-ci-a-tion (kon sō´sē ā´shan) *n.* Association in; fellowship; an association or union of churches.

con-so-la-tion (kon´so lā´shan) *n.* Comfort; the act of consoling; a person who offers consolation.

con-sole (kon sōl´) *v.* To give comfort to someone. **consolable** *adj.* **consola-tion** *n.* **consolingly** *adv.*

console table *n.* A table fixed to a wall by consoles or brackets wall.

con-sol-i-date (kon sol´i dāt´) *v.* To combine in one or to form a union of; to form a compact mass. **consolidation** *n.* **consolidator** *n.*

consolidated school *n.* A public school, formed by combining schools from several districts.

con-som-mé (kon´so mā´) *n.* A strong, clear soup made from the stock of meat.

con-so-nant (kon´so nant) *n.* A sound produced by complete or partial blockage of the air from the mouth, as the sound of b, f, k, s, t; the letter of the alphabet that represents such a sound. *adj.* In agreement. **consonantal** *adj.* **consonantly** *adv.*

con-sort (kon'sort) *n.* A spouse; companion or partner. *v.* To unite or keep in company.

con-sor-ti-um (kon sor'shē um) *n. pl.* **-tia** An association with banks or corporations that require vast resources.

con-spe-cif-ic (kon'spi sif'ik) *adj.* Of the same species.

con-spec-tus (kon spek'tus) *n.* A general summary; a digest; a resume.

con-spic-u-ous (kon spik'ū us) *adj.* Noticeable. **conspicuously** *adv.*

con-spir-a-cy (kon spir'a sē) *n. pl. -ies* A plan or act of two or more persons to do an evil act.

con-spir-a-tor-ial (kon spir'a tōr'ē al) *adj.* Relating to a conspiracy or conspirators.

con-spire (kon spīr') *v.* To plan a wrongful act in secret; to work or act together, to plot against others.

con-sta-ble (kon'sta bl) *n.* A peace officer.

con-stab-u-lar-y (kon stab'ū ler'ē) *adj.* Relating to the jurisdiction of a constable.

con-stant (kon'stant) *adj.* Faithful; unchanging; steady in action, purpose, and affection. *Math.* A quantity that remains the same throughout a given problem. **constancy,** **constantly** *adv.*

con-ster-na-tion (kon'ster nā'shan) *n.* Sudden confusion or amazement.

con-sti-pa-tion (kon'sti pā'shan) *n.* A condition of the bowels characterized by difficult or infrequent evacuation.

con-stit-u-en-cy (kon stich'ö en sē) *n. pl. -cies* A group of voters that is represented by an elected legislator.

con-stit-u-ent (kon stich'ö ent) *adj.* Having the power to elect a representative. *n.* A necessary element or part.

con-sti-tu-tion (kon'sti tö'shan) *n.* The fundamental laws that govern a nation; structure or composition. **constitutional** *adj.* **constitutionality** *n.*

con-sti-tu-tion-al (kon'sti tö'sha nal) *adj.* Pertaining or relating to the composition of a thing; essential. *n.* Exercise taken to benefit one's health.

con-sti-tu-tion-al-ism (kon'sti tö'sha na liz'um) *n.* The adherence, theory or principle of constitutional rule or authority.

con-sti-tu-tive (kon'sti tö'tiv) *adj.* Having the power to form, compose, enact, or establish.

con-strain (kon strān') *v.* To restrain by physical or moral means.

con-straint (kon strānt') *n.* The threat or use of force; confinement; restriction.

con-strict (kon strikt') *v.* To squeeze,

compress, or contract. **constriction** *n.* **constrictive** *adj.* **constrictively** *adv.*

con-stric-tor (kon strik'tėr) *n.* One that constricts; a snake that crushes its prey in its coils.

con-struct (kon strukt') *v.* To create, make, or build. **constructor** *n.*

con-struc-tion (kon struk'shan) *n.* The act of constructing or building something. *Gram.* The arrangement of words in a meaningful clause or sentence. **constructional** *adj.*

con-struc-tive (kon struk'tiv) *adj.* Useful; helpful; building, advancing, or improving; resulting in a positive conclusion.. **constructiveness** *n.*

con-strue (kon strö') *v.* To interpret; to translate; to analyze grammatical structure.

con-sul (kon'sul) *n.* An official that resides in a foreign country and represents his or her government's commercial interests and citizens.

con-sul-ate (kon'su lit) *n.* The official premises occupied by a consul.

con-sult (kon sult') *v.* To seek advice or information from; to compare views. **consultant** *n.* **consultation** *n.*

con-sult-ant (kon sul'tant) *n.* A person who consults; one who offers professional advice or services for a fee.

con-sume (kon söm') *v.* To ingest; to eat or drink; to destroy completely; to absorb; to engross. **consumable** *n.*

con-sum-er (kon sö'mėr) *n.* A person who buys services or goods.

con-sum-mate (kon'su māt') *v.* To conclude; to make a marriage complete by the initial act of sexual intercourse.

con-sump-tion (kon sump'shan) *n.* Fulfillment; the act of consuming; the quantity consumed; tuberculosis.

con-sump-tive (kon sump'tiv) *adj.* Tending to destroy or waste away; affected with or pertaining to pulmonary tuberculosis. **consumptively** *adv.* **consumptiveness** *n.*

con-tact (kon'takt) *n.* The place, spot, or junction where two or more surfaces or objects touch; the connection between two electric conductors. **contacts** Contact lens; thin lens of plastic or glass with an optical prescription, worn directly on the cornea of the eye.

contact lens *n.* A prescription lens for correcting vision, which is applied directly to the cornea of the eye.

con-ta-gion (k on tā'jon) *n.* The transmitting of a disease by contact. **contagious** *adj.* **contagiously** *adv.*

con-ta-gi-um *n.* A virus by which a contagious disease is communicated.

con-tain (kon tān') *v.* To include or enclose; to restrain or hold back. **containable** *adj.* **containment** *n.*

con-tain-er (kon tā´nẽr) v. Something that holds or carries, as a box or can.

con-tain-er-i-za-tion (kon tā´nẽr i zā´shon) n. The procedure of shipping a large amount of goods in one container.

container ship n. A ship that is designed to carry containerized cargo.

con-tam-i-nate (kon tam´i nāt´) v. To pollute or make inferior by adding undesirable elements; to taint; to infect; to make dirty or to soil. **contaminant** n. **contamination** n.

con-tam-i-na-tion (kon tam´i nā´shon) n. The act or state of contaminating, or of being contaminated.

con-temn (kon tem´) v. To scorn or despise.

con-tem-plate (kon´tem plāt´) v. To look over; to ponder; to consider thoughtfully. **contemplative, -tion** n.

con-tem-pla-tion (kon´tem plā´shon) n. The act of serious contemplating; thoughtful; attentive consideration.

con-tem-po-ra-ne-ous(kon tem´po rā´nē us) adj. Occurring or living at the same time; contemporary. **contemporane-ously** adv. **contemporaneousness** n.

con-tempt (kon tempt´) n. The act of viewing something as mean, vile, or worthless scorn; legally, the willful disrespect or disregard of authority. **contemptible** adj.

con-tempt-i-ble (kon temp´ti bl) adj. Worthy of contempt; deserving scorn.

con-temp-tu-ous (kon temp´chö us) adj. Feeling or showing contempt. **-ly** adv.

con-tend (kon tend´) v. To dispute; to fight; to debate; to argue. **-er** n.

con-tent (kon´tent) n. Something contained within; the subject matter of a book or document; the proportion of a specified part. adj. Satisfied. **contentment** n. **-edly** adv. **-ed** adj.

con-tent-ed (kon ten´tid) adj. Satisfied with one's circumstances, possessions, or status.

con-ten-tion (kon ten´shon) n. Competition; rivalry; controversy; argument. **contentious** adj. **contentiously** adv.

con-tent-ment (kon tent´ment) n. Feeling of or being contented; a satisfaction of mind.

con-ter-mi-nous (kon tër´mi nus) adj. Having the same or common boundaries or limits.

con-test (kon´test) n. A competition; strife; conflict. v. To challenge. **contestable** adj. **contestant** n.

con-text (kon´tekst) n. A sentence, phrase, or passage so closely connected to a word or words that it affects their meaning; the environment in which an event occurs.

con-tex-ture (kon teks´chẽr) n. The act of interweaving several parts into a

whole.

con-tig-u-ous (k on tig´ū us) adj. Situated next to or near in time; meeting or joining at the surface or border.

con-ti-nent (kon´ti nent) n. One of the seven large masses of the earth: Asia; Africa; Australia; Europe; North America; South America; and Antarctica.

con-ti-nen-tal (kon´ti nen´tal) adj. Of or characteristic of a continent.

continental divide n. A divide separating rivers or streams that flow to opposite sides of a continent.

con-tin-gent (kon tin´jent) adj. Likely to happen; happening by chance.

con-tin-u-al (kon tin´u al) adj. Continuing indefinitely; proceeding without interruption; not intermittent.

con-tin-u-a-tion (kon tin´ū ā´shon) n. The act of continuing or prolonging; extension or carrying on after an interruption.

con-tin-ue (kon tin´ū) v. To maintain without interruption a course or condition; to resume; to postpone or adjourn a judicial proceeding. **continuance** n. **continuer** n.

continued fraction n. A fraction with a denominator which contains a fraction and a numerator which contains a fraction.

con-tin-u-ing (kon tin´ū ing) adj. Enduring or lasting; continuous.

con-ti-nu-i-ty (kon´ti nö´i tē) n. pl. **-ties** The quality of being continuous.

con-tin-u-ous (kon tin´ū us) adj. Uninterrupted. **continuously** adv.

con-tort (kon tort´) v. To severely twist out of shape.

con-tort-ed (kon tor´tid) adj. Twisted to an extreme degree or violent manner.

con-tor-tion-ist(kon tor´sha nist) n. An acrobat who exhibits unnatural body positions.

con-tour (kon´tur) n. The outline of a body, figure, or mass.

contour line n. A line on a map carried along the surface connecting points that have the same elevation.

contour map n. A topographic map where with contour lines are shown by the relative spacing of lines known as contour intervals.

con-tra-band (kon´tra band´) n. Illegal or prohibited traffic; smuggled goods.

con-tra-bass (kon´tra bās´) n. A double bass, also called a contrabassoon.

con-tra-cep-tion (kon´tra sep´shon) n. The voluntary prevention of impregnation. **contraceptive** n.

con-tract (kon´trakt) n. A formal agreement between two or more parties to perform the duties as stated; an oral, written, or implied agreement between two or more persons.

con-trac-tile (kən trak´tĭl) *adj.* Having the power to contract.

con-trac-tion (kən trak´shən) *n.* The act of contracting; a shortening of a word by omitting a letter or letters and replacing it with an apostrophe (').

con-trac-tor (kon´trak tèr) *n.* A person who contracts to perform work at a certain price or rate.

con-trac-ture (kən trak´chèr) *n.* A permanent shortening of a muscle or tendon producing deformity.

con-tra-dict (kon´tra dĭkt´) *v.* To express the opposite side or idea; to be inconsistent. **contradictable** *adj.* **contradictory** *adj.* **contradicter** *n.*

con-tra-dic-tion (kon´tra dĭk´shən) *n.* A statement that implies by the truth and falseness about something; direct opposition.

con-tra-dic-to-ry (kon´tra dĭk´to rē) *adj.* Opposite; being inconsistent with one another; opposite.

con-trail (kon´trāl) *n.* The visible water vapor left in the sky by a plane.

con-tral-to (kən tral´tō) *n. pl.* **-tos** The lowest female singing voice.

con-trap-tion (kən trap´shən) *n.* A gadget.

con-tra-puntal (kon´tra pun´tal) *adj.* Relating to counterpoint.

con-tra-ri-wise (kon´trer ē wīz´) *adv.* In a contrary manner; vice versa; on the contrary.

con-trar-y (kon´trer ē) *adj.* Unfavorable; incompatible with another. **contrarily** *adv.* **contrariness** *n.*

con-trast (kon trast´) *v.* To note the differences between two or more people, things, or any item. **contrastable** *adj.*

con-tra-vene (kon´tra vēn´) *v.* To be contrary; to violate; to oppose; to go against.

con-tre-danse (kon´tri dans´) *n.* A graceful folk dance, in which the partners stand opposite one another in two lines.

con-trib-ute (kən trib´ūt) *v.* To give something to someone; to submit for publication. **contribution** *n.* **contributor** *n.* **contributive** *adj.* **contributory** *adj.* **contributively** *adv.*

con-tri-bu-tion (kon´trĭ bū´shən) *n.* The act of contributing or something contributed.

con-trib-u-to-ry (kən trib´ū tŏr´ē) *adj.* Contributing to a common fund; furnishing something toward a result.

con-trite (kən trīt´) *adj.* Grieving for sin or shortcoming. **contritely** *adv.*

con-triv-ance (kən trī´vəns) *n.* The act of or thing contriving, devising, or planning.

con-trol (kən trōl´) *v.* To have the authority or ability to regulate, direct, or dominate a situation. **-able** *adj.*

con-trol-ler (kən trō lèr) *n.* The chief accounting officer of a business, also called the comptroller.

controlling interest *n.* The majority stock ownership in a corporation, which exerts control over policy.

control tower *n.* A lookout tower at an airfield or airport having the necessary equipment and personnel to direct air and ground traffic in takeoffs and landings.

con-tro-ver-sy (kon´tro vèr´sē) *n.* A dispute; a debate; a quarrel **controversial** *adj.*

con-tro-vert (kon´tro vert´) *v.* To contradict.

con-tu-ma-cy (kon´tu ma sē) *n.* Stubborn rebelliousness to authority.

con-tu-me-li-ous (kon´tu mē´lē us) *adj.* Indicating or expressing humiliation.

con-tu-me-ly (kon´tu me lē) *n. pl.* **-lies** Rude treatment. **contumelious** *adj.*

con-tuse (kən tōz´) *v.* To injure the body without breaking the flesh.

con-tu-sion (kən tō´zhen) *n.* A severe bruise or injury to the body; without breaking of the skin.

co-nun-drum (ko nun´drəm) *n.* A riddle with an answer that involves a pun; a question or problem with only a surmise for an answer.

con-va-lesce (kon´va les´) *v.* To grow strong after a long illness, recovery time. **convalescence** *n.*

con-va-les-cence (kon´va les´ens) *n.* Gradual recovery of health and strength after a sickness.

con-vect (kon vekt´) *v.* To move or transfer heat by convection.

con-vec-tion (kon vek´shən) *n.* The transfer of heat by the movement of air, gas, or heated liquid between areas of unequal density, upward flow of warm air. **convectional** *adj.*

con-vec-tor (kon vek´tèr) *n.* A heating unit for circulating heat by convection.

con-vene (kon vēn´) *v.* To meet or assemble formally; meeting.

con-ven-ience (kən vēn´yans) *n.* The quality of being convenient or suitable.

con-ve-nient (kon vē´nyant) *adj.* Suitable and agreeable to the needs or purpose.

con-vent (con´vent) *n.* A local house or community of a religious order, a home for nuns.

con-ven-ti-cle (kon ven´ti kl) *n.* A secret meeting for religious study or worship.

con-ven-tion (kon ven´shan) *n.* A formal meeting; a regulatory meeting between people, states, or nations on matters that affect all of them.

con-ven-tion-al (kon ven´sha nal) *adj.* Commonplace, ordinary.

con-ven-tu-al (kon ven´chö al) *n.* A

member of a conventual community or monastery.

con-verge (kən vėrj´) v. To come to a common point. **covergence** n.

con-vers-a-ble (kən vėr´sa bl) adj. Pleasant and easy to talk to.

con-ver-sa-tion (kon´vėrsā´shan)n. An informal talk, verbal discussion with someone or a group of people, oral communication. **conversational** adj. **conversationally** adv.

converse (kən vėrs´) v. To involve oneself in conversation with another.

con-ver-sion (kən vėr´zhan) n. The act or state of changing to adopt new opinions or beliefs; a formal acceptance of a different religion. **-al** adj.

con-vert-er (kən vėr´tėr) n. One who converts; a machine or device that accepts in-formation in one form and converts to another.

con-vert-i-ble (kən vėr´ti bl) adj. A car with a top that folds back or can be removed completely.

convertible life insurance n. A limited type of life insurance, such as group or term that allows the policy holder to change the policy into an expanded or more permanent form.

convertible stock n. Preferred stock which may upon exercise of the owner's option, be exchanged for common stock

con-vex (kon´veks) adj. Curved outward like the outer surface of a ball.

con-vex-o–con-cave (kən veksō kon kāv´) adj. Convex on one side greater than on the other side, as an eyeglass lens.

con-vey (kən vā´) v. To transport; to pass information on to someone else; to conduct. **conveyable** adj.

con-vey-ance (kən vā´ans) n. The action of conveying; the legal transfer of property or the document effecting it.

con-vict (kən vikt´) v. To prove someone guilty. n. A prisoner.

con-vic-tion (kən vik´shan) n. The act of being convicted.

con-vince (kən vins´) v. To cause to believe without doubt. **-ingly** adv.

con-viv-i-al (kən viv´ē al) adj. Relating to entertainment and good company.

con-vo-ca-tion (kon´vo kā´shan) n. A formal or ceremonial assembly or meeting.

con-voke (kən vōk´) v. To call together for a formal meeting.

con-vo-lute (kon´vo lōt´) adj. Twisted; rolled up together.

con-vo-lu-tion (kon´vo lō´shan) n. A rolling, folding or coiling together; a rolled up or coiled condition.

con-voy (kon´voi) n. A group of cars, trucks, etc., traveling together. v. To escort or guide.

con-vulse (kən vuls´) v. To move or shake violently. **convulsive** adj.

con-vul-sion (kən vul´shan) n. A violent involuntary muscular contraction.

cook (kuk) v. To apply heat to food before eating; to prepare food for a meal. n. A person who prepares food.

cook-book (kuk´buk´) n. A book containing directions for preparing and cooking food.

cook-ie (kuk´ē) n. A sweet, flat cake.

cool (kōl) adj. Without warmth; indifferent or unenthusiastic. Slang Firstrate; composure.

cool-ant (kō´lant) n. The cooling agent that circulates through a machine.

Coolidge, John Calvin n. (1872-1933) The thirtieth president of the United States from 1923-1929.

coon (kōn) n., Informal A raccoon.

coop (kōp) n. A cage or enclosed area to contain animals, as chickens.

co–op (kō´op) n. A cooperative.

co-op-er-ate (kō op´e rāt´) v. To work together toward a common cause. **cooperation** n. **cooperator** n.

co-op-er-ation n. The action of cooperating; the combination of persons for purposes of production, or distribution for their joint benefit and success; a common effort.

co-op-er-a-tive (kō op´e rā´tiv) adj. Willing to cooperate in working with others. **cooperatively** adv. **cooperativeness** n.

co–opt (kō opt´) v. To elect or choose as a new member.

co-or-di-nate (kō or´di nāt´) v. To be equal in rank, importance, or degree; to plan a wardrobe or outfit so that it goes well together. n. Any of a set of numbers which establishes position on a graph, map, chart, etc. **coordinately** adv. **coordinator** n.

co-or-di-na-tion (kō or´di nā´shan) n. The state of being coordinated.

coot (kōt) n. A short-winged bird. Slang A silly old man.

coot-ie (kō´tē) n., Slang A body louse.

cop (kop) n., Informal A police officer.

co-pal (kō´pal) n. A hard, fossil resin from various tropical trees, used in making varnishes.

co-par-ce-nar-y (kō pär´se nėr´ē) n. Joint ownership; joint heirship.

co-part-ner (kō pärt´nėr) n. A partner with others; a sharer.

cope (kōp) v. To strive; to struggle or contend with something. n. The long cape worn by a priest on special ceremonial occasions.

cop-ier (kop´ē ėr) n. A machine that makes copies of original material.

co-pi-lot (kō´pī´ot) n. The assistant pilot on an aircraft.

co-pi-ous adj. Yielding something in

large quantity; abundant. **copiously** *adv.*

cop–out *n. Slang* A way to avoid responsibility; a person who cops out.

cop-per (kop´ẽr) *n.* A metallic element that is a good conductor of electricity and heat, reddish-brown in color.

cop-per-plate (kop´ẽr plāt) *n.* A copper plate on which something is engraved.

cop-ra (kop´ra) *n.* Dried coconut meat that yields coconut oil.

copse (kops) *n.* A thicket made up of trees or small bushes.

cop-ter (kop´tẽr) *n., Slang* A helicopter.

cop-u-la (kop´ũ la) *n., Gram.* A word or words which connect a subject and predicate.

cop-u-late (kop´ũ lāt) *v.* To have sexual intercourse. **copulation** *n.*

copy (kop´ē) *v. pl. -ies* To reproduce an original. *n.* A single printed text.

cop-y-boy (kop´ē boi) *n.* A person, usually employed in a newspaper office, who carries copy and runs errands.

copy edit *v.* To edit and correct a written copy for publication. **copy editor** *n.*

copy-right (kop´ē rīt) *n.* The statutory right to sell, publish, or distribute a literary or artistic work.

co-quette (kō ket´) *n.* A woman who flirts. **coquettish** *adj.*

co-qui-na (kō kē´na) *n.* A small clam used for making broth or chowder.

cor-a-cle (kor´a kl) *n.* A small boat made by covering a wicker frame with hide or leather.

cor-a-coid (kor´a koid) *adj.* Relating or referring to a bony process or cartilage in various vertebrates, as birds and reptiles.

cor-al (kor´al) *n.* The stony skeleton of a small sea creature, often used for jewelry.

coral reef *n.* A marine mound formed chiefly of broken pieces and grains of coral that have become a hard mass.

cor-beil (kor´bel) *n.* A sculptured basket of flowers and fruits.

cor-bi-na *n.* A spotted whiting fish of the California coast.

cord (cord) *n.* A string or twine; an insulated wire used to supply electricity to another source; a measurement for firewood that equals 128 cubic feet; a raised rib of fabric, as corduroy. **corder** *n.*

cord-age (kor´dij) *n.* Cords or ropes used on the rigging of ship.

cor-dial (kor´jal) *adj.* Warm-hearted and sincere. *n.* A liqueur. **cordiality** *n.*

cor-di-er-ite (kor´dē e rīt´) *n.* A silicate of aluminum, iron, and magnesium in shades of blue, having a vitreous luster.

cor-di-form (kor´di form´) *adj.* Heart-shaped.

cord-ing (kor´ding) *n.* A heavy cord used for ornamental purposes.

cord-ite (kor´dīt) *n.* A smokeless gunpowder.

cor-don (kor´don) *n.* A circle of men or ships positioned to guard or enclose an area; an ornamental ribbon or braid worn as an insignia of honor.

cor-du-roy (kor´du roi´) *n.* A durable cotton fabric which has a ribbed pile.

core (kōr) *n.* The innermost or central part of something; the inedible center of a fruit that contains the seeds. *v.* To remove the core from a piece of fruit.

co-re-op-sis (kōr´ē op´sis) *n.* A familiar garden herb grown for its showy flowers.

co-re-spon-dent (kō´ri spon´dent) *n.* A person charged with having committed adultery with the defendant in a divorce case.

co-ri-a-ceous (kōr´ē ā´shus) *adj.* Consisting of or resembling leather.

co-ri-an-der (kōr´ē an´dẽr) *n.* A herb plant of the carrot family.

co-ri-um (kōr´ē um) *n.* The vascular layer of the skin beneath the epidermis.

cork (kork) *n.* The elastic bark of the oak tree used for bottle stoppers and craft projects.

cork-age (kor´kij) *n.* The fee that must be paid when one consumes a bottle of liquor not purchased on the premises.

cork-screw (kork´skrō) *n.* A pointed metal spiral attached to a handle used for removing corks from bottles.

cork-wood (kork´wüd) *n.* The light and porous wood of certain trees and shrubs of the southeastern United States.

cor-mo-rant (kor´mẽr ant) *n.* Any bird of the voracious water birds having a long neck, webbed feet, and a pouch under the mouth for holding and catching fish.

corn (korn) *n.* An American cultivated cereal plant bearing seeds on a large ear or cob; the seed of this plant; a horny thickening of the skin, usually on the toe.

cor-na-ceous (kor nā´shus) *adj.* A family of plants, mostly trees and shrubs that include the dogwood and the tupelo.

cor-ne-a (kor´nē a) *n.* The transparent membrane of the eyeball. **corneal** *adj.*

cor-ner (kor´nẽr) *n.* The point formed when two surfaces or lines meet and form an angle; the location where two streets meet.

corner-stone (kor´nẽr stōn´) *n.* A stone that forms part of the corner of a building, usually laid in place with a special ceremony.

cor-net (kor net´) *n.* A three valved, brass musical instrument. **cornetist** *n.*

cor-nice (kor´nis) *n.* The horizontal

projecting molding which finishes a wall or building.

cor-niche (kor´nish) *n*. A road built along the edge of a cliff.

cor-nu (kor´nū) *n*. A horn-shaped structure.

cor-nu-co-pi-a (kor´nu kō´pē *a*) *n*. A curved goat's horn overflowing with flowers, fruit, and corn to signify prosperity.

cor-nute (kor nōt´) *adj*. Having horns; horn-shaped.

cor-ol-lary (kor´oler˝ē) *n*. *pl*. -ies Something that naturally or incidentally follows or accompanies.

cor-o-nar-y (kor´o ner˝ē) *adj*. Of or relating to the two arteries that supply blood to the heart muscles.

coronary thrombosis *n*. A blocking of the coronary artery of the heart.

cor-o-ner *n*. A public officer, of a county or municipality, whose chief function is to investigate, any death not clearly due to natural causes.

cor-o-net (kor´o nit) *n*. A small, lessor, or inferior crown.

co-ro-no-graph (ko rō´no graf) *n*. A telescope used for observing and photographing the corona of the sun.

cor-po-ral (kor´pēr al) *n*. The lowest non-commissioned officer. *adj*. Relating to or affecting the body.

cor-po-rate (kor´pēr it) *adj*. Combined into one joint body; relating to a corporation.

cor-po-ra-tion (kor´po rā´shan) *n*. A group of merchants united in a trade guild; any group or persons that act as one.

cor-po-re-al (kor pōr´ē al) *adj*. Of a physical nature.

corps (kōrps) *n*. *pl*. **corps** A branch of the armed forces; the body of persons under common direction.

corpse (korps) *n*. A dead body.

cor-pu-lent (kor´pū lent) *adj*. Having a large or bulky body.

corpus callosum *n*. The large band of nervous tissue uniting the two cerebral hemispheres in the brain of man and other mammals.

cor-pus-cle (kor´pu sel) *n*. A minute particle or living cell, especially as one in the blood. **corpuscular** *adj*.

corpus delicti (kor´pus di lik´tī) *n*. The essential evidence pertaining to a crime.

cor-rade (ko rād´) *v*. To rub together; to wear away by abrasion.

cor-ral (ko ral´) *n*. An enclosure for containing animals. *v*., *Slang* To take possession of.

cor-rect (ko rekt´) *v*. To make free from fault or mistakes. **corrective** *n*.

cor-re-spond (kor´i spond´) *v*. To communicate by letter or written words; to be harmonious, equal or similar.

correspondingly *adv*.

cor-re-spond-ent (kor´i spond´) *n*. Something that corresponds to something else; a person who has regular business dealings with another.

cor-ri-dor (kor´i dèr) *n*. A long hall with rooms on either side; a piece of land that forms a passage through a foreign land.

cor-ri-gen-dum (kor´i jen´dum) *n*. *pl*. -da An error in print that is accompanied by its correction.

cor-ri-gi-ble (kor´i ji bl) *adj*. Able to correct; capable of being corrected.

cor-ri-val (ko rī´val) *n*. A competitor.

cor-rob-o-rate (k o rob´o rāt´) *v*. To support a position or statement with evidence. **corroboration** *n*.

cor-rode (ko rōd´) *v*. To eat away through chemical action. **corrosive** *n*. **corrodible** *adj*. **corrosion** *n*.

cor-ro-sion (ko rō´zhan) *n*. The process of corroding, eating, or wearing away; the chemical effect of acids on metals.

cor-ro-sive (ko rō´siv) *n*. That which has the power or quality of wearing away gradually.

cor-ru-gate (kor´u gāt´) *v*. To form, draw or bend into folds or alternate grooves and ridges.

corrugated iron *n*. Galvanized sheet iron or sheet steel, shaped and strengthened by bending into equal parallel grooves and ridges.

cor-rupt (ko rupt´) *adj*. Dishonest; evil. *v*. To become or make corrupt.

cor-rup-tion (ko rup´shan) *n*. Impaired of integrity.

cor-sage (kor säzh´) *n*. A small bouquet of flowers worn on a woman's shoulder or wrist.

cor-sair (kor´sâr) *n*. A pirate; a fast moving vessel.

cor-set (kor´sit) *n*. An undergarment that is tightened with laces and reinforced with stays, worn to give shape and support to a woman's body.

cor-tege (kor tezh´) *n*. A ceremonial procession; a funeral procession.

cor-tex (kor´teks) *n*. *pl*. -tices The external layer of an organ, especially the gray matter that covers the brain; the bark of trees and the rinds of fruits.

cor-ti-sone (kor´ti sōn´) *n*. A hormone produced by the adrenal cortex, used in the treatment of rheumatoid arthritis.

co-run-dum (ko run´dum) *n*. An aluminum oxide used as an abrasive.

cor-us-cate (kor´u skät´) *v*. To sparkle. **coruscation** *n*.

cor-vette (kor vet´) *n*. An armed warship smaller than a destroyer, used as an escort vessel.

cor-vine (kor´vīn) *adj*. Birds including and resembling the crow, and ravens.

co-ry-za (ko rī´za) *n*. An acute inflamma

tion of the upper respiratory system.

co-sign (kō sig´n) v. To sign a document jointly.

co-sig-na-to-ry (kō sig´na tōr´ē) n. pl. -ies One who jointly cosigns a document.

cos lettuce n. A kind of lettuce; romaine.

cos-met-ic (koz met´ik) n. A preparation designed to beautify the face.

cos-mic (koz´mik) adj. Of or relating to cosmos; forming a part of the material universe.

cosmic dust n. Very fine particles existing in or of the universe.

cosmic ray n. An extremely high frequency and energy content that comes from outer space and bombards the atoms of the earth's atmosphere.

cos-mog-o-ny (koz mog´o nē) n. The creation of the universe.

cos-mog-ra-phy n. The general science description of the heavens and the earth, dealing with the whole makeup of nature.

cos-mo-naut (koz mo not) n. A Soviet astronaut.

cos-mop-o-lis (koz mop´o lis) n. A city inhabited by people from many lands.

cos-mo-pol-i-tan (koz´mo pol´i tan) adj. Being at home anywhere in the world.

cos-mop-o-lite (koz mop´o līt´) n. A cosmopolitan person.

cos-mos (koz´mos) n. An orderly and harmoniously systematic universe.

cos-set (kos´it) v. To pamper; pet.

cost (kost) n. The amount paid or charged for a purchase. **cost** v. **costly** adj.

cos-ta (kos´ta) n. A part of a leaf or the interior wing of an insect that most resembles a rib.

cos-tive (kos´tiv) adj. Affected with or causing constipation.

cost-mar-y (kost´mâr´ē) n. A perennial plant, with fragrant leaves, used as a pot-herb, in salads.

cos-tume (kos´tōm) n. A suit, dress, or set of clothes characteristic of a particular season or occasion; clothes worn by a person playing a part or dressing up in a disguise.

cot (kot) n. A small, often collapsible bed.

cote (kōt) n. A shelter for small animals as a coop or shed.

co-til-lion (kō til´yan) n. A dance that consists of beautiful and intricate patterns.

cot-tage (kot´ij) n. A small house, usually for vacation use.

cot-ton (kot´on) n. A plant or shrub cultivated for the fiber surrounding its seeds; a fabric created by the weaving of cotton fibers; yarn spun from cotton fibers.

cotton candy n. Spun sugar candy.

cot-ton-seed (kot´on sēd´) n. The seed of the cotton plant, the oil of which can be used as a substitute for olive oil and in cooking.

couch (kouch) n. A piece of furniture, such as a sofa or bed on which one may sit or recline for rest or sleep. v. To phrase in a certain manner; to lie in ambush.

cou-gar (kō´gér) n. A large brown cat, also called a mountain lion, panther, and puma.

cough (kof) v. To suddenly expel air from the lungs with an explosive noise.

could (kūd) v. Past tense of can.

could-n't (kūd´ent) contr. Could not.

cou-lisse (kō lēs´) n. A piece of wood, with a groove in which something slides.

cou-loir (kōl wär´) n. A gully or mountainside gorge.

cou-lomb (kō´lom) n. The unit of quantity used to measure electricity; the amount conveyed by one ampere in one second.

cou-ma-rone n. A colorless liquid compound, found in coal tar and used to form thermoplastic resins used in printing inks, and adhesives.

coun-cil (koun´sil) n. A group of people assembled for consultation or discussion; an official legislative or advisory body. **councilman,** n.

coun-sel (koun´sel) n. Professional advice given through consultation; a lawyer en-gaged in a trial or management of a court case.

coun-sel-ing (koun´se ling) n. The act or process of giving professional advice.

coun-sel-or (koun´se lér) n. One who gives advice; a lawyer.

count (kount) v. To name or number so as to find the total number of units involved; to name numbers in order; to take account of in a tally or reckoning; to rely or depend on something or someone; to have significance. n. A nobleman found in various countries throughout Europe, having rank corresponding to that of a British earl; a tally.

count-down (kount´doun´) n. An audible counting in descending order to mark the time remaining before an event.

coun-te-nance (koun´te nans) n. The face as an indication of mood or character; bearing or expression that would suggest approval or sanction.

coun-ter (koun´tér) n. A level surface over which transactions are conducted, on which food is served, or on which articles are displayed; a person or device that counts to determine a number or amount. v. To move or act in a contrary, or opposing direction or wrong way.

coun-ter-act (koun´tẽr akt´) v. To oppose and, by contrary action, make ineffective.

coun-ter-attack (koun´tẽr a tak´) n. An attack made in response to an enemy attack. **counterattack** v.

coun-ter-bal-ance (koun´tẽr bal´ans) n. A force or influence that balances another; a weight that balances another.

coun-ter-bore (koun´tẽr bōr´) v. To bore out a hole for creating a flat-bottomed enlargement for the head of a screw.

coun-ter-claim (koun´tẽr klām´) n. A contrary claim made to offset another.

coun-ter-clock-wise (koun´tẽr klŏk´wīz´) adj. & adv. In a direction contrary to that in which the hands of a clock move.

coun-ter-cul-ture (koun´tẽr kul´chẽr) n. A culture with values opposite those of traditional society.

coun-ter-es-pi-o-nage (koun´tẽr es´pē o näzh´) n. Espionage aimed at discovering and thwarting enemy espionage.

coun-ter-feit (koun´tẽr fit) v. To closely imitate or copy with the intent to deceive; to forge. adj. Marked by false pretense. n. Something counterfeit.

coun-ter-foil (koun´tẽr foil´) n. A stub, as on a check or ticket, usually serving as a record of the transaction.

coun-ter-in-tel-ligence (koun´tẽr in tel´i jens) n. An intelligence agency function designed to block information, deceive the enemy, prevent sabotage, and gather military and political material and information.

coun-ter-ir-ri-tant (koun´tẽr ir´i tant) n. An irritation that diverts attention from another. **counterirritant** adj.

coun-ter-man (koun´tẽr man) n. One who works at a counter.

coun-ter-mand (koun´tẽr mand´) v. To reverse or revoke a command by issuing a contrary order. n. An order which reverses or contradicts a previous order.

coun-ter-of-fensive (koun´tẽr o fen´siv) n. A military offensive designed to thwart an enemy attack.

coun-ter-pane (koun´tẽr pān´) n. A covering.

coun-ter-part (koun´tẽr pärt´) n. One that matches or complements another.

coun-ter-plea (koun´tẽr plē) n. A plea made in answer to a previous plea.

coun-ter-plot (koun´tẽr plot´) n. A plot that prevents another from occurring.

coun-ter-point (koun´tẽr point´) n., Mus. The combining of melodies into a harmonic relationship while retaining the linear character.

coun-ter-poise (koun´tẽr poiz´) n. An equal and opposing force or power.

coun-ter-pose (koun´tẽr pōz´) v. To place in opposition.

coun-ter-pro-duc-tive (koun´tẽr pro duk´tiv) adj. Tending to hinder rather than aid in the attainment of a goal.

coun-ter-pro-pos-al (koun´tẽr pro pō´zal) n. A return proposal for one that has been rejected.

coun-ter-punch (koun´tẽr punch) n. A punch given in quick retaliation, as a boxing punch.

coun-ter-re-vo-lu-tion (koun´tẽr rev´o lōo´shan) n. A revolution designed to overthrow a government previously seat-ed by a revolution.

coun-ter-shaft (koun´tẽr shaft´) n. A shaft driven by a belt or gearing from a main shaft and transmits motion to a working part.

coun-ter-sign (koun´tẽr sīn´) n. A signature confirming the authenticity of a document already signed by another; a sign or signal given in response to another. **countersign** v.

coun-ter-spy (koun´tẽr spī´) n. A spy against the espionage actions of a country.

coun-ter-ten-or (koun´tẽr tĕn´ẽr) n. An adult tenor with a very high range, and able to sing in an alto range.

coun-tri-fy (kun´tri fī´) v. To imply country life; rustic; unsophisticated.

coun-try (kun´trē) n. pl. -ies A given area or region; the land of one's birth, residence, or citizenship; a state, nation, or its territory.

coun-try-man (kun´trē man) n. A compatriot; one living in the country or having country ways.

country music n. Music derived from the folk style of the southern United States and from the cowboy.

coun-try-side (kun´trē sīd´) n. A rural area or its inhabitants.

coun-ty (kun´tē) n. pl. -ies A territorial division for local government within a state.

coup (kö) n. A brilliant, sudden move that is usually highly successful.

cou-ple (kup´l) n. A pair; something that joins two things together; a few. v. To join in marriage or sexual union.

cou-pler (kup´lẽr) n. One who or that which couples; a device that transfers electrical energy from one circuit to another.

cou-plet (kup´lit) n. Two rhyming lines of poetry in succession.

cou-pling (kup´ling) n. A mechanical devices for uniting or connecting parts or things.

cou-pon (kö´pon) n. A statement of interest due, to be removed from a bearer bond and presented for payment when it is payable; a form surrendered to obtain a product, service, or discount on same; a form to be clipped from a magazine or paper and mailed for discounts or gifts.

cour-age (kür´ij) *n.* Mental or moral strength to face danger without fear. **courageous** *adj.* **courageously** *adv.*

cou-ri-er (kür´ē ér) *n.* A messenger; a person who carries contraband for another.

course (kōrs) *n.* The act of moving in a path from one point to another; the path over which something moves; a period of time; a series or sequence; a series of studies.

court (kört) *n.* The residence of a sovereign or similar dignitary; a sovereign's family and advisors; an assembly for the transaction of judicial business; a place where trials are conducted; an area marked off for game playing. *v.* To try to win favor or dispel hostility.

cour-te-ous (kér´tē us) *adj.* Marked by respect for and consideration of others.

cour-te-san (kōr´ti zan) *n.* A prostitute; one who associates with or caters to high-ranking or wealthy men.

cour-te-sy (kér´ti sē) *n. pl.* **-ies** Courteous behavior; general allowance despite facts.

court-house (kört´hous´) *n.* A building for holding courts of law.

court-i-er (kör´tē ér) *n.* One in attendance at a royal court.

court-ly (kört´lē) *adj.* Dignified; elegant; polite.

court of appeals *n.* A court that hears appeals from a lower court.

court-room (kört´röm´) *n.* A room for holding a court of law.

court-ship (kört´ship) *n.* The act or period of courting.

court-yard (kört´yärd´) *n.* An open space enclosed by walls.

cous-in (kuz´in) *n.* A child of one's uncle or aunt; a member of a culturally similar race or nationality.

couth (kōth) *adj.* Having breeding, polish, or refinement.

cou-ture (kö tür´) *n.* The business of designing and selling women's clothing; dressmaker.

covalent bond *n.* The nonionic chemical bond produced by the sharing of an electron pair by two atoms in a chemical process.

cove (kōv) *n.* A small inlet or bay, generally sheltered; a deep recess or small valley in the side of a mountain.

cov-e-nant (kuv´e nant) *n.* A formal, binding agreement; a promise or pledge.

cov-er (kuv´ér) *v.* To place something on or over; to lie over; to spread over; concealment; to guard from attack; to hide or conceal, book binding. *Slang* To be all-encompassing; to act as a

stand-in during another's absence; to have within one's gun sights.

cov-er-age (kuv´ér ij) *n.* A provision for something by contract; that which is covered.

cov-er-all (kuv´ér al´) *n.* A loose one-piece outer garment used to cover other clothing.

cover charge *n.* A charge, at night clubs or restaurants, in addition to the bill for food and drink, used to pay for the entertainment.

cover crop *n.* A crop planted to prevent soil erosion.

covered wagon *n.* A canvas covered wagon with high curved hoops supported by bowed strips of metal or wood.

cov-er-let (kuv´ér lit) *n.* A bedspread.

cov-et (kuv´it) *v.* To wish for enviously; to crave possession of that which belongs to someone else.

cov-ey (kuv´ē) *n.* A small group of birds, especially quail or partridges.

cow (kou) *n. pl.* **cows** The mature female of cattle or of any species when the adult male is referred to as a bull.

cow-ard (kou´ard) *n.* One who shows great fear or timidity. **cowardice** *n.*

cow-bane (kou´bān´) *n.* Any of several poisonous parsley-like plants, as the water hemlock.

cow-boy (kou´boi) *n.* A man who tends cows and horses on a large ranch or farm and does this work while on horseback.

cow-hide (kou´hīd´) *n.* The hide of a cow from which leather is made.

cowl (koul) *n.* A hood or long hooded cloak such as that of a monk; a covering for a chimney that is designed to improve the air draft; the top portion at the front of an automobile where the windshield and dashboard are attached.

cow-lick (kou´lik´) *n.* A lock of hair growing in a different direction than the other hair.

cowl-ing (kou´ling) *n.* A removable metal covering for an engine.

cox-a (kok´sa) *n.* The joint of the hip.

cox-comb (koks´kōm) *n.* A conceited foolish person.

cox-swain (kok´san) *n.* One who steers a boat or racing shell.

coy (koi) *adj.* Quieting or shy, or to pretending to be so. **coyness** *n.*

coy-o-te (kī ō´tē) *n.* A small wolf-like animal that is native to North America.

co-yo-til-lo (kō´yō tēl´yō) *n.* A small shrub of the southwestern United States and Mexico, bearing poisonous fruit.

coy-pu (koi´pö) *n.* A beaver-like, semiaquatic mammal, valued for its soft brown fur.

coz-en (kuz´en) *v.* To swindle, cheat, deceive, win over, or induce to do something by coaxing or trickery.

co-zy (kō´zē) *adj.* Comfortable and warm; snug. **cozy** *n.* A cover placed over a teapot to retain the warmth. **cozily** *adv.*

crab (krab) *n. pl.* **crabs** Any one of numerous chiefly marine crustaceans with a short, broad shell, four pairs of legs, and one pair of pincers; sideways motion of an airplane headed into a crosswind. **crabs** Infestation with crab lice.

crab-bed (krab´id) *adj.* Morose or peevish; difficult to read or understand. **crabbedly** *adv.* **crabbedness** *n.*

crab-by (krab bē) *adj.* Cross and ill-tempered.

crab-grass (krab gras) *n.* A grass with stems that root freely and is often a weedy pest in lawns.

crack (krak) *v.* To make a loud explosive sound; to break, snap, or split apart; to break without completely separating; to go at a good speed; to break with a sudden, sharp sound; to solve; to reduce petroleum compounds to simpler forms by heating. *n.* A sharp, witty remark; a weakness caused by decay or age; an attempt or try. *Slang* A highly dangerous and addictive form of cocaine.

crack down *n.* The sudden act of disciplinary actions.

crack-le (krak´el) *v.* To make sharp, sudden, repeated noises; to develop a network of fine cracks.

crack-pot (krak´pot´) *n., Slang* An eccentric person.

crack–up (krak´up´) *n.* A breakdown of a person's health, especially mental and emotional.

cra-dle (krād´el) *n.* A small bed for infants, usually on rockers or rollers.

craft (kraft) *n.* A special skill or ability; a trade that requires dexterity or artistic skill.

cram (kram) *v.* To pack tightly or stuff; to thrust in a forceful manner; to eat in a greedy fashion; to prepare hastily for an exam.

cram-bo (kram´bō) *n.* A game in which one person gives a word or a line of verse to which another finds a rhyme.

cramp (kramp) *n.* A painful involuntary contraction of a muscle; sharp abdominal pain.

cram-pon (kram´pon) *n.* A hooked apparatus used to raise objects.

cran-age (krā´nij) *v.* To load or unload goods from a ship by using a crane.

cran-dall (kran´dal) *n.* A hammer-like tool for working with soft stone.

crane (krān) *n.* A large bird with long legs and a long neck; a machine used for lifting or moving heavy objects. *v.* To strain or stretch the neck.

cranial index *n.* The ratio multiplied by 100 of the full breadth of the skull to its maximum or full length.

cranial nerve *n.* Any of the nerves that originate in the lower part of the brain and come through openings in the skull.

cra-ni-ol-o-gy (krā´nē ol´o jē) *n.* The science that deals with the size, shape, and other characteristics of human skulls.

cra-ni-um (krā´nē um) *n. pl.* **crania** The skull, especially the part in which the brain is enclosed. **cranial** *adj.*

crank (krangk) *n.* An arm bent at right angles to a shaft and turned to transmit motion; an eccentric person; a bad-tempered person; a grouch. *v.* To operate or start by crank.

crank-case (krangk´kās´) *n.* The housing of a crankshaft.

crank-shaft (krangk´shaft´) *n.* A shaft propelled by a crank.

crank-y (krang´kē) *adj.* Grouchy, irritable.

cran-ny (kran´ē) *n. pl.* **-ies** A small break or crevice; an obscure nook or corner.

crap-pie (krap´ē) *n.* A small sunfish of the central parts of the United States.

craps (kraps) *v.* A gambling game played with two dice.

crap-shoot-er (krap´shö´tēr) *n.* A person who plays craps.

crap-u-lous *adj.* Associated with drunkenness, sick from excessive consumption of liquor.

crass (kras) *adj.* Insensitive and unrefined.

crate (krāt) *n.* A container, usually made of wooden slats, for protection during ship-ping or storage. **crate** *v.*

cra-ter (krā´tēr) *n.* A bowl-shaped depression at the mouth of a volcano; a depression formed by a meteorite; a hole made by an explosion.

cra-vat (kra vat´) *n.* A necktie.

crave (krāv) *v.* To desire intensely.

cra-ven (krā´ven) *adj.* Completely lacking courage.

crav-ing (krāv ing) *n.* A great desire; an intense longing.

craw (kro) *n.* The crop of a bird; the stomach of a lower animal.

craw-fish (kro´fish´) *n.* A crayfish.

crawl (krol) *v.* To move slowly by dragging the body along the ground in a prone position; to move on hands and knees; to progress slowly.

cray-on (krā´on) *n.* A stick of white or colored chalk or wax used for writing or drawing.

craze (krāz) *v.* To make insane or as if insane; to become insane; to develop a fine mesh of narrow cracks. *n.* Something that lasts for a short period of time; a fad.

cra-zy (krā´zē) *adj.* Insane; impractical;

unusually fond. **craziness** n.

crazy bone n. The elbow; the funny bone.

crazy quilt n. A patch quilt without a particular pattern.

creak (krēk) v. A squeaking or grating noise. **creaky** adj. **creakily** adv.

crease (krēs) n. A line or mark made by folding and pressing a pliable substance. **crease** v.

creas-er (krēs´ėr) n. A sewing machine attachment for creasing leather or cloth.

cre-ate (krē āt´) v. To bring something into existence; to give rise to.

cre-a-tion (krē ā´shan) n. The act of creating; something that is created; the universe.

cre-a-tive (krē ā´tiv) adj. Marked by the ability to create; inventive; imaginative. **creatively** adv. **creativeness** n.

crea-tor (krē ā´tėr) n. One that creates. **Creator.** God.

crea-ture (krē´chėr) n. Something created; a living being.

cre-dence (krēd´ens) n. Belief.

cre-den-dum (kri den´dum) n. Something to be believed; an article of faith.

cre-den-za (kri den´za) n. A buffet or sideboard, usually without legs.

cred-i-ble (kred´i bl) adj. Offering reasonable grounds for belief, confidence in truth and reliance. **credibility** n. **credibly** adv.

cred-it (kred´it) n. An amount at a person's disposal in a bank; recognition by name for a contribution; acknowledgment; recognition by a learning institution that a student has completed a requirement leading to a degree.

cred-u-lous (krej´u lus) adj. Gullible; ready to believe on slight or uncertain evidence; easily deceived. **credulously** adv. **credulousness** n.

creed (krēd) n. A brief authoritative statement of religious belief.

creek (krēk) n. A narrow stream. **up the creek** In a difficult or perplexing situation.

creel (krēl) n. A wicker basket for holding fish.

creep (krēp) v. To advance at a slow pace; to go timidly or cautiously; to grow along a surface, clinging by means of tendrils or aerial roots.

cre-mate (krē´māt) v. To reduce to ashes by burning.

cre-ma-tor (krē´ma tėr) n. A person who cremates; the furnace where bodies are cremated.

cre-o-sol (krē´o līzd´) n. A colorless oily liquid from wood tar and guaiacum resin.

cre-o-sote (krē´o sōt´) n. An oily liquid mixture obtained by distilling coal tar, used especially as a wood preservative.

crepe paper n. A decorative paper, with a puckered or wrinkled texture.

crepe rubber n. A synthetic rubber in the form of crinkled sheets used for shoe soles.

crept v. The past tense of creep.

cre-pus-cu-lar (kri pus´kū lėr) adj. Of, resembling, or relating to twilight.

cre-pus-cule (kri pus´kūl) n. Pertaining to twilight; glimmering; dusk.

cre-scen-do (kri shen´dō) adv. In music, gradually increasing in loudness.

cres-cent (kres´ent) n. The shape of the moon in its first and fourth quarters, defined with a convex and a concave edge.

cres-cive (kres´iv) adj. Increasing or growing.

cress (kres) n. Any of numerous plants with sharp-tasting edible leaves.

cres-set (kres´it) n. A lamp or fire pan mounted as a torch or carried on a pole as a lantern.

crest (krest) n. A tuft or comb on the head of a bird or animal; the top line of a mountain or hill.

crest-fall-en (krest´fo´len) adj. Dejected; discouraged; having a hanging head.

cre-ta-ceous (kri tā´shus) adj. Composed of, or having the qualities of chalk.

cre-tin (krē´tin) n. One afflicted with cretinism; a person with marked mental deficiency.

cre-tin-ism (krēt´e niz´um) n. A condition marked by physical stunting and mental deficiency.

cre-tonne (kri ton´) n. A strong cotton or linen cloth, used especially for curtains and upholstery; a cotton cloth with various textures of surface printed with pictorial and other patterns.

cre-vasse (kre vas´) n. A deep crack or crevice.

crev-ice (krev´is) n. A narrow crack.

crew (krö) n. A group of people that work together; the whole company belonging to an aircraft or ship.

crew-el (krö´el) n. Slackly twisted worsted yarn, used in embroidery.

crib (krib) n. A small bed with high sides for an infant; a feeding bin for animals.

crib-bage (krib´ij) n. A game of cards, for two, three or four players.

crib-ri-form (krib´ri form´) adj. Having the form of a sieve; pierced with many small openings.

crick (krik) n. A painful muscle spasm condition of the neck or back.

cri-er (krī´ėr) n. One who calls out public notices.

crime (krīm) n. An act or the commission of an act that is forbidden by law.

crim-i-nal (krim´i nal) adj. Relating to a crime. n. A person who commits a crime.

criminal law n. The law of crimes and punishment.

crim-i-nate (krim´i nāt´) v. To involve in a crime.

crim-i-nol-o-gy (krim´i nol´o jē) n. Scientific study of crime.

crimp (krimp) v. To cause to become bent or crinkled; to pinch in or together.

crim-son (krim´zon) n. A deep purplish color. v. To make or become crimson.

cringe (krinj) v. To shrink or recoil in fear.

crin-kle (kring´kl) v. To wrinkle. **crinkle** n. **crinkly** adj.

crin-o-line (krin´o lin) n. An open-weave fabric used for lining and stiffening garments.

cri-o-sphinx (krī´o sfingks´) n. A sphinx with the head of a ram.

crip-ple (krip´l) n. One who is lame or partially disabled; something flawed or imperfect. adj. Being a cripple. v. To deprive one of the use of a limb or limbs.

cri-sis (krī´sis) n. pl. **crises** An unstable or uncertain time or state of affairs, the outcome of which will have a major impact; the turning point for better or worse in a disease or fever, hectic situation.

crisp (krisp) adj. Easily broken; brittle; brisk or cold; sharp; clear. v. To make or become crisp. **crisply** adv. **-ness** n.

cri-te-ri-on (krī tēr´ē on) n. pl. **criteria** A standard by which something can be judged.

crit-ic (krit´ik) n. A person who is critical; a person who examines a subject and expresses an opinion as to its value; a person who judges or evaluates art or artistic creations, as a theatre critic.

crit-i-cal (krit´i kal) adj. Very important, as a critical decision; tending to criticize harshly. **critically** adv.

crit-i-cism (krit´i siz´um) n. The act of criticizing, usually in a severe or negative fashion.

crit-i-cize (krit´i sīz´) v. To be a critic; to find fault with; to judge critically; to blame.

cri-tique (kri tēk´) n. A written estimate of the merits of a performance.

croak (krōk) n. A hoarse, raspy cry such as that made by a frog. v. To utter a croak. Slang To die.

cro-chet (krō shā´) n. The needlework achieved by looping thread with a hooked needle.

crock (krok) n. An earthenware pot or jar most often used for cooking or storing food.

crock-et (krok´it) n. An ornament in the form of curved and bent foliage.

croc-o-dile (krok´o dīl´) n. Any of various large, thick-skinned, long-bodied reptiles of tropical and subtropical regions.

crocodile tears n. Insincere or false grief.

cro-cus (krō´kus) n. pl. **crocuses** A plant having solitary, long-tubed flowers and slender, linear leaves.

croft (kroft) n. A small piece of ground or farm worked by the tenant who lives on the property.

crois-sant (krwä sän´) n. A crescent-shaped roll of flaky bread dough.

crone (krōn) n. A witch-like, withered old woman.

cro-ny (krō´nē) n. pl. **cronies** A close friend.

crook (kruk) n. A bent or hooked implement; a bend or curve; a person given to dishonest acts. **crook** v. To bend or curve.

crook-ed (kruk´id) adj. Dishonest; bent; not straight; deformed.

croon (krōn) v. To sing in a gentle, low voice; to make a continued moaning sound.

crop (krop) n. A plant which is grown and then harvested for use or for sale; a riding whip. v. To cut off short; to appear unexpectedly.

cro-quet (krō kā´) n. An outdoor game played by driving wooden balls through hoops with long-handled mallets.

cro-quette (krō ket´) n. A small patty or roll of minced food that is breaded and deep fried.

cro-qui-gnole (krō´ki nōl) n. A method of styling the hair by winding the hair toward the head on curlers, in a circular style.

cross-current (kros´kèr´ent) n. A current flowing against another; a conflicting tendency.

crotch (kroch) n. The angle formed by the junction of two parts, such as branches, part of the human body where the legs join, a pair of pants where the legs meet. **crotched** adj.

crotch-et (kroch´it) n. A peculiar opinion or preference.

crouch (krouch) v. To bend at the knees and lower the body close to the ground.

croup (krōp) n. A spasmodic laryngitis, especially of children, marked by a loud, harsh cough and difficulty in breathing. **croupy** adj.

crou-pi-er (krō´pē ér) n. One who collects and pays bets at a gambling table.

crous-tade (krō städ´) n. A crisp shell, either fried or baked, in which to serve foods.

crou-ton (krō´ton) n. A small piece of toasted or fried bread.

crow (krō) n. A large, black bird. **crow** v. To brag; to boast.

crow-bar (krō´bär) n. A steel or iron bar with a forked end, used as a lever.

crowd (kroud) n. A large group of people gathered together. v. To assemble in large numbers; to press close.

cru-cial (krō´shal) *adj.* Extremely important; critical.

cru-ci-ble (krō´si bl) *n.* A vessel used for melting and calcining materials at high temperatures; a severe or hard test of someone.

cru-ci-fy (krō´si fī´) *v.* To put to death by nailing to a cross; to treat cruelly; to torment.

crude (krōd) *adj.* Unrefined; lacking refinement or tact; haphazardly made. *n.* Unrefined petroleum. **crudely** *adv.*

cruel (krō´el) *adj.* Inflicting suffering; causing pain. **cruelly** *adv.* **cruelty** *n.*

cru-et (krō´it) *n.* A small glass bottle normally used as a container for oil or vinegar.

cruise (krōz) *v.* To drive or sail about for pleasure; to move about the streets at leisure; to travel at a speed that provides maximum efficiency.

crul-ler (krul´er) *n.* A light, sweet cake cut in a twisted circular form and fried in deep fat.

crumb (krum) *n.* A small fragment of material, particularly bread.

crum-ble (krum´bl) *v.* To break into small pieces. **crumbly** *adj.*

crump (krump) *v.* To crunch with the teeth. *n.* A crunching sound

crum-ple (krum´pel) *v.* To bend or crush out of shape; to cause to collapse; to be crumpled.

crunch (krunch) *v.* To chew with a crackling noise; to run, walk, etc., with a crushing noise. **crunch** *n.*

cru-ral (krūr´al) *adj.* Pertaining to the thigh or leg.

crus (krus) *n.* The part of the leg or hind limb between the femur or thigh and the ankle.

cru-sade (krō sād´) *n.* Any of the military expeditions undertaken by Christian leaders during the 11th, 12th, and 13th centuries to recover the Holy Land from the Moslems. **crusade** *v.*

crush (krush) *v.* To squeeze or force by pressure so as to damage or injure.

crust (krust) *n.* The hardened exterior or surface of bread; a hard or brittle surface layer.

crus-ta-cean (kru stā´shan) *n.* Any one of a large class of aquatic arthropods, including lobsters and crabs, with a segmented body and paired, jointed limbs.

crutch (kruch) *n.* A support usually designed to fit in the armpit and to be used as an aid in walking; any support or prop.

crux (kruks) *n.* An essential or vital moment; a main or central feature.

cry (krī) *v.* To shed tears; to call out loudly; to utter a characteristic call or sound; to proclaim publicly.

cry-o-gen (krī´ō jen) *n.* A substance for producing or obtaining low temperatures.

cry-o-lite *n.* A fluoride of sodium-aluminum and used to make aluminum and soda.

cry-om-e-ter (krī om´i ter) *n.* A thermometer for measuring low temperatures.

cry-o-phyte (krī´ō fīt) *n.*, *Bot.* A plant that grows on snow and ice, usually an alga, but sometimes a moss, or fungus.

crypt (kript) *n.* An underground chamber or vault primarily used to bury the dead.

crypt-a-nal-y-sis (krip´ta nal´i sis) *n.* The study of solving written codes or ciphers.

cryp-tic (krip´tik) *adj.* Intended to be obscure; serving to conceal.

cryp-tog-ra-phy (krip tog´ra fē) *n.* The writing and deciphering of messages in secret code. **cryptographer** *n.*

crys-tal (kris´tal) *n.* Quartz that is transparent or nearly transparent; a body that is formed by the solidification of a chemical element; a clear, high-quality glass. **crystalline** *adj.*

crystal ball *n.* A glass globe foretell the future.

crys-tal-lize (kris´ta līz´) *v.* To cause to form crystals or assume crystalline form; to cause to take a definite form; to coat with crystals, especially sugar crystals.

cten-o-phore (ten´o fōr´) *n.* Any of the free-swimming aquatic animals.

cub (kub) *n.* The young of the lion, wolf, or bear; an awkward child or youth.

cu-ba-ture (kū´ba cher) *n.* The determination of the cubic contents.

cub-by-hole (kub´e hōl´) *n.* A small enclosed area.

cube (kūb) *n.* A regular solid with six equal squares, having all its angles right angles.

cu-beb (kū´beb) *n.* The spicy fruit or dried unripe berry of an East Indian climbing shrub of the pepper family.

cube root *n.* A number whose cube is a given number.

cubic (kū´bik) *adj.* Having the shape of a cube; having three dimensions; having the volume of a cube with the edges of a specified unit.

cu-bi-cle (kū´bi kl) *n.* A small partitioned area.

cu-bit (kū´bit) *n.* An ancient unit of measurement that equals approximately eighteen to twenty inches.

cu-cu-li-form (kū kū´li form) *adj.* Pertaining to birds, which includes road runners and cuckoos.

cu-cum-ber (kū´kum ber) *n.* A fruit with a green rind and white, seedy flesh.

cu-cur-bit (kū kėr´bit) *n.* A plant from the gourd family.

cud (kud) *n.* Food forced up into the mouth of a ruminating animal from the first stomach and chewed again.

cud-dle (kud´l) *v.* To caress fondly and hold close; to snuggle. **cuddle** *n.*

cudg-el (kuj´el) *n.* A short, thick stick; a heavy club.

cue (kū) *n.* A signal given to an actor or someone making a speech, letting him know it is his turn; a long rod for playing pool and billiards.

cues-ta (kwes´ta) *n.* A hill with a gradual incline on one face and a steep incline on the other.

cuff (kuf) *n.* The lower part of a sleeve; the part of the pant legs which is turned up. *v.* To strike someone.

cuffs (kufs) *n.* Handcuffs.

cui-rass (kwi ras´) *n.* A piece of armor for the breast and back, used for protection.

cui-sine (kwi zēn´) *n.* A style of cooking and preparing food; the food prepared.

cu-let (kū´lit) *n.* The small flat facet forming the bottom of a gem.

cu-lex (kū´leks) *n.* A large group of mosquitoes found in North America and Europe.

cu-li-nar-y (kū´li ner´ē) *adj.* Relating to cooking.

cull (kul) *v.* To select the best from a group, to gather only the best.

culm (kulm) *n.* Coal dust or refuse coal; slack.

cul-mi-nate (kul´mi nāt´) *v.* To reach or rise to the highest point. **culmination** *n.*

cu-lotte (kö lot´) *n.* A woman's full pants made to look like a skirt.

cul-pa-ble (kul´pa bl) *adj.* Meriting blame. **culpability** *n.*

cul-prit (kul´prit) *n.* A person guilty of a crime.

cult (kult) *n.* A group or system of religious worship. **cultic** *adj.*

cul-ti-vate (kul´ti vāt´) *v.* To improve land for planting by fertilizing and plowing; to improve by study; to encourage. **cultivatable** *adj.* **cultivation** *n.* **cultivator** *n.*

cul-ture (kul´chėr) *n.* The act of developing intellectual ability with education; a form of civilization, particularly the beliefs, arts, and customs. *Biol.* The growth of living material in a prepared nutrient media. **culture** *v.*

cul-vert (kul´vėrt) *n.* A drain that runs under a road or railroad.

cum-ber (kum´bėr) *v.* To burden someone.

cum-ber-some (kum´bėr sum) *adj.* Clumsy; awkward. **cumbersomely** *adv.* **cumbersomeness** *n.*

cum-in (kum´im) *n.* A small plant of the parsley family cultivated for its aromatic.

cum-mer-bund (kum´ėr bund´) *n.* A wide sash worn by men in formal attire.

cu-mu-late (kū´mū lāt´) *v.* To heap or build up; amass; accumulate.

cu-mu-la-tive (kū´mū lā´tiv) *adj.* Increasing by successive additions.

cu-mu-lus (kū´mū lus) *n. pl.* **cumuli** A white, fluffy cloud with a rounded top and a flat base.

cu-ne-ate (kū´nē it) *adj.* Narrowly triangular and tapering to a point at the base.

cu-ne-i-form (kū nē´i form´) *n.* Wedge-shaped characters used in ancient Babylonian, Assyrian, and Sumerian writing.

cun-ning (kun´ing) *adj.* Crafty; sly.

cup (kup) *n.* A small, open container with a handle, used for drinking; a measure of capacity that equals 1/2 pint, 8 ounces, or 16 tablespoons.

cu-pel (kū´pel) *n.* A small, cup-like porous vessel, usually made of bone ash, used in assaying, to separate gold and silver from lead.

cu-pid-ity (kū pid´i tē) *n.* An excessive desire for material gain.

cu-po-la (kū´po la) *n.* A rounded roof; a small vaulted structure that usually rises above a roof.

cu-pre-ous (kū´prē us) *adj.* Consisting of copper.

cur (kėr) *n.* A mongrel; a dog of mixed breeds.

cu-rate (kūr´it) *n.* A member of the clergy that assists the priest.

cu-ra-tor (kū ra´tėr) *n.* A person in charge of a museum.

curb (kėrb) *n.* Something that restrains or controls; the raised border along the edge of a street. **curb** *v.*

curd (kėrd) *n.* The coagulated portion of milk used for making cheese.

cure (kėr) *n.* Recovery from a sickness; a medical treatment; the process of preserving food with the use of salt, smoke, or aging.

cur-few (kėr´fū) *n.* An order for people to clear the streets at a certain hour; the hour at which an adolescent has been told to be home by his or her parents.

cu-ri-o (kūr´ē ō´) *n.* An unusual or rare object.

cu-ri-o-sa (kūr´ē ō´sa) *n.* Books written on unusual or erotic subjects.

cu-ri-os-i-ty (kūrē os´i tē) *n.* The strong desire to know something; something that arouses interest.

cu-ri-ous (kūr´ē us) *adj.* Questioning; inquisitive; eager for information. **curious-ity** *n.* **curiously** *adv.*

cu-ri-um (kūr´ē um) *n.* An artificially

produced radioactive trivalent element.

curl (kürl) v. To twist into curves; shape like a coil. n. A ringlet of hair. **curler** n. **curliness** n. **curly** adj.

cur-lew (kür´lö) n. A migratory bird with long legs and a long slender curved bill.

cur-mudg-eon (kèr muj´on) n. An ill-tempered person.

curn (kürn) n. A grain; a small quantity.

cur-rant (kür´ant) n. A small seedless raisin.

cur-ren-cy (kür´en sē) n. pl. **currencies** Money in circulation.

cur-rent (kür´ent) adj. Belonging or occurring in the present time. n. Water or air that has a steady flow in a definite direction. **currently** adv.

current assets n. The assets of a company that can be readily converted to cash.

current liabilities n. Debts of a business or corporation.

cur-ri-cle (kèr´i kl) n. A two-wheeled carriage, drawn by two horses.

cur-ric-u-lum (ku rik´ū lum) n. pl. -la, -lums The courses offered in a school.

curse (kürs) n. A prayer or wish for harm to come to someone or something. **cursed** adj. **curse** v.

cur-sive (kèr´siv) n. A flowing writing in which the letters are joined together.

cur-sor (kür´sor) n. In computer science, the flashing square, underline, or other indicator on the CRT screen of a computer that shows where the next character will be deleted or inserted.

cur-so-ry (kür´so rē) adj. Rapidly done, often without care and not paying attention to details.

curt (kèrt) adj. Abrupt; rude, as in manner or speech. **curtly** adv.

cur-tail (kèr´tāl´) v. To shorten.

cur-tain (kür´tan) n. A piece of material that covers a window and can be either drawn to the sides or raised.

cur-tate (kür´tāt) adj. Shortened or reduced; abbreviated.

cur-ti-lage (kür´ti lij) n. The piece of land occupied by a house and its yard.

curt-sy (kürt´sē) n. pl -sies A respectful gesture made by bending the knees and lowering the body. **curtsy** v.

curve (kürv) v. A continuously curved line without angles.

cush-ion (küsh´on) n. A pillow with a soft filling. v. To absorb the shock or effect.

cus-pid (kus´pid) n. A pointed canine tooth, cuspidate tooth.

cus-pi-dor (kus´pi dor´) n. A spittoon.

cuss (kus) v. To use profanity.

cus-tard (kus´tèrd) n. A mixture of milk, eggs, sugar, and flavoring that is baked.

cus-to-dy (kus´to dē) n. pl. -dies The act of guarding; the care and protection of a minor.

cus-tom (kus´tom) n. An accepted practice of a community or people; the usual manner of doing something. **customs** The tax one must pay on imported goods. **customary** adj.

cut (kut) v. To penetrate with a sharp edge, as with a knife; to omit or leave something out; to reap or harvest crops in the fields. Slang To cut class; to share in the profits.

cute (küt) adj. Attractive in a delightful way.

cu-vette (kö vet´) n. A small vessel or tube used in a laboratory.

cy-cla-mate (sī´kle māt) n. A sweetener used as a substitute for sugar, based on salts of calcium or sodium.

cyc-la-men (sik´la men) n. A plant with red, white, or pink flowers.

cy-cle (sī´kl) n. A recurring time in which an event occurs repeatedly; a bicycle or motorcycle. **cyclical** adj.

cy-clist (sī´klist) n. A person who rides a cycle.

cy-clone (sī´klōn) n. A storm with wind rotating about a low pressure center, accompanied by destructive weather.

cy-clo-tron (sī´klo tron´) n. Machine that obtains high-energy electrified particles by whirling at a high speed in a strong magnetic field.

cyg-net (sig´nit) n. A young swan.

cyl-in-der (sil´in dèr) n. A long, round body that is either hollow or solid.

cym-bal (sim´bal) n. A pair of brass plates which produce a clashing tone when struck together.

cyn-ic (sin´ik) n. One who believes that all people have selfish motives. **cynical** adj. **cynicism** n.

cy-no-sure (sī´no shör´) n. A person or object that attracts admiration and interest.

cyst (sist) n. An abnormal sac or vesicle which may collect and retain fluid.

cystic fibrosis n. A congenital disease, that usually develops in childhood and results in disorders of the lungs and pancreas.

cys-ti-tis (si stī´tis) n. An inflammation of the bladder.

cy-to-gen-e-sis (sī´to jen´i sis) n. The origin, development, and changes of cells in animal and vegetable structures.

cy-tol-o-gy (sī tol´o jē) n. The scientific study of cell formation, function, and structure, life cycle of a cell. **cytological** adj. **cytologic** adj. **cytologist** n.

cy-tol-y-sis (sī tol´i sis) n. The degeneration of cells.

cy-to-plasm (sīto plaz´um) n. The living substance or protoplasm of a cell external to the nuclear membrane.

czar (zär) n. An emperor or king or one of the former emperors or kings of Russia. Slang One who has authority.

D, d (dē) The fourth letter of the English alphabet; the Roman numeral for 500.

dab (dab) v. To touch quickly with light, short strokes. **dab** n.

dab-ble (dab´l) v. To play in a liquid, as water, with the hands; to work in or play with in a minor way.

dace (dās) n. A small freshwater fish.

dachs-hund (daks´heud˝) n. A small dog with very short legs, drooping ears, and a long body.

dac-ty-lol-o-gy (dak˝ti lol´o jē) n. The art of communicating thoughts or ideas by using the hands and fingers; the language of the deaf.

dad (dad) n., pl. **dads** Father.

dae-dal (dēd´al) adj. Having and showing artistic skill.

daf-fo-dil (daf´o dil) n. A bulbous plant with solitary yellow flowers.

daft (daft) adj. Insane; crazy, or mad; foolish. **daftly** adv. **daftness** n.

da-guerre-o-type (da ger´o tīp´) n. A very early photographic process which used silver-coated metallic plates that were sensitive to light.

dah (dä) n. The dash used in the code of telegraphy or radio, represented by a tone interval approximately three times as long as the dot.

dai-ly (dā´lē) adj. To occur, appear, or happen every day of the week. **daily** n. A newspaper which is published daily.

dain-ty (dān´tē) adj. Having or showing refined taste; delicately beautiful. **daintily** adv. **daintiness** n.

dai-qui-ri (dī´ki rē) n. A cocktail made with rum and lime juice.

dair-y (dâr´ē) n., pl. **dairies** A commercial establishment which processes milk for resale.

dale (dāl) n. A small valley.

dal-ly (dal´ē) v. To waste time; to dawdle; to flirt. **dallier** n. **dalliance** n.

dal-ton-ism (dal´to niz˝um) n. Color blindness; unable to differentiate between red and green.

dam (dam) n. A barrier constructed for controlling or raising the level of water; female animal who has had offspring.

dam-age (dam´ij) n. An injury to person or property; in law, the compensation given for loss or injury. **damage** v. **damageable** adj. **damagingly** adv.

dam-an (dam´an) n. A small, rabbit-like animal.

dam-a-scene (dam´a sēn˝) v. To form designs in metal, by inlaying with gold or other precious metals, or by etching.

dam-ask (dam´ask) n. An elaborately patterned, reversible fabric, originally made of silk.

dame (dām) n. A mature woman or matron. *Slang* A woman. **Dame** *Brit.* A title given to a woman, the female equivalent of a British Lord.

dam-mar (dam´ér) n. A resin from various coniferous trees which is used for making colorless varnish.

damp (damp) adj. Between dry and wet; of or relating to poisonous gas or foul air found in a mine. **dampish** adj.

dam-sel (dam´zel) n. A maiden; a young unmarried woman.

dance (dans) v. To move rhythmically to music using improvised or planned steps and gestures. **dancer** n.

dan-dle (dan´dl) v. To move a child or infant up and down on the knees or in the arms with a gentle movement.

dan-ger (dān´jér) n. An exposure to injury, evil, or loss.

dan-ger-ous (dān´jér us) adj. Unsafe. **dangerously** adv. **dangerousness** n.

dan-gle (dang´gl) v. To hang loosely and swing to and fro; to have an unclear grammatical relation in a sentence.

dank (dangk) adj. Uncomfortably damp; wet and cold. **-ly** adv. **dankness** n.

dan-seuse (dän soez˝) n., pl. **danseuses** A female ballet dancer.

dap-per (dap´ér) adj. Stylishly dressed.

dap-ple (dap´l) v. To make variegated or spotted in color.

dar-by (där´bē) n. A tool for leveling a plaster surface.

dare (dâr) v. To have the boldness or courage to undertake an adventure; to challenge a person as to show proof of courage. **dare** n. **daring** adj.

dark (därk) adj. Dim; to have little or no light; to be difficult to comprehend; of a deep shade of color, as black or almost black. **in the dark** Done in secret; in a state of ignorance. **-ly** adv.

Dark Ages n. The early part of the Middle Ages from about 476 to 1000 A.D.

dar-kle (där´kl) v. To darken or grow dark.

dar-ling (där´ling) n. A favorite person; someone who is very dear; a person tenderly loved. **darlingly** adv.

darn (därn) v. To mend a hole by filling the gap with interlacing stitches.

dart (därt) n. A pointed missile either shot or thrown. **darts** pl. The game of throwing darts at a usually round target.

dash (dash) n. A punctuation mark setting apart a separate thought or dividing a compound word. v. To break or shatter with a striking violent blow; to move quickly; to rush; to finish or perform a duty in haste. **dasher** n.

das-tard (das´térd) n. A coward; a sneak. **dastardliness** n. **dastardly** adj.

da-ta (dā´ta) n., pl. of datum Figures or facts from which conclusions may be drawn. In *computer science,* information processed by the computer.

data bank n. In *computer science,* the

location in a computer where information is stored.

database *n*. In *computer science*, a collection of related information.

database file *n*. In *computer science*, a file comprised of records of information in distinct, related fields.

data block *n*. In *computer science*, a selection of data based on a specific search criterion.

data conversion *n*. In *computer science*, an altering of selected data for transfer to a different program or format, as from a database file to a spreadsheet file.

data entry *n*. In *computer science*, the recording or updating of information in a computer file.

data field *n*. In *computer science*, any of the areas in a database dedicated to a particular item of information, as a date or name.

data format *n*. In *computer science*, the type of data acceptable in a particular field, as date, number, or alphameric.

data link *n*. In *computer science*, a connection between computer systems that allow information sharing; a validation formula in a spreadsheet or database that limits entry of data into cell or field base on a previous entry; a link between documents containing similar information that automatically updates all documents when one is changed.

data management *n*. In *computer science*, the process of recording and manipulating data in the conduct of a business.

data parsing *n*. In *computer science*, breaking a data string down to its basic elements for conversion to another file format, as from database fields to spreadsheet cells.

data processing *n*. In *computer science*, the business of handling and storing information using computer hardware and software.

data record *n*. In *computer science*, the set of fields that compromise a unique entry in a database file.

data transmission *n*. In *computer science*, the transfer of information through a computer system or between computer systems.

date (dāt) *n*. A particular point in time; a day, month, or year; the exact time at which something happens; a social engagement; a person's partner on such an occasion.

date-line (dāt´līn´) *n*. The line or phrase at the beginning of a periodical giving the date and place of publication; **date** line the 180th meridian on a map or globe which is where a day begins.

date number *n*. In *computer science*, the

numeric value for a specific date, as by the number of the day, month, and year or the number of days from a base date.

date palm *n*. A palm that bears dates.

da-tum (dā´tum) *n*., *pl*. **data** A single piece of information.

daub (dob) *v*. To coat or smear with grease, plaster, or an adhesive substance; to defile; to put on without taste. **dauber** *n*.

daugh-ter (do´tĕr) *n*. The female offspring of a man or woman; a female descendant of any age. **daughterly** *adj*.

daughter–in–law *n*. A son's wife.

daunt (dont) *v*. To intimidate or discourage.

dav-en-port (dav´en pōrt´) *n*. A large sofa or couch.

dav-it (dav´it) *n*. A small crane on the side of a ship, for lifting its boats.

da-vy (dā´vē) *n*. A miner's lamp.

daw-dle (dod´l) *v*. To waste time; to take more time than is needed. **dawdler** *n*.

dawn (don) *n*. The beginning of a new day; to begin to understand, expand, or develop; to grow lighter. **-ing** *n*.

day (dā) *n*. The period of time that falls between dawn and nightfall; the time that is represented by one rotation of the earth upon its axis, twenty-four hours; the large portion of a day spent in a particular way.

day-care (dā´ kâr) *n*. A service provided for working mothers and fathers, offering daytime supervision, training, and safekeeping for their children while they work.

Day of Atonement *n*. Yom Kippur.

daze (dāz) *v*. To bewilder or stun with a heavy blow or shock. **dazedly** *adv*.

DCA *abbr*. In *computer science*, Document Content Architecture; a word processing file format.

dea-con (dē´kon) *n*. The clergy person who ranks immediately below a priest. **deaconry** *n*. **deaconship** *n*.

de-ac-ti-vate (dē ak´ti vāt´) *v*. To cause to become inactive.

dead (ded) *adj*. Without life; no longer in existence or use; dormant; quiet; in law, no longer in force.

deaf (def) *adj*. Totally or partially unable to hear; refusing or unwilling to listen.

deal (dēl) *v*. To distribute or pass out playing cards; to be occupied or concerned with a certain matter; to discuss, consider, or take affirmative action. *n*. An indefinite amount; a business transaction. **dealer** *n*.

dean (dēn) *n*. The head administrator of a college, high school, or university supervising students. **deanship** *n*.

dear (dēr) *adj*. Greatly cherished; loved. **dearly** *adv*. **dearness** *n*.

death (deth) *n*. Termination; permanent

cessation of all vital functions.

deb (deb) *n.* A debutante.

de-ba-cle (dā bä´kl) *n.* A sudden downfall, failure, or collapse.

de-bar (di bär´) *v.* To bar from a place; to preclude; to prohibit.

de-bark (di bärk´) *v.* To disembark.

de-base (di bās´) *v.* To lower in character or value; demean. **debasement** *n.*

de-bate (di bāt´) *v.* To discuss or argue opposing points; to consider; to deliberate. **debate** *n.* **debatable** *adj.* **debatably** *adv.* **debater** *n.*

de-bauch (di boch´) *v.* To lead away from morality; to corrupt or pervert **de-bauchery** *n.* **debauchment** *n.*

de-bauch-er-y *n.* The excessive indulgence in sensual pleasures.

de-ben-ture (di ben´chér) *n.* A voucher given as an acknowledgment of debt.

de-bil-i-tate (di bil´i tāt´) *v.* To make feeble or weak. **debilitation** *n.*

deb-it (deb´it) *n.* A debt or item recorded in an account *v.* To enter a debt in a ledger; to charge someone with a debt.

deb-o-nair (deb´o nâr´) *adj.* Characterized by courtesy and charm.

dé-bride-ment (di brēd´ment) *n.* Removal of contaminated tissue from a wound in order to prevent the spread of infection.

de-brief (dē brēf´) *v.* To interrogate or question in order to obtain information.

de-bris (de brē´) *n.* Scattered or discarded remains or waste.

debt (det) *n.* That which someone owes, as money, services, or goods; an obligation to pay or render something to another.

debt-or (det´ér) *n.* A person owing a debt to another.

de-bug (dē bug´) *v.* To find and remove a concealed electronic listening device; in computer science, to remove errors in a computer program. In *computer science*, to find and correct errors in a computer program or the operation of a piece of equipment.

de-bunk (di bungk´) *v.* To expose false pretensions, to show the error in false opinions, statements or claims.

de-but (dā bū´) *n.* A first public appearance; the formal introduction to society; the beginning of a new career. **debut** *v.*

deb-u-tante (deb´ū tänt´) *n.* A young woman making her debut in society.

dec-ade (dek´ād) *n.* A period of ten years; a set or group of ten.

de-ca-dence (dek´a dens) *n.* A process of decay or deterioration; a period or condition of decline, as in morals.

dec-a-dent (dek´a dent) *adj.* Deteriorating; being in a state of decline. *n.* One who is decadent.

dec-a-gon (dek´a gon´) *n. Geom.* A polygon with ten sides and ten angles. **decagonal** *adj.* **decagonally** *adv.*

dec-a-gram *or* **dek-a- gram** (dek´a gram´) *n.* In the metric system, a measure of weight equal to 10 grams.

de-cal (dē´kal) *n.* A design or picture transferred by decalcomania.

de-cal-co-ma-nia (di kal´ko mā´nē a) *n.* The process of transferring pictures or designs printed on special paper to glass, wood, and other materials.

dec-a-li-ter *or* **dek-a-li-ter** (dek´a lē´tèr) *n.* In the metric system, a measure of capacity equal to 10 liters.

dec-a-logue *or* **dec-a-log** (dek´a log´) *n.* The Ten Commandments.

dec-a-me-ter *or* **dek-a-me-ter** (dek´a mē´tèr) *n.* In the metric system, a measure of length equal to 10 meters.

de-cam-e-ter (dē kam´ét ėr) *n.* A line of verse or consisting of ten metrical feet.

de-camp (di kamp´) *v.* To break camp; to leave or depart suddenly.

de-cant (di cant´) *v.* To pour off liquid with-out disturbing the sediments; to pour from one container to another.

de-cap-i-tate (di kap´i tāt´) *v.* To cut off the head; to behead **decapitation** *n.*

de-car-bon-ize (dē kär´bo nīz) *v.* To remove carbon from a substance or motor.

de-cath-lon (di kath´lon) *n.* An athletic event with ten different track and field events in all of which each contestant participates; an Olympic event.

de-cay (di kā´) *v.* To decline in quantity or quality; to rot. *Phys.* To diminish or disintegrate by radioactive decomposition.

de-cease (di sēs´) *v.* To die; to reach life's end.

de-ceit (di sēt´) *n.* Deception; falseness; the quality of being deceptive; concealment. **deceitful** *adj.* **-fully** *adv.*

de-ceive (di sēv´) *v.* To mislead by falsehood; to lead into error; to delude. **deceivable** *adj.* **deceiver** *n.*

de-cel-er-ate (dē sel´e rāt) *n.* To decrease in velocity. **deceleration** *n.*

De-cem-ber (di sem´bér) *n.* The twelfth month of the year, having 31 days.

de-cen-ni-al (di sen´ē al) *adj.* Happening once every 10 years; continuing for ten years. **decennially** *adv.*

de-cent (dē´sent) *adj.* Adequate; satisfactory; kind; generous; characterized by propriety of conduct, speech, or dress; respectable. *Informal* Properly or adequately clothed; respectable. **decently** *adv.* **-ness** *n.*

de-cen-tral-ize (dē sen´tra līz´) *v.* To divide the administrative functions of a central authority among several local authorities; to reorganize into smaller and more dispersed parts. **-ation** *n.*

de-cep-tion (di sep´shən) *n.* The act of deceiving; the fact or state of being deceived; anything which deceives or deludes.

de-cep-tive (di sep´tiv) *adj.* Having the tendency or power to deceive. **deceptively** *adv.* **deceptiveness** *n.*

dec-i-are (des´ē âr´) *n.* In the metric system, ten square meters.

de-ci-bel (des´i bl´) *n.* A measurement of sound; one tenth of a bel.

de-cide (di sīd´) *v.* To settle; to determine, as a controversy or contest; to determine the conclusion or issue of; to make up one's mind. **decider** *n.*

de-cid-ed *adj.* Definite or unquestionable; exhibiting determination, resolute. **decidedly** *adv.* **decidedness** *n.*

de-cid-u-ous (di sij´ŏ us) *adj.* *Biol.* Shedding or falling off at maturity or at a certain season, such as fruit, leaves, petals, antlers, or snake skins.

dec-i-gram (des´i gram´) *n.* In the metric system, the tenth part of a gram.

dec-i-li-ter (des´i lē´tēr) *n.* In the metric system, the tenth part of a liter.

de-cil-lion (di sil´yon) *n.* In the U.S., the cardinal number written as one followed by thirty-three zeros.

dec-i-mal (des´i mal) *n.* A proper fraction based on the number 10 and indicated by the use of a decimal point; every decimal place indicating a multiple of a power of 10; a number with a decimal point; a decimal fraction or one of its digits.

decimal number In *computer science,* a value represented in a base 10.

decimal point *n.* A period placed to the left of a decimal fraction.

dec-i-mate (des´i māt´) *v.* To destroy or kill a large proportion of something; to select by lot and kill one out of every ten. **decimation** *n.*

dec-i-meter (des´i mē´tēr) *n.* In the metric system, the tenth part of a meter.

de-ci-pher (di sī´fēr) *v.* To determine the meaning of something obscure, as a poor handwriting; to translate from code or cipher into plain text; to decode.

de-ci-sion (di sizh´an) *n.* The act of deciding; a judgment or conclusion reached by deciding.

de-ci-sive (di sī´siv) *adj.* Ending uncertainty or dispute; conclusive; characterized by firmness; unquestionable; unmistakable. **decisively** *adv.*

dec-i-stere (des´i stēr´) *n.* In the metric system, a cubic decimeter, or the tenth part of a stere.

de-claim (di klām´) *v.* To speak or deliver loudly and rhetorically; to give a formal speech; to attack verbally. **declamation** *n.* **declamatory** *adj.*

de-clar-ant (di klâr´ant) *n.* One who makes a declaration.

de-clare (di klâr´) *v.* To make known or clear; to state formally or officially; to say emphatically; to avow; to assert; to make full claim to, as goods liable to duty; to proclaim an opinion or choice for or against something. **declarer, declaration** *n.*

de-class (dē klas´) *v.* To remove from one's class; to lose standing.

de-clas-si-fy (dē klas´i fī´) *v.* To remove the security classification of a document, information considered important to national security of a nation. **declassification** *n.*

de-clen-sion (di klen´shan) *n.* A descent; a sloping downward; a decline; a deviation, as from a belief. *Gram.* The inflection of nouns, pronouns, and adjectives according to case, number, and gender **declensional** *adj.*

dec-li-nate (dek´li nāt´) *adj.* Bending downward.

dec-li-na-tion (dek´li nā´shan) *n.* The act of bending downward or inclining; deviation, as in conduct or direction; the angle formed between the direction of a compass needle and the true north; a polite refusal.

de-cline (di klīn´) *v.* To reject or refuse something; to grow frail gradually, as in health; to bend or incline to the side or downward; to refuse politely. *Gram.* To give the inflected forms of a noun, pronoun, or adjective. **decline** *n.* The act or result of deterioration, a decline in heath. **declinable** *adj.* **declination** *n.* **decliner** *n.*

de-cliv-i-ty (di klīv´i tē) *n., pl.* **declivities** A steep downward slope or surface. **declivitous** *adj.*

de-coct (di kokt´) *v.* To extract by boiling; to condense. **decoction** *n.*

de-code (dē kōd´) *v.* To convert from a coded message into plain language. **decoder** *n.*

de-col-or-a-tion (dē kul´ér ā´shan) *n.* The removal or loss of color.

de-com-pen-sa-tion (dē´kom pen sā´shan) *n.* The inability of the heart to sustain a constant heart beat.

de-com-pose (dē´kom pōz´) *v.* To decay; to separate into constituent parts. **decomposable** *adj.* **decomposer** *n.*

de-com-pound (dē´kom pound´) *adj.* Having compound parts.

de-com-press (dē´kom pres´) *v.* To relieve of pressure; to bring persons back to normal air pressure, as divers or caisson workers or high-altitude flyers.

de-con-ges-tant (dē´kon jes tant´) *n.* An agent that relieves congestion.

de-con-tam-i-nate (dē´kon tam´i nāt) *v.* To make free of contamination by destroying or neutralizing poisonous chemicals, radioactivity, or other harmful elements. **decontamination** *n*. **decontaminator** *n*.

de-con-trol (dē´kon trōl´) *v*. To free from the control of, especially from governmental control.

de-cor (dā kor´) *n*. The style of decorating a room, office, or home.

dec-o-rate (dek´o rāt´) *v*. To adorn or furnish with fashionable or beautiful things; to confer a decoration or medal upon. **decorator** *n*.

dec-o-rous (dek´ér us) *adj*. Marked by decorum; seemly; proper, as dress or speech. **decorously** *adv*. **-ness** *n*.

de-cor-ti-cate (dē kor´ti kāt´) *v*. To strip or remove the bark; to peel.

de-co-rum (di kōr´um) *n*. Proper behavior; good or fitting conduct.

de-crease (di krēs´) *v*. To grow or cause to grow gradually less or smaller; to diminish. *n*. The process or act of decreasing or the resulting state; a decline.

de-cree (di krē) *n*. An authoritative and formal order or decision; a judicial judgment. **decree** *v*.

dec-re-ment (dek´re ment) *n*. The process or act of decreasing; the amount lost by gradual waste or diminution.

de-crep-it (di krep´it) *adj*. Broken down or worn out by old age or excessive use. **decrepitly** *adv*. **decrepitude** *n*.

de-cre-scen-do (dē´kri shen´dō) *n*., *pl*. **decrescendos** *Music* A gradual decrease in force or loudness.

de-crim-i-nal-ize (dē´krim inal īz) *v*. To remove the criminal classification of; to no longer prohibit.

de-cry (di krī´) *v*. To disparage or condemn openly; to denounce.

de-cum-bent (di kum´bent) *adj*. Lying down; reclining.

dec-u-ple (dek´ū pel) *adj*. Tenfold; containing groups of ten.

de-curved (dē kûrvd´) *adj*. Bent or curved downward.

de-cus-sate (di kus´āt) *v*. To arrange in pairs at acute angles; X-shaped.

de-daus (*de* dāns) *n*. The open gallery for spectators' viewing, as provided to view a tennis match.

ded-i-cate (ded´i kāt´) *v*. To set apart, as for sacred uses; to set apart for special use, duty, or purpose; to address or inscribe a work of literature, art or music to someone; to commit oneself to a certain cause, course of action, or thought; to unveil or open to the public, a book inscribed to a person or cause.

ded-i-ca-tion (ded´i kā´shan) *n*. The act of dedicating or devotion to a sacred use or meaning.

de-duce (di dōs´) *v*. To derive a conclusion by reasoning.

de-duct (di dukt´) *v*. To subtract or take away from; to subtract or separate, in numbering, estimating, or calculating.

de-duc-tion (di duk´shan) *n*. The act of deducing or subtracting; an amount that is or may be deducted; the process or act of deducting. **deductive** *adj*. **deductively** *adv*.

deed (dēd) *n*. Anything performed or done; a notable achievement or feat; in law, a legal document, especially one relating to the transference of property. **deedless** *adj*.

deem (dēm) *v*. To judge or consider.

de-es-ca-late (dē es´ka lāt) *v*. To decrease or be decreased gradually, as in intensity, scope, or effect.

de-face (di fās´) *v*. To spoil or mar the appearance or surface of something.

de fac-to (dē fak´tō) *adj*. Really or actually exercising authority.

de-fal-cate (di fal´kāt) *v*. To embezzle; to misuse funds. **defalcation** *n*.

def-a-ma-tion (def´a mā´sham) *n*. The publishing of slanderous words in order to injure someone's reputation.

de-fame (di fām´) *v*. To slander or libel. **defamation** *n*. **defamatory** *adj*.

de-fault (di folt´) *v*. To neglect to fulfill an obligation or requirement, as to pay money due or to appear in court; to forfeit by default. *n*. The failure to participate or compete in a competition. In *computer science*, the preset action for a function key or command.

de-fea-sance (di fē´zans) *n*. A condition of rendering null or void.

de-feat (di fēt´) *v*. To win a victory; to beat; to prevent the successful outcome of; to frustrate; to baffle; in law, to make void; to annul. **defeat** *n*.

def-e-cate (def´e kāt´) *v*. To discharge feces from the bowels. **defecation** *n*.

de-fect (dē´fekt) *n*. The lack of something desirable or necessary for completeness or perfection; a fault or imperfection. **defector** *n*.

de-fend (di fend´) *v*. Protect.

de-fend-ant (di fen´dant) *n*. The person charged in a criminal or civil lawsuit.

de-fense (di fens´) *n*. The action of defending against attack.

de-fer (di fer´) *v*. To delay or postpone, to put off doing. **deferment** *n*.

de-fer-ves-cence (dē´fér ves´ens) *n*. A reducing of fever.

de-fi-ance (di fī´ans) *n*. The instance or act of defying; a challenge. **defiant** *adj*.

deficiency disease *n*. A disease due to the lack of dietary elements, such as vitamins or minerals.

de-fi-cient (di fish´ent) *adj*. Lacking in a necessary element.

def-i-cit (def´i sit) *n*. Shortage in amount.

deficit spending *n*. The practice of spending public funds beyond income.

de-file (di fīl´) v. To soil or make unclean; violate one's reputation.

de-fine (di fīn´) v. To identify the essential qualities; to make clear. In computer science, to set a value for a symbol or variable.

de-fin-i-en-dum (di fin´ē en´dum) n. The term or expression to be defined, defining as in a dictionary entry.

de-fin-i-ens (di fin´ē enz) n. A description, expression or statement that defines something.

def-i-nite (def´i nit) adj. Clearly defined; having distinct limits; not vague or general.

de-fin-i-tive (di fin´i tiv) adj. Serving to provide a final solution.

def-i-nit-ize (def´i ni tīz´) v. To make final or definite.

def-la-grate (def´le grāt´) v. To set fire to; to cause to burn rapidly with intense heat.

de-flate (di flāt´) v. To cause to collapse by removing gas or air; to remove self-esteem or conceit. To reduce or restrict money or spending so that prices decline. **deflation** n.

de-flect (di flekt´) v. To turn aside; to swerve from a course. **deflective** adj. **deflection, deflector** n.

de-flow-er (di flou´ér) v. To rob of one's virginity; to violate; to rob of charm or beauty.

de-form (di form´) v. To distort the form of; to be distorted; to mar the beauty or excellence of; to spoil the natural form of. **deformative** adj. **-ity** n.

de-fraud (di frod´) v. To cheat; to swindle. **defrauder** n.

de-fray (di frā´) v. To provide for or to make payment on something. **defrayable** adj. **defrayal** n.

de-frock (dē frok´) v. To deprive a priest or minister of the right to practice the functions of his office.

deft (deft) adj. Skillful and neat in one's actions. **deftly** adv. **deftness** n.

de-funct (di fungkt´) adj. Deceased; dead; no longer in use. **-ness** n.

de-fuse (dē fūz) v. To remove the fuse from; to make less dangerous or hostile.

de-fy (di fī´) v. To confront or resist boldly and openly; to challenge someone to do, or not to do, something; to dare, to provoke. **defier** n.

de-gauss (dē gous´) v. To neutralize the magnetic field of something.

de-gen-er-ate (di jen´e rāt´) v. To decline in quality, value, or desirability; to deteriorate; to become worse. adj. Morally depraved or sexually deviant. **degenerative** adv. **degeneracy** n.

de-glu-ti-tion (dē´glü tish´an) n. The act or process of swallowing.

de-grade (dē grād´) v. To reduce in rank, status, or grade; to demote; to reduce

in quality or intensity. **degraded** adj. **degradedly** adv. **degradedness** n.

de-gree (di grē´) n. One of a succession of stages or steps; relative manner, condition or respect; the academic title given by an institution of learning upon completion of a course of study or as an honorary distinction; a unit on a temperature or thermometer scale; in law, a measure of severity, as murder in the first degree. *Gram.* A form used in the comparison of adjectives and adverbs. **by degrees** Little by little. **to a degree** Somewhat.

de-hisce (di his´) v. To open, along a natural line, as the capsules or seedpods of a plant.

de-horn (dē horn) v. To remove the horns from an animal.

de-hu-man-ize (dē hū´ma nīz´) v. To deprive of human qualities, especially to make mechanical and routine.

de-hu-mid-i-fy (dē´hū mid´i fī´) v. To re-move moisture from.

de-hy-drate (dē hī´drāt) v. To cause to lose moisture or water.

de-hyp-no-tize v. To bring out of the hypnotic state.

de-ice (dē īs´) v. To rid of or keep free of ice. **deicer** n.

deic-tic (dīk´tik) adj. Demonstrating or pointing out directly.

de-i-fy (dē´i fī´) v. To glorify or idealize; to raise in high regard; to worship as a god or a divine being. **-ication** n.

deign (dān) v. To think it barely worthy of one's dignity; to condescend.

Dei gratia adv. By the grace of God.

de-ism (dē´iz um) n. A belief in the existence of God but a denial of the validity of revelation.

de-ist (dē´ist) n. One who believes in the existence of God.

de-i-ty (dē´i tē) n. The essential nature or rank of a god; divine character.

dé-jà vu (dā zhä vy´) n. The feeling of having experienced something at a prior time when actually experiencing something for the first time.

de-ject (di jekt´) v. To lower the spirits; to dishearten, downcast. **dejection** n. **dejectedness** n. **dejectedly** adv.

de-jec-tion (di jek´shan) n. The state or condition of being dejected; depression; melancholy.

de ju-re (dē jer´ē) adv. By right; legally or rightfully.

dek-a-stere n. In the metric system, a measure of volume equal to 10 steres.

del abbr. Delete.

de-lam-i-nate (dē lam´i nāt´) v. To split into thin layers.

Del-a-ware (del´a wâr´) n. A state located on the eastern coast of the United States, statehood December 7, 1787, state capital Dover.

de-lay (di lā´) v. To put off until a later time; to defer; to cause to be late or detained; to linger; to waste time; to procrastinate. **delay** n.

de-le (dē´lē) n., Printing A mark in typesetting which indicates something is to be deleted or taken out of the manuscript.

de-lec-ta-ble (di lek´ta bl) adj. Giving great pleasure; delightful; savory; delicious. **delectability.** n.

de-lec-ta-tion (dē´ lek tā´shan) n. Enjoyment or pleasure.

del-e-gate (del´e git) n. A person with the power to act as a representative for another; a deputy or agent; a person appointed or elected to represent a territory in the House of Representatives, where he may speak but not vote; a member of the lower legislature in Maryland, Virginia, and West Virginia. v. To entrust and commit to another.

de-lete (di lēt´) v. To cancel; to take out, eliminate; to mark out. **deletion** n.

del-e-te-ri-ous (del´i tēr´ē us) adj. Causing moral or physical injury; harmful. **deleteriously** adv.

delft (delft) n. A glazed earthenware, usually blue and white in color, originating in Delft, Holland, in 1653.

del-i (del ē) n. Slang A delicatessen.

de-lib-er-ate (di lib´e rāt´) v. To say or do something intentionally; to plan in advance; to hold formal discussions. **deliberate** adj. Premeditated; leisurely or slow in manner or motion. **deliberately** adv. **deliberateness** n.

de-lib-er-a-tion (di lib´e rā´shan) n. The act of careful consideration before making a decision. **deliberative** adj.

del-i-ca-cy (del´i ka sē) n., pl. delicacies A select or choice food; the quality or state of being delicate; sensitiveness.

del-i-cate (del´i kit) adj. Pleasing to the senses; exquisite and fine in workmanship, texture, or construction; pleasing, as in color, taste, or aroma; sensitive and subtle in perception, feeling, or expression; frail in constitution; easily broken or damaged; considerate of the feelings of others. **delicately** adv.

de-li-cious (di lish´us) adj. Extremely enjoyable and pleasant to the taste. **deliciously** adv. **deliciousness** n.

de-li-cious (di lish´us) n. A variety of red, sweet apples.

de-lict (di likt´) n. An offense; a misdemeanor.

de-light (di līt´) n. A great joy or pleasure. v. To give or take great pleasure; to rejoice; to gratify or please highly. **delighted** adj. **delightedly** adv.

de-light-ful (di līt´ful) adj. Extremely pleasing. **delightfully** adv.

de-lim-it (di lim´it) v. To give or prescribe the limits of.

de-lin-e-ate (di lin´ē āt) v. To represent by a drawing; to draw or trace the outline of something; to sketch; to represent in gestures or words.

de-lin-quent (di ling´kwent) adj. Neglecting to do what is required by obligation or law; falling behind in a payment. n. A juvenile who is out of control, as violating the law.

de-lir-i-ous (di lēr´ē us) adj. Having the characteristic of or pertaining to delirium.

de-lir-i-um (di lēr´ē um) n. A temporary or sporadic mental disturbance associated with fever, shock, or intoxication and marked by excitement, incoherence, and hallucination; uncontrolled excitement and emotion.

de-liv-er (di liv´ér) v. To surrender; to hand over; to set free; to liberate; to give or send forth; to assist in the birth of an offspring; to do what is expected or desired; to take to the intended recipient. To give a speech. **-er** n.

de-louse (dē lous´) v. To free from parasitic lice.

delta ray n. An electron ejected by an ionizing particle as it passes through matter.

de-lude (di lōd´) v. To mislead the mind or judgment; to deceive; to cause to be deceived.

del-uge (del´ūj) v. To flood with water; to overwhelm; to destroy. **deluge** n. A great flood.

de-lu-sion (di lō´zhan) n. A false, fixed belief held in spite of contrary evidence; false impression. **-al** adj.

de luxe or **de-luxe (de leks´)** adj. High elegance or luxury.

delve (delv) v. To search for information with careful investigation.

de-mag-net-ize (dē mag´ni tīz´) v. To remove the magnetic properties of. **demagnetization, demagnetizer** n.

dem-a-gogue (dem´a gog´) n. A person who leads the populace by appealing to emotions and prejudices. **demagoguery** n. **demagogy** n.

de-mand (di mand´) v. To ask for in a firm tone; to claim as due; to have the need or requirement for; in law, to summon to court; to make a formal claim to property. Econ. The ability and desire to purchase something; the quantity of merchandise wanted at a certain price. **in demand** Sought after; desired. **on demand** On request or presentation; a note payable whenever the lender demands it.

de-mar-cate (di mär´kāt) v. To set boundaries or limits; to separate or limit.

de-mar-ca-tion (dē´mär kā´shan) n. The act of defining the limits or boundaries of something.

de-mean (di mēn´) v. To behave or conduct oneself in a particular manner; to degrade; to humble oneself or another.

de-mean-or (di mē ner) n. A person's conduct toward others; a person's general behavior.

de-ment-ed (di men´tid) adj. Insane.

de-men-tia (di men´sha) n. A deterioration of intellectual faculties.

de-mer-it (dē mer´it) n. A fault; a defect; a mark against one's record, especially for bad conduct in school.

de-mise (di mīz´) n. Death; in law, a transfer of an estate by lease or will.

de-mis-sion (di mish´an) n. Resignation or relinquishment.

dem-o (dem´ ō) n., pl. **demos** Slang A demonstration to show product use and purpose of an item.

de-mo-bi-lize (dē mō´bi līz´) v. To disband; to release from military service.

de-moc-ra-cy (di mok´ra sē) n., pl. **democracies** A form of government exercised either directly by the people or through their elected representatives; rule by the majority; the practice of legal, political, or social equality.

de-mod-ed (dē mō´did) adj. Out of fashion.

de-mod-u-late (dē moj´u lāt´) v. To detect or intercept a modulated signal.

de-mog-ra-phy (di mog´ra fē) n. Study of the characteristics of human population, such as growth, size, and vital statistics. **demographic** adj. **demographically** adv.

de-mol-ish (di mol´ish) v. To tear down; to raze; to completely do away with; to end. **demolishment** n.

dem-o-li-tion (dem´o lish´an) n. The process of demolishing, especially destruction with explosives.

de-mon (dē´mon) n. An evil spirit; a devil. Informal A person of great skill or zeal..

de-mon-e-tize (dē mon´i tīz´) v. To deprive the currency of its standard value; to withdraw currency from use.

de-mo-ni-ac (di mō´nē ak´) adj. Like or befitting a demon; to be influenced or possessed by or as by demons; of, resembling, or suggestive of a demon.

de-mon-ol-o-gy (dē´mo nol´o jē) n. The belief in or study of demons.

de-mon-stra-ble (di mon´stra bl) adj. Obvious or apparent, proven. **demonstrability** n. **demonstrably** adv.

dem-on-strate (dem´on strāt´) v. To show or prove by reasoning or evidence; to teach by using examples and exhibits; to make a public protest; to march or picket to seek public attention; to prove beyond doubt.

de-mor-al-ize (di mor´a līz´) v. To

undermine the morale or confidence of someone; to degrade; to corrupt. **demoralization** n. **demoralizer** n.

de-mote (di mōt´) v. To reduce in rank, grade, or position. **demotion** n.

de-mount v. To remove from its mounting, setting, or place of support.

de-mul-cent (di mul´sent) n. A soothing substance; any medicine which lessens the effects of irritation, as mucilaginous substances,. **demulcent** adj.

de-mur (di mėr´) v. To take issue; to object. **demurral** n.

de-mure (di mūr´) adj. Reserved and modest; coy. **demurely** adv.

de-murrer (di mėr´ėr) n. In law, a plea to dismiss a lawsuit on the grounds that the plaintiff's statements are insufficient to prove claim.

den (den) n. The shelter for a wild animal; a small room in a home used for private study or relaxation.

den-a-ry (den´arē) adj. Pertaining to the number ten.

de-na-tion-al-ize (dē nash´a na līz´) v. To deprive a person of national status, attachments or characteristics.

de-na-ture (dē nā´chėr) v. To change the nature or natural qualities of, especially to make unfit for consumption, without impairing its usefulness. **denaturant** n. **denaturation** n.

den-dri-form adj. Having the form or appearance of a tree.

den-drite (den´drīt) n. Physiol. The branching process of a nerve cell which conducts impulses toward the cell body. **dendritic** adj. **dendritically** adv.

den-drol-o-gy (den drol´o jē) n. Bot. The study of trees.

de-ne-go-ti-ate (dē´ni gō´shē āt´) v. To negotiate the ending of agreements of an economic or political nature.

den-gue (deng´gä) n., Pathol. An infectious tropical disease transmitted by mosquitoes, characterized by severe joint pains and fever.

de-ni-al (di nī´al) n. A refusal to comply with a request; refusal to acknowledge the truth of a statement; abstinence; self-denial.

den-i-grate (den´i grāt´) v. To slander; to defame, to degrade.

den-i-zen (den´i zen) n. An inhabitant or a person who frequents a place.

de-no-ta-tion (dē´nō tā´shan) n. The meaning of, or the object or objects designated by a word; an indication, as a sign. **denotative** adj.

de-note (di nōt´) v. To make known; to point out; to indicate; to signify; to designate; to mean, said of symbols or words. **denotative** adj.

de-nounce (di nouns´) v. To attack or condemn openly and vehemently; to accuse formally; to announce the ending of something in a formal way.

dense (dens) *adj.* Compact; thick; as in a forest or jungle; close; slow to understand; stupid; hardheaded. **densely** *adv.* **denseness** *n.*

den-si-tom-e-ter (den´si tom´ite) *n.* An instrument for determining optical or photographic density.

dent (dent) *n.* A small surface depression made by striking or pressing. **dent** *v.* To put a dent in something; to make meaningful progress or headway.

den-tal (den´tal) *adj.* Pertaining to the teeth; of or pertaining to dentistry.

den-ti-cle (den´ti kl) *adj.* Having a small pointed projection.

den-ti-frice (den´ti fris) *n.* A preparation in powder or paste form for cleaning the teeth.

den-ti-lin-gual (den´ti ling´gwɑl) *adj.* Of speech sounds that are uttered with the cooperation of the tongue and teeth.

den-tine *or* **den-tin (den´tin)** *n.* The hard, calcified part of the tooth beneath the enamel, containing the pulp chamber and root canals.

den-tist (den´tist) *n.* A licensed person whose profession is the diagnosis, treatment, and prevention of diseases of the gums and teeth.

den-tist-ry (den´ti strē) *n.* The profession of a dentist, one that deals with the diagnosis, prevention, and treatment of the teeth and malformations of the mouth and gums.

den-ti-tion (den tish´an) *n.* The kind, number, and arrangement of teeth, as in humans and other animals; the process of cutting teeth.

den-ture (den´chēr) *n.* A set of artificial teeth either partial or full; also called a dental plate.

de-ny (di nī´) *v.* To declare untrue; to refuse to acknowledge or recognize; to withhold; to refuse to grant. **deny oneself** To refuse oneself something desired; self-denial.

de-o-dar (dē´o dä) *n.* A species of an East Indian cedar tree valued for its wood.

de-o-dor-ant (dē o´dēr ant) *n.* A product designed to prevent, mask, or destroy unpleasant odors.

de-o-dor-ize (dē ō´do rīz´) *v.* To destroy, modify, or disguise the odor of. **deodorization** *n.* **deodorizer** *n.*

de-on-tol-o-gy (dē´on tol´o jē) *n.* The study of moral obligation.

de-ox-i-dize (dē ok´si dīz´) *v.* To remove the oxygen from; to reduce from the state of an oxide. **deoxidization** , **deoxidate** *n.* **deoxidizer** *n.*

de-ox-y-ri-bo-nu-cle-ic a-cid (dē ok´siri´bō nō klē´ik as´id) *n.* A nucleic acid which forms a principal constituent of the genes and is known to play a role of importance in the genetic action of the chromosomes, also known as DNA.

dep *abbr.* Depart; deposit; deputy.

de-part (di pärt´) *v.* To leave; to go away; to deviate; to die. **departed** *adj.*

de-par-ture (di pär´chēr) *n.* The act of taking leave or going away; a divergence; a deviation; the act of starting out on a new course of action or going on a trip.

de-paup-er-ate (di po´pėr it) *adj.* Poorly developed in physical form or size.

de-pend (di pend´) *v.* To rely on; to trust with responsibilities; to be determined or conditioned.

de-pict (di pikt´) *v.* To represent in a sculpture or a picture; to describe or represent in words. **depiction** *n.*

dep-i-late (dep´i lāt´) *v.* To remove the hair from. **depilation** *n.* **depilator** *n.*

de-pil-a-to-ry (di pil´a tōr´ē) *n.* A chemical which removes hair.

de-plane (dē plān´) *v.* To disembark or leave an aircraft.

de-plete (di plēt´) *v.* To exhaust, empty, or use up a supply of something.

de-plor-a-ble (di plōr´a bl) *adj.* Grievous; lamentable; very bad; wretched, **deplorability** *n.*

de-plore (di plōr´) *v.* To have, show, or feel great disapproval of something.

de-ploy (di ploi´) *v.* To spread out; to place or position according to plans.

de-plume (dē plōm´) *v.* To deprive of feathers or plumage; to pluck.

de-pone (di pōn´) *v.* To testify; depose.

de-po-nent (di pō´nent) *n.* A person who testifies under oath giving sworn testimony, especially in writing.

de-pop-u-late (dē pop´ū lāt´) *v.* To quickly remove or lower the population greatly, as by massacre or disease.

de-port (di pōrt´) *v.* To banish or expel someone from a country; to behave in a specified manner. **deportation** *n.*

de-pose (di pōz´) *v.* To remove from a powerful position or office; in law, to declare or give testimony under oath. **deposable** *adj.* **deposal** *n.*

de-pos-it (di poz´it) *v.* To put, place, or set something down; to entrust money to a bank; to put down in the form of a layer, as silt; to give as security or partial payment, mineral masses, such as oil, coal or ores. **depositor** *n.*

de-pot (dē´pō) *n.* A railroad station; a warehouse or storehouse. *Milit.* The place where military materials are manufactured, stored, and repaired; an installation for processing personnel.

dep-ra-va-tion (dep´ra vā´shan) *n.* The act of corrupting; state of being depraved.

de-prave (di prāv´) *v.* To render bad or worse; in morals, to corrupt or pervert. **depraved** *adj.* **depravity** *n.*

dep-re-cate (dep´re kāt´) v. To express regret for or disapproval of; to belittle. **deprecating** adv. **deprecation** n.

de-pre-ci-ate (di prē´shē āt´) v. To lessen in value or price. **depreciator** n. **depreciatory** adj. **depreciatory** adj.

de-pre-ci-a-tion (di prē´shē āt´) n. A loss in efficiency or value resulting from age or usage; the decline in the purchasing value of money.

de-press (di pres´) v. To make gloomy; to lower the spirits of; to lessen in energy or vigor; to press down; to lower; to diminish in value or price.

de-pres-sion (di presh´an) n. The state of being or the act of depressing; a severe decline in business, accompanied by increasing unemployment and falling prices. *Psych.* A condition of deep dejection characterized by lack of response to stimulation and withdrawal.

dep-ri-va-tion (dep´ri vā´shan) n. The act or state of being deprived.

de-prive (di prīv´) v. To take something away from; to keep from using, acquiring, or enjoying. **deprivable** adj.

depth (depth) n. The degree or state of being deep; the distance or extent backward, downward, or inward; the most intense part of something; intensity or richness of sound or color; the range of one's comprehension. **depths** pl. A deep part or place; an intense state of feeling or being.

dep-u-ta-tion (dep´ū tā´shan) n. A person or persons who are acting for another or others; the act of deputing or the state of being deputed.

de-pute (de pūt´) v. To appoint as a deputy, an agent, or other figure of authority; to delegate; to transfer.

de-rac-in-ate (di ras´i nāt´) v. To uproot. **deracination.** n.

de-rail (dē rāl´) v. To run off the rails; to cause a train to run off the rails. *Slang* To change a plan or program.

de-range (di rānj´) v. To disturb the arrangement or normal order of; to unbalance the reason; to make insane.

de-reg-u-late (dē´reg ye lāt´) v. To decontrol or remove from regulation or control.

der-e-lict (der´e likt) adj. Neglectful of obligations; remiss. n. Abandoned or deserted, as a ship at sea; a vagrant; a social outcast.

der-e-lic-tion (der´e lik´shan) n. Voluntary neglect, as of responsibility; the fact or state of being abandoned.

de-ride (di rīd´) v. To ridicule; to treat with scornful mirth. **derider** n. **derision** n. **deridingly** adv. **derisive** adj.

de ri-gueur (de ri ger´) adj. Prescribed or required by manners, custom, or fashion.

der-i-va-tion (der´i vā´shan) n. The act of or process of deriving; the process used to form new words by the addition of affixes to roots, stems, or words.

de-rive (di rīv´) v. To receive or obtain from a source. *Chemical* To produce a compound from other substances by chemical reaction.

der-mal (der´mel) adj. Relating to or of the skin.

der-ma-ti-tis (der´ma tī´tis) n., Pathol. An inflammation of the skin.

der-mat-o-gen (der mat´o jen) n. The cellular layer at the tip of a plant root where the epidermis is produced.

der-ma-tol-o-gy (der´ma tol´o jē) n. The medical study of the skin and the diseases related it. **dermatologist** n.

der-ma-to-sis (dür´ma tō´sis) n. A disease of the skin or skin tissue.

der-o-gate (der´o gāt´) v. To take or cause to take away from; to detract; to cause to become inferior.

de-rog-a-tory (di rog´a tōr´ē) adj. Having the effect of belittling; lessening. **derogatorily** adv.

der-ri-ere (der´ē ār) n. The buttocks.

der-ring–do (der´ing dö´) n. A courageous or daring action or spirit.

der-ris (der´is) n. An East Indian plant that is the source of an insecticide.

de-salt (dēsot´) v. To remove the salt from sea or saline water.

des-cant (des´kant) v. To play or sing a varied melody.

de-scend (di send´) v. To move from a higher to a lower level; to pass through inheritance; to come from a particular family; to sink in status; to worsen in condition or reputation.

descending sort In *computer science,* an alphabetical or numerical arrangement from highest to lowest.

de-scent (di sent´) n. A slope; lowering or decline, as in level or status.

de-scribe (di skrīb´) v. To explain in written or spoken words; to draw or trace the figure of. **describable** adj.

de-scrip-tion (di skrip´shan) n. The technique or act of describing; an account or statement that describes. **descriptive** adj.

de-scry (di skrī´) v. To catch sight of; to discover by observation.

des-e-crate (des´e krāt´) v. To violate something sacred, turning it into something common or profane.

de-seg-re-gate (dē seg´re gāt´) v. To remove or eliminate racial segregation in work, school, and other activities. **desegregation** n.

de-sen-si-tize (dē sen´si tīz´) v. To make less sensitive; to eliminate the sensitivity of an individual, tissue, or organ to an allergen.

des-ert (de sert´) v. To abandon or

forsake. *Milit.* To be absent without leave with the plan of not returning, AWOL. **desert (des'ért)** *n.* A dry, barren region incapable of supporting any considerable population or vegetation without an artificial water supply.

de-serve (di zėrv') *v.* To be worthy of or entitled to.

des-ic-cant (des'i kant) *n.* A silica gel used to absorb moisture; any material used to that has drying qualities.

des-ic-cate (des'i kāt') *v.* To preserve by drying, such as food; dehydrate. **desiccation** *n.* **desiccative** *adj.*

de-sid-er-a-tum (di sid'e rā'tum) *n. pl.* **-ta** A desired and necessary thing.

de-sign (di zīn') *v.* To draw and sketch preliminary outlines; to invent or create in the mind; to have as an intention or goal. **design** *n.* An artistic or decorative piece of work; a project; a plan; a well thought out intention.

des-ig-nate (dez'ig nāt') *v.* To assign a name or title to; to point out; to specify; to appoint or select, as to an office, to set apart. **designative** *adj.* **-ion** *n.*

des-i-nence *n.* Termination or ending, as of a line of verse.

de-sir-a-ble (di zīėr'a bl) *adj.* Pleasing, attractive, or valuable; worthy of desire. **desirability** *n.* **desirableness** *n.*

de-sire (di zīėr') *v.* To long for; to wish; to crave; to request or ask for; to have sexual appetite.

de-sir-ous (di zīėr'us) *adj.* Having a craving or strong desire.

de-sist (di zist') *v.* To stop doing something; to cease to act.

desktop computer In *computer science,* a personal or micro computer, designed to fit on a desk.

desktop publishing In *computer science,* creation of type and graphics on a desktop computer.

des-mid (des'mid) *n.* Microscopic, unicellular freshwater green algae.

des-o-late (des'o lit) *adj.* Made unfit for habitation; useless; forlorn; forsaken.

des-o-la-tion (des'o la'shan) *n.* A wasteland; the condition of being ruined or deserted; loneliness.

de-spair (di spâr') *v.* To lose or give up hope; to abandon all purpose. **despair** *n.* **despairing** *adj.* **despairingly** *adv.*

des-per-ate (des'pėr it) *adj.* Rash, violent, reckless, and without care, as from despair; intense; overpowering.

des-per-a-tion (des'pe rā'shan) *n.* The state of being desperate.

des-pi-ca-ble (des'pi ka bl) *adj.* Deserving scorn or contempt. **-bly** *adv.*

de-spise (di spīz') *v.* To regard with contempt or as worthless. **despiser** *n.*

de-spite (di spīt') *prep.* Not withstanding; in spite of.

de-spite-ful *adj.* Full of spite; malicious.

de-spoil (di spoil') *v.* To rob; to strip of property or possessions by force. **despoiler** *n.* **despoilment** *n.*

de-spond (di spond') *v.* To lose hope, courage, or spirit. **despondently** *adv.*

de-spon-den-cy (di spon'den sē) *n.* A dejection of spirits from loss of courage or hope.

de-spond-ent (di spon'dent) *adj.* Having the feeling of extreme discouragement.

des-pot (des'pot) *n.* An absolute ruler; a tyrant. **despotic** *adj.* **despotically** *adv.*

des-pot-ism (des'po tiz'um) *n.* A system where a ruler has unlimited power or authority.

des-qua-mate (des'kwa māt) *v.* To come off in scales, as the epidermis in certain diseases; to peel off.

des-sert (di zėrt') *n.* A serving of sweet food, as pastry, ice cream, or fruit, as the last course of a meal.

des-ti-na-tion (des'ti nā'shan) *n.* The point or place to which something or someone is directed; the purpose or end for which something is created or intended. In computer science, the file, computer, or peripheral to which data is being transmitted.

des-tine (des'tin) *v.* To be determined in advance; to design or appoint a distinct purpose.

des-ti-ny (des'ti nē) *n., pl.* **destinies** The inevitable fate to which a person or thing is destined; fate; a predetermined course of events.

des-ti-tute (des'ti töt') *adj.* Extremely poor; utterly impoverished; not having; without the necessities of life.

de-stroy (di stroi') *v.* To ruin; to tear down; to demolish; to kill; to make useless or ineffective.

de-struct (di strukt') *n., Aeron.* The deliberate destruction of a defective or dangerous missile or rocket after launch.

des-ue-tude (des'wi tōd') *n.* A condition or state of disuse.

des-ul-to-ry (des'ul tōr'ē) *adj.* Something that occurs by chance; lacking continuity; aimless.

de-tach (di tach') *v.* To unfasten, disconnect, or separate; to extricate oneself; to withdraw.

de-tail (di tāl') *n.* A part or item considered separately. *Milit.* Military personnel selected for a particular duty.

de-tain (di tān') *v.* To stop; to keep from proceeding; to delay.

de-tect (di tekt') *v.* To find out or perceive; to expose or uncover, as a crime. **detectible** *adj.* **detection** *n.*

de-tec-tive (di tek'tiv) *n.* A person whose work is to investigate crimes, discover evidence, and capture criminals.

de-tent (di tent') *n.* A pawl; a lock.

de-ten-tion (di ten´shan) *n*. The act of or state of being detained; in law, a time or period of temporary custody which precedes disposition by a court.

de-ter (di ter´) *v*. To prevent or discourage someone from acting by arousing fear, uncertainty, intimidation, or other strong emotion. **determent** *n*.

de-terge *v*. To cleanse; to wash or clear away unclean or offending matter from.

de-te-ri-o-rate (di tēr´ē o rāt´) *v*. To worsen; to depreciate; to reduce in quality and value, degenerate or decompose. **deterioration** *n*.

de-ter-mi-na-ble (di tür´mi na bl) *adj*. Capable of being determined, definitely decided. **determinably** *adv*.

de-ter-mi-nate (di ter´mi nit) *adj*. Definitely fixed or limited; conclusive. *Bot*. Terminating in a bud or flower, often at each axis of an inflorescence.

de-ter-mi-na-tion (di tür´mi nā´shan) *n*. The act of deciding definitely; a firm resolution; adherence to purposes or aims.

de-ter-mine (di ter´min) *v*. To settle or decide conclusively or authoritatively; to limit to extent or scope; to fix or ascertain; to give direction or purpose to; to come to a conclusion after investigation; *law* to bring to an end.

de-ter-rent (di ter´ent) *n*. Something which deters. *adj*. Serving to deter; restrain from doing. **deterrently** *adv*.

de-test (di test´) *v*. To dislike strongly. **detestable** *adj*. **detestably** *adv*.

de-tes-ta-tion (dē´te stā´shan) *n*. Extreme dislike or hatred; abhorrence.

de-throne (dē thrōn´) *v*. To remove from the throne, to depose, as a king.

det-i-nue (det´i nö) *n*. The unlawful detention of a person's property, or a common-law action to recover the personal property so detained.

det-o-nate (det´o nāt´) *v*. To explode suddenly and violently.

det-o-na-tor (det´o nā´tėr) *n*. The device, such as a fuse or percussion cap, used to detonate an explosive.

de-tour (dē´ter) *n*. A road used temporarily instead of a main road; a deviation from a direct route or course of action.

de-tox-i-fy (dē tok´si fī´) *v*. To free one from dependence on drugs or alcohol, to remove poisonous effects from one's system. **detoxification** *n*.

de-tract (di trakt´) *v*. To take away from; to diminish; to divert. **detraction** *n*. **detractor** *n*. **detractive** *adj*.

de-train (dē trān´) *v*. To leave or cause to leave a railroad train. **-ment** *n*.

det-ri-ment (de´tri ment) *n*. Damage; injury; loss; something which causes damage, injury, or loss. **detrimental** *adj*. **detrimentally** *adv*.

de-tri-tus (di trī´tus) *n*. Loose fragments or particles formed by erosion, glacial action, and other forces; debris.

de-trun-cate (di trung´kāt) *v*. To cut off; to shorten.

deuce (dös) *n*. Two; a playing card or the side of a die with two spots or figures; in tennis, a tie in which each side has a score of 40 points. *Informal* The devil, bad luck, or a mild oath.

De-us *n*. God.

deu-te-ri-um (dö tēr´ē um) *n*. The isotope of hydrogen which has twice the mass of ordinary hydrogen.

de-val-u-ate (dē val´ū āt´) *v*. To reduce or lessen the value of. **devaluation** *n*.

dev-as-tate (dev´a stāt´) *v*. To destroy; to ruin; to overwhelm; to overpower. **devastation** *n*.

de-vel-op (di vel´up) *v*. To bring out or expand the potentialities; to make more elaborate; to enlarge; to evolve; to advance from a lower to a higher stage or from an earlier to a later stage of maturation. *Photog*. To process an image upon a sensitized plate that has been exposed to light. **developer** *n*. **developmental** *adj*.

de-vest (di vest´) *v*. To deprive of a right; to take away; divest.

de-vi-ate (dē´vē āt´) *v*. To turn away from a specified prescribed behavior or course, to be different from the normal patterns of a person or thing.

de-vi-a-tion (dē´vē ā´shan) *n*. The act of turning aside from the right way or course; variation from a standard..

de-vice (di vīs´) *n*. Something constructed and used for a specific purpose, as a machine; a crafty or evil scheme or plan; an ornamental design; a motto or an emblem. In computer science, any component or peripheral that is a part of a computer system.

device driver In *computer science*, a program that interprets instructions for the operation of a peripheral, such as a printer.

dev-il *or* **Devil** (dev´il) *n*. The spirit of evil, the ruler of Hell; Satan; a wicked or malevolent person; a daring, clever, and energetic person; a printer's apprentice, also called a printer's devil.

de-vi-ous (dē´vē us) *adj*. Leading away from the straight, regular, or direct course; rambling; straying from the proper way; tricky; underhanded. **deviously** *adv*. **deviousness** *n*.

de-vise (di vīz´) *v*. To form in the mind; to contrive; to plan; to invent; in law, to transmit or give by will. **devise** *n*. The act of bequeathing lands; a clause in a will conveying real estate.

de-vi-see (di vīzē´) *n*. In law, the person to whom a devise is made.

de-vi-sor (di vī´zėr) *n*. In law, the person

who devises property.

de-vi-tal-ize (dē vīt´a līz´) v. To make weak; to destroy the vitality.

de-void (di void´) adj. Empty; utterly lacking; without.

de-voir (de vwär´) n. The act or expression of courtesy or respect; duty or responsibility.

dev-o-lu-tion (dev´o lō´shan) n. The act of devolving; passage onward from stage to stage; the passing of property by succession or inheritance.

de-volve (di volv´) v. To pass duty or authority on to a successor.

de-vote (di vōt´) v. To apply time or oneself completely to some activity, purpose, or cause.

de-vour (di vour´) v. To destroy or waste; to eat up greedily; to engulf.

de-vout (di vout´) adj. Extremely and earnestly religious; showing sincerity; displaying piety or reverence, a devotion to religion and religious activities. **devoutly** adv.

dew (dö) n. Moisture condensed from the atmosphere in minute drops onto cool surfaces; something which is refreshing or pure. **dewy** adj.

dew point n. The temperature at which condensation of vapor occurs.

dex-ter (dek´stèr) adj. Pertaining to or situated on the right side.

dex-ter-i-ty (dek ster´i tē) n. Proficiency or skill in using the hands or body; cleverness.

dex-ter-ous or **dex-trous** (dek´strus) adj. Skillful or adroit in the use of the hands, body, or mind. **dexterously** adv.

dex-tran (dek´stran) n. A white gum-like substance, produced by bacterial action and used as a plasma substitute.

dex-trin (dek´strin) n. A group of water soluble gummy substances obtained from starch by the action of heat or weak acids and used as an adhesive.

dex-trose (dek´strōs) n. Sugar found in animal blood and in plant tissue and derived synthetically from starches.

di-a-base (dī´a bās´) n. A minor intrusive rock.

di-a-be-tes (dī´a bē´tis) n., Pathol. A metabolic disorder characterized by deficient insulin secretion, leading to excess sugar in the urine and blood, extreme hunger, and thirst.

di-a-bet-ic (dī´a bet´ik) adj., Med. Pertaining to, or affected with diabetes.

di-a-bol-ic or **di-a-bol-i-cal** (dī´a bol´ik) adj. Wicked; proceeding from the devil; satanic or infernal. **diabolically** adv. **diabolicalness** n.

di-a-chron-ic (dī´a kron´ik) adj. Dealing with the phenomena or study of language changes over a period of time.

di-a-crit-ic (dī´a krit´ik) n. A mark near or through a phonetic character or

combination of characters, to indicate a special phonetic value or to distinguish words otherwise graphically identical. **diacritical** adj. **diacritic** adj.

di-a-dem (dī´a dem´) n. A crown or headband worn to symbolize or indicate royalty or honor.

di-ag-no-sis (dī´ag nō´sis) n. pl. diagnoses An analysis and examination to identify a disease; the conclusion reached. **diagnostician** n.

di-ag-nos-tics adj. Branch of medicine dealing with diagnosis.

di-ag-nos-tic (dī´ag nos´tik) adj. A symptom by which a disease is known. In computer science, a description of a system to detect and isolate errors or malfunction in programs or equipment.

diagnostic message n. In computer science, an error message that describes the source of the error.

di-ag-o-nal (dī ag´o nal) adj. In mathematics, joining two opposite corners of a polygon which are not adjacent. n. A diagonal or slanting plane or line; in a diagonal pattern.

di-a-gram (dī´a gram´) n. A sketch, plan, drawing, or outline designed to demonstrate or clarify the similarity among parts of a whole or to illustrate how something works. **diagram** v., **diagrammatic, diagrammatical** adj.

di-a-lect (dī´a lekt´) n. Manner of speaking; a form of a language prevailing in a particular region or area.

di-a-lec-tic (dī´a lek´tik) n. The act or practice of argument or exposition in which the conflict between contradictory facts or ideas is resolved. **dialectic** adj. **dialectically** adv.

di-a-lec-tol-o-gy (dī´a lek tol´o jē) n. The systematic study of dialects.

di-a-logue or **di-a-log** (dī´a log´) n. A conversation involving two or more persons; a conversational passage in a literary work.

dialog box n. In computer science, a panel that appears on screen as a part of a program to furnish instructions, information or to request user input.

di-al-y-sis (dī al´i sis) n. pl. -ses The separation of substances in solution, which is accomplished by passing them through membranes or filters. **dialysis** A form of dialysis used to cleanse the blood of impurities and wastes when the kidneys are unable to perform this function.

di-a-mag-net-ic (dī´a mag net´ik) adj. Pertaining to a class of substances which are slightly repelled by a magnet.

di-am-e-ter (dī am´i tèr) n. In mathematics, a straight line which passes through the center of a circle or sphere and stops at the circumference or surface;

a measurement of that distance.

di-a-pa-son (dī′a pā′zon) *n.* The full range of a voice or an instrument; in a pipe organ, either of two principal stops which form the tonal basis for the entire scale.

di-a-pe-de-sis (dī′a pi dē′sis) *n.* The passage of blood cells through the capillary walls into the tissues.

di-a-per (dī′pèr) *n.* A folded piece of soft, absorbent material placed between a baby's legs and fastened at the waist. *v.* To put a diaper on.

di-aph-a-nous (dī af′a nus) *adj.* Of such fine texture as to be transparent or translucent; delicate; almost totally transparent. **diaphanously** *adv.*

di-a-phone (dī′a fōn′) *n.* A low-pitched fog horn, that produces a blast of two tones, the sound of which can be heard from a distance.

di-a-phragm (dī′a fram′) *n. Anat.* The muscular wall which separates the chest and abdominal cavities; a dividing membrane. A contraceptive device usually made of rubber-like material shaped like a cap to cover the uterine cervix. *Photog.* The disk with an adjustable aperture that can control the amount of light which passes through the lens of a telescope, camera, etc.

di-a-pos-i-tive (dī′a poz′i tiv) *n.* A transparent photograph.

di-a-rist (dī′a rist) *n.* A person who keeps a diary.

di-ar-rhe-a *or* **di-ar-rhoe-a** (dī′arē′a) *n.* A disorder of the intestines causing frequent, loose bowel movements.

di-ar-thro-sis (dī′ār thrō′sis) *n.* A freely movable joint in which the bones revolve in every direction, as in the shoulder or hip joint.

di-a-ry (dī′a rē) *n. pl.* **-ries** A daily record, especially a personal record of one's activities, experiences, or observations; a journal; a book for keeping such records.

di-as-ta-sis (dī as′ta sis) *n.* Dislocation of bones without a fracture.

di-as-to-le (dī as′to lē′) *n. Physiol.* The normal rhythmic dilatation of the heart cavities during which they fill with blood. **diastolic** *adj.*

di-as-tro-phism (dī as′tro fiz′um) *n. Geol.* Any process through which the earth's crust is changed into formations such as mountains and continents.

di-a-ther-my (dī′a ther′mē) *n., pl.* **diathermies** *Med.* The generation of heat in body tissues by high-frequency electromagnetic waves; the application of electric current to produce heat in tissues below the skin for therapeutic purposes. **diathermic** *adj.*

di-ath-e-sis (dī ath′i sis) *n.* Predisposition toward a condition or certain diseases

rather than to others.

di-a-tom (dī′a tom) *n.* Any of various tiny planktonic algae whose walls contain silica.

di-a-tom-ic (dī′a tom′ik) *adj.* Having two atoms in a molecule.

di-a-ton-ic (dī′a ton′ik) *adj., Music* Relating to a standard major or minor scale of eight tones without the chromatic intervals.

di-a-tribe (dī′a trīb′) *n.* A bitter, often malicious criticism or denunciation.

di-chot-o-mous (di kot′o mus) *adj.* Dividing into two parts.

di-chot-o-my (di kot′o mē) *n., pl.* **dichotomies** Division into two mutually exclusive subclasses. *Bot.* The branching of something in which each successive axis forks into two equally developed branches.

di-cot-y-le-don (dī kot′a lēd′on) *n.* A plant which has two seed leaves. **dicotyledonous** *adj.*

di-crot-ic (dī krot′ik) *adj.* Having a double arterial beat for one heartbeat.

dic-tate (dik′tāt) *v.* To read or speak aloud for another to record or transcribe; to give commands, terms, rules, or other orders with authority. **dictate** *n.* A directive or guiding principle.

dic-ta-tor (dik′tā tèr) *n.* A person having absolute authority and supreme governmental powers; one who dictates. **dictatorship** *n.*

dic-tion-ar-y (dik′sha ner′ē) *n., pl.* **dictionaries** A reference book or data base containing alphabetically arranged words together with their definitions and usages.

dic-tum (dik′tum) *n., pl.* **dictums** *or* **dicta** An authoritative or positive utterance; a pronouncement; a saying.

did (did) *v.* Past tense of do.

di-dac-tic *or* **didactical** (dīdak′ti kal) *adj.* Being inclined to teach or moralize excessively. **didacticism** *n.*

did-dle (did l) *v.* To cheat; to swindle; to waste valuable time.

did-n't (did′ant) *contr.* Did not.

did-y-mous (did′i mus) *adj.* Produced in pairs; twin.

die (dī) *v.* To expire; to stop living; to cease to exist; to fade away; to cease operation or functioning, as an engine. **die hard** To resist defeat or death to the end; to be determined not to give up. **die off** To be removed one after another by death. **die out** To become extinct.

diel-drin (dēl′drin) *n.* A highly toxic chlorinated compound which is used as an insecticide.

di-e-lec-tric (dī′i lek′trik) *n. Elect.* A non—conductor of electricity.

di-er-e-sis (dī er′i sis) *n., pl.* **-ses** The

mark over a vowel indicating that it is to be pronounced in a separate syllable.

die-sel (dē´zel) *n.* A diesel engine or a vehicle driven by a diesel engine.

di-et (dī´it) *n.* A regulated selection of food and drink, especially one followed for medical or hygienic reasons; something that is taken or provided regularly; an assembly or legislature.

dif-fer (dif´ēr) *v.* To have different opinions; to disagree; to be unlike.

dif-fer-ence (dif´ēr ens) *n.* The quality, state, or degree of being different or unlike; a controversy or cause for a disagreement; in mathematics, the amount by which a number or quantity is less or greater than another.

dif-fer-ent (dif´ēr ent) *adj.* Not the same; separate; other; marked by a difference; unlike; differing from the ordinary. **differently** *adv.* **differentness** *n.*

dif-fer-en-tia (dif´e ren´shē a) *n. pl.*-tiae A specific difference; something that distinguishes a species from others of the same genus.

dif-fer-en-tial (dif´e ren´shal) *adj.* Relating to or showing a difference or differences. *n.* The amount or degree to which similar things differ.

differential calculus *n.* In mathematics, the difference or variation of a function with respect to changes in independent variables.

dif-fi-cult (dif´i kult´) *adj.* Hard to do, deal with, or accomplish; hard to please.

dif-fi-dence (dif´i dens) *n.* Lack of self-confidence.

dif-fi-dent (dif´i dent)*adj.* Lacking confidence in oneself; unsure; unassertive. **diffidence** *n.* **diffidently** *adv.*

dif-flu-ent (dif´lö ent) *adj.* Having the tendency to flow away.

dif-fuse (di füz´) *v.* To pour out and spread freely in all directions; to scatter.

dig (dig) *v.* To turn up, break up, or remove the earth with a shovel; to discover or learn by investigation or research. *Slang* To understand, like, appreciate or enjoy. *Informal* To work intensively.

dig-a-my (dig´a mē) *n.* Second marriage; the act of marrying after the first marriage has been legally ended.

di-gas-tric (dī gas´trik) *n.* A double muscle separated by a median tendon, that pulls the lower jaw downward and backward.

di-gest (di jest´) *v.* To change ingested food into usable form; to mentally assimilate; to endure; to tolerate patiently; to decompose or soften with moisture or heat. **digestibility** *n.* **digestible** *adj.* **digestive** *adj.*

dig-it (dij´it) *n.* A toe or finger; the Arabic numerals 0 through 9. In computer science, a symbol representing an integer in a numbering system, as 0-9 in decimal notation or 0-F in hexadecimal.

dig-i-tal (dij´i tal) *adj.* Pertaining to or like the fingers or digits; expressed in digits, especially for computer use; reading in digits, as a clock. In computer science, represented by a distinct value.

digital camera In *computer science,* a camera that records images in digital format for downloading and viewing on a computer screen.

digital computer *n.* In *computer science,* a computer using data that is represented as digits to perform operations.

digital data In *computer science,* information recorded in a system of numbers, as binary for the computer.

digital recording In *computer science,* sounds recorded as discrete values.

dig-i-tal-is (dij´i tal´is) *n.* The foxglove plant; a drug prepared from dried leaves of foxglove, used as a heart stimulant.

di-glot (dī´glot) *adj.* Using two languages; bilingual.

dig-ni-fied (dig´ni fīd´) *adj.* Showing or possessing dignity; poised.

dig-ni-fy (dig´ni fī´) *v.* To give dignity or distinction to something.

dig-ni-tary (dig´ni ter´ē) *n., pl.* **dignitaries** A person of high rank, notability, and influence.

dig-ni-ty (dig´ni tē) *n., pl.* **dignities** The quality or state of being excellent; the quality of being poised or formally reserved in appearance and demeanor; a high rank, office, or title.

di-graph (dī´graf) *n.* A pair of letters, as the *ea* in seat or *oa* in boat, that represent a single sound.

di-gress (di gres´) *v.* To turn away from the main subject in a discourse; to wander. **digression** *n.* **digressive** *adj.*

dik–dik (dik´dik´) *n.* A very small African antelope.

dike (dīk) *n.* An embankment made of earth, built to hold and control flood waters, also known as a levee; also used in irrigation of crops.

di-lap-i-date (di lap´i dāt´) *v.* To cause to decay or fall into partial ruin through neglect.

di-lap-i-dat-ed (di lap´i dā´tid) *adj.* Being in a state of decay or disrepair.

dil-a-ta-tion (dil´a tā shan) *n.* The state of being expanded or distended; something which is dilated. *Med.* Enlargement of a passageway for medical examination.

di-late (dī lāt´) *v.* To become or make enlarged; to expand; extend in all directions. **dilatable** *adj.* **dilation** *n.*

di-lat-ed (dī lā´tid) *adj.* Expanded in all directions; broadened.

dil-a-tom-e-ter (dil˝a tom´i tėr) *n.* An instrument for measuring thermal expansion of substances.

dil-a-to-ry (dil´a tōr˝ē) *adj.* Tending to cause delay; slow; tardy. **dilatorily** *adv.*

di-lem-ma (di lem´a) *n.* A predicament requiring a choice between equally undesirable alternatives.

dil-et-tante (dil´i tan˝tē) *n., pl.* **dilettantes** One who has an amateurish and superficial interest in something.

dil-i-gence (dil´i jens) *n.* The constant effort to accomplish what is undertaken.

dil-i-gent (dil´i jent) *adj.* Showing painstaking effort and application in whatever is undertaken; industrious; constant in effort to accomplish what is undertaken. **diligently** *adv.*

dill (dil) *n.* An herb with aromatic leaves and seeds used as seasoning.

dil-ly (dil ē) *n., pl.* **dillies** *Slang* Someone or something that is remarkable or extraordinary.

dil-ly-dal-ly (dil´ē dal˝ē) *v.* To waste time with indecision or hesitation.

di-lute (di lōt´) *v.* To weaken, thin, or reduce the concentration of by adding a liquid; reduce strength. **dilution** *n.*

dim (dim) *adj.* Dull; lacking sharp perception or clarity of understanding.

dime (dīm) *n.* A United States coin worth ten cents or one tenth of a dollar.

dime novel *n.* A melodramatic paperback novel.

di-men-sion (di men´shan) *n.* A measurable extent, as length, thickness, or breadth. **dimensions** *pl.* The magnitude or scope of something. **dimensional** *adj.* **dimensionality** *n.*

dim-er-ous (dim´ėr us) *adj.* Consisting of two parts.

di-min-ish (di min´ish) *v.* To become or make smaller or less; to reduce in power, rank, or authority; to decrease; to taper. **diminishment** *n.*

dim-in-ished (di min´isht) *adj.* Reduced; lessened.

di-min-u-en-do (di min´ū en˝do) *adj. & adv.* Gradually lessening in volume. **diminuendo** *n.*

di-min-u-tive (di min´ū tiv) *adj.* Very small; tiny.

dim-is-so-ry (dim´i sōr˝ē) *adj.* Granting leave to depart.

dim-mer (dim´ėr) *n.* A rheostat used to reduce the intensity of an electric light.

dim-wit (dim´wit) *n.* A simple-minded or stupid person. **dimwitted** *adj.* **dimwittedly** *adv.* **dimwittedness** *n.*

din (din) *n.* A loud, confused, harsh noise.

dine (dīn) *v.* To eat dinner.

ding (ding) *v.* To sound as a bell when struck; to make a ringing sound.

ding–a–ling *n., Slang* A silly person.

din-ghy (ding´gē) *n., pl.* **dinghies** A small rowboat; an inflatable rubber raft.

din-ner (din´ėr) *n.* The main meal of the day; a formal meal honoring someone.

di-no-saur (dī´no sor˝) *n. Paleontology* A group of extinct reptiles from the Mesozoic period; some were the largest land animals known to exist.

di-no-there (dī´no thėr˝) *n.* A huge, extinct, two-tusked mammal closely associated with the elephant.

dint (dint) *n.* Means; force; effort. **dint** *v.* To drive with force.

di-ode (dī´ōd) *n.* An electron tube which permits electrons to pass in only one direction, used as a rectifier.

di-o-ra-ma (dī´o ram˝a) *n.* A miniature scene in three dimensions.

dip (dip) *v.* To let or put down into a liquid momentarily; to lift up and out by scooping or bailing; to make candles by repeatedly immersing wicks in wax or tallow; to sink or go down suddenly. **dip** *n.* A downward motion; a sauce made of liquid, into which something is to be dipped; a depression or hollow. *Slang* A silly person.

diph-the-ri-a (dif thėr˝ē a) *n. Pathol.* An acute contagious disease caused by bacillus and characterized by formation of a false membrane in the throat and accompanied by weakness and by fever.

diph-thong (dif´thong) *n.* A blend of a single speech sound which begins with one vowel sound and moves to another in the same syllable, as *oi* in oil and coil or *oy* in boy and toy.

diph-y-o-dont (dif´ē o dont˝) *adj.* Having the successive development of two sets of teeth; as humans do.

di-plex (dī´pleks) *adj.* Pertaining to sending two simultaneous signals over the same communications path.

di-plo-ma (di plō´ma) *n.* A document issued by a college, school, or university testifying that a student has earned a degree or completed a course of study.

di-plo-ma-cy (di plō´ma sē) *n., pl.* **diplomacies** The practice of conducting international negotiations; skill and tact in dealing with people.

dip-ter-ous (dip´tėr us) *adj.* Pertaining to animals having a single pair of wings such as the fly, gnat, and mosquito.

dire (dīr) *adj.* Dreadful or terrible; threatening disastrous consequence. **direly** *adv.* **direfully** *adv.* **direness** *n.*

di-rect (dī rekt´) *v.* To control or regulate the affairs of; to command or order; to or tell someone the way; to cause something to move in a given course; to indicate the destination of a letter;

to supervise or instruct the performance of a job; to move or lie in a straight line; to do something immediate. **direct** *adj.* Without compromise; absolute; in the exact words of a person, as a directquote; straightforward; referring to the shortest, least complicated route..

di-rec-tion (di rek´shan) *n.* The act of directing; an order or command; the path or line along which something points, travels or lies. **directional** *adj.*

di-rec-tive (di rek´tiv) *n.* A regulation or order from someone with authority.

di-rect-ly (di rekt´lē) *adv.* Immediately; at once; in a direct manner or line; doing without an agent or go-between.

di-rec-tor (di rek´tėr) *n.* A person who manages or directs; one of a group of persons who supervises the affairs of an institute, corporation or business.

di-rec-to-ry (di rek´to rē) *n., pl.* **directories** A book listing data, alphabetically or classified, containing the names and addresses of a specific group, persons, organizations, inhabitants, or businesses. In computer science, in the hierarchical file structure, a division that holds related program or data files and sub-directories.

direct tax *n.* A tax which is charged directly to the taxpayer.

dirge (dėrj) *n.* A slow mournful song; a funeral hymn.

dir-i-gi-ble (dir´i ji bl) *n.* A lighter-than-air plane which may be steered by means of its own motor power.

dirk (dėrk) *n.* A dagger.

dirn-dl (dėrn´dl) *n.* A lady's full-skirted dress with a gathered waistband.

dirt (dėrt) *n.* Soil or earth; obscene or profane language; scandalous or hateful gossip.

dis-a-bil-i-ty (dis´a bil´i tē) *n.* The condition or state of being mentally or physically disabled or unable.

dis-a-ble (dis ā bl) *v.* To make powerless or incapacitate; to disqualify legally.

dis-a-buse (dis´a būz´) *v.* To free from misunderstanding, misconception, or delusion.

dis-ac-cord *n.* Disagreement.

dis-ad-van-tage (dis´ad van´tij) *n.* A circumstance that is unfavorable; loss or damage; detriment.

dis-af-fect (dis´a fekt´) *v.* To weaken or destroy the affection or loyalty of. **disaffection** *n.* **disaffected** *adj.*

dis-af-firm (dis´a fėrm´) *v.* To deny; to refuse to confirm.

dis-af-for-est (dis´a fot´ist) *v.* To strip trees from the forest.

dis-a-gree (dis´a grē´) *v.* To vary in opinion; to differ; to argue; to quarrel; to be unfavorable or unacceptable.

dis-a-gree-able (dis´a grē´a bl) *adj.*

Offensive or unpleasant.

dis-al-low (dis´a lou´) *v.* To refuse to allow; to reject as invalid or untrue.

dis-ap-pear (dis´a pēr´) *v.* To vanish; to drop from sight. **disappearance** *n.*

dis-ap-point (dis´a point´) *v.* To fail to satisfy the desires, hopes, or expectations of. **disappointing** *adj.*

dis-ap-pro-ba-tion (dis´ap ro bā´shan) *n.* Disapproval; condemnation.

dis-ap-prove (dis´a prōv´) *v.* To refuse to approve; to reject; to condemn.

dis-arm (dis ärm´) *v.* To make harmless; to deprive or take away the weapons or any means of attack or defense.

dis-ar-range (dis´a ränj´) *v.* To disturb the order of something.

dis-ar-ray (dis´a rā´) *n.* A state of confusion or disorder; an upset or turmoil.

dis-as-sem-ble (dis´a sem´bl) *v.* To take apart.

dis-as-so-ci-ate (dis´a sō´shēat´) *v.* To break away from or to detach oneself from an association. **-ion** *n.*

dis-as-ter (di zas´tėr) *n.* An event that causes great ruin or distress; a sudden and crushing misfortune. **-ous** *adj.*

dis-a-vow (dis´a vou´) *v.* To disclaim or deny any responsibility for or knowledge of. **disavowal** *n.*

dis-band (dis band´) *v.* To disperse; to break up. **disbandment** *n.*

dis-bar (dis bär´) *v.* In law, to expel officially from membership in the bar or the legal profession. **-ment** *n.*

dis-be-lieve (dis´bi lēv´) *v.* To refuse to believe in something. **disbelief** *n.*

dis-burse (dis bėrs´) *v.* To pay out; to give out; to spread out. **-ment** *n.*

disc or **disk** (disk) *n. Informal* A phonograph record.

dis-card (di skärd´) *v.* To remove a playing card from one's hand; to throw out. **discard** *n.* The act of discarding; something which is rejected or cast aside. **discarder** *n.* **discardable** *adj.*

dis-cern (di sėrn´) *v.* To detect differences visually or with other senses or the intellect; to perceive as separate and distinct. **discerner** *n.* **discernment** *n.* **discernible** *adj.*

dis-cerp-ti-ble *adj.* Capable of being torn apart; divisible.

dis-charge (dis chärj´) *v.* To relieve of a charge, duty, load, or burden; to release as from confinement, custody, care, or duty; to dismiss from employment; to send forth; to shoot or fire a weapon; to get rid of; to release from service or duty; to fulfill an obligation, duty, or debt. **discharge** *n.* The act of discharging or the condition of being discharged.

dis-ci-ple (di sī´pl) *n.* One who accepts and assists in spreading doctrines of another. **Disciple** One of Christ's followers.

dis-ci-pline (dis´i plin) *n.* Training which corrects, molds, or perfects the mental faculties or moral character; behavior which results from such training; obedience to authority or rules; punishment meant to correct poor behavior. **discipline** *v.* To train or develop by teaching and by control; to bring order to; to penalize.

dis-claim (dis klãm´) *v.* To disavow any claim to or association with; to deny the authority of ; to renounce or give up a claim on. **disclaimer** *n.*

dis-close (dis klõz´) *v.* To make known; to bring into view. **disclosure** *n.*

dis-co (dis kõ) *n., pl.* **discos** Discotheque; a nightclub for dancing.

dis-cog-ra-phy (dis kog´ra fē) *n.* A systematic and descriptive list of phonograph records; as to the performer and date released.

dis-coid (dis´koid) *adj.* Having the form of or related to a disk; flat and circular.

dis-color (dis kul´ér) *v.* To alter or change the color of. **discoloration** *n.*

dis-com-fit (dis kum´fit) *v.* To defeat in battle; to make upset or uneasy.

dis-com-fort (dis kum´fért) *n.* Physical or mental uneasiness; pain; an inconvenience. **discomfort** *v.* To make uncomfortable.

dis-com-mend (dis´ko mend) *v.* To blame; to cause to be viewed unfavorably.

dis-com-mode (dis´ko mõd´) *v.* To inconvenience.

dis-com-pose (dis´kom põz´) *v.* To disrupt the composure or serenity of; to unsettle; to destroy the order of. **discomposure** *n.*

dis-con-cert (dis´kon sért´) *v.* To upset; to discompose; to perturb.

dis-con-nect (dis´ko nekt´) *v.* To sever or break the connection of or between; to detach. **disconnection** *n.*

dis-con-nect-ed (dis´kon nek´tid) *adj.* Not connected; separate.

dis-con-so-late (dis kon´so lit) *adj.* Without consolation; dejected; cheerless; sorrowful. **disconsolately** *adv.*

dis-con-tent (dis´kon tent´) *n.* Lack of contentment; dissatisfaction. **discontent** *v.* To make unhappy. **discontentedly** *adv.* **discontentment** *n.*

dis-con-tent-ed (dis´kon ten´tid) *adj.* Not pleased with one's circumstances.

dis-con-tin-ue (dis´kon tin´ū) *v.* To come or bring to an end; to break the continuity of; to interrupt; to stop trying, taking, or using.

dis-cord (dis´kord) *n.* Lacking accord or harmony; a harsh combination of musical sounds. **discordant** *adj.*

dis-cord-ance *n.* Disagreement; opposition.

dis-co-theque (dis´kō tek´) *n.* A nightclub where music is provided for dancing.

dis-count (dis´kount) *v.* To sell or offer for sale at a price lower than usual; to leave out of account; to disregard.

dis-cour-age (di skér´ij) *v.* To deprive or be deprived of enthusiasm or courage; to hinder by disfavoring; deterring or dissuading. **-ment** *n.*

dis-course (dis´kōrs) *n.* A conversation; a formal and lengthy discussion of a subject. *v.* To write or converse extensively. **discourser** *n.*

dis-cour-te-ous (dis kér´tē us) *adj.* Lacking consideration or courteous manners. **discourtesy** *n.*

dis-cov-er (di skuv´ér) *v.* To make known or visible; to observe or learn of for the first time; to explore. **discoverable** *adj.* **discovery** *n.*

dis-cred-it (dis kred´it) *v.* To mar the reputation of or disgrace someone or something; to injure the reputation of. **discredit** *n.* Loss of credit or reputation; doubt; disbelief. **discreditable** *adj.* **discreditably** *adv.*

dis-creet (di skrēt´) *adj.* Tactful; careful of appearances; modest. **discreetly** *adv.*

dis-crep-an-cy (di skrep´an sē) *n., pl.* **discrepancies** A difference in facts.

dis-crete (di skrēt´) *adj.* Separate; made up of distinct parts.

dis-cre-tion (di skresh´shan) *n.* The quality or act of being discreet; the ability to make responsible choices; power to decide; the result of separating or distinguishing.

dis-crim-i-nate (di skrim´i nāt´) *v.* To distinguish or differentiate between someone or something on the basis of race, sex, class, or religion; to detect differences.

dis-cus (dis´kus) *n.* A heavy disk made of wood, rubber, or metal, which is hurled for distance in athletic competitions; a brightly-colored, disk-shaped freshwater fish of South America.

dis-cuss (di skus´) *v.* To investigate by argument or debate; to consider or examine something through discourse.

dis-cus-sant (di skus´ant) *n.* A participant in a discussion.

dis-cus-sion (di skush´an) *n.* The act of discussing between two or more people about a subject that they may or may not agree on.

dis-dain (dis dān´) *v.* To treat contemptuously; to look on with scorn.

dis-ease (di zēz´) *n.* A condition of the living animal, plant body, or any parts which impairs normal functioning; a condition of ill health. **diseased** *adj.*

dis-em-bark (dis´em bärk´) *v.* To go

or put ashore from a ship; unload.

dis-em-bod-y (dis'em bod'ē) v. To release or free the soul from physical existence.

dis-em-bow-el (dis'em bou'el) v. To remove the bowels or entrails; to eviscerate. **disembowelment** n.

dis-en-chant (dis'en chant') v. To free from false beliefs or enchantment. **disenchanting** adj.

dis-en-cum-ber (dis'en kum'bèr) v. To relieve of hardships; to free from encumbrance; unburden.

dis-en-gage (dis'en gāj') v. To free from something that holds or otherwise engages; to set free. **-ment** n.

dis-en-tan-gle (dis'en tang'gl) v. To relieve of entanglement, confusion, etc; unravel. **disentanglement** n.

dis-e-qui-lib-ri-um (dis ē kwi lib'rē um) n. The lack of balance.

dis-es-tab-lish (dis'e stab'lish) v. To deprive of the privileges of an establishment; bring about the end.

dis-es-teem (dis'e stēm') v. To regard with little esteem. n. The lack of esteem.

dis-fa-vor (dis fā'vèr) n. Disapproval; the state of being disliked.

dis-fig-ure (dis fig'ūr) v. To mar, deface, or deform the appearance of something or someone. **disfigurement** n.

dis-grace (dis grās') n. The state of having lost grace, favor, respect, or honor; something that disgraces.

dis-grun-tle (dis grun'tl) v. To make dissatisfied or discontented.

dis-gust (dis gust') v. To affect with nausea, repugnance, or aversion; to cause one to become impatient or lose attention. n. A marked aversion to something distasteful; repugnance.

dis-ha-bille (dis'a bēl') n. The state of being carelessly dressed; undress.

dis-har-mo-ny (dis här'mo nē) n. Lack of harmony or agreement; discord.

di-shev-el (di shev'el) v. To mess up or disarrange; to throw into disorder or disarray.

dis-hon-est (dis on'ist) adj. Lack of honesty; arising from or showing fraud or falseness. **dishonesty** n.

dis-hon-or (dis on'ér) n. The deprivation of honor; disgrace; the state of one who has lost honor; a cause of disgrace; failure to pay a financial obligation. **dishonor** v. To bring disgrace on something or someone; to fail to pay.

dis-il-lu-sion (dis'i lö'zhan) v. To deprive of illusion; to disenchant.

dis-in-cline (dis'in klin') v. To make unwilling; to cause to be not interested.

dis-in-fect (dis'in fekt') v. To cleanse and make free from infection, especially by destroying harmful microorganisms; to sterilize. **disinfection** n.

dis-in-gen-u-ous (dis'in jen'ū us) adj. Lacking frankness, sincerity, or simplicity; crafty; not straightforward.

dis-in-her-it (dis'in her'it) v. To deliberately deprive of inheritance; to depose of previously held privileges.

dis-in-te-grate (dis in'te grāt') v. To break or reduce into separate elements, parts, or small particles; to destroy the unity or integrity of; to explode; to undergo a change in structure, as an atomic nucleus. **disintegration** n. **disintegrator** n.

dis-in-ter (dis'in tèr) v. To exhume or dig up something buried; to bring to light, disclose, uncover, or expose.

dis-in-ter-est-ed (dis in'tèr ist ed) adj. The state of being unbiased, impartial, unselfish, or not interested; free from selfish motive or interest. **disinterest** n. **disinterestedly** adv.

dis-join (dis join') v. To end the joining of; to become detached; to disconnect.

dis-junct (dis jungkt') adj. Disjoined; separated; discontinuous.

disk or **disc** (disk) n. A thin, flat, circular object. In computer science, a round, flat plate coated with a magnetic substance on which data for a computer is stored; a fairly flat, circular, metal object used to break up soil; the implement employing such tools.

disk crash n. In computer science, the destruction of a disk and the data it holds as a result of the read/write head coming in contact with the surface of the disk; any disk failure, sometimes recoverable.

disk drive n. Computer hardware on which files are stored; **hard disk** is storage within the computer and **floppy disk** is any storage medium external to the computer.

diskette n. In computer science, a floppy or removable disk.

disk formatting n. In computer science, a series of reference points recorded on a disk that allow orderly storage and retrieval of data.

disk fragmentation n. In computer science, a condition that occurs after many reads and writes to a disk in that data for a single file is scattered throughout the disk rather than being stored in contiguous sectors.

disk operating system n. In computer science, the software which controls the computer operations, disk drives and disk accessing; abbreviated as DOS.

disk sector n. In computer science, a section of a disk track.

disk tracks n. In computer science, concentric circles of a disk or a diskette where data is stored.

dis-like (dis līk') v. To regard with

dis-lo-cate (dis´lō kāt´) v. To put out of place or proper position. *Medical* To displace a bone from a socket or joint.

dis-lodge (dis loj´) v. To remove or drive out from a dwelling or position; to force out of a settled position.

dis-loy-al (dis loi´al) adj. Not loyal; untrue to personal obligations or duty. **disloyally** adv. **disloyalty** n.

dis-mal (diz´mal) adj. Causing gloom or depression; depressing; lacking in interest or merit. **dismalness** n.

dis-may (dis mā´) v. To deprive or be deprived of courage or resolution through the pressure of sudden fear or anxiety. **dismay** n. **dismayingly** adv.

dis-mem-ber (dis mem´bėr) v. To cut, pull off or disjoin the limbs, members, or parts of. **dismemberment** n.

dis-miss (dis mis´) v. To discharge or allow to leave; to remove from position or service as an employee; to bar from attention or serious consideration; in law, to disallow or reject any further judicial consideration on a claim or action. **dismissal** n. **dismissive** adj.

dis-o-bey (dis´o bā´) v. To refuse or fail to obey; to be rebellious. **disobedient** adj. **disobediently** adv.

dis-or-gan-ize (dis or´ga nīz´) v. To destroy or break up the organization, unity, or structure of.

dis-o-ri-ent (dis ōr´ē ent) v. To cause to lose one's bearings.

dis-own (dis ōn´) v. To refuse to acknowledge or claim as one's own.

dis-par-age v. To bring reproach or discredit upon; lower the estimation of.

dis-pa-rate (dis´pėr it) adj. Altogether dissimilar; unequal. **disparately** adv.

dis-par-i-ty (di spar´i tē) n. Inequality; difference in condition or excellence.

dis-pas-sion-ate (dis pash´o nit) adj. Free from bias or passion; impartial.

dis-pel (di spel´) v. To drive off or away.

dis-pen-sa-ble (di spen´sa bl) adj. Capable of being dispensed; not essential.

dis-pen-sa-ry (di spen´sa rē) n. A place where medicine is dispensed.

dis-pense (di spens´) v. To give out; to distribute; to administer; to let go or exempt. **dispense with** To get rid of; to forgo. **dispensation** n. **-er** n.

dis-place (dis plās´) v. To change the position of; to take the place of; to discharge from an office; to cause a physical displacement. **-ment** n.

dis-play (di splā´) v. To put forth or spread; to put in view; to show off. **display** n. The content of a display. In *computer science*, a device which gives information in a visual form such as a computer screen or a cathode-ray

tube (CRT).

dis-please (dis plēz´) v. To cause the disapproval or annoyance of; to cause displeasure. **displeasure** n.

dis-pose (di spōz´) v. To put in place; to finally settle or come to terms. **dispose of** To get rid of; to attend to or settle; to transfer or part with, as by selling. **disposal** n. **disposable** adj.

dis-po-si-tion (dis´po zish´an) n. Prevailing mood, temper or emotion; final arrangements.

dis-pos-sess (dis´po zes´) v. To deprive of possession or ownership of land, property, or other possessions.

dis-prove (dis pröv´) v. To prove to be false or erroneous.. **disprovable** adj.

dis-put-a-ble (di spū´ta bl) adj. Capable of being disputed. **disputably** adv.

dis-pu-ta-tion (dis´pū tā´shan) n. The act of disputing; a debate.

dis-pute (di spūt´) v. To debate or argue; to question the validity of; to strive against or to resist. **dispute** n. A verbal controversy; a quarrel. **disputant** n.

dis-qual-i-fy (dis kwol´i fī´) v. To deprive of the required properties or conditions; to deprive of a power or privilege; to make ineligible for a prize or further competition. **disqualification** n.

dis-qui-si-tion (dis´kwi zish´on) n. A formal inquiry into or discussion of a subject.

dis-re-gard (dis´ri gärd´) v. To ignore; to neglect; to pay no attention to; to treat without proper attention. **disregard** n. **disregardful** adj.

dis-re-la-tion (dis´ri lā´shan) n. The lack of a fitting or suitable connection.

dis-re-pair (dis´ri pâr´) n. The state of being in need of repair.

dis-re-pute (dis´ri pūt´) n. A state of being held in low esteem; loss of a good reputation; disgrace. **-able** adj.

dis-re-spect (dis´ri spekt´) n. Lack of respect or reverence. **disrespect** v.

dis-re-spect-ful adj. Displaying a lack of respect. **disrespectfully** adv.

dis-robe (dis rōb´) v. To undress.

dis-rupt (dis rupt´) v. To throw into disorder or confusion; upset; to cause to break down. **disrupter, disruption** n. **disruptive** adj.

dis-sat-is-fac-tion (dis´sat is fak´shan) n. The feeling of discontent; a lack of satisfaction.

dis-sect (di sekt´) v. To cut into pieces; to expose the parts of something, such as an animal, for examination; to analyze in detail. **dissection** n.

dis-sem-ble (di sem´bl) v. To conceal or hide the actual nature of; to put on a false appearance; to conceal facts, intentions or motives. **dissembler** n.

dis-sem-i-nate (di sem´i nāt´) v. To scatter or spread, as if by sowing, over

aversion or disapproval. n. Distaste.

a wide area. **dissemination** *n.*
disseminator *n.*

dis-sem-i-nule (di sem′i nūl′) *n.* The regenerative part of a plant.

dis-sen-sion (di sen′shan) *n.* Difference of opinion; discord; strife.

dis-sent (di sent′) *v.* To differ in opinion or thought. **dissent** *n.* Difference of opinion; refusal to go along with an established church.

dis-sep-i-ment (di sep′i ment) *n.* A partition between cells of animals and plants.

dis-ser-ta-tion (dis′ĕr tā′shan) *n.* A formal written discourse or treatise, especially one submitted for a doctorate.

dis-serv-ice (dis sĕr′vis) *n.* An ill turn; an ill service, injury, or harm.

dis-sev-er (di sev′ĕr) *v.* To sever; to divide; to separate. **disseverance** *n.*

dis-si-dent (dis′i dent) *adj.* Strong and open difference with an opinion or group. **dissident** *n.* **dissidence** *n.*

dis-sil-i-ent (di sil′ēent) *adj.* Bursting open with force.

dis-sim-i-lar (di sim′i lĕr) *adj.* Different; not the same; unlike. **dissimilarity** *n.*

dis-si-mil-i-tude (dis′si mil′i töd′) *n.* Lack of resemblance; unlikeness.

dis-sim-u-late (di sim′ū lāt′) *v.* To conceal under a false appearance; to dissemble.

dis-si-pate (dis′i pāt′) *v.* To disperse or drive away; to squander or waste; to separate into parts and scatter or vanish; to become dispersed; to lose irreversibly. **dissipation** *n.*

dis-so-ci-ate (di sō′shē āt′) *v.* To break from the association with another person or organization.

dis-sol-u-ble (di sol′ū bl) *adj.* Capable of being dissolved.

dis-so-lute (dis′o lŏt′) *adj.* Loose in morals; lacking moral restraint. **dissolutely** *adv.* **dissoluteness** *n.*

dis-so-lu-tion (dis′o lō′shan) *n.* The act or process of changing from a solid to a fluid form; termination of a business; the separation of body and soul; death.

dis-solve (di zolv′) *v.* To pass into solution, such as dissolving sugar in water; to overcome, as by emotion; to fade away; to become decomposed; to terminate. **dissolvable** *adj.*

dis-so-nance (dis′o nans) *n.* Lack of agreement; a conflict. *Music* A harsh or disagreeable combination of sounds; discord. **dissonant** *adj.*

dis-tal (dis′tal) *n.* Relatively remote from the point of attachment or origin; farthest from the center. **distally** *adv.*

dis-tance (dis′tans) *n.* Separation in time or space; the degree of separation between two points; the space that

separates any two specified points in time; the quality or state of being distant; aloofness. **distance** *v.* To put space between; to keep at a distance.

dis-tant (dis′tant) *adj.* Apart or separated by a specified amount of time or space; coming from, going to, or located at a distance; remotely related. **distantly,**

dis-tend (di stend′) *v.* To expand from internal pressure; to swell. **distensible** *adj.* **distention** *n.*

dis-tich (dis′tik) *n.* A couplet; a few lines of poetic verse that make sense alone.

dis-til-la-tion (dis′ti lā′shan) *n.* The act or process of heating a liquid or other substance until it sends off a gas or vapor and then cooling the gas of vapor until it returns to a liquid or solid form, thus separating impurities.

dis-tinct (di stingkt′) *adj.* Distinguished from all others; separated or distinguished by some feature; not the same in number or kind; different; clearly seen; unquestionable; one of a kind.

dis-tin-guish (di sting′gwish) *v.* To recognize as being different; to discriminate; to make something different or noticeable. **distinguishable** *adj.* **distinguished** *adj.*

dis-tort (di stort′) *v.* To twist or bend out of shape; to twist the true meaning of; to give a misleading account of. *Slang* Blow out of shape. **-ion** *n.*

dis-tract (di strakt′) *v.* To draw or divert one's attention away from something; to cause one to feel conflicting emotions. **distract** *n.*

dis-trac-tion (di strak′shan) *n.* The act of distracting; that which distracts.

dis-trait (di strā′) *adj.* Absent-minded.

dis-traught (di strot′) *adj.* Deeply agitated with doubt or anxiety; crazed.

dis-tress (di stres′) *v.* To cause suffering of mind or body. **distress** *n.* Pain or suffering; severe physical or mental strain; a very painful situation.

dis-trib-ute (di strib′ūt) *v.* To divide among many; to deliver or give out; to classify. **distribution** *n.*

dis-trib-u-tor (di strib′ūt ĕr) *n.* One who distributes, as a wholesaler; a device that directs electrical current to spark plugs of an engine.

dis-trict (dis′trikt) *n.* An administrative or political section of a territory; a distinctive area. **district** *v.*

district attorney *n.* The public prosecuting officer of a judicial district.

District of Columbia *n.* The capital of the United States of America; the only part of the continental United States which is not a state, is not part of a state, and does not have a voting congress person in the House of Representatives or an elected senator.

dis-trust (dis trust´) n. Suspicion; doubt. distrust v. To doubt; to suspect; to question someone or thing. distrustful adj. distrustfully adv.

dis-turb (di sterb´) v. To destroy the tranquillity or composure of; to unsettle mentally or emotionally; to interrupt or interfere with; to bother. -er n.

dis-un-ion (dis ūn´yon) n. The termination of a union; separation.

dis-u-nite (dis´ū nīt´) v. To divide or separate.

dis-u-ni-ty (dis´ū nit´ē) n. Discord; lack of unity.

dis-use (dis ūs´) n. The state of not using; out of use.

dis-u-til-i-ty (dis´ū til´i tē) n. The state of causing inconvenience or fatigue; harm; counterproductive.

di-syl-la-ble (dī´sil a bl) n. A word having two syllables.

dith-er (dith´ėr) n. A state of nervousness or indecision; commotion.

dit-to (dit´ō) n., pl. dittos An exact copy; the same as stated before. ditto mark The pair of marks (") used to substitute for the word ditto. ditto adv.

dit-ty (dit´ē) n. A short, simple song.

ditty bag n. A small bag used by sailors to hold small articles, such as thread, buttons, and other small personal effects.

di-u-ret-ic (dī´ū ret´ik) adj. Tending to cause an increase in the flow of urine. diuretic n. A drug given to increase the amount of urine produced.

di-ur-nal (di er´nal) adj. Having a daily cycle or recurring every day; of, relating to, or occurring in the daytime; opening in the daytime and closing at night.

di-va (dē´vä) n., pl. divas or dive A prima donna; a female opera star.

di-van (di van´) n. A long, backless and armless sofa or couch.

di-var-i-cate (dī var´i kāt) v. To spread apart; branch off.

di-verge (di vėrj´) v. To move or extend in different directions from a common point; to differ in opinion or manner. divergence n. divergent adj.

di-vers (dī´vėrz) adj. Various; several.

di-verse (di vers´) adj. Different; unlike in characteristics; having various forms or qualities. diversely adv.

di-ver-si-fy (di ver´si fī´) v. To give variety to something; to engage in varied operations; to distribute over a wide range of types or classes. .

di-ver-sion (di ver´zhan) n. The act of diverting from a course, activity or use; something that diverts or amuses. diversionary adj.

di-ver-sion-ist n. A person characterized by political deviation; one engaged in diversionary activities.

di-ver-si-ty (di ver´si tē) n., pl. diversities A difference; variety; unlikeness.

di-vert (di vert´) v. To turn from a set course; to give pleasure by distracting the attention from something that is burdensome or oppressive. diverting adj. divertingly adv.

di-vest (di vest´) v. To undress or strip, especially of clothing or equipment; to deprive or dispossess of property, authority, or title; to take away from a person. divestment n.

di-vide (di vīd´) v. To separate into parts, areas, or groups; to separate into pieces or portions and give out in shares; to cause to be apart; in mathematics, to perform mathematical division on a number. divide n. An act of dividing; a dividing ridge between drainage areas. dividable adj.

div-i-dend (div´i dend´) n. An individual share of something distributed; a bonus; a number to be divided; a sum or fund to be divided and distributed.

div-i-na-tion (div´i nā´shan) n. The act or practice of foretelling future events, or discovering obscure things.

di-vine (di vīn´) adj. Of, relating to, preceding from, or pertaining to God. Informal Extremely pleasing. divine n. A clergyman or theologian. divine v. To foretell. divinely adv.

di-vi-sion (di vizh´on) n. Separation; something which divides, separates, or marks off; the act, process, or instance of separating or keeping apart; the condition or an instance of being divided in opinion; in mathematics, the process of discovering how many times one quantity is contained in another. Military A self-sufficient tactical unit capable of independent action.

di-vi-sive (di vī´siv) adj. Tending to create dissension or disunity. divisiveness n.

di-vi-sor (di vī´zėr) n. In mathematics, the number by which a dividend is to be divided.

di-vorce (di vōrs´) n. The legal dissolution of a marriage; the complete separation of things. divorce v. divorce n. Divorced man. divorcee n. Divorced woman.

di-vulge (di vulj´) v. To reveal or make known; to disclose; to reveal a secret.

di-vul-sion (di vul´shan) n. The act of pulling apart; violent separation.

di-zy-got-ic (dī´zī got´ik) adj. Describing fraternal twins.

do (dö) v. To bring to pass; to bring about; to perform or execute; to put forth; to exert; to bring to an end. do n. A festive get-together; a command to do something. Mus. The first tone of a scale. **do away with** To destroy; to kill. **do in** To tire completely; to kill. **do up** To adorn or dress lavishly; to wrap and tie.

do-cent (dō´sent) *n.* A teacher at a college or university; a guide or lecturer in a museum.

doc-ile (dos´il) *adj.* Easily led, taught, or managed. **docility** *n.*

dock-et (dok´it) *n.* A brief written summary of a document; an agenda; an identifying statement about a document placed on its cover.

doc-tor (dok´tèr) *n.* A person trained and licensed to practice medicine, such as a physician, surgeon, veterinarian, or dentist; a person holding the highest degree offered by a university. **doctor** *v.* To restore to good condition; to practice medicine; to administer medical treatment; to tamper with; to alter for a desired end and self gain. **doctoral** *adj.*

doc-tor-ate (dok´tèr it) *n.* The degree, status, or title of a doctor.

doc-tri-naire (dok´tri när´) *n.* One who tries to put something into effect with little regard to practical difficulties.

doc-trine (dok´trin) *n.* Something taught as a body of principles; a statement of fundamental government policy, esp. in international relations.

doc-u-ment (dok´ū ment) *n.* An official paper utilized as the basis, proof, or support of something. **document** *v.* To furnish documentary evidence of; to prove with, support by, or provide by documents.

doc-u-men-ta-ry (dok´ū men´ta rē) *adj.* Relating to or based on documents; an artistic way of presenting facts.

doc-u-men-ta-tion (dok´ū men tā´shan) *n.* The act or use of documentary evidence. In *computer science,* information or instructions relating to a program, procedure, etc.

document retrieval In *computer science,* a system for identifying and retrieving data stored in the computer.

dod-der (dod´èr) *v.* To tremble, shake, or totter from weakness or age. **dodder** *n. Bot.* A parasitic, twining vine.

do-dec-a-gon (dō dek´agon) *n.* A polygon with twelve sides and twelve angles.

does-n't (duz´ent) *contr.* Does not.

dog-ma (dog´ma) *n.* A rigidly held doctrine proclaimed to be true by a religious group; a principle or idea considered to be the absolute truth.

dog-mat-ic (dog mat´ik) *adj.* Marked by an authoritative assertion of unproved or unprovable principles.

dol-drums (dōl´drumz) *n.* A period of listlessness or despondency. *Naut.* The ocean region near the equator where there is very little wind.

dole (dōl) *n.* The distribution of food, money, or clothing to the needy; a grant of government funds to the unemployed; something portioned out and distributed bit by bit. **dole** *v.*

dole-ful (dōl´ful) *adj.* Filled with grief or sadness. **dolefully** *adv.*

dol-er-ite (dol´e rīt´) *n.* An igneous rock, similar to basalt, whose composition cannot be determined without a microscope.

dol-i-cho-ce-phal-ic (dol´i kō se fal´ik) *adj.* Having a long head; with the width of the skull small in proportion to the length from back to front.

dol-lar (dol´èr) *n.* A coin, note, or token representing 100 cents; the standard monetary unit of the United States.

dol-lop (dol´op) *n.* A lump or blob of a semi-liquid substance; an indefinite amount or form.

dol-men (dōl´man) *n.* A prehistoric monument made up of a huge stone set on upright stones.

dol-or-ous (dol´èr us) *adj.* Marked by grief or pain; sad; mournful. **dolorously** *adv.* **dolorousness** *n.*

dolt (dōlt) *n.* A stupid person.

do-main (dō mān´) *n.* A territory under one government; a field of activity or interest.

dome (dōm) *n.* A roof resembling a hemisphere; something suggesting a dome.

do-mes-tic (do mes´tik) *adj.* Of or relating to the home, household or family life; interested in household affairs and home life; tame or domesticated; of or relating to policies of one's country; originated in a particular country. **domestic** *n.* A household servant. **domestically** *adv.*

dom-i-cile (dom´i sīl´) *n.* A dwelling place, house, or home; residence. **domicile** *v.* **domiciliary** *adj.*

dom-i-nant (dom´i nant) *adj.* Having the most control or influence; most over-whelming; in genetics, producing a typical effect even when paired with an unlike gene for the same characteristic. **dominance** *n.* **dominantly** *adv.*

do-min-ion (do min´yan) *n.* The power of supreme authority; controlling.

domino theory *n.* The theory that if a certain event occurs, a series of similar events will follow.

do-na-tion (dō nā´shan) *n.* The act of giving or bestowing a gift especially to needy or to charity. **donate** *v.*

done (dun) *adj.* Completely finished or through; doomed to failure, defeat, or death; cooked adequately.

do-nee (dō nē´) *n.* A recipient of a gift.

done for *adj.* Mortally stricken; doomed; left with no opportunity for recovery;

ruined.

don't (dōnt) *contr.* Do not.

dood-le (dŏdel) *v.* To scribble, design, or sketch aimlessly, especially when preoccupied. **doodle** *n.*

doom (dŏm) *n.* A pronounced judgment, particularly an official condemnation to a severe penalty or death; an unhappy destiny. **doom** *v.* To condemn; to make certain the destruction of.

dor-mant (dor'mant) *adj.* Asleep; in a state of inactivity or rest.

dor-mi-to-ry (dor'mi tŏr'ē) *n.* A large room that contains a number of beds, as at a college.

dor-nick (dor'nik) *n.* A small stone, or a chunk of rock.

dor-sal (dor'sal) *adj.* Of, relating to, or situated on or near the back.

dor-si-ven-tral (dor'si ven'tral) *adj.* Having distinct differences in the dorsal and ventral surfaces.

dor-sum (dor'sum) *n.* The back; the whole surface of an animal's back.

do-ry (dŏr'ē) *n., pl.* **dories** A small flat-bottomed boat with high, flaring sides and a sharp bow.

DOS *abbr. & n.* Disk operating system; a program that controls all of the basic operations of the computer.

dos-age (dō'sij) *n.* The administration of medicine in a measured dose; the amount administered.

dose (dōs) *n.* The measured quantity of a therapeutic agent to be taken at one time or at stated intervals. *Med.* The prescribed amount of radiation to which a certain part of the body is exposed.

dos-si-er (dos'ē ā') *n.* A complete file of documents or papers giving detailed information about a person or affair.

dot (dot) *n.* A small round spot; a mark made by or as if by a writing implement; a small round mark used in punctuation; a precise moment in time; a short click or buzz forming a letter or part of a letter in the Morse code.

dot-age (dō'tij) *n.* Feebleness or imbecility, especially in old age.

dot matrix In computer science, printing in which characters are formed by numerous dots arranged according to the pattern established for the character.

dote (dōt) *v.* To show excessive affection or fondness; to exhibit mental decline, especially as a result of senility. **doter** *n.* **doting** *adj.* **dotingly** *adv.*

dou-ble (dub'l) *adj.* Twice as much; composed of two like parts; designed for two. *Bot.* Having more than the usual number of petals. **double** *n.* An actor who takes the place of another for scenes calling for special skill; in baseball, a two-base hit. **double** *v.* In baseball, to make a double; to make or become twice as great; to fold in

two; to turn and go back; to serve an additional purpose. **doubly** *adv.*

double click In *computer science,* pressing and releasing a button of a mouse twice in succession, used to activate a selection in some programs.

double density disk In *computer science,* a diskette on which data is packed in order to double its capacity.

double-sided disk In *computer science,* a diskette on which data is stored on both sides.

doubt (dout) *v.* To be uncertain or mistrustful about something; to distrust. **doubt** *n.* **doubter** *n.* **doubtful** *adj.*

dour (der) *adj.* Stern and forbidding; morose and ill-tempered.

douse (dous) *v.* To plunge into liquid; to throw water on; to drench; to extinguish. **douser** *n.*

dove (duv) *n.* Any of numerous pigeons; a gentle, innocent person. **dovish** *adj.*

dow-el (dou'el) *n.* A round wooden pin which fits tightly into an adjacent hole to fasten together the two pieces.

download In *computer science,* the transfer or data to another computer or peripheral device.

downer *n.* A depressant or sedative drug; a barbiturate; something depressing.

dow-ry (dou'rē) *n.* The money, goods, or estate which a woman brings to her husband in marriage; a gift.

dowse (douz) *v.* To search for with a divining rod to find underground water or minerals. **dowser** *n.*

dpi *abbr. & n.* In *computer science,* dots per inch; a measure of the quality of image from scanner or printer' the more dots per inch, the finer the image appears to the eye.

drab (drab) *adj.* Of a light, dull brown or olive brown color; commonplace or dull. **drabness** *n.*

draft (draft) *n.* A current of air; a sketch or plan of something to be made; a note for the transfer of money; the depth of water a ship draws with a certain load. *Milit.* A mandatory selection of men for service. **draft** *v.* To draw a tentative plan or sketch. **draft** *adj.* The drawing of a liquid from a keg or tap.

drag (drag) *v.* To pull along or haul by force; to move with painful or undue slowness; to bring by force; to proceed slowly; to lag behind; to trail on the ground. **drag** *n.* Something which retards motion or action; a tool used under water to detect or collect objects; something which is boring or dull. *Slang* Someone or something that is boring or bothersome; a street; a race. In computer science, to press and hold the mouse button down while moving the cursor, thereby moving the image under the cursor. **dragger** *n.*

drag-on-et (drag´*o* net´) *n*. A little dragon; any small, brightly colored marine fish found in shallow tropical waters.

drain (drān) *n*. To draw off liquid; to use up; to exhaust physically or emotionally; to flow off gradually. **drain** *n*. A means, such as a trench or channel, by which liquid matter is drained; something which causes depletion. **drainer** *n*.

drainage *n*. A system, process or act of draining.

drainpipe *n*. A pipe for draining.

drake (drāk) *n*. A male duck.

DRAM *abbr. & n.* In *computer science*, Dynamic Random Access Memory; memory that must be constantly refreshed to be retained and that is erased when the power is off.

dram (dram) *n*. A small drink; a small portion; a measurement equaling approximately .06 ounces.

dra-ma (drä´ma) *n*. A composition in prose or verse, especially one to be presented on the stage, recounting a serious story; a play. **dramatic** *adj*.

dra-mat-ics (dra mat´iks) *n*. Amateur theatrical productions; the study of theatrical arts; excessive emotional behavior.

dram-a-tist (dram´a tist) *n*. Playwright.

drank *v*. Past tense of drink.

drape (drāp) *v*. To cover or adorn with something; to arrange or hang in loose folds. **drape** *n*. The manner in which a cloth hangs or falls; curtain or drapery.

dras-tic (dras´tik) *adj*. Being extremely harsh or severe. **drastically** *adv*.

draught (draft) *n. v.* A variation of draft.

draughts (drafts) *n*. British term for the game of checkers.

draw-er (dror) *n*. One that draws pictures; a sliding box or receptacle in furniture. **drawers** *n*. An article of clothing for the lower body.

drawl (draul) *v*. To speak slowly with prolonged vowels.

drawn *adj*. Haggard.

dray (drā) *n*. A low, heavy cart without sides, used for hauling.

dread (dred) *v*. To fear greatly; to anticipate with alarm, anxiety, or reluctance. **dread** *n*. A great fear.

dread-ful (dred´ful) *adj*. Inspiring dread; very distasteful or shocking; awful. **dreadfully** *adv*. **dreadfulness** *n*.

dream (drēm) *n*. A series of thought images, or emotions which occur during the rapid eye movement or REM state of sleep; an experience in waking life that has the characteristics of a dream; a daydream; something notable for its beauty or enjoyable quality; something that is strongly desired;

something that fully satisfies a desire. **dreamy** *adj*. **dreamily** *adv*.

drea-ry (drēr´ē) *adj*. Bleak and gloomy; dull. **drearily** *adv*. **dreariness** *n*.

dredge (drej) *n*. An apparatus used to remove sand or mud from the bottom of a body of water; a boat or barge equipped with a dredge. **dredge** *v*. To dig, gather, or deepen with a dredging machine; to use a dredge; in cooking, to coat with a powdered substance, especially flour or cornmeal.

dregs (dregz) *n*. The sediment of a liquid; the least desirable part.

drench (drench) *v*. To wet thoroughly; to throw water on. **drencher** *n*.

dress (dres) *n*. An outer garment for women and girls; covering or appearance appropriate to a particular time. **dress** *v*. To set straight; to put clothes on; to arrange in a straight line at proper intervals; to provide with clothing; to kill and prepare for market; to put on or wear formal clothes.

dressmaker *n*. A person who makes or alters women's clothing.

dress rehearsal *n*. A rehearsal, complete with costumes and stage props.

drew *v*. Past tense of draw.

drib-ble (drib´l) *v*. To drip; to slobber or drool; to bounce a ball repeatedly; to move in short bounces. **dribbler** *n*.

dried—up (drīd´up´) *adj*. Lacking moisture; wrinkled and shriveled.

drink (dringk) *v*. To take liquid into the mouth and swallow; to take in or suck up; to receive into one's consciousness; to partake of alcoholic beverages. **drink** *n*. A liquid suitable for swallowing; alcoholic beverages; a sizable body of water. **drinkable** *adj*. **drinker** *n*.

drip (drip) *v*. To fall in drops. **drip** *n*. Liquid or moisture that falls in drops; the sound made by falling drops. *Slang* A dull or unattractive person.

drive designation In *computer science*, the letter assigned to a drive in order to identify it for sourcing.

driv-el (driv´el) *v*. To slobber; to talk nonsensically. **drivel** *n*.

driver In *computer science*, a program or routine that translates and conveys messages between a computer and a peripheral.

driz-zle (driz´el) *n*. A fine, quiet, gentle rain. **drizzle** *v*.

droit (droit) *n*. A legal right or claim.

droll (drōl) *adj*. Whimsically comical.

drone (drōn) *n*. A male bee, especially a honey bee, which has no sting, performs no work, and produces no honey; a person who depends on others for his survival.

drool (drōl) *v*. To let saliva dribble from the mouth. *Slang* To make an exaggerated expression of desire.

droop (drŏp) v. To hang or bend downward; to become depressed. **droop** n. **droopingly** adv. **droopy** adj.

drop (drop) n. A tiny, pear-shaped or rounded mass of liquid; a small quantity of a substance; the smallest unit of liquid measure; the act of falling; a swift decline; the vertical distance from a higher to a lower level; a delivery of something by parachute. **drop** v. To fall in drops; to descend from one area or level to another; to fall into a state of collapse or death; to pass into a given state or condition; to end or terminate an association or relationship with; to deposit at a specified place. **drop behind** To fall behind. **drop by** To pay a brief visit. **drop out** To quit school without graduating; to withdraw from society.

drop-sy (drop'sē) n. Med. A diseased condition in which large amounts of fluid collect in the body tissues and cavities.

dross (dros) n. An impurity which forms on the surface of molten metal; inferior, trivial, or worthless matter.

drought (drowt) n. A prolonged period of dryness that affects crops; a chronic shortage of something.

drove (drōv) n. A herd being driven in a body; a crowd in motion. **drove** v. Past tense of drive.

drown (drown) v. To kill or die by suffocating in a liquid; to overflow; to cause not to be heard by making a loud noise; to drive out.

drowse (drouz) v. To doze. **drowse** n.

drows-y (drou'zē) adj. Sleepy; tending to induce sleep. **drowsiness** n.

drub (drub) v. To hit with a stick; to abuse with words; to defeat decisively.

drudge (druj) n. A person who does tiresome or menial tasks. **drudgeries, drudgery** n. **drudge** v.

drug (drug) n. A substance used in the treatment of disease or illness; a narcotic. **drug** v. To take drugs for narcotic effect; to mix or dose with drugs. **drugged** adj.

drug-get (drug'it) n. A durable cloth of wool and other fibers used chiefly as a floor covering.

drug-gist (drug'ist) n. A pharmacist; the owner or operator of a drugstore.

drunk (drungk) adj. Intoxicated with alcohol which impairs the physical and mental faculties of a person; overwhelmed by strong feeling or emotion. **drunk** n. A drunkard.

drunk-ard (drungk'kėrd) adj. A person who is often intoxicated by liquor.

drunk-om-e-ter (drung kom'i tėr) n. An instrument for measuring the alcoholic content in the bloodstream by testing the breath.

drupe (drōp) n. A fruit, as the peach, usually having one large pit or seed.

du-al (dō'al) adj. Made up or composed of two parts; having a double purpose.

dub (dub) v. To confer knighthood upon; to nickname; to give a new sound track to; to add to a film, radio, or television production; to transfer sound already recorded. **dub** n. **dubber** n.

du-bi-ous (dō'bē us) adj. Causing doubt; unsettled in judgment; reluctant to agree; questionable as to quality or validity; verging on impropriety. **dubiousness** n. **dubiously** adv.

du-cal (dō'kal) adj. Pertaining to a duke or dukedom.

duch-ess (duch'is) n. The wife or widow of a duke; a female holding a ducal title in her own right.

duct (dukt) n. A bodily tube or canal, especially one carrying a secretion; a tubular passage through which something flows.

duc-tile (duk'til) adj. Capable of being drawn into a fine strand or wire; easily influenced or persuaded.

dud (dud) n. Informal A bomb, shell, or explosive round which fails to detonate; something which turns out to be a failure. **duds** Slang Clothing; personal belongings.

dude (dōd) n. Informal A city person vacationing on a ranch; a man who is a fancy dresser. Slang A fellow.

dudg-eon (duj'on) n. A sullen, displeased, or indignant mood.

due (dō) adj. Owed; payable; owed or owing as a natural or moral right; scheduled or expected to occur. **due** n. Something that is deserved or owed. **dues** A fee or charge for membership.

du-el (dō'el) n. A premeditated combat between two people, usually fought to resolve a point of honor; a struggle which resembles a duel. **duelist** n.

du-et (dō et') n. A musical composition for two performers or musical instruments.

duff (duf) v. To manipulate so as to make anything pass for something new or different; misrepresent.

duf-fel (duf'el) n. A coarse woolen material with a thick nap.

duffer n. An incompetent or clumsy person; something counterfeit or worthless.

dug (dug) n. The nipple of a female mammal.

duke (dōk) n. A noble ranking below a prince and above a marquis. **dukes** pl. Slang The fists. **dukedom** n.

dul-cet (dul'sit) adj. Melodious; pleasing to the ear; having an agreeable, soothing quality.

dul-ci-mer (dul'si mėr) n. A musical stringed instrument played with two small hammers or by plucking.

dun (dun) *v.* To press a debtor for payment. **dun** *n.* A brownish gray to dull grayish brown color. **dun** *adj.*

dunce (duns) *n.* A slow-witted person.

dune (dūn) *n.* A ridge or hill of sand that has been blown or drifted by the wind.

dung (dung) *n.* The excrement of animals; manure.

dun-ga-ree (dun´ga rē´) *n.* A sturdy, coarse, cotton fabric, especially blue denim; pants or overalls made from this material.

dun-geon (dun´jon) *n.* A dark, confining, underground prison chamber.

dunk (dungk) *v.* To dip a piece of food into liquid before eating; to submerge someone in a playful fashion.

du-o (dō´ō) *n., pl.* **duos** A musical duet; two people in close association.

du-o-de-num (dū´o dē´num) *n., pl.* **duodena** *or* **duodenums** The first portion of the small intestine, extending from the lower end of the stomach to the jejunum. **duodenal** *adj*

du-pli-cate (dō´pli kit) *adj.* Identical with another; existing in or consisting of two corresponding parts. **duplicate** *n.* Either of two things which are identical; an exact copy of an original. **duplicate** *v.* To make an exact copy of. **duplication** *n.*

du-plic-i-ty (dō plis´i tē) *n.* The practice of contradictory speech or thoughts with the intent to deceive; double-dealing.

du-ra-ble (der´a bl) *adj.* Able to continue for a prolonged period of time without deterioration; long-lasting.

du-ra ma-ter (dor´a mā´tēr) *n.* The tough fibrous membrane that covers the brain and spinal cord.

du-ra-tion (de rā´shan) *n.* The period of time during which something exists or lasts; continuance in time.

du-ress (de res´) *n.* Constraint by fear or force; in law, coercion illegally applied; forced restraint.

dur-ing (dur´ing) *prep.* Throughout the time of; within the time of.

duty (dō´tē) *n. pl.* **duties** Something which a person must or ought to do; a moral obligation; a service, action, or task assigned to one, especially in the military; a government tax on imports. **dutiful** *adj.*

dwell (dwel) *v.* To live, as an inhabitant; to continue in a given place or condition; to focus one's attention on.

dwin-dle (dwin´dl) *v.* To waste away; to become steadily less.

dye (dī) *v.* To fix a color in or to stain materials; to color with or become colored by a dye. **dye** *n.* A color imparted by a dye; a coloring matter or material.

dy-ing (dī´ing) *adj.* Coming to the end of life; about to die.

dy-nam-ic (dī nam´ik) *adj.* Marked by energy and productive activity or change; of or relating to energy, motion, or force. **dynamically** *adv.*

dy-nam-ics (dī nam´iks) *n.* The part of physics which deals with force, energy, and motion and the relationship between them.

dy-na-mism (dī´na miz´um) *n.* A kind of theory that explains the universe in terms of forces. **dynamist** *n.* **dynamistic** *adj.*

dy-na-mite (dī´na mīt´) *n.* An explosive composed of nitroglycerin and an absorbent material, often packaged in stick form. **dynamite** *v.* To blow up with or as if with dynamite.

dy-na-mo (dī´na mō´) *n.* A person who is very energetic; a generator.

dy-na-mom-e-ter (dī´no mom´i tēr) *n.* A type of device that is used for the purpose of measuring mechanical force. **dy-namometric** *adj.*

dy-na-mo-tor (dī´na mō´tēr) *n.* A combined electrical motor and generator.

dy-nap-o-lis (dī nap´ō lis) *n.* A type of city that has been planned for orderly growth along a traffic artery.

dy-nas-ty (dī´na stē) *n., pl.* **dynasties** A succession of rulers from the same family; a family or group which maintains great power, wealth, or position for many years. **dynastic** *adj.*

dys-cra-sia (dis krā´zha) *n.* A condition of the body that is abnormal.

dys-en-ter-y (dis´en ter´ē) *n.* An infection of the lower intestinal tract which produces pain, fever, and severe diarrhea. **dysenteric** *adj.*

dys-func-tion (dis fungk´shan) *n.* An abnormal functioning; not working proper. **dysfunctional** *adj.*

dys-gen-e-sis (dis´jen e sis´) *n.* The defective development of the gonads of one's body such as in Turner's syndrome.

dys-gen-ic (dis´jen ik) *adj.* Being biologically defective.

dys-lex-i-a (dis lex´ēa) *n.* An impairment in one's ability to read; unable to read.

dys-men-or-rhea (dis´men or ē´a) *n.* Abnormal, painful menstruation. **dysmenorrheic, dysmenorrheal** *adj.*

dys-pep-sia (dis pep´sha) *n.* Indigestion. **dyspeptic** *adj.*

dys-pro-si-um (dis prō´sē um) *n.* A metallic element used in nuclear research, symbolized by Dy.

dys-tro-phy (is´tro fē) *n.* Atrophy of muscle tissue; any of various neuromuscular disorders, especially muscular dystrophy. **dystrophic** *adj.*

dz *abbr.* Dozen.

E, e (ē) The fifth letter of the English alphabet. *Mus.* The third tone in the natural scale of C.

each (ēch) *adj.* Everyone of two or more considered separately. **each** *adv.* To or for each; apiece. **each** *pron.* Each one.

each other *pron.* Each in reciprocal action or relation; one another.

ea-ger (ē´gĕr) *adj.* Marked by enthusiastic interest or desire; having a great desire or wanting something very much; earnest. **eagerly** *adv.*

ear (ēr) *n. Anat.* The hearing organ in vertebrates, located on either side of the head; any of various organs capable of detecting vibratory motion; the ability to hear keenly; attention; something that resembles the external ear. **be all ears** Listen closely. **play by ear** Play without reference to written music.

earn (ern) *v.* To receive payment in return for work done or services rendered; to gain as a result of one's efforts. **earner** *n.*

ear-nest (er´nĭst) *n.* A serious mental state; payment in advance to bind an agreement; a pledge. *adj.* Characterized by an intense and serious state of mind; having serious intent. **earnestly** *adv.*

earth (erth) *n.* The third planet from the sun, on which there is life; the outer layer of the world; ground; soil; dirt.

earth-quake (erth´kwāk´) *n.* A trembling or violent shaking of the crust of the earth.

ease (ēz) *n.* A state of being comfortable; freedom from pain, discomfort, or care; freedom from labor or difficulty; an act of easing or a state of being eased. **ease** *v.* To free from pain or discomfort; to lessen the pressure or tension; to make less difficult; to move or pass with freedom. **at ease** Standing silently with the feet apart, as in a military formation.

ea-sel (ē´zel) *n.* A frame used by artists to support a canvas or picture.

eas-i-ly *adv.* Without difficulty.

east (ēst) *n.* The direction opposite of west; the direction in which the sun rises. **eastward** *adv. & adj.*

Easter (ē´stĕr) *n.* A Christian festival celebrating the resurrection of Christ, observed the first Sunday after the full moon on or next after March 21st.

ea-sy (ē´zē) *adj.* Capable of being accomplished with little difficulty; free from worry or pain; not hurried or strenuous; something readily obtainable. **easily** *adv.* **easiness** *n.*

eat (ēt) *v.* To chew and swallow food; to erode; to consume with distress or agitation; to take a meal. **eat crow** To accept what one has been fighting against. **eat one's heart out** To grieve bitterly. **eat one's words** To retract what has been said. **one's** *n.* **eater** *n.*

eave (ēvz) *n.* The overhanging edge of a roof.

EBCDIC *abbr. & n. in computer science,* Extended Binary Coded Decimal Interchange Code; a standard code for numeric representation of alphanumeric characters.

ebb (eb) *n.* The return of the tide towards the sea; a time of decline. *v.* To recede, as the tide does; to fall or flow back; to weaken.

eb-bet *n.* A type of green newt.

ebb tide *n.* The tide while at ebb; a period of decline.

eb-o-nite (eb´o nīt´) *n.* A type of hard rubber.

eb-o-ny (eb´o nē) *n., pl.* **ebonies** The dark, hard, colored wood from the center of the ebony tree of Asia and Africa. **ebony** *adj.* Resembling ebony; black.

e-bul-lient (i bul´yent) *adj.* Filled with enthusiasm. **ebullience** *n.*

eb-ul-li-tion (eb´u lish´an) *n.* The process of boiling or bubbling; a sudden release of emotion.

ec-cen-tric (ik sen´trik) *adj.* Differing from an established pattern or accepted norm; deviating from a perfect circle; not located at the geometrical center. **eccentric** *n.* An odd or erratic person; a disk or wheel with its axis not situated in the center. **eccentricity** *n.*

ec-chy-mo-sis *n.* The escaping of blood into the surrounding tissues.

ec-cle-si-as-ti-cal (i klē´zē as´tik) *n.* A clergyman; a person officially serving a church. *adj.* Of or relating to a church.

ec-cle-si-ol-o-gy (i klē´zē ol´a jē) *n.* A study of the architecture of a church.

ec-crine *adj.* To be producing a fluid secretion which does not remove cytoplasm for the secreting cell.

eccrine gland *n.* A sweat gland that produces an eccrine secretion.

ec-dy-sis (ek´di sis) *n.* The act of shedding the outer cuticular layer such as occurs in the insects.

e-ce-sis (i sē´sis) *n.* An establishment of animals in a new habitat.

e-chid-na (i kid´na) *n.* A type of toothless spiny-coated nocturnal mammal found in Australia that feeds mainly on ants.

e-chi-no-derm (i kī´no dĕrm´) *n.* A member of the phylum Echinodermata having a radially symmetrical shape such as the starfish.

ech-o (ek´ō) *n., pl.* **echoes** Repetition of a sound by reflecting sound waves from a surface; the sound produced by such a reflection; a repetition; reflection of transmitted radar signals by an object.

echo *v.* To repeat or be repeated by; to imitate. In *computer science*, in a DOS program, command or information lines that are displayed on the screen.

ec-lamp-si-a (i klamp´sē a) *n.* A form of toxemia marked by convulsions, often happening during pregnancy.

ec-lec-tic (i klek´tik) *adj.* Having components from diverse sources or styles. **eclectically** *adv.* **eclectic** *n.*

e-clipse (i klips´) *n.* A total or partial blocking of one celestial body by another. **eclipse** *v.* To fall into obscurity or decline; to cause an eclipse of; to overshadow.

e-clip-tic (i klip´tik) *n. Astron.* The circle formed by the intersection of the plane of the earth's orbit and the celestial sphere.

ec-logue (ek´log) *n.* A short pastoral poem in the form of a dialogue.

e-clo-sion (i klō´zhan) *n.* The act of hatching from an egg of a larva.

ec-o-cide *n.* The deliberate destruction of the natural environment by pollutants.

e-col-o-gy (i kol´o jē) *n.* The branch of science studying the relationship between living organisms and their environments. **ecological, ecologic** *adj.* **ecologically** *adv.* **ecologist** *n.*

ec-o-nom-ic (ē´ko nom´ik) *adj.* Relating to the development, production, and management of material wealth; relating to the necessities of life.

ec-o-nom-i-cal (ē´ko nom´i kal) *adj.* Not wasteful; frugal; operating with little waste. **economically** *adv.*

e-con-o-my (i kon´o mē) *n., pl.* **economies** Careful management of money, materials, and resources; a reduction in expenses; a system or structure for the management of resources and production of goods and services. **economy** *adj.*

e-co-sphere (ek´ō sfēr´) *n.* The parts of the universe habitable by living beings.

ec-o-tone *n.* A transition area between two adjacent plant communities where organisms of both communities compete for dominance.

ec-ru (ek´rō) *n.* A light yellowish brown, as the color of unbleached linen.

ec-sta-sy (ek´sta sē) *n., pl.* **ecstasies** The state of intense joy or delight. **ecstatic** *adj.* **ecstatically** *adv.*

ec-to-derm (ek´to dėrm´) *n.* The outer cellular membrane of a jellyfish.

ec-to-morph (ek´to morf´) *n.* A body structure, characterized by angularity and leanness. **ectomorphic** *adj.*

ec-to-par-a-site *n.* An external parasite.

ec-top-ic (ek´top ik) *adj.* Occurring in an abnormal place or position.

ec-to-therm *n.* An animal which is classified as cold-blooded.

ec-ze-ma (ek´se ma) *n.* A noncontagious inflammatory skin condition, marked by itching and scaly patches.

e-daph-ic (i daf´ik) *adj.* Pertaining to or relating to the soil. **edaphically** *adv.*

ed-dy (ed´ē) *n., pl.* **eddies** A current, as of water, running against the direction of the main current, especially in a circular motion. **eddy** *v.*

e-e-ma (i dē´ma) *n.* An accumulation of serous fluid in the connective tissue that is abnormal. **edematous** *adj.*

e-den-tate (ē den´tāt) *n.* Any of the mammals that have few or no teeth, such as the anteater or sloth.

e-den-tu-lous (ē den´che lus) *adj.* Without teeth; toothless..

edge (ej) *n.* The thin, sharp, cutting side of a blade; keenness; sharpness; the border where an object or area begins or ends; an advantage. **edge** *v.* To furnish with an edge or border; to sharpen; to move gradually. **on edge** Tense.

e-dict (ē´dikt) *n.* A public decree; an order or command officially proclaimed.

ed-if-i-ca-to-ry *adj.* To be suitable for improvement in mind or morals.

ed-i-fice (ed´i fis) *n.* A massive building or structure.

ed-i-fy (ed´i fī´) *v.* To benefit and enlighten, morally or spiritually. **edification** *n.*

ed-it (ed´it) *v.* To prepare, alter, and correct anything for presentation, such as a publication, a speech, or a film; to compile for an edition. In *computer science*, to make changes, as additions or deletions, to a file or document.

edit commands *n.* In *computer science*, commands in a program that facilitate the process of editing, such as *move, copy, paste,* etc.

e-di-tion (i dish´an) *n.* The form in which a book is published; the total number of copies printed at one time; one similar to, but altered from, an earlier version.

edit key *n.* In *computer science*, any of the special keyboard keys, such as insert, or delete, used to edit text.

ed-i-tor *n.* A person who edits or prepares literary matter as a profession.

ed-i-to-ri-al (ed´i tōr´ē al) *n.* An article in a newspaper or magazine which expresses the opinion of a publisher or editor. **editorial** *adj.* Of or relating to an editor or an editor's work; being or resembling an editorial.

ed-u-ca-ble *adj.* Capable of being educated.

ed-u-cate (ej´e kāt´) *v.* To provide with training; to teach; to supervise the mental or moral growth of.

ed-u-ca-tion (ej´e kā´shan) *n.* The

process of educating or of being educated; the knowledge resulting from the process; the field of study of methods of teaching.

e-duce (i dōs´) *v.* To call forth or bring out; to develop from given facts.

e-dul-co-rate (i dul´ko rāt´) *v.* To make something pleasant; to remove acid.

eel (ēl) *n.* A snake-like fish without scales or pelvic fins.

ee-rie *or* **ee-ry** (ēr´ē) *adj.* Suggesting the supernatural or strange; weird; frightening. **eerily** *adv.* **eeriness** *n.*

ef-face (i fās´) *v.* To remove or rub out. **effacer** *n.* **effacement** *n.*

ef-fect (i fekt´) *n.* Something produced by a cause; the power to produce a desired result; the reaction something has on an object; a technique which produces an intended impression. **take effect** To become operative.

ef-fec-tive (i fek´tiv) *adj.* Producing an expected effect or proper result.

ef-fem-i-nate (i fem´i nit) *adj.* Having woman-like qualities unsuitable to a man. **effeminacy** *n.* **effeminately** *adv.*

ef-fen-di (i fend´ē) *n.* A man who has an education or property.

ef-fer-ent (ef´ēr ent) *adj. Physiol.* Carrying outward from a central organ or part; conveying nervous impulses to an effector. **efferent** *n.* **efferently** *adv.*

ef-fer-vesce (ef´ēr ves´) *v.* To foam and hiss as gas escapes; to exhibit liveliness or exhilaration. **effervescently** *adv.* **effervescence** *n.* **effervescent** *adj.*

ef-fete (i fēt´) *adj.* Exhausted of effectiveness or force; worn-out; decadent.

ef-fi-ca-cious (ef´i kā´shus) *adj.* Producing an intended effect. **-ly** *adv.*

ef-fi-cien-cy (i fish´en sē) *n.* The quality or degree of being efficient.

ef-fi-cient (i fish´ent) *adj.* Adequate in performance with a minimum of waste or effort; productive without waste.

ef-fi-gy (ef´i jē) *n., pl.* **effigies** A life-size sculpture or painting representing a crude image or dummy of a hated person.

ef-flo-resce (ef´lo res´) *v.* To become covered by a powdery crust; to bloom.

ef-flo-res-cence (ef´lo res´ens) *n.* A time of flowering; fullness of development; powdery crust. **efflorescent** *adj.*

ef-flu-ence (ef´lö ens) *n.* An act of flowing out; something that flows out or forth. **effluent** *n.*

ef-flu-vi-um (i flö´vē um) *n., pl.* **effluvia** *or* **effluviums** An unpleasant vapor from something. **effluvial** *adj.*

ef-flux (ef´luks) *n.* Something passing away or expiring. **effluxion** *n.*

ef-fort (ef´ērt) *n.* Voluntary exertion of physical or mental energy; a difficult exertion; a normally earnest attempt or achievement; something done

through exertion. *Phys.* A force applied against inertia.

ef-fron-ter-y (i frun´te rē) *n., pl.* **effronteries** Shameless boldness; impudence.

ef-ful-gent *adj.* Shining brilliantly; radiant. **effulgence** *n.* **effulge** *v.*

ef-fuse (i fūz´) *v.* To give off; to pour out.

ef-fu-sion (i fū´zhan) *n.* A flow of liquid or gas through a small opening; an unrestrained outpouring of feeling. **effusive** *adj.* **effusively** *adv.*

EGA In *computer science,* Enhanced Graphics Adapter; a standard for the display on a color monitor screen.

e-gad *interj.* An exclamation expressing surprise.

egal-i-tar-i-an (i gal´i târ´ē an) *adj.* Exhibiting belief in human equality. **egalitarian** *n.* **egalitarianism** *n.*

egest (ē jest´) *v.* To defecate; to rid the body of waste. **egestion** *n.*

egg (eg) *n.* The hard-shelled reproductive cell of female animals, especially one produced by a chicken, used as food; the reproductive ovum of an animal. **egg on** *v.* To incite to action.

eg-lan-tine (eg´lan tīn´) *n.* The sweetbrier, a type of rose.

e-go (ē´gō) *n.* The self thinking, feeling, and acting distinct from the external world. *Psychology* The conscious aspect that most directly controls behavior and is most in touch with reality.

e-go-cen-tric (ē´gō sen´trik) *adj.* Thinking, observing, and regarding oneself as the center of all experiences; self-centered. **egocentric** *n.*

ego—de-fense *n.* A mechanism that is psychological and protects the self-image.

e-go-ma-ni-a (ē´gō mā´nē a) *n.* Self obsession. **egomaniacal** *adj.*

e-gre-gious (i grē´jus) *adj.* Outstandingly or remarkably bad; flagrant. **egregiously** *adv.* **egregiousness** *n.*

e-gress (ē´gres) *n.* The act of coming out; emergence; a means of departing; exit.

e-gret (ē´grit) *n.* Any of several species of white wading birds having long, drooping plumes.

eh *interj.* An utterance used to ask for confirmation of something just spoken.

ei-det-ic (ī det´ik) *adj.* Involving vivid recall.

ei-do-lon (ī dō´lon) *n.* An image that is unsubstantial.

eight (āt) *n.* The cardinal number equal to 7 + 1; the symbol 8. **eight** *adj.*

ein-korn *n.* The type of wheat that can be grown in Europe and has one grain.

ein-stein-i-um (īn stī´nē um) *n.* A synthetic, radioactive, metallic element.

Eisenhower, Dwight David *n.* (1890-

the United States from 1953-1961.

ei-ther (ē'thėr) *pron.* One or the other. **either** *conj.* Used before the first of two or more alternatives linked by or. **either** *adj.* One or the other of two. **either** *adv.* Likewise; also.

e-jac-u-late (i jak'ū lāt') *v.* To eject abruptly, usually referring to a bodily fluid; to utter suddenly and briefly; to exclaim. **ejaculation** *n.*

e-ject (i jekt') *v.* To throw out; to expel. **ejection** *n.* **ejectable** *adj.*

e-ject-ment (i jekt'ment) *n.* An act for a recovery of possession of real property.

eke out (ēk' out) *v.* To obtain with great effort; to make do.

e-kis-tics (i'kis tiks) *n.* The science which deals with the settlements of humans.

e-lab-o-rate (i lab'o rāt') *adj.* Planned or done with great detail; very complex; intricate. **elaborate** *v.* To work out or complete with great detail; to give more detail. **elaboration** *n.*

e-lapse (i laps') *v.* To slip or glide away; to pass away silently.

e-las-tase *n.* The enzyme in the pancreatic juice which will digest elastin.

e-las-tic (i las'tik) *adj.* Adapting with changing circumstances; capable of easy expansion and contraction. **elastic** *n.* A rubber fabric; a rubber band.

elas-tin (i las'tin) *n.* A type of protein which is similar to collagen.

elas-to-mer (i las'tamėr) *n.* Any elastic substance which resemble rubber.

e-late (i lāt') *v.* To make proud; to bring joy. **elated** *adj.* **elatedly** *adv.*

el-a-ter (el'a tėr) *n.* Structure of a plant which aids in the distribution of spores.

e-lat-er-ite (i lat'erit') *n.* A rubberlike mineral resin which is dark brown and occurs in flexible masses.

e-la-tion *n.* A quality or state of exaltation or joy; a feeling of great happiness.

E layer *n.* The layer in the ionosphere above the earth that is able to reflect radio waves.

el-bow (el'bō) *n.* A sharp turn, as in a river or road, which resembles an elbow. *Anat.* The outer joint of the arm between the up-per arm and forearm. **elbow** *v.* To push or shove aside with the elbow.

eld-er (el'dėr) *adj.* Older. *n.* One who is older than others; a person of great influence; an official of the church. *Bot.* A shrub bearing red or purple fruit.

e-lect (i lekt') *v.* To choose or select by vote, as for an office; to make a choice. **elect** *adj.* Singled out on purpose; elected but not yet inaugurated. **elect** *n.* One chosen or set apart, especially for spiritual salvation.

e-lec-tric *or* **e-lec-tri-cal** (i lek'trik) *adj.* Relating to electricity; emotionally exciting. **electrically** *adv.*

e-lec-tri-fy (i lek'tri fī') *v.* To charge something or someone with electricity; to supply with electric power; to excite intensely, as if with an electric shock.

e-lec-tro-a-nal-y-sis *n.* The chemical analysis by electrolysis.

e-lec-tro-car-di-o-gram (i lek'trō kär'dēo gram') *n.* The record produced by an electrocardiograph; EKG.

e-lec-tro-cute (i lek'tro kūt') *v.* To kill or execute by the use of electric current or shock. **electrocution** *n.*

e-lec-trode (i lek'trōd) *n.* A conductor

e-lec-tro-dy-na-mom-e-ter *n.* Instrument used to measure electric currents.

e-lec-tro-mag-net (i lek'trō mag'nit) *n.* A magnet consisting of a soft iron core magnetized by an electric current passing through a wire which is coiled around the core.

e-lec-tron (i lek'tron) *n. Elect.* A sub-atomic particle with a negative electric charge found outside of an atom nucleus.

electronic bulletin board In *computer science*, a computer message center.

electronic mail In *computer science*, messages exchanged with the use of a computer through an internal network or the services of an outside vendor.

electronic spreadsheet In *computer science*, a computer version of a worksheet with data organized in rows and columns.

e-lec-tron-ics *n.* The branch of physics that deals with the behavior and effects of the flow of electrons in vacuum tubes, gases, and semiconductors.

e-lec-tro-va-lence (i lek'trō vā'lens) *n.* The number of charges transferred in an atom that result in the formation of ions. **electrovalent** *adj.*

el-e-doi-sin *n.* A protein that comes from the salivary glands of the octopus.

el-ee-mos-y-nar-y (el'e mos'i ner'ē) *adj.* Pertaining to or contributed as charity.

el-e-gance (el'e gans) *n.* Refinement in appearance, movement, or manners; elegant quality.

el-e-gant *adj.* Marked by elegance; tasteful or luxurious in dress or manners; gracefully refined, in habits, tastes, or a literary style.

e-le-git *n.* The writ of execution by which any or all of a defendant's goods or property are held by his creditor until the debt is paid.

el-e-gy (el'i jē) *n., pl.* **elegies** A poem expressing sorrow and lamentation for one who is dead.

el-e-ment (el'e ment) *n.* A constituent part. *Chem. & Phys.* A substance not separable into less complex substances by chemical means. **elements** The conditions of the weather.

el-e-men-ta-ry (el´e men´ta rē) adj. Fundamental, essential; referring to elementary school, the first introduction of fundamental principles.

el-e-mi (el´emē) n. A fragrant oleoresin which is obtained from tropical trees and is used in inks and varnishes.

e-len-chus n. An argument which contradicts another argument by proving the contrary to its conclusion.

el-e-phant (el´e fant) n. A large mammal having a long, flexible trunk and curved tusks.

el-e-vate (el´e vāt´) v. To lift up or raise; to promote to a higher rank.

el-e-vat-ed (el´e vā´tid) adj. Exalted; above something such as the ground; elated.

elf (elf) n., pl. **elves** An imaginary being with magical powers, often mischievous; a small, mischievous child.

e-lic-it (i lis´it) v. To bring or draw out; to evoke.

e-lide (i līd´) v. To omit, especially to slur over in pronunciation, as a vowel, consonant, or syllable. **elidible** adj.

el-i-gi-ble (el´i ji bl) adj. Worthy of being chosen. **eligibility** n.

e-lim-i-nate (i lim´i nāt´) v. To get rid of, remove; to leave out, to omit; to excrete, as waste. **elimination** n. **eliminator** n. **eliminative** adj.

e-li-sion n. The act of omitting something, such as an unstressed vowel or syllable in pronunciation or verse.

e-lite (i lēt´) n. The choice part; a small, powerful group; a type size yielding twelve characters to the inch. **elite** adj.

e-lix-ir (i lik´sėr) n. A sweetened aromatic liquid of alcohol and water, used as a vehicle for medicine; a medicine regarded as a cure-all; a sovereign remedy.

ell (el) n. An extension of a building at right angles to the main structure.

el-lipse (i lips´) n. A closed curve, somewhat oval in shape.

el-lip-sis (i lip´sis) n. An omission of a few words which are obviously understood in a sentence; a mark that indicates an ellipsis, such as ... or ***.

el-o-cu-tion (el´o kū´shan) n. The art of effective public speaking. **elocutionary** adj. **elocutionist** n.

e-lon-gate (i long´gāt) v. To stretch out in length; to extend.

e-lon-ga-tion n. State of being elongated or stretched out in length; an extension.

e-lope (i lōp´) v. To run away, especially in order to get married. **elopement** n.

el-o-quence n. The practice of using language with fluency.

el-o-quent (el´o kwent) adj. Having the ability to speak fluently and persuasively; vividly expressive. **eloquence** n. **eloquently** adv.

else (els) adj. Different; other; more; additional. adv. Otherwise; besides.

else-where (els´hwâr´) adv. To or in another place.

e-lu-ci-date (i lū´si dāt´) v. To make clear, to clarify; to explain. **elucidator** n. **elucidation** n. **elucidative** adj.

e-lu-cu-brate (i lu´kya brāt) v. To work something out with studious effort.

e-lude (i lūd´) v. To evade or avoid; to escape understanding.

e-lu-sive (i lū´siv) adj. Tending to evade something or someone. **elusively** adv.

e-lute (ē lūt´) v. Chem. To remove material from what has absorbed it with the use of a solvent. **elution** n.

e-lu-tri-ate (i lū´trē āt´) v. To remove or separate by washing. **elutriator** n.

e-lu-vi-al adj. Related to eluviation.

e-lu-vi-a-tion (i lū´vēā´shan) n. Shifting of dissolved material that is in the soil by the movement of water.

e-lu-vi-um n. Rock debris produced by the decomposition and weathering of rock; fine sand or soil deposited by the wind.

em n. Printing A unit of measure for printed matter that is equal to the width of the letter M.

e-ma-ci-ate (i mā´shē āt´) v. To become or cause to become extremely thin. **emaciated** adj. **emaciation** n.

e—mail n. Electronic mail; messages sent over the Internet or a network.

em-a-nate (em´a nāt´) v. To come out from a source; to emit. **emanation** n.

e-man-ci-pate (i man´si pāt´) v. To set free from bondage; to liberate. **emancipation** n. **emancipator** n.

e-mar-gin-ate (i mär´ji nāt) adj. To have a notched margin; having a shallow notch at the apex. **emargination** n.

e-mas-cu-late (i mas´kū lāt´) v. To castrate; to deprive of masculine vigor. **emasculation** n. **emasculator** n.

em-balm (em bäm´) v. To treat a corpse with preservatives in order to protect it from decay. **embalmer** n.

em-bar-go (em bär´gō) n., pl. **embargoes** A prohibition or restraint on trade, as a government order forbidding the entry or departure of merchant vessels; for example,.the oil embargo of 1973.

em-bark (em bärk´) v. To board a ship; to start a venture. **embarkation** n.

em-bar-rass (em bar´as) v. To cause to feel self-conscious; to confuse; to burden with financial or other difficulties.

em-bas-sage n. The commission which has been entrusted to an ambassador.

em-bat-tle (em bat´l) v. To prepare or arrange in order for battle.

em-bay (em bā´) v. To shelter.

em-bay-ment n. The formation of a bay.

em-bed (em bed´) v. To fix or enclose tightly in a surrounding mass.

embedded commands In *computer science*, program instructions that establish and maintain the appearance, position and special characteristics of a text or graphics element.

embedded object In *computer science*, a drawing, chart, sound recording, etc. that is fixed in a text or graphics element.

em-bel-lish (em bel´ish) v. To adorn or make beautiful with ornamentation; to decorate; to heighten attractiveness with ornamentation. -ment n.

em-ber (em´bėr) n. A small piece of glowing coal or wood, as in a dying fire. embers pl. The smoldering ashes or remains of afire.

em-bez-zle (em bez´l) v. To take money or other items fraudulently.

em-bit-ter (em bit´ėr) v. To arouse bitter or hostile feelings. embitterment n.

em-blaze (em blāz´) v. To set something ablaze; to provide light with a fire.

em-bla-zon (em blā´zon) v. To decorate in bright colors or with heraldic signs.

em-blem (em´blem) n. A symbol of something; a distinctive design; anything used as an identifying mark. emblematic adj. emblematical adj.

em-bod-y (em bod´ē) v. To give a bodily form to; to personify. embodiment n.

em-bold-en (em bōl´den) v. To encourage; to make bold.

em-bo-lism (em´bo liz´um) n. The blockage of a blood vessel, as by an air bubble or a detached clot.

em-bo-lus n. An abnormal particle such as an air bubble that circulates in the bloodstream.

em-bos-om v. To enclose; to shelter closely; to cherish.

em-boss (em bos´) v. To shape or decorate in relief; to represent in relief.

em-bou-chure (äm´be sher´) n. Mus. The mouthpiece of a wind instrument; the position of the lips used to produce a musical tone.

em-bowed adj. Bent or curved outward.

em-brace (em brās´) v. To clasp or hold in the arms; to hug; to surround; to take in mentally or visually. n. The act of embracing; a hug. embraceable adj.

em-brac-er-y n. An attempt to influence or corrupt a jury by bribes or promises.

em-bran-gle v. To entangle; to confuse.

em-bro-cate (em´brō kāt´) v. To moisten and rub an injured part of the body with a liquid medicine. embrocation n.

em-broi-der (em broi´dėr) v. To decorate with ornamental needlework; to add fictitious details. embroidery n.

em-broil (em broil´) v. To involve in contention or violent actions; to throw into confusion. embroilment n.

em-bry-o (em´brē ō´) n.,pl. embryos An organism in its early developmental stage before it has a distinctive form; in the human species, the first eight weeks of development; a young plant within the seed; a rudimentary stage.

em-cee (em´sē´) n. Informal A master of ceremonies. emcee v.

e-mend (i mend´) v. To correct or remove faults. emendation n. emender n.

em-er-ald (em´ėr ald) n. A bright-green, transparent variety of beryl, used as a gemstone.

e-merge (i mėrj´) v. To rise into view; to come into existence.

e-mer-gen-cy (i mėr´jen sē) n., pl. emergencies A sudden and unexpected situation requiring prompt action.

e-mer-gent adj. Emerging; unexpected; rising into view.

e-mersed adj. Standing out of or rising above the surrounding water surface.

em-er-y (em´e rē) n. A grainy, mineral substance having impure corundum, used for polishing and grinding.

e-met-ic (e met´ik) adj. A medicine used to induce vomiting. emetic n.

em-e-tine n. An alkaloid that is extracted from the ipecac root used as an expectorant.

em-i-grate (em´i grāt´) v. To move from one country or region to settle elsewhere. emigrant n. emigration n.

e-mi-gré (em´i grā´) n. A refugee.

em-i-nent (em´i nent) adj. High in esteem, rank, or office; conspicuous; outstanding. eminently adv.

eminent domain n. The right of a government to take or control property for public use.

em-is-sar-y (em´i ser´ē) n.,pl. emissaries A person sent out on a mission.

e-mis-sion n. The act of emitting; something emitted.

e-mit (i mit´) v. To send forth; to throw or give out. emitter n.

e-mol-lient (i mol´yent) n. A substance for the soothing and softening of the skin. emollient adj.

e-mol-u-ment (i mol´ū ment) n. Profit; returns arising from employment; compensation, as a salary or perquisite.

e-mote (i mōt´) v. To show emotion, as in acting.

e-mo-tion (i mō´shan) n. A strong surge of feeling; any of the feelings of fear, sorrow, joy, hate, or love; physical and psychological reaction to feelings.

em-pa-thy (em´pa thē) n. Psychol. Identification with and understanding of the feelings of another person. empathetic adj. empathic adj.

em-pha-sis (em´fa sis) n., pl. emphases Significance or importance attached to anything.

em-phat-ic (em fat´ik) *adj.* Expressed or spoken with emphasis. **-ally** *adv.*

em-phy-se-ma *n.* A condition characterized by air-filled expansions of tissues of the body; a lung condition that can result in heart impairment.

em-pire (em´pīr) *n.* The territories or nations forming a political unit governed by a single supreme authority.

em-pir-ic (em pir´i k) *n.* One who relies on practical experience.

em-pir-i-cal (em pir´i kəl) *adj.* Depending on or gained from observation or experiment rather than from theory and science. **empirically** *adv.*

em-place *v.* To put into place or position.

em-place-ment *n.* A platform for guns or military equipment.

em-ploy (em ploi´) *v.* To engage the service or use of; to devote time to an activity.

em-ploy-ee *or* **em-ploy-e** (em ploi´ē) *n.* A person who works for another in return for salary or wages.

em-poi-son *v.* To embitter.

em-po-ri-um (em pōr´ē um) *n., pl.* **emporiums** *or* **emporia** A large store which carries general merchandise.

em-pow-er (em pou´ér) *v.* To authorize; to delegate; to license.

emp-ty (emp´tē) *adj.* Containing nothing; vacant; lacking substance. **empty** *v.* To empty. **emptily** *adv.* **emptiness** *n.*

em-py-e-ma (em´pi ē ma) *n.* The collection of pus in a body cavity.

em-py-re-an (em´pi rē´an) *n.* Pertaining to the highest part of heaven; the sky.

em-u-late (em´ū lāt´) *v.* To strive to equal, especially by imitating.

e-mul-sion (i mul´shən) *n.* *Chem.* A suspended mixture of small droplets, one liquid within the other. *Photog.* A light-sensitive coating on photographic paper, film, or plates.

en-a-ble (en ā´bl) *v.* To supply with adequate authority, knowledge, or power; to give legal power to another. In computer science, allowing to operate, as by computer command.

en-act (en akt´) *v.* To make into law; to decree. **enactment** *n.*

e-nam-el (i nam´el) *n.* A decorative or protective coating fused on a surface, as of pottery; a paint that dries to a hard, glossy surface; the hard outermost covering of a tooth. **enamel** *v.* To apply, inlay, or decorate with enamel.

en-am-or (en am´ér) *v.* To inflame with love; to charm.

en-an-ti-o-morph (i nan´tē o morf´) *n.* A pair of chemical compounds having molecular structures that are mirror images.

en-cap-su-late (en kap´su lāt´) *v.* To enclose or encase in a capsule.

en-cap-su-lat-ed *adj.* Surrounded with a membranous envelope.

en-case (en kās´) *v.* To close within a case.

en-ceinte *n.* A wall or enclosure around a town.

en-ce-phal-ic (en´se fal´ik) *adj.* Pertaining to the brain.

en-ceph-a-li-tis (en sef´a li´tis) *n.* *Pathol.* Inflammation of the brain.

en-ceph-a-log-ra-phy *n.* The technique or act of taking X-ray photographs of the brain after replacing the spinal fluid with a gas.

en-ceph-a-lo-my-eli-tis (en sef´a lō mī e lī´tis) *n.* The inflammation of the spinal cord and the brain.

en-chant (en chant´) *v.* To put under a spell; to bewitch; to charm; to delight greatly. **enchanter** *n.*

en-chase (en chās´) *v.* To carve a relief into something; to set a gem in an ornamental setting.

en-chi-rid-i-on (en´kī rid ē en) *n.* A handbook; a manual.

en-ci-pher (en sī´fér) *v.* To convert anything such as a message into a cipher.

en-cir-cle (en sér´kl) *v.* To form a circle around; surround. **encirclement** *n.*

en-clasp (en klasp´) *v.* To hold onto someone or something.

en-clave (en´klāv) *n.* A country surrounded by a foreign country; a cultural group living within a larger group.

en-clit-ic *adj.* Pertaining to a word connected to a preceding word, and so closely related that it has no independent accent; such as the word *cannot.*

en-close (en klōz´) *v.* To surround on all sides; to put in the same envelope or package with something else.

en-clo-sure *n.* The action of enclosing something; state of being enclosed; the item that is enclosed.

en-code (en kōd´) *v.* To convert or change a message into a code. **encoder** *n.*

en-co-mi-ast (en kō´mē ast´) *n.* A person who praises. **encomiastic** *adj.*

en-com-pass (en kum´pəs) *v.* To surround; to form a circle; to enclose.

en-core (äng´kōr) *n.* An audience's demand for a repeat performance; a performance in response to an encore. **encore** *v.* To call for an encore.

en-coun-ter (en koun´tér) *n.* An unplanned or unexpected meeting or conflict. **encounter** *v.* To come upon unexpectedly; to confront in a hostile situation.

en-cour-age (en kér´ij) *v.* To inspire with courage or hope; to support. **encouraging** *adj.* **encouragingly** *adv.*

en-croach (en krōch´) *v.* To intrude upon

the rights or possessions of another.
encroacher *n.* **encroachment** *n.*

en-crust (en krust´) *v.* To cover with a crust; to form a crust. **-ation** *n.*

encryption In *computer science*, jumbling or coding of sensitive data for security purposes.

en-cum-ber (en kum´bér) *v.* To hinder or burden with difficulties or obligations.

en-cy-clo-pe-di-a (en sī´klo pē´dēa) *n.* A comprehensive work with articles covering a broad range of subjects.

en-cyst (en sist´) *v.* To become enclosed in a sac. **encystment** *n.*

end (end) *n.* A part lying at a boundary; the terminal point at which something concludes; the point in time at which something ceases; a goal; a fragment; a remainder; in football, either of the players in the outermost positions on the line of scrimmage. **end** *v.* To come or bring to a termination; to stop; to ruin or destroy; to die. In computer science, a program code indicating that final command.

en-dam-age (en dam´ij) *v.* To cause damage to something or to someone.

en-da-moe-ba (en´da mē´ba) *n.* Member of the genus that contains amoebas that are parasitic in the intestines.

en-dan-ger (en dān´jér) *v.* To expose to danger; to imperil.

end-ar-ter-ec-to-my *n.* The removal of the inner layer of an artery with surgery.

en-deav-or (en dev´ér) *n.* An attempt to attain or do something.

en-dem-ic (en dem´ik) *adj.* Peculiar to a particular area or people.

en-der-mic (en dér´mik) *adj.* To act through the skin. **endermically** *adv.*

end-ex-ine *n.* A membranous inner layer of the spores of the exine.

end key In *computer science,* a cursor movement key that sends the cursor to the end of a line of text and, used in conjunction with other keys, to the bottom right of the screen, the bottom of the page or the end of a file.

en-do-bi-ot-ic (en´dō bī´t´ik) *adj.* To be living within the host's tissues.

en-do-car-di-um (en´dō kär´dē um) *n.* The membrane lining the cavities of the heart.

en-do-carp *n.* Inner layer of a fruit wall.

en-do-chon-dral *adj.* Occurring in the cartilage of the long bone.

en-do-crine (en´do krin) *adj.* Making secretions which are distributed in the body by the blood or lymph.

en-do-derm (en´do dérm´) *n.* The innermost germ layer in an embryo that becomes the epithelium of the digestive tract.

en-do-der-mis (en´do dér´mis) *n.* The

most inner layer in the cortex of a plant.

en-do-en-zyme (en´dō en´zīm) *n.* A kind of enzyme which functions inside the cell.

en-do-er-gic *adj.* To be absorbing energy.

en-dog-a-my (en dog´a mē) *n.* The marriage custom that requires choosing a mate from within a specific group.

en-dog-e-nous (en doj´e nus) *adj. Biol.* Originating or growing from within the cell. **endogeny** *n.*

en-do-lymph *n.* A clear watery fluid in the labyrinth of the ear.

en-do-me-tri-um *n.* The membrane that lines the woman's uterus.

en-dor-phin *n.* Hormones with pain-killing and tranquilizing capabilities secreted by the brain.

en-dorse (en dors´) *v.* To write one's signature on a document, such as the back of a check to obtain the cash indicated on the front, or on the back of a deed or car title, so as to show transfer of ownership; to publicly endorse a person or a thing. **-ment** *n.*

en-do-scope (en´do skōp´) *n. Med.* An instrument used to examine a bodily canal or hollow organ. **endoscopic** *adj.*

en-do-skel-e-ton (en´dō skel´i ton) *n.* A skeleton which is on the inside of one's body.

en-do-tox-in (en´dō tok´sin) *n.* A kind of poisonous substance found in bacteria.

en-do-tra-che-al *adj.* Located within the trachea of the body.

en-dow-ment (en dou´) *v.* The income of an institution derived form donations; a natural ability or capacity.

en-due (en dö´) *v.* To provide; to put on.

en-dure (en der´) *v.* To undergo; to sustain; to put up with; to tolerate; to bear.

en-dur-ing *adj.* Lasting.

en-e-ma (en´e ma) *n.* The injection of a liquid into the rectum for cleansing; the liquid injected.

en-e-my (en´e mē) *n., pl.* **enemies** One who seeks to inflict injury on another; a foe; a hostile force or power.

en-er-gy (en´ér jē) *n., pl.* **energies** Vigor; strength; capacity or tendency for working or acting; vitality of expression. *Phys.* The capacity for doing work; usable heat or electric power.

en-er-vate (en´ér vāt´) *v.* To deprive of vitality or strength; to weaken.

en-fee-ble (en fē´bl) *v.* To weaken; to make feeble. **enfeeblement** *n.*

en-fet-ter (en fet´ér) *v.* To tie up in fetters.

en-fi-lade (en´fi lād´) *n.* An arrangement of things where they are in parallel and opposite rows such as rooms off a hall.

en-fleu-rage (än floe räzh´) *n.* The process used to extract perfumes from flowers.

en-fold (en fōld´) v. To enclose; to wrap in layers; to embrace.

en-force (en fōrs´) v. To compel obedience; to impose by force. **enforceable** adj. **enforcement** n. **enforcer** n.

en-fran-chise (en fran´chīz) v. To grant civil rights, as the right to vote; to give a franchise to. **enfranchisement** n.

en-gage (en gāj´) v. To employ or hire; to secure or bind, as by a contract; to pledge oneself, especially to marry; to undertake conflict; to participate. Mech. To interlock.

en-gen-der (en jen´dèr) v. To give rise to; to exist; to cause.

en-gild (in gild´) v. To make something bright with light.

en-gine (en´jin) n. A machine which converts energy into mechanical motion; a mechanical instrument; a locomotive. **engine** v.

en-gi-neer (en´jī nēr´) n. Person who works in the field of engineering.

en-gird v. To encompass.

en-gla-cial adj. To be frozen or embedded within a glacier.

en-glut v. To gulp or swallow down.

en-gorge (en gorj´) v. To swallow greedily. Pathol. To fill an artery with blood. **engorgement** n.

en-graft (en graft´) v. Bot. To join or fasten, as if by grafting.

en-grail v. To decorate or indent the edge of something with concave curves or notches. **engrailed** adj.

en-grav-ing (en grā´ving) n. Technique or act of one who engraves; impression printed from an engraved plate.

en-gross (en grōs´) v. To occupy the complete attention of; to copy or write in a large, clear hand. **engrossing** adj.

en-gulf (en gulf´) v. To enclose completely; to submerge; to swallow.

en-hance (en hans´) v. To make greater; to raise to a higher degree.

e-nig-ma (e nig´ma) n. One that baffles; anything puzzling; a riddle; something difficult to explain. **enigmatic** adj.

en-isle v. To make an island of; to isolate.

en-jamb-ment or **en-jambe-ment** (en jam´ ment) n. Construction of a sentence flowing from one line of a poem to the next, allowing related words to fall on different lines.

en-join (en join´) v. To command to do something; to prohibit, especially by legal action. **enjoinder** n.

en-joy (en joi´) v. To feel joy or find pleasure in; to have the use or possession of. **enjoyable** adj. **enjoyably** adv. **enjoyment** n.

en-kin-dle v. To kindle; to set on fire; to make bright.

en-lace v. To encircle; to entwine.

en-large (en lärj´) v. To make larger;

to speak or write in greater detail. **enlargeable** adj. **enlarger** n.

en-light-en (en līt´en) v. To give broadening or revealing knowledge; to give spiritual guidance or light to.

en-list (en list´) v. To secure the help or active aid of. Milit. To sign up for service with the armed forces.

en-liv-en (en lī´ven) v. To make livelier, cheerful or vigorous.

en masse (än mas´) adv. All together; in a group.

en-mi-ty (en´mi tē) n., pl. **enmities** Deep hatred; hostility.

en-ne-ad n. A collection or group of nine.

en-ne-a-gon (en´ē a gon´) n. A closed plane figure having nine angles and nine sides.

en-ne-a-he-dron (en´ē a hē´dron) n. A solid figure with nine faces.

en-nui (än wē´) n. Boredom; weariness.

e-nol-o-gy n. The science that deals with wine and wine making.

e-nor-mi-ty (i nor´mi tē) n., pl. **enormities** Excessive wickedness; an outrageous offense or crime; the state of being huge.

e-nor-mous (i nor´mus) adj. Very great in size or degree. **enormously** adv. .

e-nough (i nuf´) adj. Adequate to satisfy demands or needs. **enough** adv. To a satisfactory degree. **enough** n. A sufficient amount.

en-quire (en kwïer´) v. Variation of inquire.

en-rage (en rāj´) v. To put or throw into a rage.

en-rap-ture (en rap´chèr) v. To transport into a state of rapture; to delight.

en-rich (en rich´) v. To make rich or richer; to make more productive.

en-roll or **en-rol** (en rōl´) v. To enter or write a name on a roll, register, or record; to place one's name on a roll, register, or record. **enrollment** n.

en route adv. On or along the way.

en-sconce (en skons´) v. To settle securely; to shelter.

en-scroll v. To write or record on a scroll.

en-sem-ble (än säm´bl) n. A group of complementary parts that are in harmony; a coordinated outfit of clothing; a group of people performing together; music for two or more performers.

en-shrine (en shrīn´) v. To place in a shrine; hold sacred. **enshrinement** n.

en-shroud (en shroud´) v. To cover with a shroud.

en-slave (en slāv´) v. To make a slave of; to put in bondage. **enslavement** n.

en-snare (en snâr´) v. To catch; to trap.

en-snarl v. To tangle or involve in a snarl.

en-sphere (en sfēr´) v. To enclose in or make into a sphere.

en-sue (en sö´) v. To follow as a

consequence.

en-sure (en sher´) v. To make certain of.

en-ta-ble-ment n. A platform that supports a statue above a pedestal.

en-tail (en tāl´) v. To have as a necessary accompaniment or result; to restrict the inheritance of property to a certain line of heirs. **entailment** n.

en-tan-gle (en tang´gl) v. To tangle; to complicate; to confuse; to involve in a tangle. **entanglement** n.

en-tente (än tänt´) n. A mutual agreement between governments for cooperative action; the parties to an entente.

en-ter (en´tėr) v. To go or come into; to penetrate; to begin; to become a member of or participant in; to make a record of; to join in a competition. In *computer science*, to add information, as text to a document, records to a database, etc.

enter key In *computer science*, a function key used to signal the end of a block of copy or enable a selected command; also expressed as CR or carriage return or Return.

en-ter-prise (en´tėr priz´) n. A large or risky undertaking; a business organization; boldness and energy in practical affairs.

en-ter-tain (en´tėr tān´) v. To harbor or give heed to; to accommodate; receive as a guest; to amuse. **entertainer** n.

en-ter-tain-ment n. The act of entertaining; the accommodating of guests.

en-thrall (en throl´) v. To fascinate; to captivate. **enthrallment** n.

en-throne (en thrōn´) v. To place on a throne. **enthronement** n.

en-thuse v. To arouse enthusiasm; to exhibit enthusiasm.

en-thu-si-asm (en thö´zē az´um) n. Intense feeling for a cause; eagerness; zeal; keen interest.

en-tice (en tīs´) v. To attract by arousing desire. **enticer** n. **enticement** n.

en-tire (en tīer´) adj. Having no part left out; whole; complete. **entirely** adv.

en-ti-tle (en tī´tl) v. To give a name to; to furnish with a right. **entitlement** n.

en-ti-ty (en´ti tē) n., pl. **entities** The fact of real existence; something that exists alone.

en-to-mos-tra-can adj. A subclass of crustaceans which have a moderately simple organization.

en-tou-rage n. One's associates; retinue.

en-to-zo-on n. An internal parasite; an intestinal worm.

en-trails (en´trālz) pl. n. Internal organs of humans or animals.

en-trance (en trans´) v. To fascinate; enchant. **entrancement** n.

en-trance (en´trans) n. The act of

entering; the means or place of entry; the first appearance of an actor in a play; the act of entering into a place; the power or liberty of entering; admission. **entranceway** n.

en-trant (en´trant) n. One beginning a new course in life; one becoming a new member of an association.

en-trap (en trap´) v. To catch in a trap.

en-treat (en trēt´) v. To make an earnest request of or for. **entreaty** n.

en-trée (än´trā) n. A dish served as the main course.

en-tre-mets n. A side dish served at the table.

en-trench (en trench´) v. To dig a trench, as for defense; to fix or set firmly; to fortify. **entrenchment** n.

en-tre-pre-neur (än´tre pre nėr´) n. A person who launches or manages a business venture. **entrepreneurial** adj.

en-tre-sol n. One lower story positioned between two others of greater height.

en-trust (en trust´) v. To transfer to another for care or performance; to give as a trust or responsibility.

en-try (en trē´) n., pl. **entries** An opening or place for entering; an item entered in a book, list, register, or computer.

en-twine (en twīn´) v. To twine about or twist together.

e-nu-mer-ate (i nö´me rāt´) v. To count off one by one. **enumeration** n.

e-nun-ci-ate (i nun´sē āt´) v. To pronounce with clarity; to announce; to proclaim; to declare.

en-u-re-sis n. Incontinence; the involuntary discharge of urine.

en-vel-op (en vel´up) v. To cover, as by wrapping or folding; to enwrap or wrap up; to surround entirely.

en-ve-lope (en´ve lōp´) n. Something that covers or encloses; a paper case, especially for a letter, having a flap for sealing; the bag on an air balloon.

en-ven-om (en ven´om) v. To make poisonous; to embitter.

en-vi-a-ble (en´vē a bl) adj. Highly desirable. **enviably** adv.

en-vi-ron v. To surround; to encircle.

en-vi-ron-ment (en vī´ron ment) n. The surroundings; the combination of external conditions which affect the development and existence of an individual, group, or organism. In *computer science*, the operating system, the peripherals and programs that make up a computer system. **environmental** adj. **environmentally** a

en-vi-rons (en vī´ronz) n., pl. A surrounding region; a place; outskirts, especially of a city; the vicinity.

en-vis-age (en viz´ij) v. To have or form a mental image of; to visualize.

en-vi-sion (en vizh´an) v. To picture in one's mind, or to one's self.

en-voy (en´voi) *n.* A messenger or agent; a diplomatic representative who is dispatched on a special mission.

en-vy (en´vē) *n., pl.* **envies** A feeling of discontent or resentment over someone else's possessions or advantages; any object of envy. **envy** *v.* To feel envy or jealousy about.

en-wind (en wīnd´) *v.* To coil about.

en-wreathe (en rēth´) *v.* To encircle.

en-zo-ot-ic (en´zō ot´ik) *n.* A disease affecting the animals of an area.

en-zyme (en´zīm) *n. Biochem.* A protein produced by living organisms that functions as a biochemical catalyst in animals and plants. **enzymatic** *adj.*

E-o-cene (ē´o sēn´) *adj.* Pertaining to the epoch of Tertiary which is between the Oligocene and the Paleocene time periods.

e--o-li-an (ē ō´lē *a*n) *adj.* Caused by or transmitted by the wind.

e-o-lith (ē´o lith) *n.* A kind of flint which is very crudely chipped.

e-on (ē´*o*n) *n.* An indefinitely long period of time.

e-o-sin (ē´o sin) *n.* A type of red dye that is obtained with the action of bromine on fluorescein.

e-o-sin-o-phil (ē´o sin´o fil) *n.* A type of leukocyte which has cytoplasmic inclusions.

e-o-sin-o-phil-ia *n.* An abnormal increase in the number of eosinophils of the blood that can be caused by an allergic state or infection.

e-pact (ē´pakt) *n.* A period of time which has been added to harmonize the lunar with the solar calendar.

ep-ar-chy (ep´är kē) *n.* The diocese of the Eastern church.

ep-ei-rog-e-ny (ep´ī roj´e nē) *n.* A deformation in the crust of the earth which causes the broader features of relief to form.

e-pen-the-sis (e pen´thi sis) *n.* An insertion of a sound into the body of a word.

e-pergne (i pėrn´) *n.* An ornamental centerpiece for holding flowers or fruit, used on a dinner table.

ep-ex-e-ge-sis (ep ek´si jē´sis) *n.* The additional explanatory matter.

e-phah *n.* The ancient Hebrew unit of dry measure, equal to a little over a bushel.

e-phebe (i-fēb´) *n.* A youth, especially one entering manhood.

e-phem-er-al (i fem´ėr al) *adj.* Referring to something that lasts for a very short time. **ephemerally** *adv.*

e-phem-er-al (i fem´ėr al) *n.* Anything living for a short time.

e-phem-er-al-i-ty (i fem´ėr al´it ē) *n.* The state of being ephemeral.

e-phem-er-id (i fem´ėr id) *n.* A short-

lived insect; a mayfly.

e-phem-er-is (i fem´ėr is) *n.* A statement of the positions of a celestial body at regular intervals.

eph-or (ef´ėr) *n.* A Spartan magistrate who had power over the king.

epi- *prefix* Attached to; upon.

ep-i-blast (ep´i blast´) *n.* The layer which is the outside of the blastoderm.

e-pib-o-ly (i pib´o lē) *n.* The process of one part growing around another part.

ep-ic (ep´ik) *n.* A long narrative poem in dignified style that reports the deeds and adventures of a legendary or historical hero; a book or play resembling an epic. **epic** *adj.* Resembling an epic; extending beyond the ordinary in size or scope. **epical** *adj.*

ep-i-ca-lyx (ep´i kā´liks) *n.* An involucre which resembles the calyx.

ep-i-can-thic fold (ep´e kan´thik fōld) *n.* A fold of the upper eyelid skin over the inner angle or both angles of the eye.

ep-i-car-di-um (ep´i kär´dē *u*m) *n.* The visceral part of the pericardium that closely covers the heart. **-ial.** *adj.*

ep-i-cene (ep´i sēn) *adj. Gram.* Of a noun that has only one form to indicate either sex. Having the characteristics that are typical of the other sex.

ep-i-cen-ter (ep´i sen´tėr) *n.* The part of the earth's surface directly above the focus of an earthquake.

ep-i-chlo-ro-hy-drin *n.* A toxic liquid that has a chloroform odor.

ep-i-con-ti-nen-tal *adj.* Being located on a continent or a continental shelf.

ep-i-cot-yl *n.* The part of a seedling stem that lies immediately above the first leaves.

ep-i-cure (ep´i kūr´) *n.* One having refined tastes, esp. in food and wine.

ep-i-cur-ism *n.* The taste of an epicure.

ep-i-cy-cle (ep´i sī´kal) *n.* The path or circle in which a plane will move; a small circle, the center of which moves around in the circumference of a larger circle.

ep-i-dem-ic (ep´i dem´ik) *adj.* Breaking out suddenly and affecting many individuals at the same time in a particular area, especially referring to a contagious disease; alluding to anything that is temporarily widespread, as a fad. **epidemic** *n.*

ep-i-de-mi-ol-o-gy (ep´i dē´mē ol´o jē) *n.* The science concerned with the control and study of epidemic diseases.

ep-i-den-drum (ep´e den´drum) *n.* A member of the genus that contains the tropical American orchids.

ep-i-der-mis (ep´i dėr´mis) *n. Anat.* The outer, nonvascular layer of the skin of a vertebrate. **epidermal** *adj.*

e-pi-der-moid *adj.* Being similar to the

epidermal cells.

e-pi-dia-scope (ep´i dīa skōp´) *n.* Projector which is used for opaque objects or transparencies.

ep-i-did-y-mis (ep´i did´i mis) *n.* The convoluted efferent tubes at the back of the testis.

ep-i-dote (ep´dōt´) *n.* A green mineral which occurs in metamorphic rock and is sometimes used as a gem.

ep-i-du-ral *adj.* Being outside the dura mater.

ep-i-fau-na *n.* The benthic fauna which live on the sea floor.

ep-i-fo-cal *adj.* Directly above the true center of disturbance of an earthquake.

ep-i-gas-tric (ep´i gas´trik) *adj.* Being over the stomach.

ep-i-ge-al (ep i jē´al) *adj.* Growing above the surface of the ground.

ep-i-gene *adj.* Formed on the surface of the earth.

ep-i-ge-net-íc (ep´i je net´ik) *adj.* Being formed after the laying of rock due to outside influences.

ep-i-glot-tis (ep´i glot´is) *n. Anat.* The leaf-shaped, elastic cartilage at the base of the tongue that covers the windpipe during the act of swallowing.

ep-i-gone (ep´i gōn´) *n.* An imitative follower. **epigonic** *adj.*

ep-i-gram (ep´i gram´) *n.* A clever, brief, pointed remark or observation; a terse, witty poem or saying.

ep-i-gram-ma-tize (ep´i gram´a tīz´) *v.* To make or create an epigram.

ep-i-graph (ep´i graf) *n.* An inscription on a tomb, monument, etc.; a motto or quotation placed at the beginning of a literary work.

e-pig-ra-phy (i pig´ra fē) *n.* The study and interpretation of inscriptions.

e-pig-y-nous *adj. Bot.* Being attached to the ovary surface and appearing to grow from the top.

ep-i-la-tion *n.* The removal of hair.

ep-i-lep-sy (ep´i lep´sē) *n. Pathol.* A nervous disorder marked by attacks of unconsciousness with or without convulsions. **epileptic** adj.

ep-i-lep-ti-form (ep´i lep´ti form´) *adj.* To be resembling epilepsy.

ep-i-lep-to-gen-ic *adj.* Tending to be able to produce epilepsy.

ep-i-lep-toid (ep´ilep´toid) *adj.* Showing symptoms of epilepsy.

ep-i-logue *or* **ep-i-log** (ep´i log´) *n.* A short speech given by an actor to the audience at the end of a play; an appended chapter placed at the end of a novel or book, etc.

ep-i-mor-pho-sis *n.* A type of regeneration, in invertebrate animals, which involves cell proliferation and subsequent differentiation.

e-pi-my-si-um (ep´i miz´ē um) *n.* The

connective tissue sheath of a muscle.

e-pi-nas-ty (ep´i nas´tē) *n.* A movement where the leaf of a plant is bent down and outward.

ep-i-neph-rine *or* **ep-i-neph-rin** (ep´i nef´rin) *n.* A hormone secreted by the adrenal medulla of the adrenal glands that raises the blood pressure and quickens the pulse, used in synthesized form as a cardiovascular stimulant.

e-pi-neu-ri-um (ep´i ner´ē um) *n.* The connective sheath of a nerve trunk.

ep-i-phan-ic (ep i fan´ik) *adj.* To have the character of an epiphany.

e-piph-a-ny (i pif´a nē) *n.* The Christian festival held on January 6th, celebrating the manifestation of Christ to the Gentiles as represented by the Magi; also known as the Twelfth Day; appearance of a divine being.

ep-i-phe-nom-e-nal (ep´ē fe nom´i nal) *adj.* Pertaining to a secondary event accompanying or caused by another.

e-piph-o-ra (e pif´ér a) *n.* The excessive flow of tears due to a disorder of the lacrimal glands.

e-piph-y-se-al (ep´i fiz´ē al) *adj.* Of or pertaining to an epiphysis.

e-piph-y-sis (i pif´i sis) *n.* A part or section of a bone which is separated from the main body of the bone by a layer of cartilage, and which later becomes united with the bone through further ossification.

ep-i-scope *n.* The projector which is used for items that are opaque.

ep-i-sode (ep´i sōd´) *n.* A section of a poem, novel, film, or other narrative that is complete in itself; an occurrence; an incident. **episodic** *adj.*

ep-i-some *n.* The gene that can replicate autonomously in the bacterial cytoplasm. or as an integral part of the chromosomes.

ep-i-ster-num (ep´i stèr´num) *n.* An anterior part of the sternum.

ep-i-taph (ep´i taf´) *n.* An inscription, as on a tomb or gravestone, in memory of a deceased person.

e-pit-a-sis (i pit´a sis) *n.* The portion of a play that develops the main action and leads it to a catastrophe.

ep-i-tha-la-mi-um (ep´e tha lā´mē um) *n.* A song or poem in the honor of the groom and the bride.

ep-i-the-li-o-ma (ep´i thē´lē ō´ma) *n.* A tumor either malignant or benign that is derived from epithelial tissue.

ep-i-the-li-um (ep´i thē´lē um) *n., pl.* **epitheliums** *or* **epithelia** *Biol.* The thin, membranous tissue consisting of one or more layers of cells, forming the covering of the outer bodily surface and most of the internal surfaces and organs. **epithelial** *adj.* **epithelioid** *adj.*

ep-i-the-lize *v.* To convert to epithelium.

ep-i-thet (ep´i thet´) n. A term, word, or phrase used to characterize a person or thing; an abusive phrase or word.

e-pit-o-me (i pit´o mē) n. A concise summary, as of a book; a typical or ideal example.

e-pit-o-mize (i pit´o mīz´) v. To serve as a perfect example.

ep-och (ep´ok) n. A point in time marking the beginning of a new era; a division of time. **epochal** adj.

ep-ode (ep´ōd) n. Type of lyric poem.

ep-o-nym (ep´o nim) n. The person that something is named for. **eponymic** adj.

ep-o-pee (ep´o pē´) n. A type of epic poem.

ep-ox-ide n. A kind of epoxy compound.

ep-ox-i-dize v. To change something into an epoxide.

ep-ox-y (e pok´sē) n., pl. **epoxies** Chem. A durable, corrosion-resistant resin used especially in surface glues and coatings. **epoxy** v.

ep-si-lon (ep´si lon´) n. The fifth letter of the Greek alphabet.

eq-ua-ble (ek´wa bl) adj. Not changing or varying; free from extremes; evenly proportioned; uniform; not easily upset.

e-qual (ē´kwal) adj. Of the same value, measurement, or quantity as another; having the same privileges or rights of others. **equal** v. To be equal to another; to match.

e-qual-i-tar-i-an n. A person who adheres to the doctrine of equality for all men.

e-qua-nim-i-ty (ē´kwa nim´i tē) n. Composure; calmness under stress.

e-quate (i kwāt´) v. To consider or make equal.

e-qua-tion (i kwā´zhan) n. The act or process of being equal; a mathematical statement expressing the equality of two quantities, usually shown as (=). In computer science, an expression of equality, as in a spreadsheet formula.

e-qua-tion-al adj. To be involving an equation. **equationally** adv.

e-qua-tor (i kwā´tėr) n. The great imaginary circle around the earth; a line lying in a plane perpendicular to the earth's polar axis and dividing the earth's surface into the northern and southern hemispheres. **equatorial** adj.

equatorial plane n. The plane in a cell which is perpendicular to a spindle of a cell and between the poles when it is dividing.

e-ques-tri-an (i kwes´trē an) adj. Relating or pertaining to horsemanship. **equestrian** n. The person who rides or performs on a horse.

e-qui-an-gu-lar (ē´kwē ang´gū lėr) adj. Geom. Having all angles equal.

e-qui-ca-lor-ic (ē´kwi ka lor´ik) adj. Able to yield equal amounts of energy in the body.

e-qui-dis-tant (ē´kwi dis´tant) adj. Being equal distances from some point. **equidistance** n. **equidistantly** adj.

e-qui-lat-er-al (ē´kwi lat´ėr al) adj. Having all sides equal.

e-qui-lat-er-al hy-per-bo-la n. A type of hyperbola, which is a plane curve, that has the straight lines associated with the curve at right angles.

e-quil-i-brant (i kwil i brant) n. A system of forces that counterbalance to produce equilibrium.

e-qui-li-brate (i kwil´i brāt´) v. To keep something in equilibrium.

e-qui-li-brist (i kwil´i brist) n. A person who can balance himself in positions which are unnatural and dangerous.

e-qui-lib-ri-um (ē´kwi lib´rē um) n., pl. **equilibriums** Phys. The state of balance between two opposing influences or forces; any state of compromise, adjustment, or balance.

e-qui-mol-al (ē´kwi mō´lal) adj. To have an equal concentration of moles.

e-qui-mo-lar adj. Pertaining to an equal amount or number of moles.

e-quine (ē´kwīn) adj. Pertaining to or like a horse. **equine** n.

e-qui-nox (ē´kwi noks´) n. Either of the two times a year when the sun crosses the celestial equator and the days and nights are equal in time.

e-quip (i kwip´) v. To furnish or fit with whatever is needed for any undertaking or purpose; to dress for a certain purpose or reason.

e-quip-ment (i kwip´ment) n. The state or act of being equipped; the material one is provided with for a special purpose.

e-qui-poise (ē´kwi poiz´) n. A state of balance.

e-qui-pol-lence (ē´kwi pol´ens) n. Equality of power or force.

e-qui-pol-lent (ē´kwi pol´ent) adj. To have the same effect. **equipollent** n.

e-qui-pon-der-ant adj. To be balanced equally.

e-qui-po-tent (ē´wi pōt´ent) adj. To have equal effects for development of something. **equipotential** n.

e-qui-prob-able adj. To have the same degree of mathematical probability.

e-qui-se-tum (ēk´wi sē tum) n. A type of perennial plant which can spread by creeping rhizomes, such as the scouring rush.

eq-ui-ta-ble (ek´wi ta bl) adj., pl. **equitabilities** Being impartial in treatment or judgment. **equitableness** n. **equitably** adv.

eq-ui-tant (ek´wi tant) adj. Of leaves, overlapping one another at the base, such as is seen in the iris.

eq-ui-ta-tion (ek´wi tā´shan) n. The art or act of horse riding.

eq-ui-ty (ek´wi tē) *n., pl.* **equities**
Fairness or impartiality; the value of property beyond a mortgage or liability; in law, justice based on the concepts of fairness and ethics.

e-quiv-a-lent (i kwiv´a lent) *adj.* Being equal or virtually equal, as in effect or meaning. **equivalence** *n.* **equivalency** *n.* **equivalent** *n.*

e-quiv-o-cal (i kwiv´o kal) *adj.* Ambiguous; questionable; doubtful; signification. **equivocally** *adv.*

e-quiv-o-cate (i kwiv´o kāt´) *v.* To intentionally use evasive or vague language. **equivocation** *n.*

e-qui-voque (ek´wi vōk´) *n.* A double meaning.

-er *suff.* A thing or person that performs the action of the root verb; a person concerned with a trade or profession, as a banker, teacher, etc.; one who lives in or comes from a certain area, as a northerner, mid-westerner, etc.; used to form the comparative usage degree of adverbs and adjectives.

e-ra (ēr´a) *n.* An extended period of time that is reckoned from a specific date or point in the past and used as the basis of a chronology; a period of time with distinctive characteristics, such as the Victorian era..

e-rad-i-cate (i rad´i kāt´) *v.* To destroy utterly; to remove by the roots. **eradicator** *n.* **eradication** *n.* **-able** *adj.*

e-rase (i rās´) *v.* To remove something written; to rub or scratch out. *Slang* To kill. **erasable** *adj.* In computer science, to delete, as a block of copy or a file, from storage.

e-ras-er *n.* An implement, such as a piece of cloth or rubber, used to erase or remove writing or other marks.

er-bi-um (ér bē um) *n. Chem.* A soft, metallic, silvery, rare-earth element, symbolized by Er.

ere (âr) *prep.* Prior to; before.

e-rect (i rekt´) *adj.* In a vertical position; standing up straight. *Physiol.* Being in a state of erection, as through an influx of blood. **erect** *v.* To construct; to build. **erectly** *adv.* **erectness** *n.* **erector** *n.* **erection** *n.*

ere-long (âr long´) *adv. Archaic* Before long.

er-e-mite (er´em mīt´) *n.* A hermit.

e-rep-sin *n.* A proteolytic mixture that contains peptidases and is found in intestinal secretions.

er-e-thism *n.* The abnormal irritability in any organ or tissue.

erg (erg) *n. Phys.* A unit of work.

er-go (er´gō) *conj. & adv.* Consequently; therefore.

er-go-graph *n.* An implement used to measure and record muscular work completed.

er-gos-ter-ol (er gos´te rōl´) *n. Biochem.* A steroid alcohol synthesized by yeast from sugars, converted under ultraviolet radiation to vitamin D.

er-got (er´got) *n.* The disease of rye and other cereal plants; a drug used to contract involuntary muscles and to control hemorrhage.

er-got-a-mine *n.* An alkaloid extracted from ergot, used in treating migraines and stimulating labor contractions.

er-got-ism (er´go tiz´um) *n.* The toxic condition that is produced by eating grain products or grasses that have been infected with ergot fungus.

er-is-tic *adj.* Pertaining to controversy; controversial.

e-rode (i rōd´) *v.* To wear away gradually by constant friction; to corrode; to eat away.

e-rog-e-nous (i roj´e nus) *adj.* Responsive to sexual stimulation.

e-ro-sion (i rō´zhan) *n.* The state or process of being eroded. **erosional** *adj.*

e-ro-sive (i rō´siv) *adj.* Eroding or tending to erode. **erosiveness** *n.*

e-rot-ic (i rot´ik) *adj.* Pertaining to or promoting sexual desire.

err (er) *v.* To make a mistake; to sin.

er-rand (er´and) *n.* A short trip to carry a message or to perform a specified task, usually for someone else.

er-rant (er´ant) *adj.* Wandering or traveling about in search of adventure; straying from what is proper or customary. **errantry** *n.*

er-rat-ic (i rat´ik) *adj.* Lacking a fixed course. *Med.* Irregular; inconsistent.

er-ra-tum (i rä´tum) *n., pl.* **errata** An error in printing or writing.

er-ro-ne-ous (e rō´nē us) *adj.* To have or contain an error. **erroneously** *adv.*

er-ror (er´or) *n.* Something said, believed, or done incorrectly; a mistake; the state of being wrong or mistaken; in baseball, a misplay by a team member who is not batting.

errorlevel In *computer science,* in a program or batch file, a value that is tested to signal a branch.

error message In *computer science,* a message from an operating system or program displayed on the monitor or printer indicating that an error in processing has occurred, of citing the source of the error.

er-satz (er´zäts) *adj.* A substitute that is usually inferior; artificial.

erst-while (érst´hwil´) *adj. Archaic* Former.

er-u-bes-cence *n.* The instance of turning red; blushing.

e-ruct (i rukt´) *v.* To belch.

e-ruc-tate *n.* The act of belching wind from the stomach.

er-u-dite (er´ū dīt´) *adj.* Scholarly.

er-u-di-tion (er´ū dish´an) *n*. Great learning.

e-rum-pent *adj*. Bursting forth.

e-rupt (i rupt´) *v*. To burst forth violently and suddenly; to explode with steam, lava, etc., as a volcano or geyser; to break out in a skin rash or pimples.

-ery *n. suff*. A business, or a place where something is performed or done, as a bakery; the collection of things; practice or act of something; the qualities or characteristics of something; as slavery.

e-ryn-go *n*. The genus of coarse herbs having toothed or spiny leaves.

er-y-sip-e-las (er´i sip´e las) *n*. An acute, inflammatory, and very uncomfortable skin disease resulting from streptococcus.

e-ryth-ro-cyte (i rith´ro sīt´) *n*. A disk-shaped blood cell that contains hemoglobin and is responsible for the red color of blood.

es-ca-lade (es´ka lād´) *n*. A scaling or mounting by means of ladders.

es-ca-late (es´ka lāt´) *v*. To intensify, increase, or enlarge. **escalation** *n*.

es-ca-la-tor (es´ka lā´tėr) *n*. A moving stairway with steps attached to an endless belt.

es-cal-lop (e skol´op) *n. & v*. Variation of scallop.

es-ca-pade (es´ka pād´) *n*. Reckless or playful behavior; a prankish trick.

es-cape (e skāp´) *v*. To break free from capture, confinement, restraint, etc; to fade from the memory; to enjoy temporary freedom from unpleasant realities. In *computer science*, to discontinue processing or to return to a previous menu or operating level. **escape** *n*. **escapee** *n*.

escape hatch *n*. Emergency exit.

escape key (Esc) In *computer science*, a function key that triggers the escape command.

es-cape-ment (e skāp´ment) *n*. *Mech*. A device used in timepieces to control the movement of the wheel and supply energy impulses to a pendulum or balance; a typewriter mechanism that controls the horizontal movement of the carriage.

escape velocity *n*. *Phys*. The minimum velocity that a rocket or any body must attain to escape or overcome the earth's gravitational field.

es-carp-ment (e skärp´ment) *n*. A steep slope or drop; a long cliff formed by erosion.

-escence *n. suff*. Process of becoming, as in phosphorescence.

-escent *adj. suff*. Beginning to be; giving off light in a special way, as in phosphorescent.

es-chew (es chö´) *v*. To shun or avoid.

es-cort (es´kort) *n*. A group or individual person accompanying another so as to give protection or guidance; a male who accompanies a female in public.

es-cri-toire (es´kri twär´) *n*. A writing desk.

es-crow (es´krō) *n*. In law, a written deed, contract, or money placed in the custody of a third party until specified conditions are met.

es-cu-lent (es´kū lent) *adj*. Fit for eating.

es-cutch-eon (e skuch´on) *n*. A shield-shaped surface with an emblem bearing a coat of arms; a protective plate, as for a keyhole.

-ese *n. & adj. suff*. An inhabitant or native of; in the language or style of.

E-SIGN *n*. Electronic Signatures in Global and National Commerce; Act of Congress establishing a standard for electronic signatures so that they are valid under the law, passed in 1999.

e-soph-a-gus (i sof´a gus) *n., pl.* **esophagi** *Anat*. The muscular, membranous tube through which food passes on the way from the mouth to the stomach. **esophageal** *adj*.

es-o-ter-ic (es´o ter´ik) *adj*. Confidential; kept secret; understood or meant for only a particular, often very small, group

es-par-to *n*. Any of two or three types of grass used to make cord and paper.

es-pe-cial (e spesh´al) *adj*. Having a very special place; apart from or above others; exceptional. **especially** *adv*.

es-pi-al (e spī´al) *n*. Observation; discovery.

es-pi-o-nage (es´pē o näzh´) *n*. The act of spying or the hiring of spies to obtain secret information about a competing company or a foreign government.

es-pla-nade (es´pla näd´) *n*. A flat, open stretch of land along a shoreline.

es-pou-sal (e spou´zal) *n*. Support or adoption, as of a cause; a wedding.

es-pouse (e spouz´) *v*. To make something one's own; to take as a spouse; to marry; to give in marriage.

es-prit (e sprē´) *n*. Spirit; wit; mental liveliness.

es-prit de corps (e sprē´ de kor´) *n*. A group's spirit of enthusiasm and devotion to the common goals of the group.

es-py (e spī) *v*. To catch a quick view or sight of.

-esque *adj. suff*. Resembling.

es-quire (e skwier´) *n*. A title of courtesy or respect; sometimes written as Esq. be-hind a man's last name.

-ess *n. suff*. Female.

es-say (es´ā) *n*. A short composition that deals with a single topic and expresses the author's viewpoint on a subject;

an effort or attempt. **essayer** *n.*

es-sence (es´ens) *n.* The real nature of something; the most important element; an immaterial spirit; being; a perfume.

es-sen-tial (*e* sen´shal) *adj.* Necessary; indispensable; containing, of, or being an essence. **essential** *n.* **essentiality** *n.* **essentialness** *n.* **essentially** *adv.*

es-sen-tial-ism *n.* The theory that there are definite traditional concepts, standards, and procedures that are indispensable to a society.

es-so-nite *n.* A yellow to brown gem.

est *abbr.* Established; estimate.

-est *adj. & adv. suff.* Used to form the superlative degree of adverbs and adjectives.

es-tab-lish (e stab´lish) *v.* To make permanent, stable, or secure; to install; to create or find; to cause to be accepted or recognized; to prove.

es-tab-lish-ment (e stab´lish ment) *n.* The state of being established; a place of business or residence; those collectively who occupy positions of influence and status in a society.

es-tate (e stāt´) *n.* A usually large or extensive piece of land containing a large house; in law, the nature, degree, and extent of ownership or use of property.

es-teem (e stēm´) *v.* To regard with respect.

es-ter (es´tėr) *n. Chem.* Any of a class of organic compounds formed by the reaction of an acid with an alcohol.

es-the-sia (es thē´zha) *n.* Sensibility; feeling.

es-thet-ic (es thet´ik) *adj.* Variation of aesthetic.

es-ti-ma-ble (es´ti ma bl) *adj.* Worthy of respect or admiration. **estimableness** *n.* **estimably** *adv.*

es-ti-mate (es´ti māt´) *v.* To form or give an approximate opinion or calculation. **estimate** *n.* A preliminary opinion or statement of the approximate cost for certain work. **estimator** *n.*

es-ti-ma-tion (es´ti mā´shan) *n.* Judgment; the act of estimating or appraising something.

es-ti-val (es´ti val´) *adj.* Pertaining to or of summer.

es-ti-vate (es´ti vāt´) *v.* To pass the summer in a state of dormancy.

es-trange (e stranj´) *v.* To arouse hatred or indifference where there had been love and caring; to disassociate or remove oneself. **estrangement** *n.*

es-tro-gen (es´tro jen) *n. Biochem.* Any of various steroid hormones that regulate female reproductive functions and secondary sex characteristics.

es-tu-ar-y (es´chö er´ē) *n., pl.* **estuaries** The wide mouth of a river where the current meets the sea and is influenced

by tides.

et al *abbr.* And others.

et-a-mine *n.* A lightweight fabric of cotton, silk, or wool.

etc *abbr.* And so forth.

etch (ech) *v.* To engrave or cut into the surface by the action of acid; to sketch or outline by scratching lines with a pointed instrument. **etcher** *n.*

e-ter-nal (i tėr´nal) *adj.* Existing without beginning or end; unending; meant to last indefinitely. **eternalness** *n.*

e-ter-ni-ty (i tėr´ni tē) *n., pl.* **eternities** Existence without beginning or end; forever; the immeasurable extent of time; the endless time after a person dies.

eth-ane (eth´ān) *n. Chem.* An odorless, colorless, gaseous hydrocarbon from the methane series that is contained in crude petroleum and in natural gas.

eth-a-nol (eth´a nōl´) *n. Chem.* The alcohol obtained after the distillation of certain fermented sugars or starches; the intoxicant in liquors, wines, and beers; alcohol.

e-ther (ē´thėr) *n. Chem.* A highly flammable liquid compound with a characteristic odor, used as a solvent and an anesthetic; the clear upper regions of space.

e-the-re-al (i thėr´ē al) *adj.* Very airy and light; highly refined; delicate; heavenly. **ethereally** *adv.*

eth-ic (eth´ik) *n., pl.* **ethics** The system of moral values; the principle of right or good conduct.

eth-i-cal (eth´i kal) *adj.* Relating to or of ethics; conforming to right principles of conduct as accepted by a specific profession, as medicine. **ethically** *adv.*

eth-moid (eth´moid) *adj.* Pertaining to a bone of the skull located at the root of the nose, containing a number of perforations for the filaments of the olfactory nerve.

eth-nic (eth´nik) *adj.* Relating to or of a national, cultural, or racial group.

eth-no-cen-tric (eth´nō sen´trik) *adj.* Pertaining to the belief that a person's own culture is better than other ethnic groups.

e-thos *n.* The characteristic spirt of people; character or disposition.

eth-yl (eth´il) *n. Chem.* An organic radical occurring in ether and alcohol; a univalent hydrocarbon radical; any gasoline that is treated with tetraethyl lead to reduce engine knock.

eth-yl-ene (eth´i lēn´) *n. Chem.* A colorless, flammable gas refined from natural gas and petroleum and used as a fuel.

et-i-quette (et´i kit) *n.* The prescribed rules, forms and practices, established for behavior in polite society or in official or professional life.

-ette *n. suff.* Small; female.

e-tui (ā twē´) *n.* A small ornamental case holding pins or other small articles.

et-y-mol-o-gy (et´i mol´o jē) *n., pl.* **etymologies** The history of a word as shown by breaking it down into basic parts, tracing it back to the earliest known form, and indicating its changes in form and meaning; the branch of linguistics that deals with etymologies. **etymological** *adj.* **etymologist** *n.*

et-y-mon (et´i mon´) *n., pl.* **etymons** *or* **etyma** The earlier form of a word in the same language or in the ancestral language.

eu-di-om-e-ter *n.* An instrument used in the analysis and volume measurement of gases.

eu-di-om-e-try *n.* The measurement and analysis of gases using a eudiometer.

eu-gen-ics (ū jen´iks) *n.* The science of improving the physical and mental qualities of human beings through genetics. **eugenic** *adj.* **eugenicist** *n.*

eu-gle-na *n.* Microscopic green protozoa having a single flagellum and a red eyespot, having both animal and plant traits and used in biological research.

eu-la-mel-li-branch (ū´la mel´i brank) *n.* Bivalve mollusk, such as the clam, oyster, and fresh-water mussel.

eu-lo-gize (ū´lo jīz´) *v.* To deliver a eulogy for; to speak in commendation of another. **eulogist** *n.* **eulogizer** *n.*

eu-lo-gy (ū´lo jē) *n., pl.* **eulogies** A speech that honors a person or thing, usually delivered at a funeral; high praise. **eulogistic** *adj.*

eu-nuch (ū´nuk) *n.* A castrated man.

eu-pep-sia *n.* Good digestion.

eu-phe-mism (ū´fe miz´um) *n.* A substitution for a word or expression that is thought to be too strong, blunt, or painful for another person. **euphemistic** *adj.* **euphemistically** *adv.*

eu-pho-ni-um *n.* A musical instrument that resembles the baritone tuba, but has a higher range and mellower tone.

eu-pho-ny (ū´fo nē) *n., pl.* **euphonies** The agreeable sound of spoken words. **euphonious** *adj.* **euphoniously** *adv.*

eu-pho-ri-a (ū fōr´ē a) *n.* A very strong feeling of elation or well-being.

eu-phu-ism (ū´fū iz´um) *n.* An ornate style of writing with frequent use of alliteration, antitheses, and mythological similes.

eu-re-ka (ū rē´ka) *interj.* An expression of triumph or achievement.

eu-rhyth-mics *n.* The art of graceful bodily movements in harmony with music, often improvisational.

eu-ri-pus *n.* An area where the tide flows with dangerous and violent force.

eu-ry-therm *n.* An organism with the ability to adjust physically to widely varying degrees of heat and cold.

eu-sta-chian tube (ū stā´shan tōb) *n.* *Anat.* The passage between the middle ear and the pharynx that equalizes the air pressure between the tympanic cavity and the atmosphere.

eu-tha-na-sia (u´tha nā´zha) *n.* The act or practice of putting to death painlessly a person suffering from an incurable disease; also called mercy killing.

eu-then-ics (ū then´iks) *n.* The study of improving the physical and mental qualities of human beings by controlling the environmental factors.

eu-the-ri-an *adj.* Referring to a large group.

eu-tro-phy *n.* Healthful, normal nutrition.

e-vac-u-ate (i vak´ū āt´) *v.* To leave a threatened area, town, building, etc.; to empty; to remove the contents. *Physiol.* To discharge or eject, as from the bowels. **evacuative** *adj.*

e-vac-u-a-tion (i vak´ū ā´shan) *n.* The process of evacuating.

e-vac-u-ee (i vak´ū ē´) *n.* A person who is evacuated from a hazardous place.

e-vade (i vād´) *v.* To baffle; to elude; to get away from by using cleverness or tricks.

e-val-u-ate (i val´ū āt´) *v.* To examine carefully; to determine the value of; to appraise. **evaluation** *n.*

ev-a-nesce (ev´a nes´) *v.* To disappear; to fade away.

ev-a-nes-cent (ev´a nes´ent) *adj.* Vanishing or passing quickly; fleeting. **evanescence** *n.* **evanescently** *adv.*

e-van-gel-ist *or* **Evangelist** (i van´je list) *n.* One of the four writers of the New Testament Gospels: Matthew, Mark, Luke, and John; a zealous Protestant preacher or missionary.

e-van-ish *v.* To vanish.

e-vap-o-rate (i vap´o rāt´) *v.* To convert into vapor; to remove the liquid or moisture from fruit, milk, etc., so as to concentrate or dry it. **evaporative** *adj.* **evaporator** *n.* **evaporation** *n.*

e-vap-o-tran-spi-ra-tion *n.* The process by which the earth's surface loses moisture by evaporation.

e-va-sion (i vā´zhan) *n.* The act or means of evading.

e-va-sive (i vā´siv) *adj.* Being intentionally vague; equivocal. **evasively** *adv.*

eve (ēv) *n.* The evening before a special day or holiday; the period immediately preceding some event; evening.

e-vec-tion (i vek´shan) *n.* The perturbation of the orbital motion of the moon that is caused due to the attraction of the sun.

e-ven (ē´ven) *adj.* Having a flat, smooth, and level surface; having no irregularities; smooth; on the same line or plane; equally matched; not owing or having anything owed to one; exactly divisible by 2; opposed to odd. **even** *v*. To make even. **break even** *Informal* To end with neither profit or loss, as in business. **get even** Get one's full measure of revenge. **evenly** *adv*.

eve-ning (ēv′ning) *n*. The time between sunset and bedtime.

e-vent (i vent′) *n*. A significant occurrence; something that takes place; the actual or possible set of circumstances; a real or contingent situation; the final outcome; one of the parts of a sports program. **eventfulness** *n*.

e-vent-ful (i vent′ful) *adj*. Momentous; full of events.

e-ven-tide (ē′ven tīd′) *n*. Evening.

e-ven-tu-al (i ven′chō al) *adj*. Happening or expected to happen in due course of time. **eventually** *adv*.

e-ven-tu-al-i-ty (i ven′chō al′i tē) *n*., *pl*. **eventualities** A likely or possible occurrence; the conceivable outcome.

e-ven-tu-ate (i ven′chō āt′) *v*. To result ultimately; to come out eventually.

ev-er (ev′ér) *adv*. At any time; on any occasion; by any possible chance or conceivable way; at all times; throughout the entire course of time.

ev-er-more (ev′ér mōr′) *adv*. *Poet*. For all time to come; always.

e-vert (i vért′) *v*. To turn inside out or outward.

e-ver-tor *n*. A muscle that causes an outward rotation of a part.

eve-ry *adj*. Referring to each part of a group without exception. **every which way** *adv*. *Informal* In every way or direction and with very little order.

eve-ry-bod-y (ev′rē bod′ē) *pron*. Every person.

eve-ry-day (ev′rē dā′) *adj*. Happening every day; daily; suitable for ordinary days.

eve-ry-one (ev′rē wun′) *pron*. Everybody; every person.

eve-ry-place *adv*. Everywhere.

eve-ry-thing (ev′rē thing′) *pron*. All things; whatever exists; whatever is needed, relevant, or important; the essential thing; the only thing that really matters.

eve-ry-where (ev′rē hwâr′) *adv*. In, at, or to everyplace.

e-vict (i vikt′) *v*. To put out or expel a tenant by legal process. **eviction** *n*.

ev-i-dence (ev′i dens) *n*. Signs or facts on which a conclusion can be based; that which makes evident an indication of something. **evidence** *v*. To indicate clearly; to offer evidence.

ev-i-dent (ev′i dent) *adj*. Easily understood or seen; obvious.

e-vil (ē′vil) *adj*. Morally wrong or bad;

causing injury or any other undesirable result; marked by misfortune or distress; low in public esteem. **Evil One** Satan.

e-vince (i vins′) *v*. To demonstrate or indicate clearly; to give an outward sign of having a quality or feeling.

e-vis-cer-ate (i vis′e rāt′) *v*. To remove the vital part of something; to remove the entrails. **evisceration** *n*.

e-voke (i vōk′) *v*. To call or summon forth; to draw forth or produce a reaction; to summon up the spirits by or as by incantations. **evocation** *n*. **evocative** *adj*. **evocatively** *adv*.

ev-o-lu-tion (ev′o lö′shan) *n*. The gradual process of development or change. *Biol*. The theory that all forms of life originated by descent from earlier forms. **evolutionary** *adj*. **evolutionism** *n*. **evolutionist** *n*.

e-volve (i volv′) *v*. To develop or change gradually. *Biol*. To be developed by evolutionary processes; to develop or work out. **evolvement** *n*.

e-vul-sion *n*. The act of pulling out.

ewe (ū) *n*. A female sheep.

ex *n*. The letter x. *Slang* A former spouse. *abbr*. Example; exchange.

ex- (eks) *pref*. Out of; former.

ex-ac-er-bate (ig zas′ér bāt′) *v*. To make more severe or worse; to aggravate.

ex-act (ig zakt′) *adj*. Perfectly complete and clear in every detail; accurate in every detail with something taken as a model; similar. **exact** *v*. To be demanding about accuracy and detail; to force unjustly for the payment of something; to insist upon as a strict right or obligation; to call for or require. **exactness** *n*. **exactly** *adv*.

ex-ac-tion *n*. Extortion; fees, or contributions levied with injustice.

ex-act-i-tude (ig zak′ti töd′) *n*. The quality of being exact.

ex-ag-ger-ate (ig zaj′e rāt′) *v*. To look upon or to represent something as being greater than it really is; to make greater in intensity or size than would be normal or expected. **exaggerated** *adj*. **exaggerative** *adj*. **exaggerator** *n*.

ex-alt (ig zolt′) *v*. To raise in character, honor, rank, etc.; to praise or glorify; to increase the intensity of. **exalted** *adj*. **exalter** *n*. **exaltation** *n*.

ex-am (ig zam′) *n*. *Slang* An examination.

ex-am-i-na-tion (ig zam′i nā′shan) *n*. A test of skill or knowledge; the act of examining or the state of being examined; medical testing and scrutiny.

ex-am-ine (ig zam′in) *v*. To observe or inspect; to test by questions or exercises, as to fitness or qualification. **examinee** *n*. **examiner** *n*.

ex-ample (ig zam′pl) *n*. One that is

representative as a sample; one worthy of imitation; an object or instance of punishment, reprimand, etc.; a previous instance or case that is identical with or similar to something that is under consideration; a problem or exercise in algebra, arithmetic, etc. **set an example** *v.* To act in such a way as to arouse others to imitation.

ex-an-the-ma *n.* An eruption or rash on the skin; one with fever.

ex-as-per-ate (ig zas′pê rāt′) *v.* To make frustrated or angry; to irritate. **exasperatingly** *adv.* **exasperation** *n.*

ex-ca-vate (eks′ka vāt′) *v.* To dig a hole or cavity; to form or make a tunnel, hole, etc., by digging, scooping, or hollowing out; to remove or uncover by digging; to unearth. **excavation** *n.*

ex-ceed (ik sēd′) *v.* To surpass in quality or quantity; to go beyond the limit; to be superior.

ex-ceed-ing *adj.* Great in extent, quantity, or degree..

ex-cel (ik sel′) *v.* To surpass or to do better than others.

ex-cel-lence (ek′se lens) *n.* The state or quality of being superior or excellent; a superior trait or quality.

ex-cel-lent (ek′se lent) *adj.* The best quality; exceptionally good. **-ly** *adv.*

ex-cept (ik sept′) *prep.* With the omission or exclusion of; aside from; not including; leaving out.

ex-cept-ing (ik sep′ting) *prep.* With the exception that.

ex-cep-tion (ik sep′shan) *n.* The act of or state of being excepted; something that is excluded from or does not conform to a general class, rule, or principle; criticism or objection.

ex-cep-tion-a-ble (ik sep′sha nal) *adj.* Open to objection or exception. **exceptionability** *n.* **exceptionably** *adv.*

ex-cep-tion-al (ik sep′sha nal) *adj.* Being an exception to the rule; unusual; well above average. **exceptionally** *adv.*

ex-cerpt (ik sėrpt′) *n.* A passage from a book, speech, etc. **excerpt** *v.* To select and cite; to take extracts from..

ex-cess (ik ses′) *n.* The amount or condition of going beyond what is necessary, usual, or proper; overindulgence, as in drink or food.

ex-ces-sive (ik ses′iv) *adj.* Exceeding what is usual, necessary, or proper; extreme. **excessiveness** *n.*

exch *abbr.* Exchange.

ex-change (iks chānj) *v.* To give in return for something else; to trade; to return as unsatisfactory and get a replacement. **exchange** *n.* The substitution of one thing for another; a place where brokers meet to buy, sell, or trade; the mutual receiving and giving of equal sums or money. **exchangeable** *adj.*

exchange rate *n.* The value of the currency from one country to another.

ex-cheq-uer (eks′chek ėr) *n.* The treasury of a nation or organization; financial resources; funds. *Slang* One's total financial resources.

ex-cide (ik sīd′) *v.* To cut out.

ex-cip-i-ent *n.* Inert substance, as sugar or jelly, used as a vehicle for an active medicine.

ex-cise (ek′ sīz) *n.* The indirect or internal tax on the production, consumption, or sale of a commodity, such as liquor or tobacco, that is produced, sold, and used or transported within a country.

ex-cise (ik sīz′) *v.* To remove surgically.

ex-cit-a-ble (ik sī′ta bl) *adj.* Reacting to a stimulus; easily excited. **excitably** *adv.* **excitability** *n.* **excitableness** *n.*

ex-cit-ant *n.* A stimulant.

ex-ci-ta-tion *n.* The act of exciting.

ex-cit-a-tive *adj.* Having power to excite; tending to excite.

ex-cite (ik sīt′) *v.* To stir up strong feeling, action, or emotion; to stimulate the emotions of; to bring about; to induce. **excitement** *n.*. **excitingly** *adv.*

ex-cit-ed *adj.* Emotionally stimulated; having strong feelings. **excitedly** *adv.*

ex-cit-ing *adj.* Producing excitement; thrilling.

ex-claim (ik sklām′) *v.* To cry out abruptly; to utter suddenly, as from emotion.

ex-cla-ma-tion (ek′skla mā′shan) *n.* An abrupt or sudden forceful utterance.

exclamation point *n.* A punctuation mark (!) used after an interjection or exclamation.

ex-clo-sure *n.* An area closed off; a fenced area.

ex-clude (ik sklōd′) *v.* To keep out; to omit from consideration; to put out.

ex-clu-sion (ik sklō′shan) *n.* Excluding or the state of being excluded; that which is excluded or expelled.

ex-clu-sive (ik sklō′siv) *adj.* Intended for the sole use and purpose of a single individual or group; intended for or possessed by a single source; having no duplicate; the only one; complete; undivided. **exclusively** *adv.* **exclusive-ness** *n.* **exclusivity** *n.*

ex-cog-i-tate (eks koj′i tāt) *v.* To contrive; devise.

ex-com-mu-ni-cate (eks′ko mū′n/kāt′) *v.* To deprive of the right of church membership. **excommunication** *n.*

ex-co-ri-ate (ik skōr′ē āt′) *v.* To tear the skin or wear off; to censure harshly.

ex-cre-ment (ek′skre ment) *n.* Bodily waste, especially feces.

ex-cres-cent (ik skres′ent) *adj.* Growing abnormally out of something else.

ex-cre-ta (ik skrē′ta) *n.* Excretions from the body such as sweat, urine, etc.

ex-cru-ci-ate *v.* To cause extreme pain to.

ex-cru-ci-at-ing (ik skrö'shē ā'ting) *adj.* Intensely painful; agonizing.

ex-cul-pate (ek'skul pāt') *v.* To free from wrongdoing; to prove innocent of guilt. **exculpation** *n.* **exculpatory** *adj.*

ex-cur-sion (ik sker'zhan) *n.* A short trip, usually made for pleasure; a trip available at a special reduced fare. *Phys.* The oscillating movement between two points; also, the total distance traveled. **excursionist** *n.*

ex-cur-sive (ik sker'siv) *adj.* To go in one direction and then another; rambling; digressive.

ex-cus-a-to-ry *adj.* Making an excuse.

ex-cuse (ik skūz') *v.* To ask forgiveness or pardon for oneself; to grant pardon or forgiveness; to overlook or accept; to apologize for; to justify; to allow one to leave; to release. **excuse** *n.* A reason, justification, or explanation. **poor excuse** *Informal* An inferior example for something. **excusable** *adj.*

ex-ec (ig zek') *abbr.* Executive; executor.

ex-e-cra-ble (ek'si kra bl) *adj.* Extremely bad; detestable; revolting.

ex-e-crate (ek'si krāt') *v.* To detest; to feel or express detestation for; to abhor. **execration** *n.* **execrator** *n.*

ex-e-cute (ek'se kūt') *v.* To carry out; to put into effect; to validate, as by signing; to carry out what has been called for in a will; to put to death by the legal authority. In computer science, to carry out an instruction or set of instructions.

ex-ec-u-tive (ig zek'ū tiv) *n.* A manager or administrator in an organization; the branch of the government responsible for activating or putting the laws of a country into effect and for carrying out plans or policies.

ex-ec-u-tor (ig zek'yu tėr) *n.* The person appointed to carry out the reading and execution of a will. **executorial** *adj.*

ex-ec-u-to-ry *adj.* Executive; pertaining to what is yet to be performed.

ex-e-ge-sis (ek'si jē'sis) *n., pl.* **exegeses** An interpretation or explanation of a text. **exegetic** *adj.* **exegetically** *adv.*

ex-e-get-ics *n.* The science that lays down the principles and art of scriptural interpretation.

ex-em-plar (ig zem'plėr) *n.* Something that serves as a worthy model for imitation; a typical example.

ex-em-plum *n.* An anecdote or story narrated to illustrate a moral.

ex-empt (ig zempt') *v.* To free or excuse from an obligation or duty to which others are subject. **exemption** *n.*

ex-en-ter-ate (ek sen'te rāt') *v.* To surgically remove the contents of a body cavity.

ex-er-cise (ek'sėr sīz') *n.* The act of performing drills; the act of training or developing oneself; something that is done to maintain or increase a skill, such as practice on the piano. **exercises** A ceremony, such as a graduation. **exercise** *v.* **exerciser** *n.*

ex-ert (ig zėrt') *v.* To put into action, as influence or force; to put oneself through a strenuous effort. **-ion** *n.*

ex-ha-la-tion *n.* The process of exhaling; that which is exhaled or emitted.

ex-hale (eks hāl') *v.* To breathe out; the opposite of inhale; to breathe forth or give off, as air, vapor, or aroma.

ex-haust (ig zost') *v.* To make extremely tired; to drain oneself of resources, strength, etc.; to eliminate all possibilities **exhaust** *n.* The escape or discharge of waste gases, working fluid, etc.; the waste gases, etc. that escape; the device through which waste gases are released or expelled. **exhaustible** *adj.*

ex-haust-ed *adj.* Completely consumed; tired.

ex-haus-tion *n.* Extreme fatigue.

ex-haus-tive (ig zos'tiv) *adj.* Tending to exhaust or that which exhausts; thoroughly analyzed. **exhaustively** *adv.*

ex-hib-it (ig zib'it) *v.* To display, as to put up for public view; to bring documents or evidence into a court of law. **exhibit** *n.* The presentation of something for public viewing. **exhibition** *n.* **exhibitor, exhibiter** *n.*

ex-hil-a-rate (ig zil'a rāt') *v.* To elate, make cheerful, or refresh. **exhilaration** *n.* **exhilarative** *adj.*

ex-hort (ig zort') *v.* To urge by earnest appeal or argument; to advise or recommend strongly. **exhortatory** *n.*

ex-hume (ig zöm') *v.* To dig up and remove from a grave; to disinter.

ex-i-gen-cy (ek'si jen sē) *n., pl.* **exigencies** The quality or state of being urgent. *usually pl.* A pressing need or needs. **exigence** *n.*

ex-i-gent (ek'si jent) *adj.* Urgent; demanding prompt attention or action.

ex-ig-u-ous (ig zig'ū us) *adj.* Extremely small; scanty. **exiguity** *n.*

ex-ile (eg'zīl) *n.* The separation by necessity or choice from one's native country or home; banishment; one who has left or been driven from his or her country. **exile** *v.* To banish or expel from one's native country or home.

ex-ist (ig zist') *v.* To have actual being or reality; to live.

ex-is-tence (ig zis'tens) *n.* The fact or state of existing, living, or occurring; the manner of existing. **existent** *adj.*

ex-is-ten-tial (eg'zi sten'shal) *adj.* Based on experience; of or relating to existentialism. **existentially** *adv.*

ex-is-ten-tial-ism (eg'zi sten'sha liz'um)

n. A philosophy that stresses the active role of the will rather than of reason in facing problems posed by a hostile universe. **existentialist** *n.*

ex-it (eg´zit) *n.* A way or passage out; the act of going away or out; the departure from a stage, as in a play. **exit** *v.* In computer science, a program branch that returns control to the next higher level; to leave a subroutine and return to the main application program or to leave an application and return to the operating system.

ex-o-bi-ol-o-gy (ek´sō bī ol´o jē) *n.* The search for and study of extraterrestrial life and environments.

ex-o-crine *adj.* Secreting externally through a duct.

ex-o-don-tia *n.* The branch of dentistry that deals with tooth extraction.

ex-o-dus (ek´so dus) *n.* A going forth; a departure of large numbers of people, as that of Moses and the Israelites as described in Exodus, the second book of the Old Testament.

ex-o-en-zyme (ek´sō en´zīm) *n.* The enzyme that performs its function outside the cell which produced it.

ex officio (eks *o* fish´ē ō´) *adj. & adv.* By virtue of or because of office or position.

ex-og-e-nous (ek soj´e nus) *n. Biol.* Growing by additions on the outside.

ex-on-er-ate (ig zon´e rāt´) *v.* To free or clear one from accusation or blame; to relieve or free from responsibility.

ex-or-bi-tant (ig zor´bi tant) *adj.* Beyond usual and proper limits, as in price or demand. **exorbitance** *n.*

ex-or-cise (ek´sor sīz´) *v.* To cast out or expel an evil spirit by prayers or incantations; to free from an evil spirit. **exorciser** *n.* **exorcism** *n.* **exorcist** *n.*

ex-or-di-um (ig zor´dē um) *n.* The beginning of anything, such as a speech..

ex-o-skel-e-ton *n.* An external protective covering, as the shell of crustaceans, the carapace of turtles, and the scales and plates of fish.

ex-o-sphere (ek´sō sfēr´) *n. Meteor.* The outermost region of the earth's atmosphere starting about 400 miles up.

ex-o-ter-ic (ik´so ter´ik) *adj.* Pertaining only to the external; not belonging to the inner or select circle.

ex-o-ther-mic (ek´sō ther´mik) *adj.* Releasing rather than absorbing heat.

ex-ot-ic (ig zot´ik) *adj.* Belonging by nature or origin to another part of the world; foreign; strange, different, and fascinating. **exotically** *adv.*

ex-ot-i-cism *n.* The tendency to adopt what is exotic.

exp *abbr.* Expenses; export; express;

experience..

ex-pand (ik spand´) *v.* To increase the scope, range, volume, or size; to open up or spread out; to develop more fully in form or details. **expandable** *adj.* .

ex-panse (ik spans´) *n.* A wide, open stretch; something spread out over a wide area.

ex-pan-sion (ik span´shan) *n.* The act of or state of being expanded; the amount of increase in range, size, or volume.

expansion card In *computer science,* a board that is installed in the computer to provide additional memory or functions.

expansion slots In *computer science,* positions in the computer reserved for the installation of expansion or control boards.

ex-pan-sive (ik span´siv) *adj.* Capable of expanding or inclined to expand; characterized by expansion; broad and extensive; open and generous; outgoing. **expansively** *adv.*

ex par-te (eks pär´tē) *adj. & adv.* In law, giving only one side or point of view.

ex-pa-ti-ate (ik spā´shē āt´) *v.* To elaborate; to talk or write at length.

ex-pect (ik spekt´) *v.* To look forward to something as probable or certain; to look for as proper, right, or necessary; to presume or suppose.

ex-pec-ta-tion (ek´spek tā´shan) *n.* The state or act of expecting; something that is expected and looked forward to; something looked forward to in the future; anticipation.

ex-pec-to-rant (ik spek´to rant) *adj.* Helping to promote the discharge of mucus from the respiratory tract. **expectorant** *n.* Any medicine that is used to promote expectoration.

ex-pe-di-en-cy (ik spē´dē en sē) *n. pl.* **expediencies** The state or quality of being expedient.

ex-pe-di-ent (ik spē´dē ent) *adj.* Promoting narrow or selfish interests; pertaining to or prompted by self-interest rather than by what is right.

ex-pe-dite (ek´spi dīt´) *v.* To speed up the progress or process of something; to facilitate; to do with quick efficiency. **expediter** *n.*

ex-pe-di-tion (ek´spi dish´an) *n.* A journey of some length for a definite purpose; the person or group and equipment that engage in such a journey; efficient promptness.

ex-pe-di-tion-ar-y *adj.* Relating to an expedition; sent on military service abroad.

ex-pe-di-tious (ek´spi dish´us) *adj.* Quick; speedy. **expeditiousness** *n.*

ex-pel (ik spel´) *v.* To drive out, as to

dismiss from a school; to force out, as gas from a well. **expellable** *adj.*

ex-pend (ik spend´) *v.* To consume; to pay out or use up.

ex-pend-a-ble (ik spen´da bl) *adj.* Available for spending. **expendables** *Milit.* Equipment or supplies that can be sacrificed. **expendability** *n.*

ex-pen-di-ture (ik spen´di chër) *n.* An amount spent; the act or process of expending.

ex-pense (ik spens´) *n.* The outlay or consumption of money; the amount of money required to buy or do something. **expenses** The funds that have been allotted or spent to cover incidental costs; the charges incurred by an employee while at work or necessary to work; the reimbursement for such charges incurred.

ex-pen-sive (ik spen´siv *adj.* Costing a lot of money; high-priced.

ex-pe-ri-ence (ik spër´ē ens) *n.* The actual participation in something or the direct contact with; the knowledge or skill acquired from actual participation or training in an activity or event; one's total judgments or reactions based on one's past learning.

ex-per-i-ment (ik sper´i ment) *n.* The act or test performed to demonstrate or illustrate a truth. **experiment** *v.* To conduct tests or to perform operations to examine proposed truths or theories. **experimental** *adj.*

ex-pert (ik spert´) *n.* A person having great knowledge, experience, or skill in a certain field. **expert** *adj.* Skilled as the result of training or experience.

ex-per-tise (ek´spër tēz´) *n.* A specialized knowledge, ability, or skill in a particular area.

ex-pi-ate (ek´spē āt´) *v.* To atone for; to make amends for. **expiation** *n.* **expiator** *n.* **expiatory** *adj.*

ex-pi-ra-tion *n.* The act of breathing out; emission of breath; exhalation.

ex-pire (ik spīr´) *v.* To come to an end; to die; to breathe out, as from the nose or mouth; to exhale. **expiration** *n.*

ex-plain (ik splān´) *v.* To make understandable; to clarify; to give reasons for; to account for; to give an explanation; to interpret. **explainable** *adj.* **explanatory** *adj.* **explainer** *n.*

ex-pla-na-tion *n.* The act of explaining; the clearing up of a misunderstanding.

ex-plant *v.* To transfer, as live fragments of plant or animal tissue, to a nutrient material for tissue culture.

ex-ple-tive (ek´sple tiv) *n.* An exclamation, often profane, such as *oh!*; a word added merely to fill out a sentence.

ex-pli-ca-ble (ek´spli ka bl) *adj.* Capable of explanation.

ex-pli-cate (ek´spli kāt´) *v.* To clear up

the meaning of. **explication** *n.*

ex-plic-it (ik splis´it) *adj.* Plainly expressed; specific; unreserved in expression; straightforward. **explicitly** *adv.* **explicitness** *n.*

ex-plode (ik splōd´) *v.* To cause to burst or blow up violently with a loud noise; to increase rapidly without control; to show to be false.

ex-ploit (ek´sploit) *n.* A deed or act that is notable. **exploit** *v.* To use to the best advantage of; to make use of in a selfish or unethical way. **exploitable** *adj.* **exploitative** *adj.* **exploitation** *n.*

ex-plo-ra-tion *n.* Travel for purposes of discovery; a systematic search for facts or reasons to aid understanding..

ex-plore (ik splōr´) *v.* To examine and investigate in a systematic way; to travel in unfamiliar territory.

ex-plor-er *n.* One who explores unknown areas.

ex-plo-sion (ik splō´zhan) *n.* A sudden, violent release of energy; the sudden, violent outbreak of personal feelings.

ex-plo-sive (ik splō´siv) *adj.* Marked by or pertaining to an explosion. *n.* A chemical preparation that explodes. **explosively** *adv.* **explosiveness** *n.*

ex-po-nent (ik spō´nent) *n.* A person who represents or speaks for a cause or group. *Mathematics* A number that indicates the number of times a factor is to be multiplied by itself.

ex-port (ik spōrt´) *v.* To carry or send merchandise or raw materials to other countries for resale or trade. **export** *n.* A commodity exported.

ex-por-ta-tion *n.* The conveying of gods and commodities abroad.

ex-pose (ik spōz´) *v.* To lay open, as to criticism or ridicule; to lay bare and uncovered; to reveal the identity of someone; to deprive of the necessities of heat, shelter, and protection. *Photog.* To admit light to a sensitized film or plate. **exposer** *n.*

ex-po-sé (ek´spō zā´) *n.* The reporting of something discreditable or shameful.

ex-po-si-tion (ek´spo zish´an) *n.* A statement of intent or meaning; a detailed presentation of subject matter; a commentary or interpretation; a large public exhibition. **expository** *adj.*

ex-pos-i-tor *n.* A person who explains.

ex post facto (eks´ pōst´fak´tō) *adj.* After the fact and retroactive.

ex-pos-tu-late (ik spos´cha lāt´) *v.* To reason earnestly with someone in an effort to dissuade that person from certain actions or to correct previous actions. **expostulatory** *adj.*

ex-po-sure (ik spō´zhër) *n.* The act or state of being exposed; an indication of which way something faces, such as a direction. *Photog.* The act of exposing a sensitive plate or film; the time required for the film or plate to be exposed to develop a picture.

ex-pound (ik spound´) v. To give a detailed statement of something; to explain the meaning at length.

ex-press (ik spres´) v. To formulate in words; to verbalize; to state; to communicate through some medium other than words or signs; to squeeze or press out, as juice from fruit; to send something by a fast or rapid means of delivery. **express** adj. Explicit; precise; fast. **expressly** adv.

ex-pres-sion (ik spresh´an) n. Communication of opinion, thought, or feeling; the outward indication or manifestation of a condition, feeling, or quality; a particular phrase or word from a certain region of the country; a facial aspect or look that conveys a feeling; in mathematics, a symbol, sign, or set that indicates something meaningful. In *computer science*, a symbol or symbols that describe a mathematical operation.

ex-pres-sive (ik spres´iv) adj. Of or characterized by expression; serving to indicate or express; full of expression. **expressively** adv.

ex-pro-pri-ate (eks prō´prē āt´) v. To transfer or take property from the owner for public use; to deprive a person of property or ownership.

ex-pul-sion (ik spul´shan) n. The act of expelling or the state of being expelled.

ex-punge (ik spunj´) v. To delete or remove; to erase. **expunger** n.

ex-pur-gate (ek´spėr gāt´) v. To remove obscene or objectionable material from a play, book, etc., before it is available to the public. **expurgation** n.

ex-qui-site (ek´skwi zit) adj. Delicately or intricately beautiful in design or craftsmanship; highly sensitive; keen or acute, as in pain or pleasure. **exquisitely** adv. **exquisiteness** n.

ex-san-gui-nate (eks sang´gwa nāt´) v. To remove the blood from.

ex-scind v. To cut off.

ex-sert-ed adj. Standing out; projected, beyond an encompassing part.

ext abbr. Exterior; external; extention.

ex-tant (ek´stant) adj. Still in existence; not lost or destroyed; surviving.

ex-tem-po-ra-ne-ous (ik stem´po rā´nē us) adj. Acting or performing with little or no advance preparation; delivering carefully prepared material without using notes or exact memorization.

ex-tem-po-rize (ik stem´po rīz´) v. To make, do, or perform with little or no advance preparation; to improvise to meet circumstances.

ex-tend (ik stend´) v. To stretch or open to full length; to make longer, broader, or wider; to continue; to prolong; to

put forth or hold out, as the hand; to exert to full capacity; to offer something.

ex-ten-sion (ik sten´shan) n. The act or state of being extended; an agreement with a creditor that allows a debtor further time to pay a debt. *Phys.* The property whereby matter occupies space.

ex-tent (ik stent´) n. The degree, dimension, or limit to which anything is extended; the area over which something extends; the size.

ex-ten-u-ate (ik sten´ū āt´) v. To minimize the seriousness of something as a crime or fault. **extenuation** n.

ex-te-ri-or (ik stēr´ē ėr) adj. Pertaining to or of the outside; the outer layer.

ex-te-ri-or-ize v.To expose, as an internal organ from the body for surgery.

ex-ter-mi-nate (ik stėr´mi nāt´) v. To annihilate; to destroy completely. **extermination** n. **exterminator** n.

ex-tern or **externe** (ek´stėrn) n. A person that is associated with but not officially residing in a hospital or an institution.

ex-ter-nal (ik stėr´nal) adj. For, of, or on the outside; acting from the outside; pertaining to foreign countries; outside; exterior. **externals** Outward or superficial circumstances. **externally** adv.

ex-tinct (ik stingk´) adj. Inactive; no longer existing; extinguished.

ex-tinc-tion n. The act of extinguishing; a coming to an end.

ex-tine n. The outer coat of a pollen grain.

ex-tin-guish (ik sting´gwish) v. To put an end to; to put out; to make extinct. **extinguishable** adj. **extinguisher** n.

ex-tir-pate (ek´stėr pāt´) v. To pull up by the roots; to destroy wholly, completely. **extirpation** n.

ex-tol or **ex-toll** (ik stō´) To praise highly. **extoller** n. **extolment** n.

ex-tort (ik stort´) v. To obtain money from a person by threat, oppression, or abuse of authority. **extortionist** n.

ex-tor-tion n. The practice of extorting money; illegal compulsion to pay money.

ex-tra (ek´stra) adj. Over and above what is normal, required, or expected. **extra** n. A special edition of a newspaper that covers news of special importance; a performer hired for a small part in a movie.

ex-tract (ik strakt´) v. To pull or draw out by force; to obtain in spite of resistance; to obtain from a substance as by pressure or distillation. *Mathematics* To determine the root of a number. **extract** n. A passage taken from a larger work; a concentrated substance used in cooking. **extractable, extractible** adj. **extractor** n.

ex-trac-tion (ik strak´shan) n. The

process or act of extracting; that which is extracted; one's origin or ancestry.

ex-trac-tive *n.* That which may be extracted.

ex-tra-cur-ric-u-lar (ek´stra ka rik´ūlėr) *adj.* Pertaining to activities not directly a part of the curriculum of a school or college; outside the usual duties.

ex-tra-dite (ek´stra dīt´) *v.* To obtain or surrender by extradition.

ex-tra-di-tion (ek´stra dish´an) *n.* The legal surrender of an alleged criminal to the jurisdiction of another country, government, or state for trial.

ex-tra-dos (ek´stra dos´) *n., pl.* **extrados** *or* **extradoses** The exterior or upper curve of an arch.

ex-tra-ga-lac-tic (ek´stra ga lak´tik) *adj.* Coming from beyond the galaxy; situated beyond the Milky Way.

ex-tra-ju-di-cial *adj.* Out of the ordinary course of a legal procedure.

ex-tra-mu-ral (ek´stra mūr´al) *adj.* Taking place outside of an educational building or institution; involving teams from different schools.

ex-tra-ne-ous (ik strā´ne us) *adj.* Coming from without; foreign; not vital or essential. **extraneously** *adv.*

ex-tra-or-di-nar-y (ik stror´di ner´ē) *adj.* Beyond what is usual or common; remarkable. **extraordinarily** *adv.*

ex-trap-o-late (ik strap´o lāt´) *v.* To infer the possibility beyond the strict evidence of a series of events, facts, or observations. *Mathematics* To infer the unknown information by projecting or extending known information. **extrapolation** *n.* **extrapolative** *adj.*

ex-tra-sen-so-ry (ek´stra sen´so rē) *adj.* Beyond the ordinary senses.

extrasensory perception *n.* The ability to foresee something before it actually happens; the ability to know something without any factual knowledge.

ex-tra-ter-res-tri-al (ek´stra te res´trē al) *adj.* Occurring or originating outside the earth or its atmosphere.

ex-tra-ter-ri-to-ri-al (ek´stra ter´itōr´ē al) *adj.* Outside of the jurisdiction of a territory, such as one's country of residence..

ex-tra-ter-ri-to-ri-al-i-ty *n.* An exemption from local legal jurisdiction, as that extended to foreign diplomats.

ex-trav-a-gant (ik strav´a gant) *adj.* Overly lavish in expenditure; wasteful; exceeding reasonable limits; immoderate; unrestrained. **extravagance** *n.*

ex-tra-vas-cu-lar *adj.* Outside of the blood vessels or the vascular system.

ex-tra-ve-hic-u-lar (ek´stra vē hik´ūlar) *adj.* Occurring or done outside a vehicle, especially a spacecraft in flight.

ex-treme (ik strēm´) *adj.* Greatly exceeding; going far beyond the bounds of moderation; exceeding what is considered moderate, usual, or reasonable; final; last; of the highest or utmost degree; one of the two ends of farthest limits of anything; a drastic measure. *Mathematics* The first or last term of a proportion or series. **extremely** *adv.* **extremeness** *n.*

ex-trem-ist *n.* A person who advocates or resorts to extreme measures or holds extreme views. **extremism** *n.*

ex-trem-i-ty (ik strem´i tē) *n., pl.* **extremities** The utmost or farthest point; the greatest degree of distress or peril; an extreme measure; an appendage or limb of the body; a hand or foot.

ex-tri-cate (ek´stri kāt´) *v.* To free from hindrance, entanglement, or difficulties; to disengage. **extrication** *n.*

ex-trin-sic (ik strin´sik) *adj.* Not inherent; outside the nature of something; from the outside; external. **extrinsically** *adv.*

ex-trorse *adj. Bot.* Facing outward, or directed away from the axis.

ex-tro-vert *or* **extravert** (ek´strō vėrt´) *n. Psychol.* A person who is more interested in people and things outside himself than in his own private feelings and thoughts. **extroversion** *n.*

ex-trude (ik strōd´) *v.* To push or thrust out; to shape by forcing through dies under pressure; to project or protrude. **extrusion** *n.* **extrusive** *adj.*

ex-u-ber-ance *n.* An expression in speech of being enthused or exuberant.

ex-u-ber-ant (ig zō´bėr ant) *adj.* Full of high spirits, vitality, vigor, and joy; plentiful; abundant. **exuberantly** *adv.*

ex-ude (ig zōd´) *v.* To give off; to ooze or trickle forth, as sweat.

ex-ult (ig zult´) *v.* To be jubilant; to rejoice greatly. **exultant** *adj.*

ex-ur-bi-a (eks ėr´bē a) *n.* The often well-to-do residential area outside the suburbs of a large city. **exurbanite** *n.*

ey-as (ī´as) *n.* A type of bird which is unfledged.; a nestling hawk

eye (ī) *n.* An organ of sight consisting of the cornea, iris, pupil, retina, and lens; a look; gaze; the ability to judge, perceive, or discriminate; the center part. **eye of the storm** *Meteor.* The central area of a hurricane or cyclone. **eye of the wind** *Naut.* The direction from which the wind blows. **eye** *v.* To watch closely. **see eye to eye** To be in complete agreement.

eye-sight (ī´sīt´) *n.* The faculty or power of sight; the range of vision.

eye-tooth (ī´tōth´) *n., pl.* **eyeteeth** One of the canine teeth of the upper jaw.

eye-wit-ness (ī´wit´nis´) *n.* A person who has seen something and can testify to it as a firsthand witness.

F, f (ef) The sixth letter of the English alphabet; in music, the fourth tone in the scale of C major; a failing grade.

fa-ba-ceous *adj.* Related to or belonging to the bean family of plants.

fa-ble (fā´bl) *n.* A brief, fictitious story embodying a moral and using persons, animals, or in animate objects as characters; a falsehood; a lie.

fab-ric (fab´rik) *n.* A cloth produced by knitting, weaving, or spinning fibers; a structure or framework, as the social fabric.

fab-ri-cate (fab´ri kāt´) *v.* To make or manufacture; to build; to construct by combining or assembling parts; to make up in order to deceive; to invent, as a lie or story. **fabrication** *n.* **-or** *n.*

fab-u-lous (fab´ya lus) *adj.* Past the limits of belief; incredible. *Slang* Very successful or pleasing. **fabulously** *adv.*

fa-cade (fa säd´) *n., Arch.* The face or front of a building; an artificial or false appearance.

face (fās) *n.* The front surface of the head from ear to ear and from forehead to chin; external appearance, look, or aspect; the value written on the printed surface of a note or bond; the principal, front, finished, or working surface of anything; the most prominent or significant surface of an object. *v.* To confront with awareness. **face up** To recognize the existence of something and confront it bravely. **facing** *v.*

fac-et (fas´it) *n.* One of the flat, polished surfaces cut upon a gemstone; the small, smooth surface on a bone or tooth; a phase, aspect, or side of a person or subject.

fa-ce-ti-ae (fa sē´shē ē´) *n.* Humorous or witty writings or remarks.

fa-ce-tious (fa sē´shus) *adj.* Given to or marked by playful jocularity; humorous. **facetiously** *adv.*

face value *n.* The apparent value of something; the value printed on the face of a bill or bond.

fa-cial (fā´shal) *adj.* Near, of, or for the face; a massage or other cosmetic treatment for the face. **facially** *adv.*

fac-ile (fas´il) *adj.* Requiring little effort; easily achieved or performed; arrived at without due care, effort, or examination; superficial. **facilely** *adv.*

fa-cil-i-tate (fa sil´i tāt´) *v.* To make easier. **facilitation** *n.* **facilitator** *n.*

fa-cil-i-ty (fa sil´i tē) *n. pl.* **-ies** Ease in performance, moving, or doing something; something that makes an operation or action easier.

fac-ing (fā´sing) *n.* The lining or covering sewn to a garment; any outer protective or decorative layer applied to a surface.

fac-sim-i-le (fak sim´i lē) *n.* An exact copy, as of a document; the method

of transmitting drawings, messages, or such by an electronic method.

fact (fakt) *n.* Something that actually occurred or exists; something that has real and demonstrable existence; actuality.

fac-tion (fak´shan) *n.* A group or party within a government that is often self-seeking and usually in opposition to a larger group; conflict within a party; discord. **factional** *adv.*

fac-ti-tious (fak tish´us) *adj.* Produced artificially; lacking authenticity or genuineness. **factitiously** *adv.*

fac-tor (fak´tēr) *n.* One who transacts business for another person on a commission basis; one of the elements or causes that contribute to produce the result; in mathematics, one of two or more quantities that when multiplied together give or yield a given product; in biology, a gene. **factorship** *n.* **factorable** *adj.* **factorage** *n.*

fac-to-ry (fak´to rē) *n. pl.* **-ies** An establishment where goods are manufactured; a plant.

fac-to-tum (fak tō´tum) *n.* An employee who performs all types of work.

fac-tu-al (fak´chō al) *adj.* Containing or consisting of facts, literal and exact.

fac-tu-al-ism *n.* An adherence to factual evidence; a theory that places great emphasis on fact.

fac-u-la *n.* Any bright patch on the sun's surface.

fac-ture (fak´chēr) *n.* The process, manner or act of construction; making.

fac-ul-ty (fak´ul tē) *n. pl.* **-ies** A natural ability or power; the inherent powers or capabilities of the body or mind; the complete teaching staff of a school or any other educational institution.

fad (fad) *n.* A temporary fashion adopted with wide enthusiasm. **faddish** *adj.* **faddishness** *n.* **faddist** *n.*

fade (fād) *v.* To lose brightness, brilliance, or loudness gradually; to vanish slowly; to lose freshness, vigor, or youth; to disappear gradually.

fa-er-ie (fā´e rē) *n., variation of* fairy.

fag-ot-ing (fag´o ting) *n.* A method of ornamenting cloth by pulling out horizontal threads and tying the remaining vertical threads into hourglass-shaped bunches.

Fahr-en-heit (far´en hīt´) *adj.* Of or relating to the temperature scale in which the freezing point of water is 32 degrees and the boiling point of water is 212 degrees under normal atmospheric pressure.

fa-ience (fī äns´) *n.* Earthenware that is decorated with a colorful opaque glaze.

fail (fāl) *v.* To be totally ineffective, unsuccessful; to go bankrupt; to receive an academic grade below the acceptable standards; to issue such a grade; to omit or neglect. **failing, failed** v.

faille (fĭl) n. A ribbed material of cotton, silk, or rayon.

fail–safe (fāl´sāf´) adj. Of or relating to a system designed to prevent equipment failure or to compensate automatically for a mechanical failure; guaranteed not to fail.

fail-ure (fāl´yĕr) n. The fact or state of failing; a breaking down in health, action, strength, or efficiency; a situation in which a business becomes insolvent or bankrupt; in school, a failing grade.

faint (fānt) adj. Having little strength or vigor; feeble; lacking brightness or clarity; dim. n. A sudden, temporary loss of consciousness; a swoon. **faintly** adv. **faintness** n.

fair (fâr) adj. Visually light in coloring; pleasing to the eye; beautiful; impartial; free from blemish or imperfection; moderately large or good; not stormy; without precipitation. n. A periodic gathering for the buying and selling of goods and merchandise; a competitive exhibit of agricultural products, livestock, machinery, and other goods; a fund-raising event for a charity.

fairy tale n. An incredible or fictitious tale of fanciful creatures; a tale about fairies.

fait accompli n. An accomplished fact or deed that is irreversible.

faith (fāth) n. A belief in the value, truth, or trust worthiness of someone or something; belief and trust in God, the Scriptures, or other religious writings; a system of religious beliefs.

faith-ful (fāth´fŭl) adj. True and trustworthy in the performance of duty, the fulfillment of promises or obligations, etc. **faithfully** adv.

fake (fāk) adj. Having a false or misleading appearance; not genuine. v. To make a brief, deceptive movement in order to mislead one's opponent in certain sports. **faker** n. **fakery** n.

fal-cate (fāk) adj. Hooked like a sickle; curved.

fal-chion n. A broad, short and slightly curved sword used in medieval times.

fall (fol) v. To drop down from a higher place or position due to the removal of support or loss of hold or attachment; to collapse; to become less in rank or importance; to drop when wounded or slain; to be overthrown by another government; to come as though descending as night falls; to pass into a specified condition, as to fall asleep; to cut down or fell, as a tree; to surrender, as a city or fort. **on** To recede; to retreat. **on** To fail in. **for** To be deceived by. **in** the military, to meet and go along with. **out** In the mil-

itary, to leave ranks. **of** To fail to meet a standard or to reach a particular place. **under** To be classified, as to be included. **man** The disobedience of Adam and Eve that began or resulted in original sin. A moral lapse or loss of innocence; autumn. **fall back** n. **fall down** n. **short** n.

fal-la-cious (fa lā´shus) adj. Containing or based on fundamental errors in reasoning; deceptive; misleading. **fallaciousness** n. **fallaciously** adv.

fal-la-cy (fal´a sē) n. pl. **fallacies** A deception; an error.

fal-li-ble (fal´i bl) adj. Capable of making an error; liable to be deceived or misled; apt to be erroneous.

fal-lo-pi-an tube (fa lō´pē an) n. One of a pair of long, slender ducts serving as a passage for the ovum from the ovary to the uterus.

fal-low (fal´ō) n. Ground that has been plowed but left unseeded during the growing season. adj. Light yellowish-brown in color. **fallowness** n.

false (fols) adj. Contrary to truth or fact; incorrect; deliberately untrue or deceptive; treacherous; unfaithful; not natural or real; artificial; in music, an incorrect pitch. adv. Faithless in manner. **falsely** adv. **falseness** n.

fal-set-to (fol set´ō) n. A high singing voice, usually male, that is artificially high. **falsetto** adv.

fal-si-fy (fol´si fī´) v. To give an untruthful account of; to misrepresent; to alter or tamper with in order to deceive; to forge. **falsifying, falsified** v. **falsifier** n.

fal-ter (fol´tĕr) v. To be uncertain or hesitant in action or voice; to waver; to move with unsteadiness.

fame (fām) n. Public esteem; a good reputation. **famed** adj.

fa-mil-iar (fa mil´yĕr) adj. Being well-acquainted with; common; having good and complete knowledge of something; unconstrained or informal. n. A close friend or associate.

fam-i-ly (fam´i lē) n. pl. **-ies** Parents and their children; a group of people connected by blood or marriage and sharing common ancestry; the members of a household; a group or class of like things; in science, a taxonomic category higher than a genus and below an order.

fam-ine (fam´in) n. A widespread scarcity of food; a drastic shortage of or scarcity of anything; severe hunger; starvation.

fam-ish (fam´ish) v. To starve or cause to starve. **famished** adj.

fa-mous (fā´mus) adj. Well-known; renowned. Slang Excellent; admirable. **famously** adv. **famousness** n.

fan (fan) *n.* A device for putting air into motion, especially a flat, lightweight, collapsible, wedge-like shape; a machine that rotates thin, rigid vanes. *Slang* An enthusiastic devotee or admirer of a sport, celebrity, diversion, etc. **fan** *v.* To move or stir up air with a fan; to direct air upon; to cool or refresh with or as with a fan; to spread like a fan; in baseball, to strike out.

fa-nat-ic (fa nat´ik) *n.* One who is moved by a frenzy of enthusiasm or zeal. **fanatical** *adj.* **fanaticism** *n.*

fa-nat-i-cism *n.* Excessive vigor, behavior marked by such zeal or enthusiasm.

fan-cy (fan´sē) *n., pl.* **fancies** Imagination of a fantastic or whimsical nature; a notion or idea not based on evidence or fact; a whim or caprice; judgment or taste in art or style **fancy** *adj.* Adapted to please the fancy; highly decorated. **fancy** *v.* To imagine; to visualize; to believe without proof or conviction; to suppose; to breed animals for unconventional traits.

fan-ta-sia (fan´tä´zha) *n.* A composition structured according to the composer's fancy and not observing any strict musical form.

fan-ta-sied *adj.* Present only in one's imagination.

fan-ta-size *v.* To create mental fantasies; to imagine or indulge in fantasies. **fantasizing, fantasized** *v.*

fan-tas-tic (fan tas´tik) *adj.* Existing only in the fancy; unreal; wildly fanciful or exaggerated; impulsive or capricious; coming from the imagination or fancy. *Slang* Superb; wonderful.

fan-ta-sy (fan´ta sē) *n., pl.* **fantasies** A creative imagination; a creation of the fancy; an unreal or odd mental image; a whimsical or odd notion; a highly or ingeniously imaginative creation; in psychology, the sequence of pleasant mental images fulfilling a wish.

far (fär) *adv.* From, to, or at a considerable distance; to or at a certain distance, degree, or point; very remote in time, quality or degree. **far** *adj.& adv.* Remote in space or time; extending widely or at great lengths; extensive or lengthy. **far and away** Decidedly. **far and wide** Everywhere. **far be it from me** Having no audacity or desire. **in so far as** To the extent that. **to go far** To accomplish a lot; to have success; to last a long time or to cover a great extent.

farce (färs) *n.* A theater comedy employing exaggerated or ludicrous situations; a ridiculous situation or action; a seasoned stuffing.

far-cy *n.* A disease of the lymphatic glands and skin, affecting horses and cattle.

fare (fâr) *v.* To be in a specific state; to turn out. **fare** *n.* A fee paid for hired transportation; food or a variety of foods.

fa-ri-na (fa rē´na) *n.* A fine meal obtained chiefly from nuts, cereals, potatoes, or Indian corn, used as a breakfast food or in puddings.

far-i-na-ceous (far´inä shus) *adj.* Made from or rich in starch; mealy.

far-off (fär´of´) *adj.* Distant; remote.

far-out *adj. Slang* Very unconventional.

far-a-go (fa rä´gō) *n., pl.* **faragoes** A confused mixture.

far-ther (fär´ther) *adv.* To or at a more distant point. **farther** *adj.* More remote or distant.

far-ther-most *adj.* Most distant; farthest.

far-thest (fär´thist) *adj.* To or at the greatest distance.

fas-ci-cle *n.* A small bundle; a single part of a book published in installments.

fas-ci-nate (fas´i nāt´) *v.* To attract irresistibly, as by beauty or other qualities; to captivate; to hold motionless; to spellbind. **fascinating** *adj.* **fascinatingly** *adv.* **fascination** *n.*

fas-cism (fash´iz um) *n.* A one-party system of government marked by a centralized dictatorship, stringent social and economic controls, and often belligerent nationalism. **fascist** *n.,*

fash-ion (fash´an) *n.* The mode or manner of dress, living, and style that prevails in society, especially in high society; good form or style; current style or custom; a piece of clothing made up in the current style. **fashion** *v.* To make into a given shape or form; to make fitting. **fashionable** *adj.* **fashionably** *adv.*

fast (fäst) *adj.* Swift; rapid; performed quickly; constant; steadfast; firmly secured; sound or deep, as sleep; permitting or suitable for quick movement; requiring rapidity of motion or action; acting or moving quickly. **fast** *v.* To give up food, especially for a religious reason. **fast** *n.* A period prescribed for fasting.

fas-tid-i-ous (fa stid´ē us) *adj.* Exceedingly delicate or refined; hard to please in matters of taste.

fas-tig-i-ate *adj.* Pointed at the top; tapering upward to a point.

fat (fat) *adj.* Having superfluous flesh or fat; obese; plump; containing much fat or oil; rich or fertile; as land; abundant; plentiful; profitable; thick; broad. **a fat chance** *Slang* Very little or no chance at all. *n.* Any of a large class of yellowish to white, greasy liquid or solid substances that are widely distributed in animal and plant tissues; consisting of various fatty acids and glycerol, generally odorless, tasteless, and colorless, the richest or most desirable part. **fatty** *adj.*

fat-al (fāt´al) *adj.* Causing death; deadly; bringing ruin or disaster; destructive; decisively important; fateful; brought about by fate; destined; inevitable.

fa-tal-ism (fāt´a liz´um) *n.* The belief that events or things are predetermined by fate and cannot be altered. **fatalist** *n.* **fatalistic** *adj.* **fatalistically** *adv.*

fa-tal-i-ty (fā tal´i tē) *n., pl.* **fatalities** Death caused by a disaster or accident; the capability of causing death or disaster; the quality or state of being subject to or determined by fate.

fate (fāt) *n.* The force or power held to predetermine events; fortune; inevitability; the final result or outcome; unfortunate destiny; doom. **fated** *adj.* **fateful** *adj.* Determining destiny; governed by fate; bringing death or disaster. **fatefully** *adv.* .

fa-ther (fä´thër) *n.* The male parent; any male forefather; ancestor; a male who establishes or founds something. **Father** A priest; one of the early Christian writers who formulated doctrines and codified observances. To beget; to act as a father toward. **fatherhood** *v.* **fatherly** *adj.*

fath-om (fath´om) *n.* A unit of length that is equal to six feet or approximately 1. 83 m., used mostly in measuring marine depths. **fathom** *v.* To understand fully.

fath-om-less *adj.* Too deep to measure; too difficult to understand.

fa-tigue (fa tēg´) *n.* The state or condition of extreme tiredness or weariness from prolonged physical or mental exertion. **fatigues** Military clothes for heavy work and field duty. **fatigue** *v.* To become or make tired; to exhaust.

fats-hed-era *n.* An ornamental foliage plant with glossy leaves.

fat-sol-u-ble *adj.* Pertaining to something soluble in fat or oil.

fa-tu-i-ty (fa tö´i tē) *n.* Stupidity; foolishness.

fat-u-ous (fach´ö us) *adj.* Silly and foolish in a self-satisfied way. **fatuously** *adv.* **fatuousness** *n.*

fau-ces *n.* The passage at the back of the mouth to the pharynx, formed by the membranous, muscular arches extending downward from each side of the soft palate. **faucial** *adj.*

fau-cet (fo´sit) *n.* A fixture with an adjustable valve used to draw liquids from a pipe or cask.

faugh (fo) *interj.* An exclamation of contempt or disgust.

fault (folt) *n.* An impairment or defect; a weakness; a minor offense or mistake; a break in the earth's crust allowing adjoining surfaces to shift in a direction

parallel to the crack; a bad serve, as in tennis. *v.* To criticize. **at fault** Open to blame; in the wrong. **faultily** *adv.* **faultless** *adj.* **faulty** *adj.*

faux pas (fō pä´) *n.* A false step; a social blunder.

fa-vor (fā´vër) *n.* A helpful or considerate act; the attitude of friendliness or approbation; the condition of being held in high regard; approval or support. **favors** Consent to sexual intimacy, especially as granted by a woman; a token of love or remembrance; a small gift given to each guest at a party. **favor** *v.* To benefit; to give advantage; to prefer or like one more than another; to support or approve; to look like or resemble; to treat with special care. **favorer** *n.*

fa-vor-ite (fā´vër it) *n.* Anything regarded with special favor or preferred above all others; in sports, the contestant considered to be the most likely winner.

fa-vus *n.* A fungus that attacks the scalp of humans and the skin of fowls and mammals.

fax *n.* In *computer science*, a facsimile, a copy of a document sent to a remote terminal by a fax machine or computer over telephone lines; a facsimile machine. **fax** *v.* To send a fax copy.

fay (fā) *n.* A fairy or elf.

faze (fāz) *v.* To worry; to disconcert.

fe-al-ty (fē´al tē) *n., pl.* **fealties** The obligation of allegiance owed to a feudal lord by his vassal or tenant; faithfulness; loyalty.

fear (fēr) *n.* An agitated feeling caused by the anticipation or realization of danger; uneasy feeling that something might happen contrary to one's hopes; a feeling of deep, reverential awe and dread. **fear** *v.* To be apprehensive; to suspect. **fearfulness** *n.* **fearful** *adj.* **fearfully** *adv.*

fea-si-ble (fē´zi bl) *adj.* Capable of being put into effect or accomplished; practical. **feasibility** *n.*

feast (fēst) *n.* A delicious meal; a banquet; a day or days of celebration set aside for a religious purpose or in honor of some person, event, or thing. **feast** *v.* To provide with pleasure.

feat (fēt) *n.* A notable act or achievement.

fea-ture (fē´chër) *n.* The appearance or shape of the face; the main presentation at a movie theater; a special article in a magazine or newspaper that is given special prominence. **feature** *v.*

feb-ri-fuge (feb´ri füj´) *n.* A medicine used to reduce fever.

feb-rile (fē´bril) *adj.* Feverish.

Feb-ru-ary (feb´rö er´ē) *n.* The second month of the year, having 28 days or, in a leap year, 29 days.

fe-ces (fē´sēz) *pl. n.* Waste that is excreted

from the bowels; excrement. **fecal** *adj*.

fe-cund (fē´kund) *adj*. Fruitful; productive. **fecundity** *n*.

fe-cun-date (fē´kun dāt´) *v*. To make fertile. **fecundation** *n*.

fed *v*. Past tense of feed.

fed *v. abbr*. Federal, federated.

fed-er-al (fed´ér al) *adj*. Of, relating to, or formed by an agreement between two or more states or groups in which each retains certain controlling powers while being united under a central authority; of or pertaining to the United States central government. **Federal** Pertaining to or of the central government of Canada; of or supporting the Union in the American Civil War.

fed-er-ate (fed´e rāt´) *v*. To unite in a federal union or alliance.

fe-do-ra (fi dōr´a) *n*. A soft hat with a low crown creased lengthwise and a brim that can be turned up or down.

fee (fē) *n*. A fixed charge, compensation, or payment for something; a charge for professional services; an inherited estate in land.

fee-ble (fē´bl) *adj*. Very weak; lacking in strength; lacking force; ineffective. **feebleness** *n*. **feebly** *adv*.

feed (fēd) *v*. To supply with food; to consume food; to keep supplied, as with fuel for a fire; to draw support or encouragement. In *computer science,* to enter data into a computing machine. **feed** *n*. The mechanical part, as of a sewing machine, that keeps supplying material to be worked on. *Slang* A meal.

feed-back (fēd´bak´) *n*. The return to the input of a portion of the output of a machine; the return of data for corrections or control.

feel (fēl) *v*. To examine, explore, or perceive through the sense of touch; to perceive as a physical sensation; to believe; to consider; to be aware of; to be emotionally affected by; to think; to suppose; to judge; to experience the full force or impact of; to produce a sensory impression of being soft, hard, hot or cold; to produce an indicated overall condition, impression, or reaction. **feeling** *n*.

feet *n*. The plural of foot.

feign (fān) *v*. To make a false show of; to dream up a false story and tell it as the truth; to fabricate; to imitate so as to deceive. **feigned** *adj*.

feint (fānt) *n*. A deceptive or misleading movement intended to draw defensive action away from the real target.

feist *n*. A small dog.

feist-y *adj*. Excited; agitated; frisky and exuberant; quarrelsome.

feld-spar (feld´spär´) *n*. Any of a large group of crystalline materials largely made up of silicates of aluminum.

fe-lic-i-tate (fi lis´i tāt´) *v*. To congratulate; to wish happiness.

fe-lic-i-tous (fi lis´i tus) *adj*. Most appropriate; well chosen; pertinent or effective in manner or style.

fe-lic-i-ty (fi lis´i tē) *n., pl*. **felicities** Happiness; bliss; an instance or source of happiness; an agreeably pertinent or effective style.

fe-line (fē´līn) *adj*. Of or relating to cats, including wild and domestic cats; resembling a cat, as in stealth or agility. **feline** *n*. **felinely** *adv*.

fell (fel) *v*. Past tense of fall; to strike or cause to fall down; to finish a seam with a flat, smooth strip made by joining edges, then folding under and stitching flat. **fell** *n*. Timber cut down during one season; an animal's hide; pelt. *adj*. Cruel and fierce; lethal.

fel-lah (fel´a) *n. pl*. **fellahin** *or* **fellaheen** An Arab peasant or laborer.

fel-low (fel´ō) *n*. A boy or man; an associate, comrade; the counterpart; one of a pair. *Informal* A boyfriend.

fel-low-ship (fel´ō ship´) *n*. A friendly relationship; the condition or fact of having common interests, ideals, or experiences; the status of being a fellow at a college or university, also the financial grant made to a fellow.

fel-ly (fel´ē) *n. pl*. **fellies** The rim of a wooden wheel, into which spokes are inserted.

fel-on (fel´on) *n*. A person who has committed a felony; an inflammation in the terminal joint or at the cuticle of a finger or toe.

felt (felt) *v*. Past tense of feel. *n*. An unwoven fabric made from pressed animal fibers, as wool or fur; a piece of fabric or material made of felt.

fe-male (fē´māl) *n*. The sex that produces ova or bears young; a plant with a pistil but no stamen, which is capable of being fertilized and producing fruit. **female** *adj*. Of or relating to the sex that produces ova or bears young; suitable to this sex; having a bore, slot, or hollow part designed to receive a projecting part, as a plug or prong.

fem-i-nine (fem´i nin) *adj*. Pertaining to or of the female sex; female; characterized by qualities generally attributed to women; lacking in manly qualities. *Gram*. Applicable to females only or to persons or things classified as female. **feminist** *n*.

fe-mur (fē´mér) *n., pl*. **femurs** *or* **femora** The bone extending from the pelvis to the knee. **femoral** *adj*.

fen (fen) *n*. A low, marshy land; a bog.

fend (fend) *v*. To ward off or to keep off; to offer resistance. **fending** *v*.

fe-nes-tra *n*. A natural hole in the bone

between the tympanum and the inner ear; a small transparent area often found in wings of butterflies.

fen-es-tra-tion (fen´ĭ strā´shan) *n.* The design and position of doors and windows in a building.

fe-ral (fēral) *adj.* Not tame nor domesticated; returned to a wild state; existing in an untamed state.

fer-ment (fer ment´) *n.* Any substance or agent producing fermentation, as yeast, mold, or enzyme; excitement; unrest; agitation. **fermentable** *adj.*

fer-men-ta-tion (fe´men tā´shan) *n.* The decomposition of complex organic compounds into simpler substances; the conversion of glucose into ethyl alcohol through the action of zymase; great agitation; commotion.

fer-mi-on *n.* An artificially produced radioactive metallic element.

fer-mi-um (fer´mē um) *n.* A metallic radioactive element, symbolized by Fm.

fe-ro-cious (fe rō´shus) *adj.* Extremely savage, fierce, cruel, or blood thirsty. *Slang* Very intense. **ferociously** *adv.* **ferociousness** *n.* **ferocity** *n.*

fer-ret (fer´it) *n.* A small, red-eyed polecat of Europe, often domesticated and trained to hunt rodents or rabbits. **ferret** *v.* To search out by careful investigation; to drive out of hiding.

fer-ric (fer´ik) *adj.* Pertaining to or containing iron.

ferric oxide *n.* A dark compound that occurs as hematite ore and rust.

fer-rif-er-ous *adj.* Producing or containing iron.

fer-ro-con-crete *n.* A building material made of concrete and embedded steel rods.

fer-ro-mag-net-ic (fer´ō mag net´ik) *adj.* Relating to or being typical of substances, as iron and nickel, that are readily magnetized.

fer-rous (fer´us) *adj.* Pertaining to or containing iron.

fer-tile (fer´tĭl) *adj.* *Biol.* Having the ability to reproduce; rich in material required to maintain plant growth. **fertility** *n.* **fertileness** *n.*

fer-til-iz-er (fer´ti lī´zĕr) *n.* A material that fertilizes, such as nitrates or manure which enriches soil.

fer-ule (fer´ul) *n.* A flat stick sometimes used to punish children. **ferule** *v.*

fer-vent (fer´vent) *adj.* Passionate; ardent; very hot. **fervency** *n.*

fer-vid (fer´vid) *adj.* Fervent to an extreme degree; impassioned; very hot; burning. **fervidly** *adv.* **fervidness** *n.*

fer-vor (fer´vĕr) *n.* Great emotional warmth or intensity.

fes-cue (fes´kū) *n.* A type of tough grass, often used as pasturage.

fes-tal (fes´tal) *adj.* Pertaining to or typical of a festival, holiday, or feast.

fes-ter (fes´tĕr) *v.* To develop or generate pus; to be a constant source of irritation or resentment.

fes-ti-val (fes´ti val) *n.* A particular holiday or celebration; a regularly occurring occasion. **festive** *adj.*

fe-tal (fēt´al) *adj.* Relating to or like a fetus.

fetch (fech) *v.* To go after and return with; to draw forth; to elicit; to bring as a price; to sell for; to strike a blow. **fetching,** *adj.* **fetcher** *n.*

fete (fāt) *n.* A festival or feast; a very elaborate outdoor celebration. **fete** *v.*

fet-e-ri-ta *n.* A grain sorghum with compact heads of large white seeds, raised in the U.S. for grain and forage.

fet-id (fet´id) *adj.* Having a foul odor; stinking. **fetidly** *adv.* **fetidness** *n.*

fet-ish (fet´ish) *n.* An object that is regarded as having magical powers; something that one is devoted to excessively or irrationally. *Psychiatry* A nonsexual object that arouses or gratifies sexual desires. **fetishist** *n.*

fet-lock (fet´lok´) *n.* A tuft of hair that grows just above the hoof at the back of the leg of a horse.

fe-tol-o-gy *n.* The medical study of a fetus. **fetologist** *n.*

fet-ter (fet´ĕr) *n.* A chain or other bond put around the ankles to restrain movement, preventing escape; anything that prevents free movement.

fet-tle (fet´l) *n.* State; the condition of something.

fe-tus (fē´tus) *n.* The individual unborn organism carried within the womb from the time major features appear; in humans, the unborn young after the eighth week of development.

feud (fūd) *n.* A bitter quarrel between two families, usually lasting over a long period of time. **feud** *v.*

feu-dal (fūd´al) *adj.* Relating to or characteristic of feudalism. **feudalism** *n.* **feudally** *adv.*

fe-ver (fē´vĕr) *n.* Abnormally high body temperature and rapid pulse; a craze; a heightened emotion or activity. **feverish** *adj.* **feverishly** *adv.*

fever blister *n.* A cold sore.

few (fū) *adj.* Small in number; not many. *n.* A select or limited group.

few-er *adj.* Pertaining to a smaller number.

fey (fā) *adj.* Seemingly spellbound; having clairvoyance; acting as if under a spell.

fi-an-ce (fē´än sā´) *n.* A man to whom a woman is engaged to be married.

fi-as-co (fē äs´kō) *n. pl.* **fiascoes** A complete or total failure.

fi-at (fī´at) *n.* A positive and authoritative

order or decree.

fib (fĭb) *n*. A trivial lie. **fibber** *n*.

fi-ber (fī´bĕr) *n*. A fine, long, continuous piece of natural or synthetic material made from a filament of asbestos, spun glass, textile, or fabric; internal strength; character. **fibrous** *adj*.

fi-ber-glass (fī´bĕr glas´) *n*. A flexible, nonflammable material of spun glass used for textiles, insulation, and other purposes.

fiber optics *n*. *pl*. Light optics transmitted through very fine, flexible glass rods by internal reflection. **fiber optic** *adj*.

fi-bril *n*. A very fine filament.

fi-bril-lar *adj*. Pertaining to fibers

fib-ril-la-tion (fĭ´brĭ lā´shən) *n*. *Pathol*. Rapid and uncoordinated contraction of the muscle fibers of the heart.

fi-brin (fī´brĭn) *n*. *Biochem*. An insoluble protein that promotes the clotting of blood. **fibrinous** *adj*.

fi-brin-o-gen (fī brĭn´o jen) *n*. *Biochem*. A complex blood plasma protein that is converted to fibrin during the process of blood clotting.

fi-broid (fī´broid) *adj*. Made up or resembling fibrous tissue.

fi-bro-vas-cu-lar *adj*. Composed of a fibrous conductive tissue which conveys fluid from one part to another.

fib-u-la (fĭb´ū la) *n*. *Anat*. The outer and smaller bone of the lower limb or hind leg, in humans located between the knee and ankle.

-fic *adj*. *suffix* Making; causing; rendering.

-fication *n*. *suffix* Making; production.

fick-le (fĭk´l) *adj*. Inconstant in purpose or feeling; changeable. **fickleness** *n*.

fic-tile *adj*. Capable of being molded; relating to soft clay or earthenware.

fic-tion (fĭk´shən) *n*. Something that is created or imaginary; a literary work that is produced by the imagination and not based on fact. **fictional** *adj*.

fic-tion-al-i-za-tion *n*. The procedure of narrating an actual event in a fictional form.

fic-tion-eer *n*. An author who writes inferior fiction in large quantities.

fic-ti-tious (fĭk tĭsh´us) *adj*. Nonexistent; imaginary; not genuine; false; not real. **fictitiously** *adv*. **fictitiousness** *n*.

fid-dle (fĭd´l) *n*. A violin. **fiddle** *v*. To play the violin; to fidget or make nervous or restless movements; to spend time in a careless way. *Naut*. A rack used at the table to prevent things from sliding off. **fit as a fiddle** To enjoy good or perfect health. **second fiddle** In a position subordinate to that of another. **fiddler** *n*.

fi-de-ism *n*. A tenet that certain premises, as of religion and philosophy, need no rational explanation but should be accepted on faith.

fi-del-i-ty (fĭ del´i tē) *n*., *pl*. **fidelities** Faithfulness or loyalty to obligations, vows, or duties. *Elect*. The degree to which a phonograph, tape recorder, or other electronic equipment receives and transmits input signals without distortion.

fidg-et (fĭj´it) *v*. To move nervously or restlessly. **fidgets** *n*. *pl*. The condition of being nervous or restless. **fidgeter** *n*. **fidgetiness** *n*. **fidgety** *adj*.

fi-du-ci-ar-y (fī dū´shē er ē) *adj*. Relating to or pertaining to the holding of something in trust. *n*. An agent; a trustee.

fie (fī) *interj*. An expression of disgust or impatience in response to an unpleasant surprise.

fief (fēf) *n*. A feudal estate in land.

field (fēld) *n*. A piece of land with few or no trees; a cultivated piece of land devoted to the growing of crops; an area in which a natural resource such as oil is found.

fiend (fēnd) *n*. An evil spirit or demon; a person who is totally engrossed in something. *Slang* An addict. **fiendish** *adj*. **fiendishly** *adv*. **fiendishness** *n*.

fierce (fērs) *adj*. Savage and violent in nature. *Slang* Disagreeable or very difficult. **fiercely** *adv*. **fierceness** *n*.

fier-y (fīĕr´ē) *adj*. Containing or composed of fire; brightly glowing; blazing; hot and inflamed; full of spirit or intense with emotion. **fieriness** *n*.

fi-es-ta (fē es´ta) *n*. A religious holiday or festival.

fife (fīf) *n*. A small, shrill-toned instrument similar to a flute.

fifth (fĭfth) *n*. The ordinal of five; one of five equal parts. *Mus*. The space between a tone and another tone five steps from it. **fifth** *adj*. *&* *adv*.

Fifth Amendment *n*. An amendment to the United States Constitution, ratified in 1791, guaranteeing due process of law and that no person "shall be forced to testify against himself."

fig (fĭg) *n*. A tree or shrub bearing a sweet, pear-shaped, edible fruit; the fruit of the fig tree.

fight (fīt) *v*. To struggle against; to quarrel; to argue; to make one's way by struggling; to participate in wrestling or boxing until a final decision is reached. *n*. A physical battle; struggle; strife; conflict; combat.

fig-ment (fĭg´ment) *n*. An invention or fabrication.

fig-ur-a-tion *n*. The process of shaping into a particular figure; the resulting figure or shape.

fig-u-ra-tive (fĭg´ūr *a* tiv) *adj*. Based on, like, or containing a figure of speech; metaphorical; representing by means

figure 168 **film**

of a figure or symbol. **-ly** *adv*.

fig-ure (fĭg´ūr) *n*. A symbol or character that represents a number; anything other than a letter; the visible form, silhouette, shape, or line of something; the human form or body; an individual, especially a prominent one; the impression or appearance that a person makes; a design or pattern, as in a fabric; a figure of speech; a series of movements, as in a dance. **figures** In mathematics, calculations; an amount shown in numbers. **figure** *v*. To represent; to depict; to compute.

fig-ure-head (fĭg´ūr hed´) *n*. A person with nominal leadership but no real power; a carved figure on a ship's bow.

figure of speech *n*. An expression, as a metaphor or hyperbole, where words are used in a more forceful, dramatic, or illuminating way.

fil-a-ment (fĭl´a ment) *n*. A very thin, finely spun fiber, wire, or thread; the fine wire enclosed in an electric lamp bulb which is heated electrically to incandescence. **filamentous** *adj*.

fi-lar *adj*. Of or pertaining to a thread; *Optics* Having threads across the field of vision.

fil-a-ture *n*. The act of forming into threads; the reeling of silk cocoons; a reel for drawing off silk from cocoons; an establishment for reeling silk.

fil-bert (fĭl´bért) *n*. The edible nut of the hazel tree or the tree it grows on.

filch (fĭlch) *v*. To steal. **filcher** *n*.

file (fĭl) *n*. A device for storing papers in proper order; a collection of papers so arranged; a line of persons, animals, or things placed one behind another; a hard, steel instrument with ridged cutting surfaces, used to smooth or polish. In *computer science*, a set of related information, as spreadsheets, databases, etc., identified by name and manipulated as a unit. **file** *v*. To march as soldiers; to submit documents.

file attributes *n*. In *computer science*, special nature of a file for identification or protection, such as read-only, archived or hidden.

file conversion In *computer science*, the transfer of a file's formatting codes to allow access by another program.

file maintenance *n*. In *computer science*, correcting and updating files and directories to reflect the most recent data available and purging the system of outdated files.

file management In *computer science*, the organization and tracking of files by the operating system and the user.

file manager *n*. In *computer science*, a software utility designed to simplify the task of locating and organizing files.

file name *n*. In *computer science*, the designation that identifies a data file.

file name extension *n*. In *computer science*, a tag of up to three characters following a file name that aids in identification by the operating system, a program or the user.

file protection *n*. In *computer science*, a file attribute that identifies a data file as read-only; a device on a floppy disk that can be set to make the files on the disk read-only.

file server *n*. In *computer science*, a computer that stores a library of program and data files for a number of users in a network.

fi-let (fĭ lā´) *n*. A filet of meat or fish; lace or net with a pattern of squares.

fil-i-al (fĭl´ē al) *adj*. Of or relating to a son or daughter; pertaining to the generation following the parents.

fil-i-buster (fĭl´i bus´tér) *n*. An attempt to prolong, prevent, or hinder legislative action by using delaying tactics such as long speeches; using time. **filibuster** *v*. **filibusterer** *n*.

fil-i-gree (fĭl´i grē´) *n*. Delicate, lace-like ornamental work made of silver or gold intertwisted wire. **filigree** *v*. & *adj*.

fil-ing (fĭ´ling) *n*. *also* **filings** Particles removed by a file.

fill-er (fĭl´ér) *n*. Something that is added to increase weight or bulk or to take up space; a material used to fill cracks, pores, or holes in a surface before it is completed.

fil-let *or* **fi-let** (fĭl´ĭt) *n*. A narrow ribbon or band for holding the hair; a strip of boneless fish or meat. **fillet** *v*. To slice, bone, or make into fillets.

fill-in *n*. A person or thing that fills the place of another; a review usually, orally of important information.

fil-lip (fĭl´ĭp) *n*. A snap of the finger that has been pressed down by the thumb and then suddenly released; something that arouses or excites. **fillip** *v*.

fil-lis-ter *n*. A plane for grooves; a groove on a window sash that holds the glass and putty.

Fillmore, Millard *n*. (1800-1874) The thirteenth president of the United States from 1850-1853.

fil-ly (fĭl´ē) *n*. A young female horse less than four years of age; a young girl.

film (film) *n*. A thin covering, layer, or membrane. *Photog*. A photosensitive strip or sheet of flexible cellulose material that is used to make photographic negatives or transparencies; the film containing the pictures projected on a large screen; the motion picture itself. **film** *v*. To cover with or as if with a film; to make a movie; to record on film.

film-dom (film´dom) *n.* The movie industry or business.

film-strip (film´strip´) *n.* A strip of film containing graphic matter for still projection on a screen.

fil-ose *adj.* Threadlike.

fil-ter (fil´tér) *n.* A device, as cloth, paper, charcoal, or any other porous substance, through which a liquid or gas can be passed to separate out suspended matter. *Photog.* A colored screen that controls the kind and intensity of light waves in an exposure.

filth (filth) *n.* Anything that is dirty or foul; something that is considered offensive.

fil-trate (fil´trāt) *v.* To pass or cause to pass through something. **filtrate** *n.* Anything which has passed through the filter. **filtration** *n.*

fin (fin) *n.* A thin membranous extension of the body of a fish or other aquatic animal, used for swimming and balancing. *Slang* A five dollar bill.

fi-na-gle (fi nā´gl) *v. Slang* To get something by trickery or deceit. **finagling** *adj.* **finagler** *n.*

fi-nal (fin´al) *adj.* Pertaining to or coming to the end; last or terminal. **finality** *n.*

finals *n.* Something decisively final, as the last of a series of athletic contests; the final academic examination.

fi-nal-ize (fin´a līz´) *v.* To put into final and complete form. **finalization** *n.*

fi-nance (fi nans´) *n.* The science of monetary affairs. **finances** Monetary resources; funds. **finance** *v.* To supply the capital or funds for something; to sell or provide on a credit basis. **financial** *adj.* **financially** *adv.*

fin-an-cier (fin´an sēr´) *n.* An expert who deals with large-scale financial affairs; one who makes loans.

find (find) *v.* To come upon unexpectedly; to achieve; to attain; to ascertain; to determine; to consider; to regard; to recover or regain something; to detect the true identity or nature of something or someone.

fine (fin) *adj.* Superior in skill or quality; very enjoyable and pleasant; light and delicate in workmanship, texture, or structure; made up or composed of very small parts. *Slang* To be in good health; very well. **fine** *n.* The sum of money required as the penalty for an offense. **fineness** *n.* **fine** *v.* **finely** *adj.*

fi-ne (fē´na) *n., Mus.* The end.

fi-nesse (fi nes´) *n.* A highly refined skill; the skillful handling of a situation.

fin-ger (fing´gér) *n.* One of the digits of the hand, usually excluding the thumb; that part of a glove made to fit the finger; anything resembling the finger. *Mus.* The use of the fingers in playing an instrument. **finger** *v.*

fin-i-al (fin´ē al) *n.* The ornamental projection or terminating part, as on a lamp shade.

fin-i-cal *adj.* Finicky.

fin-ick-y (fin´i kē) *adj.* Hard to please; choosy. **finickiness** *n.*

fi-nis (fin´is) *n.* The end.

fin-ish (fin´ish) *v.* To bring to an end; to conclude; to reach the end; to consume all. *Slang* To kill or destroy. **finish** *n.* The last stage or conclusion of anything; the perfection or polish in manners, speech, or education; the surface quality or appearance of paint, textiles, or other materials. **finish** *adj.* Having a glossy polish.

fi-nite (fi´nit) *adj.* Having bounds or limits; of or relating to a number which can be determined, counted, or measured. **finitely** *adv.* **finiteness** *n.*

fink (fingk) *n. Slang* A person that breaks a strike; an unsavory person.

fin-ny (fin´ē) *adj.* Having or suggesting fins or fin-like extensions.

fire (fíer) *n.* The chemical reaction of burning, which releases heat and light. **fire** *v.* To inspire enthusiasm; to ignite or cause to become ignited; to bake in a kiln; to discharge a firearm or explosive; to let a person go from a job; to dismiss. **firing** *adj.*

fire escape *n.* A structure, often metal, used as an emergency exit from a building.

fire-man (fíer´man) *n., pl.* **firemen** A person employed to prevent or extinguish fires; one who tends fires.

fire station *n.* A building used to house firefighting equipment and firemen.

fire-works (fíer´werks´) *n.* Explosives used to generate colored lights, smoke, and noise for entertainment and celebrations.

firm (ferm) *adj.* Relatively solid, compact, or unyielding to pressure or touch; steadfast and constant; strong and sure. *n.* A partnership of two or more persons for conducting a business. *v.* To become or make firm or firmer.

fir-ma-ment (fer´ma ment) *n.* The expanse of the heavens; the sky.

firn (firn) *n.* Snow that is partially consolidated by thawing and freezing but has not converted to glacial ice.

first (ferst) *adj.* Preceding all others in the order of numbering; taking place or acting prior to all others; earliest; ranking above all in importance or quality; foremost. **first** *adv.* Above or before all others in time, order, rank, or importance; for the very first time. **first** *n.* The ordinal number that matches the number 1 in a series, symbol 1st; the lowest transmission gear in an automotive vehicle.

first aid *n.* The emergency care given

to a person before full treatment and medical care can be obtained.

First Amendment n. The amendment to the Constitution of the United States which forbids Congress to interfere with religion, free speech, free press, the right to assemble peaceably, or the right to petition the government, ratified in 1791.

first-hand (ferst´hand´) adj. Coming directly from the original source.

firth (ferth) n. A narrow inlet of the sea.

fis-cal (fis´kal) adj. Relating to or of the finances or treasury of a nation or a branch of government; financial.

fish (fish) n., pl. fish or fishes An aquatic animal having fins, gills for breathing, and usually scales; the flesh of fish used as food. **like a fish out of water** Not at ease or comfortable. fish v. To try to catch fish; to seek or find one's way; to grope; to try and obtain something in an artful or indirect way.

fis-sile (fis´il) adv. Capable of being separated or split in the direction of the grain. Physics Fissionable.

fis-sion (fish´an) n. The process or act of splitting into parts. Physics The exploding of the nucleus of an atom that leads to the formation of more stable atoms and the release of large quantities of energy. **fissionable** adj.

fis-si-ped (fis´i ped´) adj. Having toes that are separated.

fis-sure (fish´ėr) n. A narrow opening, crack, or cleft in a rock. fissure v.

fist (fist) n. The hand closed tightly with the fingers bent into the palm.

fis-tu-la (fis´che la) n. pl. fistulas or fistulae Pathol. A duct or other passage formed by the imperfect closing of a wound or abscess and leading either to the body surface or to another hollow organ. **fistulous** adj.

fit (fit) v. To be the proper size and shape; to be in good physical condition; to possess the proper qualifications; to be competent; to provide a time or place for something; to belong. adj. Adapted or adequate for a particular circumstance or purpose. Med. A convulsion; an impulsive and irregular exertion or action. **fitter, fitness** n.

fitch (fich) n. The polecat of the Old World or its fur.

fit-ful (fit´ful) adj. Characterized by irregular actions; capricious; restless.

five (fiv) n. The cardinal number equal to 4 + 1; any symbol of this number, as 5; anything with five units, parts, or members. **five** adj.

fix (fiks) v. To make stationary, firm, or stable; to direct or hold steadily; to place or set definitely; to make rigid; to arrange or adjust; to prepare, as a meal. **fix** n. A position of difficulty or

embarrassment. Naut. The position of a ship determined by observations, radio, or bearings. Slang The injection of a narcotic such as heroin.

fix-a-tion (fik sā´shan) n. The act or state of being fixed; a strong, often unhealthy preoccupation. **fixate** v.

fixed disk n. In computer science, a computer disk that is permanently mounted in its drive.

fixed asset n. An item of value having a relatively permanent nature, used in operating a business, but not intended to be converted to cash

fix-i-ty (fik´si tē) n. The quality or state of being fixed or stable.

fix-ture (fiks´chėr) n. Anything that is fixed or installed, as an appendage of a house; any article of personal property affixed to realty to become a part of and be governed by the law of real property.

fizz (fiz) n. A hissing or bubbling sound; effervescence; tiny gas bubbles.

fiz-zle (fiz´l) v. To fail after making a promising start. **fizzle** n. A hissing or sputtering sound.

flab (flab) n. Excessive, loose, and flaccid body tissue. **flabby** adj. **flabbiness** n.

flac-cid (flak´sid) adj. Lacking resilience or firmness. **flaccidity** n. **flaccidly** adv.

flac-on (flak´on) n. A small, stoppered decorative bottle.

flag (flag) n. A piece of cloth, usually oblong, bearing distinctive colors and designs to designate a nation, state, city, or organization. Bot. Any of various iris or cattail plants with long blade-shaped leaves. flag v. To adorn with flags for identification or ornamentation; to grow weak or tired.

Flag Day n. June 14, 1777, the day on which Congress proclaimed the Stars and Stripes the national standard of the United States.

flag-el-lant (flaj´e lant) n. One who whips himself or has himself whipped by another for religious motives or for sexual excitement. **flagellation** n.

flag-el-late (flaj´e lāt´) v. To punish by whipping; to scourge.

flag-eo-let (flaj´o let´) n. A small flute-like wind instrument, with a tubular mouthpiece and six or more holes.

flag-on (flag´on) n. A vessel or container with a handle, spout, and hinged lid, used for holding wines or liquors.

fla-grant (flā´grant) adj. Obvious; glaring; disgraceful; notorious; outrageous. **flagrantly** adv.

flair (flâr) n. An aptitude or talent for something; a dashing style.

flak (flak) n. Antiaircraft fire; abusive or excessive criticism.

flake (flāk) n. A small, flat, thin piece which has split or peeled off from a

surface. *Slang* Odd-ball; eccentric.
flake *v.* **flakily** *adv.* **flakiness** *n.* **-y** *adj.*

flam-boy-ant (flam boi´ant) *adj.* Extravagantly ornate; showy; florid; brilliant and rich in color. **flamboyance** *n.* **flamboyancy** *n.* **flamboyantly** *adv.*

flame (flām) *n.* A mass of burning vapor or gas rising from a fire, often having a bright color and forming a tongue-shaped area of light; something that resembles a flame in motion, intensity, or appearance; a bright, red-yellow color; violent and intense emotion. *Slang* A sweetheart. **flame** *v.*

fla-men-co (flä meng´kō) *n.* A fiery percussive dance of the Andalusian gypsies with strong and often improvised rhythms.

flam-ma-ble (flam´a bl) *adj.* Capable of being easily ignited and burning rapidly. **flammability** *n.*

flange (flanj) *n.* A projecting rim or collar used to strengthen or guide a wheel or other object, keeping it on a fixed track.

flank (flangk) *n.* The fleshy part between the ribs and the hip on either side of the body of an animal or human being; the lateral part of something. *Milit.* The right or left side of a military bastion or formation. *v.* To be stationed at the side of something. **flanker** *n.*

flan-nel (flan´el) *n.* A woven fabric made of wool or a wool, cotton, or synthetic blend.

flan-nelet-te *n.* Cotton flannel.

flap (flap) *v.* To move up and down; to cause to swing or sway loosely, as in the wind; to strike with something flexible; to flutter; to beat or strike a blow with something broad and flexible. **flap** *n.* Something that hangs loose or swings freely.

flare (flâr) *v.* To blaze up or burn with a bright light; to break out suddenly or violently, as with emotion or action; to open or spread outward.

flash (flash) *v.* To burst forth repeatedly or suddenly into a brilliant fire or light; to occur or appear briefly or suddenly. **flash** *n.* A short and important news break or transmission. **flashy** *adj.*

flash-o-ver (flash´ō´vér) *n.* A disruptive abnormal electrical discharge through the air or around the surface of a liquid.

flask (flask) *n.* A small container made of glass and used in laboratories.

flat (flat) *adj.* Extending horizontally with no curvature or tilt; stretched out level, prostrate or prone; lacking flavor or zest; deflated. *Mus.* Below the correct pitch. **flat** *n.* An apartment that is entirely on one floor of a building. **flat broke** Having little or no money. **fall flat** Fail to achieve. **flatly** *adv.*

flat-ter (flat´ér) *v.* To praise extrava-

gantly, especially without sincerity; to gratify the vanity of; to portray favorably; to show as more attractive. **flatterer** *n.* **flattering** *adj.*

flat-ter-y (flat´e rē) *n.* Excessive, often insincere compliments.

flat-u-lent (flach´u lent) *adj.* Marked by or affected with gases generated in the intestine or stomach; pretentious without real worth or substance. **flatulence** *n.* **flatulently** *adv.*

flaunt (flont) *v.* To display showily.

flau-tist (flo´tist) *n.* A flutist.

fla-vor (flā´vér) *n.* A distinctive element in the taste of something; a distinctive, characteristic quality; a flavoring. *v.* To impart flavor to. **flavorful** *adj.*

fla-vor-ing (flā´vér ing) *n.* A substance, as an extract or something else that is used to increase the flavor.

flaw (flo) *n.* A defect or blemish that is often hidden and that may cause failure under stress; a weakness in character; a fault in a legal paper that may nullify it. **flaw** *v.*

flax (flaks) *n.* A plant with blue flowers and seeds that yield linseed oil and slender stems from which a fine textile fiber is derived.

flay (flā) *v.* To remove the skin of; to scold harshly.

flea (flē) *n.* A small, wingless, bloodsucking, parasitic jumping insect; a parasite of warm-blooded animals.

fleam (flēm) *n., Surg.* A sharp instrument used in surgery for opening veins.

flea market *n.* A place where antiques and used items and goods are sold.

fleck (flek) *n.* A tiny spot or streak; a small flake or bit. **fleck** *v.* To mark with flecks.

fledg-ling *or* **fledge-ling** (flej´ling) *n.* A young bird with newly acquired feathers; a person who is inexperienced; a beginner.

flee (flē) *v.* To run away; to move swiftly away. **fleer** *n.*

fleece (flēs) *n.* A coat of wool covering a sheep; the soft wool covering a sheep. **fleece** *v.* To shear the fleece from; to swindle; to cover with fleece. **fleeciness** *n.* **fleecily** *adv.* **fleecy** *adj.*

fleer (flēr) *v.* To laugh or grimace in a coarse or mocking manner; jeer.

fleet (flēt) *n.* A number of warships operating together under the same command; a number of vehicles, as taxicabs or fishing boats, operated under one command. **fleet** *adj.* Moving rapidly or nimbly. **fleetly** *adv.*

flesh (flesh) *n.* Soft tissue of the body of a human or animal, especially skeletal muscle; the meat of animals as distinguished from fish or fowl; the pulpy substance of a fruit or vegetable; the body as opposed to the mind or soul; mankind in general; one's family.

flesh v. To arouse the hunting instinct of dogs by feeding fresh meat.

flew v. Past tense of *fly*.

flex (fleks) v. To bend the arm repeatedly; to contract a muscle.

flex-i-ble (flek´si bl) adj. Capable of being bent or flexed; pliable; responsive to change; easily yielding. **flexibility** n. **flexibly** adv.

flex-or (flek´sèr) n. A muscle that serves to bend a body joint.

flex time n. A system which allows employees to set their own work schedules within a wide range of hours.

flex-ure (flek´shèr) n. The state of being flexed or bent; a bent part.

flick (flik) n. A light, quick snapping movement or the sound accompanying it. *Slang* A movie. **flick** v. To strike or hit with a quick, light stroke; to cause to move with a quick movement.

flick-er (flik´èr) v. To burn or shine unsteadily, as a candle. **flicker** n. A wavering or unsteady light; a North American woodpecker having a brownish back and a spotted breast.

fli-er or **fly-er** (flī´èr) n. One who or that which flies, especially an aviator; a daring or risky venture; a printed advertisement or handbill for mass distribution.

flight (flīt) n. The act or manner of flying; a scheduled airline trip; a group that flies together; a swift or rapid passage or movement, as of time; a group of stairs leading from one floor to another; an instance of fleeing.

flim-flam (flim´flam´) n. *Slang* A swindle; trick; hoax. **flimflam** v.

flim-sy (flim´zē) adj. Lacking in physical strength or substance; unconvincing. **flimsiness** n. **flimsily** adv.

flinch (flinch) v. To wince or pull back, as from pain; to draw away.

flin-ders n. Fragments; splinters.

fling (fling) v. To throw or toss violently; to throw oneself completely into an activity. **fling** n. An act of casting away; a casual attempt; a period devoted to self-indulgence; unrestraint.

flint (flint) n. A hard quartz that produces a spark when struck by steel; an implement used by primitive man; an alloy used in lighters to light the fuel.

flip (flip) v. To turn or throw suddenly with a jerk; to strike or snap quickly and lightly. *Slang* To go crazy; to become upset or angry; to react enthusiastically. **flip** n. **flipper** n.

flirt (flert) v. To make teasing romantic or sexual overtures; to act so as to attract attention; to dart. **flirt** n. A person who flirts; a snappy, quick, jerky movement. **flirtation, flirtatiousness** n. **flirtatious** adj.

flit (flit) v. To move rapidly or abruptly.

flit-ter (flit´èr) v. To flutter. **flitter** n.

float (flōt) n. An act or instance of floating; something that floats on the surface of or in a liquid; a device used to buoy the baited end of a fishing line; a floating platform anchored near a shoreline, used by swimmers or boats; a vehicle with a platform used to carry an exhibit in a parade; a drink consisting of ice cream floating in a beverage. **float** v. To be or cause to be suspended within or on the surface of a liquid; to be or cause to be suspended in or move through the air as if supported by water; to drift randomly from place to place; to move lightly and easily; to place a security on the market; to obtain money for the establishment or development of an enterprise by issuing and selling securities. **floating** adj.

flock (flok) n. A group of animals of all the same kind, especially birds, sheep, geese, etc., living, feeding or kept together; a group under the direction of a single person, especially the members of a church; a large number. **flock** v. To travel as if in a flock.

floe (flō) n. A large, flat mass of floating ice or a detached part of such a mass.

flog (flog) v. To beat hard with a whip or stick. **flogger** n.

flood (flud) n. The great deluge depicted in the Bible; an overflow of water onto land that is normally dry; an overwhelming quantity. **flood** v. To overwhelm with or as if with a flood; to fill abundantly or overwhelm; to supply the carburetor of an engine with an excessive amount of fuel; in football, to send more than one pass receiver into the same defensive area.

floor (flōr) n. The level base of a room; the lower inside surface of a structure; a ground surface; the right, as granted under parliamentary rules, to speak to a meeting or assembly; an area dividing a building into stories. **floor** v. To cover or furnish with a floor; to knock down; to overwhelm; to puzzle; to press the accelerator of a vehicle to the floorboard.

floo-zy (flö´zē) n., pl. **floozies** *Slang* A sleazy, loose woman; a prostitute.

flop (flop) v. To fall down clumsily; to move about in a clumsy way. *Slang* To completely fail; to go to bed.

flop-py (flop´ē) adj. Flexible and loose. **floppily** adv. **floppiness** n.

floppy disk n. In *computer science*, a flexible plastic disk coated with magnetic material, used to record and store computer data.

flo-ra (flōr´a) n., pl. **floras** or **florae** Plant life growing in a specific region, season, or historic period.

flo-ral (flōr´al) *adj*. Of or pertaining to flowers.

flo-res-cence (flō res´ens) *n*. A state or process of flourishing. **florescent** *adj*.

flor-id (flōr´id) *adj*. Flushed with a rosy color or redness; ornate. **floridness** *n*.

Flor-id-a *n*. A state located on the southeastern coast of the United States, statehood March 3, 1845, state capital Tallahassee.

flo-rif-er-ous *adj*. Producing flowers; blooming.

flo-rist (flōr´ist) *n*. One who grows or sells live flowers and artificial ones made of silk or silk-like fibers.

flo-ris-tics *n*. A branch of the science dealing with the distribution and study of plants upon the earth.

floss (flos) *n*. A loosely twisted embroidery thread; a soft, silky fiber, such as the tassel on corn; a thread. for dental hygiene. **floss** *v*. To clean between the teeth with dental floss.

flo-ta-tion (flō tā´shan) *n*. The act or state of floating.

flot-sam (flot´sam) *n*. Any goods remaining afloat after a ship has sunk.

flounce (flouns) *n*. A gathered piece of material attached to the upper edge of another surface, as on a curtain. **flounce** *v*. To move with exaggerated tosses of the body. **flouncy** *adj*.

floun-der (floun´dėr) *v*. To struggle clumsily, as to gain footing; to act or speak in a confused way. **flounder** *n*. Any of various edible marine flatfish.

flour-ish (flėr´ish) *v*. To thrive; to fare well; to prosper and succeed. **flourish** *n*. A decorative touch or stroke, especially in handwriting; a dramatic act or gesture; a musical fanfare, as of trumpets.

flout (flout) *v*. To have or show open contempt for. **floutingly** *adv*.

flow (flō) *v*. To move freely, as a fluid; to circulate, as blood; to proceed or move steadily and easily; to rise; to derive; to be abundant in something; to hang in a loose, free way. **flow** *n*.

flow-age (flō´ij) *n*. An overflowing; a flooded condition; flood water.

flow chart. A diagram that shows the progress of a series of operations on a particular project.

flow-ing (flō´ing) *adj*. Moving at a smooth steady pace; moving with ease, smoothly and gracefully; having a bountiful supply. **flowingly** *adv*.

flu (flō) *n*. *Informal* Influenza.

flub (flub) *v*. To bungle or botch; to make a mess of. **flub** *n*.

fluc-tu-ant *adj*. Unstable; moving in waves; fluctuating. *Med*. Of a boil or abscess, having a compressible semiliquid center which requires lancing.

fluc-tu-ate (fluk´chō āt´) *v*. To shift irregularly; to change; to undulate.

flue (flō) *n*. A conduit or passage through which air, gas, steam, or smoke can pass.

flu-ent (flō´ent) *adj*. Having an understanding of a language use; flowing smoothly and naturally; flowing or capable of flowing. **fluency** *n*. **fluently** *adv*.

flu-id (flō´id) *n*. A substance, as water or gas, capable of flowing. **fluid** *adj*. Changing readily, as a liquid. **fluidity**, **fluidness** *n*. **fluidly** *adv*.

fluid ounce *n*. A United States unit of liquid capacity that is equal to one-sixteenth pint.

fluke (flōk) *n*. A flatfish, especially a flounder; a flattened, parasitic trematode worm; the triangular head of an anchor at the end of either of its arms; a barb or point on an arrow; an unexpected piece of good luck.

flung *v*. Past tense of fling.

flunk (flungk) *v*. *Slang* To fail in, as an examination or course; to give a failing grade to.

flu-o-res-cence (flō˝o res´ens) *n*. *Chem. & Phys*. Emission of electromagnetic radiation, usually as visible light, resulting from and occurring during the absorption of radiation from another source; the radiation emitted. **fluoresce** *v*. **fluorescent** *adj*.

fluor-i-date *v*. To add a fluoride to water in order to prevent tooth decay.

fluor-i-da-tion (flür´i dā´shan) *n*. The addition of fluoride to drinking water to help prevent tooth decay.

flu-o-ride (flō´o rīd´) *n*. A compound of fluorine with another element or a radical.

flu-o-rine (flō´o rēn´) *n*. A pale yellow, corrosive, and extremely reactive gaseous element, symbolized by F.

flur-ry (flur´ē) *n*., *pl*. **flurries** A sudden gust of wind; a brief, light fall of snow or rain, accompanied by small gusts; a sudden burst of activity or commotion. **flurry** *v*. To cause to become agitated.

flush (flush) *v*. To flow or rush out suddenly and abundantly; to become red in the face; to blush; to glow with a reddish color; to purify or wash out with a brief, rapid gush of water; to cause to flee from cover, as a game animal or bird. **flush** *n*. Glowing freshness or vigor; a hand in certain card games, as poker, in which all the cards are the same suit. **flush** *adj*. Having a heightened reddish color; abundant; affluent, prosperous; having surfaces that are even; arranged with adjacent sides close together; having margins aligned with no indentations.

flush *adv.* In an even position with another surface; in a direct way, as a direct blow.

flus-ter (flus´tĕr) *v.* To make or become nervous or confused.

flute (floot) *n.* A high-pitched, tubular woodwind instrument equipped with finger holes and keys; a decorative groove in the shaft of a column; a small grooved pleat, as in cloth. **fluting** *n.*

flut-ist *n.* A flute player.

flut-ter (flut´ĕr) *v.* To flap or wave rapidly and irregularly; to fly as with a light, rapid beating of the wings; to beat erratically, as one's heart; to move about in a restless way. **flutter** *n.*

flutter kick *n.* An alternate kicking motion in swimming.

flux (fluks) *n.* A flowing or discharge; a constant flow or movement; a state of constant fluctuation or change; a substance that promotes the fusing of metals and prevents oxide formation. **flux** *v.* To make fluid; to melt; to apply a flux to.

fly (flī) *v.* To move through the air on wings or wing-like parts; to travel by air; to float or cause to float in the air; to escape; to flee; to pass by swiftly or quickly; to hit a fly ball. **fly** *n.* A folded piece of cloth that covers the fastening of a garment, especially trousers; a fly ball one has batted over the field; any of numerous winged insects, including the housefly and the tsetse; a fishing lure that resembles an insect. **fly off the handle** To react explosively.

fly-by-night (flī´bī nīt´) *adj.* Unstable or temporary; financially unsound.

flying saucer *n.* An unidentified disk-shaped or saucer-shaped flying object reported as being seen in the air.

foal (fōl) *n.* The young animal, as a horse, especially one under a year old. **foal** *v.* To give birth to a foal.

foam (fōm) *n.* A mass of bubbles produced on the surface of a liquid by agitation; froth; a firm, spongy material used especially for insulation and upholstery. **foam** *v.* To cause to form foam. **foam at the mouth** To be very angry.

foam rubber *n.* A spongy rubber, of fine texture which is whipped prior to vulcanization, used in pillows and mattresses.

fob (fob) *n.* A chain or ribbon attached to a pocket watch and worn dangling from a pocket; an ornament or seal worn on a fob. **fob** *v.* To dispose of by fraud, deceit, or trickery; to put off by excuse.

focal infection *n. Pathol.* A persistent bacterial infection, localized in an area or organ which may enter the

bloodstream and cause symptoms in other parts of the body.

focal length *n.* The distance to the focus from a lens surface or concave mirror.

fo-cus (fō´kus) *n., pl.* **focuses** *or* **foci** A point in an optical system at which rays converge or from which they appear to diverge; the clarity with which an optical system delivers an image; adjustment for clarity; a center of activity or interest **focus** *v.* To produce a sharp, clear image of; to adjust a lens in order to produce a clean image; to direct; to come together at a point of focus. **focal** *adj.* **focally** *adv.*

fod-der (fod´ĕr) *n.* A coarse feed for livestock, made from chopped stalks of corn and hay.

foe (fō) *n.* An enemy in war; an opponent or adversary.

foe-tal (fēt´al) *adj. Var.* of fetal.

foe-tus (fē´tus) *n. Var.* of fetus.

fog (fog) *n.* A vapor mass of condensed water which lies close to the ground; a state of mental confusion or bewilderment. **fog** *v.* To obscure or cover over, as if with fog. **foggily** *adv.* **foggy** *adj.*

foi-ble (foi´bl) *n.* A minor flaw, weakness, or failing.

foil (foil) *v.* To prevent from being successful; to thwart. **foil** *n.* A very thin, flexible sheet of metal; one that serves as a contrast; a fencing sword having a light, thin, flexible blade and a blunt point.

foist (foist) *v.* To pass off something as valuable or genuine.

fold (fōld) *v.* To double or lay one part over another; to bring from an opened to a closed position; to put together and intertwine; to envelop or wrap; to blend in by gently turning one part over another. *Slang* To give in; to stop production; to fail in business. **fold** *n.* A line, layer, pleat or crease formed by folding; a folded edge; an enclosed area for domestic animals; a flock of sheep; a people united by common aims and beliefs; a church and its members.

fol-de-rol (fol´de ro´´) *n.* Nonsense; a pretty but useless ornament.

folding door *n.* A door made of hinged sections that can be folded together.

fo-li-age (fō´lē ij) *n.* The leaves of growing plants and trees; a cluster of flowers and branches.

fo-li-o (fō´lē ō´) *n.* A large sheet of paper folded once in the middle; a folder for loose papers; a book that consists of folios; a page number.

folk (fōk) *n., pl.* **folk** *or* **folks** An ethnic group of people forming a nation or tribe; people of a specified group; a person's parents, family, or relatives.

folk tale *n.* A traditional, anonymous

legend originating and passed down orally from one generation to another.

fol-li-cle (fol´i kl) *n.* A small anatomical cavity or sac.

fol-low (fol´ō) *v.* To proceed or come after; to pursue; to follow the course of; to obey; to come after in time or position; to ensue; to result; to adhere to closely; to understand the meaning of. **follower** *n.*

follow out *v.* To carry to a conclusion; to follow to the end.

follow through *v.* To extend or carry through, as the part of the stroke after the ball has been hit; to pursue an activity, especially to completion.

follow–up *n.* The act of following up; a letter sent to enhance a previous communication or notice. **follow up** *v.* To pursue closely to a conclusion.

fol-ly (fol´ē) *n., pl.* **follies** Lack of good judgment; an instance of foolishness; an excessively costly and often unprofitable undertaking.

fo-ment (fō ment´) *v.* To rouse; to incite; to treat therapeutically with moist heat. **foment, fomentation** *n.*

fond (fond) *adj.* Affectionate liking; cherished with great affection; deeply felt. **fondness** *n.*

fon-dant (fon´dӑnt) *n.* A sweet, soft preparation of sugar used in candies and icing; a candy made chiefly of fondant.

fon-dle (fon´dl) *v.* To stroke, handle, or caress affectionately and tenderly.

fond-ly (fond´lē) *adv.* In an affectionately manner.

fon-due (fon dö) *n.* A preparation of melted cheese, with white wine; a dish consisting of small pieces of food dipped into hot liquid.

font (font) *n.* A receptacle in a church that holds baptismal or holy water; an assortment of printing type of the same size and face. In *computer science*, traditionally descriptive of one type face and style in one size; with the introduction of scalable fonts, one font often refers to a type face in a single style in a wide range of sizes.

food (fŏd) *n.* A substance consisting essentially of carbohydrates and protein used to sustain life and growth in the body of an organism; nourishment, as in solid form; something that sustains or nourishes. **food for thought** Something to think about, something to ponder.

food chain *n.* A sequence of plants and animals in which each uses the next usually smaller or lower member as a food source.

food poisoning *n.* An acute gastrointestinal ailment caused by bacteria or toxic products produced by the bacteria that contaminate food.

food-stuff (fŏd´stuff´) *n.* A substance having food value.

fool (fōl) *n.* One lacking good sense or judgment; one who can easily be tricked or made to look foolish. **fool** *v.* To dupe; to act in jest; to joke. *Slang* To amuse oneself.

fool-er-y (fō´le rē) *n.* Foolish conduct; a foolish action.

fool-ish (fō´lish) *adj.* Marked by a lack of good sense; unwise. **foolishly** *adv.* **foolishness** *n.*

fool-proof *adj.* Infallible.

foot (fŭt) *n., pl.* **feet** The lower extremity of the vertebrate leg upon which one stands; a unit of measurement equal to 12 inches; a basic unit of verse meter that consists of a group of syllables; the end lower or opposite the head; the lowest part. **foot** *v.* To go on foot; to walk or run. **foot the bill** To pay for all. **on foot** Walking rather than riding.

foot-age *n.* Length expressed in feet, as the footage of a film; the total number of running feet; as board footage.

foot–and–mouth disease *n.* A highly contagious febrile virus disease of cattle and other hoofed animals marked by ulcerating blisters in the mouth, around the hooves, and on the udder.

foot-ball (fŭt´bol) *n.* A game played by two teams on a long rectangular field having goals at either end whose object is to get the ball over a goal line or between goal posts by running, passing or kicking; the oval ball used in the game of football.

foot-board (fŭt´bōrd´) *n.* A small platform to support the feet; a board forming the upright piece across the foot of a bed.

foot-bridge (fŭt´brij´) *n.* A bridge for pedestrians.

foot-ed (fŭt´id) *adj.* Having a foot or feet; having a certain number of feet: often used in compound words, as a four-footed animal.

foot-fall (fŭt´fol´) *n.* A footstep; the sound of a footstep.

foot-gear (fŭt´gēr´) *n.* Articles used to cover and protect the feet, as shoes or boots.

foot-hill (fŭt´hil´) *n.* A low hill at or near the foot of a mountain or a higher hill.

foot-hold (fŭt´hōld´) *n.* A place providing support for the foot, as in climbing; a position usable as a base for advancement.

foot-ing (fŭt´ing) *n.* Secure and stable position for placement of the feet; a foundation.

foot-less *adj.* Without feet.

foot-lights *n., pl. Theater* A row of lights positioned across the front of a stage; the theater as a profession.

foot-lock-er (fŭt´lok˝ėr) n. A small trunk for personal belongings, designed to be placed at the foot of a bed.

foot-loose (fŭt´lŏs˝) adj. Free to move as one pleases; having no ties.

foot-note (fŭt´nōt˝) n. A note of reference, explanation, or comment usually below the text on a printed page; a commentary. **footnote** v.

foot-pace (fŭt´pās˝) n. A walking pace; a platform or stair landing.

foot-pad (fŭt´pad˝) n. A person who goes on foot and robs other pedestrians.

foot-path (fŭt´path˝) n. A narrow path for people on foot.

foot-print (fŭt´print˝) n. The outline or impression of the foot on a surface; the area within which a spacecraft is expected to land.

foot-rest (fŭt´rest˝) n. A support for the feet used for resting the feet.

foot soldier n. An infantryman.

foot-sore (fŭt´sōr˝) adj. Having sore or tender feet.

foot-stalk (fŭt´stok˝) n. Zool. A supportive structure that resembles a stalk. Bot. A stem.

foot-step (fŭt´step˝) n. A footprint; the distance covered by a step.

foot-stool (fŭt´stŏl˝) n. A low stool for resting the feet.

foot-wear (fŭt´wâr˝) n. Articles, as shoes or boots, worn on the feet.

foot-work (fŭt´werk˝) n. The use of the feet, as in boxing.

fop (fop) n. A man unduly concerned with his clothes or appearance; a dandy. **foppery, foppishness** n. **foppish** adj.

for (for) prep. Used to indicate the extent of something; used to indicate the number or amount of; considering the usual characteristics of; on behalf of someone; to be in favor of. **for** conj. Because; in as much as; with the purpose of.

for-age (for´ij) n. Food for cattle or other domestic animals; a search for supplies or food. **forage** v. To make a raid so as to find supplies; to plunder or rummage through, especially in search of provisions.

for-as-much as conj. In view of the fact that; since.

for-ay (for´ā) n. A raid to plunder; act of war. **foray** v.

for-bade or **for-bad** v. Past tense of forbid.

for-bear (for´bâr˝) v. To refrain from; to use self-restraint; to be patient.

for-bear-ance (for bâr´ans) n. The act of forbearing; a refraining from something, as a debt or obligation.

for-bid (fer bid´) v. To command someone to do something; to prohibit by law; to prevent.

for-bid-den adj. Prohibited; not permitted.

forbidden fruit n. Bib. Fruit of the tree of knowledge of good and evil in the Garden of Eden which Adam and Eve ate although it was forbidden; an illegal pleasure or immoral indulgence.

forbidding (fer bid´ing) adj. Very difficult; disagreeable.

force (fors) n. Energy or power; strength; the use of such power; intellectual influence; a group organized for a certain purpose. Phys. Something that changes the state of rest or the body motion or influence. **force** v. To compel to do something or to act; to obtain by coercion; to bring forth, as with effort; to move or drive against resistance; to break down by force; to press or impose, as one's will. **in force** In large numbers; in effect. **forceful** adj. **forcer** n. **forcefully** adv.

force-feed v. To force food by employing force; to force to take.

force-meat (fors´mēt˝) n. Finely ground meat, fish, or poultry, used in stuffing or served separately.

for-ceps (for´seps) n., pl. An instrument resembling a pair of tongs used for manipulating, grasping or extracting, especially in surgery.

force pump n. A pump which draws and forces a liquid by means of pressure or force directly applied, in contrast to a lift pump.

forc-i-ble (fōr´si bl) adj. Accomplished or achieved by force; marked by force. **forcibly** adv.

ford (fōrd) n. A shallow place in a body of water that can be crossed without a boat. **ford** v. To wade across a body of water. **fordable** adj.

Ford, Gerald Rudolph n. (1913-) The thirty-eighth president of the United States from 1974-1977.

Ford, Henry n. (1863-1947) American automobile maker.

for-do, fore-do (for dō) v. To overpower or destroy; to overcome with fatigue.

fore (fōr) adj. & adv. Situated in, at, or toward the front; forward. **fore** n. The front of something. **fore** interj. A cry used by a golfer to warn others that a ball is about to land in their direction.

fore-and-aft (fōr´and aft´) adj. Lying or going lengthwise on a ship; from stem to stern.

fore-arm (fōr ärm˝) v. To prepare in advance, as for a battle. **forearm** n. The part of the arm between the elbow and the wrist.

fore-bear or **for-bear** (fōr´bâr˝) n. An ancestor.

fore-bode (fōr bōd´) v. To give an indication or warning in advance; to have a premonition of something evil. **foreboding** n. **forebodingly** adv.

fore-brain (fōr´brān´) n. Anat. The anterior of the three primary divisions of the developing vertebrate brain, or the corresponding segments of the adult vertebrate brain.

fore-cast (fōr´kast´) v. To estimate or calculate in advance, especially to predict the weather. **forecaster** n.

fore-cas-tle (fōk´sal) n. The part of a ship's upper deck located forward of the foremast; living quarters for the crew at the bow of a merchant ship.

fore-close (fōr klōz´) v. To recall a mortgage in default and take legal possession of the mortgaged property; to exclude or shut out. **foreclosure** n.

fore-go (fōr gō´) v. To go before; to precede in time, place, etc. **-going** adj.

foregone conclusion n. An inevitable result; a conclusion determined before argument or consideration of evidence.

for-eign (for´in) adj. Situated outside one's native country; belonging to; located in or concerned with a country or region other than one's own; involved with other nations; occurring in a place or body in which it is not normally located. **foreigner** n.

foreign affairs n. Diplomatic, commercial, or other matters having to do with international relations.

fore-knowl-edge (fōr´nol´ij) n. Prior knowledge of something; knowledge beforehand.

fore-most (fōr´mōst´) adj. & adv. First in rank, position, time, or order.

fo-ren-sic (fo ren´sik) adj. Of, relating to, or used in courts of justice or formal debate. **forensically** adv.

forensic medicine n. A science dealing with the application of medicine in legal problems.

fore-or-dain (fōr´or dān´) v. Appoint or dispose of in advance; predestine.

fore-quar-ter n. The front portion of the body of an animal, as of lamb or beef.

fore-short-en (fōr´shor´ten) v. To shorten parts of an object in order to give the illusion of depth.

fore-sight (fōr´sīt´) n. The act or capacity of foreseeing; the act of looking forward; concern for the future; prudence. **foresighted** adj.

fore-skin (fōr´skin´) n. A fold of skin that covers the glans of the penis.

for-est (for´ist) n. A large tract of land covered with trees.

fore-stall (fōr stol´) v. To exclude, hinder, or prevent by prior measures.

fore-tell (fōr tel´) v. To tell about in advance; to predict. **foreteller** n.

fore-thought (fōr´thot´) n. Prior thought or planning; a plan for the future.

fore-to-ken (fōr tō´ken) v. To warn beforehand. **foretoken** n.

for-ev-er (for ev´ér) adv. For eternity; without end.

fore-warn (fōr worn´) v. To warn in advance.

fore-word (for´werd) n. Preface.

for-feit (for´fit) n. Something taken away as punishment; a penalty; something that is placed in escrow and redeemed on payment of a fine; a forfeiture. **forfeit** v. To lose or give up the right to by some offense or error.

for-fei-ture n. The act of forfeiting; something forfeited; a penalty.

for-gath-er (for gath´ér) v. To come together; to convene; to assemble.

forge (fōrj) n. A furnace where metals are heated and wrought; a smithy; a workshop that produces wrought iron. **forge** v. To form by heating and hammering; to give shape to; to imitate falsely; to advance slowly but steadily; to defraud; to counterfeit. **forger, forgery** n.

for-get (fér get´) v. To lose the memory of; to fail to become mindful or aware of at the right time. **forgetful** adj. **forgettable** adj. **forgetfulness** n.

for-give (fér giv´) v. To pardon; to give up resentment of; to cease to feel resentment against. **forgiveness** n.

for-giv-ing adj. Disposed to forgive; inclined to overlook offenses; compassionate.

for-go or **fore-go** (for gō´) To give up or refrain from. **forgoer** n.

for-lorn (for lorn´) adj. Abandoned or left in distress; hopeless; being in a poor condition. **forlornly** adv.

form (form) n. The shape or contour of something; a body of a living being; the basic nature of or particular state of something; the way in which something exists; variety; manner, as established by custom or regulation; the style or manner determined by etiquette or custom; performance according to established criteria; fitness with regard to training or health; procedure of words, as in a ceremony; a document having blanks for insertion of information; style in musical or literary composition; the design or style of a work of art. In computer science, a document designed for the orderly entry of data; the configuration or arrangement of data in a report. **form** v. To construct or conceive in the mind. **form** suffix Having the form or shape of; cuneiform

for-mal (for´mal) adj. Of or pertaining to the outward aspect of something; relating to or concerned with the outward form of something; adhering to convention, rule, or etiquette; based on accepted conventions. **formally** adv.

for-mal-de-hyde (for mal´de hīd) n. A colorless, gaseous chemical used chiefly as a preservative and disinfectant in synthesizing other compounds.

for-mal-i-ty *n.* The condition or state of being formal; an established form that is required.

for-mat (for´mat) *n.* A general style of a publication; the general form or layout of a publication. **format** *v.* In *computer science*, to produce data in a specified form.

for-ma-tion (for ma´shan) *n.* The act or process of forming or the state of being formed; the manner in which something is formed; a given arrangement, as of troops, as a square or in a column.

for-ma-tive (for´ma tiv) *adj.* Forming or having the power to form; of or pertaining to formation, growth, or development.

for-mer (for´mèr) *adj.* Previous; preceding in place; being the first of two persons or things mentioned or referred to.

for-mer-ly *adv.* Previously.

form-fit-ting (form´fit´ing)*adj.* Closely following the contours of the body.

for-mi-da-ble (for´mi da bl) *adj.* Extremely difficult; exciting fear by reason of size or strength. **-bly** *adv.*

form letter *n.* A standardized format of an impersonal letter sent to different people or to a large number of people.

for-mu-la (for´mū la) *n., pl.* **formulas** *or* **formulae** A prescribed method of words or rules for use in a certain ceremony or procedure; a nutritious food for an infant in liquid form. *Math.* A combination or rule used to express an algebraic or symbolic form. *Chem.* A symbolic representation of the composition of a chemical compound. In *computer science*, a string of symbols that calculate to a value, as in a spreadsheet cell that calls for the total of the values in other specified cells, or that calculates to a logical true or false, as in a conditional branch command. **formulaic** *adj.*

for-mu-late (for´mū lāt´) *v.* To state or express as a formula. **formulation** *n.*

for-ni-ca-tion (for´ni kā´shan) *n.* Voluntary sexual intercourse between two unmarried people. **fornicator** *n.*

for-sake (for sāk´) *v.* To abandon or renounce; to give up. **forsaken** *adj.*

for-sooth (for sōth´) *adv.* In truth; certainly.

for-swear (for swâr´) *v.* To renounce emphatically or upon oath; to forsake; to swear falsely; to perjure oneself.

fort (fōrt) *n.* A fortified structure or enclosure capable of defense against an enemy; a permanent army post.

forte (fōrt´ē) *n.* An activity one does with excellence; a person's strong point;

the part of a sword blade between the middle and the hilt.

forth (fōrth) *adv.* Out into plain sight, as from seclusion; forward in order, place, or time.

forth-com-ing (fōrth´kum´ing) *adj.* Ready or about to appear or occur; readily available.

forth-right (fōrth´rīt´) *adj.* Direct; straightforward; frank. **forthrightly** *adv.* **forthrightness** *n.*

forth-with (fōrth´with´) *adv.* At once; promptly; immediately.

for-ti-fi-ca-tion *n.* The act of fortifying; something that fortifies, strengthens, or defends; a fortified place as a fort.

for-ti-fy (for´ti fī´) *v.* To strengthen and secure with military fortifications; to provide physical strength or courage to; to strengthen; to enrich food, as by adding vitamins, minerals, etc.

for-tis-si-mo (for tis´i mō´) *adv. Mus.* Very loudly, as a direction.

for-ti-tude (for´ti tōd´) *n.* Strength of mind in adversity, pain, or peril, allowing a person to withstand pain.

fort-night (fort´nīt´) *n.* A period of two weeks. **fortnightly** *adj. & adv.*

FOR-TRAN (for´tran) *n.* In *computer science*, a programming language for problems that are expressed in several different algebraic terms.

for-tress (for´tris) *n.* A fort.

for-tu-i-tous (for tō´i tus) *adj.* Occurring by chance; lucky; fortunate.

for-tu-nate (for´chu nit) *adj.* Brought about by good fortune; having good fortune. **fortunately** *adv.*

for-tune (for´chan) *n.* A hypothetical force that unpredictably determines events and issues favorably and unfavorably; success that results from luck; possession of material goods; a very large amount of money.

fortune hunter *n.* A person who seeks wealth through marriage.

for-tune-tell-er (for´chan tel´ér) *n.* A person who claims to predict the future. **fortune-telling** *n. & adj.*

for-ty *n. & adj.* Number equal to 4x10.

for-ty-nin-er (for´tē nī´nér)*n.* A United States pioneer in the 1849 California gold rush.

forty winks *n. Slang* A short nap.

fo-rum (fōr´um) *n., pl.* **forums** *or* **fora** A public marketplace in an ancient Roman city, where most legal and political business was transacted; a judicial assembly; a group discussion on any subject.

for-ward (for´wèrd) *adj.* At, near, or toward a place or time in advance; overstepping the usual bounds in an insolent or presumptuous way; extremely unconventional, as in political opinions; socially advanced.

forward *n*. A player in football at the front line. **forward** *v*. To send forward or ahead; to help advance onward. **forwardly** *adv*. **forwardness** *n*.

forward pass *n*. *Football* An offensive pass thrown in the direction of the opponent's goal.

fos-sil (fos´ il) *n*. The remains of an animal or plant of a past geologic age preserved in the crust of the earth's surface; one that is outdated. **fossilization** *n*. **fossilize** *v*.

fos-ter (fo´stĕr) *v*. To give parental care to; to nurture; to encourage. **foster** *adj*. Giving or receiving parental care.

foster child *n*. A child supported financially and cared for by someone who is not the natural parent.

foster parent *n*. A person who financially supports and cares for a child who is not his own.

foul (foul) *adj*. Revolting to the senses; spoiled or rotten; covered with offensive matter; morally offensive; vulgar or obscene; unfavorable; dishonorable; indicating the limiting lines of a playing area. **foul** *v*. To physically contact or entangle; to become foul or dirty; to dishonor; to obstruct; to entangle; to make or hit a foul. **foul up** *Slang* To make a mistake. **foully** *adv*. **foulness** *n*.

fou-lard *n*. A soft, lightweight silk usu. decorated with a printed pattern.

foul ball *n*. A batted baseball that lands outside specified lines.

foul-mouthed *adj*. Using profane, vile, or obscene language.

foul play *n*. A violent act, often murder; an infringement of sporting rules.

found (found) *v*. To establish; to set up, often with funds to permit continuation and maintenance; to establish the basis or lay the foundation of; to melt metal and pour into a mold; to make by casting molten metal. **founder** *n*.

foun-da-tion (foun dā´shan) *n*. The act of founding or establishing; the basis on which anything is founded; an institution supported by an endowment; a cosmetic base for makeup.

foun-dry (foun´drē) *n*., *pl.* **foundries** An establishment where metal is cast.

fount (fount) *n*. A fountain; an abundant source.

foun-tain (foun´tan) *n*. A natural spring or jet of water coming from the earth; an artificially created spray of water; a basin-like structure from which such a stream comes; a point of origin or source.

fountain pen *n*. A pen having a reservoir of ink that automatically feeds the writing point.

four (fōr) *n*. The cardinal number that equals 3 + 1; anything consisting of four units. **four** *adj. & pron.*

four-fold *adj*. Consisting of four units; quadruple.

four-hand-ed *adj*. Involving four players, as a game of cards; engaged in by four people.

four-poster *n*. A bed having four tall posts, one at each corner, originally for the support of a canopy.

four-score (fōr´skōr´) *adj*. Being four times twenty; eighty.

four-teen (fōr´tēn´) *n*. The cardinal number that equals 13 + 1; anything consisting of fourteen units. **fourteen** *adj. & pron.* **fourteenth** *n., adj. & adv.*

fourth (fōrth) *n*. The ordinal number matching the number four in a series; the fourth forward gear of a transmission in a motor vehicle.

Fourth of July *n*. American Independence Day celebrated as a national holiday.

four-wheel *adj*. Automotive transmission in which all four wheels are linked to the source of driving power.

fowl (foul) *n., pl.* **fowl** *or* **fowls** A bird used as food or hunted as game, as the duck etc.; the edible flesh of a fowl. **fowl** *v*. To hunt or catch wild fowl.

fox (foks) *n*. A wild mammal having a pointed snout, upright ears, and a long bushy tail; the fur of a fox; a sly or crafty person. *v*. To outwit; to trick.

fox-hole (foks´hōl´) *n*. A shallow pit dug by a soldier as protection against enemy fire.

fox-hound (foks´hound´) *n*. A large dog breed developed for fox hunting.

fox-ing *n*. The pieces or piece of leather used to cover the upper front portion of a shoe.

fox terrier *n*. Small dog with a wiry or smooth white coat and dark markings.

fox trot *n*. A ballroom dance in 4/4 or 2/4 time consisting of a variety of rhythmic steps.

fox-y (fok´sē) *adj*. Like a fox; sly or crafty; sharp; cunning. *Slang* Very pretty. **foxily** *adv*.

foy-er (foi´ér) *n*. The public lobby of a hotel, theater, etc.; an entrance hall.

fpm *abbr*. Feet per minute.

fps *abbr*. Feet per second.

Fr *abbr*. Father (clergyman); French.

fra-cas (frā´kas) *n*. A noisy quarrel or disturbance; fight or dispute.

frac-tion (frak´shan) *n*. A small part; a disconnected part or fragment of anything. *Mathematics* An indicated quantity less than a whole number that is expressed as a decimal. *Chem*. A component of a compound separated from a substance by distilling.

frac-tion-al *adj*. Relating or pertaining to a fraction or fractions.

frac-ture (frak´chér) *n*. The act of

breaking; the state of being broken. *Med.* The breaking or cracking, as in a bone.

frag-ile (fraj´il) *adj.* Easily damaged or broken; frail; tenuous; flimsy. **fragilely** *adv.* **fragility** *n.*

frag-ment (frag´ment) *n.* A part detached or broken; part unfinished or incomplete. **fragment** *v.* To break into fragments.

frag-men-tal *adj. Geol.* Fragmentary; pertaining to rocks made up of fragments of older rocks.

frag-men-tary *adj.* Composed of fragments.

frag-men-tate *v.* To fragment.

fragmentation *n.* Broken into parts. In *computer science*, a condition wherein files on a disk are recorded to scattered rather than contiguous segments.

frag-ment-ed *adj.* Being reduced to fragments; lacking unity.

fra-grance *n.* The quality of being fragrant.

fra-grant (frā´grant) *adj.* Having an agreeable, especially sweet odor. **fragrantly** *adv.*

frail (frāl) *adj.* Delicate; weak; easily damaged. **frailly** *adv.* **frailness** *n.*

frame (frām) *v.* To put into a frame, as a picture; to build; to design; to adjust or adapt for a given purpose; to provide with a frame. *Slang* To incriminate so as to make a person appear guilty. **frame** *n.* Something made up of parts and joined together, such as a skeletal structure of a body or the timbers of a building; the pieces of wood or metal which surround a picture, photograph, or work of art; general structure; one exposure on a roll of film. In *computer science*, a window on a monitor screen that provides a view of information displayed by a program. **frame-up** *Slang* Actions which serve to make someone appear guilty whether he is not. **framer** *n.*

frame-work *n.* A structure composed of parts fitted together; the structure of ideas in a written composition.

fram-ing *n.* The act, process, or manner of constructing or contriving anything.

fran-chise (fran´chiz) *n.* A privilege or right granted to a person or group by a government; the constitutional right to vote; authorization to sell a manufacturer's products; the territory within which a privilege or immunity is authorized. **franchisee, -er** *n.*

fran-gi-ble (fran´ji bl) *adj.* Breakable.

frank (frangk) *adj.* Sincere and straightforward. **frank** *v.* To mark mail officially so that no charge is made for delivery. **frank** *n.* The right to send mail without charge; a signature or mark on mail indicating that mail can

be sent without charge; mail sent without charge. **frankly** *adv.*

frank-furt-er (frangk´fér tér) *n.* A smoked sausage made of beef or beef and pork; a hot dog.

frank-in-cense (frang´kin sens´) *n.* An aromatic gum resin obtained from African and Asian trees used as incense and in medicine.

Franklin, Benjamin *n.* (1706-1790) American statesman, scientist and inventor.

fran-tic (fran´tik) *adj.* Emotionally out of control with worry or fear. **frantically** *adv.*

fra-ter-nal (fra ter´nal) *adj.* Pertaining to or relating to brothers; of, pertaining to, or befitting a fraternity. *Biol.* Of or relating to a twin or twins that developed from separately fertilized ova. **fraternalism** *n.* **fraternally** *adv.*

fra-ter-ni-ty *n.* The relationship of a brother; a class of men associated for a common interest.

frat-er-nize (frat´er niz´) *v.* To associate with others in a friendly way; to mingle intimately with the enemy, often in violation of military law. **fraterniza-tion** *n.*

frat-ri-cide (fra´tri sid´) *n.* The killing of one's brother or sister; one who has killed his brother or sister. **-al** *adj.*

fraud (frod) *n.* A deliberate and willful deception perpetrated for unlawful gain; a trick or swindle; an impostor; a cheat.

fraud-u-lent (fro´ju lent) *adj.* Marked by or practicing fraud. **fraudulence** *n.* **fraudulently** *adv.*

fraught (frot) *adj.* Full of or accompanied by something specified.

fray (frā) *n.* A brawl, or fight; a heated argument or dispute. *v.* To wear out by rubbing; to irritate one's nerves.

fraz-zle (fraz´el) *v. Slang* To wear out; to completely fatigue. **frazzle** *n.*

freak (frēk) *n.* A seemingly capricious event; a whimsical quality or disposition. *Slang* A drug addict; a highly individualistic rebel; a person with an extreme physical abnormality; a fan or enthusiast. **freak out** To experience hallucinations or paranoia induced by a drug; to make or become highly excited. **freak, freakish, freaky** *adj.* **freakily** *adv.*

freck-le (frek´l) *n.* One of the small, brownish spots on the skin due to precipitation of pigment, usually increasing in number and intensity upon exposure to the sun.

free (frē) *adj.* Not imprisoned; not under obligation; politically independent; possessing political liberties; not affected by a specified circumstance or condition; exempt; costing nothing;

not being occupied or used; too familiar; forward; liberal, as with money. **free** *adv.* In a free way; without charge. **free** *v.* To set at liberty; to release or rid; to untangle. **freely** *adv.*

free-dom (frē'dom) *n.* The condition or state of being free; political independence; possession of political rights; boldness of expression; liberty; unrestricted access or use.

free enterprise *n.* A doctrine or type of economy under which private business is allowed to operate with minimal governmental control; capitalist economy.

free-hand *adv.* Drawn by hand without the assistance of any measuring or guiding instruments.

free lance (frēlans) *n.* One whose services are without long-term commitments to any one employer.

free-spoken *adj.* Speaking freely without reserve; outspoken.

free-standing (frē'stan'ding) *adj.* Standing alone without any support; free of any apparent support or attachments.

free trade *n.* International exchange between nations or states which is unrestricted.

freeze (frēz) *v.* To become ice or a similar solid through loss of heat; to preserve by cooling at an extremely low temperature; to become nonfunctional through the formation of ice or frost; to feel uncomfortably cold; to make or become rigid; to become suddenly motionless, rigid or inactive, as though through fear; to set prices at a certain level; to forbid further use of. **freeze** *n.* An act of freezing or the state of being frozen; a cold snap.

freeze-dry (frēz'drī) *v.* To preserve by drying in a frozen state under a high vacuum. **freeze-dried** *adj.*

freezer (frēz'ér) *n.* Anything that freezes or keeps cold; an insulated cabinet for freezing and storing perishable foods.

freight (frāt) *n.* A service of transporting commodities by air, land or water; the price paid for such transportation; a train that transports goods only. **freight** *v.* To carry as cargo.

freight-age *n.* Freight; the transportation of goods.

freight-er (frā'tér) *n.* A ship used for transporting cargo.

fren-zy (fren'zē) *n.*, *pl.* **frenzies** A state of extreme excitement or violent agitation; temporary insanity or delirium.

fre-quen-cy *n.* The state of occurring often; the number of times an event is repeated.

fre-quent (frē'kwent) *adj.* Happening or appearing or reappearing often or time after time. **frequent** *v.* To go to a place repeatedly. **frequenter** *n.* **frequently** *adv.*

fres-co (fres'kō) *n.*, *pl.* **-coes** or **-cos** The art of painting on moist plaster with water-based paint; a picture so painted.

fresh (fresh) *adj.* Newly made, gathered, or obtained; not spoiled, musty, or stale; new; different; not soiled; pure and clean; having just arrived; refreshed; revived. *Slang* Impudent; disrespectful. **freshly** *adv.*

fresh-en *v.* To make fresh; to revive; renew.

fresh-wa-ter *adj.* Pertaining to water without salt.

fret (fret) *v.* To be anxious or irritated; to wear away; to make by erosion; to ripple water. **fret** *n.* An ornamental design, composed of repeated symmetric figures; a ridge of metal fixed across the fingerboard of a stringed instrument, as a guitar.

fret-ful *adj.* Irritable.

fret saw *n.* A small saw used to cut curved lines.

fret-work *n.* Ornamental work.

fri-a-ble (frī'a bl) *adj.* Easily crumbled or pulverized; brittle. **friableness** *n.*

fri-ar (frī'ér) *n.* A member of a mendicant Roman Catholic order.

fric-as-see (frik'a sē') *n.* A dish of meat or poultry stewed in gravy.

fric-tion (frik'shan) *n.* The rubbing of one surface or object against another; a conflict or clash. *Phys.* A force that retards the relative motion of two touching objects. **frictional** *adj.*

Fri-day (frī'dā) *n.* The sixth day of the week.

friend (frend) *n.* Someone who is personally well-known by oneself and for whom one holds warm regards; a supporter of a cause or group. **Friend** A member of the Society of Friends; a Quaker. **friendship** *n.*

friend-ly *adj.* Characteristic of a friend; like a friend; showing kindness and goodwill. **friendliness** *n.*

frieze (frēz) *n.* A decorative horizontal band along the upper part of a wall in a room.

frig-ate (frig'it) *n.* A square-rigged warship of the 17th to mid-19th centuries; U.S. warship smaller than a cruiser but larger than a destroyer.

fright (frīt) *n.* Sudden violent alarm or fear; a feeling of alarm. *Slang* Something very unsightly or ugly.

fright-ful *adj.* Causing intense fright or alarm. **frightfully** *adv.*

fright-en (frīt'en) *v.* To fill with fear; to force by arousing fear. **frightening** *adj.* **frighteningly** *adv.*

frig-id (frij'id) *adj.* Very cold; lacking warmth of feeling or emotional warmth;

sexually unresponsive. **frigidity** *n.*
frigidness *n.* **frigidly** *adv.*

frill (fril) *n.* A decorative ruffled or
gathered border. *Slang* A superfluous
item. **frilly** *adj.*

fringe (frinj) *n.* An edging that consists
of hanging threads, cords, or loops.

fringe benefit *n.* Any employment
benefit, such as paid holidays,
pensions, or insurance, given in
addition to salary.

frip-per-y (frip´e rē) *n., pl.* **fripperies**
Showy and often cheap ornamentation;
a pretentious display.

frisk (frisk) *v.* To skip or leap about
playfully; to search someone for a
concealed weapon by running the hands
over the clothing quickly.

frit-ter (frit´ér) *v.* To squander or waste
little by little. **fritter** *n.* A small fried
cake made of plain batter, often
containing fruits, vegetables, or fish.

fri-vol-i-ty *n.* The quality of being
frivolous.

friv-o-lous (friv´o lus) *adj.* Trivial;
insignificant; lacking importance; not
serious; silly. **frivolousness** *n.*
frivolously *adv.*

frizz (friz) *v.* To form into small, tight
curls. **frizziness** *n.* **frizzy** *adj.*

friz-zly *adj.* Frizzed, as hair; very curly.

fro (frō) *adv.* Away from; back, as
running to and fro.

frock (frok) *n.* A smock or loose-fitting
robe; a robe worn by monks.

frog (frog) *n.* Any of various small,
smooth-skinned, web-footed, largely
aquatic, tailless, leaping amphibians;
an ornamental braid, cord, or fastener;
an arrangement of intersecting railroad
tracks designed to permit wheels to
pass over the intersection without
difficulty; a perforated holder for
flower stems. *Slang* Hoarseness in the
throat.

frol-ic (frol´ik) *n.* Merriness; a playful,
carefree occasion. *v.* To romp about
playfully; to have fun. **frolicsome** *n.*

from (frum) *prep.* Starting at a
particular time or place; used to
indicate a specific point; used to
indicate a specific source; used to
indicate separation or removal; used
to indicate differentiation, as in
knowing right from left.

frond (frond) *n.* A large leaf, as of a
tropical fern, usually divided into
smaller leaflets.

front (frunt) *n.* The forward surface of
an object or body; the area or position
located before or ahead; a position of
leadership; the area of action in a war;
a field of activity for disguising
objectionable or illegal activities; an
apparently respectable person, group,
or business used as a cover for illegal

or secret activities. *Meteor.* The line
of separation between air masses of
different temperatures. **frontal** *adj.*
frontally *adv.*

front money *n.* Money paid in advance
for a service or product that has been
promised.

fron-tier (frun tēr´) *n.* A part of an
international border or the area adjacent
to it; an unexplored area of knowledge
or thought. **frontiersman** *n.*

fron-tis-piece (frun´tis pēs´) *n.* An
illustration that usually precedes the
title page of a book or periodical.

front office *n.* The executive staff of an
organization.

front-ward *adv.* Toward the front.

frost (frost) *n.* A feathery covering of
minute ice crystals on a cold surface;
the act or process of freezing. **frost** *v.*
To cover with frost; to apply frosting
to a cake. **frostily** *adv.* **frostiness** *n.*

frost-bite (frost´bīt´) *n.* The local
destruction of bodily tissue due to
exposure to freezing temperatures,
often resulting in gangrene.

froth (froth) *n.* A mass of bubbles on
or in a liquid, resulting from agitation
or fermentation; a salivary foam, as
of an animal, resulting from disease
or exhaustion; anything unsubstantial
or trivial. **froth** *v.* To expel froth.
frothily *adv.* **frothiness** *n.* **frothy** *adj.*

frou-frou (frö´frö´) *n.* A rustling sound,
as of silk; a frilly dress or decoration.

fro-ward (frō´wérd) *adj.* Obstinate;
contrary. **frowardly** *adv.*

frown (froun) *v.* To contract the brow
as in displeasure or concentration; to
look on with distaste or disapproval.
frowningly *adv.* **frowning** *adj.*

frow-zy *or* **frow-sy (frou´zē)** *adj.*
Appearing unkempt.

fro-zen (frō´zen) *adj.* Covered with,
changed into, surrounded by, or made
into ice; extremely cold, as a climate;
immobilized or made rigid, as by fear;
coldly reserved; unfriendly; kept at a
fixed level, as wages; not readily
available for withdrawal, sale, or
liquidation, as from a bank.

fruc-tu-ous (fruk´chö us) *adj.* Fruitful;
productive.

fru-gal (frö´gal) *adj.* Economical; thrifty.
frugality, frugalness *n.* **frugally** *adv.*

fruit (fröt) *n., pl.* **fruit** *or* **fruits** The
ripened, mature, seed bearing part of
a flowering plant, as a pod or berry;
the edible, fleshy plant part of this kind,
as an apple or plum; the fertile structure
of a plant that does not bear seeds; the
outcome or result. **fruit** *v.* To produce
or cause to produce fruit.

fru-i-tion (frö ish´an) *n.* Achievement
or accomplishment of something
worked for or desired; the state of

bearing fruit.

frump-y (frump´ē) *adj.* Unfashionable; dowdy. **frump, frumpiness** *n.*

frus-trate (frus´trāt) *v.* To keep from attaining a goal or fulfilling a desire; to thwart; to prevent the fruition of; to nullify. **frustration** *n.* **frustratingly** *adv.* **frustrating** *adj.*

fub-sy *adj.* To be chubby and squat.

fuch-sia (fū´sha) *n.* A chiefly tropical plant widely grown for its drooping, four-petaled flowers of purple, red, or white; a vivid reddish to purple color.

fuch-sine (fek´sin) *n.* A type of dye that is made by the oxidation of a mixture of aniline and toluidines which is a bright red.

fu-coid (fū´koid) *adj.* Pertaining to or being like seaweed or rock weeds.

fu-cose *n.* A type of aldose sugar.

fu-co-xan-thin *n.* A type of brown pigment occurring especially in the ova of brown algae.

fu-cus (fū´kus) *n.* A type of brown algae.

fud-dle (fud´l) *v.* To make someone or something confused.

fud-dy–dud-dy *n. pl.* **fuddy-duddies (fud´ē dud´ē)** An old-fashioned person.

fudge (fuj) *n.* A soft, cooked candy containing sugar, butter, and a flavoring, as chocolate. **fudge** *v.* To falsify; to adjust, make, or fit together in a clumsy way; to evade.

fuel (fū´el) *n.* A combustible matter consumed to generate energy, especially a material such as wood, coal, or oil burned to generate heat. **fuel** *v.* To take in or supply with fuel; stimulate, as an argument. **fueler** *n.*

fuel cell *n.* A kind of cell which will change the chemical energy of a fuel to an electrical energy.

fuel injection *n.* The forced spraying of fuel into the combustion chamber of an engine.

fuel oil *n.* An oil used for fuel, esp. one used as a substitute for coal.

fug (fug) *v.* To hang around or loll indoors in an atmosphere that is stuffy.

fu-ga-cious (fū gā´shus) *adj.* Lasting for only a short time. **fugacity** *n.*

fu-gal (fū´gal) *adj.* To be pertaining to the style of a musical fugue.

fu-gi-tive (fū´ji tiv) *adj.* Fleeing or having fled, as from arrest or pursuit. **fugitive** *n.* One who flees or tries to escape.

fu-gle *v.* To act as a model for proper behavior of soldiers. **fugleman** *n.*

fugue (fūg) *n. Mus.* A musical composition in which the theme is elaborately repeated by different voices or instruments; a psychological disturbance in which actions are not remembered after one returns to a normal state.

fu-ji *n.* A type of spun silk fabric that was first made in Japan.

-ful *adj. suffix* Having the qualities of something; to be filled with or full of.

ful-crum (fel´krum) *n.* The point on which a lever turns.

ful-fill *or* **ful-fil (fel fil´)** *v.* To convert into actuality; to effect; to carry out; to satisfy. **fulfillment** *n.*

ful-gent (ful´jent) *adj.* To be very bright or dazzling bright.

ful-gu-rant (fil´gur ant) *adj.* To be flashing like lightening flashes.

ful-gu-ra-tion *n.* The flashing as of lightning.

ful-gu-rite (ful´gū rīt) *n.* A type of tubular crust that is formed by the fusion of rock by lightning.

ful-gu-rous *adj.* To be giving off flashes like that of lightning.

fu-lig-i-nous (fū lij´i nus) *adj.* Being murky or to have a color that is dark.

full (fel) *adj.* To have in something the maximum amount that the thing is able to hold. **fullness** *n.*

full blood *n.* Pure extraction; an unmixed ancestry.

full moon *n.* A phase of the moon where the whole side of the disk is visible.

ful-mar (fel´mer) *n.* A type of arctic seabird which is related to the petrels.

ful-mi-nate (ful´mi nāt) *v.* To condemn severely; to explode. **fulmination, fulminator** *n.*

ful-some (fel´som) *adj.* Offensively insincere. **fulsomely** *adv.* **-ness** *n.*

ful-vous (ful´vus) *adj.* Yellow; tawny.

fum-ble (fum´bl) *v.* To handle idly; to blunder; to mishandle a baseball or football. **fumble** *n.* The act of fumbling; a fumbled ball. **fumbler** *n.*

fume (fūm) *n.* An irritating smoke, gas, or vapor. **fume** *v.* To treat with or subject to fumes; to show or feel anger or distress.

fu-mi-gate (fū´mi gāt´) *v.* To subject to fumes in order to exterminate vermin or insects. **fumigation, fumigator** *n.*

fun *n.* That which is amusing or mirthful; entertaining; recreation or play, relaxing

func-tion (fungk´shan) *n.* The characteristics or proper activity of a person or thing; specific occupation, duty, or role; an official ceremony; something depending upon or varying with another. *Math.* A quantity whose value is dependent on the value of another. **function** *v.* To serve or perform a function as required or expected.

func-tion-al *adj.* Of or pertaining to functions; able to perform a regular function. **functionally** *adv.*

function code *n.* In *computer science*, any symbol or set of symbols that generates an instruction to the computer.

function keys (*abbr.* **Fn**) *n.* In *computer science*, where *n* equals a number, one of a set of ten or twelve keys that alone or in conjunction with either the Ctrl, Alt or Shift key execute commands in certain programs.

fund (fund) *n.* A source of supply; a sum of money or its equivalent reserved for a specific purpose. **fund** *v.* To convert into long-term arrangements for paying something off; to furnish or accumulate a fund for.

fun-da-men-tal (fun´da men´tal) *adj.* Basic or essential; of major significance; anything serving as the primary origin; most important. **fundamental** *n.* **fundamentally** *adv.*

fu-ner-al (fū´nėr al) *n.* The service performed in conjunction with the burial or cremation of a dead person.

funeral director *n.* A person who manages funerals.

funeral home *n.* The establishment where a dead person is prepared for burial or cremation and for viewing of the body.

fu-ne-re-al *adj.* Pertaining to or relating to a funeral.

fun-gus (fung´gus) *n., pl.* **-gi** *or* **-guses** Any of numerous spore-bearing plants which have no chlorophyll, including yeasts, molds, mildews, and mushrooms. **fungous** *adj.* **fungal** *adj.*

fu-nic-u-lar (fū nik´ū lėr) *n.* A cable railway along which cable cars are drawn up a mountain, especially one with ascending and descending cars that counterbalance one another.

fun-nel (fun´el) *n.* A cone-shaped utensil having a tube for channeling a substance into a container. **funnel** *v.* To pass or cause to pass through a funnel.

fur *n.* The skin of certain animals, the hairy coating on such a skin; such skins that are used as a material for lining or trimming, or for entire garments.

fur-be-low (fer´be lō´) *n.* A ruffle or frill on clothing; a piece of showy decoration or ornamentation.

fur-bish (fer´bish) *v.* To make bright, as by rubbing; to polish; to renovate.

fu-ri-ous (fer´e us) *adj.* Extremely angry; marked by rage or activity.

furl (ferl) *v.* To roll up and secure to something, as a pole or mast; to curl or fold.

fur-long (fer´long) *n.* A distance equal to approximately 201 meters or 230 yards.

fur-lough (fer´lō) *n.* Permission granted to be absent from duty, especially to members of the armed forces.

fur-nace (fer´nis) *n.* A large enclosure designed to produce intense heat.

fur-nish (fer´nish) *v.* To outfit or equip, as with fittings or furniture.

fur-ni-ture (fer´ni chėr) *n.* Movable articles, such as chairs and tables, used in a home, office, etc.

fu-ror (fūr´or) *n.* Violent anger; rage; great excitement; commotion; an uproar.

fur-row (fer´ō) *n.* A long, narrow trench in the ground, made by a plow or other tool; a deep wrinkle in the skin, especially of the forehead. **furrow** *v.*

fur-ther *adv.* At a more advanced point in time or space.

fur-ther-more *adv.* Moreover.

fur-ther-most *adj.* Most distant.

fur-tive (fer´tiv) *adj.* Done in secret; surreptitious;obtainedunderhandedly; stolen.

fu-ry (fūr´e) *n., pl.* **furies** Uncontrolled anger; turbulence; an angry or spiteful woman.

fuse (fūz) *n.* An electrical safety device containing a wire or strip of fusible metal that melts and interrupts the circuit's flow when the current exceeds a particular amperage; a mechanical, electrical, or electronic device used to detonate explosives, such as bombs or grenades.

fu-see *or* **fu-zee** (fū zē´) *n.* A large-headed friction match capable of burning in the wind; a colored signal flare used as a railroad signal.

fu-se-lage (fū´se lij) *n.* The central section of an airplane, containing the wings and tail assembly.

fu-si-ble *adj.* Capable of being melted.

fu-si-lade *n.* A quickly repeated or simultaneous discharge of a number of firearms.

fu-sion (fū´zhan) *n.* The act or procedure of melting together by heat; a blend produced by fusion; a nuclear reaction in which nuclei of a light element combine to form more massive nuclei, with the release of huge amounts of energy.

fuss *n.* An excessive display of restless activity.

fus-tian (fus´chan) *n.* A sturdy, stout cotton cloth. **fustian** *adj.* Pompous, pretentious language; bombastic.

fus-ti-gate *v.* To criticize.

fu-tile (fūt´il) *adj.* Ineffectual; being of no avail; without useful result; serving no useful purpose.

fu-ture (fū´chėr) *n.* The time yet to come; a prospective condition regarding advancement or success; the future tense or a verb form in the future tense.

fuzz (fuz) *n.* A mass of fine, loose particles, fibers, or hairs.

fuzz-y *adj.* Covered with fuzz; lacking in clarity.

FYI *abbr.* For your information.

G, g (jē) The seventh letter of the English alphabet. *Mus.* The fifth tone in the scale of C major. *Slang* One thousand dollars; a grand. *Physiol.* A unit of force equal to that due to the earth's gravity.

g *abbr.* Gravity, gram.

gab (gab) *v. Slang* To talk or chat idly.

gab-ble (gab´l) *v.* To speak rapidly or incoherently. **gabble** *n.*

gab-bro (gab´rō) *n.* A granular igneous rock. **gabbroic, gabbroid** *adj.*

gab-fest *n.* Informal gathering or meeting where people engage in prolonged, general talk.

ga-ble (gā´bl) *n. Arch.* The portion of a building enclosed by the sloping ends.

gad (gad) *v.* To wander about restlessly with little or no purpose. **gadder** *n.*

gad-a-bout (gad´a bout´) *n. Slang* One who goes about seeking excitement and fun.

gadg-et (gaj´it) *n. Slang* A small device or tool used in performing miscellaneous jobs, especially in the kitchen.

ga-doid (gā´doid) *adj.* Resembling or related to the cod family.

gad-o-lin-i-um (gad´o lin´ē um) *n.* A metallic element, silvery-white in color, of the rare-earth series, which is highly magnetic.

ga-droon (ga drön´) *n.* The ornamental carving on a rounded molding.

gad-wall (gad´wal´) *n.* A grayish brown duck.

gaff (gaf) *n.* A sharp iron hook used for landing fish. *Naut.* A spar on the top edge of a fore-and-aft sail. *Slang* Abuse or harsh treatment. **gaff** *v.* To land or hook with a gaff; to deceive.

gaffe (gaf) *n.* A social blunder; mistake; a faux pas.

gaf-fer (gaf´êr) *n.* An old man; a lighting electrician.

gag (gag) *n.* Something, as a wadded cloth, forced into or over the mouth to prevent someone from speaking or crying out; an obstacle to or any restraint of free speech, such as by censorship. *Slang* A practical joke or hoax. **to pull a gag** To perform a practical joke on someone. **gag** *v.* To keep a person from speaking out by means of a gag; to choke on something.

ga-ga (gä´gä) *adj. Slang* Crazy; silly; wildly enthusiastic..

gage (gāj) *n.* Something that is given as security for an action to be performed; a pledge; anything, as a glove, thrown down as a challenge to fight or a challenge for combat.

gag-gle (gag´l) *n.* A flock of geese; a group; a cluster.

gag rule *n.* A law or rule that prevents discussion or expression of an opinion.

gag-ster *n.* A person who plays practical jokes.

gahn-ite *n.* A dark-colored mineral containing zinc and aluminum.

gai-e-ty (gā´i tē) *n., pl.* **gaieties** The state of being happy; cheerfulness; fun, festive activity.

gai-ly (gā´lē) *adj.* A gay or cheerful manner; showily or brightly.

gain (gān) *v.* To earn or acquire possession of something; to succeed in winning a victory; to develop an increase of; to put on weight; to secure as a profit; to improve progress; to draw nearer to.

gait (gāt) *n.* A way or manner of moving on foot; one of the foot movements in which a horse steps or runs.

gai-ter (gā´têr) *n.* A covering, as of leather or canvas, that covers the leg and extends from the knee to the instep; an old-fashioned shoe with a high top and elastic sides.

gal (gal) *n. Slang* A girl.

ga-la (gā´la) *n.* A festive celebration; party. **gala** *adj.*

ga-lac-tic (ga lak´tic) *adj.* Relating to a galaxy, especially the Milky Way.

ga-lac-tose (ga lak´tōs) *n.* The sugar typically occurring in lactose.

ga-la-go *n.* A nocturnal African primate with a long tail and long hind limbs enabling them to leap at great lengths.

ga-lah (ga lä´) *n.* A showy Australian cockatoo that is very destructive in wheat growing areas.

gal-an-tine (gal´an tēn´) *n.* A cold dish that consists of fish or meat that has been poached, stuffed, and covered with aspic.

ga-lax (gā´lax) *n.* An evergreen herb of the southeastern United States, whose leaves are widely used by florists.

gal-ax-y (gal´ak sē) *n., pl.* **galaxies** *Astron.* Any of the very large systems of stars, nebulae, or other celestial bodies that constitute a universe; a brilliant, distinguished group or assembly. **Galaxy** The Milky Way.

gal-ba-num (gal´ba num) *n.* A greenish or brown aromatic, bitter gum resin used for medicinal purposes.

gale (gāl) *n. Meteor.* A very powerful wind stronger than a stiff breeze; an outburst, as of hilarity.

ga-le-na (ga lē´na) *n.* A metallic, dull gray mineral that is the principal ore of lead.

gal-i-ma-ti-as (gal´i mā´shē as) *n.* A confused mixture of words.

gal-i-ot *or* **gal-li-ot** *n.* A small galley or sailing ship, moved by oars and sails.

gall (gol) *n. Physiol.* The bitter fluid secreted by the liver; bile; bitterness of feeling; animosity; impudence; something that irritates. **gall** *v.* To injure the skin by friction; to chafe.

gal-lant (gal´ənt) *adj.* Dashing in dress or appearance; majestic; stately; chivalrously attentive to women; courteous; having a fine appearance; courage; heroic. **gallantly** *adv.*

gal-lant-ry (gal´ən trē) *n., pl.* **gallantries** Nobility and bravery; a gallant act.

gall-blad-der *or* **gall bladder** *n.* The small sac under the right lobe of the liver that stores bile.

gal-le-on (gal´ē on) *n.* A large, three-masted sailing ship.

gal-ley *n., pl.* **galleys** (gal´ē) A long medieval ship that was propelled by sails and oars; the long tray used by printers to hold set type; a printer's proof made from composed type, used to detect and correct errors.

gallic acid *n.* A slightly yellow crystalline acid found in plant galls and used as a developer in photography.

gal-li-gas-kins *n.* Very loose-fitting trousers of the 16th century.

gal-li-mau-fry (gal´i mo´frē) *n.* A hodgepodge; a jumbled mixture.

gal-li-nip-per *n.* A large mosquito.

gall-ing (gä´ling) *adj.* Being very irritated; annoying; vexing.

gal-li-um (gal´ē um) *n.* A silvery metallic element used in semiconductor technology and as a component of various alloys that melt at low temperatures, symbolized by Ga.

gal-li-vant (gal´i vant) *v.* To roam about in search of amusement or pleasure; to flirt; to run about.

gal-lon (gal´on) *n.* A liquid measurement used in the United States, equal to 4 quarts; in Great Britain, a liquid measurement which equals 4 imperial quarts; a dry measurement that equals 1/8 bushel.

gal-loon (ga lön´) *n.* A trimming of lace, or embroidery with metallic threads.

gal-lows (gal´ōz) *n.* A framework of two or more upright beams and a cross-beam, used for execution by hanging.

gall-stone (gol´stōn´) *n. Pathol.* A small, hard concretion of cholesterol crystals that sometimes forms in the gall bladder or bile passages.

ga-loot (ga löt´) *n.* A strange or foolish person.

ga-lore (ga lōr´) *adj.* In great numbers; abundant; plentiful.

ga-losh (ga losh´) *n., pl.* **galoshes** A waterproof overshoe which is worn in bad weather.

ga-lumph (ga lumph´) *v.* To bump or gallop along clumsily.

gal-van-ic (gal van´ik) *adj.* Produced by or pertaining to galvanism; stimulating or shocking.

gal-va-nism (gal´və niz´um) *n.* Electricity that is produced by chemical action. *Med.* A therapeutic application of continuous electric current from voltaic cells.

gal-va-nom-e-ter (gal´və nom´i tèr) *n. Electr.* An apparatus for detecting the presence of an electric current and for determining its strength and direction.

gal-va-no-scope (gal´və no skōp´) *n.* An instrument used to detect the direction and presence of an electric current by the deflecting of a magnetic needle.

gam *n.* A school of whales.

gam-bit (gam´bit) *n.* In chess, an opening in which a piece is sacrificed for a favorable position; a maneuver that is carefully planned.

gam-ble (gam´bl) *v.* To take a chance on an uncertain outcome as in a contest or by buying a lottery number. **gamble** *n.* Any risky venture. **gambler** *n.*

gam-boge (gam bōj´) *n.* A gum resin that is orange to brown in color and is used as a yellow pigment.

gam-bol (gam´bol) *v.* To frolic, skip, or leap about in play. **gambol** *n.* Frolic; a playful leap or skip.

gambrel roof *n. Archit.* A ridged roof with the slope broken on each side, the lower slope steeper than the upper.

gam-bu-sia *n.* Any of various surface-feeding fishes which are stocked in fresh waters to eliminate mosquito larvae.

game (gām) *n.* A contest governed by specific rules; a way of entertaining oneself; amusement; a calculated way to do something; animals, fish, or birds that are hunted for sport or food.

gamely *adv.* In a courageous manner.

gam-e-tan-gi-um *n.* An organ or cell in which gametes are developed or produced.

gam-ete (gam´ēt) *n. Biol.* Either of two mature reproductive cells, an ovum or a sperm, which produce a zygote when united.

gam-in (gam´in) *n.* A homeless child who wanders the streets of a town or city.

gam-ma (gam´a) *n.* The third letter of the Greek alphabet. **gamma** *adj.* In the third position in the structure of a molecule.

gamma globulin *n. Biochem.* A globulin that is present in blood plasma and contains antibodies effective against certain infectious diseases.

gam-ma ray *n. Phys.* A radiation quantity or a photon emitted by a radioactive substance.

gam-mer (gam´ėr) *n.* An elderly woman.

gam-mon (gam´on) *n.* A cured ham; in the game of backgammon, a double victory in which a player removes all his pieces before the other player removes any.

gam-ut (gam´ut) *n.* The whole range,

series, or extent of anything.

gam-y (gā´mē) *adj.* Having the strong flavor of game, especially when slightly tainted; scandalous. **gaminess** *n.*

ga-nef (gä´nef) *n. Slang* Petty thief; rascal; an unscrupulous person.

gang (gang) *n.* A group of persons who are organized and work together or socialize regularly; a group of adolescent hoodlums or criminals. **gang up on** To attack as a group.

gan-gling (gang´gling) *adj.* Awkwardly tall and thin; lanky and loosely built.

gan-gli-on (gang´glē an) *n., pl.* **ganglia** *Physiol.* A collection of nerve cells located outside the spinal cord or brain.

gan-grene (gang´grēn) *n. Pathol.* The death and decay of tissue in the body caused by a failure in the circulation of the blood supply. **gangrenous** *adj.*

gang-ster (gang´stėr) *n.* A member of a criminal gang; a racketeer; a mobster.

gap (gap) *n.* An opening or wide crack, as in a wall; a cleft; a deep notch or ravine in a mountain ridge, offering passage.

gape (gāp) *v.* To open the mouth wide, as in yawning; to stare in amazement with the mouth wide open; to become widely separated or open. **gape** *n.*

gar (gär) *n.* A fish having a spear-like snout and elongated body covered with bony plates; a garfish.

garb (gärb) *n.* Clothing; a particular way of dressing. **garb** *n.*

gar-bage (gär bij) *n.* Food wastes, consisting of unwanted or unusable pieces of meat, vegetables, and other food products; any unwanted or worthless material; trash.

gar-ble (gär´bl) *v.* To mix up or confuse; to change or distort the meaning of with the intent to mislead or misrepresent. **garble** *n.* The act or process of garbling. **garbler** *n.*

gar-den (gär´den) *n.* A place for growing flowers, vegetables, or fruit; a piece of ground commonly used as a public recreation area. **garden** *v.* To work in or make into a garden. **garden** *adj.* Produced in a garden; referring to a garden. **gardener** *n.*

Garfield, James Abram *n.* (1831-1881) The twentieth president of the United States from March through September of 1881, assassinated.

gar-gan-tu-an (gär gan´chö an) *adj.* Of enormous size; immense.

gar-gle (gär´gl) *v.* To force air from the lungs through a liquid held in the back of the mouth and throat. **gargle** *n.* A liquid preparation used to wash the mouth and throat. **gargle** *n.*

gar-goyle (gär´goil) *n.* A waterspout made or carved to represent a grotesque animal or human figure, projecting

from a gutter to throw rain away from the wall of a building.

gar-ish (gâr´ish) *adj.* Too showy and bright; gaudy. **garishly** *adv.*

gar-lic (gär´lik) *n.* A plant related to the onion with a compound bulb which contains a strong odor and flavor, used as a seasoning. **garlicky** *adj.*

garlic salt *n.* A condiment made of salt and ground dried garlic.

gar-ment (gär´ment) *n.* An article of clothing.

gar-ner (gär´nėr) *v.* To gather and store; to accumulate; to collect; to acquire.

gar-net (gär´nit) *n.* A dark red silicate mineral used as a gemstone and as an abrasive.

garnet paper *n.* An abrasive paper coated with crushed garnet.

gar-ni-er-ite *n.* A mineral consisting of hydrous nickel magnesium silicate; an important ore of nickel.

gar-nish (gär´nish) *v.* To add something to, as to decorate or embellish; to add decorative or flavorful touches to food or drink. **garnish** *n.*

gar-ret (gar´it) *n.* A room in an attic.

gar-ri-son (gar´i son) *n.* The military force that is permanently placed in a fort or town; a military post.

gar-ron (gar´on) *n.* A small workhorse.

gar-ru-lous (gar´a lus) *adj.* Given to continual talkativeness; chatty. very talkative. **garrulousness** *n.*

gar-ter (gär´tėr) *n.* A band or strap that is worn to hold a stocking in place; a band that holds up a sleeve. **garter**

garth (gärth) *n.* A small yard.

gas (gas) *n., pl.* **gases** A form of matter capable of expanding to fill a container and taking on the shape of the container; a combustible mixture used as fuel; gasoline; a gas used to produce an irritating, poisonous, or asphyxiating atmosphere. **gas** *v.* **gassy** *adj.*

gas-con (gas´kon) *n.* A boastful person.

gash (gash) *n.* A deep cut. **gash** *v.* To make a deep cut in.

gas-ket (gas´kit) *n. Mech.* A rubber seal or ring used between machine parts or around pipe joints to prevent leakage.

gas-o-hol *n.* A fuel blended from unleaded gasoline and ethanol.

gas-o-line (gas´o lēn´) *n.* A colorless, highly flammable mixture of liquid hydrocarbons made from crude petroleum and used as a fuel and a solvent.

gasp (gasp) *v.* To inhale suddenly and sharply, as from fear or surprise; to make labored or violent attempts to breathe. **gasp** *n.*

gas-tral (ga stral´) *adj.* Relating to the stomach or digestive tract.

gas-trec-to-my *n.* The surgical removal

of the stomach or a part of it.

gas-tric (gas´trik) *adj.* Of or pertaining to the stomach.

gastric juice *n. Biochem.* The digestive fluid secreted by the stomach glands, containing several enzymes.

gastric ulcer *n. Pathol.* An ulcer formed on the stomach lining, often caused by excessive secretion of gastric juices.

gas-tri-tis (ga strī´tis) *n. Pathol.* Inflammation of the stomach lining.

gas-tro-en-ter-ol-o-gy (gas tro ent´er ŏl o jē) *n.* The medical study of the pathology and diseases of the stomach and intestines. **gastroenterologist** *n.*

gas-tro-in-tes-ti-nal *adj.* Relating to or affecting the stomach and intestines.

gas-tron-o-my (ga stron´o mē) *n.* The art of good eating. **gastronome** *n.* **gastronomic** *adj.* **gastronomical** *adj.*

gas-tro-scope *n.* An instrument for viewing the interior of the stomach.

gas-tro-vas-cu-lar *adj.* Functioning in both circulation and digestion.

gat (gat) *n. Slang* A pistol; short for Gatling gun.

gate (gāt) *n.* A movable opening in a wall or fence, commonly swinging on hinges, that closes or opens; a valve-like device for controlling the passage of gas or water through a conduit or dam; the total paid admission receipts or number of attendees at a public performance.

gath-er (gath´ĕr) *v.* To bring or come together into one place or group; to harvest or pick; to increase or gain; to accumulate; to fold or pleat a cloth by pulling it along a thread. **gather** *n.*

gath-er-ing *n.* The act of assembling; that which is gathered.

gauche (gōsh) *adj.* Socially awkward; clumsy; boorish. **gauchely** *adv.*

gau-cho (gow chō´) *n.* A cowboy of South America.

gaud *n.* An ornament or trinket.

gaud-y (gaw´dē) *adj.* Too decorated to be in good taste. **gaudiness** *n.*

gauge (gāg) *n.* A standard measurement, dimension, or capacity; an instrument used for measuring, testing, or registering; the distance between rails of a railroad; the diameter of the bore of a shotgun barrel. **gauge** *v.* To determine the capacity, contents or volume of; to estimate; to evaluate.

gaug-er *n.* A customs official who measures and inspects dutiable bulk goods.

gaunt (gont) *adj.* Thin and bony; haggard; gloomy or desolate in appearance.

ga-vage (ga väzh´) *n.* Forced feeding of nutrients into the stomach, by means of a flexible stomach tube and a force pump.

gave *v.* Past tense of give.

gav-el (gav´el) *n.* A mallet used to call for order or attention. **gavel** *v.*

ga-vi-al (gā´vē al) *n.* A large crocodile found in India, with long, slender jaws.

ga-votte (ga vot´) *n.* A dance performed by lifting the feet rather than sliding them. **gavotte** *v.*

gawk (gawk) *v.* To gape; to stare stupidly.

gay (gā) *adj.* Merry; happy and carefree; brightly ornamental or colorful; homosexual. **gay** *n.* A homosexual.

gaze (gāz) *v.* To look steadily or intently at something in admiration or wonder; to stare.

ga-zelle (ga zel´) *n.* A small, gracefully formed antelope of Asia and Africa, having curved horns and large eyes.

ga-zette (ga zet´) *n.* A newspaper; an official publication. **gazette** *v.* To publish or announce in a gazette.

gaz-et-teer (gaz´i tēr´) *n.* A dictionary consisting of geographical facts.

gaz-pa-cho (gaz pä´chō) *n.* A cold soup made from vegetables, spices, oils, etc.

gds *abbr.* Goods.

ge-an-ti-cline (jē ant´ē klīn) *n.* A great upward fold of the earth's surface.

gear (gēr) *n.* A toothed wheel which interacts with another toothed part to transmit motion; an assembly of parts that work together for a special purpose; equipment. **gear** *v.* To regulate, match, or suit something.

gee (jē) *v.* A command given to horses or other work animals, directing them to turn right. **gee** *interj.* An expression of surprise or shock.

geese *n.* Plural of goose.

gee-zer (gēzĕr) *n. Slang* An old, odd, or eccentric man.

ge-gen-schein *n.* A faint, round patch of light sometimes seen in the sky at night.

Geiger counter (gī´gĕr koun´tĕr) *n. Phys.* An instrument used to measure, detect, and record cosmic rays and nuclear radiation.

gel (jel) *n. Chem.* A colloid that is in a more solid than liquid form. **gel** *v.*

geld (geld) *v.* To castrate or spay an animal, especially a horse.

gel-id (jel´id) *adj.* Very cold; frigid. .

gel-ig-nite (jel´ig nīt´) *n.* Dynamite with an absorbent base of potassium or sodium nitrate and some wood pulp.

gem (jem) *n.* A cut and polished precious or semiprecious stone; a person or thing that is highly treasured. **gem** *v.* To decorate with or as with gems.

gem-i-nate (jem´i nāt) *v.* To become paired or arrange in pairs.

gem-mip-a-rous *adj.* Reproducing by buds.

gem-mule (jem´ūl) *n.* A small bud.

gem-ol-o-gy (je mol´o jē) *n.* The study of gems. **gemological** *adj.*

gems-bok *n.* A large antelope of southern Africa, strikingly marked and having long straight horns and a long tail.

gem-stone *n.* A mineral or petrified material which can be refined by cutting and polishing and used in jewelry.

gen *abbr.* Gender; general; generally.

gen-darme (zhän´därm) *n.* A policeman in France.

gen-der (jen´dèr) *n. Gram.* A member of a category, such as feminine, masculine, and neuter, into which words are divided and which determine agreement with or selection of modifiers or grammatical forms; the quality of being of the male or female sex.

gene (jēn) *n. Biol.* A functional hereditary unit which occupies a fixed location on a chromosome and controls or acts in the transmission of hereditary characteristics.

ge-ne-al-o-gy (jē´nē ol´o jē) *n., pl.* **genealogies** A record, table, or account showing the descent of a family, group, or person from an ancestor; the study of ancestry. **genealogical** *adj.*

gene mutation *n.* Alteration in an organism due to a chemical rearrangement within the molecules of a gene.

gen-er-a-ble *adj.* Capable of being generated or produced.

gen-er-al-i-za-tion (jen´èr a lizā´shan) *n.* Something arrived at by generalizing, such as a broad, overall statement or conclusion.

gen-er-ate (jen´e rāt´) *v.* To cause to be; to produce; to bring into existence, especially by a chemical or physical process. **generative** *adj.*

gen-er-a-tor (jen´e rā´tèr) *n. Mech.* A machine that changes mechanical energy into electrical energy.

gen-er-a-trix *n.* A point, line, or surface whose motion generates a line, surface, figure, or solid.

ge-ner-ic (je ner´ik) *adj.* Relating to or characteristic of an entire class or group; pertaining to a class or relating to a class of merchandise that does not have a trademark. **generically** *adv.*

gen-er-ous (jen´èr us) *adj.* Sharing freely; abundant; overflowing. **generosity** *n.* **generously** *adv.*

gen-e-sis (jen´i sis) *n., pl.* **geneses** The act or state of originating. **Genesis** The first book of the Old Testament.

ge-net-ic (je net´ik) *adj.* Of or pertaining to the origin or development of something; of or relating to genetics.

genetic code *n. Biochem.* The biochemical basis of heredity that specifies the amino acid sequence in the synthesis of proteins and on which heredity is based.

ge-net-ics *n.* The science that deals with the hereditary and evolutionary differences and similarities of related organisms, as produced by the interaction of genes.

ge-ne-va (je nē´va) *n.* An alcoholic liquor flavored with juniper berries.

Ge-ne-va Con-ven-tion *n.* The international agreement signed in 1864 at Geneva which governs the wartime treatment of prisoners of war and of the wounded, sick, and the dead in battle.

gen-ial (je nē´al) *adj.* Cheerful, kind, pleasant and good-humored in disposition or manner. **geniality** *n.* **genially** *adv.*

gen-ic (jen´ik) *adj.* Pertaining to a gene or genes.

ge-nic-u-late (je nik´yu lat) *adj.* Bent at an angle like the knee.

ge-nie (jē´nē) *n.* A supernatural creature, capable of taking on human form, who does one's bidding.

gen-i-tal (jen´i tal) *adj.* Of or pertaining to the reproductive organs or the process of reproduction.

genitals (jen´i talz) *n., pl.* The external sexual organs. **genitalia** *n.*

gen-i-tive (jen´i tiv) *adj. Gram.* Indicating origin, source, or possession. **genitive** *n.* The genitive case.

gen-i-tor *n.* A male parent.

gen-i-to-u-ri-nar-y (jen´i tō yer´iner´ē) *adj. Anat.* Of or pertaining to the genital and urinary organs or their functions.

gen-ius (jēn´yus) *n., pl.* **geniuses** Exceptional intellectual ability or creative power; a strong, natural talent; a person who exerts powerful influence over another.

gen-o-cide (jen´o sīd´) *n.* The deliberate and systematic extermination or destruction of a political, racial, or cultural group.

ge-nome (jē´nŏm) *n. Biol.* One of the two sets of chromosomes in a zygote.

gen-re *n.* A category of a specific artistic or literary accomplishment characterized by a particular form, technique, style, or subject matter.

gens (jenz) *n., pl.* **gentes** In ancient Rome, a clan that included families of the same name that have descended through the male line.

gent (jent) *n. Slang* A gentleman.

gen-teel (jen tēl´) *adj.* Elegant; refined or well-bred; polite; stylish or fashionable. **genteelly** *adv.*

gen-tile (jen´tīl) *n.* A person who is not a Jew, especially a Christian; among Mormons, of or relating to non-Mormons; a heathen or pagan.

gen-til-i-ty (jen til´i tē) n. The quality of being genteel; the members of the upper class; well-born or well-bred persons collectively.

gen-tle (jen´tl) adj. Moderate; not harsh, severe, rough, or loud; easily handled or managed; docile; not sudden or steep. **gentle** v. To tame; to calm. **gently** adv. **gentleness** n.

gen-try (jen´trē) n. People of good family or high social standing; the aristocracy; in England, the social class that is considered the upper ranks of the middle class.

gen-u-flect (jen´ū flekt´) v. To bend down on one knee, as in worship.

gen-u-ine (jen´ū in) adj. Real; authentic; not counterfeit or spurious; not hypocritical; sincere. **genuinely** adv.

ge-nus (jē´nus) n., pl. **genera** Biol. A group or category of plants or animals usually including several species that share certain specific characteristics.

geo- prefix Ground; earth; soil.

ge-o-cen-tric (jē´ō sen´trik) adj. Of or relating to the earth's center; formulated on the assumption that the earth is the center of the universe. **geocentrically** adv. **geocentrical** adj.

ge-o-chem-is-try (jē´ō kem´i strē) n. A branch of chemistry that deals with the chemical composition of the earth's crust. **geochemical** adj.

ge-ode (jē´ōd) n. Geol. A hollow rock having a cavity lined with crystals.

geodesic dome n. A vaulted or domed structure of lightweight straight elements that form interlocking polygons.

geodesic line (jē ō des´ik) n. Math. The shortest line between two fixed points on a sphere or other defined surface.

ge-od-e-sy (jē od´i sē) n. The geologic science dealing with the determination of the shape, area, and curvature of the earth. **geodesist** n. **geodetic** adj.

ge-og-no-sy (jē og´ne sē) n. That branch of geology that deals with the constituent parts of the earth, its description of land, air and water, its crust, and interior.

ge-og-ra-phy (jē og´ra fē) n. The science that deals with the earth's natural climate, resources, and population. **geographer** n. **geographic, geographical** adj. **geographically** adv.

ge-oid n. The surface around or within the earth which coincides with the mean sea level over the ocean and its extension under the continents.

ge-ol-o-gy (jē ol´o jē) n., pl. **geologies** The science that deals with the history, origin, and structure of the earth. **geologic, geological** adj.

ge-o-mag-net-ic adj. Relating to the earth's magnetism. **geomagnetism** n.

ge-om-e-ter n. A geometrid moth or its larva; a specialist in geometry.

ge-o-met-ric (jē´ō me´trik) adj. According to or pertaining to the rules and principles of geometry; increasing in a geometric progression.

geometric progression n. A sequence of numbers, as 4, 8, 16, 32 where each term is the product of a constant factor and the term that precedes it.

ge-om-e-trid n. A small, slender-bodied, delicate moth having broad wings, whose larvae are commonly called inchworms.

ge-om-e-try (jē om´i trē) n. The branch of mathematics that deals with the measurement, properties, and relationships of lines, angles, points, surfaces and solids.

ge-o-mor-phic adj. Relating to the form or surface features of the earth.

ge-o-mor-phol-o-gy n. The science that deals with the origin, development, and characteristics of the surface features of the earth.

ge-oph-a-gy n. The practice of eating earthy substances such as clay.

ge-o-phys-ics (jē´ō fiz´iks) n. The science of the earth and its relation to forces acting on it; it includes meteorology, magnetism, volcanology, and radioactivity.

ge-o-pol-i-tics (jē´ō pol´i tiks) n. The study of the influence of economic and geographical factors on the politics and policies of a nation or region.

geor-gette n. A fine transparent variety of silk crepe woven from hard-twisted yarns to give a dull pebbly surface.

Georgia n. A state located in the southeastern part of the United States; statehood January 2, 1788; state capital Atlanta.

ge-o-strat-e-gy n. A group of factors, geographical, political, and strategic, that are characteristic of a specific area.

ge-o-stroph-ic adj. Relating to the deflective force caused by the earth's rotation.

ge-o-tec-ton-ic adj. Relating to the structure, form, and arrangement of the earth's crust due to faulting or folding.

ge-o-ther-mal or **ge-o-ther-mic (jē´ō ther´ mal)** adj. Relating to the internal heat of the earth.

ge-ot-ro-pism n. The tendency to turn gravitationally toward the earth.

ge-ra-ni-ol n. An unsaturated alcohol, chiefly used in soaps and perfumes.

ge-ra-ni-um (ji rā´ne um) n. A plant having rounded leaves and clusters of pink, red, or white flowers; a plant of the genus Pelargonium, with divided leaves and purplish or pink flowers.

ge-rar-di-a n. An herb belonging to the

figwort family, having showy purple, pink, or yellow flowers with distended bases.

ger-a-tol-o-gy *n.* The study that addresses the decline of life of animals threatened with extinction.

ger-bil (jer´bil) *n.* An animal of the rodent family found in the desert regions of Africa and Asia Minor, having long hind legs and a long tail; a popular pet.

ger-i-at-rics (jer´e a´triks) *n.* The medical study that deals with the structural changes, diseases, physiology, and hygiene of old age. **geriatric** *adj.* **geriatrician** *n.*

germ (jerm) *n.* A small cell or organic structure from which a new organism may develop; a microorganism which causes disease. *Biol.* A reproductive cell.

Ger-man (jer´man) *n.* The language of Germany; an inhabitant or native of Germany.

ger-mane (jèr mān) *adj.* Relevant to what is being considered or discussed.

Ger-man-ic (jèr man´ik) *adj.* Relating to the language or customs of the Dutch, German, English, Afrikaans, Flemish, or Scandinavians.

ger-ma-ni-um (jèr mā´nē um) *n.* A grayish-white element widely used in electronics and optics, symbolized by Ge.

Ger-man meas-les *n.* *Med.* A contagious viral disease accompanied by sore throat, fever, and a skin rash; a disease capable of causing defects in infants born to mothers infected during the first stages of pregnancy.

German Shepherd *n.* A large breed of dog, which is often trained to help the police and the blind.

Germany *n.* A country in western Europe.

germ cell *n.* An egg or sperm cell.

ger-mi-cide (jer´mi sīd´) *n.* An agent used to destroy microorganisms or disease germs. **germicidal** *adj.*

ger-mi-nal (jer´mi nal) *adj.* Of or relating to a germ or germ cell; of or in the earliest stage of development.

ger-mi-nant *adj.* Having the ability to gradually grow and develop.

ger-mi-nate (jer´mi nāt´) *v.* To begin to grow, develop, or sprout. **germination** *n.* **germinative** *adj.*

germ plasm *n.* *Biol.* The part of the protoplasm of a germ cell containing the chromosomes and genes.

ger-on-tol-o-gy (jer´on tol´o jē) *n.* The study of the processes and phenomena of aging. **gerontological** *adj.* **gerontologic** *adj.* **gerontologist** *n.*

ger-ry-man-der (jer´i man´dèr) *v.* To divide a voting area so as to advance unfairly the interests of a political

party; to adjust or adapt to one's advantage.

ger-und (jer´und) *n.* *Gram.* A verb form that is used as a noun, such as *walking*.

ges-so (jes´ō) *n.* Plaster of Paris prepared with glue used in painting, etc.

gest (jest) *n.* A notable deed or feat.

ge-stalt (ge shält´) *n.* A pattern as a unified whole, with properties which cannot be derived by summation of its individual parts.

ge-sta-po (ge stä´pō) *n.* The secret police in Germany under the Nazi regime, known for its brutality.

ges-tate (jes´tāt) *v.* To conceive and gradually mature in the mind; to carry in the womb during pregnancy.

ges-ta-tion (je stä´shan) *n.* The carrying of a developing offspring in the uterus; pregnancy. **gestational** *adj.*

ges-tic *adj.* Pertaining to motions or gestures of the body.

ges-tic-u-late (je stik´ū lāt´) *v.* To make expressive or emphatic gestures, as in speaking. **gesticulation** *n.*

ges-ture (jes´chèr) *n.* A bodily motion, especially with the hands in speaking, to emphasize some idea or emotion. **gesture** *v.* To make gestures.

ge-sund-heit (ge zun´hīt) *interj.* A German phrase used to wish good health to a person who has just sneezed.

GET In computer science, a program instruction to fetch data, a file or command from a non-contiguous source.

get (get) *v.* To come into possession of, as by receiving, winning, earning, or buying. **to get ahead** To attain success. **to get back at** To revenge oneself on. **to get by** To manage; to survive. **to get one's goat** To make somebody angry.

get-a-ble *adj.* Accessible; procurable; obtainable.

get-a-way (get´a wā´) *n.* The act of or instance of escaping by a criminal; a start, as of a race.

get-to-geth-er (get´to geth´ér) *n.* A small, informal family or social gathering.

get-up (get´up´) *n.* An outfit; a costume.

ge-um *n.* A perennial herb of the rose family with white, purple, or yellow flowers.

gew-gaw (gū´go) *n.* A little ornamental article of small value.

gey-ser (gī´zér) *n.* A natural hot spring that intermittently ejects hot water and steam.

ghast-ly (gast´lē) *adj.* Horrible; terrifying; very unpleasant or bad; ghost-like in appearance; deathly pale.

ghat (gät) *n.* A broad flight of steps that leads down to the edge of a river.

gher-kin (ger´kin) *n.* A very small,

prickly cucumber pickled as a relish.

ghet-to (get´ō) *n.* A run-down section of a city in which a minority group lives because of poverty or social pressure.

ghost (gōst) *n.* The spirit of a dead person which is believed to appear to or haunt living persons; a spirit; a ghostwriter; a false, faint secondary television image.

ghost-ly *adj.* Pertaining to or relating to a ghost; suggestive of ghosts.

ghost town *n.* A town that once flourished but is now deserted.

ghost-writer *n.* A person hired to write for another person and to give credit for the writing or speaking to that other person.

ghoul (gōl) *n.* A person who robs graves; in Moslem legend, an evil spirit which plunders graves and feeds on corpses. **ghoulish** *adj.* **ghoulishly** *adv.*

GI (jē´ī´) *n., pl.* **GIs** *or* **GI's** An enlisted person in the United States armed forces. **GI** *adj.* In conformity with military regulations or customs. **GI** *v.* To clean or scrub in preparation for or as if for a military inspection. **GI** *abbr.* Government issue; general issue; gastrointestinal.

gi-ant (jī´ant) *n.* A legendary man-like being of supernatural size and strength; one of great power, importance, or size; large. **giant** *adj.*

giant powder *n.* A form of dynamite made of nitroglycerin and kieselguhr.

gib (gib) *n.* A thin plate of metal or other material to hold parts together or in place.

gib-ber (jib´ér) *v.* To talk or chatter incoherently or unintelligibly.

gib-ber-ish (jib´ér ish) *n.* Meaningless speech.

gib-bet (jib´it) *n.* A gallows. **gibbet** *v.* To execute by hanging on a gibbet.

gib-bon (gib´on) *n.* A slender, long-armed Asian ape.

gib-bous (gib´us) *adj.* The moon or a planet which is seen with more than half but not all of the apparent disk illuminated. **gibbously** *adv.* **gibbousness** *n.*

gibe (jīb) *v.* To ridicule or make taunting remarks. **gibe** *n.*

gib-let (jib´lit) *or* **giblets** *n.* The heart, liver, and gizzard of a fowl.

gid *n.* A disease of sheep caused by infestation of the brain caused with a larval tapeworm.

gid-dy (gid´ē) *adj.* Affected by a reeling or whirling sensation; dizzy; frivolous and silly; flighty. **giddily** *adv.* **giddiness** *n.*

gift (gift) *n.* Something that is given from one person to another; a natural aptitude; a talent.

gift-ed *adj.* The state of having a special ability.

gig (gig) *n.* A light, two-wheeled carriage drawn by one horse. *Naut.* A speedy, light rowboat; a spear with forks or prongs used for fishing. *Slang* A job, especially an engagement to play music. *Milit. Slang* A demerit; a punishment to military personnel.

gigabyte In computer science, one thousand million (one billion) bytes.

gi-gan-tic (jī gan´tik) *adj.* Of tremendous or extraordinary size; large; huge. **gigantically** *adv.*

gig-gle (gig´l) *v.* To laugh in high-pitched, repeated, short sounds. **giggle** *n.* **giggler** *n.* **giggly** *adj.*

gig-o-lo (jig´o lō´) *n.* A man who is supported by a woman not his wife; a man who is paid to be an escort or dancing partner.

gigue (zhēg) *n.* A lively dance step.

Gila monster (hē´la mon´ster) *n.* A large, venomous lizard of the southwestern United States desert areas having an orange and black body.

gild (gild) *v.* To coat with a thin layer of gold; to brighten or adorn. **gild** *v.* To add unnecessary ornamentation. **gilded** *adj.* **gilder** *n.*

gild-ing *n.* A thin coating of gold leaf; a superficially attractive appearance.

gill (gil) *n. Zool.* The organ, of fishes and various other aquatic invertebrates, used for taking oxygen from water. **gill** *n.* A liquid measure that equals 1/4 pint.

gilt (gilt) *adj.* Covered with gold; of the color of gold. **gilt** *n.* A thin layer of gold or a gold-colored substance which is applied to a surface.

gilt-edge *or* **gilt-edged (gilt´ejd´)** *adj.* Of the highest value or the best quality.

gim-bals (jim´balz) *n.* A three-ringed device that keeps an object supported on its level, as the compass of a ship.

gim-crack (jim´krak´) *n.* A showy and useless object of little or no value.

gim-let (gim´lit) *n.* A small, sharp tool with a bar handle and a pointed, spiral tip which is used for boring holes.

gim-mal *n.* A series of interlocked rings.

gim-mick (gim´ik) *n.* A tricky feature that is obscured or misrepresented; a tricky device, especially when used dishonestly or secretly; a gadget. **gimmickry** *n.* **gimmicky** *adj.*

gimp (gimp) *n. Slang* A person who walks with a limp; a cripple. **gimp** *v.* **gimpy** *adj.*

gin (jin) *n.* An aromatic, clear alcoholic liquor distilled from grain and flavored with juniper berries; a machine used to separate seeds from cotton fibers; a snare or trap for game. **gin** *v.* To remove the seeds from cotton with a gin; to trap game in a gin.

gin-ger (jin´jér) *n.* A tropical Asian plant that has a pungent, aromatic root, used in medicine and cooking. **ginger** *v.*

ginger ale *n.* An effervescent soft drink flavored with ginger.

ginger beer *n.* A sweet, nonalcoholic, effervescing drink flavored with ginger.

gin-ger-bread (jin´jér bred) *n.* A dark, ginger and molasses flavored cake or cookie.

gin-ger-ly (jin´jér lē) *adv.* Doing something very cautiously and carefully. **gingerliness** *n.* **gingery** *adj.*

gin-ger-snap (jin´jér snap´) *n.* A brittle molasses and ginger cookie.

ging-ham (ging´am) *n.* A cotton fabric woven in solid colors and checks.

gin-gi-li (jin´ji lē) *n.* The sesame plant or its oil.

gin-gi-val *adj.* Referring to the gums.

gin-gi-vi-tis (jin´ji vī´tis) *n. Pathol.* Inflammation of the gums.

gink-go (gingk´gō) *n., pl.* **ginkgoes** A large Chinese shade tree cultivated in the United States, with edible fruit or nuts.

gin rummy *n.* A variety of the card game rummy.

gin-seng (jin´seng) *n.* An herb native to China and North America with an aromatic root believed to have medicinal properties.

Gip-sy (jip´sē) *n. & adj.* Variation of gypsy.

gi-raffe (ji raf´) *n., pl.* **giraffes** *or* **giraffe** The tallest of all mammals, having an extremely long neck and very long legs, living in Africa.

gir-an-dole *n.* Radiating and showy fireworks; an ornamented branched candlestick; a central jewel in a pendant.

gir-a-sol *n.* A variety of opal showing a reddish color when turned toward the light.

gird (gerd) *v.* To surround, encircle, or attach with or as if with a belt.

gird-er (ger´dér) *n.* A strong, horizontal beam, as of steel or wood, which is the main support in a building.

gir-dle (ger´dl) *n.* A cord, sash, or belt worn around the waist; a supporting undergarment to give support and to shape of the lower body. *Anat.* The pelvic arch of the body. **girdle** *v.*

girl (gerl) *n.* A female child or infant; a young, unmarried woman; any woman of any age; one's sweetheart. **girlish** *adj.* **girlishly** *adv.* **girlishness** *n.* **girlhood** *n.*

girl Friday *n.* A woman employee responsible for a variety of tasks.

girl friend *n.* A female friend; a regular or frequent female companion of a boy or man.

girl scout *n.* A member of the Girl Scouts

of the United States; an organization for girls between 7 and 17 years of age.

girth (gerth) *n.* The circumference or distance around something; a strap that encircles an animal's body to secure something on its back, as a saddle.

gis-mo *n. Slang* A part or device whose name is unknown or forgotten; a gadget.

gist (jist) *n.* The central or main substance, as of an argument or question.

git-tern *n.* A medieval guitar strung with wire.

give (giv) *v.* To make a present of; to bestow; to accord or yield to another; to put into the possession of another; to convey to another; to donate or contribute; to apply; to devote; to yield as to pressure; to collapse; to furnish or provide; to deliver in exchange for pay. **give away** To hand over the bride to the bridegroom at a wedding ceremony. **give out** To collapse; to be exhausted. **give in** To surrender; to submit oneself. **give** *n.* **giver** *n.*

give–and–take *n.* To make a mutual exchange, as of conversation or opinions.

give-a-way (giv´awā´) *n.* Something that is given free as a premium; something that betrays, generally unintentionally

giv-en (giv´n) *adj.* Bestowed; presented; specified or assumed.

given name *n.* The name bestowed or given at birth or baptism.

give up *v.* To surrender; to cease to do; hand over; to abandon all hope; quit.

giz-zard (giz´érd) *n.* The second stomach in birds, where partly digested food is finely ground.

gla-brous (glā´brus) *adj. Biol.* Having no hair or down; having a smooth surface. **glabrousness** *n.*

gla-cial (glā´shal) *adj.* Of or pertaining to, caused by, or marked by glaciers; extremely cold. **glacially** *adv.*

glacial epoch *n. Geol.* A portion of geological time when ice sheets covered the Northern Hemisphere.

gla-ci-ate *v.* To convert into or cover with a glacier; to produce glacial effects.

gla-cier (glā´shėr) *n.* A large mass of ice formed from compacted snow that moves slowly down mountains into valleys or across land surfaces.

gla-ci-ol-o-gy *n.* Any branch of geology dealing with snow or ice accumulation; geographical distribution, movement, or the effects of glaciers.

glad (glad) *adj.* Displaying, experiencing, or affording joy and pleasure; a state of being happy; being willing to help; grateful. **glad** *n.* Short for gladiolus.

glad-den (glad´n) *v.* To make glad.

glade (glād) *n.* A clearing in a forest or

woods.

glad hand n. A warm welcome to people you meet. **glad-hand** v.

glad-i-a-tor (glad´ē ā´tér) n. An ancient Roman slave, captive, or paid freeman who entertained the public by fighting, often to the death; one who is engaged in an intense struggle or controversy. **gladiatorial** adj.

glad-i-o-lus (glad´ē ō´lus) n., pl. **gladioli** or **gladioluses** A plant with fleshy bulbs, sword-shaped leaves, and spikes of colorful flowers.

glad-some (glad´som) adj. Giving cheer; showing joy. **gladsomely** adv. **gladsomeness** n.

glam-or-ize or **glam-our-ize** (glam´o rīz´) v. To make glamorous; to portray or treat in a romantic way.

glamour girl n. A woman considered to be beautiful who leads a glamorous life.

glam-our or **glam-or** (glam´ér) n. Alluring, fascinating charm. **glamorous** adj. **glamourous** adj.

glance (glans) v. To take a brief or quick look at something; to obliquely strike a surface at an angle and be deflected; to give a light, brief touch; to brush against. **glancing** adj. **glance** n.

gland (gland) n. Anat. Any of the body's organs that excrete or secrete substances.

glan-du-lar adj. Relating to or involving glands.

glare (glâr) v. To stare fiercely or angrily; to shine intensely; to dazzle. **glare** n. An uncomfortably harsh or bright light; angry look.

glar-ing (glâr´ing) adj. Shining with an extremely bright light; painfully obvious. **glaringly** adv. **glaringness** n.

glass (glas) n. A hard, amorphous, brittle, usually transparent material which is formed in a molten state and then hardened by rapid cooling; any substance made of or resembling glass; a mirror, tumbler, window pane, lens, or other material made of glass. **glasses** A pair of eyeglasses used as an aid to vision; glassware. **glass** adj. **glassy** adj.

glass blowing n. The art or process of shaping objects from molten glass by gently blowing air into them through a glass tube. **glassblower** n.

glass-ine n. A dense, translucent paper highly resistant to air, water, or oil.

glass-mak-er (glas´mā´kér) n. A person who makes glass or glassware.

glass-ware n. Articles made of glass.

glass wool n. Glass fibers in a mass being used for thermal insulation and air filters.

glass-work n. The manufacture of glass and glassware; the fitting of glass; glazing; articles of glass.

glass-wort (glas´würt´) n. A succulent, leafless plant of the goosefoot family, living in salt water marshes as well as alkaline regions.

glau-co-ma (glo kō´ma) n. Pathol. A disease of the eye characterized by abnormally high pressure within the eyeball and gradual loss of vision.

glau-cous (glo´kus) adj. Yellowish green.

glaze (glāz) n. A thin, smooth coating, like the gloss applied on ceramics. **glaze** v. To become covered with a thin glassy coating of ice; to coat or cover with a glaze; to fit with glass, as to glaze a window. **glazer** n.

gla-zier (glā´zhér) n. A person who sets glass. **glaziery** n.

glaz-ing (glā´zing) n. The process of furnishing or fitting with glass; the act of applying glaze.

gleam (glēm) n. A ray or beam of light; a glow. **gleam** v. To shine or emit light softly; to appear briefly but clearly. **gleamy** adj.

glean (glēn) v. To collect or gather facts by patient effort; to collect part by part; to pick bits of a crop left by a reaper. **gleaner** n.

glean-ings n. Things acquired a little at a time, or in slow stages; field leftovers.

glede n. A bird of prey.

glee (glē) n. Joy; merriment; gaiety; an unaccompanied musical composition. **gleeful** adj. **gleefully** adv.

glee club n. A singing group that is organized to sing short pieces of choral music.

gleet (glēt) n. An abnormal, transparent mucous discharge of the urethra, caused by gonorrhea.

glen (glen) n. A small, secluded valley.

glen-gar-ry (glen gar´ē) n. A woolen cap worn by the Scottish people.

glen plaid n. A twill pattern of checks.

gli-a-din n. Any simple protein found in gluten, from wheat and rye.

glib (glib) adj. Spoken easily and fluently; superficial. **glibly** adv. **glibness** n.

glide (glīd) v. To pass or move smoothly with little or no effort; to fly without motor power. **glidingly** adv. **glide** n.

glid-er (glī´dér) n. One that glides; a swing gliding in a metal frame. Aeron. An aircraft without an engine, constructed to soar on air currents.

glim-mer (glim´ér) n. A faint suggestion; an indication; a dim unsteady light. **glimmer** v. To give off a faint or dim light.

glimpse (glimps) n. A momentary look.

glint (glint) n. To be reflected; to give off a flash or gleam. **glint** n. A brief, bright flash of light; a brief indication of recognition.

glis-sade (gli säd´) *n.* A gliding ballet step; a controlled slide in either a sitting or standing position, helps descend a steep, snowy, or icy incline.**-ssade** *v.*

glis-san-do (gli sän´dō) *n., pl.* **glissandi** *Mus.* A rapid passing from one tone to another by a continuous change of pitch.

glis-ten (glis´en) *v.* To shine softly as if reflected by light; to shine or glow with a luster. **glisten** *n.*

glitch (glich) *n.* A minor mishap or malfunction. *Elect.* A false signal caused by an unwanted surge of power.

glit-ter (glit´ér) *n.* A brilliant sparkle; small bits of light-reflecting material used for decoration. **glitter** *v.* To sparkle with brilliance. **glittery** *adj.*

gloam-ing (glō´ming) *n.* Twilight; the dusk of early evening.

gloat (glōt) *v.* To express, feel, or observe with great malicious pleasure or self-satisfaction. **gloater** *n.* **gloatingly** *adv.*

glob (glob) *n.* A drop of something; a rounded, large mass of something.

glob-al (glō´bal) *adj.* Spherical; involving the whole world. **globalize** *v.*

globe (glōb) *n.* A spherical object; anything that is perfectly rounded; the earth; anything like a sphere, such as a fish bowl; a spherical representation of the earth, usually including geographical and political boundaries. **globular** *adj.*

globe-fish *n.* Fish with the capabilities to inflate themselves into a globular form.

globe-trotter *n.* One who travels all over the world.

glob-ule *n.* A very small particle of matter in the form of a ball.

glob-u-lin (glob´ū lin) *n. Biochem.* Any of a class of simple proteins found widely in blood, milk, tissue, muscle and plant seeds.

glo-chid-i-ate (glō kid´ē it) *adj.* Barbed at the tip; bearing barbs.

glom-er-ate (glom´ér it) *adj.* Gathered into a round mass; congregated.

glom-er-ule (glom e rōl) *n.* A compact cluster, as of a single flower cluster that contains several flowers.

gloom (glōm) *n.* Partial or total darkness; depression of the mind or spirits. **gloomily** *adv.* **gloominess** *n.*

gloom-y *adj.* Partially or totally dark; low in spirits; lacking illumination.

glop (glob) *n. Slang* A messy mixture of food; something that is considered worthless.

glo-ri-fy (glōr´i fī˝) *v.* To worship and give glory to; to give high praise.

glo-ri-ole (glōr´ē ōl) *n.* A halo.

glo-ri-ous (glōr´ē us) *adj.* Magnificent; resplendent; delightful; illustrious; full of glory. **gloriously** *adv.*

glory (glōr´ē) *n., pl.* **glories** Distinction, praise or honor; exalted reputation; adoration and praise offered in worship; a wonderful asset; the height of one's triumph, achievement, or prosperity. **glory** *v.* To rejoice with jubilation.

gloss (glos) *n.* The sheen or luster of a polished surface; a deceptively or superficially attractive appearance; a note that explains or translates a difficult or hard to understand expression. **gloss** *v.* To cover over by falsehood in an attempt to excuse or ignore.

glos-sa-ry (glos´a rē) *n., pl.* **glossaries** A list of words and their meanings.

gloss-y (glos´ē) *adj.* Having a bright sheen; lustrous; superficially attractive. **glossy** *n.* A photo print on smooth, shiny paper. **glossily** *adv.* **-iness** *n.*

glost *n.* Ceramic glaze used on clay pottery.

glot-tis (glot´is) *n., pl.* **glottises** *or* **glottides** *Anat.* The opening or cleft between the vocal cords at the upper part of the larynx. **glottal** *adj.*

glove (gluv) *n.* A covering for the hand with a separate section for each finger; an oversized protective covering for the hand, as that used in baseball, boxing, or hockey. **glove** *v.* To protect the hand or any object with a covering like a glove; to provide with gloves; to catch a baseball in a hand protected by a glove. **gloved** *adj.*

glow (glō) *v.* To give off heat and light, especially without a flame; to have a bright, warm, ruddy color. **glow** *n.* A warm feeling of emotion. **glowing** *adj.*

glow-er (glou´ér) *v.* To look sullenly or angrily at; to glare. **glower** *n.*

glow-ing (glō´ng) *adj.* Brilliantly luminous; experiencing feelings of heat or exuberance..

glow lamp *n.* Gas-discharged electric lamp in which electrons ionize a gas, emitting a glow.

glow-worm (glō´werm˝) *n.* A European beetle; the luminous larva or grub-like female of an insect which displays phosphorescent light; the firefly.

glox-in-i-a (glok sin´ē a) *n.* A tropical South American plant with large, bell-shaped flowers.

glu-ca-gon *n.* A protein hormone that increases the content of sugar in the blood by increasing the rate of breakdown of glycogen in the liver.

glu-cose (glō´kōs) *n. Chem.* A substance less sweet than cane sugar, found as dextrose in plants and animals and obtained by hydrolysis; a yellowish to colorless syrupy mixture of dextrose, maltose, and dextrins with a small amount of water, used especially in making confectionery and in baking.

glue (glö) *n.* Any of various adhesives in the form of a gelatin, made from animal substances, as bones or skins, and used to stick and hold items together. **glue** *v.* **gluey** *adj.*

glum (glum) *adj.* Moody and sullen. **glumly** *adv.* **glumness** *n.*

glut (glut) *v.* To feed or supply beyond capacity; to provide with a supply that exceeds demand. **glut** *n.* An oversupply; an overabundance.

glutamic acid *n.* An amino acid that occurs in plant and animal proteins, used in the form of a sodium salt substitute and flavor enhancer.

glu-ten (glöt´en) *n.* A mixture of plant proteins that is used as an adhesive and as a substitute for flour. **glutenous** *adj.*

glu-te-us *n.* The large muscles of the buttock.

glut-ton (glut´n) *n.* Someone who eats immoderately; one who has a large capacity for work or punishment.

glut-ton-ous *adj.* Marked by excessive eating; greedy. **gluttonously** *adv.*

gluttony *n.* The habit of eating and drinking excessively. **glutton** *n.*

glyc-er-ol (glis´e röl´) *n. Chem.* A sweet, oily, syrupy liquid derived from fats and oils and used as a solvent, sweetener, antifreeze, and lubricant.

gly-co-pro-tein (glī´kō prō´tēn) *n.* A group of conjugated proteins containing a protein and a carbohydrate.

gly-co-side (glī´ko sīd´) *n. Chem.* Any of a group of carbohydrates which, when decomposed, produce glucose or other sugar.

glyph (glif) *n.* Any symbol that conveys meaning without using words; an ornamental channel carved on a column or frieze; a symbolic figure or character carved in relief.

gly-phog-ra-phy (gli fog´ra fē) *n.* Electrotype process where a plate having a raised surface appropriate for printing is made from an engraved plate.

glyp-tic *n.* The art of carving or engraving on precious gems or related stones.

glyp-to-dont *n.* An extinct mammal that resembled an armadillo.

G-man (jē´man´) *n., pl.* **G-men** An agent of the Federal Bureau of Investigation; a Government man.

gnarl (närl) *n.* A hard, protruding knot on a tree. **gnarled** *adj.*

gnash (nash) *v.* To grind or strike the teeth together, as in rage or pain.

gnat (nat) *n.* A small, winged insect, especially one that bites or stings.

gnat-catch-er *n.* Any of several American insectivorous birds, genus Polioptila.

gnath-ic (nath´ik) *adj.* Pertaining or relating to the jaw or jaws.

gnaw (naw) *v.* To bite or eat away with persistence; to consume or wear away. **gnawer** *n.*

gnaw-ing *n.* A constant, often severe, pain.

gneiss (nīs) *n.* A banded, coarse-grained rock with minerals arranged in layers.

gnome (nōm) *n.* In folklore, a dwarf-like creature who lives underground and guards precious metals and treasures.

gno-mon (nō´mon) *n.* An object that by, the position of its shadow, is an indicator of the hour of the day; a sundial.

GNP *abbr.* Gross national product.

gnu (nö) *n., pl.* **gnus** or **gnu** South African antelope with an ox-like head, curved horns, a long tail, and a mane.

go (gō) *v.* To proceed or pass along; to leave; to move away from; to follow a certain course of action; to function; to function correctly; to be in operation; to pass from one to another by award or lot; to have recourse; to resort to; to pass, as of time; to be abolished or given up; to pass to someone, as by a will. **go** *n.* An attempt; a try. **go back on** To abandon **go for** To try; to try to obtain. **go places** To be on the road to success. **go under** To suffer destruction or defeat; **on the go** Always busy.

goad (gōd) *v.* To drive cattle to move; to incite or arouse. **goad** *n.*

go-a-head (gō´a hed´) *n.* Permission; a signal to move ahead or proceed.

goal (gōl) *n.* A purpose; the terminal point of a race or journey; in some games, the area, space, or object into which participants must direct play in order to score.

goal-ie *n.* A goalkeeper.

goal-keep-er (gōl´kē pér) *n.* The player responsible for defending the goal in hockey, soccer, and other games, preventing the ball or puck from passing over the goal for a score; a goal tender.

goal-post *n.* Two vertical poles with a crossbar which constitutes the goal line in some sports, especially football..

goat (gōt) *n.* A horned, cud chewing mammal related to the sheep; a lecherous man. *Slang* One who is a scapegoat. **goatish** *adj.* **goatishly** adv.

goat-ee (gō tē´) *n.* A short, pointed beard on a man's chin.

goat-skin (gōt´skin´) *n.* The skin of a goat, often used for leather products.

gob (gob) *n.* A piece or lump of something. *Slang* A sailor.

gob-ble (gob´l) *v.* To eat and swallow food greedily; to take greedily; to grab.

gob-ble-dy-gook (gob´l dē gek´) *n. Informal* Wordy and often unintelligible language.

gob-bler (gob´lér) *n.* A male turkey.

go-be-tween (gō´bi twēn´) *n.* A person who acts as an agent between two parties.

gob-let (gob´lit) *n.* A drinking glass, typically with a base and stem.

gob-lin (gob´lin) *n.* In folklore, an ugly, grotesque creature said to be mischievous and evil.

go-bo (gō´bō) *n.* A dark screen to shield a television camera from light.

go-by (gō´bē) *n.* A small freshwater fish, often having the pelvic fins attached to form a ventral sucking cup enabling it to cling to rocks.

go-cart *n.* A small, gasoline-powered car, used for recreation or racing.

god (god) *n.* Someone considered to be extremely important or valuable; an image, symbol, or statue of such a being.

God (god) *n.* The Supreme Being; the ruler of life and the universe.

god-child (god´chīld´) *n.* A child for whom an adult serves as sponsor at baptism, circumcision, and other rites.

god-daughter *n.* A female godchild.

god-dess (god´is) *n.* A female of exceptional charm, beauty, or grace.

go-dev-il *n.* A small, gasoline car used on railroad tracks to transport workers and supplies.

god-father (god´fä ther) *n.* A man who sponsors a child at his or her baptism or other such ceremony.

god-for-sak-en (god´fèr sā´ken) *adj.* In a remote desolate place.

god-head (god´hed´) *n.* Godhood; divinity; the essential and divine nature of a god. **Godhead** Supreme being.

god-less (god´lis) *adj.* Not recognizing a god. **godlessness** *n.*

god-ly (god´lē) *adj.* Filled with love for God.

god-mother (god´muth èr) *n.* A woman who sponsors a child at his or her baptism or other such ceremony.

god-par-ent(god´pâr´ent)*n.* A godfather or godmother.

god-send (god´send´) *n.* Something received unexpectedly that is needed or wanted.

god-son *n.* A male godchild.

God-speed (god´spēd´) *n.*Best wishes for someone's venture or journey.

god-wit *n.* A long-billed wading bird related to snipes.

gof-fer *n.* An ornamental ruffled piece of lace used on women's clothing.

go-get-ter (gō´get´èr) *n.* An enterprising, aggressive person.

gog-gle (gog´l) *v.* To stare with bulging eyes.

gog-gles (gog´lz) *n.* Spectacles or eyeglasses to protect the eyes against dust, wind, sparks, and other debris.

go-ing (gō´ing) *n.* The act of moving, leaving, or departing; the condition of roads or ground that affects walking, riding, and other movement; a condition influencing activity or progress. **goings on** Actions or behavior that causes one to express disapproval.

goi-ter (goi´tèr) *n. Pathol.* Any abnormal enlargement of the thyroid gland, visible as a swelling in the front of the neck. **goitrous** *adj.*

gold (gōld) *n.* A soft, yellow, metallic element that is highly ductile and resistant to oxidation; used especially in coins and jewelry; a precious metal; a bright, vivid yellow; money; the element symbolized by Au.

gold-en-rod (gōl´den rod´) *n.* A North American plant with small yellow flowers; the state flower of Alabama, Kentucky, and Nebraska.

golden rule *n.* The principle of treating others as one wants to be treated.

gold standard *n.* The monetary system based on gold of a specified weight and fineness as the unit of value and exchange.

golf (golf) *n.* A game played outdoors with a hard ball and clubs, on a grassy course with 9 or 18 holes. **golfer** *n.*

gon-ad (gō´nad) *n. Anat.* The male or female sex gland where the reproductive cells develop; an ovary or testis. **gonadal, gonadial, gonadic** *adj.*

gon-do-la (gon´do la) *n.* A long, narrow, flat-bottomed boat propelled by a single oar or a motor and used on the canals of Venice. **gondolier** *n.*

gone (gon) *adj.* Past; bygone; dead; beyond hope; marked by faintness or weakness. **far gone** Exhausted; wearied; almost dead.

gon-er (go´nèr) *n. Slang* One that is ruined, close to death, or beyond all hope of being saved.

gon-fa-lon (gon´fa lon) *n.* A banner hung from a cross piece and cut so as to end in streamers.

gong (gong) *n.* A heavy metal disk which produces a deep resonant tone when struck with a padded stick.

go-ni-om-e-ter *n.* An instrument used for measuring angles.

gon-o-coc-cus (gon´o kok´us) *n., pl.* **gonococci** The bacterium which causes gonorrhea. **gonococcic** *adj.*

gon-or-rhe-a (go´´o rē´a) *n. Pathol.* A contagious venereal infection transmitted chiefly by sexual intercourse.

goo (gö) *n.* Any sticky substance.

goo-ber (gö´bèr) *n. Regional* A peanut.

good (ged) *adj.* Having desirable or favorable qualities or characteristics; morally excellent; virtuous; well-behaved; tractable; proper; excellent in degree or quality; unspoiled; fresh; healthy; striking or attractive. **goods** Merchandise or wares; personal belongings; cloth; fabric. **for good** Forever; permanently.

Good Book *n.* The Bible.

good–by *or* **good–bye (ged˝bī´)** *interj.* Used to express farewell. **good-by, good-bye** *n.* A farewell; a parting word; an expression of farewell. **good-by, good-bye** *adj.* Final.

good fellow *n.* A good natured person.

good–for–nothing (ged´fer nuth´ing) *n.* A person of little worth or usefulness.

Good Friday *n.* The Friday before Easter, a day observed by Christians to commemorate the crucifixion of Jesus.

good–heart-ed (ged´här´tid) *adj.* Having a kind and generous disposition.

good–hu-mored *adj.* Having a cheerful temper or mood; amiable.

good-ness (ged´nis) *n.* The state or quality of being good; kindness; integrity.

good-will *n.* A desire for the well-being of others; the pleasant relationship between a business and its customers.

goof (göf) *n. Slang* A stupid or dull-witted person; a mistake. **goof** *v.* To blunder; to make a mistake.

goof–off *n.* A slacker; one who shuns responsibility or work. **goof-off** *v.* To be doing something else when there is work to be done.

gook (gek) *n. Slang* A slimy, sludgy, or dirty substance.

goon (gön) *n. Slang* A thug or hoodlum hired to intimidate or injure someone; a person hired to break strikes; a stupid person.

goose (gös) *n., pl.* **geese** A large water bird related to swans and ducks; a female goose. *Informal* A silly person.

go–pher (gö´fer) *n.* A burrowing North American rodent with large cheek pouches.

gore (gōr) *v.* To stab or pierce. **gore** *n.* Clotted blood; a triangular or tapering piece of cloth in a sail or skirt.

gorge (gorj) *n.* A deep, narrow ravine; deep or violent disgust. **gorge** *v.* To eat or devour greedily. **gorger** *n.*

gor-geous (gor´jus) *adj.* Beautiful; dazzling; extremely beautiful; magnificent. **gorgeously** *adv.*

go–ril-la (go ril´a) *n.* A large African jungle ape, having a massive, stocky body, long arms, and tusk-like canine teeth. *Slang* A brutish person.

gorse (gors) *n.* A spiny plant bearing fragrant yellow flowers.

go–ry (gōr´ē) *adj.* Covered or stained with blood; resembling gore.

gosh *interj.* An expression of surprise.

gos–hawk (gos´hok˘) *n.* A large, short-winged hawk formerly used in falconry.

gos–ling (goz´ling) *n.* A young goose.

gos–pel *or* **Gos-pel (gos´pel)** *n.* The teachings of Christ and the apostles; any information which is accepted as unquestionably true; any of the first four books of the New Testament.

gospel music *n.* American religious music based on simple folk melodies blended with rhythmic and melodic elements of spirituals and jazz.

gos–port *n.* A flexible one-way speaking tube used for communications between people in separate airplane cockpits.

gos–sa-mer (gos´a mer) *n.* The fine film or strands of a spider's web floating in the air; anything sheer, delicate, light, or flimsy.

gos–san (gos´an) *n.* Decomposed rock or vein material of a reddish or rusty color, often forming a large part of the outcrop of an iron-bearing vein.

gos–sip (gos´ip) *n.* Idle, often malicious talk; a person who spreads sensational rumors or intimate facts. **gossip** *v.* To spread or engage in gossip. **gossiper** *n.* **gossipy** *adj.*

got *v.* Past tense of get.

gouache (gwäsh) *n.* A method of painting with opaque watercolors.

gouge (gouj) *n.* A chisel with a scoop-shaped blade used for wood carving; a groove or hole made with or as if with a gouge **gouge** *v.* To make a hole or groove with a gouge; to cheat, to charge exorbitant prices. **gouger** *n.*

gou–lash (gö´läsh) *n.* A stew made from beef or veal and vegetables seasoned chiefly with paprika.

gourd (gōrd) *n.* A vine fruit such as the pumpkin, squash, and cucumber; an inedible fruit with a hard rind, which can be used as a drinking or storage vessel when it is dried and hollowed.

gour–mand (ger´mand) *n.* A person who takes excessive pleasure in eating.

gour–met (ger´mā) *n.* Someone who appreciates and understands fine food and drink.

gout (gout) *n. Pathol.* A disease caused by a defect in metabolism and characterized by painful inflammation of the joints.

gov *abbr.* Government; governor.

gov–ern (guv´ern) *v.* To guide, rule, or control by right or authority; to control or guide the action of something; to restrain. **governable** *adj.*

gov–ern–ment (guv´ern ment) *n.* The authoritative administration of public policy and affairs of a nation, state or city; the system or policy by which a political unit is governed; any governed territory, district, or area. **governmental** *adj.* **governmentally** *adv.*

gov-er-nor (guv'ẽr nẽr) *n.* Someone who governs, as the elected chief executive of a state in the United States; an official appointed to exercise political authority over a territory. *Mech.* A device which will automatically control the speed of a machine. **-ship** *n.*

govt *abbr.* Government.

gow-an *n.* A yellow or white field flower.

gown (goun) *n.* A woman's dress, especially for a formal affair; any long, loose-fitting garment; a robe worn by certain judges, officials, scholars, and clergymen.

grab (grab) *v.* To snatch or take suddenly; to take possession of by force or by dishonest means. *Slang* To capture the attention of someone or something. **grabber** *n.* **grabby** *adj.*

grab-ble *v.* To search with the hand; grope.

gra-ben (grä'ben) *n. Geol.* An elongated depression in the earth, caused by the downward pressure of two or more faults.

grace (grās) *n.* Seemingly effortless beauty, ease, and charm of movement, proportion, or form; a charming quality; an attractive characteristic. **graceful** *adj.* **gracefully** *adv.*

grace-less *adj.* Lacking of grace or any pleasing quality.

grace period *n.* A time, after the actual due date of a payment when one may make payment without penalties.

gra-cious (grä'shus) *adj.* Marked by having or showing kindness and courtesy; full of compassion; merciful. **graciously** *adv.* **graciousness** *n.*

grack-le (grak'l) *n.* Any of various American blackbirds having long tails and iridescent black plumage.

grad *abbr.* Graduate; graduated.

gra-date (grä'dāt) *v.* To shade into the next color or stage.

gra-da-tion (grä dā'shan) *n.* A gradual and orderly arrangement or progression according to quality, size, rank, or other value; the act of grading.

grade (grād) *n.* A step or degree in a process or series; a group or category; a level of progress in school, usually constituting a year's work; a letter or number indicating a level of achievement in school work; the degree to which something slopes, as a road, track, or other surface. *Milit.* Rank.

grade school *n.* Elementary school, usually from kindergarten to grade 5, 6, or 8.

gra-di-ent (grä'dē ent) *n.* A slope or degree of inclination. *Phys.* A rate of change in variable factors, as temperature or pressure.

gra-din (grä'din) *n.* One in a series of steps.

grad-u-al (graj'e al) *adj.* Moving or changing slowly by degrees; not steep or abrupt. **gradually** *adv.*

grad-u-ate (graj'ŏ āt') *v.* To receive or be granted an academic diploma or degree upon completion of a course of study; to divide into categories, grades or steps. **graduate** *n.* A person who holds an academic degree; a container or beaker marked in units or degrees, used for measuring liquids.

graduate student A student who has received a college degree and is working toward an advanced or higher degree.

grad-u-a-tion (gra'ŏ ā'shan) *n.* The state of graduating; a commencement ceremony issuing diplomas or degrees.

gra-dus (grä'dus) *n.* A dictionary to assist in writing Greek or Latin verses.

graf-fi-to (gra fē'tō) *n., pl.* **graffiti** An inscription or drawing made on a public wall, subway train, rock, or any other surface.

graft (graft) *v.* To insert a shoot from a plant into another living plant so that the two will grow together as a single plant. *Surg.* To transplant a piece of tissue or an organ. **graft** *n.* Living tissue or skin used to replace damaged or destroyed tissue or skin; the act of acquiring or getting personal profit or advantage by dishonest or unfair means through one's public position.

gra-ham (grä'am) *n.* Whole wheat flour.

graham cracker *n.* A semisweet cracker made of whole wheat flour.

grail (grāl) *n.* The legendary cup used by Christ at the Last Supper; also called the *Holy Grail.*

grain (grān) *n.* A small, hard seed or kernel of cereal, wheat, or oats; the seeds or fruits of such plants as a group.

gral-la-to-ri-al *adj.* Pertaining to large, long-legged wading birds.

gram (gram) *n.* A metric unit of mass and weight equal to 1/1000 kilogram and nearly equal to one cubic centimeter of water at its maximum density.

gra-ma *n.* Any of several pasture grasses of the western United States.

gra-mer-cy *interj.* Used to express thanks; an exclamation of astonishment or sudden feeling of surprise.

gram-i-ci-din *n.* Germicide used against bacteria in local infections.

gra-min-e-ous *adj.* Like or relating to grass.

gram-i-niv-o-rous *adj.* Surviving on grains or similar food.

gram-mar (gram'ẽr) *n.* The study and description of the classes of words, their relations to each other, and their arrangement into sentences; the inflectional and syntactic rules of a language. **grammarian** *n.*

grammar checker In *computer science,* a program that inspects a file or document for grammatical errors, advises the user of the error and suggests alternatives.

gram-mat-i-cal *adj.* Relating to or conforming to the rules of grammar. **grammatically** *adv.*

gram mol-e-cule (gram´mo lek´ū lĕ) *n. Chem.* The quantity of a compound, expressed in grams, that is equal to the molecular weight of that compound.

gram-pus *n.* A large, marine mammal related to the whale family.

gran-a-ry (grā´na rē) *n., pl.* **granaries** A building for storing threshed grain; an area or region where grain grows in abundance.

grand (grand) *adj.* Large in size, extent, or scope; magnificent; of high rank or great importance; lofty; admirable; main or principal; highly satisfactory; excellent. grand *A. Slang* A thousand dollars. **grandly** *adv.* **grandness** *n.*

gran-deur (gran´jer) *n.* The quality or condition of being grand; splendor; magnificence.

gran-di-flo-ra *n.* A rose bush producing both single blooms and clusters of blooms on the same plant due to crossbreeding tea roses and floribunda.

gran-dil-o-quent (gran dil´o kwent) *adj.* Speaking in or characterized by a pompous or bombastic style.

gran-di-ose (gran´dē ōs´) *adj.* Impressive and grand; pretentiously pompous; bombastic. **grandiosely** *adv.*

grand jury *n.* A jury that listens to accusations against people and, if just cause exists, makes formal charges for trials.

grand mal (gran´mal´) *n. Pathol.* A form of epilepsy characterized by severe convulsions and loss of consciousness.

grand-moth-er (gran´muth´ĕr) *n.* The mother of one's father or mother; a female ancestor.

grand opera *n.* A form of opera having a serious and complex plot with the complete text set to music.

grand-par-ent (gran´pâr´ent) *n.* A parent of one's mother or father.

grand piano *n.* A piano with the strings arranged horizontally in a curved, wooden case.

grand-son (gran´sun´) *n.* A son of one's son or daughter.

grand-stand (gran´stand´) *n.* A raised stand of seats, usually roofed, for spectators at a racetrack or sports event.

grange *n.* A farmhouse and the buildings around it; a granary.

grang-er-ize *v.* To illustrate a book using illustrations or prints taken from other

sources.

gran-ite (gran´It) *n.* A hard, coarse-grained igneous rock composed chiefly of quartz, mica, and orthoclase, which is used for building material and in sculpture.

gran-ite-ware (gran´It wâr´) *n.* Ironware utensils coated with hard enamel.

gra-niv-o-rous (gra niv´ĕr us) *adj.* Feeding on seeds or grain.

gran-ny *or* **gran-nie** (gran´ē) *n.* An old woman; a grandmother; a fussy person.

gra-no-la *n.* Rolled oats mixed with dried fruit and seeds and eaten as a snack.

gran-o-lith (gran´o lith) *n.* An artificial stone made of crushed granite and cement.

gran-o-phyre *n.* Igneous rocks in which the ground mass is chiefly a mixture of quartz and feldspar crystals.

Grant, Ulysses S. *n.* (1822-1885) The eighteenth president of the United States from 1869-1877.

grant (grant) *v.* To allow; to consent to; to admit something as being the truth; in law, to transfer property by a deed. **grant** *n.* That which is granted. **grantee, grantor** *n.*

grant-in-aid *n., pl.* **grants-in-aid** Financial support or subsidy for public use paid by a central government to local government for a public program or project.

gran-u-lar (gran´ū lĕr) *adj.* The state of being composed of grains or containing grains or granules.

gran-u-lar (gran´ū lĕr) *adj.* The state of being composed of or seeming to be com-posed or containing grains or granules. **granularity** *n.*

gran-u-late (gran´ū lāt´) *v.* To make or form into granules or crystals; to become or cause to become rough and grainy.

gran-u-la-tion *n.* Tissue made up of minute projections of flesh that form in the process of healing.

gran-ule (gran´ūl) *n.* A very small grain or particle; part of a larger unit.

gran-u-lo-cyte *n.* A white blood cell whose cytoplasm containing granules.

gran-u-lo-ma (gran´ūlō´ma) *n.* A nodular growth of inflamed tissue associated with the process of infection.

grape (grāp) *n.* Any of numerous woody vines bearing clusters of smooth-skinned, juicy, edible berries, having a dark purplish blue, red, or green color, eaten raw or dried; also used in making wine.

graph (graf) *n.* A diagram representing the relationship between sets of things. In computer science, a chart that displays the relative magnitude of associated elements as bars, columns, or sections of a pie.

graph-eme *n*. The smallest written unit of an alphabet, a single letter as used to represent one phoneme as the *d* in *drop*.

graph-ic *or* **graph-i-cal** (graf'ik) *adj*. Describing in full detail; of or pertaining to drawings or blueprints, as in architecture. **graphically** *adv*.

graphic display In computer science, the depiction of graphic elements on a computer monitor screen.

graph-ite (graf'it) *n*. A soft black form of carbon having a metallic luster and slippery texture, used in lead pencils, lubricants, paints, and coatings. **graphitic** *adj*.

graph-i-tize *v*. To change into graphite, as part of the carbon in steel.

graph-ol-o-gy (gra fol'o je) *n*. The study of handwriting for the purpose of analyzing a person's character or personality. **graphologist** *n*.

graph paper *n*. Paper ruled with lines for drawing graphs.

grap-nel (grap'nel) *n*. A small anchor with several flukes at the end.

grasp (grasp) *v*. To seize and grip firmly; to comprehend; to understand. **grasp** *n*. The power to seize and hold. **graspable** *adj*. **grasper** *n*.

grasp-ing (gras'ping) *adj*. Urgently desiring material possessions; greedy. **graspingly** *adv*. **graspingness** *n*.

grass (gras) *n*. Any of numerous plants having narrow leaves and jointed stems; the ground on which grass is growing. *Slang* Marijuana.

grate (grāt) *v*. To reduce, shred or pulverize by rubbing against a rough or sharp surface; to make or cause to make a harsh sound or a rasping noise. **grater** *n*. **grating** *adj*. **gratingly** *adv*.

grate (grāt) *n*. A framework or bars placed over a window or other opening; an iron frame to hold burning fuel in a fireplace or furnace.

grate-ful *adj*. The state of being thankful or appreciative for benefits or kindness; expressing gratitude. **gratefully** *adv*.

grat-i-cule (grat'i kūl') *n*. The network of lines of latitude and longitude from which maps are drawn.

grat-i-fi-ca-tion *n*. The state of being gratified; that which affords pleasure, or enjoyment.

grat-i-fy (grat'i fī') *v*. To give pleasure or satisfaction to; to fulfill the desires of; to indulge. **gratifying** *adj*.

gra-tin (grat'in) *n*. A brown crust formed on food cooked with a topping of crumbs or grated cheese.

grating (grā'ting) *n*. A grate.

grat-is (grat'is) *adv*. & *adj*. Without requiring payment; free.

grat-i-tude (grat'i tōd') *n*. The state of appreciation and gratefulness;

thankfulness.

gra-tu-i-tous (gra tō'i tus) *adj*. Given or obtained without payment; unjustified; unwarranted. **gratuitously** *adv*. **gratuitousness** *n*.

gra-tu-i-ty (gra tō'i tē) *n*., *pl*. **gratuities** A gift, as money, given in return for a service rendered; a tip.

grau-pel *n*. Granules of soft hail or sleet.

gra-va-men (gra vā'men) *n*., *pl*. **gravamens** *or* **gravamina** In law, the part of an accusation or charge weighing most heavily against the accused.

grave (grāv) *n*. A burial place for a dead body, usually an excavation in the earth. **grave** *adj*. Very serious or important in nature; filled with danger; critical. **grave** *v*. To sculpt or carve; to engrave. **gravely** *adv*. **graver** *n*.

grav-e (gräv ā') *adj*. *Music* Solemn and slow.

grav-el (grav'el) *n*. Loose rock fragments often with sand. *Pathol*. The deposit of sand-like crystals that form in the kidneys; also known as kidney stones.

grave-stone (grāv'stōn') *n*. A stone that marks a grave; a tombstone.

grave-yard (grāv'yärd') *n*. An area set aside as a burial place; a cemetery.

graveyard shift *n*. *Slang* A work shift that usually begins at midnight.

gra-vim-e-ter (gra vim'i tėr) *n*. An implement for determining specific gravity. **gravimetry** *n*.

grav-i-tate (grav'i tāt') *v*. To be drawn as if by an irresistible force; to sink or settle to a lower level.

grav-i-ta-tion (grav'i tā'shan) *n*. *Physics* The force or attraction any two bodies exert towards each other. **gravitational**, **gravitative** *adj*. **gravitationally** *adv*.

grav-i-ty (grav'i tē) *n*., *pl*. **gravities** The gravitational force manifested by the tendency of material bodies to fall toward the center of the earth; gravitation in general; weight; importance; seriousness.

gra-vy (grā'vē) *n*., *pl*. **gravies** The juices exuded by cooking meat; a sauce made by seasoning and thickening these juices. *Slang* Money or profit which is easily acquired.

gray (grā) *n*. & *adj*. A neutral color between black and white; gloomy; dismal; having gray hair, characteristic of old age. **grayish** *adj*. **grayness** *n*.

gray matter *n*. The grayish-brown nerve tissue of the spinal cord and brain, consisting mainly of nerve cells and fibers; brains.

gray scale In *computer science*, a graduated series of dot patterns to depict various shades of gray on the monitor.

graze (grāz) *v*. To feed upon growing

grasses or herbage; to put livestock to feed on grass or pasturage; to brush against lightly in passing; to abrade or scrape slightly.

gra-zier (grā´zhẽr) n. One who grazes cattle.

grease (grēs) n. Melted or soft animal fat; any thick fatty or oily substance, as a lubricant. **grease** v. To lubricate or coat with grease. **greasiness** n.

greasy spoon n. A small cheap restaurant.

great (grāt) adj. Very large in size or volume; prolonged in duration or extent; more than ordinary; considerable; remarkable; impressive; eminent; renowned; very good or first-rate; a generation removed from a relative. **greatly** adv. **greatness** n.

greave (grēv) n. An armor for the leg worn below the knee.

grebe (grēb) n. Any of various swimming and diving birds having partially webbed feet, a very short tail, and a pointed bill.

greed (grēd) n. Selfish desire to acquire more than one needs or deserves.

greed-y (grē´dē) adj. Excessively eager to acquire or gain something; having an excessive appetite for drink and food; gluttonous. **greedily** adv.

green (grēn) adj. Of the color between yellow and blue in the spectrum; not fully matured or developed; lacking in skill or experience. **green** n. A grassy plot or lawn, especially an area of closely mowed grass at the end of a golf fairway. **greenish** adj.

green-horn (grēn´horn´) n. An inexperienced person; a beginner; a person who is easily fooled.

green-house (grēn´hous´) n. An enclosed structure equipped with heat and moisture built for the cultivation of plants.

greet (grēt) v. To address someone in a friendly way; to welcome; to meet or receive in a specified manner. .

gre-gar-i-ous (gri gâr´ē us) adj. Habitually associating with others as in groups, flocks, or herds; enjoying the company of others; sociable. **gregariously** adv. **gregariousness** n.

greige (grāzh) n. Woven fabric in an unbleached undyed state.

grei-sen n. A crystalline rock composed chiefly of quartz and mica.

grem-lin (grem´lin) n. A mischievous elf said to cause mechanical trouble in airplanes.

gre-nade (gri nād´) n. A small explosive device detonated by a fuse and thrown by hand or projected from a rifle.

gren-a-dine (gren´a dēn´) n. A syrup made from pomegranates or red currants and used as a flavoring in mixed drinks.

grew v. Past tense of grow.

grey (grā) n. & adj. Variation of gray.

grey-hound (grā´hound´) n. One of a breed of slender, swift-running dogs with long legs.

grib-ble (grib´l) n. A small marine crustacean which destroys submerged timber.

grid (grid) n. An arrangement of regularly spaced bars; the system of intersecting parallel lines that divide maps, charts, and aerial photographs, used as a reference for locating points.

grid-dle (grid´l) n. A flat pan used for cooking.

grid-dle cake (grid´l kāk´) n. A pancake.

grid-i-ron (grid´Īẽrn) n. A metal framework used for broiling meat, fish, and other foods; a football field.

grief (grēf) n. Deep sadness or mental distress caused by a loss, remorse, or bereavement.

griev-ance (grē´vans) n. A real or imagined wrong which is regarded as cause for complaint or resentment; a complaint of unfair treatment.

grieve (grēv) v. To feel grief or sorrow.

griev-ous (grē´vus) adj. Causing grief, sorrow, anguish, or pain; causing physical suffering. **grievously** adv.

grif-fin or **grif-fon** (grif´on) n. In Greek mythology, a fabulous beast with a lion's body, an eagle's head, and wings.

grift v. Slang To obtain money by dishonest schemes, swindling, or cheating.

grig (grig) n. A lively young person.

grill (gril) n. A cooking utensil made from parallel metal bars; a gridiron; food cooked on a grill; a restaurant where grilled foods are a specialty. **grill** v. To broil on a grill.

gril-lage (gril´ij) n. A framework of lumber or steel for support in marshy soil.

grille or **grill** (gril) n. A grating with open metal work used as a decorative screen or room divider.

grilse n. A young, mature salmon returning from the sea to spawn for the first time.

grim (grim) adj. Stern or forbidding in appearance or character; unyielding; relentless; grisly; gloomy; dismal. **grimly** adv. **grimness** n.

grim-ace (grim´as) n. A facial expression of pain, disgust, or disapproval.

grime (grīm) n. Dirt, especially soot, clinging to or coating a surface. **griminess** n. **grimy** adj.

grin (grin) v. To smile broadly. **grin** n.

grind (grīnd) v. To reduce to fine particles; to sharpen, polish, or shape by friction; to press or rub together; to work or study hard. **grind** n. A person who works hard or who studies very hard.

grind-er (grīn´dèr) n. One that grinds.

grind-stone (grīnd´stōn´) n. A flat, circular stone which revolves on an axle and is used for polishing, sharpening, or grinding.

grip (grip) n. A firm hold; a grasp; the ability to seize or maintain a hold; the mental or intellectual grasp; a suitcase. **grip** v. To grasp and keep a firm hold on; to capture the imagination or attention. **gripper** n. **grippingly** adv.

gripe (grīp) v. To cause sharp pain or cramps in the bowels; to anger; to annoy; to complain.

grippe (grip) n. Influenza. **grippy** adj.

gri-saille (gri-sāl) n. A method of decorating in single colors especially in various shades of gray, making objects appear as three-dimensional.

gris-ly (griz´lē) adj. Ghastly; gruesome.

grist (grist) n. Grain that is to be ground; a batch of such grain.

gris-tle (gris´l) n. Cartilage of meat.

grist-mill n. A mill for grinding grain.

grit (grit) n. Small, rough granules, as of sand or stone; having great courage and fortitude. **grit** v. To clamp the teeth together. **gritty** adj.

grits (grits) n. Coarsely ground hominy; coarse meal; eaten primarily in the southern states of the United States.

griz-zle (griz´l) v. To become or cause to become gray.

grizzly bear n. A large, grayish bear of western North America. Also called **grizzly**; pl. **grizzlies.**.

groan (grōn) v. To utter a deep, prolonged sound of or as of disapproval or pain. **groan** n. **groaningly** adv.

groat (grōt) n. A former British coin worth four pence; any grain without its hull; a tiny sum.

gro-cer (grō´sèr) n. A storekeeper who deals in foodstuffs and various household supplies.

gro-cer-ies n. The merchandise sold in a grocery.

gro-cer-y (grō´se rē) n., pl. **groceries** A store in which foodstuffs and household staples are sold.

grog (grog) n. Any alcoholic liquor, usually rum, mixed with water.

grog-gy (grog´ē) adj. Feeling dazed, weak, or not fully conscious, such as from a blow or exhaustion; drunk. **groggily** adv. **grogginess** n.

gro-gram (grog´ram) n. A loosely woven fabric of silk and mohair or silk and wool.

grog-shop n. A low-class barroom.

groin (groin) n. Anat. The crease or fold where the thigh meets the abdomen. Arch. The curved edge of a building formed by two intersecting vaults.

grom-met (grom´it) n. A reinforcing

eyelet through which a rope, cord, or fastening may be passed. Naut. A ring of rope or metal used to secure the edge of a sail.

grom-well n. Any plant of the borage family having hairy herbs and smooth, stony nuts.

groom (grōm) n. A person hired to tend horses; a stableman; a bridegroom. **groom** v. To make neat in appearance; to prepare for a particular position, as for a political office.

grooms-man (grōmz´man) n., pl. **groomsmen** Best man at a wedding; any of a bridegroom's attendants.

groove (grōv) n. A long, narrow channel or indentation; a fixed, settled habit or routine; a rut. **groove** v.

groovy (grō´vē) adj. Slang A state or condition of being wonderful; delightful.

grope (grōp) v. To feel about with or as with the hands, as in the dark; to look for uncertainly or blindly. **grope** n. **groper** n.

gros-beck (grōs´bēk´) n. Any of several colorful birds related to the finch, with a stout, conical beak.

gros-grain (grō´grān´) n. A heavy, horizontally corded silk or rayon fabric, woven as a ribbon.

gross (grōs) adj. Exclusive of deductions; of or relating to the total amount received; excessively large or fat; lacking refinement or delicacy; coarse; vulgar. **gross** n. The entire amount without deduction; an amount that equals 12 dozen or 144 items. **gross** v. **grossly** adv. **grossness** n.

gross national product n. The total market value of all goods and services produced by a nation in a year.

gross profit n. The total business receipts less cost of goods sold, before operating expenses and taxes are deducted.

gross-su-lar-ite n. A garnet of red, brown, yellow, green, or white.

gro-tesque (grō tesk´) adj. Distorted, incongruous or ludicrous in appearance or style; bizarre; outlandish. **grotesque, grotesqueness** n. **grotesquely** adv.

gro-tes-quer-y n. A grotesque representation; a group of absurdly represented characters.

grot-to (grot´ō) n., pl. **grottoes** or **grottos** A cave or cave-like structure.

grouch (grouch) n. An habitually irritable or complaining person. **grouchily** adv. **grouchiness** n. **grouchy** adj.

ground (ground) n. The surface of the earth; soil, sand, and other natural material at or near the earth's surface; the connecting of an electric current to the earth through a conductor.

ground (ground) v. Past tense of grind.

ground ball *n.* A batted baseball that bounds or rolls along the ground.

ground cherry *n.* A plant with round pulpy berries enclosed in a ribbed papery husk.

ground connection *n.* A grounding connection with the earth.

ground cover *n.* A plant that forms a dense, extensive ground cover, often used to control erosion; the low-growing plants in a forest.

ground crew *n.* The mechanics who maintain and service an airplane.

ground glass *n.* Glass that has been treated so that it is not fully transparent.

ground hog *n.* A woodchuck.

Groundhog Day *n.* February 2, the day on which the groundhog either sees its shadow, predicting six more weeks of winter, or not, predicting an early spring.

ground ivy *n.* A trailing mint with rounded leaves and purple flowers.

ground-less (ground'lis) *adj.* Without foundation or basis.

ground plan *n.* A floor plan of a building; any first or basic plan.

ground rent *n.* Rent paid by a lessee for the use of land.

ground rule *n.* A basic rule; the rule in sports that modifies play on a particular field, course, or court.

grounds *n.* The land that surrounds a building; the basis for an argument, action or belief; the sediment at the bottom of a liquid, such as coffee.

ground sheet *n.* A waterproof cover to protect an area of ground, used under a sleeping bag.

ground swell *n.* Deep rolling of the sea, caused by a distant storm or gale.

ground wave *n.* A radio wave along the surface of the earth.

ground zero *n.* The point on the ground vertically beneath or above the point of detonation of an atomic bomb.

group (grōp) *n.* A collection or assemblage of people, objects, or things having something in common.

grou-per (grō'pėr) *n.* A large fish related to the sea bass.

group-ie *n. Slang* A female follower of a rock group, especially when it is on tour.

group therapy *n.* Psychotherapy which involves sessions guided by a therapist and attended by several patients who discuss their problems.

grout (grout) *n.* A material used to fill cracks in masonry or spaces between tiles. **grout** *v.* **grouter** *n.*

grove (grōv) *n.* A small group of trees, lacking undergrowth.

grov-el (gruv'l) *v.* To lie or crawl face downward, as in fear; to act with abject humility. **groveler** *n.* **grovelingly** *adv.*

grow (grō) *v.* To increase in size, develop, and reach maturity; to expand; to increase; to come into existence; to be produced by natural processes; to increase gradually; to cause to grow; to cultivate. **grower** *n.*

growl (groul) *v.* To utter a deep, guttural, threatening sound, as that made by a hostile or agitated animal. **growl** *n.*

grown (grōn) *adj.* Fully matured; cultivated in a specified way, as in *home-grown.*

grown-up (grōn'up') *n.* A mature adult.

growth (grōth) *n.* The act or process of growing; a gradual increase in size or amount. *Pathol.* An abnormal formation of bodily tissue, as a tumor.

growth factor *n.* A substance that enhances the growth of an organism.

growth stock *n.* The common stock of a company with potential increase in business and profits.

grub-stake (grub'stāk') *n.* Funds and supplies furnished to a miner for a share of his findings until he can fend for himself.

grudge (gruj) *n.* A feeling of ill will, rancor, or deep resentment. **grudge** *v.* To be displeased, resentful, or envious of the possessions or good fortune of another person. **grudging** *adj.* **grudgingly** *adv.*

gru-el (grō'el) *n.* A thin liquid made by boiling meal in water or milk.

gru-el-ing (grō'e ling) *adj.* Very tiring; exhausting. **gruelingly** *adv.*

grue-some (grō'som) *adj.* Causing horror or fright or repulsion. **gruesomely** *adv.* **gruesomeness** *n.*

gruff (gruf) *adj.* Brusque and rough in manner; harsh in sound; hoarse. **gruffly** *adv.* **gruffness** *n.*

grum-ble (grum'bl) *v.* To complain in low, throaty sounds; to growl. **grumble** *n.* **grumbler** *n.*

grump-y (grum'pē) *adj.* Irritable and moody; ill-tempered. **grumpily** *adv.*

grun-gy *adj. Slang* Dirty, rundown, or inferior in condition or appearance.

grunt (grunt) *n.* The deep, guttural sound of a hog. **grunt** *v.*

grun-tle *v.* To put in a good mood.

gua-ca-mo-le (gwa'ka mō'lā) *n.* Mashed avocado seasoned with condiments.

gua-co (gwä'kō) *n.* A tropical climbing plant of America, whose leaves contain a substance that is used as an antidote for snake bites.

gua-neth-i-dine *n.* A drug used in treating severe high blood pressure.

gua-no (gwä'nō) *n.* The excrement of sea birds used as a fertilizer.

guar *abbr.* Guaranteed.

guar-an-tee (gar'an tē') *n.* The promise or assurance of the durability or quality of a product; something held or given as a pledge or security. **guarantee** *v.* To assume responsibility for the default or debt of; to certify; to vouch for.

guar-an-tor (gar´an tor´) *n.* One who gives a guarantee or guaranty.

guar-an-ty (gar´an tē) *n., pl.* **guaranties** A pledge or promise to be responsible for the debt, duty, or contract of another person in case of default; something that guarantees.

guard (gärd) *v.* To watch over or shield from danger or harm; to keep watch as to prevent escape, violence, or indiscretion. **guard** *n.* A defensive position, as in boxing or fencing; in football, one of two linemen on either side of the center; in basketball, one of the two players stationed near the middle of the court; a device or piece of equipment that protects against damage, loss, or harm. **guarded** *adj.*

guard hair *n.* The coarse, long outer hair forming a protective coating over the soft underfur of certain animals.

guard-i-an (gär´dē an) *n.* One who is legally assigned responsibility for the care of the person and property of an infant, minor or person unable to do for himself because of physical or mental disability. **guardianship** *n.*

gub-ba *v. Slang* To tickle the neck area, especially of young children and babies. **gubba** *n.* The area that is tickled.

gu-ber-na-to-ri-al (gö´bér natōr´ē al) *adj.* Of or pertaining to a governor.

gudgeon (guj´on) *n.* A small European freshwater fish related to the carp.

gue-non (ge non´) *n.* A long-tailed arboreal African monkey.

guern-sey (gern´zē) *.,* A breed of brown and white dairy cattle.

guer-ril-la (ge ril´la) *n.* A member of an irregular military force that is capable of great speed and mobility, often operating behind enemy lines. **guerrilla** *adj.*

guess (ges) *v.* To make a judgment or form an opinion on uncertain or incomplete knowledge; to suppose; to believe.

guess-ti-mate (ges´ti mät´) *n. Slang* An estimate made without all the facts.

guest (gest) *n.* One who is the recipient of hospitality from another; a customer who pays for lodging.

guff (guf) *n. Slang* Nonsense or empty talk.

guf-faw (gu fo´) *n.* A loud burst of laughter. **guffaw** *v.*

guid-ance (gid´ans) *n.* The act, process, or result of guiding or counseling.

guide *n.* One who leads or directs another, as in a course of action; a person employed to conduct others on trips, through museums, or on sightseeing tours. **guidable** *adj.*

guide-book (gid´bek´) *n.* A handbook containing directions and other information for tourists and visitors.

guided missile *n. Mil.* An unmanned missile that can be controlled by radio signals while in flight.

guide-line *n.* Any suggestion, statement, or outline of policy or procedure; a rope or cord to guide a person over a difficult point.

guide-post *n.* A post to which a sign is attached for giving direction.

gui-don (gī´don) *n.* A small flag carried by a military unit as a unit marker.

guild (gild) *n.* An association of persons of the same trade or occupation.

guile *n.* Craft; duplicity; deceit.

guil-le-mot *n.* A bird of the auk family, native to the northern Atlantic coast.

guil-loche *n.* Architectural ornament composed of two or more strands interlacing or combining other patterns.

guil-lo-tine (gil´ō tēn´) *n.* An instrument of capital punishment in France, used for beheading condemned prisoners.

guilt (gilt) *n.* The condition or fact of having committed a crime or wrongdoing; the feeling of responsibility for having done something wrong.

guilt-less *adj.* A state or condition of being without guilt; innocent.

guilt-y (gil´tē) *adj.* Deserving of blame for an offense that has been committed; convicted of some offense; pertaining to, involving or showing guilt. **guiltily** *adv.* **guiltiness** *n.*

guin-ea (gin´ē) *n.* Formerly, a British gold coin worth one pound and five pence.

guinea fowl (gin´ē foul) *n.* A widely domesticated bird of African origin with dark gray plumage speckled with white.

guinea hen *n.* The female guinea fowl.

guinea pig (gin´ē pig) *n.* A small, domesticated rodent widely used for biological experimentation.

guinea worm *n.* A slender parasitic which can causes illness in man and animals.

gui-pure (gi pur´) *n.* Heavy laces in which the pattern is connected by bars instead of worked on a net or a mesh ground.

guise *n.* External appearance in dress; garb; an assumed appearance.

gui-tar (gi tor´) *n.* A musical instrument with six strings, played by plucking or strumming.

gu-lar *adj.* Pertaining or relating to, or situated on, the throat.

gulch (gulch) *n.* A deep cleft or ravine caused by the action of water.

gulf (gulf) *n.* A large area of ocean or sea partially enclosed by land; a wide, impassable separation, as in social position or education.

gulf-weed *n.* A coarse branching olive-brown seaweed, found in tropical American waters.

gull (gul) *n.* A long-winged, web-footed sea bird, usually white and gray with a hooked upper mandible; a gullible person; one who is easily tricked.

gul-let (gul'ît) *n. Pathol.* The passage from the mouth to the stomach; esophagus; the throat; the pharynx.

gul-li-ble (gul'i bl) *adj.* Easily cheated or fooled. **gullibility** *n.,* **gullibly** *adv.*

gul-ly (gul'ē) *n., pl.* **gullies** A ditch or channel cut in the earth by running water.

gulp (gulp) *v.* To swallow rapidly or in large amounts; to gasp or choke, as in nervousness; to swallow quickly or in large quantities. **gulp** *n.*

gum-mo-sis *n.* A plant disease that causes an abnormal gummy discharge.

gump-tion (gump'shan) *n. Slang* Boldness; initiative; enterprise; personal initiative; practical sense.

gum resin *n.* Various natural mixtures of gum and resin, extruded from certain plants.

gun (gun) *n.* A weapon made of a tube from which a projectile is thrown by the force of an explosion; a portable firearm. **gun** *v.* To shoot; to open up the throttle of an engine in order to accelerate. **gun for** To try to ruin, catch, or acquire.

gunk *n.* Obnoxious sticky material; greasy or messy material.

gun-smith (gun'smith') *n.* A person who makes or repairs guns.

gur-gle (ger'gl) *v.* To flow in a broken, uneven current, making low, bubbling sounds. **gurgle** *n.* **gurgling** *adj.*

gur-nard *n.* A marine fish with a spiny head and three pairs of pectoral rays.

gush (gush) *v.* To flow or rush forth in volume and with sudden force; to be overly sentimental or enthusiastic. .

gush-er *n.* An oil well with a plentiful natural flow of oil; a person who gushes.

gus-set (gus'ît) *n.* An insert in the seam of a garment or object to allow for expansion or to strengthen.

gust (gust) *n.* A sudden, violent rush of wind or air; a sudden outburst, as of emotion. **gust** *v.* **gustily** *adv.* **gustiness** *n.* **gusty** *adj.*

gus-ta-to-ry (gus'ta tō'rē) *adj.* Of or pertaining to the sense of taste or the act of tasting.

gust-o (gus'tō) *n.* Hearty enjoyment or enthusiasm.

gut (gut) *n.* The alimentary canal or part of it; the prepared intestine of certain animals, used to make strings for musical instruments and tennis rackets.

gut *v.* To disembowel; to plunder.

gut-ta-per-cha *n.* A tough plastic from the latex of Malaysian trees that resembles rubber but has more resin and is used for electrical insulation and in dentistry.

gut-tate *adj.* Spotted, discolored by drops or drop-like spots.

guy (gī) *n. Slang* A man; a fellow.

guz-zle (guz'l) *v.* To drink greedily, continually, or to excess. **guzzler** *n.*

gym (jim) *n.* A gymnasium; an assortment of outdoor play equipment such as a seesaw, rings and a swing.

gym-no-spore *n.* A spore that does not have a protective covering.

gy-nan-dro-morph *n.* An abnormal individual exhibiting physical features characteristic of both sexes.

gy-nan-dry *n.* Hermaphroditism; the condition in an animal or plant where both male and female reproductive organs exist.

gy-ne-coid (jin'ekoid') *adj.* Having female characteristics; being typical of a woman.

gy-ne-col-o-gy (gī'ne kol'o jē) *n.* The branch of medicine dealing with the female reproductive organs, female diseases, and female functions. **gynecological** *adj.* **gynecologist** *n.*

gyp (jip) *v. Informal* To swindle, cheat, or defraud. **gyp** *n.* A fraud. **gypper** *n.*

gyp-sum (jip'sum) *n.* A mineral, hydrous calcium sulfate, used to make plaster of Paris, gypsum plaster, and plasterboard.

gypsy moth *n.* A moth whose larvae are destructive to foliage.

gy-rate (jī'rāt) *v.* To rotate or revolve around a fixed point or axis; to move or turn in a spiral motion. **gyrate** *adj.* Coiled or winding about. **gyration** *n.* **gyrator** *n.* **gyratory** *adj.*

gyr-fal-con (jer'fol'kon) *n.* A large falcon with color phases ranging from black to white.

gy-ro-com-pass (jī'rō kum'pas) *n.* A compass that has a motor-driven gyroscope so mounted that its axis of rotation maintains a constant position with reference to the true or geographic north.

gy-ro-plane *n.* An airplane balanced and supported by the aerodynamic forces, such as a helicopter, having windmill-like wings that rotate horizontally.

gy-ro-scope (jī'ro skōp') *n.* A spinning wheel or disk whose spin axis maintains its angular orientation when not subjected to external torques. .

gy-ro-sta-bi-liz-er (jī'rō stā'bi lī'zer) *n.* A gyroscopic instrument designed to reduce the rolling motion of ships.

gyve (jīv) *n.* A shackle for the legs. *v.* To chain; to shackle.

H, h (āch) The eighth letter of the English alphabet.

ha (hä) *interj.* An exclamation denoting joy, wonder, sudden emotion or surprise.

ha-ba-ne-ra (hä´b*a* när´a) *n.* Cuban dance.

ha-be-as cor-pus (hā´bē *a*s kor´p*u*s) *n.* In law, a writ commanding a person to appear before a judge or court for the purpose of releasing that person from unlawful detention or restraint.

hab-er-dash-er (hab´ĕr dash´ĕr) *n.* A person who deals in men's clothing and men's accessories.

hab-ile (hab´il) *adj.* Having skill; able.

ha-bil-i-ment (h*a* bil´i m*e*nt) *n.* Clothing characteristic of an office, rank, or occasion.

ha-bil-i-tate (h*a* bil´i tāt´) *v.* To furnish money or equipment for development of a mine.

hab-it (hab´it) *n.* Involuntary pattern of behavior acquired by frequent repetition; manner of conducting oneself; an addiction; clothing that indicates membership or rank in a religious order or activity; *Biol.* the characteristic form of a plant or animal.

hab-it-a-ble (hab´i t*a* bel) *adj.* Suitable for habitation. **habitability**, **habitable-ness** *n.* **habitably** *adv.*

ha-bi-tant (hab´i t*a*nt) *n.* An inhabitant or settler; resident of a place.

hab-i-tat (hab´i tat´) *n.* The region in which an animal or plant lives or grows; the place of residence of a person or group.

hab-i-ta-tion (hab´i tä´sh*a*n) *n.* A place of residence; a house or other dwelling where people or animals dwell.

hab-it-form-ing (hab´it for´ming) *adj.* Producing uncontrollable addiction.

ha-bit-u-al (h*a* bich´ō *a*l) *adj.* Practicing by or acting according to habit; resorted to on a regular basis; regular. **habitually** *adv.* **habitualness** *n.*

ha-bit-u-ate (h*a* bich´ō āt´) *v.* To make familiar; to accustom.

ha-chure (h*a* shur´) *n.* Shading used to denote surfaces in relief on a map.

ha-ci-en-da (hä´sē en´d*a*) *n.* A large estate or ranch in South American countries; the main building of a hacienda; a stock raising ranch.

hack (hak) *v.* To cut with repeated irregular blows; to manage successfully. *Computer Science* To look for ways to get past security on Internet sites to get at private data. **hack** *n.* A tool used for hacking; a rough, dry cough; a taxi or a taxi driver.

hack-er *n. Computer Science* A person who looks for ways to invade Internet sites to get private data or to damage the sites.

hack-le (hak´l) *n.* One of the long, slender, often narrow glossy feathers on the neck of a rooster; the hair on the back of the neck, especially of a dog, that rises in anger or fear.

hack-ney (hak´nē) *n.* A horse of medium size for ordinary driving or riding; a carriage or coach available for hire. **hackney** *v.* To make common or frequent use of.

had *v.* Past participle and past tense of have.

had-n't (had´nt) *contraction* Had not.

hae-ma-tox-y-lon (hē´m*a* tok´si lon´) *n.* A small, tropical American tree with thorns.

haf-ni-um (haf´nē *u*m) *n.* A metallic element resembling zirconium chemically and is found in zirconium ores.

haft (haft) *n.* A handle of a weapon or tool.

hag (hag) *n.* A malicious, ugly old woman; a witch. **haggish** *adj.*

hag-gard (hag´ĕrd) *adj.* A worn-out, exhausted, and gaunt look, as from hunger or fatigue; appearing wasted by suffering or want. **haggardly** *adv.*

hag-gle (hag´l) *v.* To argue or bargain on price or terms. *n.* The process or act of haggling someone. **haggler** *n.*

hag-i-og-ra-phy *n.* Biography of the lives of saints or revered persons; an idolizing biography. **hagiographer** *n.* **hagiographic, hagiographical** *adj.*

haik (hīk) *n.* An oblong piece of usually white clothing used to cover the head and body, used as an outer garment in northern Africa.

hai-ku (hī´kö) *n.* An unrhymed Japanese verse form, having three short un-rhymed lines; a poem using this style.

hail (hāl) *n.* Precipitation of small, hard lumps of ice and snow; a hailstone; an exclamation, greeting, acclamation **hail** *v.* To pour down as hail; to call loudly in greeting or welcome; to shout with enthusiasm; to signal in order to draw attention.

hake (hāk) *n.* An edible marine food fish related to the cod.

ha-kim (hä kēm) *n.* A Muslim physician, ruler or governor.

ha-la-tion *n.* A light that spreads beyond its proper boundaries in a developed photographic image.

hal-cy-on (hal´sē on) *n.* A bird said to have the power of calming waves and winds during the winter solstice. **halcyon** *adj.* Calm and tranquil; peaceful; prosperous.

hale (hāl) *adj.* Healthy and robust, free from disease; free from defect. **hale** *v.* To compel to obey. **haleness** *n.*

half (haf) *n., pl.* **halves** One of two equal parts into which a thing is divisible; part of a thing approximately equal to the remainder; one of a pair.

half *adj*. Being one of two equal parts; being partial or incomplete.

half binding *n*. A style of binding books in which the back and corners are leather and the sides are paper or cloth.

half-breed (haf´brēd´) *n*. The offspring of an American Indian and a white person; offspring of parents from different races.

half-caste (haf´kast´) *n*. A person having one European and one Asian parent.

half-mast (haf´mast´) *n*. A point or position halfway down or less below the top of a ship mast, or flag pole; the position of a flag in respect for the dead. **half-mast** *v*. To hang a flag at half-mast.

half note *n*. *Mus*. A note with the time value equivalent to one half of a whole note.

hal-i-but (hal´i but) *n*. Any of the edible flat fishes of the North Atlantic or Pacific waters.

hal-ide (hal´īd) *n*. *Chem*. A binary compound formed by the direct union of a halogen with a more electropositive element or radical.

hal-ite (hal´īt) *n*. Large crystal or masses of salt; rock salt.

hal-i-to-sis (hal´i tō´sis) *n*. A condition of having bad breath.

hal-le-lu-jah (hal´e lō´ya) *interj*. An expression of joy, praise, or jubilation.

hal-lu-ci-nate (ha-lō´si-nāt´) *v*. To affect with imaginary perceptions; to have a hallucination.

hal-lu-ci-na-tion (ha lō´si nā´han) *n*. An illusion of seeing something that is nonexistent; something one thinks is seen during a hallucination; a delusion. **hallucinatory** *adj*.

hal-lu-ci-no-gen (ha lō´si no jen´) *n*. A drug or other agent which causes hallucination. **hallucinogenic** *adj*.

hal-lu-ci-no-sis (ha-lō´si-nō´sis) *n*. *Psychi*. A mental disorder marked by hallucinations.

hal-lux (hal´uks) *n*. The innermost of the digits of the hind foot of air-breathing vertebrates; in man, the great toe.

hall-way (hol´wā´) *n*. A corridor; an entrance hall.

ha-lo (hā´lō) *n*. A ring of colored light surrounding the head; an aura of glory.

hal-o-gen (hal´o jen) *n*. Any of the group of nonmetallic elements including fluorine, chlorine, bromine, iodine, and astatine. **halogenous** *adj*.

hal-o-gen-ate (hal´o je-nāt´) *v*. *Chem*. To combine or treat with a halogen. **halogenation** *n*.

hal-o-ge-ton (hal o´je tan´) *n*. An annual herb of the goosefoot family found in western America.

hal-oid (hal´oid) *adj*. A substance that resembles common table salt in composition; formed by the mixture of a halogen and a metal.

hal-o-mor-phic (hal´o-mor´fik) *adj*. Influenced by the presence of an alkali or a neutral salt, or both.

hal-o-phile (hal´o fil) *n*. An organism that grows in a salty environment.

hal-o-phyte (hal´o-fit) *n*. A plant that grows in a salty soil.

halt (holt) *v*. To bring to a stop.

hal-ter (hol´tèr) *n*. A rope or strap for leading or tying an animal; a noose for hanging a person; a woman's upper garment tied behind the neck and across the back.

hal-vah *n*. A flaky confection of sesame seeds in a base of syrup or honey.

halve (hav) *v*. To divide into two equal parts; to lessen by half; to share equally.

hal-yard (hal´yèrd) *n*. A rope for hoisting or lowering a sail, flag, or yard.

ham (ham) *n*. The meat of a hog's thigh; the back of the knee or thigh. **ham** *v*.

ham-burg-er (ham´ber´gèr) *n*. A patty of ground beef on a bun.

hame (hām) *n* One of two curved projections attached to the collar of a draft horse to which the traces are attached.

ham-let (ham´lit) *n*. A small rural village or town.

ham-mock (ham´ok) *n*. A hanging bed or couch of fabric or heavy netting, suspended from supports at each end.

ham-per (ham´pèr) *v*. To interfere with movement or progress. **hamper** *n*. A large receptacle, usually covered with a lid, used to store dirty laundry or to pack articles .

ham-string (ham´string´) *n*. Either of two tendons located at the back of the human knee; the large tendon at the back of the hock of four-footed animals. **hamstring** *v*. To cripple by cutting the hamstring; to frustrate.

ham-u-lus (ham´ū lus) *n*. A small hook or a hooked process.

hand (hand) *n*. The part of the arm below the wrist, consisting of the palm, four fingers and a thumb; a unit of measure, four inches, used especially to state the height of a horse; a pointer on a dial, as of a clock, meter, or gauge; the cards dealt to or held by a player in one round of a game; a manual laborer, worker, or employee. **hand** *v*. To give, offer, or transmit with the hand; direct with the hands.

hand-craft (hand´kraft´) *v*. To make or create an item by hand. **-ed** *adj*.

hand-cuff (hand´kuf´) *v*. To put handcuffs on; to make ineffective. **handcuffs** *n*. A pair of circular metal shackles chained together that can be fastened around the wrists.

hand down v. To pass on in succession, from one relative to another; to deliver a court decision.

hand-i-cap (han´dē kap˝) n. A race or contest in which advantages or penalties are given to individual contestants to equalize the odds; any disadvantage that makes achievement unusually difficult; physical disability; an obstacle. **handicap** v. To give a handicap to.

hand-i-craft or **hand-craft** (han´dē kraft˝) n. Skill and expertise in working with the hands; an occupation requiring manual dexterity; skilled work produced by the hands.

hand-i-work (han´dē-wûrk˝) n. Work exhibiting the hand skills of its maker.

han-dle (han´dl) v. To touch, pick up, or hold with the hands; to represent; to trade or deal in. **handle, handler** n. **handleable** adj.

hand-made adj. Made by hand or by a hand process.

hand-maid or **hand-maid-en** n. A female maid or personal servant.

hand-some (han´som) adj. Very good-looking or attractive; very generous, as with money. **handsomely** adv. **handsomeness** n.

hand–to–mouth (hand´to mouth˝) adj. Having barely enough to exist.

hand-writ-ing (hand´rī ting) n. Writing performed with the hand, especially cursive; the type of writing of a person. **handwriting on the wall** An omen of one's fate, usually unpleasant.

hand-y (han´dē) adj. Easy to use or reach; helpful or useful. **handiness** n.

hang (hang) v. To be attached to from above and unsupported from below; to fasten or be suspended so as to swing freely; to be put to death by hanging by the neck; to fasten or attach something, as a picture to a wall. **hang out** Slang To spend one's time in a particular place. **hang up** To end a telephone conversation by replacing the receiver on its cradle. **hang-up** A psychological or emotional problem; an obsession.

han-gar (hang´ér) n. A building for housing aircraft.

han-ger (hang´ér) n. A device from which something may be hung or on which something hangs.

hang-o-ver (hang´ō˝vér) n. Something remaining from what has passed; the effects of excessive alcohol intake.

hank (hangk) n. A loop, coil, or piece of hair, thread, or yarn.

han-ker (hang´kér) v. To have a yearning or craving for something. **-er,** n.

han-som (han´som) n. A two-wheeled covered carriage with the driver's seat elevated behind the cab.

Ha-nuk-kah or **Ha-nu-kah** (hä´nu ka) n. An eight-day Jewish holiday remembering the rededication of the Temple in Jerusalem.

hao-le (how´lē) n. A person who is not of the Hawaiian race, especially a Caucasian.

hap (hap) n. Chance or fortune.

hap-haz-ard (hap´haz´érd) adj. Occurring by accident; happening by chance or at random; hit or miss. **haphazardly** adv. **haphazardness** n.

hap-less adj. Unfortunate; unlucky. **haplessly** adv. **haplessness** n.

hap-log-ra-phy (hap-log´ra-fē) n. The unintentional omission of a letter or letters in writing.

hap-ly (hap´lē) adv. By luck or chance; by accident; perhaps.

hap-pen (hap´n) v. To occur or come to pass; to take place; to discover by chance; to turn up or appear by chance.

hap-pen-ing (hap´e ning) n. A spontaneous event or performance; an important event.

hap-pen-stance (hap´en stans˝) n. An event occurring by chance.

hap-pi-ness (hap e-nis) n. The quality of being content; pleasure.

hap-py (hap´ē) adj. Enjoying contentment and well-being; glad, joyous, satisfied or pleased. **happily** adv.

happy-go-luck-y (hap´ē gō luk´ē) adj. Carefree and unconcerned.

hap-ten (hap´ten) n. A substance which reacts with an antibody only when they are together in a synthetic environment.

ha-rangue (ha rang´) n. A long, extravagant speech; a lecture.

ha-rass (har´as) v. To disturb or annoy constantly; to torment persistently. **harassment** n. **harasser** n.

har-bin-ger (här´bin˝jér) n. A person that initiates or pioneers a major change; something that foreshadows what is to come.

har-bor (här´bér) n. A place of refuge or shelter; a bay or cove; an anchorage for ships. **harbor** v. To provide shelter; to entertain, as a feeling or thought. **harborage, harborer** n.

hard (härd) adj. Difficult to perform, endure, or comprehend; solid in texture or substance; resistant to cutting or penetration; containing salts which make lathering with soap difficult; high in alcoholic content. **hardness** n.

hard–boiled (härd´boild˝) adj. Boiled or cooked in the shell to a hard or solid state.

hard copy n. In computer science, the printed information or data from a computer.

hard disk n. In computer science,

magnetic storage consisting of a rigid disk of aluminum coated with a magnetic recording substance; contained within a removable cartridge or mounted in the hard disk assembly of a microcomputer.

hard-en (här′den) v. To make or become hard or harder; to make or become physically or mentally tough; to make or become callous or unsympathetic.

har-di-hood (här′dē hed) n. Resolute courage; audacious boldness; vitality; vigor.

har-di-ment (här′dē ment) n. A bold deed.

Harding, Warren G. n. (1865-1923) The twenty-ninth President of the United States from 1921-1923, died in office.

hard-line (härd′līn′) adj. Holding fast to a rigid principle; favoring forceful action.

hard-ware (härd′wâr′) n. Manufactured machine parts; tools and utensils; the mechanical components of a computer installation.

har-dy (här′dē) adj. Bold and robust; able to survive very unfavorable conditions, as extreme cold; daring. **hardiness** n. **hardily** adv.

hare (hâr) n. Various mammals related to the rabbits but having longer ears and legs.

har-em (hâr′em) n. The women living in a Muslim residence; the living quarters of a harem.

har-i-cot (har′i-kō′) n. A kind of thick mixture of meat and vegetables; the kidney bean or its pod or seed.

hark (härk) v. To listen closely.

har-le-quin (här′le kwin) n. A jester; a clown. **harlequin** adj. Patterned with vividly colored diamond shapes.

har-lot (här′lot) n. A prostitute.

harm (härm) n. Emotional or physical damage or injury. **harm** v. To cause harm to. **harmful** adj. **harmfully** adv.

har-mat-tan (här′ma-tan′) n. A seasonal dust-laden wind occurring on the west coast of Africa.

harm-less (härm′lis) adj. Without harm; lacking ability to injure or harm.

har-mon-ic (här mon′ik) adj. Relating to musical harmony; in harmony; concordant. **harmonically** adv.

har-mon-i-ca (här mon′i ka) n. A small, rectangular musical instrument having a series of tuned metal reeds that vibrate with the player's breath.

har-mon-i-con (här-mon′i-kon) n. A harmonica or mouth organ.

har-mo-ni-ous (här mō′nē us) adj. Pleasing to the ear; characterized by agreement and accord; having components agreeably combined. **harmoniously** adv. **-ousness** n.

har-mo-nize (här′mo-nīz′) v. To be in

harmony; to bring into agreement. *Mus.* To perform in harmony.

har-mo-ny (här′mo nē) n., pl. **harmonies** Complete agreement, as of feeling or opinion; an agreeable combination of component parts; pleasing sounds; a combination of musical tones into chords. **-izer** n.

har-ness (här′nis) n. The working gear, other than a yoke, of a horse or other draft animal.

harness racing n. A racing sport in which horses are harnessed to a two-wheeled sulky with a driver.

harp (härp) n. A musical instrument having a triangular upright frame with strings plucked with the fingers. **harp** v. To play a harp. **harp on** To write or talk about excessively. **harpist** n.

harp-si-chord (härp′si kord′) n. A pianolike instrument whose strings are plucked by using quills or leather points connected to keys.

har-py (här′pē) n., pl. **harpies** A vicious woman; a predatory person.

har-ri-dan (har′i dan) n. A mean, hateful old woman.

har-ri-er (har′ē ėr) n. A slender hawk with narrow wings that preys on small animals; a hunting dog; a cross-country runner.

Harrison, Benjamin n. (1833-1901) The twenty-third president of the United States from 1889-1893.

Harrison, William Henry n. (1773-1841) The ninth president of the United States from March 4th to April 4th 1841; died in office.

har-row (har′ō) n. A cultivating tool with sharp teeth and spikes for breaking up and smoothing soil. **harrow** v. To cultivate the soil with a harrow which is drawn across plowed soil to smooth.

har-row-ing adj. Causing distress.

har-ry (har′ē) v. To harass.

harsh (härsh) adj. Disagreeable; extremely severe. **harshness** n.

hart (härt) n. A fully grown male deer.

harte-beest (här′te bēst′) n. A large African antelope.

har-um−scar-um (hâr′um skar′um) adj. Reckless; irresponsible.

har-vest (här′vist) n. The process or act of gathering a crop; the season or time for gathering crops. To reap; to obtain as if by gathering. **harvester** n.

harvest moon n. The full moon closest to the time of the September equinox.

has−been (haz′bin′) n. One who has passed the period of his greatest effectiveness, achievement, or popularity.

ha-sen-pfef-fer (häsen fef′ėr) n. A highly seasoned stew made from rabbit meat.

hasp (hasp) n. A clasp or hinged fastener that passes over a staple and is secured

has-sle (has´l) *n. Slang* A type of quarrel or argument. **hassle** *v.*

has-sock (has´ok) *n.* A firm upholstered cushion used as a footstool.

haste (hāst) *n.* Speed; swiftness of motion or action; excessive eagerness to act. **haste** *v.* To make haste; to hurry.

has-ten (hā´sen) *v.* To act or move with haste or speed.

hast-y (hā´stē) *adj.* Rapid; swift; made or done with excessive speed. **hastily** *adv.* **hastiness** *n.*

hat (hat) *n.* A covering for the head, often with a crown and brim.

hatch (hach) *n.* A small opening or door, as in a ship's deck. **hatch** *v.* To bring forth, as young from an egg; to devise; to produce; to contrive secretly.

hatch-er-y (hach´e-rē) *n., pl.* **hatcheries** A place for hatching eggs such as fish or poultry eggs.

hate (hāt) *v.* To feel hostility or animosity toward; to dislike intensely. **hateful** *adj.* **hatefully** *adv.* **-fulness, hater** *n.*

hau-berk (haw´berk) *n.* A tunic of chain worn as defensive armor.

haugh-ty (haw´tē) *adj.* Arrogantly proud; disdainful. **haughtily** *adv.*

haul (hawl) *v.* To pull or draw with force; to move or transport, as in a truck or cart. **haul** *n.* The distance over which someone travels or something is transported; an amount collected at one time.

haul-age (haw´lij) *n.* The process or act of hauling; a charge for hauling.

haunch (hawnch) *n.* The hip; the buttock and upper thigh of a human or animal; the loin and leg of a four-footed animal.

haunt (hawnt) *v.* To appear to or visit as a ghost or spirit; to visit frequently; to linger in the mind. **haunting** *adj.*

hau-sen (haw´zn) A large white fish, an outstanding source for caviar.

haus-tel-lum (ho-stel´um) *n.* The sucking organ of insects, adapted to suck juices of plants or to suck blood.

haut-bois *or* **haut-boy (hō´boi, ō´boi)** *n.* An oboe; a double reed wind instrument made of wood.

haute couture *n.* Designers who create exclusive fashions for women.

hau-teur (hō ter´) *n.* A disdainful arrogance.

have (hav) *v.* To hold or own, as a possession or a property. **have to** Need to; must. **have had it** Suffered or endured all that one can tolerate.

have-lock (hav´lok) *n.* A cap with a flap that covers the neck, protecting the neck from sun.

ha-ven (hā´ven) *n.* A place that offers a safe refuge; a harbor or port; an inlet which provides a place for ships to anchor.

hav-er-sack (hav´er sak´) *n.* A bag for carrying supplies on a hike or march.

hav-oc (hav´ok) *n.* Mass confusion; widespread destruction; devastation.

haw (haw) *interj.* A hesitating sound made by a speaker who is groping for words. **haw** *v.* To hesitate in speaking; to falter in speaking.

Ha-wai-i *or* **Ha-wai-ian Is-lands** *n.* A state of the United States, which is an island group, located in the central Pacific, statehood August 21, 1959, state capital Honolulu.

hawk (hok) *n.* Any of several predatory birds with a short, hooked bill and strong claws for seizing small prey; one who advocates a warlike foreign policy; one having an aggressive attitude. **hawkish** *adj.* **hawkishly** *adv.*

haw-ser (ho´zėr) *n.* A heavy cable or rope for towing or securing a ship.

haw-thorn (ho´thorn´) *n.* A thorny shrub or tree bearing white or pink flowers and red fruit.

hay (hā) *n.* Alfalfa or grass that has been cut and dried for animal food.

hay-cock (hākok´) *n.* A rounded pile of hay that is stacked and kept outdoors; a haystack.

Hayes, Rutherford Birchard *n.* (1822-1893) The nineteenth president of the United States from 1877-1881.

hay fever *n.* An acute allergy to certain airborne pollens, marked by severe irritation of the upper respiratory tract and the eyes.

hay-wire (hā´wiėr´) *adj.* Broken; emotionally out of control; crazy.

haz-ard (haz´ėrd) *n.* A risk; chance; an accident; danger or source of danger. **hazard** *v.* To take a chance on; to venture. **hazardous** *adj.*

haze (hāz) *n.* A fog-like suspension of dust, smoke, and vapor in the air; a confused or vague state of mind. **haze** *v.* To harass with disagreeable tasks.

ha-zel (hā´zel) *n.* A small tree or shrub bearing edible brown nuts with smooth shells; a light brown or yellowish brown. **hazel** *adj.*

haz-y (hā´zē) *adj.* Lacking clarity; vague. **hazily** *adv.* **haziness** *n.*

he (hē) *pron.* Third person singular masculine or generic pronoun used as the subject of a sentence.

he'd (hēd) *contr.* He had; he would.

he'll (hēl) *contr.* He will.

he's (hēz) *contr.* He has; he is.

he-man (hē´man´) *n. Slang* A man marked by strength; a muscular man.

head (hed) *n.* The upper part of a human or animal body containing the brain, the principal nerve centers, the eyes, ears, nose and mouth. **headed** *adj.*

head-ache (hed´āk´) *n.* A pain or ache in the head. *Slang* A bothersome problem. **headachy** *adj.*

head cold *n.* A common cold or viral infection that centers primarily in the nasal passages.

head-line (hed´li´n´) *n.* A title, caption, or summarizing words of a newspaper story or article printed in large type. **headline** *v.* To provide with a headline; to serve as the star performer.

head-note (hed´nōt´) *n.* A prefixed note of explanation, such as a statement preceding the report of a legal case.

head wind (hed´wind´) *n.* A wind blowing in the direction opposite the course of a ship or aircraft.

head-y (hed´ē) *adj.* Tending to intoxicate; affecting the senses; headstrong. **headily** *adv.* **headiness** *n.*

heal (hēl) *v.* To restore to good health; to mend. **healer** *n.*

health (helth) *n.* The overall condition or function of a living organism at a particular time; freedom from disease or defect. **healthful** *adj,* **healthfully** *adv.* **healthfulness** *n.*

heap (hēp) *n.* A haphazard assortment of things; a large number or quantity. **heap** *v.* To throw or pile into a heap.

hear (hēr) *v.* To perceive by the ear; to listen with careful attention; to be informed of; to listen to officially or formally, as in a court of law.

hear-ing (hēr´ing) *n.* One of the five senses; the range by which sound can be heard; an opportunity to be heard; in law, a preliminary examination of an accused person.

hearing aid *n.* An electronic device used to amplify the hearing of partially deaf persons.

heark-en (här´ken) *v.* To listen carefully.

hear-say (hēr´sā´) *n.* Information heard from another; common talk; rumor.

hearse (hers) *n.* A vehicle for conveying a dead body to the place of burial.

heart (härt) *n.* The hollow, primary muscular organ of vertebrates which circulates blood throughout the body; the emotional center, such as in love, hate, consideration, or compassion; the most essential part of something.

heart-ache (härt´āk´) *n.* Emotional grief; sorrow.

heart attack *n.* An acute malfunction or interrupted heart function.

heart-beat (härt´bēt´)*n.* A pulsation of the heart, consisting of one contraction and one relaxation.

heart block *n.* An impairment of the ventricular beats of the heart.

heart-break (härt´brāk´) *n.* Great sorrow; deep grief. **heartbreaking** *adj.* **heartbreakingly** *adv.*

heart-brok-en (härt´brōken) *a.* Deeply grieved; overcome by sadness.

heart-burn (härt´bern´) *n.* A sensation of burning in the stomach and esophagus, usually caused by excess acid in the stomach.

heart disease *n.* An abnormality of the heart or circulation.

heart-en (här´ten) *v.* To give courage to.

heart-felt (härt´felt´) *adj.* Deeply felt; sincere.

hearth (härth) *n.* The floor of a fireplace or furnace; the stone that forms the front of a fireplace.

heart-y (här´tē) *adj.* Marked by exuberant warmth; full of vigor; nourishing; substantial. **heartily** *adv.* **heartiness** *n.*

heat (hēt) *n.* A quality of being hot or warm; a degree of warmth; depth of feeling; a period of sexual ardor in female animals. *Slang* Pressure or stress. **heat** *v.* To make or become warm or hot. **heater** *n.*

heath (hēth) *n.* An open tract of uncultivated wasteland covered with low-growing shrubs and plants.

hea-then (hē´then) *n.* A person or nation that does not recognize the God of Christianity, Judaism, or Islam; in the Old Testament, a Gentile; non-Jew. **heathen, heathenish** *adj.*

heath-er (heth´ėr) *n.* A shrub that grows in dense masses and has small evergreen leaves and small pinkish flowers. **heather, heathery** *adj.*

heave (hēv) *v.* To raise or lift, especially forcibly; to hurl or throw. *Naut.* To push, pull, or haul, as by a rope. *Slang* To vomit. **heave** *n.* The act of throwing.

heav-en (hev´en) *n.* The sky; the region above and around the earth; the abode of God, the angels, and the blessed souls of the dead; a state or place of blissful happiness. **heavenliness** *n.* **heavenward** *adv.* & *adj.*

heav-en-ly (hev´en-lē) *adj.* Relating to heaven; celestial; delightful; holy.

heav-y (hev´ē) *adj.* Of great weight; very thick or dense; forceful; powerful; rough and violent, as stormy weather; of great significance; grave; painful, as bad news; oppressive.

heavy water *n.* Water that contains more than the usual hydrogen in its heavier isotopic form, deuterium, used for scientific experiments.

heb-do-mad (heb´do mad´) *n.* A period of seven days.

he-be-phre-nia (hē´be frē´nē a) *n.* A schizophrenic reaction causing silliness, hallucinations and regression.

heb-e-tate (heb´i-tāt´) *v.* To dull; to become dull or blunt.

He-brew (hēbrö) *n.* A member of a Semitic people claiming descent from Abraham, Isaac, and Jacob; the modern form of the language of the Hebrews.

heck (hek) *interj.* & *n.* *Slang* An

expression of disappointment, as in *oh heck*.

heck-le (hek´l) *v.* To badger or annoy, as with questions, comments, or gibes.

hec-tic (hek´tik) *adj.* Intensely active, rushed, or excited; marked by a persistent and fluctuating fever caused by a disease, such as tuberculosis; feverish; flushed.

hec-to-graph (hek´to graf) *n.* A machine for making copies of a drawing on a gelatin surface.

hec-tor (hek´tér) *n.* A bully; domineering person. **hector** *v.* To intimidate, to bully.

bed-dle (hed´l) *n.* A set of parallel cords or wires that guide warp threads in a loom.

hedge (hej) *n.* A boundary or fence formed of shrubs or low-growing trees; a means to guard against financial loss; a deliberately ambiguous statement.

he-don-ics *n.* Branch of ethics relating to pleasure. **hedonic** *adj.*

he-don-ism (hēd´o niz´um) *n.* The doctrine devoted to the pursuit of pleasure; the philosophy that pleasure is the principal good in life. **hedonist** *n.* **hedonistic** *adj.*

heed (hēd) *v.* To pay attention; to take notice of something. **heed** *n.* Attention. **heedful** *adj.* **heedfully** *adv.*

heed-less (hēd´lis) *adj.* Without heed; inconsiderate; careless.

heel (hēl) *n.* The rounded back part of the human foot under and behind the ankle; the part of a shoe supporting or covering the heel; a lower or bottom part; the crusty ends of a loaf of bread. **heel** *v.* To follow along at one's heels.

heft (heft) *n.* Weight; bulk; importance. **heft** *v.* To gauge or estimate the weight of by lifting; to lift up.

heft-y (hef´tē) *adj.* Bulky; heavy; sizable.

he-gem-o-ny (hi jem´o nē) *n.* Dominance or leadership, as of one country over another.

he-gi-ra (hi jī´ra) *n.* A journey or departure to flee an undesirable situation.

heif-er (hef´ér) *n.* A young cow, particularly one that has not produced a calf.

height (hīt) *n.* The quality of being high; the highest or most advanced point; the distance from the base of something; the apex; the distance above a specified level; altitude; the distance from head to foot.

height-en (hīt´en) *v.* To increase or become high in quantity or degree; to raise or lift.

Heimlich maneuver *n.* An emergency maneuver used to dislodge food from a choking person's throat; the closed fist is placed below the rib cage and

pressed inward to force air from the lungs upward.

hei-nous (hā´nus) *adj.* Extremely wicked; hateful or shockingly wicked. **heinously** *adv.* **heinousness** *n.*

heir (âr) *n.* A person who inherits another's property or title.

heir apparent *n.* An heir who is legally assured of his right to inherit if he survives his ancestor.

heir-ess *n.* A female heir, especially to a large fortune.

heir-loom (âr´lōm´) *n.* A family possession handed down from generation to generation; an article of personal property acquired by legal inheritance.

heist (hīst) *v.* To take from; to steal. **heist** *n.* A robbery.

he-li-an-thus (hō-lō-an´thus) *n.* Herbaceous plants, some of which are sunflowers.

hel-i-cal (hel´i kal) *adj.* Of or pertaining to the shape of a helix. **helically** *adv.*

hel-i-con (hel´i kon´) *n.* A large, circular tuba that encircles the player's shoulder.

hel-i-cop-ter (hel´i kop´tér) *n.* An aircraft propelled by rotors which can take off vertically rather than needing an approach or a rolling start.

he-li-o-cen-tric (hē´lē-ō-sen´trik) *adj.* Referred to, measured or as seen from the sun's center.

he-lio-graph (hē´lē o graf´) *n.* An apparatus for sending messages using the sun's rays reflected from a mirror.

he-li-o-trope (hē´lē-ō-trōp´) *n.* A garden plant having small, fragrant, purple flowers.

he-li-um (hē´lē um) *n.* An extremely light, nonflammable, odorless, gaseous element, symbolized by He.

he-lix (hē´liks) *n.* Something that is spiral in form; a spiral line, as of wire winding around a tube; a coil.

hell *or* **Hell (hel)** *n.* The abode of the dead souls condemned to eternal punishment; a place of evil, torment, or destruction; great distress; anguish; a cause of trouble or misery. **hellish** *adj.* **hellishly** *adv.*

hel-lo (he lō´) *n.* An expression of greeting.

helm (helm) *n.* A wheel or steering apparatus for a ship; a position or any place of control or command.

hel-met (hel´mit) *n.* A protective covering for the head made of metal, leather, or plastic.

hel-minth (hel´minth) *n.* An intestinal worm, as the tapeworm.

helms-man (helmz´man) *n.* One who guides a ship.

hel-ot *n.* A serf; a slave. **helotry** *n.*

help (help) *v.* To assist or aid. **help** *n.*

Assistance; relief; one that assists; one hired to help. **helper** *n.* **helpful** *adj.*

help-ing (hel´ping) *n.* A single serving of food.

hel-ter–skel-ter (hel´tèr skel´tèr) *adv.* In a confused or hurried manner; in an aimless way. **helter-skelter** *adj.* Rushed and confused. **helter-skelter** *n.* Great confusion; a tumult.

helve (helv) *n.* A handle on a tool such as an axe or hatchet.

hem (hem) *n.* A finished edge of fabric folded under and stitched. **hem** *interj.* A sound made as in clearing the throat, used especially to attract attention or to fill a pause in speech. **hem** *v.* To fold under and stitch down the edge of. **hem in** to confine and surround.

he-mal (hē´mal) *adj.* Pertaining to the blood or blood vessels; noting, pertaining to, or situated on that side of the spinal column containing the heart and great blood vessels.

hem-an-gi-o-ma (hē man´jē o˝ma) *n.* A benign tumor that occurs as a reddish elevated area on the skin.

hem-a-tin-ic (hem´a tin´ik) *n.* A medicine that tends to stimulate blood cell formation or increases the hemoglobin in the blood

he-ma-tol-o-gy (hem´a tol´o jē) *n.* The branch of biological science that deals with blood and blood-generating organs. **hematologist** *n.*

he-ma-to-ma *n.* A tumor containing blood.

hem-i-cel-lu-lose (hem´i sel´ū lōs˝) *n.* A natural carbohydrate less complex than cellulose, found mainly in the woody tissue of plants.

hem-i-cy-cle (hem´i sī˝kl) *n.* A curved or half circle; a semicircular structure or building.

hem-i-ple-gia *n.* The paralysis of one half of the body or part of it resulting from injury to the motor center of the brain.

hem-i-sphere (hem´i sfēr˝) *n.* A half sphere that is divided by a plane passing through its center; either symmetrical half of an approximately spherical shape; the northern or southern half of the earth divided by the equator or the eastern or western half divided by a meridian.

hem-line (hem´lin˝) *n.* The line formed at the lower edge of a garment such as a skirt or dress.

he-mo-cy-to-me-ter (hē˝mō sī tom´i tèr) *n.* The instrument used in counting blood corpuscles.

he-mo-dy-nam-ics *n.* The branch of physiology that deals with the circulation of the blood.

he-mo-glo-bin (hē˝mo glō˝bin) *n.* The iron-containing respiratory pigment occurring in red corpuscles of

vertebrates.

he-mo-ly-sin *n.* A substance which causes the dissolution of red blood cells.

he-mo-phil-i-a (hē˝mo fil´ē a) *n. Pathol.* An inherited blood disease characterized by severe, protracted, sometimes spontaneous bleeding.

hem-or-rhage (hem´ér ij) *n.* Bleeding, especially excessive bleeding. .

hem-or-rhoid (hem´o roid˝) *n. Pathol.* A painful mass of dilated veins in swollen anal tissue. Also called *hemorrhoids* or *piles.*

he-mo-stat (hē˝mo stat´) *n.* An agent that stops bleeding; a clamp-like instrument for preventing or reducing bleeding.

hemp (hemp) *n.* An Asian herb; hashish and marijuana are produced from the female plant and coarse fabrics and rope are made from the tough fibers of the male plant. **hempen** *adj.*

hem-stitch (hem´i stik˝) *n.* The decorative border stitch used in sewing.

hen (hen) *n.* A mature female bird, especially an adult female domestic fowl.

hence (hens) *adv.* From this place or time; from this source.

hence-forth (hens´ fōr-th´) *adv.* From this time on. Also *henceforward.*

hen-dec-a-gon (hen dek´a gon˝) *n.* A plane figure with eleven sides and the same number of angles.

hen-e-quen (hen´e kin) *n.* A strong fiber obtained from the leaves of a tropical American plant, used for binder twine and course fabrics.

hen-na (hen´a) *n.* An Asian and North African ornamental tree bearing fragrant white or reddish flowers; a brownish red dye derived from henna leaves and used as a cosmetic dye; a strong reddish brown.

heno-the-ism (hen´o thē iz˝um) *n.* The worship of one god although not denying the existence of other gods.

hep (hep) *adj. Slang* Knowledgeable about the styles or tends.

hep-a-rin (hep´a rin) *n. Biochem* A substance found especially in liver tissue having the power to slow or prevent blood clotting.

he-pat-ic (hi pat´ik) *adj.* Of or like the liver.

hep-a-ti-tis (hep´a tī´tis) *n. Pathol.* Inflammation of the liver causing jaundice.

hep-a-tize (hep´a tīz˝) *v. Pathol.* To convert, as the spongy lung tissue, into liver-like tissue, caused by congestion.

hep-tad (hep´tad) *n.* A group of seven.

hep-ta-gon (hep´ta gon˝) *n.* A polygon with seven angles and sides.

hep-tam-er-ous (hep tam´ér us) *adj.*

Containing seven parts.

her *pron.* The objective case and the possessive case of the feminine pronoun *she.*

her-ald (her´ald) *n.* A person who announces important news; one that comes before as a sign of what is to follow. **herald** *v.* To announce; to introduce. **heraldic** *adj.*

her-ald-ry (her´al drē) *n., pl.* **heraldries** The art or science of tracing genealogies and devising and granting coats of arms.

herb (erb) *n.* A soft-stemmed plant without woody tissue that usually withers and dies each year; an often pleasant-smelling plant.

her-ba-ceous (her bā´shus) *adj.* Like, or consisting of herbs; green and leaf-like.

herb-age (hur´bij) *n.* Herbs collectively; herbaceous vegetation; the succulent parts of herbaceous plants, as leaves and stems.

her-bal (hur´bal, ur´bal) *n.* A book on plants or herbs with reference to their medicinal properties.

herb-al-ist (her´ba list) *n.* One who gathers, grows, and deals in herbs.

her-bar-i-um (her bâr´ē um) *n., pl.* **herbariums** *or* **herbaria** A collection of dried plant specimens that are scientifically arranged for study; a place housing an herbarium.

her-bi-cide (er´bi sīd´) *n.* A chemical agent used to kill weeds.

her-bi-vore (her´bi vō´) *n.* A plant-eating animal.

her-biv-o-rous (her biv´ér us) *adj.* Feeding chiefly on plant life or vegetables. **herbivorously** *adv.*

her-cu-le-an (hèr´kū lē´an) *adj.* Of unusual size, force, or difficulty; having great strength.

herd (hèrd) *n.* A number of cattle or other animals of the same kind, kept or staying together as a group; a large crowd of people. **herd** *v.* To bring together in a herd. **herdsman** *n.*

here (hēr) *adv.* In or at this place; in a present life or state.

here-af-ter (hēr af´tèr) *adv.* From now on; at some future time. **hereafter** *n.* Existence after death.

here-by (hēr bī´) *adv.* By means or by virtue of.

her-e-dit-a-ment (her´i dit´a ment) *n.* Any heritable property.

he-red-i-tar-y (he red´i ter´ē) *adj.* Passing or transmitted from an ancestor to a legal heir; having an inherited title or possession; genetically transmitted from parent to offspring.

he-red-i-ty (he´red´i tē) *n.* The genetic transmission of traits from parents to offspring.

here-in (hēr in´) *adv.* In or into this place.

here-of (hēr uv´) *adv.* Relating to or in regard to.

her-e-sy (her´i sē) *n., pl.* **heresies** A belief in conflict with orthodox religious beliefs; any belief contrary to set doctrine.

her-e-tic (her´i tik) *n.* A person holding opinions different from orthodox beliefs, especially religious beliefs.

here-to (hēr tō´) *adv.* To this matter, proposition, or thing.

here-with (hēr with´) *adv.* Together or along with this; hereby.

her-i-ta-ble (her´i ta bl) *adj.* Capable of being inherited. **heritably** *adv.*

her-i-tage (her´i tij) *n.* Property that is inherited; something handed down from past generations; a legacy.

herm (hèrm) *n.* Monument or statue, in the form of a square stone pillar, consisting of a head or bust.

her-maph-ro-dite (hèr maf´ro dīt´) *n.* A person, animal, or plant having both male and female reproductive organs. **hermaphroditic** *adj.*

her-me-neu-tics (hur´me nō´tiks) *n.* The art of interpretation of Bible scriptures.

her-met-ic *or* **her-met-i-cal** (her met´ik) *adj.* Tightly sealed against air and liquids; made impervious to outside influences. **hermetically** *adv.*

her-mit (hèr´mit) *n.* A person who lives in seclusion, often for religious reasons.

her-ni-a (hèr´nē a) *n.* The protrusion of a bodily organ, as the intestine, through an abnormally weakened wall that usually surrounds it; a rupture.

he-ro (hēr´ō) *n., pl.* **heroes** A person of outstanding valor; a figure in mythology and legend renowned for exceptional courage and fortitude.

he-ro-ic (hi rō´ik) *adj.* Relating or pertaining to heroes; impressive in power, size or extent; a great intensity; extreme. **heroically** *adv.*

heroic couplet *n.* A verse consisting of two rhyming lines of iambic pentameter.

her-o-in (her´ō in) *n.* A highly addictive narcotic derivative of morphine.

her-o-ine (her´ō in) *n.* A woman of heroic character; the principal female character in a story or play.

her-o-ism (her´ō iz´um) *n.* Heroic behavior.

her-on (her´on) *n.* A bird having a long slender bill, long legs, and a long neck.

her-pes (hèr´pēz) *n. Pathol.* A viral infection, characterized by small blisters on the skin or mucous membranes. **herpetic** *adj.*

her-pe-tol-o-gy (hèr´pi tol´o jē) *n.* The scientific study and treatment of reptiles and amphibians. **herpetologic**, **herpetological** *adj.* **herpetologically**

adv. **herpetologist** *n.*

her-ring-bone (her´ing bōn´) *n.* A pattern utilizing rows of short slanted parallel lines with connected rows slanting in the opposite direction.

herring gull *n.* The most common large gull in North America, living on both the seashore and inland waters.

hertz *n.* A unit of frequency equaling one cycle per second.

hes-i-tant (hez´i tənt) *adj.* Given to hesitating; lacking decisiveness.

hes-i-tate (hez´i tāt´) *v.* To pause or to be slow before acting, speaking, or deciding; to be uncertain.

hes-i-ta-tion (hez´i tā´shən) *n.* The act of hesitating; a state of doubt or pausing.

het-er-o-chro-mat-ic (het´ér o krō mat´ ik) *adj.* Of or relating to or containing different colors; made up of different frequencies or wavelengths.

het-er-o-cy-clic (het´ér o sī´klik) *adj.* Relating to or characterized by an organic compound having a ring containing one or more atoms other than carbon.

het-er-o-dox (het´ér o doks´) *adj.* Not in accord with established beliefs or religious doctrine; holding unorthodox opinions or beliefs. **heterodoxy** *n.*

het-er-oe-cious (het´e rē´shus) *adj.* Of a parasite, passing through the different stages in the life cycle on often different hosts, as certain fungi.

het-er-on-o-my (het´e ron´o mē) *n.* Subordination to another.

het-er-o-nym (het´ér o nim´) *n.* A word having the same spelling as another but a different meaning and pronunciation.

het-er-o-plas-ty (het´ér o plas´tē) *n.* An operation in where lesions are repaired with grafted tissue taken from another organism or person.

het-er-o-sex-u-al (het´ér o sek´shö al) *adj.* Of or having sexual desire toward the opposite sex; involving different sexes. **heterosexuality** *n.*

het-er-o-sis (het´e rō´sis) *n.* An increased vigor or capacity for growth, often as the result of cross-breeding of plants or animals.

het-er-o-troph-ic (het´ér o trof´ik) *adj. Biol.* Using organic matter as a source of food.

het-er-o-zy-gote (het´ér o zī´gōt) *n.* A hybrid plant or animal that does not breed true because it contains at least one pair of genes with different characteristics.

heu-ris-tic (hū ris´tik) *adj.* Involving a teaching method that utilizes self-educating or a method of trial and error to improve performance.

hew (hū) *v.* To make or shape with or as

if with an axe; to adhere strictly; to conform.

hex (heks) *n.* One held to bring bad luck; a jinx. **hex** *v.* To put under an evil spell; to bewitch.

hex-a-gon (hek´sa gon´) *n.* A polygon having six sides and six angles. **hexagonal** *adj.* **hexagonally** *adv.*

hex-a-gram (hek´sa gram´) *n.* A six-pointed starlike figure formed by placing two equilateral triangles concentrically with their sides parallel and on opposite sides of the center.

hex-am-e-ter (hek sam´i tér) *n.* A line of verse containing six metrical feet.

hex-a-pod (hek´sa pod´) *n.* Arthropods having six feet, comprising the true insects.

hey (hā) *interj.* An exclamation used to express surprise or joy and used to call attention to something.

hey-day (hā´dā´) *n.* A time of great power, prosperity or popularity; a peak.

hi-a-tus (hī ā´tus) *n.* A gap, break, or lapse in time from which something is missing; a break; a break between shooting of television shows; a break in continuity.

hi-ba-chi *n., pl.* **hibachis** (hē bä´chē) A deep, portable charcoal grill used for cooking food.

hi-ber-nac-u-lum (hī´bér nak´ü lum) *n.* A shelter occupied during the winter by a dormant animal.

hi-ber-nal (hī bur´nəl) *adj.* Relating to or belonging to the winter season; wintry.

hi-ber-nate (hī´bér nāt´) *v.* To pass the winter in an inactive, dormant, sleep-like state. **hibernation** *n.*

hick (hik) *n. Slang* A clumsy, unsophisticated country person. **hick** *adj.*

hick-o-ry (hik´o rē) *n., pl.* **hickories** A North American tree with a smooth or shaggy bark, hard edible nuts, and heavy, tough wood.

hid-den (hidən) *adj.* Out of sight; away from the public eye.

hide (hīd) *v.* To put or keep out of sight; to keep secret; to obscure from sight; to conceal oneself. **hide** *n.* The skin of an animal.

hid-e-ous (hid´ē us) *adj.* Physically repulsive; extremely ugly. **hideously** *adv.* **hideousness** *n.*

hi-dro-sis (hi drō´sis) *n.* Perspiration, especially the excretion of sweat due to drugs, or a disease characterized by sweating.

hi-er-ar-chy (hī´e rär´kē) *n., pl.* **hierarchies** An authoritative body or group of things or persons arranged in successive order; a ranked series of persons or things. **hierachic** *adj.*

hi-er-o-glyph (hī´ér o glif´) *n.* A symbol.

hi-er-o-glyph-ic (hī´ér o glif´ik) *n.* A

pictorial symbol representing an idea, object, or sound. **hieroglyphically** *adv.*

hi-er-o-phant (hī´ĕr o fant˝) *n.* A priest in ancient Greece; one who interprets the rites of religion.

hi-fi (hī´fī˝) *n.* High fidelity; electronic equipment capable of reproducing high fidelity sound. **hi-fi** *adj.*

hig-gle (hig´l) *v.* To bargain; to argue or haggle often over petty details.

high (hī) *adj.* Extending upward; located at a distance above the ground; more than normal in degree or amount; expensive.

higher education *n.* An education beyond the secondary level; college education.

high fidelity *n. Electronics* The reproduction of sound with minimal distortion, as on records or tapes.

high frequency *n.* A radio frequency in the band from three to thirty megacycles.

high-road (hī´rōd˝) *n.* A main road; a direct or guaranteed method or course.

high-strung (hī´strung´) *adj.* Very nervous and excitable.

high tech *n.* An interior design that incorporates industrial materials or motifs; high technology.

high-way (hī´wā˝) *n.* A main or principal road or thoroughfare of some length which connects towns and cities and is open to the public.

hi-jack *or* **high-jack** (hī´jak˝) *v.* To seize illegally or steal while in transit; to coerce or compel someone; to commandeer a vehicle, especially an airplane in flight. **highjacker** *n.*

hike (hīk) *v.* To walk for a lengthy amount of time usually through rugged terrain or woods; to pull up clothing with a sudden motion. **hike** *n.* **hiker** *n.*

hi-lar-i-ous (hi lâr´ē us) *adj.* Boisterously happy or cheerful. **hilariously** *adv.* **hilarity** *n.*

hill (hil) *n.* A rounded elevation of the earth's surface, smaller than a mountain; a pile or heap; a small pile or mound, as of soil. **hill** *v.* To surround or cover with hills, as potatoes.

hill-ock (hil´ok) *n.* A small or low hill or mound. **hillocky** *adj.*

hill-top *n.* The summit or top of a hill.

hilt (hilt) *n.* The handle of a dagger or sword. **to the hilt** Fully; completely; thoroughly.

him (him) *pron.* The objective case of the masculine pronoun *he.*

hi-mat-i-on (hi mat´ē on˝) *n.* A rectangular cloth draped over the left shoulder and body and worn as a garment in Greece.

him-self (him self´) *pron.* The identical male one; reflexive form of the third person masculine pronoun.

hind (hīnd) *adj.* Located at or toward the rear part; posterior.

hind-brain (hīnd´brān˝) *n.* The posterior of the three primary divisions of the vertebrate brain including the pons, cerebellum, and medulla oblongata.

hin-der (hin´dĕr) *v.* To interfere with the progress or action of. **hinderer** *n.*

hind-most (hīnd´mōst˝) *adj.* Farthest to the rear or back.

hin-drance (hin´drans) *n.* The act of hindering or state of being hindered.

hind-sight (hīnd´sīt˝) *n.* Comprehension or understanding of an event after it has happened.

hinge (hinj) *n.* A jointed device which allows a part, as a door or gate, to swing or turn on another frame. **hinge** *v.* To attach by or to equip with a hinge or hinges; to be dependent on a single consideration or point.

hin-ny (hin´ē) *n.* The hybrid offspring of a stallion and female donkey.

hint (hint) *n.* An indirect indication or suggestion. **hint** *v.* To make something known by a hint.

hin-ter-land (hin´tĕr land˝) *n.* A region remote from cities; an inland area adjacent to a coastal area.

hip (hip) *n.* The part of the human body that projects outward between the waist and thigh; the hip joint; the bright, red seed case of a rose. **hip** *adj. Slang* Said to be aware of or informed about current happenings.

hip-bone (hip´bōn˝) *n.* The large, flat bone which forms a lateral half of the pelvis.

hip joint *n.* The joint between the hipbone and the thighbone.

hip-pie *or* **hip-py** (hip´ē) *n., pl.* **hippies** A young person who adopts unconventional dress and behavior along with the use of drugs to express withdrawal from middle class life and indifference to its values.

hire (hīer) *v.* To obtain the service of another for pay. **hirer** *n.*

hir-sute (her´sōt) *adj.* Covered with hair.

his (hiz) *pron.* The possessive case of the masculine or generic pronoun *he.*

His-pan-ic (hi span´ik) *adj.* Of or relating to the language, people, or culture of Spain or Latin America.

his-pid (his´pid) *adj.* Rough, shaggy, or covered with stiff bristles.

hiss (his) *n.* A sound resembling a prolonged, sibilant sound, as that of *sss.* **hiss** *v.* To emit such a sound as an expression of disapproval.

hist (hist) *interj.* A sibilant exclamation used to attract attention or command silence.

his-ta-mine (his´ta mēn˝) *n. Biochem.* A white, crystalline compound that is found in plant and animal tissue, responsible for reducing blood pressure and having a dilating effect which plays a major role in reducing the symptoms of allergies. **histaminic** *adj*.

his-to-gen-e-sis (his´to jen´i sis) *n*. The origin, development, and formation of tissues.

his-tol-o-gy (hi stol´o jē) *n*., *pl*. **histologies** The study of the minute structures of animal and plant tissues as seen through a microscope.

his-tol-y-sis (hi stol´i sis) *n*. The dissolution and breaking down of bodily tissues.

his-tone (his´tōn) *n*. Any of a class of protein substances that, on hydrolysis, yield amino acids.

his-to-ri-an (hi stōr´ē an) *n*. A person who specializes in the writing or study of history.

his-tor-ic (hi stor´ik) *adj*. Significant or famous in history; historical.

his-tor-i-cal (hi stor´i kal) *adj*. Relating to or taking place in history; serving as a source of knowledge of the past; historic. **historically** *adv*.

his-to-ry (his´to rē) *n*., *pl*. **histories** Past events, especially those involving human affairs; an account or record of past events that is written in chronological order, especially those concerning a particular nation, people, activity, or knowledge; the study of the past and its significance.

hit (hit) *v*. To give a blow to; to strike with force; to come forcibly in contact with; to collide with; to inflict a blow on; to move or set in motion by striking; in baseball, to make a successful hit while at bat. **hitter** *n*.

hitch (hich) *v*. To fasten or tie temporarily, with a hook or knot. *Slang* To unite in marriage; to obtain a ride by hitchhiking. **hitch** *n*. A delay or difficulty. *Milit*. A period of time in the armed forces.

hitch-hike (hich´hīk´) *v*. To travel by signaling and obtaining rides from passing drivers. **hitchhiker** *n*.

hith-er (hith´ér) *adv*. To this place. **hither** *adj*. Situated toward this side.

hith-er-to (hith´ér tö´) *adv*. Up to now.

hive (hīv) *n*. A natural or man-made structure serving as a habitation for honeybees; a beehive.

hives (hīvz) *n*., *pl*. Any of various allergic conditions marked by itching welts.

ho (hō) *interj*. An exclamation expressing surprise; a call used to attract attention; exultation.

hoar (hōr) *adj*. Having white or gray hair; grayish or white, as with frost.

hoard (hōrd) *n*. The accumulation of something stored away for safekeeping or future use. **hoard** *v*. To amass and hide or store valuables, money, or

supplies. **hoarder** *n*.

hoarse (hōrs) *adj*. Having a husky, gruff, or croaking voice. **hoarsely** *adv*.

hoars-en *v*. To become or make hoarse.

ho-at-zin (hō at´sin) *n*. A crested, olive-colored bird of South America, smaller than a pheasant and noted for the claws which grow out of its wings.

hoax (hōks) *n*. A trick or deception. **hoax** *v*. To deceive by a hoax. **hoaxer** *n*.

hob (hob) *n*. The projection at the side or interior of a fireplace used to keep things warm; an elf or hobgoblin.

ho-bo (hō´bō) *n*., *pl*. **hoboes** *or* **hobos** A vagrant who travels aimlessly about; a tramp.

hock (hok) *n*. The joint of the hind leg of a horse, ox, or other animal which corresponds to the ankle in man.

hock-ey (hok´ē) *n*. A game played on ice between two teams of skaters whose object is to drive a puck into the opponent's goal using curved wooden sticks; a similar kind of hockey played on a field with a small ball instead of a puck.

ho-cus-po-cus (hō´kus pō´kus) *n*. Any deception or trickery, as misleading gestures; nonsense words or phrases used in conjuring or sleight of hand.

hod (hod) *n*. A V-shaped trough held over the shoulder to carry loads, as bricks or mortar.

hodge-podge (hoj´poj´) *n*. A jumbled mixture or collection.

Hodgkin's disease *n*. *Pathol*. A disease characterized by progressive enlargement of the lymph nodes, lymphoid tissue, and spleen, generally fatal.

hoe (hō) *n*. A tool with a long handle and flat blade used for weeding, cultivating, and loosening the soil. **hoe** *v*. **hoer** *n*.

hoe-down (hō´dou´´) *n*. A lively country square dance; party.

hog (hog) *n*. A pig, especially one weighing more than 120 pounds and raised for the market; a greedy, selfish, or dirty person. **hog** *v*. To take something selfishly; to take more than one's share. **hoggish** *adj*. **hoggishly** *adv*. **hoggishness** *n*.

ho-gan (hō´gon) *n*. A building made of logs and mud and used as a dwelling by the Navaho Indians.

hog-back (hag´bak´) *n*. A sharply crested ridge of land with steeply sloping sides.

hoi pol-loi (hoi´ po loi´) *n*. The common people; the masses.

hoist (hoist) *v*. To haul or raise up. **hoist** *n*. A machine used for raising large objects.

ho-kum (hō´kum) *n*. Material introduced into a speech or a device used to evoke laughter or a desired audience response.

hold (hōld) *v*. To take and keep as in one's hand; to grasp; to possess; to put or keep in a particular place, position, or relationship; to suppress; to keep under control. **hold** *n.* A cargo storage area inside a ship or aircraft. **hold back** To withhold; retain. hold down To suppress. **hold in** To restrain or repress. **hold off** To keep from touching; to delay. **hold on** To continue, to endure, to cling to. **hold together** To remain united.

holding company *n.* A company which owns controlling stock or interest in securities of other companies.

hole (hōl) *n.* A cavity or opening in a solid mass or body. **hole** *v.*

hol-i-day (hol´i dā´) *n.* A day set aside by law to commemorate a special person or event; a day set aside for religious observance; a day free from work; any day of rest.

ho-li-ness (hō´lē nis) *n.* The state of being holy.

ho-lism (hō´liz um) *n.* The theory that a living being has an identity other than the sum of its parts.

hol-land (hol´and) *n.* An unbleached, linen or cotton fabric used in the manufacture of window shades, clothing and bookbindings.

hol-lan-daise sauce (hol´an dāz´ sos) *n.* A creamy sauce made from butter, egg yolks, and lemon juice or vinegar.

hol-ler (hol´ėr) *v.* To shout loudly; to yell. **holler** *n.*

hol-low (hol´ō) *adj.* Having a cavity or space within; concave or sunken; lacking significance or substance; not genuine; empty; meaningless. **hollowly** *adv.* **hollow** *n.*

hol-ly (hol´ē) *n.*, *pl.* **hollies** A tree or shrub that bears glossy spiny leaves and bright-red berries.

hol-ly-hock (hol´ē hok´) *n.* A tall, cultivated plant of the mallow family, widely cultivated for its tall spikes of large, variously colored flowers.

hol-o-caust (hol´o kost´) *n.* A widespread or total destruction, especially by fire.

hol-o-graph (hol´o graf´) *n.* A handwritten document, as a letter or will, signed by the person who wrote it. **holographic, holographical** *adj.*

ho-lo-gram (hō´lo gram) *n.* A three-dimensional picture made on a photographic plate without the use of a camera and viewed with coherent light from behind.

hol-o-type (hol´o tīp´) *n.* A single specimen selected for descriptive and taxonomical purposes to represent the entire species. **holotypic** *adj.*

Hol-stein (hōl´stīn) *n.* A breed of dairy cattle with black and white coloring.

hol-ster (hōl´stėr) *n.* A leather case designed to hold a pistol or gun. **holstered** *adj.*

ho-ly (hō´lē) *adj.* Regarded as having divine power; sacred; spiritually pure.

Holy Communion *n.* The Christian rite during which the Eucharist is received.

Holy Ghost *n.* The third person of the Christian Trinity.

Holy Spirit *n.* The Holy Ghost.

ho-ly-stone (hō´lē stōn´) *n.* A soft sandstone used by seamen to scrub the decks of ships.

hom-age (hom´ij) *n.* Great respect or honor, especially when expressed publicly.

hom-burg (hom´berg) *n.* A man's felt hat having a stiff brim and high crown creased lengthwise.

home (hōm) *n.* The place where one resides; a place of origin; one's birthplace or residence during the formative years; a place one holds dear because of personal feelings or relationships; a place of security and comfort. **home** *n. & adj.*

home economics *n.* The study of the principles of home management.

ho-me-op-a-thy (hō´mē op´a thē) *n.* A system of treating a disease with minute doses of medicines that produce the symptoms of the disease being treated. **homeopath** *n.* **homeopathic** *adj.*

ho-me-o-sta-sis (hō´mē o stā´sis) *n. Biol.* A state of equilibrium that occurs between different but interdependent elements.

hom-i-cide (hom´i sīd´) *n.* The killing of one person by another; a person who kills another.

hom-i-let-ic (hom´i let´ik) *n.* Pertaining to the nature of a sermon.

hom-i-ly (hom´i lē) *n.*, *pl.* **homilies** A sermon, particularly a discourse on moral behavior.

homing pigeon *n.* A pigeon trained to find its way home from great distances.

hom-i-ny (hom´i nē) *n.* Kernels of hulled and dried corn, often ground into a coarse white meal and boiled.

ho-mo-cer-cal (hō´mo sur´kal) *adj.* Having the lobes of the tail fin of approximately equal size, and the vertebral column ending near the base.

ho-mo-ge-ne-ous (hō´mo jē´nē us) *adj.* Of a similar nature or kind. **homogeneity, homogeneousness** *n.*

ho-mog-e-nize (ho moj´e nīz´) *v.* To process milk by breaking up fat globules and dispersing them uniformly. **homogenization,** *n.*

ho-mog-o-nous (ho mog´o nus) *adj.* Pertaining to a type of flower with equally long stamens and pistils.

ho-mo-graft (hō´mo graft´) *n.* A tissue taken from an individual and grafted to another of the same species.

hom-o-graph (ho´mo graf´) *n.* A word that is identical to another in spelling, but different from it in origin and meaning.

ho-moi-o-ther-mal (hō moi´o thur´mal) *adj.* Having a relatively constant body temperature independent of the surroundings.

ho-mol-o-gate (ho mol´o gāt´) *v.* To approve; to ratify.

ho-mol-o-gous (ho mol´o gus) *adj.* Related or similar in structure, nature, position, or value.

ho-mo-mor-phic(hō´mo mar´fik,hom´o mar´fik) *adj.* Having the same external form.

hom-o-nym (hom´o nim) *n.* A word that has the same sound and often the same spelling as another but a different meaning and origin.

hom-o-phone (hom´o fōn´) *n.* One of two or more words that have the same sound but different spelling, origin, and meaning.

Ho-mo sa-pi-ens (hō´mō sā´pēenz) *n.* The scientific name for the humankind.

ho-mo-sex-u-al (hō´mo sek´shō al) *adj.* Having sexual attraction or desire for persons of the same sex. **homosexual, homosexuality** *n.*

hon-cho *n., pl.* **honchos** The main person in charge; the boss; the manager.

hone (hōn) *n.* A fine-grained stone used to sharpen cutting tools, such as knives or razors. **hone** *v.* To perfect something; to sharpen.

hon-est (on´ist) *adj.* Not cheating, or stealing; free from fraud; truthful; honorable. **honestly** *adv.*

hon-es-ty (on´i stē) *n.* The quality of being honest; free from deceit or fraud; straightforwardness.

hon-ey (hun´ē) *n., pl.* **honeys** A sweet, sticky substance made by bees from the nectar gathered from flowers; sweetness. *Slang* Dear; darling.

hon-ey-bee (hun´ē bē´) *n.* Any of various bees living in colonies and producing honey.

hon-ey-moon (hun´ē mōn´) *n.* A trip taken by a newly married couple. **honeymoon** *v.* **honeymooner** *n.*

honk (hongk) *n.* The harsh, loud sound made by a goose; the sound made by an automobile horn. **honker** *n.*

hon-ky-tonk (hong´ē tongk´) *n.* A cheap bar or nightclub.

hon-or (on´ėr) *n.* High regard or respect; personal integrity; reputation; privilege; a title for mayors and judges. **honor** *v.* To accept something as valid; to treat with respect. **honorer** *n.*

hon-or-a-ble (on´ėr a bl) *adj.* Worthy of esteem.

hon-o-rar-i-um (on´o râr´ē um) *n.* A payment or reward given in recognition for a service performed for which custom or propriety discourages a fixed fee.

hon-or-ar-y (on´o rer´ē) *adj.* Relating to an office or title bestowed as an honor, without the customary powers, duties, or salaries.

hon-or-if-ic (on´o rif´ik) *adj.* Granting honor; an expression of respect in addressing someone in a superior position.

honor system *n.* A system of management, whereby one is trusted to obey the regulations without supervision.

hood (hed) *n.* A covering for the head and neck, often attached to a garment; the movable metal hinged cover of an automobile engine.

-hood *suffix* The quality or state of; sharing a given quality or state.

hoof (hef) *n., pl.* **hooves** The horny covering of the foot in various mammals, as horses, cattle, and oxen. **hoof it** *v. Slang* To dance; to walk. **on the hoof** Alive; not butchered.

hook (hek) *n.* A curved or bent piece of metal used to catch, drag, suspend, or fasten something; in golf, a stroke that sends the ball curving to the left; in boxing, to strike with a short, swinging blow; in hockey, to check illegally with the hockey stick. *Naut. Slang* An anchor. **hook** *v. Slang* To cause to become dependent or addicted. **by hook or by crook** In one way or another. **hook, line, and sinker** Unreservedly; entirely. **to hook up with** To marry; to form an association.

hoo-li-gan (hō´li gan) *n.* A street hoodlum.

hoop (hōp) *n.* A circular band of metal or wood used to hold staves of a cask or barrel together; in basketball, the basket.

hoop-la (hōp´lä) *n. Slang* Noise and excitement.

hoot (hōt) *n.* The loud sound or cry of an owl; *Slang* A very insignificant amount. **hooter** *n.* **hoot** *v.*

hoot-en-an-ny (hōt´e nan´ē) *n., pl.* **hootenannies** An informal gathering of folk singers for a public performance.

Hoover, Herbert Clark *n.* (1874-1964) The thirty-first president of the United States from 1929-1933.

hop (hop) *n.* A perennial herb with lobed leaves and green flowers that resemble pine cones; the dried flowers of the plant, containing an oil used in brewing beer. *Slang* A dance; a quick trip on a plane. **hop** *v.* To move by making short leaps on one foot; to move with light springing motions.

hope (hōp) *v.* To want or wish for something with a feeling of confident expectation. **to hope against hope** To continue hoping for something even when it appears hopeless. **hopeful** *adj.& n.* **hopefully** *adv.*

horde (hōrd) *adj.* A large crowd.

ho-ri-zon (ho rī´zon) *n.* The line along which the earth and sky seem to meet; the bounds or limit of one's knowledge, experience or interest.

hor-mone (hor´mōn) *n. Physiol.* An internal secretion carried by the bloodstream to other parts of the body where it has a specific effect.

horn (horn) *n.* A hard, bonelike, permanent projection on the heads of certain hoofed animals, as cattle, sheep, or deer.

hor-net (hor´nit) *n.* Any of various social wasps which can inflict a severe sting.

hor-o-loge (har´o lōj) *n.* A mechanism for keeping time; an older timepiece, as the sundial.

ho-rol-o-gy (ho rol´ojē) *n.* The science of measuring time; the craft of making devices to measure time.

hor-o-scope (hor´o skōp´) *n.* A chart or diagram of the relative positions of the planets and signs of the zodiac at a certain time, as that of a person's birth, used to predict the future.

hor-ren-dous (ha ren´dus) *adj.* Dreadful; terrible.

hor-ri-ble (hor´i bl) *adj.* Shocking; inducing or producing horror. *Informal* Excessive; inordinate. **horribly** *adv.*

hor-rip-i-la-tion (ha rip´i lā´shan) *n.* The standing on end of the hair as a result of fear in dogs and cats.

hor-ror (hor´ẽr) *n.* The painful, strong emotion caused by extreme dread, fear, or repugnance. *Informal* Something that is disagreeable or ugly.

hors d'oeuvre (or derv´) *n.* An appetizer served with cocktails before dinner.

horse (hors) *n.* A large, strong, hoofed quadruped mammal with a long mane and tail, used for riding and for pulling heavy objects; a device that generally has four legs, used for holding or supporting something; in gymnastics, a wooden block of wood four legs, used for vaulting and other exercises.

horse-car (hars´kär´) *n.* A streetcar that was formerly drawn by horses; a car equipped for transporting horses.

horse-pow-er (hors´pow´ẽr) *n. Mech.* A unit of power that is equal to 746 watts and nearly equivalent to the gravitational unit that equals 550 foot-pounds per second.

horst (horst) *n.* A block of the earth's crust separated by faults from an adjacent block.

hort *abbr.* Horticultural; horticulture.

hor-ti-cul-ture (hor´ti kul˘chẽr) *n.* The art or science of raising and tending fruits, vegetables, flowers, or ornamental plants. **horticultural** *adj.* **horticul-**

turist *n.*

hor-tus sic-cus *n.* A collection of plant specimens carefully dried and preserved.

ho-san-na (hō zan´a) *interj.* Expression to praise or glorify God.

hose (hōz) *n.. pl. hose or hoses* A sock; a stocking; a flexible tube for carrying fluids or gases under pressure. **hose** *v.* To wash; to water; to squirt with a hose.

ho-sel (hō´zel) *n.* The socket in the head of a golf club that encloses the shaft.

ho-sier-y (hō´zhe rē) *n.* Stockings and socks.

hos-pice (hos´pis) *n.* A lodging for travelers or the needy often maintained by a religious order.

hos-pi-ta-ble (hos´pi ta bl) *adj.* Treating guests with warmth and generosity; receptive. **hospitably** *adv.*

hos-pi-tal (hos´pi tal) *n.* An institution where the injured or sick receive medical, surgical, and emergency care.

host (hōst) *n.* One who receives or entertains guests; one who provides a room or building for an event or function; a large number of people or things. *Biol.* A living organism, as a plant or an animal, on or in which a parasite lives. **host** *v.*

hos-tage (hos´tij) *n.* A person held as security that promises will be kept or terms met by a third party.

hos-tel (hos´tel) *n.* A low-priced, supervised lodging for young travelers.

hos-tel-ry *n.* An inn or hotel.

host-ess (hō´stis) *n.* A woman who entertains socially; a woman who greets patrons at a restaurant and escorts them to their tables.

hos-tile (hos´til) *adj.* Of or relating to an enemy; antagonistic. **hostilely** *adv.*

hos-til-i-ties (ho stil´i tēs) *n.* War; acts of war.

hos-til-i-ty (ho stil´i tē) *n., pl. hostilities* Deep-seated opposition or hatred; war.

hot (hot) *adj.* At a high temperature; having heat that exceeds normal body temperature; sexually excited or receptive; electrically charged, as a *hot* wire. *Slang* Recently or illegally obtained.

hot air *n. Slang* Idle talk.

hot-bed (hot´bed´) *n.* A glass-covered bed of soil heated by fermenting manure and used for raising seedlings; an environment that is conductive to rapid growth or development.

hot-el (hō tel´) *n.* A business that provides lodging, meals, entertainment, and other services for the public.

hour (our) *n.* A measure of time equal to 60 minutes; 1/24th of a day; the time of day or night.

hour-ly (our´lē) *adj.* Something that

happens or is done every hour.

house (hous) *n*. A building that serves as living quarters for one or more families; home; the shelter or refuge for a wild animal; a business firm; a legislative body of the U.S. government. **house** *v*. To provide work space or living space.

house of correction *n*. An institution where persons who have committed minor offenses are housed until they are released back into society.

hov-el (hev´el) *n*. A small dirty house.

hov-er (hev´ér) *v*. To remain suspended over something.

how (hou) *adv*. In what manner or way; to what effect; in what condition or state; for what reason; with what meaning.

how-dy *interj*. A word used to express a greeting. **howdy** *n*.

how-ev-er (hou ev´ér) *adv*. In whatever manner or way. *conj*. Nevertheless.

how-it-zer (hou´it sér) *n*. A short cannon that fires projectiles at a high trajectory.

howl (houl) *v*. To utter a loud, sustained, plaintive sound, as the wolf. **howl** *n*.

howl-er (hou´lér) *n*. One that howls; a ridiculous or stupid blunder.

how-so-ev-er (hou´so ev´ér) *adv*. To whatever degree or extent; in whatever way.

hua-ra-che (wä rä´che) *n*. A sandal with a low heel and an upper made of interwoven leather thongs.

hub (hub) *n*. The center of a wheel; the center of activity.

hub-bub (hub´ub) *n*. Confusion; a tumult; uproar.

hub-cap *n*. The removable metal cap that covers the end of an axle, such as one used on the wheel of a motor vehicle.

hu-bris (hü´bris, hö´bris) *n*. Arrogance cause by inordinate pride.

huck-le-ber-ry (huk´l ber´e) *n*. A type of bush, related to the blueberry and bearing glossy, blackish, usually acidic berries.

hud-dle (hud´le) *n*. A crowd together; in football, a brief meeting of teammates to prepare for the next play. **huddle** *v*. To nestle or crowd together; to confer.

hue (hü) *n*. A gradation of color; the attribute of a color that defines its place on the color spectrum; a particular color; a shade. **hued** *adj*.

huff (huf) *n*. A fit of resentment or of ill temper. **huff** *v*. To exhale or breathe heavily, as from extreme exertion. **huffily** *adv*. **huffiness** *n*. **huffy** *adj*.

hug (hug) *v*. To embrace; to hold fast; to keep, cling, or stay close to. **huggable** *adj*. **hugger** *n*.

huge (hüj) *adj*. Of great quantity, size, or extent. **hugely** *adv*. **hugeness** *n*.

hu-la (hö´la) *n*. A Hawaiian dance characterized by beautiful rhythmic movement of the hips and gestures with the hands.

hulk (hulk) *n*. A heavy, bulky thing; the body of an old ship no longer fit for service.

hulk-ing *adj*. Unwieldy or awkward.

hull (hul) *n*. The outer cover of a fruit or seed; the framework of a boat; the external covering of a rocket, spaceship, or guided missile.

hul-la-ba-loo (hul´a ba lö´) *n*. A confused noise; a great uproar.

hum (hum) *v*. To make a continuous low-pitched sound; to be busily active; to sing with the lips closed.

hu-man (hü´man) *adj*. Of, relating to, or typical of man; having or manifesting human form or attributes. **humanly** *adv*. **humanness** *n*.

hu-mane (hü mān´) *adj*. Marked by compassion, sympathy, or consideration for other people or animals; merciful.

hu-man-i-tar-i-an (hü man´i târ´e an) *n*. A person who is concerned for human welfare, especially through philanthropy. **humanitarian** *adj*.

hu-man-oid (hü´ma noid´) *adj*. Of human form or characteristics.

hum-ble (hum´bl) *adj*. Marked by meekness or modesty; unpretentious; lowly. *v*. To make humble. **humbleness** *n*. **humbler** *n*. **humbly** *adv*.

hum-bug (hum´bug´) *n*. A misleading trick, hoax, fraud, or pretense; a person who seeks to deceive others; something foolish.

hum-drum (hum´drum´) *adj*. Boring; dull. **humdrum** *n*.

hu-mec-tant (hü mek´tant) *n*. A substance, as glycerol, that promotes moisture retention.

hu-mer-us (hü´mér us) *n., pl*. **humeri** Long bone of the upper arm or forelimb extending from the shoulder to the elbow.

hu-mid (hü´mid) *adj*. Containing or characterized by a lot of moisture; damp.

hu-mid-i-fy (hü mid´i fï´) *v*. To make humid or more moist. **humidifier** *n*.

hu-mid-i-stat (hü mid´i stat´) *n*. An instrument that controls or maintains the degree of humidity.

hu-mid-i-ty (hü mid´i te) *n*. A moderate amount of wetness in the air; dampness.

hu-mi-dor (hü´mi dor´) *n*. A container used to keep cigars in which the air is kept properly humidified by a special device.

hu-mil-i-ate (hü mil´e ät´) *v*. To reduce one's dignity or pride to a lower position. **humiliation, humility** *n*.

hum-ming-bird (hum´ing berd´) *n*. A

very small bird with narrow wings, long primary feathers, a slender bill, and an extensible tongue.

hum-mock (hum´ok) n. A rounded knoll or hill of snow or dirt. **hummocky** adj.

hu-mor (hū´mér) n. Something that is or has the ability to be comical or amusing. *Physiol.* Fluid contained in the body such as blood or lymph. **humor, humorous** adj.

hu-mor-ist (hū´mér ist) n. A person who has a sense of humor; one who uses humor to amuse others.

hump (hump) n. The rounded lump or protuberance, as on the back of a camel; a small hill. **over the hump** To be past the difficult or most critical state.

hu-mus (hū´mus) n. A complex material resulting from partial decomposition of plant or animal matter forming the organic portion of soil.

hunch (hunch) n. A strong, intuitive feeling about a future event or result. v. To bend into a crooked position or posture.

hunch-back (hunch´bak´) n. A back deformed by a convex curvature of the spine, a person with this disorder.

hun-dred (hun´drid) n. The cardinal number equal to 10 x 10, symbol 100.

hun-ger (hung´gér) n. A strong need or desire for food; a craving for food. **hunger** v. **hungrily** adv. **hungry** adj.

hunk-y–dor-y (hung´kē dōr´ ē) adj. *Slang* All right; quite satisfactory; comfortable.

hunt (hunt) v. To search or look for food; to pursue with the intent of capture; to look in an attempt to find. **hunt** n.

hur-dle (hér´dl) n. A portable barrier used to jump over in a race; an obstacle one must overcome. **hurdle** v. To leap over.

hur-dy-gur-dy (hér´dē ger´dē) n. A musical instrument where the sound is produced by turning a crank.

hurl (hérl) v. To throw something with great force; in baseball, to pitch. **hurl** n. **hurler** n.

hur-rah (hu rä´) interj. Used to express approval, pleasure, or exultation.

hur-ri-cane (her´i kān´) n. A tropical cyclone with winds exceeding 74 miles per hour, usually accompanied by rain, thunder, and lightning.

hurricane lamp n. A lamp or candlestick with a glass chimney to protect the flame against wind.

hur-ry (her´ē) v. To move or cause to move with haste. n. The act of hurrying. **hurriedly** adv. **hurriedness** n.

hurt (hért) v. To experience or inflict with physical pain; to cause physical or emotional harm to; to damage. **hurtful** adj. **hurtfully** adv. **hurt** n.

hur-tle (hér´tl) v. To move rapidly and

often noisily; to hurl with force..

hus-band (huz´band) n. A man who is married.

hus-band-ry (huz´ban drē) n. Agricultural cultivation, production of plants and animals, especially through scientific control and management.

hush (hush) v. To make or become quiet; to calm; to keep secret; to suppress. **hush** n. A silence.

husk (husk) n. The dry or membranous outer cover of certain vegetables, fruits, and seeds, often considered worthless.

hus-tings n. A platform used when making political speeches.

hus-tle (hus´el) v. To urge or move hurriedly along; to work busily and quickly. *Slang* To make energetic efforts to solicit business or make money. **hustle, hustler** n.

hut (hut) n. A small and simply constructed dwelling or shack a cabin.

hutch (huch) n. A enclosed area for confining small animals.

huz-zah, huz-za (hu zä´) interj. An expression of appreciation or approval.

hy-a-cinth (hī´a sinth) n. A bulbous plant that has a cluster of variously colored, highly fragrant, bell-shaped flowers.

hy-a-lite (hī´a lit´) n. A colorless opal, sometimes whitish and sometimes transparent like glass.

hy-a-lu-ron-i-dase (hī´a lu ron´i dās´) n. An enzyme that breaks down the molecules that hold cells together.

hy-brid (hī´brid) n. An offspring of two dissimilar plants or of two animals or different races, breeds, varieties, or species; something made up of mixed origin or makeup. **hybrid** adj.

hybrid computer A system which consists of a combination of analog and digital computer systems.

hy-brid-ize (hī´bri diz´) v. To cross, interbreed; to cause to form in a hybrid manner. **hybridization** n.

hy-da-tid (hī´da tid) n. A fluid-filled cyst that is formed in the bodies of men and certain animals by the tapeworm larva.

hy-dran-gea (hī drān´ ja) n. A shrub cultivated for its showy clustered pink, white, or sometimes blue flowers.

hy-drant (hī´drant) n. A pipe with a valve and spout which supplies water from a main source.

hy-drate (hī´drāt) n. A chemical compound formed by the union of water with another substance in definite proportions. **hydrate** v. **hydration** n.

hy-drau-lic (hī dro´lik) adj. Operated, moved, or effected by the means of water; hardening or setting under water. **hydrau-lically** adv.

hy-drau-lics (hī dro´liks) n. pl. The scientific study that deals with practical applications of liquids in motion and the laws that govern their actions.

hy-dric (hī′drik) *adj.* Characterized by or pertaining to, containing, or requiring moisture.

hy-dro-elec-tric (hī′drō i lek′trik) *n.* Relating to the production of electricity by the use of waterpower.

hy-dro-foil (hī′drō foil′) *n.* A motorboat built with metal plates and fins attached by struts for lifting the hull clear of the water as speed is attained.

hy-dro-gen (hī′drо jen) *n.* A colorless, normally odorless, highly flammable gas that is the simplest and lightest of the elements, symbolized by H.

hy-dro-gen-ate (hī′drо je nāt′) *v.* To combine or treat with hydrogen.

hydrogen bomb *n.* A bomb that is extremely destructive, with an explosive power obtained from the rapid release of atomic energy.

hydrogen peroxide *n.* A colorless, unstable, liquid compound that is used as an antiseptic solution and as a bleach.

hy-dro-me-te-or (hī′drō mē′tē ēr) *n.* Any of the various products formed by condensation of atmospheric water vapors, as rain, hail, or fog.

hy-dro-phil-ic (hī′drо fil′ik) *a.* Having a strong attraction for water; having the ability of dissolving in water.

hy-dro-pho-bi-a (hī′drо fō′bē a) *n.* A fear of water; rabies. -**ic** *adj.*

hy-dro-phone (hī′drо fōn′) *n.* A device for locating causes and transmitting sound under water.

hy-dro-pon-ics (hī′drо pon′iks) *n.* The method of growing plants in chemical solutions instead of soil.

hy-dro-scope (hī′drо skōp′) *n.* A mirror device which enables a person to see at a considerable distance below the surface of the water.

hy-dro-ski (hī′drō skē′) *n.* A hydrofoil, affixed to the fuselage of a seaplane in order to accelerate speed during takeoffs.

hy-dro-sphere (hī′drо sfēr′) *n.* The water on the surface of the globe in oceans, lakes, and all other waters, and the water vapor in the atmosphere.

hy-dro-stat (hī′drо stat′) *n.* The electrical device that detects the presence of water, as from leakage.

hy-dro-tax-is (hī′drо tak′sis) *n.* The reflex movement by an organism in the direction of or away from water.

hy-dro-ther-a-py (hī′drо ther′ a pē) *n.* The scientific use of water in the treatment of disease.

hy-dro-ther-mal (hī′drо thėr′mal) *adj.* Referring or relating to heated water, esp. the action of heated water that dissolves or redistributes minerals.

hy-dro-tho-rax (hī′drо thōr′aks) *n.* The presence of excess serous fluid in the pleural cavities; especially the effusion that results from failing circulation of the heart or lungs. **hydrothoric** *adj.*

hy-drot-ro-pism (hī drо′trо piz′um) *n. Biol.* A curving or growing toward or away from moisture.

hy-drous (hī′drus) *adj.* Containing water; containing water in a type of chemical union as in hydroxides or hydrates.

hy-drox-ide (hī drok′sī) *n. Chem.* A compound that is formed by the union of an element with one or more hydroxyl groups.

hydroxy acid *n. Chem.* An organic acid composed of a hydroxyl group and a carboxyl group that exhibits characteristics of an alcohol and an acid.

hy-drox-yl (hī drok′sil) *n. Chem.* A radical containing oxygen and hydrogen, found in alcohols, glycols, and hydroxides. **Hydroxylic** *adj.*

hy-dro-zo-an (hī drо zō an) *n.* Class of coelenterate aquatic marine animals.

hy-e-na (hī ē′na) *n.* Any of several strong carnivorous mammals of Africa and Asia, with coarse hair and very powerful jaws, having nocturnal habits and feeding mostly on carrion.

hy-e-tal (hī′i tal) *adj.* Relating to rain and its distribution with reference to different regions.

hy-giene (hī′jēn) *n.* The science of the establishment and maintenance of good health and the prevention of disease. **hygienic** *adj.* **hygienically** *adv.*

hy-gi-en-ics (hī′jē en′iks) *n.* The science of cleanliness and health; hygiene.

hy-gro-graph (hī′grо graf′) *n.* An instrument used to record automatically the variations of moisture content of the atmosphere.

hy-grom-e-ter (hī grom′itėr) *n.* Instrument for measuring the degree of moisture of the atmosphere.

hy-gro-scope (hī′grо skōp′) *n.* Instrument for indicating the presence and approximate amount of moisture in the atmosphere.

hy-gro-ther-mo-graph (hī′grо thėr′mo graf′) *n. Meteor.* The instrument used to register both relative humidity and the temperature on one chart.

hy-la (hī′la) *n.* The tree frog.

hy-men (hī′men) *n.* The thin membrane that partly closes the external vaginal orifice.

hymn (him) *n.* A song of praise giving thanks to God; a song of joy.

hym-nal (him′nal) *n.* A book that contains hymns for worshiping.

hym-no-dy (him′no dē) *n.* The singing or composition of hymns; the collective hymns of a specific locality, era, or denomination. **hymnodist** *n.*

hym-nol-o-gy (him nol′o jē) *n.* The

study, classification, and history of old hymns; the composition of hymns; humns in general. **hymnological** adj.

hy-oid (hī´oid) adj. Referring or relating to the U-shaped movable bone between the root of the tongue and larynx.

hype v. Slang To put on; to stimulate; to promote or publicize extravagantly.

hy-per- pref. Excessive in anything that is performed or done.

hy-per-ac-tive (hī´pêr ak´tiv) adj. Excessively or abnormally active.

hyperbaric chamber n., Med. The airtight chamber that forces oxygen under pressure to a patient's heart and lungs.

hy-per-bo-le (hīpêr´bo lē) n. Deliberate exaggeration used to cause an effect, not to be taken literally. **hypobolic** adj.

hy-per-chro-mic a-ne-mi-a (hī´pêr kro´mik a nē´mē a) n. An anemia which has an increase in the hemoglobin and a reduction in the number of red blood cells.

hy-per-crit-i-cal (hī´pêr krit´i kal) adj. Being excessively critical.

hy-per-ga-my n. The act of marrying into an equal or higher social group.

hy-per-gly-ce-mia n. An excessive amount of sugar in the blood.

hy-per-gol-ic (hī´pêr ga´lik) adj. Referring to a rocket propellant that ignites upon contact of components without external aid.

hy-per-li-pe-mia n. The presence of excessive fat in the blood.

hy-perm-ne-sia n. The ability of having complete memory or recall of the past.

hy-per-os-to-sis n. An excessive thickening of bone tissue.

hy-per-pha-gia n. An abnormal desire for the consumption of food associated with injury to the hypothalamus.

hy-per-pnea n. Abnormally rapid breathing. **hyperpneic** adj.

hy-per-ten-sion (hī´pêr ten´shan) n. The condition of abnormally high blood pressure especially in the arteries.

hy-per-ven-ti-la-tion n. An excessive rate of respiration leading to loss of carbon dioxide from the blood.

hy-per-vi-ta-min-osis n. An abnormal condition resulting from the excessive use of one or more vitamins.

hy-phen (hī´fen) n. A punctuation mark (-) used to show connection between the parts of a word. **hyphen** v.

hy-phen-ate (hī´fe nāt´) v. To separate or join with a hyphen.

hyp-no-sis (hip nō´sis) n. pl. **hypnoses** A state that resembles sleep but is brought on or induced by another person whose suggestions are accepted by the subject.

hyp-not-ic (hip not´ik) adj. Inducing sleep. n. An agent, such as a drug, which induces sleep. **hypnotically** adv.

hyp-no-tize (hip´no tīz´) v. To induce hypnosis; to be dazzled by; to be overcome by suggestion.

hy-po (hī´pō) n. pl. **hypos** Slang A hypodermic needle or syringe.

hy-po-chon-dri-a (hī´po kon´drē a) n. A mental depression accompanied by imaginary physical ailments.

hy-po-der-mic sy-ringe (hī´po dêr´mik) n. A syringe and hypodermic needle used for injecting a substance into one's body.

hy-po-gly-ce-mia n. An unusual decrease of sugar in the blood.

hy-po-ten-sion (hī´po ten´shan) n. A condition marked by unusually low blood pressure.

hy-pot-e-nuse (hī pot´e nōs´) n. That side of a right triangle which is opposite the right angle.

hy-po-thal-a-mus (hī´po thal´a mus) n. Anat. The part of the posterior section of the forebrain that composes the floor or base of the third ventricle.

hy-po-the-sis (hī poth´i sis) n. An assumption made in order to draw out and test the logical consequences.

hy-po-thet-e-cal (hī´po thet i cal) adj. Concerning a statement or idea that is not actual fact; theoretical.

hy-po-thy-roid-ism n. A condition which lowers the metabolic rate of the thyroid gland causing loss of vigor.

hy-po-xi-a (hī pok´sē a) n. A condition of a deficiency of oxygen reaching the tissues of the body.

hyp-sog-ra-phy (hip sog´rafē) n. The branch of geography which deals with the measurement of the varying elevations of the earth's surface.

hyp-som-e-ter (hip som´i têr) n. An instrument used to measure altitude by determining the boiling point of a liquid at the given height.

hyp-som-e-try (hip som´i trē) n. The measuring of elevations or altitudes, as related to sea level.

hy-rax (hī´raks) n. A small ungulate mammal with a thickset body, short legs and ears, and a rudimentary tail.

hys-sop (his´op) n. An aromatic herb from the mint family.

hys-ter-ec-to-my (his´te rek´to mē) n., pl. **hysterectomies** Surgery on a female which partially or completely removes the uterus.

hys-ter-ia (hi stēr´ē a) n. A psychological condition characterized by emotional excess and or unreasonable fear.

hys-ter-ic n. A person suffering from hysteria.

hys-ter-i-cal adj. Emotionally out of control. **hysterically** adv.

hys-ter-ics n. A fit of uncontrollable laughter or crying; hysteria.

I, i (ī) The ninth letter of the English alphabet; the Roman numeral for one.

I (ī) *pron.* The person speaking or writing. *n.* The self; the ego.

i-amb *or* **i-am-bus** (ī´am) *n.* A metrical foot consisting of a short or unstressed syllable followed by an accented syllable. **iambic** *adj. & n.*

i-at-ric (ī at´rik) *adj.* Pertaining to medicine or a physician.

i-at-ro-gen-ic (ī a´tro jen´ik) *adj.* Induced inadvertently by a physician or his treatment. **iatrogenically** *adv.*

i-bex (ī´beks) *n.* An Old World mountain goat with long curved horns.

i-bi-dem (ib´i dem) *adv.* Used in footnotes to indicate a part of literary work that was just mentioned.

i-bis (ī´bis) *n.* A long-billed wading bird related to the heron and stork.

ice (īs) *n.* Solidly frozen water; a dessert of crushed ice which is flavored and sweetened. *Informal* Extreme coldness of manner. **ice** *v.* To change into ice; to cool or chill; to cover with icing. **icily** *adv.* **iciness** *n.* **icy** *adj.*

ice age *n. Geol.* A time of widespread glaciation.

ice cap (īs´kap´) *n.* An extensive perennial covering of ice and snow that covers a large area of land.

ice cream *n.* A smooth mixture of milk, cream, flavoring, sweeteners, and other ingredients, beaten and frozen.

ich-neu-mon (ik nö´mon) *n.* An animal that feeds on snakes and rodents; a mongoose.

ich-nite (ik´nīt) *n.* A fossil footprint.

ich-nog-ra-phy (ik nog´ra fē) *n.* The ground plan; the study or art of drawing ground plans.

ich-nol-o-gy (ik nol´o jē) *n.* The study of fossil footprints of animals.

ich-thy-oid (ik´thē oid´) *adj.* Exhibiting fish-like characteristics. **ichthyoid** *n.* A fish-like organism. **ichthyoidal** *adj.*

ich-thy-ol-o-gy (ik´thē ol´o jē) *n.* The zoological study of fishes. **ichthyologic, -yological** *adj.* **ichthologist** *n.*

ich-thy-or-nis (ik´thē ar´nis) *n.* An extinct bird with a genus of vertebrae like those of fish and with teeth.

ich-thy-o-sis (ik´thē ō´sis) *n.* A hereditary skin disorder represented by thick, scaly skin.

i-ci-cle (ī´si kl) *n.* A hanging spike of ice formed by dripping water that freezes.

i-ci-ly (ī´si lē) *adv.* In an icy manner; coldly, having no warmth.

i-ci-ness (ī´sē nis) *n.* The state of being very cold or icy.

ic-ing (ī´sing)*n.* A sweet preparation for frosting cakes and cookies.

i-con *or* **i-kon** (ī´kon) *n.* A Christian pictorial representation of Jesus Christ, the Virgin Mary, or other sacred figures. In computer science, a graphic image on a monitor screen that represents a directory, file, utility, etc. and that can be selected with a mouse click.

i-con-o-clasm (ī kon´o klaz´um) *n.* The attitude or practice of an iconoclast.

i-con-o-clast (ī kon´o klast´) *n.* One who opposes the use of sacred images; one who attacks traditional or cherished beliefs. **iconoclastic** *adj.*

i-co-nog-ra-phy (ī´ko nog´ra fē) *n.* A pictorial material illustrating a subject; a published work dealing with iconography.

i-co-nol-a-ter (ī´ko nol´a tėr) *n.* A person who worships images or icons.

i-con-o-scope (ī kon´o skōp´) *n.* A cathode ray tube in a television camera that converts light rays into electrical signals.

ic-ter-us (ik´tėr us) *n.* A yellow appearance of certain plants after being exposed to cold and excess moisture; jaundice.

ic-tus (ik´tus) *n. Pathol.* A stroke, seizure, or fit.

id (id) *n. Psych.* The unconscious part of the psyche associated with instinctual needs and drives.

I'd *contr.* I had; I should, I would.

I-da-ho *n.* A state located in the northwest part of the United States; statehood July 3, 1890; state capital Boise.

i-de-a (ī dē´a) *n.* Something existing in the mind; conception or thought; an opinion; a plan of action.

i-de-al (ī dē´al) *n.* A concept or imagined state of perfection; highly desirable; perfect; an ultimate objective; an honorable principle or motive. **ideal** *adj.* Conforming to absolute excellence.

i-de-ate (ī´dē āt´) *v.* To make an idea of something; to think.

i-de-a-tion (ī dē ā´shan) *n.* The act of forming ideas.

i-dem (ī´dem) *pron. & adj.* The same; used to indicate a previously mentioned reference.

i-dem-po-tent (ī´dem pō´tent) *adj.* Pertaining to a mathematical quantity that is not zero when every positive power equals itself.

i-den-tic (ī den´tik) *adj.* Identical; constituting an expression in which governments follow precisely the same course.

i-den-ti-cal (ī den´ti kal) *adj.* Being the same; exactly equal or much alike; designating a twin or twins developed from the same ovum. **identically** *adv.*

i-den-ti-fi-a-ble (ī den´ti fī´a bl) *adj.* Having the capability of being identified or recognized. **-y** *adv.*

i-den-ti-fi-ca-tion (ī den´ti fī ka´shan) *n.* The act of identifying; the state of being identified; a means of identity.

i-den-ti-fy (ī den´ti fī´) v. To recognize the identity of; to establish as the same or similar; to equate; to associate oneself with an individual or group.

i-den-ti-ty (ī den´ti tē) n. pl. **identities** The condition or state of being a specific person or thing and recognizable as such; the condition or fact of being the same as something else; individuality.

id-e-o-gram or **id-e-o-graph** (id´ē o gram´) n. A pictorial symbol used in a writing system to represent an idea or thing, as Chinese characters; a graphic symbol, as $ or %.

id-e-og-ra-phy (id´ē og´ra fē) n. A representation of some ideas by the use of graphic symbols.

i-de-o-log-i-cal (ī dē o loj´i kal) adj. Concerned with ideas.

i-de-ol-o-gist (ī dē ol´o gist) n. A supporter of a particular ideology.

Ides (īdz) n. In the ancient Roman calendar, the fifteenth day of March, May, July, and October or the thirteenth day of the other months.

-i-din noun suffix A chemical compound that is related in structure to another compound.

id-i-o comb. form Personal; distinct; separate.

id-i-o-graph-ic (id´ē o graf´ik) adj. Pertaining to the concrete or unique.

id-i-o-lect (id´ē o´lekt) n. The speech pattern of an individual at a period of time in his life. **idiolectal** adj.

id-i-om (id´ē om) n. A form of expression having a meaning that is not readily understood from the meaning of its component words; the dialect of people or a region; a kind of language or vocabulary. **idiomaticness** n.

id-i-o-mat-ic (id´ē o mat´ik) adj. Pertaining to an idiom; being peculiar to a group.

id-i-o-mor-phic (id´ē o mor´fik) adj. To have the right or proper shape.

id-i-o-path-ic (id´ē a path´ik) adj. To be peculiar to an individual.

id-i-ot (id´ē ot) n. A mentally deficient person; an extremely foolish or stupid person.

id-i-ot-ic (id´ē ot´ik) adj. Showing of complete lack of thought or common sense by someone. **idiotically** adv. .

i-dle (īd´l) adj. Doing nothing; inactive; moving lazily; slowly; running at a slow speed or out of gear; unemployed or inactive. **idleness** n. **idler** n.

id-lesse (id´les) n. The state of being idle.

i-do-crase (ī´do krās´) n. A type of mineral which is a complex silicate of calcium, iron, magnesium, and aluminum.

i-dol (īd´ol) n. A symbol or representation of a god or deity that is worshiped; a person or thing adored.

i-dol-a-ter (ī dol´a tėr) n. One who worships idols; blind adoration; devotion.

i-dol-ize (īd´o līz´) v. To admire with excessive admiration or devotion; to worship as an idol. **idolization** n.

i-dyll or **i-dyl** (īd´il) n. A poem or prose piece about country life; a scene, event, or condition of rural simplicity; a romantic interlude. **idyllic** adj.

-ie suff. Little; dear.

if (if) conj. On the condition that; allowing that; supposing or granting that.

if-fy (if´ē) adj. Slang Marked by unknown qualities or conditions.

ig-loo (ig´lō) n. A dome-shaped Eskimo dwelling often made of blocks of snow.

ig-ne-ous (ig´nē us) adj. Geol. Relating to fire; formed by solidification from a molten magma.

ig-nes-cent (ig nes´ent) adj. Being capable of giving off sparks.

ignis fatuus (ig´nis fach´o us) n. A type of light which will appear over marshy ground in the night; it is often attributable to the combustion of gas from organic matter that is decomposed.

ig-nite (ig nīt´) v. To start or set a fire; to render luminous by heat.

ig-ni-tion (ig nish´an) n. An act or action of igniting; a device or means for igniting the fuel mixture in an engine.

ig-no-min-i-ous (ig´no min´ē us) adj. Mark-ed by or characterized by shame or disgrace; dishonorable. **ignominiousness** n. **ignominiously** adv.

ig-no-min-y (ig´no min´ē) n. A disgraceful conduct or action; dishonor; shame.

ig-no-ra-mus (ig´no rā´mus) n. A totally ignorant person.

ig-no-rant (ig´nėr ant) adj. Lacking education or knowledge; not aware; lacking comprehension.

ig-no-ra-tio e-len-chi (ig´ne rät´ē ō i len´kē) n. An argument to prove or disprove something that is not an issue.

ig-nore (ig nōr´) v. To pay no attention to; to reject. **ignorable** adj.

i-gua-na (i gwä´na) n. A large, dark-colored , herbaceous tropical American lizard that is a food source for the native inhabitants.

i-guan-o-don (i gwä´no don´) n. A member of the genus of the gigantic herbivorous dinosaurs which are from the early Cretaceous period of England.

ike-ba-na (ik´ä bän´e) n. A Japanese art of arranging flowers that emphasizes balance and form.

-ile suffix Capable of; segment of.

il-e-i-tis (il´ē ī´tis) n. Inflammation of the ileum.

il-e-um (il´ē um) *n. pl.* **ilea** The lower part of the small intestine between the jejunum and the large intestine.

il-e-us (il´ē us) *n.* A functional obstruction of the bowel.

i-lex (ī´lex) *n.* A type of European evergreen; the genus of holly related shrubs.

il-i-ac (il´ē ak) *n.* Pertaining to the ilium.

Il-i-ad (il´ē ad) *n.* An epic in the Homeric tradition; a series of disastrous events.

il-i-um (il´ē um) *n.* The largest bone of each internal half of the pelvis.

ilk (ilk) *n.* Sort; kind.

ill (il) *adj.* Not healthy; sick; destructive in effect; harmful; hostile; unfriendly; not favorable; not up to standards. **ill** *adv.* In an ill manner; with difficulty; scarcely. **ill** *n.* Evil; injury or harm; something causing suffering.

I'll *contr.* I will; I shall.

ill-ad-vised (il´ad vīzd´) *adj.* Done without careful thought or sufficient advice.

il-la-tive (i lā´tiv) *n.* A word or phrase which introduces an inference. **illatively** *adv.* **illative** *adj.*

il-laud-a-ble (il lad´dabl) *adj.* To be deserving no praise. **illaudably** *adv.*

ill-bred *adj.* Ill-mannered; impolite; rude; raised improperly.

il-le-gal (i lē´gal) *adj.* Contrary to law or official rules; unlawful.

il-le-gal-ize (i lē´gal īz´) *v.* To declare illegal. **illegalization** *n.*

il-le-git-i-mate (il´i jit´i mit) *adj.* Against the law; unlawful; born out of wedlock. **illegitimacy** *n.* **illegitimately** *adv.*

il-lic-it (i lis´it) *adj.* Not permitted by tradition or by law; unlawful.

il-lim-it-a-ble (i lim´i ta bl) *adj.* Incapable of being bounded or limited in any way. **illimitably** *adv.*

Il-li-nois *n.* A state located in the central part of the northern United States; statehood December 3, 1818; state capital Springfield.

il-lite (il´īt´) *n.* A clay mineral that has essentially the crystal structure of muscovite. **illitic** *adj.*

il-lit-er-ate (i lit´ėr it) *adj.* Unable to read and write; uneducated; having or showing a lack of knowledge of fundamentals on a particular subject. **illiteracy** *n.* **illiterately** *adv.*

ill-mannered *adj.* Lacking or showing a lack of good manners; rude.

ill-natured *adj.* Disagreeable or unpleasant disposition. **ill-naturedly** *adv.*

ill-ness (il´nis) *n.* Sickness; a state of being in poor health; the unhealthy condition of one's body or mind.

il-log-ic (i loj´ik) *n.* The state or quality of being illogical.

il-log-i-cal (i loj´i kal) *adj.* Contrary to the principles of logic; not logical.

illogicality *n.* **illogically** *adv.*

ill-tempered *adj.* Having or showing a cross temper or disposition.

ill-treat *v.* To treat someone or something improperly or cruelly. **l-treatment** *n.*

il-lu-mi-nate (il ū´me nāt) *v.* To give light; to make clear; to provide with under-standing; to decorate with pictures or designs; to be or to make spiritually or intellectually enlightened.

il-lu-mi-nism (il ū´me niz´em) *n.* A claim to a personal enlightenment which is not accessible to mankind in general.

il-lu-sion (i lö´zhan) *n.* A misleading perception of reality; an overly optimistic idea or belief; misconception; the action of deceiving; a misleading image presented to ones vision. **illusive, -usory, illusional** *adj.*

il-lus-trate (il´a strāt´) *v.* To explain or clarify, especially by the use of examples; to clarify by serving as an example; to provide a publication with explanatory features. **illustrator** *n.*

il-lus-tra-tion (il´es trā´shen) *n.* The act of illustrating; an example or comparison used to illustrate; a picture or graph to clarify text.

il-lus-tra-tive (il´es tre tiv) *adj.* Serving to illustrate. **illustratively** *adv.*

il-lus-tri-ous (i lus´trē us) *adj.* Greatly celebrated; renowned.

il-lu-vi-a-tion (il ū´vē ā´shen) *n.* A gathering of dissolved soil materials in an area as the result of lenching from another.

il-lu-vi-um (il ū´vē em) *n.* The material that is leached from one soil horizon to another soil horizon.

ill will *n.* Unfriendly or hostile feelings; malice.

I'm (īm) *contr.* I am.

im-age (im´ij) *n.* A representation of the form and features of someone or something; an optically formed representation of an object made by a mirror or lens; a mental picture of something imaginary. **image** *v.* To make a likeness of; to reflect; to depict vividly in language.

image enhancement In *computer science*, altering or improving a graphic image as art or a photograph by use of a computer program.

im-ag-er-y (im´ij rē) *n. pl.* **imageries** Mental pictures; images existing in the imagination; figurative language.

im-ag-i-nar-y (i maj´i ner´ē) *adj.* Existing only in the imagination.

imaginary number *n.* A complex number whose imaginary part is not zero, as in $2 + 6i$. Where i is the symbol.

imaginary part *n.* The portion of a complex number which has an imaginary unit as a factor, such as the $3i$ in $7 + 3i$.

imaginary unit *n.* The positive square root of negative one (-1).

im-ag-i-na-tion (i maj´i nā´shən) *n.* The power of forming mental images of unreal or absent objects; such power used creatively; resourcefulness. **imaginative** *adj.* **imaginatively** *adv.*

im-ag-ine (im aj´in) *v.* To form a mental picture or idea of; to suppose; to guess.

imaging In computer science, to create or modify a graphic representation with the use of a computer.

i-ma-go (i mā´gō) *n. pl.* **imagoes** or **imagines** An insect in its sexually mature adult stage; the idealized image of self or another person.

i-mam (i mäm´) *n.* A prayer leader of Islam; rulers that claim descent from Muhammad.

im-bal-ance (im bal´əns) *n.* A lack of functional balance; defective coordination.

im-be-cile (im´bi sil) *n.* A mentally deficient person. **imbecilic** *adj.*

im-bibe (im bīb´) *v.* To drink; to take in. **imbiber** *n.*

im-bri-cate (im´bri kāt) *adj.* With edges overlapping in a regular arrangement, as roof tiles or fish scales.

im-bri-ca-tion (im´bri kā´shen) *adj.* A pattern which shows overlapping or a regular arrangement.

im-bro-glio (im brōl´yō) *n. pl.* **imbroglios** A complicated situation or disagreement; a confused heap; a tangle.

im-brue (im brü´) *v.* To drench something.

im-brute (im brüt´) *v.* To degrade someone to the level of that of a brute.

im-bue (im bū´) *v.* To saturate or penetrate, as with a stain or dye.

imdtly *abbr.* Immediately.

im-ip-ra-mine (im ip´re mēn´) *n.* A kind of antidepressant drug.

im-i-ta-ble (im´et a bl) *adj.* Capable or worthy of imitation.

im-i-tate (im´e tāt) *v.* To copy the actions or appearance of another; to adopt the style of; to duplicate; to appear like.

im-i-ta-tion (im´e tā´shan) *n.* An act of imitating; something copied from an original. **imitation** *adj.*

im-i-ta-tive (im´e tāt´iv) *adj.* To be marked by imitation. **imitatively** *adv.*

im-mac-u-la-cy (im ak´ū le sē) *n.* The state of something being immaculate.

im-mac-u-late (im ak´ū lit) *adj.* Free from sin, stain, or fault; impeccably clean; without flaw.

im-mane (im ān´) *adj.* To be large or monstrous in character.

im-ma-nent (im´a nent) *adj.* Existing within; restricted to the mind; subjective; inherent. **immanency** *n.*

im-ma-nent-ism (im´a nent iz´em) *n.* A theory according to which God or other spirit is immanent in the world.

im-ma-te-ri-al (im´a tēr´ē al) *adj.* Lacking material body or form; of no importance or relevance. **immaterially** *adv.* **immaterialness** *n.*

im-ma-ture (im´a ter´) *adj.* Not fully grown; undeveloped; suggesting a lack of maturity. **immaturity** *n.*

im-meas-ur-a-ble (i mezh´ėr a bl) *adj.* Not capable of being measured.

im-me-di-a-cy (i mē´dē a sē) *n. pl.* **immediacies** The quality of being immediate; directness; something of urgent importance.

im-me-di-ate (i mē´dē it) *adj.* Acting or happening without an intervening object, agent, or cause; directly perceived; occurring at once; close in time, location, or relation.

im-me-mo-ri-al (im´e mōr´ē al) *adj.* Beyond the limits of memory, tradition, or records. **immemorially** *adv.*

im-mense (i mens´) *adj.* Exceptionally large. **immensely** *adv.*

im-merge (im erj´) *v.* To plunge or immerse something or oneself into a medium such as water.

im-me-thod-i-cal (im´e thäd´i kel) *adj.* Not being methodical.

im-mi-grant (im´i grant) *n.* One who leaves his country to settle in another.

im-mi-grate (im´i grāt´) *v.* To leave one country and settle in another.

im-mi-nent (im´i nent) *adj.* About to happen. **imminence** *n.* **imminently** *adv.*

im-min-gle (im in´gl) *v.* To intermingle or to blend into something such as a group; to intermix.

im-mis-ci-ble (im is´i bl) *adj* To be incapable of attaining homogeneity or mixing.

im-mix (im iks´) *v.* To mix intimately; commingle. **im-mixture** *n.*

im-mo-bile (i mō´bil) *adj.* Not moving or incapable of motion **-bility** *n.*

im-mod-er-a-cy (im mäd´er a sē) *adj.* The lack of moderation.

im-mod-er-ate (i mod´ėr it) *adj.* Exceeding normal bounds.

im-mod-est (i mod´ist) *adj.* Lacking modesty; indecent; boastful. **immodestly** *adv.* **immodesty** *n.*

im-mo-late (im´o lāt) *v.* To kill, especially by fire, as a sacrifice; to destroy completely. **immolator** *n.*

im-mor-al (im or´al) *adj.* Not moral.

im-mo-ral-i-ty (im´o ral´i tē) *n. pl.* **immoralities** Lack of morality; an immoral act or practice.

im-mor-tal (i mort´l) *adj.* Exempt from death; lasting forever, as in fame. **immortal** *n.* A person of lasting fame.

im-mor-tal-ize (i mort´l īz) *v.* To make something immortal. **immortlizer** *n.*

im-mo-tile (im ōt´l) *adj.* Lacking motility; incapable of self movement.

im-mune (i mūn´) *adj.* Not affected or responsive; resistant, as to a disease.

im-mu-no-as-say (im´ū nō as´ā) *n.* An identification of a substance by the way it acts as an antigen.

im-mu-no-dif-fu-sion (im´ū nō dif füzhen) *n.* Separation of antigen complexes into parts by passing them through a semipermeable membrane.

im-mu-no-glob-u-lin (im´ū nō glåb´ū lin) *n.* A type of protein which is made up of heavy and light chains and is used as an antibody by the body.

immunol *abbr.* Immunology.

im-mu-no-sup-pres-sion (im´ū nō se presh´en) *n.* The suppression of the body's natural immune responses.

im-mu-no-ther-a-py (im´ū nō ther´e pē) *n.* The treatment of disease by the means of antigenic preparations or with antigens.

im-mure (i mūr´) *v.* To confine by or as if by walls; to build into a wall.

im-mu-ta-ble (i mū´ta bl) *adj.* Unchanging or unchangeable. **immutability** *n.* **immutably** *adv.*

imp (imp) *n.* A mischievous child.

im-pact (im´pakt) *n.* A collision; the impetus or force produced by a collision; an initial, usually strong effect. **impact** *v.* To pack firmly together; to strike or affect forcefully.

im-pair (im pâr´) *v.* To diminish in strength, value, quantity, or quality. **impairment** *n.* **impairer** *n.*

im-pan-el (im pan´el) *v.* To enroll on a panel; to select a jury.

im-par-a-dise (im par´e dīs) *v.* To enrapture.

im-par-i-ty (im par´itē) *n.* Disparity; inequality.

im-part (im pärt´) *v.* To grant; to bestow; to make known; to communicate. **impartment** *n.* **impartation** *n.*

im-par-tial (im pär´shal) *adj.* Not partial; unbiased; not favoring one over another. **impartiality** *n.*

im-part-i-ble (im pär´ti bl) *v.* Being not subject to partition. **impartibly** *adv.*

im-pass-a-ble (im pas´a bl) *adj.* Impossible to travel over or across. **impassableness** *n.* **impassably** *adv.*

im-passe (im´pas) *n.* A road or passage having no exit; a difficult situation with no apparent way out; a deadlock.

im-pas-si-ble (im pas´i bl) *adj.* Impervious to an injury; not to be moved by passion or sympathy; emotionless.

im-pas-sion (im pash´an) *v.* To arouse the passions of another.

im-paste (im pāst´) *v.* To make or form something into a crust or a paste

im-pas-to (im pas´tō) *n.* A kind of raised decoration on ceramic ware; a heavy layering of paint.

im-pa-tient (im pā´shent) *adj.* Unwilling to wait or tolerate delay; expressing irritation at having to wait; restlessly eager; intolerant. **impatiently** *adv.*

im-pawn (im pän´) *v.* To put or place something in pawn.

im-peach (im pēch´) *v.* To charge with misconduct in public office before a proper court of justice; to make an accusation against. **impeachment** *n.*

im-pec-ca-ble (im pek´abl) *adj.* Having no flaws; perfect; not capable of sin. **impeccably** *adv.* **impeccability** *n.*

im-ped-ance (im pēd´ans) *n.* A measure of the total opposition to the flow of an electric current, specifically in an alternating current circuit.

im-pede (im pēd´) *v.* To obstruct or slow down the progress of.

im-pel (im pel´) *v.* To spur to action; to provoke; to drive forward; to propel.

im-pend (im pend´) *v.* To hover threateningly; to be about to happen.

im-pend-ent (im pend´ent) *adj.* To be near at hand; imminent.

im-pen-e-tra-bil-i-ty (im pen´i tra bil´i tē) *n.* The inability of two parts of anything to occupy the same space at exactly the same time.

im-pen-e-tra-ble (im pen´i tra bl´) *adj.* Not capable of being penetrated; not capable of being seen through or understood; unfathomable.

im-pen-i-tent (im pen´i tent) *adj.* Not sorry; unrepentant. **impenitently** *adv.*

im-per-a-tive (im per´a tiv) *adj.* Expressing a command or request; empowered to command or control; compulsory. **imperative** *n.* **imperatively** *adv.*

im-per-cep-ti-ble (im´per sep´ta bl) *adj.* Not perceptible by the mind or senses; extremely small or slight. **imperceptibly** *adv.* **imperceptibility** *n.*

im-per-cep-tive (im´per sep´tiv) *adj.* Not being perceptive.

im-per-cip-i-ence (im´pér sip´ē ens) *n.* The state of being imperceptive.

imperf *abbr.* Imperfect; imperforate.

im-per-fect (im per´fikt) *adj.* Not perfect; of or being a verb tense which shows an uncompleted or continuous action or condition. **imperfect** *n.* The imperfect tense. **imperfectly** *adv.*

im-per-fo-rate (im per´fer it) *adj.* To have no opening; lacking a normal opening.

im-pe-ri-al (im pēr´ē al) *adj.* Of or relating to an empire or emperor; designating a nation or government having dependent colonies; majestic; regal. **imperial** *n.* A pointed beard on the lower lip or chin. **im-perially** *adv.*

im-per-il (im per´il) *v.* To put in peril; endanger.

im-pe-ri-ous (im pēr´ē us) *adj.* Commanding; domineering; urgent.

imperiousness *n.* **imperiously** *adv.*

im-per-ish-a-ble (im per´i sha bl) *adj.* Not perishable; permanently enduring.

im-pe-ri-um (im pēr´ē *u*m) *n.* An absolute dominion; the right to employ the force of the state.

im-per-ma-nent (im per´ma nent) *adj.* Not permanent; not enduring; temporary; transient.

im-per-son-al (im per´so nal) *adj.* Having no personal reference or connection; showing no emotion or personality. **impersonally** *adv.*

im-per-son-ate (im per´so nāt´) *v.* To assume the character or manner of. **impersonation** *n.* **impersonator** *n.*

im-per-ti-nence (im pûr´ti nens) *n.* The instance of impertinence; rudeness in actions or speech.

im-per-ti-nent (im per´ti nent) *adj.* Overly bold or disrespectful; not pertinent; irrelevant; rude.

im-per-turb-a-ble (im´pêr ter´ba bl) *adj.* Not easily perturbed or agitated. **imperturbability** *n.*

im-per-vi-ous (im per´vē us) *adj.* Incapable of being emotionally affected or influenced by argument. **imperviously** *adv.* **imperviousness** *n.*

im-pe-ti-go (im´pi tī´gō) *n.* A contagious skin disease marked by pustules.

im-pe-trate (im´pi trāt´) *v.* To obtain something by a request.

im-pet-u-ous (im pech´ū us) *adj.* Marked by sudden action or emotion; impulsive. **-ousness** *n.* **impetuously** *adv.*

im-pe-tus (im´pi t*u*s) *n.* A driving force; an incitement; a stimulus; momentum.

im-pi (im´pē) *n. pl.* **impies, impis** A brigade or large body of soldiers.

im-pi-ous (im´pē us) *adj.* Not pious; irreverent; disrespectful. **-ly** *adv.*

imp-ish (im´pish) *adj.* Mischievous. **impishly** *adv.* **impishness** *n.*

im-pla-ca-ble (im plak´a bl) *adj.* Not capable of being placated or appeased. **implacability** *n.* **implacably** *adv.*

im-plant (im plant´) *v.* To set in firmly; to fix in the mind; to insert surgically. **implant** *n.* **implantation** *n.*

im-plau-si-ble (im plo´zi bl) *adj.* Difficult to believe; unlikely.

im-plead (im plēd´) *v.* To prosecute by law.

im-ple-ment (im´ple ment) *n.* A utensil or tool. **implement** *v.* To put into effect; to carry out; to furnish with implements. **implementation** *n.*

im-pli-cate (im´pli kāt´) *v.* To involve, especially in illegal activity; to imply.

im-pli-ca-tion (im´pli kā´shan) *n.* The act of implicating or state of being implicated; the act of implying; an indirect expression; something implied.

im-plic-it (im plis´it) *adj.* Contained in the nature of someone or something but not readily apparent; understood but not directly expressed; complete; absolute.

im-plode (im plōd´) *v.* To collapse or burst violently inward. **implosive** *adj.*

im-plore (im plōr´) *v.* To appeal urgently to; to entreat; to beg; to pray pervently. **implorer** *n.* **imploringly** *adv.*

im-plo-sion (im plō´shan) *n.* The action of bringing to a center. **implosive** *adj.*

im-ply (im plī´) *v.* To involve by logical inference; to express indirectly; to suggest.

im-po-lite (im´po līt´) *adj.* Rude; uncivil. **impoliteness** *n.* **impolitely** *adv.*

im-pol-i-tic (im pol´i tik) *adj.* Not expedient; tactless. **impolitically** *adv.*

im-pon-der-a-ble (im pon´dêr a bl) *adj.* Incapable of being weighed or evaluated precisely. **imponderable** *n.*

im-port (im pōrt´) *v.* To bring in goods from a foreign country for trade or sale; to mean; to signify; to be significant. **import** *n.* Something imported; meaning; significance; importance. **importer** *n.* **importable** *adj.*

im-por-tance (im pr´tans) *n.* The quality of being important; significance.

im-por-tant (im pr´tant) *adj.* Likely to determine or influence events; significant; having fame or authority; prominent. **im-portantly** *adv.*

im-por-tu-nate (im par´cha nit) *adj.* Urgent or persistent in pressing demands or requests; pertinacious. .

im-por-tune (im´par tön´) *v.* To press with repeated requests; to harass or beset with solicitations; to beg or beg for urgently or persistently.

im-por-tu-ni-ty (im´par tö´ni tē) *n.* State of being importunate; persistence.

im-pose (im pōz´) *v.* To enact or apply as compulsory; to obtrude or force oneself on another; to take unfair advantage; to palm off. **imposer** *n*

im-pos-si-ble (im pos´i bl) *adj.* Not capable of existing or happening; unlikely to take place or be done; unacceptable; difficult to tolerate or deal with. **impossibility** *n.* **-ly** *adv.*

im-post (im´pōst) *n.* A tax or duty.

im-pos-tor *or* **im-pos-ter** (im pos´têr) *n.* One who assumes a false identity or title for the purpose of deception.

im-pos-tume (im pos´chüm´) *n.* A type of abscess.

im-pos-ture (im pos´chêr) *n.* Deception by the assumption of a false identity.

im-po-tent (im´po tent) *adj.* Without strength or vigor; having no power; ineffectual; incapable of sexual intercourse. **impotence** *n.* **impotency** *n.*

im-pound (im pound´) *v.* To confine in or as if in a pound; to seize and keep in legal custody; to hold water, as in a reservoir.

im-pov-er-ish (im pov´ĕr ish) v. To make poor; to deprive or be deprived of natural richness or fertility.

im-prac-ti-cal (im prak´ti kal) adj. Unwise to put into effect; unable to deal with practical or financial matters efficiently. **impracticality** n.

im-pre-cate (im´pre kāt´) v. To utter curses or to invoke evil on someone or something.

im-preg-na-ble (im preg´na bl) adj. Incapable of being taken by force.

im-preg-nate (im preg´nāt) v. To make pregnant; to fertilize, as an ovum; to fill throughout; to saturate.

im-pre-sa-ri-o (im´pri sär´ē ō´) n. A theatrical manager or producer, especially the director of an opera company.

im-pre-scrip-ti-ble (im pri skrip´ti bl) adj. Not subject to prescription; referring to rights, not legally to be withdrawn or revoked.

im-press (im pres´) v. To apply or produce with pressure; to stamp or mark with or as if with pressure; to fix firmly in the mind; to affect strongly and usually favorably; to force into public service. **impress** n. The act of impressing; a mark made by impressing; a stamp or seal for impressing.

im-pres-sive (im pres´iv) adj. Making a strong impression; striking. **impressively** adv. **impressiveness** n.

im-pri-ma-tur (im´pri mä´tĕr) n. Official permission to print or publish; authorization.

im-pri-mis (im pri´mis) adv. In the first place.

im-print (im print´) v. To make or impress a mark or design on a surface; to make or stamp a mark on; to fix firmly in the mind. **imprint** n. A mark or design made by imprinting; a lasting influence or effect; a publisher's name, often with the date and place of publication, printed at the bottom of a title page.

im-pris-on (im priz´on) v. To put in prison. **imprisonment** n.

im-prob-a-ble (im prob´a bl) adj. Not likely to occur or be true. **improbability** n. **improbably** adv.

im-pro-bi-ty (im prō´bi tē) n. Lack of principle; dishonesty.

im-promp-tu (im promp´tö) adj. Devised or performed without prior planning or preparation. **impromptu** n. Something said or done without prior thought. **impromptu** adv. Offhandedly; extemporaneously.

improper fraction n. A fraction having a numerator larger than or the same as the denominator.

im-pro-pri-ate (im prō´prē āt´) v. To place valuables, such as the profits of church property, in the hands of a layman. **impropriate** adj.

im-pro-pri-e-ty (im´pro prī´i tē) n., pl. **improprieties** The quality or state of being improper; an improper act or remark.

im-prove (im prōv´) v. To make or become better; to increase something's productivity or value. **improvable** adj.

im-pro-vise (im´pro vīz´) v. To make up, compose, or perform without preparation; to make from available materials. **improviser** n.

im-pru-dent (im prōd´ent) adj. Not prudent; unwise. **imprudence** n.

im-pu-dent (im´pū dent) adj. Marked by rude boldness or disrespect.

im-pu-dic-i-ty (im´pū dis´i tē) n. Shamelessness; immodesty.

im-pugn (im pūn´) v. To attack as false; to cast doubt on. **impugner** n.

im-puis-sance (im pū´i sans) n. Weakness; impotence.

im-puis-sant (im pū´i sant) adj. Being weak; powerless.

im-pulse (im´puls) n. A driving force or the motion produced by it; a sudden spontaneous urge; a motivating force; a general tendency. Physiol. A transfer of energy from one neuron to another.

im-pul-sive (im pul´siv) adj. Acting on impulse rather than thought; resulting from impulse; uncalculated. **impulsively** adv. **impulsiveness** n.

im-pu-ni-ty (im pū´ni tē) n. Exemption from punishment.

im-pure (im pūr´) adj. Not pure; unclean; unchaste or obscene; mixed with another substance; adulterated; deriving from more than one source or style.

im-pute (im pūt´) v. To attribute something, such as a mistake, to another; to charge.

in (in) prep. A function word that expresses inclusion or presence within a time, place, or circumstances. **in** abbr. Inch. **in** adv. Into a place, state, position, or a relationship; on the inside of a building.

in-a-bil-i-ty (in´a bil´i tē) n. A lack of sufficient power or capacity.

in ab-sen-tia (in´ ab sen´chē a) adv. In the absence of.

in-ac-ces-si-ble (in´ak ses´i bl) adj. Not to be reached or approached. **inaccessibility** n. **inaccessibly** adv.

in-ac-cu-ra-cy (in ak´yĕr a sē) n. The state of being inaccurate. **inaccurately** adv.

in-ac-cu-rate (in ak´yĕr it) adj. Not correct; not according to the truth.

in-ac-tion (in ak´shan) n. The lack of activity or action.

in-ac-ti-vate (in ak´ti vāt´) v. To make someone or something inactive.

in-ac-tive (in ak´tiv) adj. Not active or

inclined to be active; out of current use or service. **inactively** *adv.* **inactivity** *n.* **inactiveness** *n.*

in-ad-e-qua-cy (in ad´e kwi sē) *n., pl.* **inadequacies** The instance of being inadequate; insufficiency.

in-ad-e-quate (in ad´e kwit) *adj.* Not adequate; deficient. **inadequately** *adv.*

in-ad-mis-si-ble (in´ad mis´i bl) *adj.* Not admissible; not proper to be allowed, admitted, or received.

in-ad-ver-tence (in´ad ver´tens) *n.* The action of something being inadvertent; an oversight or careless mistake.

in-ad-ver-tent (in´ad ver´tent) *adj.* Unintentional; accidental; inattentive. **inadvertently** *adv.*

in-ad-vis-a-ble (in´ad vī´za bl) *adj.* Not advisable; unwise. **inadvisability** *n.*

in-al-ien-a-ble (in āl´ya na bl) *adj.* Not capable of being given up or transferred. **inalienably** *adv.*

in-al-ter-a-ble (in al´tēr a bl) *adj.* Being not alterable. **inalterability** *n.*

in-am-o-ra-ta (in am´o rä´ta) *n.* The person with whom a person is in love.

in-and-in *adj. & adv.* Being in repeated generations of the same related stock families.

in-ane (i nān´) *adj.* Without sense or substance. **inanely** *adv.*

in-an-i-mate (in an´i mit) *adj.* Not having the qualities of life; not animated. **inanimately** *adv.*

in-a-ni-tion (in´a nish´an) *n.* Exhaustion, especially from malnourishment.

in-an-i-ty (i nan´i tē) *n., pl.* **inanities** The quality of being inane; the lack of substance, sense or ideas; senselessness; emptiness; silliness.

in-ar-gu-a-ble (in-är´gü e bl) *v.* Being not arguable. **inarguably** *adv.*

in-ar-tic-u-late (in´är tik´ū lit) *adj.* Not uttering or forming intelligible words or syllables; unable to speak; speechless; unable to speak clearly or effectively;unexpressed.**inarticulately** *adv.* **inarticulate-ness** *n.*

in-ar-ti-fi-cial (in är´ti fish´al) *adj.* Not artificial; natural.

in-ar-tis-tic (in´är tis´tik) *adj.* Not artistic; lacking artistic appreciation; uninformed on the principles of art.

in-as-much as (in´az much´ az´) *conj.* Because of the fact that; since.

in-at-ten-tion (in´a ten´shan) *n.* The failure to pay attention.

in-at-ten-tive (in´a ten´tiv) *adj.* Not attentive; neglectful; heedless.

in-au-di-ble (in a´di bl) *adj.* Not audible; incapable of being heard.

in-au-gu-rate (in i´gü rāt´) *v.* To put into office with a formal ceremony; to begin officially. **inauguration** *n.*

in-aus-pi-cious (in´a spish´us) *adj.* Not auspicious; unlucky; unfavorable.

in-be-tween (in´bē twēn´) *adj.* Intermediate. **in-between** *n.* An intermediate or intermediary.

in between *adv. & prep.* Between.

in-bound (in´bōund´) *adj.* Incoming.

in-bounds (in´bōunds´) *adj.* Pertaining to putting the ball into play by throwing or passing it onto a court in the game of basketball.

in-breeding (in´brē´ding) *n.* The act of interbreeding individuals which are closely related in order to preserve desirable characteristics of the stock or thing being bred; as animals in the food chain.

in-cal-cu-la-ble (in kal´kya la bl) *adj.* Not calculable; indeterminate; unpredictable; very large. **incalculably** *adv.*

in-can-des-cent (in´kan des´ent) *adj.* Giving off visible light when heated; shining brightly; ardently emotional or intense.

in-can-ta-tion (in´kan tä´shan) *n.* A recitation of magic charms or spells; a magic formula for chanting or reciting.

in-ca-pa-ble (in kā´pa bl) *n.* Lacking the ability for doing or performing.

in-ca-pac-i-tate (in´ka pas´i tāt´) *v.* To render incapable; to disable; in law, to disqualify. **incapacitation** *n.*

in-car-cer-ate (in kär´se rāt´) *v.* To confine; enclose.

in-car-na-tion (in´kär nā´shan) *n.* The act of incarnating or state of being incarnated; the embodiment of God in the human form of Jesus; one regarded as personifying a given abstract quality or idea.

in-cen-di-ary (in sen´dē er´ē) *adj.* Causing or capable of causing fires; of or relating to arson; tending to inflame; inflammatory. **incendiary** *n.*

in-cense (in´sens) *n.* To make angry; to perfume with incense; to burn or offer incense. **incense** *n.* A substance, as a gum or wood, burned to produce a pleasant smell; the smoke or odor produced from incense.

in-cen-tive (in sen´tiv) *n.* Something inciting one to action or effort; a stimulus; a motive. **incentive** *adj.* Inciting to action; provocative.

in-cep-tion (in sept´) *n.* A beginning; an origin. **inceptive** *adj.*

in-cer-ti-tude (in ser´ti tōd´) *n.* Uncertainty; lack of confidence; instability.

in-ces-sant (in ses´ant) *adj.* Occurring without interruption; continuous; ongoing. **incessantly** *adv.*

in-cest (in´sest) *n.* Sexual intercourse between persons so closely related that they are forbidden by law to marry. **incestuous** *adj.* **incestuously** *adv.*

inch (inch) *n.* A unit of measurement

equal to 1/12th of a foot. *v.* To move slowly.

in-ci-dence (in´si dens) *n.* The extent or rate of occurrence; the matter of being incident; falling upon; the range of influence.

in-ci-dent (in´si dent) *n.* An event; an event that disrupts normal procedure or causes a crisis.

in-ci-den-tal (in´si den´tal) *adj.* Occurring or likely to occur at the same time or as a result of something; minor; subordinate. **incidental** *n.* A minor attendant occurrence or condition.

in-cin-er-ate (in sin´e rāt´) *v.* To burn up. **incineration** *n.*

in-cip-i-ent (in sip´ē ent) *adj.* Just beginning to appear or occur. **incipience** *n.* **incipiently** *adv.*

in-cise (in sīz´) *v.* To make or cut into with a sharp tool; to carve into a surface; to engrave.

in-ci-sion (in sizh´an) *n.* The act of incising; a cut or notch, especially a surgical cut.

in-ci-sive (in sī´siv) *adj.* Having or suggesting sharp intellect; penetrating; cogent and effective; telling. **incisively** *adv.* **incisiveness** *n.*

in-ci-sor (in sī´zėr) *n.* A cutting tooth at the front of the mouth.

in-cite (in sīt´) *v.* To provoke to action. **incitement** *n.* **inciter** *n.*

in-clem-ent (in klem´ent) *adj.* Stormy or rainy; unmerciful. **inclemency** *n.*

in-clin-a-ble (in klī´na bl) *adj.* Having an inclination; favorably disposed.

in-cli-na-tion (in´kli nā´shan) *n.* An attitude; a disposition; a tendency to act or think in a certain way; a preference; a bow or tilt; a slope.

in-cline (in klīn´) *v.* To deviate or cause to deviate from the horizontal or vertical; to slant; to dispose or be disposed; to bow or nod; to cause to bend or lean. **incline** *n.* An inclined surface.

in-cli-nom-e-ter (in´kli nom´i tėr) *n.* An apparatus for indicating the direction of the earth's magnetic field in reference to the plane of the horizon.

in-clude (in klöd´) *v.* To have as a part or member; to contain; to put into a group or total. **included** *adj.*

in-clu-sion (in klö´zhan) *n.* The act or state of including; that which is included.

in-clu-sive (in klö´siv) *adj.* Embracing; comprehensive; including a great deal; covering the specified costs or limits. **inclusively** *adv.* In *computer science*, incorporating as part of the whole, such as the part of a formula in which terms or values joined by the reserved word *AND*, often enclosed by parenthesis, must both be considered in evaluating the formula. **inclusiveness** *n.*

in-co-er-ci-ble (in´kō ûr´si bl) *adj.* Not coercible; incapable of being confined or controlled.

in-cog-ni-to (in kog´ni tō´) *adj.* Having a hidden or assumed identity; unknown. *adv.* With the real identity concealed. **incognito** *n.* A person who is in disguise.

in-cog-ni-zant (in kog´ni zant) *adj.* Lacking awareness.

in-co-her-ence (in´kō hēr´ens) *n.* The quality of being incoherent; something incoherent or disorganized.

in-co-her-ent (in´kō hēr´ent) *adj.* Lacking order, connection, or harmony; unable to think or speak clearly or consecutively. **incoherently** *adv.*

in-come (in´kum) *n.* Money or its equivalent received in return for work or as profit from investments.

income tax *n.* A tax on income earned by an individual or business.

in-com-ing (in´kum´ing) *adj.* Coming in or soon to come in.

in-com-men-su-ra-ble (in´kō men´shėr a bl) *adj.* Lacking a basis of comparison; utterly disproportionate.

in-com-men-su-rate (in´kō men´shėr it) *adj.* Not commensurate; disproportionate; inadequate.

in-com-mode (in´kō mōd´) *v.* To inconvenience; to disturb.

in-com-mu-ni-ca-ble (in´kō mū´ni ka bl) *adj.* Not communicable; incapable of being communicated; ineffable.

in-com-pa-ra-ble (in kom´pėr a bl) *adj.* Incapable of being compared; without rival. **incomparably** *adv.*

in-com-pat-i-ble (in´kom pat´a bl) *adj.* Not suited for combination or association; inconsistent. **incompatibility** *n.* **incompatibly** *adv.*

in-com-plete (in´kom plēt´) *adj.* Not complete; unfinished. **incompletely** *adv.* **incompleteness** *n.*

in-com-pre-hen-si-ble (in´kom pri hen´si bl) *adj.* Unable to be understood; unintelligible. **-ibility** *n.*

in-com-pre-hen-sion (in´kom pri hen´shan) *n.* Lack of understanding.

in-com-put-a-ble (in´kom pū´ta bl) *adj.* Incapable of being computed.

in-con-ceiv-a-ble (in´kon sē´va bl) *adj.* Not imaginable; unthinkable; impossible to understand. **inconceivably** *adv.*

in-con-clu-sive (in´kon klö´siv) *adj.* Having no definite result; indefinite.

in-con-den-sa-ble (in´kon den´sa bl) *adj.* Incapable of being condensed.

in-con-dite (in kon´dit) *adj.* Being put together badly; crude.

in-con-gru-i-ty (in´kong grö´i tē) *n. pl.* **incongruities** The quality or state of being incongruous; that which seems out of place.

in-con-gru-ous (in kong´grö us) *adj.*
Not corresponding; disagreeing; made
up of diverse or discordant elements;
unsuited to the surroundings or setting;
inappropriate. **incongruously** *adv.*

in-con-sec-u-tive (in˝kon sek´ü tiv) *adj.*
Not successive.

in-con-se-quent (in kon´se kwent˝) *adj.*
Not logical; irrelevant; disconnected.
inconsequently *adv.*

in-con-se-quen-tial (in´kon se
kwen´shal) *adj.* Without importance;
petty. **inconsequentially** *adv.*

in-con-sid-er-a-ble (in´kon sid´ér a bl)
adj. Not worthy of consideration;
unimportant; trivial.

in-con-sid-er-ate (in´kon sid´ér it) *adj.*
Not considerate for the feelings of
others; thoughtless. **inconsiderately**
adv. **inconsiderateness** *n.*

in-con-sis-tent (in´kon sis´tent) *adj.*
Lacking firmness, harmony, or
compatibility; incoherent in thought
or actions; not consistent.

in-con-sol-a-ble (in´kon sō´la bl) *adj.*
Not capable of being consoled; sad;
brokenhearted. **inconsolably** *adv.*

in-con-so-nant (in kon´so nant) *adj.* Not
in harmony; discordant.

in-con-spic-u-ous (in´kon spik´ü us) *adj.*
Not readily seen or noticed. **inconspic-
uously** *adv.* **inconspicuousness** *n.*

in-con-stant (in kon´stant) *adj.* Likely
to change; unpredictable; faithless;
fickle. **inconstancy** *n.*

in-con-trol-la-ble (in˝kon trō´la bl) *adj.*
Uncontrollable; unmanageable.

in-con-ven-ience (in´kon vēn´yens) *n.*
The quality or state of being inconvenient; something inconvenient.
inconvenience *v.* To cause inconvenience to; to bother.

in-con-vert-i-ble (in˝kon vür´ta bl) *adj.*
Incapable of being exchanged;
currency that cannot be exchanged for
that of another country.

in-con-vin-ci-ble (in˝kon vin´si bl) *adj.*
Incapable of being convinced.

in-cor-po-rate (in kor´po rāt˝) *v.* To
combine into a unified whole; to unite;
to form or cause to form a legal
corporation; to give a physical form
to; to embody. **incorporation** *n.*

in-cor-rect (in˝ko rekt˝) *adj.* Not correct;
inaccurate; not true; wrong; improper.

in-cor-rupt-i-ble (in´ko rup´ti bl) *adj.*
Not capable of being corrupted morally;
not subject to decay. **incorruptibility**
n. **incorruptibly** *adv.*

in-cras-sate (in-kras´āt) *v.* To make
thicker by evaporation or by adding
another substance. **incrassate** *adj.*

in-crease (in krēs˝) *v.* To make or
become greater or larger; to have
offspring; to reproduce. **increase** *n.*
The act of increasing; the amount or

rate of increasing; something that is
added. **increasingly** *adv.*

in-cred-i-ble (in kred´i bl) *adj.* Too
unlikely to be believed; unbelievable;
extraordinary; astonishing. **incredibil-
ity** *n.* **incredibly** *adv.*

in-cred-u-lous (in krej´u lus) *adj.*
Skeptical; disbelieving; expressive of
disbelief. **incredulity** *n.*

in-cre-ment (in´kre ment) *n.* An
increase; something gained or added,
especially one of a series of regular
additions. **incremental** *adj.*

in-crim-i-nate (in krim´i nāt˝) *v.* To
involve in or charge with a wrongful
act, as a crime. **incrimination** *n.*

in-cu-bus (in´kü bus) *n., pl.* **incubuses**
or **incubi** An evil spirit believed to
seize or harm sleeping persons; a
nightmare; a nightmarish burden.

in-cul-cate (in kul´kāt) *v.* To impress
on the mind by frequent repetition or
instruction. **inculcation** *n.*

in-cul-pa-ble (in kul´pa bl) *adj.* Not
culpable; free from guilt or blame.

in-cul-pate (in kul´pāt) *v.* To incriminate.

in-cum-bent (in kum´bent) *adj.* Lying
or resting on something else; imposed
as an obligation; obligatory; currently
in office. **incumbent** *n.* A person who
is currently in office. **incumbency** *n.*

in-cur (in ker´) *v.* To become liable or
subject to, especially because of one's
own actions. **incurrence** *n.*

in-cur-a-ble (in kür´a bl) *adj.* Unable
to be cured by medical means.

in-cu-ri-ous (in kür´ē us) *adj.* Lacking
interest; detached. **incuriously** *adv.*

in-cur-rent (in kür´ent) *n.* A current that
flows inward.

in-cur-sion (in kür´zhan) *n.* A sudden
hostile intrusion into another's territory.

in-cus (ing´kus) *n. pl.* **incudes** An
anvil-shaped bone in the middle ear
of mammals.

in-cuse (in küz´) *v.* To form or impress
by striking or stamping. **incuse** *n.*

in-da-mine (in´da mēn˝) *n.* Basic organic
compounds which form blue and green
salts, used to manufacture dyes.

in-debt-ed (in det´id) *adj.* Obligated to
another, as for money or a favor;
beholden. **indebtedness** *n.*

in-de-cent (in dē´sent) *adj.* Morally
offensive or contrary to good taste.
indecency *n.* **indecently** *adv.*

in-de-ci-pher-a-ble (in´di sī´fėr a bl)
adj. Not capable of being deciphered
or interpreted; unreadable..

in-de-ci-sion (in´di sizh´an) *n.* Inability
to make up one's mind; irresolution.

in-de-ci-sive (in´di sī´siv) *adj.* Without
a clear-cut result; marked by indecision.
indecisively *adv.* **indecisiveness** *n.*

in-de-clin-a-ble (in´di klī´na bl) *adj.*
Gram. Not being inflected for case,

number, etc..

in-dec-o-rous (in dek´ẽr us) *adj.* Lacking good taste or propriety. **indecorously** *adv.* **indecorousness** *n.*

in-deed (in dēd´) *adv.* Most certainly; without doubt; in reality; in fact. **indeed** *interj.* Used to express surprise, irony, or disbe-lief.

in-de-fat-i-ga-ble (in´di fat´i ga bl) *adj.* Tireless. **indefatigably** *adv.*

in-de-fen-si-ble (in´di fen´si bl) *adj.* Incapable of being justified; not able to protect against a physical fight.

in-def-i-nite (in def´i nit) *adj.* Not decided or specified; vague; unclear; lacking fixed limits. **indefinitely** *adv.* **indefiniteness** *n.*

in-del-i-ble (in del´i bl) *adj.* Not able to be erased or washed away; permanent. **indelibility** *n.* **indelibly** *adv.*

in-del-i-cate (in del´i kit) *adj.* Lacking sensitivity; tactless or crude. **indelicacy** *n.* **indelicately** *adv.*

in-dem-ni-fy (in dem´ni fī´) *v.* To secure against hurt, loss, or damage; to make compensation for hurt, loss, or damage. **indemnification** *n.* **indemnifier** *n.*

in-dent (in dent´) *v.* To set in from the margin, as the first line of a paragraph; to notch the edge of; to serrate; to make a dent or depression in; to impress; to stamp. **indent** *n.* An indentation.

in-den-ture (in den´chẽr) *n.* A legal deed or contract; a contract obligating one party to work for another for a specified period of time. **indenture** *v.* To bind into the service of another.

in-de-pend-ence (in´di pen´dens) *n.* The quality or state of being independent.

Independence Day *n.* July 4, a legal holiday in the United States, commemorating the adoption of the Declaration of In-dependence in 1776.

in-de-pend-ent (in´di pen´dent) *adj.* Politically self-governing; free from the control of others; not committed to a political party or faction; not relying on others, especially for financial support; providing or having enough income to enable one to live without working. **independent** *n.* One who is independent, especially a candidate or voter not committed to a political party. **independently** *adv.*

in-depth *adj.* Thorough; detailed.

in-de-scrib-a-ble (in´di skrī´ba bl) *adj.* Surpassing description; incapable of being described. **indescribably** *adv.*

in-de-struc-ti-ble (in´di struk´ti bl) *adj.* Unable to be destroyed.

in-de-ter-mi-na-ble (in´di tẽr´mi na bl) *adj.* Unable to determine as certain or fixed; not able to be decided.

in-de-ter-mi-nate (in´di tẽr´mi nit) *adj.* Not determined; not able to be determined; unclear or vague.

in-de-ter-min-ism (in´di tẽr´mi niz˝um) *n.* The theory maintaining that not every event has a cause; belief in free will.

in-dex (in´deks) *n., pl.* **indexes** *or* **indices** A list for aiding reference, especially an alphabetized listing in a printed work which gives the pages on which various names, places, and subjects are mentioned; something serving to guide or point out, especially a printed character calling attention to a paragraph or section.

index number *n.* A number which indicates change in a factor, as the cost of living, from one year or reference point chosen arbitrarily to another specified time.

index of refraction *n.* The quotient of the speed of light in a vacuum divided by the speed of light in a medium under consideration.

In-di-an-a (in´dē an a) *n.* A state located in the central part of the northern United States; statehood December 11, 1816; state capital Indianapolis.

Indian Ocean *n.* An ocean that extends from southern Asia to Antarctica and from eastern Africa to southeastern Australia.

in-di-cate (in´di kāt´) *v.* To point out; to show; to serve as a sign or symptom; to signify; to suggest the advisability of; to call for. **indicator** *n.*

in-dic-a-tive (in dik´a tiv) *adj.* Serving to indicate; of or being a verb mood used to express actions and conditions that are objective facts. **indicative** *n.* The indicative mood; a verb in the indicative mood. **indicatively** *adv.*

in-dict (in dīt´) *v.* To accuse of an offense; to charge; to make a formal accusation against by the findings of a grand jury. **indictable** *adj.* **indicter** *n.* **indictor** *n.* **indictment** *n.*

in-dif-fer-ence (in dif´ẽr ens) *n.* Lack of interest; apathy.

in-dif-fer-ent (in dif´ẽr ent) *adj.* Having no marked feeling or preference; impartial; neither good nor bad; without interest. **indifferently** *adv.*

in-di-gence (in´di jens) *n.* The condition of real hardship; poverty.

in-dig-e-nous (in dij´e nus) *adj.* Living or occurring naturally in an area; native.

in-di-gent (in´di jent) *adj.* Impoverished; needy.

in-di-ges-tion (in´di jes´chan) *n.* Difficulty or discomfort in digesting food.

in-dig-nant (in dig´nant) *adj.* Marked by or filled with indignation; showing displeasure. **indignantly** *adv.*

in-dig-na-tion (in´dig nā´shan) *n.* Anger aroused by injustice, unworthiness, or unfairness; feelings of disgust.

in-dig-ni-ty (in dig′ni tē) *n. pl.* **indignities** Humiliating treatment; something that offends one's pride.

in-di-go (in′di gō′) *n. pl.* **indigos** *or* **indigoes** A blue dye obtained from a plant or produced synthetically; a dark blue.

in-di-rect (in′di rekt′) *adj.* Not taking a direct course; not straight to the point. **indirection** *n.* **indirectly** *adv.*

in-dis-creet (in′di skrēt′) *adj.* Lacking sound judgment; imprudent; not discreet. **indiscreetly** *adv.*

in-dis-crete (in′di skrēt′) *adj.* Not consisting of distinct parts.

in-dis-cre-tion (in′di skresh′an) *n.* The condition of being indiscreet; want of discretion; lack of discretion.

in-dis-pose (in′di spōz′) *v.* To make or render unfit; to disqualify.

in-dis-posed *adj.* Mildly ill.

in-dis-tinct (in′di stingkt′) *adj.* Not distinct; not sharply outlined; blurred; not clear; confused. **indistinctly** *adv.*

in-dis-tinc-tive (in′di stingk′ tiv) *adj.* Without distinctive characteristics.

in-dite (in dīt′) *v.* To write; to compose; to put down in writing. **inditer** *n.*

in-di-vid-u-al (in′di vij′ŏ al) *adj.* Of, for, or relating to a single human being. **individually** *adv.* **individual** *n.*

in-di-vis-i-ble (in′di viz′i bl) *adj.* Not able to be divided.

in-doc-tri-nate (in dok′tri nāt′) *v.* To instruct in a doctrine or belief; to train to accept a system of thought uncritically. **indoctrination** *n.*

in-do-lent (in′do lent) *adj.* Disinclined to exert oneself; lazy. **indolence** *n.*

in-dom-i-ta-ble (in dom′i ta bl) *adj.* Incapable of being subdued or defeated.

in-door (in′dōr′) *adj.* Occurring inside a building or house rather than outdoors.

in-duce (in dōs′) *v.* To move by persuasion or influence; to cause to occur; to infer by inductive reasoning.

in-duce-ment (in dōs′ment) *n.* The act of inducing; something that induces.

in-duct (in dukt′) *v.* To place formally in office; to admit as a new member; to summon into military service.

in-duc-tile (in duk′til) *adj.* Not pliable; unyielding.

in-duc-tion (in duk′shan) *n.* The act of inducting or of being inducted; reasoning in which conclusions are drawn from particular instances or facts; the generation of electromotive force in a closed circuit by a magnetic field that changes with time; the production of an electric charge in an uncharged body by bringing a charged body close to it.

in-dulge (in dulj′) *v.* To give in to the desires of, especially to excess; to yield to; to allow oneself a special pleasure. **indulgent** *adj.* **indulger** *n.*

in-dul-gence (in dul′jens) *n.* The practice of indulging; an indulgent act.

in-du-rate (in′dū rāt′) *v.* To make stubborn; to make hardy; to become hard. **indurative** *adj.* **induration** *n.*

in-du-si-um (in dōˈzē um) *n.* The covering or outgrowth of a fern.

in-dus-tri-al (in dusˈtrē al) *adj.* Of, relating to, or used in industry; involved in industrial products.

in-dus-tri-ous (in dusˈtrē us) *adj.* Working steadily and hard; diligent.

in-dus-try (in′du strē) *n., pl.* **industries** The commercial production and sale of goods and services; a branch of manufacture and trade; industrial management as distinguished from labor; diligence.

in-e-bri-ant (in ēˈbrē ant) *n.* Anything that intoxicates.

in-e-bri-ate (in ēˈbrē at′) *v.* To make drunk; to intoxicate. **inebriate** *n.* **inebriated** *adj.* **inebriation** *n.*

in-ed-i-ble (in ed′i bl) *adj.* Not edible; not useful as food.

in-ed-it-ed (in ed′i tid) *adj.* Not edited; unabridged.

in-ef-fa-ble (in ef′a bl) *adj.* Beyond expression; indescribable.

in-ef-fec-tive (in′i fek′tiv) *adj.* Not producing intended or desired results; inefficient. **ineffectiveness** *n.*

in-ef-fi-ca-cy (in ef′i ka sē) *n.* Lack of the means or force to achieve the desired results.

in-ef-fi-cient (in′i fish′ent) *adj.* Wasteful of time, energy, or materials. **inefficiency** *n.* **inefficiently** *adv.*

in-el-e-gant (in el′e gant) *adj.* Not elegant; lacking in grace or refinement.

in-el-o-quent (in el′ō kwent) *adj.* Not eloquent; not fluent in speech.

in-e-luc-ta-ble (in′i luk′ta bl) *adj.* Not capable of being avoided or overcome.

in-ept (in ept′) *adj.* Awkward or incompetent; not suitable. **ineptitude** *n.* **ineptness** *n.* **ineptly** *adv.*

in-e-qual-i-ty (in′i kwol′i tē) *n. pl.* **inequalities** The condition or quality of being unequal; the lack of evenness.

in-eq-ui-ty *n. pl.* **inequities** Injustice; unfairness.

in-e-qui-valve (in ēˈkwi valv′) *adj.* Having valves unequal in size and form, used in reference to a bivalve mollusk.

in-ert (in ert′) *adj.* Not able to move or act; slow to move or act; sluggish; displaying no chemical activity.

in-er-tia (in erˈsha) *n.* The tendency of a body to remain at rest or to stay in motion unless acted upon by an external force; resistance to motion or change. **inertial** *adj.* **inertially** *adv.*

in-es-cap-a-ble (in´e skā´pa bl) *adj.* That which is unavoidable.

in-es-sen-tial (in´i sen´shal) *adj.* Not necessary or essential.

in-es-ti-ma-ble (in es´ti ma bl) *adj.* Unable of being estimated or computed; too great to be fully appreciated.

in-ev-i-ta-ble (in ev´i ta bl) *adj.* Not able to be avoided or prevented. **inevitability** *n.* **inevitably** *adv.*

in-ex-cus-a-ble (in´ik skü´za bl) *adj.* Unpardonable; indefensible.

in-ex-haust-i-ble (in´ig zas´ti bl) *adj.* Not exhaustible; unfailing; tireless.

in-ex-ist-ence (in´ig zis´tens) *n.* Nonexistence.

in-ex-is-tent *adj.* Not existent.

in-ex-o-ra-ble (in ek´sėr a bl) *adj.* Not capable of being moved by entreaty; unyielding. **inexorably** *adv.*

in-ex-pe-di-ent (in´ik spē´dē ent) *adj.* Not expedient; inappropriate.

in-ex-pen-sive (in´ik spen´siv) *adj.* Not expensive; cheep.

in-ex-pe-ri-ence (in´ik spėr´ē ens) *n.* The lack of experience; without knowledge.

in-ex-pert (in eks´pėrt) *adj.* Unskilled.

in-ex-pi-a-ble (in eks´pē a bl) *adj.* Incapable of being expiated; unpardonable.

in-ex-pli-ca-ble (in eks´pli ka bl) *adj.* Not capable of being explained; unable to be interpreted. **inexplicably** *adv.*

in-ex-pli-cit (in´ik splis´it) *adj.* Not explicit; not clearly stated.

in-ex-pres-sive (in´ik spres´iv) *adj.* Not expressive; wanting in meaning.

in-ex-pug-na-ble (in´ik spug´na bl) *adj.* Cannot be overcome or taken by force; impregnable.

in-ex-tin-guish-a-ble (in ik sting´gwisha bl) *adj.* Not to be extinguished.

in ex-tre-mis (in ex trēm´is) *adv.* At the point of death.

in-fal-li-ble (in fal´i bl) *adj.* Not capable of making mistakes; not capable of failing; never wrong. **infallibility** *n.*

in-fa-mous (in´fa mus) *adj.* Having a very bad reputation; shocking or disgraceful. **infamously** *adv.*

in-fant (in´fant) *n.* A child in the first period of life; a very young child; in law, a minor.

in-fan-ti-cide (in fan´ti sīd´) *n.* The killing of an infant.

in-fan-ti-lism (in´fan ti liz˝um) *n.* Abnormal recurrence of childish characteristics; a lack of mature emotional development.

in-farct (in färkt´) *n.* An area of dead tissue caused by an insufficient supply of blood. **infarcted** *adj.* **infarction** *n.*

in-fat-u-ate (in fach´ū ät´) *v.* To arouse an extravagant or foolish love in. **infatuated** *adj.* **infatuation** *n.*

in-fect (in fekt´) *v.* To contaminate with disease-producing organisms; to transmit a disease to; to affect as if by contagion. **infecter** *n.*

in-fec-tion (in fek´shan) *n.* Invasion of a bodily part by disease-producing organisms; the condition resulting from such an invasion; an infectious disease.

in-fec-tious (in fek´shus) *adj.* Causing infection; communicable by infection, as diseases; contagious; catching.

in-fe-cund (in fē´kund) *adj.* Barren; not fruitful.

in-fe-lic-i-tous *adj.* Not happy; unfortunate; not apt, as in expression.

in-fe-lic-i-ty (in´fe lis´i tē) *n. pl.* **infelicities** The state of being unhappy.

in-fer (in fer´) *v.* To conclude by reasoning; to deduce; to have as a logical consequence; to lead to as a result or conclusion. **inferable** *adj.*

in-fer-ence (in´fer ens) *n.* A conclusion based on facts and premises.

in-fe-ri-or (in fēr´ē ėr) *adj.* Located under or below; low or lower in order, rank, or quality. **inferiority** *n.*

inferiority complex *n.* An acute sense of personal inferiority resulting in withdrawal from social contact or aggression.

in-fer-tile (in fėr´til) *adj.* Not fertile or fruitful; barren. **infertility** *n.*

in-fest (in fest´) *v.* To spread so as to be harmful or offensive, as a swarm of mosquitos. **infestation** *n.*

in-fi-del (in´fi del) *n.* One who has no religion; an unbeliever in a religion.

in-fi-del-i-ty (in´fi del´i tē) *n., pl.* **infidelities** The lack of faith or belief; unfaithfulness to a moral obligation; adultery.

in-fi-nite (in´fi nit) *adj.* Without boundaries; limitless; immeasurably great or large; in mathematics, greater in value than any specified number, however large; having measure that is infinite.

in-fin-i-tes-i-mal (in´fin i tes´i mal) *adj.* Immeasurably small. **-lly** *adv.*

in-fin-i-tive (in fin´i tiv) *n.* A verb form which expresses the meaning of the verb without specifying number or person; it can function as a noun, usually preceded by *to.*

in-fin-i-ty (in fin´i tē) *n. pl.* **infinties** The quality or state of being infinite; unbounded space, time, or amount; an inde-finitely large number.

in-firm (in ferm´) *adj.* Physically weak, especially from age; feeble; in law, not sound or valid.

in-fir-ma-ry (in fer´ma rē) *n. pl.* **infirmaries** An institution for the care of the sick or disabled.

in-flam-ma-ble (in flam´a bl) *adj.* Tending to catch fire easily; easily excited.

in-flam-ma-tion (in´fla mā´shan) n. Localized redness, swelling, heat, and pain in response to an injury or infection.

in-flam-ma-to-ry (in flam´a tōr¯ē) adj. Tending to excite or anger, to inflame, anger. Med. Causing inflammation, usually accompanied by heat.

in-fla-tion (in flā´shan) n. The act or process of inflating; a period during which there is an increase in the monetary supply, causing a continuous rise in the price of goods. -nary adj.

in-flict (in flikt´) v. To cause to be suffered; to impose. inflicter n. inflictor n. infliction n.

in-flo-res-cence (in´flō res´ens) n. A characteristic arrangement of flowers on a stalk. inflorescent adj.

in-flu-ence (in´flōō ens) n. The power to produce effects, especially indirectly or through an intermediary; the condition of being affected; one exercising indirect power to sway or affect. influence v. To exert influence over; to modify. influential adj.

in-flu-en-za (in´flōō en´za) n. An acute, infectious viral disease marked by respiratory inflammation, fever, muscular pain, and often intestinal discomfort; the flu.

in-flux (in´fluks´) n. A stream of people or things coming in.

in-for-mal (in for´mal) adj. Not in usual form; unofficial; casual or relaxed.

in-form-ant (in for´mant) n. One who discloses or furnishes information which should remain secret.

in-for-ma-tion (in´fér mā´shan) n. The news communicated by word or in writing; data or facts; knowledge gained from reading or instruction, or gathered in another way. In computer science, any data that can be stored, retrieved and manipulated by a computer.

information management In computer science, the systems and techniques involved in effectively compiling and manipulating useful data.

information processing In computer science, the manipulation of compiled data and the compilation of reports from the data.

information retrieval In computer science, descriptive of the techniques for accessing data from storage in the form or pattern that the user desires.

information theory n. The statistical study or theory that deals with the processes and efficiency of transmitted messages, as in a computer or telecommunications.

in-for-ma-tive (in for´ma tiv) adj. Providing information; instructive.

in-frac-tion (in frak´shan) n. A violation of a rule.

in-fran-gi-ble (in fran´ji bl) adj. Not capable of being broken into parts; unbreakable.

in-fra-son-ic (in´fra son´ik) adj. Producing or using frequencies below those of audible sound.

in-fra-struc-ture (in´fra struk´chér) n. An underlying base or foundation; the basic facilities needed for the functioning of a system.

in-fre-quent (in frē´kwent) adj. Seldom; not occurring frequently; rare; occasional. infrequently adv.

in-fringe (in frinj´) v. To break a law; to violate; to encroach; to trespass.

in-fun-dib-u-lum (in´fun dib´ū lum) n. The funnel-shaped portion of the third ventricle in the brain that leads to the pituitary gland; the calyx of a kidney; the funnel-shaped abdominal opening of the fallopian tube.

in-fu-ri-ate (in fūr´ē āt´) v. To make very angry or furious; to enrage. infuriatingly adv. infuriation n.

in-fuse (in fūz´) v. To pour into; introduce, instill or inculcate, as principles; to obtain a liquid extract by soaking a substance in water.

-ing suffix Used in forming nouns and adjectives from verbs showing activity or action; the result or a product of an action.

in-gem-i-nate (in jem´i nāt´) v. To repeat.

in-gen-ious (in jēn´yus) adj. Showing great ingenuity; to have inventive ability; clever. ingeniously adv.

in-ge-nu-i-ty (in´je nōō´i tē) n., pl. ingenuities Cleverness; inventive skill.

in-gen-u-ous (in jen´ū us) adj. Frank and straightforward; lacking sophistication.

in-gest (in jest´) v. To take or put food into the body by swallowing. ingestion n. ingestive adj.

in-got (ing´got) n. A mass of cast metal shaped in a bar or block.

in-gre-di-ent (in grē´dē ent) n. An element that enters into the composition of a mixture; a part of anything.

in-gress (in´gres) n. A going in or entering of a building; an entrance. ingression n. ingressive adj.

in-grown (in´grōn´) adj. Growing into the flesh; growing abnormally within or into. ingrowing adj.

in-gur-gi-tate (in gur´ji tāt´) v. To swallow greedily or in great quantity.

in-hab-it (in hab´it) v. To reside in; to occupy as a home; where people live or work. inhabitability n. inhabiter n. inhabitation n. inhabitable adj.

in-hab-i-tant (in hab´i tant) n. A person who occupies a residence permanently, as distinguished from someone who visits.

in-hal-ant (in hā´lant) n. Something that

is inhaled. *adj.* Inhaling; used for inhaling.

in-hale (in´hāl´) *v.* To breathe or draw into the lungs, as air or tobacco smoke; the opposite of exhale.

in-her-ent (in hĕr´ent) *adj.* Forming an essential element or quality of something. **inherently** *adv.*

in-her-it (in her´it) *v.* To receive something, as property, money, or other valuables, by legal succession or will. *n, Biol.* To receive traits or qualities from one's ancestors or parents. **inheritable** *adj.* **inheritor** *n.*

in-he-sion (in hē´zhən) *n.* The fact of becoming a permanent part of something.

in-hib-it (in hib´it) *v.* To restrain or hold back; to prevent full expression. **inhibitor** *n.* **inhibiter** *n.* **inhibitive** *adj.*

in-hi-bi-tion (in´i bish´ən) *n.* The act of restraining, especially a self-imposed restriction on one's behavior; a mental or psychological restraint.

in-hos-pi-ta-ble (in hos´pi ta bl) *adj.* Not showing hospitality; not friendly or receptive; uninviting. **inhospitable-ness** *n.* **inhospitably** *adv.*

in-hu-mane (in´hū mān´) *adj.* Lacking compassion or pity; cruel. **-ly** *adv.*

in-hu-man-i-ty (in´hū man´i tē) *n. pl.* **inhumanities** The lack of compassion or pity; an inhumane or cruel act.

in-iq-ui-ty (i nik´wi tē) *n. pl.* **iniquities** The grievous violation of justice; wickedness; sinfulness. **iniquitous** *adj.*

in-i-tial (i nish´al) *adj.* Of or pertaining to the beginning. **initial** *n.* The first letter of a name or word. **initial** *v.* To mark or sign with initials. **initially** *adv.*

initialize In *computer science*, to format a disk to accept data; to boot up a computer by loading the system files it needs to become functional.

in-i-ti-a-tive (i nish´ē a tiv) *n.* The ability to originate or follow through with a plan of action; the action of taking the first or leading step. *Govt.* The power or right to propose legislative measures.

in-ject (in jekt´) *v.* To force a drug or fluid into the body through a blood vessel or the skin with a syringe; to throw in or introduce a comment abruptly. **injection** *n.* **injectable** *adj.*

in-ju-di-cious (in´jō dish´us) *adj.* To act without discretion or sound judgment; unwise. **injudiciously** *adv.*

in-junc-tion (in jungk´shən) *n.* An authoritative command or order; in law, a court order requiring a person to refrain from some specified action.

in-jure (in´jėr) *v.* To cause physical harm, damage, or pain.

in-ju-ri-ous (in jer´ē us) *adj.* Causing injury, damage or hurt; slanderous; abusive. **injuriously** *adv.*

in-ju-ry (in´je rē) *n., pl.* **injuries** Damage or harm inflicted or suffered.

in-jus-tice (in jus´tis) *n.* The violation of another person's rights; an unjust act; a wrong; lack of fairness.

ink jet printer In *computer science*, a printer that forms images from tiny jets of ink sprayed on paper.

in-laid (in lād´) *adj.* Ornamented with wood, ivory, or other materials embedded flush with the surface.

in-law (in´law) *n.* A relative by marriage.

in-lay (in lā´) *v.* To set or embed something, as gold or ivory, into the surface of a decorative design. **inlay** *n.* An inlaid surface; a filling cemented into a tooth cavity.

in-let (in´let) *n.* A bay or stream that leads into land; a passage between nearby islands.

in-most (in´mōst´) *adj.* Farthest or deepest within; farthest from the surface or outside; secret, as feelings..

inn (in) *n.* A place of lodging where a traveler may obtain meals and lodging for the night.

in-nards (in´ėrdz) *n.* The internal parts of the body; the inner parts of a machine.

in-nate (i nāt´) *adj.* Inborn and not acquired; having as an essential part; inherent. **innately** *adv.*

in-ner (in´ėr) *adj.* Situated or occurring farther inside; relating to or of the mind or spirit; internal.

in-ner-vate (i nur´vāt) *v.* To supply with nerves or nervous energy.

in-ner-va-tion (i nur vā shun) *n.* The communicating of nervous energy by means of nerves; the stimulation of some part or organ through its nerves.

in-no-cent (in´o sent) *adj.* Free from sin, evil, or moral wrong; pure; legally free from blame or guilt; not maliciously intended; lacking in experience or knowledge; naive. **innocence** *n.*

in-no-vate (in´o vāt´) *v.* To introduce or begin something new. **innovative** *adj.* **innovator** *n.* **innovation** *n.*

in-nu-en-do (in´ū en´dō) *n. pl.* **innuen-dos** *or* **innuendoes** An indirect or oblique comment, suggestion or hint.

in-nu-mer-a-ble (i nō´mėr a bl) *adj.* Too numerous; too much to be counted; countless. **innumerableness** *n.*

in-oc-u-late (i nok´ū lāt´) *v.* To introduce a mild form of a disease or virus to a person or animal in order to produce immunity. **inoculation** *n.*

in-op-er-a-ble (in op´ėr a bl) *adj.* Unworkable; incapable of being treated or improved by surgery.

in-op-er-a-tive (in op´ėr a tiv) *adj.* Not working; not functioning.

in-op-por-tune (in op´ėr tōn´) *adj.* Inappropriate; untimely; unsuitable.

in-or-di-nate (in ir´di nit) *adj.* Exceeding proper or normal limits; not regulated; unrestrained. **inordinately** *adv.*

in-or-gan-ic (in´ir gan´ik) *adj.* Not having or involving living organisms, their remains, or products.

in-os-cu-late (in os´ku lāt´) *v.* To unite into a continuous system by connecting open ends, as nerve fibers and arteries.

in-pa-tient (in´pā´shent) *n.* A patient admitted to a hospital for medical treatment.

in-per-so-nam (in per sō´nam) *adv.* Referring to a legal action against a person and not against specific things.

in-put (in´pút´) *n.* The amount of energy delivered to a machine; in computer science, information that is put into a data processing system. *Elect.* The voltage, current, or power that is delivered to a circuit. **input** *n.* In *computer science,* to supply data for processing.

input device In *computer science,* any equipment linked to the computer that enters source data, such as a keyboard, an optical scanner or a modem.

in-quest (in´kwest) *n.* A legal investigation into the cause of death.

in-quire (in kwïer´) *v.* To ask a question; to make an investigation. **inquirer** *n.*

in-quir-y (in kwïer´ē) *n. pl.* **inquiries** The act of seeking or inquiring; a request or question for information; a very close examination; an investigation or examination of facts or evidence.

in-quis-i-tive (in kwiz´i tiv) *adj.* Curious; probing; questioning. **inquisitively** *adv.*

in-sane (in sān´) *adj.* Afflicted with a mental disorder impairing a person's ability to function; showing the characteristics of a person who is not sane. **insanely** *adv.*

in-sa-tia-ble (in sā´sha bl) *adj.* Incapable of being satisfied. **insatiability, insatiableness** *n.* **insatiably** *adv.*

in-scribe (in skrïb´) *v.* To write, mark, or engrave on a durable surface; to enter a name in a register or on a formal list; to write a short note on a card. *Geometry* To enclose one figure in another so that the latter encloses the former. **inscriber** *n.*

in-sect (in sekt´) *n. Zool.* Any of a numerous class of small to minute winged arthropods with three pairs of legs, a segmented body, and usually two pairs of wings; a contemptible person.

in-se-cure (in´si kūr´) *adj.* Troubled by anxiety and apprehension; threatened; not securely guarded; unsafe; liable to break, fail, or collapse; precarious. **insecurely** *adv.* **insecurity** *n.*

in-sem-i-nate (in sem´i nāt´) *v.* To introduce semen into the uterus of; to make pregnant; to sow or implant seed.

in-sen-sate (in sen´sāt) *adj.* Showing a lack of humane feeling; unconscious; unable to experience sensations.

in-sen-si-ble (in sen´si bl) *adj.* Deprived of consciousness; unconscious; incapable of perceiving or feeling; unmindful; unaware. **insensibility** *n.*

in-sep-a-ra-ble (in sep´ėr a bl) *adj.* Incapable of being separated or parted. **inseparability** *n.* **inseparably** *adv.*

in-sert (in sert´) *v.* To put in place; to set. **insert** *n.* In printing, something inserted or to be inserted. **-tion** *n.*

in-side (in´sïd´) *n.* The part, surface, or space that lies within. **insides** *n. pl.* The internal parts or organs. **inside** *adj.*

in-sid-er (in´sï´dėr) *n.* One having special knowledge or access to confidential information.

in-sid-i-ous (in sid´ē us) *adj.* Cunning or deceitful; treacherous; seductive; attractive but harmful. **insidiously** *adv.*

in-sight (in´sït´) *n.* Perception into the true or hidden nature of things. **insightful** *adj.* **insightfully** *adv.*

in-sig-nif-i-cant (in´sig nif´i kant) *adj.* Lacking meaning importance, influence, or character; unimportant.

in-sin-cere (in´sin sēr´) *adj.* Not sincere; hypocritical. **insincerely** *adv.*

in-sin-u-ate (in sin´ū āt´) *v.* To suggest something by giving a hint; to introduce by using ingenious and sly means. **insinuating** *adv.*

in-sist (in sist´) *v.* To demand or assert in a firm way; to dwell on something repeatedly, as to emphasize. **insistence** *n.* **insist-ent** *adj.* **insistently** *adv.*

in-so-bri-e-ty (in´so brï´e tē) *n.* The lack of moderation; drunkenness.

in-so-far (in´so fär´) *adv.* To such an extent.

in-so-lent (in´so lent) *adj.* To be insultingly contemptuous in one's speech; overbearing. *n.* A rude disrespectful person. **insolently** *adv.*

in-sol-vent (in sol´vent) *adj.* In law, unable to meet debts; bankrupt.

in-som-ni-a (in som´nē a) *n.* The chronic inability to sleep. **insomniac** *n.*

in-sou-ci-ant (in sö´sē ant) *adj.* Lighthearted and cheerful; unconcerned; not bothered. **insouciance** *n.*

in-spect (in spekt´) *v.* To examine or look at very carefully for flaws; to examine or review officially. **inspection** *n.*

in-spec-tor (in spek´tėr) *n.* One who reviews or examines something critically.

in-spi-ra-tion (in´spi rā´shan) *n.* The stimulation within the mind of some idea, feeling, or impulse which leads to creative action; a divine or holy presence which inspires; the act of inhaling air. **inspirational** *adj*.

in-spire (in spïer´) *v*. To exert or guide by a divine influence; to arouse and create high emotion; to exalt; to inhale; breathe in. **inspirer** *n*. **inspiringly** *adv*.

in-sta-bil-i-ty (in´sta bil´i tē) *n*. *pl*. **instabilities** Lacking stability.

installation In *computer science*, the process of setting up and configuring a computer system or program; the computer system so installed.

in-stall-ment (in stal´ment) *n*. One of several payments due in specified amounts at specified intervals.

in-stance (in´stans) *n*. An illustrative case or example; a step in proceedings. **instance** *v*. To illustrate.

in-stant (in´stant) *n*. A very short time; a moment; a certain or specific point in time. **instant** *adj*. Instantaneously; immediate; urgent.

in-stan-ta-ne-ous (in´stan tā´nē us) *adj*. Happening with no delay; instantly; completed in a moment.

in-stant-ly (in´stant lē) *adv*. Immediately; at once.

in-stead (in sted´) *adv*. In lieu of that just mentioned.

in-sti-gate (in´sti gāt´) *v*. To urge forward; to stir up; to foment; to provoke. **instigation** *n*. **instigator** *n*.

in-still (in stil´) *v*. To introduce by gradual instruction or effort; to pour in slowly by drops. **instillation** *n*.

in-stinct (in´stingkt) *n*. The complex and normal tendency or response of a given species to act in ways essential to its existence, development, and survival. **instinctive** *adj*. **instinctively** adv.

in-sti-tute (in´sti tōt´) *v*. To establish or set up; to find; to initiate; to set in operation; to start. **institute** *n*. An organization set up to promote or further a cause; an institution for educating.

in-sti-tu-tion (in´sti tō´shan) *n*. The principle custom that forms part of a society or civilization; an organization which performs a particular job or function, such as research, charity, or education; a place of confinement such as a prison or mental hospital. **Institutionalize** *v*. **institutional** *adj*.

in-struct (in strukt´) *v*. To impart skill or knowledge; to teach; to give orders or direction. **instructive** *adj*.

in-struc-tion (in struk´shan) *n*. The act of teaching or instructing; important knowledge; a lesson; an order or direction. In *computer science*, a direction to the computer to set a parameter or execute an operation.

instruction format In *computer science*, the syntax required by a particular program for issuing a command.

in-struc-tor (in struk´tẽr) *n*. One who

instructs; a teacher; a low-rank college teacher, not having tenure.

in-stru-ment (in´stru ment) *n*. A mechanical tool or implement; a device used to produce music; a person who is controlled by another; a dupe; in law, a formal legal document, deed, or contract.

in-stru-men-ta-tion (in´stru men tā´shan) *n*. The use of instruments or work performed with instruments. *n.*, *Mus*. The arrangement of music for instruments.

in-sub-or-di-nate (in´su bor´di nit) *adj*. Not obedient; not obeying orders. **insubordinately** *adv*. **-tion** *n*.

in-sub-stan-tial (in´sub stan´shal) *adj*. Lacking substance or material nature; slight; imaginary; unreal; lacking firmness.

in-suf-fer-a-ble (in suf´ẽr a bl) *adj*. Not to be suffered; unendurable; intolerable.

in-suf-fi-cient (in´su fish´ent) *adj*. Inadequate; not enough. **insufficiently** *adv*. **insufficiency** *n*.

in-su-late (in´su lāt´) *v*. To isolate; to wrap or surround with nonconducting material in order to prevent the passage of heat, electricity, or sound into or out of; to protect with wrapping or insulation. **insulation** *n*. **insulator** *n*.

in-su-lin (in´su lin) *n.*, *Biochem*. The hormone released by the pancreas, essential in regulating the metabolism of sugar; a preparation of this hormone removed from the pancreas of a pig or an ox, used in the treatment of diabetes.

in-sult (in´sult) *v*. To speak or to treat with insolence or contempt; to abuse verbally. **insult** *n*. An act or remark that offends someone. **insulter** *n*. **insulting** *adj*. **insultingly** *adv*.

in-sup-press-i-ble (in´su pres´i bl) *adj*. Incapable of being concealed or suppressed.

in-sur-ance (in shur´ans) *n*. Protection against risk, loss, or ruin; the coverage an insurer guarantees to pay in the event of death, loss, or medical bills; a contract guaranteeing such protection on future specified losses in return for annual payments; any safeguard against risk or harm.

in-sur-mount-a-ble (in´sẽr moun´ta bl) *adj*. Incapable of being overcome.

in-sur-rec-tion (in´su rek´shan) *n*. An open revolt against an established government. **insurrectionary** *adj*. & *n*. **insurrectional** *adj*. **-tionist** *n*.

in-sus-cep-ti-ble (in´su sep´ta bl) *adj*. Immune; incapable of being infected. **insusceptibility** *n*.

in-tact (in takt´) *adj*. Remaining whole and not damaged in any way.

in-take (in´tāk´) *n*. The act of taking in

or absorbing; the amount or quantity taken in or absorbed.

in-tan-gi-ble (in tan´ji bl) *adj.* Incapable of being touched; vague or indefinite to the mind. **intangibility** *n.* **intangibleness** *n.* **intangibly** *adv.*

in-te-ger (in´ti jèr) *n.* Any of the numbers 1, 2, 3, etc., including all the positive whole numbers and all the negative numbers and zero; a whole entity.

in-te-gral (in´te gral) *adj.* Being an essential and indispensable part of a whole; made up, from, or formed of parts that constitute a unity.

integral calculus *n.* A branch of mathematical concerned with integrals and integration, their use in the solution of differential equations and problems that involve lengths, volumes, and areas.

in-te-grate (in´te grāt´) *v.* To make into a whole by joining parts together; to unify; to be open to people of all races or ethnic groups. **integration** *n.*

integrated circuit In *computer science,* an electronic device that contains a number of circuit elements working together.

integrated software In *computer science,* descriptive of applications that are able to share data; a program package that offers a combination of features, such as a word processor, spreadsheet, and database capability.

integrated system In *computer science,* a combination of computers and peripherals that are compatible.

in-teg-ri-ty (in teg´ri tē) *n.* Uprightness of character; honesty; the condition, quality, or state of being complete or undivided.

in-tel-lect (in´te lekt´) *n.* The power of the mind to understand and to accept knowledge; the state of having a strong or brilliant mind; a person of notable intellect.

in-tel-li-gent (in tel´i jent) *adj.* Having or showing intelligence.

in-tel-li-gi-ble (in tel´i ji bl) *adj.* Having the capabilities of being understood; understanding.

in-tem-per-ance (in tem´pèr ans) *n.* The lack of moderation, as in satisfying of the appetite or of one's passion for something; excess in anything.

in-tend (in tend´) *v.* To have a plan or purpose in mind; to design for a particular use. **intender** *n.*

in-ten-er-ate (in ten´e rāt´) *v.* To cause or to make something tender or softer than it was to begin with.

in-tense (in tens´) *adj.* Extreme in strength, effect, or degree; expressing strong emotion, concentration, or strain; profound. **intensely** *adv.* **-ness** *n.*

in-ten-si-fy (in ten´si fī) *v.* To become

or make more intense or acute.

in-ten-si-ty (in ten´si tē) *n. pl.* **intensities** The quality of being intense or acute; a great effect, concentration, or force.

in-tent (in tent´) *n.* A purpose, goal, aim, or design. **intently** *adv.* **intentness** *n.*

in-ten-tion-al (in ten´shan al) *adj.* Deliberately intended or done. **intentionality** *n.* **intentionally** *adv.*

in-ter- (in ter´) *prefix.* Mutually; with each other; together; among or between.

in-ter-act (in´tèr akt´) *v.* To act on each other or with each other. **-active** *adj.*

interactive system In *computer science,* a combination of computers and peripherals that are compatible.

interactive program In *computer science,* an application that responds to each user command as it is entered, then waits for the next command.

in-ter-breed (in´tèr brēd´) *v.* To breed together by crossing one variety of plant or animal with another.

in-ter-cede (in´tèr sēd) *v.* To argue or plead on another's behalf. **-er** *n.*

in-ter-cept (in´tèr sept´) *v.* To interrupt the path or course of; to seize or stop.

in-ter-cep-tion (in´tèr sep´shan) *n.* The state of being intercepted.

in-ter-change (in´tèr chänj´) *v.* To put each in the place of another; to give and receive in return. **interchange** *n.* The intersection of a highway which allows traffic to enter or turn off without obstructing other traffic. **interchangeably** *adv.* **-er** *n.*

in-ter-change-a-ble (in´tèr chänj´a bl) *adj.* To be capable of being interchanged with something; an alternate; exchange. **interchangeableness** *n.*

in-ter-clav-i-cle (in´tèr klav´i kl) *n.* The bone which is located between the clavicles and in front of the sternum of reptiles. **interclavicular** *adj.*

in-ter-com (in´tèr kom´) *n., Informal* A two-way communication system, as used in different areas of a home or business.

in-ter-con-nect (in´tèr ko nekt´) *v.* To connect two or more things with one another. **interconnection** *n.*

in-ter-con-ti-nen-tal (in´tèr kon´ti nen´tal) *adj.* Pertaining to or involving two or more continents.

in-ter-course (in´tèr kōrs´) *n.* Mutual exchange between persons or groups; communication; sexual intercourse.

in-ter-cur-rent (in´tèr kür´ent) *adj.* To be happening in the midst of a process.

in-ter-de-part-men-tal (in´tèr dē´pärt men´tal) *adj.* To be involving or to be between different departments in a company or government. **-ally** *adv.*

in-ter-dis-ci-pli-nar-y (in´tèr dis´i pli nèr ´ē) *adj.* To be involving or containing two or more artistic, academic, or scientific disciplines.

in·ter·est (in´tèr ist) *n.* Curiosity or concern about something; that which is to one's benefit; legal or financial right, claim, or share, as in a business; a charge for a loan of money, usually a percent of the amount borrowed.

in·ter·est·ing (in´tèr i sting) *adj.* Stimulating interest, attention, or curiosity. **interesting** *adv.*

in·ter·face (in´tèr fās´) *n.* A surface forming a common boundary between adjacent areas; in *computer science*, the software or hardware connecting one device or system to another.

in·ter·fere (in´tèr fēr´) *v.* To come between; to get in the way; to be an obstacle or obstruction. **interferer** *n.*

in·ter·fer·ence (in´tèr fēr´ens) *n.* The process of interfering in something.

in·ter·file (in´tèr fīl´) *v.* To place in or fit into an existing file.

in·ter·flu·ent (in´tèr flō´ent) *adj.* The flowing or intermingling into each other.

in·ter·fuse (in´tèr fūz´) *v.* To make or to cause something to pass into another. **interfusion** *n.*

in·ter·gov·ern·men·tal (in´tèr gov´èrn ment l) *adj.* To be happening between two or more governments.

in·ter·im (in´tèr im) *n.* A time between events or periods. **interim** *adj.* Temporary.

in·te·ri·or (in tēr´ē èr) *adj.* Of, or contained in the inside; inner; away from the coast or border; inland; private; not exposed to view.

in·ter·ject (in´tèr jekt´) *v.* To go between other parts or elements; to add something between other things. **interjector** *n.* **inter·jectory** *adj.*

in·ter·jec·tion (in´tèr jek´shan) *n.* A word used as an exclamation to express emotion, as *Oh! Heavens! Super!*

in·ter·lay·er (in´tèr lā´èr) *n.* The layer that is placed in between other layers.

in·ter·leaf (in´tèr lēf´) *n. pl.* **interleaves** A blank sheet of paper that is bound or inserted between two other pages of a book.

in·ter·line (in´tèr līn´) *v.* To mark or insert between the lines; to write between lines already written or printed.

in·ter·link (in´tèr lĭngk´) *v.* To put togther or to link things together.

in·ter·lock (in´tèr lok´) *v.* To join closely.

in·ter·lo·cu·tion (in´tèr lo kū shan) *n.* The interchange of speech with others; conversation; a dialogue or colloquy.

in·ter·lope (in´tèr lōp´) *v.* To intrude or interfere in the rights of others.

in·ter·lude (in´tèr lŏd´) *n.* A period of time that occurs in and divides some

longer process; light entertainment between the acts of a show, play, or other more serious entertainment.

in·ter·lu·nar (in´tèr lō´nèr) *adj.* To be pertaining to the interval that is between the new and old moon, where the moon is in·visible.

in·ter·me·di·ar·y (in´tèr mē´dē er´ē) *n. pl.* **intermediaries** A mediator. **intermediary** *adj.* Coming between; intermediate.

in·ter·mez·zo (in´tèr met´sō) *n.* The musical composition coming between the main sections or divisions of and extended musical work.

in·ter·min·a·ble (in tür´mi na bl) *adj.* To seem to have no end.

in·ter·min·gle (in´tèr ming´gl) *v.* To blend or become mixed together.

in·ter·mis·sion (in´tèr mish´an) *n.* A temporary interval of time between events or activities; the pause in the middle of a performance.

in·ter·mit (in´tèr mit´) *v.* To cause something to cease for a certain amount of time.

in·ter·mit·tent (in´tèr mit´ent) *adj.* Ceasing from time to time; coming at intervals.

in·tern (in´tèrn´) *n.* A medical school graduate undergoing supervised practical training in a hospital. **intern** *v.* To confine as in wartime. **-ship** *n.*

in·ter·nal (in ter´nal) *adj.* Of or pertaining to the inside; pertaining to the domestic affairs of a country; intended to be consumed by the body from the inside.

internal storage In *computer science*, data storage that is built into, and directly accessible by, the computer.

in·ter·nal·ize (in ter´na līz) *adj.* To incorporate within oneself.

in·ter·na·tion·al (in´tèr nash´a nal) *adj.* Pertaining to or involving two or more nations. **internationally** *adv.*

in·tern·ee (in´tèr nē´) *n.* A person who is confined or interned.

internet In *computer science*, the information super highway connecting computers.

in·ter·nist (in´tür nist) *n.* A physician who is a specialist in internal medicine.

in·tern·ment (in tèrn´ment) *n.* The state of something being interned.

in·ter·nun·ci·o (in´tèr nun´shē ō´) *adj.* The messenger who is between two parties.

in·ter·pel·late (in´tèr pel´āt) *v.* To question; to call upon formally; to ask for an explanation of an official action.

in·ter·pen·e·trate (in´tèr pen´i trāt´) *v.* To penetrate mutually; to penetrate between throughout, or within; to penetrate each other.

in·ter·per·son·al (in´tèr pers´nel) *adj.*

To be relating to or pertaining to relations between people.

in-ter-plan-e-tar-y (in´tër plan´i ter˝ē) *adj.* To be happening or operating between the planets.

in-ter-plant (in´tër plant´) *v.* To plant or place a crop between other crops.

in-ter-play (in´tër plā´) *n.* Action, movement, or influence between or among people.

in-ter-po-late (in ter´po lāt´) *v.* To insert between other things or elements; to change something by introducing additions or insertions. **interpolation** *n.* **interpolative**-*adj.*

in-ter-pose (in´tër pōz´) *v.* To put between parts; to put in or inject a comment into a conversation or speech; to intervene. **interposer** *n.*

in-ter-pret (in ter´prit) *v.* To convey the meaning of something by explaining or restating; to present the meaning of something, as in a picture; to take words spoken or written in one language and put them into another language. **interpretable** *adj.* **interpre-tation, interpreter** *n.*

in-ter-pu-pil-lar-y (in´ter´pyü˝pi ler˝ē) *adj.* To be located or extending between the pupils of one's eyes.

in-ter-ra-cial (in´tër rā´shal) *adj.* Between, among, or affecting different races.

in-ter-reg-num (in´tër reg´num) *n. pl.* **nums** An interval between two successive reigns; a break in continuity.

in-ter-re-late (in´tër ri lāt´) *v.* To have or bring into a mutual relationship. **interrelation, interrelationship** *n.*

in-ter-re-lat-ed (in´tër ri lāt´d) *adj.* To have a mutual relation with someone or something. **interrelatedly** *adv.*

in-ter-ro-gate (in ter´o gāt´) *v.* To question formally. **interrogation** *n.*

in-ter-rog-a-tive (in´te rog´a tiv) *adj.* Asking or having the form of a question. *n.* A word used to ask a question. **interrog-atively** *adv.*

in-ter-rupt (in´te rupt´) *v.* To break the continuity of something; to intervene abruptly while someone else is speaking or performing. **interrupter** *n.* **interruption** *n.* **interruptive** *adj.*

in-ter se (in´ter sā´) *adj. or adv.* To be between or among friends.

in-ter-sect (in´tër sekt´) *v.* To divide by cutting through or across; to form an intersection; to cross.

in-ter-sec-tion (in´tër sek´shan) *n.* A place of crossing; a place where streets or roads cross; in mathematics, the point common to two or more geometric elements.

in-ter-ses-sion (in´ter sesh en) *n.* The period that is between two academic sessions that can be used for brief,

concentrated courses.

in-ter-space (in´tër spās´) *n.* A space between things; an intervening space or interval. *v.* To fill a space

in-ter-sperse (in´tër spers´) *v.* To scatter among other things. **interspersion** *n.*

in-ter-sta-di-al (in´tër stād´ē el) *n.* The subdivision that is within a glacial stage and marking a temporary retreat of the ice.

in-ter-state (in´tër stāt´) *adj.* Between, involving, or among two or more states.

in-ter-stel-lar (in´tër stel´ér) *adj.* Among or between the stars.

in-ter-stice (in tür´stis) *n.* The small space between things.

in-ter-sti-tial (in´tër stish´ al) *adj.* To be situated within a tissue or an organ.

in-ter-till (in´tër til´) *v.* To cultivate the ground between the rows of a crop.

in-ter-trop-i-cal (in´tër trop´i kal) *adj.* To be located between the tropics.

in-ter-twine (in´tër twīn´) *v.* To unite by twisting together.

in-ter-val (in´tër val) *n.* The time coming between two points or objects; a period of time between events or moments. *Mus.* The difference in pitch between two tones.

in-ter-vene (in´tër vēn) *v.* To interfere or take a decisive role so as to modify or settle something; to interfere with force in a conflict. **intervention** *n.*

in-ter-ven-or (in´tër vēn ér) *n.* A person who will intervene.

in-ter-ven-tion-ism (in´tër ven´shan izm) *n.* The practice of intervening in something. **interventionist** *n.*

in-ter-ver-te-bral (in´tër vert´e bral) *adj.* To be situated between the vertebrae, such as a disk.

in-ter-view (in´tër vū´) *n.* A conversation conducted by a reporter to elicit information from someone; a conversation led by an employer who is trying to decide whether to hire someone. **interview** *v.* **interviewer** *n.*

in-ter vi-vos (in´tër vē˝vōs) *adj. & adv.* To be between living people; from one living person to another.

in-ter-vo-cal-ic (in´tër vō kal´ik) *n.* To be preceded and followed immediately by a vowel.

in-ter-weave (in´tër wēv´) *v.* To weave together; to intertwine.

in-ter-zon-al (in´tër zōn´l) *adj.* To be carried on between two or more zones.

in-tes-tate (in tes´tāt) *adj.* Having made no valid will; not disposed of by a will.

intestinal fortitude *n.* Stamina of a person; courage.

in-tes-tine *or* **intestines** (in tes´tin) *n., Anat.* The section of the alimentary canal from the stomach to the anus.

in-tim-a (in´ti ma) *n.* The covering of an organ which is the innermost and is made up of an endothelial layer and is backed by connective tissue.

in-ti-mate (in´ti mit) *adj.* Characterized by close friendship or association. **intimate** *n.* **intimately** *adv.* **intimacy** *n.* **intimateness** *n.*

in-tim-i-date (in tim´i dāt´) *v.* To make timid or fearful; to frighten; to discourage or suppress by threats or by violence. **intimidation** *n.*

in-tim-i-da-tor-y (in tim´i de´tōr ¯e) *adj.* Tending to intimidate others.

in-tine (in tēn´) *n.* The layer that is innermost of a spore and is a cellular wall.

intitule (in tit´ūl) *v.* To give or furnish with a title.

intl *abbr.* International.

in-to (in´tö) *prep.* To the inside of; to a form or condition of; to a time in the midst of.

in-tol-er-a-ble (in tol´ër *a* bl) *adj.* Not tolerable; unbearable. **intolerability** *n.* **intolerableness** *n.* **intolerably** *adv.*

in-tol-er-ant (in tol´ër *ant*) *adj.* Not able to endure; not tolerant of the rights or beliefs of others; bigoted. **intolerance** *n.* **intolerantly** *adv.*

in-to-nate (in´tö nāt´) *v.* To utter something.

in-to-na-tion (in´tö nā´sh*a*n) *n.* The manner of speaking, especially the meaning and melody given to speech by changing levels of pitch.

in-tone (in tōn´) *v.* To utter or recite in a monotone; to chant. **intoner** *n.*

in-tort (in tort´) *v.* To curl; to twist inward.

in-tor-tion (in tor´sh*a*n) *n.* A winding or twisting, usually inward, around an axis, as of a plant stem around a pole.

in-to-to (in tö´tö) *adv.* Totally.

in-tox-i-cate (in tok´si kāt´) *v.* To make drunk; to elate or excite. **intoxicant** *n.* **intoxication** *n.*

in-tox-i-cat-ed (in tok´si kāt´d) *adj.* To be affected by alcohol.

in-tra- *prefix* Within.

in-tra-ar-te-ri-al (in´tr*a* är tir´¯e al) *adj.* To be located or situated within an artery.

in-tra-car-di-ac (in´tr*a* kär´dē ak) *adj.* To be occurring within a being's heart.

in-tra-cel-lu-lar (in´tr*a* sel´ū lër) *adj.* To be occurring within a cell or cells.

in-tra-cra-ni-al (in´tr*a* krā nē *a*l) *adj.* To be occurring within the skull.

in-trac-ta-ble (in trak´t*a* bl) *adj.* Hard to manage; difficult to cure or treat. **intractableness, intractability** *n.*

in-tra-cu-ta-ne-ous (in´tr*a* kū tā´nē us) *adj.* To be occurring between the layers of a being's skin.

in-tra-der-mal (in´tr*a* dür´m*a*l) *adj.* To be done within the layers of a being's skin.

in-tra-mu-ral (in´tr*a* mür´*a*l) *adj.* Taking place within a school, college, or institution; competition limited to a school community.

in-tra-mus-cu-lar (in´tr*a* mus´kū lër) *adj.* Within a muscle.

in-trans *abbr.* Intransitive.

in-tran-si-gence (in tran´si jens) *n.* The state of something being intransigent.

in-tran-si-gent (in tran´si jent) *adj.* Refusing to moderate a position; uncompromising or unbending. **intransigency** *n.* **intransigent** *n.*

in-tran-si-tive (in tran´si tiv) *adj.* To be not transitive. **intransitiveness** *n.*

in-trant (in trant´) *n.* A person who is entering or going into a learning institution.

in-tra-oc-u-lar (in´tr*a* ok´ū lër) *adj.* To be located within the eyeball.

in-tra-per-i-to-ne-al (in´tr*a* per´e ton ē´al) *adj.* To be going into the peritoneal cavity of the body.

in-tra-per-son-al (in´tr*a* per´son al) *adj.* To be taking place among the members of a population.

in-tra-pop-u-la-tion (in´tr*a* päp´ū lā´sh*a*n) *adj.* To be taking place between the members of a population.

in-tra-psy-chic (in´tr*a* sī´kik) *adj.* Arising or occurring within the psyche, mind, or personality.

in-tra-spe-cif-ic (in´tr*a* spi sif´ik) *adj.* Occurring among or within a species or involving the members of the same species.

in-tra-state (in´tr*a* stāt´) *adj.* Within a state.

in-tra-u-ter-ine (in´tr*a* ū´tër in) *adj.* Within the uterus.

in-tra-vas-cu-lar (in´tr*a* vas´kūler) *adj.* To be occurring within a vessel such as a blood vessel.

in-tra-ve-nous (in´tr*a* vē´nus) *adj.* To be occurring within a vein. **intravenously** *adv.*

in-tra-vi-tam (in´tr*a* vī´tam) *adj.* Happening during one's life; used on a living subject.

in-trep-id (in trep´id) *adj.* Courageous; unshaken by fear; bold. **intrepidly** *adv.* **intrepidness** *n.*

in-tri-ca-cy (in´tri k*a* sē) *n.* The state of something being intricate.

in-tri-cate (in´tri kit) *adj.* Having many perplexingly entangled parts or elements; complex; difficult to solve or understand. **intricately** *adv.*

in-tri-gant (in´tri g*a*nt) *n.* Someone or something that will intrigue.

in-trigue (in trēg´) *v.* To arouse the curiosity or interest; to fascinate; to plot; to conspire; to engage in intrigues. **intrigue** *n.* A secret or illicit love affair; a secret plot or plan. **intriguer** *n.*

in-tri-gu-ing (in tri´ging) *adj.* To be

engaging the interest of something or of someone to a marked degree.

in-trin-sic (in trin´sik) *adj.* Belonging to the true or fundamental nature of a thing; inherent. **intrinsically** *adv.*

in-tro-duce (in´tro dōs´) *v.* To present a person face to face to another; to make acquainted; to bring into use or practice for the first time; to bring to the attention of. **introductory** *adj.*

in-tro-duc-tion (in´tro duk´shan) *n.* A passage of a book that will introduce the story or the content of the book; something which introduces.

in-tro-gres-sion (in´tro gresh´en) *n.* The introduction of a gene from one gene complex to another gene complex.

in-tro-it (in´trō it) *n.* A hymn or psalm sung at the beginning of a Roman Catholic Mass; a piece of music played at the be-ginning of a religious service.

in-tro-ject (in´tro jekt´) *n.* To unconsciously incorporate ideas into someone's personality.

in-tro-mis-sion (in´tro mish´in) *n.* The process of intromitting.

in-tro-mit (in´tro mit) *v.* To put something in; insert.

in-trorse (in trors´) *adj.* To be facing inward.

in-tro-spect (in´tro spekt´) *v.* To examine reflectively; to look into one's own feelings or thoughts. **introspection** *n.*

in-tro-ver-sion (in´tro vür´zhan) *n.* The state of being introverted.

in-tro-vert (in´tro vert´) *n., Psychol.* A person who directs his interest to himself and not to friends or social activities. **introversive** *adj.* **-ed** *adj.*

in-trude (in trōd´) *v.* To thrust or push oneself in; to come in without being asked or wanted.

in-tru-sion (in trö´zhan) *n.* The act of intruding.

in-tru-sive (in trö´siv) *adj.* To be intruding where a person is not wanted or welcome. **intrusiveness** *n.* **-ly** *adv.*

in-tu-ba-tion (in´tü bā´shan) *n.* The act of placing a tube in a hollow organ or orifice. **intubate** *v.*

in-tu-it (in tö´it) *v.* To understand through intuition. **intuitable** *adj.*

in-tu-i-tion (in´to ish´an) *n.* The direct knowledge or awareness of something without conscious attention or reasoning; knowledge that is acquired in this way. **intuitive** *adj.*

in-tu-i-tion-ism (in´to ish´a niz˝um) *n.* A type of doctrine that states that objects of one's perception are intuitively known to be real.

in-tu-mesce (in´tü mes´) *v.* To enlarge.

in-tu-mes-cence (in´tü mes´ns) *n.* The swelling or the bubbling that can be caused by heat. **intumescent** *adj.*

in-tus-sus-cept (in´tus su sept´) *v.* To undergo an intussusception.

in-tus-sus-cep-tion (in´tus su sep´shan) *n.* The pulling or drawing in of something, such as with the intestines in one's body. **intussusceptive** *adj.*

in-u-lin (in´ū lin) *n.* A type of white polysaccharide which can be found in the sap of the roots of composite plants.

in-unc-tion (in´ungk´shan) *n.* The act of placing ointment on a body part.

in-un-date (in´un dāt´) *v.* To overwhelm with abundance or excess, as with work. **inundation** *n.* **inundatory** *adj.*

in-ure (in ūr´) *v.* To become used to accepting something which is undesirable. **inurement** *n.*

in-u-tile (in ū´til) *adj.* To be unusable or useless.

in va-cu-o (in vak´ū ō´) *adv.* To be done in a vacuum.

in-vade (in vād´) *v.* To enter by force with the intent to conquer or pillage; to penetrate and overrun harmfully; to violate; to encroach upon.

in vag-i-nate (in vaj´i nāt´) *v.* To sheathe something; to undergo an invagination.

in-va-lid (in´va lid) *n.* A chronically sick, bedridden, or disabled person.

in-val-id (in val´id) *adj.* Not valid; unsound; having no force; without legal force or void, as a contract. **invalidity** *n.* **invalidly** *adv.*

in-val-i-date (in val´i dāt´) *v.* To nullify; to make invalid. **invalidation** *n.* **invalidator** *n.*

in-va-lid-ism (in´va´li diz˝um) *n.* A type of condition, which is chronic, of being an invalid.

in-val-u-a-ble (in val´ū a bl) *adj.* Priceless; of great value; to be of great help or use. **invaluably** *adv.*

in-var-i-a-ble (in vâr´ē a bl) *adj.* Constant and not changing.

in-var-i-ance (in vâr´ē ans) *n.* The state of being invariable; constancy.

in-va-sion (in vā´zhan) *n.* The act of invading; an entrance made with the intent of overrunning or occupying.

in-va-sive (in vā´siv) *adj.* To be characterized by or to be similar to military aggression; intruding..

in-vec-tive (in vek´tiv) *adj.* To be characterized by abuse or insult. **invectively** *adv.*

in-veigh (in vā´) *v.* To angrily protest something. **inveigher** *n.*

in-vei-gle (in vā´gl) *v.* To win over by flattery. **inveiglement** *n.* **inveigler** *n.*

in-vent (in vent´) *v.* To devise or create by original effort or design.

in-ven-tion (in ven´shan) *n.* The act or process of inventing; a new process, method, or device conceived from study and testing.

in-ven-tive (in ven´tiv) *adj.* Skillful at invention or contrivance; ingenious.

inventively adv. **inventiveness** n.

in-ven-to-ry (in´ven tōr´ē) n. pl.
inventories A list of items with
descriptions and quantities of each;
the process of making such a list.

in-ver-ness (in´vèr nes´) n. A type of
loose belted coat with a cape.

in-verse (in vers´) adj. Reversed in order
or sequence; inverted. **inverse** n.
Something opposite. **inversely** adv.

in-ver-sion (in ver´zhan) n. The act of
inverting or the state of being inverted;
that which is inverted.

in-ver-sive (in ver´siv) adj. To be marked
or characterized by inversion.

in-vert (in vert´) v. To turn upside down;
to reverse the position, condition, or
order of something. **invertible** adj.

in-vert-ase (in ver´tās) n. A type of
enzyme which is capable of inverting
sucrose.

in-ver-te-brate (in vür´te brit) adj.
Lacking a backbone or spinal column.

inverted comma n. A type of comma that
is inverted to be upside down and is
placed at the top of a line.

in-vert-er (in vert´èr) n. Someone or
something that will invert.

in-vert-i-ble (in vert´i bl) adj. To be
capable of being inverted.

invert sugar n. A type of dextrose that
can be obtained from starch.

in-vest (in vest´) v. To use money for the
purchase of stocks or property in order
to obtain profit or interest; to place in
office formally; to install; to make an
investment. **investor** n.

in-ves-ti-gate (in ves´ti gāt) v. To search
or inquire into; to examine carefully.
investigative adj. **investigation** n.
investigator n.

in-ves-ti-ture (in ves´ti chèr) n. The
ceremony or act of investing or
installing someone in a high office.

in-vest-ment (in vest´ment) n. The act
of investing money or capital to gain
interest or income; property acquired
and kept for future benefit.

in-vet-er-a-cy (in vet´èr a sē) n. The state
of being persistent.

in-vet-er-ate (in vet´èr it) adj. To be
confirmed in a habit. **inveterate** adv.

in-vi-a-ble (in vī´abl) adj. To be unable
to survive. **inviability** n.

in-vid-i-ous (in vid´ē us) adj. To be
causing animosity or discontent.

in-vig-o-rate (in vig´o rāt) v. To give
strength or vitality to. **invigoratingly**
adv. **invigoration** n.

in-vin-ci-ble (in vin´si bl) adj. Incapable
of being defeated. **invincibility** n.

in-vi-o-la-ble (in vī´o la bl) adj. Secure
from profanation; safe from assault.
inviolability n. **inviolably** adv.

in-vi-o-late (in vī´o lit) adj. Not violated.
inviolately adv. **inviolateness** n.

in-vis-cid (in vis´id) adj. To have zero
viscosity.

in-vis-i-ble (in viz´i bl) adj. Not capable
of being seen; not visible; not open to
view; hidden. **invisibility** n. **-ly** adv.

in-vi-ta-tion (in´vi tā´shan) n. The act
of inviting; the means or words that
request someone's presence or
participation.

in-vi-ta-to-ry (in vī´ta tōr´ē) adj.
Intending to invite; containing an
invitation; to convey an invitation.

in-vite (in vīt´) v. To request the presence
or participation of; to make a formal
or polite request for; to provoke; to
entice; to issue an invitation.

in-vi-tee (in vi tē´) n. The person who
is being invited to something or
somewhere.

in-vit-ing (in vīt ing) adj. Tempting;
attractive. **invitingly** adv.

in vi-tro (in vē´trō) adv. To be done
outside the body, such as fertilization.

in vi-vo (in vē´vō) adv. To be done in the
living body of an animal or in a plant.

in-vo-cate (in´vo kāt´) v. To invoke
someone or something into doing
something.

in-vo-ca-tion (in´vo kā´shan) n. An
appeal to a deity or other agent for
inspiration, witness, or help; a prayer
used at the opening of a ceremony or
service.

in-voice (in´vois) n. An itemized list of
merchandise shipped or services
rendered, including prices, shipping
instructions, and other costs; a bill. .

in-voke (in vōk´) v. To call upon for aid,
support, or inspiration; to conjure.
invoker n.

in-vol-u-cel (in vol´ū sel´) n. A small
involucre often at the base of an
individual flower or a small cluster of
flowers.

in-vo-lu-cre (in´vo lō´kèr) n. One or
more whorls of bracts that are situated
below and close to a flower cluster or
fruit.

in-vo-lu-crum (in´vo lū´krum) n. A type
of surrounding sheath.

in-vol-un-tar-y (in vol´un ter´ē) adj. Not
done by choice or willingly. **involuntary** n., Physiol. Muscles which
function with-out an individual's
control. **involuntariness** n.

in-vo-lute (in´vo lōt´) v. To return to the
former condition; to be cleared up.

in-vo-lu-tion (in´vo lō´shan) n. The
process where something returns itself
to its former condition or state.

in-volve (in volv´) v. To include as a part;
to make a participant of; to absorb; to
engross. **involvement** n.

in-volved (in volvd´) n. To be complex
in an extreme manner; not easily
understood.

in-vul-ner-a-ble (in vul´nẻr a bl) *adj.* To be immune to attack; impregnable; not able to be physically injured or wounded. **invulnerability** *n.* **invulnerably** *adv.*

in-wall (in wal´) *v.* To enclose within a wall. **inwall** *n.* interior wall.

in-ward (in´wẻrd) *adj.* Situated toward the inside, center, or interior; of or existing in the mind or thoughts. **inwardness** *n.*

in-weave (in wēv´) *v.* To interlace something.

in-wrought (in rot´) *adj.* To have the decoration worked in, such as with embroidery.

I/O In *computer science,* Input/Output.

I/O buffer In *computer science,* a portion of memory dedicated to the temporary storage of data received or to be sent by the computer- the buffer compensates for differences in communication speeds between devices the prevents the interruption of other operations.

I/O bus In computer science, a group of lines that carries signals between devices.

I/O port In computer science, the physical connector between the computer and its peripherals.

IOC *abbr.* International Olympic Committee.

i-o-date (i´o dāt´) *v.* To treat something with iodine. **iodation** *n.*

i-od-ic (i´od´ik) *adj.* To be pertaining to or containing iodine.

iodic acid *n.* An oxidizing solid that is formed by the oxidation of iodine.

i-o-dide (i´o dīd´) *n.* A type of iodine compound that has a more electropositive element.

i-o-din-ate (i´o din āt´) *v.* To cause a compound to combine with iodine.

i-o-dine (i´o dīn´) *n.* A grayish-black, corrosive, poisonous element, symbolized by I; a solution made up of iodine, alcohol, and sodium or potassium iodide used as an antiseptic.

i-o-dize (i´o dīz´) *v.* To treat something with iodine or to treat with an iodide.

i-o-do-form (i o´do form´) *n.* A type of yellow compound that has a penetrating, persistent odor and is used as an antiseptic dressing.

i-o-do-phor (i o´do for´) *n.* A type of complex iodine and organic compound that will release iodine gradually and is used as a disinfectant.

i-o-dous (i o´dus) *adj.* Pertaining to or containing iodine.

i-o-lite (i´o līt´) *n.* A mineral of a violet-blue color.

i-o moth (i´o moth´) *n.* A type of yellow American moth that has a large ocellated spot on both of its hind legs.

i-on (i´on) n., *Physics* An atom or group

of atoms which carries a positive or negative electric charge as a result of having lost or gained one or more electrons.

-ion *n. suffix* A process; a condition.

i-on-ize(i´on iz´) *v.* To convert completely or partially into ions. **ionizer** *n.* **ionization** *n.* **ionizable** *adj.*

i-on-o-sphere (i on´o sfẻr´) *n.* An ionized region of the atmosphere; the earth's atmosphere beginning at an altitude of about 30 miles and a latitude of 300 miles above the earth's surface and extends upward approximately 200 miles.

i-o-ta (ī ō´ta) *n.* The ninth letter in the Greek alphabet; a small amount.

I-o-wa (ī ō´wa) *n.* A state which is located in the north central part of the United States.

ipecac (ip´e kak´) *n.* A type of South American creeping plant that has flowers which droop and is found in tropical areas; the extract from its roots that is used as an emetic and expectorant.

i-pro-ni-a-zid (ī´pro nī´a zid) *n.* A type of derivative of isoniazid that was formerly used to treat tuberculosis.

ip-se dix-it (ip´sē dik´set) *n* A type of assertion that is made but not proven.

ip-si-lat-er-al (ip´si lat´ẻr al) *adj.* To be appearing on the same side of the body.

ip-so fac-to (ip´sō fak´tō) *adv.* By that very fact or act.

IQ *abbr.* Intelligence quotient.

i-ras-ci-ble (i ras´i bl) *adj.* Easily provoked to anger; quick-tempered. **irascibly** *adv.* **irascibility** *n.* **irascibleness** *n.*

i-rate (ī´rāt) *adj.* Raging; angry. **irately** *adv.* **irateness** *n.*

IRBM *abbr.* Intermediate range ballistic missile.

ire (īẻr) *n.* Anger; wrath.

i-ren-ic (ī ren´ik) *adj.* To be operating toward peace.

ir-i-da-ceous (ir´i dā´shus) *adj.* To be pertaining to the iris family of flowers.

ir-i-des-cent (ir´i des´ent) *adj.* Displaying the colors of the rainbow in shifting hues and patterns. **iridescence** *n.*

i-rid-ic (i rid´ik) *adj.* To be pertaining to iridium or to the iris of the eye.

i-rid-i-um (i rid´ē um) *n.* A type of silver-white brittle and very hard metallic element of the platinum group.

ir-i-dos-mine (ir´i doz´min) *n.* A compound of iridium and osmium alloy, that often contains some platinum and rhodium.

i-ris (ī´ris) *n. pl.* **irises** *or* **irides** The pigmented part of the eye which regulates the size of the pupil by contracting and expanding around it.

Bot. A plant with narrow sword-shaped leaves and handsome flowers, as the gladiolus and crocus.

iris diaphragm *n.* Adjustable diaphragm made of thin opaque plates that is turned by a ring, so as to change the diameter of a central opening such as the aperture of a lens.

I-rish (ī´rish) *n.* Pertaining to Ireland and its people or their language.

Irish coffee *n.* A type of hot, sweetened coffee that contains Irish whiskey and whipped cream.

Irish confetti *n.* A brick, rock, or fragment of either, used as a missile.

Irish Gaelic *n.* The Celtic language that has been used in Ireland since the end of the medieval period.

I-rish-ism (ī´rish iz´im) *n.* A phrase or a word that is characteristic of the Irish.

Irish mail *n.* A child's toy with three or four wheels that is activated by a hand lever.

Irishman *n.* A male person who is native to or an inhabitant of Ireland.

Irish moss *n.* Red alga that has been dried and is used for thickening or emulsifying.

Irish setter *n.* A type of bird dog that has a chestnut or reddish coat.

Irish stew *n.* A type of stew that contains meat (lamb, beef, or mutton) onions, and potatoes.

Irish terrier *n.* A type of medium-sized terrier dog that was developed in Ireland and has a reddish wiry coat.

Irish whiskey *n.* A type of whiskey, mainly of barley, that is made in Ireland.

Irish wolfhound *n.* A very large hound that resembles the Scottish deerhound but is much stronger and larger.

Irish woman *n.* A female person who was born in Ireland or is of Irish descend.

irk (erk) *v.* To annoy or to weary someone or something.

irk-some (erk´sum) *adj.* Tending to annoy someone or something; aggravating.

i-ron (ī´ern) *n.* A type of heavy, malleable, ductile and magnetic element that is silver-white and will rust easily in moist air. **iron** *v.* To smooth with an iron.

Iron Age *n.* The most recent of three early stages of human progress, following the Stone Age and the Bronze Age.

i-ron-bound (ī´ern bound´) *adj.* Bound with iron; unyielding.

i-ron-clad (ī´ern klad´) *adj.* Covered with protective iron plates; strict; unbreakable.

iron curtain *n.* An impenetrable political and ideological barrier between the Soviet bloc and the rest of the world.

i-ron-er (ī´ēr nēr) *n.* A person who irons things, such as clothing.

i-ron-fis-ted (ī´ern fis´tid) *adj.* To be ruthless and mean.

iron gray *n.* A type of color which is neutral and slightly greenish dark gray.

iron hand *n.* The rigorous control of someone or of something. **ironhanded-ness** *n.* **ironhanded** *adj.*

ironhearted *adj.* To be hardhearted and cruel.

iron horse *n.* The engine of a train.

i-ron-ic (ī ron´ik) *adj.* Marked by or characterized by irony. **ironical** *adj.*

i-ron-ing (ī´ern ing) *n.* The process or action of pressing or smoothing with a heated iron; clothes that have been ironed or are to be ironed.

i-ro-nist (ī´ro nist) *n.* A person who uses irony in developing of a literary work.

iron lung *n.* A tank which encloses the entire body with the exception of the head and regulates the respiration of a patient by alternately increasing and decreasing air pressure.

i-ron-ma-ster (ī´ern mä´ster) *n.* The manufacturer of iron.

iron out *v.* To make harmonious or tolerable by modification of extremes.

i-ron-smith (ī´ern smith´) *n.* A person who works with iron, as a blacksmith.

i-ron-stone (ī´ern stōn´) *n.* A heavy, white, glazed pottery.

i-ron-ware (ī´ern wâr´) *n.* Utensils, tools, and other articles made of iron; hardware.

i-ron-work (ī´ern wurk) *n.* Any object that has been made from iron.

i-ro-ny (ī´ro nē) *n. pl.* **ironies** A literary device for conveying meaning by saying the direct opposite of what is really meant.

ir-ra-di-ance (i rā´dē ans) *n.* A ray of light or anything of such luster or splendor.

ir-ra-di-ate (i rā´dē āt´) *v.* To subject to ultraviolet light, radiation, or similar rays. **irradiation** *n.* **irradiator** *n.*

ir-ra-tion-al (i rash´a nel) *adj.* Unable to reason; contrary to reason; absurd; in mathematics, a number which is not expressible as an integer or a quotient of integers. **irrationality** *n.* **irrationally** *adv.*

ir-rec-on-cil-a-ble (i rek´on sī´la bl) *adj.* Not willing or able to be reconciled. **irreconcilability** *n.* **irreconcilably** *adv.*

ir-re-cov-er-a-ble (ir´i kuv´ēr a bl) *adj.* Incapable of being regained or recovered; not capable of being remedied or restored.

ir-re-cu-sa-ble (ir´i kū´za bl) *adj.* Not to be objected to.

ir-re-deem-a-ble (ir´i dē´ma bl) *adj.* Not capable of being recovered, bought back, or paid off; not convertible into coin.

ir-re-den-ta (ir´i den´ta) *n.* Any region whose people are connected ethnically or historically to one country or area, but who are forced to accept the political jurisdiction of another state.

ir-re-duc-i-ble (ir´i dö´si bl) *adj.* Incapable of being reduced or simplified; not reducible.

ir-ref-ra-ga-ble (i ref´ra ga bl) *adj.* Incapable of being disproved; undeniable. **irrefragably** *n.*

ir-re-fran-gi-ble (ir´i fran´ji bl). Not to be violated; not to be broken.

ir-ref-ut-able (i ref´ü ta bl) *adj.* Cannot be disproved as truth. **irrefutability** *n.* **irrefutably** *adv.*

ir-reg-u-lar (i reg´ü lèr) *adj.* Not according to the general rule or practice; not straight, uniform, or orderly; uneven. **irregular** *n.* One who is irregular. **irregularity** *n.*

ir-rel-a-tive (i rel´a tiv) *adj.* Not relative; without relationship; not related.

ir-rel-e-vant (i rel´e vant) *adj.* Not pertinent or related to the subject matter. **irrelevantly** *adv.* **irrelevance** *n.* **irrele-vancy** *n.*

ir-re-lig-ious *adj.* Lacking in religion; opposed to religion. **irreligiously** *adv* **irreligiousness** *n.* **irreligion** *n.*

ir-re-me-di-a-ble (ir´i mē´dē a bl) *adj.* Incapable of being cured or remedied incurable.

ir-re-mis-si-ble (ir´i mis´a bl) *adj.* Unpardonable, as for sin.

ir-re-mov-a-ble (ir´i mö´va bl) *adj.* Not removable. **irremovably** *adv.*

ir-rep-a-ra-ble (i rep´ér a bl) *adj.* Unable to be set right or repaired. **irreparability** *n.* **irreparably** *adv.*

ir-re-peal-a-ble (ir´i pē´la bl) *adj.* Impossible to revoke or repeal.

ir-re-place-a-ble (ir´i plä´sa bl) *adj.* Unable to be replaced.

ir-re-press-i-ble (ir´i pres´i bl) *adj.* Impossible to hold back or restrain. **irrepressibility** *n.* **irrepressibly** *adv.*

ir-re-proach-a-ble (ir´i prö´cha bl) *adj.* Blameless; not meriting reproach. **irreproachableness** *n.* **-ably** *adv.*

ir-re-sist-i-ble (ir´i zis´ti bl) *adj.* Completely fascinating; impossible to resist. **irresistibility** *n.* **-y** *adv.*

ir-res-o-lu-ble (i re´zol´ü bl) *adj.* Admitting or having no explanation or solution.

ir-res-o-lute (i rez´o löt´) *adj.* Lacking resolution; indecisive; lacking firmness of purpose; hesitant. **irresolutely** *adv.* **irresoluteness** *n.*

ir-re-spec-tive (ir´i spek´tiv) *adj.* Regard-less of; not related to certain conditions. **irrespective of** *prep.* Without regard to anything.

ir-re-spon-si-bil-i-ty (ir´i spon´si bil´i tē) *n.* The quality of being irresponsible.

ir-re-spon-si-ble (ir´i spon´si bl) *adj.* Lacking in responsibility; not accountable. **irresponsibly** *adv.*

ir-re-spon-sive (ir´i spon´siv) *adj.* Unable to react or respond.

ir-re-triev-a-ble (ir´i trē´va bl) *adj.* Unable to be retrieved or recovered.

ir-rev-er-ence (i rev´ér ens) *n.* A lack of reverence; a disrespectful action.

ir-rev-er-ent (i rev´ér ent) *adj.* Lacking the proper respect. **irreverently** *adv.*

ir-re-vers-i-ble (ir´i ver´si bl) *adj.* Impossible to reverse. **irreversibility** *n.* **irreversibly** *adv.*

ir-rev-o-ca-ble (i rev´o ka bl) *adj.* Unable or incapable of being turned in the other direction; incapable of being repealed, annulled or undone. **irrevocability** *n.* **irrevocably** *adv.*

ir-ri-gate (ir´i gät´) *v.* To water the land or crops artificially, as by means of ditches or sprinklers; to refresh with water. *Med.* To wash out with a medicated fluid or water. **irrigation** *n.* **irrigator** *n.* **irrigational** *adj.*

ir-ri-ta-ble (ir´i ta bl) *adj.* Easily annoyed; ill-tempered. *Pathol.* To respond abnormally to stimuli. **irritability** *n.* **irritableness** *n.*

ir-ri-tate (ir´i tät´) *v.* To annoy or bother; to provoke; to be sore, chafed, or inflamed. **irritant** *adj.* & *n.* **irritator** *n.* **irritation** *n.* **irritatingly** *adv.*

ir-ri-ta-tive (ir´i tä´tiv) *adj.* Serving to excite or irritate; produced or accompanied by an irritant or irritation.

ir-rupt (i rupt´) *v.* To burst or rush in; to invade. **irruption** *n.* **irruptive** *adj.* **irruptively** *adv.*

IRS *abbr.* Internal Revenue Service.

is (iz) *v.* Third person, singular, present tense of the verb to be.

i-sa-gog-ic (ī´sa goj´ik) *adj.* To introduce one to the Bible. *pl.* **isagogics** *n.* The introductory study to the critical interpretation of the sacred writings of the Bible.

is-al-lo-bar (ī sal´o bär´) *n.* A line on a chart which connects the locations of equal change of atmospheric pressure.

is-ba (iz bä´) *n.* The Russian log hut.

is-che-mi-a (i skē´mē a) *n.* The tissue anemia that is localized due to an obstruction of the inflow of arterial blood.

is-chi-um (is´kēm um) *n. pl.* **ischia** The posterior bone of the pelvis at the hip joint of the body.

is-en-tro-pic (īs´en trö´pik) *adj.* To be related to constant entropy.

-ish *suffix* Of or belonging to a nationality or ethnic group; characteristic of; the approximate age of; the approximate time of; somewhat.

is-land (ī´land) *n.* A piece of land smaller than a continent, completely surrounded by water.

is-land-er(ī´lan dêr) *n.* A person who makes his home on an island.

island universe *n.* Any galaxy other than the Milky Way.

isle (īl) *n.* A small island.

is-let (ī´lit) *n.* A small island.

-ism *suffix* Practice; process; a manner of behavior characteristic of person or thing; a system of principles.

is-n't (iz´ont) *contr.* Is not.

iso-ag-glu-ti niŋ (ī´sō a glŏt´i niŋ) *n.* A clotting agent from one individual organism, effective in the cells of other individuals of the same species.

is-o-bar (ī´so bär´) *n.* An imaginary line or a line drawn on a map connecting places on the surface of the earth where the barometric pressure is the same for a given time.

is-o-bath (ī´so bath´) *n.* An imaginary line, or a line drawn on a map, connecting points that have the same depth below sea level.

is-o-cli-nal (ī´so klīn´al) *adj.* To be having an equality of inclination.

is-o-cy-clic (ī´sō sī´klik) *adj.* Having a ring composed of atoms of only one element.

is-o-di-a-met-ric (ī´so dī´a me´trik)*adj.* Having equal axes or diameters; having a similar diameter throughout.

is-o-e-lec-tron-ic (ī´sō i lek tron´ik)*adj.* To have the same number of electrons.

is-o-gen-ic (ī´sō jen´ik) *adj.* To be characterized by having identical genes.

is-o-ge-o-therm (ī´so jē´o thurm´) *n.* The imaginary line under the earth's surface which passes through points with the same mean temperature.

is-o-gloss (ī´so glŏs´) *n.* A boundary line that divides areas which differ in a particular linguistic feature.

is-o-gon-ic (ī´so gon´ik) *adj.* Growing so that sizes of parts remain equivalent.

is-o-gram (ī´so gram´) *n.* A line on a map or chart showing all points having constant value in relation to any climatic variable.

is-o-late (ī´so lāt´) *v.* To set apart from the others; to put by itself; to place or be placed in quarantine. **isolation** *n.*

iso-la-tion-ism (ī´so lā´sha niz´um) *n.* A national policy of avoiding political or economic alliances or relations with other countries. **isolationist** *n.*

is-o-mer (ī´so mêr) *n.* A compound having the same kinds and numbers of atoms as another compound but differing in chemical or physical properties due to the linkage or arrangement of the atoms.

isosceles triangle *n.* A triangle which

has two equal sides.

is-o-therm (ī´so therm´) *n.* A line on a map linking points that have the same temperature. **isothermal** *adj.*

is-o-tope (ī´so tōp´) *n.* Any of two or more species of atoms of a chemical element which contain in their nuclei the same number of protons but different numbers of neutrons.

is-o-trop-ic (ī´so trop´ik) *adj.* Having the same value in all directions.

is-sue (ish´ŏ) *n.* The act of giving out; something that is given out or published; a matter of importance to solve. *Med.* A discharge as of pus or blood. **issue** *v.* To come forth; to flow out; to emerge; to distribute or give out, as supplies. **issuable** *adj.*

it (it) *pron.* Used as a substitute for a specific noun or name when referring to places, things, or animals of unspecified sex; used to refer to the general state of something.

i-tal-ic (i tal´ik) *adj.* A style of printing type in which the letters slant to the right. **italics** *n. pl.* Italic typeface.

i-tal-i-cize (i tal´i sīz´) *v.* To print in italics.

itch (ich) *n.* A skin irritation which causes a desire to scratch; a contagious skin disease accompanied by a desire to scratch; a restless desire or craving. **itch** *v.* **itchiness** *n.* **itchy** *adj.*

-ite *suffix* A native or inhabitant of; an adherent of; a sympathizer or follower; a descendant of; a rock or mineral.

i-tem (ī´tem) *n.* A separately noted unit or article included in a category or series; a short article, as in a magazine.

i-tem-ize (ī´te mīz´) *v.* To specify by item; to list. **-er** *n.* **itemization** *n.*

it-er-ate (it´e rāt´) *v.* To state or do again; to repeat. **iteration** *n.*

i-tin-er-ant (ī tin´ êr ant) *adj.* Traveling from place to place; wandering around.

i-tin-er-ar-y (ī tin´e rer´ē) *n. pl.* **itineraries** A scheduled route of a trip.

it'll (it´il) *contr.* It will; it shall.

it's (its) *contr.* It is; it has.

its (its) *adj.* The possessive case of the pronoun it.

-ity *n. suffix* Quality or state.

i-vied (ī´vēd) To be overgrown with ivy.

i-vo-ry (ī´vo rē) *n.* A hard, smooth, yellowish-white material which forms the tusks of elephants, walruses, and other animals; a yellow to creamy-white color. **ivories** The teeth; the keys on a piano. **ivory** *adj.*

i-vy (ī´vē) *n. pl.* **ivies** A climbing plant having glossy evergreen leaves.

-ization *suffix* The process, action, or result of doing a specified thing.

-ize *suffix* To cause to become or resemble.

iz-zard (iz´êrd) *n.* The letter Z.

J, j (jā) The tenth letter of the English alphabet.

JA *abbr.* Joint account; judge advocate.

jab (jab) *v.* To poke or thrust sharply with short blows; a rapid punch.

jab-ber (jab´ẽr) *v.* To speak quickly or without making sense.

jab-i-ru (jab´i rö) *n.* A wading bird of the stork family, usually white in color.

jab-ot (zha bō´) *n.* A ruffle or decoration on the front of a blouse, dress, or shirt; a lace decoration that was formerly worn by men.

ja-cal (ha käl´) *n.* A small hut found in the southwestern United States and Mexico, with walls made of rows and rows of thin vertical poles filled in with mud.

jac-a-mar (jak´a mär´) *n.* A tropical, brilliantly colored, insectivorous bird of tropical America.

ja-ca-na (zhä´sa nä´) *n.* A small aquatic bird having long, straight claws that are adapted for walking on floating objects such as aquatic plants.

jac-a-ran-da (jak´a ran´da) *n.* A tall tropical tree; or the fragrant wood of such a tree.

jack-a-napes (jak´a näps) *n.* An impudent person, an impudent child.

jack-ass (jak´as´) *n.* A male donkey or ass; a stupid person or one who acts in a stupid fashion.

jack-boot (jak´böt´) *n.* A heavy military boot which reaches above the knee.

jack-daw (jak´do´) *n.* A glossy, black, crow-like bird.

jack-et (jak´it) *n.* A short coat worn by men and women; an outer protective cover for a book; the skin of a cooked potato. **jacketed, jacketless,** *adj.*

Jackson, Andrew *n.* (1767-1845) The seventh president of the United States from 1829-1837.

jac-ti-ta-tion (jak´ti tā´shɐn) *n.* An untrue statement which is insulting to another.

jac-u-late (jak´ū lāt´) *v.* To throw outwards; to hurl.

jade (jād) *n.* A hard, translucent, green gem-stone; an old, worn-out, unmanageable horse; a mean old woman; hussy. **jade** *adj.* Worn-out; exhausted.

jad-ed (jā´did) *adj.* Tired; worn-out; bored.

jag (jag) *n.* A very sharp projection or point. *Slang* A binge or spree.

jag-ged *adj.* Having jags or sharp notches; serrated. **jaggedly** *adv.* **jaggedness** *n.*

jag-ger-y (jag´e rē) *n.* A brown sugar made from palm tree sap.

jag-uar (jag´wär) *n.* A large feline mammal of tropical America with a tawny coat and black spots.

ja-gua-run-di (jä´gwa run´dē) *n. pl.*

jaguarundis A type of wildcat that is short-legged and slender.

jai alai (hī lī´) *n.* A game similar to handball in which players catch and throw a ball with long, curved, wicker baskets strapped to their arms.

jail (jāl) *n.* A place of confinement for incarceration.

ja-lop-y (ja lop´ē) *n. pl.* **jalopies** *Slang* An old, run-down automobile.

ja-lou-sie (jal´o sē´) *n.* A window, blind, or door having adjustable horizontal slats.

jam (jam) *v.* To force or wedge into a tight position; to apply the brakes of a car suddenly; to be locked in a position; to block; to crush. *Mus.* To be a participant in a jazz session. *Slang* To be in a difficult situation or to be crowded together, as of people, cars; a difficult situation. **jam** *n.* A preserve of whole fruit boiled with sugar.

jamb (jam) *n.* The vertical sidepiece of a door.

jam-ba-lay-a (jum´ba lī´a) *n.* A dish of rice that is cooked with vegetable, and various kinds of fish, meat, but usually shrimp or ham.

jam session *n.* An informal gathering of a group of jazz musicians, usually for their own enjoyment.

jan-gle (jang´gl) *v.* To make a harsh, unmusical sound; to dispute something in an angry way; to cause to become angry, tense or mad. **jangle** *n.* A discordant sound; a dispute or quarrel. **jangle, jangler** *n.*

jan-i-tor (jan´i tẽr) *n.* A person who cleans and cares for a building, office, school, apartment, etc. **janitorial** *adj.*

Jan-u-ar-y (jan´ū er´ē) *n.* The first month of the year, having thirty-one days.

jape (jāp) *v.* To joke; to make fun of or mock by words or actions. **jape, japer, japery** *n.*

Jap-o-nism (jap´oniz´um) *n.* To adapt to Japanese styles or methods; any manner-ism or trait that is characteristic of the Japanese.

jar (jär) *n.* A deep, cylindrical vessel with a wide mouth; a harsh sound. **jar** *v.* To strike against or bump into; to affect one's feelings unpleasantly.

jar-di-niere (jär´di nēr´) *n.* A decorative pot or stand for flowers or plants; a garnish for meat made from cooked and diced vegetables.

jar-gon (jär´gon) *n.* The technical or specialized vocabulary used among members of a particular profession. a type of speech containing pretentious or unfamiliar words; unintelligible writing or speech; gibberish.

jas-mine *or* **jes-sa-mine (jaz´min)** *n.* A shrub with fragrant yellow or white flowers.

jas-per (jas´pėr) *n.* An opaque red, brown, or yellow variety of quartz, having a high polish and often used for jewelry and vases.

ja-to (jā´tō) *n.* A takeoff of an airplane which is assisted by an auxiliary rocket engine.

jaun-dice (jon´dis) *n., Pathol.* A diseased condition of the liver due to the presence of bile pigments in the blood and characterized by yellowish staining of the eyes, skin, and body fluids.

jaunt (jont) *n.* A short journey for pleasure. *v.* To make a short journey, trip, or excursion.

jaunting car *n.* A light weight, open air cart that has two seats, set back to back or facing each other, with an area in front for the driver.

jaun-ty (jon´tē) *adj.* Having a buoyantly carefree and self-confident air or manner about oneself. **jauntily** *adv.*

jave-lin (jav´lin) *n.* A light spear thrown as a weapon; a long spear with a wooden shaft, used in competitions of distance throwing.

jave-lin throw *v.* To wound or strike with a javelin.

jaw (jo) *n., Anat.* Either of the two bony structures forming the framework of the mouth and the teeth.

jaw-bone (jo´bōn´) *n.* One of the bones of the jaw, especially the lower jaw or mandible.

jazz (jaz) *n.* A kind of music which has a strong rhythmic structure with frequent syncopation and often involving ensemble and solo improvisation. *Slang* Lying and exaggerated talk; idle and foolish talk; liveliness. **jazz up** To make more interesting; to enliven. **jazzer** *n.* **jazzy** *adj.*

jazz band *n.* A musical band that plays jazz, and typically uses the saxophone, clarinet, piano, trombone, and drums.

jeal-ous (jel´us) *adj.* Suspicious or fearful of being replaced by a rival; resentful or bitter in rivalry; demanding exclusive love. **jealously** *adv.*

jeal-ous-y (jel´o sē) *n.* Envy; resentment against a rival or someone who possesses any coveted advantage.

Jefferson, Thomas *n.* (1743-1826) The third president of the United Stated from 1801-1809.

Je-ho-vah (ji hō´va) *n.* God, in the Christian translations of the Old Testament.

je-june (ji jön´) *adj.* Lacking in substance or nourishment; immature.

je-ju-num (ji jö´num) *n., Anat.* The part of the small intestine which extends from the duodenum to the ileum.

jel-ly (jel´ē) *n. pl.* **jellies** Any food preparation made with pectin or gelatin and having a somewhat elastic consis-

tency; a food made of boiled and sweetened fruit juice and used as a filler or spread. **jelly** *v.* To make into jelly; to become or take the form of jelly; to become gelatinous; to assume or cause to assume definite form.

jen-net (jen´It) *n.* Name for a female donkey or a small Spanish horse.

jeop-ard-ize *v.* To put in jeopardy; to expose to loss or danger.

jeop-ard-y (jep´ėr dē) *n.* Exposure to loss or danger.

je-quir-i-ty (je kwir´i tē) *n.* The beans or seeds of the Indian licorice plant, black and scarlet in color, which contain abrin, a po-tent poison released when the seeds are broken open; the plant itself.

jer-e-mi-ad (jer´e mī´ad) *n.* A lament or prolonged complaint.

jerk (jerk) *v.* To give a sharp twist or pull to. **jerk** *n.* A sudden movement, as a tug or twist. *Physiol.* An involuntary contraction of a muscle resulting from a reflex action. *Slang* An annoying or foolish person. **jerky, jerkily** *adv.* **jerkiness** *n.*

jer-kin (jer´kin) *n.* A close-fitting jacket, usually sleeveless.

jerk-wa-ter (jerk´wo˝tėr) *adj.* Of little importance.

jer-o-boam (jer´o bō´am) *n.* An extra-large wine bottle.

jer-ry-build (jer´ē bild´) *v.* To build flimsily and cheaply. **jerrybuilt** *adj.*

jer-sey (jer´zē) *n. pl.* **jerseys** A soft ribbed fabric of wool, cotton, or other material; a knitted sweater, jacket, or shirt; fawn-colored, small dairy cattle which yield milk rich in butter fat.

Je-ru-sal-lem *n.* Capital of Israel.

jess (jes) *n.* A leather strap tied around each of the legs of a hawk, to which the falconer's leash is attached.

jest (jest) *n.* An action or remark intended to provoke laughter; a joke; a playful mood. **jester** *n.*

Jesus (jē´zus) *n.* The founder of Christianity, son of Mary and regarded in the Christian faith as Christ the son of God, the Messiah; also referred to as Jesus Christ or Jesus of Nazareth.

jet (jet) *n.* A sudden spurt or gush of liquid or gas emitted through a narrow opening; a jet airplane; a hard, black mineral which takes a high polish and is used in jewelry; a deep glossy black.

jet-ty (jet´ē) *n. pl.* **jetties** A wall, made by piling rocks or other material, which extends into a body of water to protect a harbor or influence the current; a pier.

Jew (jö) *n.* A descendant of the ancient Hebrew people; a person believing in Judaism.

jew-el (jö´el) *n.* A precious stone used for personal adornment; a person or

thing of very rare excellence or value.
jewel *v.* To furnish with jewels.

jew-el-er (jō´e lėr) *n.* A person who makes or deals in jewelry.

jew-fish (jō´fish˝) *n.* A large fish of the sea bass family, found in the tropical waters of the Atlantic Ocean.

Jew-ish (jo´lsh) *adj.* Of, relating to, or resembling the Jews, their customs, or their religion. **Jewishness** *n.*

jib (jib) *n., Naut.* A triangular sail set on a stay extending from the outer end of a jib boom. **jib** *v.* To swing or shift from one side of a vessel to the other.

jibe (jīb) *v.* To sail a course so that a vessel shifts from one side to the other; to be in agreement or in harmony.

jif-fy (jif´ē) *pl.* **jiffies** A very short time.

jig (jig) *n.* Any of a variety of fast, lively dances; the music for such a dance. *Mech.* A device used to hold and guide a tool.

jig-ger (jig´ėr) *n.* A small measure holding 1-1/2 oz. used for measuring liquor. *Naut.* A small sail in the stern of a sailing craft. *Slang* A small item which does not have a particular name.

jig-gle (jig´l) *v.* To move or jerk lightly up and down. **jiggle** *n.* A jerky, unsteady movement.

jig saw *n.* A saw having a slim blade set vertically, used for cutting curved or irregular lines.

jig-saw puz-zle *n.* A puzzle consisting of many irregularly shaped pieces which fit together and form a picture.

jilt (jilt) *v.* To discard a lover. **jilt** *n.* A woman who discards a lover.

jim-jams (jim´jamz˝) *n., Slang.* Feelings of nervousness; delirium tremors.

jim-my (jim´ē) *n. pl.* **jimmies** A short crowbar, used by a burglar. **jimmy** *v.* To force open or break into with a jimmy.

jin-go (jing´gō) *n.* Self-proclaimed patriot who advocates a tough, warlike foreign policy. **jingoish** *adj.*

jin-go-ism *n.* Extreme nationalism which is marked by a belligerent foreign policy. **jingoist** *n.* **jingoistic** *adj.*

jink (jingk) *v.* To move with agility; to make a quick, evasive turn.

jinn (jin) *n. pl.* **jinni** or **jinn** In Moslem legend, a spirit with supernatural powers.

jin-rik-i-sha (jin rik´sha) *n.* A two-wheeled vehicle used in the Orient, which is pulled by one or more men.

jinx (jingks) *n., Slang* A person or thing thought to cause bad luck; a period of bad luck.

jit-ter (jit´ėr) *v., Slang* To be intensely nervous. **jittery** *adj.*

jit-ter-bug (jit´ėr bug˝) *n., Slang* A lively dance or one who performs this dance. **jitterbug** *v.*

jit-ters *n.* Nervousness.

jive (jīv) *n., Slang* Jazz or swing music and musicians.

job (job) *n.* Anything that is done; work that is done for a set fee; the project worked on; a position of employment. **jobless** *adj.* **joblessness** *n.*

job-ber (job´ėr) *n.* One who buys goods in bulk from the manufacturer and sells them to retailers; a person who works by the job; a pieceworker.

job-ber-y (job´e rē) *n.* Graft; dishonest use of a public office for private gain.

job-hold-er (job´hōl˝dėr) *n.* Someone who is working at a steady job.

job-hop-ping (job´hop˝ing) *n.* The act of changing jobs at short intervals; often for better pay. **job-hopper** *n.*

job lot *n.* A mixed set of goods sold in a single deal, often at a reduced price.

job-name *n.* In *computer science,* a code that is assigned to a specific job instruction in a computer program, for the operator's use.

job processing In *computer science,* the execution of a particular task or series of tasks by the computer.

job work *n.* Work done by the job.

jock (jok) *n., Slang* A male athlete in college; a person who participates in athletics.

jock-ey (jok´ē) *n.* A person who rides a horse as a professional in a race; one who works with a specific object or device.

jo-cose (jō kōs´) *adj.* To be joking and jesting; causing laughter; merry; playful.

joc-u-lar (jok´ūlėr) *adj.* Joking; playful. **jocularity** *n.* **jocularly** *adv.*

joc-und (jok´and) *adj.* Cheerful; merry; suggestive of high spirits and lively mirthfulness. **jocundity** *n.*

jodh-pur (jod´pėr) *n.* Riding breeches that are wide at the hips, narrow at the knees and fit tightly to the ankles.

jog (jog) *n.* A slight movement or a slight shake; the slow steady trot of a horse, especially when exercising or participating in a sport; a projecting or retreating part in a surface or line. **jog** *v.* To shift direction abruptly; to exercise by running at a slow but steady pace. **jogger** *n.*

jog-gle (jog´l) *v.* To move or shake slightly. **joggle** *n.*

Johnson, Andrew *n.* (1808-1875) The seventeenth president of the United States from 1865-1869.

Johnson, Lyndon Baines *n.* (1908-1973) The thirty-sixth president of the United States from 1963-1969.

John the Baptist *n.* The baptizer of Jesus Christ.

join (join) *v.* To bring or put together so as to form a unit; to become a member of an organization; to participate.

join-er (joi´nêr) n. A person whose occupation is to build articles by joining pieces of wood; a cabinet maker; a carpenter.

joint (joint) n. The place where two or more things or parts are joined; a point where bones are connected. *Slang* A disreputable or shabby place of entertainment. **joint** *adj*. Marked by cooperation, as a joint effort; shared by two or more.

joint res-o-lu-tion n. A resolution that is approved by the two houses of a legislature, which becomes law when signed by the chief executive.

joist (joist) n. Any of a number of small parallel beams set from wall to wall to support a floor.

joke (jōk) n. Something said or done to cause laughter, such as a brief story with a punch line; something not taken seriously. **joke** v. To tell or play jokes. **jokingly** *adv*.

jok-er (jō´kêr) n. A person who jokes; a playing card, used in certain card games as a wild card; an unsuspected or unap-parent fact which nullifies a seeming advantage.

jol-li-fi-ca-tion n. Merrymaking; festivity.

jol-ly (jol´ē) *adj*. Full of good humor; merry. **jollity** n. **jolly** v.

jolt (jōlt) v. To knock or shake about. **jolt** n. A sudden bump or jar, as from a blow.

jon-quil (jong´kwil) n. A widely grown species of narcissus related to the daffodil, having fragrant white or yellow flowers and long narrow leaves.

jo-rum (jōr´um) n. A large drinking vessel.

josh (josh) v., *Slang* To make good-humored fun of someone; to tease; to joke.

joss (jos) n. A Chinese idol or image.

joss stick n. A stick of incense burnt by the Chinese.

jos-tle (jos´l) v. To make one's way through a crowd by pushing, elbowing, or shoving. **jostler** n.

jot (jot) v. To make a brief note of something. **jot** n. A tiny bit.

jounce (jouns) v. To bounce; to bump; to shake. **jounce** n. **jouncy** *adj*.

jour *abbr*. Journal.

jour-nal (jer´nal) n. A diary or personal daily record of observations and experiences; in bookkeeping, a book in which daily financial transactions are recorded. *Mech.* The part of an axle which rotates in or against a bearing.

jour-nal-ese (jer´na lēz´) n. The vocabulary and style of writing supposedly characteristic of most newspapers.

jour-nal-ism (jer´na liz˝um) n. The

occupation, collection, writing, editing, and publishing of newspapers and other periodicals. **journalist** n. **journalistic** *adj*. **journalistically** *adv*.

jour-ney (jer´nē) n. A trip from one place to another over a long distance; the distance that is traveled. **journey** v. to make a trip; to travel a long distance.

jour-ney-man (jer´nē man) n. pl. **journey-men** A worker who has served an apprenticeship in a skilled trade.

jo-vi-al (jō´vē al) *adj*. Good-natured; good-humored; jolly. **joviality** n.

jowl (joul) n. The fleshy part of the lower jaw; the cheek. **jowly** *adj*.

joy (joi) n. A strong feeling of great happiness; delight; a state or source of contentment or satisfaction; anything which makes one delighted or happy. **joyful, joyless** *adj*. **joyfully** *adv*. **joyfulness** n. **joylessly** *adv*.

joy-ous (joi´us) *adj*. Joyful; causing or feeling joy. **joyously** *adv*.

joy stick *Slang* The control stick of an airplane or video game.

jub-bah (jub´ba) n. An outer garment worn in Muslin countries by both men and women, which is long and has sleeves.

ju-bi-lant (jō´bi lant) *adj*. Exultantly joyful or triumphant; expressing joy. **jubilance** n. **jubilantly** *adv*.

ju-bi-la-tion (jō´bi lā´shan) n. Rejoicing; exultation.

ju-bi-lee (jō´bi lē´) n. A special anniversary of an event; any time of rejoicing.

judge (juj) v., *Law* A public officer who passes judgment in a court. **judge** v. To decide authoritatively after deliberation.

judg-ment (juj´ment) n. The ability to make a wise decision or to form an opinion; the act of judging. *Law* The sentence or de-termination of a court.

ju-di-ca-ble (jō´di ka bl) *adj*. Able to be judged or tried.

ju-di-ca-to-ry (jō´di ka tōr´ē) *adj*. Pertaining to the administration of justice. **judicatory** n. A court of justice; a person or persons having judicial authority; processes used to administer justice.

ju-di-ca-ture (jō´di kā˝chêr) n. The function of administration of justice; law, courts, or judges as a whole.

ju-di-cial (jō dish´al) *adj*. Pertaining to the administering of justice, to courts of law, or to judges; enforced or decreed by a court of law.

ju-di-cious (jō dish´us) *adj*. Having, showing, or exercising good sound judgment. **judiciously** *adv*. **-ness** n.

ju-do (jō´dō) n. A system or form of self-defense, developed from jujitsu in Japan in 1882, which emphasizes principles of balance and leverage.

ju-do-gi (jō dō´ gē) n. A loosely fitted white cotton costume, worn by judo wrestlers.

jug (jug) n. A small pitcher or similar vessel for holding liquids. *Slang* A jail.

ju-gal (jō´gal) adj. Relating to the bony arch of the cheek.

jug-ger-naut (jug´ĕr not´) n. Any destructive force or object.

jug-gle (jug´l) v. To keep several objects continuously moving from the hand into the air; to practice fraud or deception.

ju-glan-da-ceous (jō´glan dā´shus) adj. Belonging to the tree family that includes walnuts and hickories.

jug-u-lar (jug´ū lĕr) adj., Anat. Of or pertaining to the throat or the jugular vein.

jugular vein n., Anat. One of the large veins on either side of the neck.

ju-gu-late (jō´gū lāt) v. To use extreme measures in order to suppress disease; to slit the throat.

ju-gum (jō´ gum) n. In some insects, an area at the base of the forewings which locks the forewings and backwings together during flight.

juice (jōs) n. The liquid part of a vegetable, fruit, or animal. *Slang* Electric current. **juice** v.

juic-er (jō´sĕr) n. A device for extracting juice from fruit.

juic-y (jō´sē) adj. Full of; abounding with juice; full of interest; richly rewarding, especially financially. **juiciness** n.

ju-jit-su (jō jit´sō) n. A Japanese system of using holds, throws, and stunning blows to subdue an opponent.

juke-box (jōk´boks´) n. A large, automatic, coin-operated record player equipped with push buttons for the selection of records.

ju-lep (jū´lip) n. A mint julep.

ju-li-enne (jō´lē en´) adj. Cut into thin strips. **julienne** n. A clear meat soup containing vegetables chopped or cut into thin strips.

Ju-ly (jū lī´) n. The seventh month of the year, having 31 days.

jum-ble (jum´bl) v. To mix in a confused mass; to throw together without order; to confuse or mix something up in the mind. **jumble** n.

jum-bo (jum´bō) n. A very large person, animal, or thing. **jumbo** adj. Very large.

jump (jump) v. To spring from the ground, floor, or other surface into the air by using a muscular effort of the legs and feet; to move in astonishment; to leap over; to increase greatly, as prices. *Informal* To attack by surprise. *Computer Science* To move from one set of instructions in a program to another set further behind or ahead.

jump-er (jum´pĕr) n. One who or that which jumps; a sleeveless dress, usually worn over a blouse. *Electr.* A short wire used to bypass or join parts of a circuit.

jump-ing bean n. The seed of certain shrubs from Mexico which jumps about due to the movements of the larva inside.

jump seat n. An extra seat, often folding, found in a limousine or a taxicab.

jump shot n. In basketball, a shot made at the highest point of a jump.

jump-start v. To start an automobile by connecting a jumper cable from its battery to one of another automobile and turning the engine over.

jump suit n. Originally, a uniform for parachutists; now, any one-piece garment.

jump-y adj. Nervous; jittery.

jun-co (jung´kō) n. Any of various small birds of North America, having mainly gray plumage.

junc-tion (jungk´shan) n. The place where lines or routes meet, as roads or railways; the process of joining or the act of joining.

junc-ture (jungk´chĕr) n. The point where two things join; a crisis; an emergency; a point in time.

June (jūn) n. The sixth month of the year, having 30 days.

jun-gle (jung´gl) n. A densely covered land with tropical vegetation, usually inhabited by wild animals. **jungle** adj.

jungle fever n. A disease that is commonly found in tropical regions; a severe, recurring fever.

jun-ior (jōn´yĕr) adj. Younger in years or rank, used to distinguish the son from the father of the same first name; the younger of two. **junior** n. The third year of high school or college.

ju-ni-per (jō´ni pĕr) n. An evergreen shrub or tree of Europe and America with dark blue berries, prickly foliage, and fragrant wood.

junk (jungk) n. Discarded material, as glass, scrap iron, paper, or rags; a flat-bottomed Chinese ship with battened sails; rubbish; worthless matter. *Slang* Heroin, narcotics or dope.

jun-ket (jung´kit) n. A party, banquet, or trip; a trip taken by a public official with all expenses paid for by public funds; a custard-like dessert of flavored milk set with rennet. **junket** v.

junk-ie (jung´kē) n., *Slang* A drug addict that uses heroin.

jun-ta (hen´ta) n. A body of men or persons, as military officers, in power following a coup d'etat.

Ju-pi-ter (jō´pi tĕr) n., Astron. The fifth planet from the sun; the largest planet in the solar system.

ju-ral (jur´al) adj. Pertaining to law;

legal; pertaining to rights and obligations.

ju-rat (jur´at) *n., Law* The description on an affidavit that states when, where, before whom, and by whom the affidavit was made.

ju-ra-to-ry (jur´a tōr´ē) *adj.* Referring to an oath.

ju-rid-i-cal (je rid´i kal) *adj.* Of or pertaining to the law and to the administration of justice.

ju-ris-con-sult (jur´is kon sult´) *n.* An expert who gives opinions in cases of law.

ju-ris-dic-tion (jer´is dik´shan) *n.* The lawful right or power to interpret and apply the law; the territory within which power is exercised.

ju-ris-pru-dence (jur´is prōd´ens) *n.* The record of court decisions that are the basis for the formal principles upon which laws are based; the science of law.

ju-ror (jer´ėr) *n.* A person who serves on a jury.

ju-ry (jer´ē) *n. pl.* **juries** A group of legally qualified persons summoned to serve on a judicial tribunal to give a verdict ac-cording to evidence presented.

just (just) *adj.* Fair and impartial in acting or judging; morally right; merited; deserved; based on sound reason. **just** *adv.* To the exact point; precisely; exactly right. **justly** *adv.* **justness** *n.*

jus-tice (jus´tis) *n.* The principle of moral or ideal rightness; conformity to the law; the abstract principle by which right and wrong are defined; a judge.

justice of the peace *n.* A local magistrate having limited jurisdiction with authority to try minor cases, administer oaths, and perform marriages.

jus-ti-ci-a-ble (ju stish´ē a bl) *adj.* Expected to be settled by court action or within the legal system.

jus-ti-fi-a-ble (jus´ti fī a bl) *adj.* Able to be defended or proven to be right.

justified margin *n.* A typing or type-setting margin with all the characters at the ends of the lines vertically aligned.

jus-ti-fy (jus´ti fī´) *v.* To be just, right, or valid; to declare guiltless; to adjust or space lines to the proper length. **justifiably** *adv.* **justification** *n.*

jut (jut) *v.* To extend beyond the main portion; to project.

jute (jöt) *n.* A tall, annual Asian herb of the linden family, yielding a strong, coarse fiber used to make sacking and rope.

ju-ve-nile (jö´ve nil) *adj.* Young; youthful; not yet an adult. **juvenile** *n.* A young person; an actor who plays youthful roles; a child's book.

juvenile court *n.* A court which deals only with cases involving dependent, neglected, and delinquent children.

juvenile delinquent *n.* A person who is guilty of violations of the law, but is too young to be punished as an adult criminal; a young person whose behavior is out of control.

juvenile officer *n.* A police officer who specializes in investigating, prosecuting, and looking after juvenile delinquents.

ju-ve-nil-i-a (jö´ve nil´ē a) *n.* Works of art, such as writings or paintings, produced while young; any writings or artistic works intended to appeal to the young.

ju-ve-nil-i-ty (jö´ve nil´i tē) *n.* Youthful looks or actions; a childish act; behaving in an immature manner.

jux-ta-pose (juk´sta pōz´) *v.* To put side by side; to place together. **juxtaposed** *adj.* **juxtaposition** *n.*

K

K, k (kā) The eleventh letter of the English alphabet.

K *abbr., Computer science* A unit of storage capacity equal to 1024 bytes.

ka-bob (ka bob´) *n.* Cubed meat and mushrooms, onions, and tomatoes placed on a skewer usually marinated, and broiled over an open fire.

ka-bu-ki (kä bö´kē) *n.* A traditional Japanese drama in which dances and songs are performed in a stylized fashion.

kaf-fee klatsch (kä´fā kläch´) *n.* An informal get-together to drink coffee and talk.

kaf-ir (kaf´ėr) *n.* A grain sorghum that is cultivated in dry areas having a tough leafy stalk and is used for fodder.

kai-nite (kī´nīt) *n.* A mineral that is used as a fertilizer and a source of magnesium and potassium.

ka-ka (kä´ka) *n.* A New Zealand parrot, having an olive-brown color.

ka-ka-po (kä´kä pō´) *n.* A large parrot.

kale (kāl) *n.* A green cabbage having crinkled leaves which do not form a tight head.

ka-lei-do-scope (ka lī´do skōp´) *n.* A tubular instrument rotated to make successive symmetrical designs by using mirrors reflecting the changing patterns made by pieces of loose, colored glass at the end of a tube; a series of continuously changing colors; changing events or phases. **kaleido-scopic** *adj.* **kaleidoscopical** *adj.*

kaleyard school (kāl´yärd´skōl) *n.* A school of writers from the 19th century who wrote about Scottish life in a very sentimental manner, using heavy dialect.

kal-mi-a (kal'mē *a*) *n.* An evergreen shrub of North America, having pink, white, or purple flowers.

kame (kām) *n.* A short ridge of gravel and sand that remains after glacial ice melts.

kam-ik (käm'ik) *n.* Boot made of sealskin, knee-high in length and worn in the eastern arctic regions.

ka-mi-ka-ze (kä'mi kä'zē) *n.* A Japanese pilot in World War II trained to make a suicidal crash; an aircraft loaded with ex-plosives used in a suicide attack.

kam-pong (käm'pong) *n.* A group of dwellings or a local village in countries that speak Malay.

kan-ga-roo (kang''g*a* rō') *n. pl.* **kangaroos** *or* **kangaroo** Any of various herbivorous marsupials of Australia with short forelegs, large hind limbs capable of jumping, and a large tail.

kangaroo court *n.* A self-appointed, illegal court, usually marked by incompetence or dishonesty where the laws are deliberately totally disregarded or misinterpreted.

Kan-sas *n.* A state in the central United States; statehood January 29, 1861; state capital Topeka.

ka-o-lin *or* **ka-o-line** (kā'o lin) *n.* A fine clay which remains white after firing, used in ceramics and in manufacturing high quality porcelain.

ka-pok (kā'pok) *n.* A silky fiber manufactured from the fruit of the silk-cotton tree and used for stuffing cushions and life preservers, pillows, and sleeping bags and also used for insulation.

ka-put (kä pet') *adj., Slang* Destroyed or out of order; something with no possibility of success.

kar-a-kul (kar'*a* kul) *n.* Any of a breed of fat-tailed sheep of central Asia, having a narrow body and coarse, wiry, brown fur.

kar-at (kar'at) *n.* A unit of measure for the fineness of gold; a measure of weight for precious gems.

ka-ra-te (k*a* rä'tē) *n.* A Japanese art of self-defense, in which a person uses his elbows, feet, and knees in quick, damaging blows to his opponent.

ka-ross (k*a* ros') *n.* Animal skins sewn together into the shape of a square and worn by natives; a throw rug made from animal skins.

kar-y-o-lymph (kar'ē o limf') *n., Biol.* The transparent substance surrounding the nucleus of a cell.

kar-y-o-type (kar'ē o tīp') *n.* The characteristics of the nucleus of a cell, including its size, form, and chromosome number.

ka-ty-did (kā'tē did) *n.* Any of various green insects related to grasshoppers and crickets having specialized organs on the wings of the male that make a shrill sound when rubbed together.

katz-en-jam-mer (kat'sen jam'ér) *n.* A feeling of uneasiness, worry, or nervousness that follows intoxication.

kau-ri (kou'rē) *n.* A New Zealand tree which is the source of valuable resin used in varnish and timber used in construction.

ka-va (kä-*v*a) *n.* A pepper shrub from Polynesia; a beverage made from this shrub that can be intoxicating.

kay-ak (kī'ak) *n.* A watertight Eskimo boat, having a circular hole in the top for the occupant, and made from a light wooden frame with a sealskin cover.

kay-o (kā'ō') *v.* To knock out an opponent, in boxing. **kayo** *n.* A knockout.

ka-zoo (k*a* zō') *n.* A toy musical instrument with a paper membrane which vibrates simultaneously when a player hums into the tube.

ke-a (kā'*a*) *n.* A New Zealand parrot.

kedge (kej) *n.* A small anchor. **kedge** *v.* To pull a ship by the rope of an anchor.

keel (kēl) *n.* The central main stem on a ship or aircraft, which runs lengthwise along the center line from bow to stern, on which a frame is built upwards. **keel** *v.* To capsize. **keel over** To fall over suddenly; to turn upside down.

keel-age (kē'lij) *n.* A fee for mooring a ship in port.

keel-boat (kēl'bōt') *n.* A boat used on rivers; a shallow boat used for freight.

keel-haul (kēl'hol') *v.* To drag a person under the keel of a ship as a form of punishment.

keel-son (kēl'son) *n., Naut.* A structural member fastened above and parallel to the keel to give additional strength.

keen (kēn) *adj.* Having a sharp edge or point; acutely painful or harsh; intellectually acute; strong; intense. *Slang* Great. **keen** *v.* Wailing lament, especially for the dead. **keen** *v.* **keenly** *adv.* **keenness, keener** *n.*

keep (kēp) *v.* To have and hold; to not let go; to maintain, as business records; to know a secret and not divulge it; to protect and defend.

keep back *v.* To withhold things; to prevent one from coming forward.

keep-er (kē'pér) *n.* One who keeps, guards, or maintains something; a person who respects or observes a requirement; a device for holding something in place, as a latch, or clasp.

keep-ing (kē'ping) *n.* Charge or possession; conformity or harmony; maintenance or support.

keep off *v.* To fend or avert off. **keep**

off v. To stay back or remain at a distance.

keep-sake (kēp´sāk˝) n. A memento or souvenir; a token or remembrance of friendship.

keep up v. To persist in, sustain, or continue. To remain equal or even to; to stay informed; to continue without interruption.

kef (kāf) n. A tranquil and dreamy state; a narcotic.

keg (keg) n. A small barrel usually having the capacity of five to ten gallons; the unit of measure for nails which equals 100 pounds.

keg-ler (keg´lêr) n. A bowler.

ke-loid (kē´loid) n. A scar formed from fibrous growth in the connective skin tissue.

kelp (kelp) n. Any large brown seaweed.

kel-pie (kel´pē) n. A sheep dog originally bred in Australia.

kemp n. A coarse hairlike fiber used in the making of carpet.

Kennedy, John Fitzgerald n. (1917-1963) The thirty-fifth president of the United States from 1961-1963; assassinated while in office.

ken-nel (ken´el) n. A shelter for or a place where dogs or cats are bred, boarded, or trained. **kennel** v.

ke-no (kē´nō) n. A game of chance resembling bingo; a lottery game.

kent-ledge (kent´lij) n. Ship ballast for a ship made of pig iron.

Ken-tuck-y n. A state located in the east central United States; statehood June 1, 1792; state capital Frankfort.

kep-i (kā´pē) n. A French military cap having a flat, round top and a visor.

ker-a-tin (ker´a tin) n. A fibrous protein which forms the basic substance of nails, hair, horns, and hooves.

ker-a-to-plas-ty (ker´a tō plas´tē) n., Med. An operation that replaces damaged corneal tissue with healthy corneal tissue. **keratoplastic** adj.

ker-a-to-sis (ker´a tō´sis) n. An area of skin overgrown with horny tissue.

ker-chief (kêr´chif) n. A piece of cloth worn around the neck or on the head; scarf; a handkerchief.

kerf (kêrf) n. A slit or notch made by a saw or other cutting tool; the place where a branch is cut across.

ker-mes (kêr´mēz) n. A red dye consisting of the dried bodies of female scaled insects found in the Mediterranean area.

ker-mis (ker´mis) n. An annual fair of the Netherlands.

ker-nel (ker´nel) n. A grain or seed, as of corn, enclosed in a hard husk; the inner substance of a nut; the central, most important part. **kernally** adj.

ker-o-sene or **ker-o-sine** (ker´o sēn˝) n. An oil distilled from petroleum or coal and used for illumination.

ker-ri-a (ker´ē a) n. A shrub of Japan, having ridged, green stems and double or single flowers that are yellow in color.

ker-sey (ker´zē) n. A coarse cloth made from wool and cotton used mainly for rugged garments and outer wear.

ker-sey-mere (ker´zi mēr) n. A twill weave cloth made from fine wool; also cassimere.

ke-ryg-ma (ki rig´ma) n. The apostolic preaching of the life and teachings of Jesus Christ.

kes-trel (kes´trel) n. A small falcon that hovers in the air with its head in the direction of the wind, having a gray and brown plumage, common in Europe, inhabiting coasts, moors, and farms.

ketch (kech) n. A small sailing vessel with two masts, one large mainmast toward the bow of the ship, and a smaller mizzenmast in the direction of the stern but before the rudder.

ketch-up (kech´up) n. A thick, smooth sauce made from tomatoes. *Also* catsup

ke-tene (kē´tēn) n. A gas which is colorless and poisonous, having a penetrating odor.

ke-to (kē´tō) adj. Having or pertaining to a ketone.

ke-tol (kē´tol) n. Organic compound having both a ketone and alcohol group.

ke-tone (kē´tōn) n. An organic compound; used as a solvent; acetone. **ketonic** adj. **ketosis** n.

ket-tle (ket´l) n. A pot or vessel, usually made of metal, used for stewing or boiling liquids.

ket-tle-drum (ket´l drum˝) n. A musical instrument with a parchment head which can be tuned by adjusting the tension.

ket-tle of fish n. A mess; an awkward situation; matter of consideration.

key (kē) n. An object used to open a lock; button or level pushed on a keyboard of a typewriter, piano, etc; the crucial or main element; an island. **key** v.

key-board (kē´bōrd˝) n. A bank of keys, as on a piano, typewriter, or computer terminal. **keyboard** v. To set by means of a keyed typesetting machine; to generate letters by means of a word processor. **keyboarder** n.

key-note (kē´nōt˝) n., Mus. The first and harmonically fundamental tone of a scale; main principle or theme.

key-punch n. A machine operated from a keyboard that uses punched holes in tapes or cards for data processing systems. **keypunch** v. **keypuncher** n.

key-stroke n. A stroke of a key, as of a

typewriter or computer keyboard.

key-way (kē'wā') *n.* A slot cut in a wheel hub or shaft for the reception of a key.

key word *n.* A word having special significance in relation to other phrases, words, or concepts.

kg *abbr.* Kilogram.

khad-dar (kä'dèr) *n.* Cloth made from cotton.

khak-i (kak'ē) *n.* A yellowish brown or olive-drab color; a sturdy cloth which is khaki in color. **khakis** *n. pl.* A uniform of khaki cloth. **khaki** *adj.*

khan (kän) *n.* An Asiatic title of respect; a medieval Turkish, Mongolian or Tartar ruler. **khanate** *n.*

khe-dive (ke dēv') *n.* A ruler of Egypt from 1867 to 1914, governing as a viceroy of the sultan of Turkey.

ki *abbr.* Kiloliter.

kib-ble (kib'l) *n.* A bucket used in the shaft of a mine for hoisting ore.

kib-butz (ki buts') *n.* In Israel, a settlement or farm operated as a collective system.

kibe (kīb) *n.* An ulcerated chilblain, usually on the heel.

kib-itz (kib'its) *v., Slang* To look on and offer meddlesome advice to others. **kibitzer** *n.*

ki-bosh (kī' bosh) *n., Slang* Something that acts as a check or stop.

kick (kik) *v.* To strike something with a force by the foot. **kick in** To put in money. **kick out** To expel with force.

kick-back (kik'bak') *n.* A secret payment to a person who can influence a source of income; repercussion; a strong reaction.

kick-shaw (kik'sha') *n.* Something of little substance or value; a trinket.

kid (kid) *n.* A young goat; leather made from the skin of a young goat. *Slang* A child; youngster. **kid** *v.* To mock or tease playfully; to deceive for fun; to fool. **kiddish** *adj.*

kid-nap (kid'nap) *v.* To seize and hold a person unlawfully, often for ransom. **kidnapper** *n.* **kidnapping** *n.*

kid-ney (kid'nē) *n. pl.* **kidneys** Either of two organs situated in the abdominal cavity of vertebrates whose function is to keep proper water balance in the body and to excrete wastes in the form of urine.

kid-skin (kid'skin') *n.* A soft, pliable leather made from the skin of a young goat.

kidvid *n., Slang* Television programming for children.

kiel-ba-sa *n.* A smoked Polish sausage.

kier (kēr) *n.* A large-capacity tub or boiler used for bleaching and dyeing jobs.

kil-der-kin (kil'dèr kin) *n.* A measure of capacity of half a barrel; a vessel

that holds this amount.

kill (kil) *v.* To put to death; to nullify; to cancel; to slaughter for food; to deprive of life; to neutralize or destroy the active qualities.

kil-lick (kil'ik) *n.* An anchor for a boat usually consisting of a stone secured by wood.

kil-li-fish (kil'ē fish') *n.* A fish found in the bays and rivers of N. America.

kill-joy (kil'joi') *n.* One who spoils the enjoyment of others.

kiln (kil) *n.* An oven or furnace for hardening or drying a substance, especially one for firing ceramics and pottery.

ki-lo (kil'ō) *n.* A kilogram.

kil-o-bit *n.* In Computer Science, one thousand binary digits.

kilobyte (KB) In Computer Science, one thousand bytes.

kil-o-cal-o-rie (kil'o kal'o rē) *n.* One thousand gram calories.

ki-lo-cy-cle (kil'o sī'kl) *n.* A unit equal to one thousand cycles; one thousand cycles per second.

kil-o-gram (kil'o gram') *n.* A measurement of weight in the metric system equal to slightly more than one third of a pound.

kil-o-li-ter (kil'o lē'tèr) *n.* Metric measurement equal to one thousand liters.

kil-o-me-ter (kil'o mē'tèr) *n.* Metric measurement equal to one thousand meters.

kil-o-ton (kil'o tun') *n.* One thousand tons; an explosive power equal to that of one thousand tons of TNT.

kil-o-volt (kil'o vōlt') *n.* One thousand volts.

kil-o-watt (kil'o wot') *n.* A unit of power equal to one thousand watts.

kil-o-watt–hour (kil'o wot'our') *n.* A unit of electric power consumption of one thousand watts throughout one hour.

kilt (kilt) *n.* A knee-length wool skirt with deep pleats, usually of tartan, worn especially by men in the Scottish Highlands.

kil-ter (kil'tèr) *n.* Good condition; proper or working order.

ki-mo-no (ko mō'no) *n.* A loose Japanese robe with a wide sash; a loose robe.

kin (kin) *n.* One's relatives by blood; relatives collectively.

ki-nase (kī'nās) *n.* A catalyst that assists in changing a zymogen into an enzyme.

kind (kīnd) *n.* A characteristic; a particular variety of sort.

kind (kīnd) *adj.* Of a friendly or good-natured disposition; coming from a good-natured readiness to please others.

kin-der-gar-ten (kin'dèr gär'ten) *n.* A school or class for young children from the ages of four to six to further their social, mental and physical development.

kin-der-gart-ner (kin´dẻr gärt´nẻr) n. A child who attends kindergarten.

kind-heart-ed (kīnd´här´tid) adj. Having much generosity and kindness.

kin-dle (kin´dl) v. To ignite; to catch fire; to stir up; to arouse; to excite, as the feelings.

kind-less (kīnd´lis) adj. Mean, cruel, unkind, unfriendly. **kindlessly** adv.

kin-dling (kind´ling) n. Easily ignited material, such as sticks, wood chips, or paper, used to start a fire.

kind-ly (kīnd´lē) adv. A kind nature, disposition, or character; benevolent. **kindliness** n.

kind-ness (kīnd´nis) n. An act of good will; state or quality of being kind; a kind act.

kin-dred (kin´drid) n. A person's relatives by blood. **kindred** adj. Having a like nature; similar. **kindredness** n.

kin-e-mat-ics (kin´ē mat´iks) n. The branch of dynamics that deals with motion, considered apart from force and mass. **kinematic** adj.

kln-e-scope (kin´i skōp´) n. A cathode-ray tube in a television set which translates received electrical impulses into a visible picture on a screen; a film of a television broad-cast.

ki-ne-sics (ki nē´siks) n. To study the relation-ship between communication and nonverbal body language. **kinesic** adj. **kinesically** adv.

ki-ne-si-ol-o-gy (ki nē´sē ol´o jē) n. Science that investigates organic and anatomy process in reference to human motion.

kin-es-the-sia (kin´is thē´zha) n. The sense of muscular movement or effort. **kinesthesis** n. **kinesthetic** adj.

ki-net-ic (ki net´ik) adj. Of, pertaining to, or produced by motion.

ki-net-ic art n. The type of modern abstract art that attempts to present or indicate a sense of motion.

kinetic theory n, Physics The theory of matter that hypothesizes that the minute particles of matter are constantly in very rapid random motion.

kin-folk (kin´fōk´) n. Relatives; family.

king (king) n. One who rules over a country; a male ruler; a playing card with a picture of a king; the main piece in the game of chess; a crowned checker in the game of checkers.

King James Bible n. An English translation of the Bible from Hebrew and Greek, published in 1611, authorized by King James I of England.

kink (kingk) n. A tight twist or knot-like curl; a sharp, painful muscle cramp; a mental quirk. **kink** v. To form or

cause to form a kink.

kink-a-jou (king´ka jö´) n. A tropical American mammal having large eyes, brown fur, and a long, prehensile tail.

kink-y adj. Tightly curled; sexually uninhibited. **kinkily** adv., **-iness** n.

kin-ship (kin´ship) n. Family relationship; common blood bond.

kins-man (kinz´man) n. A blood relative, especially a male relative.

kins-wo-man (kinz´wum´an) n. A female blood relation.

ki-osk (kē osk´) n. A small building used as a refreshment booth or newsstand.

kip (kip) n. The untanned skin of a calf, a lamb and or an adult of any small breed; a bundle of such hides.

kip-per (kip´ẻr) n. A salted and smoked herring or salmon. **kipper** v. To cure by salting, smoking, or drying.

kirk (kerk) n. The Presbyterian Church of Scotland as opposed to the Episcopal Church of Scotland.

kirsch (kẻrsh) n. A brandy made from the fermented juice of black cherries.

kir-tle (ker´tl) n. A woman's long skirt or petticoat; a man's tunic or coat.

kis-met (kiz´mit) n. Fate; appointed lot.

kiss (kis) v. To touch two lips together in greeting; between two people.

kit (kit) n. A collection of tools, supplies, or items for a special purpose.

kitch-en (kich´en) n. A room in a house or building used to prepare and cook food.

kite (kīt) n. A light-weight framework of wood and paper designed to fly in a steady breeze at the end of a string; any of various predatory birds of the hawk family having long, usually forked tails.

kith (kith) n. Acquaintances or family.

kitsch (kich) n. Anything that is pretentious and in poor taste.

kit-ten (kit´en) n. A young cat. **kittenish** adj. **kittenishly** adv.

kit-ty (kit´ē) n. A small collection of objects or money; a young cat or kitten.

kit-ty-cor-nered (kit´ē kor´nẻr) adj. Diagonally; catty-cornered.

ki-va (kē´va) n. A Pueblo Indian chamber, used in ceremonies, often underground.

klatch or **klatsch** (klach) n. A social gathering devoted primarily to small talk and gossip.

klep-to-ma-ni-a (klep´to mā´nē a) n. Obsessive desire to steal or impulse to steal, especially without economic motive. **klep-tomaniac** n.

kloof (klöf) n. A ravine; gorge; deep mountain cleft.

kludge n. A computer system that is made up of poorly matched components.

klutz n., Slang A stupid or clumsy person. **klutziness** n. **klutzy** adj.

km *abbr.* Kilometer.

knack (nak) *n.* A natural talent; aptitude; dexterity.

knave (năv) *n.* Tricky or dishonest person; a rascal. **knavish** *adj.* **knavishly** *adv.* **knavishness** *n.*

knead (nēd) *v.* To work dough into a uniform mass; to shape by or as if by kneading. **kneader, kneadability** *n.* **kneadable** *adj.*

knee (nē) *n.* The joint in the human body which connects the calf with the thigh.

kneel (nēl) *v.* To go down upon one's knees.

knell (nel) *v.* To sound a bell, especially when rung for a funeral; to toll. **knell** *n.* An act of knelling; a signal of disaster.

knick-ers (nik´ėrz) *n. pl.* Short, loose-fitting pants gathered at the knee.

knick-knack (nik´nak´) *n.* A trinket; trifling article.

knife (nif) *n.* An instrument used to cut an item. **knife** *v.*

knish *n.* Baked or fried dough stuffed with meat, cheese, or potatoes.

knit (nit) *v.* To form by intertwining thread or yarn by interlocking loops of a single yarn by means of needles; to fasten securely; to draw together; to furrow the brow. **knitting** *n.*

knob (nob) *n.* A rounded protuberance; a lump; a rounded mountain; a rounded handle. **knobbed, knobby** *adj.*

knock (nok) *v.* To hit or strike with a hard blow; to criticize; to collide; to make a noise, as that of a defective engine. **knock out** To render unconscious.

knoll (nōl) *n.* A small, round hill; a mound.

knot (not) *n.* An intertwining of string or rope; a fastening made by tying together lengths of material, as string; a unifying bond, especially of marriage; a hard node on a tree from which a branch grows. *Naut.* A unit of speed, also called a nautical mile, which equals approximately 1.15 statute miles per hour. **knot** *v.* **knottiness** *n.*

knout (nout) *n.* A whip or scourge for flogging criminals. **knout** *v.*

know (nō) *v.* To perceive directly as fact or truth; to believe to be true; to be certain of; to be familiar with or have experience of. **knowable** *adj.*

know–how (nō´hou´) *n.* Knowing how to do something.

know-ing (nō´ing) *adj.* To be astute; to know secret knowledge. **-ingly** *adv.*

knowl-edge (nol´ij) *n.* Acquainted with facts and areas of study; having ability to know facts, information.

knowl-edge-a-ble (nol´i jǝ bl) *n.* The state of being intelligent.

know–nothing (nō´nuth´ing) *n.* An extremely stupid person.

knuck-le (nuk´l) *n.* On the finger; the joint of the finger. **knuckly** *adj.*

knuck-le-ball *n.* A pitch used in baseball that is a slow pitch.

knuck-le-bone (nuk´l bōn´) *n.* The bone of the finger which forms the knuckle.

knuck-le-head (nuk´l hed´) *n.* A person who is not very smart; dumb.

knuck-le joint *n.* A finger joint; a machine joint formed like a knuckle.

knur (ner) *n.* A lump or knot of a tree.

knurl (nûrl) *n.* A ridge. **knurled, knurly** *adj.*

kohl (kōl) *n.* Dark powder used as cosmetics to darken under the eyes.

kohl-ra-bi (kōl rä´bē) *n. pl.* **kohlrabies** A variety of cabbage having a thick stem and eaten as a vegetable.

koi-ne (koi nā´) *n.* Any regional language or dialect which becomes the standard language of a larger region.

ko-la (kō´la) *n.* The tree which produces the kola nut.

ko-la nut *n.* The brownish nut used as a tonic or stimulant.

ko-lin-sky (ko lin´skē) *n.* A mink found in Asia.

kook (kōk) *n. Slang* A crazy or eccentric person. **kookiness** *n.* **kooky** *adj.*

Ko-ran (kō rän´) *n.* The sacred book of Islam, accepted as containing the revelations made to Mohammed by Allah through the angel Gabriel.

ko-sher (kō´shėr) *adj.* Serving food prepared according to Jewish dietary laws. *Slang* Appropriate; proper.

kow-tow (kou´tou´) *v.* To show servile deference.

kraal (kräl) *n.* A village of southern African natives; an enclosure for animals in southern Africa.

krill (kril) *n.* A small crustacean living in open ocean waters and an important food source for whales.

kryp-ton (krip´ton) *n.* A white, inert gaseous chemical used mainly in fluorescent lamps, symbolized by Kr.

ku-chen (kō´chen) *n.* Any coffee cake made with a sweetened yeast-dough.

ku-dos (kō´dōs) *n.* Acclaim or prestige resulting from notable achievement or high position; glory; recognition; renown.

kum-quat (kum´kwot) *n.* A small, round orange fruit having a sour pulp and edible rind; the tree bearing this fruit..

kwash-i-or-kor *n.* Severe malnutrition, especially in children, caused by protein deficiency.

kwh *abbr.* Kilowatt-hour.

ky-mo-graph (kī´mo graf´) *n.* A device for graphically recording variations in motion or pressure; a blood pressure graph.

ky-pho-sis (kī fō´sis) *n.* Abnormal curving of the spine; hunchback.

L, l (el) *n*. The twelfth letter of the English alphabet; the Roman numeral for fifty.

lab (lab) *n*. Laboratory.

la-bel (lā'bel) *n*. Something that identifies or describes. **label** *v*. To attach a label to.

la-bi-al (lā'bē el) *adj*. Pertaining to or of the labia or lips.

la-bi-um (lā'bē um) *n*. *pl*. **labia** Any of the four folds of the vulva.

la-bor (lā'bér) *n*. Physical or manual work done for hire. *Med*. The physical pain and effort involved in childbirth. *v*. To work; to progress with great effort. **laborer** *n*.

lab-o-ra-to-ry (lab'ro tōr'ē) *n*. *pl*. **laboratories** A place equipped for conducting scientific experiments, research, or testing; a place where drugs and chemicals are produced.

lab-ra-dor-ite (lab'ra da rīt') *n*. A kind of plagioclase feldspar mineral, distinguished by its iridescent colors.

la-bret (lā btet) *n*. A decoration or ornament worn through a hole in the lip.

la-bur-num (la bur'nam) *n*. A small ornamental tree; from the legume family, grown for its yellow flowers.

lab-y-rinth (lab'e rinth) *n*. A system of winding, intricate passages; a maze. **labyrinthian** *adj*.

lab-y-rin-thine (lab'e rin then) *adj*. Resembling or related to a labyrinth.

lac (lak) *n*. The resinous secretion left on certain trees by the lac insect and used in making paints and varnishes.

lac-co-lith (lak'e lith) *n*. A body of igneous rock between beds of overlying strata that causes the formation of domes.

lac-er-ate (las'e rāt') *v*. To open with a jagged tear; to wound the flesh by tearing. **laceration** *n*.

lac-er-a-tion (las e'rā shan) *n*. The act of tearing; a jagged tear caused by lacerating.

lach-es (lach'iz) *n*. Inexcusable delay in completing a duty or claiming a legal right.

lach-ry-mal *or* **lac-ri-mal** (lak'ri mal) Relating to or producing tears; relating to the glands that produce tears.

lach-ry-ma-to-ry (lak'ri ma tōr'ē) *n*. A small vase found in ancient tombs that is said to have held tears from mourners.

lach-ry-mose (lak'ri mō) *adj*. Tearful; crying; trying to provoke tears.

lack (lak) *n*. The deficiency or complete absence of something. *v*. To have little of something or to be completely without.

lack-a-dai-si-cal (lak'a dā'zi kal) *adj*. Lacking life, interest, or spirit; melancholy. **lackadaisically** *adv*.

lack-a-day (lak'a dā') *interj*. Exclamation used to express sorrow or regret.

lack-ey (lak'ē) *n*. A male servant of very low status.

lack-lus-ter (lak'lus'tér) *adj*. Lacking sheen; dull.

la-con-ic (la kon'ik) *adj*. Short; concise; brief and to the point; expressing a great deal in a few words.

lac-quer (lak'ér) *n*. A transparent varnish which is dissolved in a volatile solution and dries to give surfaces a glossy finish. **lac-quer** *v*. lacrimator

lac-tase (lak'tās) *n*. An enzyme in intestinal juices in young mammals and in yeasts that catalyzes the production of galactose and glucose from lactose.

lac-tate (lak'tāt) *v*. To secrete or to milk. **lactation** *n*.

lac-te-al (lak'tēl) *adj*. Of, resembling, or like milk. *n*., *Anat*. Any of the lymphatic vessels carrying chyle from the small in-testine to the blood.

lac-tes-cent (lak tes'ent) *adj*. Being or becoming milky; producing milk.

lactic acid *n*. A limpid, syrupy acid that is present in sour milk, molasses, some fruits, and wines.

lac-tif-er-ous (lak'tif e res) *adj*. Producing milk or a milky liquid substances.

lac-tone (lak'tōn) *n*. Any of a class of cyclic esters derived from hydroxy acids.

lac-tose (lak'tōs) *n*. A white, odorless, crystalline sugar that is found in milk.

la-cu-na (la kū'na) *n*. *pl*. **-nas, -nae** A space from which something is missing; a gap.

la-cu-nar (la kū'nèr) *n*. A ceiling with recessed panels.

la-cus-trine (lakus'trin) *adj*. Pertaining to a lake; living or formed in lakes, as various plants and animals.

lad (lad) *n*. A boy or young man.

lad-der (lad'ér) *n*. An implement used for climbing up or down in order to reach another place or area.

lade *v*. To load down, as with cargo or a burden; to dip or lift out.

lad-en (lād'en) *adj*. Heavily burdened; oppressed; weighed down; loaded.

la-di-da (lā'dē dā') *adj*. An expression of ridicule aimed at pretentious or elegant manners.

la-dy (lā'dē) *n*. *pl*. **ladies** A woman showing refinement, cultivation, and often high social position; the woman at the head of a household; an address or term of reference for any woman.

lag (lag) *v*. To stray or fall behind; to move slowly; to weaken gradually. **lag** *n*. The process or act of retardation or falling behind; the amount or period of lagging.

lag-an (lag en**)** *n.* Something sunk at sea, but attached to a buoy in order to recover it.

la-ger (lä´ gér) *n.* A light beer originated in Germany, which is brewed by slow fermentation and matured or aged under refrigeration.

lag-gard (lag erd) *adj.* Slow; backward; lagging. *n.* A person who lags behind everyone else; a loiterer.

lag-ging (lag´ing) *n.* A material used for thermal insulation; a plank used to prevent cave-ins of earth walls; a support during construction

la-gniappe (lan yap´) *n.* A small gift which is given to a purchaser by a storekeeper; anything given as an extra bonus.

la-goon (la gün**)** *n.* A body of shallow water separated from the ocean by a coral reef or sandbars. **lagoonal** *adj.*

la-i-cism (lā e **siz** em**)** *n.* A governmental system which is free from ecclesiastical in-fluence or jurisdiction.

laid *v.* Past tense of lay.

laid back *adj., Slang* Casual or relaxed in character.

lain *v.* Past tense of lie.

lair (leer) *n.* The den or bed of a wild animal. **lair** *v.* To lie in a lair; to place in a lair.

lais-sez–faire (le sä´faer) *n.* A policy stating that a government should exercise very little control in trade and industrial affairs; non-interference.

la-i-ty (lā´i tē) *n.* Laymen, the people of a religious group or faith as distinguished from clergy.

lake (lāk) *n.* A large inland body of either salt or freshwater.

lak-er (lā´kér) *n.* One connected or associated with lakes; a fish living in or taken from a lake.

lake trout *n.* Any of various species of trout found in freshwater lakes.

lam (lam) *v., Slang* To beat; to thrash; to run or flee quickly. **lam** *n., Slang* A trip to escape; the escape.

Lamaze method *n.* A method of childbirth in which the mother is prepared psychologically and physically to give birth without the use of drugs.

lamb (lam) *n.* A young sheep; the meat of a lamb used as food; a gentle person.

lam-baste *or* **lambast (lam bāst´)** *v., Slang* To thrash or beat.

lam-bent (lam´bent) *adj.* Lightly and playfully brilliant; flickering gently; softly radiant. **lambency** *n.*

lame (lām) *adj.* Disabled or crippled, especially in the legs or feet so as to impair free movement; weak; ineffective; unsatisfactory. **lamely** *adv.*

la-mel-la (la mel´a) *n. pl.* **lamellae** A thin flat plate or scale; one composing the thin plates of the gills of certain mollusks.

la-mel-li-branch (lamel´i brangk´) *n.* A species of mollusks, that include the oyster, mussel and clam.

la-ment (la ment´) *v.* To express sorrow; to mourn. *n.* An expression of regret or sorrow. **lamentable** *adj.*

lam-en-ta-tion (lam´en tā shan) *n.* A wailing or expression of sorrow.

lam-i-na (lam´i na) *n. pl.* **laminae** *or* **laminas** A thin scale or layer. *Bot.* The blade or flat part of a leaf.

lam-i-nate (lam´i nāt´) *v.* To form or press into thin sheets; to form layers by the action of pressure and heat. **lamination** *n.* **laminated** *adj.*

lamp (lamp) *n.* A device for generating heat or light.

lamp-black (lamp´biak´) *n.* A black soot of very fine texture of pure carbon.

lamp-light-er (lamp´lī´tér) *n.* A person who lights street lamps; a torch or device for lighting lamps.

lam-poon (lam pün´) *n.* A satirical, but often humorous, attack in verse or prose, especially one that ridicules a group, person, or institution.

lam-prey (lam´prē) *n. pl.* **lampreys** An eel-like fish having a circular, suctorial mouth with rasping teeth and no jaw.

lam-ster (lam´stér) *n., Slang* A person who is fleeing from the law.

LAN In *computer science,* Local Area Network; a group of computers that are linked to share common programs, data, output devices, etc.

la-nate (lā´nāt) *adj.* Covered with a substance or growth that resembles wool.

lan-ce-o-late (lan´sē o lāt´) *adj.* Shaped like a lance head; widening above the base and tapering to the apex.

lanc-er (lan´sér) *n.* One such as a soldier who is armed with a lance.

lan-cet (lan´sit, län´sit) *n.* A small surgical instrument having a sharp pointed generally two-edged blade, used to open veins, abscesses or tumors.

lan-cet-ed (lan´si tid) *adj.* Characterized by lancet arches or lancet windows.

lancet window *n.* A narrow window characterized by a pointed apex.

lance-wood (lans´wud´) *n.* Elastic wood that is used for fishing rods and archery bows.

lan-ci-nate (lan´si nāt´) *v.* Pierce or stab; to tear. **lancination** *n.*

land (land) *n.* The solid, exposed surface of the earth as distinguished from the waters. **land** *v.* To arrive at a destination; to catch a fish; to get a new job. **land grant** *n.* A grant of land made by a government, especially for railroads, roads, or agricultural colleges.

lane (lān) *n*. A small or narrow path between walls, fences, or hedges.

lang-syne (lang´zīn´) *n*. The time long ago; times past.

lan-guage (lang´gwij) *n*. The words, sounds, pronunciation and method of combining words used and understood by people.

lan-guet (lang´gwet) *n*. Something that resembles a tongue in shape, form or function.

lan-guid (lang´gwid) *adj*. Lacking in energy; drooping; weak. **languidly** *adv*. **languid-ness** *n*.

lan-guish (lang´gwish) *v*. To become weak; to be or live in a state of depression. **languisher** *n*. **-ment** *n*.

lan-guor (lang´gėr) *n*. Feebleness; physical exhaustion; listlessness; oppressive stillness. **languorous** *adj*. **languorously** *adv*.

la-ni-ar-y (lā´nē er´ē) *n. pl.* **laniaries** A canine tooth, of a carnivorous animal.

la-nif-er-ous (la nif´ėr us) *adj*. Woolly.

lank (langk) *adj*. Slender; lean.

lan-o-lin (lan´o lin) *n*. Wool grease obtained from sheep's wool and refined for use in ointments and cosmetics.

lan-tern (lan´tėrn) *n*. A portable light having transparent or translucent sides.

lantern jaw *n*. A thin, long and projecting lower jaw.

lanthanide series *n*. The series of rare elements of increasing atomic numbers that start with lanthanum and ending with lutetium.

lan-tha-num (lan´tha num) *n*. The white soft metallic element of the rare-earth series, that has a valence of three, and is allied to aluminum.

la-nu-gi-nose or la-nu-gi-nous(la nŏ´ji nōs´) *adj*. Downy; to be covered with down or fine soft hair.

la-nu-go (la nŏ´gō) *n., Biol.* A wooly or dense downy growth, as on the surface of a leaf or the hair that covers a newborn of some mammals.

lan-yard (lan´yėrd) *n*. A piece of rope or line used to secure objects on ships.

lap (lap) *n*. The surface of the upper thighs of the legs when a person is seated. **lap** *v*. To twist or wrap around; to enfold; to fold over; to lay a part above; to overlap.

lap-a-rot-o-my (lap´arot´o mē) *n*. The cutting of the abdominal wall.

lap board (lap´bŏrd´) *n*. A thin board used on the lap as a writing surface or table.

la-pel (la pel´) *n*. The front part of a garment, especially that of a coat, that is turned back, usually a continuation of the collar.

lap-i-dar-y (lap´i der´ē) *n. pl.* **lapidaries** A craftsman who polishes, cuts, and engraves precious stones and or gems.

lap-i-date (lap´i dāt´) *v*. To pelt someone or something with stones; to stone to death.

la-pil-lus (la pil´us) *n*. A glassy volcanic fragment ejected during an eruption.

lap-in (lap´in) *n*. Rabbit fur that is sheared and dyed.

lapis lazuli *n*. A semiprecious stone that is azure blue in color, used in making jewelry

lap-pet (lap´it) *n*. A flap or fold on a headdress or on a garment.

lapse (laps) *n*. A temporary deviation or fall to a less desirable estate.

lap strake (lap´strāk´) *adj*. A boat, constructed with each plank overlapping the one below it.

laptop computer In *computer science*, a portable computer complete with monitor and keyboard as a unit, smaller in size than a desktop, larger than a notebook computer.

lar-ce-ny (lär´se nē) *n*. The unlawful taking of another person's property.

lard (lärd) *n*. The soft, white, solid or semi- solid fat obtained after rendering the fatty tissue of the hog.

lar-der (lär´dėr) *n*. A place, such as a pantry or room, where food is stored.

large (lärj) *adj*. Greater than usual or average in amount or size. **at large** To be free and not confined.

lar-gess or lar-gesse (lär jes´) *n*. Liberal or excessive giving to an inferior; generosity.

lar-go (lär´gō) *adv., Mus*. In a very slow, broad, and solemn manner.

lar-i-at (lar´ē at) *n*. A long, light rope with a running noose at one end to catch live-stock.

lark (lärk) *n*. A bird having a melodious ability to sing; a merry or carefree adventure.

lar-ri-kin (lar´i kin) *n. Slang*. A rough and rowdy person. *adj*. Disorderly; rough.

lar-rup (lar´up) *v*. To flog or whip. **larrup** *n*. A blow; whipping.

lar-va (lär´va) *n. pl.* **larvae** The immature, wingless, often worm-like form of a newly hatched insect; the early form of an animal that differs greatly from the adult, such as the tadpole. **larval** *adj*.

lar-vi-cide (lär´vi sīd´) *n*. A chemical agent used to kill larvae.

la-ryn-ge-al (la rin´jē al) *adj*. Of or pertaining to the larynx. *n*. The sound made in the larynx.

lar-yn-gi-tis (lar´in jī´tis) *n*. Inflammation of the larynx.

lar-yn-gol-o-gy (lar´ing gol´o jē) *n*. The study or branch of medicine that deals with the larynx and its diseases.

lar-yn-got-o-my (lar˝ing got´o mē) *n*.
The surgical removal of the larynx.

lar-ynx (lar´ingks) *n*. *pl*. **larynxes**
The upper portion of the trachea which
contains the vocal cords. **larynges** *adj*.

la-sa-gna *or* **la-sa-gne** (le zän ye) *n*. The
traditional Italian dish of wide flat
noodles baked with a sauce of
tomatoes, meat, and cheese.

la-ser (lā´zĕr) *n*. A device which utilizes
the natural oscillations of molecules
or atoms between energy levels for
generating coherent electromagnetic
radiation in the visible, ultraviolet, or
infrared parts of the spectrum.

laser disk In *computer science*, a storage
disk that is read using laser technology.

laser printer In *computer science*, an
electrostatic printer that uses laser
technology to create images on paper.

lash (lash) *v*. To strike or move violently
or suddenly; to attack verbally; to whip.
n. Eyelash. **lasher** *n*.

lass (las) *n*. A young girl or woman.

las-si-tude (las´i tüd´) *n*. A condition
of weariness; fatigue.

las-so (las´ō) *n*. *pl*. **-sos, -soes** A long
rope or long leather thong with a
running noose used to catch horses and
cattle. **lasso** *v*.

last (last) *adj*. Following all the rest; of
the final stages, as of life; worst; lowest
in rank. **last** *adv*. After all others in
sequence or chronology. **last** *v*. To
continue. **last** *n*. A form in the shape
of a foot used to hold a shoe while it
is repaired or to shape a shoe as it is
being made.

latch (lach) *n*. A device used to secure
a gate or door, consisting of a bar that
usually fits into a notch. **onto** To grab
onto.

late (lāt) *adj*. Coming, staying, happening
after the proper or usual time; having
recently died. **lateness** *n*. **lately** *adv*.

la-tent (lāt´ent) *adj*. Not apparent or
visible although present and capable
of becoming; not manifested.

la-ter (lā´tēr) *adv*. After the present; late
in a greater degree.

lat-er-al (lat´ĕr al) *adj*. Relating to or
of the side. *n*. In football, an underhand
pass thrown sideways or away from
the line of scrimmage. **laterally** *adv*.

lat-er-ite (lat´e rīt´) *n*. A porous residual
product of rock decay, reddish in color
having heavy concentrations of iron
and aluminum hydroxides.

la-tex (lā´teks) *n*. The milky, white fluid
that is produced by certain plants, such
as the rubber tree; a water emulsion
of synthetic rubber or plastic globules
used in paints and adhesives.

lath (lath) *n*. A thin, narrow strip of wood
nailed to joists, rafters, or studding and
used as a supporting structure for

plaster.

lathe (lāth) *n*. A machine for holding
material while it is spun and shaped
by a tool.

lath-er (lath´ĕr) *n*. A foam formed by
detergent or soap and water.

lath-y (lath´ē) *adj*. Thin.

lat-i-cif-er-ous (lat´i sif´ĕr us) *adj*.
Containing latex, as in a plant cell.

lat-i-tude (lat´i tüd´) *n*. The angular
distance of the earth's surface north
or south of the equator, measured in
degrees along a meridian; freedom to
act and to choose.

lat-i-tu-di-nar-i-an (lat´i tŏd´in är´ēan)
adj. Permitting free and liberal thought
and conduct, in religious beliefs.

lat-ten (lat´en) *n*. A brass-like alloy
formed in thin sheets.

lat-ter (lat´ĕr) *adj*. Being the second of
two persons or two things.

laud (lod) *v*. To praise; to extol. **laudable**
adj. **laudably** *adv*.

laud-a-ble (la´da bl) *adj*. Worthy of
praise; commendable.

laud-a-to-ry (la´da tŏr´ē) *adj*. Containing
relating to or expressing praise.
laudative, laudatorily, *adv*.

laugh (laf) *v*. To express or show joy,
merriment, or amusement; to display
ridicule or to show a degree of
contempt; to become amused; to
produce the sound of laughter; to
express by laughing; to compel with
laughter. **laugh** *n*. The sound expressing amusement, joy, or ridicule.
laugher *n*. **laughingly** *adv*.

laugh-ter (laf´tĕr) *n*. The expression,
sound, or act produced by laughing.

launch (lonch) *v*. To push or move a
vessel into the water for the first time;
to set a rocket or missile into flight;
to put into operation.

laun-der (lon´dĕr) *v*. To wash clothes
or other materials in soap and water;
to wash and iron. **launderer** *n*.

laun-dry (lon´drē) *n*. *pl*. **laundries** An
establishment where laundering is done
professionally; clothes or other articles
to be or that have been laundered.

lau-re-ate (lor´ē it) *n*. A person honored
for his accomplishment. **laureate** *v*.

lau-rel (lar´el) *n*. A small lauraceous
evergreen tree having alternate leaves
and small flowers.

la-va (lā´va) *n*. Molten rock which erupts
or flows from an active volcano; the
rock formed after lava has cooled and
hardened.

lav-age (la väzh´) *n*. The washing out;
the process of cleansing an organ by
injection.

la-va-tion (la vā´shan) *n*. A cleansing
or washing.

lav-a-to-ry (lav´a tŏr´ē) *n*. *pl*. **-ies** A
room with permanently installed

washing and toilet facilities.

lave (lāv) v. To bathe; of a river or the sea, to flow along or against.

la-ver (lā´vėr) n. Any of several edible seaweeds or sea lettuce.

lav-ish (lav´ish) adj. Generous and extravagant in giving or spending. **lavisher** n. **lavishly** adv.

law (lo) n. A rule of conduct or action, recognized by custom or decreed by formal enactment, considered binding on the members of a nation, community, or group; a system or body of such rules.

law-ful (la´ful) adj. To be in harmony with the law; allowed by law; agreeable to law; legitimate, rightful. **lawfully** adv. **lawfulness** n.

lawn (lon) n. A stretch of ground near a house, park, or building covered with grass that is mowed regularly.

law-ren-ci-um (lo-ren´sē um) n. A short-lived radioactive element, symbolized by LR.

law-yer (lo´yèr) n. A person trained in the legal profession who acts for and advises clients or pleads in court.

lax (laks) adj. Lacking disciplinary control; lacking rigidity or firmness. **laxity** n. **laxness** n. **laxly** adv.

lax-a-tion (lak sā´shan) n. The state of being relaxed; a loosening.

lax-a-tive (lak´sa tiv) n. A medicine taken to stimulate evacuation of the bowels. **laxative** adj.

lax-i-ty (lak´si-tē) n. The state or quality or being lax or loose; looseness.

lay (lā) v. To cause to lie; to place on a surface; past tense of lie.

lay-er (lā´er) n. A single thickness, coating, or covering that lies over or under another. **layered** adj. **layer** v.

laz-ar (laz´ėr) n. A person afflicted with a repulsive disease; a leper.

laz-a-ret-to (laz´a ret´ō) n. pl. **lazarettos** A hospital for persons afflicted with contagious diseases; a ship, building or hospital used for quarantine purposes.

laze (lāz) v. To pass time lazily; to lounge or relax. **laze** n.

laz-u-lite (laz´a līt´) n. An azure blue crystalline that is a phosphate of aluminum, magnesium and iron.

la-zy (lā´zē) adj. Unwilling to work; moving slowly; sluggish. **lazily** adv.

lea (lē) n. ,Poetic A grassy field or meadow.

leach (lēch) v. To cause a liquid to pass through a filter; to remove or wash out by filtering. **leachable** adj.

lead (lēd) v. To go ahead so as to show the way; to control the affairs or action of. **lead** n. A soft, malleable, heavy, dull gray metallic element symbolized by Pb, used in solder, paints, and bullets; a graphite stick used as the writing material in pencils; in printing, the thin strip of type metal used to provide space between printed lines.

lead poisoning (led poi´zo ning) n. Poisoning of a person's system by the absorption of lead or any of its salts.

lead time (lēd tīm) n. The amount of time required from the beginning of a process to the end results.

leaf (lēf) n. pl. **leaves** A flat out-growth from a plant structure or tree, usually green in color and functioning as the principal area of photosynthesis; a single page in a book. v. To turn the pages of a book. **leafless** adj. **leafy** adj.

league (lēg) n. An association of persons, organizations, or states for common action or interest; an association of athletic com-petition; an underwater measurement of distance that equals 3 miles or approximately 4.8 km.

leak (lēk) n. An opening, as a flaw or small crack, permitting an escape or entrance of light or fluid. **leaky,**

lean (lēn) v. To rest or incline the weight of the body for support; to rest or incline anything against a large object or wall; to rely or depend on; to have a tendency or preference for; to tend towards a suggestion or action. **lean** adj. having little or no fat; thin.

leap (lēp) v. To rise or project oneself by a sudden thrust from the ground with a spring of the legs; to spring, to jump. **leap** n. **leaper** n.

leap year n. A year containing 366 days, occurring every 4th year, with the extra day added to make 29 days in February

learn (lern) n. The process of acquiring knowledge, understanding, or mastery of a study or experience. **learner** n.

learn-ed (lur´nid) adj. Characterized by or associated with learning; acquired or obtained by study.

lease (lēs) n. A contract for the temporary use or occupation of property or premises in exchange for payment of rent. **lease** v.

leash (lēsh) n. A strong cord or rope for restraining a dog or other animal.

least-wise (lēst wīz) adv., Slang At least; at any rate.

leath-er (leth´ėr) n. An animal skin or hide with the hair removed, prepared for use by tanning.

leave (lēv) v. To go or depart from; to permit to remain behind or in a specified place or condition; to forsake; to abandon; to bequeath, as in a will. **leave** n. Official permission for absence from duty.

leav-en (lev´en) n. An agent of fermentation, as yeast, used to cause batters and doughs to rise; any pervasive influence that produces a significant change.

leav-ing (lē´ving) n. Residue; something that is left. **leavings** Refuse or remains.

lec-i-thin (les´i thin) n. Any of a group of phosphorus containing compounds found in plant and animal tissues, commercially derived from egg yolks, corn, and soybeans, and used in the production of foods, cos-metics, pharmaceuticals, and plastics.

lec-tern (lek´tērn) n. A stand or tall desk, usually with a slanted top, on which a speaker or instructor may place books or papers.

lec-tion (lek´shan) n. A variant reading of a text or passage in a manuscript.

lec-ture (lek´chēr) n. A speech on a specific subject, delivered to an audience for information or instruction. v. To give a speech or lecture; to criticize or reprimand.

led v. Past tense of lead.

ledge (lej) n. A narrow, shelf-like projection forming a shelf, as on a wall or the side of a rocky formation.

ledg-er (lej´ēr) n. A book in which sums of money received and paid out are recorded.

leech (lēch) n. Any of various carnivorous or bloodsucking worms; a person who clings or preys on others.

leek (lēk) n. A culinary herb of the lily family, related to the onion, with a slender, edible bulb.

leer (lēr) n. A sly look or sideways glance expressing desire or malicious intent.

lee tide n. A tide running in the same direction in which the wind is blowing.

lee-ward (lē´wērd) adj., Naut. Pertaining to the side of a ship which is sheltered from the wind; opposite to windward. **leeward** n. A sheltered side.

lee-way (lē´wā´) n., Naut. The lateral drift of a plane or ship away from the correct course.

left (left) adj. Pertaining to or being on the side of the body that faces north when the subject is facing east.

left-hand (left´hand´) adj. Situated on or to the left; left-handed.

leg (leg) n. A limb or appendage serving as a means of support and movement in animals and man; a part or division of a journey or trip.

leg-a-cy (leg´a sē) n. pl. -ies Personal property, money, and other valuables that are bequeathed by will; anything that is handed down from an ancestor, predecessor, or earlier era.

le-gal (lē´gal) adj. Of, pertaining to, or concerned with the law or lawyers; some-thing based on or authorized by law. **legality** n. **-ization** n. **legalize** v.

le-ga-tion (li gā´shan) n. The official diplomatic mission in a foreign country, headed by a minister; the official residence or business premises of a diplomatic minister of lower rank than an ambassador.

le-ga-to (le gä´tō) adv., Music Smooth and flowing with successive notes connected. **legato** n.

leg-end (lej´end) n. An unverifiable story handed down from the past; a body of such stories, as those connected with a culture or people.

leg-i-ble (lej´i bl) adj. Capable of being read or deciphered. **legibility** n.

leg-is-la-tion (lej´is lā´shan) n. The act or procedures of passing laws; lawmaking; an officially enacted law.

leg-is-la-tive (lej´is lā´tiv) adj. Of or pertaining to legislation or a legislature; having the power to legislate.

leg-is-la-tor (lej´is lā´tēr) n. A lawmaker; a member of a legislative body.

leg-is-la-ture (lej´is lā´chēr) n. A body of persons officially constituted and empowered to make and change laws.

le-git-i-mate (li jit´imit) adj. Accordant with the laws and established rules or principles; to conform to accepted standards; born of parents legally married; of the regular type; genuine; in accordance with established laws or reasoning.

leg-ume (leg´ūm, li gūm´) n. A simple, one-cell, dried, dehiscent, fruit which splits along two seams that are attached to a ventral suture.

le-gu-min (li gū´min) n. A protein resembling casein, obtained from the seeds of leguminous plants.

leg-work n., Slang A chore, task, or gathering of information accomplished by going about on foot.

leis-ter (lē´stēr) n. A barbed spear used to catch fish.

lei-sure (lē´zhēr) n. The time of freedom from work or duty.

lei-sure-ly (lē´zhēr lē) adv. Acting, without haste.

lem-nis-cus (lem nis´kus) n. A long band of nerve fibers of the brain.

lend (lend) v. To allow the temporary use or possession of something with the understanding that it is to be returned; to offer oneself as to a specific purpose.

length (lengkth) n. The linear extent of something from end to end, usually the longest dimension of a thing as distinguished from its thickness and width; the measurement of something to estimate distance. **lengthy** adj.

length-en (lengk´then) v. To make longer or to become longer.

length-wise (lengkth´wīz´) adv. & adj. Of or in the direction or dimension of length; longitudinally.

le-ni-ent (lē´nē ent) adj. Gentle, forgiving, and mild; merciful; undemanding; tolerant. **leniency** n.

len-i-tive (len'i tiv) *adj.* Having the ability to softening or moderate, as with medicines. **lenitive** *n.*

lens (lenz) *n.* In optics, the curved piece of glass or any other transparent substance that is used to refract light rays so that they converge or diverge to form an image; the transparent structure in the eye, situated behind the iris, which serves to focus an image on the retina.

lent (lent) *v.* Past tense of lend.

Lent (lent) *n.* The period of forty days, excluding Sundays, of fasting and penitence observed by many Christians from Ash Wednesday until Easter.

len-tan-do (len tän'dō) *adj.* In a slackening manner; getting slower.

len-ti-cel (len'ti sel) *n.* A pore in shape, in the bark of woody stems through which the gases are exchanged between the stem tissue and the atmosphere.

len-ti-go (len tī'gō) *n.* A freckle or a freckly condition.

len-til (len'til) *n.* A leguminous plant, having broad pods that contain edible seeds and leafy stalks used as fodder.

le-o-tard (lē'o tärd') *n.* A close-fitting garment worn by dancers and acrobats.

lep-er (lep'ér) *n.* One who suffers from leprosy.

lep-i-dop-ter-an (lep'i dop'tèr an) *n.* Any insects comprising the butterfly, moth, or skipper.

lep-i-dote (lep'i dōt) *adj.* Covered with scurf or scurfy spots or scales.

lep-re-chaun (lep're kon') *n.* A mischief-making elf of Irish folklore, supposed to own hidden treasure.

lep-ro-sy (lep'ro sē) *n., Pathol.* A chronic communicable disease characterized by nodular skin lesions and the progressive destruction of tissue. **leprous** *adj.*

lep-ton (lep'ton) *n.* A small coin; small in mass, as an electron.

les-bi-an (lez'bē an) *n.* A homosexual woman. **lesbian** *adj.*

lese majesty *n.* An offense against a ruler or supreme power of state.

le-sion (lē'zhan) *n.* An injury; a wound; any well-defined bodily area where the tissue has changed in a way that is characteristic of a disease.

less (les) *adj.* Smaller; of smaller or lower importance or degree. **less** *prep.* With the subtraction of; minus.

-less *suffix* Without; lacking.

les-see (le sē') *n.* One who leases a property.

less-en (les'en) *v.* To decrease or make smaller or less; to become smaller; to diminish.

les-son (les'on) *n.* An instance from which something is to be or has been learned; an assignment to be learned

or studied as by a student.

les-sor (les'or) *n.* One who grants a lease to another.

let (let) *v.* To give permission; to allow. **let** *n.* An invalid stroke in a game such as tennis, that must be repeated because of some interruption or hindrance of playing conditions. **let's** (lets) *contr.* Let us.

le-thal (lē'thal) *adj.* Pertaining to or being able to cause death. **lethally** *adv.*

lethal gene *n.* A gene that may affect, prevent development, or cause death of an organism at any stage of its life.

le-thar-gic (le thär'jik) *adj.* Affected with or characterized by lethargy; sluggish; inclined to sleep; dull.

leth-ar-gy (leth'ér jē) *n., Pathol.* A state of excessive drowsiness or abnormally deep sleep; laziness. **lethargic** *adj.*

let-ter (let'ér) *n.* A standard character or sign used in writing or printing to represent an alphabetical unit or speech sound; a written or printed means of communication sent to another person.

let-up (let'up') *n.* A pause or lessening of intensity.

leu-co-ma-ine (lōkō'ma ēn') *n.* A poisonous nitrogen compound that is present in animal tissue as a by-product of metabolism.

leu-ke-mi-a (lü kē'mē a) *n., Pathol.* A generally fatal disease of the blood in which white blood cells multiply in uncontrolled numbers. **leukemic** *adj.*

le-vant-er (li van'tér) *n.* A forceful wind that blows in an easterly direction.

le-vee (lev'ē) *n.* An embankment along the shore of a body of water, especially a river, built to prevent overflowing.

lev-el (lev'el) *n.* A relative position, rank, or height on a scale; a standard position from which other heights and depths are measured. *adj.* Balanced in height; even. *v.* To make or become flat or level. **leveler** *n.* **levelness** *n.*

level-headed (lev'el hed'id) *adj.* Showing good judgment and common sense. **level-headedness** *n.*

lev-i-gate (lev'i gāt') *v.* To make a smooth paste; to rub or grind to a fine smooth powder.

lev-i-tate (lev'i tāt') *v.* To rise and float in the air in apparent defiance of gravity. **levitation** *n.*

lev-i-ty (lev'i tē) *n. pl.* **-ies** Lack of seriousness; frivolity; lightness.

le-vo-ro-ta-tion (lē'vō rō tā'shan) *n.* Rotation toward the left; a counter-clockwise rotation or direction.

lev-y (lev'ē) *v.* To impose and collect by authority or force, as a fine or tax; to draft for military service; to prepare for, begin, or wage war. **levy** *n.*

lewd (lüd) *adj.* Preoccupied with sex; lustful. **lewdly** *adv.* **lewdness** *n.*

lex-i-cal (lek´si kəl) *adj.* Pertaining or relating to words or vocabulary of a language, as distinguished from its construction and grammar.

lex-i-con (lek´si kon´) *n.* A dictionary; a vocabulary or list of words that relate to a certain subject, occupation, or activity. **lexical** *adj.*

li (lē) *n.* A Chinese linear unit of measure equivalent to about ⅓ mile or 0.5 kilometer.

li-a-bil-i-ty (lī´a bil´i tē) *n. pl.* **-ies** The condition or state of being liable; that which is owed to another.

li-a-ble (lī´a bl) *adj.* Legally or rightly responsible.

li-ai-son (lē´ā zon´) *n.* A communication, as between different parts of an armed force or departments of a government; a close connection or relationship; an illicit love affair.

li-ar (lī´ér) *n.* A person who tells falsehoods.

li-bel (lī´bel) *n., Law* A written statement in published form that damages a person's character or reputation.

lib-er-al (lib´ér al) *adj.* Characterized by generosity or lavishness in giving; abundant; ample; inclining toward opinions or policies that favor progress or reform, such as religion or politics. **liberalism** *n.* **liberality** *n.* **-lize** *v.*

liberal arts *n. pl.* Academic courses that include literature, philosophy, history, languages, etc., which provide general cultural information.

lib-er-ate (lib´e rāt´) *v.* To set free, as from bondage, oppression, or foreign control. **liberation** *n.*

lib-er-tar-i-an (lib´ér târ´ē an) *n.* A person who upholds the doctrine of the free will; one who advocates unrestricted liberty.

li-ber-ti-cide (li bur´ri sīd´) *n.* The destruction of liberty; a destroyer of liberty.

lib-er-tine (lib´ér tēn´) *n.* A person lacking moral or sexual restraint; one who leads a unscrupulous life.

lib-er-ty (lib´ér tē) *n. pl.* **-ies** The state of being free from oppression, tyranny, confinement, or slavery; freedom; in Navy terms, the permission to be absent from one's ship or duty for less that 48 hours.

li-bi-do (li bē´dō) *n.* One's sexual desire or impulse; the psychic energy drive that is behind all human activities. **libidinal** *adj.* **libidinous** *adj.*

li-brar-i-an (lī brer´ē en) *n.* A person in charge of a library; one who specializes in library work.

li-brar-y (lī´brer´ē) *n. pl.* **libraries** A collection of books, pamphlets, magazines, and reference books kept for reading, reference, or borrowing; a commercial establishment, usually in connection with a city or school, which lends or rents books.

lice *n.* Plural of louse.

li-cense (lī´sens) *n.* An official document that gives permission to engage in a specified activity or to perform a specified act. **licensee** *n.* **licenser** *n.*

li-cen-tious (lī sen´shus) *adj.* Lacking in moral restraint; immoral. **licentiously** *adv.* **licentiousness** *n.*

lic-it (lis´it) *adj.* Lawful. **licitly** *adv.*

lick (lik) *v.* To pass the tongue over or along the surface of. *Slang* To beat; to thrash.

lid (lid) *n.* A hinged or removable cover for a container; an eyelid. **lidded** *adj.*

li-dar (lī där) *n.* A radar system that emits pulsed laser light instead of microwaves.

lie (lī) *v.* To be in or take a horizontal recumbent position; to recline. *n.* A false or untrue statement.

liege (lēj) *n.* A feudal lord or sovereign. *adj.* Loyal; faithful.

lien (lēn) *n.* The legal right to claim, hold, or sell the property of another to satisfy a debt or obligation.

li-en-ter-y (lī´en ter´ē) *n.* A condition or type of diarrhea, where the food is discharged undigested.

lieu (lü) *n.* Place; instead of; in place of.

life (līf) *n. pl.* **lives** The form of existence that distinguishes living organisms from dead organisms or inanimate matter in the ability to carry on metabolism, respond to stimuli, reproduce, and grow.

life-support system *n.* A system giving a person all or some of the items, such as oxygen, water, food, and control of temperature, necessary for a person's life and health while in a spacecraft or while exploring the surface of the moon; a system used to sustain life in a critical health situation.

lift (lift) *v.* To raise from a lower to a higher position; to elevate; to take from; to steal. **lift** *n.* The act or process of lifting; force or power available for lifting; an elevation of spirits; a device or machine designed to pick up, raise, or carry something; an elevator.

lift-off (lift´of´) *n.* The vertical take off or the instant of takeoff of an aircraft or spacecraft.

lig-a-ment (lig´a ment) *n.* A tough band of tissue joining bones or holding a body organ in place. **ligamentous** *adj.*

li-gate (lī´gāt) *v.* To tie with a ligature.

lig-a-ture (lig´a chèr) *n.* Something, as a musical cord, that is used to bind; a thread used in surgery; something that unites or connects; a printing character that combines two or more letters.

light (līt) *n.* Electromagnetic radiation that can be seen by the naked eye; brightness; a source of light; spiritual illumination; enlightenment; a source of fire, such as a match. *adj.* Having light; bright; of less force, quantity, intensity, weight, than normal; having less calories or alcoholic content; dizzy; giddy. **light** *v.* **lightness** *n.*

light-year *or* **light year (līt´yēr´)** *n.* A measure equal to the distance light travels in one year, approximately 5.878 trillion miles.

lig-ne-ous (lig´nē us) *adj.* Of or resembling wood; woody.

lig-ni-fy (lig´ni fī´) *v.* To make or become woody or wood-like.

lig-nin (lig´nin) *n.* An organic substance associated with cellulose that forms the woody cell walls of plants.

lg-nite (lig´nīt) *n.* A brownish-black soft coal, especially one in which the texture of the original wood is distinct.

lig-no-cel-lu-lose (lig´nō sel´ū lōs´) *n.* An association of lignin and cellulose that contains the essential part of woody cell walls and the fibrous tissue in plants.

lig-ro-in (lig´rō in) *n.* A volatile, flammable fraction of petroleum used as a solvent.

like (līk) *adj.* Of the same form, appearance, kind, character, or amount. *n.* A counter-part one that is like a another; the match or equal.

li-lac (lī´lak) *n.* A shrub widely grown for its large, fragrant purplish or white flower cluster; a pale purple. **lilac** *adj.*

lilt (lilt) *n.* A light song; a rhythmical way of speaking.

lil-y (lil´ē) *n. pl.* **lilies** Any of various plants bearing trumpet-shaped flowers; a plant similar or related to the lily, as the water lily.

limb (lim) *n.* A large bough of a tree; an animal's appendage used for movement or grasping; an arm or leg.

lim-bate (lim´bāt) *adj.* Bordered, in color as a leaf or flower with one color surrounded by an edging of another.

lim-ber (lim´bér) *adj.* Bending easily; pliable; moving easily; agile. **limber** *v.* To make or become limber.

lim-bo *or* **Lim-bo (lim´bō)** *n.* The abode of souls kept from entering Heaven; a place or condition of oblivion or neglect.

lime (līm) *n.* A tropical citrus tree with evergreen leaves, fragrant white flowers, and edible green fruit; calcium oxide.

lim-er-ick (lim´ér ik) *n.* A humorous verse of five lines.

lime-stone (līm´stōn´) *n.* A form of sedimentary rock composed mainly of calcium carbonate which is used in building and in making lime and cement.

lim-it (lim´it) *n.* A boundary; a maximum or a minimum number or amount; a restriction on frequency or amount. *v.* To restrict; to establish bounds or boundaries. **able** *adj.*

lim-i-ta-tion (lim´i tā´shan) *n.* The instance or act of limiting; that which limits; a certain period of time that limits.

limn (lim) *v.* To describe; to depict by drawing. **limner** *n.*

li-mo-nite (lī´mo nīt´) *n.* A natural iron oxide used as an ore of iron.

lim-ou-sine (lim´o zēn´) *n.* A luxurious large vehicle; a small bus used to carry passengers to airports and hotels.

limp (limp) *v.* To walk lamely. *adj.* Lacking or having lost rigidity; not firm or strong. **limply** *adv.* **limpness** *n.*

lim-pid (lim´pid) *adj.* Transparently clear. **limpidity** *n.* **limpidly** *adv.*

lin-age (lī´nij) *n.* The number of printed or written lines on a page.

linch-pin (linch´pin´) *n.* A locking pin inserted through a shaft to keep a wheel from slipping off.

Lincoln, Abraham *n.* (1809-1865) The sixteenth president of the United States from 1861-1865.

lin-den (lin´den) *n.* Any of various shade trees having heart-shaped leaves.

line (līn) *n.* A mark made with a pencil, pen, or other writing tool, on a surface; the spoken words of a play; a short written note. *Math.* The shortest distance between two points. **line-up** A line of persons formed for the purpose of inspection or identification; the members of a team who take part in a game; a group of television programs that are aired sequentially.

lin-e-age (lin´ē ij) *n.* A direct line of descent from an ancestor.

lin-e-a-ment (lin´ē a ment) *n.* A contour, shape, or feature of the body and especially of the face.

lin-e-ar (lin´ē ér) *adj.* Of, pertaining to, or resembling a line; long and narrow.

linear accelerator *n., Phys.* A device for accelerating charged particles in a straight line by successive impulses from a series of electric fields.

lin-en (lin´en) *n.* Thread, yarn, or fabric made of flax; household articles, such as sheets and pillow cases, made of linen or a similar fabric. **linen** *adj.*

line of sight *n.* The imaginary line that extends from the viewer's eye to the distant point to which he is looking.

ling (ling) *n.* Any of various marine food fishes related to the cod.

lin-ger (ling´gér) *v.* To be slow in parting or reluctant to leave; to be slow to act;

to procrastinate. **lingerer** *n.* **-ingly** *adv.*

lin-ge-rie (län´zhe rā´) *n.* Women's undergarments.

lingo (ling´gō) *n. pl.* **goes** Language that is unfamiliar; a specialized vocabulary.

lin-gual (ling´gwal) *adj.* Relating or pertaining to the tongue; relating to the surface of the tooth laying next to the tongue.

lin-guist (ling´gwist) *n.* One who is fluent in more than one language; a person specializing in linguistics.

lin-i-ment (lin´i ment) *n.* A liquid or semi-liquid medicine applied to the skin.

li-nin (lī´nin) *n., Biol.* The substance that forms the net-like formation which connects the chromatin granules in a cell nucleus.

lin-ing (lī´ning) *n.* A material which is used to cover an inside surface.

link (lingk) *n.* One of the rings forming a chain; something in the form of a link; a tie or bond; a cuff link. *v.* To connect by or as if by a link or links.

link-age (ling´kij) *n.* The act or process of linking; a system of connecting structures.

linked documents In *computer science*, records or files that are connected so that data from one will be automatically entered in another, such as billing records that are automatically added to the accounts receivable file.

linking verb *n., Gram.* A verb which links a subject to the predicate of a sentence: as *become, be, feel, seem.*

links (lingks) *n. pl.* A golf course.

link-work (lingk´wurk´) *n.* Work that is composed of links, as a chain.

li-no-le-um (li nō´lē um) *n.* A floor covering consisting of a surface of hardened linseed oil and a filler, as wood or powdered cork, on a canvas or burlap backing.

lin-seed (lin´sēd´) *n.* The seed of flax, used in paints and varnishes.

linsey–woolsey (lin´zē wel´zē) *n.* A coarse, sturdy fabric of wool and linen or cotton.

lin-stock (lin´stok´) *n.* A staff with a fork tip and formally used to hold a lighted match.

lin-tel (lin´tel) *n.* A horizontal beam across the top of a door which supports the weight of the structure above it.

lint-er (lin´tėr) *n.* A machine used to remove fibers that remain on cotton seeds after the first ginning.

li-pase (lī´pās, lip´ās) *n., Biochem.* An enzyme, that occurs in the liver and pancreas that accelerates the breaking down of fats into fatty acids and glycerin.

li-pid (lī´pid) *n., Biochem.* Substances of an organic material, including

sterols, fats, and waxes, that are insoluble in water but are able to be metabolized.

lip-oid (lip´oid) *adj., Biochem.* Resembling fat.

liq-ue-fac-tion (lik´we fak´shan) *n.* The act of making liquid or becoming liquid.

liq-ue-fy (lik´ we fī´) *v.* To convert or reduce to a liquid state.

li-queur (li ker´) *n.* A sweet alcoholic beverage flavored with fruit, spices or nuts; a cordial.

liq-ui-date (lik´wi dāt´) *v.* To settle a debt by payment or other settlement; to close a business by settling accounts and dividing up assets; to get rid of, especially to kill. **liquidation** *n.*

liq-uor (lik´ėr) *n.* A distilled alcoholic beverage; a liquid substance, as a watery solution of a drug.

lisle (līl) *n.* A fine, tightly twisted cotton thread.

lisp (lisp) *n.* A speech defect or mannerism marked by lisping. **lisp** *v.* To mispronounce the s and z sounds, usually as th.

lis-some (lis´om) *adj.* Nimble. **lissomely** *adv.* **lissomeness** *n.*

list (list) *n.* A series of numbers or words; a tilt to one side. **list** *v.*

list-ed (lis´tid) *adj.* Set down or to make a list, as a telephone number.

lis-ten (lis n) *v.* To monitor or tune in to conversation or a broadcast.

list-ing (lis´ting) *n.* The act or process of making or putting in a list; the entry on a list; a directory.

list-less (list´lis) *adj.* Lacking energy or enthusiasm. **listlessly** *adv.*

lit (lit) *abbr.* Literary; literature.

lit-a-ny (lit´e nē) *n. pl.* **litanies** A prayer in which phrases, recited by a leader are alternated with answers from the congregation.

li-tchi *or* **li-chee** (lē´chē) *n.* A Chinese tree, bearing edible fruit; the fruit of the tree.

lit-er-a-c y (lit´ėr a sē) *n.* The state or quality of being literate, having the skills of reading and writing.

lit-er-al (lit´ėr al) *adj.* Conforming to the exact meaning of a word; concerned primarily with facts; without embellishment or exaggeration. **literally** *adv.*

lit-er-ar-y (lit´e rer´ē) *adj.* Pertaining to literature; appropriate to or used in literature; of or relating to the knowledge of literature. **literarily** *adv.*

lit-er-ate (lit´ėr it) *adj.* Having the ability to read and write; showing skill in using words. **literacy** *n.* **literate** *n.*

lit-er-a-ture (lit´ėr a chėr) *n.* Printed material, as leaflets for a political campaign; written words of lasting excellence.

li-tharge (lith´ärj) *n.* The yellowish-red oxide of lead, that is used for glazing earthenware.

lithe (līth) *adj.* Bending easily; supple. **lithely** *adv.* **litheness** *n.*

li-thi-a-sis (li thī´a sis) *n., Pathol.* The formation of stony solid concretions in any part of the body, as in the gallbladder.

lith-ic (lith´ik) *adj.* Pertaining or relating to or consisting of stone; *Pathol.* Pertaining to stones in the body, as in the bladder.

lith-i-um (lith´ē um) *n.* A metallic element, the lightest metal know.

li-thog-ra-phy (li thog´ra fē) *n.* A printing process in which a flat surface is treated so that the ink adheres only to the portions that are to be printed. **lithograph** *n. & v.* **lithographer** *n.* **lithographic** *adj.* **lithographical** *adj.*

li-thol-o-gy (li thol´o jē) *n.* The microscopic study and classification of rocks.

lith-o-marge (lith´o märj´) *n.* A compact clay.

lith-o-sphere (lith´o sfēr´) *n.* The crust or outer surface of the solid earth, thought to be approximately 50 miles thick.

lit-i-gate (lit´i gāt´) *v.* To conduct a legal contest by judicial process. **litigant** *n.* **litigation** *v.* **litigator** *n.*

lit-mus (lit´mus) *n.* A blue powder obtained from lichens which turns red in acid solutions and blue in alkaline solutions, used as an acid-base indicator.

lit-ter (lit´ėr) *n.* A covered and curtained couch, mounted on shafts and used to convey a single passenger; a stretcher used to carry a sick or injured person; material used as bedding for animals; the offspring at one birth of a multiparous animal; an accumulation of waste material. **litter** *v.* **litterer** *n.*

lit-tle (lit´l) *adj.* Small in size or extent; not large; short in time; small in amount or quantity.

Little Dipper *n.* Ursa Minor.

lit-to-ral (lit´ėr al) *adj.* Relating to or existing on a shore. *n.* A shore.

lit-ur-gy (lit´ėr jē) *n. pl.* **-ies** A prescribed rite or body of rites for public worship. **liturgical** *adj.*

liv-a-ble (liv´abl) *adj.* Endurable; suitable for living in.

live (liv) *v.* To have life; to be alive; capable of performing vital functions; to remain effective; not to perish; to pass through or spend life in a particular manner.

live (līv) *adj.* Being in life, living, or alive; of or pertaining to life or living beings.

liv-er (liv´ėr) *n.* The large, very vascular, glandular organ of vertebrates which secretes bile.

live-stock (līv´stok´) *n.* Farm animals raised for human use.

live wire *n., Slang* An energetic person.

liv-id (liv´id) *adj.* Discolored from a bruise; very angry.

liv-ing (liv´ing) *n.* The act or condition of being alive; one who or that which lives; manner or course of life.

load (lōd) *n.* A mass or weight that is lifted or supported; anything, as cargo, put in a ship, aircraft, or vehicle for conveyance; something that is a heavy responsibility; a burden. **loader** *n.* **loading** *n.* **load** *v.*

load-ed (lō´did) *adj.* Intended to trick or trap. *Slang* Drunk; rich.

loaf (lōf) *n. pl.* **loaves** A food, especially bread, that is shaped into a mass. To spend time in idleness.

loam (lōm) *n.* Soil that consists chiefly of sand, clay, and decayed plant matter.

loan (lōn) *n.* Money lent with interest to be repaid; something borrowed for temporary use. *v.* To lend.

loath (lōth) *adj.* Averse.

loathe (lōth) *v.* To dislike intensely.

loath-ing (lō´thing) *n.* Intense dislike; abhorrence.

loath-some (lōth´som) *adj.* Arousing disgust. **loathsomely** *adv.*

lob (lob) *v.* To hit or throw in a high arc; to move in an arc. **lob** *n.*

lob-by (lob´ē) *n. pl.* **lobbies** A foyer, as in a hotel or theater; a group of private persons trying to influence legislators. **lobbyist** *n.* **lobby** *v.*

lobe (lōb) *n.* A curved or rounded projection or division, as the fleshy lower part of the ear. **lobar** *adj.*

lo-bot-o-my (lō bot´o mē) *n. pl.* **lobotomies** Surgical severance of nerve fibers by incision into the brain.

lob-ster (lob´stėr) *n.* Any of several large, edible marine crustaceans with five pairs of legs, the first pair being large and claw- like.

lob-ule (lob´ūl) *n.* A small lobe; a subdivision of a lobe. **lobular** *adj.*

lo-cal (lō´kel) *adj.* Pertaining to, being in, or serving a particular area or place.

lo-cale (lō kal´) *n.* A locality where a particular event takes place; the setting or scene, as of a novel.

lo-cate (lō´kāt) *v.* To determine the place, position, or boundaries of; to look for and find; to establish or become established; to settle. **locator** *n.*

lo-ca-tion (lō kā´shan) *n.* The process or act of locating; a place where something is or can be located; a site outside a motion picture or television studio where a movie is shot.

loch (lok) *n.* A lake.

lock (lok) *n.* A device used, as on a door,

to secure or fasten; a part of a waterway closed off with gates to allow the raising or lowering of boats by changing the level of the water; a strand or curl of hair. **lock** v.

lo-co (lō'kō) adj., Slang Insane.

lo-co-mo-tion (lō'ko mō'shan) n. The act or power of moving from place to place.

lo-co-mo-tive (lō'ko mō'tiv) n. A self-propelled vehicle that is generally electric or diesel-powered and is used for moving railroad cars.

lo-co-weed (lō'kō wēd') n. Any of several plants found throughout the western and central United States which are poisonous to livestock.

loc-u-late (lok'ūlāt') adj., Biol. Composed or divided into cells or loculi.

lo-cus (lō'kus) n. pl. **lo-ci** or **lo-ca** A place; locality; the center of activity.

lo-cust (lō'kust) n. Any of numerous grasshoppers which often travel in swarms and damage vegetation; any of various hard- wooded leguminous trees, such as carob, black locust, or honey locust.

lo-cu-tion (lōkū'shan) n. A particular form of a phrase; a style of verbal expression.

lode-star (lōd'stär) n. The North Star, used as reference point or guiding star.

lodge (loj) n. A house, such as a cabin, used as a temporary or seasonal dwelling or shelter; an inn; the den of an animal, such as a beaver; a local chapter of a fraternal organization; the meeting hall of such a chapter.

lod-i-cule (lod'i kūl) n., Bot. One of the delicate membranous scales at the base of a grass.

loft (loft) n. One of the upper, generally unpartitioned floors of an industrial or commercial building, such as a warehouse; an attic; a gallery in a church or hall.

log (lag, log) n. A bulky piece of timber either from a branch or a tree trunk. The record of a ship or aircraft travel.

loge (lōzh) n. A small compartment, especially a box in a theater; a small partitioned area, as a separate forward section of a theater mezzanine or balcony.

log-gi-a (loj'a) n. A roofed but open arcade along the front of a building; an open balcony in a theater.

log-ic (loj'ik) n. The science dealing with the principles of reasoning, especially of the method and validity of deductive reasoning; something that forces a decision apart from or in opposition to reason.

log-i-cal (loj'i kal) adj. Relating to; or in accordance with logic; something

marked by consistency of reasoning. **logically** adv.

log in or **log on** In computer science, to type the password that allows access to the computer.

lo-gi-on (lō'gē on') n. pl. **logions** or **logia** Traditional saying attributed to Jesus.

lo-gis-tics (lō jis'tiks) n. The methods of procuring, maintaining, and replacing material and personnel, as in a military operation. **logistic** adj.

log-jam (lag'jam') n. A jumble or group of logs wedged together in a river; deadlock.

lo-gom-a-chy (lō gom'a kē) n. pl. **logomachies** A dispute over or about words; a verbal disagreement

lo-go-type (lo'go tīp') n. Identifying symbol for a company or publication.

log-roll (lag'rōl') v. To promote successfully passage of a bill; rolling of logs in water.

lo-gy (lō'gē) adj. Something marked by sluggishness. **loginess** n.

loin (loin) n. The area of the body located between the ribs and pelvis; a cut of meat from an animal.

loin-cloth (loin'kloth') n. A cloth worn about the loins.

loins (loinz) n. The thighs and groin; the reproductive organs.

loi-ter (loi'tér) v. To stay for no apparent reason; to dawdle or delay.

loll (lol) v. To move or act in a lax, lazy or indolent manner; to hang loosely or laxly. **loller** n.

lol-ly-gag (lol ē gag) v., Slang To fool around.

lo-ment (lō'ment) n., Bot. A dry indehiscent one-cell fruit, produced from a single ovary, which separates at maturity into numerous segments.

lone (lōn) adj. Single; isolated; sole; unfrequented.

lone-ly (lōn'lē) adj. Being without companions; dejected from being alone.

lon-er (lō ner) n. A person who avoids the company of others.

long (lang, long) adj. Having a greater length than usual; considerable extent; not short; unusually great; prolonged past the usual time. n. A long length of time; a long sounding syllable.

long abbr. Longitude.

long distance n. The service handling by telephone communications; calls between a location and out of state or out of country. **long distance** adv. Connecting distant places; over a long distance.

long division n., Math. Arithmetical division, where several steps are involved in finding the answer, in which all steps are indicated in writing.

lon-gev-i-ty (lon jev'i tē) n. Long duration; length or duration of life; long continuance; length of service.

lon-gi-tude (lon´ji tūd´) *n.* The angular distance that is east and west of the prime meridian at Greenwich, England.

lon-gi-tu-di-nal (lon´ji tūd´i nal) *adj.* Of or relating to the length; relating to longitude. **longitudinally** *adv.*

lon-gueur (lang gur´) *n.* A tedious section passage in a book.

look (lek) *v.* To examine with the eyes; to see; to glance, gaze, or stare at. **look** *n.* The act of looking; the physical appearance of something or someone.

loom (lūm) *v.* To come into view as a image; to seem to be threatening. *n.* A machine used for interweaving thread or yarn to produce cloth.

loon (lōn) *n.* An idle or worthless man; a crazy person; a fish-eating diving bird of the northern hemisphere.

loo-ny *or* **loo-ney (lü´nē)** *n.* Crazy; foolish.

loop (lüp) *n.* A circular length of line folded over and joined at the ends; a loop-shaped pattern, figure, or path. **loop** *v.* To form into a loop; to join, fasten, or encircle with a loop.

loop-hole (lüp´hōl´) *n.* A means of escape; a legal way to circumvent the intent of a law.

loose (lüs) *adj.* Not tightly fastened; not confined or fitting; free.

loose end *n.* Something left unattached or hanging loose; unfinished business.

loose-jointed (lōs´join´tid) *adj.* Having loose joints of unusually free movement.

loos-en (lōs´en) *v.* To make looser, or less firm, compact, or tight; to relax.

loot (lüt) *n.* Goods, usually of significant value, taken in time of war; goods that have been stolen. **loot** *v.* To plunder; to steal. **looter** *n.*

lop (lop) *v.* To remove branches from; to trim; to cut off with a single blow.

lope (lōp) *v.* To run with a steady gait. **lope** *n.* **lopper** *n.*

lop-eared (lop´ērd´) *adj.* Having ears that droop or hang down.

lop-sid-ed (lop´sī´did) *adj.* Larger or heavier on one side than on the other; tilting to one side. **lopsidedly** *adv.*

lo-qua-cious (lō kwā´shus) *adj.* Talkative; given to excessive or continual talking; **loquaciously** *adv.*

lo-quat (lō´kwot, lō´kwat) *n.* A small Asian evergreen tree.

lo-ran (lōr´an) *n.* A system by which a navigator determines the position of his airplane or ship based in part on the measurement of arrival times and signals sent out by ground stations.

Lord (lord) *n.* God. A man having dominion and power over other people; the owner of a feudal estate.

lore (lōr) *n.* Traditional fact; knowledge that has been gained through education or experience.

lor-gnon (lor nyon´) *n.* A pair of eyeglasses or opera glasses.

lorn (larn) *adj.* Forsaken; abandoned; desolate.

lose (loz) *v.* To mislay; to fail to keep; misplace. **loser** *n.*

loss (los) *n.* The suffering or damage used by losing; someone or something that is lost. **losses** *pl.* Killed, wounded, or captured soldiers; casualties.

loss ratio *n.* The ratio between insurance premiums and insurance losses in a given period of time.

lost (lost) *adj.* Unable to find one's way.

lot (lot) *n.* Fate; fortune; a parcel of land having boundaries; a plot.

lo-ta (lō ta) *n.* A small spherical water vessel of copper or brass used in India.

lo-tic (lō´tic) *adj.* Living in or related to actively moving water.

lo-tion (lō´shan) *n.* A liquid medicine for external use on the hands and body.

lot-ter-y (lot´e rē) *n. pl.* **-ies** A contest in which winners are selected by a random drawing.

lot-to (lot´ō) *n.* A game of chance that resembles bingo.

loud (loud) *adj.* Marked by intense sound and high volume. **loudly** *adv.*

Lou-is-i-an-a n. A state located in the south central part of the United States, statehood April 30, 1812, state capital Baton Rouge.

lounge (lounj) *v.* To move or act in a lazy, relaxed manner. *n.* A room, as in a hotel or theater, where people may wait; a couch. **lounger** *n.*

loupe (lōp) *n.* A small magnifying glass, that attaches to eyeglasses, or is held close to the eye for viewing an object up close.

louse (lous) *n. pl.* **lice** A small, wingless sucking and biting insect that lives on various animals as well as human beings. *Slang* A contemptible person.

louse up *v., Slang.* To botch or mess up.

lous-y (lou´zē) *adj.* Lice- infested. *Slang* Mean; poor; inferior; abundantly supplied. **lousily** *adv.*

lout (lout) *n.* An awkward, stupid person. **loutish** *adj.*

lou-ver *or* **lou-vre (lü´ver)** *n.* An opening in a wall fitted with movable, slanted slats which let air in, but keep precipitation out; one of the slats used in a louver. **louvered** *adj.*

love (luv) *n.* Intense affection for another arising out of kinship or personal ties; a strong feeling of attraction resulting from sexual desire; enthusiasm or fondness; a score of zero in tennis. **love** *v.* **lovable** *adj.* **loving** *adj.*

low (lō) *adj.* Not high; being below or under normal height, rank, or level;

depressed or lacking in health or vigor; soft in pitch; small in number; cheap in price. **low** v. To moo, as a cow.

low-er (lō´ér) adj. Relatively low in position; in a position considered inferior to others in value or rank; located beneath or under something. **lower** v. To make lower in position; to reduce the value of.

low-er-case (lō´ēr kās´) adj. Having as its typical form a, b, c, or u, v, w rather than A, B, C, or U, V, W.

lowest common denominator n. The least common multiple of the denominators of a set of fractions.

low frequency n. A radio-wave frequency between 30 and 300 kilohertz.

low-key (lō´kē´) adj. Restrained.

low-land (lō´land) n. Land that is lower than the adjacent neighboring country; level or low country.

low-lev-el (lō´lev´el) adj. Being of minor importance; done, placed or occurring at a low level.

low-pres-sure (lō´presh´ēr) adj. Having or operation under a low degree of steam or water pressure.

low profile n. A deliberately inconspicuous lifestyle or posture.

low-ten-sion (lō´ten´shan) adj. Having a low voltage; built to be used at low voltage.

lox (loks) n. Smoked salmon; liquid oxygen.

loy-al (loi´al) adj. Faithful in allegiance to one's country and government; faithful to a person, cause, ideal, or custom. **loyalty** n.

loy-al-ist (loi´ al ist) n. One who is or remains loyal to a political cause, party, government, or sovereign.

loz-enge (loz´inj) n. Small medicated candy, normally having the shape of a lozenge.

LSD (el´es´dē´) n. Lysergic acid diethylamide, a hallucinogenic drug that induces psychotic symptoms, producing changes in thought, perception, mood, and behavior.

lu-au (lü ou´) n. A traditional Hawaiian feast.

lub-ber (lub´ér) n. An awkward, clumsy or stupid person; an inexperienced sailor.

lu-bri-cant (lü´bri kant) n. A material, as grease or oil, applied to moving parts to reduce friction.

lu-carne (lö kärn´) n. A window set vertically in a steeple.

lu-cid (lü´sid) adj. Easily understood; mentally clear; rational; shining. **lucidity** n. **lucidness** n. **lucidly** adv.

luck (luk) n. Good fortune; the force or power which controls odds and which brings good fortune or bad fortune. **lucky** adj. **luckily** adv. **luckiness** n.

lu-cra-tive (lü´kra tiv) adj. Producing profits or great wealth. **lucratively** adv.

lu-cre (lü´kēr) n. Money; profit.

lu-cu-brate (lü´kü brāt´) v. To study or work laboriously.

lu-di-crous (lü´di krus) adj. Amusing or laughable through obvious absurdity; ridiculous. **ludicrously** adv.

luff (luf) v. To turn a sailing vessel toward the wind.

lug (lug) n. An ear-like handle or projection used as a hold; a tab. **lug** v. To carry with difficulty.

luge (lüzh) n. A small sled similar to a toboggan which is ridden in a supine position and used in competitions like the Olympics..

lug-gage (lug´ij) n. Something that is lugged, especially suitcases or a traveler's baggage.

lu-gu-bri-ous (le gü´brē us) adj. Mournful; dejected; especially exaggeratedly or affectedly so. **lugubriously** adv. **lugubriousness** n.

luke-warm (lük´worm´) adj. Mildly warm; tepid; unenthusiastic; soothing. **lukewarm-ly** adv.

lull (lul) v. To cause to rest or sleep; to cause to have a false sense of security. **lull** n. A temporary period of quiet.

lul-la-by (lul´a bī´) n. pl. **lullabies** A song to lull a child to sleep.

lum-ba-go (lum bā´gō) n. Painful rheumatic pain of the muscles and tendons of the lumbar region.

lum-bar (lum´bēr) adj. Part of the back and sides between the lowest ribs and the pelvis.

lum-ber (lum´bér) n. Timber, sawed or split into boards. v. To walk clumsily.

lu-mi-nar-y (lü´mi ner´ē) n. pl. -ies A celestial body, as the sun; a notable person.

lu-mi-nes-cence (lü´mi nes´ens) n. An emission of light without heat, as in fluorescence.

lu-mi-nous (lü´mi nus) adj. Emitting or reflecting light; bathed in steady light; illuminated; easily understood; clear. **luminously** adv.

luminous paint n. A paint that glows in the dark.

lum-mox (lum´uks) n. A clumsy oaf.

lump (lump) n. A projection; a protuberance; a swelling, as from a bruise or infection. **lump** v. To group things together.

lum-pen (lum´pen adj. Relating to groups of people who have been uprooted from their normal routine or economic status.

lump-ish (lum´pish) adj. Stupid or dull. **lumpishly** adv. **lumpiness** n.

lump-y (lum´pē) adj. Covered or full of lumps.

lu-na-cy (lü´na sē) n. pl. **lunacies**

Insanity.

lu-nar (lü´nēr) adj. Of, relating to, caused by the moon.

lunar eclipse n. An eclipse where the moon passes partially or wholly through the umbra of the earth's shadow.

lu-nate (lö´nāt) adj. Having the form or shape like the half-moon; crescent-shaped.

lu-na-tic (lü´na tik) n. A crazy person.

lunatic fringe n. Members of a political or extremist expressing extreme or eccentric views.

lunch (lunch) n. A meal served between breakfast and supper.

lunch-eon (lun´chon) n. A lunch.

lunch-room (lunch´röm¯) n. Room in a school, business or establishments where individual may eat lunch.

lung (lung) n. One of the two spongy organs that constitute the basic respiratory organ of air breath-ing vertebrates.

lunge (lunj) n. A sud-den forward movement. **lunge** v.

lu-pine (lö´pīn) adj. To be wolf-like; wolfish.

lu-pu-lin (lö´pü lin) n. A yellow powder that is obtained from hops and used as a sedative.

lu-pus (lü´pus) n. A bacterial disease of the skin.

lurch (lürch) v. To heave something to one side.

lure (ler) n. A decoy; something appealing; an artificial bait to catch fish. **lure** v. To attract or entice with the prospect of reward or pleasure.

lu-rid (lür´id) adj. Sensational; shining with a fiery glare; fierce passion. **luridly** adv. **luridness** n.

lurk (lerk) v. To lie in concealment, as in an ambush.

lus-cious (lush´us) adj. Very pleasant to smell or taste; appealing to the senses. **lusciously** adv. **-ness** n.

lush (lush) adj. Producing luxuriant growth or vegetation. Slang An alcoholic. **lushly** adv. **lushness** n.

lust (lust) n. Intense sexual desire; an intense longing; a craving. **lustful** adj.

luster (lus´tēr) n. A glow of reflected light; sheen; brilliance or radiance; brightness. **lustrous** adj. **lusterless** adj.

lus-ter-ing (lus´tēr ing) n. The process that gives a luster to cloth.

lus-ter-ware (lus´tēr wâr¯) n. A glossy and often iridescent piece of pottery.

lust-ful (lust´ful) adj. Having a strong desire for sexual satisfaction.

lus-trate (lus´trāt) v. To purify by a ceremony.

lus-trous (lus´trus) adj. Characterized by sheen; bright; luminous. **lustrously** adv. **lustrousness** n.

lust-y (lus´tē) adj. Vigorous; healthy; robust; lively. **lustily** adv.

lusus naturae (lö´sus na tür´ē) n. An abnormally formed animal, person, or plant; a freak of nature.

lu-tan-ist (löt´a nist) n. A person who plays the lute.

lute (lüt) n. A medieval musical stringed instrument with a fretted fingerboard, a pear-shaped body, and a bent neck.

lute-string (löt´string) n. A glossy silk fabric formerly used for women's ribbons and dresses.

lu-te-ti-um or **lu-te-ci-um** (lü tē´shē um) n. A silvery rare-earth metallic element symbolized by Lu.

lux-ate (luk´sāt) v. To dislocate a limb, as a shoulder, arm, or hip.

lux-u-ri-ant (lug zher´ē ant) adj. Growing or producing abundantly; lush; plentiful. **luxuriance** n.

lux-u-ri-ate (lug zher´ē āt) v. To enjoy luxury or abundance; to grow abundantly; pleasure.

lux-u-ry (luk´sha rē) n. pl. **-ies** Something desirable but costly or hard to get; something which adds to one's comfort or pleasure but is not absolutely necessary; sumptuous surroundings or living.

ly-can-thro-py (lī kan´thro pē) n. An insanity where the patient supposes himself to be a wolf; the delusional trans-formation of a human into the form of a wolf.

ly-ce-um (lī sē´um) n. A hall where public programs are presented; an organization which sponsors such programs as lectures and concerts.

lye (lī) n. A powerful caustic solution yielded by leaching wood ashes; potassium hydroxide; sodium hydroxide.

ly-ing-in (lī´ing in´) n. Confinement in childbirth.

lymph node n. A roundish body of lymphoid tissue; lymph gland.

lym-pho-ma (lim´fo´ma) n. pl. **lympho-mas** Pathol. A tumor located in the lymphoid tissue.

lynch (linch) v. To execute without authority or the due process of law.

lynx (lingks) n. A wildcat. **lynx-eyed** adj. Having acute eyesight.

lyre (līer) n. A harp-like stringed instrument of Ancient Greece.

lyr-ic (lir´ik) adj. Concerned with thoughts and feelings; romantic; appropriate for singing. n. A lyric poem. **lyrics** The words of a song. **lyrical** adj. **lyrically** adv.

lysergic acid diethylamide n. An organic compound which induces psychotic symptoms similar to those of schizophrenia; LSD.

ly-sis (lī´sis) n., Med. The gradual decline of a disease.

M, m (em) The thirteenth letter of the English alphabet; the Roman numeral for 1,000.

m *abbr.* Mile.

ma (mä) *n., Slang* Mother.

ma'am (mam) *n.* Madam.

mac *n.* An address for a man whose name is unknown.

ma-ca-bre (ma kab´re) *adj.* Suggesting death and decay.

mac-ad-am (ma kad´am) *n.* Pavement for roads consisting of layers of compacted, broken stone, usually cemented with asphalt and tar.

mac-a-ro-ni (mak´a rō´nē) *n.* Dried pasta made into short tubes and prepared as food.

ma-caw (ma ko´) *n.* Any of various tropical American parrots with long tails, brilliant plumage, and harsh voices.

mac-e-doine (mas´i dwän´) *n.* A jellied salad; mixture of diced vegetables or fruits.

mace (mäs) *n.* An aromatic spice made by grinding the cover of the nutmeg.

mac-er-ate (mas´e rāt´) *v.* To make a solid substance soft by soaking in liquid; to cause to grow thin. **macerater** *or* **macerator** *n.* **maceration** *n.*

ma-chet-e (ma shet´ē) *n.* A large, heavy knife with a broad blade, used as a weapon.

mach-i-nate (mak´i nāt´) *v.* To plot. **machination** *n.* **machinator** *n.*

ma-chine (ma shēn´) *n.* A device or system built to use energy to do work; a political organization. *v.* To produce precision tools.

ma-chin-ist (ma shē´nist) *n.* One skilled in the operation or repair of machines.

ma-chis-mo *n.* An exaggerated sense of masculinity **macho** *Slang* Exhibiting machismo.

ma-cho *adj., Slang* Exhibiting machismo.

mack-er-el (mak´ér el) *n.* A fish with dark, wavy bars on the back and a silvery belly, found in the Atlantic Ocean.

mack-le (mak´l) *n.* To become blurred.

ma-cle *n.* The double crystal of a diamond.

mac-ra-me (mak´ra mä´) *n.* The craft or hobby of tying knots into a pattern.

macro In *computer science*, a set of computer instructions that are executed by a single command or a hot key combination.

mac-ro-bi-ot-ic *adj.* Relating to or being on an extremely restricted diet to promote longevity, consisting mainly of whole grain, vegetables and fish.

mac-ro-cosm *n.* A large scale model of something that is smaller. **-ic** *adj.*

mac-ro-cyte *n.* A red blood cell that is larger than normal. **macrocytic** *adj.*,

mac-ro-graph *n.* A drawing or photograph that is at least life-size or larger.

ma-crog-ra-phy *v.* To investigate something by the use of the naked eye.

ma-cron *n.* A short mark (-) placed over a vowel to indicate the pronunciation as a long sound.

ma-cron (mā´kron) *n.* A mark (-) placed over a vowel to indicate a long sound.

mac-ro-scop-ic *or* **macroscopical** (mak´-ro skop´ik) *adj.* Large enough to be seen by the naked eye. **macroscopical, macroscopically** *adv.*

mac-u-la (mak´ū la) *n.* A discolored spot on the skin, an anatomical spot. **macular** *adj.*

mad (mad) *adj.* Angry; afflicted with a mental disorder; insane.

mad-am (mad´am) *n.* A title used to address a married woman; used without a name as a courtesy title when addressing a woman.

mad-cap *adj.* Impulsive, rash or reckless; hare brained.

mad-den *v.* To craze; to enrage; to make mad. To become mad.

mad-ding *adj.* Behaving senselessly; acting mad; inducing madness.

made (mād) *v.* Past tense of make. *adj.* Constructed not natural; invented or construct-ed.

mad-e-moi-selle *n.* An unmarried French girl or woman.

made–to–order *adj.* Custom-made.

made–up (mād´up´) *adj.* Fabricated; invented; having makeup on.

mad-house (mad´hous´) *n. Slang* A place of confusion and disorder.

Madison, James *n.* (1751-1836) The fourth president of the United States from 1809-1817.

mad-man *n.* A lunatic.

mad-ness *n.* The state of being mad; extreme excitement.

mad-ri-gal (mad´ri gal) *n., Music* An unaccompanied song, usually for four to six voices, developed during the early Renaissance.

mael-strom (māl´strom) *n.* Any irresistible or dangerous force; a whirlpool off the coast of Norway.

maes-tro (mī´strō) *n.* A person mastering any art, but especially a famous conductor of music.

mag-a-zine (mag´a zēn´) *n.* A publication with a paper cover containing articles, stories, illustrations and advertising; the part of a gun which holds ammunition ready for feeding into the chamber.

ma-gen-ta (ma jen´ta) *n.* A purplish-red color.

mag-got (mag´ot) *n.* The legless larva of any of various insects, as the housefly, often found in decaying matter.

mag·ic (maj´ik) *n.* The art which seemingly controls natural events and forces by means of supernatural agencies. **magic** *adj.* **magical** *adj.*

magician *n.* A person who is skilled in magic and performs magic.

mag·is·te·ri·al *adj.* Pertaining to the office or a magistrate; arrogant; pompous; authoritative.

mag·is·trate (maj´i strãt´) *n.* A civil officer with the power to enforce the law.

mag·ma (mag´ma) *n. pl.*-**mas** -**mata** *or Geol.* The molten rock beneath the earth's surface from which igneous rocks are formed.

Magna Carta (mag´na kär´ta) *n.* The Great Charter of English liberties which the barons forced King John to sign in June 1215; any document constituting a guarantee of rights and privileges.

mag·nan·i·mous (mag nan´i mus) *adj.* Generous in forgiving insults or injuries. **magnanimity** *n.* **magnanimously** *adv.*

mag·nate (mag´nãt) *n.* A person notable or powerful, especially in business.

mag·ne·sia (mag nē´zha) *n., Chem.* A light, white powder used in medicine as an antacid and laxative.

mag·ne·si·um (mag nē´zē um) *n.* A light, silvery metallic element which burns with a very hot, bright flame and is used in lightweight alloys, symbolized by Mg.

mag·net (mag´nit) *n.* A body having the property of attracting iron and other magnetic material. **magnetism** *n.*

magnetic field *n.* The area in the neighborhood of a magnet or of an electric current, marked by the existence of a detectable magnetic force in every part of the region.

mag·ne·to (mag nē´tõ) *n.* A small alternator which works by means of magnets that are permanently attached, inducing an electric current for the spark in some engines.

mag·ne·tom·e·ter (mag´ni tom´i tẽr) *n.* An instrument used for measuring the direction and intensity of magnetic forces.

mag·ne·to·sphere (mag nē´to sfẽr´) *n. Physics.* A region of the upper atmosphere extending from about 500 to several thousand km above the surface, forming a band of ionized particles trapped by the earth's magnetic field.

mag·ni·fi·ca·tion *n.* The act of magnifying; magnified reproduction.

mag·nif·i·cent (mag nif´i sent) *adj.* Having an extraordinarily imposing appearance; beautiful; outstanding; exceptionally pleasing.

mag·ni·fy (mag´ni fī´) *v.* To increase in size; to cause to seem more important or greater; to glorify or praise someone or something. **magnification** *n.*

mag·nil·o·quent (mag nil´o kwent) *adj.* Speaking or spoken in a lofty and extravagant manner. **magniloquence** *n.* **magniloquently** *adv.*

mag·ni·tude (mag´ni tõd´) *n.* Greatness or importance in size or extent. *Astron.* The relative brightness of a star expressed on a numerical scale, ranging from one for the brightest to six for those just visible.

mag·no·lia (mag nōl´ya) *n.* An ornamental flowering tree or shrub with large, fragrant flowers of white, pink, purple, or yellow.

Magnolia State *n.* Nickname of the state of Mississippi.

mag·num (mag´num) *n.* A wine bottle holding about two quarts or approximately 2/5 gallon.

magnum o·pus *n.* A great work of art; literary or artistic masterpiece; the greatest single work of an artist, writer, or other creative person.

mag·pie (mag´pī´) *n.* Any of a variety of large, noisy bird found the world over having long tapering tails and black and white plumage.

ma·ha·ra·ja *or* **ma·ha·ra·jah** (mä´harä´ja) *n.* A king or prince who rules an Indian state.

ma·ha·ra·ni *or* **ma·ha·ra·nee** (mä´harä´ nē) *n.* The wife of a maharajah.

ma·hat·ma (ma hät´ma) *n.* In some Asian religions, a person venerated for great knowledge; a title of respect.

ma·hog·a·ny (ma hog´a nē) *n. pl.* -**ies** Any of various tropical trees having hard, reddish-brown wood, much used for cabinet work and furniture.

maid (mãd) *n.* A young unmarried woman or girl; a female servant.

mail (mãl) *n.* Letter, printed matter, or parcel handled by the postal system. *v.* To send something through the mail; to put in a mailbox for delivery.

mail·box *n.* A box used to deposit mail waiting for delivery and collection; a box at a private residence that receives mail.

mail order *n.* Goods which are ordered and sent by mail.

maim (mãm) *v.* To disable or to deprive of the use of a body part; to impair.

main (mãn) *adj.* Being the most important part of something. *n.* A large pipe used to carry water, oil, or gas. **mainly** *adv.*

Maine *n.* A state located in the northeastern corner of the United States; statehood March 15, 1820; state capital Augusta.

main·tain (mãn tãn´) *v.* To carry on or to keep in existence; to preserve in a desirable condition. **maintenance** n.

maj-es-ty (maj'i stē) n., pl. **-ties** Stateliness; dignity. **majestic** adj.

ma-jor (mā'jėr) adj. Greater in importance, quantity, number, or rank.

ma-jor-i-ty (ma jor'i tē) n. pl. **-ies** The greater number of something; more than half; the age at which a person is considered to be an adult, usually 21 years old; a number of voters in agreement; a political party group with the most votes.

majority rule n. A majority vote that consists of at least one vote over half of the total.

make (māk) v. To cause something to happen; to create; to provide, as time; to manufacture a line of goods. n. A brand name, as a make of a car. **with To carry off. hay** To take advantage of a given opportunity in the early stages. **bones** To perform unhesitating. **make away** v. **make** n. **maker** n.

make–be-lieve (māk'bi lēv') n. A pretending to believe. v. To pretend.

make–up (māk'up') n. The manner in which something is formed together or assembled; constructions; the qualities of physical or mental constitution; cosmetics. v. To invent a story.

mal-ad-min-is-ter v. To conduct dishonestly. **maladministration** n.

mal-a-droit (mal'a droit') adj. Lacking skill; awkward; clumsy. **maladroitly** adv. **maladroitness** n.

mal-a-dy (mal'a dē) n. pl. **-ies** A chronic disease or sickness.

mal-aise (ma lāz') n. The vague discomfort sometimes indicating the beginning of an illness.

mal-a-prop-ism (mal'a prop iz'um) n. A foolish misuse of a word. **malaprop, malapropian** adj.

mal-ap-ro-pos (mal'ap ro pō') adj. Not appropriate. **malapropos** adv.

ma-lar-i-a (ma lâr'ē a) n., Pathol. The infectious disease introduced into the blood by the bite of the infected female anopheles mosquito and characterized by cycles of fever, chills, and profuse sweating.

ma-lar-key (ma lär'kē) n., Slang Foolish or insincere talk; nonsense.

mal-con-tent (mal'kon tent') adj. Unhappy with existing conditions or affairs. **malcontent** n.

mal de mer n. Seasickness.

male (māl) adj. Of or belonging to the sex that has organs to produce spermatozoa. Bot. A plant with stamens but no pistil. n. A male person or animal. **maleness** n.

mal-e-dic-tion (mal'i dik'shan) n. A curse; execration. **maledictory** adj.

mal-e-fac-tor (mal'e fak'ter) n. A person

who commits a crime or an unlawful act; a criminal. **malefaction** n.

ma-lef-i-cent n. Harmful; doing evil or wrong. **maleficence** n.

ma-lev-o-lent (ma lev'o lent) adj. Full of spite or ill will for another; malicious. **malevolence** n.

mal-for-ma-tion (mal'for mā'shan) n. Defective structure or form.

mal-func-tion (mal fungk'shan) n. Failure to function correctly.

mal-ice (mal'is) n. The direct intention or desire to harm others. Law The willfully formed design to injure another without just reason or cause.

ma-lign (ma līn') v. To speak slander or evil of. **maligner** n.

ma-lig-nant (ma lig'nant) adj., Pathol. Of or relating to tumors and abnormal or rapid growth, and tending to metastasize; opposed to benign; causing death or great harm. **malignancy** n. **malignity** n. **malignantly** adv.

ma-lin-ger (ma ling'gėr) v. To pretend injury or sickness so as to avoid responsibility or work. **malingerer** n.

mall (mol) n. A walk or other shaded public promenade; a street with shops, restaurants, and businesses which is closed to vehicles.

mal-le-a-ble (mal'ē a bl) adj. Able to be bent, shaped, or hammered without breaking; capable of being molded, altered, or influenced. **malleability** n. **malleableness** n. **malleably** adv.

mal-le-us (mal'ē us) n., Anat. The club-shaped bone of the middle ear or the largest of three small bones; also called the hammer.

mal-nour-ished (mal'ner'isht) adj. Undernourished.

mal-nu-tri-tion (mal'nö trish'an) n. Insufficient nutrition.

mal-o-dor n. An offensive stench; odor.

mal-oc-clu-sion (mal'o klö'zhan) n. Improper alignment of the teeth.

mal-o-dor-ous (mal ō'dèr us) adj. Having a disagreeable or foul odor.

mal-po-si-tion n., Pathol. Wrong position as of a fetus in the uterus or a body organ.

mal-prac-tice (mal prak'tis) n. Improper treatment of a patient by his doctor during surgery or treatment which results in damage or injury; failure to perform a professional duty in a proper, careful, or correct fashion, resulting in injury, loss, or other problems.

malt (molt) n. Grain, usually barley, used chiefly in brewing and distilling; an alcoholic beverage.

mal-tose (mol'tōs) n. A white, crystalline sugar found in malt.

mal-treat (mal trēt') v. To treat badly, unkindly, or roughly. **-ment** n.

mal-ver-sa-tion n. Improper behavior

in a position of trust.

ma-ma (mam'a) *n.* Mother.

mam-bo (mäm'bō) *n.* A dance resembling the rumba of Latin America.

mam-mal (mam'al) *n.* Any member of a class whose females secrete milk for nourishing their young, including man.

mam-ma-ry gland (mam'a rē) *n.* The milk-producing organ of the female mammal, consisting of small cavity clusters with ducts ending in a nipple.

mam-mog-ra-phy *n.* An x-ray examination of the breast for early detection of cancer.

mam-moth (mam'oth) *n.* An extinct, early form of elephant whose tusks curved upwards and whose body was covered with long hair; any thing of great or huge size.

man (man) *n. pl.* **men** An adult or fully-grown male; the human race; Husband; an expression of pleasure or surprise.

man-a-cle (man'a kl) *n.* A device for re-straining the hands; handcuffs.

man-age (man'ij) *v.* To direct or control the affairs or use of; to organize. **manageability** *n.* **manageable** *adj.*

man-age-ment *n.* The act of directing, or managing for a purpose; administration; a group of managers.

man-date (man'dāt) *n.* An authoritative order or command. *Law* A judicial order issued by a higher court to a lower one. **mandate** *v.*

man-da-to-ry (man'da tōr'ē) *adj.* Required by, having the nature of, or relating to a mandate; obligatory.

man-di-ble (man'di bl) *n.* The lower jaw bone. *Biol.* Either part of the beak of a bird. **mandibular** *adj.*

man-do-lin (man'do lin) *n.* A musical instrument having a pear-shaped body and a fretted neck.

man-drake (man'drāk) *n.* A plant having purplish flowers and a branched root sometimes resembling the human form.

man-drel *or* **mandril** (man'drel) *n.* A spindle or shaft on which material is held for working on a lathe.

ma-nege (ma nezh') *n.* The art of training and riding horses; the performance of a horse so trained.

ma-neu-ver (ma nö'vèr) *n., Milit.* A planned strategic movement or shift, as of warships, or troops; any planned, skillful, or calculated move. **maneuverability** *n.* **maneuverable** *adj.*

man-ga-nese (mang'ga nēs') *n.* A hard, brittle, gray-white metallic element which forms an important component of steel alloys, symbolized by Mn.

mange (mänj) *n.* A contagious skin disease of dogs and other domestic animals caused by parasitic mites and marked by itching and hair loss.

man-ger (mān'jér) *n.* A trough or box which holds livestock feed.

man-gle (mang'gl) *v.* To disfigure or mutilate by bruising, battering, or crushing; to spoil. **mangler** *n.*

ma-ni-a (mā'nē a) *n.* An extraordinary enthusiasm or craving for something; intense excitement and physical over activity, often a symptom of manic depressive psychosis.

-mania *suffix* Unreasonable or intense desire or infatuation with.

ma-ni-ac (mā'nē ak') *n.* A violently insane person. **maniac** *adj.*

man-ic-de-pres-sive (man'ik di pres'iv) *adj.* Of a mental disorder characterized by alternating periods of manic excitation and depression.

man-i-cot-ti *n.* Pasta shaped like a tube, filled with meat or ricotta cheese and served with hot tomato sauce.

man-i-cure (man'i kūr) *n.* The cosmetic care of the hands and finger nails. **manicure** *v.* **manicurist** *n.*

man-i-fest (man'i fest') *adj.* Clearly apparent; obvious. *v.* To display, reveal or show. *n.* A list of cargo or passengers. **manifestly** *adv.*

man-i-fes-ta-tion (man'i fe stā'shan) *n.* The act or state of being manifest; making clear to the understanding; display; that which reveals; a person who participates in public demonstrations.

man-i-fes-to (man'i fes'tō) *n. pl.* **-toes** *or* **-tos** A public or format explanation of principles or intentions, usually of a political nature

man-i-fold (man'i fōld') *adj.* Having many and varied parts, forms, or types; having an assortment of features. *Mech.* A pipe with several or many openings, as for the escaping of exhaust gas. **manifoldly** *adv.* **manifoldness** *n.*

man-i-kin *or* **mannikin** (man'i kin) *n.* A little man; a dwarf; a mannequin.

ma-nip-u-late (ma nip'ū lāt') *v.* To handle or manage shrewdly and deviously for one's own profit. **manipulation** *n.* **manipulator** *n.*

manned (mand) *adj.* Operated by a human being.

man-ne-quin (man'e kin) *n.* A life-sized model of a human figure, used to fit or display clothes; a woman who models clothes.

man-ner (man'ér) *n.* The way in which something happens or is done; an action or style of speech; one's social conduct and etiquette. **mannered** *adj.*

man-ner-ism (man'e riz'um) *n.* A person's distinctive behavioral trait or traits. **mannerist** *n.*

man-ner-ly (man'ér lē) *adj.* Well-behaved; polite. **mannerliness** *n.*

ma-nom-e-ter (ma nom'i tèr) *n.* An instrument used to measure pressure, as of gases or liquids. **manometric** *adj*.

man-or (man´ẻr) *n*. A landed estate; the house or hall of an estate.

man-que *adj*. Lacking fulfillment; frustrated.

man-sard (man´särd) *n*., *Archit*. A curved roof with the lower slope almost vertical and the upper almost horizontal.

manse (mans) *n*. The house of a clergyman.

man-sion (man´shẚn) *n*. A very large, impressive house.

man-size *or* **man-sized** (man´sīzd´) *Slang* Quite large.

man-slaugh-ter (man´slo´tẻr) *n*., *Law* The unlawful killing without malice of a person by another.

man-slay-er *n*. One who murders or kills a human being.

man-ta (man´tẚ) *n*. A rough-textured cotton fabric; any of several very large fishes having large, very flat bodies with wing-like fins.

man-teau (man´tō) *n*. *pl*. **-teaus** *or* **-teaux** A robe or cloak.

man-tel *also* **mantle** (man´tl) A shelf over a fireplace; the ornamental brick or stone around a fireplace.

man-til-la (man til´ẚ) *n*. A light scarf worn over the head and shoulders by women in Latin America and Spain.

man-tis (man´tis) *n*. *pl*. **mantises** *or* **mantes** A tropical insect with a long body, large eyes, and swiveling head, which stands with its forelegs folded as if in prayer.

man-tle (man´tl) *n*. A loose-fitting coat which is usually sleeveless; something that covers or conceals; a device consisting of a sheath of threads, used in gas lamps to give off brilliant illumination when heated by a flame. **mantle** *v*.

man-u-al (man´ū ẚl) *adj*. Used or operated by the hands. *n*. A small reference book which gives instructions on how to operate or work something. **manually** *adv*.

man-u-fac-ture (man´ū fak´chẻr) *v*. To make a product; to invent or produce something. **manufacturer** *n*.

ma-nure (mẚ ner´) *n*. The fertilizer used to fertilize land, obtained from animal dung. **manure** *v*.

man-u-script (man´ū skript´) *n*. A typed or written material copy of an article, book, or document, which is being prepared for publication.

many (men´ē) *adj*. A mounting to a large or indefinite number or amount.

man-y-sid-ed *adj*. Having many aspects or sides, talents or capabilities.

map (map) *n*. A plane surface representation of a region. *v*. To plan anything in detail. **mapmaker** *n*. **mapper** *n*.

maple (mā´pl) *n*. A tall tree having lobed leaves and a fruit of two joined samaras; the wood of this tree, amber-yellow in color when finished and used for furniture and flooring.

maple sugar *n*. Sugar made from the sap of the maple tree.

maple syrup *n*. The refined sap of the sugar maple.

mar *v*. To scratch or deface; to blemish; to ruin; to spoil.

mar-a-bou (mar´ẚ bö´) *n*. A stork of Africa, whose soft down is used for trimming women's garments.

ma-ra-ca (mẚ rä´kẚ) *n*. A percussion instrument made from gourds containing dried beans or pebbles.

mar-a-schi-no (mar´ẚ skē´nō) *n*. A cherry preserved in a cordial distilled from the fermented juice of the small wild cherry and flavored with cracked cherry pits.

mar-a-thon (mar´ẚ thon´) *n*. A foot race of 26 miles, usually run on the streets of a city; any contest of endurance.

mar-ble (mär´bl) *n*. A limestone which is partly crystallized and irregular in color. *v*. To contain sections of fat, as in meat. **marbles** A game played with balls of glass. A person's common sense or sanity.

march (märch) *v*. To walk with measured, regular steps in asolemn or dignified manner. *Mus*. A musical composition.

March (märch) *n*. The third month of the year, containing 31 days.

mare (mâr) *n*. The female of the horse and other equine animals.

ma-re (mär´ẚ) *n*. *pl*., *Astron*. Any of the dark areas on the surface of the moon.

mare clausum *n*. The body of water that is controlled by one nation.

ma-re li-be-rum *n*. A body of water that is available to all nations for travel and navigation.

mar-ga-rine (mär´jẻr in) *n*. A butter substitute made from vegetable oils and milk.

mar-gin (mär´jin) *n*. The edge or border around the body of written or printed text; the difference between the selling price and cost of an item.

mar-gi-na-li-a *n*. *pl*. The notes in the margin of a book.

mar-i-jua-na *or* **marihuana** (mar´i wä´nẚ) *n*. Hemp; the dried flower tops and leaves of this plant, capable of producing disorienting or hallucinogenic effects when smoked in cigarettes or ingested.

ma-ri-na (mẚ rē´nẚ) *n*. A docking area for boats, furnishing moorings and supplies for small boats.

mar-i-nade (mar´i näd´) *n*. A brine made

from vinegar or wine and oil with various herbs and spices for soaking meat, fowl, or fish before cooking.

mar-i-nate (mar´i nāt´) v. To soak meat in a marinade.

ma-rine (ma rēn´) adj. Of, pertaining to, existing in, or formed by the sea. n. A soldier trained for service on land and at sea. **Marine** A member of the Marine Corps.

mar-i-tal (mar´i tal) adj. Pertaining to marriage. **maritally** adv.

mar-i-time (mar´i tĭm´) adj. Located or situated on or near the sea; pertaining to the sea and its navigation and commerce.

mark (märk) n. A visible impression, trace, dent, or stain; an identifying seal, inscription, or label.

mar-ket (mär´kit) n. The trade and commerce in a certain service or commodity; a public place for purchasing and selling merchandise; the possible consumers of a particular product. v. To sell. **marketability** n.

mar-ma-lade (mär´ma lād´) n. A preserve made from the pulp and rind of fruits.

ma-roon (ma rŏn´) v. To put ashore and abandon on a desolate shore. n. A dull purplish red.

mar-que-try (mär´ki trē) n. Inlaid work of wood or ivory used for decorating furniture.

mar-quis (mär´kwis) n. The title of a nobleman ranking below a duke.

mar-qui-sette (mär´ki zet´) n. A fabric of cotton, silk, nylon, or a combination of these, used in curtains, clothing, and mosquito nets.

mar-riage (mar´ij) n. The state of being married; wedlock; the act of marrying or the ceremony entered into by a man and woman so as to live together as husband and wife. **marriageability** n. **marriageable** adj.

mar-row (mar´ō) n. The soft, vascular tissue which fills bone cavities; the main part or essence of anything.

mar-row-bone n. A bone that is rich in marrow.

mar-ry (mar´ē) v. To take or join as husband or wife; to unite closely.

Mars (märz) n. The 4th planet from the sun.

marsh (märsh) n. An area of low, wet land; a swamp. **marshy** adj.

mar-su-pi-al (mär sō´pē al) n. An animal, such as a kangaroo, koala, or opossum, which has no placenta, but which in the female has an abdominal pouch with teats to feed and carry the off spring.

mar-tial (mär´shal) adj. Of, pertaining to, or concerned with war or the military life.

martial arts n. pl. Oriental arts of self-defense, such as karate or judo, which are practiced as sports.

martial law n. Temporary rule by military forces over the citizens in an area where civil law and order no longer exist.

mar-tin (mär´tin) n. A bird of the swallow family with a tail that is less forked than that of the common swallow.

mar-ti-ni (mär tē´nē) n. pl. -nis A cocktail of gin and dry vermouth, served with an olive or lemon peel.

mar-tyr (mär´tĕr) n. A person who would rather die than renounce his religious principles; one making great sacrifices to advance a cause, belief, or principle. **martyrdom** n.

mar-vel (mär´vel) n. Anything causing surprise, wonder, or astonishment.

mar-vel-ous or **marvellous (mär´ve lus)** Informal Excellent; very good, admirable. **marvelously** adv.

Mary-land n. A state located on the eastern coast of the United States; statehood April 28, 1788; state capital Annapolis.

mar-zi-pan (mär´zi pan´) n. A confection of grated almonds, sugar, and egg whites.

mas-car-a (ma skar´a) n. A cosmetic preparation used for coloring or darkening the eyelashes.

mas-cot (mas´kot) n. A person, animal, or object thought to bring good luck.

mas-cu-line (mas´kū lin) adj. Of or pertaining to the male sex; male; the masculine gender.

ma-ser (mā´zĕr) n., Physics One of several devices which are similar to the laser but which operate with microwaves rather than light.

mask (mask) n. A covering used to conceal the face in order to disguise or protect. v. To hide or conceal.

mas-o-chism (mas´o kiz´um) n. A condition in which sexual gratification is marked by pleasure in being subjected to physical pain or abuse. **masochist** n. **masochistic** adj.

mas-quer-ade (mas´ke rād´) n. A costume party in which the guests are masked and dressed in fancy costumes. v. To disguise oneself.

mass (mas) n. A body of matter that does not have definite shape but is relatively large in size; physical volume; the measure of a body's resistance to acceleration.

Mass or **mass (mas)** n. A celebration in the Roman Catholic and some Protestant churches; the service including this celebration.

Mass-a-chu-setts n. A state located in the northeastern part of the United

States; statehood February 6, 1788; state capital Boston.

mas-sa-cre (mas´a kér) n. The indiscriminate and savage killing of human beings in large numbers. **massacre** v.

mas-sage (ma säzh´) n. The manual or mechanical manipulation of the skin to improve circulation and to relax muscles. **massage** v.

mas-seur (ma ser´) n. A man who gives massages.

mas-seuse (ma sös´) n. A woman who gives massages.

mas-sive (mas´īv) adj. Of great intensity, degree, and size. **massively** adv. **massiveness** n.

mast (mast) n. The upright pole or spar which supports the sails and running rigging of a sail boat.

mas-tec-to-my (ma stek´to mē) n. pl. -ies The surgical removal of breast.

mas-ter (mas´tér) n. A person with control or authority over others; one who is exceptionally gifted or skilled in an art, science, or craft; the title given for respect or in address. v. To learn a skill, craft, or job; to overcome defeat. **mastership** n.

mas-ti-cate (mas´ti kāt´) v. To chew.

mas-to-don (mas´to don´) n. A large, extinct mammal which resembles an elephant.

mas-toid (mas´toid) n., Anat. The nipple shaped portion at the rear of the temporal bone behind the ear.

mas-tur-ba-tion (mas´tér bā´shan) n. The act of stimulating the sexual organs by hand or other means without sexual intercourse. **masturbate** v.

mat (mat) n. A flat piece of material made of fiber, rubber, rushes, or other material and used to cover floors; the border around a picture, which serves as a contrast between the picture and the frame.

match (mach) n. Anything that is similar or identical to another; a short, thin piece of wood or cardboard with a specially treated tip which ignites as a result of friction. v. To equal; to oppose successfully. **matchable** adj.

mate (māt) n. A spouse; something matched, joined, or paired with another; in chess, a move which puts the opponent's king in-jeopardy. Naval A petty officer. **mate** v.

ma-te-ri-al (ma tēr´ē al) n. The substance from which anything is or may be composed or constructed of; anything that is used in creating, working up, or developing something.

ma-ter-nal (ma ter´nal) adj. Relating to a mother or motherhood; inherited from one's mother.

ma-ter-ni-ty (ma ter´ni tē) n. The state of being a mother; the qualities of a mother; the department in a hospital for the prenatal and postnatal care of babies and their mothers.

math (math) n. Mathematics.

math-e-mat-ics (math´e mat´iks) n. The study of form, arrangement, quantity, and magnitude of numbers and operational symbols. **mathematical** adj. **mathematician** n.

mat-i-nee (mat´i nā´) n. An afternoon performance of a play, concert, movie, etc.

mat-ri-cide (ma´tri sīd´) n. The killing of one's own mother; one who kills his mother. **matricidal** adj.

ma-tric-u-late (ma trik´ū lāt´) v. To enroll, or to be admitted into a college or university. **matriculation** n.

mat-ri-mo-ny (ma´tri mō´nē) n. The condition of being married; the act, sacrament, or ceremony of marriage. **matrimonial** adj. **matrimonially** adv.

ma-trix (mā´triks) n., pl. **matrixes** or **matrices** Something within which something else develops, originates, or takes shape; a mold or die.

ma-tron (mā´tron) n. A married woman or widow of dignity and social position; the woman supervisor in a prison. **matronly** adv. **matronliness** n.

mat-ter (mat´ér) n. Something that makes up the substance of anything; that which is material and physical, occupies space, and is perceived by the senses; something that is sent by mail; something that is written.

mat-u-rate (mach´e rāt´) v. To ripen or mature. **maturation** n.

ma-ture (ma ter´) adj. Completely developed; at full growth; something, as a bond at a bank, that is due and payable. **mature** v. **maturely** adv.

mat-zo (mät´sa) n. pl. -zos or -zot A large, flat piece of unleavened bread eaten during Passover.

maud-lin (mod´lin) adj. Overly sentimental; tearfully and overwhelmingly emotional.

maun-der (mon´dér) v. To wander or talk in an incoherent manner.

mau-so-le-um (mo´so lē´um) n. pl.-leums or -lea A large and stately tomb.

mauve (mōv) n. A purplish rose shade; a moderately reddish to gray purple.

mav-er-ick (mav´ér ik) n. An unbranded or orphaned calf or colt. Slang A person who is unorthodox in his ideas or attitudes.

mawk-ish (mo´kish) adj. Disgustingly sentimental; sickening or insipid. **mawkishly** adv. **mawkishness** n.

max abbr. Maximum.

max-i n. A floor-length garment, such as a skirt or coat.

max-il-la (mak sil´a) n, pl. -lae or -las

The upper jaw or jawbone.

max-im (mak´sim) *n*. A brief statement of truth, general principle, or rule of conduct.

max-i-mize (mak´si mīz´) *v*. To increase as greatly as possible; to intensify to the maximum.

max-i-mum (mak´si mum) *n*. *pl*. **-mums** *or* **-ma** The greatest possible number, measure, degree, or quantity.

may (mā) *v*. To be permitted or allowed; used to express a wish, purpose, desire, contingency, or result.

May (mā) *n*. The fifth month of the year, having 31 days.

may-be (mā´bē) *adv*. Perhaps; possibly.

may-hem (mā´hem) *n*., *Law* The offense of injuring a person's body; any situation brought on by violence, confusion, noise, or disorder.

may-on-naise (mā´o nāz´) *n*. A dressing for salads, made by beating raw egg yolk, oil, lemon juice or vinegar, and seasonings.

may-or (mā´ér) *n*. The chief magistrate of a town, borough, municipality, or city. **mayoral** *adj*. **mayoralty** *n*.

maze (māz) *n*. A complicated, intricate network of passages or pathways; a labyrinth; a state of uncertainty, bewilderment, or perplexity. **maze** *v*.

McKinley, William. (1843-1901) The twenty-fifth president of the United States from 1897- 1901; assassinated.

me (mē) *pron*. The objective case of the pronoun I.

mead (mēd) *n*. An alcoholic beverage made from fermented honey and water with yeast and spices added.

mead-ow (med´ō) *n*. A tract of grassland used for grazing or growing hay.

mea-ger *or* **mea-gre** (mē´gér) *adj*. Thin; lean; deficient in quantity, richness, vigor, strength or fertility. **meagerly** *adv*. **meagerness** *n*.

meal (mēl) *n*. The edible seeds of coarsely ground grain; any powdery material; the food served or eaten at one sitting at certain times during the day; the time or occasion of taking such food. **mealy** *adj*.

mean (mēn) *v*. To have in mind as a purpose or intent; to be of a specified importance or significance. *adj*. Poor or inferior in appearance or quality. *n*. The middle point. **means** The method or instrument by which some end is or may be accomplished; the available resources.

me-an-der (mē an´dér) *v*. To wander about without a certain course or a fixed direction. **meander** *n*.

mean-ing (mē´ning) *n*. That which is meant or intended; the aim, end, or purpose; the significance; an interpretation. **meaningful** *adj*. **-fulness** *adj*.

mean-time (mēn´tīm´) *n*. The time or period between or during the intervening time.

mean-while (mēn´hwīl´) *adv*. During the intervening time.

mea-sles (mē´zelz) *n*. A contagious viral disease usually occurring in children, characterized by the eruption of red spots.

mea-sly (mē´zlē) *adj., Slang* Very small; meager.

meas-ure (mezh´ér) *n*. The range, dimension, extent, or capacity of anything. *Mus*. The group of beats marked off by regularly recurring primary accents; the notes and rests between two successive bars on a musical staff. *v*. To determine the range, dimension, extent, volume, or capacity of anything. **measurable** *adj*. **measurably** *adv*. **measurer** *n*.

meat (mēt) *n*. The flesh of an animal which is used as food; the core or essential part of something..

me-chan-ic (me kan´ik) *n*. A person skilled in the making, operation, or repair of machines or tools.

me-chan-i-cal (me kan´i kal) *adj*. Involving or having to do with the construction, operation, or design of tools or machines; produced or operated by a machine. **mechanically** *adv*.

mechanical drawing *n*. A drawing done with the aid of squares, compasses, or other instruments.

med-al (med´al) *n*. A small piece of metal with a commemorative image or inscription which is presented as an award.

med-al-ist (med´a list) *n*. A person who designs, collects, or makes medals; one who has been awarded or received a medal.

me-dal-lion (me dal´yan) *n*. A large circular or oval medal which is used as a decorative element.

med-dle (med´l) *v*. To interfere or participate in another person's business or affairs. **meddler** *n*. **meddlesome** *adj*.

med-i-a (mē´dē a) *n*. *pl*. The instruments of news communication, as radio, television, and newspapers.

me-di-al (mē´dē al) *adj*. Pertaining to or situated in the middle; ordinary.

me-di-an (mē´dē an) *n*. Something that is halfway between two different parts. *adj*. Relating to or constituting the median of a set of numbers.

median strip *n*. The strip which divides highway traffic lanes which are going in opposite directions.

me-di-ate (mē´dē āt´) *v*. To help settle or reconcile opposing sides in a dispute. **mediation** *n*. **mediator** *n*.

med-ic (med´ik) *n*. *Slang* A physician

or intern; a medical student; in the armed forces, a corpsman or enlisted person trained to give first aid.

med-i-cal (med´i kal) *adj.* Relating to the study or practice of medicine.

medical examiner *n.* A physician who is authorized by a governmental body to ascertain causes of death.

med-i-cine (med´i sin) *n.* Any agent or substance used in the treatment of disease or in the relief of pain; the science of diagnosing and treating disease; the profession of medicine.

me-di-e-val *or* **mediaeval** (mē´dēē´val) *adj.* Like or characteristic of the Middle Ages.

me-di-o-cre (mē´dēō´kėr) *adj.* Common; fair; undistinguished.

med-i-tate (med´i tāt´) *v.* To be in continuous, contemplative thought; to think about doing something. **meditative** *adj.* **meditation** *n.*

me-di-um (mē´dē um) *n. pl.* **-dia** *or* **-ums** Something which occupies a middle position between two extremes; the means of communicating information or ideas through publishing, radio, or television.

med-ley (med´lē) *n.* A mixture or confused mass of elements; a jumble. *Music* A musical composition made up of parts of different songs.

me-dul-la (mi dul´a) *n.,* **Anat.** The center of certain vertebrate structures, such as bone marrow.

medulla oblongata (mi dul´a ob´longgä´ta) *n.* The mass of nerve tissue found at the base of the brain, controlling bodily functions such as breathing and circulation.

meek (mēk) *adj.* Showing patience and a gentle disposition; lacking spirit or backbone; submissive. **meekly** *adv.*

meet (mēt) *v.* To come upon; to encounter; to come into conjunction or contact with someone or something; to cope or deal with; to handle; to fulfill an obligation or need.

meet-ing (mē´ting) *n.* An assembly or gathering of persons; a coming together.

meg-a-bucks *n.,* **Slang** One million dollars; a lot of money.

megabyte (MB) In *computer science,* one million bytes.

meg-a-hertz *n. pl.* **-hertz** *Physics.* One million cycles per second, used as a radio-frequency unit.

meg-a-lo-ma-ni-a (meg´a lō mā´nēa) *n.* A mental disorder marked by fantasies of power, wealth, or omnipotence. **mega-lomaniac** *n.* **megalomaniacal** *adj.*

meg-a-lop-o-lis (meg´a lop´o lis) *n.* A very large urban complex.

meg-a-phone (meg´a fōn´) *n.* A

funnel-shaped device which is used to amplify or direct the voice.

meg-a-ton (meg´a tun´) *n.* One million tons; the unit equal to the explosive power of one million tons of TNT.

meg-a-watt (meg´a wot´) *n.* A unit of electrical power equal to one million watts.

mel-an-cho-li-a (mel´an kō´lē a) *n.* **Psychi.** A mental disorder of great depression of spirits and excessive brooding without apparent cause.

mel-an-chol-y (mel´an kol´ē) *adj.* Excessively gloomy or sad.

me-lange (mā länzh´) *n.* A medley or mixture.

mel-a-nin (mel´a nin) *n.,* **Biochem.** The brownish-black pigment which is contained in animal tissues, as the hair and skin.

mel-a-nism (mel´a niz´um) *n.* An abnormally dark pigmentation of the skin.

mel-a-no-ma (mel´a nō´ma) *n., pl.* **-mas** *or* **-mata** A dark-colored tumor or malignant mole.

meld (meld) *v.* In pinochle and other card games, to declare or announce a combination of cards for inclusion in one's total score. *n.* The card or combination of cards declared for a score.

me-lee (mā´lā) *n.* The confused and tumultuous mingling of a crowd.

mel-io-rate (mel´ya rāt´) *v* To cause to improve or to make better. **meliorative** & *n.* **melioration** *n.*

mel-lif-er-ous (me lif´ėr us) *adj.* Producing or bearing honey.

mel-lo *adj.* Sweet and soft; rich and full-flavored; rich and soft in quality, as in sounds or colors.

me-lo-di-ous (me lō´dē us) *adj.* Characterized by a melody; tuneful; pleasant to hear. **melodiously** *adv.*

mel-o-dra-ma (mel´o drä´ma) *n.* A very dramatic presentation which is marked by suspense and romantic sentiment; sensational and highly emotional language or behavior. **melodramatic** *adj.* **melodramatically** *adv.*

mel-o-dy (mel´o dē) *n. pl.* **-ies** An agreeable succession of pleasing sounds. **melodic** *adj.* **melodically** *adv.*

mel-on (mel´on) *n.* The large fruit of any of various plants of the gourd family, as the watermelon.

melt (melt) *v.* To change from a solid to a liquid as a result of pressure or heat.

melt-down *n.* The melting of a nuclear-reactor core.

mem-ber (mem´bėr) *n.* A person who belongs to a society, party, club, or other organization. *Biol.* An organ or part of an animal or person's body, especially a limb.

mem-ber-ship (mem´bér ship´) *n*. The state or fact of being a member.

mem-brane (mem´brān) *n*. A thin, pliable, sheet-like layer of tissue which covers body surfaces and separates or connects body-parts. **membranous** *adj*.

me-men-to (me men´tō) *n*. *pl*. **-tos** or **-toes** A keepsake.

mem-o (mem´ō) *n*. A memorandum.

mem-oir (mem´wär) *n*. Personal records or reminiscences; an autobiography.

mem-o-ra-ble (mem´ér a bl) *adj*. Worth remembering or noting.

mem-o-ran-dum (mem´o ran´dum) *n*. *pl*. **-dums** or **-da** A brief, informal note written as a reminder.

me-mo-ri-al (me mōr´ē al) *n*. Something that serves to keep in remembrance, as a person or event. *adj*. Perpetuating remembrance. **memorialize** *v*.

Memorial Day *n*. The holiday that recognizes members of the armed forces killed in wars, celebrated on the last Monday in May.

mem-o-rize (mem´o rīz´) *v*. To commit something to memory. **memorization** *n*. **memorizer** *n*.

mem-ory (mem´o rē) *n*. *pl*. **-ries** The mental function or capacity of recalling or recognizing something that has been previously learned or experienced.

men *n*. *pl*. The plural of man.

men-ace (men´is) *n*. Something or someone who threatens; an annoying person. **menace** *v*. **menacingly** *adv*.

me-nar-che *n*. The beginning or the first occurrence of menstruation.

mend (mend) *v*. To fix; to repair; to correct.

men-da-cious (men dā´shus) *adj*. Prone to lying; deceitful; untrue; false. **mendaciously** *adv*. **mendacity** *n*.

men-de-le-vi-um (men´de lē´vē um) *n*. A short-lived radioactive element of the actinide series, symbolized by Md.

me-ni-al (mē´nē al) *adj*. Relating to a household servant or household chores requiring little responsibility or skill.

men-in-gi-tis (men´in jī´tis) *n*., *Pathol*. An inflammation of the membranes which enclose the brain and spinal cord.

me-ninx (mē´ningks) *n*. *pl*. **meninges** The membrane which encloses the spinal cord and brain. **meningeal** *adj*.

men-o-pause (men´o poz´) *n*., *Physiol*. The time of final menstruation, occurring normally between the ages of 45 and 50. **menopausal** *adj*.

men-ses (men´sēz) *n*. *pl*. The blood and dead cell debris which are discharged from the uterus through the vagina by women who are not pregnant; menstruation, occurring at monthly intervals between puberty and menopause.

men-stru-ate (men´strō āt´) *v*. To discharge the menses, approximately every 28 days. **menstrual** *adj*.

men-stru-a-tion (men´strō ā´shan) *n*. *Physiol*. The process, act, or periodical flow of bloody fluid from the uterus, also called period.

-ment *suffix* The result or product of achievement; action; process.

men-tal (men´tal) *adj*. Relating to or of the mind. **mentally** *adv*.

mental deficiency *n*. Subnormal intellectual development, marked by deficiencies ranging from impaired learning ability to social incompetence.

men-tal-i-ty (men tal´i tē) *n*. *pl*. **-ies** Mental faculties or powers; mental activity; habit of mind.

men-thol (men´thōl) *n*., *Chem*. The white, waxy crystalline alcohol which is obtained from and has the odor of peppermint oil. **mentholated** *adj*.

men-tion (men´shan) *v*. To refer to incidentally, in passing, or briefly. **mentionable**, **mentioner** *adj*.

men-tor (men´tér) *n*. A wise and trusted person.

men-u (men´ū) *n*. A list of food or dishes available at a restaurant; in computer science, a list of options displayed on the screen from which the operator may choose.

me-ow (mē ou´) *n*. The cry of a cat.

me-phi-tis (me fī´tis) *n*. A sickening or foul smell; a stench emitted from the earth.

mer-can-tile (mer´kan tēl´) *adj*. Of or relating to merchants, trading, or commerce.

mer-ce-nar-y (mer´se ner´ē) *n*. A person who is concerned only with making money and obtaining material gain; a person paid to serve as a soldier in a foreign country. **mercenary** *adj*.

mer-chan-dise (mer´chan dīz´) *n*. Commodities or goods that are bought and sold. *v*. To buy and sell.

mer-chant (mer´chant) *n*. A person who operates a retail business for profit.

mer-chant-man (mer´chant man) *n*. A ship used for commercial shipments.

mer-cu-ry (mùr´kū rē) *n*. A silvery, metallic, liquid element used in thermometers and barometers, symbolized by Hg.

mer-cy (mer´sē) *n*. *pl*. **-ies** Compassionate and kind treatment. **merciful** *adj*. **merciless** *adj*. **mercifully** *adv*. .

mere (mēr) *adj*. Absolute; no more than what is stated. **merest** *adj*. **merely** *adv*.

merge (merj) *v*. To unite or bring together as one; in computer science, to combine two or more files into one, retaining the internal order of both.

merger (mer´jér) *n*. The act of combining two or more corporations into one.

me-ringue (me rang´) *n.* A mixture of stiffly beaten egg whites and sugar, used as a topping for cakes and pies or baked into crisp shells.

mer-it (mer´it) *n.* A characteristic act or trait which is worthy of praise. **merit** *v.* To earn; to be worthy of.

mer-i-toc-ra-cy *n. pl.* **-ies** A system which bases advancement on ability or achievement.

mer-i-to-ri-ous (mer´i tōr´ē us) *adj.* Deserving honor, praise or reward.

mer-ry (mer´ē) *adj.* Delightful; gay; entertaining; festive; happy; joyous. **merrily** *adv.* **merriness** *n.*

mer-ry-go-round (mer´ē gō round´) *n.* A circular, revolving platform often with benches and animal figures, usually found in circuses and amusement parks.

me-sa (mā´sa) *n.* A flat-topped hill or small plateau with steep sides.

mesh (mesh) *n.* Open spaces in a thread, wire or cord net; something that entraps or snares; the fitting or coming together of gear teeth for transmitting power.

mes-mer-ize (mez´me rīz´) *v.* To hypnotize or put into a trance.

mes-quite (me skēt´) *n.* A thorny, deep-rooted shrub or small tree which grows in the southwestern United States and in Mexico.

mess (mes) *n. pl.* **messes** A disorderly or confused heap; a jumble; a dish or portion of soft or liquid food; a meal eaten by a group of persons, usually in the military.

mes-sage (mes´ij) *n.* Any information, command, or news transmitted from one person to another.

mes-sen-ger (mes´en jėr) *n.* A person who carries a message or does an errand for another person or company.

Mes-si-ah (mi sī´a) *n.* The anticipated or expected king of the Jews; Jesus Christ.

mess-y *adj.* Untidy; upset; dirty; lacking neatness. **messily** *adv.* **messiness** *n.*

met *v.* Past tense of meet.

me-tab-o-lism (me tab´o liz´um) *n.* The chemical and physical changes in living cells which involve the maintenance of life. **metabolic** *adj.*

meta-car-pus (met´a kär´pus) *n.* The part of the forefoot or hand which connects the bones of the toes or fingers to the ankle or wrist.

met-a-gal-ax-y (met´a gal´ak sē) *n.* The universe; the entire system of galaxies.

metal (met´al) *n.* One of a category of opaque, fusible, ductile, and typically lustrous elements. **metallic** *adj.*

met-al-lur-gy (met´a ler´jē) *n.* The technology and science which studies methods of extracting metals from their ores and of preparing them for use.

metallurgical *adj.* **metallurgist** *n.*

met-a-mor-pho-sis (met´a mor´fo sis) *n.* The transformation and change in the structure and habits of an animal during normal growth, as the metamorphosis of a tadpole into a frog. **metamorphism** *n.* **metamorphose** *v.*

met-a-phor (met´a for´) *n.* A figure of speech in which the context demands that a word or phrase not be taken literally, such as 'the sun is smiling'; a comparison which doesn't use *like* or *as*.

me-tas-ta-sis (me tas´ta sis) *n.* A spread of cancer cells from the original tumor to one or more additional sites within the body. **metastasize** *v.*

met-a-tar-sus (met´a tär´sus) *n. pl.* **-si** The part of the human foot which forms the instep and contains five bones between the ankle and the toes; the hind foot of four-legged animals.

me-te-or (mē´tē ėr) *n.* A moving particle in the solar system which appears as a trail or streak in the sky as it comes into contact with the atmosphere of the earth.

me-te-or-ic (mē´tē or´ik) *adj.* Of or relating to a meteor or meteors; resembling a meteor in speed, brilliance, or brevity.

me-te-or-ite (mē´tē o rīt´) *n.* A stony or metallic mass of a meteor which reaches the earth after partially burning in the atmosphere.

me-te-or-ol-o-gy (mē´tē o rol´ojē) *n.* The science concerned with the study of weather, weather conditions and weather forecasting. **meteorological** *adj.* **meteorologic** *adj.* **meteorologically** *adv.* **meteorologist** *n.*

me-ter (mē´tėr) *n.* The arrangement of words, syllables, or stanzas in verse or poetry; a measure equaling 39.37 inches.

meth-a-done (meth´a dōn´) *n.* A man-made narcotic used in the treatment of heroin addiction.

meth-ane (meth´ān) *n.* A colorless, odorless flammable gas used as a fuel; a product of the decomposition of organic matter.

meth-a-nol (meth´a nōl´) *n.* A colorless, odorless flammable alcohol that is used as an antifreeze, as a fuel, and as a raw material in chemical synthesis.

me-thinks (mi thingks´) *v.* It seems to me.

meth-od (meth´od) *n.* A manner, a process, or the regular way of doing something; the orderly arrangement, development, or classification. **methodical** *adj.* **methodically** *adv.*

meth-yl (meth´il) *n.* An alkyl radical derived from methane which occurs in several organic compounds.

me-tic-u-lous (me tik´ū lus) *adj.* Very precise; careful; concerned with small details. **meticulously** *adv.*

me-tis (mā tēs´) *n.* A person of mixed blood, usually of French and Indian ancestry.

met-ric (me´trik) *adj.* Of or relating to the metric system. **metrical** *adj.* Pertaining to rhythm. **metrication** *n.*

metric system *n.* A decimal system of weights and measures based on the meter as a unit of length and the kilogram as a unit of mass, originated in France around 1790.

met-ro (me´trō) *n.* A subway system for transportation.

met-ro-nome (me´tro nōm´) *n.* An instrument designed to mark time by means of a series of clicks at exact intervals. **metronomic** *adj.*

me-trop-o-lis (me trop´o lis) *n.* A large or capital city of a state, region, or country. **metropolitan** *adj.*

mew (mū) *n.* A hideaway; a secret place.

mez-za-nine (mez´a nēn´) *n.* A low story between two main stories of a building; the lowest balcony in a theater.

mice *pl. n.* The plural of mouse.

Mich-i-gan *n.* A state located in the on the northern border of the central United States; statehood January 26, 1837; state capital Lansing.

mi-crobe (mī´krōb) *n.* A germ, plant, or animal so small that is can be seen only with the aid of a microscope.

mi-cro-ceph-a-ly *n.* A condition of abnormal smallness of the head, usually associated with mental defects.

mi-cro-cir-cuit *n.* An electronic circuit composed of very small components.

mi-cro-com-put-er *n.* A computer which uses a microprocessor.

mi-cro-film (mī´kro film´) *n.* A film used to photograph printed matter at a greatly reduced size.

micro-or-gan-ism(mī´krōor´ganiz´um) *n.* An organism too small to see without the aid of a microscope.

mi-cro-phone (mī´kro fōn´) *n.* An instrument which converts acoustical waves into electrical signals and feeds them into a recorder, amplifier or broadcasting transmitter.

mi-cro-proc-es-sor *n.* In *computer science*, a semiconductor processing unit which is contained on an integrated circuit chip.

mi-cro-scope (mī´kro skōp´) *n.* An optical instrument consisting of a lens or combination of lenses, used to produce magnified images of very small objects.

mi-cro-scop-ic (mī´kro skop´ik) *adj.* Too small to be seen by the eye alone. **microscopical** *adv.*

mi-cro-sur-ger-y *n.* Surgery performed by means of a microscope and laser beam. **microsurgical** *adj.*

mi-cro-wave (mī´krō wāv´) *n.* A very short electromagnetic wave.

mid (mid) *adj.* In the middle or center; central.

mid-den *n.* A refuse heap or dunghill.

mid-dle (mid´l) *adj.* Being equally distant from extremes or limits; the central. *n.* Anything which occupies a middle position; the waist.

midg-et (mij´it) *n.* A very small person.

mid-i *n., Slang* A dress, skirt, or coat which extends to the calf.

midst (midst) *n.* The central or middle part or position; a person positioned among others in a group.

miff (mif) *n.* Ill humor; displeasure. **miff** *v.*

might (mīt) *n.* Force, power, or physical strength. *v.* To indicate a present condition contrary to fact; to ask permission politely.

might-y (mī´tē) *adj.* Showing or having great power.

mi-graine (mī´grān) *n.* A condition of severe, recurring headaches often accompanied by nausea.

mi-grant (mī´grant) *n.* A person who moves from one place to another to find work in the fields.

mi-grate (mī´grāt) *v.* To move from one place to another or from one climate to another. **migration** *n.* **migrational** *adj.* **migratory** *adj.*

mike (mīk) *n., Slang* Microphone.

mil (mil) *n.* A unit of measure equal to 1/1000 of an inch, used in measuring wire.

mild (mild) *adj.* Gentle in manner, behavior, or disposition; not severe or extreme. **mildly** *adv.* **mildness** *n.*

mil-dew (mil´dō´) *n.* A fungal growth which is usually white in color.

mile (mīl) *n.* A unit of measurement equaling 5,280 feet.

mil-i-tant (mil´i tant) *adj.* Engaged in warfare or combat; aggressive. .

mil-i-ta-rize (mil´i ta rīz´) *v.* To train or equip for war.

mil-i-tar-y (mil´i ter´ē) *adj.* Of or related to arms, war, or soldiers. *n.* A nation's armed forces. **militarily** *adv.*

milk (milk) *n.* A whitish fluid produced by the mammary glands of all mature female mammals as a source of food for their young. *v.* To draw milk from the breast or udder. *Slang* To take advantage of every possibility in a given situation. **milky** *adj.*

Milky Way (mil´kē) *n.* The broad, luminous galaxy in which the solar system is located.

mill (mil) *n.* A building housing machinery for grinding grain into meal or flour; any of various machines which grind, crush, or press; a unit of money which equals 1/1000 of a United States dollar. **mill** v. To grind. **miller** A person who operates, works, or owns a grain mill; a moth whose wings are covered with a powdery substance.

mil-li-ner (mil´i nėr) n. Someone who designs, sells, or makes women's hats.

mil-lion (mil´yon) n. A very large number equal to 1,000 x 1,000. **million** adj.

mil-lion-aire (mil´ya nâr´) n. A person whose wealth is estimated at $1,000,000 or more.

mime (mīm) v. To act a part or performance without using words. n. An actor who portrays a part, emotion, or situation using only gestures and body language. **mimer** n.

mim-e-o-graph (mim´ē o graf´) n. A duplicating machine that makes duplicates of typed or drawn information from a stencil through which ink is pressed.

mim-ic (mim´ik) v. To imitate another person's behavior or speech.

mince (mins) v. To cut or chop something into small pieces.

mind (mīnd) n. The element of a human being which controls perception, thought, feeling, memory, and imagination. v. To obey; to take care of; to bring; to remember; to object to.

mine (mīn) n. A pit or underground excavation from which metals or coal can be uncovered and removed. The one that belongs to me. **miner** n.

mine pron. The one that belongs to me.

mine-lay-er n. A navy ship used to lay underwater mines.

min-er-al (min´ėr al) n. A solid inorganic substance, such as silver, diamond, or quartz, which is taken from the earth. **mineral** adj. **mineralize** v.

min-e-stro-ne (min´i strō´nē) n. A very thick vegetable soup that may contain pasta and beans.

min-gle (ming´gl) v. To mix or come together. **mingler** n.

min-i-a-ture (min´ē a chėr) n. A copy or model of something that has been greatly reduced in size.

min-i-com-put-er n. In computer science, a computer designed on a very small scale.

min-i-mize v. To reduce something to a minimum.

min-i-mum (min´i mum) n. pl., -ums or -uma The least, smallest, or lowest amount, degree, number, or position.

min-is-ter (min´i stėr) n. The pastor of a Protestant church; a high officer of state who is in charge of a governmental division.

mink (mingk) n. pl. mink or minks A semiaquatic animal of the weasel family whose thick, lustrous fur is used for making fur coats.

Min-nes-o-ta n. A state located in the north central part of the United States; statehood May 11, 1858; state capital St. Paul.

min-now (min´ō) n. A small, freshwater fish used as bait.

mi-nor (mī´nėr) adj. Not of legal age; lesser in degree, size or importance.

mi-nor-i-ty (mi nor´i tē) n. pl. -ies The smaller in number of two groups making a whole; a part of the population that differs, as in race, sex, or religion.

min-ster (min´stėr) n. A large cathedral or church.

min-strel (min´strel) n. A medieval traveling musician or poet.

mint (mint) n. A place where coins are made by a government; any of a variety of aromatic plants used for flavoring; candy flavored by such a plant.

min-u-end (min´ū end´) n. A number of quantity from which another is to be subtracted.

min-u-et (min´ū et´) n. A slow, stately dance.

mi-nus (mī´nus) prep. Reduced, by subtraction. n. The minus sign (-); a negative number.

mi-nus-cule (min´u skūl´) n. Small in size; a lowercase letter.

min-ute (min´it) n. The unit of time which equals 60 seconds.

mi-nute (mī nöt´) adj. Extremely small in size.

mir-a-cle (mir´a kl) n. A supernatural event or happening regarded as an act of God.

mi-rage (mi räzh´) n. An optical illusion in which nonexistent bodies of water with reflections of objects are seen.

mire (mīer) n. Soil or heavy mud.

mir-ror (mir´ėr) n. A polished surface which reflects light, forming the image of an object.

mirth (merth) n. Merriment or joyousness expressed by laughter.

mis- prefix Wrong, bad, or ill.

mis-ad-ven-ture (mis´ad ven´chėr) n. An unlucky mishap; a misfortune.

mis-an-thrope (mis´an thrōp´) n. Someone who hates mankind.

mis-ap-pre-hend (mis´ap ri hend´) v. To understand something incorrectly; to misunderstand.

mis-ap-pro-pri-ate (mis´a prō´prēat´) v. To embezzle money; to use wrongly for one's own benefit.

mis-car-riage (mis kar´ij) n. The premature birth of a fetus from the uterus.

mis-ce-ge-na-tion (mis´i je nā´shan) n. The marriage between two people of different races.

mis-cel-la-ne-ous (mis´e lā´nē us) *adj.* Consisting of a mixed variety of parts, elements, or characteristics.

mis-chance (mis chans´) *n.* Bad luck or mishap.

mis-chief (mis´chif) *n.* Behavior which causes harm, damage, or annoyance.

mis-chie-vous (mis´chi vus) *adj.* Tending to behave in a playfully annoying way. **mischievously** *adv.*

mis-ci-ble (mis´i bl) *adj., Chem.* Capable of being mixed.

mis-con-ceive (mis´kon sēv´) *v.* To misunderstand the meaning. **misconceiver** *n.* **misconception** *n.*

mis-con-duct (mis kon´dukt) *n.* Improper conduct or behavior; bad management.

mis-count (mis kount´) *v.* To count incorrectly; to miscalculate.

mis-cre-ant (mis´krē ant) *n.* A person who is involved in criminal or evil acts; a heretic. **miscreant** *adj.*

mis-cue (mis kū´) *n.* An error; a mistake.

mis-deed (mis dēd´) *n.* A wrong or improper act; an evil deed.

mis-de-mean-or (mis´di mē´nėr) *n., Law* A crime less serious than a felony.

mis-er (mī´zėr) *n.* A person who hoards money; a person who lives a meager life in order to hoard his money.

mis-er-a-ble (miz´ėr a bl) *adj.* Very uncomfortable or unhappy; causing misery. **miserably** *adv.*

mis-er-y (miz´e rē) *n.* A state of great unhappiness, distress, or pain.

mis-feed *n.* In *computer science*, the failure of paper or other media to pass through a printer or other device properly.

mis-fit (mis fit´) *n.* A person who is not adjusted to his environment; anything which does not fit correctly.

mis-for-tune (mis for´chan) *n.* Bad luck or fortune.

mis-giv-ing (mis giv´ing) *n.* A feeling of doubt.

mis-guide (mis gīd´) *v.* To guide incorrectly; to misdirect. **misguidance** *n.* **misguidedly** *adv.*

mis-han-dle (mis han´dl) *v.* To handle clumsily; to manage inefficiently.

mis-hap (mis´hap) *n.* An unfortunate accident; bad luck.

mish-mash (mish´mash´) *n.* A jumble or hodgepodge.

mis-in-ter-pret (mis´in ter´prit) *v.* To understand or explain incorrectly. **misinterpretation** *n.*

mis-judge (mis juj´) *v.* To make a mistake in judgment **misjudgment** *n.*

mis-lay (mis lā´) *v.* To lose; to put something in a place and not remember where.

mis-lead (mis lēd´) *v.* To lead in a wrong direction; to deliberately deceive. **misleader** *n.* **misleading** *adj.*

mis-no-mer (mis nō´mėr) *n.* A wrong or inappropriate name.

mis-pro-nounce (mis´pro nouns´) *v.* To pronounce a word incorrectly.

mi-sog-a-my (mi sog a mē) *n.* Hatred of marriage.

mi-sog-y-ny (mi soj´i nē) *n.* Hatred of women.

mis-place (mis plās´) *v.* To mislay; to put in a wrong place.

mis-rep-re-sent (mis´rep ri zent´) *v.* To represent wrongly, misleadingly, or falsely. **misrepresentation** *n.*

mis-rule (mis rōl´) *n.* Misruling; the condition of being misruled; disorder.

Miss (mis) *n.* The proper title for an unmarried woman or girl. *v.* To fail to hit, reach, or make contact with something; to omit; to feel the absence or loss of.

mis-shape (mis shāp´) *v.* To deform; to shape badly; to distort. **misshapen** *adj.*

mis-sile (mis´il) *n.* An object that is thrown or shot at a target.

mis-sion (mish´an) *n.* An instance or the act of sending; an assignment or task to be carried out.

mis-sion-ar-y (mish´a ner´ē) *n. pl.* **-ies** A person sent to do religious or charitable work, usually in a foreign country.

Miss-i-ssip-pi *n.* A state located in the south central part of the United States; statehood December 10, 1817; state capital Jackson.

Miss-ou-ri *n.* A state located in the central part of the United States; statehood August 10, 1821; state capital Jefferson City.

mis-spell (mis spel´) *v.* To spell a word incorrectly. **misspelling** *n.*

mis-take (mi stāk´) *n.* A wrong statement, action, or decision. **mistaken** *adj.* **mistakable** *adj.* **mistakably** *adv.*

Mis-ter (mis´tėr) *n.* A courtesy title used before a man's name, abbreviated as Mr.

mis-tle-toe (mis´l tō´) *n.* A parasitic plant with thick leaves, small yellowish flowers and white berries.

mis-treat (mis trēt´) *v.* To treat badly or wrongly. **mistreatment** *n.*

mis-tress (mis´tris) *n.* A woman having authority, ownership, or a position of control; a woman having a sexual relationship with a man who is not her husband.

mis-tri-al (mis trī´al) *n.* A trial that is invalid because of an error during the procedure.

mis-trust (mis trust´) *v.* To have doubt; to lack trust in something or someone. **mistrust** *n.* **mistrustful** *adj.*

mis-un-der-stand (mis´un dėr stand´) *v.* To interpret incorrectly; to fail to understand. **misunderstanding** *n.*

mite (mīt) *n*. A very small insect; a small amount of money.

mi-ter (mī'tĕr) *n*. A joint made by cutting two pieces at an angle and then fitting them together.

mit-i-gate (mit'i gāt') *v*. To make or become less severe or painful.

mi-to-sis (mī tō'sis) *n*. *pl*. **mitoses** A process of cell division in which chromatin divides into chromosomes.

mitt (mit) *n*. A women's glove that covers only the wrist and hand, leaving the fingers exposed; in baseball, a glove for a catcher or first baseman made in the style of a mitten.

mix (miks) *v*. To blend or combine into one; to come or bring together.

mixed number *n*. A number representing the sum of an integer and a fraction, such as 5 1/2.

mix-ture (miks'chĕr) *n*. The state of being mixed; the process or act of mixing; a combination of two or more substances.

mix-up (miks'up') *n*. An instance or state of confusion.

mo *abbr*. Money order; mail order.

moan (mōn) *n*. A very low, dull sound indicative of pain or grief. *v*. To make a moan.

moat (mōt) *n*. A deep and wide trench surrounding a castle, usually filled with water.

mob (mob) *n*. A large, unruly crowd. *v*. To overcrowd.

mo-bi-lize (mō'bi līz') *v*. To put into motion; to make ready as in preparing an Army. **mobilization** *n*.

moc-ca-sin (mok'a sin) *n*. A heelless shoe or slipper made of a soft leather.

mo-cha (mō'ka) *n*. An Arabian coffee of superior quality; a flavoring with coffee, often used with chocolate.

mock (mok) *v*. To treat with contempt or scorn; to imitate a mannerism or sound closely; to mimic. *adv*. In an insincere manner. *n*. An imitation; a copy. **mockingly** *adv*.

mock-er-y (mok'e rē) *n*. *pl*. **-ies** Insulting or contemptuous action or speech; a subject of laughter or sport; a false or counterfeit appearance; something that's ridiculous.

mock–he-ro-ic (mok'hi rō'ik) *n*. A satirical imitation of the heroic manner or style.

mock-up or **mock–up** (mok'up') *n*. A model of a structure used for study, testing, or demonstration.

mod *n*. A modern and unusual style of dress. *adj*. Modern.

mode (mōd) *n*. A way or method of doing something; a particular manner or form; the value or score that occurs most frequently in a set of data; the current fashion or style, as in dress.

mod-el (mod'el) *n*. A small representation of an object; a pattern that something will be based on; a design or type; one serving as an example; one who poses for an artist or photographer. **model** *v*. **modeler** *n*.

modem In Computer Science, modulator/demodulator; a device for translating digital signals to telephone signals and back, used to communicate between computers via telephone lines.

mod-er-ate (mod'ĕr it) *adj*. Not excessive; tending toward the mean or average extent or quality; opposed to extreme political views.

mod-ern (mod'ĕrn) *adj*. Typical of the recent past or the present; advanced or up-to-date. **modern** *n*. **modernity** *n*. **modernly** *adv*.

mod-ern-ize (mod'ĕr nīz') *v*. To make or become modern. **-ation** *n*.

mod-est (mod'ist) *adj*. Placing a moderate estimate on one's abilities or worth; retiring or reserved; limited in size or amount. **modesty** *n*.

mod-i-cum (mod'i kum) *n*. A small amount.

mod-i-fy (mod'i fī') *v*. To alter; to make different in character or form; to change to less extreme; to moderate. **modified** *adj*. **modifiable** *adj*. **modification** *n*.

mod-ish (mō'dish) *adj*. Fashionable. **modishly** *adv*. **modishness** *n*.

mo-diste (mō dēst') *n*. A person dealing in fashionable clothing for women.

mod-u-late (moj'u lāt') *v*. To soften; to temper; to vary the intensity of. *Music* To change from one key to another; to vary the tone or intensity of. **modulation** *n*. **modulator** *n*. **modulative** *adj*. **modulatory** *adj*.

mod-ule (moj'ōl) *n*. One of a series of standardized components which work together in a system. *Electr*. A self-contained subassembly of electronic components, as a computer stage; the self-contained area of a spacecraft for performing a particular task. **modular** *adj*.

mod-us op-er-an-di (mō'dus op'eran'dī) *n*. A method of operating or proceeding.

mod-us vi-ven-di (mō'dus vi ven'dī) *n*. A compromise which avoids difficulties.

mo-gul (mō'gul) *n*. A very great or important person; a small hill or bump of ice and snow on a ski slope.

mo-hair (mō'hâr') *n*. The fabric or yarn made from the silky hair of the Angora goat.

Mo-ham-med *n*. The Arab founder of Islam.

moi-e-ty (moi'e tē) *n*. A half; any portion; part or share.

moil (moil) *v*. To work hard; to drudge.

moi-re (mwä rā´) *n.* Fabric, especially silk or rayon having a wavy pattern.

moist (moist) *adj.* Slightly wet; damp; saturated with moisture or liquid. **moistly** *adv.* **moistness** *n.*

mois-ten (moi´sen) *v.* To make or become moist or slightly wet. **moistener** *n.*

mois-ture (mois´chër) *n.* Liquid diffused or condensed in a relatively small quantity; dampness. **moisturize** *v.*

mol (mōl) *abbr.* Molecular; molecule.

mo-lar (mō´lër) *n.* A grinding tooth which has a broad surface for grinding food, located in the back of the mouth. **molar** *adj.*

mo-las-ses (mo las´iz) *n.* A thick, dark syrup produced when sugar is refined.

mold (mōld) *n.* A superficial, often woolly growth produced on damp or decaying organic matter or on living organisms; a fungus that produces such a growth; crumbling, soft, pliable earth suited to plant growth; distinctive nature or character; the frame on or around which an object is constructed; a cavity in which an object is shaped; general shape; form. **mold** *v.*

mole (mōl) *n.* A pigmented spot or mark on the human skin; a small, insectivorous mammal that lives mostly underground and has an arrow snout, small eyes, and silky fur; a large wall of stone or masonry used as a breakwater or pier.

mo-lec-u-lar (mō lek´ū lër) *adj.* Of, relating to, or caused by molecules.

molecular biology *n.* The branch of biology dealing with the structure and development of biological systems which are studied in terms of their molecular constituents.

mol-e-cule (mol´e kūl´) *n.* The simplest structural unit into which a substance can be divided and still retain its identity.

mo-lest (mo lest´) *v.* To bother, annoy, or persecute; to accost sexually. **molestation** *n.* **molester** *n.*

mol-li-fy (mol´i fī´) *v.* To make less angry; to soften; to make less intense or severe. **mollification** *n.*

mol-lusk *or* **mol-lusc (mol´usk)** *n.* Any of various largely marine invertebrates, including the edible shellfish.

mol-ly-cod-dle (mol´ē kod´l) *v.* To spoil by pampering; to coddle.

molt (mōlt) *v.* To cast off or shed an external covering, as horns, feathers, or skin, which is periodically replaced by new growth. **molt** *n.*

mol-ten (mōl´ten) *adj.* Transformed to liquid form by heat.

mo-lyb-de-num (mo lib´de num) *n.* A hard, gray metallic element used to harden steel alloys, symbolized by Mo.

mo-men-tar-i-ly (mō´men târ´ïlē) *adv.*

For just a moment; soon; from moment to moment.

mo-men-tar-y (mō´men ter´ē) *adj.* Lasting just a moment; occurring presently or at every moment.

mo-men-tous (mō men´tus) *adj.* Of great importance or consequence; significant. **momentously** *adv.* **-ness** *n.*

mo-men-tum (mō men´tum) *n., pl.* **-ta** *or* **-tums** A property of a moving body which determines the length of time required to bring it to rest when under the action of a constant force.

mon-arch (mon´ärk) *n.* A person who reigns over a kingdom or empire; a large orange and black butterfly. **monarchic** *adj.* **monarchical** *adj.*

mon-as-ter-y (mon´a ster´ē) *n. pl.* **-ies** A house for persons under religious vows. **monasterial** *adj.*

mo-nas-tic (mo nas´tik) *adj.* Of, relating to, or typical of monasteries, monks, or life in monasteries.

mo-nas-ti-cism (mo nas´ti siz´um) *n.* The monastic lifestyle or system.

mon-au-ral (mon är´al) *adj.* Of or relating to a system of transmitting or recording sound by techniques in which one or more sources are channeled into one carrier.

mon-e-tar-y (mon´i ter´ē) *adj.* Of or relating to money or how it is circulated. **monetarily** *adv.*

mon-ey (mun´ē) *n.* Anything which has or is assigned value and is used as a medium of exchange.

mon-ey-lend-er *n.* Someone whose business is lending money to others with interest.

mon-ger (mung´gër) *n.* One who attempts to stir up or spread something that is undesirable; one who deals.

mon-goose (mong´gōs´) *n. pl.* **-ses** A chiefly African or Asian mammal which has the ability to kill venomous snakes.

mon-grel (mung´grel) *n.* An animal or plant, especially a dog, produced by interbreeding.

mo-ni-tion (mō nish´an) *n.* A caution or warning, as for an impending danger.

mon-i-tor (mon´i tër) *n.* A student assigned to assist a teacher; a receiver used to view the picture being picked up by a television camera; the image being generated by a computer.

mon-i-to-ry (mon´i tōr´ē) *adj.* Giving a caution or conveying a warning.

monk (mungk) *n.* A man who is a member of a religious order and lives in a monastery. **monkish** *adj.*

mon-o *n.* Mononucleosis.

mon-o-chro-mat-ic (mon´o krōmat´ik) *adj.* Of, consisting of, or having one color. **monochromatically** *adv.*

mon-o-cle (mon´o kl) *n.* An eyeglass for

one eye.

mon-o-cot-y-le-don (mon´o kot´ĭlēd´on) n. Any of various plants having a single embryonic seed leaf appearing at germi-nation. **monocotyledonous** adj.

mo-noc-u-lar (mo nok´ū lêr) adj. Of, relating to, or having one eye.

mo-nog-a-my (mo nog´a mē) n. Marriage or sexual relationship with only one person at a time. **monogamist** n. **monogamous** adj.

mon-o-gram (mon´o gram´) n. A design consisting of one or more initials.

mon-o-graph (mon´o graf´) n. A scholarly pamphlet or book on a particular and usually limited subject. **monographic** adj.

mon-o-lin-gual (mon´o ling´gwal) adj. Knowing only one language.

mon-o-lith (mon´o lith) n. A single block of stone, as one used in architecture or sculpture. **monolithic** adj.

mon-o-logue or **mon-o-log** (mon´o log´) n. A speech by one person which precedes conversation; a series of jokes and stories delivered by a comedian. **monologist** n.

mon-o-ma-ni-a (mon´o mā´nē a) n. A pathological obsession or mental disorder in which a person is totally obsessed with a single idea. **monomaniac** n. **monomaniacal** adj.

mo-no-mi-al (mō nō´mē al) n. An algebraic expression consisting of only one term. **monomial** adj.

mon-o-nu-cle-ar (mon´o nō´klē êr) adj. Having only one nucleus.

mon-o-nu-cle-o-sis (mon´o nō´klēo´sis) n. An infectious disease marked by an abnormal increase white blood cells caused by a virus.

mon-o-nu-cle-o-tide n. A compound containing one molecule each of a phosphoric acid, a pentose, and either a purine or pyrimidine base.

mon-o-phon-ic (mon´o fon´ik) adj. Having only one part; a solo voice with accompaniment, as a piano.

mon-o-plane (mon´o plān´) n. An aircraft with one wing or one set of wings.

mo-nop-o-ly (mo nop´o lē) n. pl., -ies Exclusive ownership or control, as of a service or commodity, by a single group, person, or company; a group, person, or company having a monopoly; exclusive possession; a service or commodity controlled by a single group. **monopolist** n. **monopolization** n. **monopolistic** adj. **monopolize** v.

mon-o-rail (mon´o rāl´) n. A single rail serving as a track on which a wheeled vehicle can travel; a vehicle that travels on such a rail.

mon-o-so-di-um glu-ta-mate (mon´o sō´dēum glō´ta māt´) n. Sodium glutamate used as a seasoning,

abbreviated as MSG.

mon-o-syl-la-ble (mon´o sil´a bl) n. A word of one syllable. **monosyllabic** adj. **monosyllabically** adv.

mon-o-the-ism (mon´o thē iz´um) n. The belief that there is just one God. **monotheist** n. **monotheistic** adj.

mon-o-tone (mon´o tōn´) n. The utterance of sounds, syllables, or words in a single unvarying tone.

mo-not-o-nous (mo not´o nus) adj. Spoken in a monotone; lacking in variety. **monotonously** adv.

mon-ox-ide (mon ok´sīd) n. An oxide that contains one oxygen atom per molecule.

Monroe, James n. (1758-1831). The fifth president of the United States from 1817-1825.

mon-soon (mon sōn´) n. A periodic wind, especially in the Indian Ocean and southern Asia; the season of the monsoon in India and parts of Asia.

mon-ster (mon´stêr) n. An animal or plant having an abnormal form or structure; an animal, plant, or object having a frightening or deformed shape; one unusually large for its kind. **monstrosity** n. **monstrousness** n. **monstrous** adj. **monstrously** adv.

mon-tage (mon täzh´) n. A composite picture made by combining several separate pictures or parts of several pictures; a rapid succession of images in a motion picture, designed to illustrate an association of ideas.

Mon-tan-a n. A state located in the northwestern United States; statehood November 8, 1889; state capital Helena.

month (munth) n. One of the twelve divisions of a calendar year.

month-ly (munth´lē) adj. Occurring, done, or payable each month. n. A publication issued once a month. **monthly** adv.

mon-u-ment (mon´ū ment) n. An object, such as a statue, built as a memorial to a person or an event; a burial vault; an area set aside for public use by a government because of its aesthetic, historical, or ecological significance.

mon-u-men-tal (mon´ū men´tal) adj. Serving as or similar to a monument; massive; extremely important.

mooch (mōch) v., Slang To acquire by begging; to steal. **moocher** n.

mood (mōd) n. A conscious yet temporary state of mind or emotion; the prevailing spirit; a verb form or set of verb forms inflected to show the understanding of the person speaking regarding the condition expressed.

mood-y (mō´dē) adj. Subject to moods, especially depression; gloomy.

moon (mōn) n. The earth's only natural

satellite; a natural satellite which revolves around a planet. *v.* To dream.

moon shot *n.* The launching of a spacecraft to the moon or its vicinity.

moor (mer) *v.* To make fast with cables, lines, or anchors. *n.* An expanse of open, rolling, infertile land.

moose (mös) *n. pl.* **moose** A very large North American deer having a large broad muzzle.

moot (möt) *v.* To bring up as for debate or discussion; to argue. *adj.* Open to debate; having no legal significance.

mope (möp) *v.* To be uncaring or dejected; to move in a leisurely manner.

mo-raine (mo rān´) *n.* An accumulation of earth and stones carried and finally deposited by a glacier.

mor-al (mor´al) *adj.* Of or pertaining to conduct or character from the point of right and wrong; teaching a conception of right behavior. *n.* The lesson to be learned from a story, event, or teaching. **morals** Standards of right and wrong.

mo-rale (mo ral´) *n.* An individual's state of mind with respect to the tasks he or she is expected to perform; esprit decorps.

mor-al-ist (mor´a list) *n.* Someone concerned with moral principles and questions; someone who practices morality. **moralism** *n.* **moralistic** *adj.*

mo-ral-i-ty (mo ral´i tē) *n. pl.* **-ies** The quality of being morally right; moral behavior.

mo-rass (mo ras´) *n.* A marsh or bog; low-lying wet, soft ground; something which hinders or overwhelms.

mor-a-to-ri-um *n. pl.* **-iums** *or* **-ia** A temporary pause in activity; an authorization given legally to a debtor to suspend payments for a period of time.

mo-ray (mōr´ā) *n.* Any of various marine eels found usually in tropical waters.

mor-bid (mor´bid) *adj.* Of, pertaining to, or affected by disease; suggesting an unhealthy mental state of being; gruesome. **morbidity** *n.* **morbidness** *n.* **morbidly** *adv.*

mor-da-cious (mor dā´shus) *adj.* Violent in action; prone to biting.

mor-dant (mor´dant) *adj.* Biting and caustic in thought, manner, or style. **mordancy** *n.* **mordantly** *adv.*

more (mōr) *adj.* Greater number, size, or degree; additional. *n.* An additional or greater number, degree, or amount. *adv.* To a greater extent or degree; in addition. *pron.* Additional things or persons.

mo-rel (mo rel´) *n.* An edible mushroom having a sponge-like cap or hood.

more-o-ver (mōr ō´vèr) *adv.* Furthermore; besides.

mo-res (mōr´āz) *n. pl.* The moral customs and traditional customs of a social group.

morgue (morg) *n.* A place in which dead bodies are kept until claimed or identified; the reference file at a newspaper or magazine office.

mor-i-bund (mor´i bund´) *adj.* Approaching extinction; at the point of death. **moribundity** *n.*

morn (morn) *n.* Morning.

morn-ing (mor´ning) *n.* The early part of the day; the time from midnight to noon.

morning star *n.* A planet seen in the eastern part of the sky just before or at sunrise.

mo-roc-co (mo rok´ō) *n.* A soft, textured leather made of goatskin.

mo-ron (mōr´on) *n.* An adult exhibiting an intelligence equal to that of a seven to twelve year old child; a very stupid person. **moronic** *adj.* **moronically** *adv.*

mo-rose (mo rōs´) *adj.* Having a sullen disposition; marked by gloom. **morosely** *adv.* **moroseness** *n.*

mor-pheme (mor´fēm) *n.* A meaningful unit which cannot be divided into smaller meaningful parts. **morphemic** *adj.* **morphemically** *adv.*

mor-phi-a (mor´fē a) *n.* Morphine.

mor-phine (mor´fēn) *n.* A highly addictive narcotic derived from opium which can be used as either a sedative or to dull pain.

mor-phol-o-gy (mor fol´o jē) *n.* The study of the form and structure of living organisms, considered separate from function; the study and description of word formation in a language. **morphological** *adj.* **morphologically** *adv.* **morphologist** *n.*

mor-ris (mor´is) *n.* An old English folk dance.

mor-row (mor´ō) *n.* The next day.

mor-sel (mor´sel) *n.* A small piece or quantity of food; a tasty dish.

mor-tal (mor´tal) *adj.* Having caused or about to cause death; fatal; subject to death; very tedious or prolonged; unrelentingly hostile; of, relating to, or connected with death. *n.* A human being. **mortally** *adv.*

mor-tal-i-ty (mor tal´i tē) *n. pl.* **-ies** The state or condition of being mortal; the death rate; deaths.

mor-tar (mor´tèr) *n.* A strong vessel in which materials can be crushed or ground with a pestle; a muzzle-loading cannon for firing shells at short ranges and at high angles; a mixed building material, as cement with sand and water, which hardens and is used with masonry or plaster.

mor-tar-board (mor´tèr bōrd´) *n.* A square-board with a handle, for holding mortar; an academic cap topped by a stiff, flat square.

mort-gage (mor´gij) n. A temporary conveyance of property to a creditor as security for the repayment of a debt; a contract or deed defining the terms of a mortgage. v. To pledge or transfer by means of a mortgage. **mortgagee** n. **mortgagor** n.

mor-ti-cian (mor tish´an) n. An undertaker.

mor-ti-fy (mor´ti fī´) v. To destroy the strength or functioning of; to subdue or deaden through pain or self-denial; to subject to severe humiliation; to become gangrenous. **mortification** n.

mor-tise (mor´tis) n. A usually hollowed out rectangular hole in a piece of wood which receives a tenon of another piece to form a joint.

mor-tu-ar-y (mor´chö er´ē) n. pl. -ies A place in which dead bodies are temporarily held until burial or cremation.

mo-sa-ic (mözā´ik) n. A decorative inlaid design of small pieces, as of colored glass or tile, in cement. **mosaic** adj.

mo-sey (mö´zē) v., Slang To move slowly; to shuffle along.

mosque (mosk) n. A Moslem house of worship.

mos-qui-to (mo skē´tö) n. pl. -toes or -tos Any of various winged insects of which the females suck the blood of animals or humans.

mosquito net n. A fine net or screen to keep out mosquitoes.

moss (mos) n. Delicate, small green plants which of ten form a dense, mat-like growth. **mossiness** n.

moss-back (mos´bak´) n. An old-fashioned person.

moss rose n. An old-fashioned garden rose which has a glandular, mossy calyx and flower stalk.

most (möst) adj. The majority of. n. The greatest amount. pron. The largest part or number. adv. In or to the highest degree.

most-ly (möst´lē) adv. For the most part; principally.

mot (mö) n. A short, witty saying.

mote (möt) n. A particle, as of dust; a speck of dust.

mo-tel (mö tel´) n. A temporary, roadside dwelling for motorists with rooms opening directly onto a parking area.

mo-tet (mö tet´) n. A polyphonic vocal composition, based on a religious text and usually sung without accompaniment.

moth (moth) n. A usually nocturnal insect having antennae that are often feathered, duller in color and with wings smaller than the butterflies.

moth-ball (moth´bol´) n. A ball, usually of camphor, used to repel moths from clothing during storage. **in mothballs** A condition of protective storage.

moth–eat-en (moth´ēt´en) adj. Partially eaten by moths; in a state of disrepair.

moth-er (muth´ër) n. A female parent; one who holds a maternal relationship toward another; an old or elderly woman; a woman in a position of authority. adj. Of, relating to, or being a mother. v. To give birth to; to care for or protect like a mother. **mother-hood** n. **motherliness** n.

mother-board n. In computer science, the primary circuit board in a computer.

mother–in–law (muth´ër in lo´) n. The mother of one's spouse.

mother-land (muth´ër land´) n. The country or land of one's birth.

moth-er–of–pearl (muth´ër ov perl´) n. The pearly iridescent internal layer of a mollusk shell.

mo-tif (mö tēf´) n. An underlying main element or theme that recurs in a musical, artistic, or literary work.

mo-tile (mö´til) adj. Exhibiting or capable of movement.

mo-tion (mö´shan) n. The act or process of changing position; a purposeful movement of the body or a bodily part; a formal proposal or suggestion that action be taken. **motionless** adj.

motion picture n. A sequence of filmed pictures that gives the illusion of continuous movement, when projected on a screen.

motion sickness n. Dizziness; nausea brought on by motion as traveling by land or water.

mo-ti-vate (mö´ti vāt´) v. Causing to act.

mo-tive (mö´tiv) n. Something, as a need or desire, which causes a person to act; a musical motif. adj. Causing or having the power to cause motion.

mot-ley (mot´lē) adj. Composed of a variety of components.

mo-tor (mö´tër) n. Any of various devices which develop energy or impart motion. adj. Imparting or producing motion; driven by or equipped with a motor; of, relating to or designed for motor vehicles; of, relating to, or involving muscular movement. v. To travel or transport by motor vehicle.

motor-bike (mö´tër bīk´) n. A small motorcycle.

mo-tor-boat (mö´tër böt´) n. A boat propelled by an internal-combustion engine or an electric motor.

mo-tor-cade (mö´tër kād´) n. A procession of motor vehicles.

mo-tor-car (mö´tër kär´) n. An automobile.

mo-tor-cy-cle (mö´tër sī´kl) n. A two-wheeled automotive vehicle. **motorcy-cle** v. **motorcyclist** n.

motor home *n*. A motor vehicle built on a truck frame and equipped to provide a self-contained home during travel.

mo-tor-ize (mō´*to* rīz´) *v*. To equip with a motor; to supply with motor-propelled vehicles. **motorization** *n*.

mo-tor-man (mō´tèr *man*) *n*. An operator of a locomotive engine, streetcar, or sub-way train.

motor scooter *n*. A small two-wheeled vehicle similar to a scooter but having a low-powered gasoline engine.

motor vehicle *n*. A motor-powered vehicle which travels freely without the need for rails.

mot-tle (mot´l) *v*. To mark or be marked with spots or streaks of different colors or shades; to blotch. *n*. A blotch.

mot-to (mot´ō) *n. pl*. **-toes** *or* **-tos** A sentence, phrase, or word expressing purpose, character, or conduct; an appropriate phrase inscribed on something.

moue (mö) *n*. A grimace, as of disapproval or disdain.

mound (mound) *n*. A small hill of earth, sand, gravel or debris; the slightly elevated ground in the middle of a baseball diamond on which the pitcher stands.

mount (mount) *v*. To rise or ascend; to get up on; climb upon; to increase in amount or extent; to organize and equip; to launch and carry out. *n*. A horse or other animal used for riding; a support to which some-thing is fixed.

moun-tain (moun´tin) *n*. A land mass that rises above its surroundings and is higher than a hill.

mountain ash *n*. Any of various deciduous trees bearing clusters of small white flowers and orange-red berries.

moun-tain-eer (moun´ta nēr´) *n*. An inhabitant of a mountainous region; one who climbs mountains for sport. **mountaineer** *v*.

mountain goat *n*. A long-haired Rocky Mountain goat.

mountain laurel *n*. A low-growing evergreen shrub with poisonous leaves and clusters of pink or white flowers.

mountain lion *n*. A large wildcat; puma.

moun-tain-ous (moun´ta nus) *adj*. Of or relating to a region with many mountains.

moun-tain-side (moun´tan sīd´) *n*. The side of a mountain.

moun-tain-top (moun´tan top´) *n*. The top of a mountain.

moun-te-bank (moun´te bangk´) *n*. A quack doctor; a false and boastful pretender; a charlatan.

Mountie Mounty *n*. A member of the Canadian Mounted Police.

mount-ing (moun´ting) *n*. A supporting frame or structure of an article.

mourn (mōrn) *v*. To express grief; to feel grief or sorrow; to follow the religious customs and rituals surrounding the death of a loved one.

mouse (mous) *n., pl*. **mice** A small rodent that frequents human habitations; a timid person.

mousse (mös) *n*. A light frozen dessert.

mouth (mouth) *n., pl*. **mouths** The bodily opening through which nutrients are taken.

mouth-off *v*. To speak disrespectfully.

mouth-to-mouth (mouth´tō mouth´) *adj*. Pertaining to a method of artificial resuscitation.

move (möv) *v*. To set in motion; to change one's place or location; to make a recommendation in a formal manner. **movable** *adj*. **moveable** *adj*.

move-ment (möv´ment) *n*. The act of moving; a part of a musical composition; an excretion of the bowels.

mov-er *n*. One that moves; a person employed to help in moving the contents of a home or business.

mov-ie (mö´vē) *n*. A motion picture; motion picture industry.

mow (mō) *v*. To cut down, as with a machine. *n*. The part of the barn where hay or grain is stored. **mower** *n*.

moz-za-rel-la *n*. A soft white cheese with a mild flavor.

Mr *abbr*. Mister.

Mrs *abbr*. Mistress.

Ms *abbr*. A form of address used for a woman when her marital status is irrelevant or unknown.

much (much) *adj*. In great amount, quantity, degree, or extent. *adv*. To a great extent. *n*. Something impressive.

mu-ci-lage (mū´si lij) *n*. A sticky substance that is similar to plant gums.

muck (muk) *n*. Moist farmyard manure; moist, sticky soil or filth. *v*. To dirty with or as with muck. **mucky** *adj*.

muck-rake (muk´rāk´) *v*. To search out and publicly expose real or apparent misconduct on the part of well-known persons. **muckraker** *n*.

mu-co-sa (mū kō´sa) *n*. A mucous membrane.

mu-cous (mū´kus) *adj*. Of, pertaining to, or secreting mucus.

mucous membrane *n*. A membrane secreting mucus which lines bodily channels that come into contact with air.

mu-cus (mū´kus) *n*. The viscous liquid secreted by glands by the mucous membrane.

mud (mud) *n*. A mixture of water and earth. *Slang* A slanderous remark. **muddy** *& v*. **muddily** *adv*.

mud-dle (mud´l) *v*. To make muddy; to mix up or confuse; to make a mess of;

to think or act in a confused way. **muddler** *n*.

mud-guard (mud´gärd´) *n*. A piece of material applied to a wheel well to prevent mud from splashing onto a vehicle.

mud-sling-er *n*. One who makes malicious statements or charges against a political opponent. **mudslinging** *n*.

muff (muf) *n*. An arm, tubular covering for the hands; a bungling performance. *v*. To handle awkwardly; to act or do something stupidly or clumsily.

muf-fin (muf´in) *n*. A soft, cup-shaped bread that is cooked in a muffin pan and often served hot.

muf-fle (muf´l) *v*. To wrap up so as to conceal or protect; to deaden the sound of; to suppress.

muf-fler (muf´lėr) *n*. A scarf worn around the neck; a device which deadens noise, especially one forming part of the exhaust system of an automotive vehicle.

mug (mug) *n*. A large drinking cup; a person's face; a photograph of someone's face. *v*. To make funny faces; to assault viciously, usually with the intent to rob. **mugger** *n*.

mug-gy (mug´ē) *adj*. Warm, humid and sultry. **muggily** *adv*. **mugginess** *n*.

mug-wump (mug´wump´) *n*. A defector from the Republican Party in 1884; anyone who acts independently, especially in politics.

muk-luk (muk´luk) *n*. A boot made from the skin of seals or reindeer, worn by Eskimos; a slipper that resembles a mukluk.

mu-lat-to (mu lat´ō) *n*. *pl*. **-tos** *or* **-toes** A person with one white parent and one black parent; a person of mixed black and white ancestry.

mul-ber-ry (mul´ber´ē) *n*. Any of several trees having an edible, berry-like fruit.

mulch (mulch) *n*. A loose protective covering, as of sawdust or compost, or wood chips spread on the ground to prevent moisture evaporation, to protect roots from freezing, and to retard the growth of weeds. **mulch** *v*.

mulct (mulkt) *n*. A financial penalty or fine. *v*. To punish by fining; to obtain by fraud or theft.

mule (mul) *n*. A hybrid animal that is the offspring of a female horse and a male ass. *Slang* A stubborn person. **mulish** *adj*. **mulishly** *adv*.

mule deer *n*. A long-eared deer of western North America, heavier built and larger than the white-tail deer.

mule–foot *adj*. Having a solid foot; not cleft.

mule-skinner *n*. A muleteer.

mu-le-teer (mū´le tēr´) *n*. A person who drives mules.

mu-ley (mū´lē) *adj*. Naturally without horns.

mull (mul) *v*. To mix or grind thoroughly; to ponder; to think about.

mul-lah (mul´a) *n*. A Muslim leader and clergyman.

mul-lein (mul´en) *n*. A plant having yellow flowers and downy leaves.

mul-let (mul´it) *n*. An edible marine and freshwater fish.

mul-li-gan stew (mul´i gan) *n*. A stew made of various vegetables and meats.

multi- *prefix* Much, many, multiple; more than two.

mul-ti-dis-ci-plin-ary *adj*. Using or related to a combination of several disciplines for a common cause.

mul-ti-far-i-ous (mul´ti fâr´ē us) *adj*. Having much diversity. **-ously** *adv*.

mul-ti-form (mul´ti form´) *adj*. Having many appearances or forms. **multiformity** *n*.

mul-ti-lane *adj*. Having several lanes.

mul-ti-lat-er-al (mul´ti lat´ėr al) *adj*. Having many sides; involving or participated in by more than two parties or nations. **multilaterally** *adv*.

mul-ti-lin-gual (mul´ti ling´gwal) *adj*. Expressed in several languages.

mul-ti-mil-lion-aire (mul´tē mil´yanâr´) *n*. A person whose fortune is worth many millions of dollars.

mul-ti-na-tion-al *adj*. Involving or relating to several countries.

mul-tip-a-rous *adj*. Producing more than one at a birth.

mul-ti-ple (mul´ti pl) *adj*. Relating to or consisting of more than one individual, part, or element. *Math*. A number into which another number can be divided with no remainders.

multiple–choice (mul´ti pl chois´) *adj*. Offering several answers from which the correct one is to be chosen.

multiple sclerosis *n*. A degenerative condition marked by patches of hardened tissue in the spinal cord or the brain.

multi-plex (mul´ti pleks) *n*. A communications system in which two or more messages can be transmitted simultaneously on the same circuit. **multiplex** *v*. **multiplexor** *n*.

mul-ti-pli-ca-tion (mul´ti plikā´shan) *n*. The mathematical operation by which a number indicates how many times another number is to be added to itself.

mul-ti-plic-i-ty (mul´ti plis´i tē) *n*. *pl*. **-ies** A large number or variety.

mul-ti-pli-er (mul´ti plī´ėr) *n*. A number that is or is to be multiplied by another number.

mul-ti-ply (mul´ti plī´) *v*. To increase in amount or number; to combine by multiplication.

mul-ti-sense *adj.* Having several meanings.

mul-ti-stage (mul´ti stãj´) *adj.* Consisting of propulsion units which operate in turn.

mul-ti-tude (mul´ti tõd´) *n.* A very large amount or number. **multitudinous** *adj.*

mul-ti-vi-ta-min *n.* A pill containing several vitamins that are essential to health.

mum (mum) *adj.* Silent, not speaking.

mum-ble (mum´bl) *v.* To speak or utter in a low, confused manner. **mumble** *n.* **mumbler** *n.*

mum-ble-ty-peg (mum´bl tẽ peg´) *n.* A game in which players try to throw a knife from various positions so that the blade will stick into the ground.

mum-bo jum-bo (mum´bõ jum´bõ) *n.* A complicated or obscure ritual; a confusing and complicated language or activity.

mum-mer (mum´ẽr) *n.* A performer who acts in a pantomime.

mum-mery (mum´e rẽ) *n., pl.* **-ies** A hypocritical or ridiculous ceremony.

mum-mi-fy (mum´i fī´) *v.* To dry and embalm a mummy; to cause to shrivel and dry up. **mummification** *n.*

mum-my (mum´ẽ) *n. pl.* **-ies** A body embalmed or treated for burial in the manner of the ancient Egyptians.

mumps (mumps) *n., pl.* An acute, contagious viral disease marked by fever and swelling of the salivary glands.

mun *abbr.* Municipal; municipality.

munch (munch) *v.* To chew noisily. **muncher** *n.*

mun-dane (mun dãn´) *adj.* Pertaining to or relating to the world; characterized by the ordinary and practical. **mundanely** *adv.*

mu-nic-i-pal (mũ nis´i pal) *adj.* Relating to or typical of a municipality; having self-government in local affairs. **municipally** *adv.* **municipality** *n.*

mu-nif-i-cent (mũ nif´i sent) *adj.* Very liberal in giving; lavish. **munificence** *n.* **munificently** *adv.*

mu-ni-tions *n. pl.* Guns and ammunition. **munition** *v.*

mu-ral (mer´al) *n.* A painting created on a wall. **muralist** *n.*

mur-der (mer´dẽr) *n.* The crime of unlawfully killing a person. *Slang* Something very dangerous, difficult, or uncomfortable. *v.* To kill a person unlawfully and with premeditated malice. **murderer** *n.*

mur-der-ous (mer´dẽr us) *adj.* Intending or having the purpose or capability of murder. **murderously** *adv.*

murk (merk) *n.* Darkness; gloom. **murkily** *adv.* **murkiness** *n.*

mur-mur (mer´mẽr) *n.* A low, indistinct, and often continuous sound; a gentle or soft utterance. **murmur** *v.*

mur-mur-ous *adj.* Characterized by murmurs. **murmurously** *adv.*

Murphy bed (mer´fẽ bed) *n.* A bed which folds into a closet.

mur-rain (mer´in) *n.* A plague affecting plants or domestic animals.

mur-rey (mer´ẽ) *n.* Mulberry colored; purplish-black.

mus *abbr.* Museum; musical; musician.

muscae volitantes A condition of spots before the eyes due to cells and cell fragments in the vitreous humor and lens.

mus-cle (mus´l) *n.* Bodily tissue which consists of long cells that contract when stimulated. **muscle** *v.*

mus-cle-bound (mus´l bound´) *adj.* Having muscles which are overdeveloped and lack the capacity to flex fully, usually caused by too much exercise.

mus-cu-lar (mus´kũ lẽr) *adj.* Relating to or consisting of muscle; brawny; having well-developed muscles. **muscularity** *n.*

muscular dystrophy *n.* A noncontagious hereditary disease characterized by gradual but irreversible muscular deterioration.

mus-cu-la-ture (mus´kũ la chẽr) *n.* The muscles of an animal's body.

muse (mũz) *n.* A state of deep thought.

mu-sette (mũ zet´) *n.* A small bagpipe having a soft, sweet tone or sound; a small bag with a shoulder strap.

mush (mush) *n.* A thick porridge of corn meal boiled in water or milk; soft matter. **mushiness** *n.* **mushy** *adj.*

mush-room (mush´rõm) *n.* A fungus having an umbrella-shaped cap on a stalk. *v.* To grow or multiply quickly.

mu-sic (mu´zik) *n.* Organized tones in sequences and combinations which make up a continuous composition. **musical** *adj.*

music box *n.* A box enclosing an apparatus which produces music when activated.

mu-si-cian (mũ zish´an) *n.* A composer or performer of music. **musicianly** *adj.* **musicianship** *n.*

mu-si-col-o-gy (mũ´zi kol´o jẽ) *n.* The scientific and historical study of music. **musicological** *adj.* **musicologist** *n.*

musk (musk) *n.* A substance with a strong, powerful odor which is secreted by the male musk deer. **muskiness** *n.* **musky** *adj.*

mus-keg (mus´keg) *n.* A bog formed by moss, leaves, and decayed matter resembling peat.

mus-ket (mus´kit) *n.* A heavy, large-caliber shoulder gun with a long barrel.

musk-mel-on (musk´mel´on) *n.* A sweet

melon having a rough rind and juicy, edible flesh.

musk-rat (musk´rat´) *n.* A rodent of North America with brown fur.

Mus-lim (muz´lim) *n.* A follower of Islam. **Muslim** *adj.*

mus-lin (muz´lin) *n.* A plain-woven, sheer, or coarse fabric.

muss (mus) *v.* To make messy or untidy. *Slang* A confused conflict.

mus-sel (mus´el) *n.* A freshwater bivalve mollusk.

must (must) *v.* To be forced to; to have to; to be obligated to do something; to be necessary to do something. *n.* A requirement; absolute; something indispensable.

mus-tache *also* **moustache** *n.* The hair growing on the human upper lip, especially on the male upper lip.

mus-tang (mus´tang) *n.* A wild horse of the western plains.

mus-tard (mus´terd) *n.* A condiment or medicinal preparation made from the seeds of the mustard plant.

mustard gas *n.* An irritating liquid chemical used as a war gas.

mus-ter (mus´ter) *v.* To come or bring together; to convene; to bring or call forth. *n.* The act of examining or inspecting critically.

mustn't *contr.* Must not.

mus-ty (mus´te) *adj.* Moldy or stale in odor or taste. **mustily** *adv.*

mu-ta-ble (mu´ta bl) *adj.* Prone to or capable of change. **mutability** *n.* **mutableness** *n.*

mu-tant (mut´ant) *n.* An individual or organism which differs from the parental strain as a result of mutation.

mu-tate (mu´tat) *v.* To undergo or cause to undergo mutation. **mutative** *adj.*

mute (mut) *adj.* Unable to speak. *n.* A person who cannot speak. **mutely** *adv.*

mu-ti-late (mut´i lat´) *v.* To deprive of an essential part, as a limb of the body; to maim or cripple; to make imperfect. **mutilation** *n.* **mutilator** *n.*

mu-ti-ny (mut´i ne) *n. pl.* **-ies** Open revolt against lawful authority. **mutineer** *n.* **mutinous** *adj.*

mutt (mut) *n.*, *Slang* A mongrel; a dog of mixed breed.

mut-ter (mut´er) *v.* To speak or utter in a low voice; to grumble; to complain.

mut-ton (mut´on) *n.* The flesh of a fully grown sheep, used for food.

mu-tu-al (mu´cho al) *adj.* Having the same relationship; received and directed in equal amounts.

mutual fund *n.* An investment company which invests its shareholders' money in diversified ways.

muu-muu *n.* A dress which hangs loosely, originally given to the native women of Hawaii by missionaries.

muz-zle (muz´l) *n.* The projecting mouth of certain animals; the open end or mouth of an implement such as the barrel of a gun. **muzzler** *n.*

my (mi) *adj.* Relating to or of myself or one. *interj.* Used to express surprise, dismay, or pleasure.

my-ce-li-um (mi se´le um) *n. pl.* **-lia** A mass of interwoven filaments which form the main growing structure of a fungus. **mycelial** *adj.*

my-col-o-gy (mi kol´o je) *n.* A branch of botany; the scientific study of fungi. **mycological** *adj.* **mycologist** *n.*

my-e-li-tis *n.* An inflammation of the spinal cord or bone marrow.

my-elo-ma *n.* A tumor of the bone marrow.

myo-car-dio-graph (mi´o kär´deograf´) *n.* A recording tool which traces the action of the heart muscles.

myo-car-di-um *n.* The muscular layer of the heart, located in the middle of the heart wall. **myocardial** *adj.*

my-o-pia (mi o¯´pe a) *n.* A visual defect in which visual images come to a focus in front of the retina of the eye rather than on the retina, causing fuzzy images. **myopic** *adj.* **myopically** *adv.*

myr-tle (mer´tl) *n.* An evergreen shrub.

my-self (mi self´) *pron.* The one identical with me; used reflexively; my normal, healthy state or condition.

mys-te-ri-ous (mi ster´e us) *adj.* Relating to or being a mystery; impossible or difficult to comprehend. **mysteriously** *adv.* **mysteriousness** *n.*

mys-ter-y (mis´te re) *n. pl.* **-ies** Something not understood; a problem or puzzle; an enigma; a Christian sacrament.

mys-tic (mis´tik) *adj.* Relating to mystics, mysticism, or mysteries. *n.* A person practicing or believing in mysticism. **mystical** *adj.* **mystically** *adv.*

mys-ti-cism (mis´ti siz´um) *n.* The spiritual discipline of communion with God or the spirit world.

mys-ti-fy (mis´ti fi) *v.* To perplex, to bewilder. **mystification** *n.*

myth (mith) *n.* A traditional story dealing with supernatural ancestors; a person or thing having only an unverifiable or imaginary existence. **mythical** *adj.* **mythic** *adj.* **mythically** *adv.*

my-thol-o-gy (mi thol´o je) *n. pl.* **-ies** A body of myths dealing with gods and heroes. **mythological** *adj.* **mythologist** *n.*

my word *interj.* An expression of astonishment or surprise.

myx-e-de-ma *n.* A disease that is caused by the decreased activity of the thyroid gland and marked by the loss of mental and physical vigor; dry skin and hair. **myxedematous** *adj.*

N, n (en) The fourteenth letter of the English alphabet.

nab (nab) *v. Slang* To seize; to arrest; to catch suddenly.

na-celle (na sel´) *n.* The housing of an airplane that usually contains the engine.

na-dir (nā´dėr) *n.* The lowest point.

nag (nag) *v.* To bother by scolding or constant complaining. **nag** *n.* A worthless horse. **nagging** *adj.*

na-ga-na (na gä´na) *n.* A disease of horses caused by flies.

nai-ad (nā´ad) *n., Mythol.* A nymph presiding over and living in springs, brooks, and fountains.

na-ive (nä ēv´) *adj.* Simple and trusting; not sophisticated. **naively** *adv.*

na-ked (nā´kid) *adj.* Without clothes on the body; nude; exposed; uncovered. **nakedly** *adv.* **nakedly, nakedness** *n.*

nam-by-pam-by(nam´bēpam´bē)*adj.* Weak; indecisive; lacking in substance or character.

name (nām) *n.* A title or word by which something or someone is known. *v.* To give a name. **namable** *n.*

name-sake (nām´sāk´) *n.* A person named after someone with the same name.

nap (nap) *n.* A short rest or sleep, often during the day. *v.* The surface of a piece of leather or fabric.

na-palm (nā´päm) *n.* A mixture of aluminum soaps used in jelling gasoline for use in bombs or by flame throwers.

nape (nāp) *n.* The back of the neck.

na-per-y (nāp´e rē) *n.* Linens in general that are used for domestic purposes.

naph-tha (naf´tha) *n.* A volatile, colorless, liquid, that is used especially as a solvent or fuel.

na-pi-form (nāpi form´) *adj.* Having the globular shape of a turnip.

nap-kin (nap´kin) *n.* A cloth or soft paper, used at the dinner table for wiping the lips and fingers.

na-po-le-on (na pō´lē an) *n.* A pastry of several flaky layers filled with custard cream.

nap-py (nap´ē) *n. pl.* **nappies.** A small rimless, shallow serving.

na-prap-a-thy (na prap´a thē) *n.* A system of treatment of a disease, that is based on the theory that an illness is caused by dis-ordered connective tissues, and that using massage, manipulation, and dietary measures, healing is achieved.

nar-cis-sus (när sis´us) *n.* A widely grown type of bulbous plant which includes the jonquil, narcissus, and daffodil.

nar-co-ma-ni-a (när´o mä´nē a) *n.* The abnormal craving for a narcotic.

nar-co-sis (när kō´sis) *n.* A deep

drug-induced state of stupor or unconsciousness.

nar-cot-ic (när kot´ik) *n.* A drug which dulls the senses, relieves pain, and induces a deep sleep; if abused, it can become habit-forming and cause convulsions or comas.

nard (närd) *n.* An aromatic medical, ointment that is obtained from the rhizomes of an East Asian plant.

nar-is (när´is) *n,. pl.* **nares** The nasal passage or opening; the nostril.

nar-rate (när´rāt) *v.* To tell a story or give a description in detail. **-tion** *n.*

nar-row (när´ō) *adj.* Slender or small in width; of less than standard width. **narrowly** *adj.* **narrowness** *n.*

narrow−mind-ed (när´ō mīn´did) *adj.* Lacking sympathy or tolerance.

nar-y (när´ē) *adj.* Never a; not a; not; not one.

na-sal (nā´zal) *adj.* Of or pertaining to the nose; producing a nasal speech sound.

na-sal-ize (nā´za līz´) *v.* To produce or speak in a nasal manner.

nas-tic (nas´tik) *adj., Bot.* Relating to the movement of a plant part, as a result of changing cellular pressure on the surface.

na-stur-tium (na ster´shim) *n.* A five-petaled garden plant usually having red, yellow, or orange flowers.

nas-ty (nas´tē) *adj.* Dirty, filthy, or indecent; unpleasant. **nastily** *adv.*

na-tal (nāt´al) *adj.* Pertaining to or associated with birth.

na-tant (nāt´ant) *adj.* Swimming or floating; in or on water.

na-ta-tion (nā tā´shan) *n.* The act or part of swimming. **natator** *n.* A swimmer.

na-ta-to-ri-al (nā´ta tōr´ē al) *adj.* Pertaining to, adapted for, or characterized by swimming.

na-ta-to-ri-um (nā´ta tōr´ē um) *n. pl.* **natatoriums** An indoor swimming pool.

na-tes (nā´tēz) *n. pl.* The buttocks.

na-tion (nā´shan) *n.* A group of people made up of one or more nationalities under one government. **national** *adj.*

na-tion-al (nash´a nal) *adj.* Pertaining or relating to a nation or people; maintained by a nation as an independent political unit; devoted totally to one's own nation, welfare, and interests; to be patriotic.

na-tion-al-i-ty (nash´a nal´i tē) *n.* The fact or condition of belonging to a nation.

na-tive (nā´tiv) *n.* A person born in a country or place. *adj.* Belonging to one by nature or birth.

na-tiv-ism (nā´ti viz´um) *n.* The policy of protecting and favoring native inhabitants from immigrants.

na-tiv-i-ty (*na* tiv´i tē) *n.* Birth, circumstances, or conditions; the birth of Christ.

nat-ro-lite (na´tro līt´) *n.* A hydrolous silicate of sodium and aluminum, that occurs occasionally in white, needle-shaped crystals.

na-tron (nā´tron) *n.* Native carbonate of soda found in solution found in some mineral springs and lakes, used in previous times as an embalming agent.

nat-ty (nat´ē) *adj.* Tidy; neatly dressed; of a neat appearance.

nat-u-ral (nach´ér al) *adj.* Produced or existing by nature; not artificial. *Mus.* A note that is not sharp or flat. **naturalness, naturally** *adv.*

na-ture (nā´chér) *n.* The universe and its phenomena; kind, sort, or type; one's own character or temperament.

naught (not) *n.* Nothing; the number 0; zero.

naugh-ty (no´tē) *adj.* Unruly; not proper; ill-behaved. **naughtily** *adv.*

nau-se-a (no´zē a) *n.* An upset stomach with a feeling that one needs to vomit. **nauseous** *adj.* **nauseate** *v.* **nauseatingly** *adv.*

nau-se-ate (na´ze āt´) *v.* To feel nausea or be sick to ones stomach; to be inclined to vomit.

nau-seous (na´shus) *adj.* Disgusting, nauseating; to cause a feeling of nausea. **nauseously** *adj.* **nauseousness** *n.*

nau-ti-cal (no´ti kal) *adj.* Pertaining to ships or seamanship. **nautically** *adv.*

na-val (nā´val) *adj.* Of or relating to ships; maritime.

na-vel (nā´vel) *n.* A small mark or scar on the abdomen where the umbilical cord was attached.

na-vic-u-lar (na vik´ū lér) *adj.* Having the shape of a boat. *n.* The bone of the ankle or wrist.

nav-i-gate (nav´i gāt´) *v.* To plan the course of a ship or aircraft; to steer a course. **navigator** *n.* **navigation.**

nav-i-ga-tion (nav´i gā´shan) *n.* The act or science of navigating ships; the science of determining the location, speed, destination, and direction of airplanes and other crafts and moving them from place to place.

na-vy (nā´vē) *n.* One of a nation's organizations for defense; a nation's fleet of ships; a very dark blue.

neap tide (nēp) *n.* A tide in the minimum range which occurs during the first and third quarter of the moon or twice a month.

near (nēr) *adv.* At, to, or within a short time or distance. *adj.* Closely or intimately related. **nearness** *n.*

near-by (nēr´bī´) *adj. & adv.* Close by; near at hand; adjacent.

near-sight-ed (nēr´sī´tid) *adj.* Able to see clearly at short distances only.

neat (nēt) *adj.* Tidy and clean; free from disorder and dirt. *Slang* Great, fine, or wonderful. **neatly** *adv.* **neatness** *n.*

neb-bish (neb´ish) *n.* A timid, ineffectual person.

Neb-ras-ka *n.* A state located in the central part of the United States; statehood March 1, 1867; state capital Lincoln.

neb-u-lize (neb´ū liz´) *v.* Reduce to fine spray .

neb-u-lous (neb´ū lus) *adj.* Confused or vague; hazy, cloudy, or misty.

nec-es-sar-y (nes´i ser´ē) *adj.* Unavoidable; required; essential; needed.

ne-ces-si-tate (ne ses´i tāt´) *v.* To make necessary; to oblige; to require; to force or be forced.

ne-ces-si-ty (ne ses´i tē) *n.* *pl.* -ies The condition of being necessary; the condition making a particular course of action necessary; a requirement; something inevitable.

neck (nek) *n.* The part of the body which connects the head and trunk; a narrow part or projection, as of land, a stringed instrument, or bottle. *v.* To caress and kiss.

ne-crol-o-gy (ne krol´o jē) *n.* *pl.* **ne-crol-o-gies** A death notice or list of the most recent dead.

nec-tar (nek´tér) *n.* A good-tasting beverage; a sweet fluid in various flowers, gathered by bees to help make honey.

nec-tar-ine (nek´ta rēn´) *n.* A variety of the common peach, whose fruit at maturity is smooth like a plum.

nee (nā) *n.* Born; the surname a woman was born with.

need (nēd) *n.* The lack of something desirable, useful, or necessary; misfortune or poverty; a necessity.

nee-dle (nēd´l) *n.* A slender, pointed steel implement which contains an eye through which thread is passed. *v.* To tease.

need-n't (nēd´ant) Need not.

ne-far-i-ous (ni fâr´ē us) *adj.* Extremely wicked; despicable.

ne-gate (ni gāt´) *v.* To nullify; to deny; to rule out. **negation** *n.*

neg-a-tive (neg´a tiv) *adj.* Expressing denial or disapproval; not positive. *n.* In photography, a negative photo. **negatively** *adj.* **negativeness** *n.*

neg-a-tron (neg´a tron´) *n.* An electron.

neglect (ni glekt´) *v.* To ignore; to pay no attention to; to fail to perform.

neg-li-gee (neg´li zhā´) *n.* A woman's loose fitting dressing gown.

neg-li-gence (neg´li jens) *n.* The act or condition of being negligent, an act of being habitually neglectful.

neg-li-gent (neg´li jent) *adj.* To neglect

what needs to be done; neglectful.

ne-go-ti-a-ble (ni gō´shē *a* bl) *adj.* Capable of being negotiated.

ne-go-ti-ate (ni gō´shē āt´) *v.* To confer with another person to reach an agreement; to accomplish successfully.

ne-gus (nēg*u*s) *n.* A beverage made of wine, hot water, sugar, lemon and nutmeg or other spices.

neigh (nā) *v.* To make the cry of a horse.

neigh-bor (nā´bėr) *n.* One who lives near another; fellowman. **neighboring** *adj.*

neigh-bor-hood (nā´bėr hed´) *n.* A section or small region that possesses a specific quality; the people living in such a region.

nei-ther (nē´thėr) *adj.* Not one or the other. *pron.* Not the one or the other. *conj.* Not either; also not.

nek-ton (nek´ton) *n.* Free-swimming aquatic animals in the middle depths of the sea, that are independent of wave patterns and cur-rents.

nem-a-to-cyst (nem´*a to* sist) *n.* A minute stinging apparatus of coelenterate animals, that is used in kill its prey.

ne-o-clas-sic (nē´ō klas´ik) *adj.* Pertaining to a renewal of a classic style, as literature.

neo-dym-i-um (nē´ō dim´ē *u*m) *n.* A metallic element of the rare-earth group, symbolized by Nd.

ne-ol-o-gism (nē ol´o jiz´*u*m) *n.* A new word or phrase; that is often disapproved of because of its newness.

ne-o-my-cin (nē´ō mī´sin) *n.* An antibiotic, developed from microorganisms, and used in a variety of local skin infections.

ne-on (nē´on) *n.* An inert gaseous element used in lighting fixtures, symbolized by Ne.

ne-o-nate (nē´o nāt´) *n.* A newborn child less than a month old.

ne-o-na-tol-o-gy *n.* The medical study of the first 60 days of a baby's life.

neo-phyte (nē´o fīt´) *n.* A novice; a beginner.

ne-o-plasm (nē´o plaz´*u*m) *n.* A tumor tissue serving no physiologic function.

ne-ot-e-ny (nē ot´e nē) *n.* The achievement of sexual maturity during the larval stage.

neph-e-line (nef´e li nit´) *n.* A heavy, dark-colored rock of volcanic origin.

neph-ew (nef´ū) *n.* The son of one's sister, brother, sister-in-law, or brother-in-law.

ne-phrid-i-um (ne frid´ē *u*m) *n. pl.* **nephridia** A primitive excretory organ or structure in annelids, mollusks, and other invertebrates, like the kidney and functioning in some cases in reproduction.

neph-rite (nef´rīt) *n.* A white to dark green variety of actinolite, a form of jade.

ne-phrit-ic *adj.* Relating to the kidneys; afflicted with an inflammation of the kidneys.

nep-o-tism (nep´o tiz´*u*m) *n.* The act of showing favoritism to relatives or friends in the work force. **nepotist** *n.*

nep-tu-ni-um (nep tö´nē *u*m) *n.* A radioactive metallic element, symbolized by Np.

ne-rit-ic (ne rit´ik) *adj.* Of or pertaining to the region of shallow water immediately adjoining the seacoast.

nerve (nerv) *n.* The bundles of fibers which convey sensation and originate motion through the body. *Slang* Impudent.

nerve cell *n.* Any of the cells constituting the cellular element of nerve tissue; neuron.

nerv-ous (ner´vus) *adj.* Affecting the nerves or the nervous system; agitated; worried. **nervously** *adv.* **-ness** *n.*

nervous breakdown *n.* Nervous exhaustion; emotional or mental weakness, that results from extended mental strain.

nervous system *n., Physiol.* The body system that coordinates, regulates, and controls the various internal functions and responses to stimuli.

ner-vure (nür´vür) *n.* The vein of a leaf.

nes-cience (nesh´ens) *n.* The lack of knowledge; ignorance

nest (nest) *n.* A place, shelter, or home built by a bird to hold its eggs and young.

nes-tle (nes´l) *v.* To settle snugly; to lie close to. **nestler** *n.*

nest-ling (nest´ling) *n.* A young bird still living in the nest.

net (net) *n.* A meshed fabric made of cords, ropes, threads, or other material knotted or woven together; the profit, weight, or price which remains after all additions, subtractions, or adjustments have been made.

neth-er (neth´ėr) *adj.* Situated below or beneath.

net-tle (net´l) *n.* A plant having toothed leaves covered with stinging hairs. *v.* To provoke; to sting.

net-work (net´werk´) *n.* A system of interlacing tracks, channels, or lines; an interconnected system; a group of broadcasting stations.

network server In *computer science*, a computer that stores and manages programs and data for other computers in the network.

neu-ral (ner´al) *adj.* Relating to a nerve or the nervous system.

neu-ral-gia (ne ral´ja) *n.* Pain that occurs along the course of a nerve.

neu-ri-lem-ma (nur´i lem´a) *n.* The delicate plasma membrane sheath of a nerve fiber.

neu-ri-tis (ne rī'tis) *n.* An inflammation of a nerve which causes pain, the loss of reflexes, and muscular decline.

neu-ro-cir-cu-la-to'-ry (nur'ō sur'kū la tōr'e) *adj.* Pertaining to the circulatory and nervous systems of the human body.

neu-ro-fi-bril (nūr'o fī'bril) *n., Anat.* The minute fibrils in the nerve cells.

neu-ro-gen-ic (nūr'o jen'ik) *adj., Med.* Beginning in a nerve or the nerve tissue.

neu-rog-li-a (nü rog'lē a) *n.* The delicate connective tissue that binds together and supports the necessary parts of the nervous tissue.

neu-rol-o-gy (ne rol'o jē) *n.* The medical and scientific study of the nervous system and its disorders. **neurological** *adj.* **neurologist** *n.*

neu-ro-ma (nü rō'ma) *n. pl.* **neuromas** *Pathol.* A tumor or mass that is growing from or comprised of nerve tissue.

neu-ron *or* **neu-rone (ner' on)** *n., Anat.* A granular cell nerve which is the main functional unit of the nervous system.

neu-rop-ter-an (nü rop'ter an) *n.* Insects having two pairs of net-like membranous wings.

neu-ro-sis (ne rō'sis) *n.* Any one of various functional disorders of the mind or emotions having no physical cause. **neurotic** *adj.* **neurotically** *adv.*

neu-ro-tox-ic (nūr'ō tok'sik) *adj.* Poisonous to nerves or to nerve tissue such as the brain.

neu-ter (nö'tēr) *adj.* Neither feminine nor masculine. *n.* A castrated animal.

neu-tral (nö'tral) *adj.* Not supporting either side of a debate, quarrel, or party; a color which does not contain a decided hue. *Chem.* Neither alkaline nor acid. **neutrality** *n.* **neutrally** *adv.*

neu-tral-ize (nö'tra līz') *v.* To make or declare neutral.

neu-tri-no (nö trē'nō) *n., Phys.* The uncharged elementary particle having a mass nearing zero.

neu-tron (nö'tron) *n.* An uncharged particle in the nucleus of an atom present in all atomic nuclei except the hydrogen nucleus.

Ne-va-da *n.* A state located in the western part of the United States; statehood October 31, 1864; state capital Carson City.

nev-er (nev'ēr) *adv.* Not ever; absolutely not.

nev-er-more (nev'ēr mōr') *adv.* Never again.

nev-er-nev-er (nev'ēr nev'ēr) *adj.* Imaginary.

nev-er-the-less (nev'ēr the les') *adv.* Nonetheless; however.

ne-vus (nē'vus) *n., pl.* **nevi** A congenital pigmented mark, or blemish; a birthmark.

new (nö) *adj.* Not used before; unaccustomed; unfamiliar. **newness** *n.*

New Deal *n.* The legislative and social programs of President F. D. Roosevelt designed for relief, economic recovery, and social security during the 1930's.

New Hampshire *n.* A state located in the northeastern part of the United States; statehood June 21, 1788; state capital Concord.

New Jersey *n.* A state located on the eastern coast of the United States; statehood December 18, 1787; state capital Trenton.

New Mexico *n.* A state located in the southwestern part of the United States; statehood January 6, 1912; state capital Santa Fe.

news (nöz) *n. pl.* Current happenings; matter considered newsworthy.

news-pa-per (nöz'pā'pēr) *n.* A weekly or daily publication which contains recent news and information.

New Testament *n.* The second part of the Christian Bible containing the Gospels, Acts, Epistles, and the Book of Revelation.

New Year's Day *n.* January 1st, the first day of the year.

New York *n.* A state located on the eastern coast of the United States; statehood July 26, 1788; state capital Albany.

next (nekst) *adj.* Immediately following or proceeding; nearest in space or position.

nex-us (nek'sus) *n. pl.* **nexus** A connected group; connection; connector; a linked series.

nib-ble (nib'l) *v.* To bite a little at a time; to take small bites. **nibble, nibbler** *n.*

nic-co-lite (nik'o līt') *n.* A pale copper-red mineral with a metallic luster that consists mainly of nickel arsenide.

nice (nīs) *adj.* Pleasing; enjoyable; polite and courteous; refined. **nicely** *adv.*

ni-ce-ty (nī'si tē) *n. pl.* **niceties** A delicate point; a fine destination. The characteristic of being nice; precision.

niche (nich) *n.* A recess or alcove in a wall, usually used for displays.

nick (nik) *n.* A small chip or cut on a surface; the final critical moment.

nick-el (nik'el) *n.* A hard, silver, metallic element used in alloys and symbolized by Ni; a United States coin worth five cents.

nick-name (nik'nām') *n.* The familiar form of a proper name, expressed in a shortened form. **nickname** *v.*

nic-o-tine *or* **nicotin (nik'o tēn')** *n.* A poisonous alkaloid found in tobacco and used in insecticides and medicine.

nic-ti-tate (nik´ti tāt´) v. To wink.

ni-dic-o-lous (nī dik´o lus) adj. Sharing the nest of another; raised for a time in a nest.

ni-dif-u-gous (nī dif´ū gus) adj. Indicating a bird that leaves a nest soon after it is hatched.

ni-dus (nīdus) n. A nest or breading place; a place where insects deposit their eggs.

niece (nēs) n. A daughter of one's sister or brother or one's sister-in-law or brother-in- law.

ni-el-lo (nē el´ō) n. The art of decorating silverplates with incised designs filled with a black metallic composition.

nig-gle (nig´l) v. To triffle; to find fault in a petty way; to work ineffectively.

nigh (nī) adv. Near in relationship, time, or space.

night (nīt) n. The time between dusk and dawn or the hours of darkness.

night blindness n. A condition of the eyes where the visual capacity is reduced in faint or dim light.

ni-gres-cent (nī gres´ent) adj. Blackish; a shade of black. **nigrescence** n.

nig-ri-tude (nig´ri tŏd´) n. Complete darkness.

ni-gro-sine (nī´gro sēn´) n. A blue-black dye that is used commercially as a dyeing agent.

ni-hil-ism (nī´i liz´um) n. An extreme form of skepticism where traditional values and beliefs are unfounded; the total disbelief in religion or moral obligations and principles.

nil (nil) v. Nothing.

nill (nil) v. To be unwilling.

nim-ble (nim´bl) adj. Marked by a quick, light movement; quick-witted. **nimbleness** n. **nimbly** adv.

nim-bo-stra-tus (nim´bō strātus) n. pl. **nimbostratus** Meteor. A low, dark gray cloud often producing rain.

nin-com-poop (nin´kom pōp´) n. A silly or stupid person.

nine (nīn) n. The cardinal number that is equal to 8+1. **nine** adj. & pron.

nin-ny (nin´ē) n. pl. **ninnies** A fool; a simpleton.

ni-non (nē non´) n. A smooth sheer fabric, as chiffon, used for curtains, and women's clothing.

ni-o-bi-um (nī ō´bē um) n. A gray, metallic element used in alloys, symbolized by Nb.

nip (nip) v. To pinch, bite, or grab something. n. A pinch, bite, or grab; a sharp, stinging feeling caused by cold temperatures. **nipper** n.

ni-pa (nē´pa) n. A fruit-bearing palm; a shelter made from the leaves of the nipa palm.

nip-ple (nip´l) n. The small projection of a mammary gland through which milk passes; an artificial teat usually made from a type of rubber which a bottle-fed baby nurses.

nip-py (nip´ē) adj. Inclined to be biting cold, as chilly weather.

Ni-sei (nē´sā´) n. A native American of Japanese ancestry.

ni-sus (nīsus) n., pl. **nisus** Endeavor; effort; striving; an impulse.

nit (nit) n. The egg of a louse or other similar parasitic insects.

nit-id (nit´id) adj. Bright; shining; lustrous.

nit–pick (nit´pik´) v. Slang To be overly critical with unimportant details.

ni-trate (nī´trāt) n. Chem. A salt or ester of nitric acid; potassium or sodium nitrate, used as a fertilizer.

ni-tro-gen (nī´tro jen) n. A nonmetallic gaseous element which is essential to life, symbolized by N.

nitrogen balance n. Equivalent of the intake and loss of nitrogen in an organism or in soil.

ni-tro-glyc-er-in (nī´tro glis´ér in) n. A highly flammable, explosive liquid, used to make dynamite and in medicine, to dilate blood vessels.

nit-wit (nit´wit´) n. A stupid person.

ni-val (nīval) adj. Pertaining to snow.

nix (niks) n. A water spirit usually small and either good or bad.

Nixon, Richard M. n. (1913-1994) The thirty-seventh president of the United States from 1969-1974; resigned August 9, 1974 due to Watergate scandal.

no (nō) adv. Used to express rejection, disagreement, or denial; not so; not at all.

no-bel-i-um (nō bē´lē um) n. A radioactive element, symbolized by No.

Nobel prize (nō bel´ prīz) n. An award given to people with achievements in literature, economics, medicine, and other fields, established by the last will and testament of Alfred Nobel.

no-bil-i-ty (nō bil´i tē) n. The state or quality of being noble; the rank or status of a noble.

no-ble (nō´bl) adj. Morally good; superior in character or nature; of high quality or class. n. A person of rank or noble birth. **nobleman** ,-**ness** n.

no-blesse (nō bles´) n. Nobility; person of noble rank collectively.

noblesse oblige n. The obligation of people of wealth and social position to behave with honor and generosity.

no-bod-y (nō´bod´ē) pron. Not anybody; no person.

no-cent (nō sent) adj. Harmful; hurtful, or injurious.

noc-tur-nal (nok ter´nal) adj. Pertaining to or occurring during the night; active at night and quiet during the daylight hours. **nocturnally** adv.

noc-u-ous (nok′ū us) adj. Harmful; injurious.

nod (nod) n. A quick downward motion of the head as one falls off to sleep; a downward motion of the head indicating acceptance or approval. v. To move the head down and then up again.

node (nōd) n. A swollen or thickened enlargement; a knot.

nod-ule (noj′ŏl) n. A little knot or lump.

no-dus (nō′dus) n. A difficult situation.

no-el (nō el′) n. A Christmas carol.

no-et-ic (nō et′ik) adj. Pertaining to the mind or intellect.

nog (nog) n. A wooden peg or block; a strong ale.

nog-gin (nog′in) n. A small mug or cup; a small quantity of a beverage.

no-how (nō′hou′) adv. In no way or manner; not at all.

noil (noil) n. A short fiber of wool, cotton, or silk often separated during combing and separately spun into yarn.

noise (noiz) n. A sound which is disagreeable or loud; in computer science, un-wanted data in an electronic signal.

noi-some (noi′som) adj. Offensive to the sense of smell; noxious; harmful.

nois-y (noi′zē) adj. Making an excessive amount of noise; abounding in or attended with noise.

no-mad (nō′mad) n. A member of a group of people who wander from place to place. **nomadic** adj. **nomadism** n.

nom de guerre (nom′ de gâr′) n. An assumed name under which one pursues a profession.

no-men-cla-tor (nōmen klā′tér) n. An inventor of names.

no-men-cla-ture (nō′men klā′chér) n. The set of names used to describe the elements of art, science, and other fields.

nom-i-nal (nom′i nal) adj. Of or relating to something that is in name or form only. **nominally** adv.

nom-i-nate (nom′i nāt′) v. To select a candidate for an elective office; to appoint or designate to a position. **nomination, nominator** n.

nom-i-nee (nom′i nē′) n. A person nominated for a position or office.

no-mism (nō′miz um) n. Conduct based on moral or religious beliefs.

no-mol-o-gy (nō mol′ojē) n. The science of the formulation of law; the science that deals directly with the laws of reason.

non- prefix Not.

non-a-bra-sive (non′a brā′siv) adj. Not causing wear by friction.

non-ab-sorb-ent (non′ab sor′bent) adj.

Unable to absorb liquids.

non-ac-cept-ance (non′ak sep′tans) n. Failure to accept.

non-ad-he-sive (non′ad hē′siv) adj. Not having the quality to adhere.

non-ad-min-is-tra-tive (non′ad min′i strā′ tiv) adj. Not pertaining to the executive staff of an organization.

non-a-ge-nar-i-an (non′a je nâr′ēan) adj. A person between the ages of 90 and 100 years.

non-a-gon (non′a gon′) n. A geometric figure with nine sides and nine angles.

non-al-co-hol-ic (non′al ko ho′lik) adj. Not containing alcohol.

non-ap-pear-ance (non′a pēr′ans) n. The failure to appear.

non-be-liev-er (non′bi lē′vér) n. One who does not believe; a person who does not believe in God.

non-cha-lant (non′sha länt′) adj. Giving an effect of casual unconcern. **nonchalance** n. **nonchalantly** adv.

non-col-le-gi-ate (non′ko lē′jit) adj. Not belonging to a college.

non-com-bus-ti-ble (non′kom bus′ti bl) adj. Not easily ignitable.

non-com-mu-ni-ca-ble (non′ka mū′i ka bl) adj. Not transmissible through personal contact, as a disease.

non com-pos men-tis (non kom′pos men′tis) adj. Mentally unbalanced; not of sound mind.

non-con-duc-tor (non′kon duk′tér) n. A substance which conducts with difficulty or in a very small degree, such as electricity, heat, or sound.

non-con-form-ist (non′kon for′mist) n. One who does not feel compelled to follow or accept traditions.

non-con-tagious (non′kon tā′jus) adj., Med. Of a disease, not transmissible by contact.

non-co-op-er-a-tion (non′kō op′e rā shon) n. Failure to cooperate with an individual, party, or organization.

non-cor-ro-sive (non′ko rō′sive) adj. Unable to corrode, as certain acids.

non-de-duct-i-ble (non′di duk′ti bl) adj. Unable to subtract.

non-de-script (non′di skript′) n. A person or something not easily classed or described.

non-de-struct-ive (non′di stuk′tiv) adj. Not causing destruction, or ruin.

non-dis-tinc-tive (non′di stingk′tiv) adj. Not distinctive.

none (nun) adj. Not any; not one.

non-ef-fec-tive (non′i fek′tiv) adj. Without the necessary power to cause or produce effect.

non-en-ti-ty (non en′ti tē) n. pl. **nonentities**. Nonexistence; something that does not exist.

non-es-sen-tial (non′isen′shal) adj. Not essential; not absolutely necessary. n.

An unnecessary person or thing.

non-ex-empt (nun´ig zempt´) adj. Not exempt from liability.

non-sense (non´sens) n. Something that seems senseless or foolish; something which is very unimportant.

non seq-ui-tur (non sek´wi tĕr) n. An inference that does not follow as the logical result of what has preceded it.

non-sex-ist adj. Not discriminating on the basis of gender.

noo-dle (nŏd´l) n. A flat strip of dried dough made with eggs and flour. Slang The head.

nook (nek) n. A corner, recess, or secluded place.

noon (nŏn) n. The middle of the day; 12: 00 o'clock.

noose (nŏs) n. A loop of rope secured by a slipknot, allowing it to decrease in size as the rope is pulled.

nor (nor) conj. Not either; or not.

norm (norm) n. A rule, model, or pattern typical for a particular group.

nor-mal (nor´mal) adj. Ordinary, average, usual; having average intelligence; standard. **normalcy**, **normality** n. **normally** adv.

north (north) n. The direction to a person's left while facing east.

North Carolina n. A state located in the southeastern part of the United States; statehood November 21, 1789; state capital Raleigh.

North Dakota n. A state located in the north central part of the United States; statehood November 2, 1889; state capital Bismarck.

nose (nŏz) n. The facial feature containing the nostrils; the sense of smell. v. To discover by smell.

no-sol-o-gy (nŏ sol´o jē) n. pl. nosologies A systematic list of diseases; the branch of medical science that deals with the grouping of diseases.

nos-tal-gia (no stal´ja) n. A yearning to return to the past. **nostalgic** adj.

nos-tril (nos´tril) n. The external openings of the nose.

nos-trum (nos´trum) n. A secret remedy for a medical condition.

nos-y or **nos-ey (nŏ´zē)** adj. Snoopy; inquisitive; prying.

not (not) adv. In no manner; used to express refusal or denial.

no-ta-ble (nŏ´ta bl) adj. Remarkable, distinguished. n. A person or thing which is notable. v. To acknowledge and certify as a notary public. -ly adv.

notary public n. A person who is legally authorized as a public officer to witness and certify documents.

no-ta-tion (nŏ tā´shan) n. A process or system of figures or symbols used in specialized fields to represent quantities, numbers, or values.

notch (noch) n. A v-shaped indentation or cut. **notch** v.

note (nŏt) n. A record or message in short form. Mus. A tone or written character.

not-ed (nŏ´tid) adj. Famous; well-known.

note-wor-thy (nŏt´wûr´thē) adj. Significant; worthy of observation or attention. **noteworthily** adv.

noth-ing (nuth´ing) n. Not anything; no part or portion. adv. In no way; not at all.

no-tice (nŏ´tis) n. An announcement; a notification. v. To give notice; to become aware of. **noticeable** adj.

no-ti-fi-ca-tion (nŏ´ti fĭ kā´shan) n. The act of notifying; a notice in words of writing; anything which gives information.

no-ti-fy (nŏ´ti fī´) v. To give notice of; to announce. **notifier**, **notification** n.

no-tion (nŏ´shan) n. An opinion; a general concept; an idea. pl. Small useful articles, such as thread or buttons.

no-tion-al (nŏ´sha nal) adj. Referring to or expressing ideas, concepts.

no-to-ri-ous (nŏ tŏr´ē us) adj. Having a widely known and usually bad reputation.

not-with-stand-ing (not´with stan´ding) In spite of. adv. Nevertheless; anyway. conj. Although.

nou-gat (nŏ´gat) n. A confection made of sugar , honey, or corn syrup, contains nuts and fruit pieces.

noun (noun) n. A word which names a person, place, or thing.

nour-ish (ner´ish) v. To furnish with the nutriment and other substances needed for growth and life; to support. **nourishing** adj. **nourishment** n.

nour-ish-ment (nûr´ish ment) n. Food, the act of nourishing.

nou-veau riche (nŏ´vŏ rēsh´) n. A person who has recently become rich.

no-va (nŏ´va) n. pl. -vae or -vas A star which flares up and fades away after a few years or months.

nov-el (nov´el) n. An inventive narrative dealing with human experiences; a book. **novelist** n.

nov-el-ty (nov´el tē) n. pl. -ies Something unusual or new.

No-vem-ber (nŏ vem´bĕr) n. The 11th month of the calendar year, having 30 days.

nov-ice (nov´is) n. A person who is new and unfamiliar with an activity or business.

now (nou) adv. At the present time; immediately.

now-a-days (nou´a dāz´) adv. At the present time.

no-way (nŏ´wā´) adv. Not at all.

no-where (nŏ´hwâr´) adv. Not in or at any place.

nox-ious (nok´shus) adj. Harmful;

obnoxious; corrupt.

noz-zle (noz´l) *n.* A projecting spout or vent of something.

nu-ance (nö´äns) *n.* A gradation or variation by which a color passes from the lightest possible shade to its darkest shade.

nub (nub) *n.* A knob; a small piece or lump.

nub-bin (nub´in) *n.* A small piece.

nu-bile (nö´bil) *adj.* Suitable or ready for marriage; of the right age for marriage.

nu-bi-lous (nö´bi lus) *adj.* Cloudy; foggy; vague.

nu-cha (nö´ka) *n. pl.* **nuchae** The nape of the neck.

nu-cle-ar (nö´klē ėr) *adj.* Pertaining to and resembling a nucleus; relating to atomic energy.

nuclear force *n.* The powerful and explosive interaction between the nucleons which holds the atomic nuclei together.

nu-cle-ase (nö´klē ās´) *n.* An enzyme which breaks down nucleic acids.

nu-cle-ate (nö´klē āt) *v.* To form into a nucleus; to gather round or form a nucleus. *adj.* Having a nucleus.

nu-cle-on (nö´klē on´) *n.*, *Phys.* An elementary particle of the atomic nucleus, a proton or neutron.

nu-cle-on-ics *n. pl.* The science dealing with the practical application of nuclear physics.

nu-cle-us (nö´klē us) *n.* The main element around which all other elements group; the central core of an atom.

nude (nöd) *adj.* Unclothed; naked. **nudity**, **nudist** *n.*

nu-di-cau-lous (nö´di ko´lus) *adj.*, *Bot.* having leafless stems.

nu-ga-to-ry (nö´ga tōr´ē) *adj.* Trifling; worthless; inoperative.

nudge (nuj) *v.* To poke or push gently.

nug-get (nug´it) *n.* A lump, as of precious metal.

nui-sance (nö´sans) *n.* A source of annoyance or inconvenience.

null (nul) *adj.* Invalid; having no value or consequence. **nullification** *n.*

nul-li-fy (nul´i fī) *v.* To counteract.

numb (num) *adj.* Lacking physical sensation; paralyzed or stunned. **numb** *v.* **numbness** *n.*

num-ber (num´bėr) *n.* A word or symbol which is used in counting or which indicates how many or which one in a series.

nu-men (nö´min) *n. pl.* **numina** A divine spiritual force or influence, one thought to dwell within an object.

nu-mer-al (nö´mėr al) *n.* A symbol, figure, letter, word, or a group of these which represents a number.

nu-mer-a-tion (nö˝me rā´shan) *n.* The act of numbering or calculating.

nu-mer-a-tor (nö´me rā´tėr) *n.* The term in mathematics indicating how many parts are to be taken; the number in a fraction which appears above the line.

nu-mer-ous (nö´mėr us) *adj.* Consisting or made up of many units, things, or individuals.

num-mu-lar (num´ūlėr) *adj.* Characterized by circular lesions.

nun (nun) *n.* A woman who has joined a religious group and has taken vows to give up worldly goods and never to marry.

nup-tial (nup´shal) *adj.* Of or pertaining to a wedding. **nuptials** *n. pl.* A wedding.

nurse (ners) *n.* A person who is specially trained to care for disabled or sick persons. **nurse** *v.* To feed a baby from a mother's breast; to provide care to a sick or disabled person.

nur-ture (ner´chėr) *n.* The upbringing, care, or training of a child. **nurture** *v.* **nurturer** *n.*

nut (nut) *n.* A hard-shelled fruit or seed which contains an inner, often edible kernel. *Slang* A person who does crazy or silly things.

nu-ta-tion (nö tā´shan) *n.* The involuntary nodding of the head.

nu-tri-ent (nö´trē ent) *n.* A substance which nourishes. **nutrient** *adj.*

nu-tri-tion (nö trish´an) *n.* The process by which a living being takes in food and uses it to live and grow. **nutritive**, **nutritional** *adj.* **nutritionally** *adv.* **nutritionist** *n.*

nu-tri-tious (nö trish´us) *adj.* Containing or serving as nourishment.

nuts (nuts) *adj.*, *Slang* Foolish, crazy.

nuz-zle (nuz´l) *v.* To gently rub against something with the nose; to cuddle.

nyc-ta-lo-pi-a (nik´ta lō´pē a) *n.* A condition of the eyes where the sight is good during day or bright light but abnormally poor at night or in dim light; night blind-ness.

ny-lon (nī´lon) *n.* A strong, elastic material; yarn or fabric made from nylon. *pl.* **nylons** Stockings made of nylon.

nymph (nimf) *n.* Nature goddesses who lived in woods, rivers, and trees; various immature insects, especially the larva which undergoes incomplete metamorphosis.

O

O, o (ō) The 15th letter of the English alphabet.

O (ō) *n.* A word used before a name when addressing that person; an interjection.

oaf (ōf) *n.* A stupid or clumsy person.

oar (ōr) *n.* A long pole, flat at one end, used in rowing a boat.

oasis (ō ā'sis) *n., pl.* **oases** A fertile section in the desert which contains water; anything that can provide refuge.

oat (ōt) *n.* A cultivated cereal grass whose grain or seed is used as food for humans as well as animals.

oath (ōth) *n.* A solemn promise in the name of God or on a Bible that a person will speak only the truth.

oat-meal (ōt'mēl') *n.* A cooked cereal food made from rolled oats.

ob-du-rate (ob'de rit) *adj.* Stubborn; hard-hearted; not giving in.

o-be-di-ent (ō bē'dē ent) *adj.* Obeying or willing to do what one is told.

ob-e-lisk (ob'e lisk) *n.* A tall, four-sided stone pillar which slopes from a pointed top.

o-bese (ō bēs') *adj.* Very fat. **obesity** *n.*

o-bey (ō bā') *v.* To carry out instructions; to be guided or controlled; to follow directions. **obeyer** *n.*

o-bit-u-ar-y (ō bich'ö er'ē) *n. pl.* **-ies** A published announcement that a person has died, often containing a short biography of the person's life.

ob-ject (ob jekt') *v.* To voice disapproval; to protest. *n.* Something that is visible or can be touched. A word in a sentence which explains who or what is acted upon.

ob-jec-tion (ob jek'shan) *n.* A feeling of opposition or disagreement, etc.; the reason for a disagreement.

ob-jec-tive (ob jek'tiv) *adj.* Pertaining to or dealing with material objects rather than mental concepts. *n.* Something that one works toward, a goal; a purpose. **objectivity** *n.*

ob-la-tion (o blā'shan) *n.* A religious offering or the act of sacrifice; that which is offered.

ob-li-ga-tion (ob'li gā'shan) *n.* A promise or feeling of duty; something one must do because one's conscience or the law demands it; a debt which must be repaid.

o-blige (o blīj') *v.* To constrain; to put in one's debt by a service or favor; to do a favor. **obliger** *n.* **obligingly** *adv.*

o-blique (o blēk') *adj.* Inclined; not level or straight up and down; slanting; indirect. **obliqueness** *n.* **obliquity** *n.*

o-blit-er-ate (o blit'e rāt') *v.* To blot out or eliminate completely; to wipe out. **obliteration** *n.* **obliterator** *n.*

o-bliv-i-on (o bliv'ē an) *n.* The condition of being utterly forgotten; the act of forgetting.

ob-liv-i-ous (o bliv'ē us) *adj.* Not aware or conscious of what is happening; unmindful. **obliviously** *adv.*

ob-long (ob'long') *adj.* Rectangular; longer in one direction than the other;

normally, the horizontal dimension; the greater in length. **oblong** *n.*

ob-nox-ious (ob nok'shus) *adj.* Very unpleasant; repugnant.

o-boe (ō'bō) *n.* A double reed, tube-shaped woodwind instrument. **oboist** *n.*

ob-scene (ob sēn') *adj.* Indecent; disgusting. **obscenity** *n.*

ob-scure (ob skūr') *adj.* Remote; not clear; faint. *v.* To make dim; to conceal by covering. **obscurity** *n.*

ob-ser-va-tion (ob'zer vā'shan) *n.* The act of observing something; that which is observed; a judgment or opinion. **observational** *adj.*

ob-ser-va-to-ry (ob zer'vatör'ē) *n. pl.* **-ies** A building or station furnished with instruments for studying the natural phenomenon; a high tower affording a panoramic view.

ob-serve (ob zerv') *v.* To pay attention; to watch. **observable** *adj.* **observant** *adj.* **observably** *adv.* **observer** *n.*

ob-sess (ob ses') *v.* To preoccupy the mind with an idea or emotion; to be abnormally preoccupied. **-ion** *n.*

ob-so-lete (ob'so lēt') *adj.* No longer in use; out-of-date; no longer current. **obsolescence** *n.* **obsolescent** *adj.*

ob-sta-cle (ob'sta kl) *n.* An obstruction; anything which opposes or stands in the way of.

ob-ste-tri-cian (ob'sti trish an) *n.* A physician who specializes in the care of a woman during pregnancy and childbirth.

ob-stet-rics (ob ste'triks) *n.* The branch of medicine which deals with pregnancy and childbirth.

ob-sti-nate (ob'sti nit) *adj.* Stubbornly set to an opinion or course of action; difficult to control or manage; hardheaded. **obstinacy** *n.* **-ately** *adv.*

ob-strep-er-ous (ob strep'ėr us) *adj.* Noisy, unruly, or boisterous in resistance to advice or control. **obstreperously** *adv.* **-ness** *n.*

ob-struct (ob strukt') *v.* To block, hinder or impede. **obstructor** *n.* **-tion** *n.*

ob-tain (ob tān') *v.* To acquire or gain possession of. **obtainable** *adj.*

ob-trude (ob trōd') *v.* To thrust forward without request or warrant; to call attention to oneself.

ob-tuse (ob tōs') *adj.* Lacking acuteness of feeling; insensitive; not distinct or clear to the senses, as pain or sound. *Bot.* Rounded or blunt at the end, as a petal or leaf.

ob-vi-ate (ob'vē āt') *v.* To counter or prevent by effective measures; to provide for.

ob-vi-ous (ob'vē us) *adj.* Easily seen, discovered, or understood.

oc-ca-sion (o kā'zhan) *n.* The time an event occurs; the event itself; a

oc-ca-sion-al (*o kā´zha nal*) *adj.* Appearing or occurring irregularly or now and then; intended, made, or suitable for a certain occasion; incidental.

oc-cip-i-tal bone (*ok sip´i tal*) *n., Anat.* The bone which forms the back of the skull.

oc-cult (*o kult´*) *adj.* Concealed. *n.* The action or influence of supernatural agencies or secret knowledge of them.

oc-cu-pan-cy (*ok´kū pan sē*) *n.* The state or act of being occupied; the act of holding in possession; the time or term during which something is occupied.

oc-cu-pa-tion (*ok´ū pā´shan*) *n.* A job, profession, or vocation; a foreign military force which controls an area.

oc-cu-py (*ok´ū pī´*) *v.* To take and retain possession of; to live in. **occupier** *n.*

oc-cur (*o ker´*) *v.* To suggest; to have something come to mind; to happen.

o-cean (*o´shan*) *n.* An immense body of salt water which covers 3/4 of the earth's surface; one of the oceans.

o'clock (*o klok´*) *adv.* Of, or according to the clock.

oc-ta-gon (*ok´ta gon´*) *n.* A polygon with eight angles and eight sides. **octagonal octagonally** *adv.*

oc-tave (*ok´tiv*) *n., Music* A tone on the eighth degree above or below another tone.

Oc-to-ber (*ok to´bèr*) *n.* The 10th month of the calendar year, having 31 days.

oc-to-ge-nar-i-an (*ok´to je när´ēan*) *n.* A person between 80 and 90 years.

oc-to-pus (*ok´to pus*) *n. pl.* **-es** *or* **-pi** A cephalopod with a sac-like body and eight tentacles containing double rows of suckers.

oc-u-lar (*ok´ū lèr*) *adj.* Of or relating to the eye; perceived or done by the eye.

OD *n., Slang* An overdose of a drug; one who has taken an overdose. *v.* To overdose; to die from an overdose.

odd (*od*) *adj.* Unusual; strange; singular; left over; not even. **oddly** *adv.*

odds (*odz*) *n.* An equalizing advantage given to a weaker opponent; a ratio between the probability against and the probability for something happening or being true.

ode (*ōd*) *n.* A lyric poem usually honoring a person or event.

o-dom-e-ter (*ō dom´i tèr*) *n.* A device in a vehicle used to measure distance traveled. **odometry** *n.*

o-dor (*ō´dèr*) *n.* A smell; a sensation which occurs when the sense of smell is stimulated.

od-ys-sey (*od´i sē*) *n.* A long voyage marked by many changes of fortune; a spiritual quest.

of (*uv*) *prep.* Proceeding; composed of; relating to; at a distance from.

off (*of*) *adv.* From a position or place; no longer connected or on. *adj.* Canceled. *prep.* Away from.

of-fend (*o fend´*) *v.* To make angry; to arouse resentment; to break a law; to insult. **offender** *n.*

of-fense (*o fens´*) *n.* A violation of a duty, rule, or propriety; the act of causing dis-pleasure; the act of assaulting or attacking; in football and other sports, the team having possession of the ball.

of-fen-sive (*o fen´siv*) *adj.* Disagreeable; causing resentment; insulting.

of-fer (*o´fèr*) *v.* To present for acceptance or rejection; to present as an act of worship; to make available; to present in order to satisfy a requirement.

of-fice (*o´fis*) *n.* A place where business or professional duties are conducted; an important job, duty, or position.

of-fi-cial (*o fish´al*) *adj.* Something derived from proper authority. *n.* One who holds a position or office; a person who referees a game such as football, basketball, or soccer. **officially** *adv.*

of-fi-ci-ate (*o fish´ē at´*) *v.* To carry out the duties and functions of a position or office.

of-ten (*o´fen*) *adv.* Frequently; many times.

oh (*ō*) Used to express surprise, fear, or pain.

O-hi-o *n.* A state in the north central section of the United States; statehood March 1, 1803; state capital Columbus.

ohm (*ōm*) *n.* A unit of electrical resistance equal to the resistance of a conductor in which one volt produces a current of one ampere.

oil (*oil*) *n.* Any of various substances, usually thick, which can be burned or easily melted; a lubricant. *v.* To lubricate.

oint-ment (*oint´ment*) *n.* An oily substance used on the skin as an aid to healing or to soften the skin.

Ok-la-ho-ma *n.* A state in the south central part of the United States; statehood November 16, 1907; state capital Oklahoma City.

ok-tane (*ok´tän*) *n.* Any of several hydrocarbon compounds which occur in petroleum.

old (*ōld*) *adj.* Having lived or existed for a long time; of a certain age.

old–fash-ioned (*ōld´fash´ond*) *adj.* Pertaining to or characteristic of former times or old customs; not modern or up-to-date.

Old Glory *n.* The flag of the United States of America.

Old Testament *n.* The first of two parts of the Christian Bible, containing the history of the Hebrews, the laws of Moses, writings of the prophets, and the Scriptures of Judaism.

ol-fac-tory (ol fak´to rē) *adj.* Pertaining to the sense of smell.

oli-gar-chy (ol´i gär´kē) *n., pl.* **-ies** A government controlled by a small group for corrupt and selfish purposes; the group exercising such control.

ol-ive (ol´iv) *n.* A small oval fruit from an evergreen tree with leathery leaves and yellow flowers, valuable as a source of oil.

om-buds-man (om´bödz man´) *n.* **-men** A government official appointed to report and receive grievances against the government.

om-e-let *or* **om-e-lette** (om´e lit) *n.* A dish made from eggs and other items, such as bacon, cheese, and ham, and cooked until set.

o-men (ō´men) *n.* A phenomenon which is thought of as a sign of something to come, whether good or bad.

om-i-nous (om´i nus) *adj.* Foreshadowed by an omen or by a presentiment of evil; threatening.

o-mis-sion (ō mish´an) *n.* The state or act of being omitted; anything neglected or left out.

o-mit (ō mit´) *v.* To neglect; to leave out; to overlook.

om-ni-bus (om´ni bus´) *n.* A public vehicle designed to carry a large number of people; a bus. *adj.* Covering a complete collection of objects or cases.

om-nip-o-tent (om nip´o tent) *adj.* Having unlimited or infinite power or authority.

om-nis-cient (om nish´ent) *adj.* Knowing all things; having universal or complete knowledge.

om-niv-or-ous (om niv´ér us) *adj.* Feeding on both vegetable and animal substances; absorbing everything. **omnivorously** *adv.*

on (on) *prep.* Positioned upon; indicating proximity; indicating direction toward; with respect to. **on** *adv.* In a position of covering; forward.

once (wuns) *adv.* A single time; at any one time. *conj.* As soon as.

on-col-o-gy (ong kol´o jē) *n.* The study of tumors. **oncological, oncologic** *adj.*

one (wun) *adj.* Single; undivided. *n.* A single person; a unit; the first cardinal number (1).

oneself *pron.* One's own self.

one-sid-ed (wun´sī´did) *adj.* Partial to one side; unjust. **one-sidedness** *n.*

on-line (on´līn´) *adj., computer science* Controlled directly by a computer.

on-ly (ōn´lē) *adj.* Sole; for one purpose alone. *adv.* Without anyone or anything else. *conj.* Except; but.

on-to (on´tö) *prep.* To a position or place; aware of.

o-nus (ō´nus) *n.* A burden; a responsibility or duty which is difficult or unpleasant; the blame.

on-ward (on´wérd) *adv.* Moving forward in time or space. **onwards** *adj.*

on-yx (on´iks) *n.* A gemstone; a chalcedony in layers of different colors.

oo-dles (öd´lz) *n., pl. Slang* A great or large quantity.

ooze (öz) *n.* A soft deposit of slimy mud on the bottom of a body of water; muddy or marshy ground; a bog. *v.* To flow or leak slowly; to disappear little by little.

o-pal (ō´pal) *n.* A translucent mineral composed of silicon, often marked with an iridescent play of colors.

o-paque (ō pāk´) *adj.* Not transparent; dull; obscure. **opacity** *n.* **-ness** *n.*

o-pen (ō´pen) *adj.* Having no barrier; not covered, sealed, locked, or fastened. **open** *n.* A contest for both amateurs and professionals. **open** *v.* To begin or start. **openness** *n.* **openly** *adv.*

open-and-shut (ō´pen an shut´) *adj.* Easily settled; simple to decide.

op-er-a (ō´pèr a) *n.* Drama having music as a dominant factor, an orchestral accompaniment, acting, and scenery.

op-er-ate (op´e rāt´) *v.* To function, act, or work effectively; to perform an operation, as surgery. **operative** *adj.*

op-er-a-tion (op´e rā´shan) *n.* The process of operating; the system or method of operating; a series of acts to effect a certain purpose; a process; a procedure performed on the human body with surgical instruments to restore health; various mathematical or logical processes.

oph-thal-mol-o-gy (of´thal mol´o jē) *n.* A branch of medical science dealing with diseases of the eye, its structure, and functions.

o-pin-ion (o pin´yan) *n.* A judgment held with confidence; a conclusion held without positive knowledge.

o-pi-um (ō´pē um) *n.* A bitter, highly addictive drug; a narcotic.

op-po-nent (o pō´nent) *n.* An adversary; one who opposes another.

op-por-tune (op´ér tön´) *adj.* Occurring at the right or appropriate time. **opportunist** *n.* **opportunely** *adv.*

op-por-tu-ni-ty (op ér tö´ni tē) *n., pl.* **opportunities** A favorable opportunity; a chance for advancement.

op-pose (o pōz´) *v.* To be in direct contention with; to resist; to be against. **opposable** *adj.* **opposition** *n.*

op-po-site (op´o zot) *adj.* Situated or placed on opposing sides.

op-press (o pres´) *v.* To worry or trouble the mind; to weigh down; to burden as if to enslave. **oppression** *n.*

op-ti-cal (op´ti kal) *adj.* Pertaining to

sight; constructed or designed to assist vision. **optically** *adv.*

op-ti-cian (op tish´an) *n.* A person who makes eyeglasses and other optical articles.

op-ti-mism (op´ti miz´um) *n.* A doctrine which emphasizes that everything is for the best.

op-ti-mum (op´ti mum) *n., pl.* **optima** The degree or condition producing the most favorable result. *adj.* Conducive to the best result.

op-tion (op´shan) *n.* The act of choosing or the power of choice; a choice.

op-tion-al *adj.* Left to one's decision; elective; not required.

op-tom-e-try (op tom´i trē) *n.* The occupation or profession of examining the eyes and prescribing corrective lenses.

op-u-lence (op´ū lens) *n.* Wealth in abundance; affluence.

or (or) *conj.* A word used to connect the second of two choices or possibilities, indicating uncertainty.

-or *suffix* Indicating a person or thing which does something.

or-a-cle (or´a kl) *n.* A seat of worship where ancient Romans and Greeks consulted the gods for answers; a person of unquestioned wisdom.

o-ral (ōr´al) *adj.* Spoken or uttered through the mouth; taken or administered through the mouth. **orally** *adv.*

oral contraceptive *n.* A pill containing hormones, taken monthly to prevent pregnancy.

o-rate (ō rāt´) *v.* To speak in an elevated manner.

orb (orb) *n.* A globe or sphere.

or-bit (or´bit) *n.* The path of a celestial body or a manmade object. *v.* To revolve or move in an orbit; to circle.

or-chard (or´chėrd) *n.* Land that is devoted to the growing of fruit trees.

or-ches-tra (or´ki stra) *n.* A group of musicians performing together on various instruments. **orchestral** *adj.*

or-dain (or dān´) *v.* To appoint as a minister, priest, or rabbi by a special ceremony; to decree.

or-deal (or dēl´) *n.* A painful or severe test of character or endurance.

or-der (or´dėr) *n.* A condition where there is a logical arrangement or disposition of things; sequence or succession; method; an instruction for a person to follow; a request for certain objects. *v.* To command; to demand.

orderly (or´dėr lē) *adj.* Neat, tidy.

or-di-nance (or´di nans) *n.* A command, rule, or order; a law issued by a municipal body.

or-di-nar-y (or´di ner´ē) *adj.* Normal; having no exceptional quality; common; average; plain.

ore (ōr) *n.* A natural underground substance, as a mineral or rock, from which valuable matter is extracted.

o-reg-a-no (o reg´a nō) *n.* A bushy perennial herb of the mint family, used as a seasoning for food.

Or-e-gon (or´e gon) *n.* A state in the northwestern part of the United States; statehood February 14, 1859; state capital Salem.

or-gan-dy *or* **or-gan-die** (or´gan dē) *n.* A translucent, stiff fabric of cotton or silk.

or-gan-ic (or gan´ik) *adj.* Effecting or pertaining to the organs of an animal or plant. **organically** *adv.*

or-gan-i-za-tion (or´ga ni zā´shan) *n.* The state of being organized or the act of organizing; a group of people united for a particular purpose.

or-gan-ize (or´ga nīz´) *v.* To assemble or arrange with an orderly manner; to arrange by planning.

or-gasm (or´gaz um) *n. Physiol.* Intensive emotional excitement; the culmination of a sexual act.

o-ri-ent (ōr´ē ent´) *v.* To determine the bearings or right direction with respect to another source.

or-i-fice (or´i fis) *n.* An opening through which something may pass; a mouth.

or-i-gin (er´i jin) *n.* The cause or beginning of something; the source; a beginning place.

o-rig-i-nal (o rij´i nal) *adj.* Belonging to the first or beginning. *n.* A new idea produced by one's own imagination; the first of a kind. **originality** *n.*

or-na-ment (or´na ment) *n.* A decoration. *v.* To adorn or beautify. **ornamental** *adj.* **ornamentation** *n.*

or-nate (or nāt´) *adj.* Excessively ornamental; elaborate; showy, as a style of writing.

or-phan (or´fan) *n.* A child whose parents are deceased. **orphanage** *n.*

or-ris (or´is) *n.* Any of several species having a fragrant root and used in medicine, perfumes, and cosmetics.

or-tho-don-tics (or´tho don´tiks) *n.* The branch of dentistry dealing with the correction and prevention of irregularities of the teeth.

or-tho-dox (or´tho doks´) *adj.* Following established traditions and beliefs, especially in religion.

or-tho-pe-dics *or* **or-tho-pae-dics** (or´thōpe´diks) *n.* A branch of surgery that deals with correcting skeletal deformities.

os-cil-late (os´i lāt) *v.* To swing back and forth with regular motion, as a pendulum. **oscillation** *n.* **oscillator** *n.*

os-mi-um (oz´mē um) *n.* A hard but brittle metallic element symbolized as OS.

os-mo-sis (oz mō´sis) *n.* The tendency of fluids separated by a semipermeable membrane to pass through it and become mixed and equal in strength.

os-ten-ta-tion (os´ten tā´shən) *n.* The act of displaying pretentiously in order to excite.

osteo *n., comb. form* Bone; pertaining to the bones.

os-te-op-a-thy (os´tē op´a thē) *n.* A medical practice based on the theory that diseases are due chiefly to abnormalities of the body, which can be restored by manipulation of the parts by therapeutic measures.

os-teo-po-ro-sis *n.* A disorder causing gradual deterioration of bone tissue, usually occurring in older women.

os-tra-cize (os´tra sīz) *v.* To exile or exclude from a group; to shut out.

oth-er (uth´ér) *adj.* Additional; alternate; different from what is implied or specified. **other** *pron.* A different person or thing.

oth-er-wise (uth´ér wīz´) *adv.* Under different conditions of circumstances.

ot-ter (ot´ér) *n., pl.* **otter** *or* **otters** Web-footed aquatic mammals, related to the weasel.

ouch (ouch) *n. & interj.* An exclamation to express sudden pain.

ought (ot) *v.* Used to show or express a moral duty or obligation; to be advisable or correct.

ounce (ouns) *n.* A unit of weight which equals 1/16 of a pound.

our (our) *adj.* Of or relating to us ourselves. **our** *pron.* The possessive case of the pronoun *we*.

oust (oust) *v.* To eject; to remove with force.

out (out) *adv.* Away from the center or inside. *adj.* Away. *n.* A means of escape. *prep.* Through; forward from.

out-break (out´brāk´) *n.* A sudden outburst; an occurrence.

out-cast (out´kast´) *n.* A person who is excluded; a homeless person.

out-come (out´kum´) *n.* A consequence or result.

out-let (out´let) *n.* An exit.

out-line (out´līn´) *n.* A rough draft showing the main features of something. **outline** *v.*

out-put (out´pet´) *n.* Production or yield during a given time.

out-stand-ing (out´stan´ding) *adj.* Excellent; prominent; unsettled, as a bill owed; projecting.

o-val (ō´val) *adj.* Having the shape of an egg; an ellipse.

o-va-ry (ō´va rē) *n., pl.* -ies One of the pair of female reproductive glands.

o-va-tion (o vā´shən) *n.* An enthusiastic display of approval for a person or a performance; applause.

ov-en (uv´en) *n.* An enclosed chamber used for baking, drying, or heating.

o-ver (ō´vèr) *prep.* Above; across; upon. *adv.* Covering completely; thoroughly; again; repetition. *adj.* Higher; upper. *prefix* Excessive, as overcrowded.

over-act (ō´vèr akt´) *v.* To act in an exaggerated way.

over-all (ō´vèr ol´) *adj.* Including or covering everything; from one side or end to another; generally. *n.* Pants with a bib and shoulder straps.

over-con-fi-dence (ō´vèr kon´fi dens) *n.* Extreme or excessive confidence.

over-do (ō´vèr dō´) *v.* To do anything excessively; to overcook.

over-dose (ō´vèr dōs´) *n.* To take an excessive dose of medication, especially narcotics.

over-due (ō´vèr dō´) *adj.* Past the time of return or payment.

overload *n.* In *computer science,* a condition that can cause a crash, due to an attempt to transfer more data than memory can hold or transferring data faster than the CPU can process it.

over-ride (ō´vèr rīd´) *v.* To disregard; to take precedence over; to declare null and void.

over-sight (ō´vèr sīt´) *n.* A mistake made inadvertently.

overt (ō vert´) *adj.* Open to view.

overwrite *v.* In *computer science,* to save information to storage already occupied, obliterating the old data.

o-void (ō´void) *adj.* Having the shape of an egg.

ov-u-late (ō´vū lāt´) *n.* To discharge or produce eggs from an ovary.

o-vum (ō´vum) *n. pl.* **ova** The female reproductive cell.

owe (ō) *v.* To be in debt for a certain amount; to have a moral obligation.

owl (oul) *n.* A predatory nocturnal bird, having large eyes, a short, hooked bill, and long powerful claws. **owlish** *adj.*

own (ōn) *adj.* Belonging to oneself. **own** *v.* To possess; to confess; to admit; to have, as property. **owner** *n.*

ox (oks) *n., pl.* **oxen** A bovine animal used domestically in much the same way as a horse; an adult castrated bull.

ox-ide (ok´sīd) *n.* A compound of oxygen and another elements.

ox-y-gen (ok´si jen) *n.* A colorless, odorless, tasteless gaseous element essential to life, symbolized by O.

oys-ter (oi´stèr) *n.* An edible marine mollusk having an irregularly shaped shell.

oyster bed *n.* A breading area or place for oysters.

o-zone (ō´zōn) *n.* A pale-blue gas formed of oxygen with an odor like chlorine, formed by an electrical discharge in the air. *Slang* Fresh air.

P, p (pē) The 16th letter of the English alphabet.

pab-u-lom (pan´ū lum) n. Type of food such as an absorbable solution.

pa-ca (pä´ka) n. A large brown with white spots, rodent from Central and South America.

pace (pās) n. A person's step in walking or the length of a person's step; stride; the gait of a horse in which the legs on the same side are moved at the same time. **pacer** n.

pace-mak-er (pās´mā´kėr) n. The person who sets the pace for another in a race; a surgically implanted electronic instrument used to stabilize or stimulate the heartbeat.

pa-chi-si (pa chē´zē) n. Another name for the game Parcheesi; ancient board game played with dice.

pach-y-derm (pak´i dürm´) n. A group of animals including the elephant, the rhinoceros, and hippo; animals having thick skins. **pachydermal** adj.

Pa-cif-ic (pa sif´ik) n. The largest ocean on the earth, extending from North & South America westward to Asia and Australia.

pa-cif-i-ca-tion (pas´i fi kā´shan) n. The state of something being pacified or calmed.

pac-i-fism (pas´i fiz˝um) n. The policy dealing with the establishment of universal peace between all nations; opposition to violence or war as a means of settling problems or disputes.

pac-i-fy (pas´i fī) v. To quiet or soothe anger or distress; to calm.

pack (pak) n. A bundle; a group or number of things tied or wrapped up; a full set of associated or like things, such as a pack of cards; a group of wolves or wild dogs that hunt together. v. To put things together in a trunk, box, or suitcase; to put away for storage. **packing** Material used to make a tight connection, as in steam pipes.

package (pak´ij) n. Something tied up, wrapped or bound together.

pack-et (pak´it) n. A type of parcel or package that is small in size and can be used to carry or hold small items.

pact (pakt) n. An agreement between nations, groups, or people.

pad (pad) n. Anything stuffed with soft material and used to protect against blows; a cushion; a drawing or writing tablet of paper gummed together at one edge; the cushion-like part of the foot on some animals, as the dog. Slang A person's home. v. To stuff, line, or protect with soft material; to extend or lengthen something by inserting unnecessary matter; to travel by foot in a soft and nearly inaudible way.

pad-ding (pad ing) n. The material, as cotton, or synthetic fibers, which is used for the purpose of protecting something.

pad-dle (pad´l) n. A broad-bladed implement usually made from wood, used to steer and propel a small boat; a tool used for mixing, turning, or stirring; a small wooden, rounded racket used in table tennis. **paddle** v.

pad-dy (pad´ē) n. Land usually in China, which is flooded with water and used for the purpose of growing rice.

pad-lock (pad´lok) n. A detachable lock, having a pivoted u-shaped hasp which can be inserted through a ring and then locked. **padlock** v.

pa-dre (pä´drä) n. A title used in Spain and Italy for a priest.

pa-dro-ne (pa drō´nē) n. The person who is master of a vessel; the owner or operator of a business; an innkeeper.

pad-u-a-soy (paj´ō a soi´) n. A corded, rich silk fabric.

pae-an (pē´an) n. A song of praise or joy.

pae-do-gen-e-sis (pē´do jen´i sis) n. The reproduction by immature animals.

pae-on (pē´on) n. A type of metrical foot that is made up of four syllables, one long and three short.

pa-gan (pā´gan) n. A person who does not acknowledge God in any religion; a heathen. **pagan** adj. **paganism** n.

page (pāj) n. A person hired to deliver messages or run errands; one side of the leaf of a book or letter. In computer science, a unit of memory used by the computer to manipulate data in storage; a single sheet of output from the printer. **page** v. To call or summon a person.

pag-eant (paj´ent) n. An elaborate exhibition or spectacular parade for public celebration; anything having a showy appearance.

pag-eant-ry (paj´en trē) n. A type of exhibition that is showy; a spectacle.

pag-i-nate (paj´i nāt´) v. To number or to place numbers on a page showing the order in which they should be placed in order to read.

pa-go-da (pa gō´da) n. A sacred Buddhist tower, built as a memorial or shrine.

paid v. Past tense of pay.

pail (pāl) n. A cylindrical container usually having a handle; a bucket.

pail-ful (pāl´fūl´) adj. The total amount that a pail is able to hold.

pail-lasse (pal yas´) n. A type of mattress that is filled with wood shavings and can be used under another mattress for support.

pail-lon (pä yän´) n. A type of metallic foil which is used for the purpose of enamel work.

pain (pān) n. The unpleasant feeling

resulting from injury or disease; any distress or suffering of the mind; sorrow. *v.* To cause or experience pain.

pain-kill-er (pān kil´ẽr) *n.* Medication that relieves pain. **painkilling** *adj.*

pains-tak-ing (pānz´tā´king) *adj.* To be given to taking pains; done with carefulness and diligence.

paint (pānt) *n.* A mixture of colors or pigments which are spread on a surface as protection or as a decorative coating; makeup for the face, as rouge. *v.* To apply paint to a surface; the practice of using paint to express oneself on canvas. **painter** *n.* **painting** *n.*

paint-ing (pān´ting) *n.* The piece of art that is made by a painter and can be hung on one's wall for decoration.

pair (pâr) *n. pl.* **pairs** *or* **pair** Two things which are similar and used together; something made of two parts which are used together; two persons or animals which live or work together.

pais-ley (pāz´lē) *adj.* To have colors that are bright and patterned into a design which is typical of paisley.

pa-ja-mas (pạ jäm´az) *n. pl.* A loose fitting garment for sleeping, consisting of a jacket and pants.

pal (pal) *n.* A good friend.

pal-ace (pal´is) *n.* The royal residence of a sovereign, as of a king; a mansion.

pal-a-din (pal´ạ din) *n.* One who is an eminent hero.

pa-laes-tra (pạ les´trạ) *n.* A type of school of ancient Greece that was used to teach athletics.

pal-at-a-ble (pal´ạ tạ bl) *adj.* Pleasant to the taste; agreeable to one's feelings or mind.

pal-a-tal (pal´ạ tal) *adj.* To be pertaining or to be related to the palate.

pal-ate (pal´it) *n.* The muscular tissue at the roof of a person's mouth, opposite the tongue; sense of taste.

pa-la-tial (pạ lā´shal) *adj.* Pertaining to a palace. **palatialness** *n.*

pal-a-tine (pal´ạ tīn˝) *adj.* To be related to the palate of one's mouth. *n.* A lord invested with royal privileges within his territory.

pa-lav-er (pạ lav´ẽr) *n.* A type of discussion; superfluous talk.

pale (pāl) *n.* The pointed stake of a fence; a picket; an area that is enclosed within bounds. *adj.* Having a whitish or lighter than normal complexion; pallid; weak.

pa-le-eth-nol-o-gy (pā˝lē eth nol´o jē) *n.* A part or branch of ethnology which deals with the earliest human races known.

pa-le-o-bot-a-ny (pā˝lē ō bot´ạ nē) *n.* A study of plants which are discovered in their fossilized state or condition.

pa-le-og-ra-phy (pā˝lē og´rạ fē) *n.* The study of ancient writings. **paleog-**

raphically *adv.* **paleographer** *n.*

pa-le-o-lith (pā˝lē ọ lith) *n.* A stone implement that is from the Paleolithic period.

pa-le-on-tol-o-gy (pā˝lē ọn tol´ọ jē) *n.* The study and the science which deals with ancient life and how they lived.

pa-le-o-zo-ol-o-gy (pā˝lē ō zō ol´ọ jē) *n.* The science or the study of the fossil animals.

pal-ette (pal´it) *n.* A thin oval board with a hole for the thumb, on which an artist lays and mixes colors.

pal-frey (pol´frē) *n.* A type of small horse that is used by a lady.

pal-imp-sest (pal´imp sest˝) *n.* A piece of writing paper from which something has been erased and another writing has been written over, leaving the first faintly visible.

pal-in-drome (pal´in drōm˝) *n.* A word, number, or sentence which reads the same backward or forward, such as toot or 1991.

pal-ing (pā´ling) *n.* A type of fence which is made from pales or pickets.

pal-in-gen-e-sis (pal´in jen´i sis) *n.* The regeneration or the rebirth of someone or something. **palingenetically** *adv.*

pal-i-node (pal´i nōd˝) *n.* A poem that contains something from a previous piece; a recantation. **palinodist** *n.*

pal-i-sade (pal´i sād˝) *n.* A fence made of stakes for protection. **palisade** *v.*

pall (pol) *n.* A heavy cloth used to cover a bier or coffin; a very gloomy atmosphere.

pal-la-di-um (pạ lā´dē um) *n.* A silvery-white metallic element symbolized by Pd.

pal-let (pal´it) *n.* A wooden platform on which material for freight shipments can be moved or stored.

pal-li-al (pal´ē al) *adj.* To be related to or pertaining to pallium.

pal-li-ate (pal´ē āt˝) *v.* To conceal something with an excuse.

pal-lid (pal´id) *adj.* Deficient in color; lacking sparkle.

pal-lor (pal´ẽr) *n.* Lacking color.

palm (päm) *n.* The inner area of the hand between the fingers and wrist; any of a large group of tropical evergreen trees, having an unbranched trunk with a top or crown of fan-like leaves. *v.* To hide something small in or about the hand.

pal-mar (pal´mẽr) *adj.* To be located or situated in the palm of one's hand.

pal-met-to (pal met´ō) *n.* A type of palm tree that has fan-shaped leaves. *Palmetto* The nickname for the state of South Carolina.

palm-is-try (pä´mi strē) *n.* The practice of fortune telling by the configurations of the palms of the hands.

palmitic acid *n*. A type of fatty acid that is used for the making of soap.

pal-mi-tin (pal´mi tin) *n*. A type of colorless compound that is found in palm oil and can be used in the making of soap.

palm-y (pä´mē) *adj*. To be prosperous.

pal-my-ra (pal mī´ra) *n*. A type of palm that is used for the making of stiff brushes.

pal-o-min-o (pal´o mē´nō) *n*. A type of horse that has a coat which is golden in color and a mane that is flaxen.

pal-pa-ble (pal´pa bl) *adj*. To be capable of being touched or felt by someone or something; easily detected; obvious; plain. **palpably** *adv*. **palpability** *n*.

pal-pate (pal´pāt) *v*. To check something through the use of touch, such as a doctor would examine a patient.

pal-pe-bral (pal´pe bral) *adj*. To be located near the eyelid of someone or something.

pal-pus (pal´pus) *n*. A type of organ found on certain insects and is used for the purpose of sensing.

pal-sy (pol´zē) *n*. *pl*. **-ies** Paralysis; the loss of ability to control one's movements. **palsy** *v*.

pal-ter (pol´tẽ) *v*. To haggle over something, such as the price of a good.

pal-try (pol´trē) *adj*. To be worthless or inferior. **paltriness** *n*.

pa-lu-dal (pa löd´al) *adj*. To be related to or referring to a marsh.

pal-u-drine (pal´ū drēn˘) *n*. A type of drug which is used for the purpose of treating malaria in people.

pam-pas (pam´paz) *n*. The grassy plains that can be found in South America.

pam-per (pam´pẽr) *v*. To treat with extreme care.

pam-pe-ro (päm pâr´ō) *n*. The strong and cold wind that blows in the pampas of South America and coming from the Andes mountain chain.

pam-phlet (pam´flit) *n*. A brief publication which is not permanently bound.

pan (pan) *n*. A type of vessel that is usually made of metal and is used for the cooking of foods over heat.

pan-a-ce-a (pan´a sē´a) *n*. A remedy for all diseases, difficulties, or ills; a cure-all.

pa-nache (pa nash´) *n*. A type of showy plume that is worn on a cap.

pan-cake (pan´kāk´) *n*. A thin, flat cake made from batter and fried on a griddle, served with butter, powdered sugar, syrup, and other toppings.

pan-chro-mat-ic (pan´krō mat´ik) *adj*. To be sensitive to the light of all of the colors.

pan-cra-ti-um (pan krā´shē a) *n*. A type of gymnastic context that was held in ancient Greece and contained a combination of wrestling and boxing.

pan-cre-as (pan´krē as) *n*., *Anat*. A large, irregularly shaped gland situated behind the stomach which releases digestive enzymes and produces insulin. **pancreatic** *adj*.

pan-cre-at-ec-to-my (pan´krēt omē) *n*. The surgical removal of any part or all of the pancreas.

pan-de-mo-ni-um (pan´de mō´nē um) *n*. A place marked with disorder and wild confusion; disorder; confusion.

pan-der *or* **panderer** (pan´dẽr) *n*. A go-between in sexual affairs; a pimp; one who profits from the base desires or passions of others. *v*. To act as a panderer for someone.

pan-dit (pan´dĕt) *n*. A man who is respected highly.

pan-dow-dy (pan dou´dē) *n*. A type of deep-dish pie that has been made with apples.

pan-e-gry-ic (pan´i jir´ik) *n*. A type of writing about a person that praises them.

pan-el (pan´el) *n*. A flat, rectangular piece of material, often wood, which forms a part of a surface; a group of people selected to participate in a discussion group or to serve on a jury. **panelist** *n*. **panel** *v*.

pan-eling (pan´el ing) *n*. A type of wood that has been made into panels and is used to cover walls for decoration.

pan-e-tel-la (pan´i tel´a) *n*. A type of cigar that has one end that is slender.

pang (pang) *n*. A sudden and sharp pain that does not last for very long.

pan-go-lin (pang gō´lin) *n*. A type of scaled mammal that has a pointed tail and eats ants, found in Africa.

pan-han-dle (pan´han´dl) *n*. A projecting strip of land that is not a peninsula, such as the state of Texas.

pan-ic (pan´ik) *n*. A sudden unreasonable fear which overpowers. *v*. To cause or to experience panic. **panicky** *adj*.

pan-ic–strick-en (pan´ik strik˘en) *adj*. To be overcome by great fear.

panne (pan) *n*. A type of light-weight velvet.

pan-nier (pan´yẽr) *n*. One of a pair of large baskets which are carried on either side of an animal or over a person's back.

pan-ni-kin (pan´i kin) *n*. A small cup or pan.

pan-o-cha (pa nō´cha) *n*. A type of sugar that has a course grade and can be found in Mexico.

pan-o-ply (pan´o plē) *n*. *pl*. **-lies** The complete equipment of a warrior, including his armor and weapons.

pan-o-ram-a (pan´o ram´a) *n*. An unlimited or complete view in all directions of what is visible.

pan-sy (pan´zē) *n.* A garden plant with flowers bearing blossoms in a variety of colors.

pant (pant) *v.* To breathe in rapid or short gasps; to yearn. *n.* A short breath.

pan-ta-lets (pan´ta lets´) *n.* A type of underpants that are long and have a fringed bottom.

pan-tech-ni-con *n.* A type of storehouse that is used to store furniture.

pan-the-ism (pan´thē iz´um) *n.* The belief that the laws and forces of nature are all manifestations of God. **pantheist** *n.* **pantheistic** *adj.*

pan-the-on (pan´thē on´) *n.* A type of building or temple that was built in order to honor all the gods.

pan-ther (pan´thèr) *n.* A black leopard in its unspotted form. **pantheress** *n.*

pan-ther-ess (pan´thèr is) *n.* The female panther.

pan-to-mime (pan´to mīm´) *n.* Communication done solely by means of facial and body gestures. *v.* To express or act in pantomime.

pan-to-then-ic ac-id (pan´to then´ik as´id) *n.* A type of vitamin belonging to the B complex that promotes cell growth.

pan-try (pan´trē) *n.* A closet or room for the storage of food, dishes, and other kitchen items.

pants (pants) *n.* Trousers; underpants.

pan-zer (pan´zér) *n.* A type of German tank.

pap (pap) *n.* A soft food for invalids or babies.

pa-pa-cy (pā´pa sē) *n.* The dignity or jurisdiction of a pope; a pope's term in office.

pa-pa-in (pa pā´in) *n.* A type of enzyme that is found in the juice of the unripe fruit of the papaya tree.

pa-pa-ya (pa pa´ya) *n.* A type of tropical tree that will yield melon-like fruits.

pa-per (pā´pèr) *n.* A substance made of pulp from wood and rags, formed into sheets for printing, wrapping and writing.

pa-per-back (pā´pèr bak´) *n.* A book with its cover made of paper.

pa-pier–ma-che (pā´pèr ma shā) *n.* A material consisting of paper mixed with glue or paste which can be molded when wet and becomes hard when dry.

pap-il-lo-ma (pap´i lō´ma) *n.* A type of benign tumor that exists on mucous membranes or the skin.

pa-poose (pa pös´) *n.* A North American Indian child or baby.

pa-pri-ka (pa prē´ka) *n.* A dark red seasoning powder made by grinding red peppers.

Pap test *n.* A test in which a smear of bodily secretion from the uterus is examined for the early detection of cancer.

pap-ule (pap´ūl) *n.* A type of elevation in the skin that does not contain pus, but is inflammatory. **papular** *adj.*

pa-py-rus (pa pī´rus) *n.* A reed-like plant used as paper in early Egypt, to write upon.

par-a-bi-o-sis (par´a bī ō´sis) *n.* The joining or fusion of two separate organisms, such as Siamese twins.

par-a-ble (par´a bl) *n.* A short, fictitious story which illustrates a moral lesson.

par-a-chute (par´a shöt´) *n.* A folding umbrella-shaped apparatus of light fabric used to make a safe landing after a free fall from an airplane. **-ist** *n.*

pa-rade (pa rād´) *n.* An organized public procession; a march. **parader** *n.*

par-a-di-chlor-ben-zene (par´adīklör´ ben´zēn) *n.* A white compound used as an insecticide.

par-a-dise (par´a dīs´) *n.* A state or place of beauty, bliss or delight; heaven. **paradisiac** *adj.* **paradisiacal** *adj.*

par-a-dox (par´a doks´) *n.* A statement which seems opposed to common sense or contradicts itself, but is perhaps true. **paradical** *adj.*

par-aes-the-sia (par´is thē´zha) *n.* An abnormal sensation, as the prickling of the skin.

par-af-fin (par´a fin) *n.* A white, waxy sub-stance derived from petroleum and used to make lubricants, candles, and sealing materials. **paraffin** *v.*

par-a-gen-e-sis (par´a jen´i sis) *n.* A type of formation of minerals where they are too close together and impact on one another's development. **paragenetic** *n.* **paragenetically** *adv.*

par-ago-ge (par´a gō´jē) *n.* An addition of a letter or syllable to the end of a word that is incorrect.

par-a-gon (par´a gon´) *n.* A pattern or model of excellence or perfection.

par-a-graph (par´a graf´) *n.* A section of a composition dealing with a single idea, containing one or more sentences with the first line usually indented.

par-al-de-hyde (pa ral´de hīd´) *n.* A type of colorless liquid that can be used in medicine as a hypnotic.

par-al-lel (par´a lel´) *adj.* Moving in the same direction but separated by a distance, as railroad tracks. *n.* A parallel curve, line, or surface; a comparison; one of the imaginary lines which circle the earth paralleling the equator and mark the latitude. In computer science, descriptive of operations that occur simultaneously. **parallelism** *n.*

parallel bars *n.* One pair of bars that are horizontal and supported by uprights.

par-al-lel-o-gram (par´a lel´o gram´) *n.* A four-sided figure having parallel opposite sides which are equal.

parallel interface *n.* In *computer science*, a multichannel interface that allows the transfer of a full computer word at one time.

parallel port *v.* In *computer science*, a connection on the computer for communicating with a peripheral device, such as a printer.

pa-ral-o-gism (pa ral´o jiz˝um) *n.* A type of argument that is fallacious.

pa-ral-y-sis (pa ral´i sis) *n., pl.* **paralyses** Complete or partial loss of the ability to feel sensation or to move.

par-a-lyze (par´a līz˝) *v.* To cause to be inoperative or powerless.

par-a-mat-ta (par´a mat´a) *n.* A type of light twilled fabric that can be used for the making of dresses.

par-a-med-ic (par´a med´ik) *n.* A person trained to give emergency medical treatment until a doctor is available.

par-am-ne-sia (par´am nē˝zha) *n.* The illusion of remembering things that have not yet been experienced.

parameter *n.* In *computer science*, a limit or characteristic, as of a program or operating system. *Math.* A term in a mathematical expression.

par-a-mount (par´a mount´) *adj.* Superior to all others in rank, importance, and power.

par-a-mour (par´a mür) *n.* An unlawful lover.

pa-rang (pä´räng) *n.* A type of knife that is large and heavy.

par-a-noi-a (par´a noi´a) *n.* Mental insanity marked by systematic delusions of persecution or grandeur.

par-a-noid (par´a noid˝) *adj.* To be marked by paranoia.

par-a-nor-mal (par´a nor´mal) *adj.* To be supernatural in character.

par-a-pet (par´a pit) *n.* A type of covering or wall that is used to protect the soldiers from the attacks of the enemy in front of them.

par-a-pher-na-lia (par´a fèr nāl´ya) *n.* Personal effects or belongings; the apparatus or articles used in some activities; equipment.

par-a-phrase (par´a fräz˝) *v.* To put something written or spoken into different words while retaining the same meaning.

par-a-phras-tic (par´a fras´tik) *adj.* To be making or forming a paraphrase.

par-a-ple-gi-a (par´a plē´jē a) *n.* The paralysis of the lower trunk and of both legs.

par-a-site (par´a sīt´) *n. Biol.* An organism which lives, grows, feeds, and takes shelter in or on another organism; a person depending entirely on another without providing something in return.

par-a-sit-i-cide (par´a sit´i sīd˝) *n.* A

type of agent that is used to destroy parasites.

par-a-si-tize (par´a si tīz˝) *v.* To live upon another object as a parasite.

par-a-sol (par´a sol´) *n.* A small umbrella used as protection from the sun.

par-a-thi-on (par´a thī´on) *n.* A type of insecticide that is very poisonous.

parathyroid gland *n.* The four glands that are located in or near the thyroid gland and are used for the control of calcium in the blood.

par-a-troops (par´a trö˝ps) *n.* Troops which are equipped and trained to parachute behind enemy lines.

par-a-ty-phoid (par´a tī´foid) *n.* A type of very infectious bacterial disease that has symptoms which are like those of typhoid fever.

par-boil (pär´boil´) *v.* To precook something in boiling water.

par-cel (pär´sel) *n.* A wrapped package; a bundle; a portion or plat of land.

parch (pärch) *v.* To become very dry from intense heat; to become dry from thirst or the lack of water.

parch-ment (pärch´ment) *n.* Goatskin or sheepskin prepared with a pumice stone and used as a material for writing or drawing.

par-don (pär´don) *v.* To forgive someone for an offense; in law, to allow a convicted person freedom from the penalties of an office or crime. **pardonable** *adj.* **pardonably** *adv.*

pare (pâr) *v.* To cut away or remove the outer surface gradually. **parer** *n.*

par-e-go-ric (par´e gor´ik) *n.* A medication used to relieve stomach pains.

par-ent (pâr´ent) *n.* A mother or father; a forefather; an ancestor; a source.

par-ent-age (pâr´en tij) *n.* The origin or birth of someone.

par-en-ter-al (pa ren´tèr al) *adj.* To be introduced into the body by means other than the digestive tract.

pa-ren-the-sis (pa ren´thi sis) *n., pl.* **parentheses** One of a pair of curved lines ( ) used to enclose a qualifying or explanatory remark.

pa-re-sis (pa rē´sis) *n.* A type of paralysis that is incomplete and affecting only movement. **paretic** *adj.*

par-fleche (pär´flesh) *n.* The hide of an animal that has been dried upon a frame, such as the buffalo.

par-get (pär´jit) *v.* To cover something with plaster.

pa-ri-ah (pa rī´a) *n.* A person who is thought of as an outcast.

pa-ri-e-tal (pa rī´i tal) *adj.* Referring to the two bones of the skull which form the side and the top.

par-ing (pâr´ing) *n.* The action of cutting or of paring a piece of a vegetable off, such as with a potato.

par-ish (par´ish) *n*. In association with the Roman Catholic Church, the district under the charge of a priest; the members of a parish.

par-i-ty (par´i tē) *n*. Equal in amount, character, or status; the fact of having borne children.

park (pärk) *n*. A tract of land used for recreation. **park** *v*. To leave something temporarily in a parking garage or lot, as a car.

par-ka (pär´ka) *n*. A cloth jacket with an attached hood.

par-lia-ment (pär´li ment) *n*. The assembly which constitutes the law making body of various countries, as the United Kingdom.

par-lia-men-ta-ry *adj*. To be relating or pertaining to a parliament.

par-lor (pär´lėr) *n*. A room for entertaining visitors or guests; a business offering a personal service, as beauty parlor, ice cream parlor, or funeral parlor.

par-lous *adj*. To be dangerous; clever.

pa-ro-chi-al (pa rō´kē al) *adj*. Belonging to a local parish; having to do with a parish.

pa-ro-chi-al-ism (pa rō´kē a liz˝um) *n*. A condition or state of being parochial.

parochial school *n*. A type of school which is maintained by the parish.

par-o-dy (par´o dē) *n., pl*. **-ies** A composition, song, or poem which mimics another in a ridiculous way.

pa-rol (pa rōl´) *n*. An oral statement.

pa-role (pa rōl´) *n*. The conditional release of a prisoner before his sentence expires. **parole** *adj*.

parotid gland *n*. A type of salivary gland that is located in front of each ear.

pa-rot-i-di-tis (pa rot´i dī´tis) *n*. The swelling and inflammation of the parotid glands.

par-ox-ysm (par´ok siz´um) *n*. A violent attack or outburst; a spasm.

par-quet (pär kā) *n*. A main floor of the theater which will extend back from the orchestra pit.

parquet circle *n*. Those seats which are located at the rear of the main floor in a theater.

parr (pär) *n*. A type of salmon when it is young and has not yet entered the salt waters.

par-ri-cide (par´i sīd´) *n*. One who murders his mother or father; the crime of murdering parents. **parricidal** *adj*.

par-rot (par´ot) *n*. A brightly colored, semitropical bird with a strong, hooked bill. **parrot** *v*. To imitate or repeat.

par-rot-fish (par´ot fish´) *n*. A type of fish that is tropical and has bright colors.

par-ry (par´ē) *v*. To avoid something;

to turn aside. **parry** *n*.

parse (pärs) *v*. To identify the parts of speech in a sentence and to indicate their relationship to each other.

par-si-mo-ny (pär´si mō´nē) *n*. Extreme reluctance to use one's resources or to spend money. **parsimonious** *adj*. **parsimoniously** *adv*.

pars-ley (pärs´lē) *n*. An herb with curly leaves which is used for seasoning and garnishing.

par-son (pär´son) *n*. A pastor or clergyman.

parsonage (pär´so nij) *n*. The home provided by a church for its parson.

part (pärt) *n*. A segment, portion, or division of a whole; a component for a machine; the role of a character, as in a play; the line which forms where the hair is parted by combing or brushing. **part** *v*. To leave or go away from; to be separated into pieces; to give up control or possession.

par-take (pär tāk´) *v*. To have a share or part; to take; to take a part in something.

par-tial (pär´shal) *adj*. Incomplete; inclined to favor one side more than the other. **partiality** *n*. **partially** *adv*.

par-tic-i-pate (pär tis´i pāt´) *v*. To join in or share; to take part. **participant** *n*. **participation** *n*. **participator** *n*.

par-ti-cle (pär´ti kl) *n*. A very small piece of solid matter. *Gram*. A group of words, such as articles, prepositions, and conjunctions which convey very little meaning but help to connect, specify, or limit the meanings of other words.

par-tic-u-lar (pėr tik´ū lėr) *adj*. Having to do with a specific person, group, thing, or category; noteworthy; precise.

part-ing (pär´ting) *n*. A division; a separation; the place where a division or separation occurs. *adj*. Done, given, or said on departing.

par-ti-tion (pär tish´an) *n*. A separation or division. *v*. To divide. In computer science, as on a disk for file management or for processing a database sort.

part-ner (pärt´nėr) *n*. One who shares something with another.

part-ner-ship (pärt´nėr ship) *n*. Two or more persons who run a business together and share in the profits and losses.

par-tridge (pär´trij) *n*. A plump or stout-bodied game bird.

par-ty (pär´tē) *n. pl*. **-ies** A group of persons who gather for pleasure or entertainment; a group of persons associated together for a common purpose; a group which unites to promote or maintain a policy, a cause, or other purposes, as a political group; *n*. in law, a person or group of people involved in a legal proceeding.

pass (pas) *v.* To proceed; to move; to transfer; to go away or come to an end; to get through a course, trial or test; to approve; to vote for; to give as an opinion or judgment; to hit or throw a ball to another player. **pass** *n.* A ticket or note that allows a person to come and go freely. **come to pass** To happen. **pass away** To die or cease to live. **pass over** To leave out, to ignore.

pas-sage (pas'ij) *n.* The act of going, proceeding, or passing; the enactment by a legislature of a bill into law; a small portion or part of a whole book or speech; something, as a path or channel, through, over or along which something else may pass.

pas-sen-ger (pas'en jẽr) *n.* One who travels in a vehicle, car, plane, boat, or other conveyance.

pas-sion (pash'an) *n.* A powerful feeling; lust; sexual desire; an outburst of strong feeling; violence or anger. **Passion** The suffering of Christ which followed the Last Supper to the time of his death. **passionless** *adj.* **passionate** *adj.*

pas-sive (pas'iv) *adj.* Not working, acting, or operating; inactive; acted upon, influenced, or affected by something external. *Gram.* Designating the form of a verb which indicates the subject is receiving the action. **passively** *adv* **passivity** *n.* **-ness** *n.*

Pass-o-ver (pas'ō'vẽr) *n.* The Jewish holiday which commemorates the Exodus from Egypt.

pass-port (pas'pōrt) *n.* An official permission issued to a person allowing him to travel out of this country and to return; a document of identification.

past (past) *adj.* Having to do with or existing at a former time. **past** *n.* Before the present time; a person's history or background. **past** *adv.* To go by. **past** *prep.* After; beyond in time; beyond the power, reach, or influence.

paste (pāst) *n.* A mixture usually made from water and flour, used to stick things together; dough used in making pastry; a brilliant glass used in imitating precious stones. **paste** *v.*

pas-tel (pa stel') *n.* A crayon made of ground pigments; a drawing made with crayons of this kind. **pastel** *adj.* Pale and light in color or shade.

pas-teur-i-za-tion (pas'che rĩ'zẽr) *n.* The process of killing disease-producing microorganisms by heating the liquid to a high temperature for a period of time.

pas-time (pas'tīm') *n.* Spending spare time in a pleasant way; a diversion.

pas-tor (pas'tẽr) *n.* A Christian clergyman in charge of a church or congregation.

past participle *n.* A participle used with reference to actions and conditions in the past.

pas-try (pā'strē) *n.* Food made with dough or having a crust made of dough, as pies, tarts, or other desserts.

pas-ture (pas'chẽr) *n.* An area for grazing of domestic animals. **pastured** *v.* **pasturing** *v.* **pasturage** *n.*

pat (pat) *v.* To tap lightly with something flat. *n.* A soft, caressing stroke.

patch (pach) *n.* A piece of fabric used to repair a weakened or torn area in a garment; a piece of cloth with an insignia which represents an accomplishment. *v.* To repair or put together hastily. **patchy** *adj.* **patchable** *adj.*

pat-ent (pat'ent) *n.* A governmental protection assuring an inventor the exclusive right of manufacturing, using, exploiting, and selling an invention. **patent** *adj.* Evident; obvious. **patentee,** **patency** *n.* **patently** *adv.*

pa-ter-nal (pa ter'nal) *adj.* Relating to or characteristic of a father; inherited from a father. **paternally** *adv.*

path (path) *n.* A track or course; a route; a course of action or life. In *computer science*, the course followed by the computer in seeking programs and files.

pa-thet-ic (pa thet'ik) *adj.* A rousing pity, tenderness, or sympathy.

pa-thol-o-gy (pa thol'o jē) *n.* The science that deals with facts about diseases, their nature and causes. **pathologic** *adj.* **pathological** *adj.* **pathologist** *n.*

pa-thos (pā'thos) *n.* A quality in a person that evokes sadness or pity.

pa-tience (pā'shens) *n.* The quality, state, or fact of being patient; the ability to be patient.

pa-tient (pā'shent) *adj.* Demonstrating uncomplaining endurance under distress. *n.* A person under medical care.

pa-tri-arch (pā'trē ärk') *n.* The leader of a tribe or family who rules by paternal right; a very old and revered man. **patriarchal** *adj.* **patriarchy** *n.*

pa-tri-ot (pā'trē ot) *n.* A person who loves and defends his country. **patriotic** *adj.* **patriotically** *adv.* **patriotism** *n.*

pa-trol (pa trōl') *n.* Walking around an area for the purpose of maintaining or observing security; a person or group carrying out this action. **patrol** *v.*

pa-tron (pā'tron) *n.* A person who fosters, protects, or supports some person, enterprise, or thing; a regular customer. **patroness** *n.*

pat-sy (pat'sē) *n., pl.* **patsies** *Slang* A person who is taken advantage of.

pat-tern (pat'ẽrn) *n.* Anything designed or shaped to serve as a guide in making something else; a sample. **pattern** *v.* To make according to a pattern.

pat-ty (pat´ē) n., pl. **patties** A small, flat piece of chopped meat.

pau-per (po´pér) n. A very poor person who depends on charity. **pauperism** n. **pauperize** v.

pause (poz) v. To linger, hesitate, or stop for a time. **pause** n.

pave (pāv) v. To surface with gravel, concrete, asphalt, or other material.

pa-vil-ion (pa vil´yon) n. A large, roofed structure used for shelter.

paw (po) n. The foot of an animal. **paw** v. To handle clumsily or rudely.

pawn (pon) n. Something given as security for a loan; a hostage; a chessman of little value. **pawn** v.

pay (pā) v. To give a person what is due for a debt, purchase, or work completed; to compensate; to suffer the consequences.

pay-ment (pā´ment) n. The act of paying.

pay-roll (pā´rōl) n. The amount of money to be paid to a list of employees.

PC abbr. & n. In computer science, personal computer, a microcomputer originally designed for individual use at home or in business.

pea (pē) n. A round edible seed contained in a pod and grown on a vine.

peace (pēs) n. A state of physical or mental tranquillity; calm; serenity; the absence of war; the state of harmony between people. **peaceable** adj. **peaceful** adj. **peaceably** adv.

peak (pēk) n. A projecting edge or point; the summit of a mountain; the top. **peak** v. To bring to the maximum.

peal (pēl) n. The ring of bells; the long, loud sound of thunder or laughter. **peal** v. To ring.

pea-nut (pē´nut´) n. A nut-like seed which ripens underground; the plant bearing this nut.

pearl (perl) n. A smooth, rounded deposit formed around a grain of sand in the shell of various mollusks, especially the oyster; anything which is precious, rare, or fine. **pearly** adj.

peas-ant (pez´ant) n. A farmhand or rustic workman; an uneducated person of the lowest class. Slang Uneducated or uncouth.

peat (pēt) n. The black substance formed when plants begin to decay in wet ground, as bogs. **peaty** adj.

peb-ble (peb´l) n. A small, smooth stone. v. To treat, as to give a rough texture.

pe-can (pi kän´) n. A large tree of the central and southern United States with an edible oval, thin-shelled nut.

peck (pek) v. To strike with the beak; to eat without any appetite, taking only small bites. **peck** n. A measure which equals 1/4 of a bushel.

pec-tin (pek´tin) n. A complex carbohydrate found in ripe fruits and used in making jelly. **pectic** adj.

pe-cu-liar (pi kūl´yèr) adj. Odd; strange. **peculiarity** n. **peculiarly** adv.

ped-al (ped´al) n. A lever usually operated by the foot. **pedal** v.

ped-dle (ped´l) v. To travel around in an attempt to sell merchandise.

ped-es-tal (ped´i stal) n. A support or base for a statue. **pedestal** v. To set on or provide with a pedestal.

pe-des-tri-an (pe des´trē an) n. A person traveling by foot.

pe-di-at-rics (pē´dē a´triks) n. The branch of medicine dealing with the care of children and infants. **pediatric** adj. **pediatrician** n.

ped-i-cure (ped´i kūr´) n. The cosmetic care of the toenails and feet.

ped-i-gree (ped´i grē´) n. A line of ancestors, especially of an animal of pure breed.

ped-i-ment (ped´i ment) n. A broad, triangular architectural or decorative part above a door.

pe-dom-e-ter (pe dom´i tèr) n. An instrument which indicates the number of miles one has walked.

pe-dun-cle (pi dung´kl) n. Biol. A stalk-like support in some plants and animals.

peek (pēk) v. To look shyly or quickly from a place of hiding; to glance.

peel (pēl) n. The natural rind or skin of a fruit. v. To pull or strip the skin or bark off; to remove in thin layers. Slang To undress. **peeler** n.

peep (pēp) v. To utter a very small and weak sound, as of a young bird.

peer (pēr) v. To look searchingly; to come partially into one's view. **peer** n. An equal; a member of the British nobility, as a duke or earl.

pee-vish (pē´vish) adj. Irritable in mood; cross. **peevishly** adv. **peevishness** n.

peg (peg) n. A small pin, usually of wood or metal; a projecting pin on which something may be hung. Slang An artificial leg, often made of wood.

pei-gnoir (pān wär´) n. A woman's loose fitting dressing gown.

pe-koe (pē´kō) n. A superior black tea made from young or small leaves.

pel-let (pel´it) n. A small round ball made from paper or wax; a small bullet or shot.

pelt (pelt) n. The skin of an animal with the fur.

pel-vis (pel´vis) n., pl. **pelvises** or **pelves** The structure of the vertebrate skeleton which rests on the lower limbs, supporting the spinal column.

pen (pen) n. An instrument used for writing.

pe-nal (pēn´al) adj. Of or pertaining to punishment or penalties.

pen-al-ty (pen´al tē) n., pl. **penalties** The

legal punishment for an offense or crime; something which is forfeited when a person fails to meet a commitment; in sports, a punishment or handicap imposed for breaking a rule.

pen-ance (pen´ans) *n.* A voluntary act to show sorrow or repentance for sin.

pen-cil (pen´sil) *n.* A writing or drawing implement made from graphite. *v.* To make, write, or draw with a pencil.

pend-ing (pen´ding) *adj.* Not yet decided; imminent. *prep.* During; until.

pen-du-lous (pen´ja lus) *adj.* Hanging downward so as to swing; wavering.

pen-du-lum (pen´ja lum) *n.* A suspended object free to swing back and forth.

pen-e-trate (pen´i trāt´) *v.* To force a way through or into; to pierce; to enter; to pass through something. **penetrable** *adj.* **penetrating** *adj.* **penetration** *n.*

pen-guin (pen´gwin) *n.* A web-footed, flightless, marine bird of the southern hemisphere.

pen-i-cil-lin (pen´i sil´in) *n.* A powerful antibiotic derived from mold and used to treat certain types of bacterial infections.

pen-in-su-la (pe nin´sa la) *n.* A piece of land projecting into water from a larger land mass. **peninsular** *adj.*

pe-nis (pē´nis) *n., pl.* **penises** The male sex organ; the male organ through which urine leaves the body.

pen-i-tent (pen´i tent) *adj.* Having a feeling of guilt or remorse for one's sins or misdeeds; sorry. **penitence** *n.*

Penn-syl-va-nia *n.* A state located in the mideastern part of the United States; statehood December 12, 1787; state capital Harrisburg.

pen-ny (pen´ē) *n., pl.* **pennies** A United States coin worth 1/10th of a dollar or one cent ($.01).

pen-sion (pen´shan) *n.* The amount of money a person receives regularly after retirement. **pension** *v.* To pay a person his pension.

pen-sive (pen´siv) *adj.* Involved in serious, quiet reflection; causing melancholy thought. **pensively** *adv.*

pen-ta-gon (pen´ta gon´) *n.* Any object or building having five sides and five interior angles. **Pentagon** The five-sided office building in Arlington, Va. which houses the Defense Department.

peo-ple (pē´pl) *n., pl.* **people** Human beings; a body of persons living in the same country, under the same government, and speaking the same language; one's relatives or family.

pep-per (pep´ér) *n.* A strong, aromatic condiment. *v.* To pelt or sprinkle.

pep-tic (pep´tik) *adj.* Pertaining to or aiding digestion.

per an-num (pèr an´um) *adv.* For, by,

or in each year; annually.

per-cale (pèr kāl´) *n.* A closely woven cotton fabric.

per cap-i-ta (pèr kap´i ta) *adj. & adv.* Of each individual.

per-ceive (pèr sēv´) *v.* To become aware of by the senses; to understand; to feel or observe. **perceivable** *adj.*

per-cent-age (pèr sen´tij) *n.* The rate per hundred; a part or proportion in relation to a whole. *Slang* Profit; advantage.

per-cept (per´sept) *n.* A mental impression of something perceived; the immediate knowledge obtained from perceiving.

perch (perch) *n.* A place on which birds rest or light; any place for standing or sitting; a small, edible freshwater fish having tender white meat.

per-cip-i-ent (pèr sip´ent) *adj.* Having the power of perception. **percipience** *n.* **percipiency** *n.*

per-co-late (per´ko lāt´) *v.* To pass or cause to pass through a porous substance; to filter. **percolation** *n.*

per-cus-sion (pèr kush´an) *n.* The sharp striking together of one body against another; the striking of a cap in a firearm. *Music* An instrument which makes music when it is struck, as a drum or cymbal.

per-en-ni-al (pe ren´ē al) *adj.* Lasting from year to year; perpetual. *n.* A plant which lives through the winter and blooms again in the spring.

per-fect (per´fikt) *adj.* Having no defect or fault; flawless; accurate; absolute. *v.* To make perfect. **perfectly** *adv.*

per-form (pèr form´) *v.* To execute or carry out an action; to act or function in a certain way; to give a performance or exhibition. **performable** *adj.* **performer, performance** *n.*

per-fume (per´fūm) *n.* A fragrant substance which emits a pleasant scent; one distilled from flowers.

per-haps (pèr haps´) *adv.* Possibly; maybe; not sure.

per-i-gee (per´i jē´) *n.* The point of an orbit when a satellite of the earth is closest to the earth; the lowest part of an orbit.

per-il (per´il) *n.* A source of danger; exposure to the chance of injury; danger. **perilous** *adj.* **perilously** *adv.*

pe-ri-od (pēr´ē od) *n.* An interval of time marked by certain conditions; an interval of time that is regarded as a phase in development; menstruation; the punctuation mark (.) which indicates the end of a sentence or an abbreviation.

pe-riph-er-y (pe rif´e rē) *n., pl.* **-ies** The outer part, boundary, or surface.

peripheral *n.* In *computer science*, a

device that is connected to a computer and controlled by it.

pe·riph·er·al program *n.* In *computer science*, a utility; a program that adds to the capabilities of a computer or another program, such as a memory manager or grammar checker.

per·ish (per'ish) *v.* To ruin or spoil; to suffer an untimely or violent death.

per·i·win·kle (per'i wing'kl) *n.* Any of several edible marine snails; a trailing evergreen plant with blue and sometimes white flowers.

per·jure (per'jer) *v.* To give false testimony while under oath. **-jury** *n.*

per·ma·nent (per'ma nent) *adj.* Continuing in the same state; lasting indefinitely; enduring. **permanent** *n.* A hair wave which gives long lasting curls or body to the hair. **permanence, permanency** *n.* **permanently** *adv.*

permanent memory *n.* In *computer science*, a storage medium, such as a computer disk, that retains its memory when power is off.

per·me·ate (per'me at') *v.* To spread through; to pervade; to pass through the pores. **permeation** *n.*

per·mis·sion (per mish'an) *n.* The act of permitting something; consent.

per·mit (per mit') *v.* To consent to; to allow. *n.* An official document giving permission for a specific activity.

per·ni·cious (per nish'us) *adj.* Very harmful; malicious. **perniciously** *adv.*

per·ox·ide (pe rok'sīd) *n.* *Chem.* Oxide containing the highest proportion of oxygen for a given series; a chemical used with other ingredients to bleach the hair.

per·pen·dic·u·lar (per'pen dik'ū ler) *adj.* Being at right angles to the plane of the horizon. *Math.* Meeting a plane or given line at right angles. **perpendicular** *n.* **perpendicularity** *n.*

per·pe·trate (per'pi trāt') *v.* To perform; to commit; to be guilty. **perpetration** *n.* **perpetrator** *n.*

per·pet·u·al (per pech'ö al) *adj.* Lasting or continuing forever or an unlimited time. **perpetually** *adv.*

per·plex (per pleks') *v.* To confuse or be confused; to make complicated. **perplexing** *adj.* **perplexingly** *adv.*

per·se·cute (per'se kūt') *v.* To harass or annoy persistently; to oppress because of one's religion, beliefs, or race. **persecution** *n.* **persecutor** *n.*

per·se·vere (per'se vēr') *v.* To persist in any purpose or idea; to strive in spite of difficulties or obstacles. **perseverance** *n.* **perseveringly** *adv.*

per·sim·mon (per sim'on) *n.* A tree having reddish-orange, edible fruit.

per·sist (per sist') *v.* To continue firmly despite obstacles; to endure. **persis-**

tence *n.* **persistency** *n.* **persistent** *adj.*

per·son (per'son) *n.* A human being; an individual; the personality of a human being. *Law* Any human being, corporation, or other entity having legal rights and duties.

per·son·al (per'so nal) *adj.* Belonging to a person or persons; of the body or person; relating to oneself; done by oneself.

per·son·nel (per'so nel') *n.* The body of people working for a business or service.

per·spec·tive (per spek'tiv) *n.* A painting or drawing technique in which objects seem to have depth and distance.

per·spi·ra·tion (per'spi rā shan) *n.* The salty fluid excreted from the body by the sweat glands.

per·spire (per spīer') *v.* To give off perspiration.

per·suade (per swād') *v.* To cause to convince or believe by means of reasoning or argument. **persuader** *n.* **persuasiveness** *n.* **persuasive** *adj.*

per·tain (per tān') *v.* To relate to; to refer to; to belong as a function, adjunct or quality; to be appropriate or fitting.

per·ti·na·cious (per'ti na'shus) *adj.* Adhering firmly to an opinion, belief, or purpose; stubbornly persistent. **pertinaciously** *adv.* **pertinacity** *n.*

per·ti·nent (per'ti nent) *adj.* Relating to the matter being discussed; or the matter at hand.

per·turb (per terb') *v.* To disturb, make anxious, or make uneasy; to cause confusion. **perturbation** *n.*

per·vade (per vād') *v.* To spread through every part of something; to permeate.

per·ver·sion (per ver'zhan) *n.* The act of being led away from the accepted course; a deviant form of sexual behavior.

per·vert (per vert') *v.* To lead away from the proper cause; to use in an improper way. *n.* A person practicing or characterized by sexual perversion. **perverted** *adj.* **pervertible** *adj.*

pes·si·mism (pes'i miz'um) *n.* The tendency to take a gloomy view of affairs or situations and to anticipate the worst. **pessimist** *n.* **pessimistic** *adj.*

pest (pest) *n.* A person or thing which is a nuisance; an annoying person or thing; a destructive insect, plant, or animal.

pes·ter (pes'ter) *v.* To harass with persistent annoyance; to bother.

pes·ti·cide (pes'ti sīd') *n.* A chemical substance used to destroy rodents, insects, and pests. **pesticidal** *adj.*

pes·ti·lence (pes'ti lens) *n.* A widespread and often fatal infectious disease, as bubonic plague or cholera.

pet·al (pet'al) *n.* *Bot.* One of the leaf-like parts of a flower.

pe-tite (pe tēt´) *adj.* Small in size; little.

pet-it four (pet´ē fōr´) *n., pl.* **petit fours** A small decorated cake.

pe-ti-tion (pe tish´an) *n.* A solemn request or prayer; a formal written request addressed to a group or person in authority. **petitioner** *n.*

pet-ri-fy (pe´tri fī´) *v.* To convert into a stony mass; to make fixed or immobilize, as in the face of danger or surprise. **petrification** *n.*

pe-tro-le-um (pe trō´lē um) *n.* An oily, thick liquid which develops naturally below the ground surface, used in products such as gasoline, fuel oil, and kerosene.

pew (pū) *n.* A row of bench-like seats for seating people in church.

pew-ter (pū´tėr) *n.* An alloy of tin with copper, silver-gray in color and used for tableware and kitchen utensils.

pfen-nig *n., pl.* **-nigs** *or* **-nige** A small coin of Germany, equal to one hundredth of a Deutschemark.

phal-lus (fal´us) *n., pl.* **-li** *or* **-luses** A representation of the penis, often as a symbol of generative power.

phan-tasm (fan´taz um) *n.* The creation of an imaginary image; a fantasy; a phantom. **phantasmal** *adj.*

phan-tom (fan´tom) *n.* Something which exists but has no physical reality; a ghost.

phar-ma-cy (fär´ma sē) *n., pl.* **pharmacies** A place of business which specializes in preparing, identifying, and disbursing drugs; a drugstore.

phar-ynx (far´ingks) *n., pl.* **-ynges** *or* **-ynxes** The part of the throat located between the palate and the esophagus, serving as a passage for air and food.

phase (fāz) *n.* Any decisive stage in development or growth. *Astron.* One of the forms or appearances of a planet.

pheas-ant (fez´ant) *n.* A long-tailed game bird noted for the beautiful plumage of the male.

phe-nom-e-non (fi nom´e non´) *n., pl.* **phenomena** *or* **phenomenons** Something that can be observed or perceived; a rare occurrence. *Slang* An outstanding person with remarkable power, ability, or talent.

phi-lan-der (fi lan´dėr) *v.* To make love without feeling or serious intentions.

phi-lat-e-ly (fi lat´e lē) *n.* The collection and study of postage stamps and postmarked material. **philatelic** *adj.*

phil-har-mon-ic (fil´här mon´ik) *adj.* Pertaining to a symphony orchestra.

phi-los-o-phy (fi los´o fē) *n. pl.* **-ies** The logical study of the nature and source of human knowledge or human values; the set of values, opinions, and ideas of a group or individual.

pho-bi-a (fō´bē a) *n.* A compulsive fear of a specified situation or object.

phone (fōn) *n.* A telephone. **phone** *v.* To call or communicate by telephone.

phon-ic (fon´ik) *adj.* Pertaining to sounds in speech; using the same symbol for each sound. **phonetics** *n.*

pho-no-graph (fō no graf´) *n.* A machine which uses a needle to reproduce sound from a grooved disc or record.

pho-ny (fō´nē) *adj. Informal* Counterfeit; fraudulent; not real or genuine.

phos-phate (fos´fāt) *n., Chem.* A salt or phosphoric acid which contains mostly phosphorus and oxygen.

phos-pho-rus (fos´fėr us) *n.* A highly flammable, poisonous, nonmetallic element used in safety matches, symbolized by P.

pho-to (fō´tō) *n. Slang* A photograph.

pho-to-cop-y (fō´to kop´ē) *v.* To reproduce printed material using a photographic process. **photocopier** *n.* **photocopy** *n.*

pho-to-graph (fō´to graf) *n.* A picture or image recorded by a camera and then reproduced on a photosensitive surface.

pho-to-stat (fō´to stat´) *n.* A trademark for a camera designed to reproduce documents and graphic material.

pho-to-syn-the-sis (fō´tō sin´thi sis) *n. Biochem.* The chemical process by which plants use light to change carbon dioxide and water into carbohydrates, releasing oxygen as a byproduct.

phrase (frāz) *n. Gram.* A clear or concise expression which does not contain a predicate.

phre-nol-o-gy (fri nol´o jē) *n.* The study of or the theory that the conformation of the human skull indicates the degree of intelligence and character.

phys-i-cal (fiz´i kal) *adj.* Relating to the human body apart from the mind or emotions; pertaining to material rather than imaginary subjects. *n.* A medical exam to determine a person's physical condition. **physically** *adv.*

phy-si-cian (fi zish´an) *n.* A person licensed to practice medicine.

phys-ics (fiz´iks) *n.* The scientific study which deals with energy, matter, motion, and related areas of science.

phys-i-ol-o-gy (fiz´ē ol´o jē) *n., pl.* **-ies** The study of living animals, plants, and their activities and functions; the vital functions and processes of an organism. **physiological** *adj.*

phys-i-o-ther-a-py (fiz´ē ō ther´apē) *n.* The treatment of disease or physical defects by the use of heat and massage.

pi-an-o (pē an´ō) *n.* A musical instrument with a manual keyboard and felt-covered hammers which produce musical tones when struck upon steel wires.

pi-az-za (pē az´a) *n.* A public square or an open area in an Italian town or city.

pi-ca (pī´ka) *n.* A printer's type size of 12 points, equal to about 1/6 inch; a typewriter type size with 10 characters to an inch.

pic-co-lo (pik´o lō) *n.* A small flute with a brilliant sound pitched an octave above the flute.

pick (pik) *v.* To select or choose from a number or group

pick-et (pik´it) *n.* A pointed stake driven into the ground as support for a fence; a person positioned outside of a place of employment during a strike. *Mil.* A soldier posted to guard a camp.

pick-le (pik´l) *n.* A cucumber preserved in a solution of brine or vinegar. *Slang* A troublesome situation.

pic-nic (pik´nik) *n.* An outdoor social gathering where food is provided usually by the people attending.

pic-ture (pik´chèr) *n.* A visual representation on a surface, which is printed, drawn or photographed; the mental image or impression of an event or situation.

piece (pēs) *n.* An element, unit, or part of a whole; a musical or literary work. *Slang* A firearm.

piece-meal (pēs´mēl´) *adv.* Gradually, bit by bit.

pier (pèr) *n.* A structure extending into the water, used to secure, protect, and provide access to vessels.

pierce (pèrs) *v.* To penetrate or make a hole in something; to force into or through. **piercing** *adj.*

Pierce, Franklin *n.* (1804-1869) The fourteenth president of the United States from 1853-1857.

pi-e-ty (pī´i tē) *n., pl.* **pieties** Devoutness toward God.

pig (pig) *n.* A cloven-hoofed mammal with short legs, bristly hair, and a snout for rooting; the edible meat of a pig; pork. *Slang* A greedy or gross person.

pig-ment (pig´ment) *n.* A material used as coloring matter, suitable for making paint. *Biol.* Any substance such as melanin and chlorophyll which imparts color to vegetable tissue or animals.

pile (pīl) *n.* A quantity of anything thrown in a heap; a massive or very large building or a group of buildings.

pil-fer (pil´fèr) *v.* To steal in little quantities; to steal items of little value.

pil-grim (pil´grim) *n.* A person who travels to a sacred place; a wanderer. **Pilgrims** The English Puritans who founded the Plymouth colony in New England in the year 1620.

pill (pil) *n.* A small tablet containing medicine which is taken by mouth; someone or something which is disagreeable but must be dealt with.

pill An oral contraceptive drug taken by women.

pil-lar (pil´èr) *n.* A freestanding column which serves as a support.

pil-low (pil´ō) *n.* A cloth case filled with feathers or other soft material, used to cushion the head during sleep.

pi-lot (pī´lot) *n.* A person who is licensed to operate an aircraft; someone who is trained and licensed to guide ships in and out of port. *v.* To act or serve as a pilot.

pi-men-to (pi men´tō) *n.* A sweet pepper used as a stuffing for olives or as a relish.

pimp (pimp) *n.* A person who arranges customers for prostitutes in exchange for a share of their money.

pim-ple (pim´pl) *n.* A small eruption of the skin, having an inflamed base. **pimpled** *adj.* **pimply** *adj.*

pin (pin) *n.* A small, stiff piece of wire with a blunt head and a sharp point, used to fasten something, usually temporarily; one of the rounded wooden clubs serving as the target in bowling.

pin-a-fore (pin´a fōr´) *n.* A sleeveless apron-like garment.

pin-cers (pin´chèrz) *n.* An implement having two handles and a pair of jaws working on a pivot, used to hold objects.

pinch (pinch) *v.* To squeeze between a finger and thumb causing pain or discomfort; to be miserly. *n.* The small amount that can be held between the thumb and forefinger.

pink (pingk) *n.* Any of various plants related to the carnation, having fragrant flowers; a light or pale hue of crimson; the highest or best possible degree.

pin feed In *computer science,* a device that feeds a continuous form through a printer by engaging a series of holes along the edges of the form.

pin-na-cle (pin´a kl) *n.* The highest peak; a sharp point; a pointed summit.

pint (pīnt) *n.* A liquid or dry measurement equal to half of a quart or two cups.

pin-to (pin´tō) *n. pl.* **-tos** *or* **-toes** A horse with spots; a spotted bean of the southwestern United States.

pin-wheel (pin´hwēl´) *n.* A toy with revolving paper or plastic fastened to a stick; a fireworks display featuring a revolving wheel of colored flames.

pin-worm (pin´werm´) *n.* A nematode parasite which infests the human intestines and rectum.

pi-o-neer (pī´o nēr´) *n.* One of the first settlers of a new region or country; the first developer or investigator in a new field of enterprise, research, or other endeavor.

pi-ous (pī′us) *adj.* Reverently religious; devout. **piously** *adv.* **piousness** *n.*

pipe (pīp) *n.* A hollow cylinder for conveying fluids; a small bowl with a hollow stem for smoking tobacco. *Music* A tubular flute.

pipe-line (pīp′līn′) *n.* A pipe used to transfer gas or oil over long distances; a means for conveying information.

pique (pēk) *n.* A feeling of resentment or irritation.

pirated software *n.* In *computer science,* programs obtained outside of normal or legal channels.

pis-ta-chi-o (pi stash′ē ō′) *n.* A small tree of western Asia; the edible fruit from this tree.

pis-til (pis′til) *n.* The seed-producing female reproductive organ of a flower.

pis-tol (pis′tol) *n.* A small handheld firearm.

pis-ton (pis′ton) *n.* Mech. A solid cylinder fitted in a larger cylinder, moving back and forth under liquid pressure.

pit (pit) *n.* An artificial or manmade hole in the ground; a slight indentation in the skin, as a scar from the chicken pox; an area for refueling or repair at a car race; the stone in the middle of some fruit, as peaches. *Slang* **the pits** Anything at its worst.

pith (pith) *n. Bot.* The sponge-like soft tissue at the center of the branch or stem of many plants.

pit-i-ful (pit′i ful) *adj.* Evoking or meriting pity. **pitifully** *adv.*

pit-y (pit′ē) *n. pl.* **pities** A feeling of compassion or sorrow for another's misfortune. **pity** *v.*

piv-ot (piv′ot) *n.* A thing or person upon which development, direction, or effect depends. **pivot** *v.* To turn.

pixel *n.* In *computer science,* a picture element; a basic component of a computer screen display.

piz-za (pēt′sa) *n.* An Italian food consisting of a doughy crust covered with tomato sauce, cheese, and other toppings and then baked.

place (plās) *n.* A region; an area; a building or location used for a special purpose; the position of something in a series or sequence. **place** *v.* To put in a particular order or place.

place-ment (plās′ment) *n.* The act of being placed; a business or service which finds positions of employment for applicants.

pla-cen-ta (pla sen′ta) *n., pl.* **-tas** *or* **-tae** *Anat.* The vascular, membranous structure which supplies a fetus with nourishment before its birth.

plague (plāg) *n.* Anything that is troublesome. *Pathol.* A highly contagious and often fatal epidemic disease, as the bubonic plague.

plaid (plad) *n.* A rectangular wool cloth or garment, usually worn by men and women, having a crisscross or checkered design.

plain (plān) *adj.* Level; flat; clear; open, as in view; not rich or luxurious; not highly gifted or cultivated. **plainly** *adv.*

plain-tiff (plān′tif) *n.* A person who brings suit.

plan (plan) *n.* A scheme or method for achieving something; a drawing to show proportion and relationship to parts. **plan** *v.* To have in mind as an intention or purpose.

plane (plān) *n.* A tool for smoothing or leveling a wood surface. *Geom.* A surface as a straight line that joins any two points on it. *Slang* Airplane.

plan-et (plan′it) *n. Astron.* A celestial body which is illuminated by light from the star around which it revolves.

plan-e-tar-i-um (plan′i târ′ē um) *n. pl.-iums* or *- ia* A device for exhibiting celestial bodies as they exist at any time and for any place on earth.

plank (plangk) *n.* A broad piece of wood; one of the issues or principles of a political platform.

plant (plant) *n.* A living organism belonging to the vegetable kingdom, having cellulose cell walls. *v.* To place a living organism in the ground for growing; to place so as to deceive or to spy.

plaque (plak) *n.* A flat piece, made from metal, porcelain, ivory, or other materials, engraved for mounting; the bacteria deposit which builds up on the teeth.

plas-ma (plaz′ma) *n.* The clear fluid part of blood, used for transfusions.

plas-ter-board (plas′tĕr bõrd′) *n.* A building material of layered gypsum bonded to outer layers of paper.

plas-tic (plas′tik) *adj.* Pliable; capable of being molded. **plastic** *n.* A synthetically made material which is molded and then hardened into objects.

plastic surgery *n.* Surgery dealing with the restoration or repair of deformed or destroyed parts of the body or skin.

pla-teau (pla tō′) *n.* An extensive level of elevated land; a period of stability.

plat-form (plat′form) *n.* Any elevated or raised surface used by speakers or by other performers or for display purposes; a formal declaration of principles or policy of a political party.

plat-i-num (plat′i num) *n.* A silver-white, metallic element, corrosive resistant, used in jewelry; symbolized by Pt.

plat-ter (plat′ĕr) *n.* A large, oblong, shallow dish for serving food.

plau-si-ble (plo′zi bl) *adj.* Seeming to

be probable; appearing to be trustworthy or believable.

play (plā) *v.* To entertain, as in recreation; to take part in a game; to perform in a dramatic role; to perform with a musical instrument; in fishing, to allow a hooked fish to tire itself out; to pretend to do something. *n.* A dramatic presentation.

pla-za (plä´za) *n.* An open-air market place or square; a shopping mall.

plea (plē) *n.* An urgent request; in law, an allegation made by either party in a law suit.

plea bargaining *v.* Making a pretrial agreement to plead guilty to a lesser charge if a more serious one will be dropped.

plead (plēd) *v.* To argue for or against something in court; to ask earnestly.

pleas-ant (plez´ant) *adj.* Giving or promoting the feeling of pleasure; very agreeable. **pleasantly** *adv.*

please (plēz) *v.* To make happy; to give pleasure; to be the will or wish of; to prefer.

pleas-ur-a-ble (plezh´er a bl) *adj.* Pleasant; gratifying.

pleas-ure (plezh´er) *n.* A feeling of satisfaction or enjoyment; one's preference or wish.

pleat (plēt) *n.* A fold in a cloth made by doubling the cloth back and fastening it down.

plebe (plēb) *n.* A freshman or first year student at the United States Naval Academy.

pledge (plej) *n.* A solemn promise; a deposit of something as security for a loan; a promise to join a fraternity; a person who is pledged to join a fraternity. *v.* To promise or vow.

plen-ti-ful (plen´ti ful) *adj.* Having great abundance. **plentifully** *adv.*

plen-ty (plen´tē) *n.* An ample amount; prosperity or abundance.

pleu-ra (pler´a) *n. pl. pleurae Anat.* The membranous sac which covers the inside of the thorax membrane, which covers the lungs.

pli-a-ble (plī´a bl) *adj.* Flexible; easily controlled or persuaded. **pliability** *n.* **pliableness** *n.* **pliably** *adv.*

pli-ers (plī´erz) *n.* A pincers-like tool used for holding, bending, or cutting.

plight (plīt) *n.* A distressing circumstance, situation, or condition.

plod (plod) *n.* To walk in a heavy, slow way.

plot (plot) *n.* A small piece of ground usually used for a special purpose; the main story line in a piece of fiction; a plan; an intrigue; a conspiracy. *v.* To represent something by using a map or chart; to scheme secretly.

plow (plou) *n.* An implement for breaking up or turning over the soil. *v.* To dig out. *Slang* To hit with force.

pluck (pluk) *v.* To remove by pulling out or off; to pull and release the strings on a musical instrument. *Slang* To swindle. **plucker** *n.*

plug (plug) *n.* Anything used to stop or close a hole or drain. *Electr.* A two-pronged device attached to a cord and used in a jack or socket to make an electrical connection. **plug** *v. Slang* To advertise favorably; to give a recommendation or a piece of publicity for someone.

plum-age (plö´mij) *n.* The feathers of a bird.

plumb (plum) *n.* A lead weight tied to the end of a string, used to test the exact perpendicular line of something.

plumb-er (plum´er) *n.* A person who repairs or installs plumbing in a home or business.

plumb-ing (plum´ing) *n.* The profession or trade of a plumber; the connecting of pipes and fixtures used to carry water and waste.

plume (plöm) *n.* A feather used as an ornament.

plun-der (plun´der) *v.* To deprive of goods or property in a violent way.

plunge (plunj) *v.* To thrust or cast something, as into water; to submerge; to descend sharply or steeply.

plunk (plungk) *v.* To put down or place suddenly; to pluck or strum a banjo.

plu-ral (pler´al) *adj.* Consisting of or containing more than one. **plural** *n.*

plus (plus) *n.* The symbol (+) which indicates addition; increase; extra quantity.

plu-to-ni-um (plö tō´nē um) *n.* A radioactive metallic element symbolized by Pu.

ply (plī) *v.* To mold, bend, or shape. *n.* A layer of thickness; the twisted strands of thread, yarn, or rope.

ply-wood (plī´wed´) *n.* A structural material consisting of thin layers of wood which have been glued and pressed together.

pneu-mo-nia (ne mōn´ya) *n.* An inflammation caused by bacteria, virus of the lungs, or irritation.

poach (pōch) *v.* To cook in a liquid just at the boiling point; to trespass on another's property with the intent of taking fish or wild game. **poacher** *n.*

pock-et (pok´it) *n.* A small pouch within a garment, having an open top and used for carrying items. *v.* To put in or deposit in a pocket.

pod (pod) *n., Bot.* A seed vessel, as of a bean or pea. *Aeron.* A separate and detachable compartment in a spacecraft.

po-di-a-try *n.* Professional care and treatment of the feet.

po-di-um (pō′dē um) *n., pl.* **-ia** *or* **-iums**
A small raised platform for an orchestra
conductor or a speaker.

po-em (pō′im) *n.* A composition in verse
with language selected for its beauty
and sound.

po-et (pō′it) *n.* A person who writes
poetry.

po-et-ry (pō′i trē) *n.* The art of writing
stories, poems, and thoughts into verse.

poin-set-ti-a (poin set′ē a) *n.* A tropical
plant having large scarlet, pink, or
white leaves, used in Christmas
decorations.

point (point) *n.* The sharp or tapered end
of something; a mark of punctuation,
as a period (.); a geometric object which
does not have property or dimensions
other than location; a degree, condition,
or stage; a particular or definite spot
in time. **point** *v.* To aim; to indicate
direction by using the finger.

point and click *v.* In *computer science*,
to select an object by moving the
mouse cursor to it, then pressing and
releasing the mouse button.

poise (poiz) *v.* To bring into or hold one's
balance. **poise** *n.* Equilibrium; self-
confidence; the ability to stay calm in
all social situations.

poi-son (poi′zon) *n.* A substance which
kills, injures, or destroys. **poisoner** *n.*
poisonous *adj.*

poke (pōk) *v.* To push or prod at
something with a finger or other
implement.

pok-er (pō′kėr) *n.* A card game, played
by two or more people in which the
players bet on the cards dealt to them.

po-lar (pō′lėr) *adj.* Having to do with
the poles of a magnet or sphere; relating
to the geographical poles of the earth.

po-lar-ize (pō′la rīz′) *v.* To cause
something to vibrate in an exact
pattern; to break up into opposite
groups.

pole (pōl) *n.* Either of the two ends of
the axis of a sphere, as the earth; the
two points called the North and South
Poles, where the axis of the earth's
rotation meets the surface; a long,
slender rod.

po-lice (po lēs′) *n.* A division or
department organized to maintain
order; the members of such a department. **police** *v.* To patrol; to enforce
the law and maintain order.

po-liceman (po lēs′man) *n.* A member
of the police force. **policewoman** *n.*

pol-i-cy (pol′i sē) *n., pl.* **policies** Any
plan or principle which guides a
person's or group's decision making.

pol-i-o-my-e-li-tis (pō′lē ōmī′e lī′tis)
n. Inflammation of the spinal cord
causing paralysis; also polio.

pol-ish (pol′ish) *v.* To make lustrous and
smooth by rubbing; to become refined
or elegant.

po-lite (po līt′) *adj.* Refined, mannerly,
and courteous.

po-lit-i-cal (po lit′i kal) *adj.* Concerned
with or pertaining to government;
involved in politics.

pol-i-ti-cian (pol′i tish′an) *n.* A person
active in governmental affairs or
politics.

pol-i-tics (pol′i tiks) *n.* The activities and
methods of a political party.

Polk, James Knox *n.* (1795-1849) The
eleventh president of the United States
from 1845-1849.

poll (pōl) *n.* The recording of votes in
an election; a public survey taken on
a given topic. In *computer science*,
an I/O function that scans transmission
lines to check their status and ascertain
when data is to be sent or received. **poll**
v. To vote.

pol-len (pol′en) *n.* The yellow dust-like
powder which contains the male
reproductive cells of a flowering plant.

pol-lute (po löt′) *v.* To contaminate; to
make unclear or impure; to dirty.

po-lo (pō′lō) *n.* A game played on
horseback in which players try to drive
a wooden ball through the opposing
team's goal using long-handled mallets.

po-lo-ni-um (po lō′nē um) *n.* A
radioactive metallic element symbolized by PO.

pol-ter-geist (pōl′tėr gīst′) *n.* A
mischievous spirit which makes noise.

pol-y-es-ter (pol′ē es′tėr) *n.* A strong
lightweight synthetic resin used in
fibers.

pol-y-gon *n.* A closed figure bounded
by straight lines.

pol-y-graph (pol′ē graf′) *n.* A machine
designed to record different signals
given off by the body, as respiration,
blood pressure, or heartbeats; may be
used to detect a person who could be
lying.

pol-y-he-dron (pol′ē hē′dron) *n., pl.*
-dra *or* **-drons** *Geom.* A solid bounded
by polygons.

pom-pa-dour (pom′pa dōr′) *n.* A
hairstyle which is puffed over the
forehead.

pomp-ous (pom′pus) *adj.* A showing
or appearance of dignity or importance.

pond (pond) *n.* A body of still water,
smaller in size than a lake.

pon-der (pon′dėr) *v.* To think about very
carefully; to meditate.

pon-der-ous (pon′dėr us) *adj.* Massive;
having great weight.

pon-tiff (pon′tif) *n.* A pope.

po-ny (pō′nē) *n., pl.* **-ies** A small horse.

pool (pōl) *n.* A small body of water; the
collective stake in gambling games.

poor (per) *adj.* Lacking possessions and

money; not satisfactory; broke; needy; destitute.

pop (pop) *v.* To cause something to burst; to make a sharp, explosive sound. *Slang* Soda. **popper** *n.*

pope (pōp) *n.* The head of the Roman Catholic Church.

pop-lar (pop'lėr) *n.* A rapid growing tree having a light, soft wood.

pop-u-lar (pop'ū lėr) *adj.* Approved of; widely liked; suited to the means of the people.

pop-u-la-tion (pop'ū lā'shan) *n.* The total number of people in a given area, country, or city.

por-ce-lain (pōr'se lin) *n.* A hard, translucent ceramic which has been fired and glazed.

porch (pōrch) *n.* A covered structure forming the entrance to a house.

por-cu-pine (por'kū pīn') *n.* A clumsy rodent covered with long sharp quills.

pore (pōr) *v.* To ponder or meditate on something. **pore** *n.* A minute opening, as in the skin.

pork (pōrk) *n.* The edible flesh of swine. *Informal* Favors given by a government for political reasons and not public necessity.

por-no *n., Slang* Pornography.

por-nog-ra-phy (por nog'ra fē) *n.* Pictures, films, or writing which deliberately arouse sexual excitement.

por-poise (por'pos) *n.* An aquatic mammal with a blunt, rounded snout.

port (pōrt) *n.* A city or town with a harbor for loading and unloading cargo from ships; the left side of a ship; a dark red, sweet, fortified wine. In *computer science*, any of the connections to a computer that allow the transfer of data.

port-a-ble (pōr'ta bl) *adj.* Capable of being moved easily.

por-ter (pōr'tėr) *n.* A person hired to carry baggage.

port-fo-li-o (pōrt fō'lē ō') *n.* A carrying case for holding papers, drawings, and other flat items.

port-hole (pōrt'hōl') *n.* A small opening in the side of a ship providing light and ventilation.

por-tion (pōr'shan) *n.* A section or part of a whole; a share. **portion** *v.* To allot; to assign.

por-tray (pōr trā') *v.* To represent by drawing, writing, or acting.

pose (pōz) *v.* To place or assume a position, as for a picture.

po-si-tion (po zish'an) *n.* The manner in which something is placed; an attitude; a viewpoint; a job; employment. *v.* To place in proper order.

pos-i-tive (poz'i tiv) *adj.* Containing, expressing, or characterized by affirmation; very confident; absolutely certain; not negative. **positively** *adv.* **positiveness** *n.*

pos-se (pos'ē) *n.* A deputized group or squad.

pos-ses-sion (po zesh'an) *n.* The fact or act of possessing property; the state of being possessed, as by an evil spirit.

pos-ses-sive (po zes'iv) *adj.* Having a strong desire to possess; not wanting to share. *n.* The noun or pronoun case which indicates ownership.

pos-si-ble (pos'i bl) *adj.* Capable of being true, happening, or being accomplished. **possibility** *n.* **possibly** *adv.*

post (pōst) *n.* An upright piece of wood or metal support; a position or employment. **post** *v.* To put up information in a public place. **post** *prefix* After; later than; behind.

post-age (pō'stij) *n.* The charge or fee for mailing something.

pos-te-ri-or (po stēr'ē ėr) *adj.* Located in the back. *n.* The buttocks.

post-mor-tem (pōst mor'tem) *adj.* The examination of a body after death; an autopsy.

post-pone (pōst pōn') *v.* To put off; to defer to a later time. **postponable** *adj.* **postponement** *n.* **postponer** *n.*

post-script (pōst'skript') *n.* A short message added at the end of a letter.

pos-ture (pos'chėr) *n.* The carriage or position of the body.

pot (pot) *n.* A rounded, deep container used for cooking and other domestic purposes. *Slang* A large sum of money which is shared by all members of a group; marijuana. **potful** *n.*

po-tas-si-um (po tas'ē um) *n.* A silvery-white, highly reactive metallic element symbolized by K.

po-ta-to (po tā'tō) *n., pl.* potatoes A thick, edible, underground tuber plant native to America.

po-tent (pōt'ent) *adj.* Having great strength or physical powers; having a great influence on the mind or morals; sexually competent.

po-ten-tial (po ten'shal) *adj.* Possible, but not yet actual; having the capacity to be developed. *Electr.* The potential energy of an electric charge that depends on its position in an electric field.

pot-pour-ri (pō'pe rē') *n.* A mixture of sweet-smelling dried flower petals and spices, kept in an airtight jar.

pot-ter-y (pot'e rē) *n., pl.* -ies Objects molded from clay and fired by intense heat; place where objects are made.

pouch (pouch) *n.* A small bag or other container for holding or carrying money, tobacco, and other small articles. *Zool.* The sac-like structure in which some animals carry their young.

poul·try (pōl′trē) *n.* Domestic fowl as ducks and hens, which are raised for eggs or meat.

pound (pound) *n., pl.* **pound** A measure of weight equal to sixteen ounces; a public enclosure where stray animals are fed and housed.   To strike repeatedly or with force; to throb or beat violently or rapidly. **pound** *v.*

pov·er·ty (pov′ér tē) *n.* The condition or state of being poor and needing money.

POW (pē′ō′dub′l ū′) *abbr.* Prisoner of war.

pow·der (pou′dér) *n.* A dry substance which has been finely ground or pulverized; dust; an explosive, such as gunpowder. *v.* To dust or cover.

pow·er·ful (pou′ér ful) *adj.* Possessing energy or great force; having authority.

power of attorney A legal document in which one person gives another the authority to act for him.

power surge *n.* In *computer science*, a sudden increase in electrical energy that can damage a computer's system and files.

power up *v.* In *computer science*, to turn on a piece of equipment.

prac·ti·cal (prak′ti kal) *adj.* Serving an actual use or purpose; inclined to act instead of thinking or talking about something; useful.

pract·ice (prak′tis) *n.* A custom or habit of doing something. **practice** *v.* To work at a profession; to apply; to put into effect; to exercise or rehearse.

prai·rie (prâr′ē) *n.* A wide area of level or rolling land with grass and weeds but no trees.

praise (prāz) *v.* To express approval; to glorify.

prank (prangk) *n.* A mischievous, playful action or trick. **prankster** *n.*

pra·seo·dym·i·um (prā′zē ō dim′ēum) *n.* A metallic element of the rare-earth group, symbolized by Pr.

prawn (pron) *n.* An edible shrimp-like crustacean found in both salt and fresh water.

pray (prā) *v.* To address prayers to God; to ask or request.

prayer (prâr) *n.* A devout request; the act of praying; a formal or set group of words used in praying.

praying mantis *n.* An insect which holds its front legs folded as if in prayer.

preach (prēch) *v.* To advocate; to proclaim; to deliver a sermon. **preacher** *n.* **preachment** *n.* **preachy** *adj.*

pre·am·ble (prē′am bl) *n.* An introduction to something, as a law, which states the purpose and reasons for the matter which follows.

pre·cau·tion (pri ko′shun) *n.* A measure of caution or care taken in advance to guard against harm.

pre·cede (pri sēd′) *v.* To be or go before in time, position, or rank.

prec·e·dent (pres′i dent) *n.* An instance which may serve as a rule or example in the future.

pre·cept (prē′sept) *n.* A rule, order, or commandment meant to guide one's conduct.

pre·cinct (prē′singkt) *n.* An electoral district of a county, township, city, or town; an enclosure with definite boundaries.

pre·cious (presh′us) *adj.* Having great worth or value; beloved; cherished.

pre·cip·i·ta·tion (pri sip′i tā′shan) *n.* Condensed water vapor which falls as snow, rain, sleet or hail. *Chem.* The act of causing crystals to separate and fall to the bottom of a liquid.

pre·cip·i·tous (pri sip′i tus) *adj.* Very steep; marked with very steep cliffs.

pre·cise (pri sīs′) *adj.* Exact; definite; strictly following rules; very strict.

pre·ci·sion (pri sizh′an) *n.* Exactness; the quality of being precise; accuracy.

pre·clude (pri klōd′) *v.* To shut out; to make impossible; to prevent.

pre·co·cious (pri kō′shus) *adj.* Showing and developing skills and abilities very early in life.

pre·con·ceive (prē′kon sēv′) *v.* To form a notion or conception before knowing all the facts. **preconception** *n.*

pre·da·cious (pri dā′shus) *adj.* Living by preying on other animals.

pred·a·tor (pred′a tér) *n.* A person who lives or gains by stealing from another person; an animal that survives by killing and eating other animals.

pre·des·ti·na·tion (pri des′ti nā′shan) *n.* Destiny; fate; the act by which God has predestined all events.

pred·i·ca·ble (pred′i ka bl) *adj.* Capable of being predicated to foretell.

pred·i·cate (pred′i kāt′) *n. Gram.* The word or words which say something about the subject of a clause or sentence; the part of a sentence which contains the verb. *v.* To establish.

pre·dict (pri dikt′) *v.* To tell beforehand; to foretell; to forecast. **predictability** *n.* **predictable** *adj.* **predictably** *adv.*

pre·dom·i·nant (pri dom′i nant) *adj.* Superior in strength, authority, number, or other qualities.

pree·mie *n. Slang* A baby born before the expected due date.

pre·empt (prē empt′) *v.* To take or get hold of before someone else; to take the place of; to do something before someone else has a chance to do it. **preemption** *n.* **preemptive** *adj.*

pre·fab·ri·cate (prē fab′ri kāt′) *v.* To construct in sections beforehand.

pref·ace (pref′is) *n.* The introduction

at the beginning of a book or speech.

pre-fect (prē′fekt) *n.* A high administrative official. **prefecture** *n.*

pre-fer (pri fer′) *v.* To select as being the favorite; to promote; to present.

pref-er-ence (pref′er ens) *n.* A choice; a special liking for anything over another. **preferential** *adj.*

pre-fix (prē fiks′) *v.* To put at the beginning; to put before.

preg-nant (preg′nant) *adj.* Carrying an unborn fetus; significant.

pre-his-tor-i-cal (prē′hi stor′ik) *adj.* Of or related to the period before recorded history.

pre-judge (prē juj′) *v.* To judge before one knows all the facts. **-ment** *n.*

prej-u-dice (prej′a dis) *n.* A biased opinion based on emotion rather than reason; bias against a group, race, or creed.

pre-lim-i-nar-y (pri lim′i ner′ē) *adj.* Leading up to the main action.

prel-ude (prel′ūd) *n.* An introductory action. *Music* The movement at the beginning of a piece of music.

pre-ma-ture (prē′ma ter′) *adj.* Occurring or born before the natural or proper time. **prematurely** *adv.*

pre-med-i-tate (pri med′i tāt′) *v.* To plan in advance or beforehand.

pre-mi-er (pri mēr′) *adj.* First in rank or importance. *n.* The chief executive of a government. **premiership** *n.*

pre-mi-um (prē′mē um) *n.* An object offered free as an inducement to buy; the fee or amount payable for insurance; an additional amount of money charged above the nominal value.

pre-na-tal (prē nāt′al) *adj.* Existing prior to birth.

pre-oc-cu-py (prē ok′ū pī′) *v.* To engage the mind or attention completely.

prep (prep) *Slang* Preparatory school; preparation.

prep-a-ra-tion (prep′a rā′shan) *n.* The process of preparing for something.

pre-par-a-to-ry (pri pâr′a tōr′ē) *adj.* Serving as preparation.

pre-pare (pri pâr′) *v.* To make ready or qualified; to equip. **preparedly** *adv.*

pre-pay (prē pā′) *v.* To pay for in advance.

pre-pon-der-ate (pri pon′de rāt′) *v.* To have superior importance, weight, force, influence, or other qualities. **preponderance** *n.* **preponderancy** *n.* **preponderantly** *adv.*

prep-o-si-tion (prep′o zish′an) *n. Gram.* A word placed in front of a noun or pronoun to show a connection with or to something or someone.

pre-pos-ter-ous (pri pos′ter us) *adj.* Absurd; ridiculous; beyond all reason.

prep-pie (prep ē) *n. Slang* A student

attending a prep school; a young adult who behaves and dresses very traditionally.

pre- *prefix* Earlier or prior to something; in front.

preprocessing *n.* In *computer science,* configuring data before entering it into a program, such as converting spreadsheet rows to comma separated values for entering into a database.

pre-rog-a-tive (pri rog′a tiv) *n.* The unquestionable right belonging to a person.

pres-age (pres′ij) *n.* An omen or indication of something to come; a premonition. **presage** *v.*

pre-school (prē′skōl′) *adj.* Of or for children usually between the ages of two and five. **preschooler** *n.*

pre-scribe (pri skrīb′) *v.* To impose as a guide; to recommend.

pre-scrip-tion (pri skrip′shan) *n. Medical* A physician's written order for medicine.

pres-ence (prez′ens) *n.* The state of being present; the immediate area surrounding a person or thing; poise.

pres-ent (prez′ent) *adj.* Now going on; not past or future. *Gram.* Denoting a tense or verb form which expresses a current state or action. **present** *v.* To bring into the acquaintance of another; to introduce; to make a gift of. **present** *n.* A gift. **presently** *adv.* Currently.

pres-en-ta-tion (prez′en tā′shan) *n.* A formal introduction of one person to another; something presented, as an exhibition, show, or product.

pre-serv-a-tive (pri zer′va tiv) *adj.* Keeping something from decay or injury. **preservative** *n.*

pre-serve (pri zerv′) *v.* To save from destruction or injury; to prepare food to prevent spoilage or decay.

preserves *n.* Fruit which has been preserved with sugar.

pre-side (pri zīd′) *v.* To have a position of authority or control; to run or control a meeting.

pres-i-dent (prez′i dent) *n.* The chief executive officer of a government, corporation, or association. **presidency** *n.* **presidential** *adj.*

press (pres) *v.* To act upon or exert steady pressure or force; to squeeze out or extract by pressure; to smooth by heat and pressure; to iron clothes. **press** *n.* A machine used to produce printed material.

pres-sure (presh′er) *n.* The act of or the state of being pressed; a constraining moral force; any burden, force, painful feeling, or influence; the depressing effect of some-thing hard to bear.

pres-tige (pre stēzh′) *n.* Importance based on one's past reputation and achievements.

pres-to (pres´tō) *adv, Music* Very fast and quick; at once.

pre-sume (pri zōm´) *v.* To take for granted; to take upon oneself without permission; to proceed overconfidently. **presumable** *adj.* **presumably** *adv.* **presumer** *n.*

pre-sump-tion (pri zump´shan) *n.* Arrogant conduct or speech; something that can be logically assumed true until disproved.

pre-tend (pri tend´) *v.* To make believe; to act in a false way. **pretender** *n.*

pre-tense (pri tens´) *n.* A deceptive and false action or appearance; a false purpose.

pre-ten-tious (pri ten´shus) *adj.* Having or making claims to worth, excellence, etc.; showy.

pre-text (prē´tekst) *n.* A motive assumed in order to conceal the true purpose.

pret-ty (prit´ē) *adj.* Pleasant; attractive; characterized by gracefulness; pleasing to look at. *Slang* **sitting pretty** In a favorable position; good circumstances. **prettify** *v.* **prettily** *adv.*

pret-zel (pret´sel) *v.* A hard, cooked dough usually twisted in a knot and sprinkled with salt.

pre-vail (pri vāl´) *v.* To succeed; to win control over something; to predominate. **prevailer** *n.* **prevailingly** *adv.*

pre-vent (pri vent´) *v.* To keep something from happening; to keep from doing something.

pre-ven-tive *or* **preventative (pri ven´tiv)** *adj.* Protecting or serving to ward off harm, disease, or other problems.

pre-view *or* **prevue (prē´vū´)** *n.* An advance showing or viewing to invited guests.

pre-vi-ous (prē´vē us) *adj.* Existing or occurring earlier. **previously** *adv.*

price (pris) *n.* The set amount of money expected or given for the sale of something.

prick (prik) *n.* A small hole made by a sharp point. **prick** *v.* To pierce something lightly.

pride (prīd) *n.* A sense of personal dignity; a feeling of pleasure because of something achieved, done, or owned.

priest (prēst) *n.* A clergyman in the Catholic church who serves as mediator between God and His worshipers.

pri-ma-ry (prī´mer ē) *adj.* First in origin, time, series, or sequence; basic; fundamental.

prime (prīm) *adj.* First in importance, time, or rank. *n.* A period of full vigor, success, or beauty. **prime** *v.* To make ready by putting something on before the final coat, as to prime wood before painting.

prim-i-tive (prim´i tiv) *adj.* Of or pertaining to the beginning or earliest time; resembling the style or manners of an earlier time. **primitive** *n.*

primp (primp) *v.* To dress or arrange with superfluous attention to detail.

prin-ci-pal (prin´sipal) *adj.* Chief; most important. **principal** *n.* The headmaster or chief official of a school; a sum of money invested or owed which is separate from the interest.

prin-ci-ple (prin´si pl) *n.* The fundamental law or truth upon which others are based; a moral standard.

print (print) *n.* An impression or mark made with ink; the design or picture which is transferred from an engraved plate or other impression. **print** *v.* To stamp designs; to publish something in print, as a book or magazine.

printer fonts *n.* In *computer science*, type fonts built into a printer or a printer cartridge.

Print Screen key *n.* In *computer science*, the function key that commands the computer to copy the data on the monitor screen to the printer.

print-out (print´out´) *n.* In *computer science* the output of a computer printed on paper.

pri-or (prī´ér) *adj.* Previous in order or time.

pri-or-i-ty (prī or´i tē) *n.* Something which takes precedence; something which must be done or taken care of first.

prism (priz´um) *n.* A solid figure with triangular ends and rectangular sides, used to disperse light into a spectrum.

pris-on (priz´on) *n.* A place of confinement where people are kept while waiting for a trial or while serving time for breaking the law; jail. **prisoner** *n.*

pri-vate (prī´vit) *adj.* Secluded or removed from the public view; secret; intimate; owned or controlled by a group or person rather than by the public or government.

priv-i-lege (priv´i lij) *n.* A special right or benefit granted to a person.

prize (prīz) *n.* An award or something given to the winner of a contest; something exceptional or outstanding.

pro (prō) *n.* An argument in favor of or supporting something. *Slang* A professional or an expert in a given field.

prob-a-bil-i-ty (prob´a bil´i tē) *n., pl.* **-ies** The state or quality of being probable; a mathematical statement or prediction of the odds of something happening or not happening.

prob-a-ble (prob´a bl) *adj.* Likely to become a reality, but not certain or proved. **probably** *adv.*

pro-bate (prō´bāt) *n.* The act of legally

proving that a will is genuine.

pro-ba-tion (prō bā´shan) *n.* A period used to test the qualifications and character of a new employee; the early release of law breakers who must be under supervision and must report as requested to a probation officer.

probe (prōb) *n.* An instrument used for investigating an unknown environment; a careful investigation or examination.

prob-lem (prob´lem) *n.* A perplexing situation or question; a question presented for consideration, solution, or discussion. **problem** *adj.* **-matic** *adj.*

pro-ce-dure (pro sē´jer) *n.* A certain pattern or way of doing something; the normal methods or forms to be followed.

pro-ceed (pro sēd´) *v.* To carry on or continue an action or process. *Law* To begin or institute legal action.

proc-ess (pros´es) *n.* The course, steps, or methods toward a desired result. *Law* Any judicial request or order. In *computer science*, the sequence of operations which gives a desired result. **process** *v.* To compile, compute, or assemble data.

processing *n.* In *computer science*, data manipulation by the computer.

pro-ces-sion (pro sesh´an) *n.* A group which moves along in a formal manner; a parade.

pro-ces-sion-al (pro sesh´a nal) *adj.* A hymn sung during a procession; the opening of a church service. **processional** *adj.* Relating to a procession.

pro-ces-sor (pros´es or) *n.* In *Computer Science*, the central unit of a computer which processes data.

pro-claim (prō klām´) *v.* To announce publicly.

proc-la-ma-tion (prok´la mā´shan) *n.* An official public declaration or announcement.

pro-cras-ti-nate (prō kras´ti nāt´) *v.* To put off, defer, or postpone to a later time. **procrastination** *n.* **-tor** *n.*

proc-tor (prok´ter) *n.* A person in a university or college whose job it is to see that order is maintained during exams. **proctorial** *adj.*

pro-cure (prō kūr´) *v.* To acquire; to accomplish.

prod (prod) *v.* To arouse mentally; to poke with a pointed instrument. **prod** *n.* A pointed implement used to prod or poke.

prod-i-gal (prod´i gal) *adj.* Wasteful expenditure of money, strength, or time; extravagant. **prodigal** *n.* One who is a spendthrift or is wasteful.

pro-duce (pro dōs´) *v.* To bear or bring forth by a natural process; to manufacture; to make; to present or bring into view. **producer** *n.*

prod-uct (prod´ukt) *n.* Something produced, manufactured, or obtained *Math.* The answer obtained by multiplying.

pro-duc-tion (pro duk´shan) *n.* The process or act of producing; something produced, as a play.

pro-fane (pro fān´) *adj.* Manifesting disrespect toward sacred things; vulgar.

pro-fess (pro fes´) *v.* To admit or declare openly; to make an open vow.

pro-fes-sor (pro fes´ér) *n.* A faculty member of the highest rank in a college or university; a highly skilled teacher.

pro-fes-sion-al (pro fesh´a nal) *adj.* Having to do with a job or profession; referring to or engaging in an occupation, usually a sport for money rather than for fun.

pro-fi-cient (pro fish´ent) *adj.* Highly skilled in a field of knowledge. **proficiency** *n.* **proficiently** *adv.*

pro-file (prō´fīl) *n.* The outline of a person's face or figure as seen from the side; a short biographical sketch indicating the most striking characteristics.

prof-it (prof´it) *n.* The financial return after all expenses have been accounted for. *v.* To gain an advantage or a financial reward. **profitable** *adj.*

pro-found (pro found´) *adj.* Deeply held or felt; intellectually penetrating.

pro-fuse (pro fūs´) *adj.* Extravagant; giving forth lavishly; overflowing. **profusely** *adv.* **profuseness** *n.*

prog-e-ny (proj´e nē) *n., pl.* **-ies** One's offspring, children, or descendants.

prog-no-sis (prog nō´sis) *n., pl.* **prognoses** A prediction of the outcome and course a disease may take.

pro-gram (prō´gram) *n.* Any prearranged plan or course; a show or performance, as one given at a scheduled time. In *computer science*, a sequence of commands which tell a computer how to perform a task or sequence of tasks. **program** *v.*

programmable *adj.* In *computer science*, descriptive of a device whose function can be altered by the user.

programmable mouse *n.* In *computer science*, a mouse whose buttons may be assigned a command or series of commands, usually in conjunction with key combinations.

programmer *n.* In *computer science*, an individual who creates or alters routines for a computer.

programming language *n.* In *computer science*, a precise system of vocabulary and syntax for writing instructions for the computer.

prog-ress (prog´res) *n.* Forward motion or advancement to a higher goal; an advance; steady improvement.

pro-hib-it (prō hib′it) v. To forbid legally; to prevent.

pro-ject (proj′ekt′) n. A plan or course of action; a proposal; a large job. v. To give an estimation on something.

pro-jec-tile (pro jek′til) n. Anything hurled forward through the air.

pro-jec-tion (pro jek′shan) n. The act or state of being projected; the state or part that sticks out.

pro-lif-er-ate (prō lif′e rāt′) v. To grow or produce with great speed, as cells in tissue formation.

pro-logue (prō′log) n. An introductory statement at the beginning of a poem, song, or play.

pro-long (pro long′) v. To extend or lengthen in time.

prom-e-nade (prom′e nād′) n. An unhurried walk for exercise or amusement; a public place for such a walk, as the deck of a ship.

prom-i-nent (prom′i nent) adj. Jutting out; widely known; held in high esteem.

pro-mis-cu-ous (pro mis′kū us) adj. Lacking selectivity or discrimination, especially in sexual relationships.

prom-ise (prom′is) n. An assurance given that one will or will not do something; a pledge. **promise** v.

promissory note n. A written document or agreement that contains a promise to pay a debt to a particular person by a specified date or on demand.

prom-on-to-ry (prom′on tōr′ē) n. A projecting rock that extends into the sea.

pro-mote (pro mōt′) v. To raise to a higher rank or position; to work on behalf of. **promotion** n.

pro-mot-er (pro mō′tēr) n. A person who encourages; one who aids in promoting a financial understanding; a person who starts or sets up a business venture.

prompt (prompt) adj. Arriving on time; punctual; immediate. **prompt** v. To suggest or inspire. **prompt** n. In computer science, a cursor; a highlight on the monitor screen that indicates where the next character will be entered; a program query or instruction.

promp-ti-tude (promp′ti tōd′) n. Promptness.

prom-ul-gate (prom′ul gāt′) v. To proclaim; to make known to the public.

prone (prōn) adj. Lying flat; face down. **pronely** adv. **proneness** n.

prong (prong) n. A pointed, projecting part, as the end of a sharp instrument or the end of an antler.

pro-nom-i-nal (prō nom′inal) adj. Sharing the nature of a pronoun.

pro-noun (prō′noun′) n. Gram. A word which can be used in the place of a noun or noun phrase.

pro-nounce (pro nouns′) v. To deliver officially; to articulate the sounds. **pronunciation** n.

pro-nounce-ment (pro nouns′ment) n. Act of pronouncing a word or letter; a decision.

pron-to (pron′tō) adv. Quickly; promptly.

proof (prōf) n. The establishment of a fact by evidence; the act of showing that something is true; a trial impression from the negative of a photograph. **proof** v. To proofread; to mark and make corrections.

prop (prop) n. A support to keep something upright. v. To sustain.

prop-a-gate (prop′a gāt′) v. To reproduce or multiply by natural causes; to pass on qualities or traits.

pro-pel (pro pel′) v. To thrust or cause to move forward; to motivate.

prop-er (prop′ēr) adj. Appropriate; especially adapted or suited; conforming to social convention; correct.

proper adjective n. An adjective whose form is obtained from that of a proper noun.

proper fraction n. A fraction with a larger denominator than numerator.

prop-er-ly (prop′ēr lē) adv. In a suitable manner; fitly; correctly.

proper noun n. A noun denoting a specific person, place, or thing which is capitalized.

prop-er-ty (prop′ēr tē) n., pl. **properties** Any object of value owned or lawfully acquired, as real estate; a piece of land. **propertied** adj.

proph-e-cy (prof′i sē) n., pl. **-ies** A prediction made under divine influence.

proph-et (prof′it) n. One who delivers divine messages; one who foretells the future. **prophetess** n.

pro-pi-ti-ate (pro pish′ē āt′) v. To win the good will of; to stop from being angry. **pro-pitiation** n.

pro-po-nent (pro pō′nent) n. One who supports or advocates a cause.

pro-por-tion (pro pōr′shan) n. The relation of one thing to another in size, degree, or amount. v. To adjust or arrange with balance and harmony. **proportional** adj.

pro-por-tion-ate adj. In proportion; a true comparative relation.

pro-pose (pro pōz′) v. To present or put forward for consideration or action; to suggest someone for an office or position; to make an offer; to offer marriage. **proposal** n.

prop-o-si-tion (prop′o zish′an) n. A scheme or plan offered for consideration; a subject or idea to be proved or discussed. **proposition** v. To make a sexual suggestion.

pro-pri-e-tor (pro prī'i tér) *n.* The person who owns property and has the exclusive title or legal right.

pro-pri-e-ty (pro prī'i tē) *n.*, *pl.* **proprieties** The quality or state of being proper in accordance with recognized principles or usage.

pro-pul-sion (pro pul'shan) *n.* The act or process of propelling. **-sive** *adj.*

pro-pul-sis *n.* The outward protuberance of an organ.

pro-rate (prō rāt') *v.* To distribute or divide proportionately. **proration** *n.*

pro-scribe (prō skrīb') *v.* To banish; to outlaw; to prohibit.

prose (prōz) *n.* Ordinary language, speech, or writing which is not poetry.

pros-e-cute (pros'e kūt') *v.* To carry on. *Law* To bring suit against a person; to seek enforcement for legal process. **prosecution** *n.*

pros-pect (pros'pekt) *n.* Something that has the possibility of future success; a possible customer. *v.* To explore. **prospective** *adj.* **prospectively** *adv.*

pros-per (pros'pér) *v.* To be successful; to achieve success. **prosperous** *adj.*

pros-tate (pros'tāt) *n.* A small gland at the base of the male bladder.

pros-ti-tute (pros'ti tōt') *n.* One who sells the body for the purpose of sexual intercourse.

pros-trate (pros'trāt) *adj.* Lying with the face down to the ground. **prostrate** *v.* To overcome; to adopt a submissive posture. **prostrative** *adj.*

pro-tect (pro tekt') *v.* To guard or shield from attack or injury; to shield. **protective** *adj.* **protectively** *adv.*

protected field *n.* In *computer science*, a block of text, formula, etc. that cannot be altered.

protected files *n.* In *computer science*, read-only files; computer memory that may be read, but cannot be altered.

pro-tein (prō'tēn) *n. Biochem.* Any of a very large group of highly complex nitrogenous compounds occurring in living matter and composed of amino acids which are essential for tissue repair and growth.

pro-test (pro test') *v.* To make a strong formal objection; to object to. *n.* The act of protesting. **protester** *n.*

pro-to-col (prō'to kol') *n.* The code and rules of diplomatic and state etiquette. In *computer science*, the rules governing the transfer of data between a computer and peripherals or another computer.

pro-ton (prō'ton) *n. Physics* A unit of positive charge equal in magnitude to an electron.

pro-tract (prō trakt') *v.* To extend in space; to protrude.

pro-trude (prō trōd') *v.* To project; to thrust outward. **protrusion** *n.*

proud (proud) *adj.* Showing or having a feeling that one is better than the others; having a feeling of satisfaction; having proper self-respect or proper self-esteem.

prove (prōv) *v.* To show with valid evidence that something is true. **provable** *adj.* **provably** *adv.*

prov-erb (prov'erb) *n.* An old saying which illustrates a truth. **Proverbs** The book contained in the Bible which has many sayings supposed to have come from Solomon and others.

pro-vide (pro vīd') *v.* To supply or furnish with what is needed.

pro-vi-dence (prov'i dens) *n.* The supervision of God over his people.

pro-vi-sion (pro vizh'an) *n.* A supply of food or needed equipment.

pro-voke (pro vōk') *v.* To cause to be angry; to annoy. **provocation** *n.*

prox-i-mate (prok'si mit) *adj.* Immediate; direct; close.

prox-y (prok'sē) *n.*, *pl.* **proxies** The authority, usually written, to act for another.

prude (prōd) *n.* A person who is very modest, especially in matters related to sex. **prudery** *n.* **prudishness** *n.*

pru-dent (prōd'ent) *adj.* Cautious; discreet; managing very carefully.

psalm (säm) *n.* A sacred hymn, taken from the Book of Psalms in the Old Testament.

psal-tery (sol'tér ē) *n.* A type of musical instrument that was used many years ago.

pseu-do (sō'dō) *adj.* Being counterfeit or fake.

pseu-do-nym (sō'do nim) *n.* A name that is a fake. **pseudonymous** *adj.*

psi (sī) *n.* The twenty-third letter that is found in the Greek alphabet.

psil-o-cy-bin (sil'o sī'bin) *n.* Hallucinogenic compound from a fungus.

pso-ri-a-sis (so rī'a sis) *n. Pathol.* A noncontagious, chronic, inflammatory skin disease characterized by reddish patches and white scales.

psych (sī'kē) *v. Slang* To prepare oneself emotionally or mentally; to outwit or outguess.

psy-chas-the-ni-a (sī'kas thē'nē a) *n.* A type of emotional disorder that is caused by morbid fears.

psych-e-del-ic (sī'kidel'ik) *adj.* Causing extraordinary alterations in the consciousness of a person.

psy-chi-a-trist (si kī'a trist) *n.* A person who is a specialist in the field of psychiatry.

psy-chi-a-try (si kī'a trē) *n.* The branch of medicine which deals with the diagnosis and treatment of mental disorders.

psy-chic (sī'kik) *adj.* Cannot be explained by natural or physical laws. *n.* A person who communicates with the spirit world.

psy-cho-a-nal-y-sis (sī'kō *a* nal'i sis) *n.* The way of studying and analyzing one's subconscious thoughts.

psy-cho-an-a-lyst (sī'kō an'*a* list) *n.* The person who has been trained and is qualified to practice psychoanalysis on others.

psy-cho-bi-ol-o-gy (sī'kō bī ol'*o* jē) *n.* The science of the study of the relationships between the body and the mind.

psy-cho-gen-e-sis (sī'kō jen'i sis) *n.* The development of the mind.

psy-chol-o-gy (sī kol'*o* jē) *n., pl.* **-gies** The science of emotions, behavior, and the mind. **psychologist** *n.*

psy-cho-path (sī'kō path') *n.* A person suffering from a mental disorder characterized by aggressive antisocial behavior. **psychopathic** *adj.*

ptar-mi-gan (tär'mi gan) *n.* A type of species of grouse that has feathered feet and can be located in the cold regions.

PT boat (pē'tē'bōt) *n.* A type of small vessel of the navy.

pter-i-dol-o-gy (ter'i dol'*o* jē) *n.* The section or part of botany concerned with the study of ferns.

pter-o-dac-tyl (ter'o dak'til) *n.* A type of flying reptile that is now extinct and is believed to have lived thousands of years ago.

pter-o-saur (ter'o sor') *n.* A type of flying reptile that is now extinct.

pto-maine (tō'mān) *n.* A type of compound that can be very poisonous and is produced by an animal.

pto-sis (tō'sis) *n.* The drooping of a body organ. **ptotic** *adj.*

pty-a-lin (tī'a lin) *n.* A type of enzyme found in saliva of man and used to digest starch into maltose and dextrin.

pty-a-lism (tī'a liz'um) *n.* The excessive production of saliva in one's mouth.

pub (pub) *n.* A type of tavern.

pu-ber-ty (pū'bér tē) *n.* The stage of development in which sexual reproduction can first occur; the process of the body which culminates in sexual maturity. **pubertal** *adj.* **puberal** *adj.*

pu-ber-u-lent (pū ber'ū lent) *adj.* To be covered or to have down.

pu-bes-cence (pū bes'ens) *n.* The arrival of the stage of puberty in a person.

pubis (pū'bis) *n.* The part of the bone that forms the pelvis which is located in the front.

pub-lic (pū'bik) *adj.* Pertaining to or affecting the people or community; for everyone's use; widely or well known.

pub-li-can (pub'li kan) *n.* A person who collects taxes in a town or city; any collector of public revenues.

pub-li-ca-tion (pub'li kā'shan) *n.* The business of publishing; any pamphlet, book, or magazine.

public defender *n.* The attorney who defends someone without charging them because they cannot afford to hire an attorney for themselves.

public domain *n.* Public property; a published work whose copyrights have expired.

public house *n.* A type of inn.

pub-li-cist (pub'li sist) *n.* A press or publicity agent; a person who is a specialist in public relations; a specialist on international law.

pub-lic-i-ty (pu blis'i tē) *n.* The state of being known to the public; common knowledge.

pub-lic-ly (pub'lik lē) *adv.* Public manner; without concealment.

public property *n.* The property which is owned by the public.

public sale *n.* A type of sale which is made after a public notice.

pub-lish (pub'lish) *v.* To print and distribute a book, magazine, or any printed matter to the public. **publishable** *adj.*

pub-lish-er (pub'li shér) *n.* A person who will publish the works of others as in books.

puce (pūs) *adj.* To be a reddish brown.

puck (puk) *n.* A hard rubber disk used in playing ice hockey.

pud-dle (pud'l) *n.* A small pool of water.

pu-den-cy (pūd'en sē) *n.* The modesty of someone.

pudg-y (puj'ē) *adj.* To be fat and short.

pueb-lo (pweb'lō) *n.* A type of village of grouped houses that can be found in New Mexico, used by the Pueblo Indians of North America.

pu-er-ile (pū'ér il) *adj.* To be childish in character and actions.

pu-er-per-al (pū ür'pér al) *adj.* To be related to childbirth.

puff (puf) *n.* A brief discharge of air or smoke. *v.* To breathe in heavy breaths.

puff adder *n.* A type of large African viper that will puff up its body when it becomes agitated.

puff-ball (puf'bol') *n.* A type of fungus that is rounded and will discharge its spores in a mass of smoke.

puff-er (puf'ér) *n.* A person or something that puffs.

puff-er-y (puf'e rē) *n.* A type of praise which is very exaggerated.

puf-fin (puf'in) *n.* A type of sea bird that has a red bill and can be found in the North Atlantic regions.

pug (pug) *n.* A type of dog which looks like a small bulldog.

pug-na-cious (pug nā'shus) *adj.* Being

inclined to fight. **pugnaciousness** n.

pug-ree (pug´re) n. A type of turban that is worn to keep the rays of the sun off one's head.

pu-is-sance (pū´i sans) n. Might; strength.

puke (pūk) v. To throw up or vomit food.

puk-ka (puk´a) adj. To be good.

pull (pel) v. To apply force; to cause motion toward or in the same direction of; to remove from a fixed place.

pul-let (pūl´it) n. A young chicken.

pull-o-ver (pūl´ō´vér) n. A type of clothing that is put on the body by pulling it over the head.

pul-lu-late (pul´ya lāt´) v. To send off or forth buds.

pul-mo-nar-y (pul´mo ner´ē) adj. To be referring to the lungs.

pulmonary artery n. The artery which is going from the heart to the lungs and is carrying unoxygenated blood.

pulmonary vein n. A vein which comes from the lungs to the heart and is carrying the blood which has received oxygen in the lungs and is ready to be pumped through the rest of the body.

pulp (pulp) n. The soft juicy part of a fruit; a moist mass; inexpensive paper.

pul-pit (pel´pit) n. The elevated platform lectern used in a church from which a service is conducted.

pulp-wood (pulp´wüd´) n. A type of soft wood which is found in the pine and spruce, and it is used for the purpose of making paper.

pul-sate (pul´sāt) v. To beat rhythmically. **pulsation** n. **pulsator** n.

pul-sa-tile (pul´sa til) adj. To be throbbing.

pul-sa-tion (pul sā´shan) n. The action or the process of beating.

pul-sa-tor (pul´sā tér) n. Something which will pulsate, such as the heart.

pulse (puls) n., Physiol. The rhythmical beating of the arteries caused by the action of the heart. pulse v.

pul-sim-e-ter (pul sim´i tér) n. A type of device that is used to measure the rate and the strength of one's pulse.

pul-ver-a-ble (pul´vér a bl) adj. To be capable of being changed or reduced to dust.

pul-ver-ize (pul´ve rīz´) v. To be reduced to dust or powder by crushing.

pul-ver-u-lent (pul ver´ya lent) adj. To be made up of fine powder.

pul-vil-lus (pul vil´us) n. A type of cushion-like mass that is found on the feet of certain insects.

pu-ma (pū´ma) n. A type of large cat that is tawny in color and is located in North and South America.

pump (pump) n. A mechanical device for moving a gas or liquid. v. To raise with a pump; to obtain information

through persistent questioning.

pum-per-nick-el (pum´pér nik´el) n. A type of coarse bread that is made from rye.

pump-kin (pump´kin) n. A large, edible yellow-orange fruit having a thick rind and many seeds.

punch (punch) n. A tool used for perforating or piercing; a blow with the fist; a drink made of an alcoholic beverage and a fruit juice or other nonalcoholic beverage. v. To use a punch on something; to hit sharply with the hand or fist.

pun-cheon (pun´chon) n. A type of tool used to punch holes into something.

pun-chi-nel-lo (pun´chon) n. A person who is grotesque.

punching bag n. A type of leather bag that is stuffed and used to punch on for practice.

punc-tate (pungk´tāt) adj. To be ending with a point; marked with dots, that are variously scattered over a surface.

punc-til-i-ous (pungk til´ē us) adj. To be formal in one's behavior.

punc-tu-al (pungk´chō al) adj. Prompt; arriving on time.

punc-tu-ate (pungk´chō āt´) v. To mark words or written material with punctuation; to give or show emphasis.

punc-ture (pungk´chér) v. To prick or pierce with a pointed instrument. n. The act or effect of puncturing.

pun-gent (pun´jent) adj. Sharp or acrid in smell or taste.

pun-ish (pun´ish) v. To subject a person to confinement or impose a penalty for a crime.

punishment (pun´ish ment) n. A penalty which is imposed for breaking the law or a rule.

pun-ster (pun´stè) n. A person who likes to make puns.

punt (punt) n. A narrow, long, flat-bottomed boat; in football, a kick of a football dropped from the hands. v. To kick a football.

pun-ty (pun´tē) n. A rod that is made of iron and is used for the making of glassworks.

pu-ny (pū´nē) adj. To be weak and underdeveloped; insignificant or petty.

pup (pup) n. A puppy, young dog, or the young of other animals.

pu-pa (pū´pa) n. The stage in the development of an insect that is between the larva and the adult stage.

pupil (pū´pil) n. A person who attends school and receives instruction by a teacher.

pu-pil-age (pū´pi lij) n. The state of being a pupil.

pup-pet (pup´it) n. A small figure of an animal or person which is manipulated by hand or by strings. **puppeteer** n.

pup-py (pup´ē) *n.* The young of a dog.

pup tent *n.* A type of tent that sleeps only a few people.

pur-blind (pûr´blīnd´) *adj.* To be lacking in insight. **purblindness** *n.*

pur-chase (per´chas) *v.* To receive by paying money as an exchange.

pure (pûr) *adj.* Free from anything that damages, weakens, or contaminates; innocent; clean. **pureness** *n.*

pur-ga-tive (pûr´ga tiv) *n.* A type of medicine that is used to clean the bowels in preparation for surgery.

purge (perj) *v.* To make clean; to free from guilt or sin; to rid of anything undesirable, as unwanted persons. *Med.* To cause or induce emptying of the bowels. **purge** *n.*

pu-ri-fy (pûr´i fī´) *v.* To make clean or pure. **purification** *n.* **purifier** *n.*

pu-ri-ty (pûr´i tē) *n.* The quality of being pure; freedom from guilt or sin.

pur-ple (per´pl) *n.* A color between red and violet. **purplish** *adj.*

pur-port (per´pôrt) *v.* To give the appearance of intending; to imply, usually with the intent to deceive.

pur-pose (per´pos) *n.* A desired goal; an intention. **purposeful** *adj.* **purposeless** *adj.* **purposely** *adv.*

purr (per) *n.* The low, murmuring sound characteristic of a cat. **purr** *v.*

purse (pers) *n.* A small pouch or bag for money; a handbag; a pocketbook; the sum of money offered as a prize.

pur-sue (pèr sö´) *v.* To seek to achieve; to follow in an attempt to capture.

pur-suit (pèr söt´) *n.* The act of pursuing an occupation.

pur-vey (pèr vā´) *v.* To supply provisions as a service. **purveyance** *n.*

pus (pus) *n.* A yellowish secretion formed in infected tissue which contains bacteria.

push (pesh) *v.* To move forward by exerting force; to force oneself through a crowd; to sell illegally. *Slang* To sell illegal drugs.

pus-sy (pŭs´ē) *adj.* To be containing or to be filled with pus.

pus-tu-late (pus´cha lāt´) *v.* To cause blisters.

put (pet) *v.* To cause to be in a location; to bring into a specific relation or state; to bring forward for debate or consideration, as to put up for. **down** To humiliate.

pu-ta-tive (pū´ta tiv) *adj.* Commonly supposed.

pu-tre-fy (pū´tre fī´) *v.* To cause to decay; to decay. **putrefaction** *n.*

putt (put) *n.* In golf, a light stroke made on a putting green to get the ball into the hole.

puz-zle (puz´l) *v.* To bewilder; to confuse. *n.* A toy, board game, or word game which tests one's patience and skills.

pyg-my (pig´mē) *n. pl.* **-ies** A very small person or animal; a dwarf.

py-lon (pī´lon) *n.* A tower serving as a support for electrical power lines.

py-or-rhe-a (pī´o rē´a) *n., Pathol.* Inflammation of the gums and sockets of the teeth. **pyorrheal** *adj.*

py-ral-i-did *n.* A type of moth that has a slender body.

pyr-a-mid (pir´a mid) *n.* A solid structure with a square base and sides which meet at a point.

pyre (pī´er) *n.* A pile of combustible material for burning a dead body.

py-ro-ma-ni-a (pī´ro mā´nē a) *n.* A compulsion to set fires.

py-rom-e-ter (pī rom´tèr) *n.* A type of device that can measure very high temperatures. **pyrometrically** *adv.*

py-rope (pī´rōp) *n.* A type of deep-red garnet.

py-ro-pho-bi-a (pī´ro fō´bē a) *n.* A fear of fire that is considered to be abnormal.

py-ro-phor-ic (pī´ro for´ik) *adj.* To be highly flammable.

pyr-rhic (pir´ik) *n.* A metrical foot containing two short syllables.

pyr-rhu-lox-i-a (pir´a lok´sē a) *n.* A type of gray grosbeak that has a rose-colored breast and crest.

py-thon (pī´thon) *n.* A large nonvenomous snake which crushes its prey.

py-u-ri-a (pi ûr´ē a) *n., Pathol.* The condition where there is pus in the urine.

pyx-ie (pik´sē) *n.* A type of evergreen plant located in the eastern United States.

pyx-is (pik´sis) *n.* A small box, used by the Romans to hold jewelry.

Q

Q, q (kū) The seventeenth letter of the English alphabet.

qat *n.* A small plant found in Africa, the fresh leaf is chewed for a stimulating effect.

qi-vi-ut *n.* Yarn spun from the fine, soft hair of the musk ox.

qt. *abbr.* Quart.

quad-ran-gle (kwod´rang´gl) *n., Math* A plane figure with four sides and four angles.

quad-rant (kwod´rant) *n.* A quarter section of a circle, subtending or enclosing a central angle of 90 degrees.

qua-draph-o-ny *n.* The recording of sound using four transmission channels.

quad-rate (kwod´rit) *adj.* Being square or almost square.

qua-drat-ics (kwo drat´iks) *n.* A branch of algebra concerned with equations.

quad-ra-ture *n.* An arrangement of two

celestial bodies with a separation of 90 degrees.

qua-dren-ni-um (kwo dren´ē um) n. A period consisting of four years.

quad-ri-cen-ten-ni-al n. An anniversary celebrating 400 years.

quad-ri-ceps (kwod´ri seps˜) n. The muscle located in the front of the thigh.

qua-dri-ga n. A chariot pulled by four horses abreast.

qua-drille n. A square dance with five or six figures executed by four couples.

quad-ril-lion (kwo dril´yon) n. A thousand trillions; one followed by fifteen zeros.

quad-ri-par-tite adj. Consisting of four persons or parts.

quad-ri-ple-gic n. A person who is paralyzed in both arms and both legs.

qua-dru-ma-na n. A group of primates distinguished by hand-shaped feet.

quad-ru-ped (kwod´re ped˜) n. Any animal having four feet.

quad-ru-ple (kwo drö´pl) adj. Consisting of four parts; multiplied by four.

qua-dru-plet (kwo drup´lit) n. One of four infants born at the same time.

qua-dru-pli-cate (kwo drö´pli kit) n. Consisting of four identical parts.

quag-ga (kwag´a) n. A wild ass of Africa related to the zebras.

quag-mire (kwag´mïer´) n. An area of soft muddy land that gives way underfoot; a marsh.

qua-hog (kwo´hog) n. A clam found in the Atlantic Ocean.

quail (kwāl) n. pl. A small game bird, about the same size as the pigeon.

quaint (kwānt) adj. Pleasing in an old-fashioned, unusual way.

quake (kwāk) v. To shake or tremble violently.

quak-er (kwā´kér) n. The religious sect called the Society of Friends.

qual-i-fi-ca-tion An act of qualifying; the ability, skill, or quality which makes something suitable for a given position.

qualifier n. In *computer science*, a symbol or set of symbols in a formula that limits or clearly defines an element.

qual-i-fy (kwol´i fï´) v. To prove something able; restrict; limit; modify.

qual-i-ty (kwol´i tē) n., pl. **qualities** A distinguishing characteristic; a high degree of excellence.

qualm (kwäm) n. A sudden feeling of sickness; sensation of uneasiness.

quan-da-ry (kwon´da rē) n. A state of perplexity.

quan-ti-ty (kwon´ti tē) n. Number; amount; bulk; weight; a portion; as a large amount.

quan-tum (kwon´tum) n., pl. **quanta** An amount or quantity.

quar-an-tine (kwor´an tēn´) n. A period of enforced isolation for a specified period of time used to prevent the spread of a contagious disease.

quar-rel (kwor´el) n. An angry disagreement; quarrel. **quarrel** v. To find fault with; to dispute or debate.

quarrier (kwor´ē ér) n. A person who works in a stone quarry.

quar-ry (kwor´ē) n., pl. **quarries** An animal hunted for food; an open pit or excavation from which limestone or other material is being extracted.

quart (kwort) n. A unit of measurement equaling four cups.

quartan (kwor´tan) n. Something happening every four years.

quar-ter (kwor´tér) n. One of four equal parts into which anything may be divided; a place of lodging, as a barracks; a United States coin equal to 1/4 of a dollar.

quar-ter-back (kwor´tér bak´) n. *football* The offensive player who directs the plays for his team.

quarterdeck n. The part of a deck used for ceremonial and official use only.

quarter horse n. A horse capable of high speed and great endurance.

quarterly adj. Payable at intervals of three months.

quar-ter-mas-ter (kwor´tér mas´tér) n. The officer in charge of supplies for army troops; a navy officer who steers a ship and handles signaling equipment.

quar-tet (kwor tet´) n. A musical composition for four voices or instruments; any group or set of four.

quartz (kworts) n. A hard, transparent crystallized mineral.

qua-sar (kwä´sär) n. One of the most distant and brightest bodies in the universe, which emits immense quantities of radio waves.

quash (kwosh) v. To nullify or suppress by judicial action.

quay (kē) n. A landing place beside water for loading and unloading ships.

quea-sy (kwē´zē) adj. Nauseated; sick. **queasiness** n.

que-bra-cho n. A tree of the sumac family, which has hard wood found in South America.

queen (kwēn) n. The wife of a king; a woman sovereign or monarch; in chess, the most powerful piece on the board, which can move any number of squares in any direction; the fertile female in a colony of social insects.

quell (kwel) v. To put down with force; to quiet; to pacify.

quench (kwench) v. To extinguish or put out; to cool metal by thrusting into water; to drink to satisfy a thirst.

quer-cit-ron n. A large oak tree rich in tannin used in dyeing and tanning.

quer-u-lous (kwer´a lus) adj. Complaining or fretting; expressing complaints.

que-ry (kwēr′ē) n. An injury; a question. v. To question. In computer science, a request for data as a record or set of records from a database.

query language n. In *computer science*, formal notation for requesting specific data, as from a database.

quest (kwest) n. A search; pursuit; an expedition to find something.

ques-tion (kwes′chan) n. An expression of inquiry which requires an answer; a problem; an unresolved matter; the act of inquiring or asking. **question** v. To ask; to inquire.

ques-tion-able adj. Being in doubt; not certain or sure.

question mark n. A mark of punctuation, (?), used in writing to indicate a question.

ques-tion-naire (kwes′cha nâr′) n. A written series of questions to gather statistical information often used for a survey.

queue (kū) n. In *computer science*, a sequence of stored programs or data on hold for processing. **queue** v. To form a line; to stand in line.

quib-ble (kwib′l) v. To raise trivial objection. **quibble** n. **quibbler** n.

quiche n. Unsweetened custard baked in a pastry shell, usually with vegetables or seafood.

quick (kwik) adj. Moving swiftly; occurring in a short time; responding, thinking, or understanding something rapidly and easily. **quickly** adv.

quick-en adj. To become faster; to increase in pace.

quick–temp-ered (kwik′tem′pèrd) adj. Being easily angered or upset.

quick–wit-ted (kwik′wit′id) adj. Being quick to understand something.

quid (kwid) n. A small portion of tobacco; a cow's cud.

qui-es-cent (kwē es′ent) adj. Being in a state of quiet repose.

qui-et (kwī′it) adj. Silent; making very little sound; still; tranquil; calm. **quiet** v. To become or make quiet. **quiet** n. The state of being quiet.

quill (kwil) n. A strong bird feather; a spine from a porcupine; a writing instrument made from a long feather.

quilt (kwilt) n. A bed coverlet made of two layers of cloth with a soft substance between and held in place by lines of stitching. v. To sew or stitch together.

quince n. A fruit resembling a yellow apple used to make marmalade, etc.

quin-i-dine n. An alkaloid used in treating cardiac rhythm irregularities.

qui-nine (kwī′nīn) n. Chem. A very bitter, colorless, crystalline powder used in the treatment of malaria.

quin-quen-ni-al adj. Happening or being

done every five years.

quin-sy (kwin′zē) n. Pathol. A severe inflammation of the tonsils, which is accompanied by fever.

quin-tes-sence (kwin tes′ens) n. The most essential and purest form of anything.

quin-tet (kwin tet′) n. A musical composition written for five people; any group of five.

quin-til-lion (kwin til′yon) n. A thousand quadrillions, one followed by eighteen zeros.

quin-tu-ple (kwin tö′pl) adj. Increased five times; multiplied by five; consisting of five parts. **quintuple** v. To make five times larger.

quip (kwip) n. A sarcastic remark.

quire (kwī′ér) n. Twenty-five sheets of paper removed from a complete ream of paper; a set of all the sheets of paper necessary to form a book.

quirk (kwerk) n. A sudden, sharp bend or twist; a personal mannerism.

quis-ling (kwiz′ling) n. A person who is a traitor, working against his own country from within.

quit (kwit) v. To cease; to give up; to depart; to resign or leave a job or position.

quite (kwīt) adv. To the fullest degree; really; actually; to a great extent.

quittance n. A document which releases someone from an obligation.

quiv-er (kwiv′ér) v. To shake with a trembling motion. n. The arrows used in archery; the case holding the arrows.

quix-ot-ic (kwik sot′ik) adj. Extravagantly romantic; impractical.

quiz (kwiz) v. To question, as with an informal oral or written examination.

quo-rum (kwōr′um) n. The number of members needed in order to validate a meeting.

quo-ta (kwō′ta) n. An allotment or proportional share; a proportion or share required from each person, state, or group in order to meet a certain number required.

quo-ta-tion (kwō tā′shan) n. The exact quoting of words as a passage; the stated current price.

quotation mark n. One of a pair of punctuation marks " " or ' ' around a direct quote.

quote (kwōt) v. To repeat exactly what someone else has previously stated; to state the price of an item.

quo-tid-i-an (kwō tid′ē an) adj. Occurring or recurring daily.

quo-tient (kwō′shent) n. Math. The amount or number which results when one number is divided by another.

QWERTY keyboard n. In *computer science*, a keyboard with letters arranged the same as those on a typewriter.

R, r (är) The eighteenth letter of the English alphabet.

ra-ba-to (ra bā´tō) n. A wide lace-edged collar of the early 17th century.

rab-bet (rab´it) n. A recess or groove along the edge of a piece of wood cut to fit another piece to form a joint. v. To join the edges of in a rabbet joint.

rab-bi (rab´ī) n. An ordained leader of Jews; the leader and teacher of a Jewish congregation. **rabbinic** adj.

rab-bin-ate n. The dignity of a rabbi.

rab-bit (rab´it) n. A burrowing mammal related to but smaller than the hare.

rab-ble (rab´l) n. A disorderly crowd; a disordered jumble. **rabble** v.

rab-ble-ment n. A rabble; a tumult.

rab-ble-rous-er (rab´l rou˝zėr) n. A person who stirs masses of people to riot; a demogogue.

rab-id (rab´id) adj. Affected with rabies; mad; furious. **rabidly** adv.

ra-bies (rā´bēz) n. An acute, infectious viral disease of the central nervous system, often fatal, which is transmitted by the bite of an infected animal.

rac-coon (ra kön´) n., pl. **raccoons**, **raccoon** A nocturnal mammal with a black, mask-like face and a black and white ringed, bushy tail.

race (räs) n. A contest which is judged by speed; any contest, such as a race for an elective office. **race** v. **racer** n.

race (räs) n. The zoological division of the human population having common origin and physical traits, such as hair form and pigmentation; a group of people having such common characteristics or appearances.

ra-ceme (rā sēm´) n. A type of plant bearing flowers along its stalk. **racemose** adj.

rac-er (rā´sėr) n. A person who takes part in a race; one who runs in a race.

ra-chis (rā´kis) n. A type of axial structure.

ra-cial (rā´shal) adj. A characteristic of a race of people. **racially** adv.

rac-ism (rā´siz um) n. A thought or belief that one race is better than another race. **racist** n. One who believes that one race is better than another race.

rack-et or **racquet** n. A lightweight bat-like object with netting stretched over an oval frame, used in striking a tennis ball or a shuttlecock.

ra-clette n. A Swiss dish with cheese melted over a fire then scraped onto bread or potatoes.

rac-on-teur n. One who is skilled in the act of telling stories.

rac-y (rā´sē) adj. Having a spirited or strongly marked quality; slightly improper or immodest. **racily** adv.

ra-dar (rā´där) n. A system which uses radio signals to detect the presence of an object or the speed the object is traveling.

ra-dar as-tron-o-my n. Astronomy that deals with investigations of the celestial bodies of the solar system by comparing characteristics of reflected radar waves with characteristics of ones transmitted from earth.

ra-dar-scope (rā´där skōp´) n. A screen or oscilloscope that serves as a visual indicator in a radar receiver.

rad-dled adj. Being in a state of confusion; broken down; worn; lacking composure.

ra-di-al (rā´dē al) adj. Pertaining to or resembling a ray or radius; developing from a center axis.

ra-di-ance (rā´dē ans) n. The quality of being shiny; the state of being radiant; relating or emitting to radiant heat.

ra-di-ant (rā´dē ant) adj. Emitting rays of heat or light; beaming with kindness or love; projecting a strong quality.

ra-di-ant en-er-gy n. The energy traveling as a wave motion.

ra-di-ant heat n. Heat that is transmitted by radiation.

ra-di-a-tion (rā´dē ā´shan) n. An act of radiating; the process of emitting radiant energy in the form of particles or waves. **radiative** adj.

ra-di-a-tor (rā´dē ā´tėr) n. Something which radiates; a system of pipes for heating or cooling external or internal substances.

rad-i-cal (rad´i kal) adj. Proceeding from a foundation or root; drastic; making extreme changes in views, conditions, or habits; carrying convictions or theories to their fullest application. **radically** adv. **radicalness** n.

rad-i-cate v. To take root.

rad-i-cle (rad´i kl) n. The lower part of a plant embryo or seedling.

ra-di-o (rā´dē ō´) n. The technique of communicating by radio waves; the business of broadcasting programmed material to the public via radio waves.

ra-di-o-ac-tiv-i-ty n. Phys. A spontaneous emission of electromagnetic radiation, as from a nuclear reaction.

ra-di-o-chem-is-try n. The part of chemistry that deals with radioactive bodies. **radiochemical** adj.

ra-di-o-fre-quen-cy (rā´dē ōfrē´kwen sē) n. A frequency which is above 15,000 cycles per second that is used in radio transmission.

ra-di-o-gram (rā´dē ō gram´) n. A type of radiograph.

ra-di-o-graph n. A picture made by rays from a radioactive substance. **-ic** adj. **radiographically** adv.

ra-di-o-lar-o-an n. A member of the group of minute marine protozoans having an amoeboid body.

ra-di-o-lo-ca-tion n. The finding of the location of something using of radar.

ra-di-ol-o-gy (rā′dē ol′o jē) n. A science which deals with rays from a radioactive substance and their uses for medical diagnosis. **radiologist** n..

ra-di-o-lu-cen-cy n. The state of being permeable to radiation.

ra-di-o-pho-to n. A picture transmitted via radio.

ra-di-o-sonde n. A miniature radio transmitter with instruments for broadcasting the humidity, pressure, and temperature.

rad-ish (rad′ish) n. The pungent, edible root of the radish plant.

ra-di-um (rā′dē um) n A radioactive metallic element symbolized by Ra.

ra-di-us (rā′dē us) n., pl. **radii** or **radiuses** A line from the center of a circle to its surface or circumference.

ra-dix n. The origin of something; a root.

ra-dome n. A plastic housing which protects the antenna assembly on an airplane.

ra-don (rā′don) n. A heavy, colorless, radioactive gaseous element symbolized by Rn.

rad-u-la (raj′e la) n. The chitinous band in a mollusk's mouth that is used to break up its food. **radular** adj.

raff (raf) n. The rabble of a group or town; riffraff.

raf-fi-a (raf′ē a) n. A fiber from an African palm tree used for making baskets, hats, and other woven articles.

raf-fi-nose (raf′i nōs′) n. A slightly sweet sugar obtained commercially from cotton seed meal.

raff-ish (raf′ish) adj. Something marked by crudeness or flashy vulgarity. **raffishly** adv. **raffishness** n.

raf-fle (raf′l) n. A game of chance; a lottery in which one buys chances to win something.

raf-fle-sia n. A type of plant that has foul-smelling flowers and appears to be stemless.

raft (raft) n. A floating structure made from logs or planks and used for water transportation.

rag (rag) n. A cloth which is useless and sometimes used for cleaning purposes.

ra-ga (rä′ga) n. Ancient melodic patterns in Indian music.

rage (rāj) n. Violent anger; intense feelings. **raging** adj.

rag-gle (rag′l) n. A small groove cut in masonry.

rag-i (rag′ē) n. East Indian cereal grass used as a staple food in the Orient.

rag-lan (rag′lan) n. A loose fitting coat with extra wide sleeves.

raglan sleeve n. A sleeve with slanted seams from the underarm to the neck.

rag-man n. A person who collects objects

which have been discarded by others.

ra-gout (ra gü′) n. A highly seasoned meat and vegetable dish with a thick sauce.

raid (rād) n. A sudden invasion or seizure. **raid** v.

rail (rāl) n. A horizontal bar of metal, wood, or other strong material supported at both ends or at intervals; the steel bars used to support a track on a railroad.

rail-ler-y n. A teasing that is good-humored.

rail-road n. A road having a line of rails providing a track for cars propelled by a locomotive. **railroader** n.

railroad worm n. A fruit fly larva.

rail-split-ter n. A person who chops logs into fence rails.

rai-ment (rā′ment) n. Garments.

rain (rān) n. The condensed water from atmospheric vapor, which falls to earth in the form of drops.

rain-bow (rān′bō′) n. An arc that contains bands of colors of the spectrum and is formed opposite the sun and reflects the sun's rays, usually visible after a light rain shower.

rain forest n. A tropical woodland that has an annual rainfall of at least 100 inches.

rain-wear n. Waterproof clothing.

raise (rāz) v. To cause to move upward; to build; to make greater in size, price, or amount; to increase the status; to grow; as plants; to rear as children; to stir one's emotions; to obtain or collect, as funds or money.

raised (rāzd) adj. Being elevated.

rai-sin (rā′zin) n. A grape dried for preservation and eating.

ra-ja (rä′ja) n. An Indian prince or chief.

ral-len-tan-do (rä′len tän′dō) adj. In music, a gradual decrease in tempo.

ral-ly (ral′ē) v. To call together for a purpose. **rally** n. A rapid recovery, as from depression, exhaustion, or any setback; in a meeting whose purpose is to rouse or create support; an automobile race over public roads at average speeds between checkpoints over a route unfamiliar to the participants.

ram (ram) n. A male sheep; an implement used to drive or crush by impact; to cram or force into place.

RAM abbr. Random access memory.

ram-ble (ram′bl) v. To stroll or walk without a special destination in mind; to talk without sequence of ideas. **ramble** n. **ramblingly** adv.

ram-bler n. A climbing rose with small flowers in large clusters.

ram-bunc-tious (ram bungk′shus) adj. Rough or boisterous; unruly.

ram-bu-tan n. A bright red spiny fruit

found on the soapberry plant.

ram-e-kin (ram´e kin) n. A dish made of cheese with bread crumbs or eggs baked in a mold; a baking dish.

ra-men-tum (ra men´tum) n. A type of scaly material that adheres to the leaves and the stems of certain ferns.

ra-met n. A member of a clone.

ra-mie (ram´ē) n. A perennial plant with strong fibers used in the manufacture of clothing.

ram-i-form (ram´i form´) adj. To have the shape of a branch.

ram-i-fy (ram´i fī´) v. To send forth branches.

ra-mose (rā´mōs) adj. To have branching.

ramp (ramp) n. An incline which connects two different levels; movable staircase allows passengers to enter or leave an aircraft.

ram-page (ram pāj´) n. A course of destruction or violent behavior. **rampage** v. To storm about in a rampage. **rampageous** adj.

ram-pan-cy (ram´pan sē) n. The state or quality of being rampant.

ram-pant (ram´pant) adj. Acting or growing without control; wild in actions; extravagant; standing on the hind legs and elevating both forelegs. **rampantly** adv.

ram-part (ram´pärt) n. An embankment raised as a fortification or barrier.

ram-pi-on n. A tuberous root bellflower with leaves which can be used in salads.

ram-rod (ram´rod´) n. A metal rod used to drive or plunge the charge into a muzzle-loading gun or pistol; the rod used for cleaning the barrels of a rifle or other firearm.

ram-shack-le (ram´shak´l) adj. Likely to fall apart from poor construction or maintenance.

rams-horn (ramz´horn´) n. A snail used in an aquarium as a scavenger.

ram-til n. A tropical herb grown for its oil seeds.

ram-u-lose (ram´ya lōs´) adj. To have small branches.

ranch (ranch) n. A large establishment for raising cattle, sheep, or other livestock; a large farm that specializes in a certain crop or animal.

ran-cid (ran´sid) adj. Having a rank taste or smell. **rancidness** n.

ran-cor (rang´kėr) n. Bitter ill will. **rancorous** adj. **rancorousness** n.

ran-dom (ran´dom) adj. Done or made in a way that has no specific pattern or purpose; to select from a group whose members all had an even chance of being chosen. **randomly** adv.

ran-dom-iz-a-tion n. An arrangement to simulate a chance distribution.

rang v. Past tense of ring.

range (rānj) n. An area over which anything moves; an area of activity; a tract of land over which animals such as cattle and horses graze; an extended line or row especially of mountains; an open area for shooting at a target; large cooking stove with burners and oven; the limits of a series. **range** v. To arrange in a certain order; to extend or proceed in a particular direction.

range finder n. Instrument that is used in gunnery to determine the distance to a target.

rang-er (rān´jėr) n. A person who is hired to tend the public forests.

rang-y (rān´jē) adj. To be adapted for moving around. **ranginess** n.

ra-ni (rä´nē) n. A Hindu queen.

ra-nid n. A large family of frogs.

rank (rank) n. A degree of official position or status. **rank** v. To place in order, class, or rank. **rank** adj. A strong and disagreeable odor, smell, or taste. **rankly** adv. **rankness** n.

ran-kle (rang´kl) v. To cause anger or deep bitterness.

ran-sack (ran´sak) v. To search or plunder through every part of something.

ran-som (ran´som) n. The price demanded or paid for the release of a kidnaped person; the payment for the release of a person or property detained. **ransom** v.

rant (rant) v. To talk in a wild, excited loud way. **ranter** n.

ran-u-la (ran´ū la) n. A type of cyst that can occur under the tongue due to a blockage in a duct.

rap (rap) v. To talk with people with similar interest and problems.

ra-pa-cious adj. Living on prey seized alive; taking by force; plundering.

rape (rāp) n. The crime of forcible sexual intercourse; abusive treatment.

rap-id (rap´id) adj. Having great speed; completed quickly or in a short time. **rapidity** n. **rapidness** n.

rap-id–fire adj. Pertaining to firing shots in close succession to one another.

rap-id trans-it n. The train system that runs within a city and in the area around it.

ra-pi-er (rā´pē ėr) n. A long, slender, straight sword with two edges.

rap-ine (rap´in) n. The forcible taking of another's property.

rap-pa-ree n. An Irish soldier or bandit.

rap-pee (ra pē´) n. A snuff made from dark tobacco leaves.

rap-pel (ra pel´) n. A descent from a cliff using a rope under one thigh, across the back and over the opposite shoulder.

rap-pi-ni (rap skal on) n. An immature turnip plant used for its greens.

rap-port (ra pōr´) *n*. A harmonious relationship.

rap-proche-ment (rä prosh män´) *n*. The establishment of cordial relations.

rap-scal-ion (rap skal´yon) *n*. A rascal.

rapt (rapt) *adj*. Deeply absorbed or carried away with something and not noticing anything else. **raptness** *n*.

rap-tor (rap´tôr) *n*. A bird of prey.

rap-to-ri-al (rap tôr´ē al) *adj*. Having the ability to seize prey.

rap-ture (rap´chėr) *n*. An experience of being carried away by emotion. **rapturous** *adj*. **rapturously** *adv*.

rare (râr) *adj*. Scarce; infrequent; often held in high esteem or admiration because of infrequency. **rareness** *n*.

rare-bit (râr´bit) *n*. A dish made of cheese poured over toast or crackers.

rar-e-fy *v*. To make thin or less dense.

rare-ly *adv*. Seldom; not often.

rar-ing *adj*. Being full of eagerness and enthusiasm.

rar-i-ty *n*. The quality of something being rare.

ras-bo-ra (raz bôr´a) *n*. A breed of brightly colored fish often kept in tropical aquariums.

ras-cal (ras´kal) *n*. A person full of mischief; a person who is not honest.

ras-cal-i-ty *n*. Behavior which is mischievous.

rash (rash) *adj*. Acting without consideration or caution. *n*. A skin irritation or eruption caused by an allergic reaction.

rash-er *n*. A thin slice of bacon; a portion of several slices of bacon.

ra-so-ri-al (ra sôr´ē al) *adj*. Scratching the ground in search of food.

rasp *n*. A file with coarse raised and pointed projections. **rasp** *v*. To scrape or rub with a coarse file; to utter something in a rough, grating voice. **rasper** *n*.

rasp-ber-ry (raz´bėr´ē) *n*. A small edible fruit, red or black in color and having many small seeds. *Slang* Contemptuous sound made by expelling air with the tongue between the lips in order to make a vibration.

rasp-y (ras´pē) *adj*. Grating; irritable.

ras-ter *n*. An area onto which an image is reproduced in a kinescope.

rat-a-fia (rat´a fē´a) *n*. A liqueur flavored with kernels of fruit and almonds.

rat-a-tat (rat´a tat´) *n*. A sharp tapping, or repeated knocking.

ratch-et (rach´it) *n*. A mechanism consisting of a pawl that allows a wheel or bar to move in one direction only.

rate (rāt) *n*. The measure of something to a fixed unit; the degree of price or value; a fixed ratio or amount. **rate** *v*. To appraise.

ra-tel (rāt´el) *n*. An African nocturnal carnivorous mammal resembling a badger.

rate of ex-change *n*. The amount of one currency which equals the given amount of another.

rathe (rāth) *adj*. To be before the normal time.

rath-er (rath´ėr) *adv*. Preferably; with more reason or justice; more accurate or precise.

rat-i-cide (rat´i sīd´) *n*. A material that is used to kill rats.

rat-i-fy (rat´i fī) *v*. To approve something in an official way.

ra-ti-ne (rat´i nā´) *n*. A nubby ply yarn made by twisting a thick and a thin yarn under pressure.

rat-ing (rā´ting) *n*. A relative evaluation or estimate of something.

ra-tio (rā´shō) *n., pl*. **ratios** The relationship between two things in amount, size, degree, expressed as a proportion.

ra-ti-o-ci-na-tion (rash˝ē os´i nā´shan) *n*. A reasoned train of thought.

ra-tion (rash´an) *n*. A fixed portion or share. **ration** *v*. To provide or allot in rations. **rationing** *n*.

ra-tion-al (rash´a nal) *adj*. Having the faculty of reasoning; being of sound mind. **rationality** *n*. **rationally** *adv*.

ra-tion-ale *n*. An explanation of principles, opinions, beliefs, or phenomena.

ra-tio-nal-ize *v*. To provide plausible but not truthful reasons for conduct.

ra-toon (ra tön´) *v*. To grow or sprout up from the root.

rat race *n*. A strenuous activity or rush.

rat-tan (ra tan´) *n*. An Asian palm whose stems are used to make wicker works.

rat-teen *n*. A woolen fabric which is coarse in texture.

rat-tle (rat´l) *v*. To make a series of rapid, sharp noises in quick succession; to talk rapidly; chatter. **rattle** *n*. A baby's toy made to rattle when shaken.

rat-tle-brain (rat´l brān´) *n*. A thoughtless person. **rattlebrained** *adj*.

rat-tle-trap (rat´l trap´) *n*. Something that is rickety or noisy; an old car.

rat-ty (rat´ē) *adj*. Shabby; unkempt.

rau-cous (ro´kus) *adj*. Loud and rowdy; having a rough, hoarse sound; disorderly. **raucously** *n*.

raun-chy *adj*. Being dirty, slovenly.

rau-wol-fi-a *n*. A type of shrub which is used as a source of the drug reserpine.

rav-age (rav´ij) *v*. To bring on heavy destruction; devastate. **ravagement** *n*. **ravager** *n*.

rave (rāv) *v*. To speak incoherently; to speak with enthusiasm. **rave** *n*. The act of raving.

rav-el (rav´el) *v*. To separate fibers or

threads; to unravel. **ravel** *n.* A loose thread; something tangled.

ra-ven (rā´ven) *n.* A large bird, with shiny black feathers. **raven** *adj.* Of or relating to the glossy sheen or color of the raven.

rav-en-ing *adj.* To be hunting in order to devour something.

rav-en-ous (rav´e nus) *adj.* Being very hungry and eager for food.

rav-in (rav´n) **1.** Something seized as prey.

ra-vine (ra vēn) *n.* A deep gorge with steep sides in the earth's surface, usually created by flowing water.

rav-ing (rav´ ing) *adj.* An incoherent, wild, or extravagant outburst.

rav-i-o-li (rav´ē ō´lē) *n.* A small piece of dough filled with meat or cheese served in a tomato sauce.

rav-ish (rav´ish) *v.* To seize and carry off; to rape. **ravishment, ravisher** *n.*

rav-ish-ing *adj.* Unusually striking.

raw (ro) *adj.* Uncooked; in natural condition; not processed; inexperienced; damp, sharp, or chilly. **rawly** *adv.* **rawness** *n.*

raw material *n.* Material that is existing in its natural form.

ray (rā) *n.* A thin line of radiation or light; a small trace or amount; one of several lines coming from a point.

ray-on (rā´on) *n.* A synthetic cellulose yarn; any fabric made from such yarn.

raze (rāz) *v.* To destroy or demolish.

ra-zor (rā´zér) *n.* A sharp cutting instrument used especially for shaving.

razz (raz) *v. Slang* To heckle; to tease.

raz-zle–daz-zle (raz´l daz´l) *n.* A state of complete confusion.

re- *prefix* Again, anew, or reverse action.

reach (rēch) *v.* To stretch out; to be able to grasp. **reach** *n.* The act of stretching out. **reachable** *adj.* **reacher** *n.*

re-act (rē akt´) *v.* To act in response to. *Chem.* To undergo a chemical change; to experience a chemical reaction; to move in a reverse direction; to cause to react.

re-ac-tant (rē ak´tant) *n.* Substance which enters into and is altered by the course of a chemical reaction.

re-ac-tion (rē ak´shən) *n.* The mental or bodily response to an activity; the process or act of reacting; the action that is induced by vital resistance to another action; exhaustion caused by excessive exertion or stimulation; an emotional disorder forming a person's response to his life; the force that a body exerts when encountering force from another body in the opposite direction; a chemical change; the state resulting from an interaction of chemical entities.

re-ac-tion-ar-y *adj.* Marked by, or relating to political reaction.

re-ac-ti-vate *v.* To activate something again. **reactively** *adv.* **reactiveness** *n.* **reactivity** *n.*

re-ac-tor (rē ak´tér) *n.* A person, object, device, or substance which reacts to something.

read (rēd) *v.* To visually go over something, as a book, and to understand its meaning; to learn or be informed; to perceive something in a meaning which may or may not actually be there; to become acquainted with or look at the contents; to recognize the nature of by observing outward expression or signs.

read-i-ly (red´i lē) *adv.* Without hesitation; without a lot of difficulty.

read-ing *n.* An interpretation of something; the act of reading; a particular interpretation or version; the indication of a state of affairs.

read-out (rēd´out´) *n.* In *computer science,* the process of removing information from a computer and displaying it in an understandable form; the process of reading something; the radio transmission of pictures or information from a space vehicle either immediately upon acquisition or by tape recording playback.

read-y (red´ē) *adj.* Prepared for use or action; quick or prompt. **readiness** *n.*

read-y-made *n.* Something made beforehand for sale to the public; something that is lacking individuality or originality.

Reagan, Ronald Wilson *n.* (1911-) The fortieth president of the United States from 1981-1989.

re-a-gent (rē ā´jent) *n.* Any substance which causes a chemical reaction.

re-ag-gre-gate *v.* To reform into a whole. **reaggregate, reaggregation** *n.*

re-al (rē´al) *adj.* Something which is existing, genuine, true, or authentic. *Law* Property which is regarded as permanent, fixed, or immovable; not illusory, artificial, or fraudulent.

real estate *n.* The property in land and buildings.

re-al-gar *n.* An orange-red mineral consisting of arsenic sulfide with a resinous luster.

re-a-li-a (rē ā´lē a) *n.* Objects used to relate classroom teaching to the real life of people studying.

re-al-ism (rē´a liz´um) *n.* Concern with actual facts and things as they really are. **realist** *n.* **realistic** *adj.*

re-al-i-ty (rē al´i tē) *n. pl.* **realities** The fact or state of being real or genuine; an actual situation or real event; something that is neither dependent nor derivative but exists necessarily.

re-al-ize (rē´a līz´) *v.* To understand

correctly; to make real; to make or cause to seem real. **realizable** *adj.* **realizer, realization** *n.*

re-al-ly (rē´a lē) *adv.* Actually; truly; indeed; unquestionably.

realm (relm) *n.* A scope or field of any power or influence.

re-al-po-li-tik *n.* Politics that are based on material and practical factors and not on ethical or theoretical objectives.

real-valued *adj.* Using only real numbers for values.

ream (rēm) *n.* A quantity of paper containing 500 sheets; a huge amount. **ream** *v.* To widen the opening of something; to shape a hole by reaming.

reap (rēp) *v.* To harvest a crop with a sickle or other implement; to cut with a scythe, sickle, or other harvesting machine.

reap-er (rē´pėr) *n.* A machine used to reap grain; one who reaps.

reap-hook *n.* An implement that is held by the hand and has a hook-shaped blade used in reaping grain.

rear (rēr) *n.* The back. **rear** *adj.* Of or at the rear. **rear** *v.* To raise up on the hind legs; to raise as an animal or child; to erect by building something.

rea-son (rē´zon) *n.* A statement given to confirm or justify a belief, promise, or excuse; the ability to decide things, to obtain ideas, to think clearly, and to make logical and rational choices and decisions. **reason** *v.* To discuss something logically. **reasoning** *adj.*

rea-son-a-ble (rē´zo na bl) *adj.* Moderate; rational; not excessive or extreme. **reasonableness** *n.*

re-as-sur-ance *n.* The act of reassuring; reinsurance.

re-as-sure (rē´a sher´) *v.* To restore confidence. **reassuringly** *adv.*

reave *v.* To carry away. **reaver** *n.*

re-bar-ba-tive *adj.* The act of being repellent. **rebarbatively** *adv.*

re-bate (rē´bāt) *n.* A deduction allowed on items sold; a discount; money which is returned to the purchaser from the original payment. **rebate** *v.* To return part of the payment. **rebater** *n.*

reb-be *n.* A Jewish spiritual leader.

re-bec *n.* An ancient musical instrument with a pear-shaped body and slender neck.

re-bel (ri bel´) *v.* To refuse allegiance; to resist any authority; to react with violence; to take arms against a government.

re-bel-lion (ri bel´yon) *n.* An organized uprising to change or overthrow an existing authority.

re-bel-lious (ri bel´yus) *adj.* Engaged in rebellion; relating to a rebel or rebellion; characteristic of a rebellion. **rebelliously** *adv.* **rebelliousness** *n.*

re-birth (rē berth´) *n.* A revival or renaissance; reincarnation; spiritual regeneration.

re-bound (ri bound´) *v.* To spring back; to recover from a setback or frustration; to gain possession of a rebound ball in basketball. **rebound** *n.* Recoil.

re-bo-zo *n.* A long scarf worn by Mexican women.

re-broad-cast (rē brod´kast´) *v.* To repeat or broadcast again at a later time or date. **rebroadcaster** *n.*

re-buff (ri buf´) *v.* To refuse abruptly; to snub.

re-build (rē bild´) *v.* To restore or make extensive changes to a building; to reconstruct; remodel.

re-buke (ri būk´) *v.* To reprimand; to criticize sharply; to turn back. **rebuke** *n.* Strong disapproval.

re-bus (rē´bus) *n.* A riddle using words or syllables whose names resemble the intended words or syllables in sound.

re-but (ri but´) *v.* To try and prove someone wrong by argument or evidence; to contradict by formal argument.

re-but-tal *n.* An argument that rebuts.

re-but-ter (ri but´ėr) *n.* The reply of a defendant to the plaintiff's surrejoinder.

re-cal-ci-trant (ri kal´si trant) *adj.* Being difficult to handle or operate.

re-cal-cu-late (rē kal´ku lāt´) *v.* To calculate again to discover an error or formulate new conclusions.

re-ca-les-cence *n.* An increase in temperature occurring while cooling metal.

re-call (ri kol´) *v.* To order or summon to return to ask for something to be returned; so that defects can be fixed or repaired; to remember; to recollect. **recallability** *n.* **recallable** *adj.*

re-cant (ri kant´) *v.* To formally admit that a previously held belief was wrong by making public confession; to withdraw; renounce. **recantation** *n.*

re-cap (rē´kap´) *v.* To restore an old tire; to review or summarize something. **recappable** *adj.*

re-cap-i-tal-i-za-tion *n.* A revision of the capital structure of a corporation.

re-ca-pit-u-la-tion *n.* A concise summary; the third section of a sonata.

re-cast (rē kast´) *v.* To cast new people in a play; to cast once again.

re-cede (ri sēd´) *v.* To move back; as flood water; to withdraw from an agreement; to grow less or smaller.

re-ceipt (ri sēt´) *n.* The written acknowledgment of something received. **receipts** An amount of money received.

re-ceiv-ables (ri sē´va blz) *n.* The amount of money received.

re-ceive (ri sēv´) *v.* To take or get something; to greet customers or guests; to accept as true or correct; to assimilate through senses.

re-ceiv-er (ri sē´vêr) n. A person that receives something.

re-cen-sion (ri sen´shan) n. A revision of a text.

re-cent (rē´sent) adj. Happening at a time just before the present; relating to a short time ago. **recently** adv. **recentness** n.

re-cep-ta-cle (ri sep´ta kl) n. Anything which holds something; an electrical outlet designed to receive a plug.

re-cep-tion (ri sep´shan) n. The act or manner of receiving something; a formal entertainment of guests, as a wedding reception.

re-cep-tion-ist (ri sep´sha nist) n. An employee who greets callers and answers the telephone for a business.

re-cep-tive (ri sep´tiv) adj. Able to receive; open and responsive to ideas. **receptively** adv. **receptivity** n.

re-cep-tor (ri sep´têr) n. A group of cells that receive stimuli.

re-cess (ri ses´) n. A break in the normal routine of something; a depression or niche in a smooth surface.

re-ces-sion (ri sesh´an) n. The act of receding; withdrawal; a period or time of reduced economic activity.

re-ces-sion-al (ri sesh´a nal) n. A musical piece at the conclusion of a service. **recessive** adj. Having a tendency to go backward. **recessively** adv.

re-charge v. To restore the active materials in a battery; to make a new attack. **recharger** n. **rechargeable** adj.

re-cheat n. A hunting call on a horn to assemble the hounds.

re-cid-i-vism n. A tendency to relapse into a previous mode of behavior.

rec-i-pe (res´i pē´) n. The directions and a list of ingredients for preparing food.

re-cip-i-ent (ri sip´ē ent) n. A person who receives.

re-cip-ro-cal (ri sip´ro kal) adj. To return the same way.

reciprocal pronoun n. A pronoun to denote mutual action between members in a plural subject.

re-cip-ro-cate (ri sip´ro kāt´) v. To give and return mutually, one gift or favor for another. **reciprocator** n.

re-cip-ro-ca-tion n. A mutual exchange; an alternating motion. **-tive** adj.

rec-i-proc-i-ty n. Mutual exchange of privileges; the state of being reciprocal.

re-cit-al (ri sit´al) n. A performance given by an individual musician or dancer. **recitalist** n.

rec-i-ta-tion n. An instance of repeating aloud; a student's oral reply to questions.

re-cite (ri sīt´) v. To repeat something from memory; give an account of

something in detail. **reciter** n.

reck-less (rek´lis) adj. State of being careless and rash when doing something. **-ness** n. **-iy** adv.

reck-on (rek´on) v. To calculate; to compute; to estimate; to consider; to assume. **reckon with** Take into consideration.

re-claim (ri klām´) v. To redeem; to reform; to recall; to change to a more desirable condition or state.

rec-la-ma-tion (rek´la mā´shan) n. The state of being reclaimed.

re-cline (ri klīn´) v. To assume a prone position.

re-clos-able adj. Capable of being shut or closed again.

rec-luse (rek´lōs) n. A person who chooses to live in seclusion.

rec-og-ni-tion (rek´og nish´an) n. An acknowledgment which is formal; the action of recognizing something; special attention or notice.

re-cog-ni-zance (ri kog´ni zans) n. An amount of money which will be forfeited for a nonperformance of an obligation.

rec-og-nize (rek´og nīz´) v. To experience or identify something or someone as having been known previously; to be appreciative. **recognizable** adj. **recognizably** adv.

re-coil (ri koil´) v. To fall back or to rebound; to spring back under pressure.

rec-ol-lect (rek´o lekt´) v. To remember or recall to the mind. **recollection** n.

rec-om-mend (rek´o mrnd´) v. To suggest to another as desirable; advise. **recommendation** n. **-able** adj.

re-com-mit (rē´ko mit´) v. To refer back to; to entrust or consign again. **recommitment, recommital** n.

rec-om-pense (rek´om pens´) v. To reward with something for a service.

re-com-pose (rē´kom pōz´) v. To restore the composure of. **recomposition** n.

rec-on-cile (rek´on sīl´) v. To restore a friendship after an estrangement. **reconcilably** adv. **reconcilable** adj. **reconciler** n. **reconcilement** n.

rec-on-dite (rek´on dīt´) adj. Being obscure. **reconditely** adv.

re-con-di-tion (rē´kon dish´an) v. To return to a good condition.

re-con-firm (rē´kon ferm´) v. Confirm something again. **reconfirmation** n.

re-con-nais-sance (ri kon´i sans) n. An observation of territory such as that of the enemy.

re-con-noi-ter (rē´ko noi´têr) v. To survey a region.

re-con-sid-er (rē´kon sid´êr) v. To think about again with a view to changing a previous action or decision. **reconsideration** n.

re-con-sti-tute v. To restore to a former condition. **reconstitution** n.

re-con-struct v. To build something again. **reconstructible, -tive** adj.

re-con-struc-tion (rē´kon struk´shan) n. Something which has been reconstructed or rebuilt.

re-con-ver-sion n. Returning back to the previous or original state.

re-con-vey v. To return back to a previous position or owner. **reconveyance** n.

re-cord (ri kord´) v. To write down for future use or permanent reference; to preserve sound on a tape or disk for replay; a phonograph record. **record** n. Information which is recorded and kept permanently.

re-cord-er (ri kor´dẽr) n. A person who records things such as official transactions.

re-cord-ing (ri kor´ding) n. The act of making a transcription of sounds.

re-count (rē kount´) v. To tell the facts; narrate or describe in detail; to count again. **recount** n. A second count to check the results of the first count.

re-coup (ri kŏp´) v. To be reimbursed; to recover. **recoupable** adj.

re-course (rē´kōrs) n. A turning to or an appeal for help; a source of help.

re-cov-er (ri kuv´ẽr) v. To regain something which was lost; to be restored to good health. Law To obtain a judgment for damages. **recoverability** n. **recoverable** adj. **recoverer** n.

re-cov-er-y (ri kuv´e rē) n. The power to regain something.

rec-re-ant (rek´rē ant) adj. Cowardly; unfaithful.

re-cre-ate (rē´krēāt´) v. To create again, to form in the imagination. **recreative** adj. **recreatable** adj. **recreative** adj.

rec-re-a-tion (rek´rē ā´shan) n. Refreshment of body and mind; a pleasurable occupation or exercise.

re-crim-i-nate v. The retaiatory charging of another. **recriminatory, recriminative** adj. **recrimination** n.

re-cru-desce (rē´krō des´) v. To break out; become raw again.

re-cruit (ri krōt´) v. To enlist someone for military or naval purposes; to look for someone as for a service or employment. n. A newly enlisted person. **recruiter, recruitment** n.

rec-tal (rek´tal) adj. Referring to the rectum of the body. **rectally** adv.

rec-tan-gle (rek´tang´gl) n. A parallelogram with all right angles. **rectangular** adj. **rectangularity** n.

rec-ti-fi-er (rek´ti fī´ẽr) n. That which rectifies something. **rectifiable** adj.

rec-ti-fy (rek´ti fī´) v. To make correct. Chem. To purify by repeated distillations. Electr. To make an alternating current a direct current. **-fication** n.

rec-ti-lin-ear (rek´ti lin´ē ẽr) adj. Made up of or indicated by straight lines; bounded by straight lines. **-ly** adv.

rec-ti-tude (rek´ti tōd´) n. Rightness in principles and conduct; correctness.

rec-to (rek´tō) n. The right hand page of a book.

rec-tor (rek´tẽr) n. A member of the clergy in charge of a parish; a priest in charge of a congregation, church, or parish; the principal or head of a school or of a college. **rectorate** n. **rectorial** adj. **rectorship** n.

rec-to-ry (rek´to rē) n. The rector's residence.

rec-trix n. The quill feathers of a bird's tail that are important in controlling flight.

rec-tum (rek´tum) n., Anat. The lower terminal portion of the large intestine connecting the colon and anus.

re-cum-bent (ri kum´bent) adj. Lying down or reclining. **recumbently** adv.

re-cu-per-ate (ri kō´pe rāt´) v. To regain strength or to regain one's health; to recover from a financial loss. **recuperation** n. **recuperative** adj.

re-cur (ri ker´) v. To happen, to return, or to appear again. **recurrence** n.

re-cur-rent (ri kŭr´ent) adj. Happening time after time. **recurrently** adv.

re-cu-san-cy n. The refusal to accept established authority.

re-cy-cle v. To return to an earlier usable condition. **recyclable** adj.

red (red) n. Having the color which resembles blood, as pigment or dye which colors red.

re-dact (ri dakt´) v. To adapt for publication. **redactional** adj.

red carpet n. A greeting reserved for very important people.

Red Cross n. An organization which helps people in need, collects and preserves human blood for use in emergencies, and responds with help in time of disaster.

rede (rēd) v. To advise or counsel.

re-dec-o-rate (rē dek´o rāt´) v. To change in appearance; to refurbish. **redecorator** n. **redecoration** n.

re-deem (ri dēm´) v. To buy back; to pay off; to turn something in, as coupons or rain checks and receive something in exchange. **redeemable** adj.

re-de-fine (v. To examine with a view to change. **redefinition** n.

re-demp-tion (ri demp´shan) n. The act of redeeming; rescue; ransom; that which redeems; salvation.

re-demp-tion-er (ri demp´shan ẽr) n. An immigrant to America who obtained passage by becoming a servant.

re-demp-tive (ri demp´tiv) adj. Relating to redemption.

re-de-ploy (rē´di ploi´) v. To move men

and equipment from one location to another.

re-de-scribe v. To give a more updated version of something.

re-de-sign (rē´di zīn´) v. To change or revise the appearance or function of something.

re-de-vel-op-ment n. The renovation of a rundown area.

red-in-gote (red´ing gōt´) n. A fitted double-breasted coat with wide flat cuffs and collar worn by men in the 18th century.

red ink n. A business loss.

red-in-te-grate (red in´te grāt´) v. To restore to a former sound state.

re-di-rect (rē´di rekt´) v. To change the course of. **redirection** n.

re-dis-trib-ute (rē´di strib´ūt) v. To spread to different areas. **redistributive** adj. **redistribution** n.

re-double v. To make something twice in size or amount.

re-doubt (ri dout´) n. A small enclosed fortification.

re-doubt-a-ble adj. To be dreaded. **redoubtably** adv.

re-dound (ri dound´) v. To have an effect on something.

red pencil v. To correct; to censor.

re-dress (ri dres´) v. To put something right; to remedy. **redresser** n.

red tide n. The presence of large numbers of dinoflagellates in seawater which is fatal to many forms of marine life.

re-duce (ri dōs´) v. To decrease; lessen in number, degree, or amount; to put into order; to lower in rank; to lose weight by dieting. **reducer** n. **-ible** adj.

re-duc-tion (ri duk´shan) n. The state of being reduced.

re-dun-dant (ri dun´dant) adj. Exceeding what is necessary; repetitive. **redundantly** adv. **redundancy** n.

re-du-pli-cate (ri dö´pli kāt´) v. To repeat something. **reduplication** n. **reduplicative** adj. **reduplicatively** adv.

re-ech-o v. To reverberate again.

reed (rēd) n. Tall grass with a slender stem, which grows in wet areas; a thin tongue of wood, metal, cane, or plastic; placed in the mouthpiece of an instrument to produce sounds by vibrating. **reediness** n. **reedy** adj.

reed-buck n. An African antelope.

re-ed-u-cate v. To train again through education; rehabilitate. **-ation** n.

reef (rēf) n. A chain of rocks, coral, or sand at or near the surface of the water.

reef knot n. A square knot used on a sail.

reek (rēk) v. To emit vapor or smoke; to give off a strong offensive odor.

reel (rēl) n. A device which revolves on an axis and is used for winding up or letting out fishing line, rope, or other string-like material; a lively and fast dance; a bobbin for sewing thread.

re-e-lect (rē´i lekt) v. The act of electing someone again for an office.

re-em-pha-size (rē em´fa sīz´) v. To stress something or an idea again.

re-em-ploy (rē´em ploi´) v. To rehire someone who previously worked for you.

re-en-act (rē´en akt´) v. To perform again; to repeat the actions of a previous event.

re-en-list v. To enlist or join a group or an armed force again. **-ment** n.

re-en-ter (rē en´tẽr) v. To enter a room or area again.

re-en-try (rē en´trē) n. The return of a space craft after a mission into outer space.

reeve (rēv) n. A medieval English manor officer responsible for overseeing feudal obligations.

re-ex-am-ine (rē´ig zam´in) v. Examine something or someone another time or again. **reexamination** n.

re-fer-to-ry (ri fek´to rē) n. The place in colleges where students dine.

re-fer (ri fer´) v. To direct for treatment, information, or help; to classify within a general category or cause.

ref-e-ree n. A person who supervises a game, making sure all the rules are followed.

ref-er-ence (ref´ẽr ens) n. The act of referring someone to someplace or to something.

reference mark n. A mark, such as an asterisk, to direct the reader's attention to a footnote.

ref-er-en-dum (ref´e ren´dum) n. A public vote on an item for final approval or for rejection.

ref-er-ent (ref´ẽr ent) n. What is referred to, such as a person; the thing that a word or sign stand for. **referent** adj.

re-fill (rē fil´) v. To fill something with an item again. **refillable** adj.

re-fine (ri fīn´) v. To purify by removing unwanted substances or material; to improve. **refined** adj. **refinement** n.

re-fin-er-y (ri fī´ne rē) n. A place or location which is used for the purpose of refining products, such as sugar.

re-fin-ish v. The act of putting a new surface onto something, such as wood.

re-fit (rē fit´) v. To repair something.

re-flect (rē flekt´) v. To throw back rays of light from a surface; to give an image, as from a mirror; to ponder or think carefully about something. **reflection, reflectiveness** n.

re-flec-tom-e-ter (rē´flek tom´i tẽr) n. A device for measuring radiant energy.

re-flec-tor n. Something which is able to reflect things, such as light.

re-flex (rē´fleks) adj. Turning, casting, or bending backward. **reflex** n. An involuntary reaction of the nervous system to a stimulus.

re-flex-ive (ri flek'siv) *adj.* A relation that exists between an entity and itself. **reflexiveness** *n.* **reflexivity** *n.*

re-flex-ol-gy *n.* The science of behavior of simple and complex reflexes.

re-flo-res-cent *adj.* Blooming again.

re-flow *v.* To flow back again.

re-fo-cus (rē fō'kus) *v.* To change the direction of.

re-forge (rē fōrj') *v.* To make over.

re-form (ri form') *v.* To reconstruct, make over, or change something for the better; improve; to abandon or give up evil ways. **reformer** *n.* **-ed** *adj.*

reformat *v.* In *computer science*, to change the style of text; to convert a file for use by a different application.

re-for-ma-to-ry *n.* A jail-like institution for young criminals.

re-fract (ri frakt') *v.* The deflecting of something, such as a ray of light. **refractive** *adj.*

re-frac-to-ry *adj.* Unmanageable; obstinate; difficult to melt; resistant to heat. **refractory** *n.* Something which does not change significantly when exposed to high temperatures. **refractorily** *adv.*

refractory period *n.* The period immediately following the response of a muscle before it recovers to make a second response.

re-frain (ri frān') *v.* To hold back; to keep oneself from following a passing impulse. **refrain** *n.* A recurring phrase at the end of each stanza of a poem or song.

re-fresh (ri fresh') *v.* To freshen something again; to restore strength. **refreshing** *adj.* **refresher** *n.*

re-fresh-ment (ri fresh'ment) *n.* Something which will refresh someone, such as a cold drink or snack.

re-frig-er-a-tor *n.* A piece of storage equipment which chills food and other materials.

re-fu-el (rē fū'el) *v.* To put fuel into something again; take on additional fuel.

ref-uge *n.* Shelter or protection from harm; any place one may turn for relief or help.

ref-u-gee (ref'ū jē') *n.* A person who flees to find safety. **refugeeism** *n.*

re-ful-gent (ri ful'jent) *adj.* State of being radiant or putting off a bright light.

re-fund (ri fund') *v.* To return or pay back; to reimburse. **refundable** *adj.*

re-fur-bish *v.* To make clean; to renovate. **refurbisher, refurbishment** *n.*

re-fus-al (ri fū'zal) *n.* The denial of something which is demanded.

re-fuse (ri fūz') *v.* To decline; to reject;

to deny.

re-fute (ri fūt') *v.* To overthrow or to disprove with the use of evidence. **refutable** *adj.* **refutably** *adv.* **-er** *n.*

re-gain (ri gān') *v.* To recover; to reach again.

re-gal (ri gāl') *adj.* Of or appropriate for royalty. **regally** *adv.*

re-gale (ri gāl') *v.* To entertain or delight; to give pleasure.

re-ga-li-a (ri gā'lē a) *n.* Something which represents royalty such as a scepter.

re-gard (ri gärd') *v.* To look upon closely; to consider; to have great affection for. **regard** *n.* Careful attention or thought; esteem or affection. **regards** Greetings or good wishes.

re-gard-less *adj.* State of being careless or showing no regard towards something or someone.

re-gat-ta (ri gat'a) *n.* A boat race.

re-gen-cy (rē'jen sē) *n.,* *pl.* **-ies** The jurisdiction or office of a regent.

re-gen-er-ate *v.* To reform spiritually or morally; to make or create anew; to refresh or to restore.

re-gent (rē'jent) *n.* One who rules and acts as a ruler during the absence of a sovereign, or when the ruler is underage.

reg-i-cide *n.* A person who kills a king.

re-gime (re zhem') *n.* An administration.

reg-i-men (rej'i men') *n.* Government control; therapy; a systematic plan to improve the health.

reg-i-ment *n.* A military unit of ground troops which is composed of several battalions. **regimental** *adj.*

re-gion (rē'jan) *n.* An administrative, political, social, or geographical area.

re-gion-al (rēja nal) *adj.* Typical of or pertaining to a geographic region; limited to a particular region.

reg-is-ter (rej'i stèr) *n.* Something which contains names or occurrences; a book of public records.

reg-is-tered (rej'i stèrd) *adj.* Recorded with the owner's name; recorded on the basis of pedigree of an animal.

reg-is-trar *n.* The person who keeps a register; an office of an educational institution which is in charge of registration, keeping academic records, and evaluating credentials.

reg-is-tra-tion *n.* An act of recording things or names.

reg-is-try *n.* The nationality of a ship in a register; an official record book.

reg-let (reg'lit) *n.* A narrow strip of molding.

re-gress *v.* To return to a previous state or condition. **regressor** *adj.* **-ive** *n.*

re-gres-sion *n.* The progressive decline of a disease; a shift toward a lower state; gradual loss of memory and acquired skills. **regressive** *adj*.

re-gret (ri gret´) *v*. To feel disappointed or distressed about; to be sorry for. **regret** *n*. A sense of loss or expression of grief; a feeling of sorrow. **regretta- bly, regretfully** *adv*. **regrettable, regretful** *adj*.

re-group (rē grōp´) *v*. To reorganize after a setback in an activity.

reg-u-lar *adj*. Usual; normal; customary; conforming to set principles, proce- dures, or discipline; well-ordered; not varying. **regularity** *n*. **regularly** *adv*.

reg-u-lar-ize (reg´ya lāt´) *v*. To conform to laws, rules, and customs.

reg-u-late (reg´ya lāt´) *v*. To adjust to a specification or requirement; to bring order or authority. **regulative** *adj*. **regulatory** *adj*. **regulator** *n*.

reg-u-la-tion *n*. A rule that is set down in order to govern an area or people.

reg-u-lus (reg´a lus) *n*. A star in the constellation Leo.

re-gur-gi-tate (ri g´ *v*. To pour something forth. **regurgitation** *n*.

re-ha-bil-i-tate *v*. To restore to a former state by education and therapy. **rehabilitation** *n*. **rehabilitative** *adv*.

re-hash (rē hash´) *v*. To rework or go over old material; to discuss again.

re-hears-al *n*. The act of practicing for a performance; a practice session.

re-hu-man-ize *v*. To restore to a full life; restore human rights and dignity.

re-hy-drate (rē hī´drāt) *v*. To return fluid lost due to dehydration.

reichs-mark *n*. A German coin.

reign (rān) *n*. The period in time when the monarch rules over an area.

re-im-burse (rē´im bers´) *v*. To repay; to make restitution. **-ment** *n*.

rein (rān) *n*. One of a pair of narrow, leather straps attached to the bit of a bridle and used to control a horse.

re-in-car-na-tion *n*. The state of rebirth in new forms of life.

re-in-force (rē´in fōrs´) *v*. To support; to strengthen with additional people or equipment. **reinforcement** *n*.

re-in-state (rē´in stāt´) *v*. To restore something to its former position or condition. **reinstatement** *n*.

re-in-te-grate *v*. To reunite with something.

re-in-vent *v*. To remake something that has already been invented.

re-in-vest (rē´in vest´) *v*. To invest money in additional securities.

re-in-vig-o-rate *v*. To restore vigor.

re-is-sue (rē ish´ö) *v*. To make available again.

re-it-er-ate *v*. To say or do something over and over again. **reiteration** *n*.

re-ject (ri jekt´) *v*. To refuse; to discard as useless. **reject** *n*. **rejection** *n*.

re-jec-tion *n*. The process in which the body rejects an organ transplant or tissue.

re-joice *v*. To fill with joy; to be filled with joy. **rejoicer** *n*. **rejoicingly** *adv*.

re-joic-ing (ri jois´ing) *n*. An occasion or expression of joy.

re-join *v*. To respond or to answer someone.

re-ju-ve-nate (ri jö´ve nāt´) *v*. To restore to youthful appearance or vigor. **rejuvenation** *n*.

re-kin-dle (rē kin´dl) *v*. To inflame something again. **rekindler** *n*.

re-lapse (ri laps´) *v*. To fall back or revert to an earlier condition. **relapser** *n*.

re-late (ri lāt´) *v*. To tell the events of; to narrate; to bring into natural association. **relater** *n*. **relatable** *adj*.

re-lat-ed *adj*. To be in the same family; connected to each other by blood or marriage.

re-la-tion (ri lā´shan) *n*. The relationship between people by marriage or blood lines; a person one is related to.

re-la-tion-ship (ri lā´shan ship´) *n*. A connection by blood or family; kinship; friendship; a natural association.

rel-a-tive (rel´a tiv) *adj*. Relevant; connected; considered in comparison or relationship to other. **relative** *n*. A member of one's family. **relatively** *adv*.

rel-a-tiv-i-ty (rel´a tiv´i tē) *n*. A condition or state of being relative.

re-lax (ri laks´) *v*. To make loose or lax; to relieve something from effort or strain; to become less formal or less reserved. **relaxation** *n*.

re-lax-a-tion (rē´lak sā´shan) *n*. A period of recreational activity or pastime.

re-laxed *adj*. Being at rest or ease. **relaxedly** *adv*. **relaxedness** *n*.

re-lay (rē´lā) *n*. A race in which a fresh team replaces another. **relay** *v*. To pass from one group to another.

re-lease *v*. To set free from confinement; to unfasten; to free; to relinquish a claim on something. *n*. A release from an obligation. **releaser** *n*.

rel-e-gate (rel´e gāt´) *v*. To banish someone or something. **relegation** *n*.

re-lent (ri lent´) *v*. To soften in temper, attitude, or determination; to slacken. **relentless, relentlessness** *adj*.

rel-e-vant (rel´e vant) *adj*. Related to matters at hand. **relevantly** *adv*.

re-li-a-ble (ri lī´a bl) *adj*. Dependable; capable of being relied upon.

re-li-ance (ri lī´ans) *n*. Confidence and trust; something which is relied upon.

re-li-ant (ri lī´ant) *adj*. State of being confident or having reliance.

re-lic (rel´ik) *n*. Something which is very old; a keepsake; an object whose cultural environment has disappeared.

re-lic-tion *n*. The recession of water from land leaving it permanently uncovered.

re-lief (ri lēf´) *n.* Anything which decreases or lessens anxiety, pain, discomfort, or other unpleasant conditions or feelings.

re-lieve *v.* To lessen or ease pain, anxiety, embarrassment, or other problems; to release or free from a duty by providing a replacement. **reliever** *n.*

re-lig-ion *n.* An organized system of beliefs, rites, and celebrations centered on a supernatural being; belief pursued with devotion. **religious** *adj.*

re-li-gi-ose *adj.* Being excessively religious.

re-lin-quish (ri ling´kwish) *v.* To release something or someone; withdraw from; to give up. **relinquishment** *n.*

rel-i-quary (rel´i kwer´ē) *n.* A shrine in which sacred relics are kept.

re-lish (rel´ish) *v.* Pleasure; a spicy condiment taken with food to lend it flavor.

re-live(rē liv´) *v.* To experience something again in the imagination or fantasy.

re-lo-cate *v.* To move to another area; establish in another place. **-tion** *n.*

re-luct (ri lukt´) *v.* To revolt; to feel opposition.

re-luc-tance *n.* An unwillingness; opposition by a magnetic substance to magnetic flux.

re-luc-tant (ri lik´tant) *adj.* Unwilling, not yielding. **reluctation** *n.*

re-lume (ri lōm´) *v.* To light again.

re-ly (ri lī´) *v.* To trust or depend; to have confidence in someone.

re-main (ri mān´) *v.* To continue without change; to stay after the departure of others.

re-main-der (ri mān dèr) *n.* Something left over. *Math* The difference which remains after division or subtraction.

re-make *v.* To revise an old movie, etc.

re-mand (ri mand´) *v.* To order back; to send to another court or agency for further action; to return to custody pending trial.

re-man-u-fac-ture *v.* To make into a new product. **remanufacturer** *n.*

re-mark (ri märk´) *n.* A brief expression or comment; to take notice; to observe; to comment.

re-mark-a-ble *adj.* Extraordinary.

re-match (rē´mach) *n.* A second contest between the same contestants or teams.

rem-e-di-a-ble (ri mē´dē a bl) *adj.* Being able to be remedied.

re-me-di-al (ri mē´dē al) *adj.* Concerned with the correction of study habits.

rem-e-dy (rem´i dē) *n., pl.* **remedies** A therapy or medicine which relieves pain; something which corrects an error or fault. **remedy** *v.* To cure or relieve a disease; to rectify.

re-mem-ber *v.* To bring back or recall to the mind; to retain in the mind carefully; to keep a person in one's thoughts; to recall a person to another as a means of greetings. **remember-ability, rememberer** *n.* **-erable** *adj.*

re-mem-brance *n.* Something which is remembered by someone.

re-mex (rē´meks) *n.* A quill feather in the wing of a bird. **remigial** *adj.*

re-mil-i-ta-rize *v.* To equip again with military installations.

re-mind (ri mīnd´) *v.* To cause or help to remember. **reminder** *n.*

rem-i-nisce (rem´i nis´) *v.* To recall the past things which have happened.

rem-i-nis-cence *n.* The practice or process of recalling the past. **reminiscent** *adj.*

re-mint *v.* To make old coins into a new coins by melting down the old coins.

re-mise (ri miz´) *v.* To grant or release a claim to.

re-miss *adj.* Lax in performing one's duties; negligent. **remissness** *n.*

re-mis-sion *n.* A forgiveness; act of remitting; a temporary state of a disease when it doesn't progress; forgiveness.

re-mit (ri mit´) *v.* To send money as payment for goods; to forgive, as a crime or sin; to slacken, make less violent, or less intense.

re-mit-tance (ri mit´ans) *n.* A sum of money sent to reduce a debt.

re-mit-tent *adj.* Marked by periods of abatement and increase of symptoms.

rem-nant (rem´nant) *n.* A small piece or a scrap of something; an unsold end of a material.

re-mod-el *v.* To reconstruct something making it like new; to alter the structure of a building or house.

re-mon-e-tize (rē mon´i tīz´) *v.* To restore to use as legal tender.

re-mon-strance *n.* Statement of reasons against an idea or something.

re-mon-strate *v.* Giving strong reasons against an act or an idea. **remonstrative** *adj.* **remonstration** *n.*

re-morse (ri mors´) *n.* Deep moral regret for past misdeeds. **remorseful** *adj.* **remorsefully** *adv.* **remorsefulness** *n.*

re-mote *adj.* Distant in time, space, or relation. **remotely** *adv.* **-ness** *n.*

remote access *n.* In *computer science,* ability of a computer to connect and interact with a computer or peripheral that is not in the immediate area.

re-mount (rē mount´) *v.* To mount something again.

re-mov-a-ble (ri mö´va bl) *adj.* Being able to be removed.

re-mov-al *n.* The change of a site or place; the act of removing from a post.

re-move (ri möv´) *v.* To get rid of; to extract; to dismiss from office; to change one's business or residence. *n.* An act of moving. **removable** *adj.*

re-mu-da (ri mö´da) n. A herd of horses from which the horses to be used for the day are chosen.

re-mu-ner-ate (ri mū´ne rāt´) v. Pay an equivalent for a service; to reward. **remunerator, remuneration** n.

ren-ais-sance n. A revival or rebirth; the humanistic revival of classical art, literature, and learning in Europe which occurred during the 14th through the 16th centuries.

re-nal adj. Of or relating to the kidneys.

re-nas-cence (ri nas´ens) n. A revival or a rebirth.

re-na-ture v. To restore to an original condition.

ren-con-tre (ren kon´tér) n. A hostile contest between forces or individuals.

ren-coun-ter (ren koun´tér) v. A casual meeting; a duel; a debate.

rend (rend) v. To remove from with violence; to split.

ren-der v. To give or make something available; to submit or give; to represent artistically; to liquify or melt fat by means of heat. **rendering** n. **renderable** adj.

ren-dez-vous n. A meeting place that has been prearranged; an appointment made between two or more people. v. To meet at a particular time and place.

ren-di-tion (ren dish´an) n. An interpretation or a translation.

ren-dzi-na n. A grayish brown intrazonal soil developed in grassy regions of high humidity; a rich limey soil.

ren-e-gade (ren´e gād´) n. A person who rejects one allegiance for another; an outlaw; a traitor. **renegade** adj.

re-nege (ri nig´) v. To fail to keep one's word. **reneger** n.

re-new (ri nö´) v. To make new or nearly new by restoring; to resume.

re-ni-tent (ri nīt´ent) adj. Resisting pressure; opposed.

ren-net (ren´it) n. An extract taken from a calf's stomach and used to curdle milk for making cheese.

ren-nin (ren´in) n. An enzyme that coagulates milk used in making cheese.

re-nom-i-nate (rē nom´i nāt´) v. To nominate for a succeeding term.

re-nounce (ri nouns´) v. To reject something. **renouncement** n.

ren-o-vate (ren´o vāt´) v. To return or to restore to a good condition; to make new. **renovation, renovator** n.

re-nown (ri noun´) n. The quality of being widely honored. **renowned** adj.

rent (rent) n. The payment made for the use of another's property. v. To obtain occupancy in exchange for payment. **rental** n. **rentable** adj.

re-nun-ci-a-tion (ri nun´sē ā´shan) n. Renouncing. **renunciative** adj.

re-o-pen (rē ö´pen) v. To resume again,

as a discussion or session.

re-or-der (rē or´dèr) n. An order for more of the same kind as previously ordered.

re-or-gan-i-za-tion(rē´orga nizā´shan) n. The process of reorganizing something.

rep (rep) n. Slang Representative. v. To represent.

re-pack-age v. To wrap into a more efficient and attractive form.

re-pair (ri pâr´) v. To restore to good or usable condition; to renew; refresh.

re-pand (ri pand´) adj. Having a slightly wavy margin.

rep-a-ra-ble adj. Being able to be corrected.

rep-a-ra-tion (rep´a rā´shan) n. The act of repairing something.

re-par-a-tive (ri par´a tiv) adj. Able to make amends.

rep-ar-tee n. A quick, witty response or reply; an interchange of clever retorts.

re-pass (rē pas´) v. To pass through again.

re-past (ri past´) n. Something taken as food; food which comprises a meal.

re-pa-tri-ate (rē pātrē āt´) v. To go back to one's own country; to return to the country of one's origin. **-ation** n.

re-pay (ri pā) v. To pay back money; to compensate; to do something in return.

re-peal (ri pel´) v. To withdraw officially; to rescind; to revoke. **repealable** adj. **repeal** n. **repealer** n.

re-peat (ri pēt´) v. To utter something again; to do an action again.

re-peat-ed adj. Recurring again and again.

re-peat-er (ri pē´tér) n. Something or someone which repeats.

re-pel (ri pel´) v. To discourage; to force away; to create aversion.

re-pel-lent (ri pel´ent) adj. Able to repel; tending to drive away or ward off.

re-pent (ri pent´) v. To feel regret for something which has occurred; to change one's sinful way. **repentance** n. **repentant** adj. **repenter** n.

re-per-cus-sion (rē´pér kush´an) n. An unforeseen effect produced by an action.

rep-er-toire (rep´ér twär´) n. The accomplishments or skills of a person.

rep-er-to-ry n. A collection of things.

rep-e-tend n. A repeated sound or refrain.

rep-e-ti-tion (rep´i tish´an) n. The act of doing something over and over again; the act of repeating.

re-pine v. To feel discontent; to complain.

re-place v. To return something to its previous place. **replaceable** adj. **replacement** n. **replacer** n.

re-plant v. To provide with new plants; to move plants to a new location.

re-play v. To play something again.

re-plen-ish (ri plen´ish) v. To add to

something to replace what has gone or been used. **replenisher** *n*. **-ment** *n*.

re-plete (ri plēt´) *adj*. Having plenty; abounding; full. **repleteness** *n*.

re-ple-tion (ri plē´shən) n. An act of eating too much food.

rep-li-ca (rep´li kə) *n*. A reproduction or copy of something. **replicate** *v*.

re-ply (ri plī´) *v*. To give an answer to either verbally or in writing. **reply** *n*.

re-port (ri pōrt´) *n*. A detailed account; usually in a formal way. **report** *v*. To tell about; to make oneself available; to give details of. **reportable** *adj*.

report card *n*. The report of a student's progress in school submitted to the parents for review.

re-pos-al (ri pō´zal) *n*. An act or action of reposing.

re-pose (ri pōz´) *n*. The act of being at rest. *v*. To lie at rest. **reposeful** *adj*.

re-pos-it (ri poz´it) *v*. To put something back into place.

re-po-si-tion (rē´pozish´an)n. The state of something being repositioned.

re-pos-i-tor-y *n*. The location where things may be placed for preservation; a side altar in a Catholic church.

re-pos-sess (rē´po zes´) *v*. To restore ownership of something.

re-pow-er *v*. To return power anew to something or someone.

rep-re-hend (rep´ri hend´) *v*. To show or express disapproval of. **reprehension** *n*. **reprehensible** *adj*.

rep-re-hen-sive (rep´ri hen ziv) *adj*. To be conveying reproof.

rep-re-sent *v*. To stand for something; to serve as the official representative for.

re-pre-sent-a-tion *n*. The act of representing. **representational** *adj*.

rep-re-sent-a-tive *n*. A person or thing serving as an example or type. *adj*. Of or relating to government by representation; typical. **representatively** *adv*.

re-press (ri pres´) *v*. To restrain; hold back; to remove from the conscious mind. **repressive** *adj*. **repressibility** *n*. **repression** *n*. **repressiveness** *n*.

re-prieve (ri prēv´) *v*. To postpone punishment; to provide temporary relief. **reprieve** *n* A temporary suspension of an execution.

rep-ri-mand (rep´ri mand) *v*. To censure severely; rebuke. **repripand** *n*.

re-print (rē print´) *n*. An additional printing of a book exactly as the previous one. **reprint** *v*. **reprinter** *n*.

re-pri-sal *n*. Retaliation with intent to inflict injury in return for injury received; a sum of money paid in restitution.

re-prise (ri prīz´) *v*. To take back by force.

re-proach (ri prōch´) *v*. To blame; to

rebuke. **reproachful** *adj*.

rep-ro-bate (rep´ro bāt´) *adj*. The state of being morally depraved. **reprobate** *v*. To condemn as unacceptable or evil.

re-pro-cess *v*. To treat in a special way in preparation for reuse.

re-pro-duce (rē´pro dōs´) *v*. To produce an image or copy. *Biol*. To produce an offspring; to recreate or produce again. **reproducer** *n*. **reproducible** *adj*. **reproduction** *n*. **reproductive** *adj*.

re-pro-gram *v*. To rewrite an existing pro-gram for a computer.

re-proof (ri prōf´) *n*. A censure.

re-prove (ri prōv´) *v*. To tell or express a disapproval of something.

rep-tile *n*. A cold-blooded, egg-laying vertebrate, as a snake, lizard, or turtle.

re-pub-lic (ri pub´lik) *n*. A political unit or state where representatives are elected to exercise the power.

Republican Party *n*. One of the two political parties in the United States.

re-pu-di-ate (ri pū´dē āt´) *v*. To cast away; to refuse to pay something.

re-pugn (ri pūn´) *v*. To offer resistance.

re-pug-nance (ri pug´nans) n. The state or condition of being opposed.

re-pug-nant (ri pug´nant) adj. Distasteful; repulsive; offensive.

re-pulse (ri puls´) *v*. To repel or drive back; to repel or reject rudely; to disgust or be disgusted. **repulsion** *n*.

re-pul-sive (ri pul´siv) *adj*. State of causing aversion. **repulsively** *adj*.

rep-u-ta-ble (rep´ū ta bl) adj. Considered to be honorable; held in high esteem. **reputably** *adv*. **reputability** *n*.

rep-u-ta-tion *n*. The commonly held evaluation of a person's character.

re-pute (ri pūt´) *v*. To account or to consider something. **reputedly** *adj*.

re-quest *v*. To ask for something.

re-qui-em (rek´wē em) *n*. The Roman Catholic mass for a deceased person.

re-quire (ri kwī´ér) *v*. To demand or insist upon. **requirement** *n*.

req-ui-site (rek´wi zit) *adj*. Absolutely needed; necessary.

req-ui-si-tion (rek´wi zish´an) n. A request; a demand by one government to another for release of prisoners.

re-quite (ri kwīt´) *v*. To reward; to repay someone. **requiter** *n*.

rere-dos (rēr´dos) *n*. An ornamental screen or partition wall behind an altar.

re-run (rē run) *n*. A television show which is shown again.

re-sale (rē´sā) *n*. The act of selling something again. **resalable** *adj*.

re-scind (ri sind´) *v*. To repeal; to void. **rescinder** *n*. **rescindment** *n*.

res-cue (res´kū) *v*. To free from danger. *n*. An act of deliverance. **rescuer** *n*.

re-search *n*. A scientific or scholarly investigation. *v*. To carefully seek out.

re-sec-tion (ri sek´shan) n. The surgical removal of a action of an organ.

re-se-da (ri sē´da) n. An herb of the mignonette family with greyish-green leaves.

re-sem-ble (ri zem´bl) v. To have similarity to something.

re-send v. To send back.

re-sent (ri zent´) v. To feel angry about. resentful adj. resentment n.

res-er-va-tion (rez´ér vā´shan) n. The act of keeping something back.

re-serve (ri zerv´) v. To save for a special reason; to set apart; to retain; to put off. n. Something that is saved for a future point in time; the portion of a country's fighting force kept inactive until called upon.

re-serve-clause n. A clause in an athlete's contract which gives the club the exclusive rights of the athletes services until he is traded or released.

res-er-voir (rez´ér vwär´) n. A body of water stored for the future; large reserve; a supply.

reset In computer science, to command a return to an original state; to restart the computer.

re-shape (rē shāp´) v. To give new form to.

re-side (ri zīd´) v. To dwell permanently; to exist as a quality or attribute; live in or at. residence n.

res-i-den-cy (rez´i den sē) n. A period of training in a medical field.

res-i-due (rez´i dö´) n. Matter remaining after treatment or removal of a part; some-thing which remains.

re-sign v. To give up; to submit to something as being unavoidable; to quit.

res-ig-na-tion n. A formal notification stating the resignation of one's job, etc.

re-sil-ience (ri zil´yens) n. The ability to recover from a shock without permanent aftereffects.

res-in n. A plant substance from certain plants and trees used in varnishes and lacquers. resinous n.

re-sist (ri zist´) v. To work against or actively oppose; to withstand. -ible adj.

re-sist-er n. A person who is opposed to the policies of the government.

re-sis-tor (ri zis´tér) n. An electrical device used in an electric circuit for protection or current control.

res-ju-di-ca-ta n. A matter decided on its merits by a court and not subject to litigation again between the same parties.

res-o-lute (rez´o löt´) adj. Coming from or characterized by determination. resolutely resolution n.

re-solve (ri zolv´) v. To make a firm decision on something; to find a solution. resolvable adj. -lution n.

res-o-nance n. The increase of sound by the vibration of other bodies.

res-o-na-tor (rez´o nā´tér) n. A device for increasing sounds of a musical instrument.

re-sort (ri zort´) v. To go frequently or customarily. n. A place, or recreation, for rest and for a vacation.

re-sound (ri zound´) v. To be filled with echoing sounds; to reverberate; to ring or sound loudly. resounding adj.

re-source (rē´sörs) n. A source of aid or support which can be drawn upon if needed. resources n. One's available capital or assets. resourceful adj.

re-spect (ri spekt´) v. To show consideration or esteem for; to relate to. n. Courtesy or considerate treatment. respectful adj. respectability n.

res-pi-ra-tion n. The process or act of inhaling and exhaling; the act of breathing; the process in which an animal or person takes in oxygen from the air and releases carbon dioxide. respirator n. respiratory adj.

re-spire (ri spīér´) v. To inhale and exhale air; take in oxygen.

res-pi-rom-e-ter n. An instrument for studying the extent and character of respiration.

res-pite (res´pit) n. A temporary postponement.

re-splen-dent (ri splen´dent) adj. Having a shining appearance. -ly adj.

re-spond (ri spond´) v. To answer or reply; to act when prompted by something or someone.

re-sponse (ri spons´) n. A reply; the act of replying. responsive adj.

re-spon-si-ble adj. Trustworthy; in charge; having authority; being answerable for one's actions or the actions of others. responsibility n.

re-spon-sum n. A formal opinion from a rabbinic authority to a submitted question or problem.

rest (rest) n. A cessation of all work, activity, or motion. Mus. An interval of silence equal in time to a note of same value. v. To stop work; to place or lay. restful adj. rester n. -fully adv.

res-tau-rant (res´tér ant) n. A place which serves meals to the public.

res-tau-ran-teur (res´tér a tür´) n. The owner of a restaurant.

res-ti-tu-tion (res´ti tö´shan) n. The act of restoring something to its rightful owner; compensation for injury, loss, or damage.

res-tive (res´tiv) adj. Nervous or impatient because of a delay; resisting control. restively adv. restiveness n.

re-store (ri stōr´) v. To bring back to a former condition or original state; to make restitution of. restoration n.

re-strain (ri strān´) v. To hold back or be held back; to control, limit, or restrict. **restrainer** n. **restraint** n.

restraining order n. A legal document issued to keep a situation unchanged.

re-strict (ri strikt´) v. To confine within limits. **restriction** n. **restrictive** adj. **restrictively** adv.

re-sult (ri zult´) v. To happen or exist in a particular way. n. The consequence of an action, course, or operation.

re-sume (rizōm´) v. To start again after an interruption. **resumption** n.

res-u-me (rez´e mā´) n. A summary of one's personal history, background, work, and education.

re-su-pi-nate (ri sö´pi nāt´) adj. To bend backward to an inverted position.

res-ur-rec-tion n. The act of Christ rising from the dead.

re-sus-ci-ate (ri sus´i tāt) v. To return to life; to revive; give mouth-to-mouth breathing technique to help a person to start breathing again. **resuscitation**, **resuscitator** n.

re-tail n. The sale of goods or commodities to the public. v. To sell to the consumer. **retail** adj. **retailer** n.

re-tain (ri tān´) v. To hold in one's possession; to remember; to employ someone, as for his services.

re-tain-er n. A person or thing that retains; a fee paid for one's services.

re-tal-i-ate (ri tal´ē āt´) v. To seek revenge against someone. **-tion** n.

re-tard (ri tärd´) v. To delay or slow the progress of. **retardant** n. & adj.

re-tar-da-tion n. A condition in which mental development is slow or delayed; a condition of mental slowness.

re-ten-tion (ri ten´shan) n. The act or condition of being retained.

re-ten-tive adj. Having the capacity of retaining knowledge with ease.

ret-i-cent (ret´i sent) adj. Being uncommunicative in speech; reserved.

re-tic-u-late (ri tik´ya lit) v. To divide or construct as to form a network.

ret-i-na (ret´i na) n. pl. **-nas, nae** The light sensitive membrane lining the inner eyeball connected by the optic nerve to the brain. **retinal** adj.

re-tire (ri tīer´) v. To depart for rest; to remove oneself from the daily routine of working. *Baseball* To put a batter out. **retirement, retiree** n.

re-tired (ri tīed´) adj. No longer working at one's profession.

re-tir-ing adj. Being shy or withdrawn.

re-tort (ri tort´) n. A witty or cutting reply to another person.

re-touch (rē tuch´) v. To alter a negative to produce a more desirable picture.

re-trace (ri trās´) v. To go back over.

re-tract (ri trakt´) v. To draw back or to take back something that has been

said. **retractable** adj. **retraction** n.

re-tral adj. Toward the back.

re-tread (rē tred´) v. To replace the tread of a worn tire. **retread** n.

re-treat n. The act of withdrawing from danger; a time of study, prayer, and meditation in a quiet, isolated location.

ret-ri-bu-tion (re´tri bū´shan) n. An act of getting revenge against another person. **retributively** adv. **-tive** adj.

re-trieve (ri trēv´) v. To regain; to find something and carry it back. **retrievable** adj. **retrieval** n.

ret-ro-ac-tive adj. Taking effect on a date prior to enactment; extending to a prior time. **retroactively** adv.

ret-ro-grade (re´tro grād´) adj. Moving backward; contrary to normal order.

ret-ro-gres-sion n. A reversal in development from a higher to a lower state.

ret-ro-pack n. A system of rockets on a spacecraft which produce thrust used to reduce speed.

ret-ro-re-flec-tor n. A device that reflects radiation.

ret-ro-rock-et n. A rocket on an airplane or spacecraft which produces thrust in the opposite direction to the motion of the craft for deceleration.

ret-ro-spect (re´tro spekt´) n. A review of things in the past. **retrospectively** adv. **retrospective** adj.

re-turn v. To come back to an earlier condition; to reciprocate. n. The act of sending, bringing, or coming back. **returns** n. A yield or profit from investments; a report on the results of an election. **returnable** adj. **returnee**, **re-un-ion** (rē ūn´yan) n. A reuniting; the coming together of a group which has been separated for a period of time.

re-us-able (rē ū´za bl) adj. Capable of using something over and over again.

re-val-u-ate (rē val´ū āt´) v. To increase the value of something.

re-val-ue (rē val´ū) v. To reappraise something as jewelry.

re-vamp (rē vamp´) v. Patch or reconstruct some thing again.

re-veal (ri vēl´) v. To disclose or make known; to expose or bring into view.

rev-eil-le (rev´e lē) n. The sounding of a bugle used to awaken soldiers in the morning.

rev-el (rev´el) v. To take great delight in. **reveler** n.

rev-e-la-tion (rev´e lā´shan) n. An act of or something revealed; a manifestation of divine truth. **Revelation** The last book in the New Testament.

re-venge (ri venj´) v. To impose injury in return for injury received. **revengeful** adj. **revenger** n.

rev-e-nue (rev´en ū´) n. Income returned by an investment.

re-verb *n.* An echo effect produced electronically in recorded music.

re-vere (ri vēr´) *v.* To honor and respect.

re-ver-sal (ri ver´sal) *n.* An act of over throwing a legal proceeding or judgment.

re-verse (ri vers´) *adj.* Turned backward in position. *n.* The opposite of something; a change in fortune usually from better to worse; change or turn to the opposite direction; to transpose or exchange the positions of. *Law* To revoke a decision. **reverser** *n.*

re-vert (ri vert´) *v.* To return to a former practice or belief. **reversion** *n.*

re-view (ri vū´) *v.* To study or look over something again; to give a report on. *n.* A reexamination; a study which gives a critical estimate of something.

re-vile (ri vīl´) *v.* To use verbal abuse.

re-vise (ri vīz´) *v.* To look over something again with the intention of improving or correcting it. **reviser, revision** *n.*

re-vi-tal-ize (rē vīt´a līz´) *v.* To give new life or energy to. **revitalization** *n.*

re-viv-al (ri vī´val) *n.* The act or condition of reviving; the return of a film or play which was formerly presented; a meeting whose purpose is religious reawakening.

re-vive (ri vīv´) *v.* To restore, refresh, or recall; to return to consciousness or life. **revivable** *adj.* **reviver** *n.*

re-voke (ri vōk´) *v.* To nullify or make void by recalling. **revocation** *n.*

re-volt (ri vōlt´) *n.* To try to overthrow authority; to fill with disgust.

rev-o-lu-tion (rev´o lō´shan) *n.* The act or state of orbital motion around a point; the abrupt overthrow of a government; a sudden change in a system.

re-volve (ri volv´) *v.* To move around a central point; to spin; to rotate.

re-volv-ing charge ac-count (ri vol´ving) *n.* A charge account in which payment is made in monthly installments.

re-vue (ri vū´) *n.* A musical show consisting of songs, dances, skits, and other similar entertainment.

re-ward (ri word´) *n.* Something given for a special service. *v.* To give a reward.

rhab-do-man-cy (rab´do man´sē) *n.* The discovery of things that are concealed in the ground by the use of a divining rod.

rham-na-ceous (ram nā´shus) *adj.* To be pertaining to or belonging to the buckthorn family of plants.

rhap-sod-ic (rap sod´ik) *adj.* To have the characteristics of a rhapsody.

rhap-so-dist (rap´so dist) *n.* A person who speaks in a rhapsodical way or manner.

rhap-so-dize (rap´so dīz´) *v.* To recite rhapsodies.

rhap-so-dy (rap´so dē) *n. pl.* **-ies** An excessive display of enthusiasm.

rhat-a-ny (rat´a nē) *n.* A type of South American shrub whose roots are used as an astringent.

rhe-ni-um (rē´nē um) *n.* A metallic element symbolized by Re.

rhe-ol-o-gy (rē ol´o jē) *n.* The study of the behavior of a liquid matter.

rhe-om-e-ter (rē om´i tėr) *n.* A type of device that is used for measuring the flow of liquids.

rhe-sus (rē´sus) *n.* A light-brown monkey that is used for laboratory tests.

rhe-tor (rē´tėr) *n.* One who is an orator.

rhet-o-ric (ret´ėr ik) *n.* Effective expression in writing or speech; language which is not sincere.

rhe-tor-i-cal (ri tor´i kal) *adj.* To be involving rhetoric. **rhetoricalness** *n.*

rhetorical question *n.* A kind of question that is used for an effect and no answer is expected.

rhet-o-ri-cian (ret´o rish´an) *n.* A person who writes elaborate prose.

rheum (rōm) *n.* A fluid that is discharged from the mucus glands of the body.

rheumatic fever *n.* A severe infectious disease that is characterized by the swelling of the heart lining and the heart valves.

rheu-ma-tism (rö´ma tiz´um) *n.* A kind of inflammation that affects the joints and muscles of the body and can be very pain-ful.

Rh fac-tor *n.* A substance found in the red blood cells of 85% of all humans; the presence of this factor is referred to as RH positive; the absence as RH negative.

rhi-nal (rīn´al) *adj.* To be referring to the nose.

rhi-ni-tis (rī nī´tis) *n.* An inflammation that occurs in the nose or the membranes of the nose.

rhi-noc-er-os (rī nos´ėr os) *n.* A very large mammal with one or two upright horns on the snout found in Africa and Asia. **rhinocerotic** *adj.*

rhi-zan-thous (rī zan´thus) *adj.* To be bearing very short-stemmed flowers.

rhi-zo-bi-um (rī zō´bē um) *n.* A type of bacteria that is important in maintaining the soil's fertility.

rhi-zo-ceph-a-lan (rī´zō sef´a lan) *n.* A kind of crustacean that lives off a host and causes the host to lose its ability to reproduce.

rhi-zoid (rī´zoid) *n.* The hair-like structure that provides a root for ferns and mosses.

rhi-zome (rī´zōm) *n.* A subterranean plant stem thickened by deposits of reserve food material which produces shoots above and roots below.

rhi-zo-mor-phous (rī'zō mor'fus) *adj.* To be shaped like a root.

rhi-zo-pus (rī'zō pus) *n.* A type of mold fungus.

rho-da-mine (rō'da mēn') *n.* A red dye.

Rhode Island *n.* A state located in the northeastern part of the United States; statehood May 29, 1790; state capital Providence.

rho-di-um (rō'dē um) *n.* A metallic element symbolized by Rh.

rho-do-chro-site (rō'do krō'sīt) *n.* A kind of mineral that is made of manganese car-bonate and is pink in color.

rho-do-den-dron (rō'do den'dron) *n.* A variety of cultivated shrubs and trees with showy flowers and evergreen leaves.

rho-do-lite (rōd'o līt') *n.* A type of garnet that is rose-red in color.

rho-do-ra (rō dōr'a) *n.* A shrub found in Canada and New England having delicate pink flowers produced before the leaves in spring.

rhom-boid (rom'boid) *n.* A parallelogram where the angles are oblique and adjacent sides are unequal. **-bic** *adj.*

rhom-bus (rom'bus) *n.* A four sided figure whose sides are equal in length.

rhon-chus (rong'kus) *n.* A type of rale that occurs in the bronchial tubes of the airway.

rhu-barb (rō'bärb) *n.* A garden plant with large leaves and edible stalks used for pies.

rhyme (rīm) *n.* A word having a sound similar to another. **rhymer** *n.*

rhy-thm (rith'um) *n.* Music, speech, or movements which are characterized by equal or regularly alternating beats. **rhythmic, rhythmical** *adv.*

rhyth-mics (rith'miks) *n.* The science of rhythms.

ri-al-to (rē al'tō) *n.* The theater district.

ri-ant (rī'ant) *adj.* To be smiling; happy.

rib (rib) *n.* One of a series of curved bones enclosed in the chest of man and animals. *Slang* To tease.

rib-ald (rib'ald) *adj.* To be using indecent humor.

rib-band (rib'band') *n.* A narrow strip used in ship building to hold frames in position during construction.

rib-bon (rib'on) *n.* A narrow band or strip of fabric, such as satin, used for trimming.

rib-bon fish (rib'on fish') *n.* A kind of marine fish that has a long and flat body.

ri-bo-fla-vin (rī'bō flā'vin) *n.* A B complex vitamin that is found in milk, leafy vegetables, and liver.

rice (rīs) *n.* A cereal grass grown extensively in warm climates.

ric-er (rī'sėr) *n.* A kitchen utensil thru which soft foods are pressed in order to produce strings about the diameter of rice grain.

rich (rich) *adj.* Having great wealth; of great value; satisfying and pleasing in voice, color, tone, or other qualities; extremely productive; as soil or land.

rich-es (rich'iz) *n.* One's wealth.

rich-ly (rich'lē) *adv.* To be done in a rich manner or way.

Richter scale *n.* An instrument which measures a seismic disturbance such as an earth-quake with 1.5 being the smallest and 8.5 being a very devastating earthquake.

ri-cin (rī'sin) *n.* A white powder that is poisonous and is used to cause the agglutination of the red corpuscles.

rick-ets (rik'its) *n.* A childhood disease which is caused by lack of inadequate sunlight or vitamin D resulting in severely deformed bones.

rick-ett-si-a (ri ket'sē a) *adj.* A microorganism that is passed from arthropods to humans.

rick-et-y (rik'i tē) *adj.* To be ready to fall apart or fall down. **ricketiness** *n.*

rick-rack (rik'rak') *n.* A zigzag braid used in trimming.

rick-sha (rik'sho') *n.* A small 2-wheeled vehicle that is pulled by one man and that originated in Japan.

ric-o-chet (rik'o shā') *n.* A glancing blow off a flat surface.

ri-cot-ta *n.* A white whey cheese of Italy resembling cottage cheese.

ric-tus (rik'tus) *n.* An opening.

rid (rid) *v.* To make free from anything objectionable. **ridable** *adj.*

rid-dance (rid'ans) *n.* The getting rid of something or someone that is unwanted.

rid-dle (rid'l) *v.* To perforate with numerous holes. **riddle** *n.* A puzzling problem or question which requires a clever solution.

ride (rīd) *v.* To travel in a vehicle or on an animal; to sit on and drive, as a motorcycle. **ride for a fall** To flirt with danger. **ride high** To experience great success. **ride roughshod over** To treat with abuse.

ridge (rij) *n.* A long, narrow crest; a horizontal line formed where two sloping surfaces meet. **ridge** *v.*

ridge-pole (rij'pōl') *n.* Timber located at the top of a roof which is horizontal.

rid-i-cule (rid'i kūl') *n.* Actions or words intended to make a person or thing the object of mockery. **ridiculer** *n.*

ri-dic-u-lous (ri dik'ū lus) *adj.* To be causing derision or ridicule; to be laughable. **ridiculousness** *n.*

ri-dot-to *n.* A place of entertainment in masquerade popular in the 18th century England.

rife (rīf) *adj.* State of being abundant or abounding. **rifely** *adv.*

rif-fle (rif´l) *n.* Rippled water which is caused by a ridge.

rif-fler *n.* A small scraping tool.

riff-raff (rif´raf´) *n.* The rabble; low persons in society; a disreputable person.

ri-fle (rī´fl) *n.* A firearm having a grooved bore designed to be fired from the shoulder.

ri-fle-man (rī´fl man) *n.* A person skilled in the shooting of a rifle.

ri-fling (rī´fling) *n.* The act of putting or cutting spiral grooves in the barrel of a gun.

rift (rift) *n.* A fault; disagreement; a lack of harmony; a shallow place in a stream.

rig (rig) *v.* To outfit with necessary equipment. *n.* The arrangement of sails, masts, and other equipment on a ship; the apparatus used for drilling water or oil wells.

rig-a-doon (rig´a dön´) *n.* A lively dance of the 17th and 18th century.

rig-a-to-ni (rig´a tō´nē) *n.* A curved macaroni with fluted edges.

rig-ging (rig´ing) *n.* The lines used aboard a ship in working sails and supporting masts and spars; ropes, etc. used to support and manipulate scenery in the theater.

right (rīt) *adj.* In accordance with or conform able to law, justice, or morality; proper and fitting; properly adjusted, disposed, or placed; orderly; sound in body or mind. *n.* The right side, hand, or direction; the direction opposite left. *adv.* Immediately; completely; according to justice, morality, or law.

right angle *n., Geom.* An angle of 90 degrees; an angle with two sides perpendicular to each other.

right-eous (rī´chus) *adj.* Free from guilt; morally right; acting in accordance with moral or divine law. **righteousness** *n.*

right tri-an-gle *n.* A type of triangle where one angle is 90 degrees.

right wing *n.* One who is a member of a conservative political party. **right-winger** *n.* **rightwing** *adj.*

rig-id (rij´id) *adj.* Not bending; inflexible; severe; stern. **-ity** *n.* **-ness** *n.*

ri-gid-i-fy (ri jid´i fī´) *v.* To make something rigid. **rigidification** *n.*

rig-ma-role (rig´ma rōl´) *n.* A mean less or complex procedure.

rig-or (rig´ėr) *n.* The condition of being rigid or stiff; stiffness of temper; harshness. **rigorous , rigorously** *adv.*

rig-or-ism (rig´o riz´um) *n.* A strictness in practice.

rig-or mor-tis (rig´ėr mor´tis) *n.* The rigidity of muscles occurring after death.

rile (rīl) *v.* To make angry.

rill-et (ril´it) *n.* A small brook.

rim (rim) *n.* The outer edge or border of something; the outer part of a wheel joined to the hub on a car. **rimless** *adj.*

rime (rīm) *n.* An accumulation of granular ice on the windward sides of exposed objects formed from super-cooled fog or clouds.

ri-mose (rī´mōs) *adj.* To be filled with fissures. **rimosity** *n.* **rimosely** *adv.*

rim-rock (rim´rok´) *n.* An overlying strata of rock on a plateau that outcrops to form a vertical face.

rind (rīnd) *n.* A tough outer layer which may be taken off or peeled off.

rin-der-pest (rin´dėr pest´) *n.* A kind of contagious disease that affects the ruminant animals.

ring (ring) *n.* A circular mark, line, or object; a small circular band worn on a finger; a group of persons acting together; especially in an illegal way. *v.* To make a clear resonant sound, as a bell when struck. *n.* The sound made by a bell.

ring-lead-er (ring´lē´dėr) *n.* The person who is the leader of a group, usually one that will violate the law.

ring-let (ring´lit) *n.* A small curl of hair.

ring-mas-ter (ring´mas´tėr) *n.* The person in charge of performances in the circus.

ring-worm (ring´werm´) *n., Pathol.* A contagious skin disease caused by fungi and marked by discolored, ring-shaped, scaly patches on the skin.

rink (ringk) *n.* A smooth area covered with ice used for hockey or ice-skating; a smooth wooden surface for roller-skating.

rinse (rins) *v.* To wash lightly with water. *n.* The act of rinsing; a hair coloring or conditioning solution. **rinsed** *v.*

rins-ing (rin´sing) *n.* The action or act of a person who rinses.

ri-ot (rī´ot) *n.* A wild and turbulent public disturbance. *Slang* An irresistibly amusing person. **riotous** *adj.* **-er** *n.*

rip (rip) *v.* To tear apart violently; to move violently or quickly. *n.* A torn place. **rip-off** To steal.

ri-par-i-an (ri pâr´ē an) *adj.* To be located on the bank by water, such as a lake.

rip cord *n.* A cord which, when pulled, releases a parachute from its pack.

rip cur-rent *n.* A strong surface current flowing outward from shore which results from the return flow of waves.

ripe (rīp) *adj.* Fully developed or aged; mature. **ripeness** *n.*

rip-en (rī´pen) *v.* To age; to develop to maturity.

ri-poste (ri pōst´) *n.* A quick return thrust

used in fencing; a verbal outbreak.

rip-per (rip´er) *n.* A machine used to break up rock, ore, etc.

rip-ping (rip´ing) *adj.* To be pertaining to the tearing of something.

rip-ple (rip´l) *v.* To cause to form small waves on the surface of water; to waver gently. **rippler** *n.*

rip rap (rip´rap´) *n.* A foundation wall of stones thrown together in random fashion.

rip-roar-ing *adj.* To be noisy and loud.

rip tide (rip´tid´) *n.* Water made rough by the meeting of opposite tides and currents.

rise (riz) *v.* To move from a lower position to a higher one; to extend upward; to meet a challenge or demand. *n.* The act of going up or rising; an elevation in condition or rank.

ris-er (ri´zer) *n.* A person who rises; the upright part of a stairway.

ris-i-bil-i-ty (riz´i bil´i te) *n.* The ability to laugh.

ris-i-ble (riz´i bl) *adj.* Being inclined to or causing laughter.

ris-ing (ri´zing) *adj.* To be growing in height; to be more active.

risk (risk) *n.* A chance of suffering or encountering harm or loss; danger; a person who is a hazard to an insurer.

risk-y (ris´ke) *adj.* To be hazardous or full of risk. **riskiness** *n.*

ri-sot-to (ri so´to) *n.* Rice cooked in meat stock, seasoned with cheese.

rite (rit) *n.* A formal religious ceremony; any formal custom or practice.

rit-u-al (rich´o al) *n.* A prescribed method for performing a religious ceremony. *adj.* Pertaining to or practiced as a rite. **ritualism** *n.* **-ly** *adv.*

ritzy (rit´se) *adj.* To be fashionable; having a high fashion.

ri-val (ri´val) *n.* One who strives to compete with another; one who equals or almost equals another.

ri-val-ry (ri´val re) *n.* Competition.

rive (riv) *v.* To tear or to rip. **river** *n.*

riv-er (riv´er) *n.* A relatively large natural stream of water, usually fed by another body of water.

river bed (riv´er bed´) *n.* The channel thru which the river flows.

riv-er-ine (riv´e rin) *adj.* To be caused or formed by a river.

riv-er-weed (riv´er wed´) *n.* A type of submerged freshwater plant.

ri-vet (riv´it) *n.* A metal bolt that is used to secure two or more objects.

riv-u-let (riv´u lit) *n.* A small stream.

roach back *n.* A back that is curved.

road (rod) *n.* A public highway used for vehicles, people, and animals; a path or course; a course toward the achievement of something.

road-a-bil-i-ty (ro´da bil´i te) *n.* In reference to a car, its ability to ride over all types of roads.

road show *n.* A theatrical show given by a traveling troupe on tour.

roam (rom) *v.* To travel aimlessly or without a purpose. **roamer** *n.*

roan (ron) *n.* The color of a horse; a sheepskin tanned with sumac.

roar (ror) *v.* To utter a deep prolonged sound of excitement; to laugh loudly; a boisterous outcry. **roar** *n.* **roarer** *n.*

roar-ing (ror´ing) *n.* A loud sound or cry that is given off by something.

roast (rost) *v.* To cook meat by using dry heat in an oven. *n.* A cut of meat.

roast-er (ro´ster) *n.* A person that roasts.

rob (rob) *v.* To take property unlawfully from another person. **robber** *n.*

ro-band *n.* A piece of woven yarn used to fasten the sail to a spar.

rob-ber (rob´er) *n.* A person who steals from others.

rob-ber fly *n.* A large predatory fly.

rob-ber-y (rob´e re) *n.* The act of larceny from a person by violence or threat.

robe (rob) *n.* A long loose garment usually worn over nightclothes; a long flowing garment worn on ceremonial occasions.

ro-ble (ro´bla) *n.* Type of white oak tree that is found mainly in California.

ro-bot (ro´bot) *n.* A machine capable of performing human duties.

ro-bot-ics *n.* In *computer science*, the development of machines that perform an human tasks.

ro-bot-ize (ro´bo tiz´) *v.* To make something automatic. **robotization** *n.*

ro-bust (ro bust´) *adj.* Full of strength and health; rich; vigorous. **robustly** *adv.* **robustness** *n.*

ro-bus-tious (ro bus´chus) *adj.* To be sturdy or strong. **robustiousness** *n.*

roc-am-bole (rok´am bol´) *n.* One type of garlic that is cultivated.

rock (rok) *n.* A hard naturally formed material. *Slang* One who is dependable. **rock** *v.* To move to and fro.

rock-et (rok´it) *n.* A device propelled with the thrust from a gaseous combustion. *v.* To move rapidly.

rocket plane *n.* An airplane propelled by rockets.

rock-et-ry (rok´i tre) *n.* The study of rockets.

rock-fish (rok´fish´) *n.* The striped bass.

rock-oon (rok´on) *n.* A research rocket carried by a balloon to a high altitude and then fired.

rock salt *n.* Salt that is artificially prepared in large crystals, sometimes used in the preparation of ice cream made at home.

rock-y (rok´e) *adj.* Unsteady or unstable; full of rocks. **rockiness** *n.*

rod (rod) *n.* A straight stick growing from

a tree or bush; a pole with a line attached for fishing. **rodlike** *adj.*

rode *v.* Past tense of ride.

ro-dent (rōd´ent) *n.* A mammal, such as a rat, mouse, or beaver having large incisors used for gnawing.

ro-den-ti-cide (rō den´ti sīd´) *n.* A material that is used to destroy rodents.

ro-de-o (rō´dē ō´) *n.* A public show, contest, or demonstration of ranching skills, as riding and roping.

rod-o-mon-tade (rō´do mon tād´) *n.* Boasting that is vain.

roe (rō) *n.* The eggs of a fish.

roent-gen-o-gram (rent´ge no gram´) *n.* Type of photograph which is made with the use of x-rays.

roent-gen-o-ther-a-py (rent´ge nōther´ ape) *n.* Kind of medical treatment using x-rays.

rogue (rōg) *n.* A scoundrel or dishonest person; a mischievous or playful person. **roguishness** *n.* **roguishly** *adv.*

roil (roil) *v.* To make one angry.

role (rōl) *n.* The position or character that an actor or actress plays.

roll (rōl) *v.* To move in any direction by turning over and over; to sway or rock from side to side, as a ship; to make a deep prolonged sound as thunder. *n.* A list of names. *Slang* A large amount of money.

roi-lick (rol´ik) *v.* To frolic about.

rolling mill *n.* A type of mill where metal is rolled into sheets.

roll up *v.* To collect items together.

ROM Read Only Memory; In *computer science*, memory, as on a compact disk, that can be accessed, but cannot be altered.

ro-maine (rō mān´) *n.* Type of lettuce that has narrow leaves.

ro-mance (rō mans´) *n.* A love affair, usually of the young, characterized by ideals of devotion and purity; a fictitious story filled with extravagant adventures. **romance** *n.*,

Roman numeral *n.* The letter of the Roman system of numbering still used in formal contexts, as: I=1, V=5, X=10, L=50, C=100, D=500, M=1000.

ro-man-tic (rō man´tik) *adj.* Very amorous; referring to romance.

romp (romp) *v.* To run, play, or frolic in a carefree way.

ron-dure (ron´jer) *n.* A form that is gracefully curved.

rood (rōd) *n.* A measurement of land which equals 1/4 acre; a cross or crucifix.

roof (rōf) *n.* The top or covering of a house or other building keeping the elements of weather out. **rooflike** *adj.*

roof garden *n.* The garden that can be found on top of a building.

roof-ing (rō´fing) *n.* The supplies and

material that are used to cover a roof.

rook-ie (rek´ē) *n.* An untrained person; a novice or inexperienced person.

room (rōm) *n.* A section or area of a build-ing set off by partitions or walls. *v.* To occupy or live in a room.

room-er (rō´mér) *n.* Person who rents a room from someone and pays rent.

room-mate (rōm´māt) *n.* A person who will share the same room with another.

Roosevelt, Franklin Delano *n.* (1882-1945) The thirty-second president of the United States from 1933-1945.

Roosevelt, Theodore *n.* (1858-1919) The twenty-sixth president of the United States from 1901-1909.

roost (rōst) *n.* A place or perch on which birds sleep or rest. **Roost** *n.* To settle into a roost or place of nest.

roost-er (rō´stér) *n.* The male chicken.

root (rōt) *n.* The part of a plant which grows in the ground. *Math* A number when multiplied by itself, will produce a given quantity. **root** *v.* To search or rummage for something; to turn up the earth with the snout, as a hog.

root out *v.* To discover something.

root rot *n.* A plant disease which is recognized by the decaying of it's roots.

root-y (rō´tē) *adj.* To have a lot of roots.

rope (rōp) *n.* A heavy cord of twisted fiber. **know the ropes** To be familiar with all of the conditions at hand.

ro-que-laure *n.* A knee-length coat that was worn in the 18th and 19th centuries.

ror-qual (ror´kwal) *n.* Large whale.

ro-sa-ry (rō´za rē) *n. pl.* -ies A string of beads for counting prayers; a series of prayers.

rose (rōz) *n.* A shrub or climbing vine having sharp prickly stems and variously colored fragrant flowers.

ro-se-ate (rō´zē it) *adj.* To be of a deep pink color. **roseately** *adv.*

rose-bud (rōz´bud´) *n.* The state of the rose just before it blooms.

rose fever *n.* The allergy that is associated to rose pollen.

ro-se-o-la (rō zē´o la) *n.* A rash that is rose colored and appearing on the skin.

Rosh Hashanah (rōsh´ ha shä´na) *n.* The Jewish New Year.

ros-i-ly (rō´zi lē) *adv.* In a cheerful manner; with a rosy color.

ros-in-weed (roz´in wēd´) *n.* A sunflower-like plant that is found in North America.

ros-ter (ros´tèr) *n.* A list of names.

ros-y (rō´zē) *adj.* To be pink, like the color of roses. **rosiness** *n.*

rot (rot) *v.* To break down or decompose.

ro-ta-ry (rō´ta rē) *adj.* Turning or designed to turn; of or relating to axial rotation.

ro-tate (rō´tāt) *v.* To turn on an axis; to

alternate something in sequence.
rotation *n*. **rotator** *n*. **rotatory** *adj*.

rote (rōt) *n*. Repetition of sounds.

ro-te-none (rōt'e nōn') *n*. Type of compound that is used as an insecticide.

ro-tis-ser-ie (rō tis'e rē) *n*. A rotation device with spits for roasting food.

ro-tor (rō'tėr) *n*. A rotating part of a mechanical device.

rot-ten (rot'en) *adj*. Decomposed; morally corrupt; very bad.

rot-ten-stone (rot'en stōn') *n*. Type of soft stone that is used for polishing brass.

rot-ter (rot'ėr) *n*. A really bad person.

ro-tund (rō tund') *adj*. Plump; rounded.

ro-tun-da (rō tun'da) *n*. A building that is round having a domed roof.

rouge (rözh) *n*. A cosmetic coloring for the cheeks.

rough (ruf) *adj*. Having an uneven surface; violent or harsh. **rough** *n*. The part of a golf course with tall grass. **rough** *v*. To treat roughly. **roughly** *adv*. In a very rude manner; approximately.

rough-age (ruf'ij) *n*. Material that is coarse in texture.

rough–and–ready (ruf'an red'ē) *adj*. Crude in method but effective in action.

rou-leau (rö lō') *n*. A trimming for hats that is rolled.

rou-lette (rö let') *n*. A gambling game in which players bet on which slot a small ball will land in.

round (round) *adj*. Curved; circular; spherical. **round** *v*. To become round; to surround. **round** *adv*. Throughout; prescribed duties, places, or actions.

rouse (rouz) *v*. To awaken or stir up.

rout (rout) *v*. To dig something up, such as a root.

route (rōt) *n*. A course of travel. **route** *v*. To send in a certain direction.

rou-tine (rö tēn') *n*. Activities done regularly. **routine** *adj*. Ordinary.

rove (rōv) *v*. To wander over a wide area. **rover** *n*. **roving** *adj*.

row (rō) *n*. A number of things positioned next to each other; a continuous line. **row** *v*. To propel a boat with oars.

row-dy (rou'dē) *n*. A person who is disorderly. **rowdily** *adv*. **-iness** *n*.

roy-al (roi'al) *adj*. Relating to a king or queen.

roy-al-ist (roi'a list) *n*. A person who supports the king.

roy-al-ty *n*. *pl*. **royalties** Monarchs and their families; a payment to someone for the use of his invention, copyright, or services.

R.S.V.P. *abbr*. Respondez s'il vous plait; please reply.

rub (rub) *v*. To move over a surface with friction and pressure; to cause to become worn or frayed.

rub-ber (rub'ėr) *n*. A resinous elastic

material obtained from the coagulated and processed sap of tropical plants or produced synthetically. **-bery** *adj*.

rubber cement *n*. A type of adhesive that is liquid and made of rubber.

rub-ber-ize (rub'e rīz') *v*. Coat or cover something with rubber.

rubber plant *n*. Type of plant that is found in East India and yields rubber.

rubber stamp *n*. A type of rubber plate which is coated with ink and used for the purpose of leaving prints on paper or other objects.

rub-bish (rub'ish) *n*. Worthless trash; nonsense.

rub-ble (rub'l) *n*. The pieces of broken material or stones.

rub-down (rub'doun') *n*. A type of quick and brisk massage.

ru-be-fa-cient (rö'be fā'shent) *n*. A type of substance which will turn the area of skin it is applied to red.

ru-bel-la (rö bel'a) *n*. The German measles.

ru-bel-lite (rö bel'īt) *n*. A red gem stone.

ru-be-o-la (rö bē'o la) *n*. The German measles. **rubeoloid** *adj*. **rubeolar** *adj*.

ru-bi-cund (rö'bi kund') *adj*. State of being of a red color or hue.

ru-bid-i-um (rö bid'ē um) *n*. A silvery, highly reactive element symbolized by Rb.

ru-bi-ous (rö'bē us) *adj*. Being red in color.

ru-bric (rö'brik) *n*. A heading, title, or initial letter of a manuscript which appears in red. **rubrically** *adv*. **-al** *adj*.

ru-bri-cate (rö'bri kāt') *v*. To color something red. **rubricator** *n*.

ru-by (rö'bē) *n*. *pl*. **-ies** A deep-red precious stone. **rubylike** *adj*.

ruby glass *n*. Type of red glass.

ru-by spi-nal *n*. A gem stone, red in color.

ruche (rösh) *n*. Piece of crimped fabric which is used to trim a woman's clothes.

ruck-sack (ruk'sak') *n*. A knapsack that is carried by hikers.

ruck-us *n*., *Slang* A noisy uproar, or com-motion.

rud-der (rud'ėr) *n*., *Naut*. A broad, flat, hinged device attached to the stern of a boat used for steering.

ru-di-ment (rö'di ment) *n*. A first step, element, skill, or principle. *Biol*. An undeveloped organ. **-tariness** *n*.

rue (rö) *v*. To repent.

rue-ful (rö'ful) *adj*. To be causing sorrow or remorse. **ruefully** *adv*.

ru-fes-cent (rö fes'ent) *adj*. To be red in color or tint. **rufescence** *n*.

ruff (ruf) *n*. A stiff collar which has pleats in it.

ruffed grouse *n*. A bird, like the chicken, and living in North America having a fan-shaped tail and tufted feathers at the neck.

ruf-fi-an (ruf'ē an) *n.* A lawless, rowdy person. **ruffianly** *adj.* **ruffianism** *n.*

ruf-fle (ruf'l) *n.* A pleated strip or frill; a decorative band. *v.* To disturb or destroy the smoothness.

ru-fous (rō'fus) *adj.* To be red in color or tint.

rug (rug) *n.* A heavy textile fabric used to cover a floor.

ru-ga (rō'ga) *n.* A wrinkle or fold in something.

rug-ged (rug'id) *adj.* Strong; rough; having an uneven or rough surface. **ruggedness** *n.* **ruggedly** *adv.*

ru-gose (rō'gōs) *adj.* To be filled with folds and wrinkles. **rugous** *adj.*

ru-in (rō'in) *n.* Total destruction. **ruin** *v.* To destroy. **ruination** *n.* **-ous** *adj.*

rule (rōl) *n.* Controlling power; an authoritative direction or statement which regulates the method of doing something; a standard procedure. **rule** *v.* To have control over; to make a straight line using a ruler; to be in command.

rule out *v.* To omit something.

rul-er (rō'lėr) *n.* A straight edge used for measuring; a person who rules as a sovereign.

rul-ing (rō'ling) *n.* A type of decision which is handed down by a judge in a trial.

rum (rum) *n.* A type of liquor made from molasses and is distilled.

rum-ble (rum'bl) *v.* To make a heavy, continuous sound. *n.* A long, deep rolling sound.

ru-men (rō'min) *n.* The first stomach of ruminant animals, such as a cow or goat.

ru-mi-nant (rō'mi nant) *n.* A cud-chewing animal; as a cow, deer, sheep, or giraffe; an animal which chews something which was swallowed. **ruminantly** *adv.*

ru-mi-nate (rō'mi nāt') *v.* To chew a cud; to ponder at length. **rumination** *n.* **ruminative** *adj.* **ruminator** *n.*

rum-mage (rum'ij) *v.* To look or search thoroughly by digging or turning things over; to ransack.

ru-mor (rō'mėr) *n.* An uncertain truth which is circulated from one person to another; gossip. **rumor** *v.* To spread by rumor.

rump (rump) *n.* The fleshy hind quarter of an animal; the human buttocks.

rum-ple (rum'pl) *v.* To form into creases or folds; to wrinkle.

rum-pus (rum'pus) *n.* A loud noise or disturbance.

rumpus room *n.* A type of room which is used for parties.

run (run) *v.* To hurry busily from place to place; to move quickly in such a way that both feet leave the ground for a portion of each step; to make a rapid journey; to be a candidate seeking an office; to drain or discharge. *Law* To be effective, concurrent with. **run** *n.* A speed faster than a walk; a streak, as of luck; the continuous extent or length of something; an outdoor area used to exercise animals. In baseball, the method of scoring a point by running the bases and returning to home plate.

run-a-way (run'a wā') *n.* A person who leaves home without telling anyone where they are going and does not plan on coming back.

rung (rung) *n.* A bar or board which forms a step of a ladder.

run-nel (run'el) *n.* A small stream.

run-ner-up (run'ėr up') *n.* A contestant who finishes second in a competition.

runt (runt) *n.* The smallest animal in a litter. **runty** *adj.* **runtiness** *n.*

run time In *computer science*, the period required for a computer to perform a particular task, such as a mail merge.

rup-ture (rup'chėr) *n.* A state of being broken; the act of bursting.

ru-ral (rer'al) *adj.* Pertaining to the country or country life. **ruralist** *n.*

ru-ral-ize (rer'a līz') *v.* The act of moving to or living in the country or the rural area. **ruralization** *n.*

rural route *n.* A mail route which runs through the country.

rush (rush) *v.* To move quickly; to hurry; to be in a hurry. **rushy** *adj.*

rust (rust) *n.* Ferric oxide which forms a coating on iron material exposed to moisture and oxygen; deterioration through neglect. **rust** *v.* To form rust.

rus-tic (rus'tik) *adj.* Characteristic of country life. **rustic** *n.* A simple person.

rus-tle (rus'l) *v.* To move making soft sounds, such as those made by leaves of a tree.

rut (rut) *n.* An indented track made by the wheels of vehicles.

ru-ta-ba-ga (rō'ta bā'ga) *n.* A vegetable of the mustard family which makes an underground white tuber.

ruth (rōth) *n.* Grief; sorrowful for another.

ru-the-ni-um (rō thē'nē um) *n.* A metallic element symbolized by Ru.

ruth-ful (rōth'ful) *adj.* To be mournful.

ruth-less (rōth'lis) *adj.* Merciless.

ru-ti-lant (rör'i lant) *adj.* To have a glow that is reddish in color or tine.

rut-ty (rut'ē) *adj.* A state of having many ruts.

rye (rī) *n.* A cultivated cereal grass used to make flour and whiskey.

rye whiskey *n.* Whiskey distilled from rye.

S, s (ess) The nineteenth letter of the English alphabet.

sab-bat (sab´at) n. The midnight assembly of the diatomists.

Sab-ba-tar-i-an n. A person who observes the Sabbath on Saturday.

Sab-bath n. The seventh day of the week; sundown on Friday to sundown on Saturday; a day set aside as the day of worship for Jews and some Christians; Sunday, the first day of the week, a day set apart as the day of worship by most Christians.

sab-bat-i-cal (sa bat´ik) adj. To be relating to the Sabbath.

saber—toothed tiger n. A type of extinct cat which was characterized by the great development of the upper canines.

sa-bin n. Unit of acoustic absorption.

sa-ble (sā´bl) n. A carnivorous mammal having soft, black or dark fur.

sa-ble-fish (sā´bl fish´) n. A type of large spiny-finned fish which is grey or black and of the Pacific coast.

sa-bot (sab´ō) n. The kind of wooden shoe which is worn by the people in various European countries.

sab-o-tage (sab´o täzh´) n. An act of malicious destruction, intended to obstruct production of war material by the opposing side.

sab-o-teur n. A person who commits sabotage.

sac (sak) n., Biol. A membranous pouch in an animal or plant, containing a liquid.

sa-ca-huis-te n. A kind of forage grass that has long linear leaves.

sac-cade n. A type of small, rapid, and jerky movement of the eye.

sac-cate (sak´it) adj. To have the form of a pouch.

sac-cha-rate n. A compound of sugar usually with a bivalent metal.

sac-char-i-fy v. To break some compound into a simple sugar.

sac-cha-rim-e-ter n. A kind of device which is used for the purpose of measuring the amount of sugar in a solution.

sac-cha-rin (sak´a rin) n. A white, crystal-line powder used as a non-caloric sugar substitute.

sac-cha-rine (sak´a rin) adj. Pertaining to or like sugar.

sac-cha-roi-dal adj. Being of fine granular texture.

sac-cha-rom-e-ter n. A type of hydrometer that has a special scale.

sac-cu-lar adj. To be resembling a sac.

sac-cu-late adj. To be formed of a series of saccular expansions.

sac-cule n. A chamber which is the smaller of the membranous labyrinth of the ear.

sac-er-do-tal (sas´ē dōt´al) adj. Pertaining to the priesthood or priests.

sa-chem (sā´chem) n. A kind of North American Indian chief.

sa-chet (sa shā´) n. A small bag of a sweet smelling powder used to scent clothes.

sack (sak) n. A strong bag for holding articles. Slang Dismissal from a position or job; sleeping bag or bed.

sacque (sak) n. A type of infant jacket that is short and fastens at the neck.

sa-cral adj. Pertaining to the sacrum.

sac-ra-ment (sak´ra ment) n. Eccl. A formal Christian rite performed in a church, as a baptism. **Sacrament** The consecrated bread and wine of the Eucharist; the Lord's Supper.

sac-ra-ment-al adj. The use of the sacramental acts or rites.

sa-crar-i-um n. An ancient Roman shrine which holds sacred articles.

sa-cred (sā´krid) adj. Dedicated to worship; holy. **sacredly** adv.

sac-ri-fice (sak´ri fis´) n. The practice of offering something, as an animal's life, to a deity. **sacrifice** v. To give up something of value for something else. **sacrificial** adj.

sa-cro-il-i-ac adj. Pertaining to the region of juncture of the sacrum and the ilium.

sa-crum n. The section or part of the vertebral column which is directly connected with the pelvis and in man is made up of five fused vertebrae.

sad (sad) adj. Marked by sorrow; unhappy; causing sorrow; deplorable. **sadly** adv. **sadness** n.

sadden v. To become or to make sad.

sad-dle (sad´l) n. A seat for a rider, as on the back of a horse or bicycle; a cut of meat which includes the backbone. **saddle** v. To put a saddle on; to load down; to burden.

saddlebag n. A covered pouch which is put across the back of the horse.

saddle leather n. A type of leather which is made from the hide of cattle that is vegetable-tanned and used for making saddles.

saddle roof n. A type of roof having one ridge and two gables.

sad-i-ron (sad Tèrn) n. A type of flatiron which is pointed at both ends.

sa-dism (sad´iz um) n. Psychol. A condition in which sexual gratification comes from inflicting pain on others; cruelty. **sadistic** adj.

sad sack n. A kind of person who is inept.

sa-fa-ri (sa fär´ē) n., pl. **safaris** A trip; a hunting expedition in Africa.

safe (sāf) adj. Secure from danger, harm, or evil; unharmed; not likely to cause harm. **safe** n. A strong metal container used to protect and store documents or money. **safely** adv.

safe—conduct n. The protection which

is given to a person that is passing through a military zone.

safe–deposit box n. A box which can be found in a bank and used for the purpose of protecting the valuables of the one who uses it.

safe-guard n. A kind of precautionary measure.

safety belt n. A type of belt that is used to prevent a person from injury or falling.

saf-ra-nine n. Any of the various mixtures of safranine salts which are used in dyeing.

saf-role n. A type of poisonous ether that is used for perfuming and flavoring.

sag v. To droop; to sink from pressure or weight; to lose strength; decline in amount.

sa-ga (sä´gạ) n. A long heroic story.

sa-ga-cious (sạ gä´shus) adj. Being of keen penetration and judgment.

sag-a-more (sag´a mŏr´) n. The subordinate chief of the Algonquian Indians who are of the north Atlantic coast.

sage (sāj) n. A person recognized for judgment and wisdom. **sage** adj.

sagebrush n. A type of North American low shrubs with a bitter juice and odor.

sag-ger (sag´ẽr) n. A type of box which is made of fireclay.

sag-it-tal adj. Pertaining to the suture between the parietal bones of the skull.

sag-it-tate (saj´i tāt´) adj. To be shaped like an arrowhead.

sa-go n. A type of powdered starch that is made from the pith of a sago palm.

sa-gua-ro n. A type of arborescent cactus which grows in the southwestern United States and Mexico.

said (sed) v. Past tense of say.

sail (sāl) n. A strong fabric used to catch the wind and cause a ship to move; a trip on a sailing vessel or boat. **sail** v. To travel on a sailing vessel.

sail-board A type of small flat sailboat made for two passengers.

sail-boat n. A type of boat which is propelled with a sail.

sail-cloth n. A type of canvas which is used for making sails.

sail-er n. A boat which has specified sailing qualities.

sail-fish n. A type of pelagic fish that has a large dorsal fin.

sailor n. The person that sails or works on a boat or ship.

sain-foin (sān´foin) n. A type of herb that has pink flowers.

saint (sānt) n. A person of great purity who has been officially recognized as such by the Roman Catholic Church; a person who has died and is in heaven.

sake (sāk) n. Motive or reason for doing something.

sal-a-ble (sā´lạ bl) adj. Fit to be sold.

sa-la-cious adj. To be appealing to sexual desire. **salaciousness** n.

sal-ad (sal´ạd) n. A dish usually made of green vegetables, fruit, or meat tossed with dressing.

sal-a-man-der (sal´a man´dẽr) n. A lizard-like amphibian with porous, scaleless skin.

sa-la-mi (sạ lä´mē) n. A spiced sausage made of beef and pork.

sa-la-ry (sal´ạ rē) n., pl. salaries A set compensation paid on a regular basis for services rendered or hours served. **salaried** adj.

sale (sāl) n. An exchange of goods for a price; disposal of items at reduced prices. **salable** adj.

sa-lep n. The dried tubers of various Old World orchids.

sal-er-a-tus n. A kind of leavening agent.

sales adj. Pertaining to selling.

sales tax n. A tax which is placed on the sale of goods.

sal-i-cin (sal´i sin) n. A bitter white glucoside that is found in the bark of willows.

sa-lic-y-late n. The ester of salicylic acid.

sa-li-ence n. The state of being salient.

sa-li-ent (sā´lē ent) adj. Projecting beyond a line; conspicuous.

sa-li-tian n. Any of the group of amphibians which consists of frogs, toads, and tree toads.

sa-lim-e-ter n. Type of hydrometer for indicating a percentage of salt in a solution.

sa-li-nize v. To impregnate with salt.

sa-li-nom-e-ter n. A type of instrument used for the purpose of measuring salt in a solution.

sa-li-va (sạ lī´va) n. Tasteless fluid secreted in the mouth which aids in digestion.

sal-i-var-y adj. Pertaining to saliva or the glands of the body that secrete saliva.

sal-i-vate v. To produce or make an abnormal flow of saliva.

Salk vaccine (salk´ vak sēn´) n. A vaccine used to immunize against polio.

sal-low (sal´ō) n. A type of Old World broad-leaved willow.

sal-ly n., pl. sallies A sudden rush to launch an assault.

sal-ma-gun-di n. A kind of salad plate made with eggs, meats, and vegetables.

sal-mi n. A ragout of roasted game that is stewed in a rich sauce.

salm-on (sam´on) n., pl. salmon or salmons A large game fish with pinkish flesh.

sal-mon-el-la n. A type of aerobic rod-shaped bacteria that causes food poisoning.

sal-mo-nel-lo-sis n. A disease that is

caused by salmonellae.

sal-mo-nid *n.* A member of the family of elongated soft-finned fishes.

sa-lon (*sa* lon') *n.* A large drawing room; a business establishment pertaining to fashion.

sa-loon (*sa* lön') *n.* A place where alcoholic drinks are sold; a barroom.

sa-loop (*sa* löp') *n.* A hot drink which is made from sassafras and dried tubers of orchids.

sal-pa *n.* An oceanic tunicate which is found to be abundant in warm seas.

sal-pin-gian *adj.* Pertaining to or relating to a fallopian or eustacian tube.

sal-pin-gi-tis *n.* The swelling or inflammation of a fallopian tube or a eustachian tube.

sal-si-fy *n.* A type of European biennial herb that has an edible root.

sal soda *n.* A crystalline hydrated sodium carbonate.

salt (solt) *n.* A white crystalline solid, mainly sodium chloride, found in the earth and sea water, used as a preservative and a seasoning. **salt** *adj.* Containing salt. **salt** *v.* To season or preserve with salt. **salty** *adj.*

sal-ta-tion (sal tā'shan) *n.* The process of jumping or leaping.

sal-ta-to-ri-al *adj.* To be adapted for leaping.

sal-ta-to-ry *adj.* Pertaining to dancing.

sal-tine (sol tēn') *n.* A crisp cracker which is sprinkled with salt.

salt-pe-ter (solt'pē'tēr) *n.* Potassium nitrate.

sa-lu-bri-ous (*sa* lö'brē us) *adj.* To be promoting well-being or health.

sa-lu-ki *n.* A type of northern African and Asiatic breed of hunting dogs.

sal-u-tar-y (sal'ü tēr'ē) *adj.* Wholesome; healthful; beneficial.

sal-u-ta-tion (sal'ū tā'shan) *n.* An expression; a greeting of good will, as used to open a letter.

sa-lu-ta-to-ri-an *n.* A student that usually has the second highest rank in the class; based on grade scores.

sa-lu-ta-to-ry *adj.* Pertaining to a salutation.

sa-lute (*sa* löt') *v.* To show honor to a superior officer by raising the right hand to the forehead. **salute** *n.* An act of respect or greeting by saluting.

salv-a-ble *adj.* Capable of being salvaged; reuseable.

sal-vage (sal'vij) *n.* Act of rescuing a ship, its cargo, or its crew; property which has been saved. **salvage** *v.* To save from destruction; to rescue.

sal-va-tion (sal vā'shan) *n.* The means which effect salvation; the deliverance from the effects of sin.

salve (sav) *n.* A medicated ointment to soothe the pain of a burn or wound.

sal-ver (sal'vēr) *n.* A type of tray which is used for serving food and drinks.

sal-ver-form *adj.* Being tubular with a spreading limb.

sal-vi-a *n.* Type of herbs of the mint family that have a two-lipped open calyx.

sal-vif-ic *adj.* Having the intent to save.

sal-vo (sal'vō) *n., pl.* **salvos** *or* **salvoes** The discharge of a number of guns at the same time.

sal volatile *n.* A solution of ammonium carbonate in alcohol.

SAM *abbr.* Surface-to-Air Missile.

Sa-mar-i-tan (*sa* mar'i tan) *n.* A person who is ready to help others in need.

sa-mar-i-um (*sa* mâr'ē *u*m) *n.* A metallic element symbolized by Sm.

sam-ba *n.* A type of Brazilian dance.

sam-bar *n.* A large Asiatic deer that has long, coarse hair on its neck.

sam-bo *n.* A type of international wrestling with judo techniques.

same (sām) *adj.* Identical; exactly alike; similar; not changing. **same** *pron.* The very same one or thing.

sa-mite (sam'ī t) *n.* A silk fabric with interwoven gold or silver threads.

sam-o-var *n.* A type of Russian urn used to boil water for making tea.

samp *n.* A coarse hominy.

sam-phire (sam'fī ēr') *n.* A common glasswort that is sometimes pickled.

sam-ple (sam'pl) *n.* A portion which represents the whole. **sample** *v.* To try a little.

sam-pler (sam'plēr) *n.* A person who collects or examines samples.

sample room *n.* the room where samples of product are storedor displayed.

sam-shu *n.* An alcoholic liquor distilled in China from millet or rice.

sam-u-rai *n.* The warrior aristocracy of Japan.

san-a-to-ri-um (san'*a* tōr'ē *u*m) *n. pl.* **sanatoriums** An institution for treating chronic diseases.

sanc-ti-fy (sangk'ti fī') *v.* To make holy. **sanctification** *n.*

sanc-ti-mo-ni-ous *adj.* To be possessing sanctity. **sanctimoniousness** *n.*

sanc-ti-mo-ny *n.* A hypocritical holiness.

sanc-tion (sangk'shan) *n.* Permission from a person of authority; a penalty to ensure compliance. **sanction** *v.* To officially approve an action.

sanc-tu-ar-y (sangk'chō er'ē) *n., pl.* **sanctuaries** A sacred, holy place, as the part of a church, where services are held; a safe place; a refuge.

sanc-tum *n.* A place which is sacred.

sand (sand) *n.* Fine grains of disintegrated rock found in deserts and on beaches; a light tan color. **sand** *v.* To smooth or polish with sandpaper; to sprinkle or toss sand.

san-dal (san´dal) *n.* A shoe which is fastened to the foot by straps attached to the sole; a low shoe or slipper with an ankle strap.

san-dar-ac (san´da rak´) *n.* A resin that is aromatic and brittle obtained from the African sandarac tree.

sand-cast (sand´kast) *v.* To make a casting by pouring the metal into a mold which is made of sand.

sand dollar *n.* A flat circular sea urchin that lives in shallow water on the sandy bottom.

sand-glass *n.* A type of instrument for measuring the passing of time with the running of sand through it.

sand-pa-per *n.* A type of paper that is covered on one side with sand used for the purpose of smoothing rough edges.

sand-wich (sand´wich) *n.* Two or more slices of bread between which a filling, such as cheese or meat, is placed.

sane (sān) *adj.* Having a healthy, sound mind; showing good judgment. **sanely** *adv.* **sanity** *n.*

san-ga-ree (sang´ga rē) *n.* An iced drink of wine, beer, ale, or liquor which has been garnished with nutmeg.

sang-froid (sän frwä´) *n.* A self-possession or imperturbability.

san-gui-nar-ia *n.* The roots and rhizome of the bloodroot which can be used as an emetic or an expectorant.

san-guine (sang´gwin) *adj.* To be relating to the blood. **sanguinely** *adv.*

san-guin-e-ous *adj.* Pertaining to bloodshed; consisting of blood.

san-guin-o-lent *adj.* To be tinged by blood or to contain blood.

san-guin-o-pu-ru-lent *adj.* Containing us and blood in the discharge.

san-i-cle *n.* A type of plants that are held to have healing powers.

san-it *abbr.* Sanitation; sanitary.

san-i-tar-i-an *n.* One who is a specialist in sanitary science and the public health.

san-i-tar-i-ly *adv.* Doing something in a sanitary manner or way.

san-i-tar-y (san´i ter´ē) *adj.* Free from bacteria or filth which endanger health. **sanitary** *n.*

san-i-tate *v.* To make a thing sanitary; clean.

san-i-ta-tion (san´i tā´shan) *n.* The process of making something sanitary.

san-i-tize (san´i tīz´) *v.* To make sanitary; to make clean or free of germs.

san-i-ty *n.* The state of being sane.

sank *v.* Past tense of sink.

san-nup (san´up) *n.* An American Indian male who is married.

sans-cu-lotte *n.* One who is considered to be from a lower class and lacking culture or refinement.

san-se-vie-ria *n.* A member of the group of tropical herbs of the lily family that yield a strong fiber.

sap (sap) *n.* The liquid which flows or circulates through plants and trees. *v.* To weaken or wear away gradually. *Slang* A gullible person; fool.

sa-pi-ent (sā´pē ent) *adj.* Wise.

sap-phire (saf´īer) *n.* A clear, deep-blue gem, used in jewelry.

sar-casm (sär´kaz um) *n.* An insulting or mocking statement or remark. **sarcastic** *adj.* **sarcastically** *adv.*

sar-dine (sär dēn´) *n.* A small edible fish of the herring family, canned in oil, mustard, or tomato sauce.

sar-don-ic (sär don´ik) *adj.* Scornful; mockingly cynical.

sa-ri (sär´ē) *n.* A garment consisting of a long piece of lightweight material wrapped around the body and over the shoulder of Hindu women.

sar-sa-pa-ril-la (sas´pa ril´a) *n.* The dried root of a tropical American plant, which is used as flavoring.

sash (sash) *n.* A band worn over the shoulder or around the waist.

sass (sas) *n.* *Slang* Rudeness; a disrespectful manner of speech. **sass** *v.* To talk with disrespect.

sas-sa-fras (sas´a fras´) *n.* The dried root of a North American tree, used as flavoring.

Sa-tan (sāt´an) *n.* The devil.

sat-el-lite (sat´e līt´) *n.* A natural or man-made object which orbits a celestial body.

sat-in (sat´in) *n.* A smooth, shiny fabric made of silk, nylon, or rayon, having a glossy face and dull back.

sat-ire (sat´īer) *n.* The use of mockery, sarcasm, or humor in a literary work to ridicule or attack human vice.

sat-is-fac-tion (sat´is fak´shan) *n.* Anything which brings about a happy feeling; the fulfillment of a need, appetite, or desire; a source of gratification. **satisfactory** *adj.*

sat-u-rate (sach´a rāt´) *v.* To make completely wet; to soak or load to capacity. **saturable** *adj.* **-tion** *n.*

sat-yr (sā´tėr) *n.* *Myth.* A Greek woodland god having a human body and the legs, horns, and ears of a goat.

sauce (sos) *n.* A liquid or dressing served as an accompaniment to food.

sau-cer (so´sėr) *n.* A small shallow dish for holding a cup.

sau-er-kraut (sour´krout´) *n.* Shredded and salted cabbage cooked in its own juices until tender and sour.

sau-na (sou´nä) *n.* A steam bath in which one is subjected to heat produced by water poured over heated rocks.

sau-sage (so´sij) *n.* Chopped meat, usually pork, which is highly seasoned, stuffed into a casing, and cooked.

sav-age (sav´ij) *adj.* Wild; not domesticated; uncivilized; brutal. **savage** *n.* A vicious or crude person. **-ery** *n.*

save (sāv) *v.* To rescue from danger, loss, or harm; to prevent waste or loss; to keep for another time in the future; to be delivered from sin. **saver** *n.*

sav-ior (sāv´yėr) *n.* One who saves.

sa-voir-faire (sav´wär fâr´) *n.* Social skill; the ability to say and do the right thing.

sa-vor (sā´vėr) *n.* The taste or smell of something. **savor** *v.* To have a particular smell; to truly enjoy. **-y** *adj.*

saw (so) *n.* A tool with a sharp metal blade edged with teeth-like points for cutting. **saw** *v.* Past tense of *see*; to cut with a saw.

sax-o-phone (sak´so fōn´) *n.* A brass wind instrument having finger keys and a reed mouthpiece.

say (sā) *v.* To speak aloud; to express oneself in words; to indicate; to show. **say** *n.* The chance to speak; the right to make a decision.

scab (skab) *n.* The stiff and crusty covering which forms over a healing wound. *Slang* One who continues to work while others are on strike.

scab-bard (skab´ėrd) *n.* A type of sheath for a bayonet or a dagger.

scab-ble *v.* To dress something, such as stone, with a rough furrowed surface.

scab-by *adj.* To be diseased with scab.

sca-bies (skā´bēz) *n.* A contagious skin disease characterized by severe itching, caused by a mite under the skin.

sca-bi-o-sa *n.* A type of herb of the teasel family.

sca-brous (skab´rus) *adj.* To be rough to the touch. **scabrousness** *n.*

scad (skad) *n.* A type of caragid fish.

scaf-fold (skaf´old) *n.* A temporary support of metal or wood erected for workers who are building or working on a large structure.

scaf-fold-ing *n.* A system of scaffolds.

scal-a-ble *adj.* Able to be scaled.

sca-lar *adj.* To have an uninterrupted series of steps such as a staircase.

sca-lar-i-form *adj.* To be like or resembling a ladder.

scal-a-wag (skal´a wag´) *n.* Rascal.

scald (skold) *v.* To burn with steam or a hot liquid; to heat a liquid to a temperature just under boiling.

scale (skāl) *n.* A flat plate which covers certain animals, especially fish and reptiles; a device for weighing; a series of marks indicating the relationship between a map or model and the actual dimensions. *Music* A sequence of eight musical notes in accordance with a specified scheme of intervals.

scale–down *n.* A kind of reduction that

is according to a fixed ratio.

sca-lene (skā lēn´) *adj.* Having three sides that are unequal in length.

scale-pan *n.* A kind of pan which is used for the purpose of weighing things.

scal-er (skā´lėr) *n.* Someone or something that scales an object.

scale–up *n.* The increase that is according to a ratio which is fixed.

scall (skol) *n.* A type of scabby disorder which can occur on the skin.

scal-lion *n.* A type of onion that will form a thick basal part but without a bulb.

scal-lop (skol´op) *n.* A marine shellfish with a fan-shaped, fluted bivalve shell; the fleshy edible muscle of the scallop.

scalp (skalp) *n.* The skin which covers the top of the human head where hair normally grows. **scalp** *v.* To tear or remove the scalp from. *Slang* To buy or sell something at an inflated price.

scal-pel (skal´pel) *n.* A small, straight knife with a narrow, pointed blade, used in surgery.

scalp lock *n.* A tuft of the hair on the crown of an otherwise shaved head.

scamp (skamp) *n.* A tricky person.

scamp-er *v.* To run playfully about.

scamp-i *n.* A type of large shrimp that is prepared with a garlic sauce.

scan (skan) *v.* To examine all parts closely; to look at quickly; to analyze the rhythm of a poem. *Electron.* To move a beam of radar in search of a target. **scanner** *n.*

scan-dal (skan´dal) *n.* Something which brings disgrace when exposed to the public; gossip.

scan-dal-ize (skan´da līz´) *v.* To offend someone in a moral sense.

scan-dal-mon-ger (skan´dal mon´gėr) *n.* One who circulates scandal.

scan-dal-ous *adj.* Being offensive to morality. **scandalously** *adv.*

scan-dal sheet *n.* A magazine or newspaper, based on gossip or scandal.

scan-dent *adj.* To be characterized by a climbing means of growth; such as a vine.

scan-di-um (skan´dē um) *n.* A metallic element symbolized by Sc.

scanner *n.* In *computer science,* an optical device for reading hard copy and translating it to digital data.

scant (skant) *adj.* Not plentiful or abundant; inadequate; give out sparingly. **scantily** *adv.*

scant-ling (skant´ling) *n.* The dimensions of material used in building, as the wood or brick.

scant-y (skan´tē) *adj.* To be somewhat less than is normal; lacking; meager.

scape (skāp) *n.* The shaft of a column; shaft of a feather. **scape** *v.* means of escape; a mistake.

scape-goat *n.* A person bearing a blame

for others.

scape-goat-ing *n.* The act of casting blame on an innocent individual.

scape-grace (skāp´grās´) *n.* A rascal.

scaph-oid *adj.* To be shaped like a boat.

scap-u-la (skap´ū la) *n.,, pl.* **-lae** One pair of large, flat, triangular bones which form the back of the shoulder.

scap-u-lar *adj.* To be pertaining to or related to the scapula or the shoulder.

scar (skär) *n.* A permanent mark which remains on the skin after a sore or injury has healed. **scar** *v.*

scar-ab *n.* The scarabaeid beetle.

scar-a-bae-id *n.* A stout-bodied beetle.

scarce (skârs) *adj.* Not common or plentiful; rare. **scarceness** *n.*

scarce-ly *adv.* Being done by a slight margin.

scar-ci-ty *n.* The state of being scarce.

scare (skâr) *v.* To become scared or to frighten someone suddenly.

scarf (skärf) *n.* A wide piece of cloth worn around the head, neck, and shoulders for warmth.

scarf-skin (skärf´skin´) *n.* The skin which forms the cuticle of the nail.

scar-i-fi-ca-tion *n.* The marks which can be made by scarifying.

scar-i-fy (skar´i fī´) *v.* To make small cuts into the skin. **scarifier** *n.*

scar-i-ous (skär´ē us) *adj.* To be membranous in texture.

scar-la-ti-na (skär´la tē´na) *n.* A mild form of scarlet fever.

scar-let (skär´lit) *n.* A bright or vivid red.

scarlet fever *n.* A communicable disease caused by streptococcus and characterized by a sore throat, vomiting, high fever, and a rash.

scar tissue *n.* A connective tissue that forms a scar and is made mostly of fibroblasts.

scar-y (skä´ē) *adj.* To be able to scare; to be easily scared.

scathe (skāth) *v.* To assail something with withering denunciation.

scath-ing (skā´thing) *adj.* To be bitterly severe. **scathingly** *adv.*

scat-ter (skat´ér) *v.* To spread around; to distribute in different directions.

scat-ter-brain *n.* A heedless person.

scat-ter-ing (skat´ér ing) *n.* The process of something being scattered.

scatter pin *n.* A pin which is worn for decoration on one's clothes.

scatter rug *n.* A small rug.

scav-enge *v.* To salvage something from being discarded; to take away from an area.

scav-en-ger (skav´in jér) *n.* An animal, as a vulture, which feeds on decaying or dead animals or plant matter.

sce-na *n.* A solo vocal that consists of a recitative.

sce-nar-i-o (si när´ē ō´) *n.* A synopsis of a dramatic plot.

sce-nar-ist (si när´ist) *n.* A person who creates and writes a scenario.

scend (send) *v.* To heave up under the influence of a natural force.

scene (sēn) *n.* A view; the time and place where an event occurs; a public display of temper; a part of a play.

scene dock *n.* An area or space which is near the stage in a theater and is used for the storage of the scenery.

scen-er-y *n.* Painted screens or other accessories that are used with a play.

scent (sent) *n.* A smell; an odor. *v.* To smell; to give something a scent.

scent-ed *adj.* To have a smell or odor.

scep-ter (sep´tér) *n.* A rod or staff carried by a king or queen as a sign of authority.

sch *abbr.* School.

scha-den-freu-de *n.* The enjoyment that is obtained through the troubles of others.

sched-ule (skej´öl) *n.* A list or written chart which shows the times at which events will happen, including a plan given for work and specified deadlines; a timetable of events.

schee-lite (shā´līt) *n.* A type of mineral that consists of the tungstate of calcium and is a source of tungsten.

sche-ma (skē´ma) *n.* A presentation which is diagrammatic.

sche-mat-ic *adj.* To be pertaining to a schema. **schematically** *adv.*

scheme (skēm) *n.* A plan of action; an orderly combination of related parts; a secret plot. **schemer** *n.*

schil-ler (shil´ér) *n.* A type of bronzy iridescent luster.

schism (siz´um) *n.* A formal separation from a religious body.

schis-mat-ic (siz mat´ik) *n.* The person who creates schism.

schis-ma-tize *v.* To take part in schism.

schist *n.* A type of metamorphic rock that has a closely foliated structure.

schis-tose *adj.* To be pertaining to schist rock.

schiz-o-carp *n.* A type of dry compound fruit that will split at its maturity.

schiz-ont *n.* A type of multinucleate sporozoan that will reproduce by schizogony.

schle-miel *n.* An unlucky bungler.

schlie-ren *n* Irregularly, shaped masses in a rock such as streaks, which differ in texture from the main mass.

schmo *n.* A foolish or boring person; a jerk; naive.

schnapps *n.* A type of distilled liquors or spirits.

schnau-zer *n.* A dog that has a long head, small ears, and a wiry coat.

schnit-zel (shnit´sel) *n.* A type of

garnished and seasoned veal cutlet.

schnor-rer *n.* A person who wheedles other people into supplying his or her wants; one who solicits unjustified help from others.

schnoz-zle *n. Slang* The nose. *Yiddish*

schol-ar (skŏl´ĕr) *n.* A student with a strong interest in learning.

schol-ar-ly (skŏl´ĕr lē) *adj.* Being suitable to learned persons.

schol-ar-ship *n.* A grant of money which is given to a students to enable them to go to school.

scho-las-tic (sko las´tik) *adj.* Pertaining to schools. **scholastically** *adv.*

scho-li-um *n.* A comment which is marginal.

school (skōl) *n.* A place for teaching and learning; a group of persons devoted to similar principles.

school age *n.* The time of one' life when one is able to attend school and required to do so by the law.

school board *n.* The board of people who are in charge of public schools.

school-book *n.* A textbook which is used for the schoolwork done in schools.

school-room (skōl´rŏm˜) *n.* A classroom that is used for teaching.

school-time *n.* The time that is designated for the beginning of a session of school.

schoon-er (skō´nĕr) *n.* A sailing vessel with two or more masts.

Schwann cell *n.* A type of cell of the neurilemma of the fiber of the nerve.

sci-ae-nid *n.* A carnivorous marine percoid fish, such as the croaker.

sci-at-ic (sī at´ik) *adj.* Being located near the hip area of the body.

sciatic nerve *n.* The largest nerve of the body that runs down both legs.

sci-ence (sī´ens) *n.* The study and theoretical explanation of natural phenomena in an orderly way; knowledge acquired through experience. **scientific** *adj.* **scientist** *n.*

sci-en-tism *n.* The attitudes that are typical of the natural scientist.

sci-fi *abbr.* Science fiction.

scil-la *n.* A type of Old World herb of the lily family that has pink, blue, or white flowers.

scim-i-tar (sim´i tĕr) *n.* A type of saber that is made of a curved blade and is used by the Turks and the Arabs.

scin-til-late (sin´ti lāt˜) *v.* To give off or emit quick flashes. **scintillator** *n.*

scir-rhus *n.* A type of malignant tumor that has a preponderance of fibrous tissue.

scis-sion (sizh´an) *n.* The process of splitting or cutting.

scis-sors (siz´ĕrz) *n.* A cutting tool consisting of two blades joined and pivoted so that the edges are close to each other.

scler-a *n.* A dense fibrous white outer coat that will enclose the eyeball except the section which is covered by the cornea.

scler-ite (sklĕr´ĭt) *n.* A type of hard chitinous plate or piece.

scle-ro-der-ma (sklĕr´o dur´ma) *n.* A disease of the skin that causes thickening of the subcutaneous tissues.

scle-rom-e-ter *n.* A device which is used for the purpose of determining the hardness of something.

scle-ro-pro-tein *n.* A type of protein that can be found in the skeletal and the connective tissues of the body.

scle-ro-sis (skli rō´sis) *n.* A hardening of a part of the body, as an artery.

scle-rot-ic *adj.* Pertaining to the sclera.

scler-o-ti-za-tion *n.* The state of being sclerotized, usually referring to the cuticle of an insect.

scler-o-tized *adj.* Being made hard by a substance other than chitin.

scoff *n.* The expression of derision or scorn. **scoffer** *n.*

scold (skōld) *v.* To accuse or reprimand harshly.

sco-lex (skōleks) *n.* A head of the tapeworm either in the larval or adult stage of its life.

sco-li-o-sis (skō´lē ō´sis) *n.* The lateral curvature of the spine. **scoliotic** *adj.*

sconce (skons) *n.* A wall bracket for holding candles.

scoop (skōp) *n.* A small, shovel-like tool. *Slang* An exclusive news report released ahead of ones competition. **scoop** *v.* To lift up or out.

scoot (skōt) *v.* To go suddenly and quickly.

scope (skōp) *n.* The range or extent of one's actions; the space to function or operate in.

-scope *suff.* A device for seeing or discovering.

sco-pol-a-mine (sko pol´a mēn˜) *n.* A kind of poisonous alkaloid that can be found in the roots of some plants belonging to the nightshade family; used as a sedative, mydriatic or truth serum.

scor-bu-tic *adj.* To be like or resembling scurvy. **scorbutically** *adv.*

scorch (skorch) *v.* To burn slightly, changing the color and taste of something; to parch with heat.

scorched *adj.* To be discolored by scorching.

scorch-er (skor´chĕr) *n. Slang* A very hot day.

score (skōr) *n.* A numerical record of total points won in a game or other contest; the result of an examination; a grouping of twenty items; a written musical composition which indicates the part to be performed by each person; a groove made with a pointed tool. **score** v. To achieve or win; to arrange a musical score for.

score-board n. A board which is used to display the score of a game.

score-card n. A card which is used for the recording of the score in a game.

sco-ria n. A refuse from the melting of metals. **scoriaceous** adj.

scorn (skorn) n. Contempt; disdain. **scorn** v. To treat with scorn; to reject with contempt.

scorn-ful adj. Being full of scorn.

scor-pae-nid n. A member of the group or family of marine spiny-finned fishes, having large mouths and sharp teeth.

scor-pi-oid adj. Curved or circular at the end like the tail of the scorpion.

scor-pi-on (skor´pē on) n. An arachnid having an upright tail tipped with a poisonous sting.

Scor-pi-us n. The southern constellation that is located partly in the Milky Way and next to Libra.

sco-ter n. A sea duck of the northern coasts of Europe and North America.

scot–free adj. To be totally free from harm or penalty.

sco-to-ma n. A dark spot in the visual field.

scoun-drel n. A villain or a robber.

scour (skour) v. To clean by rubbing with an abrasive agent; to clean thoroughly. **scourer** n.

scout (skout) v. To observe activities in order to obtain information. **scout** n. A person whose job is to obtain information; a member of the boy scouts or girl scouts.

scow (skou) n. A large barge with a flat bottom and square ends used to transport freight, gravel, or cargo.

scowl (skoul) v. To make an angry look; to frown. **scowl** n.

scrab-ble (skrab´l) v. To scratch about frantically, as if searching for something. **scrabble** n. **scrabbler** n.

scrag v. To kill or to execute by hanging.

scrag-gly (skrag´lē) adj. Messy; irregular.

scram v. To go away at once.

scram-ble v. To move with panic.

scrap (skrap) n. A small section or piece. **scrap** v. To throw away waste.

scrap-book (skrap´bük´) n. A book that contains miscellaneous items.

scrape (skrāp) v. To rub a surface with a sharp object in order to clean. Slang An embarrassing situation.

scra-pie n. A kind of viral disease of sheep where they become itchy, excited, excessively thirsty, weak, and eventually a paralysis occurs.

scratch (skrach) v. To mark or make a slight cut on; to mark with the fingernails. **scratch** n. The mark made

by scratching; a harsh, unpleasant sound. Slang Money

scratch test n. A test for allergic susceptibility that involves placing an extract of an allergy producing substance into a scratch on the skin.

scrawl (skrol) n. To write or draw quickly and often illegibly. **scrawl** n.

scraw-ny (skro´nē) adj. Very thin; skinny. **scrawniness** η.

screak v. To make or produce a shrill noise.

scream (skrēm) v. To utter a long, sharp cry, as of fear or pain. **scream** n. A long piercing cry. Slang A very funny person.

scree (skrē) n. A gathering of stones lying on a slope.

screech (skrēch) v. To make a shrill, harsh noise.

screech owl n. A type of owl that has a tuft of feathers on its head.

screed n. A piece of writing that is informal.

screen (skrēn) n. A movable object used to keep something from view, to divide, or to decorate; a flat reflecting surface on which a picture is projected. **screen** v. To keep from view.

screen saver n. In computer science, a screen blanker that displays a random, moving pattern on the screen.

screen test n. A type of short film sequence testing the abilities of a prospective movie actor.

screw (skrō) n. A metal piece that resembles a nail, having a spiral thread which is used for fastening things together; a propeller on a ship. **screw** v. To join by twisting. **screw up** To make a mess of.

scrib-ble v. To write without thought.

scribe (skrīb) n. A person whose profession is to copy documents and manuscripts.

scrib-er n. A sharp tool for the purpose of making marks in material to be cut.

scrieve v. To move along smoothly.

scrim (skrim) n. A type of durable cotton fabric used for clothing and curtains.

scrim-mage (skrim´ij) n. In football, a practice game. **scrimmage** v.

scrimp (skrimp) v. To make something too small or short.

scrim-shaw (skrim´sho´) n. The art of carving designs on whale ivory or whalebone.

scrip n. A type of small wallet; money; a receipt.

script n. The written text of a play; document.

scrip-tur-al adj. According to a sacred writing. **scripturally** adv.

scrip-ture (skrip´chėr) n. A sacred writing. **Scriptures** The Bible.

script-writ-er n. A person who writes

screenplays and other scripts.

scriv-en-er *n.* A public copyist; writer.

scrod (skrod) *n.* A type of young fish such as the haddock or the cod.

scrof-u-la (skrof´ū la) *n.* A tuberculosis of the lymph glands.

scrof-u-lous *adj.* To be affected with scrofula.

scroll (skrōl) *n.* A roll of parchment or similar material used in place of paper.

scroll-work *n.* An ornamentation that is characterized by scrolls.

scrooge *n.* A type of person who is miserly.

scro-tum (skrō´tum) *n., pl.* scrota The external sac of skin which encloses the testes. **scrotal** *adj.*

scrounge *v.* To collect by foraging.

scrub (skrub) *v.* To clean something by rubbing. *Slang* To cancel.

scrub-land *n.* An area of land which has been covered with scrub.

scruff *n.* The region on the back of the neck.

scrump-tious (skrump´shus) *adj. Slang* Delightful.

scru-ple (skrō´pl) *n.* A principle which governs one's actions.

scru-pu-los-i-ty *n.* The state of being scrupulous.

scru-pu-lous (skrō´pū lus) *adj.* Having moral integrity. **-ly** *adv.*

scru-ta-ble (skrō´ta bl) *adj.* To be able to be deciphered.

scru-ti-nize *v.* To look at or to examine something very carefully.

scru-ti-ny *n.* An inspection of something.

sct *abbr.* Scout.

scu-ba (skō´ba) *n.* An apparatus used by divers for underwater breathing; from the initials for Self-Contained Underwater Breathing Apparatus.

scuba diver *n.* One who swims under the water with the use of scuba gear.

scud *v.* To move or to go quickly.

scuff (skuf) *v.* To drag or scrape the feet while walking. **scuff** *n.*

scuf-fle (skuf´l) *v.* To struggle in a confused manner. **scuffle** *n.*

scuffle hoe *n.* A type of hoe which has both edges sharpened.

scull (skul) *n.* An oar mounted at the stern of a boat, which is moved back and forth to produce forward motion.

scul-ler-y (skul´e rē) *n.* A room used for storing and cleaning dishes.

scul-lion *n.* A type of kitchen helper.

scul-pin (skul´pin) *n.* A type of large-headed scaleless fish.

sculpt *v.* To carve; to make a sculpture.

sculp-tor (skulp´těr) *n.* A person who creates statues from clay, marble, or other material.

sculp-ture (skulp´chěr) *n.* The art of processing a hard or soft material into another form, such as a statue.

scum (skum) *n.* A thin layer of waste matter floating on top of a liquid.

scum-ble *v.* To make something less brilliant by covering it with a thin coat of color.

surf (skerf) *n.* Flaky dry skin; dandruff.

scur-ril-i-ty *n.* The state of being scurrilous.

scur-ri-lous *adj.* To be vulgar and evil.

scur-ry (sker´ē) *v.* To move quickly; to scamper.

scur-vy *n.* A type of disease that is caused by the lack of ascorbic acid and is characterized by bleeding gums and bleeding into the skin.

scut *n.* A tail which is short and erect.

scu-tage *n.* A kind of tax that is levied on a tenant of a knight's land in the place of service for the military.

scutch *v.* To separate flax or hemp from their woody fibers.

scute *n.* An external horny plate.

scu-tel-late (skū tel´it) *adj.* To be resembling scutellum.

scu-tel-lum (skū tel´um) *n.* A small shield-shaped plant structure.

scut-tle *n.* A small opening with a movable lid in the hull of a ship. **scuttle** *v.* To deliberately sink a boat or other floating object by making holes in the bottom or sides.

scy-pho-zo-an (sī´fo zō´an) *n.* A type of coelenterates of the group of jellyfish lacking a true polyp.

scythe (sith) *n.* A tool with a long handle and curved, single-dged blade, used for cutting hay, grain and grass.

sea *n.* The body of salt water which covers most of the earth; a large body of salt water.

seacoast *n.* Land that borders the sea.

seal (sēl) *n.* A device having a raised emblem, displaying word or symbol, used to certify a signature or the authenticity of a document; a tight closure which secures; a large aquatic mammal with a sleek body and large flippers; the fur or pelt of a seal. **seal** *v.* To close tightly; to mark with a seal; to hunt seals. **sealant** *n.*

sea level *n.* The level of the sea's surface, used as a standard reference point in measuring the height of land or the depth of the sea.

seam (sēm) *n.* The line formed at the joint of two pieces of material.

sear (sēr) *v.* To wither or dry up; to shrivel; to burn or scorch.

search (serch) *v.* To look over carefully; to find something; to probe.

sea-son (sē´zon) *n.* One of the four parts of the year: spring, summer, fall or autumn, and winter; a time marked by particular activities or celebrations. **season** *v.* To add flavorings or spices; to add interest or enjoyment; to age.

seat (sēt) *n.* A place or spot, as a chair, stool, or bench, on which to sit; the part of the body used for sitting; the buttocks. **seat** *v.*

se-cede (si sēd´) *v.* To withdraw from an organization. **secession** *n.*

se-clude (si klōd´) *v.* To isolate; to keep apart.

sec-ond (sek´ond) *n.* A unit of time equal to 1/60 of a minute; a very short period of time; an object which does not meet first class standards. *Math.* Unit of measure equal to 1/60 of a minute of angular measurement.

sec-on-dar-y (sek´on der ē) *adj.* Not being first in importance; inferior; pertaining to high school.

se-cret (sē´krit) *n.* Knowledge kept from others; a mystery. **secretly** *adv.* **secret** *n.* **secrecy** *n.*

sec-re-tary (sek´ri ter ē) *n. pl.* **secretaries** A person hired to write and keep records for an executive or an organization; the head of a government department. **secretarial** *adj.*

se-crete (si krēt´) *v.* To produce and give off; to release or discharge.

sec-tion (sek´shan) *n.* A part or division of something; a separate part. **section** *v.* To divide or separate into parts.

sec-tor (sek´tēr) *n.* An area or zone in which a military unit operates; the part of a circle bounded by two radii and the arc they cut. **sector** *v.*

sec-u-lar (sek´ya lēr) *adj.* Relating to something worldly; not religious.

se-cure (si kūr´) *adj.* Safe and free from doubt or fear; sturdy or strong; not likely to fail. **secure** *v.* To tie down, fasten, lock, or otherwise protect from risk or harm; to ensure. **securely** *adv.*

se-cu-ri-ty (si kūr´i tē) *n., pl.* **securities** The state of being safe and free from danger or risk; protection; an object given to assure the fulfillment of an obligation; in *computer science,* the prevention of unauthorized use of a device or program.

se-dan (si dan´) *n.* A closed automobile with a front and back seat.

se-date (si dāt´) *adj.* Serene and composed. **sedate** *v.* To keep or be kept calm through the use of drugs.

sedative *n.* A medicine to calm or help one to sleep.

sed-i-ment (sed´i ment) *n.* Material which floats in or settles to the bottom of a liquid. **sedimentary** *adj.*

se-duce (si dōs´) *v.* To tempt and draw away from proper conduct; to entice one to have sexual intercourse. **seducer** *n.* **seduction** *n.* **seductive** *adj.*

see (sē) *v.* To have the power of sight; to understand; to experience; to predict; to imagine. **see red** To be extremely angry.

seed (sēd) *n.* A fertilized plant ovule with an embryo, capable of producing an offspring. **seed** *v.* To plant seeds; to remove the seeds from.

seek (sēk) *v.* To search for; to try to reach; to attempt. **seeker** *n.*

seem (sēm) *v.* To appear to be; to have the look of. **seeming** *adj.*

seep (sēp) *v.* To leak or pass through slowly. **seepage** *n.*

seer (sē´ēr) *n.* A person who predicts the future.

see-saw (sē´so´) *n.* A board supported in the center which allows children to alternate being up and down.

seg-ment (seg´ment) *n.* Any of the parts into which a thing is divided. **segment** *v.* To divide. **-ation** *n.*

seg-re-gate (seg´re gāt´) *v.* To separate or isolate from others.

seg-re-ga-tion (seg´re gā´shan) *n.* The act of separating people based on the color of their skin.

seine (sān) *n.* A fishing net having weights on one edge and floats on the other.

seize (sēz) *v.* To grasp or take possession forcibly.

sel-dom (sel´dom) *adv.* Not often.

se-lect (si lekt´) *v.* To choose from a large group; to make a choice. **selection, select** *n.* **selector** *n.*

se-le-ni-um (si lē´nē um) *n.* An element symbolized by Se.

self (self) *n., pl.* **selves** The complete and essential being of a person; personal interest, advantage or welfare.

self-de-fense (self´di fens´) *n.* The act of defending oneself or one's belongings.

sell (sel) *v.* To exchange a product or service for money; to offer for sale.

se-man-tics (si man´tiks) *n.* The study of word meanings and the relationships between symbols and signs.

sem-a-phore (sem´a for´) *n.* A system for signaling by using flags, lights or arms in various positions.

se-men (sē´men) *n.* Secretion of the male reproductive system, thick and whitish in color, containing sperm.

se-mes-ter (si mes´tēr) *n.* One of two periods of time in which a school year is divided.

sem-i-an-nu-al (sem´ē an´ū al) *adj.* Occurring twice a year.

sem-i-co-lon (sem´i kō´lon) *n.* A punctuation mark (;) having a degree of separation stronger than a comma but less than a period.

sem-i-nar (sem´i när´) *n.* A course of study for students engaged in advanced study of a particular subject.

sem-i-nar-y (sem´i ner ē) *n., pl.* **-ies** A school that prepares ministers, rabbis, or priests for religious careers.

sen-ate (sen'it) *n*. The upper house of a legislature. **Senate** The United States upper house.

send (send) *v*. To cause something to be conveyed from one place to another; to dispatch.

se-nile (sē'nīl) *adj*. Having a mental deterioration often associated with old age. **senility** *n*.

sen-ior (sēn'yēr) *adj*. Being the older of two; of higher office or rank; referring to the last year of high school or college. **senior** *n*. One who is older or of higher rank.

sen-ior-i-ty (sēn yor'i tē) *n*. Priority over others based on the length of time or service.

sen-sa-tion (sen sā'shan) *n*. An awareness associated with a mental or bodily feeling; something causing a condition of strong interest.

sense (sens) *n*. Sensation; feeling; the physical ability which allows a person to be aware of things around him; the five senses; taste, smell, touch, sight, and hearing; an ethical or moral attitude; the meaning of a word; **sense** *v*. To feel through the senses; to have a feeling about.

sen-si-bil-i-ty (sen'si bil'i tē) *n*., *pl*. **-ies** The ability to receive sensations.

sen-si-ble (sen'si bl) *adj*. Capable of being perceived through the senses; sensitive; having good judgment.

sen-si-tive (sen'si tiv) *adj*. Capable of intense feelings; affected by the emotions or circumstances of others; tenderhearted; of or relating to secret affairs of state. **sensitively** *adv*. **sensitivity** *n*. **sensitiveness** *n*.

sen-sor (sen'sēr) *n*. A device which responds to a signal.

sen-su-al (sen'shō al) *adj*. Preoccupied with the gratification of the senses. **sensually** *adv*. **sensualist** *n*. **sensuality** *n*. **sensuous** *adj*.

sent *v*. Past tense of send.

sen-tence (sen'tens) *n*. A series of words arranged to express a single complete thought; a prison term for a convicted person, determined by a judge or jury. **sentence** *v*. To impose or set the terms of punishment.

sen-ti-ment (sen'ti ment) *n*. Feelings of affection; an idea, an opinion, a thought, an attitude based on emotion rather than reason.

sen-ti-men-tal (sen'ti men'tal) *adj*. Emotional; affected by sentiment.

sen-ti-nel (sen'ti nel) *n*. A guard.

se-pal (sē'pal) *n*. One of the leaves which forms a calyx in a flower.

sep-a-rate (sep'a rāt') *v*. To divide or keep apart by placing a barrier between; to go in different directions; to set apart from others. **separate** *adj*. Single;

individual.

sep-a-ra-tion (sep'a rā'shan) *n*. The process of separating or being separated; an interval which separates.

Sept *abbr*. September.

September *n*. The ninth month of the calendar year, having 30 days.

se-quel (sē'kwel) *n*. A new story which follows or comes after an earlier one and which uses the same characters.

se-quence (sē'kwens) *n*. A set arrangement; a number of connected events; the regular order; the order in which something is done. **sequential** *adj*.

ser-e-nade (ser'enād') *n*. Musical expression of romantic love.

se-rene (se rēn') *adj*. Calm; peaceful.

serf (serf) *n*. A slave owned by a lord during the Middle Ages.

serge (serj) *n*. A twilled, durable woolen cloth.

ser-geant (sär'jent) *n*. A noncommissioned officer who ranks above a corporal but below a lieutenant.

se-ri-al (sēr'ē al) *adj*. Arranged in a series with one part presented at a time.

se-ries (sēr'ēz) *n*. A number of related items which follow one another.

se-ri-ous (sēr'ē us) *adj*. Sober; grave; not trivial; important. **seriously** *adv*.

ser-mon (ser'mon) *n*. A message or speech delivered by a clergyman during a religious service.

ser-pent (ser'pent) *n*. A snake.

ser-rate (ser'it) *adj*. Having sharp teeth; having a notched edge.

se-rum (sēr'um) *n*., *pl*. **serums** *or* **sera** The yellowish fluid part of the blood which remains after clotting; the fluid extracted from immunized animals and used for the prevention of disease.

ser-vant (ser'vant) *n*. One employed to care for someone or his property.

serve (serv) *v*. To take care of; to wait on; to prepare and supply; to complete a term of duty; to act in a certain capacity; to start the play in some sports. **serve** *n*. The manner of serving or delivering a ball.

server *n*. In *computer science*, a computer that stores and manages programs and data for other computers in a network.

serv-ice (ser'vis) *n*. Help given to others; a religious gathering; the military; a set of dishes or utensils. **service** *v*. To repair; to furnish a service to something or someone.

ses-a-me (ses'a mē) *n*. A tropical plant and its edible seeds.

ses-sion (sesh'an) *n*. A meeting or series of meetings; a meeting set for a specific purpose; the period during the day or year during which a meeting takes place.

set (set) *v*. To put or place; to cause to do; to regulate; to adjust; to arrange;

to place in a frame or mounting; to go below the horizon; to establish or fix.

set *n.* A group of things which belong together; a piece of equipment made up of many pieces; a young plant. **set** *adj.* Established; ready.

set-ting (set'ing) *n.* The act of placing or putting something somewhere; the scenery for a show or other production; the place where a novel, play, or other fictional work takes place; a jewelry mounting.

set-tle (set'l) *v.* To arrange or put in order; to restore calm or tranquillity to; to come to an agreement on something; to resolve a problem or argument; to establish in a new home or business.

sev-en (sev'en) *n.* The cardinal number 7, which is 6 + 1. **seven** *adj. & pron.* **seventh** *adj. & n.*

sev-er (sev'ėr) *v.* To cut off or separate. **severance** *n.*

sev-er-al (sev'ėr al) *adj.* Being more than one or two, but not many; separate.

se-vere (si vēr') *adj.* Strict; stern; hard; not fancy; extremely painful; intense. **severely** *adv.* **severity** *n.*

sew (sō) *v.* To fasten or fix; to make stitches with thread and needle.

sew-age (sō'ij) *n.* The solid waste material carried away by a sewer.

sew-er (sō'ėr) *n.* A conduit or drain pipe used to carry away waste.

sex (seks) *n.* One of two divisions, male and female, into which most living things are grouped; sexual intercourse.

sex-tet (seks tet') *n.* A group of six people or things; music written for six performers.

shab-by (shab'ē) *adj.* Worn-out; ragged. **shabbily** *adv.* **shabbiness** *n.*

shack (shak) *n.* A small, poorly built building.

shack-le (shak'l) *n.* A metal band locked around the ankle or wrist of a prisoner; anything that restrains or holds. *v.* To restrain with shackles.

shade (shād) *n.* A shadow that will gather with the coming of darkness; a comparative darkness due to the interception of the rays of the sun by an object.

shad-ing *n.* A filling up with color within outlines to give the object a three-dimensional shape or look.

shad-ow (shad'ō) *n.* An area from which light is blocked. **shadow** *v.* To cast or throw a shadow on.

shad-y (shā'dē) *adj.* Being sheltered or protected from the rays of the sun.

shaft (shaft) *n.* A long, narrow part of something; a beam or ray of light; a long, narrow underground passage; a tunnel; a narrow, vertical opening in a building for an elevator.

shag *n.* A long matted fiber.

shag-gy (shag'ē) *adj.* To be covered with long, matted, or coarse hair.

shak-a-ble *n.* Being capable of being shaken.

shake (shāk) *v.* To move or to cause a back-and-forth or up-and-down motion; to tremble; to clasp hands with another, as to welcome or say farewell; to upset or disturb. **shaky** *adj.*

sha-ko (shak'ō) *n.* A stiff military hat that has a plume and high crown.

shale *n.* A fissile rock which is made by the consolidation of mud or clay having a finely stratified structure.

shale oil *n.* A type of dark oil which is obtained from oil shale by heating.

shall (shal) *v.* To expect to; to plan to; used to express future tense; to indicate promise or a command.

shal-loon *n.* The twilled fabric of wool which is used for linings of coats.

shal-lop *n.* A type of small boat that can be propelled with oars or sails.

shal-lot (sha lot') *n.* A type of perennial herb that resembles an onion and is used for seasoning.

shal-low (shal'ō) *adj.* Not deep; lacking intellectual depth.

sham (sham) *n.* A person who is not genuine but pretends to be; a cover for pillows. **sham** *v.* To pretend to have or feel something.

sham-ble (sham'bl) *v.* To walk while dragging one's feet. **shambles** A scene or state of complete destruction.

sham-bling *adj.* Characterized with or by slow awkward movements.

shame (shām) *n.* A painful feeling of embarrassment or disgrace brought on by doing something wrong; dishonor; disgrace; a disappointment.

shame-faced (shām'fāst') *adj.* To be showing shame. **shamefacedness** *n.*

shame-ful (shām'ful) *adj.* Arousing feelings of shame within someone.

shame-less (shām'lis) *adj.* Showing a lack of shame. **shamelessness** *n.*

sham-poo (sham pö') *n.* A soap used to cleanse the hair and scalp; a liquid preparation used to clean upholstery and rugs; the process of cleaning with shampoo. **shampoo** *v.*

shang-hai (shang'hī) *v.* To put someone on board a ship with the help of a drug.

shank (shangk) *n.* The portion of the leg between the ankle and the knee; a cut of meat from the leg of an animal, such as a lamb.

shap-a-ble *n.* To be capable of being shaped.

shape (shāp) *n.* The outline or configuration of something; the form of a human body; the condition of something; the finished form in which something may appear. *v.* To cause to take a particular form.

shape-less (shāp´lis) *adj.* To have no real or definite shape; without shape.

shape-ly (shāp´lē) *adj.* To have a pleasant or pleasing shape to the form.

shard (shärd) *n.* A fragment of a substance which is brittle.

share (shâr) *n.* A part or portion given to or by one person; one of equal parts, as the capital stock in a corporation. **share** *v.* To divide or distribute portions.

share-hold-er *n.* A person who holds a share in a piece of property.

shark (shärk) *n.* A large marine fish which eats other fish and is dangerous to man; a greedy, crafty person.

shark-skin *n.* The skin or hide of the shark that is made into leather goods.

sharp (shärp) *adj.* Having a thin edge or a fine point; capable of piercing or cutting; clever; quick-witted; intense; painful. **sharp** *n. Music* A note raised half a tone above a given tone. **sharpness** *n.* **sharply** *adv.*

sharp-tongued (shärp–tungd´) *adj.* To have bitter or harsh speech.

shat-ter (shat´ér) *v.* To burst suddenly into pieces.

shave (shāv) *v.* To remove a thin layer; to cut body hair, as the beard, by using a razor; to come close to. *n.* The act of shaving.

shawl (shol) *n.* An oblong or square piece of fabric worn over the head or shoulders.

she (shē) *pron.* A female previously indicated by name.

shear (shēr) *v.* To trim, cut, or remove the fleece or hair with a sharp instrument; to clip. **shearer** *n.*

sheath (shēth) *n.* A cover or case for a blade, as a sword.

sheath-bill (shēth´bil´) *n.* A white shore bird that has a horny sheath on the base of the upper mandible.

sheave *n.* A wheel that is grooved.

shed (shed) *v.* To pour out or cause to pour; to throw off without penetrating; to cast off or leave behind, esp. by a natural process. **shed** *n.* A small building for shelter or storage.

shed-der *n.* Something that sheds something such as skin.

sheen (shēn) *n.* Luster.

sheep (shēp) *n., pl.* **sheep** A cud-chewing thick-fleeced mammal, widely domesticated for meat and wool; a meek or timid person.

sheer (shēr) *adj.* Very thin; almost transparent; complete; absolute; very steep, almost perpendicular.

sheet (shēt) *n.* A large piece of cloth for covering a bed; a single piece of paper; a continuous, thin piece of anything.

sheet metal *n.* A type of metal that is in the form of a sheet.

shelf (shelf) *n. pl.* **shelves** A flat piece of wood, metal, plastic, or other rigid material attached to a wall or within another structure, used to hold or store things; something which resembles a shelf, as a ledge of rocks.

shelf ice *n.* An ice sheet that starts on land and continues out to sea and out to where it rests on the floor of the ocean.

shell (shel) *n.* The hard outer covering of certain organisms; something light and hollow which resembles a shell; the framework of a building under construction; a case containing explosives which are fired from a gun. *v.* To remove the shell from.

shel-lac (she lak´) *n.* A clear varnish used to give a smooth, shiny finish to furniture and floors. *Slang* To defeat decisively.

shel-ter (shel´tér) *n.* Something which gives protection or cover. **shelter** *v.* To give protection.

shelve (shelv) *v.* To put aside; to place on a shelf.

shelv-ing *n.* The degree of sloping of something.

shep-herd (shep´érd) *n.* A person who takes care of a flock of sheep; a person who takes care of others.

shepherd's pie *n.* A type of pie that is made with meat and has a mashed potato crust.

sher-bet (sher´bit) *n.* A sweet frozen dessert made with fruit juices, milk or water, egg white, and gelatin.

sher-iff (sher´if) *n.* A high ranking law-enforcement officer.

sher-ry (sher´ē) *n.* A type of wine of Spanish origin that has a nutty taste.

shield (shēld) *n.* A piece of protective metal or wood held in front of the body; anything which serves to conceal or protect; a badge. **shield** *v.*

shield law *n.* The law that protects journalists from being forced to reveal confidential sources.

shift (shift) *n.* A group of people who work together; a woman's loose-fitting dress. **shift** *v.* To change direction or place; to change or move the gears in an automobile.

shill *n.* A person or thing that acts as a decoy.

shim-mer (shim´ér) *v.* To shine with a faint sparkle. **shimmery** *adj.*

shin (shin) *n.* The front part of the leg from the knee to the ankle. *v.* To climb a rope or pole by gripping and pulling with the hands and legs.

shin-bone *n.* The tibia in the lower leg.

shin-dig *n.* A party or social gathering.

shine (shīn) *v.* To give off light; to direct light; to make bright or glossy; to polish shoes. *n.* Brightness.

shin-er (shī´nér) *n.* A black eye.

shin-gle (shing´gl) n. A thin piece of material used to cover a roof or sides of a house. **shingle** v.

shin-gles (shing´glz) n. Pathol. An acute, inflammatory viral infection, character-ized by eruptions along a nerve path.

shin-ing adj. To be reflecting light.

shin-splints n. The inflammation and injury to the muscles of the lower leg due to run-ning on hard surfaces.

ship (ship) n. A large vessel for deep-wat-er travel or transport. v. To send or transport.

ship-board n. A side of a ship.

ship-borne adj. To be designed to be carried or transported by a ship.

ship-build-er n. A person who builds ships. **shipbuilding** n.

ship-ment (ship´ment) n. The process of shipping goods from one port to another.

ship-worm n. A marine clam that will burrow into the wharf and wooden ships causing damage to them.

ship-wreck (ship´rek´) n. The loss of a ship; destruction; ruin. v. To destroy; wreck.

ship-wright n. The carpenter who is skilled in the repair and construction of ships.

shire (shī´er) n. The administrative division such as a county.

shire town n. The town in which is located a court of jurisdiction.

shirt (shert) n. A garment worn on the upper part of the body.

shirt-ing (shür´ting) n. The fabric which can be used to make shirts.

shirt-maker n. A person who is capable of making shirts.

shirt-tail n. The section of the shirt which falls below the waist in the back.

shiv-er (shiv´er) v. To tremble or shake with excitement or chill.

shoal (shōl) n. Large group.

shoat n. A hog less than one year old.

shock (shok) n. A sudden blow or violent impact; an unexpected, sudden upset of mental or emotional balance; a serious weakening of the body caused by the loss of blood pressure or sudden injury. **shock** v. To cause great surprise, disgust, or outrage; to give an electric shock.

shock absorber n. A device which is used for absorbing the energy of impulses to something.

shock-er (shok´er) n. Something that produces shock.

shod adj. To be equipped with a shoe.

shoe (shö) n. An outer cover for a foot; the part of a brake which presses against the drum or wheel to slow or stop the motion. v. To put on shoes.

shoot (shöt) v. To kill or wound with a missile, as a bullet, fired from a weap-on; to discharge or throw rapidly; to push forward or begin to grow by germinating.

shooting star n. A meteor that appears in the sky as a temporary streak of light.

shop (shop) n. A small business or small retail store; a place where certain goods are produced. **shop** v. To visit a store in order to examine or buy things. **shopper** n.

shop-keep-er n. A person who runs a store.

shop-lift (shop´lift´) v. To take something from a store without paying for it. **shoplifting** n.

shore (shōr) n. The land bordering a body of water.

shore-line n. A line or location where a body of water and the shore meet.

short (short) adj. Having little height or length; less than normal in distance, time, or other qualities; less than the needed amount. **shorts** Underpants or outer pants which end at the knee or above. **shortage** A lack in the amount needed. **short-change** To give less than the correct amount, as change for money. **short circuit** An electrical malfunction.

short-cut n. A type of route that is more direct than the one that is usually taken.

short-en-ing (shor´te ning) n. A fat, such as butter, used to make pastry rich and light.

short-fall (short´fol) n. The failure to accomplish a goal.

short-hand (short´hand´) n. A type of writing where words and phrases are represented by symbols.

short-lived (short´lïvd´) adj. Not lasting long or living long.

short-sight-ed (short´sï´tid) adj. To be missing or lacking one's foresight.

shot (shot) n. The discharging of a gun, rocket, or other device; an attempt; a try; an injection; a photograph. Slang Useless; ruined.

should (shed) v. Past tense of shall.

shoul-der (shōl´der) n. The part of the body located between the neck and upper arm; the side of the road. v. To use the shoulder to push or carry something; to take upon oneself.

should-n't (shed´ant) contr. Should not.

shout (shout) v. To yell. n. A loud cry.

shouting distance n. A short distance.

shove v. To push something or someone in a manner that may be rough.

shov-el (shuv´el) n. A tool with a long handle and a scoop, used for picking up material or digging. **shovel** v. To move, dig, push, or scoop up.

show (shō) v. To put within sight; to point out; to explain; to put on display. n. A display; a movie, play or similar entertainment.

show bill *n.* A poster which may be used for advertising purposes.

show-er (shou´ẽr) *n.* A short period of rain; a party with gifts given in honor of someone; a bath with water spraying down on the bather. **shower** *v.* To take a shower; to be generous; to pour down. **showery** *adj.*

shrap-nel (shrap´nel) *n. pl.* **shrapnel** A large shell containing metal fragments; fragments of metal that are exploded with great force.

shred (shred) *n.* A narrow strip or torn fragment; a small amount. *v.* To rip, tear, or cut into shreds.

shrew (shrö) *n.* A small mouse-like mammal, having a narrow, pointed snout.

shriek (shrēk) *n.* A loud, sharp scream or noise. **shriek** *v.*

shrill (shril) *adj.* A high-pitched, sharp sound.

shrimp (shrimp) *n., pl.* **shrimp** *or* **shrimps** A small, edible shellfish.

shrine (shrīn) *n.* A place for sacred relics; a place considered sacred because of an event or person associated with it.

shrink (shringk) *v.* To make or become less or smaller; to pull back from; to flinch. *Slang* A psychiatrist.

shroud (shroud) *n.* A cloth in which a body is wrapped for burial. *v.* To cover.

shrub (shrub) *n.* A woody plant which grows close to the ground and has several stems beginning at its base.

shrug (shrug) *v.* To raise the shoulders briefly to indicate doubt or indifference. **shrug** *n.*

shuck (shuk) *n.* The outer husk that covers an ear of corn. **shuck** *v.*

shud-der (shud´ẽr) *v.* To tremble uncontrollably, as from fear.

shuf-fle (shuf´l) *v.* To drag or slide the feet; to mix together in a haphazard fashion; to rearrange or change the order of cards. **shuffle** *n.*

shun (shun) *v.* To avoid deliberately.

shut (shut) *v.* To move a door, drawer, or other object to close an opening; to block an entrance; to lock up; to cease or halt operations.

shut-tle (shut´l) *n.* A device used to move thread in weaving; a vehicle, as a train or plane, which travels back and forth from one location to another.

shy (shī) *adj.* Bashful; timid; easily frightened. *v.* To move suddenly from fear. **shyly** *adv.* **shyness** *n.*

si-al-a-gogue *n.* A kind of agent that will promote the flow of saliva.

si-al-ic *adj.* Pertaining to the light rock which is rich in alumina and silica.

Siamese twin *n.* One of a pair of twins that are united at some part of the body with the other twin.

sib-ling (sib´ling) *n.* One of two or more children from the same parents.

sick (sik) *adj.* In poor health; ill; nauseated; morbid. **sickness** *n.*

sick bay *n.* A room on a ship that can be used as a hospital.

sick-en (sik´en) *v.* To become sick.

sick-en-er (sik´e nẽr) *n.* Something that disgusts or sickens.

sick-le (sik´l) *n.* A tool with a curved blade attached to a handle, used for cutting grass or grain.

sick leave *n.* The absence from one's work that is permitted due to an illness.

sick-le cell *n.* An abnormal red blood cell which will take the shape of a crescent.

sickle feather *n.* A long curved tail feather of the cock.

sick-ly *adj.* To be somewhat unwell.

side (sīd) *n.* A surface between the front and back or top and bottom of an object; either surface of a flat object; the part to the left or right of a vertical axis; the right or left portion of the human body; the space beside someone or something; an opinion or point of view which is the opposite of another. **side** *v.* To take a stand and support a particular side. *adj.* Supplementary; peripheral.

side-band *n.* A band of frequencies that are produced by modulation.

side effect *n.* The secondary effect.

side-glance *n.* A look that is directed to the side.

side issue *n.* The issue that is apart from the main point.

si-de-re-al (sī dēr´ē al) *adj.* To be pertaining to the stars.

sid-er-ite *n.* A type of ferrous carbonate that is an iron ore.

sid-er-it-ic *adj.* Pertaining to siderite.

side-split-ting *adj.* To be very funny.

side-step *v.* To step to the side.

side-stroke *n.* A swimming stroke swimmers do on their sides.

side-ward *adj.* To move toward the side.

SIDS *abbr.* Sudden Infant Death Syndrome; unexpected death of a seemingly healthy baby, occurring during sleep in the first four months of life.

siege (sēj) *n.* The action of surrounding a town or port in order to capture it; a prolonged sickness.

si-er-ra (sē er´a) *n.* A rugged chain of mountains or hills.

si-es-ta (sē es´ta) *n.* A rest; short nap.

sie-va bean *n.* A type of bean which is closely related to the lima bean.

sieve (siv) *n.* A meshed or perforated device which allows small particles to pass through but which holds back larger particles; a device for separating liquids from solids.

sieve plate *n.* A wall which is perforated located at the end of one of the cells that make up a sieve tube.

sieve tube *n*. A type of tube that is made of thin-walled cells.

sift (sift) *v*. To separate coarse particles from small or fine ones by passing through a sieve. **through** To carefully examine. **sift** *n*. **sifter** *n*.

sigh (sī) *v*. To exhale a long, deep breath, usually when tired, sad, or relieved.

sight (sīt) *n*. The ability to see with the eyes; the range or distance one can see; a view; a device mounted on a firearm used to guide the eye or aim.

sighted *adj*. To have sight.

sight gag *n*. A comic episode where the effect is created by a camera shot rather than by the words.

sight-less *adj*. Lacking or missing the sense of sight. **sightlessness** *n*.

sight-ly (sīt´lē) *adj*. To be pleasing to the sight. **sightliness** *n*.

sight-see (sīt´sē) *v*. To travel about and see sights that are of interest.

sig-il (sij´il) *n*. A word that is supposed to have occult power in magic.

sig-ma (sig´ma) *n*. The 18th letter in the Greek alphabet.

sig-moid *adj*. To be curved in two directions.

sign (sīn) *n*. A piece of paper, wood, metal, etc., with information written on it; a gesture that tells or means something. *v*. To write one's name.

sig-nal (sig´nal) *n*. A sign which gives a warning; the image or sound sent by television or radio. **signal** *v*. To make or send a signal to.

sig-nal-ize (sig´na līz´) *v*. To make signals to someone. **signalization** *n*.

sig-nal-man *n*. A person who works with signals or signals others.

sig-na-ture (sig´na chér) *n*. The name of a person, written by that person; a distinctive mark which indicates identity. *Music* A symbol indicating the time and key.

sig-net *n*. A type of seal which is used to give personal authority to a document or papers instead of using a signature.

signet ring *n*. A type of ring that is engraved with a signet.

sig-ni-fi-a-ble *adj*. Being represented with a symbol or a sign of some sort.

sig-nif-i-cance (sig nif´i kans) *n*. The quality of being important; the meaning of something which is considered important.

sig-ni-fi-er *n*. Something that signifies.

sig-ni-fy (sig´ni fī´) *v*. To express or make known by a sign; to indicate. **signification** *n*. **significant** *adj*.

sign in *v*. To record the arrival of someone at a particular time by the signing of a list or the punching of the time

clock.

sign language *n*. A means of communicating by using hand gestures; the language of deaf people.

sign manual *n*. The signature of a king which is on a royal grant and is placed at the top or beginning of the document.

sign off *v*. To tell or to announce the end of a program or of a broadcast.

sign on *v*. To tell or to announce the beginning of a broadcast for the day.

si-gnor *n*. An Italian man.

si-gno-ra *n*. An Italian woman.

si-gno-ri-na (sēn´yo rē´na) *n*. Italian woman who is not yet married.

sign out *v*. To tell of one's departure by signing a list depicting when a person left.

sign-post *n*. A post that bears signs on it for the use of giving directions.

sike (sīk) *n*. A type of stream which is small in size.

si-lage (sīlij) *n*. The fodder which is converted into feed for livestock.

si-lence (sī´lens) *n*. The state or quality of being silent; quiet. *v*. To quiet.

si-lenc-er (sī´len sér) *n*. Someone or something which will cause silence.

si-lent (sī´lent) *adj*. Making no sound; not speaking; mute; an unpronounced letter, as the "g" in *gnat*.

si-lents *n*. A kind of motion picture in which there is not a spoken dialogue.

silent treatment *n*. The act of ignoring another person completely.

sil-hou-ette (sil´ō et´) *n*. The outline of something, as a human profile, filled in with a solid color, as black; the outline of an object. **silhouette** *v*.

sil-i-con (sil´i kon) *n*. The second most common chemical element, found only in combination with another substance, symbolized as Si.

silicone rubber *n*. A type of rubber that is made from silicone elastomers and is flexible over a wide range of different temperatures.

silk (silk) *n*. A soft, thread-like fiber spun by silkworms; thread or fabric made from silk. **silken** *adj*. **silky** *adj*.

silk-a-line *n*. A type of cotton fabric with a smooth finish like that of silk.

silk cotton *n*. A type of silky covering that can be found on the seeds of various silk cotton trees.

silk-cotton tree *n*. A type of tropical tree that has large fruits with the seeds covered by silk cotton.

silk gland *n*. The gland that will produce the fluid which is excreted in filaments and then hardens into silk when it comes into contact with air.

silk oak *n*. An Australian timber tree that has mottled wood which is used for the purpose of making cabinets.

silk stocking *n*. A person who is dressed

in a fashionable manner.

silk-worm *n.* A type of larva that spins a large amount of silk in its cocoon.

sill (sil) *n.* The horizontal support that forms the bottom part of the frame of a window or door.

sil-ly (sil´ē) *adj.* Foolish; lacking good sense, seriousness, or substance.

si-lo (sī´lō) *n.* A tall, cylindrical structure for storing food for farm animals; an underground shelter or storage for guided missiles.

silt *n.* A deposit of soil and sediment that is often caused by a river.

silt-stone *n.* A type of stone which is composed of silt.

sil-va *n.* The trees of a country or region.

sil-ver (sil´vér) *n.* A soft, white metallic element used in tableware, jewelry, and coins, symbolized by Ag. *v.* To coat with silver. *adj.* Of the color silver.

silver age *n.* A period in history that is secondary to the gold age.

silver bell *n.* A type of tree located in the southeastern United States that is grown for its bell-shaped flowers.

sil-ver-ber-ry *n.* A type of shrub which is found in North America and is related to the buffalo berry.

silver fir *n.* A fir that has leaves that are silver-colored underneath.

sil-ver-fish *n.* A small wingless insect which eats clothing and paper.

silver fox *n.* A color phase of the red fox when the coat is white.

silver hake *n.* A type of hake that is found off the New England coast and is used as an important food fish.

silver lining *n.* A hopeful prospect.

silver maple *n.* A type of maple of North America that has leaves which are silvery white beneath.

sil-vern *adj.* To be made of silver.

silver paper *n.* A metallic paper, such as tinfoil, with a silver-like coating.

silver perch *n.* A type of fish with a silvery in color, resembling perch.

sil-ver-sides *n.* A fish that has a silver stripe down both sides of its body.

sil-ver-smith *n.* A person who makes goods and articles out of silver.

sil-ver-y *adj.* To have a musical tone which is clear and soft.

sil-vics *n.* A study of the characteristics and ecology of forest trees.

sim-i-lar (sim´i lér) *adj.* Almost the same, but not identical.

sim-i-lar-i-ty *n.* The state of two things or people being like or similar.

sim-i-le (sim´i lē) *n.* A structure of speech which is used to compare two things that are often unlike.

sim-mer (sim´ér) *v.* To cook just below boiling; to be near the point of breaking, as with emotion.

simmer down *v.* To calm.

si-mo-nize *v.* To polish something with wax.

si-moom *n.* A dry wind from the African and Asian deserts.

sim-ple (sim´pl) *adj.* Easy to do or understand; not complicated; ordinary; not showy; lacking intelligence or education. **simply** *adv.*

simple closed curve *n.* A type of curve that does not intersect itself.

simple fraction *n.* A type of fraction where the denominator and the numerator are of whole numbers.

simple motion *n.* A type of motion that is in a straight line.

sim-plic-i-ty (sim plis´i tē) *n.* The state of being easy to understand; naturalness; sincerity.

sim-pli-fy (sim´pli fī´) *v.* To make easy or simple. **simplification** *n.*

sim-u-late (sim´ū lāt´) *v.* To have the appearance, effect, or form of. **simulation** *n.* **simulator** *n.*

sim-u-lat-ed rank *n.* The status of a civilian that is equal to a military rank.

si-mul-ta-ne-ous *adj.* Occurring at exactly the same time. **-ly** *adv.*

sin (sin) *n.* The breaking of a religious law or a law of God. *v.* To do something which is morally wrong.

since (sins) *adv.* At a time before the present. **since** *prep.* During the time later than; continuously from the time when something occurs.

sin-cere (sin sēr´) *adj.* Honest; not deceitful; genuine; true. **-ly** *adv.*

sin-cip-i-tal *adj.* To be pertaining to the sinciput.

sin-ci-put *n.* The upper half or section of the skull.

sine *n.* A function in trigonometry.

sine qua non *n.* Something which is indispensable.

sin-ful *adj.* Being tainted with sin.

sing (sing) *v.* To use the voice to make musical tones; to make a humming or whistling sound. **singer** *n.*

singe (sinj) *v.* To slightly burn the surface of something; to remove feathers.

sin-gle (sing´gl) *adj.* Of or referring to only one, separate; individual; unmarried. *n.* A separate, individual person or item; a dollar bill; in baseball, a hit that allows the batter to progress to first base.

single-breasted *adj.* To have a center closing that has one row of buttons.

single cross *n.* The first generation hybrid between two selected lines.

sin-gle file *n.* A line where the people are one right behind each other.

single-handed *adj.* To be done by one person. **single-handedly** *adv.*

sin-gle-minded *adj.* To have one overriding purpose.

sin-gle-ness *n.* State of being single.

sin-gu-lar (sing´gŭ lĕr) *adj.* Separate; one; extraordinary; denoting a single unit, thing or person.

sin-gu-lar-i-ty (sing´gŭ lar´i tē) *n.* A unit that is separate.

sin-gu-lar-ize *v.* To make something singular.

sin-is-ter (sin´i stèr) *adj.* To be evil or causing evil. **sinisterness** *n.* **-ly** *adv.*

sink (singk) *v.* To submerge beneath a surface; to go down slowly; to become less forceful or weaker. **sink** *n.* A basin for holding water, attached to a wall and connected to a drain.

sink-er *n.* A weight that is used for the purpose of sinking a fishing line into the water.

sink-hole *n.* A type of hollow depression where drainage collects.

si-nol-o-gy *n.* A study of the Chinese and the culture, history, and language. **sinological** *adj.* **sinologist** *n.*

sin-u-ate (sin´ū it) *adj.* Having a margin with indentations. **sinuately** *adv.*

sin-u-ous (sin´ū us) *adj.* To be marked with strong lithe movements.

si-nus (sī´nus) *n., Anat.* A body cavity; one of eight air spaces in the bones of the face which drain into the nasal cavity.

si-nus-i-tis *n.* The swelling and inflammation of the sinuses of the skull.

sip (sip) *v.* To drink in small amounts.

si-phon (sī´fon) *also* **syphon** *n.* A tube through which liquid from one container can be drawn into another by forced air pressure. **siphon** *v.*

si-pho-no-phore *n.* A type of free-swimming hyfrozoans that are transparent and have specialized zooids.

sip-pet (sip´it) *n.* A small piece of toast used for garnishing.

sir (ser) *n.* A respectful term used when addressing a man.

sir-dar (sér där´) *n.* The person who holds a responsible position in India.

si-ren (sī´ren) *n.* A whistle which makes a loud wailing noise as a warning; a seductive woman.

si-re-ni-an *n.* A type of aquatic herbivorous mammal, such as the manatee.

sir-loin (sür´loin) *n.* The cut of meat that is from the hindquarter.

sis-ter (sis´tèr) *n.* A female having the same parents as another; a woman in membership with others, as in a church group or sorority. **-ly** *adj.*

sis-ter-hood *n.* Women who have a close relationship.

sis-trum *n.* A type of percussion instrument used in ancient Egypt.

sit (sit) *v.* To rest the body with the weight on the buttocks; to cover eggs for hatching; to pose for a portrait.

si-tar *n.* An Indian lute that has a long neck and varying number of strings.

site (sīt) *n.* A location of planned buildings.

sit-ting (sit´ing) *n.* An act of one that sits.

sitting duck *n.* A defenseless target.

sit-u-a-tion *n.* A way in which something or someone is placed, with its surroundings. **situationally** *adv.*

six (siks) *n.* The cardinal number 6, after five and before seven.

six-fold (siks´fōld) *adj.* To have six members.

six-pack *n.* Packaging for six cans so that they can be bought together.

six–penny nail *n.* A type of nail that is about two inches in length.

six-teen (siks´tēn´) *n.* The cardinal number 16; which is 15 + 1.

siz-a-ble (sī´za bl) *adj.* Large in size or dimensions.

size (sīz) *n.* The measurement or dimensions of something; a sticky substance used to glaze walls before applying wallpaper. **size** *v.*

siz-ed *adj.* To have a size which is specified.

siz-zle (siz´l) *v.* To make a hissing sound, as of fat frying. **sizzle** *n.*

sizzler *n.* The one that will sizzle.

skald *n.* Ancient Scandinavian poet.

skat *n.* A kind of three-handed game of cards where each player bids for the privilege to attempt any of the several contracts.

skate (skāt) *n.* A device with blades or rollers which attaches to the shoe and allows one to glide over ice or roll over a wooden or cement surface; a shoe for skating. **skater** *n.*

skate-board *n.* A narrow piece of wood with wheels attached.

ska-tole *n.* A foul smelling substance which is found in the intestines.

ske-dad-dle *v.* To leave or to run away from something or someone.

skeet *n.* The sport of trapshooting where the targets are made of clay and thrown in a way which resembles the manner in which birds fly.

skee-ter *n.* A type of iceboat that has one sail.

skein (skān) *n.* A piece of thread which is wound onto a reel.

skel-e-tal *adj.* Pertaining to or relating to the skeleton.

skel-e-ton (skel´i ton) *n.* The framework of bones that protects and supports the soft tissues and organs.

skel-e-ton-ize *v.* To reduce something to skeleton form.

skeleton key *n.* A key that is filed in order to be able to open many locks which can be used as a master key.

skep (skep) *n.* A type of hive that is doomed and has been made of twisted straw.

skep-sis *n.* A philosophic doubt as to the reality of something.

skep-tic (skep´tik) *n.* A person who doubts or questions. **skepticism** *n.* **skeptical** *adj.* **skeptically** *adv.*

sker-ry *n.* A island which is rocky.

sketch (skech) *n.* A rough drawing or outline; a brief literary composition.

sketch-book *n.* A book which is used for the purpose of sketching things.

skew (skū) *v.* To turn or slant. **skew** *n.* A slant.

skew-bald *adj.* To be marked with spots of white or another color or colors.

skew curve *n.* A type of curve which is three-dimensional and does not lie in the same plane or single plane.

skew-er *n.* A piece of metal used as a pin for the purpose of fastening foods together in order to broil them on a grill

skew lines *n.* Type of lines which are straight and do not intersect and are not located within the same plane.

skew-ness *n.* The lack of symmetry or of straightness of an object such as a line or curve.

ski (skē) *n., pl.* **skis** One of a pair of long, narrow pieces of wood worn on the feet for gliding over snow or water. **ski** *v.* **skier** *n.*

ski-a-gram *n.* The figure which is formed by shading the outline of a shadow that is created by the figure.

ski boot *n.* A rigid boot which is attached to the ski and is used to hold the ski on the foot.

skid (skid) *v.* To slide to the side of the road; to slide along without rotating.

skid-der *n.* A person who uses a skid or who skids.

skid-dy *adj.* Being likely to cause skidding.

skid road *n.* A type of road where logs are skidded along.

skill (skil) *n.* Ability gained through practice; expertise. **skilled** *adj.*

skiff (skif) *n.* A type of small and light sailing ship.

ski-ing (skē´ing) *n.* The sport of jumping and moving on skis.

ski jump *n.* Jump is made by one who is wearing skis off of a large ramp.

ski lift *n.* A conveyor used to bring the skiers to the top of a hill.

skill (skil) *n.* Ability gained through practice; expertise.

skilled (skild) *adj.* To have acquired a skill for something.

skil-let (skil´it) *n.* A type of pot that has feet and is used for the purpose of cooking foods on the hearth.

skill-ful (skil´ful) adj. To be displaying a skill. **skillfully** *adv.*

skil-ling (skil´ing) *n.* Type of old Scandinavian unit of value, such as a coin.

skill-less (skil´lis) *adj.* To have no skill for anything. **skillessness** *n.*

skim (skim) *v.* To remove the top layer; to remove floating matter; to read over material quickly; to travel over lightly and quickly. **skimmer** *n.*

ski mask *n.* A type of face covering that is made of fabric and can be worn while one is skiing for protection from the elements.

skim milk *n.* A type of milk where the cream has been taken out.

skim-ming (skim´ing) *n.* The substance or that which is skimmed from a liquid.

skimp (skimp) *v.* To economize; to hold back. **skimpy** *adj.*

skin (skin) *n.* The tough, outside covering of man and some animals; the outside layer of a vegetable or fruit; the fur or pelt of an animal. **skin** *v.* **skinless** *adj.*

skin–deep *adj.* To be as deep as the skin; very thin.

skin diving *n.* A sport that involves swim-ming under the water without a breathing device.

skin-flint (skin´flint´) *n.* A type of person who would extort or save money any way that is possible.

skin game *n.* A game that involves a trick or swindling of a person.

skin graft *n.* A section of the skin that is removed from one area and placed in an area where the skin has been removed or damaged.

skin grafting *n.* The process of placing or making a skin graft.

skin-head (skin´hed) *n.* A person whose hair is very short.

skink *v.* To serve alcoholic drinks.

skink-er *n.* One who serves liquor.

skin-ner (skin´ėr) *n.* A person who deals or sells skins.

skin-ny (slin´ē) *adj.* To be lacking a sufficient amount of flesh on the body, making one look thin.

skin-tight (skin´tīt) *adj.* To be closely fitted to one's body.

skip (skip) *v.* To move in light jumps or leaps; to go from one place to another, missing what is between. **skip** *n.*

skip-jack *n.* A type of fish that will jump above the surface of the water.

ski pole *n.* The pole used in skiing to push the skier along the snow.

skirl (skürl) *n.* The high shrill sound which is produced by a bagpipe.

skir-mish *n.* A small and minor fight.

skirt (skert) *n.* A piece of clothing that extends down from the waist. **skirt** *v.* To extend along the boundary; to avoid the issue.

skirt-ing (skür´ting) *n.* The fabric which is suitable for making skirts.

ski run *n.* The trail which is used for the sport of skiing.

skit (skit) *n.* A type of humorous story.

ski tow *n.* A conveyor used to bring skiers

to the top of the hill.

skit-tish (skit´ish) *adj.* To be frightened easily.

skiv-er (skī´vĕr) *n.* A type of thin leather that is made from sheepskin.

ski-wear *n.* The clothing that is used while one is skiing to keep warm.

skulk *v.* To conceal something out of fear; to move in a furtive way. **skulk** *n.* A person who skulks around.

skull (skul) *n.* The bony part of the skeleton which protects the brain.

skull-cap (skul´kap´) *n.* A type of cap that is close-fitting.

skull practice *n.* A type of meeting for a discussion or the exchanging of ideas.

skunk (skungk) *n.* A black mammal with white streaks down its back, which sprays an unpleasant smelling liquid when annoyed or frightened.

skunk cab-bage *n.* A type of herb that has a very foul odor and is found in the eastern part of North America.

sky (skī) *n.* *pl.* **skies** The upper atmosphere above the earth; the celestial regions.

sky blue *n.* A color which may range from light blue to pale blue.

sky-cap *n.* A person who has the job of handling the luggage at an airport.

sky-div-ing *n.* The sport of jumping out of an airplane while it is flying in the air.

sky-ey (skī´e) *adj.* Pertaining to or resembling the sky.

sky-high (skī´hī) *adv. or adj.* To be located high in the air; to do in a manner which is exorbitant.

ski-lark *n.* A type of lark which is large in size and is especially noted for its song.

sky-light *n.* The light of the sky; a window in the roof to admit natural light.

sky-line *n.* The outline of a building or other very large object against the sky.

sky-phos (skī´fos) *n.* A type of drinking vessel that was used in ancient Greece and had two handles.

sky-scrap-er (skĭskrā´pĕr) *n.* A type of building which is very tall and therefore seems to scrape the sky.

sky-ward *adj.* To be moving toward the sky.

sky-way (skī´wā´) *n.* The route which is used by airplanes.

sky-write *v.* To write letters or words in the sky.

sky-writ-ing *n.* The writing which is formed in the sky with the use of smoke.

slab (slab) *n.* A thick piece or slice.

slab-sid-ed *adj.* To have sides which are flat.

slack (slak) *adj.* Not taut or tense; sluggish; lacking in strength. *v.* To

make slack. *n.* A part of something which hangs loose. **slacks** Long pants or trousers.

slack-baked *n.* To be underdone.

slack-en *v.* To slow something down.

slack-er *n.* One who shirks an obligation.

slain *v.* Past tense of slay.

sla-lom *n.* A type of skiing where the skier zig-zags down the hill between upright obstacles such as flags.

slam (slam) *v.* To shut with force; to strike with a loud impact. **slam** *n.* A loud noise produced by an impact.

slan-der (slan´dĕr) *n.* A false statement that deliberately does harm to another's reputation. **slanderous** *adj.*

slang (slang) *n.* Informal language that contains made-up words or common words used in a different or uncommon way.

slant (slant) *v.* To lie in an oblique position; to slope; to report on something giving only one side or viewpoint. *n.* An incline or slope.

slap (slap) *n.* A sharp blow with an open hand. **slap** *v.*

slap-hap-py *adj.* To be recklessly foolish.

slap shot *n.* The shot which is taken in ice hockey that is made with a swinging stroke.

slap-stick *n.* A type of comedy that stresses or contains horseplay and silly expressions.

slash (slash) *v.* To cut with a fast sweeping stroke; to reduce or limit greatly. *n.* A long cut.

slash-ing *n.* The process of slashing something. **slashingly** *adv.*

slash pine *n.* A type of southern pine which is a source of lumber and of turpentine.

slat *n.* A narrow piece of wood.

slate (slāt) *n.* A fine grained rock that splits into thin layers, often used as a writing surface or roofing material.

slate black *n.* A color that is purplish black.

slat-er *n.* A person who slates.

slath-er *v.* To spread something in a thick manner onto something else.

slat-ing *n.* The work that is done by a slater.

slat-tern-ly (slat´ĕrn lē) *adj.* To be dirty because of neglect.

slat-y *adj.* To have the characteristic of slate.

slaugh-ter (slo´tĕr) *v.* To kill livestock for food; to kill in great numbers. *Slang* To soundly defeat. **slaughterer** *n.* **slaughterous** *adj.*

slaugh-ter-house *n.* A place where one butchers or slaughters animals.

slave (slāv) *n.* A person held against his will and made to work for another.

slave ant *n.* A type of ant that is enslaved by the slave-making ant of the colony.

slave driver *n.* A person who is the supervisor of slaves.

slave-hold-er *n.* A person who is the owner of the slaves.

slav-ish (slā´vish) *adj.* Pertaining to the characteristics of a slave.

slay (slā) *v.* To kill or to destroy something in a violent manner.

sleave (slēv) *v.* To separate something such as silk fibers into filaments.

sleave silk *n.* A type of floss silk that is easily separated into filaments.

sled (sled) *n.* A vehicle with runners, used to travel on snow or ice.

sled dog *n.* A type of dog which has been trained to pull a sledge.

sledge *n.* A kind of vehicle that has low runners and is used for the purpose of transporting loads over the snow and is pulled by dogs.

sledge-ham-mer *n.* A type of hammer which is very heavy and must be wielded with both hands.

sleek (slēk) *adj.* Smooth and shiny; neat and trim. **sleekly** *adv.* **-ness** *n.*

sleep (slēp) *n.* A natural state of rest for the mind and body. **sleep** *v.*

sleeping bag *n.* The bag which is lined and is used for sleeping.

sleep-ing car *n.* A car of a train that has accommodations allowing a person to sleep.

sleeping pill *n.* A type of drug which is taken to help a person fall asleep.

sleep-less *adj.* Being not able to get to sleep. **sleeplessness** *n.*

sleep out *v.* To sleep away in a place that is not one's home.

sleep-walk-er *n.* A person who is able to walk while still asleep.

sleep-y (slē´pē) *adj.* Pertaining to sleep; needing sleep.

sleet (slēt) *n.* Rain that is partially frozen; a combination of snow and rain. **sleet** *v.* **sleety** *adj.*

sleeve (slēv) *n.* The part of a garment which covers the arm; a case for something.

sleeve-let *n.* A kind of covering which is worn on the forearm in order to protect the clothing from dirt and wear.

sleigh (slā) *n.* A vehicle mounted on runners, usually pulled over ice and snow by horses.

sleigh bell *n.* A type of bell that is attached to a sleigh.

slen-der (slen´dėr) *adj.* Slim; inadequate in amount. **slenderly** *adv.*

slept *v.* Past tense of sleep.

sleuth *n.* A detective.

slew *n.* A large amount of something.

slice (slīs) *n.* A thin cut; a portion or share; in sports, a ball in flight that curves off to the right of its target. *v.* To cut into slices. **slicer** *n.*

slice bar *n.* A type of steel bar that has

a flat blade used for chipping.

slick (slik) *adj.* Smooth and slippery; quick; smart; clever; attractive for the present time but without quality or depth. *n.* Water with a thin layer of oil floating on top.

slick-en-side *n.* A striated surface that is produced on a rock by moving along a fault.

slick-er (slik´ėr) *n.* A raincoat made of yellow oilcloth.

slide (slīd) *v.* To move smoothly across a surface without losing contact. *n.* The act of sliding; a slanted smooth surface usually found on playgrounds; a transparent picture which can be projected on a screen; a small glass plate for examining specimens under a microscope.

slid-er *n.* Something that slides.

slide valve *n.* A kind of valve which opens and closes something such as a passageway.

slide-way *n.* The way which something slides.

slid-ing seat *n.* The rower's seat which will slide aft and fore.

slight (slīt) *adj.* Minor in degree; unimportant. *v.* To ignore. **slightly** *adv.*

slight-ing *adj.* To be characterized by disrespect. **slightingly** *adv.*

slim (slim) *adj.* Slender; meager; not much. **slimness** *n.*

slime (slīm) *n.* A wet, slippery substance. **slimy** *adj.*

slim-ming *adj.* To be giving the appearance or effect of slenderness.

sling (sling) *n.* A piece of material, as leather, or a strap which secures something; a piece of fabric worn around the neck used to support an injured hand or arm; a weapon made of a strap, used to throw a stone.

sling-shot *n.* A type of v-shaped device which has an elastic band and is used to propel objects such as rocks through the air.

slink-y (sling´ke) *adj.* To be sinuous and sleek in moving.

slip (slip) *v.* To move in a smooth, quiet way; to fall or lose one's balance. *Slang* To become less active or alert. **slip** *n.* The action of slipping; the place between two piers used for docking a boat; a woman's undergarment; a small piece of paper; a portion of a plant used for grafting.

slip-case (slip´kās´) *n.* A type of container that has one end open in order to slide books into for protection.

slip-cov-er *n.* A type of cover that can be slipped on and off of something.

slip-knot *n.* A knot that will slip along the rope of which it is made.

slip-o-ver *n.* A type of garment that will slip on and off with ease.

slip-page *n.* The process of slipping.

slip-pery (slip´e rē) *adj.* To cause something to slip. **slipperiness** *n.*

slip–sheet *v.* To put in or to insert a slip sheet between other sheets.

slip sheet *n.* A type of paper that is put between newly printed sheets.

slip-sole *n.* A type of thin insole.

slip stitch *n.* A stitch which is used for concealing folded edges in sewing.

slip up *v.* Make a blunder or mistake.

slit *v.* To cut an opening into something. **slit** *n.* A narrow opening or cut into something.

slith-er (slith´ēr) *v.* To slide or slip in an indirect manner; to move like a snake. **slithery** *adj.*

slit trench *n.* A trench which is narrow and is used as shelter in a battle from shell fragments.

sliv-er (sliv´ēr) *n.* A thin, narrow piece of something that has been broken off.

slob (slob) *n.* One who is slovenly.

slob-ber (slob´ēr) *v.* To dribble from the mouth. **slobber** *n.*

sloe gin *n.* A type of sweet liquor made of grain spirits, flavored with plums.

slog *v.* To plod along slowly and heavily.

slo-gan (slō´gan) *n.* A phrase used to express the aims of a cause.

slo-gan-ize *v.* To use something as a slogan.

sloop (slōp) *n.* A type of boat with one mast which is rigged fore-and-aft.

slop (slop) *n.* A tasteless liquid food.

slop chest *n.* The store which is on a merchant ship and supplies the crew with goods such as tobacco.

slope (slōp) *v.* To slant upward or downward. *n.* An upward or downward incline, as a ski slope.

slop jar *n.* A type of pail that is large in size and is used for the purpose of receiving and holding the waste water from a washbowl.

slop-py *adj.* To be wet so that it spatters easily.

slosh (slosh) *v.* To splash in a liquid, as water. **sloshy** *adj.*

slot (slot) *n.* A narrow, thin groove or opening. *Slang* A place or scheduled time for an event.

slot-back *n.* The offensive halfback in the game of football that lines up behind and between the tackle and the offensive end.

sloth (sloth) *n.* Laziness; a slow mammal found in South America.

sloth-ful *adj.* To be inclined to sloth. **slothfulness** *n.*

slouch (slouch) *n.* A drooping or sagging posture; a lazy person. *v.* To sit or walk with poor posture.

slouch hat *n.* A kind of hat that has a wide flexible brim.

slouch-y *adj.* To be lacking good posture.

slouchiness *n.*

slough *n.* The skin which is cast off from a snake as he sheds it.

slo-ven (sluv´en) *n.* A person who is habitually negligent of cleanliness.

slov-en-ly (sluv´en lē) *adj.* To be untidy as in one's personal appearance.

slow (slō) *adj.* Moving at a low rate of speed; requiring more time than usual; not lively; sluggish; not interesting. *adv.* At less speed; in a slow manner. **slow** *v.* To make slower.

slow–foot-ed *adj.* To be moving at a slow pace. **slow-footedness** *n.*

slow-poke *n.* A person who is slow.

slow–witted *adj.* To be mentally slow.

sludge *n.* A mass which is slushy.

slue *v.* To cause something to skid.

slug (slug) *n.* A slow animal related to the snail; a bullet or a lump of metal. *v.* To strike forcefully with the fist or a heavy object.

slug-fest *n.* A type of fight which is marked by the exchange of blows that are heavy.

slug-gard (slug´ērd) *n.* A person who is habitually lazy. **sluggardly** *adj.*

slug-ger *n.* A person who strikes with heavy blows such as a fighter.

slug-gish *adj.* To be slow to respond to a treatment or to a stimulation. **sluggishness** *n.* **sluggishly** *adv.*

sluice (slōs) *n.* A man-made ditch used to move water; a sloping trough used for floating logs. *v.* To wash with flowing water.

sluice-way (slōs´wā) *n.* A channel which is artificial and into which water is admitted from a sluice.

slum (slum) *n.* A crowded urban neighborhood marked by poverty.

slum-ber (slum´bēr) *v.* To sleep; to doze. *n.* Sleep. **slumberer** *n.*

slum-ber-ous (slum´bē us) *adj.* Being able to induce slumber.

slumber party *n.* A type of overnight gathering usually of girls at someone's house.

slum-my *adj.* To be pertaining to a slum.

slump (slump) *v.* To fall or sink suddenly. **slump** *n.*

slung *v.* Past tense of sling.

slur (slēr) *v.* To slide over without careful consideration; to pronounce unclearly. *n.* An insult. *Music* Two or more notes connected with a curved line to indicate they are to be slurred.

slurp (slūrp) *v.* To make or produce a sucking noise while one is drinking.

slur-ry (slūr´ē) *n.* A type of watery mixture of matter which is insoluble.

slush (slush) *n.* Melting snow; snow which is partially melted. **slushy** *adj.*

slut (slut) *n.* A woman of bad character; a prostitute. **sluttish** *adj.*

sly (slī) *adj.* Cunning; clever; sneaky;

underhanded. **slyly** *adv.* **slyness** *n.*
sly-boots *n.* A person who is sly.
sm *abbr.* Small.
smack (smak) *v.* To slap; to press and open the lips with a sharp noise. *n.* The act or noise of slapping something. *adv.* Directly.
smack-ing (smak´ing) *adj.* Lively.
small (smol) *adj.* Little in size, quantity, or extent; unimportant. **small** *n.* The part that is less than the other.
small ale *n.* A weak ale that is brewed with little malt and is a cheap drink.
small arm *n.* A firearm which can be fired while it is held in the hands.
small change *n.* The coins of a low denomination; thingsof little value.
small-clothes *n.* The close-fitting knee breeches which were worn in the 18th century.
small–fry *adj.* Pertaining to a child.
small hours *n.* Early morning hours.
small intestines *n.* The section of the intestines which is located between the colon and the stomach.
small-mouth bass *n.* Type of black bass which can be found in clear lakes and rivers.
small-pox (smol´poks´) *n.* An acute, contagious disease marked by high fever and sores on the skin.
small–scale *adj.* To be small in scope.
small-sword *n.* A light tapering sword that is used for thrusting in fencing.
small talk *n.* A casual conversation.
smalt-ite *n.* A type of white or grey mineral which is an arsenide of nickel and cobalt.
smal-to *n.* A type of colored glass that can be used for mosaic work.
smarm-y *adj.* Smug; self-satisfied.
smart (smärt) *adj.* Intelligent; clever. **smart-ly** *adv.* **smartness** *n.*
smart-en *v.* To make someone smarter.
smart-weed *n.* A polygonums that has a strong acid juice.
smash (smash) *v.* To break into small pieces; to move violently, as to shatter; to ruin. **smash** *n.* The sound or act of crashing. **smashing** *adj.*
smat-ter *v.* To speak with a superficial knowledge.
smaze *n.* The combination of smoke and haze that is similar to smog in its appearance only.
smear (smēr) *v.* To spread or cover with a sticky, oily, or moist substance. *Slang* To discredit one's reputation.
smear-y *adj.* Marked with smears.
smell (smel) *v.* To notice an odor by means of the olfactory sense organs. *n.* An odor; the ability to perceive an odor; the scent of something.
smel-ly (smel´ē) *adj.* To have an odor.
smelt (smelt) *v.* To heat metals or their ores to a high temperature in order to

obtain pure metallic constituents.
smelt-er *n.* Something or someone that smelts.
smew (smū) *n.* A bird of northern Europe and Asia; the male of this species has a white crest.
smid-gen (smij´en) *n.* A small amount.
smi-lax *n.* A type of twinning plant which has ovate bright green cladophylls.
smile (smīl) *n.* A grin; a facial expression in which the corners of the mouth turn upward, indicating pleasure. **smile** *v.*
smirch (smürch) *v.* To make something stained or dirty.
smirk (smerk) *v.* To smile in a conceited way. **smirk** *n.* **smirker** *n.*
smite (smīt) *v.* To hit with great force using the hand.
smith (smith) *n.* One who repairs or shapes metal.
smith-er-y *n.* The art of a smith.
smith-son-ite *n.* A type of zinc which is white.
smock (smok) *n.* A loose-fitting garment worn as a protection for one's clothes while working. *v.* To gather fabric into very small pleats or gathers.
smock frock *n.* An outer garment which is loose-fitting and is worn by workmen.
smog (smog) *n.* A mixture of smoke and fog. **smoggy** *adj.*
smoke (smōk) *n.* A cloud of vapor released into the air when something is burning. **smoke** *v.* To preserve or flavor meat by exposing it to smoke. **smoky** *adj.*
smoke-house *n.* A place or building where meat and fish are cured by using smoke.
smoke jumper *n.* A type of forest fighter who will parachute to the area of a fire that may have become hard to reach by land.
smoke out *v.* To force or drive out with the use of smoke.
smoke-stack *n.* The chimney through which gases and smoke are able to be discharged.
smoke tree *n.* A type of shrubby tree belonging to the sumac family.
smok-ing jack-et *n.* A type of jacket which is worn by the man at home.
smolder (smōl´dèr) *v.* To burn slowly without flame and with little smoke.
smolt *n.* A young sea trout or salmon.
smooth (smōyth) *adj.* Not irregular; flat; without lumps, as in gravy; without obstructions or impediments. *adv.* Evenly. *v.* To make less difficult; to remove obstructions.
smooth-en *v.* To make a thing smooth.
smooth-y *n.* A type of person who has manners which are greatly polished.
smor-gas-bord (smor´gas bōrd´) *n.* A buffet meal with a variety of foods to

choose from.

smother (smuth´ẽr) *n.* Failure to receive enough oxygen to survive. *v.* To conceal; to be overly protective.

smudge (smuj) *v.* To soil by smearing with dirt. *n.* A dirty mark or smear; a fire made to fill the air with smoke in order to protect fruit trees from frost.

smug (smug) *adj.* Complacent with oneself; self-satisfied. **smugly** *adv.* **smugness** *n.*

smug-gle (smug´l) *v.* To import or export goods illegally without paying duty fees. **smuggler** *n.*

smug-ly *adv.* To be done in a smug manner.

smut *n.* A type of matter or substance which will soil something.

smut-ty *adj.* To be tainted or soiled by smut. **smittiness** *n.*

SMV *abbr.* Slow moving vehicle.

snack (snak) *n.* A small amount of food taken between meals. **snack** *v.*

snack bar *n.* An eating place for the public that serves snacks at a counter.

snaf-fle *n.* A jointed bit used with a bridle.

sna-fu *v.* To be someone in a confused state.

snag (snag) *n.* A stump or part of a tree that is partly hidden under the surface of water; a pull in a piece of fabric. *v.* To tear on a rough place. *Slang* To catch unexpectedly; to snatch.

snail (snāl) *n.* A gastropod mollusk that can live in a spiral shell.

snail-paced *adj.* To be moving at a slow pace.

snake (snāk) *n.* Any of a large variety of scaly reptiles, having a long tapering body; an untrustworthy person.

snake-bite *n.* A bite of a snake on the skin.

snake charmer *n.* A person who exhibits his power to charm a snake.

snake-mouth *n.* A type of bog orchid that is located in eastern N. America and Japan and has pink flowers.

snake-skin *n.* The leather that has been pre-pared from the skin of a snake.

snake-weed (snā´kĕd˘) *n.* A plant that is associated with snakes and used in the treatment of snake bites.

snak-y *adj.* Entwined with snakes.

snap (snap) *v.* To break suddenly with a sharp, quick sound; to fly off under tension; to snatch something suddenly.

snap back *n.* A type of football snap; a sudden recovery.

snap bean *n.* A type of bean which is grown for its pods that are broken and cooked.

snap-drag-on *n.* A type of plant of the figwort family and having white, yellow, or crimson flowers.

snap-per (snap´ẽr) *n.* A type of fish found in warm seas.

snapper–back *n.* In the game of football, a center.

snap-pish (snap´ish) *adj.* To be given to curt irritable speech.

snap-shot *n.* A type of photograph which is made by an amateur with a small camera.

snare (snâr) *n.* Anything that entangles or entraps; a trap with a noose, used to catch small animals.

snare drum *n.* A type of drum that has snares stretched across the lower end.

snarl (snärl) *v.* To speak in an angry way; to cause confusion; to tangle or be tangled. *n.* A growl.

snatch (snach) *v.* To seize or grasp something suddenly. *n.* The act of taking something; a brief or small part.

snatch block *n.* A type of block which can be opened on one side in order to get the bight of a rope.

snaz-zy *adj.* To be flashily attractive.

sneak (snēk) *v.* To act or move in a quiet, sly way. *n.* A person who acts in a secret, underhanded way.

sneak-ing *adj.* To be characteristic of a sneak. **sneakingly** *adv.*

sneak pre-view *n.* An advance showing of a motion picture.

sneak thief *n.* A type of thief that will steal whatever he can without using violence.

sneak-y *adj.* To be marked by shiftiness.

sneer (snẽr) *v.* To express scorn by the look on one's face.

sneeze (snēz) *v.* To expel air from the nose suddenly and without control. **sneeze** *n.*

sneeze-wort *n.* A type of strong-scented herb found in Eurasia.

snee-zy *adj.* To be causing sneezing.

snick *v.* To cut at something slightly.

snide (snīd) *adj.* To be unworthy of esteem; malicious.

sniff *v.* To inhale through the nose in short breaths with a noise; to show scorn. **sniff** *n.* **sniffer** *n.*

sniff-ish *adj.* Expressing an attitude.

snif-ter *n.* A type of drink of liquor that has been distilled.

snig-gle *n.* To try to catch an eel by putting the baited hook into the place where they hide.

snip (snip) *v.* To cut off in small pieces and with quick strokes. **snip** *n.*

snipe (snīp) *n.* *pl.* snipe or snipes A bird with a long bill which lives in marshy places. *v.* To shoot at people from a hidden position. **sniper** *n.*

snip-pet (snip´it) *n.* A small part or thing.

snips *n.* A type of hand shears that can be used for the purpose of cutting metal.

sniv-el (sniv´l) *v.* To whine with snuffling.

snob (snob) *n.* A person who considers himself better than anyone else and who looks down on those he considers to be his inferiors.

snob-ber-y *n.* A snobbish conduct.

snob-bish (snob´ish) *adj.* Being like a snob.

snood (snōd) *n.* A type of band that can be worn on a woman's hair.

snook (snŏk) *n.* A type of fish that is large and can be used as food or for sport.

snook-er *n.* A type of pool which is played with six colored balls and fifteen red balls.

snoop (snŏp) *v., Slang* To prowl or spy. *n.* One who snoops.

snoop-y *adj.* To be given to snooping.

snoot (snŏt) *n.* An expression of contempt.

snooze (snŏz) *n.* To sleep for a short amount of time.

snore (snōr) *v.* To breath with a harsh noise while sleeping. **snorer** *n.*

snor-kel (snor´kel) *n.* A tube that extends above the water, used for breathing while swimming face down.

snort (snort) *n.* To force air through the nostrils with a loud, harsh noise. *Slang* To inhale a narcotic through the nose.

snort-er *n.* Someone or something that snorts.

snout (snout) *n.* A nose of an animal such as a swine.

snout beetle *n.* A type of beetle that has a head which has projected into a snout.

snow (snō) *n.* Vapor that forms crystals in cold air and falls to earth in white flakes. **snow** *v.* To fall like snow. *Slang* To deceive.

snow-ball *n.* A rounded mass of snow that is pressed together.

snow–blind (snō´blīnd´) *adj.* To be affected with snow blindness.

snow-bound (snō´bound´) *adj.* To be blocked in by a large snowfall.

snowfall *n.* The precipitation falling as snow.

snow-mo-bile (snō´mo bēl´) *n.* A vehicle used for traveling on snow.

snub (snub) *v.* To treat with contempt or in an unfriendly way. **snub** *n.*

snub-ber (snub´ėr) *n.* Someone who snubs.

snuff (snuf) *v.* To draw air in through the nostrils. **snuff** *n.*

snuff-box (snuf´boks´) *n.* A type of small box that can be used for holding snuff.

snuff-er *n.* A type of device used for dropping and holding the snuff of a candle.

snuf-fle *v.* To breathe through a nose that is obstructed producing a sniffing sound.

snug (snug) *adj.* Warm, pleasant, comfortable and safe.

snug-gle (snug´l) *v.* To curl up to someone in an affectionate manner.

so (sō) *adv.* To a degree or extent as a result; likewise; also; indeed. *conj.* In order that; therefore.

soak (sōk) *v.* To pass through something with the use of pores. **soaker** *n.*

soak-age (sōk´āj) *n.* The amount of liquid that is gained through absorption.

soap (sōp) *n.* A cleansing agent made of an alkali and a fat, and used for washing. *v.* To rub with soap.

soap-ber-ry (sōp´ber´e) *n.* A type of tropical woody plant.

soap-box (sōp´boks´) *n.* A platform that is used by an informal orator.

soap bubble *n.* A type of hollow globe which is formed by blowing a small film of soapsuds.

soap-less *adj.* Containing no soap.

soap plant *n.* A type of plant which has a part that can be used in the place of soap.

soap-y (sō´pē) *adj.* To be covered or smeared with soap.

soar (sōr) *v.* To glide or fly high without any noticeable movement; to rise higher than usual.

sob (sob) *v.* To weep with short, quick gasps.

so-ber (sō´bėr) *adj.* Not drunk or intoxicated; serious; solemn; quiet. **soberly** *adv.* **soberness** *n.*

soc-cer (sok´ėr) *n.* A game in which two teams of eleven people each try to kick a ball into the goal of the opposing team.

so-cia-ble (sō´sha bl) *adj.* Capable of friendly social relations; enjoying the company of others. **sociably** *adv.*

so-cial (sō´shal) *adj.* Having to do with people living in groups; enjoying friendly companionship with others. *n.* An informal party or gathering.

so-cial-ism (sō´sha liz´um) *n.* A system in which people as a whole, and not individuals, control and own all property.

so-ci-e-ty (so sī´i tē) *n. pl.* **-ies** People working together for a common purpose; companionship.

so-ci-ol-o-gy (sō´sē ol´o jē) *n.* The study of society and the development of human society. **sociologic** *adj.* **sociological** *adj.*

sock-et (sok´it) *n.* A hollow opening into which something is fitted.

Soc-ra-tes *n.* Greek philosopher.

so-da (sō´da) *n.* Sodium carbonate; a flavored, carbonated drink.

sod-den (sod´en) *adj.* Completely saturated; very wet; lacking in expression.

so-di-um (sō´dē um) *n.* A metallic element symbolized by Na.

sod-om-y (sod´o mē) *n.* Anal sexual

intercourse.

so-fa (sō´fa) *n.* An upholstered couch with arms and a back.

soft (soft) *adj.* Not stiff or hard; not glaring or harsh; mild or pleasant; gentle in sound.

soft-ball (soft´bol´) *n.* A game played on a smaller diamond than baseball, with a larger, softer ball.

soft-ware (soft´wâr´) *n.* In *computer science,* data, as routines, programs and languages, which is essential to the operation of computers.

sog-gy (sog´ē) *adj.* Saturated with a liquid or moisture.

sol-ace (sol´is) *n.* Comfort in a time of trouble, grief, or misfortune.

so-lar (sō´lėr) *adj.* Relating to or connected with the sun; utilizing the sun for power or light; measured by the earth's movement around the sun.

so-lar-i-um (sō lâr´ē um) *n. pl.* **-ia** *or* **-ums** A glassed-in room exposed to the sun's rays.

solar system *n.* The sun and the planets, asteroids, etc. that orbit it.

sol-der (sod´ėr) *n.* Any alloy, as lead or tin, which is melted and used to mend or join other pieces of metal. **solder** *v.* To join with solder.

sol-dier (sōl´jėr) *n.* An enlisted person who serves in the military.

sole (sōl) *n.* The bottom of a foot or shoe; single, the only one; a flat fish very popular as seafood.

sol-emn (sol´em) *adj.* Very serious; characterized by dignity; sacred. **solemnity** *n.* **solemnness** *n.*

so-lic-it (so lis´it) *v.* To try to obtain; to ask earnestly; to beg or entice a person persistently. **solicitation** *n.*

sol-id (sol´id) *adj.* Having a definite firm shape and volume; having no crevices; not hollow; having height, weight and length; without interruption; reliable, sound and upstanding. *n.* A solid substance. **solidification** *n.* **-ify** *v.*

sol-i-taire (sol´i târ´) *n.* A single gemstone set by itself; a card game played by one person.

sol-i-tude (sol´i tōd´) *n.* The act of being alone or secluded; isolation.

so-lo (sō´lō) *n.* A musical composition written for and performed by one single person or played by one instrument.

sol-stice (sol´stis) *n.* Either of the two times in a twelve month period at which the sun reaches an extreme north or south position.

sol-u-ble (sol´ū bl´) *adj.* Capable of being dissolved; able to be solved or explained. **solubility** *n.* **solubly** *adv.*

solve (solv) *v.* To find the answer to. **solvable** *adj.*

som-ber (som´bėr) *adj.* Dark; gloomy; melancholy.

some (sum) *adj.* Being an indefinite number or quantity; unspecified. *pron.* An undetermined quantity. *adv.* An approximated degree. **somebody** A person unknown. **somehow** In a way. **someday** *adv.* At an unspecified future time.

som-er-sault (sum´ėr solt´) *n.* The act or acrobatic stunt in which one rolls the body in a complete circle, with heels over head.

som-nam-bu-lism (som nam´bya liz´um) *n.* The act of walking during sleep. **somnambulant** *adj.*

son (sun) *n.* A male offspring.

so-na-ta (so nä´ta) *n.* An instrumental composition with movements contrasting in tempo and mood but related in key.

song (song) *n.* A piece of poetry put to music; the act or sound of singing.

son-ic (son´ik) *adj.* Pertaining to sound or the speed of sound.

son-net (son´it) *n.* A poem made up of fourteen lines.

soon (sön) *adv.* In a short time; in the near future; quickly.

soot (set) *n.* The black powder generated by incomplete combustion of a fuel, such as coal or wood.

soothe (söth) *v.* To make comfortable; to calm.

sop (sop) *v.* To soak up a liquid; to absorb. *n.* Anything softened by a liquid; something given as a conciliatory offering.

soph-o-more (sof´o mōr´) *n.* A second year college or high school student.

so-pran-o (so pran´ō) *n.* The highest female singing voice.

sor-cery (sor´se rē) *n.* The use of supernatural powers.

sor-did (sor´did) *adj.* Filthy, very dirty; morally corrupt.

sore (sōr) *adj.* Tender or painful to the touch, as an injured part of the body; severe or extreme. *n.* A place on the body which has been bruised, inflamed, or injured in some way. **sorely** *adv.*

sor-ghum (sor´gum) *n.* A cane-like grass grown for its sweet juices and used as fodder for animals; the syrup prepared from the sweet juices.

so-ror-i-ty (so ror´i tē) *n. pl.* **-ies** A social organization for women.

sor-rel (sor´el) *n.* Any of several herbs with sour tasting leaves, used in salads.

sor-row (sor´ō) *n.* Anguish; mental suffering; an expression of grief. **sorrowful** *adj.* **sorrowfully** *adv.*

sor-ry (sor´ē) *adj.* Feeling or showing sympathy or regret; worthless.

sort (sort) *n.* A collection of things having common attributes or similar qualities. *v.* to arrange according to class, kind, or size.

sor-tie (sor´tē) *n., Mil.* An attack on enemy forces; a combat mission flown by an aircraft.

SOS (es´ō´es´) *n.* A call for help; the international distress signal; a call made when a rescue is needed, especially by a ship or plane.

souf-fle (sō flā´) *n.* A fluffy dish made of egg yolks, whipped egg whites, and other ingredients, served as a main dish or sweetened as a dessert.

sought *v.* Past tense of seek.

soul (sōl) *n.* The spirit in man that is believed to be separate from the body and is the source of a person's emotional, spir-itual, and moral nature. *Slang* A spirit or attitude derived from Blacks and their culture.

sound (sound) *n.* A sensation received by the ears from air, water, noise, and other sources. **sound** *v.* To make a sound; to make noise. **sound** *adj.* Free from flaw, injury, disease, or damage. **soundly** *adv.*

soup (sōp) *n.* A liquid food made by boiling meat and/or vegetables, in water.

sour (sour) *adj.* Sharp to the taste; acid; unpleasant; disagreeable. *v.* To become sour or spoiled. **sourly** *adv.*

source (sōrs) *n.* Any point of origin or beginning; the beginning or place of origin of a stream or river.

source data In *computer science*, data that has been entered into the computer for manipulation.

south (south) *n.* The direction opposite of north. *adv.* To or towards the south. *adj.* From the south. **southerly** *adj.& adv.* **southern** *adj.* **southerner** *n.*

South Carolina *n.* A state located in the southeastern part of the United States; statehood May 23, 1788; state capital Columbia.

South Dakota *n.* A state located in the central northwestern part of the United States; statehood November 2, 1889; state capital Pierre.

south-paw (south´po´) *n.* A left-handed person. **southpaw** *adj.*

South Pole *n.* The southern most part of the earth.

south-west (south´west´) *n.* The direction between south and west.

sou-ve-nir (sō´ve nēr´) *n.* An item kept as a remembrance of something or someplace.

sov-er-eign (sov´rin) *n.* A ruler with supreme power; a monarch. *adj.* Possessing supreme authority.

sow (sō) *v.* To scatter seeds on the ground for growth. *n.* A female pig.

space (spās) *n.* The unlimited area in all directions in which events occur and have relative direction; an interval of time; the area beyond the earth's atmosphere.

spade (spād) *n.* A tool with a flat blade used for digging; a heavy shovel.

spa-ghet-ti (spa get´ē) *n.* Long thin pasta.

span (span) *n.* The extent of space from the end of the thumb to the end of the little finger of a spread hand; the section between two limits or supports. *v.* To extend across.

span-iel (span´yel) *n.* A dog with large drooping ears and short legs.

spank (spangk) *v.* To strike or slap the buttocks with an open hand as a means of punishment.

spare (spâr) *v.* To refrain from injuring, harming or destroying; to refrain from using; to do without. **spare** *n.* An extra, as a spare tire.

spark (spärk) *n.* A glowing or incandescent particle, as one released from a piece of burning wood or one produced by means of friction. **spark** *v.* To give off sparks.

spar-kle (spär´kl) *v.* To emit or reflect light.

spar-row (spar´ō) *n.* A small bird with grayish or brown plumage.

sparse (spärs) *adj.* Scant; thinly distributed. **sparsely** *adv.* **sparsity** *n.*

spasm (spaz´um) *n.* An involuntary muscle contraction.

spat-ter (spat´ēr) *v.* To splash or scatter a liquid.

spat-u-la (spach´a la) *n.* A kitchen utensil with a flexible blade for mixing soft substances.

spawn (spon) *n.* The eggs of fish or other water animals, as oysters or frogs. *v.* To lay eggs.

speak (spēk) *v.* To utter words; to express a thought in words.

speak-er (spē´kēr) *n.* A person who speaks, usually before an audience.

spear (spēr) *n.* A weapon with a long shaft and a sharp pointed head. *v.* To strike, pierce, or stab with a spear.

spear-mint (spēr´mint´) *n.* A plant yielding an aromatic oil; flavoring.

spe-cial-ist (spesh´a list) *n.* A person, such as a doctor, who devotes his practice to one particular field.

spe-cial-ize (spesh´a līz´) *v.* To focus one's efforts or interests in one field of activity or study.

spec-i-men (spes´i men) *n.* A sample; a representative of a particular thing.

speck (spek) *n.* Small particle; a spot.

speckle *v.* To cover or dot with specks.

spec-ta-cle (spek´ta kl) *n.* A public display of something strange and unusual. **spectacles** Eyeglasses.

spec-trum (spek´trum) *n. Physics* The band of colors produced when light is passed through a prism or by other means, separating the light into different wave lengths.

spec-u-late (spek´ū lāt´) v. To reflect and think deeply; to take a chance on a business venture in hopes of making a large profit. **speculation** n.

speech (spēch) n. The ability, manner, or act of speaking; a talk before the public. **speechless** adj.

speed (spēd) n. Rate of action or movement; quickness; rapid motion. Slang A drug used as a stimulant.

spell (spel) v. To say out loud or write in proper order the letters which make up a word; to relieve. n. The state of being controlled by magic; a short period of time; a time or period of illness; an attack.

spell-bind v. To fascinate or hold as if by magic.

spell checker In Computer Science, a feature in some word processors that checks and corrects spelling in a document.

spend (spend) v. To give out; to use up; to pay; to exhaust.

sperm (sperm) n. The male cell of reproduction; semen. **spermatic** adj.

sphere (sfēr) n., Math A round object with all points the same distance from a given point; globe, ball, or other rounded object. **spherical** adj.

sphinx (sfingks) n., pl. **sphinxes** or **sphinges** An ancient Egyptian figure having the head of a man, male sheep, or hawk and the body of a lion; a very mysterious person.

spice (spīs) n. A pungently aromatic plant used as flavoring in food, as nutmeg, cinnamon, pepper, or curry.

spi-der (spī´dėr) n. An eight-legged arachnid with a body divided into two parts that spins webs used to capture and hold its prey.

spike (spīk) n. A large, thick nail; a pointed metal piece on the sole of a shoe to prevent slipping, as on a sports shoe. **spike** v.

spill (spil) v. To allow or cause something to flow or run out of something, often accidentally. **spill** n.

spin (spin) v. To draw out fibers and twist into thread; to run something around and around; to resolve. Slang A short drive or ride in an auto. **spinner** n.

spin-ach (spin´ich) n. A widely cultivated plant with dark green leaves which are used in salads.

spin-dle (spin´dl) n. A rod with a slit in the top and a piece of wood at the other end, used to hold thread or yarn; a needle-like rod mounted on a base, used to hold papers.

spine (spīn) n. The spinal column; the backbone; the back of a bound book, inscribed with the title.

spin-ster (spin´stėr) n. An unmarried woman; an old maid.

spir-it (spir´it) n. The vital essence of man, considered divine in origin; the part of a human being characterized by personality and self-consciousness; the mind; a supernatural being, as an angel.

spir-i-tual (spir´i chö al) adj. Of the nature of spirit; relating to religion; sacred. n. A religious song originating among the Blacks of the southern United States. **spirituality** n.

spite (spīt) n. Hatred or malicious bitterness; a grudge; ill will. **spite** v. **spiteful** adj. **spitefully** adv.

spitz (spits) n. A small dog with a tail which curls over its back.

splash (splash) v. To spatter a liquid; to wet or soil with liquid; to make a splash. **splash** n. **splashy** adj.

splash-down (splash´doun´) n. The landing of a missile or spacecraft in the ocean.

spleen (splēn) n. Anat. A highly vascular, flattened organ which filters and stores blood, located below the diaphragm.

splen-did (splen´did) adj. Illustrious; magnificent.

splice (splīs) v. To join together by wearing, overlapping, and binding the ends.

splint (splint) n. A device used to hold a fractured or injured limb in the proper position for healing. **splint** v.

splotch (sploch) n. A discolored and irregularly shaped spot.

splutter (splut´ėr) v. To make a slight, short spitting sound. **splutter** n.

spoil (spoil) v. To destroy the value, quality, or usefulness; to overindulge as to harm the character. **spoils** n.

spoke (spōk) n. One of the rods that serve to connect and support the rim of a wheel. v. Past tense of speak.

spokes-man (spōks´man) n. One who speaks on behalf of another.

sponge (spunj) n. Any of a number of marine creatures with a soft, porous skeleton which soaks up liquid. v. To clean with a sponge. **spongy** adj.

spon-sor (spon´sėr) n. A person who is responsible for a debt or duty of another; a business that finances a television or radio program that in turn advertises its product. **-ship** n.

spon-ta-ne-ous (spon tā´nē us) adj. Done from one's own impulse without apparent external cause. **spontaneity** n. **spontaneously** adv.

spoof (spöf) n. A deception; nonsense.

spook (spök) n., Slang A ghost. v. To scare or frighten. **spooky** adj.

spool (spöl) n. A small cylinder for holding thread, tape or wire.

spoon (spön) n. An eating or cooking utensil; a shiny metallic fishing lure.

Slang To make love, as by kissing.

spo-rad-ic (spō rad´lk) *adj.* Occurring occasionally or at irregular intervals.

spore (spōr) *n., Bot.* The reproductive single-celled structure produced by nonflowering plants; any cell capable of developing into a new organism, seed, or germ.

sport (spōrt) *n.* An interesting diversion; a particular game or physical activity with set rules; a person who leads a fast life. **sport** *adj.* Relating or pertaining to sports.

sport-ing (spōr´ting) *adj.* Of or relating to risk taking or gambling; displaying sportsmanship.

sports-man-ship (spōrts´man ship´) *n.* Fair play; the ability to win or lose graciously.

spot (spot) *n.* A small area that differs in size, portion, or color; a dangerous or difficult situation. **spot** *v.*

spot-light (spot´lit´) *n.* A powerful light thrown directly at one area.

spouse (spous) *n.* One's husband or wife; a marriage partner.

spout (spout) *v.* To pour out forcibly, as under pressure; to cause to shoot forth. *Slang* To orate pompously.

sprain (sprān) *n.* A wrenching or twisting of a muscle or joint.

sprawl (sprol) *v.* To sit or lie in an ungraceful manner; to develop haphazardly. **sprawl** *n.* **sprawler** *n.*

spray (sprā) *n.* A liquid dispersed in a fine mist or droplets. *v.* To disperse or send forth in a spray. **sprayer** *n.*

spread (spred) *v.* To unfold or open fully; to apply or distribute over an area; to force apart; to extend.

spreadsheet *n.* In *computer science*, a document with data, arranged in rows and columns, that can be adjusted for the entry of additional data and manipulated for reporting.

spree (sprē) *n.* An excessive indulgence in an activity; a binge.

spright-ly (sprīt´lē) *adj.* Vivacious, lively. **sprightliness** *n.*

Spring-field *n.* The capital of the state of Illinois.

sprin-kle (spring´kl) *v.* To scatter in small particles or drops; to rain in small drops. **sprinkle** *n.*

sprint (sprint) *n.* A short, fast race.

sprock-et (sprok´it) *n, Mech.* A toothlike projection from the rim of a wheel.

spruce (sprös) *n.* An evergreen tree with needle-like foliage, cones, and soft wood.

spry (sprī) *adj.* Quick; brisk; energetic.

spud (spud) *n., Slang* A potato.

spur (sper) *n.* A sharp, projecting device worn on a riders boot, used to nudge a horse. *v.* To urge on.

sput-nik (spet´nik) *n.* An unmanned Soviet earth satellite.

sput-ter (sput´ér) *v.* To throw off small particles in short bursts; to speak in an agitated manner.

spu-tum (spū´tum) *n. pl.* -ta Saliva or mucus that is expectorated.

spy (spī) *n., pl.* **spies** A secret agent who obtains information; one who watches other people secretly.

squab *n.* A type of fledgling bird.

squab-ble (skwob´l) *v.* To engage in a petty argument. **squabble** *n.*

squad (skwod) *n.* A small group organized to perform a specific job.

squad car *n.* A type of police car.

squad-ron (skwod´ron) *n.* A naval unit that has two or more divisions.

squa-lene *n.* An acyclic hydrocarbon that is widely distributed in nature.

squal-id (skwol´id) *adj.* Marked by degradation from poverty or neglect.

squall (skwol) *v.* To cry out.

squa-lor *n.* The state of being squalid.

squa-ma-tion *n.* A state of being scaly or having an arrangement of scales.

squa-mo-sal)skwa mō´sal) *adj.* Pertaining to the membrane bone of the skull.

squa-mous (skwā´mus) *n.* To be consisting of scales. **squamously** *adv.*

squamous cell *n.* A type of cell which is derived from squamous epithelium.

squan-der (skwon´dér) *v.* To spend extra vagrantly or wastefully.

square (skwâr) *n.* A parallelogram with four equal sides; an implement having a T or L shape used to measure right angles. *v. Math.* To multiply a number by itself. *Slang* An unsophisticated person.

square deal *n.* A fair trade.

square knot *n.* A kind of knot that is comprised of two reverse half-knots.

square root *n.* A number which when multiplied by itself gives the given number.

squat (skwot) *v.* To sit on the heels; to crouch; to settle on a piece of land in order to obtain legal title. **-ter** *n.*

squaw (skwo) *n.* An American Indian woman.

squawk (skwok) *v.* To protest something in a loud manner.

squeak (skwēk) *v.* To utter a sharp, penetrating sound. **squeak** *n.* -y *adj.*

squeal (skwēl) *v.* To produce or to make a shrill cry. **squealer** *n.*

squea-mish (skwē´mish) *adj.* Easily shocked or nauseated. -ly *adv.*

squea-mish-ness *n.* State of being squeamish.

squee-gee (skwē´jē) *n.* A tool having a stout rubber blade across a wooden handle, used to wash windows.

squeeze (skwēz) *v.* To press together; to extract by using pressure; to hug.

squeg v. To oscillate in a manner which is irregular.

squelch (skwelch) n. The process or act of suppressing. **squelchy** adv.

squib (skwib) n. A firecracker that does not explode.

squid (skwid) n. A type of 10-armed cephalopod that has a tapered body.

squig-gle n. A short wavy line or twist.

squil-la (skwil´a) n. A type of stomatopod crustacean that digs into mud.

squinch v. To make something more compact.

squint (skwint) v. To view something through partly closed eyes; to close the eyes in this manner. **squint** n.

squint–eyed adj. To have eyes that squint.

squire (skwi´ẽr) n. An old-fashioned title for a rural justice of the peace, lawyer, or judge; a man who escorts a woman; a young man who ranks just below a knight.

squire-ar-chy (skwiẽr´är kē) n. The gentry.

squirm (skerm) n. To twist the body in a wiggling motion. **squirm** v.

squir-rel (skwer´el) n. A rodent with gray or brown fur, having a long bushy tail and dark eyes. **squirrel** v.

squir-rel cage n. A type of cage that is used for small animals and has a rotatable cylinder for exercising.

squir-rel-ly (squir rel y) adj. To be odd.

squirt (skwert) v. To eject in a thin stream or jet; to wet with a squirt. n. The act of squirting.

squirting cucumber n. A type of plant of the Mediterranean that belongs to the gourd family and will burst to eject its seeds when it is ripe.

squish-y adj. To be soft and damp.

sta-bi-lize (stā´bi liz´) v. To make firm; to keep from changing. **stabilization** n. **stabilizer** n.

sta-ble (stā´bl) n. A building for lodging and feeding horses or other farm animals. adj. Standing firm and resisting change.

stac-ca-to (sta kä´tō) adj. Music Marked by sharp emphasis.

stack (stak) n. A large pile of straw or hay; any systematic heap or pile; a chimney. **stack** v. To fix cards so as to cheat.

sta-di-um (stā´dē um) n., pl. **stadia** A large structure for holding athletic events or other large gatherings.

staff (staf) n. pl. **staffs** or **staves** A pole or rod used for a specific purpose; the people employed to assist in the day-to-day affairs of running a business, organization, or government. Mil. A group of people on an executive or advisory board. Music The horizontal lines on which notes are written. **staff** v.

stag-nant (stag´nant) adj. Not flowing; standing still; foul from not moving; inactive. **stagnate** v.

stair (stâr) n. A step or a series of steps.

staircase (stâr´kãs´) n. A series or a flight of steps that connect one level to another.

stake (stāk) n. A bet placed on a game of chance; a sharpened piece of wood for driving into the ground. **stake** v.

stale (stāl) adj. Having lost freshness; deteriorated; lacking in interest; dull; inactive.

stale-mate (stāl´māt´) n. A position in chess when a player cannot move without placing his king in check.

stalk (stok) n. Main axis of a plant. v. To approach in a stealthy manner.

stall (stol) n. An enclosure in a barn, used as a place to feed and confine animals; a sudden loss of power in an engine; a booth used to display and sell. v. To try to put off doing something; to delay.

stal-lion (stal´yan) n. An uncastrated, fully grown male horse.

sta-men (stā´men) n. pl. **stamens** Bot. The pollen-producing organs of a flower.

stam-i-na (stam´i na) n. Physical or moral endurance.

stam-mer (stam´ẽr) v. To make involuntary halts or repetitions of a sound or syllable while speaking. .

stamp (stamp) v. To put the foot down with force; to imprint or impress with a die, mark, or design. n. The act of stamping; the impression or pattern made by a stamp; a postage stamp.

stam-pede (stam pēd´) n. A sudden rush of panic, as of a herd of horses or cattle. v. To cause a stampede.

stance (stans) n. The posture or position of a standing person or animal.

stand (stand) v. To be placed in or maintain an erect or upright position; to take an upright position; to remain unchanged; to maintain a conviction; to resist. n. The act of standing; a device on which something rests; a small booth for selling or displaying items.

stand-ard (stan´dẽrd) n. A model which stands for or is accepted as a basis for comparison. **standard** adj.

stand-ing (stan´ding) n. A status, reputation, or achievement; a measure of esteem. adj. Unchanging; stationary; not moving.

sta-ple (stā´pl) n. A principle commodity grown in an area; a major element; a metal fastener designed to hold materials such as cloth or paper.

star (stär) n., Astron. A self-luminous body that is a source of light; any of the celestial bodies that can be seen in the night sky; a symbol having five or six points resembling a star.

star-board (stär′bĕrd) n. & adj. & adv. The right side of a ship or boat.

starch (stärch) n. Nutrient carbohydrates that are found in foods such as rice and potatoes. v. To stiffen clothing by using starch. **starchiness** n. **starchy** adj.

stare (stâr) v. To look with an intent, direct gaze. **stare** n. **starer** n.

stark (stärk) adj. Bare; total; complete; forbidding in appearance. **starkly** adv.

star-ling (stär′ling) n. A common black or brown bird.

star-tle (stär′tl) v. To cause a sudden surprise; to shock. **startle** n.

starve (stärv) v. To suffer or die from not having food; to suffer from the need of food, love, or other necessities.

state (stāt) n. A situation, mode, or condition of something; a nation; the governing power or authority of; one of the subdivisions or areas of a federal government, as the United States. v. To make known verbally.

stat-ic (stat′ik) adj. Not moving. n. A random noise heard on a radio.

sta-tion (stā′shan) n. The place where someone or something is directed to stand; a scheduled stopping place; the place from which radio and television programs are broadcast.

sta-tion-ar-y (stā′sha ner′ē) adj. Not movable; unchanging.

sta-tion-er-y (stā′sha ner′ē) n. Writing paper and envelopes.

sta-tis-tic (sta tis′tik) n. An estimate using an average or mean on the basis of a sample taken; numerical data.

stat-ue (stach′ō) n. A form sculpted from wood, clay, metal, or stone.

stave (stāv) n A narrow piece of wood used in forming part of a container, as a barrel. **stave** v.

stay (stā) v. To remain; to pause; to maintain a position; to halt or stop; to postpone or delay an execution. n. A short visit.

stead (sted) n. The position, place, or job of another.

stead-fast (sted′fast′) adj. Not changing or moving; firm in purpose; true; loyal. **steadfastly** adv. **-ness** n.

stead-y (sted′ē) adj. Firmly placed, fixed or set; not changing; constant; uninterrupted.

steal (stēl) v. To take another person's property; to move in a sly way; to move secretly. *Baseball* To take a base without the ball being hit. *Slang* A real bargain.

steam (stēm) n. Water in the form of vapor; the visible mist into which vapor is condensed by cooling. **steam** v. **steamy** adj.

steel (stēl) n. A various mixture of iron, carbon, and other elements; a strong

material that can be shaped when heated. **steely** adj.

stem (stem) n. The main stalk of a plant; the main part of a word to which prefixes and suffixes may be added. v. To stop or retard the progress or flow of something.

sten-cil (sten′sil) n. A form cut into a sheet of material, as cardboard or plastic, so that when ink or paint is applied, the pattern will reproduce on paper or another material.

ste-nog-ra-phy (ste nog′ra fē) n. The skill of writing in shorthand. **stenographer** n. **stenographic** adj.

step (step) n. A single completed movement in walking, dancing, or running; the distance of such a step; the part of a ladder that one places the feet on in ascending or descending. *Music* A musical scale; a degree.

ste-re-o (ster′ē ō′) n. A record player with stereophonic sound. **stereo** adj.

ste-reo-phon-ic (ster′ē o fon′ik) adj. Relating to or giving a three-dimensional effect of auditory perspective.

ster-e-o-type (ster′ē o tīp′) n. A conventional opinion or belief; a metal printing plate.

ster-ile (ster′il) adj. Free from microorganisms; sanitary; unable to reproduce.

ster-ling (ster′ling) n. An alloy of 92.5% silver and another metal, as copper.

stern (stern) adj. Inflexible; harsh. n. The rear of a boat or ship. **-ly** adv.

ster-num (ster′num) n. pl -nums or -na A long, flat bone located in the chest wall, connecting the collarbones and the cartilage of the first seven pairs of ribs. **sternal** adj.

steth-o-scope (steth′o skōp′) n. An instrument used to listen to the internal sounds of the body.

stew (stō) v. To cook slowly; to simmer; to boil. n. A dish of stewed meat and potatoes. *Slang* To worry.

stew-ard (stō′ĕrd) n. A manager of another's financial affairs; a person responsible for maintaining household affairs; a male attendant on an airplane or ship. **-ess** n. **-ship** n.

stick (stik) n. A slender piece of wood; a club, rod, or walking stick. v. To put a hole in something; to pierce; to cling; to become jammed.

stiff (stif) adj. Not flexible; not easily bent; awkward. n. *Slang* A dead body.

sti-fle (stī′fl) v. To suffocate; to cut off; to suppress; to keep back.

stig-ma (stig′ma) n. pl. -mata or -mas A mark of disgrace. **stigmata** The part of a flower where pollen is deposited at pollination; wounds resembling the crucifixion scars of Jesus Christ.

still (stil) adj. Silent; calm; peaceful; until

now or another time. *adv.* Nevertheless.
still *v.* **stillness** *n.*

still-birth (stil´berth´) *n.* The birth of a dead fetus.

stilt (stilt) *n.* One of a pair of long poles with foot supports, used for walking.

stim-u-lant (stim´ū lant) *n.* An agent which arouses or accelerates physiological activity.

stim-u-late (stim´ū lāt´) *v.* To excite to a heightened activity; to quicken. **stimulation** *n.*

stim-u-lus (stim´ū lus) *n.* Something that excites to action.

sting (sting) *v.* To prick with something sharp; to feel or cause to feel a smarting pain; to cause or feel sharp pain, either physical or mental. *n.* The act of stinging; the injury or pain caused by the stinger of a bee or wasp. **-er** *n.*

stin-gy (stin´jē) *adj.* Not giving freely; cheap.

stink (stingk) *v.* To give off a foul odor that is highly offensive.

stip-u-late (stip´ū lāt´) *v.* To settle something by agreement; to establish conditions of agreement. **-tion** *n.*

stir (ster) *v.* To mix a substance by moving round and round; to agitate or provoke. **stirrer** *n.*

stitch (stich) *n.* In sewing, a single loop formed by a needle and thread; the section of loop of thread, as in sewing. *v.* To join with a stitch.

stock (stok) *n.* A supply of goods kept on hand; animals living on a farm; a share in ownership, as in a company or corporation; the raw material or the base used to make something. *v.* To provide with stock. *adj.* Regular, common, or typical.

stock-ade (sto kād´) *n.* Barrier placed around a fort for protection.

stock-ing (stok´ing) *n.* A knitted covering for the foot.

stock-y (stok´ē) *adj.* Short and plump; built sturdily.

stole (stōl) *n.* A long, narrow scarf that is usually worn around a woman's shoulders, as a mink stole. *v.* Past tense of steal.

stom-ach (stum´ak) *n.*, *Anat.* The organ into which food passes from the esophagus; one of the primary organs of digestion. *v.* To tolerate or stand; to put up with.

stone (stōn) *n.* Rock; compacted earth or mineral matter; a gem or jewel; the seed or pit of certain fruits. *Med.* A hard rock that forms inside a body organ, as the kidney. **stoned** To be overcome by an excessive amount of alcohol or drugs.

stood *v.* Past tense of stand.

stool (stōl) *n.* A seat without a backrest and arms; a small version of this on

which to rest the feet; a bowel movement.

stoop (stöp) *v.* To bend the body forward and downward from the waist. *n.* A porch attached to a house.

stop (stop) *v.* To cease; to halt; to refrain from moving, operating, or acting; to block or obstruct; to visit for a short time. *v.* A location where a bus, train, or other means of mass transportation may pick up or drop off passengers.

stor-age (stōr´ij) *n.* The act of storing or keeping; in *computer science*, the part of a computer in which all information is held; the memory.

store (stōr) *n.* A business offering merchandise for sale; a supply to be used in the future. *v.* To supply; to accumulate.

stork (stork) *n.* A large, wading bird.

storm (storm) *n.* An atmospheric condition marked by strong winds with rain, sleet, hail, or snow. **storm** *v.* To attack with a powerful force.

sto-ry (stōr´ē) *n. pl.* **-ies** A narration of a fictional tale or account; a lie; a level in a building or house.

stout (stout) *adj.* Strong; sturdy; substantial; courageous. **stoutly** *adv.*

stove (stōv) *n.* An apparatus in which oil, electricity, gas, or other fuels are consumed to provide the heat for cooking.

stow (stō) *v.* To pack or put away.

strad-dle (strad´l) *v.* To sit or stand with the legs on either side of something; to favor both sides of an issue.

straight (strāt) *adj.* Being without bends, angles, or curves; upright; erect; honest; undiluted; unmodified; heterosexual. *n.* In poker, a numerical sequence of five cards not of the same suit. **straightly** *adv.* **straightness** *n.*

strain (strān) *v.* To stretch beyond a proper limit; to injure by putting forth too much effort; to pass through a sieve to separate small particles from larger ones.

strait (strāt) *n.* A narrow passageway which connects two bodies of water.

strand (strand) *n.* Land that borders a body of water; one of the threads that are twisted together to form a rope. *v.* To leave in a difficult situation.

strange (strānj) *adj.* Not previously known or experienced; odd; peculiar; inexperienced; alien. **strangely** *adv.*

stran-ger (strān´jèr) *n.* A person unknown; unrecognized; a newcomer; an alien.

stran-gle (strang´gl) *v.* To kill by choking. **strangler** *n.*

strap (strap) *n.* A long, narrow strip of leather or other material used to secure objects. **strap** *v.*

strat-e-gy (strat´i jē) *n. pl.* **-ies** The

skillful planning and managing of an activity. **strategic** *adj.* **strategist** *n.*

stra-tum (strā´tum) *n. pl.* **-ta** *or* **-tums** A horizontal layer, as of the earth's crust.

straw (stro) *n.* A stalk of dried and threshed grain; a slender, plastic or paper straw used to suck up a liquid. **straw** *adj.* Yellowish brown color.

straw-ber-ry (stro´ber´ē) *n.* A low plant with white flowers and red fruit; the fruit of this plant.

stray (strā) *v.* To roam or wander. *n.* A lost or wandering animal or person. *adj.* Lost. **strayer** *n.*

streak (strēk) *n.* A narrow stripe or line that is different from the surrounding area; a run of good or bad luck. **streak** *v.* To rush or move rapidly; to make a streak.

stream (strēm) *n.* A small body of flowing water; a steady or continuous succession or procession. *v.* To flow in or like a stream.

street (strēt) *n.* A public thoroughfare in a town or city with buildings on either or both sides.

strength (strengkth) *n.* The quality of being strong; power in general; degree of concentration or potency.

strength-en (strengk´then) *v.* To grow strong or stronger.

stren-u-ous (stren´ū us) *adj.* Necessitating or characterized by vigorous effort or exertion. **strenuously** *adv.*

stress (stres) *n.* Special significance; an emphasis given to a specific syllable, word, action, or plan; strain or pressure.

stretch (strech) *v.* To extend fully; to extend forcibly beyond proper limits; to prolong. *n.* The state or act of stretching. **stretchable** *adj.* **-y** *adj.*

strew (strō) *v.* To scatter about.

strick-en (strik´en) *adj.* Suffering, as from an emotion, illness, or trouble.

strict (strikt) *adj.* Holding to or observing rules exactly; imposing absolute standards. **-ly** *adv.* **-ness** *n.*

stride (strīd) *v.* To walk with a long, sweeping step. **stride** *n.*

strike *v.* To hit with the hand; to ignite, as with a match; to afflict suddenly with a disease; to discover; to conclude or make; to stop working as a protest against something or in favor of rules or demands presented to an employer.

string *n.* A strip of thin twine, wire, or catgut used on stringed musical instruments; a series of related acts, items, or events; in Computer Science, data arranged in an ascending or descending sequence according to a command within the data.

strin-gent (strin´jent) *adj.* Of or relating to strict requirements; marked by obstructions or scarcity.

strip *v.* To take off the outer layer or covering; to divest of rank; to remove one's clothes; to rob; to perform a striptease. **strip** *n.* **stripper** *n.*

stripe *n.* A streak, band, or strip of a different color or texture; a piece of material or cloth worn on the sleeve of a uniform to indicate rank, award, or service..

stroke (strōk) *n.* The movement of striking; a sudden action with a powerful effect; a single movement made by the hand or as if by a brush or pen. *Path.* A sudden interruption of the blood supply to the brain. *v.* To pass the hand over gently.

stroll (strōl) *v.* To walk in a slow, leisurely way. **stroll** *n.*

strong (strong) *adj.* Exerting or possessing physical power; durable; difficult to break. **strongly** *adv.*

stron-ti-um (stron´shē um) *n.* A metallic element symbolized by Sr.

struc-ture (struk´cher) *n.* A construction made up of a combination of related parts. **structure** *v.* **-ral** *adj.*

strug-gle (strug´l) *v.* To put forth effort against opposition. **struggle** *n.* **struggler** *n.* **strugglingly** *adv.*

strych-nine (strik´nin) *n.* An extremely poisonous alkaloid derived from certain plants, used to kill rodents and as a neural stimulant.

stub (stub) *n.* A short, projecting part; the short end of something after the main part has been removed or used. **stub** *v.*

stub-born (stub´ern) *adj.* Inflexible; difficult to control, handle, or manage. **stubbornness** *n.*

stuc-co (stuk´ō) *n. pl.* **-coes** *or* **-cos** Fine plaster used to coat exterior walls and to decorate interior walls.

stud (stud) *n.* An upright post, as in a building frame, to which sheets of wallboard or paneling are fastened; a small removable button used as an ornament; a male horse used for breeding. **stud** *v.*

stu-dent (stōd´ent) *n.* A person who studies at a school or college.

stu-di-o (stō´dē ō´) *n.* The place of work for an artist, photographer, or other creative person; a place for filming movies.

stud-y (stud´ē) *n. pl.* **-ies** The process of ap-plying the mind to acquire knowledge.

stum-ble (stum´bl) *v.* To trip and nearly fall over something; to come upon unexpectedly. **stumble** *n.*

stump (stump) *n.* The part of a tree which remains after the top is cut down. *v.* To puzzle or be puzzled; to walk heavily; to campaign.

stun (stun) *v.* To render senseless by or

as if by a blow.

stu-pen-dous (stŏo pen´dŭs) *adj.*
Astonishing or highly impressive.
stupendousness *n.* **stupendously** *adv.*

stu-pid (stō´pid) *adj.* Slow in apprehension or understanding. **-ity** *n.*

stur-dy (ster´dē) *adj.* Possessing robust strength and health. **sturdily** *adv.*
sturdiness *n.*

stur-geon (ster´jĕn) *n.* A large freshwater fish highly valued as a source of caviar.

stut-ter (stŭt´ĕr) *v.* To speak with involuntary repetitions of sound.

sty (stī) *n.,* *pl.* **sties** An inflammation of the edge of an eyelid.

style (stīl) *n.* A method, manner, or way of performing, speaking, or clothing; elegance, grace, or excellence in performance or appearance.

suave (swäv) *adj.* Ingratiating; smoothly pleasant in manner.

sub- (sub) *prefix.* Beneath, under, or below.

sub (sub) *abbr.* Substitute.

sub-con-scious (sub kon´shus) *adj.*
Below the level of consciousness.

sub-due (sub dō´) *v.* To bring under control by influence, training, persuasion or force.

sub-ject (sub´jikt) *n.* The word in a sentence that defines a person or thing; a person who is under the control of another's governing power. *v.* To subdue or gain control over.

sub-jec-tive (sub jek´tiv) *adj.* Taking place within, relating to or proceeding from an individual's emotions or mind.
-ly *adv.* **-tivity** *n.*

sub-ma-rine (sub´ma rēn´) *adj.*
Operating or existing beneath the surface of the sea. *n.* A ship that travels underwater. **submariner** *n.*

sub-merge (sub merj´) *v.* To plunge under the surface of the water.
submergible *adj.* **submergence** *n.*

sub-mit (sub mit´) *v.* To give in to or surrender to another's authority.
submission *n.* **submittal** *n.*.

sub-or-di-nate (su bor´di nit) *adj.* Being of lower class or rank; minor; inferior.
subordinate *v.* **-nation** *n.*

sub-poe-na (su pē´na) *n.* A legal document requiring a person to appear in court for testimony.

sub-se-quent (sub´se kwent) *adj.*
Following in time, place, or order.
subsequently *adv.*

sub-side (sub sīd´) *v.* To move to a lower level; to become less intense.

sub-sid-i-ar-y (sub sid´ē er´ē) *adj.*
Providing assistance in a lesser capacity. **subsidiary** *n.*

sub-si-dy (sub´si dē) *n.,* *pl.* **-dies**
Financial aid granted directly to a private commercial enterprise from the government.

sub-sist (sub sist´) *v.* To have continued existence.

sub-soil (sub´soil´) *n.* The layer of earth that is below the surface soil.

sub-stance (sub´stans) *n.* Matter or material of which anything consists.

sub-sti-tute (sub´sti tōt´) *n.* Something or someone that takes the place of another. **substitute** *v.*

sub-ten-ant (sub ten´ant) *n.* A person who rents property from a tenant.

sub-ter-ra-ne-an (sub´te rā´nē an) *adj.*
Located or occurring underground.

sub-ti-tle (sub´tīt´l) *n.* An explanatory title, as in a document, book, etc.; a written translation that appears on a foreign motion picture screen.

sub-tract (sub trakt´) *v.* To deduct or take away from.

sub-trop-i-cal (sub trop´i kal) *adj.*
Pertaining to regions adjacent to the tropics.

sub-urb (sub´erb) *n.* A residential community near a large city.

sub-way *n.* An underground electric-powered train, usually used as a means of transportation.

suc-ceed (suk sēd´) *v.* To accomplish what is attempted; to come next to or follow.

suc-cess (suk ses´) *n.* Achievement of something intended or desired; attaining wealth, fame, or prosperity.

suc-ces-sion (suk sesh´an) *n.* The act or process of following in order; sequence; series; the order, sequence, or act by which something changes hands.

suc-ces-sive (suk ses´iv) *adj.* Following in order or sequence. **successively** *adv.*
successiveness *n.*

suc-cu-lent (suk´u lent) *adj.* Juicy; full of juice or sap. **succulence** *n.* .

such (such) *adj.* Of this or that kind or thing; a great degree or extent in quality. *pron.* Of a particular degree or kind; a person or thing of such.

suck (suk) *v.* To pull liquid into the mouth by means of a vacuum created by the lips and tongue. **suck** *n.*

su-crose (sō´krōs) *n.* Sugar obtained from the sugar beet or sugar cane.

suc-tion (suk´shan) *n.* The process or act of sucking.

sud-den (sud´en) *adj.* Happening very quickly; most often without warning or notice; sharp; abrupt; marked by haste. **suddenly** *adv.* **suddenness** *n.*

suds *n.* Bubbles or soapy water. *Slang* Beer.

suede (swād) *n.* Leather with a soft, napped finish.

su-et (sō´it) *n.* The hard fat around the kidney and loins of sheep.

suf-fer (suf´ĕr) *v.* To feel pain or distress; to sustain injury or damage.

suf-fi-cient (su fish´ent) *adj.* As much

as is needed or desired. **-ciency** *n.*

suf-fix (suf´iks) *n.* A form affixed to the end of a word.

suf-fo-cate (suf´o kāt´) *v.* To kill by depriving something or someone of oxygen. **suffocation** *n.*

sugar (sheg´ér) *n.* A sweet, water soluble, crystalline carbohydrate.

sug-gest (sug jest´) *v.* To give an idea for action or consideration; to imply; hint or intimate.

sug-ges-tion (sug jes´chən) *n.* The act of suggesting; a slight insinuation; hint.

su-i-cide (sō´i sīd´) *n.* The act of taking one's own life. **suicidal** *adj.*

suit (sōt) *n.* A set of articles, as clothing, to be worn together; in cards, one of the four sets: spades, hearts, clubs, and diamonds, that make up a deck. **suit** *v.* To meet the requirements of; to satisfy.

sul-fur *also* **sul-phur** (sul´fér) *n.* A light, yellow, nonmetallic element occurring naturally in both combined and free form, used in matches, gunpowder and medicines.

sulk (sulk) *v.* To be sullenly silent.

sul-len (sul´en) *adj.* Ill-humored, melancholy; gloomy; depressing.

sul-try (sul´trē) *adj.* Hot and humid; muggy.

sum (sum) *n.* The result obtained by adding; the whole amount, quantity, or number; summary.

sum-ma-ry (sum´a rē) *n. pl.* **summaries.** Giving the sum or substance. *adj.* A statement covering the most important points or topics. **summarily** *adv.*

sum-mer (sum´ér) *n.* The warmest of the four seasons, following spring and coming before autumn. **summery** *adj.*

sum-mit (sum´it) *n.* The top and highest point, degree, or level.

sum-mons (sum´onz) *n., pl.* **summonses** An order or command to perform a duty; a notice to appear at a certain place and time.

sun (sun) *n.* The star around which other planets of the solar system orbit; the energy, visible light, and heat, that is emitted by the sun.

Sun-day *n.* The Christian holy day; the first day of the week.

sun-down (sun´doun´) *n.* The time of day the sun sets.

sunk-en (sung´ken) *adj.* Submerged or deeply depressed in.

su-per (sō´pér) *adj.* Exceeding a norm; in excessive intensity or degree; surpassing most others; superior in rank, status or position; excellent. *n., Slang* Superintendent of a building.

su-perb (se perb´) *adj.* Of first-rate quality. **superbly** *adv.*

su-per-fi-cial (sō´pér fish´al) *adj.* Pertaining to a surface; concerned only with what is not real.

su-pe-ri-or (su pēr´e ér) *adj.* Of higher rank, grade, or dignity. *n.* A person who surpasses another in rank or excellence. **superiority** *n.* **superiorly** *adv.*

su-per-la-tive (su per´la tiv) *adj.* Of the highest degree of excellence; pertaining to the degree of comparison of an adverb or adjective that shows extreme extent or level. **superlatively** adv.

su-per-nat-u-ral *adj.* An order of existence beyond the natural world; pertaining to a divine power.

su-per-sede (sō´pér sēd´) *v.* To take the place of; to set aside.

su-per-son-ic (sō´pér son´ik) *adj., Aero.* Characterized by a speed greater than that of sound.

su-per-sti-tion (sō´pér stish´ən) *n.* A belief held, despite evidence that it is irrational; a belief, resulting from faith in magic or chance. **superstitious** *adj.*

su-per-vise (sō´pér vīz´) *v.* To have charge in directing the work of other people. **supervision** *n.* **supervisor** *n.*

sup-per (sup´ér) *n.* The last or evening meal of the day.

sup-ple-ment (sup´le ment) *n.* A part that compensates for what is lacking. **supplementary** *adj.* **-al** *adj.*

sup-ply (su plī´) *v., n. pl.* **-plies** To provide with what is needed; to make available. **supplier** *n.*

sup-port (su pōrt´) *v.* To bear or hold the weight of; to tolerate; to give assistance or approval. *n.* The act of supporting. **supportive** *adj.*

sup-pose (su pōz´) *v.* To think or assume as true; to consider probable. **supposed** *adj.* **supposedly** *adv.*

sup-pos-i-to-ry (su poz´i tōr´ē) *n. pl.*-ries A medication, in solid form, that melts when inserted into the body cavity, as the rectum.

su-preme (su prēm´) *adj.* Of the highest authority, rank, or power.

sur-charge (ser´chärj´) *n.* An extra fee added to the cost of something; to overcharge.

sure (sher) *adj.* Firm and sturdy; being impossible to doubt; inevitable; not liable to fail. **surer** *adj.* **surest** *adj.*

surge (serj) *v.* To increase suddenly. *n.* A large swell of water. In Computer Science, an increase in electrical current that may damage the computer or its memory.

sur-geon (ser´jon) *n.* A physician who practices surgery.

sur-ger-y (ser´je rē) *n. pl.* -ies. The branch of medicine in which physical deformity or disease is treated by an operative procedure.

surge suppresser In *computer science,* a device that protects the computer and peripherals from power surges.

sur-mise (sèr mīz´) *v.* To guess; to conjecture.

sur-mount (sèr mount´) *v.* To overcome; to be at the top.

sur-name (ser´nām´) *n.* A person's family's last name.

sur-pass (sèr pas´) *v.* To go beyond the limits of; to be greater than.

sur-plus (ser´plus) *n.* An amount beyond what is needed.

sur-prise (sèr prīz´) *v.* To come upon unexpectedly or suddenly; to cause to feel astonished. **surprise** *n.* **sur-priser** *n.* **surprisingly** *adv.*

sur-ren-der (su ren´dèr) *v.* To give up or yield possession or power. *n.* The act of surrendering.

sur-rey (ser´ē) *n. pl.* **-reys.** A four-wheeled, horse-driven carriage.

sur-ro-gate (ser´o gāt´) *n.* A person who puts himself in the place of another.

sur-round (su round´) *v.* To extend around all edges of something; to enclose or shut in.

sur-veil-lance (sèr vā´lans) *n.* Close observation kept over one, especially as a suspect.

sur-vey (sèr vā´) *v., n. pl.* **-veys.** To examine in detail; to determine area, boundaries, or position and elevation of a section of the earth's surface.

sur-vive (sèr vīv´) *v.* To continue to exist; to outlast; to outlive. **-al** *n.*

su-shi *n.* A Japanese dish of thin slices of fresh, raw fish.

sus-pect (su spekt´) *v.* To have doubt or dis-trust; to have a suspicion or inkling of someone or something. **suspect** *n.*

sus-pend (su spend´) *v.* To bar from a privilege for a certain time, as a means of punishment; to hang so as to allow free movement.

sus-pense (su spens´) *n.* The feeling of being insecure or undecided, resulting from uncertainty.

sus-pi-cion (su spish´an) *n.* The instance of suspecting something wrong without proof. **suspicious** *adj.* **-ciously** *adv.*

sus-tain (su stān´) *v.* To hold up and keep from falling; to suffer or undergo an injury.

su-ture (sō´chèr) *n.* The stitching together or joining the edges of an incision or cut. **suture** *v.*

swab (swäb) *n.* A small stick with a wad of cotton on both ends, used to apply medication. *Slang* A sailor.

swad-dle (swäd´l) *v.* To wrap closely, using a long strip of flannel or linen.

swal-low (swäl´ō) *v.* To cause food to pass from the mouth to the stomach; to retract or take back, as words spoken. *n.* The act of swallowing.

swap (swäp) *v.* To trade something for something in return. **swap** *n.*

swarm (sworm) *n.* A large number of insects, as bees; a large group of persons or things. **swarmer** *n.*

swat (swät) *v.* To hit something with a sharp blow.

swatch (swäch) *n.* A strip of cloth cut off a larger piece, used as a sample.

swath (swoth) *n.* The area or width of grass cut by a machine. **swathe** *v.*

sway (swā) *v.* To move or swing from right to left or side to side; to exert influence or control. *n.* Dominating power.

swear (swâr) *v.* To make an affirmation under oath. **swearer** *n.*

sweat (swet) *v.* To excrete a salty moisture from the pores of the skin. *Informal* To work hard; to cause to sweat. *Slang* Being impatient; having anxiety.

sweat gland *n., Anat.* One of the tubular glands that secrete sweat externally through pores.

sweep (swēp) *v.* To touch lightly; to remove or clear away with a brush or broom; to move with an even action.

sweet (swēt) *adj.* Having a sugary, agreeable flavor; arousing pleasant emotions; a beloved or dear person.

swell (swel) *v.* To increase in size or bulk; to grow in volume. *n.* The process, effect, or act of swelling; a continuous wave that is long and billowing. *Informal* Fine; smart.

swel-ter (swel´tèr) *v.* To suffer from extreme heat.

swerve (swerv) *v.* To turn aside from the regular course.

swift (swift) *adj.* Moving with great speed; accomplished or occurring quickly. **swiftly** *adv.* **swiftness** *n.*

swim (swim) *v.* To move oneself through water by moving parts of the body, as arms, head, and legs.

swin-dle (swin´dl) *v.* To cheat out of property or money; to practice fraud. **swindle** *n.* **swindler** *n.*

swine (swīn) *n. pl.* **swine** A hoofed mammal with a snout, related to pigs and hogs; a low, despicable person.

swing (swing) *v.* To move freely back and forth; to hang or to be suspended. *n.* The act of a swing; a seat that hangs from chains or ropes. *Music* Jazz played by a large band and developed by using simple harmonic patterns. **swinger** *n.*

swirl (swerl) *v.* To move with a whirling, rotating motion. **swirly** *adj.*

switch (swich) *n.* A small, thin, flexible stick, twig or rod. *Electr.* A device for opening or closing an electric circuit; to shift to another train track by using a switch; to exchange.

swiv-el (swiv´el) *n.* A coupling device, ring, or pivot that allows attached parts to move freely. **swivel** *v.*

sword (sōrd) *n*. A weapon with a long, pointed cutting blade.

syc-a-more (sik´*a* mōr´) *n*. A North American tree that is used widely for shade.

sy-cee *n*. The silver money which was once used in China.

sy-co-ni-um *n*. A type of fleshy fruit where the ovaries are borne in an enlarged receptacle.

sy-co-phan-cy *n*. The behavior of a sycophant.

sy-co-phant *n*. A self-seeking flatterer.

sy-co-phan-tic *adj*. Pertaining to a sycophant. **sycophantically** *adv*.

sy-co-sis *n*. An inflammatory disorder of the hair follicles.

syl-la-bar-y *n*. A listing of syllables.

syl-lab-ic *adj*. Pertaining to or denoting syllables.

syl-la-bic-i-ty *n*. The state of being a syllable.

syl-la-ble (sil´*a* bl) *n*., *Phonet*. A word or part of one that consists of a single vocal impulse, usually consisting of one or more vowels or consonants.

syl-la-bub *n*. A type of desert that is made by curdling milk with an acid such as wine.

syl-la-bus *n*. An outline of a course of study.

syl-lo-gism (sil´*o* jiz´*u*m) *n*. An argument with a major premise, a minor premise and a conclusion that is logically drawn from the premises. **syllogistic** *adj*.

syl-lo-gist *n*. A person who applies syllogistic reasoning.

sylph *n*. A slender woman who is very graceful. **sylphlike** *adj*.

sylph-id *n*. A diminutive sylph.

syl-van *adj*. To be living or located in the woods.

syl-va-nite *n*. A kind of mineral which will often occur in crystals.

sym-bi-ont *n*. An organism that is living in symbiosis.

sym-bi-o-sis *n*. A living together in close union of two dissimilar organisms.

sym-bol (sim´bol) *n*. Something that stands for or represents something else. **symbolic** *adj*. **symbolical** *adj*.

sym-bol-ism *n*. The practice of using symbols.

sym-bol-ist *n*. A person who is skilled in the interpretation of symbols.

sym-bol-iz-a-tion *n*. An instance of symbolizing.

sym-bol-ize *v*. To serve as a symbol of or for something.

sym-bol-o-gy *n*. The interpretation of a symbol or symbols.

sym-met-ri-cal *adj*. Involving symmetry. **symmetricalness** *n*.

sym-me-trize *v*. To make something symmetrical in form or size.

sym-me-try (sim´i trē) *n*. *pl*. -tries Balance in form, size, and position of parts that are on two sides of an axis.

sym-pa-thet-ic (sim´pa thet´ik) *adj*. Having or showing kindness or sympathy for others. **sympathetically** *adv*. **sympathize** *v*.

sympathetic nervous system *n*. Part of the body's nervous system which when stimulated will decrease muscle tone and constriction of the blood vessels and will depress secretions.

sympathetic vibration *n*. The vibration which is produced in a body by another body.

sym-pa-thin *n*. The substance which is produced by the sympathetic nerve endings in the body.

sym-pa-thize *v*. To respond to someone or something with sympathy.

sym-pa-tho-lyt-ic *adj*. To be tending to oppose physiological results of the sympathetic nervous activity.

sym-pa-tho-mi-met-ic *adj*. To be able to simulate the sympathetic nervous system in effect and action.

sym-pa-thy (sim´pa thē) *n*. *pl*. -thies Mutual understanding or affection during a time of sadness or loss.

sym-pat-ric (sim pa´trik) *adj*. To be happening or occurring in the same area.

symphonic poem *n*. An extended composition for a symphony orchestra in a freer form than a symphony.

sym-pho-ni-ous (sim fō´nē us) *adj*. To be agreeing such as in sound.

sym-pho-nist *n*. One who composes or writes symphonies.

sym-pho-ny (sim´fo nē) *n*., *pl*. -nies A large orchestra with wind, percussion and string sections. **-nic** *adj*.

sym-phy-se-al *adj*. Pertaining to or related to a symphysis.

sym-po-di-al *adj*. To be involving the formation of a main axis from a secondary axis. **sympodially** *adv*.

sym-po-si-arch *n*. The person who will preside over a symposium.

sym-po-si-um *n*. A gathering or meeting where several specialists will give short speeches on a topic or on subjects which are related.

symp-tom (simp´*tom*) *n*. A sign of change in a bodys functions or appearance.

symp-tom-at-ic *adj*. To be having the characteristics of a particular disease but arising from something else.

symp-tom-at-ol-ogy *n*. The part of medical science that deals with symptoms of a disease or diseases.

syn *abbr*. Synonymous; synonym.

syn-aes-the-sis *n*. The harmony of opposing impulses which are produced by a piece of art.

syn-a-gogue (sin´*a* gog´) *n*. A place for

Jewish worship and prayer.

syn-a-loe-pha (sin´a lē´fa) n. A reduction to one syllable of two vowels of syllables which are adjacent.

syn-apse (sin´aps) n. A point where a nervous impulse passes from one neuron to the next neuron.

syn-ar-thro-di-al adj. Pertaining to or related to a synarthrosis.

syn-ar-thro-sis (sin´är thrō´sis) n. A joining of bones that is immovable and is united by fibrous connective tissues.

syn-car-pous adj. To have the carpels of gynoecium to unite in a compound ovary.

syn-chro-mesh adj. To be designed for effecting synchronized gear shifting.

syn-chro-nism(sing´kro niz˝um)n. The state of being synchronous.

syn-chro-ni-za-tion (sing´kro ni zā´shan) n. A result of synchronizing.

syn-chro-nize (sing´kro nīz´) v. To take place at the same time.

syn-chro-nous adj. To be existing at precisely the same time.

syn-chro-ny n. A synchronistic treatment or occurrence.

syn-cli-nal adj. Inclined down from opposite directions then meeting.

syn-co-pate (sing´ko pāt´) v. To produce by a synscope. **syncopator** n.

syn-co-pated (sing´kopā´tid) adj. To be exhibiting syncopation.

syn-cret-ism n. A combination of different beliefs or practices.

syn-cy-ti-um n. The multinucleate mass made of protoplasm which is formed from the fusion or the joining of cells.

syn-det-ic adj. To be marked by a conjunctive. **syndetically** adv.

syn-dic n. A type of municipal magistrate in other countries.

syn-di-cate (sin´di kit) n. An organization set up to carry out business transactions; a company that sells materials for simultaneous publication at several of different locations.

syn-drome (sin´drōm) n. A set of concurrent symptoms that indicate or characterize a disorder or disease.

syn-e-col-o-gy n. A section or branch of ecology which deals with the development, structure, and distribution of ecological communities.

syn-eph-rine n. A type of crystalline sympathomimetic amine.

syn-er-gism n. Cooperative action of independent units that improves the total results. **synergistic** adj.

syn-er-gy n. Combined action.

syn-o-nym (sin´o nim) n. A word that means the same or nearly the same as another. **synonymous** adj.

syn-op-sis (si nop´sis) n. pl. -ses A shortened statement or narrative.

syn-os-to-sis n. The joining or the union of bones which are separate to form a single bone.

sy-no-vi-al (si nō´vē a) adj. Pertaining to or relating to synovia, a lubricating substance that resembles the white of a egg.

sy-no-vi-tis (sin˝ovī´tis) n. The inflammation or the swelling of a synovial membrane.

syn-tax (sin´taks) n. The way in which words are put together or arranged to form sentences and phrases. **syntactic** adj. **syntactical** adj.

syn-the-sis (sin´thi sis) n., pl. A production of a substance by the joining of chemical elements.

syn-the-size v. To produce or to make with synthesis.

syn-thet-ic adj. To be involving synthesis. **synthetically** adv.

syph-i-lis (sif´i lis) n. An infectious venereal disease transmittable by direct contact and usually progressing in severity.

syph-i-lol-o-gist n. One who specializes in the treatment and the diagnosis of syphilis.

syph-i-lol-o-gy n. Med. The study and treatment of the disease syphilis.

sy-ringe (si rinj´) n. A medical instrument used to inject or draw fluids from the body. **syringe** v.

sy-rin-go-my-el-ia n. A progressive chronic disease of the spinal cord associated with muscle atrophy, spasticity, and sensory disturbances.

syr-up (sir´up) n. A thick, sweet liquid, used as a topping for food.

sys-tal-tic (si stol´tik) adj. To be marked by regular dilatation and contraction.

sys-tem (sis´tem) n. A planned method of doing something; the human body or related parts of the body that perform vital functions; an orderly arrangement. **systematic** adj. **systematically** adv.

system backup n. In computer science, a reserved copy of all of the program and data files in a computer; a second set of hardware that can replace the primary hardware in the event of equipment failure.

system resources n. In computer science, all of the elements unique to a particular computer system, as peripheral devices, type of CPU, memory, etc.

system software n. In computer science, the programs that control the operation of the computer and its peripherals.

sys-to-le (sis´to lē) n. Physiol. The regular rhythmic contraction of the heart that pumps blood through the aorta and pulmonary artery.

sy-zy-gy n. A configuration of three celestial bodies in one gravitational system such as the moon, the sun, and earth when an eclipse is taking place.

T, t (tē) The twentieth letter of the English alphabet.

tab (tab) *n.* A strip, flap, or small loop that projects from something. *Slang* A bill or total, as for a meal. In computer science, a tabulator; a user-defined position on a text line to which the cursor can be advanced with a single key stroke; to move by activating the *tab* key.

tab-ard (tabĕrd) *n.* A type of sleeveless coat that is worn as a tunic by a knight over top the armor.

tab-by (tab´ē) *n.* A type of domestic cat that has a coat which is mottled and striped.

tab-er-na-cle (tab´ĕr nak´l) *n.* A portable shelter or structure used by the Jews during their journey out of Egypt; a place of worship.

ta-bes (tāb´bēz) *n.* The wasting that comes with or is accompanying a chronic disease.

tabes forsalis *n.* A type of syphilitic disorder that affects the nervous system and is marked with wasting, incorrdination, and pain.

ta-bla (tab´la) *n.* A type of drum which is usually used in pairs of different sizes in the Hindu music.

ta-ble (tā´bl) *n.* An article of furniture having a flat top, supported by legs; a collection of related signs, values, or items. **table** *v.* To put off or postpone the discussion of something until another time.

tab-leau (tab´lō) *n. pl.* **tableaux** or **tableaus** A vivid representation; a stage scene rep-resented by motionless and silent people who stand in an appropriate arrangement.

ta-ble-land *n.* An area of land which is flat and is elevated, such as a table.

tab-let (tab´lit) *n.* A pad used for writing; a thin, flat piece of stone or wood which is fit for or has an inscription.

table tennis *n.* A type of game that is like lawn tennis and is played on a table top with a plastic ball and wooden paddles.

ta-ble-top (tā´bl top˝) *n.* A top of a table.

ta-ble-ware (tā´bl wâr˝) *n.* The utensils such as forks, knives, and plates that are used on the table to eat food with.

table wine *n.* A type of wine that is served with the food and does not have more that 14 percent alcohol.

tab-loid (tab´loid) *n.* A small newspaper with news reported by means of pictures and concise reporting.

ta-boo (*ta* bö´) *n.* A custom or rule against doing, using, or mentioning something. *adj.* Forbidden by social authority, convention, or custom.

ta-bor (tā´bĕr) *n.* A type of small drum that has one head made of calf skin.

tab-o-ret (tab´rit) *n.* A type of cylindrical seat that is without a back or arms.

tab-u-lar (tab´ū lĕr) *adj.* Pertaining to or arranged in a table or list. **-ly** *adv.*

tabula rasa *n.* A person's mind in its hypothetical empty state before receiving an impression from the outside.

tab-u-late (tab´ū lāt˝) *v.* To put something in a tabular form. **tabulation** *n.*

tab-u-la-tor (tab´ū lā˝tĕr) *n.* Something or someone that tabulates.

ta-chom-e-ter (ta kom´i tĕr) *n.* An instrument for measuring velocity and speed.

tach-y-car-dia (tak´i kär´dē a) *n.* A rapid heart beat.

tach-y-lyte (tak´ilit) *n.* A type of black basalt, glossy in appearance.

ta-chym-e-ter (ta kim´i tĕ) *n.* A device that is used to determine bearings or distances quickly.

tac-it (tas´it) *adj.* Understood; expressed or implied nonverbally; implicit. **tacitly** *adv.* **tacitness** *n.*

tac-i-turn *adj.* To be temperamentally disinclined to speak or talk.

tack (tak) *n.* A small, short nail with a flat head; a sewing stitch used to hold something temporarily; the changing of a sailboat from one direction to another. *v.* To attach or fasten with tacks; to change the direction in which a sailboat is going. **tacker** *n.*

tack-board *n.* A type of board that can be made of cork and used for the purpose of tacking notices up.

tack claw *n.* A small tool used to remove tacks.

tack-i-fy *v.* To cause or to make something tacky. **tackifier** *n.*

tack-ily *adv.* To be done in a tacky manner.

tack-i-ness *n.* The state of being tacky.

tack-le (ta´kl) *n.* Equipment used for fishing or other sports or occupations; an apparatus of ropes and pulley blocks for pulling and hoisting heavy loads; in football, a position on a football team; the lineman between the guard and end. **tackle** *v.* **tackler** *n.*

tack-y (tak´ē) *adj.* Slightly sticky; shabby; lacking style or good taste; flashy.

ta-co (tä´kō) *n., pl.* **-cos** A type of Mexican or Spanish food made of a tortilla folded over with a filling inside.

tac-o-nite *n.* A type of flint-like rock which can be considered a low-grade iron ore.

tact (takt) *n.* Having the ability to avoid what would disturb or offend someone. **tactful** *adj.* **tactfully** *adv.* **-fulness** *n.*

tac-tic (tak´tik) *n.* A way or method of working toward a goal; the art of using strategy to gain military objectives or other goals. **tactical** adj. **tactician** n.

tac-tics (tak´tiks) n., pl. The art of maneuvering forces in combat or war.

tac-til-i-ty n. The responsiveness of someone or something to stimulation of the sense of touch. **tactile** adj.

tact-less adj. To be marked by a lack of tact. **tactlessness** n. **tactlessly** adv.

tad (tad) n. A small boy; an insignificant degree or amount.

tad-pole (tad´pōl) n. The early stage in the growth of a frog or toad during which it breathes by external gills, has a long tail, and lives in the water; a polliwog.

tae-ni-a-sis n. A type of disease that can be caused by tapeworms.

taf-fe-ta (tafʹi ta) n. A stiff, smooth fabric of rayon, nylon, or silk.

taf-fe-tized adj. To have a finish that is crisp in nature.

taff-rail (tafʹrāl) n. The rail around the stern of a boat or ship.

taf-fy (tafʹē) n. A type of candy which is boiled and is made of brown sugar and is pulled until it becomes porous.

taf-i-a (tafʹē a) n. A type of rum of West India that is made from distilled sugar cane juice.

Taft, William Howard n. (1857-1930) The twenty-seventh president of the United States from 1909-1913.

tag (tag) n. A piece of plastic, metal, paper, or other material that is attached to something in order to identify it; a children's game in which one child is "it" and tries to catch another child, who then becomes "it." **tagger** n.

tag-along n. The person that follows the lead of another person.

tag-board n. A type of cardboard that is used for the making of shipping tags.

tag end n. A random bit.

tag up v. To touch the base one is occupying in the game of baseball before advancing after a fly ball is caught.

tah-sil-dar (ta sēl där´) n. One who is a revenue officer in the country of India.

tai-ga n. The moist subarctic forest which begins where the tundra ends and contains firs and spruces.

tail (tāl) n. The posterior extremity, extending from the end or back of an animal. **tails** n., pl. The opposite side of a coin from heads; formal evening dress for men. **tail** v. To follow or keep close watch on someone; to connect end to end.

tail-gate (tāl´gāt´) n. The hinged gate at the back of a truck or automobile for loading and unloading. v. To follow very closely in a car.

taille (tāl) n. A type of tax that was levied by a French king on his subjects or the land that they held in their possession.

tai-lor (tā´lėr) n. One whose profession is making, mending, and altering clothing. **tailor** v. To adapt for a specific purpose.

tai-lored (tā´lėrd) adj. Made by a tailor.

tail-or-ing (tā´lėr ing) n. The occupation of a tailor.

tail-spin (tāl´spin´) n. An emotional collapse.

taint (tānt) v. To spoil, contaminate, or pollute. n. A blemish or stain.

take (tāk) v. To seize or capture; to get possession of; to receive, swallow, absorb, or accept willingly; to attack and surmount; to move, convey, or conduct to a different place; to require; to choose or pick. Slang To cheat; to subtract. **take** n. The process of acquiring; the total receipts for admission at an event.

take back v. To make or state a retraction of something such as a statement.

take in v. To receive as a lodger; to encompass something within the limits of some-thing else.

take on v. To deal with something or someone.

talc (talk) n. A soft, fine-grained, smooth mineral used in making talcum powder.

talcum powder n. A type of powder that is made of talc and an antiseptic.

tale (tāl) n. A story or recital of relating events that may or may not be true; a malicious or false story; gossip.

tal-ent (talʹent) n. The aptitude, disposition, or characteristic ability of a person. **talented** adj.

talent scout n. A person who discovers and recruits people with talent for a specialized activity or field.

ta-ler n. A silver coin which was issued by German states in the 15th to the 19th centuries.

talk (tok) v. To communicate by words or speech; to engage in chatter or gossip. **talk** n. A speech or lecture, usually given to a group of people. Slang To boast; to brag. **talker, talkativeness** n. **talkative** adj.

talk-y (to´kē) adj. To be containing or having too much talk in something.

tall (tol) adj. Of greater than average height; of a designated or specified height; imaginary, as a tall tale.

tal-lage (talʹij) n. A fee that is paid a lord for his feudal tenant.

tall-boy (tol´boi´) n. A type of chest of drawers where the top section is smaller than the lower section.

tal-low (talʹō) n. Hard fat rendered from sheep or cattle, used to make candles, lubricants, and soap. **tallow** adj.

tal-ly (talʹē) n., pl. **tallies** A record or counting of money, amounts, or scores. **tally** v. To agree with; to reckon or a score; to count.

tal-ly-man (tal´ē man) n. The person who checks or has a record of counting.

tal-on (tal´on) n. A long, curved claw found on birds or animals, used to kill or capture prey. **taloned** adj.

ta-lus n. The slope which is formed by the gathering or accumulation of rock debris.

ta-ma-le (ta mä´lē) n. The meat that is seasoned with chili and then is rolled into a cornmeal dough and is steamed.

tam-bour (tam´bür) n. A type of frame that can be used for the purpose of embroidering.

tam-bou-rine (tam´bo rēn´) n. A percussion instrument made of a small drum with jingling metal disks around the rim.

tame (tām) adj. Not wild or ferocious; domesticated or manageable. **tame** v. To make docile or calm. **tamely** adv. **tamer** n. **tameness** n.

tame-less (tām´lis) adj. Being unable to be tamed.

tam-per (tam´pér) v. To change, meddle, or alter something; to use corrupt measures to scheme. **tamperproof** adj.

tan (tan) v. To cure a hide into leather by using chemicals. Slang To spank a child. **tan** n. A brownish skin tone caused by exposure to the sun.

tan-a-ger n. A type of American passerine bird which can be found in the woodlands.

tan-bark n. A type of bark that is rich in tannin and is used in the tanning process.

tan-dem (tan´dem) n. Any arrangement that involves two or more things, animals or persons arranged one behind the other.

tang (tang) n. A sharp, distinct taste, smell, or quality; a slender shank that projects from a tool and connects to a handle.

tan-ge-lo n. The hybrid that is between a tangerine and a pomelo or grapefruit.

tan-gent (tan´jent) n. A line that touches a curved line but does not intersect or cross it; a sudden change from one course to another. **tangency** n.

tan-ger-ine (tan´je rēn) n. A small citrus fruit with an easily peeled orange skin, resembling an orange.

tan-gi-ble (tan´ji bl) adj. Capable of being appreciated or felt by the sense of touch; capable of being realized. **tangibleness, tangibility** n.

tan-gle (tang´gl) v. To mix, twist, or unite in a confused manner making separation difficult. **tanglement** n.

tangled adj. To be in a state of disorder. **tangly** adv. To be full of tangles.

tan-go (tang´gō) n. A ballroom dance with long, gliding steps. **tango** v.

tangram n. A type of Chinese puzzle that is made by cutting a square of material into different shapes, such as five triangles, a rhomboid, and a square and they are able to be combined in different figures.

tank (tangk) n. A large container for holding or storing a gas or liquid. .

tankage n. The contents of a tank.

tan-nage (tan´ij) n. A process of tanning something.

tan-nery n. The place where tanning is done.

tan-ning (tan´ing) n. The browning of the skin with an exposure to the sun.

tan oak n. A type of evergreen oak that will yield tan bark.

tan-tal-ic (tan tal´ik) adj. To be pertaining to tantalum.

tan-ta-lite (tan´ta līt´) n. The mineral that is made of dark oxide of iron, tantalum, manganise, and columbium.

tan-ta-lize (tan´ta līz´) v. To tease or tempt by holding or keeping something just out of one's reach. **-ingly** adv.

tan-ta-liz-ing (tan´ta līz´) adj. To have a quality that stimulates an interest.

tan-ta-lum (tan´ta lūm) n. A metallic element symbolized by Ta.

tan-ta-mount (tan´ta mount´) adj. To be equivalent in effect, significance, or value.

tan-ta-ra (tan´tér a) n. A blare of the horn or trumpet.

tan-trum (tan´trum) n. A fit; an outburst or a rage of bad temper.

tan-yard n. The part of the tannery that is used to house the tanning vats.

tan-za-nite n. A type of mineral that is a blue variety of zoisite.

tap (tap) v. To strike repeatedly, usually while making a small noise; to strike or touch gently; to make secret contact with something; in medicine, to remove fluids from the body. **tapper** n.

tape backup In computer science, a reserve copy of computer programs and data on magnetic tape.

tap dance n. A type of step dance that is tapped out by the means of shoes that have metal taps on them.

tape (tāp) n. A narrow strip of woven fabric; a string or ribbon stretched across the finish line of a race.

tape measure n. A strip of cloth or other material that is marked off in units of measure and is used to measure things.

ta-per (tā´pér) n. A very slender candle. v. To become gradually smaller or thinner at one end.

ta-per-er n. The person who bears or carries a taper in a religious procession.

tap-es-tried adj. To be decorated with tapestry.

tap-es-try (tap´i strē) n. pl. **-ies** A thick fabric woven with designs and figures.

ta-pe-tum *n*. The layer of the nutritive cells that is found in the sporogenous tissue.

tape-worm (tāp´wûrm˝) *n*. A type of cestode worm that is parasitic and found in the intestine of animals and man.

tap-i-o-ca (tap´ē ō´ka) *n*. A bead-like substance used for thickening and for puddings.

ta-pis *n*. The tapestry material that is used for table coverings and hangings.

tappet hen *n*. A hen that is crested.

tap-ping *n*. Process where something is tapped.

tap-root *n*. A root that will grow vertically downward and has other lateral roots.

taps (taps) *n. pl., Milit*. A bugle call that signals lights out, also sounded at memorial and funeral services.

tap-ster (tap´stèr) *n*. The person who is hired to dispense liquors in a barroom.

tar (tär) *n*. A black bituminous viscous liquid that is made or obtained by the destructive distillation of organic matter.

tar-an-tel-la (tar˝an tela) *n*. A type of folk dance of Italy.

ta-ran-tu-la (ta ran´cha la) *n*. A type of spider which is hairy and slow and not poisonous to man.

ta-rax-a-cum (ta rak´sa kum) *n*. A dried root of the dandelion which can be used as a tonic and diuretic.

tar-dy (tär´dē) *adj*. Late; not on time. tardily, tardiness *n*.

tare (târ) *n*. An element which is undesirable.

targe *n*. A type of light shield.

tar-get (tär´git) *n*. An object marked to shoot at; an aim or goal. In computer science, objective, as a file or device to which data is to be transmitted, or a directory to which a file is to be copied or saved.

target date *n*. A date which has been set for the completion of something.

tar-iff (tar´if) *n*. Duty or tax on merchandise coming into or going out of a country.

tar-la-tan (tär´la tan) *n*. A type of cotton fabric that is heavily sized for stiffness.

tarn (tärn) *n*. A type of steep-banked mountain pool.

tar-nish (tär´nish) *v*. To become discolored or dull; to lose luster; to spoil. tarnish, tarnishable *adj*.

ta-ro *n*. A type of plant of the arum family that is grown in the tropics for its root stocks which can be eaten.

tar-ok *n*. The card game that was popular in Europe and was played with a deck of 40, 52, or 56 cards.

tar-pau-lin (tär pa´lin) *n*. A sheet of waterproof canvas used as a protective covering.

tar-ra-gon (tar´a gon˝) *n*. A type of European wood that is grown for its aromatic foliage.

tar-ry (tar´ē) *v*. To linger, delay, or hesitate.

tar-sal *adj*. To be pertaining to the tarsus.

tar-si-er *n*. A type of nocturnal mammal of East India which is related to the lemurs.

tar-sus (tär´sus) *n*. A bone of the foot or hand which makes up the ankle or the wrist.

tart (tärt) *adj*. Sharp; sour; cutting, biting in tone or meaning. -ly, tartness *n*.

tar-tan (tär´tan) *n*. A plaid fabric pattern of Scottish origin. tartan *adj*.

tar-tar (tär´tèr) *n*. The reddish, acidic, crust-like deposit which forms as grape juice turns to wine; a hard deposit which forms on the teeth, composed of secretions, food, and calcium salts.

task (task) *n*. A bit of work, usually assigned by another; a job. In computer science, a job assigned to the computer.

task-mas-ter *n*. A person who imposes labor upon another person.

tasse *n*. An overlapping plate in a suit of armor which will make a short skirt below the waist.

tas-sel (tas´el) *n*. An ornamental decoration made from a bunch of string or thread.

taste (tāst) *n*. The ability to sense or determine flavor in the mouth; a personal liking or disliking. *v*. To test or sense flavors in the mouth. tasteless, tasteful *n*.

tasty *adj*. To have a taste which is pleasing. tastiness *n*.

ta-ta-mi *n*. The straw matting which is used as a covering for the floor in the Japanese home.

tat-ter (tat´ér) *n*. A torn scrap of cloth. *v*. To become or make ragged.

tat-ter-de-ma-lion (tat´ér di mäl´yon) *n*. One who is dressed in clothing that is ragged.

tat-ting (tat´ing) *n*. A type of handmade lace.

tat-tle (tat´l) *v*. To reveal the secrets of another by gossiping. tattler *n*.

tat-too (ta tö˝) *n*. A permanent design or mark made on the skin by pricking and inserting an indelible dye.

tat-ty *adj*. To be frayed.

taught (tot) *v*. Past tense of teach.

taunt (tont) *v*. To mock or insult someone.

taupe *n*. A color which is a brownish gray.

tau-rine (tor´ēn) *adj*. To be pertaining to a bull.

taut (tot) *adj*. Tight; emotionally strained. tautly *adv*. tautness *n*.

tau-tog *n.* A type of fish that is found along the Atlantic coast of the United States.

tau-tol-o-gy (ta'tol'o jē) *n., pl.* -ies Redundancy; a statement which is an unnecessary repetition of the same idea.

tau-to-mer-ic *adj.* To be pertaining to tautomerism.

tav-ern (tav'ẽrn) *n.* An inn; an establishment or business licensed to sell alcoholic drinks. **taverner** *n.*

tav-ern-er *n.* A person who runs a tavern.

taw *v.* To dress such as skins by a dry process. **taw** *n.* A playing marble.

taw-dry (to'drē) *adj.* To be gaudy in appearance. **tawdriness** *n.*

taw-pie *n.* A person who is foolish.

tax (taks) *n.* A payment imposed and collected from individuals or businesses by the government. *v.* To strain. **taxable** *adj.* **taxation** *n.* **taxer** *n.*

tax-ex-empt (taks'ig zempt) *adj.* Exempted from tax; bearing tax-free interest on federal or state income.

tax evasion *n.* The failure, which is deliberate, to pay taxes.

tax-i (tak'sē) *v.* To move along the ground or water surface on its own power before taking off.

tax-i-cab (tak'sē kab') *n.* A vehicle for carrying passengers for money.

tax-i-der-my (tak'si dur'mē) *n.* The art or profession of preparing, stuffing, and mounting animal skins.

tax-i stand *n.* The place where a taxi will park while the driver waits for a passenger.

tax-pay-er (taks'pā'ẽr) *n.* A person who pays a tax.

tax shelter *n.* A credit or allowance that reduces taxes on current earnings for an individual investor or corporation.

tax stamp *n.* The stamp which is placed on something to show that the tax for it has been paid.

Taylor, Zachary *n.* (1784-1850) The twelfth president of the United States from 1849-1850.

tea (tē) *n.* A small tree or bush which grows where the climate is very hot and damp; a drink made by steeping the dried leaves of this shrub in boiling water.

teach (tēch) *v.* To communicate skill or knowledge; to give instruction or insight. **teaching** *n.*, **teachability** *n.*, **teachable-ness** *n.*, **teachable** *adj.*

teach-er (tē'chẽr) *n.* A person who teaches; one who instructs.

teachership *n.* A position of teaching.

teacher's pet *n.* A student in the class who gets the special attention of the teacher.

teaching aid *n.* The device which is used to help reinforce the classroom instructions.

teak *n.* A type of tall tree of East India that can be used for shipbuilding.

teal blue *n.* A color which is a dark greenish blue.

team (tēm) *n.* Two or more players on one side in a game; a group of people trained or organized to work together; two or more animals harnessed to the same implement. *v.* To join or work together.

teammate *n.* A person who is on a team with others.

team-ster (tēm'stẽr) *n.* A person who drives a team of animals or a vehicle as an occupation.

tea party *n.* A gathering that takes place in the afternoon where tea is served.

tear (tēr) *n.* A fluid secreted by the eye to moisten and cleanse. *v.* To cry.

tear (târ) *v.* To become divided into pieces; to separate; to rip into parts or pieces; to move fast; to rush. *n.* A rip or torn place.

tear-down *n.* The process of taking something apart.

tear-ful *adj.* To be accompanied by tears.

tear gas *n.* A type of gaseous substance that will blind the eyes with tears.

tear jerker *n.* A story that is pathetic.

tea-room *n.* A type of room in a restaurant that is designed for the female clientele.

tea rose *n.* A type of rose that descends from the Chinese rose.

tear-stain *n.* The streak that is left by a tear. **tearstained** *adj.*

tear up *v.* To remove or to damage something.

teary *adj.* To be stained with tears.

tease (tēz) *v.* To make fun of; to bother; to annoy; to tantalize. *n.* A person who teases. **teaser**, **teasingly** *adv.*

teasel *n.* A type of herb which is prickly and is used in the wool industry.

teat *n.* The protuberance that milk flows out of.

tech-ne-tium (tek nē'shē um) *n.* A metallic element symbolized by Tc.

tech-ne-tron-ic *adj.* To be pertaining to a society that is shaped by the impact of technology.

tech-ni-cal (tek'ni kal) *adj.* Expert; derived or relating to technique; relating to industry or mechanics.

tech-ni-cal-i-ty (tek'ni kal'i tē) *n.* The state of something being technical.

tech-ni-cian *n.* A person who is a specialist in the technical details of a subject.

tech-nique (tek nēk') *n.* A technical procedure or method of doing something.

tech-no-crat *n.* A person who is a member of a technocracy.

tech-no-crat-ic *adj.* To be pertaining to a technocracy.

technol *abbr.* Technology.

tech-nol-o-gist *n.* A person who is a specialist in technology.

tech-nol-o-gy (tek nol´*o* jē) *n., pl.* -ies The application of scientific knowledge to serve man in industry, commerce, medicine and other fields.

tec-ton-ic (tek ton´ik) *adj.* To be pertaining to the deformation of the crust of the earth. **tectonically** *adv.*

tec-ton-ics *n.* The art of construction and building of things, such as a building.

ted (ted) *v.* To turn and scatter something, such as grass for drying purposes.

ted-der (ted´ér) *n.* Someone or something that teds.

teddy bear *n.* A type of bear that is stuffed and used as a child's toy.

te-di-ous (tē´d*e* us) *adj.* Boring; taking a longtime. **tediously** *adv.*

tedium *n.* The state of being tedious.

tee (tē) *n.* A peg used to hold a golf ball on the first stroke toward a hole or goal post; a peg used to support a football during a field goal attempt. **teed off**

teem (tem) *v.* To abound; to be full of; to swarm or crowd.

teen-ag-er (tēn´ā´jèr) *n.* A young adult who is in the teen years of life, such as 13 to 19 years old.

teens (tēnz) *n. pl.* The ages between 13 and 19; the years of one's life between 13 and 19.

tee-ter (tē´tér) *v.* To move about in an unsteady manner.

teeth *n. pl.* The plural of tooth.

teethe (tēth) *v.* To grow one's teeth.

teeth-er *n.* An object which can be used by babies while they are cutting teeth.

teff *n.* A type of grass which is grown for its grain in Africa.

tel-e-cast (tel´ē kast´) *n.* A television broadcast. **telecast** *v.*

tel-e-com-mu-ni-ca-tion *n.* The communication between two points which are a great distance away from each other.

tel-e-course *n.* A school course which can be taught over the television.

tel-e-film *n.* A movie or picture which has been made or produced for television.

tel-e-gram (tel´e gram) *n.* A message sent or received by telegraph.

tel-e-graph (tel´e graf) *n.* A system for communicating; a transmission sent by wire or radio. *v.* To send messages by electricity over wire. **telegraphist**, **telegrapher** *n.* **telegraphic** *adj.*

te-le-ost *n.* The group of fishes that have a bony skeleton. **teleostean** *adj.*

te-lep-a-thy (*te* lep´*a* thē) *n.* Communication by means of mental processes rather than ordinary means. **-ic** *n.*

tel-e-phone (tel´e fōn´) *n.* A system or device for transmitting conversations

by wire. **telephone** *v.* **telephoner** *n.*

telephone number *n.* The number which has been given to a person and one is able to call this person with this number.

tel-e-phon-ic (tel´e fon´ik) *adj.* To be able to convey sound.

tel-e-pho-to (tel´ē fō´tō) *adj.* Relating to a camera lens which produces a large image of a distant object.

tel-e-pho-to (tel´e fō´tō) *adj.* Relating to a camera lens which produces a large image of a distant object.

tel-e-pho-to-graph-ic *adj.* To be pertaining to the process of telephotography.

tel-e-play (tel´e plā´) *n.* A type of play which has been written for the television.

tel-e-scope (tel´i skōp´) *n.* An instrument which contains a lens system which makes distant objects appear larger and nearer. **telescopic** *adj.*

tel-e-sis *n.* The progress which is directed and planned in an intelligent manner.

tel-e-thon (tel´e thon´) *n.* A long telecast used to raise money for a worthy cause.

tel-e-vise (tel´e vīz´) *v.* To broadcast some show with the use of a television.

tel-e-vi-sion (tel´e vizh´*an*) *n.* Reception and transmission of images on a screen with sound; the device that reproduces television sounds and images.

tel-ex *n.* Teletype communications by means of automatic exchanges.

te-lio-spore *n.* A type of chlamydospore that is thick-walled and in its final stage in the life cycle of the rust fungus.

tell (tel) *v.* To relate or describe; to command or order. **-ing**, **tellable** *n.*

tell-er *n.* A person who will relate or tell.

tell-tale *n.* The device for recording something.

tel-lu-ri-an (te lür´ē *a*n) *adj.* To be pertaining to the earth.

tel-lu-ri-um (te lur´ē um) *n.* An element symbolized by Te.

tel-lu-rom-e-ter *n.* The device that will measure a distance with the use of microwaves.

tel-lu-rous (tel´yer us) *adj.* To be pertaining to tellurium.

tem-per (tem´pér) *n.* The state of one's feelings. *v.* To modify something, making it flexible or hard.

tem-per-a-ment (tem´pér *a* ment) *n.* Personality; a characteristic way of thinking, reacting, or behaving.

tem-per-ance (tem´pér *a*ns) *n.* Moderation; restraint; moderation or abstinence from drinking alcoholic beverages.

tem-per-ate (tem´ér it) *adj.* Avoiding extremes; moderate. **temperately** *adj.*

tem-per-a-ture (tem´pér *a* cher) *n.* A measure of heat or cold in relation to the body or environment; an elevation in body temperature above the normal 98.6 degrees Fahrenheit.

tem-pest (tem´pist) *n*. A severe storm, usually with snow, hail, rain, or sleet.

tem-ple (tem´pl) *n*. A place of worship; the flat area on either side of the forehead.

tem-po (tem´po) *n. pl.* **-pos** *or* **-pi** *Mus.* The rate of speed at which a musical composition is to be played.

tem-po-rar-y (tem´po rer´ē) *adj.* Lasting for a limited amount of time; not permanent.

temporary storage In *computer science*, the computer's main memory; the area that holds program and data files that are active.

tempt (tempt) *n*. To encourage or draw into a foolish or wrong course of action; to lure. **temptation** *n*.

ten (ten) *n*. The cardinal number equal to 9 + 1; the number before eleven.

te-na-cious (*te* nā´shus) *adj.* Persistent; stubborn. **tenaciousness** *n*.

ten-ant (ten´ant) *n*. A person who pays rent to occupy another's property. **tenantless** *adj.* **tenantable** *adj.*

Ten Commandments *n*. The ten rules of moral behavior which were given to Moses by God.

tend (tend) *v*. To be inclined or disposed; to be directed; to look after.

ten-den-cy (ten´den sē) *n. pl.* **-ies** A disposition to act or behave in a particular way; a particular direction, mode, outcome, or direction.

ten-der (ten´dėr) *adj.* Fragile; soft; not hard or tough; painful or sore when touched. **tender** *n*. Something offered as a formal bid or offer; compassionate; a supply ship. **tender** *v*. To make an offer to buy or purchase; to present, as a resignation. **tenderly** *adv*. **tenderhearted** *adj.* **tenderness** *n*.

ten-der-loin (ten´dėr loin´) *n*. A cut of tender pork or beef.

ten-don *n*. A band of tough, fibrous tissues that connect, a muscle and bone.

ten-dril (ten´dril) *n*. A thread-like part of a climbing plant which attaches itself to a support. **tendriled** *adj.*

Ten-nes-see *n*. A state located in the eastern part of the United States; statehood June 1, 1796; state capital Nashville.

ten-nis (ten´is) *n*. A sport played with a ball and racket by 2 or 4 people on a rectangular court.

ten-or (ten´ėr) *n*. An adult male singing voice, above a baritone.

tense (tens) *adj.* Taut or stretched tightly; nervous; under strain. **tense** *v*.

ten-sion (ten´shạn) *n*. The condition of stretching or the state of being stretched. **tensional** *adj.* **-less** *adj.*

tent (tent) *n*. A portable shelter made by

stretching material over a supporting framework.

ten-ta-cle (ten´ta kl) *n*. A long, unjointed, flexible body part that projects from certain invertebrates, as the octopus. **tentacular** *adj.* **-ed** *adj.*

ten-ta-tive (ten´ta tiv) *adj.* Experimental; subject to change; not definite.

ten-ure (ten´yėr) *n*. The right, state, or period of holding something, as an office or property. **tenurial, tenured** *adj.* **tenurially** *adv.*

te-pee (tā´pē) *n*. A tent made of hides or bark used by the Indians of North America.

tep-id (tep´id) *adj.* Lukewarm. **tepidly** *adv.* **tepidness** *n*.

te-qui-la *n*. A type of Mexican liquor.

te-rai *n*. A type of wide-brimmed felt hat that is worn by the people in subtropical areas.

ter-a-to-log-i-cal *adj.* To be abnormal in structure of growth.

ter-a-to-ma *n*. A type of tumor that is made up of a heterogeneous mixture of the tissues. **teratomatous** *adj.*

ter-bi-um (tûr´bē ûm) *n*. A metallic element of the rare-earth group symbolized by Tb.

ter-cen-ten-a-ry (ter sen´te ner´ē) *n. pl.* **-ries** The time span of 300 years; a 300th anniversary. **tercentenary** *adj.*

ter-cet *n*. A group of three lines of verse.

ter-e-binth (ter´e binth) *n*. A type of European tree that belongs to the sumac family and yields turpentine.

ter-e-bin-thine (ter´e bin´thin) *adj.* To be pertaining to or resembling turpentine.

te-rete *adj.* To be almost cylindrical but to be tapering at both ends.

ter-gi-ver-as-tion *n*. The evasion of a clear-cut statement.

ter-gum (tûr´gum) *n*. A plate of an rthropod that is a dorsal section.

ter-i-ya-ki *n*. A Japanese dish where the ingredients are marinated in soy sauce then grilled.

term *n*. A phrase or word; a limited time or duration; a phrase having a precise meaning. *Math* The quantity of two numbers either added together or subtracted.

ter-mi-nal (ter´mi nal) *adj.* Of, forming, or located at the end; final. *n*. A station at the end of a bus line, railway, or airline; in Computer Science, the instrument through which data enters or leaves a computer.

ter-mi-nate (tûr´mi nāt´) *v*. To bring to a conclusion or end; to finish; to fire someone from a job. **termination** *n*.

ter-mite (tee´mīt) *n*. The winged or wingless insect which lives in large colonies feeding on wood.

ter-race (ter´as) *n*. An open balcony or

porch; a level piece of land that is higher than the surrounding area; a row of houses built on a sloping or raised site.

ter-ra cot-ta *n.* A hard, baked clay used in ceramic pottery.

ter-rain (*te* rān´) *n.* The surface of an area, as land.

ter-ra-pin (ter´*a* pin) *n.* An edible turtle of North America, living in both fresh and salt water.

ter-res-tri-al (*te* res´trē *a*l) *adj.* Something earthly; not heavenly; growing or living on land.

ter-ri-ble (ter´i bl) *adj.* Causing fear or terror; intense; extreme; horrid; difficult. **terribly** *adv.* **-ness** *n.*

ter-ri-er (ter´ē ėr) *n.* A very active small dog, originally bred by hunters to dig for burrowing game, now kept as a family pet.

ter-rif-ic (*te* rif´ik) *adj.* Terrifying. *Informal* Excellent; causing amazement.

ter-ri-fy (ter´i fī´) *v.* To fill with fear or terror; to frighten; to menace. **terrified** *adj.* **terrifying** *adj.*

ter-ri-to-ry (ter´i tōr´ē) *n. pl.* **-ies** An area, usually of great size, which is controlled by a particular government; a district or area assigned to one person or group. **territorial** *adj.*

ter-ror (ter´ėr) *n.* Extreme fear; one who causes terror.

ter-ror-ism *n.* The state of being terrorized or the act of terrorizing; the use of intimidation to attain one's goals or to advance one's cause.

terse (ters) *adj.* Brief; using as few words as possible without loss of force or clearness. **tersely** *adv.* **terseness** *n.*

test (test) *n.* An examination or evaluation of something or someone; an examination to determine one's knowledge, skill, intelligence or other qualities. **tester** *n.* In computer science, to subject to diagnostics or sample problems to ascertain that a hardware device or program is working properly.

tes-ta-ment (tes´ta ment) *n.* A legal document which states how one's personal property is to be distributed upon his death. **Testament** One of the two sections of the Bible; the Old Testament and the New Testament.

tes-tate (tes´tāt) *adj.* Having left a valid will.

test data In computer science, data whose output is known for a particular formula or routine.

tes-ti-fy (tes´ti fī´) *v.* To give evidence while under oath; to serve as proof.

tes-ti-mo-ni-al (tes´ti mō´nē al) *n.* A formal statement; a gift, dinner, reception, or other sign of appreciation given to a person as a token of esteem.

tes-ti-mo-ny (tes´ti mō´nē) *n. pl.* **-ies** A solemn affirmation made under oath; an outward expression of a religious experience.

tes-tis (tes´tis) *n. pl.* **testes** The sperm producing gland of the male.

test run In computer science, to operate with test data to confirm the validity of a formula or routine.

test tube *n.* A thin glass tube closed at one end, used in biology and chemistry.

test–tube baby *n.* A baby conceived outside of the womb by fertilizing an egg removed from a woman and then returning the fertilized egg to the womb.

tet-a-nus (tet´a nus) *n., Pathol* An often fatal disease marked by muscular spasms, commonly known as lockjaw.

teth-er (teth´ėr) *n.* A rope or chain which fastens an animal to something but allows limited freedom to wander within its range.

Tex-as *n.* A state located in the south central part of the United States; statehood December 29, 1845; state capital Austin.

text (tekst) *n.* The actual wording of an author's work distinguished his from notes; the main part or body of a book. In computer science, the body of a document; any set of character and symbols that conveys a message. **textual** *adj.* **textually** *adv.*

text-book (tekst´bek´) *n.* A book used by students to prepare their lessons.

text editor In computer science, a basic program for altering text without formatting.

tex-tile (teks´til) *n.* A cloth made by weaving; yarn or fiber for making cloth.

tex-ture (teks´chėr) *n.* The look, surface, or feel of something; the basic makeup. **textural** *adj.* **texturally** *adv.*

thal-li-um (thal´ē um) *n.* A metallic element resembling lead, symbolized by Tl.

than (than) *conj.* In comparison with or to something.

thank (thangk) *v.* To express one's gratitude; to credit.

thank-ful (thangk´ful) *adj.* Feeling or showing gratitude; grateful. **thankfully** *adv.* **thankfulness** *n.* **thankless** *adj.*

thanks (thangks) *n. pl.* An expression of one's gratitude.

Thanksgiving Day *n.* A United States holiday, set apart as a legal holiday for public thanksgiving, celebrated on the fourth Thursday of November.

that (that) *adj. pl.* **those** The person or thing present or being mentioned. Used to introduce a clause stating what is said.

thatch (thach) *n.* Grass, straw, or similar material used to make a roof. **thatch**

overlay or cover with or as if with thatch.

thaw (tho) v. To change from a frozen state to a liquid or soft state; to grow warmer; to melt. **thaw** n.

the-a-tre (thē´a tēr) n. A building adapted to present dramas, motion pictures, plays, or other performances; a performance.

the-at-ri-cal (thē a´tri kal) adj. Extravagant; designed for show, display, or effect. **theatricals** n.

the definite adj. or article Used before nouns and noun phrases as a determiner, designating particular persons or things. adv. Used to modify words in the comparative degree; by so much; by that much.

theft (theft) n. The act or crime of stealing; larceny.

their (thâr) adj. & pron. The possessive case of they; belonging to two or more things or beings previously named.

the-ism (thē´iz um) n. The belief in the existence of God. **theist, theistic** adj.

them (them) pron. The objective case of they.

theme (thēm) n. The topic or subject of something. Mus. A short melody of a musical composition. **thematic** adj.

them-selves (them selvz´) pron. Them or they; a form of the third person plural pronoun.

then (then) adv. At that time; soon or immediately. adj. Being or acting in or belonging to or at that time.

thence (thens) adv. From that place, event, fact, or origin.

the-oc-ra-cy (thē ok´ra sē) n. pl. -ies Government by God or by clergymen who think of themselves as representatives of God. **theocrat** n.

the-ol-o-gy (thē ol´o jē) n. pl. -ies The religious study of the nature of God, beliefs, practices, and ideas. -ian n.

the-o-rize (thē´o rīz´) v. To analyze theories. **theoretician** n. **theorization** n. **theorizer** n. **theorist** n.

the-o-ry (thē´o rē) n. pl. -ies A general principle or explanation which covers the known facts; an offered opinion which may possibly, but not positively, be true.

ther-a-peu-tics (ther´a pū´tiks) n. The medical treatment of disease.

ther-a-py (ther´a pē) n. pl. -ies The treatment of certain diseases; treatment intended to remedy an undesirable condition. **therapist** n.

there (thâr) adv. In, at, or about that place; toward, into, or to. **thereabouts** adv. **thereafter** adv. **thereby** adv. **therefore** adv. -**from** adv. **therein** adv.

ther-mal (ther´mal) adj. Having to do with or producing heat.

ther-mom-e-ter (ther mom´i tēr) n. A glass tube containing mercury which rises and falls with temperature changes. **thermometric** adj.

ther-mo-plas-tic (ther´mo plas´tik) adj. Pliable and soft when heated or warm but hard when cooled.

ther-mo-stat (ther´mo stat´) n. A device that automatically responds to temperature changes and activates equipment such as air conditioners and furnaces to adjust the temperature to correspond with the setting on the device. **thermostatic** adj.

the-sau-rus (thi so´us) n. pl. -**ruses** or -**ri** A book which contains synonyms.

these pron. The plural of this.

the-sis (thē´sis) n. pl. -**ses** A formal argument or idea; a paper written by a student that develops an idea or point of view.

they (thā) pron. The two or more beings just mentioned.

they'd (thād) contr. They had.

they'll (thāl) contr. They will.

they're (thār) contr. They are.

they've (thāv) contr. They have.

thick (thik) adj. Having a heavy or dense consistency; having a considerable extent or depth from one surface to its opposite. Slang Excessive. **thickly** adv. **thickness** n. **thicken** v.

thief (thēf) n. pl. **thieves** A person who steals.

thieve (thēv) v. To take by theft.

thigh (thī) n. The part of the leg between the hip and the knee of man.

thim-ble (thim´bl) n. A small cap-like protection for the finger, worn while sewing. **thimbleful** n.

thin (thin) adj. Having very little depth or extent from one side or surface to the other; not fat; slender. v. To make or become thin. **thinly** adv. -**ness** n.

thing (thing) n. Something not recognized or named; an idea, conception, or utterance; a material or real object.

things n. One's belongings.

think (thingk) v. To exercise thought; to use the mind; to reason and work out in the mind; to visualize. **thinkable** adj. **thinker** n.

third (therd) n. Next to the second in time or place; the last in a series of three. Mech. The 3rd forward gear in an automobile, truck, tractor, or other vehicle.

thirst (therst) n. An uncomfortably dry feeling in the throat and mouth accompanied by an urgent desire for liquids. **thirsty** adj.

this (this) pron. pl. **these** The person or thing that is near, present, or just mentioned; the one under discussion.

this-tle (this´l) n. A prickly plant usually producing a purplish or yellowish flower.

thith-er (thith´ẽr) adv. To that place; there; on the farthest side.

thong (thong) n. A narrow strip of leather used for binding.

tho-rax (thõr´aks) n. pl. -raxes or -races The section or part of the human body between the neck and abdomen, supported by the ribs and breastbone.

tho-ri-um (thõr´ē um) n. A radioactive metallic element symbolized by Th.

thorn (thorn) n. A sharp, pointed, woody projection on a plant stem. thorniness n. thorny adj.

thor-ough (ther´õ) adj. Complete; intensive; accurate; very careful; absolute. -ness n. thoroughly adv.

thor-ough-bred (ther´õbred´) adj. Being of a pure breed of stock.

thor-ough-fare (ther´õ fãr´) n. A public highway, road or street.

those adj. & pron. The plural of that.

though (thō) adv. Nevertheless; in spite of.

thought (thot) n. The process, act, or power of thinking; a possibility; an idea. thoughtful adj. thoughtless adj.

thou-sand (thou´zand) n. The cardinal number equal to 10 X 100.

thrash (thrash) v. To beat or strike with a whip; to move violently about; to defeat. thrasher n.

thread (thred) n. A thin cord of cotton or other fiber; the ridge going around a bolt, nut or screw. v. To pass a thread through, as to thread a needle.

thread-bare (thred´bãr´) adj. Shabby.

threads n. pl., Slang Clothes.

threat (thret) n. An expression or warning of intent to do harm; anything holding a possible source of danger. threaten v. threatener n.

thresh (thresh) v. To separate seed from a harvested plant mechanically; to strike severely.

thresh-old (thresh´ōld) n. A horizontal piece of wood or other material which forms a doorsill; a beginning point.

threw v. Past tense of throw.

thrice (thrīs) adv. Three times.

thrift (thrift) n. The careful use of money and other resources. thriftily adv. thriftiness n. thrifty adj.

thrill (thril) n. A feeling of sudden intense excitement, fear, or joy. thrilling adj. thrillingly adv.

thrive (thrīv) v. To prosper; to be healthy; to do well in a position.

throat (thrōt) n. The front section or part of the neck containing passages for food and air.

throb (throb) v. To beat, move, or vibrate in a pulsating way; to pulsate.

throm-bo-sis (throm bō´sis) n. pl. -ses The formation of a blood clot in a blood vessel or in the heart cavity.

throng (throng) n. A large group or crowd. v. To crowd around or into.

throt-tle (throt´l) n. The valve which controls the flow of fuel to an engine. v. To control the speed or fuel with a throttle.

through (thrö) prep. From the beginning to the end; in one side and out the opposite side. Slang Completed; finished.

through-out (thrö out´) prep., adv. In every place; everywhere; at all times.

throw (thrō) v. To toss or fling through the air with a motion of the arm; to hurl with force. Slang To entertain, as to throw a party. throw up To vomit. throw out To discard something.

thru (thrö) prep., adv., & adj. Through.

thrush (thrush) n. A small songbird having a brownish upper body and spotted breast.

thrust (thrust) v. To push; to shove with sudden or vigorous force. n. A sudden stab or push.

thru-way or throughway (thrö´wä´) n. A major highway; an expressway.

thud (thud) n. A heavy, dull thumping sound.

thug (thug) n. A tough or violent gangster. thuggish adj.

thumb (thum) n. The short first digit of the hand; the part of the glove that fits over the thumb. v. To browse through something quickly. Slang To hitchhike.

thump (thump) n. A blow with something blunt or heavy. thump v.

thun-der (thun´dẽr) n. The loud explosive sound made as air is suddenly expanded by heat and then quickly contracted again.

thun-der-show-er (thun´dẽr shou´ẽr) n. A brief rainstorm with thunder and light-ning.

thus (thus) adv. In this or that way; therefore.

thwack (thwak) v. To strike hard, using something flat.

thwart (thwort) v. To prevent from happening; to prevent from doing something. n. A seat positioned crosswise in a boat.

thy (thī) adj. Pertaining to oneself; your.

thyme (tīm) n. An aromatic mint herb whose leaves are used in cooking.

thy-roid (thī´roid) adj., Anat. Pertaining to the thyroid gland. n. The gland in the neck of man that produces hormones which regulate food use and body growth.

thy-rox-ine (thī rok´sēn) n. A hormone secreted by the thyroid gland.

ti-ar-a (tē ar´a) n. A bejeweled crown in the form of a half circle and worn by women at formal occasions.

tick (tik) n. One of a series of rhythmical tapping sounds made by a clock; a small bloodsucking parasite, many of which are carriers of disease.

tick-et (tik´it) *n.* A printed slip of paper or cardboard allowing its holder to enter a specified event or to enjoy a privilege; a list of candidates who represent a political party.

tick-le (tik´l) *v.* To stroke lightly so as to cause laughter; to amuse or delight. **tickle** *n.* **tickler** *n.*

tidal wave *n.* An enormous rise of destructive ocean water caused by a storm or earth-quake.

tid-bit (tid´bit´) *n.* A choice bit of food, news, or gossip.

tide (tīd) *n.* The rise and fall of the surface level of the ocean which occurs twice a day due to the gravitational pull of the sun and moon on the earth.

tid-ings (tī´dingz) *n. pl.* News; information about events.

ti-dy (tī´dē) *adj.* Well arranged; neat; orderly. *v.* To make orderly and neat. **tidily** *adv.* **tidiness** *n.*

tie (tī) *v.* To secure or bind with a rope, line, cord or other similar material; to make secure or fasten with a rope; to make a bow or knot in; to match an opponent's score. *n.* A string, rope, cord or other material used to join parts or hold something in place; a necktie; a beam that gives structural support. **tie** A device, as timber, laid crosswise to support train tracks.

tier (tēr) *n.* A layer or row placed one above the other. **tiered** *adj.*

ti-ger (tī´gėr) *n.* A large carnivorous cat having tawny fur with black stripes.

tight (tīt) *adj.* Set closely together; bound or securely firm; not loose; taut; difficult. *adv.* Firmly.

tight-en (tīt´en) *v.* To become or make tighter. **tightener** *n.*

tile (tīl) *n.* A thin, hard, flat piece of plastic, asphalt, baked clay, or stone used to cover walls, floors, and roofs. *v.* To cover with tile.

till (til) Until; unless or before. *v.* To cultivate; to plow. *n.* A small cash register or drawer for holding money.

tilt (tilt) *v.* To tip, as by raising one end. *n.* The state of tilting or being tilted.

tim-ber (tim´bėr) *n.* Wood prepared for building; a finished piece of wood or plank.

timber line *n.* The height on a mountain beyond which trees cannot grow.

time (tīm) *n.* A continuous period measured by clocks, watches, and calendars; the period or moment in which something happens or takes place. *adj.* Of or pertain-ing to time; pertaining to paying in, installments. *Slang* A period of imprisonment.

time–shar-ing *n.* The joint ownership of property with each individual sharing the use of the property.

time tri-al *n.* A race or competition where each participant is timed individually over a set distance.

tim-id (tim´id) *adj.* Lacking self-confidence; shy.

tin (tin) *n.* A white, soft, malleable metallic element, symbolized by Sn; a container made of tin. *adj.* Made of tin.

tinc-ture (tingk´chėr) *n.* A tinge of color; an alcohol solution of some medical substance. *v.* To tint.

tin-der (tin´dėr) *n.* A readily combustible substance or material used for kindling.

tine (tīn) *n.* A narrow pointed spike or prong, as of a fork or antler.

tinge (tinj) *v.* To impart a faint trace of color; to tint. *n.* As light trace of added color.

tin-gle (ting´gl) *v.* To feel a stinging or prickling sensation. **tingle** *n.* **-ly** *adj.*

tin-kle (ting´kl) *v.* To produce a slight, sharp series of metallic ringing sounds.

tin-ny (tin´ē) *adj.* Pertaining to or composed of tin.

tin-sel (tin´sel) *n.* Thin strips of glittering material used for decorations.

tint (tint) *n.* A slight amount or trace of color. *v.* To color.

ti-ny (tī´nē) *adj.* Minute; very small.

tip (tip) *v.* To slant from the horizontal or vertical. *n.* Extra money given as an acknowledgment of a service; a gratuity; a helpful hint.

tip-ple (tip´l) *v.* To drink an alcoholic beverage to excess.

tip-sy (tip´sē) *adj.* Partially intoxicated. **tipsiness** *n.*

ti-rade (tī´rād) *n.* A long, violent speech or outpouring, as of censure.

tire (tīer) *v.* To become or make weary; to be fatigued; to become bored. *n.* The outer covering for a wheel, usually made of rubber, serving to absorb shock and to provide traction.

tire-less *adj.* Untiring. **tirelessly** *adv.*

tis-sue (tish´ö) *n., Biol.* Similar cells and their products developed by plants and animals; a soft, absorbent piece of paper, consisting of two layers.

ti-ta-ni-um (tī tā´nē um) *n.* A metallic element symbolized by Ti.

tithe (tīth) *n.* A tenth of one's income given voluntarily for the support of a church. **tithe** *v.* **tither** *n.*

tit-il-late (tit´i lāt´) *v.* To excite or stim-ulate in a pleasurable way. **titillating** *adj.* **titillative** *adj.*

ti-tle (tīt´l) *n.* An identifying name of a book, poem, play, or other creative work; a name or mark of distinction indicating a rank or an office; in law, the evidence giving legal right of possession or control of something; in sports, a championship. *v.* To give a title or name to.

to (tŏ) *prep.* Toward, opposite or near; in contact with; as far as; used as a function word indicating an action, movement, or condition suggestive of movement; indicating correspondence, dissimilarity, similarity, or proportion; indicating the one for which something is done or exists. *adv.* In the state, direction, or condition.

toast (tōst) *v.* To heat and brown over a fire or in a toaster. *n.* Sliced bread browned in a toaster. **toasty** *adj.*

to-bac-co (tŏ bak´ō) *n.* A tropical American plant widely cultivated for its leaves, which are prepared in various ways, as for chewing or smoking.

to-bog-gan (tŏ bog´an) *n.* A long sled-like vehicle without runners, having long thin boards curved upwards at the forward end. **toboggan-ist** *n.* **toboggan** *v.*

to-day (tŏ dā´) *adv.* On or during the present day. *n.* The present time, period, or day.

tod-dle (tod´l) *v.* To walk unsteadily with short steps.

toddler *n.* A small child learning to walk.

tod-dy (tod´ē) *n. pl.* **-ies** A drink made with hot water, sugar, spices, and liquor.

toe (tō) *n.* One of the extensions from the front part of a foot; the part of a stocking, boot or shoe that covers the toes. *v.* To kick, reach, or touch with the toe or toes.

tof-fee (to´fē) *n.* A chewy candy made of butter and brown sugar.

to-geth-er (te geth´ér) *adv.* In or into one group, mass, or body; regarded jointly; in time with what is happening or going on. **togetherness** *n.*

toggle In *computer science*, a switch that may be in either of two states; to select one of two options.

toil (toil) *v.* To labor very hard and continuously. *n.* A difficult task.

toi-let (toi´lit) *n.* A porcelain apparatus with a flushing device, used as a means of disposing body wastes.

to-ken (tōk´en) *n.* A keepsake; a symbol of authority or identity; a piece of imprinted metal used in place of money. *adj.* Done as a pledge or indication.

tol-er-ate (tol´e rāt´) *v.* To put up with; to recognize and respect the opinions and rights of others; to endure; to suffer. **toleration** *n.* **tolerance** *adj.*

toll (tōl) *n.* A fixed charge for travel across a bridge or along a road. *v.* To sound a bell in repeated single, slow tones.

to-ma-to (tŏ mā´tō) *n. pl.* **-toes** A garden plant cultivated for its edible fruit; the fruit of such a plant.

tomb (tŏm) *n.* A vault for burying the dead; a grave.

tomb-stone (tŏm´stōn´) *n.* A stone used to mark a grave.

tom-cat (tom´kat´) *n.* A male cat.

to-mor-row (tŏ mor´ō) *n.* The day after the present day. *adv.* On the day following today.

ton (tun) *n.* A measurement of weight equal to 2,000 pounds. *Slang* A large amount.

tone (tōn) *n.* A vocal or musical sound that has a distinct pitch, loudness, quality, and duration; the condition of the body and muscles when at rest. *v.* To change or soften the color.

tongs (tongz) *n. pl.* An implement with two long arms joined at one end, used for picking up or lifting.

tongue (tung) *n.* The muscular organ attached to the floor of the mouth, used in tasting, chewing, and speaking; anything shaped like a tongue, as the material under the laces or buckles of a shoe.

ton-ic (ton´ik) *n.* A medicine or other agent used to restore health; in music, the first note of a scale. *Slang* Flavored carbonated soda.

to-night (tŏ nīt´) *n.* This night; the night of this day; the night that is coming. *adv.* On or during the present or coming night.

ton-sil (ton´sil) *n.* One of a pair of tissue similar to lymph nodes, found on either side of the throat.

ton-sil-lec-to-my (ton´si lek´to mē) *n.* The surgical removal of tonsils.

too (tŏ) *adv.* Also; as well; more than is needed.

tool (tŏl) *n.* An implement used to perform a task; anything needed to do one's work. *v.* To make or shape with a tool.

tooth (tŏth) *n. pl.* **teeth** One of the hard, white structures rooted in the jaw and used for chewing and biting; the small, notched, projecting part of any object, such as a gear, comb or saw. **toothless** *adj.*

top (top) *n.* The highest part or surface of anything; a covering or lid; the above ground part of a rooted plant; the highest degree; a toy having a symmetric body with a tapered end upon which it spins.

to-paz (tō´paz) *n.* A gemstone, usually yellow in color.

top-coat (top´kōt´) *n.* An outer coat.

To-pe-ka *n.* The capital of the state of Kansas.

top-ic *n.* The subject discussed in an essay, thesis, speech or other discourse; the theme.

to-pog-ra-phy (tŏ pog´ra fē) *n. pl.* **-ies** A detailed description of a region or place; a physical outline showing the features of a region or place.

top-ple (top'l) v. To fall; to overturn.

top-sy-tur-vy (top'sē ter'vē) adv. With the top side down; upside down. adj. In a con-fused state. n. Confusion.

To-rah (tōr'a) n. The body of law and wis-dom contained in Jewish Scripture and oral tradition; a parchment scroll that contains the first five books of the Old Testament.

torch (torch) n. A stick of resinous wood which is burned to give light; any portable device which produces hot flame. *Slang* To set fire to.

tor-ment (tor'ment) n. Extreme mental anguish or physical pain; a source of trouble or pain. v. To cause terrible pain; to pester, harass, or annoy. **tormentingly** adv. **tormentor** n.

tor-na-do (tor nā'dō) n., pl. **tornados** or **tornadoes** A whirling, violent windstorm accompanied by a funnel-shaped cloud that travels a narrow path over land; a whirlwind.

tor-pe-do (tor pē'dō) n., pl. **torpedoes** A large, self-propelled, underwater missile launched from a ship, containing an explosive charge.

tor-pid (tor'pid) adj. Having lost the power of motion or feeling; dormant. **torpidity** n. **torpidly** adv.

tor-rent (tor'ent) n. A swift, violent stream; a raging flood. **torrential** adj.

tor-rid (tor'id) adj. Parched and dried by the heat. **torridly** adv.

tor-sion (tor'shan) n. The act or result of twisting; the stress produced when one end is held fast and the other turned.

tor-so (tor'sō) n. pl. **-sos** or **-si** The trunk of the human body.

tort (tort) n., *Law* A wrongful act requiring compensation for damages.

tor-toise (tor'tos) n. A turtle that lives on the land; a person or thing regarded as slow.

tor-tu-ous (tor'chö us) adj. Marked by repeated bends, turns, or twists; devious. **tortuousness** n.

tor-ture (tor'chér) n. The infliction of intense pain as punishment; something causing anguish or pain. v. To subject or cause intense suffering; to wrench or twist out of shape. **torturer** n. **torturously** adv.

toss (tos) v. To fling or throw about continuously; to throw up in the air. n. A throw.

tot (tot) n. A young child; a toddler.

to-tal (tōt'al) n. The whole amount or sum; the entire quantity. adj. Absolute; complete. **total** v. **totally** adv.

to-tal-i-tar-i-an adj. Characteristic of a government controlled completely by one party; exercising complete political control. **totalitarian** n.

tote (tōt) v. To carry something on one's arm or back. n. A load.

to-tem (tō'tem) n. An animal or plant regarded as having a close relationship to some family clan or group; a representation or symbol.

tot-ter (tot'ér) v. To walk unsteadily; to shake or sway as if about to fall.

tou-can (tö'kan) n. A brightly colored tropical bird having a very large thin bill.

touch (tuch) v. To allow a part of the body, as the hands, to feel or come into contact with; to hit or tap lightly; to eat or drink; to join; to come next to; to have an effect on; to move emotionally. n. An instance or act of touching; the feeling, fact, or act of touching or being touched; a trace; a tiny amount; a method, manner, or style of striking the keys of an instrument with a keyboard. **touchable** adj.

tough (tuf) adj. Resilient and strong enough to withstand great strain without breaking or tearing; strong; hardy; very difficult; difficult to cut or chew. n. An unruly person; a thug. **toughly** adv. **toughness** n.

tou-pee (tö pā) n. A small wig piece worn to cover a bald spot on one's head.

tour (ter) n. A trip with visits to points of interest; a journey; a period or length of service at a single place or job. **tourism** n. **tourist** n.

tour-na-ment (ter'na ment) n. A contest involving a number of competitors for a title or championship.

tour-ni-quet (ter'ni kit) n. A device used to temporarily stop the flow of blood through an artery.

tou-sle (tou'zl) v. To mess up; to disarrange.

tout (tout) v. To solicit customers. *Slang* In horse racing, a person who obtains information on racehorses and sells it to bettors. **touter** n.

tow (tō) v. To drag or pull, as by a chain or rope. n. An act of being pulled; a rope or line for pulling or dragging; coarse broken flax, hemp, or jute fiber prepared for spinning.

to-ward or **towards** (tōrd) prep. In the direction of; just before; some what before; regarding; with respect to.

tow-el (tou'el) n. An absorbent piece of cloth used for drying. **towel** v.

tow-er (tou'ér) n. A very tall building or structure; a skyscraper; a place of security or defense. **towering** adj.

town (toun) n. A collection of houses and other buildings larger than a village and smaller than a city.

town-ship (toun'ship) n. A subdivision of a county having corporate powers of municipal government.

tox-e-mi-a (tok sē'mē a) n., *Pathol.*

Blood poisoning; a condition in which the blood contains toxins.

tox-ic (tok´sik) *adj.* Relating to a toxin; destructive, deadly, or harmful.

tox-in (tok´sin) *n.* A poisonous substance produced by chemical changes in plant and animal tissue.

toy (toi) *n.* An object designed for the enjoyment of children; any object having little value or importance; a small trinket; a bauble; a dog of a very small breed. *v.* To amuse or entertain oneself.

trace (trās) *n.* A visible mark or sign of a thing, person, or event; something left by some past agent or event. **trace** *v.* To follow the course or track of; to copy by drawing over the lines visible through a sheet of transparent paper; to decorate with line patterns. **traceable** *adj.* **traceably** *adv.* **tracer** *n.*

track (trak) *n.* A mark, as a footprint, left by the passage of anything; a regular course; a set of rails on which a train runs; a circular or oval course for racing or walking. **track** *v.* To follow the trail of footprints of. **trackable** *adj.* **tracker** *n.*

trackball In computer science, a hand held device, similar to a mouse, but with a fixed base holding a sphere that is manipulated to move the cursor.

tract (trakt) *n.* An extended area, as a stretch of land. *Anat.* An extensive region of the body, one comprising body organs and tissues that together perform a specialized function.

trac-tion (trak´shən) *n.* The act of drawing, as a load over a surface; the state of being drawn or pulled; rolling friction that prevents a wheel from skidding over the surface on which it runs.

trac-tor (trak´tər) *n.* A diesel or gasoline-powered vehicle used in farming to pull another piece of machinery.

tractor feed In *computer science,* a device that feeds a continuous form through a printer by engaging a series of holes along the deep edges of the form; same as *pin feed* or *sprocket feed*.

tractor trailer *n.* A large truck having a cab and no body, used to pull large trailers.

trade (trād) *n.* A business or occupation; skilled labor; a craft; an instance of selling or buying; a swap. **trade** *v.* **tradeable** *adj.* **trader** *n.*

trade-mark (trād´märk´) *n.* A brand name which is legally the possession of one company and cannot be used by another. **trademark** *v.*

trade-off *n.* A compromise of possibilities when all cannot be attained at the same time; a surrender of one

consideration in order to obtain another.

tra-di-tion (trə dish´ən) *n.* The doctrines, knowledge, practices, and customs passed down from one generation to another. **traditional** *adj.* **-ally** *adv.*

tra-duce (trə dōs´) *v.* To betray. **traducement** *n.* **traducer** *n.*

traf-fic (traf´ik) *n.* The passage or movement of vehicles; trade, buying and selling; the signals handled by a communications system. **-ker** *n.*

trag-e-dy (traj´i dē) *n.* *pl.* **-ies** An extremely sad or fatal event or course of events; a story, play, or other literary work which arouses terror or pity by a series of misfortunes or sad events.

trail (trāl) *v.* To draw, drag, or stream along behind; to follow in the tracks of; to follow slowly behind or in the rear; to let hang so as to touch the ground. *n.* Something that hangs or follows along behind; a rough path through a wooded area.

trail-er (trā´lər) *n.* One who trails; a large vehicle that transports objects and is pulled by another vehicle.

train (trān) *n.* The part of a long gown that trails behind the wearer; a long moving line of vehicles or persons; a group of railroad cars. *v.* To instruct so as to make skillful or capable of doing something; to aim; to direct. **trainable** *adj.* **trainer** *n.* **training** *n.* **trainee** *n.*

trait (trāt) *n.* A quality or distinguishing feature, such as one's character.

trai-tor (trā´tər) *n.* A person who betrays his country, a cause, or another's confidence.

tra-jec-to-ry (trə jek´to rē) *n.* *pl.* **-ies** The curved line or path of a moving object.

tram-mel (tram´el) *n.* A long, large net used to catch birds or fish; something that impedes movement. **trammeler** *n.* **trammel** *v.*

tramp (tramp) *v.* To plod or walk with a heavy step. *n.* A homeless person or vagrant who travels about aimlessly.

tram-ple (tram´pl) *v.* To tread heavily; to stomp; to inflict injury, pain, or loss by heartless or brutal treatment. **trample** *n.* **trampler** *n.*

tram-po-line (tram´po lēn´) *n.* A canvas device on which an athlete or acrobat may perform. **trampolinist** *n.*

trance (trans) *n.* A stupor, daze, mental state, or condition, such as produced by drugs or hypnosis.

tran-quil (trang´kwil) *adj.* Very calm, quiet, and free from disturbance. **tranquilly** *n.* **tranquility** *n.* **-ize** *v.*

trans-act (tran sakt´) *v.* To perform, carry out, conduct, or manage business in some way. **transact, transactor** *n.* **transactional** *adj.*

transaction file In *computer science*, a record of recent transactions, used to update a master file, such as a recording of daily sales used to update the sales account, receivables, cash account, inventory, etc.

tran-scend (tran send´) *v.* To pass beyond; to exceed; to surpass. **transcendent** *adj.* **transcendence** *n.*

tran-scribe (tran skrib´) *v.* To make copies of something; to adopt or arrange.

tran-script (tran´skript) *n.* A written copy.

trans-crip-tion (tran skrip´shan) *n.* The process or act of transcribing.

trans-fer (trans fer´) *v.* To remove, shift, or carry from one position to another. In computer science, to move data or files from one location, storage device, or computer to another. **transferable** *adj.* **transference** *n.*

trans-fig-ure (trans fig´yer) *v.* To change the outward appearance or form; to exalt; to glorify. **transfiguration** *n.*

trans-fix (trans fiks´) *v.* To pierce; to hold motionless, as with terror, awe or amazement. **transfixion** *n.*

trans-form (trans form´) *v.* To change or alter completely in nature, form or function. **transformable** *adj.* **transformation** *n.* **transformer** *n.*

trans-fuse (trans fūz´) *v.* To transfer liquid by pouring from one place to another. *Med.* To pass blood from the blood vessels of one person into the vessels of another. **transfusion** *n.* **transfuser** *n.*

trans-gress (trans gres´) *v.* To go beyond the limit or boundaries; to sin against or violate. **transgression** *n.* **transgressor** *n.* **transgressive** *adj.*

tran-sient (tran´shent) *adj.* Not staying or lasting very long; moving from one location to another. In computer science, temporary, as a file that is created by a program while it is processing, then deleted when processing is completed.

tran-sit (tran´sit) *n.* Passage or travel from one point to another; an instrument for surveying that measures horizontal and vertical angles.

trans-late (trans lāt´) *v.* To change from one language to another while retaining the orig-inal meaning; to explain. In computer science, to change signals to a different format, as from analog to digital; to adapt data files to a format that can be read by a different program. **translation** *n.* **translator** *n.*

trans-lu-cent (trans lö´sent) *adj.* Diffusing and admitting light but not allowing a clear view of the object.

trans-mis-sion (trans mish´an) *n.* The act or state of transmitting. *Mech.* The gears and associated parts of an engine which transmit power to the driving wheels of an automobile or other vehicle. In *computer science*, the transfer of signals between parts of a computer system.

transmission speed *n.* In *computer science*, the rate at which data can be sent and received.

trans-mit (trans mit´) *v.* To dispatch or convey from one thing, person, or place to another. **transmissible** *adj.* **transmittable** *adj.* **transmitter** *n.*

trans-mute (trans mūt´) *v.* To change in nature, kind, or substance.

tran-som (tran´som) *n.* A small, hinged window over a doorway; the horizontal crossbar in a window.

trans-par-ent (trans pâr´en sē) *adj.* Admitting light so that images and objects can be clearly viewed; easy to understand; obvious. In computer science, descriptive of computer processing that is taking place in the background, not under the direct supervision of, or apparent to, the user. Seen through or easily detected. **transparency** *n.* **transparently** *adv.*

tran-spire (tran spiêr´) *v.* To give off waste products through plant or animal pores in the form of vapor; to happen; to take place. **transpiration** *n.*

trans-plant (trans plant´) *v.* To remove a living plant from where it is growing and plant it in another place; to remove a body organ from one person and implant it in the body of another, as a heart or a kidney transplant; to remove skin from one area of the body and move it to another area of the body, as a skin graft. **transplant** *n.* **transplantable** *adj.*

trans-port (trans pōrt´) *v.* To carry or move from one place to another. *n.* A vessel or ship used to carry military supplies and troops; the process or act of transporting. **transportation** *n.*

trans-pose (trans pōz´) *v.* To reverse the place or order of. *Mus.* To perform or write music in a key different from the one it was originally written in.

trans-sex-u-al *n.* A person whose sex has been changed surgically.

trap (trap) *n.* A device for holding or catching animals; *v.* To catch in a trap; to place in an embarrassing position. *Slang* The mouth.

tra-peze (tra pēz´) *n.* A short horizontal bar suspended by two ropes, used for acrobatic exercise or stunts.

trau-ma (trou´ma) *n. pl.* **-mas** *or* **-mata** A severe wound caused by a sudden physical injury; an emotional shock causing lasting and substantial damage to a person's psychological develop-ment.

tra-vail (tra vāl´) *n.* Strenuous mental or physical exertion; labor in childbirth. *v.* To undergo the sudden sharp pain of childbirth.

trav-el (trav´el) *v.* To journey or move from one place to another. *n.* The process or act of traveling. **-er** *n.*

tra-verse (trav´ers) *v.* To pass over, across, or through. *n.* A path or route across; something that lies across something else. **-sable** *adj.,* **-al** *n.*

trawl (trol) *n.* A strong fishing net which is dragged through water.

tray (trā) *n.* A flat container having a low rim, used for carrying, holding, or displaying something.

treach-er-ous (trech´er us) *adj.* Disloyal; deceptive; unreliable. **treacherously** *adv.* **treachery** *n.*

tread (tred) *v.* To walk along, on, or over; to trample. *n.* The act or manner of treading; the part of a wheel which comes into contact with the ground.

trea-son (trē´zon) *n.* Violation of one's allegiance to a sovereign or country, as giving or selling state secrets to another country or attempting to overthrow the government. **treasonable** *adj.* **treasonous** *adj.*

treas-ure (trezh´er) *n.* Hidden riches; some thing regarded as valuable. *v.* To save and accumulate for future use; to value.

treasurer (trezh´er er) *n.* A person having charge and responsibilities for funds.

treas-ur-y (trezh´a rē) *n. pl.* **-ies** A place where public or private funds are kept. **Treasury** The executive department of the United States Government in charge of collection, management, and expenditure of public revenue.

treat (trēt) *v.* To behave or act toward; to regard in a given manner; to provide entertainment or food for another at one's own expense or cost. *n.* A pleasant surprise; something enjoyable which was unexpected. **treatable** *adj.*

treat-ment (trēt´ment) *n.* The manner or act of treating; medical care.

treb-le (treb´l) *adj.* Multiplied by three; having three. *Mus.* Performing or having the highest range, part, or voice. *n.* A high-pitched sound or voice.

tree (trē) *n.* A tall woody plant, usually having a single trunk of considerable height; a diagram resembling a tree, as one used to show family descent. *Slang* To get the advantage of something. In computer science, a graphic representation of a directory structure showing the directories that branch from the root directory, then their subdirectories, etc. **tree** *v.*

tre-foil (trē´foil) *n.* Any of various plants

having three leaflets with red, purple, yellow, or pink flowers.

trek (trek) *v.* To make a slow and arduous journey. **trek** *n.* **trekker** *n.*

trel-lis (trel´is) *n.* A lattice work frame used for supporting vines and other climbing plants.

trem-ble (trem´bl) *v.* To shake involuntarily, as with fear or from cold; to express or feel anxiety. **tremble** *n.* **trembler** *n.* **trembly** *adj.*

tre-men-dous (tri men´dus) *adj.* Extremely huge, large, or vast. *Slang* Wonderful.

trem-or (trem´er) *n.* A quick, shaking movement; any continued and involuntary trembling or quavering of the body.

trench (trench) *n.* A ditch; a long, narrow excavation in the ground. *v.* To cut deep furrows for protection. **trencher** *n.*

trend (trend) *n.* A general inclination, direction, or course; a fad. *v.* To have a specified direction. **-setter** *n.*

Tren-ton *n.* The capital of the state of New Jersey.

tres-pass (tres´pas) *v.* To infringe upon another's property; in law, to invade the rights, property, or privacy of another without consent or knowledge.

tri-al (trī´al) *n.* In law, the examination and hearing of a case before a court of law in order to determine the case; an attempt or effort; an experimental treatment or action to determine a result. *adj.* Pertaining to or of a trial; performed or used during an experiment or test.

tri-an-gle (trī´ang´gl) *n., Geom.* A plane figure bounded by three sides and having three angles. **triangular** *adj.*

tribe (trīb) *n.* A group of people composed of several villages, districts, or other groups which share a common language, culture, and name.

trib-u-la-tion (trib´ū lā´shan) *n.* Great distress or suffering caused by oppression.

trib-ute (trib´ūt) *n.* An action of respect or gratitude to someone; money or other goods given by one country to another showing obedience and insuring against invasion.

tri-ceps (trī´seps) *n., Anat.* The large muscle at the back of the upper arm.

trick (trik) *n.* An action meant to fool, as a scheme; a prank; a feat of magic. *v.* To deceive or cheat. **tricky** *adj.*

trick-er-y (trik´e rē) *n.* Deception.

trick-le (trik´l) *v.* To flow in droplets or a small stream. **trickle** *n.*

tri-cy-cle (trī´si kl) *n.* A small vehicle having three wheels, propelled by pedals.

tri-dent (trīd´ent) *n.* A long spear with three prongs, used as a weapon.

tried (trīd) *adj*. Tested and proven reliable or useful.

tri-en-ni-al (trī en´ē al) *adj*. Happening every third year; lasting for a time period of three years. **triennial** *n*. **triennially** *adv*.

tri-fle (trī´fl) *n*. Something of little value or importance; a dessert made with cake, jelly, wine, and custard. *v*. To use or treat without proper concern.

trig-ger (trig´ẽr) *n*. A lever pulled to fire a gun; a device used to release or start an action. *v*. To start.

trill *n*. A tremulous utterance of successive tones. *v*. To utter with a fluttering sound.

tril-lion (tril´yon) *n*. The cardinal number equal to one thousand billion.

trim (trim) *v*. To clip or cut off small amounts in order to make neater; to decorate. *adj*. Neat. **trim** *n*.

tri-ni-tro-tol-u-ene (trī nī´trōtol´ū ēn´) *n*. A very powerful explosive, abbreviated as TNT.

trin-ket (tring´kit) *n*. A small piece of jewelry.

tri-o (trē´ō) *n*. A set or group of three.

trip (trip) *n*. Travel from one place to another; a journey; a loss of balance. *v*. To stumble. *Slang* A hallucinatory effect induced by drugs.

tripe (trīp) *n*. The stomach lining of oxen or similar animals, used as food. *Slang* Nonsense.

trip-le (trip´l) *adj*. Having three parts. *v*. To multiply by three; in baseball, a three-base hit.

trip-let (trip´lit) *n*. One of three born at the same time.

trip-li-cate (trip´li kāt´) *n*. A group of three identical things. **triplicate** *v*.

tri-pod (trī´pod) *n*. A three-legged stand or frame.

trite (trīt) *adj*. Used too often; common.

tri-umph (trī´umf) *v*. To be victorious. *n*. A victory. **triumphant** *adj*.

triv-i-al (triv´ē al) *adj*. Insignificant; of little value or importance; ordinary.

trol-ley (trol´ē) *n*. A streetcar powered by electricity from overhead lines; a small container or basket used to convey material, as in an underground tunnel or mine.

trom-bone (trom bōn´) *n*. A brass musical instrument, larger and lower in pitch than a trumpet.

troop (trōp) *n*. A group or assembly of people or animals; a group of Boy Scouts or Girl Scouts having an adult leader; a military unit. **trooper** *n*.

tro-phy (trō´fē) *n. pl*. **-ies** A prize or object, such as a plaque, awarded to someone for his success, victory, or achievement.

trop-ic (trop´ik) *n*. Either of two imaginary parallel lines which constitute the Torrid Zone. **Tropics** The very warm region of the earth's surface that lies between the Tropic of Cancer and the Tropic of Capricorn. **tropical** *adj*.

tro-po-sphere (trop´o sfēr´) *n*. The lowest atmosphere between the earth's surface and the stratosphere.

trot (trot) *n*. The gait of a horse or other four-footed animal, between a walk and a run, in which the hind leg and opposite front leg move at about the same time.

troth (troth) *n*. Good faith; the act of pledging one's fidelity. **troth** *v*.

trou-ble (rub´l) *n*. Danger; affliction; need; distress; an effort; physical pain, disease or malfunction. *v*. To bother; to worry; to be bothered; to be worried. **troubler** *n*. **troublingly** *adv*.

troubleshoot In *computer science*, to attempt to locate the source of a hardware or software problem and correct it.

trough (trof) *n*. A long, narrow, shallow container, especially one that holds food or water for animals.

troupe (trōp) *n*. A group, especially of the performing arts. **troupe** *v*.

trou-sers (trou´zẽrz) *n. pl*. An outer garment that covers the body from the waist down.

trout (trout) *n*. A freshwater game or food fish.

trowel (trou´el) *n*. A flat-bladed garden tool with a pointed blade, used for digging. **trowel** *v*. **troweler** *n*.

tru-ant (trö´ant) *n*. A person who is absent from school without permission.

truce (trös) *n*. An agreement to stop fighting; a cease-fire.

truck (truk) *n*. An automotive vehicle used to carry heavy loads; any of various devices with wheels designed to move heavy loads; garden vegetables for sale. **trucker** *n*.

trudge (truj) *v*. To walk heavily; to plod.

true (trö) *adj*. In accordance with reality or fact; not false; real; loyal; faithful. *adv*. Truthfully. **truly** *adv*.

Truman, Harry S. *n*. (1884-1972) The thirty-third president of the United States from 1945-1953.

trump (trump) *n*. In cards, a suit of any cards which outrank all other cards for a selected period of time.

trum-pet (trum´pit) *n., Mus*. A brass instrument having a flared bell, valves, and a mouthpiece. *v*. To proclaim something loudly.

truncate In computer science, to shorten by eliminating less significant parts, as by rounding off a decimal number or eliminating leading zeros in the number.

trunk (trungk) *n*. The main part of a tree;

the human body, excluding the head, arms and legs; a sturdy box for packing clothing, as for travel or storage; the long snout of an elephant. **trunks** Men's clothing worn for swimming or athletics.

truss (trus) v. To fasten or tie securely. *Med.* A support or device worn to keep a hernia in place.

trust (trust) n. Confidence or faith in a person or thing; care or charge. *Law* The confidence or arrangement by which property is managed and held for the good or benefit of another person. v. To have confidence or faith in; to believe; to expect; to entrust; to depend on.

truth (trŏth) n., pl. **truths** The facts corresponding with actual events or happenings; sincerity or honesty. **truthful** adj. **truthfully** adv. **truthfulness** n.

try (trī) v. To make an attempt; to make an effort; to strain; to hear or conduct a trial; to place on trial. **trying** adj.

tsp abbr. Teaspoon.

tub (tub) n. A round, low, flat-bottomed, vessel often with handles on the side, as one used for washing.

tu-ba (tö'ba) n. A large, brass wind instrument having a low pitch.

tube (töb) n. A hollow cylinder, made of metal, rubber, glass or other material, used to pass or convey something through. **tube** adj. **tubal** adj.

tu-ber (tö'bër) n. The underground stem of certain plants, as the potato, with buds from which new plants arise.

tu-ber-cu-lo-sis n. A contagious lung disease of humans and animals caused by bacteria; abbreviated as TB.

tuck (tuk) n. A flattened fold of material, usually stitched in place. v. To sew or make a tuck in material; to put in a safe place; to make secure.

tuft (tuft) n. A small cluster of feathers, threads, hair, or other material fastened or growing closely together.

tug (tug) v. To strain and pull vigorously. n. A hard pull; a strong force.

tu-i-tion (tö ish'an) n. Payment for instruction, as at a private school or college.

tu-lip (tö'lip) n. A bulb-type plant, having upright cup-like blossoms.

tum-ble (tum'bl) v. To fall or cause to fall; to perform acrobatic rolls, somersaults, and similar maneuvers; to mix up; to turn over and over. **tumbler** n. **tumble** n.

tum-ble-down (tum'bl doun') adj. Ramshackle; in need of repair.

tu-mor (tö'mër) n., *Pathol.* A swelling on or in any part of the body; an abnormal growth which may be malignant or benign.

tu-mult (tö'mult) n. The confusion and noise of a crowd; a riot; any violent commotion. **tumultuous** adj.

tu-na (tö'na) n. pl. **-na** or **-nas** Any of several large marine food fish.

tune (tön) n. A melody which is simple and easy to remember; agreement; harmony. v. To adjust. **tunable** adj. **tunably** adv.

tu-nic (tö'nik) n. A loose garment extending to the knees, worn by ancient Romans and Greeks.

tun-nel (tun'el) n. An underground or underwater passageway. **tunnel** v.

tur-ban (ter'ban) n. A Moslem headdress that consists of a long scarf wound around the head.

tur-bine (ter'bin) n. A motor having one or more rotary units mounted on a shaft, which are turned by the force of gas or a liquid.

tur-bu-lent (ter'bya lent) adj. Marked by a violent disturbance. **turbulence** n. **turbulently** adv.

tu-reen (te rēn') n. A large dish, often covered, used to serve soup or stew.

turf (terf) n. A layer of earth with its dense growth of grass and matted roots. *Slang* Home territory or ground.

tur-key (ter'kē) n. A large game bird of North America, having a bare head and extensible tail; the meat of this bird. *Slang* A failure.

tur-moil (ter'moil) n. A state of confusion or commotion.

turn (tern) v. To move or cause to move around a center point; to revolve or rotate; to transform or change; to move so that the bottom side of something becomes the top and the top becomes the bottom.

turn-buck-le (tern'buk'l) n. A metal coupling, used to regulate the distance between two metal rods or wires.

turn-down (tern'doun') n., *Slang* A rejection or refusal.

tur-nip (ter'nip) n. An edible root from the mustard family of plants.

turn-over (tern'ō'vèr) n. The process or act of turning over; an upset; a change or reversal; the number of times merchandise is bought, sold, and restocked in a certain period of time; the number of people hired in a given period of time to replace those who have left.

tur-pen-tine (ter'pen fin') n. The thick sap of certain pine trees; a clear liquid manufactured from this sap, used to thin paint.

tur-quoise (ter'koiz) n. A blue-green gemstone; a light bluish-green color.

tur-ret (ter'it) n. A small ornamental tower on a building; a raised, usually rotating, section of a ship, tank, or plane where the gunner sits.

tur-tle (ter´tl) *n.* A scaly-skinned animal having a soft-body covered with a hard shell into which the head, legs, and tail can be retracted.

tusk (tusk) *n.* A long, curved tooth, as of an elephant or walrus.

tus-sle (tus´l) *n.* A hard fight or struggle with a problem or person. **tussle** *v.*

tu-tor (tö´tër) *n.* A person who teaches another person privately. *v.* To teach, coach, or instruct privately.

tutorial In *computer science*, an adjunct to a program that teaches the user how to use each program.

tut-ti-frut-ti (tö´të frö´të) *n.* An ice cream flavor that contains different types of can-died fruits.

tu-tu (tö´tö) *n.* A very short ballet skirt.

tux-e-do (tuk sē´dö) *n.* A semiformal dress suit worn by men.

twang (twang) *n.* A sharp, ringing sound like that of a violin or other stringed instrument. *v.* To cause or make a twang.

tweak (twēk) *v.* To pinch and twist sharply. **tweak** *n.*

tweed (twēd) *n.* A coarse woolen fabric, woven in two or more colors. **tweeds** Clothing made of tweed.

tweez-ers (twē´zërz) *n. pl.* A small, pincer-like implement used to grasp or pluck small objects.

twelve (twelv) *n.* The cardinal number equal to 11 + 1.

twen-ty (twen´tē) *n.* The cardinal number equal to 19 + 1 or 2 X 10.

twice (twīs) *adv.* Double; two times.

twid-dle (twid´l) *v.* To turn or twirl in an aimless way.

twig (twig) *n.* A small branch which grows from a larger branch on a tree.

twi-light (twī´līt´) *n.* The soft light of the sky between sunset and complete darkness.

twill (twil) *n.* A weave that produces the parallel rib on the surface of a fabric.

twin (twin) *n.* One of two persons born at the same time to the same mother; one of two similar persons or things. *adj.* Having two similar or identical parts.

twine (twīn) *v.* To weave or twist together. *n.* A strong cord or thread made by twisting many threads together.

twinge (twinj) *n.* A sudden, sharp pain; a brief emotional or mental pang.

twin-kle (twing´kl) *v.* To gleam or shine with quick flashes; to sparkle.

twirl (twerl) *v.* To rotate or cause to turn around and around. **twirl** *n.*

twist (twist) *v.* To wind two or more pieces of thread, twine, or other materials together to make a single strand; to curve; to bend; to distort or change the meaning of; to injure and wrench. *n.* The act of twisting.

twit (twit) *v.* To tease about a mistake. *n.* A taunting reproach.

twitch (twich) *v.* To move or cause to move with a jerky movement. *n.* A sudden tug.

two (tö) *n.* The cardinal number of 1 + 1; the second in a sequence.

two-bit (tö´bit´) *adj.* Insignificant. **bits** Twenty-five cents. **faced** Double-dealing. **twofold.** Being double as much or as many.

two-time (tö´tīm´) *v., Slang* To be unfaithful to. **two-timer** *n.*

ty-coon (tī kön´) *n., Slang* A business person of wealth and power.

tyke (tīk) *n.* A small child.

Tyler, John *n.* (1790-1862) The tenth president of the United States from 1841-1845.

type (tīp) *n.* A class or group of persons or things; letters, numbers, and other symbols typewritten on paper or another surface; in printing, the piece of plastic, metal, or wood having the character or characters that are printed; a model or example of. **type** *v.* To identify according to some sort of classification; to typewrite. **typecast** *v.* To use more than once or repeatedly in the same kind of role.

type-face (tīp´fās´) *n.* A style or design of printing type.

type-set-ter (tīp set´ër) *n.* A person who arranges or sets type. **typesetting** *n.*

ty-phoid (tī´foid) *n., Pathol.* An acute, infectious disease caused by germs in drink or food, resulting in high fever and intestinal hemorrhaging.

ty-phoon (tī fön´) *n.* A tropical hurricane, especially one in the western part of the Pacific Ocean.

typ-i-cal (tip´i kal) *adj.* Exhibiting the characteristics of a certain class or group. **typically** *adv.*

typ-i-fy (tip´i fī´) *v.* To be characteristic or typical of; to show all the traits or qualities of a group. **typification** *n.* **typifying** *adj.*

typ-ist (tī´pist) *n.* The operator of a typewriter.

ty-po (tī´pö) *n., Slang* An error in typewriting or in setting type; any printed error which was not the fault of the author.

ty-ran-no-sau-rus (ti ran´o sor´) *n.* A large, flesh-eating dinosaur which walked on its hind legs.

tyr-an-ny (tir´a nē) *n.* Harsh, absolute, and unfair rule by a government, king or other ruler.

ty-rant (tī´rant) *n.* An absolute, unjust, or cruel ruler; one who exercises power or control unfairly.

ty-ro *also* **ti-ro** (tīrö) *n.* A novice or a beginner.

U, u (ū) The twenty-first letter of the English alphabet.

ubiq-ui-none *n.* The quinone which is able to function as an electron transfer agent in the Kreb's cycle.

ubiq-ui-tous (ū bik´wi tus) *adj.* To be everywhere at the same point in time.

ubiq-ui-ty (ū bik´wi tē) *n.* A presence in many places or locations at the same time.

ud-der (ud´er) *n.* The milk-producing organ pouch of some female animals, having two or more teats.

ugh (öch) Used to express disgust or horror.

ug-li-fy (ug´li fī) v. To make something or someone ugly.

ug-ly (ug´lē) *adj.* Offensive; unpleasant to look at.

ug-some *adj.* To be loathsome.

uh *interj.* To express hesitation.

uh–huh *interj.* Used for the purpose of showing or indicating agreement.

uhf *abbr.* Ultra high frequency.

uh-lan (ö´län) *n.* Part of a body of the Prussian light cavalry that was originally modeled on Tartar lancers.

uin-ta-ite *n.* A type of black asphalt which can be found especially in Utah.

ukase *n.* The proclamation by a Russian government that has the force of law.

u-ku-le-le (ū´kə lā´lē) *n.* A small, four-stringed musical instrument, originally from Hawaii.

ula-ma n. Body of mullahs.

-u-lar *adj., suffix* To be relating to.

ul-cer (ul´sėr) *n.* A festering, inflamed sore on a mucous membrane or on the skin that results in the destruction of the tissue. **ulcerous** *adj.*

ul-cero-gen-ic *adj.* To be tending to develop into an ulcer.

-ule *n., suffix* Small or little one.

-u-lent *adj., suffix* That abounds in.

ulex-ite *n.* A kind of mineral that occurs in loose fibers that is able to transmit light lengthwise with very little diminished intensity.

ul-lage (ul´ij) *n.* That amount a container lacks from being full.

ul-na (ul´na) *n., Anat.* One of the two bones of the forearm.

-u-lose *n., suffix* Ketose sugar.

ulot-ri-chous (ū lo´ti kus) *adj.* To have crisp or woolly hair.

-u-lous *adj., suffix* Being slightly.

ul-ster (ul´stėr) *n.* A type of long loose overcoat that is of Irish origin and is made of heavy material.

ul-te-ri-or (ul tēr´ē ėr) *adj.* To be located or situated on the further side of something or someone.

ultima *n.* A last syllable of a word.

ul-ti-ma ra-tio *n.* A final argument or the last resort to a problem or discussion.

ul-ti-mate (ul´ti mit) *adj.* Final; ending; most extreme; maximum; most.

ul-ti-ma-tum (ul´ti mä´tum) *n. pl* **-tums, -ta** A final demand, proposal, or choice, as in negotiating.

ul-ti-mo (ul´ti mō) *adj.* To be happening or occurring in the month which precedes the present.

ul-ti-mo-gen-i-ture (ul´ti mō jen´i chėr) *n.* The system of inheritance where the youngest boy succeeds to the estate.

ultra *adj.* To be going beyond others.

ul-tra- (ul´tra) *prefix* Beyond the scope, range, or limit of something.

ul-tra-ba-sic *adj.* To be extremely basic. **ultrabasic** *n.*

ul-tra-cen-trif-u-gal *adj.* Pertaining to being obtained by the means or methods of ultra-centrifuge.

ul-tra-cen-tri-fuge (ul´tra sen´tri fūj´) *n.* A kind of high speed centrifuge that is able to sediment colloidal and other small particles.

ul-tra-cen-ser-va-tive (ul´tra kən sür´va tiv) *adj.* To be extremely cautious.

ul-tra-fash-ion-able *adj.* Being up-to-date with fashions and customs.

ul-tra-fiche *n.* A type of microfiche whose microimages are of printed matter which has been reduced 90 times or more.

ul-tra-fil-tra-tion *n.* The act of filtrating small particles through a membrane and holding back the larger particles.

ul-tra-high *adj.* To be exceedingly high.

ul-tra-ism (ul´tra iz´um) *n.* An example of radicalism. **ultraist** *n.* or *adj.*

ul-tra-lib-er-al *adj.* To be very liberal. **ultraliberal** *n.*

ul-tra-ma-rine (ul´tra ma rēn´) *adj.* To be situated beyond the sea or the ocean.

ul-tra-mi-cro *adj.* To be referring or dealing with something which is smaller than micro.

ul-tra-mi-cro-scope (ul´tra mī´kro skōp´) *n.* A type of instrument used for the purpose of viewing objects which are too small to be viewed through a regular microscope.

ul-tra-mi-cro-scop-ic *adj.* Being too small in size to be viewed with a regular microscope.

ul-tra-mi-cro-tome *n.* A type of microtome that is made or designed to cut very thin sections off of something for the purpose of examining it. **ultramicrotomy** *n.*

ul-tra-mil-i-tant *adj.* To be very militant. **ultramilitant** *n.*

ul-tra-min-ia-ture *adj.* Extremely small; below miniature; tiny.

ul-tra-mod-ern (ul´tra mod´ėrn) *adj.* Extremely advanced or modern in style or ideas.

ul-tra-na-tion-al-ism *n.* An excessive devotion to national interests.

ul-tra-pure *adj.* To be of the utmost purity. **ultrapurely** *adv.*

ul-tra-se-cret *adj.* To be highly secret.

ul-tra-short *adj.* To be short in duration.

ul-tra-son-ic (ul′tra son′ik) *adj.* Relating to sound frequencies inaudible to humans. **ultrasonically** *adv.*

ul-tra-son-ics *n.* The science of the ultrasonic happenings and phenomena.

ul-tra-so-phis-ti-cat-ed *adj.* To be very sophisticated.

ult-ra-sound *n.* The vibrations of the same physical nature as sound.

ul-tra-vi-o-let (ul′tra vī′o lit) *adj.* Producing radiation having wave lengths just shorter than those of visible light and longer than those of x-rays.

ultra vires *adv.* Beyond the scope of legal authority.

ul-u-lant *adj.* To have a howling sound or noise. **ululation** *n.*

ul-u-late *v.* To howl like a wolf of dog; to wail very loud.

um-ber *n.* A moderate brown color.

um-bil-i-cal *adj.* Pertaining to the navel.

umbilical cord *n.* The structure by which a fetus is attached to its mother, serving to supply food and dispose of waste.

um-bil-i-cate *adj.* To be depressed such as the navel in appearance.

um-bil-i-cus (um bil′i kus) *n.* A little depression occurring in the abdominal wall where the umbilical cord was attached to the embryo.

um-bles (um′belz) *n.* Entrails of an animal such as a deer which used to be used as food.

um-bo (um′bō) *n.* The elevation of the tympanic membrane of the ear.

um-bra *n.* The conical shadow that excludes all light from the given source.

um-brage (um′brij) *n.* A reason for doubt.

um-bra-geous *adj.* To be filled with shadows. **umbrageousness** *n.*

um-brel-la (um brel′a) *n.* A collapsible frame covered with plastic or cloth, held above the head as protection from sun or rain.

umi-ak (ō′mē ak′) *n.* An open flat bottom Eskimo boat propelled with broad paddles.

ump *v., Slang* To act or to behave as an umpire such as in the game of baseball.

um-pir-age *n.* An act of umpiring.

um-pire (um′pī ėr) *n.* In sports, the person who rules on plays in a game. *v.* To act as an umpire.

ump-teen (ump′tēn′) *adj., Slang* An indefinitely large number.

un- *prefix* The reverse or opposite of an act; removal or release from.

un-a-bat-ed *adj.* To be not abated.

un-able (un ā′bl) *adj.* Not having the mental capabilities.

un-abridged *adj.* To be the most complete of a group or of a class.

un-ac-cept-able (un′ak sep′ta bl) *adj.* To be not welcome. **unacceptably** *adv.*

un-ac-com-mo-dat-ed (un′a kom′o dā′tid) *adj.* To be not accommodated.

un-ac-com-pa-nied *adj.* Alone; without a companion. *Mus.* Solo.

un-ac-count-a-ble (un′a koun′ta bl) *adj.* Without an explanation; mysterious; not responsible. **unaccountably** *adv.*

un-ac-cus-tomed (un′a kus′tomd) *adj.* Not used to or in the habit of; not ordinary.

un-adorned (un′a dornd′) *n.* Being without decorations.

un-adorn-ment *n.* The state of being unadorned.

un-adul-ter-at-ed *adj.* To be pure.

un-ad-vised (un′ad vīzd′) *adj.* To do something or an action without consideration.

un-af-fect-ed (un′a fek′tid) *adj.* Not being affected in any way by something or someone.

un-af-fec-tion-ate *adj.* Without or lacking affection.

un-al-loyed (un′a loid′) *adj.* To be not alloyed; pure.

un-al-ter-able (un ol′tėr a bl) *adj.* Incapable of being changed. **unalterableness** *n.*

un-am-biv-a-lent *adj.* Being not ambivalent. **unambivalently** *adv.*

un-an-chor *v.* To remove or to loosen for an anchor, as a boat.

un-anes-the-tized *adj.* Not having been subject to the anesthetic.

u-na-nim-i-ty *n.* The state of being unanimous.

u-nan-i-mous (ū nan′i mus) *adj.* Agreed to completely; based on the agreement of all. **unanimously** *adv.*

un-an-tic-i-pat-ed *adj.* To be not anticipated. **unanticipatedly** *adv.*

un-apol-o-get-ic *adj.* To be put forward without an apology.

un-ap-peas-able *adj.* Not to be appeased.

un-ap-proach-able (un′a prō′cha bl) *adj.* To be physically inaccessible.

un-apt (un apt′) *adj.* Not likely.

un-armed (un ermd′) *adj.* Lacking means for protection.

un-ar-tic-u-lat-ed *adj.* To be not carefully reasoned before something is done.

una-ry *adj.* To consist of a single item.

un-a-shamed (un′a shāmd′) *adj.* To be without guilt. **unashamedly** *adv.*

un-as-sail-a-ble (un′a sā′la bl) *adj.* Being not liable to attack.

un-as-ser-tive (un′a sür′tiv) *adj.* Not being assertive.

un-as-sist-ed (un′a sis′tid) *adj.* To be made without being assisted by another.

un-as-sum-ing (un′a sö′ming) *adj.*

Modest and not showy.

un-at-tach-ed (un´a tacht´) *adj.* Not engaged, going steady, or married.

un-at-trac-tive *adj.* Not attractive or pretty; dull.

un-a-vail-ing (un´a vā´ling) *adj.* To be not availing.

un-a-void-able (un´a void´a bl) *adj.* Inevitable; unstoppable. **avoidably** *adv.*

un-a-ware (un´a wâr´) *adj.* Not realizing. **unawareness** *n.* **unawarely** *adv.*

un-backed *adj.* To be lacking aid or support from another.

un-bal-ance (un bal´ans) *v.* To put someone or something out of balance.

un-bal-anced (un bal´anst) *adj.* Not in balance.

un-bar-bered *adj.* To have unkempt long hair.

un-barred *adj.* Not being fixed or secured with a bar.

un-be *v.* To cease to have being.

un-bear-a-ble (un bâr´a bl) *adj.* Not possible to endure; intolerable.

un-beat-able (un bēt´a bl) *adj.* To be possessing unsurpassable qualities.

unbeaten *adj.* Being not pounded.

un-be-coming (un bi kum´ing) *adj.* Unattractive; not pleasing; not proper, polite or suitable for the situation or occasion. **unbecomingness** *n.*

un-be-known *or* **un-be-knownst (un´bin-ōnst´)** *adj.* Not known; without one's knowledge.

un-be-lief *n.* The skepticism in the matters such as one's religious faith.

un-be-liev-able (un´bi lēv´a bl) *adj.* Incredible; hard to accept; not to be believed. **unbelievably** *adv.*

un-be-liev-er (un´bi lē´vér) *n.* A person who does not believe certain things as being true.

un-belt-ed *adj.* To not be belted or furnished with a belt.

un-bend (un bend´) *v.* To make something straight. **unbendable** *adj.*

un-bend-ing (un ben´ding) *adj.* To not bend.

un-bi-ased *adj.* To be not biased.

un-bib-li-cal *adj.* To be unsanctioned by the Bible.

un-bid-den (un bid´en) *adj.* To be not bidden.

un-bind (un bīnd´) *v.* To take or remove a band from something or from someone.

un-blessed (un blest) *adj.* To be not blessed.

un-blind-ed *adj.* Existing free from illusion.

un-blink-ing *adj.* Not showing any emotions such as crying.

un-block *v.* To free something from being blocked by something else.

un-bod-i-ed (un bod´ēd) *adj.* To have no body.

un-bolt (un bōlt´) *v.* To unfasten with the withdrawal of a bolt such as with a lock on a door.

un-born (un born) *adj.* To be existing without birth.

un-bo-som (un büz´om) *v.* To disclose or tell the thoughts of oneself to another.

un-bound (un bound´) *adj.* Being free or not fastened to anything or by anything.

un-brace (un brās´) *v.* To detach as if removing a brace or a band from something or someone.

un-braid *v.* To take apart grouped strands of hair or cloth.

un-branched (un brancht´) *adj.* To have no or be without branches.

un-bred (un bred´) *adj.* Being not taught.

un-bri-dle *v.* To free from or to unfasten a bridle.

un-bro-ken (un brō´ken) *adj.* Being not violated or broken; being in one piece.

un-buck-le (un buk´l) *v.* To loosen or remove the buckle of something such as a belt.

un-budg-ing *adj.* Unable to be moved or changed.

un-build (un bild) *v.* To take down such as a house.

un-bun-dle *v.* To price or place something separately.

un-bur-den (un bür´den) *v.* To relieve from a burden; to free from fears or problems.

un-but-tered *adj.* Being without butter.

un-cage *v.* To set something or someone free from a cage or the object that holds them.

un-cal-cu-lat-ed *adj.* Not thought about or out before it occurs.

un-called for (un kåld´fâr´) *adj.* Not necessary or needed; not requested.

un-can-did *adj.* Not honest.

un-can-ny (un kan´ē) *adj.* Strange, odd, or mysterious; exceptional. **uncannily** *adv.* **uncanniness** *n.*

un-cap (un kap´) *v.* To remove covering or lid of something.

un-caused *adj.* Having no cause or reason.

un-ceas-ing *adj.* To never cease or end. **unceasingly** *adv.*

un-cel-e-brat-ed *adj.* Not being famous or well-known.

un-cer-e-mo-ni-ous (un´ser e mō´nē us) *adj.* To be informal; not ceremonious.

un-cer-tain (un ser´tan) *adj.* Doubtful; not sure; not known; hard to predict.

un-cer-tain-ty (un sür´tan tē) *n.* The state of being uncertain or unsure.

un-change-able (un chān´ja bl) *adj.* To be not changing. **-ableness** *n.*

un-changed *adj.* Having nothing new or different.

un-char-ac-ter-is-tic *adj.* Being not

typical.

un-charged (un chärjd´) *adj.* Not being charged with something.

un-char-i-ta-ble (un char´i ta bl) *adj.* To be lacking in charity. **-ness** *n.*

un-chart-ed (un chär´tid) *adj.* Not plotted such as on a map.

un-chiv-al-rous *adj.* Not being chivalrous. **unchivalrously** *adv.*

un-choke *v.* To unblock an obstruction such as a piece of food in the throat.

un-ci-al (un shē al) *n.* A style of writing used in Greek and Latin manuscripts.

un-ci-form (un´si form´) *adj.* To be hook shaped.

un-ci-nar-ia *n.* A type of parasitic worm in the shape of a hook; hookworm.

un-ci-nate (un´si nit) *adj.* To be bent at the end or the tip.

un-cir-cum-cised (un sür´kum sīzd´) *adj.* Being spiritually impure.

un-civ-il (un siv´il) *adj.* Being not civil.

un-civ-i-lized (un siv´i lizd´) *adj.* Without culture or refinement; without an established cultural and social way of living.

un-clamp *v.* To remove the clamp off of something.

un-clar-i-ty *n.* A lack of clarity.

un-clasp (un klasp´) *v.* To remove the clasp of or open the clasp of something.

un-clas-si-cal *adj.* Not being classical.

un-clas-si-fied *adj.* To not be subject to a security classification.

un-cle (ung´kl) *n.* The brother of one's mother or father; the husband of an aunt.

un-clean (un klēn´) *adj.* Immoral; dirty; not decent.

un-clench (un klench´) *v.* To open something from a clenched position.

un-climb-a-ble *adj.* Unable to be climbed. **unclimbableness** *n.*

un-cloak (un klōk´) *v.* To remove a cover from.

un-closed *adj.* Not being settled.

un-clothe (un klōth´) *v.* To uncover or undress.

un-cloud-ed *adj.* Not being covered by clouds. **uncloudedly** *adv.*

un-clut-ter (un klut´ėr) *v.* To take clutter from an area; to make neat.

un-cof-fin *v.* To take out of a coffin.

un-coil (un koil´) *v.* To release from a coiled state; to unwind.

un-coined (un koind´) *adj.* Not being minted.

un-com-fort-a-ble (un kumf´ta bl) *adj.* Disturbed; not at ease physically or mentally; causing discomfort.

un-com-mit-ted (un´ko mit´id) *adj.* Not being committed to something or to someone.

un-com-mon (un kom´on) *adj.* Rare; odd; unusual; extraordinary. **-ly** *adv.*

un-com-mu-ni-ca-ble *adj.* Being unable to communicate something.

un-com-mun-i-ca-tive (un´ko mū´ni kā´tiv) *adj.* Not able to give information about something.

un-com-pas-sion-ate *adj.* Being unfeeling; not compassionate.

un-com-pet-i-tive *adj.* Being unable to compete in a competition or sport.

un-com-plain-ing *adj.* Not complaining. **uncomplainingly** *adv.*

un-com-pli-cat-ed *adj.* To be not complex or complicated; simple.

un-com-pli-men-ta-ry (un´kom pli men´ta rē) *adj.* Not being complimentary.

un-com-pre-hend-ing (un´kom pli men´ta rē) *adj.* To be lacking in understanding of something.

un-com-pro-mis-ing (un kom´pro mī´zing) *adj.* Firm; unwilling to give in or to compromise.

un-con-cern (un´kon sern´) *n.* Lack of interest; disinterest; indifference.

un-con-cern-ed *adj.* The state of not having any interest in something or someone. **unconcernedly** *adv.*

un-con-di-tion-al (un´kon dish´a nal) *adj.* Without conditions or limits.

un-con-di-tioned *adj.* Not subject to conditioning.

un-con-form-a-ble (un´kon for´ma bl) *adj.* Not conforming to anything such as ideals.

un-con-for-mi-ty *n.* The lack of conformity.

un-con-ge-nial *adj.* Not being compatible to something or to someone.

un-con-ge-nial-i-ty *n.* The state of being uncongenial.

un-con-quer-a-ble (un kong´ke a bl) *adj.* Being unable to be conquered by someone.

un-con-scio-na-ble (un kon´sha na bl) *adj.* To be not guided by the conscience. **unconscionability,** *n.*

un-con-scious (un kon´shus) *adj.* Not mentally aware; done without thought; not on purpose.

un-con-sid-ered (un´kon sid´ėrd) *adj.* To be not worth considering.

un-con-sol-i-dat-ed *adj.* To be arranged loosely.

un-con-sti-tu-tion-al (un´kon sti tö´sha nal) *adj.* Contrary to the constitution or the basic laws of a state or country.

un-con-straint *adj.* To be free from constraint.

un-con-trol-la-ble (un´kon trō´la bl) *adj.* To exist free from the control of another.

un-con-ven-tion-al (un´kon ven´sha nal) *adj.* Not in accordance with convention.

un-con-vinc-ing *adj.* To not be convincing. **unconvincingly** *adv.*

un-cool *adj.* To be lacking or without assurance.

un-cork (un kork´) v. To release from a container that has been sealed with a cork.

un-cou-ple (un kup´l) v. To release or disconnect from railroad cars.

un-couth (un kŏth´) adj. Acting or speaking crudely, unrefined; clumsy or awkward. **uncouthness** n.

un-cov-er (un kuv´ĕr) v. To remove the cover from something; to disclose.

un-cre-at-ed (un´krē ā´tid) adj. To not exist because of creation.

un-crit-i-cal (un krit´i kal) adj. To be lacking in discrimination.

un-cross v. To remove or to change something from a crossed position.

un-crown v. To remove the crown from someone such as a king.

un-crum-ple v. To return something to its original smooth condition.

un-crush-a-ble adj. Not being able to be crushed by something or by someone.

unc-tion n. An ointment which is used for the purpose of anointing an injury.

unc-tu-ous (ungk´chŏ us) adj. To be smooth in texture; have organic matter and be easily workable.

un-curl (un kürl´) v. To straighten something from a curled position.

un-cut (un kut´) adj. Not being cut into.

un-cyn-i-cal adj. Not being cynical.

un-daunt-a-ble adj. To be incapable of being daunted.

un-daunt-ed (un don´tid) adj. Being courageously resolute. **-ly** adv.

un-de-bat-a-ble adj. Being not subject to debate. **undebatably** adv.

un-de-cid-ed (un´di sī´did) adj. Unsettled; having made no firm decision; open to change. **-edly** adv.

undecylenic acid n. Type of acid that is found in perspiration.

un-de-fend-ed adj. Being not defended or protected.

un-dem-o-crat-ic adj. To not be agreeing with the ideals of the democratic party.

un-de-mon-stra-tive (un´de mon´stra tiv) adj. Being restrained in the expression of one's feelings or emotions. **undemonstrativeness** n.

un-de-ni-a-ble (un´di nī´a bl) adj. Not open to doubt or denial; not possible to contradict. **undeniably** adv.

un-der (un´dĕr) prep. Below, in place or position; in a place lower than another; less in degree, number, or other quality; inferior in rank, quality, or character; during the reign or period; in accordance with. **under** Into; in a position underneath or below something; less than the required amount; insufficient.

under (un´dĕr) prefix Location beneath or below; lower in importance or rank, degree or amount.

un-der-a-chiev-er (un´dĕr a chē´vĕr) n. A kind of student that fails to achieve his or her scholastic potential.

un-der-act (un´dĕr akt´) v. To perform something in a feeble manner.

un-der-ac-tiv-i-ty n. A low level of activity which is thought of as not being normal.

un-der-age (un´dĕr āj´) adj. Being less than legal age.

un-der-arm (un´dĕr ärm) n. The armpit.

un-der-bel-ly (un´dĕr bel´ē) n. The parts or sections of the body which are lower.

un-der-bid (un´dĕr bid´) v. To bid for something at a level which is too low.

un-der-bred (un´dĕr bred´) adj. Being of an inferior breed.

un-der-brush (un´dĕr brush´) n. Small bushes, vines, and plants that grow under tall trees.

un-der-bud-get-ed adj. To be provided with a budget which is inadequate.

un-der-car-riage (un´dĕr kar´ij) n. The landing gear of an airplane.

un-der-charge (un´dĕr chärj´) v. To charge too little for something that one buys.

un-der-class (un´dĕr klas´) n. The class which is lower such as in high school.

un-der-class-man (un´dĕr klas´man) n. A person who is a member of the freshman class in high school.

un-der-clothes (un´dĕr klōz´) n. Clothes worn next to the skin; underwear.

un-der-coat (un´dĕr kōt) n. A jacket which can be worn under another jacket.

un-der-coating n. A kind of waterproof coating which is applied to the underside of cars for the prevention of rusting and other types of wear.

un-der-cover (un´dĕr kuv´ĕr) adj. To be executed in a secret manner; engaged in spying for one's country, etc.

un-der-croft (un´dĕr kroft´) n. A type of room which is subterranean.

un-der-cur-rent (un´dĕr kür´ent) n. The current that is located below the surface currents in the water.

un-der-cut v. To sell something at a price which is lower than the competitor's price to get the business of the one being offered the price.

un-der-de-vel-oped (un´dĕr di vel´apt) adj. Not fully mature or grown; lacking modern communications and industry.

un-der-de-vel-op-ment n. The state of being underdeveloped.

un-der-do (un´dĕr dō) v. To do something less thoroughly than one is able to do it.

un-der-done (un´dĕr dun´) adj. To be not completely cooked.

un-der-dress n. A piece of clothing which is made to be worn under the dress of a woman when the dress is sheer.

un·der·ed·u·cat·ed *adj.* Being educated poorly.

un·der·em·ployed *adj.* To have less than adequate employment.

un·der·es·ti·mate (un´dĕr es´ti māt´) *v.* To place or to put a value or price on something which is too low.

un·der·feed (un´dĕr fēd´) *v.* To feed someone or something too little food.

un·der·foot (un´dĕr fot´) *adj.* Underneath or below the feet; being so close to one's feet as to be in the way.

un·der·fur (un´dĕr fûr´) *n.* A thick and soft fur that is lying under the long and coarse hair of a mammal.

un·der·gar·ment (un´dĕr gär´ment) *n.* A kind of garment that is made to be worn under another piece of garment, such as underwear.

un·der·gird (un´dĕr gûrd´) *v.* To make the foundation of something.

un·der·glaze (un´dĕr glāz´) *adj.* Suitable for applying before glaze is applied to something.

un·der·go (un´dĕr gō´) *v.* To have the experience of; to be subjected to.

un·der·grad·u·ate (un´dĕr graj´ö it) *n.* A college or university student studying for a bachelor's degree.

un·der·ground (un´dĕr ground´) *adj.* A channel or space which is subterranean. *n.* A group which functions outside of the law.

un·der·ground·er *n.* The member of the underground.

un·der·growth *n.* A type of growth which is found growing on the floor of the forest.

un·der·hand (un´dĕr hand´) *adj.* Done deceitfully and secretly; sly; sneaky. **underhandedly** *adv.*

un·der·hung *adj.* To have an underhung jaw; protruding or projecting beyond the upper jaw.

un·der·in·sured *adj.* Being not sufficiently insured.

un·der·laid (un´dĕr lād´) *adj.* To be placed beneath something.

un·der·lay (un´dĕr lā) *v.* To cover the bottom of something.

un·der·let (un´dĕr let) *v.* To be below the real value.

un·der·lie (un´dĕr lī´) *v.* To be at the basis of something.

un·der·line (un´dĕr līn´) *v.* To draw a line directly under something.

un·der·ling (un´dĕr ling) *n.* The person who is under the orders of another person.

un·der·lip (un´dĕr lip´) *n.* The lower lip of a person's mouth.

un·der·ly·ing (un´dĕr lī´ing) *adj.* To be lying below something.

un·der·manned *adj.* Being inadequately staffed.

un·der·mine (un´dĕr mīn´) *v.* To weaken; to make less strong.

un·der·most (un´dĕr mōst´) *adj.* The lowest in position.

un·der·neath (un´dĕr nēth´) *adv.* Beneath or below; on the under side; lower. **underneath** *prep.* Under; below.

un·der·nour·ished *n.* To be supplied with less than the minimum amount of the needed food. **undernourishment** *n.*

un·der·nu·tri·tion *n.* The lacking or deficient bodily nutrition which is due to inadequate food intake.

un·der·paid *adj.* To receive less than enough or adequate pay.

un·der·pants (un´dĕr pants´) *n.* The pants that are worn under another garment.

un·der·part *n.* An auxiliary part or section.

un·der·pass (un´dĕr pas´) *n.* A road or walk that goes under another.

un·der·pin (un´dĕr pin´) *v.* To strengthen the foundation of something.

un·der·pin·ning (un´dĕr pin´ing) *n.* The material which is used for the support of a structure.

un·der·play (un´dĕr plā´) *v.* To act with restraint.

un·der·plot *n.* A kind of dramatic plot in a play that is subordinate to the main action or plot.

un·der·pow·ered *adj.* To be driven by an engine that is not sufficiently powered.

un·der·priv·i·leged (un´dĕr priv´i lijd) *adj.* Deprived of economic and social advantages.

un·der·pro·duc·tion *n.* A type of production which is unable to satisfy the demand.

un·der·pro·duc·tive *adj.* Being unable to produce something adequately.

un·der·proof *adj.* To be containing less alcohol than the proof spirit.

un·der·rate (un´dĕr rāt´) *v.* To rate or value below the true worth.

un·der·re·port *v.* To report something as being less than it actually is.

un·der·ripe (un´dĕr rīp´) *adj.* To be insufficiently ripe.

un·der·sat·u·rat·ed *adj.* To be less than normally saturated or wet with a liquid.

un·der·score (un´dĕr skōr´) *v.* To emphasize. **underscore** *n.*

un·der·sea (un´dĕr sē´) *adj.* Being carried under the sea or under the surface of the sea.

un·der·sec·re·tar·i·at *n.* The staff which is under the secretary.

un·der·sell (un´dĕr sel´) *v.* To sell for less than a competitor.

un·der·side (un´dĕr sīd´) *n.* The side or part on the bottom.

un·der·stand (un´dĕr stand´) *v.* To comprehend; to realize; to know the feelings and thoughts of.

un-der-stand-a-ble (un'dèr stan'da bl) *adj.* Able to sympathize or comprehend. **understandably** *adv.*

un-der-state (un'dèr stāt') *v.* To make too little of the actual situation. **understatement** *n.*

un-der-stood (un'dèr sted') *adj.* Agreed upon by all.

un-der-stud-y (un'dèr stud'ē) *v.* To learn, another person's part or role in order to be able to replace him if necessary. **under-study** *n.*

un-der-take (un'dèr tāk') *v.* To set about to do a task; to pledge oneself to a certain job; to attempt. **-taking** *n.*

un-der-tak-er (un'dèr tā'kèr) *n.* A person who prepares the dead for burial.

un-der-tone (un'dèr tōn') *n.* A low, quiet voice; a pale or subdued color visible through other colors.

un-der-tow (un'dèr tō') *n.* The underwater current which runs in the opposite direction of the surface current.

un-der-wa-ter (un'dèr wä'tèr) *adj.* Occurring, happening or used beneath the surface of the water.

un-der-write (un'dèr rīt') *v.* To sign or write at the end of something; to finance; to assume a risk by means of insurance. To assume responsibility for; to undertake to pay a written pledge of money. **underwriter** *n.*

un-de-sir-a-ble (un'di zī'èr a bl) *adj.* Offensive; not wanted. **-ly** *adv.*

un-do (un dö') *v.* To cancel; to reverse; to loosen or unfasten; to open a package.

un-done *adj.* Not finished; unfastened; ruined.

un-du-late (un'ja lāt') *v.* To move from side to side with a flowing motion; to have a wavy shape. **undulation** *n.*

un-dy-ing (un dī'ing) *adj.* Without end.

un-earth (un erth') *v.* To dig up from the earth; to find or discover.

unearthly (un erth'lē) *adj.* Strange; not from this world.

un-eas-y (un ē'zē) *adj.* Feeling or causing distress or discomfort; embarrassed; awkward; uncertain. **uneasily** *adv.*

un-em-ployed (un'em ploid') *adj.* Without a job; without work. **-ment** *n.*

un-en-thu-si-as-tic *adj.* Not being excited about something.

un-e-qual (un ē'kwal) *adj.* Not even; not fair; not of the same size or time; lacking sufficient ability.

un-equiv-o-cal *adj.* Being clear; having no doubt.

un-es-sen-tial *adj.* Not being important.

un-e-ven (un ē'ven) *adj.* Not equal; varying inconsistency or form; not balanced.

un-e-vent-ful (un'i vent'ful) *adj.* Lacking insignificance; calm.

un-expect-ed (un'ik spek'tid) *adj.* Surprising; happening without warning. **unexpectedly** *adv.*

un-fail-ing (un fā'ling) *adj.* Constant, unchanging.

un-fair (un fār') *adj.* Not honest; marked by a lack of justice. **unfairly** *adv.*

un-faith-ful (un fāth'ful) *adj.* Breaking a promise or agreement; without loyalty; guilty of adultery.

un-fa-mil-iar (un'fa mil'yèr) *adj.* Not knowing; strange; foreign.

un-fath-om-able *adj.* Being unable to comprehend.

un-fa-vor-able (un fā'vèr a bl) *adj.* Undesired; harmful.

un-feel-ing (un fē'ling) *adj.* Without sympathy; hardheartend; without sensation. **unfeelingly** *adv.*

un-fin-ished *adj.* At loose ends; not completed.

un-fit (un fit') *adj.* Not suitable; not qualified; in poor body or mental health.

un-fold (un fōld') *v.* To open up the folds of and lay flat; to reveal gradually. **unfoldment** *n.*

un-fore-seen (un'fōr sēn') *adj.* Not anticipated or expected.

un-for-get-ta-ble (un'fèr get'a bl) *adj.* Impossible or hard to forget; memorable. **unforgettably** *adv.*

un-for-tu-nate (un for'cha nit) *adj.* Causing or having bad luck, damage, or harm. *n.* A person who has no luck.

un-found-ed (un foun'did) *adj.* Not founded or based on fact; groundless; lacking a factual basis.

un-friend-ly (un frend'lē) *adj.* Showing a lack of kindness; not friendly; not favorable.

un-furl (un ferl') *v.* To unroll or unfold; to open up or out.

un-fur-nished (un fer'nisht) *adj.* Without furniture.

un-god-ly (un god'lē) *adj.* Wicked; evil; lacking reverence for God.

un-grate-ful (un grāt'ful) *adj.* Not thankful; showing no appreciation.

un-guent (ung'gwent) *n.* A healing or soothing salve; ointment.

un-hap-py (un hap'ē) *adj.* Sad; without laughter or joy; not satisfied or pleased. **unhappily** *adv.* **unhappiness** *n.*

un-healthy *adj.* Sickly; not enjoying good health.

un-heard (un herd') *adj.* Not heard; not listened to.

un-heard-of (un herd'uv') *adj.* Not known or done before; without precedent.

un-ho-ly *adj.* Wicked.

un-hook (un hek') *v.* To release or undo from a hook.

un-hur-ried *adj.* At a leisurely pace. **unhurriedly** *adv.*

u-ni-corn (ū′*ni* kårn′) *n.* A mythical animal resembling a horse, with a horn in the center of its forehead.

u-ni-cy-cle (ū′*ni* sī′kl) *n.* A one wheeled vehicle with pedals.

unidentified flying object *n.* A flying object that cannot be explained or identified, abbreviated as UFO.

uni-fac-to-ri-al *adj.* Controlled by a single gene.

u-ni-form (ū′*ni* form′) *n.* Identical clothing worn by the members of a group to dis-tinguish them from the general population. **uniformly** *adv.*

uniform spacing In *computer science,* a type of font in which everyday character occupies exactly the same space regardless of the width of the character itself.

u-ni-fy (ū′*ni* fī′) *v.* To come together as one; to unite.

uni-lat-er-al *adj.* Affecting only one side of a subject.

uni-lin-ear *adj.* Developing in a series of stages from primitive to advanced.

un-in-hab-it-ed *adj.* Not lived in; empty.

un-in-ter-est-ed (un in′tèr i stid) *adj.* Having no interest or concern in; not interested.

un-ion (ūn′yon) *n.* The act of joining together of two or more groups or things; a group of countries or states joined under one government; a marriage; an organized body of employees who work together to upgrade their working conditions and wages. **Union** The United States, especially the federal government during the Civil War.

u-nip-ar-ous (ū nip′èr us) *adj.* Having produced one egg or offspring at a time.

u-nique (ū nēk′) *adj.* Unlike any other; sole.

u-ni-sex *adj.* Adaptable and appropriate for both sexes.

u-ni-son (ū′ni son) *n.* In music, the exact sameness of pitch, as of a tone; harmonious agreement.

u-nit (ū′nit) *n.* Any one of several parts regarded as a whole; an exact quantity that is used as a standard of measurement; a special section or part of a machine.

u-ni-tar-i-an (ū′ni târ′ē an) *n.* A member of a denomination that believes the deity exists in one person.

u-nite (ū nīt′) *v.* To join or come together for a common purpose.

United Nations *n.* An international organization formed in 1945; comprised of nearly all the countries of the world whose purpose is to pro-mote security, economic development, and peace.

unit rule *n.* A ruling which allows a delegation to a Democratic national convention to cast its entire vote as a unit by majority vote.

u-ni-ty (ū′ni tē) *n. pl.* **unities** The fact or state of being one; accord; agreement; harmony.

u-ni-valve (ū′ni valv′) *n.* A mollusk having a one-piece shell, such as a snail.

u-ni-ver-sal (ū′ni ver′sal) *adj.* Having to do with the world or the universe in its entirety.

u-ni-verse (ū′ni vers′) *n.* The world, stars, planets, space, and all that is contained.

u-ni-ver-si-ty (ū′ni ver′si tē) *n. pl.* **universities** An educational institution offering undergraduate and graduate degrees in a variety of academic areas.

un-just (un just′) *adj.* Not fair; lacking justice or fairness. **unjustly** *adv.*

un-kempt (un kempt′) *adj.* Poorly groomed; messy; untidy.

un-kind (un kīnd′) *adj.* Harsh; lacking in sympathy, concern, or under-standing. **unkindly** *adj.* **-ness** *n.*

un-known (un nōn′) *adj.* Strange; unidentified; not known; not familiar or famous. **unknown** *n.*

un-lead-ed (un led′id) *adj.* Containing no lead.

un-like (un līk′) *adj., prep* Dissimilar; not alike; not equal in strength or quantity.

un-lim-it-ed (un lim′i tid) *adj.* Having no boundaries or limitations.

un-load (un lōd′) *v.* To take or remove the load; to unburden; to dispose or get rid of by selling in volume.

un-lock (un lok′) *v.* To open, release, or unfasten a lock; open with a key.

un-loose (un lōs′) *v.* To loosen or undo; to release.

un-luck-y (un luk′ē) *adj.* Unfortunate; having bad luck; disappointing or unsuitable. **unluckily** *adv.*

un-manned (un mand′) *adj.* Designed to operate or be operated without a crew of people.

un-mask *v.* To reveal the truth of one's identity; to expose.

un-men-tion-a-ble (un men′sha na bl) *adj.* Improper or unsuitable.

un-mis-tak-a-ble (un′mi stä′ka bl) *adj.* Very clear and evident; understood; obvious. **unmistakably** *adv.*

un-mor-al (un mor′al) *adj.* Having no moral knowledge.

un-nat-u-ral (un nach′èr al) *adj.* Abnormal or unusual; strange; artificial.

un-nec-es-sar-y (un nes′i ser′ē) *adj.* Not needed; not appropriate.

un-nerve (un nerv′) *v.* To frighten; to upset.

un-num-bered (un num′bèrd) *adj.*

Countless; not identified by number.

un-oc-cu-pied (un ok'ya pīd') *adj.* Empty; not occupied.

un-pack (un pak') *v.* To remove articles out of trunks, suitcases, boxes, or other storage places.

un-pleas-ant (un plez'ant) *adj.* Not agreeable; not pleasant. **unpleasantly** *adv.* **unpleasantness** *n.*

un-pop-u-lar (un pop'ya lèr) *adj.* Not approved or liked. **unpopularity** *n.*

un-pre-dict-a-ble (un'pri dik'ta bl) *adj.* Not capable or being foretold; not reliable. **unpredictably** *adj.*

un- *prefix* The reverse or opposite of an act; removal or release from.

un-pre-pared (un'pri pârd') *adj.* Not equipped or ready.

un-pro-fes-sion-al (un'pro fesh'a nal) *adj.* Contrary to the standards of a profession; having no professional status.

un-prof-it-a-ble (un prof'i ta bl) *adj.* Showing or giving no profit; serving no purpose.

un-qual-i-fied (un kwol'i fīd') *adj.* Lacking the proper qualifications; unreserved.

un-ques-tion-able *adj.* Being indisputable.

un-rav-el (un rav'el) *v.* To separate threads; to solve; to clarify; to come apart.

un-re-al (un rē'al) *adj.* Having no substance or reality.

un-rea-son-a-ble (un rē'zo na bl) *adj.* Not according to reason; exceeding all reasonable limits.

un-re-lent-ing *adj.* Not weakening in vigor or determination.

un-re-li-a-ble (un'ri lī'a bl) *adj.* Unable to be trusted; not dependable.

un-re-served (un'ri zervd') *adj.* Done or given without reserve; unlimited.

un-re-strained (un'ri strānd') *adj.* Not held back, forced, or affected.

un-ripe *adj.* Immature, not ready to harvest. **unripeness** *n.*

un-ruf-fled *adj.* Serene and calm in the face of setbacks.

un-ru-ly (un rö'lē) *adj.* Disorderly; difficult to subdue or control.

un-sat-is-fac-to-ry (un'sat is fak'to rē) *adj.* Unacceptable; not pleasing.

un-sa-vor-y *adj.* Disagreeable; morally offensive.

un-screw (un skrö') *v.* To loosen or unfasten by removing screws from.

un-scru-pu-lous (un skrö'pya lus) *adj.* Without morals, guiding principles, or rules. **unscrupulously** *adv.* **unscrupulousness** *n.*

un-seat (un sēt') *v.* To cause to lose one's seat; to force out of office.

un-seg-re-gat-ed *adj.* Being free from racial segregation.

un-sel-fish (un sel'fish) *adj.* Willing to share; thinking of another's well being before one's own. **unselfishly** *adv.* **unselfish- ness** *n.*

un-set-tle (un set'l) *v.* To cause to be upset or excited; to disturb. **-ed** *adj.*

un-sheathe (un shēth') *v.* To draw a sword from a sheath or other case.

un-sight-ly (un sīt'lē) *adj.* Not pleasant to look at; ugly.

un-skilled (un skild') *adj.* Having no skills or training in a given kind of work.

un-skill-ful (un skil'ful) *adj.* Lacking in proficiency. **unskillfully** *adv.*

un-sound (un sound') *adj.* Having defects; not solidly made; unhealthy in body or mind. **unsoundly** *adv.*

un-speak-a-ble (un spē'ka bl) *adj.* Of or relating to something which cannot be expressed or described. **-ably** *adv.*

un-sta-ble (un stā'bl) *adj.* Not steady or firmly fixed; having the tendency to fluctuate or change.

un-stead-y (un sted'ē) *adj.* Not secure; unstable; variable. **unsteadily** *adv.* **unsteadiness** *n.*

un-sub-stan-tial (un'substan'shal) *adj.* Lacking strength, weight, or solidity; unreal.

un-suit-a-ble (un sö'ta bl) *adj.* Unfitting; not suitable; not appropriate for a specific circumstance. **unsuitably** *adv.*

unswerving *adj.* Being loyal and steady.

un-tan-gle (un tang'gl) *v.* To free from snarls or entanglements.

un-thank-ful (un thangk'ful) *adj.* Ungrateful.

un-think-a-ble (un thing'ka bl) *adj.* Unimaginable.

un-ti-dy (un tī'dē) *adj.* Messy; showing a lack of tidiness. **untidily** *adv.*

un-tie (un tī') *v.* To unfasten or loosen; to free from a restraint or bond.

un-til (un til') *prep.* Up to the time of. *conj.* To the time when; to the degree or place.

un-time-ly (un tīm'lē) *adj.* Premature; before the expected time.

un-told (un tōld') *adj.* Not revealed; not told; inexpressible; cannot be described or revealed.

un-touch-a-ble (un tuch'a bl) *adj.* Cannot be touched; incapable of being obtained or reached.

un-true (un trö) *adj.* Not true; contrary to the truth; not faithful; disloyal.

un-used (un ūzd') *adj.* Not put to use; never having been used.

un-u-su-al (un ū'zhö al) *adj.* Not usual; uncommon. **unusually** *adv.* **-ness** *n.*

un-ut-ter-a-ble (un ut'ér a bl) *adj.* Incapable of being described or expressed; unpronounceable.

un-veil (un vāl') *v.* To remove a veil from; to uncover; to reveal.

un-war-y (un wâr´ē) *adj*. Not cautious or careful; careless.

un-wa-ver-ing (un wā´vér ing) *adj*. Steady; not moving; steadfast.

un-whole-some (un hōl´som) *adj*. Unhealthy; morally corrupt or harmful.

un-will-ing (un wil´ing) *adj*. Reluctant; not willing. **unwillingly** *adv*.

un-wind (un wīnd´) *v*. To undo or reverse the winding of; to untangle.

un-wise (un wīz´) *adj*. Lacking good judgment or common sense. **-ly** *adv*.

un-wor-thy (un wer´thē) *adj*. Not deserving; not becoming or befitting; lacking merit or worth; shameful.

up (up) *adv*. From a lower position to a higher one; on, in, or to a higher level, position, or place; to a greater degree or amount; in or into a specific action or an excited state, as they stirred up trouble; to be even with in time, degree, or space, as up to date; under consideration, as up for discussion; in a safe, protected place, as vegetables are put up in jars; totally, completely, as the building was burned up; in baseball, at bat or, as up to bat. **up front** To be honest.

up and running In *computer science*, descriptive of computers and peripherals that are on line and functioning properly.

up-beat (up´bēt´) *n*., *Mus*. The relatively unaccented beat preceding the down beat. **upbeat** *adj*. Optimistic; happy.

up-bring-ing (up´bring´ing) *n*. The process of teaching and rearing a child.

up-com-ing (up´kum´ing) *adj*. About to take place or appear.

up-date (up dāt´) *v*. To revise or bring up-to-date; to modernize. In *computer science*, to add or alter data to reflect the most recent information available.

up-grade (up´grād´) *v*. To increase the grade, rank, or standard of. *n*. An upward slope.

up-hold *v*. To support.

up-hol-ster (up hōl´stér) *v*. To cover furniture with fabric covering, cushions, and padding. **upholsterer** *n*. **upholstery** *n*.

up-keep (up´kēp´) *n*. The cost and work needed to keep something in good condition.

up-lift (up lift´) *v*. To raise or lift up; to improve the social, economic, and moral level of a group or of a society.

up-on (*u* pon´) *adv*., *prep*. On.

up-per (up´ér) *adj*. Higher in status, position or location. **upper** *n*. The part of a shoe to which the sole is attached. *Slang* A drug used as a stimulant. **case** The large or capital case of letters.

up-per-class (up´ér klas´) *adj*. Economically or socially superior.

up-per-class-man (up´ér klas´man) *n*.

A junior or senior at a high school or college.

up-right (up´rīt´) *adj*. Having a vertical direction or position; honest. **upright** *n*. Something standing vertically, such as a beam in a building.

up-ris-ing (up´rī´zing) *n*. A revolt; a rebellion; an insurrection.

up-roar (up´rōr´) *n*. A confused, loud noise; a commotion.

up-root (up rōt´) *v*. To detach completely by pulling up the roots. **uprooter** *n*.

up-set (up set´) *v*. To capsize; to turn over; to throw into confusion or disorder; to overcome; to beat unexpectedly. **upset** *adj*. Capsized; overturned; distressed; troubled.

up-stage (up´stāj´) *adj*. & *adv*. Toward or at the back part of a stage. *Slang* To steal the show or scene from.

up-stairs (up´stârz´) *adv*. Up one or more flights of stairs. **upstairs** *adj*. Situated on the upper floor.

up-stand-ing (up stan´ding) *adj*. Straightforward; honest; upright.

up-start (up´stärt´) *n*. One who has risen quickly to power or wealth, especially one who is conceited.

up-stream (up´strēm´) *adv*. Toward the origin of a stream; against the current.

up-tight *adv*. Nervous, tense, or anxious.

up time In *computer science*, the period that a computer is on line and functioning properly.

up-to-date (up´to dāt´) *adj*. Most current or recent; appropriate to the present time.

up-town (up´toun´) *adv*. Toward or in the upper part of town. *n*. The upper part of town or city. **uptown** *adv*.

up-ward *or* **up-wards** *adv*. From a lower position to or toward a higher one **upward** *adj*. Directed toward a higher position.

u-ra-ni-um (ū rā´nē um) *n*. A hard, heavy, shiny metallic element that is radioactive, used especially in research and in nuclear weapons and fuels, symbolized by U.

ura-nog-ra-phy *n*. The science concerned with the description of the heavens and the celestial bodies.

ura-nom-e-try (ūr´a nom´i trē) *n*. A chart of celestial bodies.

U-ra-nus *n*. The seventh planet of the solar system in distance from the sun.

ur-ban (er´ban) *adj*. Pertaining to a city or having characteristics of a city; living or being in a city. **urbanite** *n*.

ur-ban-ol-o-gy *n*. The study dealing with the problems of a city such as education, politics, planning, etc.

urge (erj) *v*. To encourage, push, or drive; to recommend persistently and strongly. *n*. An influence, impulse, or force.

ur-gent (er´jent) *adj*. Requiring immediate attention. **urgency** n. **-ly** adv.

urine (ūr´in) n. In man and other mammals, the yellowish fluid waste produced by the kidneys.

us (us) pron. pl. The objective case of we; used as an indirect object, direct object, or object of a preposition.

us-a-ble or **useable** (ū´za bl) adj. Fit or capable of being used. **usably** adv.

us-age (ū´sij) n. The way or act of using something; the way words are used.

use (ūz) v. To put into action; to employ for a special purpose; to employ on a regular basis; to exploit for one's own advantage. n. The state or fact of being used; the act or way of using something; the reason or purpose for which something is used; the function of something; the occupation or utilization of property. **used** adj. **useful** adj. **useless** adj.

user friendly In computer science, descriptive of a computer system or program that is intuitive, making it easier to use.

ush-er (ush´ër) n. A person who directs people to the correct seats in a theater. v. To show or escort someone to a place; to go before as a representative or sign of something that comes later.

u-su-al (ū´zhō al) adj. Ordinary or common; regular; customary. **usually** adv. **usualness** n.

u-surp (ū serp´) v. To take over by force without authority. **usurpation** n.

usu-ry n. An exorbitant rate of interest charged to a borrower.

Ut-ah n. A state located in the western part of the United States, statehood January 4, 1896, state capital Salt Lake City.

u-ten-sil (ū ten´sil) n. A tool, implement, or container, especially one for the kitchen.

u-ter-ine (ū´tër in) adj. Referring to birth by the same mother but by a different father.

u-ter-us (ū´tër us) n. An organ of female mammals within which young develop and grow before birth. **uterine** adj.

utilities In computer science, computer programs that improve performance or productivity of the computer or the user.

u-til-i-ty (ū til´i tē) n. pl. **-ies** The state or quality of being useful; a company which offers a public service, as water, heat, or electricity.

u-til-ize (ūt´i līz´) v. To make, put to use.

ut-most (ut´mōst´) adj. Of the greatest amount or degree; most distant.

u-to-pi-a (ū tō´pē a) n. A condition or place of perfection or complete harmony and peace.

ut-ter (ut´ër) v. To say or express verbally; to speak. adv. Absolute;

complete. **utterly** adv. **utterance** n.

ut-ter-most n. To do or perform to our highest ability.

u-vu-la (ū´vya la) n. The fleshy projection which hangs above the back of the tongue. **uvular** adj.

ux-or-i-cide (uk sōr´i sīd´) adj. Murder of a wife by her husband.

-V-

V, v (vē) The twenty-second letter of the English alphabet; the Roman numeral for the number 5.

va-cant (vā´kant) adj. Empty; not occupied; without expression or thought.

va-cate (vā´kāt) v. To leave; to cease to occupy.

va-ca-tion (vā kā´shan) n. A period of time away from work for pleasure, relaxation, or rest. v. To take a vacation.

vac-ci-nate (vak´si nāt´) v. To inject with a vaccine so as to produce immunity to an infectious disease, as measles or smallpox.

vac-ci-na-tion (vak´si nā´shan) n. The inoculation with a vaccine.

vac-cine (vak sēn´) n. A solution of weakened or killed microorganisms, as bacteria or viruses, injected into the body to produce immunity to a disease.

vac-u-um (vak´ū um) n. pl. **vacuums** or **vacuua** A space which is absolutely empty; a void; a vacuum cleaner. **vacuum** v. To clean with a vacuum cleaner.

vag-a-bond (vag´a bond´) n. A homeless person who wanders from place to place; a tramp; a wanderer.

va-gar-y (va găr´ē) n. pl. **-ies** An eccentric or capricious action or idea.

va-gi-na (va jī´na) n. pl. **vaginas, vaginae** Anat. The canal or passage extending from the uterus to the external opening of the female reproductive system.

vaginitis (vaj´i nī´tis) n. An inflammation of the vagina.

va-grant (vā´grant) n. A person who wanders from place to place. adj. Roaming from one area to another without a job. **vagrancy** n.

vague (vāg) adj. Not clearly expressed; not sharp or definite. **vaguely** adv.

vain (vān) adj. Conceited; lacking worth or substance; having too much pride in one-self.

val-ance (val´ans) n. A decorative drapery across the top of a window.

vale (vāl) n. A valley.

val-e-dic-to-ri-an (val´i dik tōr´ē an) n. The student ranking highest in a graduating class, who delivers a speech at the commencement.

val-en-tine (val´en tīn´) n. A card or gift

sent to one's sweetheart on Valentine's Day, February 14th.

val-et (val´it) *n.* A man who takes care of another man's clothes and other personal needs; a hotel employee who attends to personal services for guests.

val-iant (val´yant) *adj.* Brave; exhibiting valor. **valiance, valor** *n.*

val-id (val´id) *adj.* Founded on facts or truth. *Law* Binding; having legal force. **validity, validate** *n.*

val-ley (val´e) *n. pl.* **-leys** Low land between ranges of hills or mountains.

val-or (val´er) *n.* Bravery. **valorous** *adj.* **valorously** *adv.*

val-u-a-ble (val´u a bl) *adj.* Of great value or importance; having a high monetary value; having a worthy quality or value. **valuableness** *n.*

val-ue (val´u) *n.* The quality or worth of something that makes it valuable; material worth; a principle regarded as worthwhile or desirable. *Math* A calculated numerical quantity. *v.* To estimate the value or worth of; to regard very highly; to rate according to importance, worth, or usefulness.

valve (valv) *n.* The movable mechanism which opens and closes to control the flow of a substance through a pipe or other passageway. *Anat.* A membranous structure in a vein or artery that prevents or slows the backward movement of fluid. **valveless** *adj.*

va-moose (va mös´) *v., Slang* To leave in a hurry.

van (van) *n.* A large closed wagon or truck.

va-na-di-um (va nā´dē um) *n.* A metallic element symbolized by V.

Van Buren, Martin *n.* (1782-1862) The eighth president of the United States from 1837-1841.

van-dal-ism (van´da liz´um) *n.* The malicious defacement or destruction of private or public property.

vane (vān) *n.* A metal device that turns in the direction the wind is blowing; a thin rigid blade of an electric fan, propeller, or windmill.

va-nil-la (va nil´a) *n.* A flavoring extract used in cooking and baking; prepared from the vanilla bean.

van-ish (van´ish) *v.* To disappear suddenly; to drop out of sight; to go out of existence.

van-i-ty (van´i tē) *n., pl.,* **-ies** Conceit; extreme pride in one's ability, possessions, or appearance.

van-tage (van´tij) *n.* A superior position; an advantage.

va-por (vā´pėr) *n.* Moisture or smoke suspended in air, as mist or fog. **vaporish, vaporous** *adj.* **vaporize** *v.*

var-i-able (vâr´ē a bl) *adj.* Changeable; tending to vary; inconstant. *n.* A quantity or thing which can vary. In *computer science,* a symbol or code that represents a value that changes during processing. **variably** *adv.*

var-i-ance (vâr´ē ans) *n.* The state or act of varying; difference; conflict.

var-i-a-tion (vâr´ē ā´shan) *n.* The result or process of varying; the degree or extent of varying. *Mus.* A different form or version of a given theme, with modifications in rhythm, key, or melody.

var-i-e-gat-ed (vâr´ē e gāt´tid) *adj.* Having marks of different colors.

va-ri-e-ty (va rī´i tē) *n.* The state or character of being varied or various; a number of different kinds; an assortment.

var-i-ous (vâr´ē us) *adj.* Of different kinds. **variousness** *n.*

var-mint (vär´mint) *n., Slang* A troublesome animal; an obnoxious person.

var-nish (vär´nish) *n.* A solution paint used to coat or cover a surface with a hard, transparent, shiny film. *v.* To put varnish on.

var-si-ty (vär´si tē) *n. pl.* **-ies** The best team representing a college, university, or school.

var-y (vâr´ē) *v.* To change; to make or become different; to be different; to make of different kinds.

vas-cu-lar (vas´kya lėr) *adj., Biol.* Having to do with vessels circulating fluids, as blood.

va-sec-to-my (va sek´to mē) *n. pl.* **-ies** Method of male sterilization involving the surgical excision of a part of the tube which conveys semen.

vast (vast) *adj.* Very large or great in size. **vastly** *adv.* **vastness** *n.*

veg-e-ta-ble (vej´ta bl) *n.* A plant, as the tomato, greenbeans, lettuce, raised for the edible part. *adj.* Resembling a vegetable in activity; passive; dull.

veg-e-tar-i-an (vej´i târ´ē an) *n.* A person whose diet is limited to vegetables. *adj.* Consuming only plant products. **vegetarianism** *n.*

ve-hi-cle (vē´i kl) *n.* A motorized device for transporting goods, equipment, or passengers; any means by which something is transferred, expressed, or applied.

veil (vāl) *n.* A piece of transparent cloth worn on the head or face for concealment or protection; anything that conceals from view. *v.* To cover or conceal, as with a veil.

vein (vān) *n., Anat.* A vessel which transports blood back to the heart after passing through the body; one of the branching support tubes of an insect's wing; a long wavy, irregularly colored streak, as in marble, or wood. **vein.** *v.*

ve-lour (ve ler´) *n*. A soft velvet-like woven cloth having a short, thick nap.

vel-vet (vel´vit) *n*. A fabric made of rayon, cotton, or silk, having a smooth, dense pile. **velvety** *adj*.

vend-er (ven´dĕr) *n*. A person who sells, as a peddler.

ven-det-ta (ven det´a) *n*. A fight or feud between blood-related persons, involving revenge killings.

ven-er-a-ble (ven´ĕr a bl) *adj*. Meriting or worthy of respect by reason of dignity, position, or age.

venereal disease *n*. A contagious disease, as syphilis, or gonorrhea, which is typically acquired through sexual intercourse.

ven-i-son (ven´i son) *n*. The edible flesh of a deer.

ven-om (ven´om) *n*. A poisonous substance secreted by some animals, as scorpions or snakes, usually transmitted to their prey or an enemy through a bite or sting. **venomous** *adj*.

ve-nous (vē´nus) *adj*. Of or relating to veins. *Physiol*. Returning blood to the heart after passing through the capillaries, supplying oxygen for the tissues, and becoming charged with carbon dioxide. **venously** adv.

ven-ti-late (ven´ti lāt´) *v*. To expose to a flow of fresh air for refreshing, curing, or purifying purposes

ven-ture (ven´chĕr) *n*. A course of action involving risk, chance, or danger, especially a business investment. *v*. To take a risk.

ven-ue (ven´ō) *n*. The place where a crime or other cause of legal action occurs; the locale of a gathering or public event.

verb (verb) *n*. The part of speech which expresses action, existence, or occurrence.

ver-bal (ver´bal) *adj*. Expressed in speech; expressed orally; not written; relating to or derived from a verb. *n*. An adjective, noun, or other word which is based on a verb and retains some characteristics of a verb. **verbally** *adv*. **verbalize** *v*.

ver-ba-tim (vĕr bā´tim) *adv*. Word for word.

ver-be-na (vĕr bē´na) *n*. An American garden plant having variously colored flower clusters.

verge (verj) *n*. The extreme edge or rim; margin; the point beyond which something begins. *v*. To border on.

ver-min (ver´min) *n*. *pl*. **vermins** A destructive, annoying animal which is harmful to one's health.

Ver-mont *n*. A state located in the northeastern part of the United States; statehood March 4, 1791; state capital Montpelier.

ver-sa-tile (ver´sa til) *adj*. Having the capabilities of doing many different things; having many functions or uses.

verse (vers) *n*. Writing that has a rhyme; poetry; a subdivision of a chapter of the Bible. *v*. To make verse; to tell or celebrate in verse; to familiarize by close association or study.

ver-sion (ver´zhan) *n*. An account or description told from a particular point of view; a translation from another language, especially a translation of the Bible; a form or particular point of view; a condition in which an organ, such as the uterus, is turned; manual turning *n*. Of a fetus in the uterus to aid delivery. **versional** *adj*.

ver-so (ver´sō) *n. pl.* **-sos** The left-hand page.

ver-sus (ver´sus) *prep*. Against; in contrast to; as an alternative of.

ver-te-bra (ver´te bra) *n. pl.* **-brae, -bras** One of the bony or cartilaginous segments making up the spinal column.

ver-tex (ver´teks) *n. pl.* **-es, -tices** The highest or top most point; the pointed top of a triangle, opposite the base; the point at which two lines meet to form an angle.

ver-ti-cal (ver´ti kal) *adj*. In a straight up-and-down direction; being perpendicular to the plane of the horizon or to a primary axis; upright.

ver-y (ver´ē) *adv*. To a high or great degree; truly; absolutely; exactly; actually; in actual fact.

ves-per (ves´pĕr) *n*. An evening prayer service; a bell to call people to such a service.

ves-sel (ves´el) *n*. A hollow or concave utensil; as a bottle, kettle, container, or jar; a hollow craft designed for navigation on water, one larger than a rowboat. *Anat*. A tube or duct for circulating a bodily fluid.

vest (vest) *n*. A sleeveless garment open or fastening in front, worn over a shirt.

ves-tige (ves´tij) *n*. A trace or visible sign of something that no longer exists. **vestigial** *adj*. **vestigially** *adj*.

ves-try (ves´trē) *n. pl.* **vestries** A room in a church for meetings and classes.

vet (vet) *n., Slang* A veterinarian; a veteran.

vet-er-an (vet´ĕr an) *n*. A person with a long record or experience in a certain field; one who has served in the military.

Veterans Day *n*. A day set aside to commemorate the end of World War I in 1918, celebrated on November 11th of each year; national holiday.

vet-er-i-nar-i-an (vet´ĕr i nâr´ēan) *n*. One who is trained and authorized to give medical treatment to animals.

vet-er-i-nar-y (vet´ĕr i ner´ē) *adj*.

Pertaining to or being the science and art of prevention and treatment of animals.

ve-to (vē′tō) n. pl. vetoes The power of a government executive, as the President or a governor, to reject a bill passed by the legislature. v. To reject a bill passed by the legislature.

vex (veks) v. To bother; or annoy; to torment.

vexed adj. Annoyed by something.

VGA In computer science, video graphics array; a standard for high resolution display on a color monitor screen.

vi-a (vī′a) prep. By way of; by means of.

vi-a-duct (vī′a dukt′) n. A bridge, resting on a series of arches, carrying a road or railroad.

vi-al (vī′al) n. A small, closed container used especially for liquids.

vi-brate (vī′brāt) v. To move or make move back and forth or up and down.

vice (vīs) n. An immoral habit or practice; evil conduct. prefix One who takes the place of another.

vice-ge-rent n. A substitute for someone having his or her powers to make decisions on their behalf.

vi-ce ver-sa (vī′se ver′sa) adv. With the order or meaning of something reversed.

vi-cin-i-ty (vi sin′i tē) n. pl. -ies The surrounding area or district; the state of being near in relationship or space.

vi-cious (vish′us) adj. Dangerously aggressive; having the quality of immorality; unpleasantly intence. viciously adv. viciousness n.

vic-tim (vik′tim) n. A person who is harmed or killed by another; a living creature which is slain and offered as sacrifice; one harmed by circumstance or condition. victimize v.

vic-tor (vik′tēr) n. A person who conquers; the winner.

vic-to-ri-ous (vik tōr′ē us) adj. Being the winner in a contest. -ously adv.

vic-to-ry (vik′to rē) n. pl. -ies A defeat of those on the opposite side.

vid-e-o (vid′ē ō′) adj. Being, related to, or used in the reception or transmission of television.

video card In computer science, a board in the computer that controls the display on the monitor.

video disc n. A disc containing recorded images and sounds which may be played on a television set.

video game n. A computerized game displaying on a display screen, controlled by a player or players.

video terminal n., computer science A computer device having a cathode-ray tube for displaying data on a screen.

vie (vī) v. To strive for superiority.

view (vū) n. The act of examining or seeing; a judgment or opinion; the range or extent of one's sight; something that is kept in sight. v. To watch or look at attentively; to consider.

vig-il (vij′il) n. A watch with prayers kept on the night before a religious feast; a period of surveillance.

vig-or (vig′ēr) n. Energy or physical strength; intensity of effect or action.

vile (vīl) adj. Morally disgusting, miserable, and unpleasant. vilely adv.

vil-la (vil′a) n. A luxurious home in the country; a country estate.

vil-lage (vil′ij) n. An incorporated settlement, usually smaller than a town.

vil-lain (vil′an) n. An evil or wicked person; a criminal; an uncouth person. villainous adj. villainy n.

vin-di-cate (vin′di kāt′) v. To clear of suspicion; to set free; to provide a defense or justification for. -tion n.

vin-dic-tive (vin dik′tiv) adj. Showing or possessing a desire for revenge; spiteful.

vine (vīn) n. A plant whose stem needs support as it climbs or clings to a surface.

vin-e-gar (vin′e gėr) n. A tart, sour liquid derived from cider or wine and used in flavoring and preserving food.

vin-tage (vin′tij) n. The grapes or wine produced from a particular district in one season.

vi-nyl (vī′nil) n. A variety of shiny plastics, similar to leather, often used for clothing and for covering furniture.

vi-o-la (vē ō′la) n. A stringed instrument, slightly larger and deeper in tone than a violin.

vi-o-late (vī′o lāt′) v. To break the law or a rule; to disrupt or disturb a person's privacy. violation n.

vi-o-lence (vī′o lens) n. Physical force or activity used to cause harm, damage, or abuse. violent adj.

vi-o-let (vī′o lit) n. A small, low-growing plant with blue, purple, or white flowers; a purplish-blue color.

vi-o-lin (vī′o lin′) n. A small stringed instrument, played with a bow.

vi-per (vī′pėr) n. A poisonous snake; an evil or treacherous person.

vir-gin (ver′jin) n. A person who has never had sexual intercourse. adj. In an unchanged or natural state.

Vir-gin-ia n. A state located in the eastern part of the United States; statehood June 25, 1788; state capital Richmond.

vir-ile (vir′il) adj. Having the qualities and nature of a man; capable of sexual performance in the male. virility n.

vir-tu (vėr tö′) n. The love or knowledge of fine objects of art.

virtual memory In computer science,

an extension of the computer's main memory in disk storage.

vir-tue (ver´chö) *n.* Morality, goodness or uprightness; a special type of goodness. **virtuous** *adj.* **-ly** *adv.*

vi-rus (vī´rus) *n.* Any of a variety of microscopic organisms which cause diseases. In *computer science,* unauthorized instructions in the computer that disrupt its normal operation.

vi-sa (vē´za) *n.* An official authorization giving permission on a passport to enter a specific country.

vis-cid (vis´id) *adj.* Sticky; having an adhesive quality.

vise (vīs) *n.* A tool in carpentry and metal work having two jaws to hold things in position. vise n.

vis-i-bil-i-ty (viz´i bil´i tē) *n.* *pl.* **-ies** The degree or state of being visible; the distance that one is able to see clearly.

vis-i-ble (viz´i bl) *adj.* Apparent; exposed to view.

vi-sion (vizh´an) *n.* The power of sight; the ability to see; an image created in the imagination; a supernatural appearance.

vis-it (viz´it) *v.* To journey to or come to see a person or place. *n.* A professional or social call. *Slang* To chat. **visitor, visitation** *n.*

vi-sor (vī´zẽr) *n.* A brim on the front of a hat which protects the eyes from glare, the sun, wind, and rain.

vi-su-al (vizh´ö al) *adj.* Visible; relating to seeing or sight.

vi-tal (vīt´al) *adj.* Essential to life; very important. **vitally** *adv.*

vital signs *n.* *pl., Med.* The pulse rate, body temperature, blood pressure, and respiratory rate of a person.

vi-ta-min (vī´ta min) *n.* Any of various substances which are found in foods and are essential to good health.

vit-re-ous (vi´trē us) *adj.* Related to or similar to glass.

vit-ri-fy (vi´tri fī´) *v.* To convert into glass or a substance similar to glass, by heat and fusion.

vi-va-cious (vi vā´shus) *adj.* Filled with vitality or animation; lively.

viv-id (viv´id) *adj.* Bright; brilliant; intense; having clear, lively, bright colors; realistic. **vividly** *adv.*

viv-i-fy (viv´i fī´) *v.* To give life to. **vivification** *n.*

vo-cab-u-lar-y (vō kab´ya ler´ē) *n.* A list or group of words and phrases, usually in alphabetical order; all the words that a person uses or understands. In *computer science,* the collection of reserved words that are acceptable for use in a particular programming language.

vo-cal (vō´kal) *adj.* Of or related to the voice; uttered by the voice; to speak freely and loudly. *n.* A vocal sound.

vocal cords *n.* *pl.* The lower of two folds or bands in the throat which produce sound when made tighter or loosened when air is breathed out while speaking or singing.

vo-ca-tion (vō kā´shan) *n.* A career, occupation, or profession.

vo-cif-er-ate (vō sif´e rāt´) *v.* To utter or cry out loudly; to shout. **vociferation** *n.* **vociferous** *adj.* **vociferously** *adv.*

vod-ka (vod´ka) *n.* A colorless liquor of neutral spirits distilled from fermented rye or wheat mash.

vogue (vōg) *n.* The leading style or fashion; popularity. **vogue** *adj.*

voice (vois) *n.* The sounds produced by speaking; the ability or power to produce musical tones. *v.* To express; to utter; to give voice.

void (void) *adj.* Containing nothing; empty; not inhabited; useless; vain; without legal force or effect; null. *n.* Empty space; the quality or state of being lonely. *v.* To make void; to discharge; to emit.

voile (voil) *n.* A fine, soft, sheer fabric used for making light clothing and curtains.

vol-ley (vol´ē) *n.* *pl.* **-leys** A simultaneous discharge of a number of missile weapons; the shooting or eruption of similar things at one time; in the game of tennis, a shot in which the ball is hit before touching the ground.

volt-age (vōl´tij) *n.* The amount of electrical power, given in terms of the number of volts.

vol-ume (vol´ūm) *n.* The capacity or amount of space or room; a book; a quantity; the loudness of a sound.

volume label In *computer science,* the name given to a hard or floppy disk to identify it.

vol-un-tar-y (vol´an ter´ē) *adj.* Done cooperatively or willingly; from one's own choice.

vol-un-teer (vol´un tēr´) *n.* One who offers himself for a service of his own free will. *adj.* Consisting of volunteers. *v.* To offer voluntarily.

vo-lup-tuous (vo lup´chö us) *adj.* Full of pleasure; delighting the senses; sensuous; luxury. **voluptuousness** *n.*

vom-it (vom´it) *v.* To eject contents of the stomach through the mouth. *n.* The food or matter ejected from the stomach by vomiting.

voo-doo (vö´dö) *n.* A religious cult derived from African ancestor worship; a cure or spell resulting from magical powers. **voodooism** *n.*

vo-ra-cious (vō rā´shus) *adj.* Having a large appetite; insatiable. **-ly** *adv.*

vote (vōt) *n.* The expression of one's choice by voice, by raising one's hand, or by secret ballot. *v.* To express one's views. **voteless** *adj.* **voter** *n.*

vo-tive (vō'tiv) *adj.* Performed in fulfillment of a vow or in devotion.

vouch (vouch) *v.* To verify or support as true; to guarantee. **voucher** *n.*

vow (vou) *n.* A solemn pledge or promise, especially one made to God; a marriage vow. *v.* To make a vow.

vow-el (vou'el) *n.* A sound of speech made by voicing the flow of breath within the mouth; a letter representing a vowel, as a, e, i, o, u, and sometimes y.

voy-age (voi'ij) *n.* A long trip or journey.

vul-gar (vul'gėr) *adj.* Showing poor manners; crude; improper; immoral or indecent. **vulgarity** *n.*

vul-ner-a-ble (vul'nėr a bl) *adj.* Open to physical injury or attack. **vulnerability** *n.* **vulnerably** *adv.*

vul-ture (vul'chėr) *n.* A large bird of the hawk family, living on dead animals; a greedy person; one who feeds on the mistakes or bad luck of others.

W

W, w (dub'l ū') The twenty-third letter of the English alphabet.

wacky *adj.* Amusingly or absurdly irrational. **wackiness** *n.*

wad (wod) *n.* A small crumpled mass or bundle; a soft plug used to hold shot or gunpowder charge in place. *Slang* A large roll of money. **wad** *v.*

wad-able *adj.* Capable of being wadded.

wad-ding *n.* Wads or materials for making wads; a sheet of loose fibers that is used for stuffing or padding.

wad-dle (wod'l) *v.* To walk with short steps and swing from side to side. **waddle** *n.* **waddler** *n.*

wade (wād) *v.* To walk through a substance as mud or water which hampers one's steps.

wader *n.* A person that wades; a name for high top waterproof boots.

wae-sucks *interj.* A Scottish phrase used to express pity.

wa-fer (wā'fėr) *n.* A small, thin, crisp cracker, cookie, or candy.

waf-fle (wof'l) *n.* Pancake batter cooked in a waffle iron.

waft (waft) *v.* To drift or move gently, as by the motion of water or air.

waft-age *n.* The state or act of being wafted.

waf-ture *n.* A wavelike motion.

wag (wag) *v.* To move quickly from side to side or up and down. *n.* A playful, witty person. **waggish** *adj.*

wage (wāj) *n.* A payment of money for labor or services. *v.* To conduct.

wage earner *n.* A person who works for a salary or wages.

wage level *n.* The approximate position of wages at any given time.

wag-on (wag'on) *n.* A four-wheeled vehicle used to transport goods; a station wagon; a child's four-wheeled cart with a long handle.

wa-hi-ne *n.* A Polynesian girl or woman.

waif (wāf) *n.* An abandoned, homeless, or lost child; a piece of property found without the owner; a stray animal.

wail (wāl) *n.* A loud, mournful cry or weep. *n.* To make such a sound.

waist (wāst) *n.* The narrow part of the body between the thorax and hips; the middle part or section of something which is narrower than the rest.

wait (wāt) *v.* To stay in one place in expectation of; to await; to put off until a later time or date; to be ready or prepared. *n.* A time of waiting.

wait-er (wā'tėr) *n.* A man who serves food at a restaurant.

wait-ress (wā'tris) *n.* A woman who serves food at a restaurant.

waive (wāv) *v.* To forfeit of one's own free will; to postpone or dispense with.

waiv-er *n.* The act of intentionally abandoning a privilege or right.

wake (wāk) *v.* To come to consciousness, as from sleep. *n.* A vigil for a dead body; the surface turbulence caused by a vessel moving through water.

walk (wok) *v.* To move on foot over a surface; to pass over, go on, or go through by walking; in baseball, to advance to first base after four balls have been pitched. **walker** *n.*

walk-ie-talk-ie *n.* A battery-operated radio transmitting and receiving set.

wall (wol) *n.* A vertical structure to separate or enclose an area. *v.* To provide or close up, as with a wall.

wal-la-by (wol'a bē) *n.* A small or medium sized kangaroo.

wal-lah *n.* A person who performs a specific service or duty.

wal-let (wol'it) *n.* A flat folding case for carrying paper money.

wal-lop (wol'op) *n.* A powerful blow; an impact. *v.* To move with disorganized haste. **walloper** *n.*

wall-pa-per (wol'pā'pėr) *n.* Decorative paper for walls, usually having a colorful pattern.

Wall Street *n.* The street in New York City where the New York Stock Exchange is located.

wal-nut (wol'nut) *n.* An edible nut with a hard, light-brown shell; the tree on which this nut grows.

waltz (wolts) *n.* A ballroom dance in 3/4 time; music for a waltz. *v.* To dance a waltz; to advance successfully and easily.

wam-pum (wom´pum) n. Polished shells, once used as currency by North American Indians. *Slang* Money.

wand (wond) n. A slender rod used by a magician.

wan-der (won´dĕr) v. To travel about aimlessly; to roam; to stray.

wane (wān) v. To decrease in size or extent; to decrease gradually. n. A gradual deterioration.

wan-gle (wang´gl) v. To resort to devious methods in order to obtain something wanted. **wangler** n.

want (wont) v. To wish for or desire; to need; to lack; to fail to possess a required amount; to hunt in order to apprehend. n. The state of lacking a required or usual amount. **wanting** adj.

war (wor) n. An armed conflict among states or nations; a state of discord; the science of military procedures.

ward (word) n. A section in a hospital for certain patients requiring similar treatment; a person under protection or surveillance. v. To keep watch over someone or some thing.

ware (wâr) n. Manufactured items of the same general kind; items or goods for sale.

ware-house (wâr´hous´) n. A large building used to store merchandise.

warm (worm) adj. Moderate heat; neither hot or cold; comfortably established; marked by a strong feeling; having pleasant feelings.

warn (worn) v. To give notice or inform beforehand; to call to one's attention; to alert.

warp (worp) v. To become bent out of shape; to deviate from a proper course. n. The condition of being twisted or bent; threads running down the length of a fabric.

war-rant (wor´ant) n. A written authorization giving the holder legal power to search, seize, or arrest. v. To provide a reason; to give proof. **warrantable** adj. **warrantor** n.

war-ri-or (wor´ē ĕr) n. One who fights in a war or battle.

war-y (wâr´ē) adj. Marked by caution; alert to danger.

wash (wosh) v. To cleanse by the use of water; to remove dirt; to move or deposit as if by the force of water. n. A process or instance of washing; a group of soiled clothes or linens.

Wash-ing-ton n. A state located in the northwestern part of the United States, statehood November 11, 1889, state capital Olympia.

Washington, George n. (1732-1799) The first president of the United States from 1789-1797.

was-n't (wuz´ant) Was not.

wasp (wasp) n. Any of various insects,

having a slim body with a constricted abdomen, the female capable of inflicting a painful sting.

waste (wāst) v. To be thrown away; to be available but not used completely. n. A barren region; the instance of wasting; useless material produced as a by-product. *Slang* To destroy or murder. **wasteful** adj. **waster** n.

watch (woch) v. To view carefully; to guard; to keep informed. n. The act of staying awake to guard or protect; a small timepiece worn on the wrist, designed to keep the correct time of day.

watch-ful (woch´ful) adj. Carefully observant or attentive. **watchfully** adv.

watch-man (woch´man) n. A person hired to keep watch; a guard.

wa-ter (wo´tĕr) n. The clear liquid making up oceans, lakes, and streams; the body fluids as tears or urine. v. To pour or spray water on something or someone; to give water to drink; to weaken or dilute with water.

water power n. The power of energy produced by swift-moving water.

wa-ter-proof (wo´tĕr prōf´) adj. Capable of preventing water from penetrating. v. To make or treat in order to make waterproof. n. A material or fabric which is waterproof.

wa-ter-shed n. The raised area between two regions that divides two sections drained by different river sources.

wa-ter-way (wo´tĕr wā´) n. A navigable body of water; a channel for water.

watt (wot) n. A unit of electrical power represented by current of one ampere, produced by the electromotive force of one volt.

wave (wāv) v. To move back and forth or up and down; to motion with the hand. n. A swell or moving ridge of water; a curve or curl, as in the hair.

wa-ver (wā´vĕr) v. To sway unsteadily; to move back and forth; to weaken in force. **waver** n. **waveringly** adv.

wax (waks) n. A natural yellowish substance made by bees, solid when cold and easily melted or softened when heated. **waxy** adj.

way (wā) n. A manner of doing something; a tendency or characteristic; a habit or customary manner of acting or living; a direction; freedom to do as one chooses.

way-lay (wā´lā´) v. To attack by ambush; to rob.

way-ward (wā´wĕrd) adj. Unruly; unpredictable.

we (wē) pron. Used to refer to the person speaking and one or more other people.

weak (wēk) adj. Having little energy or strength; easily broken; having inadequate skills; not reasonable or convincing. **weakness** *n.* **weakly** *adv.*

wealth (welth) *n.* An abundance of valuable possessions or property; all goods and resources having monetary value.

wealth-y (wel´thē) *adj.* Having much wealth or money; abundant; rich.

wean (wēn) *v.* To accustom an infant or small child to food other than a mother's milk or bottle.

weap-on (wep´on) *n.* A device used in fighting a war; advice which can be used to harm another person.

wear (wâr) *v.* To have on or put something on the body; to display. *n.* The act of wearing out or using up; the act of wearing, as clothing. **-able** *adj.*

wea-ri-some (wēr´ē som) *adj.* Tedious, boring or tiresome.

wea-ry (wēr´ē) *adj.* Exhausted; tired; feeling fatigued. *v.* To make or become tired; to become fatigued. **wearily** *adv.*

wea-sel (wē´zel) *n.* A mammal with a long tail and short legs; a sly, sneaky person.

weath-er (weth´ér) *n.* The condition of the air or atmosphere in terms of humidity, temperature, and similar features. *v.* To become worn by the actions of weather; to survive.

weath-er-man (weth´ér man´) *n.* A man who reports or forecasts the weather.

weather vane *n.* A device that turns, indicating the direction of the wind.

weave (wēv) *v.* To make a basket, cloth, or other item by interlacing threads or other strands of material. **weaver** *n.*

web (web) *n.* A cobweb; a piece of interlacing material which forms a woven structure; something constructed as an entanglement; a thin membrane that joins the toes of certain water birds.

wed (wed) *v.* To take as a spouse; to marry.

we'd (wēd) *contr.* We had; we should.

wed-ding (wed´ing) *n.* A marriage ceremony; an act of joining together in close association.

wedge (wej) *n.* A tapered, triangular piece of wood or metal used to split logs, to add leverage, and to hold something open or ajar. *v.* To force or make something fit tightly.

wed-lock (wed´lok) *n.* Marriage; the state of being married.

Wed-nes-day *n.* The fourth day of the week.

weed (wēd) *n.* An unwanted plant which interferes with the growth of grass, vegetables, or flowers.

week (wēk) *n.* A period of seven days, beginning with Sunday and ending with Saturday; the time or days normally spent at school or work.

week-day (wēk´dā´) *n.* Any day of the week except Saturday or Sunday.

week-end (wēk´end´) *n.* The end of the week from the period of Friday evening through Sunday evening.

week-ly (wēk´lē) *adv.* Every week; once a week. *adj.* Taking place or done every week of or relating to a week.

weep (wēp) *v.* To shed tears; to express sorrow, joy, or emotion; by shedding tears; to cry. **weeper** *n.*

weigh (wā) *v.* To determine the heaviness of an object by using a scale; to consider carefully in one's mind; to be of a particular weight; to oppress or burden.

weight (wāt) *n.* The amount that something weighs; heaviness; a heavy object used to hold or pull something down; an over-powering force; the quality of a garment for a particular season. *v.* To make heavy.

weight-y (wā´tē) *adj.* Burdensome; important.

weird (wērd) *adj.* Having an extraordinary or strange character. **weirdly** *adv.*

weird-o *n., Slang* A person who is very strange.

wel-come (wel´kom) *v.* To extend warm hospitality; to accept gladly. *v.* Received warmly. *n.* A greeting upon one's arrival.

weld (weld) *v.* To unite metallic parts by applying heat and sometimes pressure, allowing the metals to bond together. *n.* A joint formed by welding.

wel-fare (wel´fâr´) *n.* The state of doing well; governmental aid to help the disabled or disadvantaged.

well (wel) *n.* A hole in the ground which contains a supply of water; a shaft in the ground through which gas and oil are obtained. *adj.* Being in good health; in an agreeable state.

we'll (wēl) *contr.* We will; we shall.

well-be-ing (wel´bē´ing) *n.* The state of being healthy, happy, or prosperous.

well-done (wel´dun´) *adj.* Completely cooked; done properly.

well-groomed (wel´grōmd´) *adj.* Clean, neat, and properly cared for.

well-known (wel´nōn´) *adj.* Widely known.

well-man-nered *adj.* Polite; having good manners.

well-mean-ing (wel´mē´ning) *adj.* Having good intentions.

well-to-do (wel´to dō´) *adj.* Having more than enough wealth.

welsh (welsh) *v., Slang* To cheat by avoiding a payment to someone; to neglect an obligation. **welsher** *n.*

welt (welt) *n.* A strip between the sole and upper part of a shoe; a light swelling on the body, usually caused by a blow to the area. *v.* To hit severely.

wel-ter-weight (wel´tér wāt´) *n.* A boxer weighing between 136 and 147 pounds.

went *v.* Past tense of go.

wept *v.* Past tense of weep.

were (wer) *v.* Past tense and subjunctive form of be.

we're (wēr) *contr.* We are.

were-n't (wernt) *contr.* Were not.

west (west) *n.* The direction of the setting sun; the direction to the left of a person standing north. *adj.* At, of, or from the west. *adv.* To or toward the west.

West Virginia *n.* A state located in the eastern part of the United States; statehood June 20, 1863; state capital Charleston.

whack (hwak) *v.* To strike with a hard blow, to slap. *n.* An attempt.

whale (hwāl) *n.* A very large mammal resembling a fish which lives in salt water. *Slang* An outstanding or impressive example.

wharf (hworf) *n.* A pier or platform built at the edge of water so ships can load and unload.

what (hwut) *pron.* Which one; which things; which type or kind. *adv.* In which way. *adj.* Which particular one.

what-ev-er (hwut ev´ẽr) *pron.* Everything or anything. *adj.* No matter what. *Slang* Which thing or things.

what's *contr.* What is.

wheat (hwēt) *n.* A grain ground into flour, used to make breads and similar foods.

wheel (hwēl) *n.* A circular disk which turns on an axle; an apparatus having the same principles of a wheel; something which resembles the motion or shape of a wheel. *v.* To move on or as if by wheels; to turn around a central axis; to rotate, pivot, or turn around.

whelk (hwelk) *v.* Any of various large water snails, sometimes edible.

when (hwen) *adv.* At what time; at which time. *pron.* What or which time. *conj.* While; at the time that; although.

whence (hwens) *adv.* From what source or place; from which.

when-ev-er (hwen ev´ẽr) *adv.* At any time; when. *conj.* At whatever time.

where (hwâr) *adv.* At or in what direction or place; in what direction or place.

where-a-bouts (hwâr´a bouts´) *adv.* Near, at, or in a particular location. *n.* The approximate location.

where-as (hwâr az´) *conj.* It being true or the fact; on the contrary.

where-by (hwâr bī´) *conj.* Through or by which.

wher-ev-er *adv.* In any situation or place.

whet (hwet) *v.* To make sharp; to stimulate.

wheth-er (hweth´ẽr) *conj.* Indicating a choice; alternative possibilities; either.

whet-stone (hwet´stōn´) *n.* A stone used to sharpen scissors, knives, and other implements.

whew (hwū) *n., interj.* Used to express relief; or tiredness.

whey (hwā) *n.* The clear, water-like part of milk that separates from the curd.

which (hwich) *pron.* What one or ones; the one previously; whatever one or ones; whichever. *adj.* What one; any one of.

which-ev-er (hwich ev´ẽr) Any; no matter which or what.

whiff (hwif) *n.* A slight puff; a light current of air; a slight breath or odor.

while (hwīl) *n.* A length or period of time. *conj.* During the time that; even though; at the same time; although.

whim (hwim) *n.* A sudden desire or impulse.

whim-per (hwim´pẽr) *v.* To make a weak, soft crying sound. **whimper** *n.*

whim-si-cal (hwim´zi kal) *adj.* Impulsive; erratic; light and spontaneous.

whine (hwīn) *v.* To make a squealing, plaintive sound; to complain in an irritating, childish fashion.

whin-ny (hwin´ē) *v.* To neigh in a soft gentle way.

whip (hwip) *v.* To spank repeatedly with a rod or stick; to punish by whipping; to move in a motion similar to whipping or beating. *n.* A flexible stick or rod used to herd or beat animals; a dessert made by whipping ingredients; the utensil used to do so. *Slang* To overcome. **whipper** *n.*

whip-lash (hwip´lash´) *n.* An injury to the spine or neck caused by a sudden jerking motion of the head.

whir (hwer) *v.* To move with a low purring sound.

whirl (hwerl) *v.* To rotate or move in circles; to twirl; to move, drive, or go very fast. *n.* A rapid whirling motion.

whisk (hwisk) *v.* To move with a sweeping motion; to move quickly or lightly. *n.* A sweeping movement; a utensil used in cooking; to stir.

whisk-er (hwis´kẽr) *n.* The hair that grows on a man's face; the long hair near the mouth of dogs, cats, and other animals. **whiskers** A man's beard.

whis-key (hwis´kē) *n.* An alcoholic beverage distilled from rye, barley, or corn.

whis-per (hwis´pẽr) *v.* To speak in a very low tone; to tell in secret. *n.* A low rustling sound; the act of whispering.

whis-tle (hwis´l) *v.* To make a clear shrill sound by blowing air through the teeth, through puckered lips, or through a special instrument. *n.* A device used to make a whistling sound.

white (hwīt) *n.* The color opposite of black; the part of something that is white or light in color, as an egg or the eyeball; a member of the Caucasian group of people. *adj.* Having a light color; pale; pure; blameless, without sin.

White House n. The official residence of the President of the United States, located in Washington, D.C.

whither (with´ér) v. To dry up or wilt from a lack of moisture; to lose freshness or vigor.

whit-tle (hwit´l) v. To cut or carve off small shavings from wood with a knife; to remove or reduce gradually.

whiz (hwiz) v. To make a whirring or buzzing sound, a projectile passing at a high rate of speed through the air. *Slang* A person having notable expertise, as with a computer.

who (hö) pron. Which or what certain individual, person, or group; referring to a person previously mentioned.

who'd contr. Who would; who had.

who-ev-er (hö ev´ér) pron. Whatever person; all or any persons.

whole (höl) adj. Complete; having nothing missing; not divided or in pieces; a complete system or unity; everything considered. *Math* Not a fraction. **wholeness** n.

whole-sale (höl´säl´) n. The sale of goods in large amounts to a retailer. adj. Relating to or having to do with such a sale. v. To sell wholesale.

whole-some (höl´som) adj. Contributing to good mental or physical health. **wholesomely** adv. **wholesomenes** n.

whole wheat (höl´hwët´) adj. Made from the wheat kernel with nothing removed.

who'll contr. Who shall; who will.

whol-ly (hö´lë) adv. Totally; exclusively.

whom (höm) pron. The form of who used as the direct object of a verb or the object of a preposition.

whom-ev-er (höm ev´ér) pron. The form of whoever used as the object of a preposition or the direct object of a verb.

whooping cough (hö´ping käf) n. An infectious disease of the throat and breathing passages in which the patient has spasms of coughing often followed by gasps for breath.

whoosh (hwösh) v. To make a rushing or gushing sound, as a rush of air.

whop-per (hwop´ér) n. Something of extra ordinary size. *Slang* A lie.

who's contr. Who is; who has.

whose (höz) pron. Belonging to or having to do with one's belongings. adj. Relating to *which* or *whom.*

why (hwī) adj. For what reason or purpose. conj. The cause, purpose, or reason for which. interj. Expressing surprise or disagreement.

wick (wik) n. The soft strand of fibers which extends from a candle or lamp and draws up the fuel for burning.

wick-er (wik´ér) n. A thin, pliable twig

used to make furniture and baskets.

wick-et (wik´it) n. A wire hoop in the game of croquet; a small door, window, or opening used as a box office.

wide (wid) adj. Broad; covering a large area; completely extended or open. adv. Over a large area; full extent.

wide-spread (wid´spred´) adj. Fully spread out; over a broad area.

wid-ow (wid´ö) n. A woman whose husband is no longer living.

wid-ow-er (wid´ö ér) n. A man whose wife is no longer living.

width (width) n. The distance or extent of something from side to side.

wield (wëld) v. To use or handle something skillfully; to employ power effectively.

wie-ner (wë´nér) n. A frankfurter; a hot dog.

wife (wif) n. A married female.

wig (wig) n. Artificial or human hair woven together to cover baldness or a bald spot on the head.

wig-gle (wig´l) v. To squirm; to move with rapid side-to-side motions.

wig-wam (wig´wom) n. An Indian dwelling place.

wild (wild) adj. Living in a natural, untamed state; not occupied by man; not civilized; strange and unusual. adv. Out of control. n. A wilderness region not cultivated or settled by man.

wil-der-ness (wil´dér nis) n. An unsettled area; a region left in its uncultivated or natural state.

wild-life (wild´lif´) n. Animals and plants living in their natural environments.

will (wil) n. The mental ability to decide or choose for oneself; strong desire or determination; a legal document stating how one's property is to be distributed after death. v. To bring about by an act of a will; to decide as by decree; to give or bequeath something in a will.

Wilson, Woodrow n. (1856-1924) The twenty-eighth president of the United States from 1913-1921.

wilt (wilt) v. To cause or to become limp; to lose force; to deprive of courage or energy.

win (win) v. To defeat others; to gain victory in a contest; to receive. n. Victory; the act of winning. **-ner** n.

winch (winch) n. An apparatus with one or more drums on which a cable or rope is wound, used to lift heavy loads.

wind (wind) n. A natural movement of air. v. To become short of breath.

wind instrument (wind´in´stru ment) n. A musical instrument which produces sound when a person forces his breath into it.

wind-pipe (wind´pip´) n. The passage in the neck used for breathing; the trachea.

wine (wīn) *n*. A drink containing 10-15% alcohol by volume, made by fermenting grapes.

wing (wing) *n*. One of the movable appendages that allow a bird or insect to fly; one of the airfoils on either side of an aircraft, allowing it to glide or travel through the air. *v*. To move as if on wings; to fly.

win-ning (win´ing) *adj*. Defeating others; captivating. *n*. Victory.

win-some (win´som) *adj*. Very pleasant; charming.

win-ter (win´tèr) *n*. The coldest season, coming between autumn and spring. *adj*. Relating to or typically of winter.

wipe (wīp) *v*. To clean by rubbing; to take off by rubbing. *n*. The act or instance of wiping.

Wis-con-sin *n*. A state located in the north central part of the United States; statehood May 29, 1848; state capital Madison.

wis-dom (wiz´dom) *n*. The ability to understand what is right, true, or enduring; good judgment; knowledge.

wise (wiz) *adj*. Having superior intelligence; having great learning; having a capacity for sound judgment marked by deep understanding.

wish (wish) *v*. To desire or long for something; to command or request. *n*. A longing or desire.

wish-ful (wish´ful) *adj*. Having or expressing a wish; hopeful. -**fully** *adv*.

wisp (wisp) *n*. A tuft or small bundle of hay, straw, or hair; a thin piece.

wit (wit) *n*. The ability to use words in a clever way; a sense of humor.

witch (wich) *n*. A person believed to have magical powers; a mean, ugly, old woman.

with (with) In the company of; near or alongside; having, wearing or bearing; in the judgment or opinion of; containing; in the possession or care of; supporting; among; occurring at the same time. *v*. To take away or back; to retreat.

with-draw (with dro´) *v*. To take away; to take back; to remove; to retreat.

with-hold (with hōld´) *n*. To hold back or keep.

with-out (with out´) *adv*. On the outside; not in possession of. *prep*. Something or someone lacking.

with-stand (with stand´) *v*. To endure.

wit-ness (wit´nis) *n*. A person who has seen, experienced, or heard something; something serving as proof or evidence. *v*. To see or hear something; to give proof or evidence of; to give testimony.

wit-ty (wit´ē) *adj*. Amusing or cleverly humorous.

wiz-ard (wiz´èrd) *n*. A very clever person; a person thought to have

magical powers. *Slang* One with amazing skill.

wob-ble (wob´l) *v*. To move unsteadily from side to side, as a rocking motion.

woe (wō) *n*. Great sorrow or grief; misfortune.

wok *n*. A convex metal cooker for stir frying food.

woke *v*. Past tense of wake.

woman (wem´an) *n*. The mature adult human female; a person who has feminine qualities.

womanhood (wem´an hed´) *n*. The state of being a woman.

womb (wōm) *n*. The uterus; the place where development occurs.

won (wun) *v*. Past tense of win.

won-der (wun´dèr) *n*. A feeling of amazement or admiration. *v*. To feel admiration; to feel uncertainty.

won-der-ment (wun´dèr ment) *n*. A feeling or state of amazement.

won-drous (wun´drus) *adj*. Wonderful; marvelous.

won't (wōnt) *contr*. Will not.

won-ton *n*. A noodle dumpling filled with minced pork and served in soup.

wood-en (wed´en) *adj*. Made of wood; resembling wood; stiff; lifeless; lacking flexibility. **woodenly** *adv*.

wool (wel) *n*. The soft, thick hair of sheep and other such mammals; a fabric made from such hair.

word (werd) *n*. A meaningful sound which stands for an idea; a comment; a brief talk; an order or command. *v*. To express orally. **wording** *n*.

word processing *n*. A system which produces typewritten documents with automated type and editing equipment.

work (werk) *n*. The action or labor required to accomplish something; employment; a job; a project or assignment; something requiring physical or mental effort. *v*. To engage in mental or physical exertion; to labor to have a job; to arrange.

work-man-ship (werk´man ship´) *n*. The skill or art of a craftsman; the quality given to something in the process of making it.

work-out (werk´out´) *n*. A period of strenuous exercise.

world (werld) *n*. The planet Earth; the universe; the human race; a field of human interest or effort.

worldly (werld´lē) *adj*. Interested in pleasure rather than religious or spiritual matters.

worm (werm) *n*. A small, thin animal having a long, flexible, rounded or flattened body. *Slang* A crude person.

worn (wōrn) *adj*. Made weak or thin from use; exhausted.

wor-ry (wer´ē) *v*. To be concerned or troubled; to tug at repeatedly; to annoy;

to irritate. *n.* Distress or mental anxiety.

wor-ship (wer´ship) *n.* Reverence for a sacred object; high esteem or devotion for a person. *v.* To revere; attend a religious service.

worst (werst) *adj.* Bad; most inferior; most disagreeable. *adv.* In the worst degree.

worth (werth) *n.* The quality or value of something; personal merit; the quantity that can be purchased for a certain amount of money.

wor-thy (wer´thē) *adj.* Valuable or useful; deserving admiration or honor.

would-n't (wed´nt) *contr.* Would not.

wound (wönd) *n.* A laceration of the skin. *v.* To injure by tearing, cutting, or piercing the skin.

wow (wou) *interj.* An expression of amazement, surprise, or excitement.

wran-gle (rang´gl) *v.* To quarrel noisily.

wrap (rap) *v.* To fold in order to protect something; to encase or enclose. *n.* A coat, shawl, or other outer protection. *Slang* To finish doing something, to finish producing or making something.

wrath (rath) *n.* Violent anger or fury.

wreak (rēk) *v.* To inflict punishment upon another person.

wreath (rēth) *n.* A decorative ring-like form of intertwined flowers, bows, and other articles.

wrest (rest) *v.* To twist or pull away in a violent way. *n.* A forcible twist.

wres-tle (res´l) *v.* To struggle with an opponent in order to pin him down. *n.* The instance of wrestling.

wretch (rech) *n.* An extremely unhappy person; a miserable person.

wrig-gle (rig´l) *v.* To squirm; to move by turning and twisting.

wring (ring) *v.* To squeeze and twist by hand or machine; to press together.

wrin-kle (ring´kl) *n.* A small crease on the skin or on fabric. *v.* To have or make wrinkles.

wrist (rist) *n., Anat.* The joint of the body between the hand and forearm; the part of a sleeve which encircles the wrist.

writ (rit) *n., Law* A written court document directed to a public official or individual ordering a specific action.

write (rīt) *v.* To form symbols or letters; to form words on a surface; to communicate by writing; to earn a living by writing books.

writhe (rīth) *v.* To twist, as in pain; to suffer greatly with pain.

writ-ing (rī´ting) *n.* A book or other written work; handwriting; the process of forming letters into words; the occupation of a writer.

wrong (rong) *adj.* Incorrect; against moral standards; not suitable; immoral; unsuitable; in appropriate. *n.* An act which is wicked or immoral. *v.* To do

wrong; to injure or hurt. **wrongly** *adv.*

wrote *v.* Past tense of write.

wrought (rot) *adj.* Fashioned; formed; beatened or hammered into shape.

wrung *v.* Past tense of wring.

Wy-o-ming *n.* A state located in the western part of the United States; statehood July 10, 1890; state capital Cheyenne.

X

X, x (eks) The twenty-fourth letter of the English alphabet.

xan-thate (zan´thāt) *n.* Ester or slat of a xanthic acid.

xan-thic (zan´thik) *adj.* The color yellow or all colors that tend toward the color yellow when relating to flowers.

xan-thin (zan´thin) *n.* A carotinoid pigment that is soluble in alcohol.

xan-thine (zan´thēn) *n.* A crystalline nitrogen compound, closely related to uric acid, found in blood, urine, and certain plant and animal tissues.

xan-tho-chroid (zan´tho kroid´) *adj.* Pertaining to the light-complexioned Caucasoid race.

xan-tho-ma (zan thō´ma) *n.* A skin condition of the eyelids marked by small, yellow, raised nodules or plates.

X chro-mo-some (eks´krō´mo sōm) *n.* The sex female chromosome, associated with female characteristics; occurs paired in the female and single in the male chromosome pair.

xe-bec (zē´bek) *n.* A small vessel with three masts having both lateen and square sails.

xe-nic *adj.* Relating to, or employing a culture medium that contains one or more unidentified organisms.

xe-non (zē´non) *n.* The colorless, odorless gaseous element found in small quantities in the air, symbolized by Xe.

xe-no-phile *n.* One attracted to foreign people, styles, manners, etc.

xen-o-phobe (zen´o fōb´) *n.* A person who dislikes, fears, and mistrusts foreigners or anything stranger.

xe-rarch (zērärk) *adj.* Originating or developing in a dry place.

xe-ric (zēr´ik) *adj.* Relating to or requiring only a small amount of moisture. **xeric-ally** *adv.*

xe-roph-i-lous (zi rof´i lus) *adj.* Tolerant or characteristic of xeric environments.

xe-roph-thal-mi-a (zēr´of thal´mē a) *n.* An itching soreness of the eyes that is caused by an insufficient amount of vita-min A.

xe-ro-phyte (zēr´o fīt´) *n.* A plant that can live in a surrounding of extreme heat and drought. **xerophytic** *adj.* **xerophytically** *adv.* **xerophytism** *n.*

X–Ra-di-a-tion *n.* Treatment with

X-rays.

X ray (eks´rā´) *n*. Energy that is radiated with a short wavelength and high penetrating power; a black and white negative image or picture of the interior of the body.

x-sec-tion *n*. Cross section of something. **x-sectional** *adj*.

xy-lo-phone (zī´lo fōn´) *n*. A musical instrument consisting of mounted wooden bars which produce a ringing musical sound when struck with two small wooden hammers. **xylophonist** *n*.

xy-lose (zī´lōs) *n., Chem*. A crystalline aldose sugar.

xy-lot-o-mous (zīlot´o mus) *adj*. Capable of cutting or boring wood.

Y

Y, y (wī) The twenty-fifth letter of the English alphabet.

yacht (yot) *n*. A small sailing vessel powered by wind or motor, used for pleasure cruises. **yacht** *v*.

yak (yak) *n*. A long haired ox of Tibet and the mountains of central Asia.

yam (yam) *n*. An edible root; a variety of the sweet potato.

Yan-kee (yang´kē) *n*. A native of the northern United States. **Yankee** *adj*.

yap (yap) *v*. To bark in a high pitched, sharp way. *Slang* To talk in a relentless, loud, or stupid manner.

yard (yärd) *n*. A unit of measure that equals 36 inches or 3 feet; the ground around or near a house or building.

yard goods *n*. Fabric that is sold by the yard.

yard-man (yärd´man) *n*. A person employed as a worker in a railroad yard.

yard-mas-ter (yärd´mas´tèr) *n*. A person in charge of a railroad yard.

yard-stick (yärd´stik´) *n*. A graduated measuring stick that equals 1 yard or 36 inches.

yarn (yarn) *n*. Twisted fibers, as of wool, used in knitting or weaving. *Slang* An involved tale or story.

yawn (yon) *v*. To inhale a deep breath with the mouth open wide. **yawner** *n*.

yawn-ing (yo´ning) *adj*. Expressing tiredness by a yawn.

Y-Chro-mo-some (wī´krō´mo sōm) *n*. The sex chromosome associated with male characteristics.

ye (yē) *pron*. You, used especially in religious contexts, as hymns.

yea (yā) *adv*. Yes; indeed; truly.

yeah *adv., Slang* Yes.

year (yēr) *n*. A period of time starting on January lst and continuing through December 31st, consisting of 365 days or 366 days in a leap year, which occurs every four years.

year-book (yēr´bük´) *n*. A book printed each year giving facts about the year; a book printed each year for a high school, college, etc.

year-ling (yēr´ling) *n*. An animal that is one year old.

year-ly (yēr´lē) *adj*. Pertaining to something that happens, appears, or comes once a year, every year.

yearn (yern) *v*. To feel a strong craving.

year-round *adj*. Lasting or continuing for an entire year.

yeast (yēst) *n*. Fungi or plant cells used to make baked goods rise or fruit juices ferment.

yell (yel) *v*. To cry out loudly. *n*. A loud cry; a cheer to show support for an athletic team.

yel-low (yel´ō) *n*. The bright color of a lemon; the yolk of an egg. *v*. To make or become yellow. *adj*. Of the color yellow. *Slang* Cowardly.

yellow fever *n*. An acute infectious disease of the tropics, spread by the bite of a mosquito.

yelp *n*. A quick, sharp, shrill cry, as from pain.

yen (yen) *n*. An intense craving or longing.

yeo-man (yō´man) *n*. The owner of a small farm; a petty officer who acts as a clerk.

yeo-man-ly *n*. The rank of a yeoman; befitting a yeoman.

Yeoman's service *n*. Useful, good, or substantial service.

yes (yes) *adv*. To express agreement or consent.

yes-ter-day (yes´tèr dē) *n*. The day before today; a former or recent time. *adv*. On the day before the present day.

yes-ter-year *n*. Time just recently past; last year.

yet (yet) *adv*. Up to now; at this time; even now; more so. *conj*. Nevertheless.

yet-i *n*. The abominable snowman.

yew (ū) *n*. An evergreen tree having poisonous flat, dark-green needles and poisonous red berries.

yield (yēld) *v*. To bear or bring forward; to give up the possession of something; to give way to. *n*. An amount that is produced; the act of producing.

yield-ing (yēl´ding) *adj*. Ready to yield, comply, or submit; unresisting. **yieldingly** *adv*.

yo-del (yōd´el) *v*. To sing in a way so that the voice changes from normal to a high shrill sound and then back again.

yo-ga (yō´ga) *n*. A system of exercises which helps the mind and the body in order to achieve tranquillity and spiritual insight.

yo-gurt (yō´gèrt) *n*. A thick custard-like

food made from curdled milk and often mixed with fruit.

yoke (yōk) *n.* A wooden bar used to join together two oxen or other animals working together; the section of a garment fitting closely around the shoulders. *v.* To join with a yoke.

yolk (yōk) *n.* The yellow nutritive part of an egg.

Yom Kip-pur (yom kip´ẽr) *n.* The Jewish holiday observed with fasting and prayer for the forgiveness of sins.

you (ū) *pron.* The person or persons addressed.

you all (ū ol´) *pron., Slang* y'all A southern variation used for two or more people in direct address.

you'd (ūd) *contr.* You had; you would.

you'll (ūl) *contr.* You will; you shall.

young (yung) *adj.* Of or relating to the early stage of life; not old. *n.* The offspring of an animal. **youngster** *n.*

your (yẽr) *adj.* Belonging to you or yourself or the person spoken to.

you're (ūr) *contr.* You are.

your-self (yẽr self´) *pron.* A form of you for emphasis when the object of a verb and the subject is the same.

youth (ūth) *n.* The appearance or state of being young; the time of life when one is not considered an adult; a young person.

you've (ūv) *contr.* You have.

yowl (youl) *v.* To make a loud, long cry or howl. **yowl** *n.*

yt-ter-bi-um (i tẽr´bē um) *n.* A metallic element of the rare-earth group symbolized by Yb.

yt-tri-um (i´trē um) *n.* A metallic element symbolized by Y.

yuc-ca (yuk´a) *n.* A tropical plant having large, white flowers and long, pointed leaves.

yule (ūl) *n.* Christmas.

yule-tide (ūl´tīd´) *n.* The Christmas season.

Z

Z, z (zē) The twenty-sixth letter of the English alphabet.

za-ny (zā´nē) *n. pl.* -nies A clown; a person who acts silly or foolish. *adj.* Typical of being clownish. **zaniness** *n.* **zanily** *adv.*

zap *v., Slang* To destroy; to do away with.

zeal (zēl) *n.* Great interest or eagerness.

zeal-ot (zel´ot) *n.* A fanatical person; a fanatic.

zeal-ous (zel´us) *adj.* Full of interest; eager; passionate. **zealously** *adv.*

ze-bra (zē´bra) *n.* An African mammal of the horse family having black or brown stripes on a white body.

zeph-yr (zef´ẽr) *n.* A gentle breeze.

ze-ro (zēr´ō) *n. pl.* -ros, -roes The number or symbol "0"; nothing; the point from which degrees or measurements on a scale begin; the lowest point. *v.* To aim, point at, or close in on. *adj.* Pertaining to zero; nonexisting.

zest (zest) *n.* Enthusiasm; a keen quality. **zestful** *adj.* **zestfully** *adv.* **zesty** *adj.*

zig-zag (zig´zag´) *n.* A pattern with sharp turns in alternating directions. *adv.* To move in a zigzag course or path.

zilch *n., Slang* Nothing; zero.

zil-lion (zil´yon) *n., Slang* An extremely large number.

zinc (zingk) *n.* A bluish-white crystalline metallic element, used as a protective coat-ing for steel and iron, symbolized by Zn.

zip (zip) *n.* To act or move with vigor or speed. *v.* To move with energy, speed, or facility; to open or close with a zipper. *Slang* Energy; zero; nothing.

zip code *n.* The system to speed the delivery of mail by assigning a five digit number, plus four to each postal delivery location in the United States.

zip-per (zip´ẽr) *n.* A fastener consisting of two rows of plastic or metal teeth that are interlocked by means of sliding a tab.

zir-co-ni-um (zẽr kō´nē um) *n.* A metallic element symbolized by Zr.

zit *n., Slang* A pimple.

zo-di-ac (zō´dē ak´) *n.* The celestial sphere; the unseen path followed through the heavens by the moon, sun, and most planets; this area divided into twelve parts or twelve astrological signs, each bearing the name of a constellation.

zone (zōn) *n.* An area or region set apart from its surroundings by some characteristic.

zoo (zō) *n., pl.* zoos A public display or collection of living animals.

zo-ol-o-gy (zō ol´o jē) *n.* The science that deals with animals, animal life, and the animal kingdom. **zoologist** *n.*

zoom (zōm) *v.* To move with a continuous, loud, buzzing sound; to move upward sharply; to move toward a subject with great speed.

zuc-chi-ni (zō kē´nē) *n. pl.* -ni A summer squash that is long and narrow and has a dark-green, smooth rind.

zy-mol-o-gy (zī mol´o jē) *n.* The branch of science dealing with ferments and fermentation. **zymologic** *n.*

zy-mo-scope (zī´mo skōp) *n.* An instrument that measures yeast's fermenting power.

zy-mot-ic (zī mot´ik) *adj.* Relating or pertaining to fermentation.

zy-mur-gy (zī´mer jē) *n.* The chemistry dealing with the fermentation process.

ENTER THE AMAZING
NEW WORLD OF

- *The caterpillars that march until they die*
- *The Assembly of the Great Peacock Moths*
- *The ingenuity of the Burying-beetles*
- *The wisdom of the Hunting Wasp*
- *The courtship of the Scorpion*
- *The mating feast of the Praying Mantis*

The discoveries of J. Henri Fabre have enriched modern science beyond measure. In the field of comparative psychology and experimental biology Fabre's harvest of facts is invaluable.

This book, ably edited and with interpretive comments by Edwin Way Teale, presents the most famous insect stories of the great French entomologist. They make absorbing and exciting reading. Here also are glimpses of Fabre himself—his childhood, his struggle against poverty—and of the carefully planned experiments which revealed to him, as to no other scientist, the fascinating insect world.

The Insect World of
J. Henri Fabre

NEWLY REVISED WITH AN INTRODUCTION
BY EDWIN WAY TEALE

A PREMIER BOOK

FAWCETT PUBLICATIONS, INC., GREENWICH, CONN.
MEMBER OF AMERICAN BOOK PUBLISHERS COUNCIL, INC.

A Premier Book published by arrangement with
Dodd, Mead & Company, Inc.

Books by J. Henri Fabre, copyright 1913, 1914, 1915, 1916, 1917,
1919, 1922, 1923, Dodd, Mead & Company, Inc.
Copyright MCMXLIX, Edwin Way Teale
Copyright 1956, Edwin Way Teale

Second Premier printing, September 1964

Premier Books are published by Fawcett World Library
67 West 44th Street, New York, New York. 10036
Printed in the United States of America.

Contents

I	A Laboratory of the Open Fields	15
II	The Pine Processionary	24
III	Insect Weather Prophets	40
IV	The Hunting Wasp	46
V	The Wisdom of Instinct	57
VI	The Ignorance of Instinct	71
VII	The Great Peacock Moth	83
VIII	The Song of the Cicada	99
IX	The Praying Mantis	102
X	Mating of the Mantis	110
XI	The Hatching of the Mantis	115
XII	How I Met the Mason-bee	120
XIII	Experiments with Mason-bees	123
XIV	Cricket Music	128
XV	Courtship of the Scorpion	131
XVI	The Cionus Weevil	138
XVII	The Burying-beetle	155
XVIII	Experiments with Burying-beetles	164
XIX	The Oil-beetle's Journey	181
XX	The Edge of the Unknown	190

Contents

I. ...
II. ...
III. ...
IV. ...
V. ...
VI. ...
VII. ...
VIII. ...
IX. ...
X. ...
XI. ...
XII. ...
XIII. ...
XIV. ...
XV. ...
XVI. ...
XVII. ...
XVIII. ...
XIX. ...
XX. ...

Foreword

IN THE FIELD OF INSECT STUDY, the works of J. Henri Fabre are classics; in the field of literature, they hold a special place of their own. The present volume brings into the compass of a single book the most famous of Fabre's studies, many of them now out of print. In some instances, material has been shortened but nothing has been added. My own comments are confined to the italicized sections at the beginning of each chapter.

In the matter of style and spelling in the text, I have followed the original translation. This, in all cases, was the work of Alexander Teixeira de Mattos, whose rendering into English of Fabre's prose cannot be too highly commended. A single instance will illustrate the feeling and skill he contributed to the work. Where another translator expressed Fabre's words as: ". . . to see whether he was rolling his manure ball, the image of the world for ancient Egypt," De Mattos phrases it: ". . . to see whether he was rolling that pellet of dung in which ancient Egypt beheld an image of the world." Without changing the meaning by a hair, his phrasing gave the line the nobility of literature.

—Edwin Way Teale

Introduction

J. HENRI FABRE, OF FRANCE, found the delights of a lifetime—adventure and fame, as well—in observing the near-at-home. He was an explorer whose jungles were weed-lots and whose deserts were sandbanks. There, with tireless enthusiasm, he studied "all those vague, unconscious, rudimentary and almost nameless little lives," as Maeterlinck called the insects. Throughout most of his long life—a life that stretched to within eight years of the century mark, from 1823 to 1915, from two years after the death of Napoleon Bonaparte on St. Helena to the days of the first World War—Fabre never lost his zest for the insect world with its multitudinous mysteries. And no man ever lived who transmitted that enthusiasm to more of his fellow-men.

All of Fabre's years were shadowed by penury. His life was an epic of struggle against the worries and irritations that beset the poor. He knew nothing of his peasant ancestors beyond the second generation. His mother could neither read nor write. Reminiscences of his youth, little biographical glimpses, sidelights on his prolonged and lonely labors, these illuminate the pages of his books. The man, Fabre, becomes as interesting to readers as the small protagonists of his insect dramas.

The author's father, Antoine Fabre, was the first of his line to leave the land for the city. An unsuccessful keeper of small cafés, he moved from failure to failure. The family was living at Saint-Léons, market town and administrative center of the canton of Vezins, on December 22, 1823, when Jean Henri Casimer Fabre was born. To make one mouth less to feed, the child was soon sent to live with his maternal grandparents at their farm at Malaval, on "the cold granite ridge of the Rouergue tableland." He was six when he returned to Saint-Léons to begin his schooling; ten when his father moved to Rodez. He never saw his birthplace again.

For a time, working as a laborer, doing odd jobs, selling lemonade at fairs, he supported himself and struggled toward a diploma. In 1842, when he was eighteen years old, Fabre left the Normal College of Avignon with this goal achieved and began his teaching career as a primary schoolmaster at Carpentras. Here his meager salary was often in arrears. At Ajaccio, Corsica, where he taught science for a few years, malaria forced him to return to the mainland. Finally, in 1852, he became a professor at the Lycée of Avignon. Here he labored for nearly twenty years at a salary that never exceeded $320 a year. When he left, his rank, his title, his salary were the same as when he began.

In 1879, when Fabre was already fifty-five years old, a long dream came true. He was able to buy a small foothold of earth, sun-scorched and thistle-ridden, unfit for grazing or agriculture, an area known locally as a *harmas,* at the edge of the village of Sérignan. It was the first bit of land Fabre had owned in his life. To him, the stony soil, arid and rusty-red, formed an Eden. It was inhabited by wasps and wild bees and all those small creatures to which he wished to devote uninterrupted study during the remaining years of his life.

His routine became fixed. He arose at six, walked about his *harmas,* ate a sparing breakfast and retired to his laboratory —a long room with whitewashed walls, a tile floor and a great walnut table supporting home-made rearing cages and the simple equipment of the experimenter. He lacked even a microscope for many years, relying on a pocket lens in his work. Late in his life, long after he was too old to use it, the state bestowed upon him the elaborate equipment of a modern laboratory. His best instruments, Fabre used to say, were Time and Patience.

Evidence of ample use of both remained when he died. In the floor of his laboratory, a path or groove had been worn in the tiles by Fabre's years of circling his table in his heavy peasant shoes. Once in his laboratory, he shut himself up "like a snail." He rarely saw callers. He rarely answered letters. To a friend who complained of a long-neglected reply to a letter, Fabre wrote: "Once I have mounted my hobby-horse, goodbye to replies, goodbye to everything."

For a quarter of a century, he had been assembling material, shaping and planning, preparing in fragments a great work on the lives of the insects. It was to be called *Souvenirs Entomologiques.* The initial volume appeared the very year that Fabre reached his *harmas* Eden. Nearly thirty years were to elapse before the tenth and final volume would come from the press in 1907. Oftentimes, Fabre felt that he had reached the end of his strength, that his grand scheme would fail of fulfillment. "Dear insects," he wrote in the final paragraph of Volume III, "my study of you has sustained me in my heaviest trials. I must take leave of you for today. The ranks are thinning around me and the long hopes have fled. Shall I be able to speak to you again?" Often despairing but working on in despair, Fabre continued through seven more volumes, containing more than 2,500 pages and nearly 850,-000 words.

As the successive volumes of *Souvenirs Entomologiques* appeared, they attracted only mild attention. Fabre worked alone. He had no connection with any large institution. He lived, in truth, more in the world of insects than in the world of men. His publisher, moreover, issued the original editions in a heavy, unattractive format. Thus, overlooked and ignored, Fabre struggled on "without masters, without guides, often without books . . . with one aim: to add a few pages to the history of the insects."

His long years of neglect, his decades of painstaking labor, ended in five exhausting years of fame. Fabre was eighty-four when the last of the ten volumes of his *magnum opus* appeared. Soon afterwards, he was suddenly discovered by such eminent literary figures as Maurice Maeterlinck, Edmund Rostand and Romain Rolland. A jubilee in his honor was held at Sérignan in 1910. Government officials and representatives of scientific institutions and societies did him homage. A statue was erected in the village. People who had never heard of the "Insect's Homer" before, began reading his books at home and abroad. Scientific societies in London, Brussels, Stockholm, Geneva and St. Petersburg elected him to membership. The government bestowed upon him an annual pension of $400. The President of France journeyed to Sérignan to meet its first citizen. After the long years of poverty, of labor, of niggardly recognition, Fabre, nearing his ninetieth year, saw with his failing eyesight the sunshine of brilliant acclaim.

But, even then, tension and sadness darkened the sunshine. Fabre's second wife died in 1912. His country began fighting for its life in 1914. On the 11th of October, 1915, fighting was heavy in the Argonne and Belgrade, in the Balkans, had just fallen to the Germans. On that day, in the village quiet of Sérignan, the long life of J. Henri Fabre came to an end.

Looking back on Fabre's work today, it is easy to see the

mistakes he made, blind spots in his approach to the larger aspects of biological research. He never accepted, for example, the theory of evolution. Although Charles Darwin called Fabre an "incomparable observer" and suggested experiments for him to do and although Fabre had the highest personal regard for the English scientist, he was so little interested in the *Origin of Species* that he never read more than a few pages. He was a realist opposed to hypotheses. His harvest was a harvest of facts rather than a harvest of conclusions. Fabre was far surer than present-day scientists of the machine-like character of instinct. He tended to overemphasize the belief that instinct sticks to its course like a train on its rails; that the creature has almost no choice in the matter. The Peckhams, experimenting with solitary wasps in America, demonstrated that instinct provides considerable latitude in the actions of many insects, a finding that has been substantiated by numerous more recent investigations.

But, when all these weaknesses are acknowledged, the greatness of Fabre towers above them. He was a pioneer, working alone, under-valued, poverty-cramped, using crude equipment that would cause a modern research worker to throw up his hands in despair. Yet, by repeating an experiment over and over again, by the endless inventiveness of his mind, he made up for the lack of adequate equipment. He produced some of the basic studies of the nature of instinct. All students of insect behavior, of comparative psychology, of experimental biology are indebted to him. His harvest of facts is invaluable still.

In the autumn of 1911, Fabre penned a short introduction for Dr. C. V. Legros' biography, *Fabre, Poet of Science*. "It seems to me," he wrote, "that in the depths of my being I can still feel rising in me all the fever of my early years, all the enthusiasm of long ago, and that I should still be no less ardent a worker were not the weakness of my eyes and the failure of my strength today an insurmountable obstacle." At the time, J. Henri Fabre was eighty-eight years old. His sense of wonder outlived his sense of sight; his interest and enthusiasm outlasted his strength.

There is an epic character, something universal and symbolic, in the story of this simple man's life, in his years of unremitting struggle to solve mysteries of the commonplace. With so little, Fabre did so much.

The Insect World of
J. Henri Fabre

I

A Laboratory of the Open Fields

The village of Sérignan, in the Department of Vaucluse, lies in the Rhone valley about fifty miles north of the Mediterranean. The nearest town is Orange. At the time of Fabre's death, the population of Sérignan was about 1,000. The soil of the region is rust-red, stony and arid, supporting, here and there, a vineyard or olive-grove. The Lygues River, flowing by the village on its way to the Rhone, is a muddy torrent in spring, a dry river of stones and pebbles in summer. The horizon to the east is formed by the foothills of the Alps.

Fabre's harmas had an area of 2.47 acres, almost exactly a Roman hectare. It was roughly rectangular in shape, with the flat-roofed, two-story house set at one end. A wall provided seclusion and paths wound among the tangles of this "Eden." Beyond the wall, a dusty road, lined with plane trees, led to Orange where the family did its weekly marketing.

Among the insects named by Fabre in this chapter, the Cicadella is a froghopper; the Scarab, Lamellicorns, Orycetes and Cetoniae are beetles; the Sphex, Ammophila, Cerceris, Stizus, Pompilus, Pelopaeus, Polistes, Eumenes, Scoliae and Bembeces are wasps; the Ephippiger is a green grasshopper and the Halicti, Megachiles, Chalcicodomae, Osmiae, Anthophorae, Anthidium, Eucerae, Macrocerae, Dasypodae and Andrenae are all wild bees. The first two paragraphs of this chapter are taken from THE GLOW-WORM; *the rest forms Chapter I of* THE LIFE OF THE FLY.

TO TRAVEL THE WORLD, by land and sea, from pole to pole; to cross-question life, under every clime, in the infinite variety of its manifestations: that surely would be glorious luck for him that has eyes to see; and it formed the radiant dreams of my young years, at the time when ROBINSON CRUSOE was my delight. These rosy illusions, rich in voyages, were

15

soon succeeded by dull, stay-at-home reality. The jungles of India, the virgin forests of Brazil, the towering crests of the Andes, beloved by the Condor, were reduced, as a field for exploration, to a patch of pebbles enclosed within four walls.

I go the circuit of my enclosure over and over again, a hundred times, by short stages; I stop here and I stop there; patiently, I put questions and, at long intervals, I receive some scrap of a reply. The smallest insect village has become familiar to me: I know each fruit-branch where the Praying Mantis perches; each bush where the pale Italian Cricket strums amid the calmness of the summer nights; each downy plant scraped by the Anthidium, that maker of cotton bags; each cluster of lilac worked by the Megachile, the leaf-cutter.

This is what I wished for, *hoc erat in votis:* a bit of land, oh, not so very large, but fenced in, to avoid the drawbacks of a public way; an abandoned, barren, sun-scorched bit of land, favoured by thistles and by Wasps and Bees. Here, without fear of being troubled by the passers-by, I could consult the Ammophila and the Sphex and engage in that difficult conversation whose questions and answers have experiment for their language; here, without distant expeditions that take up my time, without tiring rambles that strain my nerves, I could contrive my plans of attack, lay my ambushes and watch their effects at every hour of the day. Yes, this was my wish, my dream, always cherished, always vanishing into the mists of the future.

And it is no easy matter to acquire a laboratory in the open fields, when harassed by a terrible anxiety about one's daily bread. For forty years have I fought, with steadfast courage, against the paltry plagues of life; and the long-wished-for laboratory has come at last. What it has cost me in perseverance and relentless work I will not try to say. It has come; and, with it—a more serious condition— perhaps a little leisure. I say perhaps, for my leg is still hampered with a few links of the convict's chain.

The wish is realized. It is a little late, O my pretty insects! I greatly fear that the peach is offered to me when I am beginning to have no teeth wherewith to eat it. Yes, it is a little late: the wide horizons of the outset have shrunk into a low and stifling canopy, more and more straitened day by day. Regretting nothing in the past, save those whom I have lost; regretting nothing, not even my first youth; hoping nothing either, I have reached the point at which, worn out by the experience of things, we ask ourselves if life be worth the living.

Amid the ruins that surround me, one strip of wall remains standing, immovable upon its solid base: my passion for scientific truth. Is that enough, O my busy insects, to enable me to add yet a few seemly pages to your history? Will my strength not cheat my good intentions? Why, indeed, did I forsake you so long? Friends have reproached me for it. Ah, tell them, tell those friends, who are yours as well as mine, tell them that it was not forgetfulness on my part, not weariness, nor neglect: I thought of you; I was convinced that the Cerceris cave had more fair secrets to reveal to us, that the chase of the Sphex held fresh surprises in store. But time failed me; I was alone, deserted, struggling against misfortune. Before philosophizing, one had to live. Tell them that; and they will pardon me.

Others again have reproached me with my style, which has not the solemnity, nay, better, the dryness of the schools. They fear lest a page that is read without fatigue should not always be the expression of the truth. Were I to take their word for it, we are profound only on condition of being obscure. Come here, one and all of you—you, the sting-bearers, and you, the wing-cased armour-clads—take up my defence and bear witness in my favour. Tell of the intimate terms on which I live with you, of the patience with which I observe you, of the care with which I record your actions. Your evidence is unanimous: yes, my pages, though they bristle not with hollow formulas nor learned smatterings, are the exact narrative of facts observed, neither more nor less; and whoso cares to question you in his turn will obtain the same replies.

And then, my dear insects, if you cannot convince those good people, because you do not carry the weight of tedium, I, in my turn, will say to them:

"You rip up the animal and I study it alive; you turn it into an object of horror and pity, whereas I cause it to be loved; you labour in a torture-chamber and dissecting-room, I make my observations under the blue sky to the song of the Cicadas, you subject cell and protoplasm to chemical tests, I study instinct in its loftiest manifestations; you pry into death, I pry into life. And why should I not complete my thought: the boars have muddied the clear stream;

natural history, youth's glorious study, has, by dint of cellular improvements, become a hateful and repulsive thing. Well, if I write for men of learning, for philosophers, who, one day, will try to some extent to unravel the tough problem of instinct, I write also, I write above all things for the young. I want to make them love the natural history which you make them hate; and that is why, while keeping strictly to the domain of truth, I avoid your scientific prose, which too often, alas seems borrowed from some Iroquois idiom!"

But this is not my business for the moment: I want to speak of the bit of land long cherished in my plans to form a laboratory of living entomology, the bit of land which I have at last obtained in the solitude of a little village. It is a *harmas*, the name given, in this district, to an untilled, pebbly expanse abandoned to the vegetation of the thyme. It is too poor to repay the work of the plough; but the sheep passes there in spring, when it has chanced to rain and a little grass shoots up.

My *harmas,* however, because of its modicum of red earth swamped by a huge mass of stones, has received a rough first attempt at cultivation: I am told that vines once grew here. And, in fact, when we dig the ground before planting a few trees, we turn up, here and there, remains of the precious stock, half-carbonized by time. The three-pronged fork, therefore, the only implement of husbandry that can penetrate such a soil as this, has entered here; and I am sorry, for the primitive vegetation has disappeared. No more thyme, no more lavender, no more clumps of kermes-oak, the dwarf oak that forms forests across which we step by lengthening our stride a little. As these plants, especially the first two, might be of use to me by offering the Bees and Wasps a spoil to forage, I am compelled to reinstate them in the ground whence they were driven by the fork.

What abounds without my mediation is the invaders of any soil that is first dug up and then left for a long time to its own resources. We have, in the first rank, the couch-grass, that execrable weed which three years of stubborn warfare have not succeeded in exterminating. Next, in respect of number, come the centauries, grim-looking one and all, bristling with prickles or starry halberds. They are the yellow-flowered centaury, the mountain centaury, the star-thistle and the rough centaury: the first predominates. Here and there, amid their inextricable confusion, stands, like a chandelier with spreading, orange flowers for lights, the fierce Spanish oyster-plant, whose spikes are strong as nails. Above it, towers the Illyrian cotton-thistle, whose straight and solitary stalk soars to a height of three to six feet and ends in large pink tufts. Its armour hardly yields before that of the oyster-plant. Nor must we forget the lesser thistle-tribe, with first of all, the prickly or "cruel" thistle, which is so well armed that the plant-collector knows not where to grasp it; next, the spear-thistle, with its ample foliage, ending each of its veins with a spear-head; lastly, the black knap-weed, which gathers itself into a spiky knot. In among these, in long lines armed with hooks, the shoots of the blue dewberry creep along the ground. To visit the prickly thicket when the Wasp goes foraging, you must wear boots that come to mid-leg or else resign yourself to a smarting in the calves. As long as the ground retains a few remnants of the vernal rains, this rude vegetation does not lack a certain charm, when the pyramids of the oyster-plant and the slender branches of the cotton-thistle rise above the wide carpet formed by the yellow-flowered centaury saffron heads; but let the droughts of summer come and we see but a desolate waste, which the flame of a match would set ablaze from one end to the other. Such is, or rather was, when I took possession of it, the Eden of bliss where I mean to live henceforth alone with the insect. Forty years of desperate struggle have won it for me.

Eden, I said; and, from the point of view that interests me, the expression is not out of place. This cursed ground, which no one would have had as a gift to sow with a pinch of turnip-seed, is an earthly paradise for the Bees and Wasps. Its mighty growth of thistles and centauries draws them all to me from everywhere around. Never, in my insect-hunting memories, have I seen so large a population at a single spot; all the trades have made it their rallying-point. Here come hunters of every kind of game, builders in clay, weavers of cotton goods, collectors of pieces cut from a leaf or the petals of a flower, architects in pasteboard, plasterers mixing mortar, carpenters boring wood, miners digging underground galleries, workers handling goldbeater's skin and many more.

Who is this one? An Anthidium. She scrapes the cobwebby stalk of the yellow-flowered centaury and gathers a ball of wadding which she carries off proudly in the tips of her mandibles. She will turn it, under ground, into cotton-felt satchels to hold the store of honey and the egg. And these others, so eager for plunder? They are Megachiles, carrying under their bellies their black, white or blood-red reaping-brushes. They will leave the thistles to visit the neighbouring shrubs and there cut from the leaves oval pieces which will be made into a fit receptacle to contain the harvest. And these, clad in black velvet? They are Chalcicodomæ, who work with cement and gravel. We could easily find their masonry on the stones in the *harmas*. And these, noisily buzzing with a sudden flight? They are the Anthophoræ, who live in the old walls and the sunny banks of the neighbourhood.

Now come the Osmiæ. One stacks her cells in the spiral staircase of an empty snail-shell; another, attacking the pith of a dry bit of bramble, obtains for her grubs a cylindrical lodging and divides it into floors by means of partition-walls; a third employs the natural channel of a cut reed; a fourth is a rent-free tenant of the vacant galleries of some Mason-bee. Here are the Macroceræ and the Euceræ, whose males are proudly horned; the Dasypodæ, who carry an ample brush of bristles on their hind-legs for a reaping implement; the Andrenæ, so manifold in species; the slender-bellied Halicti. I omit a host of others. If I tried to continue this record of the guests of my thistles, it would muster almost the whole of the honey-yielding tribe. A learned entomologist of Bordeaux, Professor Pérez, to whom I submit the naming of my prizes, once asked me if I had any special means of hunting, to send him so many rarities and even novelties. I am not at all an experienced and, still less, a zealous hunter, for the insect interests me much more when engaged in its work than when stuck on a pin in a cabinet. The whole secret of my hunting is reduced to my dense nursery of thistles and centauries.

By a most fortunate chance, with this populous family of honey-gatherers was allied the whole hunting tribe. The builders' men had distributed here and there in the *harmas* great mounds of sand and heaps of stones, with a view to running up some surrounding walls. The work dragged on slowly; and the materials found occupants from the first year. The Mason-bees had chosen the interstices between the stones as a dormitory where to pass the night, in serried groups. The powerful Eyed Lizard, who, when close-pressed, attacks both man and dog, wide mouthed, had selected a cave wherein to lie in wait for the passing Scarab; the Black-eared Chat, garbed like a Dominican, white-frocked with black wings, sat on the top stone, singing his short rustic lay: his nest, with its sky-blue eggs, must be some-where in the heap. The little Dominican disappeared with the loads of stones. I regret him: he would have been a charm-ing neighbour. The Eyed Lizard I do not regret at all.

The sand sheltered a different colony. Here, the Bembeces were sweeping the threshold of their burrows, flinging a curve of dust behind them; the Languedocian Sphex was dragging her Ephippigera by the antennæ; a Stizus was storing her preserves of Cicadellæ. To my sorrow, the masons ended by evicting the sporting tribe; but, should I ever wish to recall it, I have but to renew the mounds of sand: they will soon all be there.

Hunters that have not disappeared, their homes being dif-ferent, are the Ammophilæ, whom I see fluttering, one in spring, the others in autumn, along the garden-walks and over the lawns, in search of a Caterpillar; the Pompili, who travel alertly, beating their wings and rummaging in every corner in quest of a Spider. The largest of them waylays the Narbonne Lycosa, whose burrow is not infrequent in the *harmas*. This burrow is a vertical well, with a curb of fescue-grass intertwined with silk. You can see the eyes of the mighty Spider gleam at the bottom of the den like little di-amonds, an object of terror to most. What a prey and what dangerous hunting for the Pompilus! And here, on a hot summer afternoon, is the Amazon-ant, who leaves her bar-rack-rooms in long battalions and marches far afield to hunt for slaves. We will follow her in her raids when we find time. Here again, around a heap of grasses turned to mould, are Scoliæ an inch and a half long, who fly gracefully and dive into the heap, attracted by a rich prey, the grubs of Lamellicorns, Oryctes and Cetoniæ.

What subjects for study! And there are more to come. The house was as utterly deserted as the ground. When man was gone and peace assured, the animal hastily seized on every-thing. The Warbler took up his abode in the lilac-shrubs; the Greenfinch settled in the thick shelter of the cypresses; the Sparrow carted rags and straw under every slate; the Serin-finch, whose downy nest is no bigger than half an apricot, came and chirped in the plane-tree-tops; the Scops made a habit of uttering his monotonous, piping note here, of an evening; the bird of Pallas Athene, the Owl, came hurrying along to hoot and hiss.

In front of the house is a large pond, fed by the aqueduct that supplies the village-pumps with water. Here, from half a mile and more around, come the Frogs and Toads in the lovers' season. The Natterjack, sometimes as large as a plate, with a narrow stripe of yellow down his back, makes his appointments here to take his bath; when the evening twilight falls, we see hopping along the edge the Midwife Toad, the male, who carries a cluster of eggs, the size of peppercorns, wrapped round his hind legs: the genial paterfamilias has brought his precious packet from afar, to leave it in the water and afterwards retire under some flat stone, whence he will emit a sound like a tinkling bell. Lastly, when not croaking amid the foliage, the Tree-frogs indulge in the most graceful dives. And so, in May, as soon as it is dark, the pond becomes a deafening orchestra: it is impossible to talk at table, impossible to sleep. We had to remedy this by means perhaps a little too rigorous. What could we do? He who tries to sleep and cannot needs become ruthless.

Bolder still, the Wasp has taken possession of the dwelling-house. On my door-sill, in a soil of rubbish, nestles the White-banded Sphex: when I go indoors, I must be careful not to damage her burrows, not to tread upon the miner absorbed in her work. It is quite a quarter of a century since I last saw the saucy Cricket-hunter. When I made her acquaintance, I used to visit her at a few miles' distance: each time, it meant an expedition under the blazing August sun. Today, I find her at my door; we are intimate neighbours. The embrasure of the closed window provides an apartment of a mild temperature for the Pelopæus. The earth-built nest is fixed against the freestone wall. To enter her home, the Spider-huntress uses a little hole left open by accident in the shutters. On the mouldings of the Venetian blinds, a few stray Mason-bees build their group of cells; inside the outer shutters, left ajar, a Eumenes constructs her little earthen dome, surmounted by a short, bell-mouthed neck. The common Wasp and the Polistes are my dinner-guests: they visit my table to see if the grapes served are as ripe as they look.

Here, surely—and the list is far from complete—is a company both numerous and select, whose conversation will not fail to charm my solitude, if I succeed in drawing it out. My dear beasts of former days, my old friends, and others, more recent acquaintances, all are here, hunting, foraging, building in close proximity. Besides, should we wish to vary the scene of observation, the mountain is but a few hundred steps away, with its tangle of arbutus, rock-roses and arborescent heather; with its sandy spaces dear to the Bembeces; with its marly slopes exploited by different Wasps and Bees. And that is why, foreseeing these riches, I have abandoned the town for the village and come to Sérignan to weed my turnips and water my lettuces.

II

The Pine Processionary

Among Fabre's insect stories, one of the most celebrated is this record of the Pine Processionary caterpillars following their charmed circle day after day, unable to turn aside even though they faced starvation. Silk-trails are important in the lives of many other social caterpillars, including the American tent caterpillar, found in wild cherries in the spring. Since Fabre's time, the Processionaries have been given a group all their own in entomological classification and christened the Thaumatopoeidae. *The species with which Fabre experimented was probably* T. processionea (Lin.). *The adults of these caterpillars are small nondescript brownish moths with a wing-spread of about an inch and a quarter. The material below originally appeared in Chapters I and III of* THE LIFE OF THE CATERPILLAR.

IN MY *harmas* laboratory, now stocked with a few trees in addition to its bushes, stand some vigorous fir-trees, the Aleppo pine and the black Austrian pine, a substitute for that of the Landes. Every year the caterpillar takes possession of them and spins his great purses in their branches. In the interest of the leaves, which are horribly ravaged, as though there had been a fire, I am obliged each winter to make a strict survey and to extirpate the nests with a long forked batten.

You voracious little creatures, if I let you have your way, I should soon be robbed of the murmur of my once so leafy pines! Today I will seek compensation for all the trouble I have taken. Let us make a compact. You have a story to tell. Tell it me; and for a year, for two years or longer, until I know more or less all about it, I shall leave you undisturbed, even at the cost of lamentable suffering to the pines.

Having concluded the treaty and left the caterpillars in peace, I soon have abundant material for my observations. In return for my indulgence I get some thirty nests within a few steps of my door. If the collection were not large enough, the pine-trees in the neighbourhood would supply me with any necessary additions. But I have a preference and a decided preference for the population of my own enclosure, whose nocturnal habits are much easier to observe by lantern-light. With such treasures daily before my eyes, at any time that I wish and under natural conditions, I cannot fail to see the Processionary's story unfolded at full length. Let us try.

Drover Dingdong's Sheep followed the Ram which Panurge had maliciously thrown overboard and leapt nimbly into the sea, one after the other, "for you know," says Rabelais, "it is the nature of the sheep always to follow the first, wheresoever it goes; which makes Aristotle mark them for the most silly and foolish animals in the world."

The Pine Caterpillar is even more sheeplike, not from foolishness, but from necessity: where the first goes all the others go, in a regular string, with no empty spaces.

They proceed in single file, in a continuous row, each touching with its head the rear of the one in front of it. The complex twists and turns described in his vagaries by the caterpillar leading the van are scrupulously described by all the others. No Greek *theoria* winding its way to the Eleusinian festivals was ever more orderly. Hence the name of Processionary given to the gnawer of the pine.

His character is complete when we add that he is a ropedancer all his life long: he walks only on the tight-rope, a silken rail placed in position as he advances. The caterpillar who chances to be at the head of the procession dribbles his thread without ceasing and fixes it on the path which his fickle preferences cause him to take. The thread is so tiny that the eye, though armed with a magnifying glass, suspects it rather than sees it.

But a second caterpillar steps on the slender footboard and doubles it with his thread; a third trebles it; and all the others, however many there be, add the sticky spray from their spinnerets, so much so that, when the procession has marched by, there remains, as a record of its passing, a narrow white ribbon whose dazzling whiteness shimmers in the sun. Very much more sumptuous than ours, their system of road-making consists in upholstering with silk instead of macadamazing. We sprinkle our roads with broken stones and level them by the pressure of a heavy steamroller; they lay over their paths a soft satin rail, a work of general interest to which each contributes his thread.

What is the use of all this luxury? Could they not, like other caterpillars, walk about without these costly preparations? I see two reasons for their mode of progression. It is night when the Processionaries sally forth to browse upon the pine-leaves. They leave their nest, situated at the top of a bough, in profound darkness; they go down the denuded pole till they come to the nearest branch that has not yet been gnawed, a branch which becomes lower and lower by degrees as the consumers finish stripping the upper storeys; they climb up this untouched branch and spread over the green needles.

When they have had their suppers and begin to feel the keen night air, the next thing is to return to the shelter of the house. Measured in a straight line, the distance is not great, hardly an arm's length; but it cannot be covered in this way on foot. The caterpillars have to climb down from one crossing to the next, from the needle to the twig, from the twig to the branch, from the branch to the bough and from the bough, by a no less angular path, to go back home. It is useless to rely upon sight as a guide on this long and erratic journey. The Processionary, it is true, has five ocular specks on either side of his head, but they are so infinitesimal, so difficult to make out through the magnifying glass, that we cannot attribute to them any great power of vision. Besides, what good would those short-sighted lenses be in the absence of light, in black darkness?

It is equally useless to think of the sense of smell. Has the Processional any olfactory powers or has he not? I do not know. Without giving a positive answer to the question, I can at least declare that his sense of smell is exceedingly dull and in no way suited to help him find his way. This is proved, in my experiments, by a number of hungry caterpillars that, after a long fast, pass close beside a pine-branch without betraying any eagerness or showing a sign of stopping. It is the sense of touch that tells them where they are. So long as their lips do not chance to light upon the pasture-land, not one of them settles there, though he be ravenous. They do not hasten to food which they have scented from afar; they stop at a branch which they encounter on their way.

Apart from sight and smell, what remains to guide them in returning to the nest? The ribbon spun on the road. In the Cretan labyrinth, Theseus would have been lost but for the clue of thread with which Ariadne supplied him. The spreading maze of the pine-needles is, especially at night, as inextricable a labyrinth as that constructed for Minos. The Processionary finds his way through it, without the possibility of a mistake, by the aid of his bit of silk. At the time for going home, each easily recovers either his own thread or one or other of the neighbouring threads, spread fanwise by the diverging herd; one by one the scattered tribe line up on the common ribbon, which started from the nest; and the sated caravan finds its way back to the manor with absolute certainty.

Longer expeditions are made in the daytime, even in winter, if the weather be fine. Our caterpillars then come down from the tree, venture on the ground, march in procession for a distance of thirty yards or so. The object of these sallies is not to look for food, for the native pine-tree is far from being exhausted: the shorn branches hardly count amid the vast leafage. Moreover, the caterpillars observe complete abstinence till nightfall. The trippers have no other object than a constitutional, a pilgrimage to the outskirts to see what these are like, possibly an inspection of the locality where, later on, they mean to bury themselves in the sand for their metamorphosis.

It goes without saying that, in these greater evolutions, the guiding cord is not neglected. It is now more necessary than ever. All contribute to it from the produce of their spinnerets, as is the invariable rule whenever there is a progression. Not one takes a step forward without fixing to the path the thread hanging from his lip.

If the series forming the procession be at all long, the ribbon is dilated sufficiently to make it easy to find; nevertheless, on the homeward journey, it is not picked up without some hesitation. For observe that the caterpillars when on the march never turn completely; to wheel round on their tight-rope is a method utterly unknown to them. In order therefore to regain the road already covered, they have to describe a zig-zag whose windings and extent are determined by the leader's fancy. Hence come gropings and roamings which are sometimes prolonged to the point of causing the herd to spend the night out of doors. It is not a serious matter. They collect into a motionless cluster. Tomorrow the search will start afresh and will sooner or later be successful. Oftener still the winding curve meets the guide-thread at the first attempt. As soon as the first caterpillar has the rail between his legs, all hesitation ceases; and the band makes for the nest with hurried steps.

The use of this silk-tapestried roadway is evident from a second point of view. To protect himself against the severity of the winter which he has to face when working, the Pine Caterpillar weaves himself a shelter in which he spends his bad hours, his days of enforced idleness. Alone, with none but the meagre resources of his silk-glands, he would find difficulty in protecting himself on the top of a branch buffeted by the winds. A substantial dwelling, proof against snow, gales and icy fogs, requires the cooperation of a large number. Out of the individual's piled-up atoms, the community obtains a spacious and durable establishment.

The enterprise takes a long time to complete. Every evening, when the weather permits, the building has to be strengthened and enlarged. It is indispensable, therefore, that the corporation of workers should not be dissolved while the stormy season continues and the insects are still in the caterpillar stage. But, without special arrangements, each nocturnal expedition at grazing-time would be a cause of separation. At that moment of appetite for food there is a return to individualism. The caterpillars become more or less scattered, settling singly on the branches around; each browses his pine-needle separately. How are they to find one another afterwards and become a community again?

The several threads left on the road make this easy. With that guide, every caterpillar, however far he may be, comes back to his companions without ever missing the way. They come hurrying from a host of twigs, from here, from there, from above, from below; and soon the scattered legion reforms into a group. The silk thread is something more than a road-making expedient: it is the social bond, the system that keeps the members of the community indissolubly united.

At the head of every procession, long or short, goes a first caterpillar whom I will call the leader of the march or file, though the word leader, which I use for want of a better, is a little out of place here. Nothing, in fact, distinguishes this caterpillar from the others: it just depends upon the order in which they happen to line up; and mere chance brings him to the front. Among the Processionaries, every captain is an officer of fortune. The actual leader leads; presently he will be a subaltern, if the file should break up in consequence of some accident and be formed anew in a different order.

His temporary functions give him an attitude of his own. While the others follow passively in a close file, he, the captain, tosses himself about and with an abrupt movement flings the front of his body hither and thither. As he marches ahead he seems to be seeking his way. Does he in point of fact explore the country? Does he choose the most practicable places? Or are his hesitations merely the result of the absence of a guiding thread on ground that has not yet been covered? His subordinates follow very placidly, reassured by the cord which they hold between their legs; he, deprived of that support, is uneasy.

Why cannot I read what passes under his black, shiny skull, so like a drop of tar? To judge by actions, there is here a small dose of discernment which is able, after experimenting, to recognize excessive roughnesses, over-slippery surfaces, dusty places that offer no resistance and, above all, the thread left by other excursionists. This is all or nearly all that my long acquaintance with the Processionaries has taught me as to their mentality. Poor brains, indeed; poor creatures, whose commonwealth has its safety hanging upon a thread!

The processions vary greatly in length. The finest that I have seen manœuvring on the ground measured twelve or thirteen yards and numbered about three hundred caterpillars, drawn up with absolute precision in a wavy line. But, if there were only two in a row, the order would still be perfect: the second touches and follows the first.

By February I have processions of all lengths in the greenhouse. What tricks can I play upon them? I see only two: to do away with the leader; and to cut the thread.

The suppression of the leader of the file produces nothing striking. If the thing is done without creating a disturbance, the procession does not alter its way at all. The second caterpillar, promoted to captain, knows the duties of his rank offhand: he selects and leads, or rather he hesitates and gropes.

The breaking of the silk ribbon is not very important either. I remove a caterpillar from the middle of the file. With my scissors, so as not to cause a commotion in the ranks, I cut the piece of ribbon on which he stood and clear away every thread of it. As a result of this breach, the procession acquires two marching leaders, each independent of the other. It may be that the one in the rear joins the file ahead of him, from which he is separated by but a slender interval; in that case, things return to their original condition. More frequently, the two parts do not become reunited. In that case, we have two distinct processions, each of which wanders where it pleases and diverges from the other. Nevertheless, both will be able to return to the nest by discovering sooner or later, in the course of their peregrinations, the ribbon on the other side of the break.

These two experiments are only moderately interesting. I have thought out another, one more fertile in possibilities. I propose to make the caterpillars describe a closed circuit, after the ribbons running from it and liable to bring about a change of direction have been destroyed. The locomotive engine pursues its invariable course so long as it is not shunted on to a branch-line. If the Processionaries find the silken rail always clear in front of them, with no switches anywhere, will they continue on the same track, will they persist in following a road that never comes to an end? What we have to do is to produce this circuit, which is unknown under ordinary conditions, by artificial means.

The first idea that suggests itself is to seize with the forceps the silk ribbon at the back of the train, to bend it without shaking it and to bring the end of it ahead of the file. If the caterpillar marching in the van steps upon it, the thing is done: the others will follow him faithfully. The operation is very simple in theory but very difficult in practice and produces no useful results. The ribbon, which is extremely slight, breaks under the weight of the grains of sand that stick to it and are lifted with it. If it does not break, the caterpillars at the back, however delicately we may go to work, feel a disturbance which makes them curl up or even let go.

There is a yet greater difficulty: the leader refuses the ribbon laid before him; the cut end makes him distrustful. Failing to see the regular, uninterrupted road, he slants off to the right or left, he escapes at a tangent. If I try to interfere and to bring him back to the path of my choosing, he persists in his refusal, shrivels up, does not budge; and soon the whole procession is in confusion. We will not insist: the method is a poor one, very wasteful of effort for at best a problematical success.

We ought to interfere as little as possible and obtain a natural closed circuit. Can it be done? Yes. It lies in our power, without the least meddling, to see a procession march along a perfect circular track. I owe this result, which is eminently deserving of our attention, to pure chance.

On the shelf with the layer of sand in which the nests are planted stand some big palm-vases measuring nearly a yard and a half in circumference at the top. The caterpillars often scale the sides and climb up to the moulding which forms a cornice around the opening. This place suits them for their processions, perhaps because of the absolute firmness of the surface, where there is no fear of landslides, as on the loose, sandy soil below; and also, perhaps, because of the horizontal position, which is favorable to repose after the fatigue of the ascent. It provides me with a circular track all ready-made. I have nothing to do but wait for an occasion propitious to my plans. This occasion is not long in coming.

On the 30th of January, 1896, a little before twelve o'clock in the day, I discover a numerous troop making their way up and gradually reaching the popular cornice. Slowly, in single file, the caterpillars climb the great vase, mount the ledge and advance in regular procession, while others are constantly arriving and continuing the series. I wait for the string to close up, that is to say, for the leader, who keeps following the circular moulding, to return to the point from which he started. My object is achieved in a quarter of an hour. The closed circuit is realized magnificently, in something very nearly approaching a circle.

The next thing is to get rid of the rest of the ascending column, which would disturb the fine order of the procession by an excess of newcomers; it is also important that we should do away with all the silken paths, both new and old, that can put the cornice into communication with the ground. With a thick hair-pencil I sweep away the surplus climbers; with a big brush, one that leaves no smell behind it—for this might afterwards prove confusing—I carefully rub down the vase and get rid of every thread which the caterpillars have laid on the march. When these preparations are finished, a curious sight awaits us.

In the uninterrupted circular procession there is no longer a leader. Each caterpillar is preceded by another on whose heels he follows, guided by the silk track, the work of the whole party; he again has a companion close behind him, following him in the same orderly way. And this is repeated without variation throughout the length of the chain. None commands, or rather none modifies the trail according to his fancy; all obey, trusting in the guide who ought normally to lead the march and who in reality has been abolished by my trickery.

From the first circuit of the edge of the tub the rail of silk has been laid in position and is soon turned into a narrow ribbon by the procession, which never ceases dribbling its thread as it goes. The rail is simply doubled and has no branches anywhere, for my brush has destroyed them all. What will the caterpillars do on this deceptive, closed path? Will they walk endlessly round and round until their strength gives out entirely?

The old schoolmen were fond of quoting Buridan's Ass, that famous Donkey who, when placed between two bundles of hay, starved to death because he was unable to decide in favour of either by breaking the equilibrium between two equal but opposite attractions. They slandered the worthy animal. The Ass, who is no more foolish than any one else, would reply to the logical snare by feasting off both bundles. Will my caterpillars show a little of his mother wit? Will they, after many attempts, be able to break the equilibrium of their closed circuit, which keeps them on a road without a turning? Will they make up their minds to swerve to this side or that, which is the only method of reaching their bundle of hay, the green branch yonder, quite near, not two feet off?

I thought that they would and I was wrong. I said to myself:

"The procession will go on turning for some time, for an hour, two hours perhaps; then the caterpillars will perceive their mistake. They will abandon the deceptive road and make their descent somewhere or other."

That they should remain up there, hard pressed by hunger and the lack of cover, when nothing prevented them from going away, seemed to me inconceivable imbecility. Facts, however, forced me to accept the incredible. Let us describe them in detail.

The circular procession begins, as I have said, on the 30th of January, about midday, in splendid weather. The caterpillars march at an even pace, each touching the stern of the one in front of him. The unbroken chain eliminates the leader with his changes of direction; and all follow mechanically, as faithful to their circle as are the hands of a watch. The headless file has no liberty left, no will; it has become mere clockwork. And this continues for hours and hours. My success goes far beyond my wildest suspicions. I stand amazed at it, or rather I am stupefied.

Meanwhile, the multiplied circuits change the original rail into a superb ribbon a twelfth of an inch broad. I can easily see it glittering on the red ground of the pot. The day is drawing to a close and no alteration has yet taken place in the position of the trail. A striking proof confirms this.

The trajectory is not a plane curve, but one which, at a certain point, deviates and goes down a little way to the lower surface of the cornice, returning to the top some eight inches farther. I marked these two points of deviation in pencil on the vase at the outset. Well, all that afternoon and, more conclusive still, on the following days, right to the end of this mad dance, I see the string of caterpillars dip under the ledge at the first point and come to the top again at the second. Once the first thread is laid, the road to be pursued is permanently established.

If the road does not vary, the speed does. I measure nine centimetres a minute as the average distance covered. But there are more or less lengthy halts; the pace slackens at times, especially when the temperature falls. At ten o'clock in the evening the walk is little more than a lazy swaying of the body. I foresee an early halt, in consequence of the cold, of fatigue and doubtless also of hunger.

Grazing-time has arrived. The caterpillars have come crowding from all the nests in the greenhouse to browse upon the pine-branches planted by myself beside the silken purses. Those in the garden do the same, for the temperature is mild. The others, lined up along the earthenware cornice, would gladly take part in the feast; they are bound to have an appetite after a ten hours' walk. The branch stands green and tempting not a hand's breadth away. To reach it they need but go down; and the poor wretches, foolish slaves of their ribbon that they are, cannot make up their minds to do so. I leave the famished ones at half-past ten, persuaded that they will take counsel with their pillow and that on the morrow things will have resumed their ordinary course.

I was wrong. I was expecting too much of them when I

accorded them that faint gleam of intelligence which the tribulations of a distressful stomach ought, one would think, to have aroused. I visit them at dawn. They are lined up as on the day before, but motionless. When the air grows a little warmer, they shake off their torpor, revive and start walking again. The circular procession begins anew, like that which I have already seen. There is nothing more and nothing less to be noted in their machine-like obstinacy.

This time it is a bitter night. A cold snap has supervened, was indeed foretold in the evening by the garden caterpillars, who refused to come out despite appearances which to my duller senses seemed to promise a continuation of the fine weather. At daybreak the rosemary-walks are all asparkle with rime and for the second time this year there is a sharp frost. The large pond in the garden is frozen over. What can the caterpillars in the conservatory be doing?

All are ensconced in their nests, except the stubborn processionists on the edge of the vase, who, deprived of shelter as they are, seem to have spent a very bad night. I find them clustered in two heaps, without any attempt at order. They have suffered less from the cold, thus huddled together.

'Tis an ill wind that blows nobody any good. The severity of the night has caused the ring to break into two segments which will, perhaps, afford a chance of safety. Each group, as it revives and resumes its walk, will presently be headed by a leader who, not being obliged to follow a caterpillar in front of him, will possess some liberty of movement and perhaps be able to make the procession swerve to one side. Remember that, in the ordinary processions, the caterpillar walking ahead acts as a scout. While the others, if nothing occurs to create excitement, keep to their ranks, he attends to his duties as a leader and is continually turning his head to this side and that, investigating, seeking, groping, making his choice. And things happen as he decides: the band follows him faithfully. Remember also that, even on a road which has already been travelled and beribboned, the guiding caterpillar continues to explore.

There is reason to believe that the Processionaries who have lost their way on the ledge will find a chance of safety here. Let us watch them. On recovering from their torpor, the two groups line up by degrees into two distinct files.

There are therefore two leaders, free to go where they please, independent of each other. Will they succeed in leaving the enchanted circle? At the sight of their large black heads swaying anxiously from side to side, I am inclined to think so for a moment. But I am soon undeceived. As the ranks fill out, the two sections of the chain meet and the circle is reconstituted. The momentary leaders once more become simple subordinates; and again the caterpillars march round and round all day.

For the second time in succession, the night, which is very calm and magnificently starry, brings a hard frost. In the morning the Processionaries on the tub, the only ones who have camped out unsheltered, are gathered into a heap which largely overflows both sides of the fatal ribbon. I am present at the awakening of the numbed ones. The first to take the road is, as luck will have it, outside the track. Hesitatingly he ventures into unknown ground. He reaches the top of the rim and descends upon the other side on the earth in the vase. He is followed by six others, no more. Perhaps the rest of the troop, who have not fully recovered from their nocturnal torpor, are too lazy to bestir themselves.

The result of this brief delay is a return to the old track. The caterpillars embark on the silken trail and the circular march is resumed, this time in the form of a ring with a gap in it. There is no attempt, however, to strike a new course on the part of the guide whom this gap has placed at the head. A chance of stepping outside the magic circle has presented itself at last; and he does not know how to avail himself of it.

As for the caterpillars who have made their way to the inside of the vase, their lot is hardly improved. They climb to the top of the palm, starving and seeking for food. Finding nothing to eat that suits them, they retrace their steps by following the thread which they have left on the way, climb the ledge of the pot, strike the procession again and, without further anxiety, slip back into the ranks. Once more the ring is complete, once more the circle turns and turns.

Then when will the deliverance come? There is a legend that tells of poor souls dragged along in an endless round until the hellish charm is broken by a drop of holy water. What drop will good fortune sprinkle on my Processionaries to dissolve their circle and bring them back to the nest? I see only two means of conjuring the spell and obtaining a release from the circuit. These two means are two painful ordeals. A strange linking of cause and effect: from sorrow and wretchedness good is to come.

And, first, shrivelling as the result of cold. The caterpillars gather together without any order, heap themselves some on the path, some, more numerous these, outside it. Among the latter there may be, sooner or later, some revolutionary who, scorning the beaten track, will trace out a new road and lead the troop back home. We have just seen an instance of it. Seven penetrated to the interior of the vase and climbed the palm. True, it was an attempt with no result, but still an attempt. For complete success, all that need be done would have been to take the opposite slope. An even chance is a great thing. Another time we shall be more successful.

In the second place, the exhaustion due to fatigue and hunger. A lame one stops, unable to go farther. In front of the defaulter the procession still continues to wend its way for a short time. The ranks close up and an empty space appears. On coming to himself and resuming the march, the caterpillar who has caused the breach becomes a leader, having nothing before him. The least desire for emancipation is all that he wants to make him launch the band into a new path which perhaps will be the saving path.

In short, when the Processionaries' train is in difficulties, what it needs, unlike ours, is to run off the rails. The side-tracking is left to the caprice of a leader who alone is capable of turning to the right or left; and this leader is absolutely non-existent so long as the ring remains unbroken. Lastly, the breaking of the circle, the one stroke of luck, is the result of a chaotic halt, caused principally by excess of fatigue or cold.

The liberating accident, especially that of fatigue, occurs fairly often. In the course of the same day, the moving circumference is cut up several times into two or three sections; but continuity soon returns and no change takes place. Things go on just the same. The bold innovator who is to save the situation has not yet had his inspiration.

There is nothing new on the fourth day, after an icy night like the previous one; nothing to tell except the following detail. Yesterday I did not remove the trace left by the few caterpillars who made their way to the inside of the vase. This trace, together with a junction connecting it with the circular road, is discovered in the course of the morning. Half the troop takes advantage of it to visit the earth in the pot and climb the palm; the other half remains on the ledge and continues to walk along the old rail. In the afternoon the band of emigrants rejoins the others, the circuit is completed and things return to their original condition.

We come to the fifth day. The night frost becomes more intense, without however as yet reaching the greenhouse. It is followed by bright sunshine in a calm and limpid sky. As soon as the sun's rays have warmed the panes a little, the caterpillars, lying in heaps, wake up and resume their evolutions on the ledge of the vase. This time the fine order of the beginning is disturbed and a certain disorder becomes manifest, apparently an omen of deliverance near at hand. The scouting-path inside the vase, which was upholstered in silk yesterday and the day before, is today followed to its origin on the rim by a part of the band and is then abandoned after a short loop. The other caterpillars follow the usual ribbon. The result of this bifurcation is two almost equal files, walking along the ledge in the same direction, at a short distance from each other, sometimes meeting, separating farther on, in every case with some lack of order.

Weariness increases the confusion. The crippled, who refuse to go on, are many. Breaches increase; files are split up into sections each of which has its leader, who pokes the front of his body this way and that to explore the ground. Everything seems to point to the disintegration which will bring safety. My hopes are once more disappointed. Before the night the file is reconstituted and the gyration resumed.

Heat comes, just as suddenly as the cold did. Today, the 4th of February, is a beautiful, mild day. The greenhouse is full of life. Numerous festoons of caterpillars, issuing from the nests, meander along the sand on the shelf. Above them, at every moment, the ring on the ledge of the vase breaks up and comes together again. For the first time I see daring leaders who, drunk with heat, standing only on their hinder prolegs at the extreme edge of the earthenware rim, fling themselves forward into space, twisting about, sounding the depths. The endeavour is frequently repeated, while the whole troop stops. The caterpillars' heads give sudden jerks; their bodies wriggle.

One of the pioneers decides to take the plunge. He slips

under the ledge. Four follow him. The others, still confiding in the perfidious silken path, dare not copy him and continue to go along the old road.

The short string detached from the general chain gropes about a great deal, hesitates long on the side of the vase; it goes half-way down, then climbs up again slantwise, rejoins and takes its place in the procession. This time the attempt has failed, though at the foot of the vase, not nine inches away, there lay a bunch of pine-needles which I had placed there with the object of enticing the hungry ones. Smell and sight told them nothing. Near as they were to the goal, they went up again.

No matter, the endeavour has its uses. Threads were laid on the way and will serve as a lure to further enterprise. The road of deliverance has its first landmarks. And two days later, on the eighth day of the experiment, the caterpillars—now singly, anon in small groups, then again in strings of some length—come down from the ledge by following the staked-out path. At sunset the last of the laggards is back in the nest.

Now for a little arithmetic. For seven times twenty-four hours the caterpillars have remained on the ledge of the vase. To make an ample allowance for stops due to the weariness of this one or that and above all for the rest taken during the colder hours of the night, we will deduct one-half of the time. This leaves eighty-four hours' walking. The average pace is nine centimetres a minute. The aggregate distance covered, therefore is 453 metres, a good deal more than a quarter of a mile, which is a great walk for these little crawlers. The circumference of the vase, the perimeter of the track, is exactly 1 m. 35. Therefore the circle covered, always in the same direction and always without result, was described three hundred and thirty-five times.

These figures surprise me, though I am already familiar with the abysmal stupidity of insects as a class whenever the least accident occurs. I feel inclined to ask myself whether the Processionaries were not kept up there so long by the difficulties and dangers of the descent rather than by the lack of any gleam of intelligence in their benighted minds. The facts, however, reply that the descent is as easy as the ascent.

The caterpillar has a very supple back, well adapted for twisting round projections or slipping underneath. He can walk with the same ease vertically or horizontally, with his back down or up. Besides, he never moves forward until he has fixed his thread to the ground. With this support to his feet, he has no falls to fear, no matter what his position.

I had a proof of this before my eyes during a whole week. As I have already said, the track, instead of keeping on one level, bends twice, dips at a certain point under the ledge of the vase and reappears at the top a little farther on. At one part of the circuit, therefore, the procession walks on the lower surface of the rim; and this inverted position implies so little discomfort or danger that it is renewed at each turn for all the caterpillars from first to last.

It is out of the question then to suggest the dread of a false step on the edge of the rim which is so nimbly turned at each point of inflexion. The caterpillars in distress, starved, shelterless, chilled with cold at night, cling obstinately to the silk ribbon covered hundreds of times, because they lack the rudimentary glimmers of reason which would advise them to abandon it.

III

Insect Weather Prophets

Another of Fabre's famous studies concerned the ability of the Pine Processionary caterpillar to predict the coming of storms. Various insects have a "weather sense" but none appears to be more accurate as a prophet than the humble subject of these experiments. This selection is taken from Chapter IV of THE LIFE OF THE CATERPILLAR.

DURING THE WHOLE WINTER, the Pine Caterpillars are active only at night. In the daytime, when the weather is fine, they readily repair to the dome of the nest and there remain motionless, gathered into heaps. It is the hour of the open-air siesta, under the pale December and January sun. As yet none leaves the home. It is quite late in the evening, towards nine o'clock, when they set out, marching in an irregular procession, to browse on the leaves of the branches hard by. Their grazing is a protracted affair. The flock returns late, some time after midnight, when the temperature falls too low.

Secondly, it is in the heart of winter, during the roughest months, that the Processionary displays his full activity. Indefatigably at this time of year he spins, adding each night a new web to his silken tent; at this time, whenever the weather permits, he ventures abroad on the neighbouring boughs to feed, to grow and to renew his skein of silk.

By a very remarkable exception, the harsh season marked by inactivity and lethargic repose in other insects is for him the season of bustle and labour, on condition, of course, that the inclemencies of the weather do not exceed certain limits. If the north wind blow too violently, so that it is like to sweep the flock away; if the cold be too piercing, so that there is a risk of freezing to death; if it snow, or rain, or if the mist thicken into an icy drizzle, the caterpillars prudently stay at home, sheltering under their weatherproof tent.

It would be convenient to some extent to foresee these inclemencies. The caterpillar dreads them. A drop of rain sets him in a flutter; a snowflake exasperates him. To start for the grazing-grounds at dark of night, in uncertain weather, would be dangerous, for the procession goes some distance and travels slowly. The flock would fare ill before regaining shelter did any sudden atmospheric trouble supervene, an event of some frequency in the bad season of the year. So that he may be informed in this particular during his nocturnal winter rambles, can the Pine Caterpillar be endowed with some sort of meteorological aptitudes? Let me describe how the suspicion occurred to me.

Divulged I know not how, my rearing of caterpillars under glass acquired a certain renown. It was talked about in the village. The forest-ranger, a sworn enemy to destructive insects, wanted to see the grazing of the famous caterpillars, of whom he had retained a too poignant memory ever since the day when he gathered and destroyed their nests in a pine-wood under his charge. It was arranged that he should call the same evening.

He arrives at the appointed hour, accompanied by a friend. For a moment we sit and chat in front of the fire; then, when the clock strikes nine, the lantern is lit and we all three enter the greenhouse. The visitors are eager for the spectacle of which they have heard such wonderful things, while I am certain of satisfying their curiosity.

But, but . . . what is this? Not a caterpillar on the nests, not one on the fresh ration of branches! Last night and on the previous nights they came out in countless numbers; tonight not one reveals himself. Can it be that they are merely late in going to dinner? Can their habitual punctuality be at fault because appetite has not yet arrived? We must be patient. . . . Ten o'clock. Nothing. Eleven. Still nothing. Midnight was at hand when we abandoned our watch, convinced that it would be vain to prolong the sitting. You can imagine what an abject fool I looked at having thus to send my guests away.

Next day I thought that I dimly perceived the explanation of this disappointment. It rained in the night and again in the morning. Snow, not the earliest of the year, but so far the most abundant, whitened the brow of the Ventoux.

Had the caterpillars, more sensitive than any of us to atmospheric changes, refused to venture forth because they anticipated what was about to happen? Had they foreseen the rain and the snow, which nothing seemed to announce, at all events to us? After all, why not? Let us continue to observe them and we shall see whether the coincidence is fortuitous or not.

On this memorable day, therefore, the 13th of December, 1895, I institute the caterpillars' meteorological observatory. I have at my disposal absolutely none of the apparatus dear to science, not even a modest thermometer, for my unlucky star continues in the ascendant, proving as unkind today as when I learn chemistry with pipe-bowls for crucibles and bottles that once contained sweets for retorts. I confine myself to visiting nightly the Processionaries in the greenhouse and those in the garden. It is a hard task, especially as I have to go to the far end of the enclosure, often in weather when one would not turn a dog out of doors. I set down the acts of the caterpillars, whether they come out or stay at home; I note the state of the sky during the day and at the moment of my evening examination.

To this list I add the meteorological chart of Europe which the *Temps* publishes daily. If I want more precise data, I request the Normal School at Avignon to send me, on occasions of violent disturbances, the barometrical records of its observatory. These are the only documents at my disposal.

Before we come to the results obtained, let me once more repeat that my caterpillars' meteorological institute has two stations: one in the greenhouse and one in the open air, on the pines in the enclosure. The first, protected against the wind and rain, is that which I prefer: it provides more regular and more continuous information. In fact, the open-air caterpillars often enough refuse to come out, even though the general conditions be favourable. It is enough to keep them at home if there be too strong a wind shaking the boughs, or even a little moisture dripping on the web of the nests. Saved from these two perils, the greenhouse caterpillars have only to consider atmospheric incidents of a higher order. The small variations escape them; the great alone make an impression on them: a most useful point for the observer and going a long way towards solving the problem for him. The colonies under glass, therefore, provide most of the material for my notes; the colonies in the open air add their testimony, which is not always quite clear.

Now what did they tell me, those greenhouse caterpillars who, on the 13th of December, refused to show themselves to my guest, the forest-ranger? The rain that was to fall that night could hardly have alarmed them: they were so well sheltered. The snow about to whiten Mont Ventoux was nothing to them: it was so far away. Moreover, it was neither snowing yet nor raining. Some extraordinary atmospheric event, profound and of vast extent, must have been occurring. The charts in the *Temps* and the bulletin of the Normal School told me as much.

A cyclonic disturbance, coming from the British Isles, was passing over our district; an atmospheric depression the like of which the season had not as yet known, had spread in our direction, reaching us on the 13th and persisting, in a more or less accentuated form, until the 22nd. At Avignon the barometer suddenly fell half an inch, to 29.1 in., on the 13th and lower still, to 29 in., on the 19th.

During this period of ten days, the garden caterpillars made no sortie on the pine-trees. True, the weather was changeable. There were a few showers of fine rain and some violent gusts of the mistral; but more frequently there were days and nights when the sky was superb and the temperature moderate. The prudent anchorites would not allow themselves to be caught. The low pressure persisted, menacing them; and so they stopped at home.

In the greenhouse things happen rather differently. Sorties take place, but the staying-in days are still more numerous. It looks as though the caterpillars, alarmed at first by the unexpected things happening overhead, had reassured themselves and resumed work, feeling nothing, in their shelter, of what they would have suffered out of doors—rain, snow and furious mistral blasts—and had then suspended their work again when the threats of bad weather increased.

There is, indeed, a fairly accurate agreement between the oscillations of the barometer and the decisions of the herd. When the column of mercury rises a little, they come out; when it falls they remain at home. Thus on the 19th, the night of the lowest pressure, 29 in., not a caterpillar appears.

As the wind and rain can have no effect on my colonies under glass, one is led to suppose that atmospheric pressure, with its physiological results, so difficult to define, is here the principal factor. As for the temperature, within moderate limits there is no need to discuss it. The Processionaries have a robust constitution, as behooves spinners who work in the open air in midwinter. However piercing the cold, so long as it does not freeze, when the hour comes for working or feeding they spin on the surface of the nest or browse on the neighbouring branches.

Another example. According to the meteorological chart in the *Temps*, a depression whose centre is near the Iles Sanguinaries, at the entrance of the Gulf of Ajaccio, reaches my neighbourhood, with a minimum of 29.2 in., on the 9th of January. A tempestuous wind gets up. For the first time this year there is a respectable frost. The ice on the large pond in the garden is two or three inches thick. This wild weather lasts for five days. Of course, the garden caterpillars do not sally forth on the pine-trees while these are battered by such a gale.

The remarkable part of the business is that the greenhouse caterpillars do not venture out of their nests either. And yet for them there are no boughs dangerously shaken, no cold piercing beyond endurance, for it is not freezing under the glass. What keeps them in can be only the passage of that wave of depression. On the 15th the storm ceases; and the barometer remains between 29.6 and 30 in. for the rest of the month and a good part of February. During this long period there are magnificent sorties every evening, especially in the greenhouse.

On the 23rd and 24th of February, suddenly the Processionaries stop at home again, for no apparent reason. Of the six nests under cover, only two have a few rare caterpillars out on the pine-branches, while previously, in the case of all six, I used every night to see the leaves bending under the weight of an innumerable multitude. Warned by this forecast, I enter in my notes:

"Some deep depression is about to reach us."

And I have guessed right. Two days later, sure enough, the meteorological record of the *Temps* gives me the following information: a minimum of 29.2 in., coming from the Bay of Biscay on the 22nd, reaches Algeria on the 23rd and spreads over the Provence coast on the 24th. There is a heavy snowfall at Marseilles on the 25th.

"The ships," I read in my paper, "present a curious spectacle, with their yards and rigging white. That is how the people of Marseilles, little used to such sights, picture Spitz-bergen and the North Pole."

Here certainly is the gale which my caterpillars foresaw when they refused to go out last night and the night before; here is the centre of disturbance which revealed itself at Sérignan by a violent and icy north wind on the 25th and the following days. Again I perceive that the greenhouse caterpillars are alarmed only at the approach of the wave of atmospheric disturbance. Once the first uneasiness caused by the depression had abated, they came out again, on the 25th and the following days, in the midst of the gale, as though nothing extraordinary were happening.

From the sum of my observations it appears that the Pine Processionary is eminently sensitive to atmospheric vicissi-tudes, an excellent quality, having regard to his way of life in the sharp winter nights. He foresees the storm which would imperil his excursions.

His capacity for seeing bad weather very soon won the confidence of the household. When we had to go into Orange to renew our provisions, it became the rule to consult him the night before; and, according to his verdict, we went or stayed at home. His oracle never deceived us.

IV

The Hunting Wasp

It was among the solitary wasps that Fabre found subjects for some of his most revealing experiments. Sphex wasps have a widespread distribution. A number of species finish the work of filling in their burrows by using a pebble as a hammer to tamp down the ground. Many are grasshopper-hunters. The Ephippiger, hunted by the Languedocian Sphex, is a long-horned green grasshopper found in the south of France. The scene of many of Fabre's wasp studies, before he retired to Sérignan, was along a deeply sunken road on the outskirts of Carpentras. This account is taken from THE HUNTING WASPS.

WHEN THE CHEMIST has fully prepared his plan of research, he mixes his reagent at the most convenient moment and lights a flame under his retort. He is the master of time, place and circumstances. He chooses his hour, shuts himself up in his laboratory, where nothing can come to disturb the business in hand; he produces at will this or that condition which reflection suggests to him: he is in quest of the secrets of inorganic matter, whose chemical activities science can awaken whenever it thinks fit.

The secrets of living matter—not those of anatomical structure, but really those of life in action, especially of instinct—present much more difficult and delicate conditions to the observer. Far from being able to choose his own time, he is the slave of the season, of the day, of the hour, of the very moment. When the opportunity offers, he must seize it as it comes, without hesitation, for it may be long before it presents itself again. And, as it usually arrives at the moment when he is least expecting it, nothing is in readiness for making the most of it. He must then and there improvise his little stock of experimenting-material, contrive his plans, evolve his tactics, devise his tricks; and he can think himself lucky if inspiration comes fast enough to allow him to profit by the chance offered. This chance, moreover, hardly ever comes except to those who look for it. You must watch for it patiently for days and days, now on sandy slopes exposed to the full glare of the sun, now on some path walled in by high banks, where the heat is like that of an oven, or again on some sandstone ledge which is none too steady. If it is in your power to set up your observatory under a meagre olive-tree that pretends to protect you from the rays of a pitiless sun, you may bless the fate that treats you as a sybarite: your lot is an Eden. Above all, keep your eyes open. The spot is a good one; and—who knows?—the opportunity may come at any moment.

It came, late, it is true; but still it came. Ah, if you could now observe at your ease, in the quiet of your study, with nothing to distract your mind from your subject, far from the profane wayfarer who, seeing you so busily occupied at a spot where he sees nothing, will stop, overwhelm you with queries, take you for some water-diviner, or—a graver suspicion this—regard you as some questionable character searching for buried treasure and discovering by means of incantations where the old pots full of coin lie hidden! Should you still wear a Christian aspect in his eyes, he will approach you, look to see what you are looking at and smile in a manner that leaves no doubt as to his poor opinion of people who spend their time in watching Flies. You will be lucky indeed if the troublesome visitor, with his tongue in his cheek, walks off at least without disturbing things and without repeating in his innocence the disaster brought about by my two conscripts' boots.

Should your inexplicable doings not puzzle the passer-by, they will be sure to puzzle the village keeper, that uncompromising representative of the law in the ploughed acres. He has long had his eye on you. He has so often seen you wandering about, like a lost soul, for no appreciable reason; he has so often caught you rooting in the ground, or, with infinite precautions, knocking down some strip of wall in a sunken road, that in the end he has come to look upon you with dark suspicion. You are nothing to him but a gipsy, a tramp, a poultry-thief, a shady person or, at the best, a madman. Should you be carrying your botanizing-case, it will represent to him the poacher's ferret-cage; and you would never get it out of his head that, regardless of the game-laws

and the rights of landlords, you are clearing all the neighbouring warrens of their rabbits. Take care. However thirsty
you may be, do not lay a finger on the nearest bunch of
grapes: the man with the municipal badge will be there, delighted to have a case at last and so to receive an explanation
of your highly perplexing behaviour.

I have never, I can safely say, committed any such mis-
demeanour; and yet, one day, lying on the sand, absorbed
in the details of a Bembex' household, I suddenly heard beside me:

"In the name of the law, I arrest you! You come along
with me!"

It was the keeper of Les Angles, who, after vainly waiting
for an opportunity to catch me at fault and being daily more
anxious for an answer to the riddle that was worrying him,
at last resolved upon the brutal expedient of a summons. I
had to explain things. The poor man seemed anything but
convinced:

"Pooh!" he said. "Pooh! You will never make me believe
that you come here and roast in the sun just to watch Flies.
I shall keep an eye on you, mark you! And, the first time
I . . . ! However, that'll do for the present."

And he went off. I have always believed that my red ribbon had a good deal to do with his departure. And I also put
down to that red ribbon certain other little services by
which I benefited during my entomological and botanical excursions. It seemed to me—or was I dreaming?—it seemed to
me that, on my botanizing expeditions up Mont Ventoux,
the guide was more tractable and the donkey less obstinate.

The aforesaid bit of scarlet ribbon did not always spare
me the tribulations which the entomologist must expect when
experimenting on the public way. Here is a characteristic
example. Ever since daybreak I have been ambushed, sitting
on a stone, at the bottom of a ravine. The subject of my ma-
tutinal visit is the Languedocian Sphex. Three women, vine-
pickers, pass in a group, on the way to their work. They give
a glance at the man seated, apparently absorbed in reflection.
At sunset, the same pickers pass again, carrying their full
baskets on their heads. The man is still there, sitting on the
same stone, with his eyes fixed on the same place. My motionless attitude, my long persistency in remaining at that
deserted spot, must have impressed them deeply. As they

passed by me, I saw one of them tap her forehead and heard her whisper to the others:

"*Un paouré inoucènt, pécaïre!*"

And all three made the sign of the Cross.

An innocent, she had said, *un inoucènt,* an idiot, a poor creature, quite harmless, but half-witted; and they had all made the sign of the Cross, an idiot being to them one with God's seal stamped upon him.

"How now!" thought I. "What a cruel mockery of fate! You, who are so laboriously seeking to discover what is instinct in the animal and what is reason, you yourself do not even possess your reason in these good women's eyes! What a humiliating reflection!"

No matter: *pécaïre,* that expression of supreme compassion, in the Provençal dialect, *pécaïre,* coming from the bottom of the heart, soon made me forget *inoucènt.*

It is in this ravine with its three grape-gathering women that I would meet the reader, if he be not discouraged by the petty annoyances of which I have given him a foretaste. The Languedocian Sphex frequents these points, not in tribes congregating at the same spot when nest-building work begins, but as solitary individuals, sparsely distributed, settling wherever the chances of their vagabondage lead them. Even as her kinswoman, the Yellow-winged Sphex, seeks the society of her kind and the animation of a yard full of workers, the Languedocian Sphex prefers isolation, quiet and solitude. Graver of gait, more formal in her manners, of a larger size and also more sombrely clad, she always lives apart, not caring what others do, disdaining company, a genuine misanthrope among the Sphegidæ. The one is sociable, the other is not: a profound difference which in itself is enough to characterize them.

This amounts to saying that, with the Languedocian Sphex, the difficulties of observation increase. No long-meditated experiment is possible in her case; nor, when the first attempts have failed, can one hope to try them again, on the same occasion, with a second or a third subject and so on. If you prepare the materials for your observation in advance, if, for instance, you have in reserve a piece of game which you propose to substitute for that of the Sphex, it is to be feared, nay, it is almost certain that the huntress will not appear; and, when she does come at last, your materials are no longer fit for use and everything has to be improvised in a hurry, that very moment, under conditions that are not always satisfactory.

Let us take heart. The site is a first-rate one. Many a time already I have surprised the Sphex here, sunning herself on a vine-leaf. The insect, spread out flat, is basking voluptuously in the heat and light. From time to time it has a sort of frenzied outburst of pleasure: it quivers with content; it rapidly taps its feet on its couch, producing a tattoo not unlike that of rain falling heavily on the leaf. The joyous thrum can be heard several feet away. Then immobility begins again, soon followed by fresh nervous commotion and by the whirling of the tarsi, a symbol of supreme felicity. I have known some of these passionate sun-lovers suddenly to leave the workyard, when the larva's cave has been half-dug, and go to the nearest vine to take a bath of heat and light, after which they would come back to the burrow, as though reluctantly, just to give a perfunctory sweep and soon end by knocking off work, unable to resist the exquisite temptation of luxuriating on the vine-leaves.

It may be that the voluptuous couch is also an observatory, whence the Wasp surveys the surrounding country in order to discover and select her prey. Her exclusive game is the Ephippiger of the Vine, scattered here and there on the branches or on any brambles hard by. The joint is a substantial one, especially as the Sphex favours solely the females, whose bellies are swollen with a mighty cluster of eggs.

Let us take no notice of the repeated trips, the fruitless searches, the tedium of frequent long waiting, but rather present the Sphex suddenly to the reader as she herself appears to the observer. Here she is, at the bottom of a sunken road with high, sandy banks. She comes on foot, but gets help from her wings in dragging her heavy prize. The Ephippiger's antennæ, long and slender as threads, are the harnessing-ropes. Holding her head high, she grasps one of them in her mandibles. The antenna gripped passes between her legs; and the game follows, turned over on its back. Should the soil be too uneven and so offer resistance to this method of carting, the Wasp clasps her unwieldy burden and carries it with very short flights, interspersed, as often as possible, with journeys on foot. We never see her undertake a sustained flight, for long distances, holding the game in her legs, as is the practice of those expert aviators, the Bembeces and Cerceres, for instance, who bear through the air for more than half a mile their respective Flies or Weevils, a very light booty compared with the huge Ephippiger. The overpowering weight of her capture compels the Languedocian Sphex, to make the whole or nearly the whole journey on foot, her method of transport being consequently slow and laborious.

The same reason, the bulk and weight of the prey, have entirely reversed the usual order which the Burrowing Wasps follow in their operations. This order we know: it consists in first digging a burrow and then stocking it with provisions. As the victim is not out of proportion to the strength of the spoiler, it is quite simple to carry it by flying, which means that the Wasp can choose any site that she likes for her dwelling. She does not mind how far afield she goes for her prey: once she has captured her quarry, she comes flying home at a speed which makes questions of distance quite immaterial. Hence she prefers as the site for her burrow the place where she herself was born, the place where her forebears lived; she here inherits deep galleries, the accumulated work of earlier generations; and, by repairing them a little, she makes them serve as approaches to new chambers, which are in this way better protected than they would be if they depended upon the labours of a single Wasp, who had to start boring from the surface each year. This happens, for instance, in the case of the Great Cerceris and the Bee-eating Philanthus. And, should the ancestral abode not be strong enough to withstand the rough weather from one year to the next and to be handed down to the offspring, should the burrower have each time to start her tunnelling afresh, at least the Wasp finds greater safety in places consecrated by the experience of her forerunners. Consequently she goes there to dig her galleries, each of which serves as a corridor to a group of cells, thus effecting an economy in the aggregate labour expended upon the whole business of the laying.

In this way are formed not real societies, for there are no concerted efforts towards a common object, but at least assemblies where the sight of her kinswomen and her neighbours doubtless puts heart into the labour of the individual. We can observe, in fact, between these little tribes, springing from the same stock, and the burrowers who do their work alone, a difference in activity which reminds us of the emulation prevailing in a crowded yard and the indifference of labourers who have to work in solitude. Action is contagious in animals as in men; it is fired by its own example.

To sum up: when of a moderate weight for its captor, the prey can be conveyed flying, to a great distance. The Wasp can then choose any site that she pleases for her burrow. She adopts by preference the spot where she was born and uses each passage as a common corridor giving access to several cells. The result of this meeting at a common birthplace is the formation of groups, like turning to like, which is a source of friendly rivalry. This first step towards social life comes from facilities for travelling. Do not things happen in the same way with man, if I may be permitted the comparison? When he has nothing but trackless paths, man builds a solitary hut; when supplied with good roads, he and his fellows collect in populous cities; when served by railways which, so to speak, annihilate distance, they assemble in those immense human hives called London or Paris.

The situation of the Languedocian Sphex is just the reverse. Her prey is a heavy Ephippiger, a single dish representing by itself the sum total of provisions which the other freebooters amass on numerous journeys, insect by insect. What the Cerceres and the other plunderers strong on the wing accomplish by dividing the labour she does in a single journey. The weight of the prey makes any distant flight impossible; it has to be brought home slowly and laboriously, for it is a troublesome business to cart things along the ground. This alone makes the site of the burrow dependent on the accidents of the chase: the prey comes first and the dwelling next. So there is no assembling at a common meeting-place, no association of kindred spirits, no tribes stimulating one another in their work by mutual example, but isolation in the particular spot where the chances of the day have taken the Sphex, solitary labour, carried on without animation though with unfailing diligence. First of all, the prey is sought for, attacked, reduced to helplessness. Not until after that does the digger trouble about the burrow. A favourable place is chosen, as near as possible to the spot where the victim lies, so as to cut short the tedious work of transport; and the chamber of the future larva is rapidly hollowed out and at once receives the egg and the victuals. There you have an example of the inverted method of the Languedocian Sphex, a method, as all my observations go to prove, diametrically opposite to that of the other Hymenoptera. I will give some of the more striking of these observations.

When caught digging, the Languedocian Sphex is always alone, sometimes at the bottom of a dusty recess left by a stone that has dropped out of an old wall, sometimes ensconced in the shelter formed by a flat, projecting bit of sandstone, a shelter much sought after by the fierce Eyed Lizard to serve as an entrance-hall to his lair. The sun beats full upon it; it is an oven. The soil, consisting of old dust that has fallen little by little from the roof, is very easy to dig. The cell is soon scooped out with the mandibles, those pincers which are also used for digging, and the tarsi, which serve as rubbish-rakes. Then the miner flies off, but with a slow flight and no sudden display of wing-power, a manifest sign that the insect is not contemplating a distant expedition. We can easily follow it with our eyes and perceive the spot where it alights, usually ten or twelve yards away. At other times it decides to walk. It goes off and makes hurriedly for a spot where we will have the indiscretion to follow it, for our presence does not trouble it at all. On reaching its destination, either on foot or on the wing, it looks round for some time, as we gather from its undecided attitude and its journeys hither and thither. It looks round; at last it finds or rather retrieves something. The object recovered is an Ephippiger, half-paralysed, but still moving her tarsi, antennæ and ovipositor. She is a victim which the Sphex certainly stabbed not long ago with a few stings. After the operation, the Wasp left her prey, an embarrassing burden amid the suspense of house-hunting; she abandoned it perhaps on the very spot where she captured it, contenting herself with making it more or less conspicuous by placing it on some grass-tuft, in order to find it more easily later; and, trusting to her good memory to return presently to the spot where the booty lies, she set out to explore the neighbourhood with the object of finding a suitable site and there digging a burrow. Once the home was ready, she came back to her prize, which she found again without much hesitation, and she now prepares to lug it home. She bestrides the victim, seizes one or both of the antennæ and off she goes, tugging and dragging with all the strength of her loins and jaws.

Sometimes, she has only to make one journey; at other times and more often, the carter suddenly plumps down her load and quickly runs home. Perhaps it occurs to her that the entrance-door is not wide enough to admit so substantial a morsel; perhaps she remembers some lack of finish that might hamper the storing. And, in point of fact, the worker does touch up her work: she enlarges the doorway, smooths the threshold, strengthens the ceiling. It is all done with a few strokes of the tarsi. Then she returns to the Ephippiger, lying yonder, on her back, a few steps away. The hauling begins again. On the road, the Sphex seems struck with a new idea, which flashes through her quick brain. She has inspected the door, but has not looked inside. Who knows if all is well in there? She hastens to see, dropping the Ephippiger before she goes. The interior is inspected; and apparently a few pats of the trowel are administered with the tarsi, giving a last polish to the walls. Without lingering too long over these delicate aftertouches, the Wasp goes back to her booty and harnesses herself to its antennæ. Forward! Will the journey be completed this time? I would not answer for it. I have known a Sphex, more suspicious than the others, perhaps, or more neglectful of the minor architectural details, to repair her omissions, to dispel her doubts, by abandoning her prize on the way five or six times running, in order to hurry to the burrow, which each time was touched up a little or merely inspected within. It is true that others make straight for their destination, without even stopping to rest. I must also add that, when the Wasp goes home to improve the dwelling, she does not fail to give a glance from a distance every now and then at the Ephippiger over there, to make sure that nothing has happened to her. This solicitude recalls that of the Sacred Beetle when he leaves the hall which he is excavating in order to come and feel his beloved pellet and bring it a little nearer to him.

The inference to be drawn from the details which I have related is manifest. The fact that every Languedocian Sphex surprised in her mining-operations, even though it be at the very beginning of the digging, at the first stroke of the tarsus in the dust, afterwards, when the home is prepared, makes a short excursion, now on foot, anon flying, and invariably finds herself in possession of a victim already stabbed, already paralysed, compels us to conclude, in all certainty, that this Wasp does her work as a huntress first and as a burrower after, so that the place of the capture decides the place of the home.

This reversal of procedure, which causes the food to be

prepared before the larder, whereas hitherto we have seen
the larder come before the food, I attribute to the weight of
the Sphex' prey, a prey which it is not possible to carry far
through the air. It is not that the Languedocian Sphex is ill-
built for flight: on the contrary, she can soar magnificently;
but the prey which she hunts would weigh her down if she
had no other support than her wings. She needs the support
of the ground for her hauling work, in which she displays
wonderful strength. When laden with her prey, she always
goes afoot, or takes but very short flights, even under conditions when flight would save her time and trouble. I will
quote an instance taken from my latest observations on this
curious Wasp.

A Sphex appears unexpectedly, coming I know not whence.
She is on foot, dragging her Ephippiger, a capture which
apparently she has made that moment in the neighbourhood.
In the circumstances, it behoves her to dig herself a burrow.
The site is as bad as bad can be. It is a well-beaten path, hard
as stone. The Sphex, who has no time to make laborious
excavations, because the already captured prize must be
stored as quickly as possible, the Sphex wants soft ground,
wherein the larva's chamber can be contrived in one short
spell of work. I have described her favourite soil, namely, the
dust of years which has accumulated at the bottom of some
hole in a wall or of some little shelter under the rocks. Well,
the Sphex whom I am now observing stops at the foot of a
house with a newly-whitewashed front some twenty to twenty-
five feet high. Her instinct tells her that up there, under the
red tiles of the roof, she will find nooks rich in old dust. She
leaves her prey at the foot of the house and flies up to the
roof. For some time, I see her looking here, there and everywhere. After finding a proper site, she begins to work under
the curve of a pantile. In ten minutes or fifteen at most, the
home is ready. The insect now flies down again. The Ephippiger is promptly found. She has to be taken up. Will this
be done on the wing, as circumstances seem to demand? Not
at all. The Sphex adopts the toilsome method of scaling a
perpendicular wall, with a surface smoothed by the mason's
trowel and measuring twenty to twenty-five feet in height.
Seeing her take this road, dragging the game between her
legs, I at first think the feat impossible; but I am soon reassured as to the outcome of the bold attempt. Getting a foot-
hold on the little roughnesses in the mortar, the plucky in-

sect, despite the hindrance of her heavy load, walks up this vertical plane with the same assured gait and the same speed as on level ground. The top is reached without the least accident; and the prey is laid temporarily on the edge of the roof, upon the rounded back of a tile. While the digger gives a finishing touch to the burrow, the badly-balanced prey slips and drops to the foot of the wall. The thing must be done all over again and once more by laboriously climbing the height. The same mistake is repeated. Again the prey is incautiously left on the curved tile, again it slips and again it falls to the ground. With a composure which accidents such as these cannot disturb, the Sphex for the third time hoists up the Ephippiger by scaling the wall and, better-advised, drags her forthwith right into the home.

As even under these conditions no attempt has been made to carry the prey on the wing, it is clear that the Wasp is incapable of long flight with so heavy a load. To this incapacity we owe the few characteristics that form the subject of this chapter. A quarry that is not too big to permit the effort of flying makes of the Yellow-winged Sphex a semisocial species, that is to say, one seeking the company of her fellows; a quarry too heavy to carry through the air makes of the Languedocian Sphex a species vowed to solitary labour, a sort of savage disdainful of the pleasures that come from the proximity of one's kind. The lighter or heavier weight of the game selected here determines the fundamental character of the huntress.

V

The Wisdom of Instinct

Continuing his questioning of the Sphex *"through the language of experiment," Fabre is seen in this chapter in the midst of classic researches into the nature of instinct. It was in this field that he made his greatest contributions to science.* THE HUNTING WASPS *is also the source of this selection.*

TO PARALYSE HER PREY, the Languedocian Sphex, I have no doubt, pursues the method of the Cricket-huntress and drives her lancet repeatedly into the Ephippiger's breast in order to strike the ganglia of the thorax. The process of wounding the nerve-centres must be familiar to her; and I am convinced beforehand of her consummate skill in that scientific operation. This is an art thoroughly known to all the Hunting Wasps, who carry a poisoned dart that has not been given them in vain. At the same time, I must confess that I have never yet succeeded in witnessing the deadly performance. This omission is due to the solitary life led by the Languedocian Sphex.

When a number of burrows are dug on a common site and then provisioned, one has but to wait on the spot to see how one huntress and now another arrive with the game which they have caught. It is easy in these circumstances to try upon the new arrivals the substitution of a live prey for the doomed victim and to repeat the experiment as often as we wish. Besides, the certainty that we shall not lack subjects of observation, as and when wanted, enables us to arrange everything in advance. With the Languedocian Sphex, these conditions of success do not exist. To set out expressly to look for her, with one's material prepared, is almost useless, as the solitary insect is scattered one by one over vast expanses of ground. Moreover, if you do come upon her, it will most often be in an idle hour and you will get nothing out of her. As I said before, it is nearly always unexpectedly, when your thoughts are elsewhere engaged, that the Sphex appears, dragging her Ephippiger after her.

This is the moment, the only propitious moment to attempt a substitution of prey and invite the huntress to let you witness her lancet-thrust. Quick, let us procure an alternative morsel, a live Ephippiger! Hurry, time presses: in a few minutes, the burrow will have received the victuals and the glorious occasion will be lost! Must I speak of my mortification at these moments of good fortune, the mocking bait held out by chance? Here, before my eyes, is matter for interesting observations; and I cannot profit by it! I cannot surprise the Sphex' secret for the lack of something to offer her in the place of her prize! Try it for yourself, try setting out in quest of an alternative piece with only a few minutes at your disposal, when it took me three days of wild running about before I found Weevils for my Cerceres! And yet I made the desperate experiment twice over. Ah, if the keeper had caught me this time, tearing like mad through the vineyards, what a good opportunity it would have been for crediting me with robbery and having me up before the magistrate! Vine-branches and clusters of grapes: not a thing did I respect in my mad rush, hampered by the trailing shoots. I must have an Ephippiger at all costs, I must have him that moment. And once I did get my Ephippiger during one of these frenzied expeditions. I was radiant with joy, never suspecting the bitter disappointment in store for me.

If only I arrive in time, if only the Sphex be still engaged in transport work! Thank heaven, everything is in my favour! The Wasp is still some distance away from her burrow and still dragging her prize along. With my forceps I pull gently at it from behind. The huntress resists, stubbornly clutches the antennæ of her victim and refuses to let go. I pull harder, even drawing the carter back as well; it makes no difference: the Sphex does not loose her hold. I have with me a pair of sharp scissors, belonging to my little entomological case. I use them and promptly cut the harness-ropes, the Ephippiger's long antennæ. The Sphex continues to move ahead, but soon stops, astonished at the sudden decrease in the weight of the burden which she is trailing, for this burden is now reduced merely to the two antennæ, snipped off by my mischievous wiles. The real load, the heavy, pot-bellied insect, remains behind and is instantly replaced by my live specimen. The Wasp turns round, lets go the ropes that now draw nothing after them and retraces her steps. She comes face to face with the prey substituted for her own. She examines it, walks round it gingerly, then stops, moistens her foot with saliva and begins to wash her eyes. In this attitude of meditation, can some such thought as the following pass through her mind:

"Come now! Am I awake or am I asleep? Do I know what I am about or do I not? That thing's not mine. Who or what is trying to humbug me?"

At any rate, the Sphex shows no great hurry to attack my prey with her mandibles. She keeps away from it and shows not the smallest wish to seize it. To excite her, I offer the insect to her in my fingers, I almost thrust the antennæ under her teeth. I know that she does not suffer from shyness; I know that she will come and take from your fingers, without hesitation, the prey which you have snatched from her and afterwards present to her. But what is this? Scorning my offers, the Sphex retreats instead of snapping up what I place within her reach. I put down the Ephippiger, who, obeying a thoughtless impulse, unconscious of danger, goes straight to his assassin. Now we shall see! Alas, no: the Sphex continues to recoil, like a regular coward, and ends by flying away. I never saw her again. Thus ended, to my confusion, an experiment that had filled me with such enthusiasm.

Later and by degrees, as I inspected an increasing number of burrows, I came to understand my failure and the obstinate refusal of the Sphex. I always found the provisions to consist, without a single exception, of a female Ephippiger, harbouring in her belly a copious and succulent cluster of eggs. This appears to be the favourite food of the grubs. Well, in my hurried rush through the vines, I had laid my hands on an Ephippiger of the other sex. I was offering the Sphex a male. More far-seeing than I in this important question of provender, the Wasp would have nothing to say to my game:

"A male, indeed! Is that a dinner for my larvæ? What do you take them for?"

What nice discrimination they have, these dainty epicures, who are able to differentiate between the tender flesh of the female and the comparatively dry flesh of the males! What an unerring glance, which can distinguish at once between the two sexes, so much alike in shape and colour! The female carries a sword at the tip of her abdomen, the ovipositor wherewith the eggs are buried in the ground; and that is about the only external difference between her and the male. This distinguishing feature never escapes the perspicacious Sphex; and that is why, in my experiment, the Wasp rubbed her eyes, hugely puzzled at beholding swordless a prey which she well knew carried a sword when she caught it. What must not have passed through her little Sphex brain at the sight of this transformation?

Let us now watch the Wasp when, having prepared the burrow, she goes back for her victim, which, after its capture and the operation that paralysed it, she has left at no great distance. The Ephippiger is in a condition similar to that of the Cricket sacrificed by the Yellow-winged Sphex, a condition proving for certain that stings have been driven into her thoracic ganglia. Nevertheless, a good many movements still continue; but they are disconnected, though endowed with a certain vigour. Incapable of standing on its legs, the insect lies on its side or on its back. It flutters its long antennæ and also its palpi; it opens and closes its mandibles and bites as hard as in the normal state. The abdomen heaves rapidly and deeply. The ovipositor is brought back sharply under the belly, against which it almost lies flat. The legs stir, but languidly and irregularly; the middle legs seem more torpid than the others. If pricked with a needle, the whole body shudders convulsively; efforts are made to get up and walk, but without success. In short, the insect would be full of life, but for its inability to move about or even to stand upon its legs. We have here therefore a wholly local paralysis, a paralysis of the legs, or rather a partial abolition and ataxia of their movements. Can this very incomplete inertia be caused by some special arrangement of the victim's nervous system, or does it come from this, that the Wasp perhaps administers only a single prick, instead of stinging each ganglion of the thorax, as the Cricket-huntress does? I cannot tell.

Still, for all its shivering, its convulsions, its disconnected movements, the victim is none the less incapable of hurting the larva that is meant to devour it. I have taken from the burrow of the Sphex Ephippigers struggling just as lustily as when they were first half-paralysed; and nevertheless the feeble grub, hatched but a few hours since, was digging its teeth into the gigantic victim in all security; the dwarf was biting into the colossus without danger to itself. This striking result is due to the spot selected by the mother for

laying her egg. I have already said how the Yellow-winged
Sphex glues her egg to the Cricket's breast, a little to one
side, between the first and second pair of legs. Exactly the
same place is chosen by the White-edged Sphex; and a similar
place, a little farther back, towards the root of one of the
large hind-thighs, is adopted by the Languedocian Sphex, all
three thus giving proof, by this uniformity, of wonderful
discernment in picking out the spot where the egg is bound to
be safe.

Consider the Ephippiger pent in the burrow. She lies
stretched upon her back, absolutely incapable of turning. In
vain, she struggles, in vain she writhes: the disordered movements of her legs are lost in space, the room being too wide
to afford them the support of its walls. The grub cares nothing for the victim's convulsions: it is at a spot where naught
can reach it, not tarsi, nor mandibles, nor ovipositor, nor
antennæ; a spot absolutely stationary, devoid of so much as
a surface tremor. It is in perfect safety, on the sole condition
that the Ephippiger cannot shift her position, turn over, get
upon her feet; and this one condition is admirably fulfilled.

But, with several heads of game, all in the same stage of
paralysis, the larva's danger would be great. Though it would
have nothing to fear from the insect first attacked, because
of its position out of the reach of its victim, it would have
every occasion to dread the proximity of the others, which,
stretching their legs at random, might strike it and rip it open
with their spurs. This is perhaps the reason why the Yellow-
winged Sphex, who heaps up three or four Crickets in the
same cell, practically annihilates all movement in its victims,
whereas the Languedocian Sphex, victualling each burrow
with a single piece of game, leaves her Ephippigers the best
part of their power of motion and contents herself with making it impossible for them to change their position or stand
upon their legs. She may thus, though I cannot say so
positively, economize her dagger-thrusts.

While the only half-paralysed Ephippiger cannot imperil
the larva, fixed on a part of the body where resistance is impossible, the case is different with the Sphex, who has to
cart her prize home. First, having still, to a great extent,
preserved the use of its tarsi, the victim clutches with these
at any blade of grass encountered on the road along which it
is being dragged; and this produces an obstacle to the hauling process which is difficult to overcome. The Sphex, al-

ready heavily burdened by the weight of her load, is liable
to exhaust herself with her efforts to make the other insect
relax its desperate grip in grassy places. But this is the least
serious drawback. The Ephippiger preserves the complete
use of her mandibles, which snap and bite with their customary vigour. Now what these terrible nippers have in front
of them is just the slender body of the enemy, at a time
when she is in her hauling attitude. The antennæ, in fact,
are grasped not far from their roots, so that the mouth of the
victim dragged along on its back faces either the thorax or the
abdomen of the Sphex, who, standing high on her long
legs, takes good care, I am convinced, not to be caught in
the mandibles yawning underneath her. At all events, a moment of forgetfulness, a slip, the merest trifle can bring her
within the reach of two powerful nippers, which would not
neglect the opportunity of taking a pitiless vengeance. In
the more difficult cases at any rate, if not always, the action
of those formidable pincers must be done away with; and the
fish-hooks of the legs must be rendered incapable of increasing their resistance to the process of transport.

How will the Sphex go to work to obtain this result? Here
man, even the man of science, would hesitate, would waste
his time in barren efforts and would perhaps abandon all hope
of success. He can come and take one lesson from the Sphex.
She, without ever being taught it, without ever seeing it practised by others, understands her surgery through and through.
She knows the most delicate mysteries of the physiology of
the nerves, or rather she behaves as if she did. She knows
that under her victim's skull there is a circlet of nervous
nuclei, something similar to the brain of the higher animals.
She knows that this main centre of innervation controls the
action of the mouth-parts and moreover is the seat of the
will, without whose orders not a single muscle acts; lastly,
she knows that, by injuring this sort of brain, she will cause
all resistance to cease, the insect no longer possessing any
will to resist. As for the mode of operating, this is the easiest
matter in the world to her; and, when we have been taught
in her school, we are free to try her process in our turn. The
instrument employed is no longer the sting; the insect, in
its wisdom, has deemed compression preferable to a poisoned
thrust. Let us accept its decision, for we shall see presently
how prudent it is to be convinced of our own ignorance in
the presence of the animal's knowledge. Lest by editing my

account I should fail to give a true impression of the sublime talent of this masterly operator, I here copy out my note as I pencilled it on the spot, immediately after the stirring spectacle.

The Sphex finds that her victim is offering too much resistance, hooking itself here and there to blades of grass. She then stops to perform upon it the following curious operation, a sort of *coup de grâce*. The Wasp, still astride her prey, forces open the articulation of the neck, high up, at the nape. Then she seizes the neck with her mandibles and, without making any external wound, probes as far forward as possible under the skull, so as to seize and chew up the ganglia of the head. When this operation is done, the victim is utterly motionless, incapable of the least resistance, whereas previously the legs, though deprived of the power of connected movement needed for walking, vigorously opposed the process of traction.

There is the fact in all its eloquence. With the points of its mandibles, the insect, while leaving uninjured the thin and supple membrane of the neck, goes rummaging into the skull and munching the brain. There is no effusion of blood, no wound, but simply an external pressure. Of course, I kept for my own purposes the Ephippiger paralysed before my eyes, in order to ascertain the effects of the operation at my leisure; also of course, I hastened to repeat in my turn, upon live Ephippigers, what the Sphex had just taught me. I will here compare my results with the Wasp's.

Two Ephippigers whose cervical ganglia I squeeze and compress with a forceps fall rapidly into a state resembling that of the victims of the Sphex. Only, they grate their cymbals if I tease them with a needle; and the legs still retain a few disordered and languid movements. The difference no doubt is due to the fact that my patients were not previously injured in their thoracic ganglia, as were those of the Sphex, who were first stung on the breast. Allowing for this important condition, we see that I was none too bad a pupil and that I imitated pretty closely my teacher of physiology, the Sphex. I confess, it was not without a certain satisfaction that I succeeded in doing almost as well as the insect with her prey.

As well? What am I talking about? Wait a bit and you shall see that I still have much to learn from the Sphex. For what happens is that my two patients very soon die: I mean, they really die; and, in four or five days, I have nothing but putrid corpses before my eyes. And the Wasp's Ephippiger? I need hardly say that the Wasp's Ephippiger, even ten days after the operation, is perfectly fresh, just as she will be required by the larva for which she has been destined. Nay, more: only a few hours after the operation under the skull, there reappeared, as though nothing had occurred, the disorderly movements of the legs, antennæ, palpi, ovipositor and mandibles; in a word, the insect returned to the condition wherein it was before the Sphex bit its brain. And these movements were kept up after, though they became feebler every day. The Sphex had merely reduced her victim to a passing state of torpor, lasting amply long enough to enable her to bring it home without resistance; and I, who thought myself her rival, was but a clumsy and barbarous butcher: I killed my prize. She, with her inimitable dexterity, shrewdly compressed the brain to produce a lethargy of a few hours; I, brutal through ignorance, perhaps crushed under my forceps that delicate organ, the main seat of life. If anything could prevent me from blushing at my defeat, it would be the conviction that very few, if any, could vie with these clever ones in cleverness.

Ah, I now understand why the Sphex does not use her sting to injure the cervical ganglia! A drop of poison injected here, at the centre of vital force, would destroy the whole nervous system; and death would follow soon after. But it is not death that the huntress wishes to obtain; the larvæ have not the least use for dead game, for a corpse, in short, smelling of corruption; and all that she wants to bring about is a lethargy, a passing torpor, which will put a stop to the victim's resistance during the carting process, this resistance being difficult to overcome and moreover dangerous for the Sphex.

The torpor is obtained by a method known in laboratories of experimental physiology: compression of the brain. The Sphex acts like a Flourens, who, laying bare an animal's brain and bearing upon the cerebral mass, forthwith suppresses intelligence, will, sensibility and movement. The pressure is removed; and everything reappears. Even so do the remains of the Ephippiger's life reappear, as the lethargic effects of a skilfully-directed pressure pass off. The ganglia of the skull, squeezed between the mandibles but without fatal contusions, gradually recover their activity and put an end to the general torpor. Admit that it is all alarmingly scientific.

Fortune has her entomological whims: you run after her and catch no glimpse of her; you forget about her and behold, she comes tapping at your door! How vainly I watched and waited, how many useless journeys I made to see the Languedocian Sphex sacrifice her Ephippigers! Twenty years pass; these pages are in the printer's hands; and, one day early this month, on the 8th of August 1878, my son Émile comes rushing into my study:

"Quick!" he shouts. "Come quick: there's a Sphex dragging her prey under the plane-trees, outside the yard!"

Émile knew all about the business, from what I had told him, to amuse him when we used to sit up late, and better still from similar incidents which he had witnessed in our life out of doors. He is right. I run out and see a magnificent Languedocian Sphex dragging a paralysed Ephippiger by the antennæ. She is making for the hen-house close by and seems anxious to scale the wall, with the object of fixing her burrow under some tile on the roof; for, a few years ago, in the same place, I saw a Sphex of the same species accomplish the ascent with her game and make her home under the arch of a badly-joined tile. Perhaps the present Wasp is descended from the one who performed that arduous climb.

A like feat seems about to be repeated; and this time before numerous witnesses, for all the family, working under the shade of the plane-trees, come and form a circle around the Sphex. They wonder at the unceremonious boldness of the insect, which is not diverted from its work by a gallery of onlookers; all are struck by its proud and lusty bearing, as, with raised head and the victim's antennæ firmly gripped in its mandibles, it drags the enormous burden after it. I, alone among the spectators, feel a twinge of regret at the sight:

"Ah, if only I had some live Ephippigers!" I cannot help saying, with not the least hope of seeing my wish realized.

"Live Ephippigers?" replies Émile. "Why, I have some perfectly fresh ones, caught this morning!"

He dashes upstairs, four steps at a time, and runs to his little den, where a fence of dictionaries encloses a park for the rearing of some fine caterpillars of the Spurge Hawkmoth. He brings me three Ephippigers, the best that I could wish for, two females and a male.

How did these insects come to be at hand, at the moment when they were wanted, for an experiment tried in vain twenty years ago? That is another story. A Lesser Grey Shrike had nested in one of the tall plane-trees of the avenue. Now a few days earlier, the mistral, the brutal northwest wind of our parts, blew with such violence as to bend the branches as well as the reeds; and the nest, turned upside down by the swaying of its support, had dropped its contents, four small birds. Next morning, I found the brood upon the ground; three were killed by the fall, the fourth was still alive. The survivor was entrusted to the cares of Émile, who went Cricket-hunting twice a day on the neighbouring grass-plots for the benefit of his young charge. But Crickets are small and the nursling's appetite called for many of them. Another dish was preferred, the Ephippiger, of whom a stock was collected from time to time among the stalks and prickly leaves of the eryngo. The three insects which Émile brought me came from the Shrike's larder. My pity for the fallen nestling had procured me this unhoped-for success.

After making the circle of spectators stand back so as to leave the field clear for the Sphex, I take away her prey with a pair of pincers and at once give her in exchange one of my Ephippigers, carrying a sword at the end of her belly, like the game which I have abstracted. The dispossessed Wasp stamps her feet two or three times; and that is the only sign of impatience which she gives. She goes for her new prey, which is too stout, too obese even to try to avoid pursuit, grips it with her mandibles by the saddle-shaped corselet, gets astride and, curving her abdomen, slips the end of it under the Ephippiger's thorax. Here, no doubt, some stings are administered, though I am unable to state the number exactly, because of the difficulty of observation. The Ephippiger, a peaceable victim, suffers herself to be operated on without resistance; she is like the silly Sheep of our slaughterhouses. The Sphex takes her time and wields her lancet with a deliberation which favours accuracy of aim. So far, the observer has nothing to complain of; but the prey touches the ground with its breast and belly and exactly what happens underneath escapes his eye. As for interfering and lifting the Ephippiger a little, so as to see better, that must not be thought of: the murderess would resheathe her weapon and retire. The act that follows is easy to observe. After stabbing the thorax, the tip of the abdomen appears under the victim's neck, which the operator forces open by pressing the nape. At this point, the sting probes with marked persistency, as if the prick administered here were more effective than elsewhere. One would be inclined to think that the nerve-centre attacked is the lower part of the œsophageal chain; but the continuance of movement in the mouth-parts —the mandibles, jaws and palpi—controlled by this seat of innervation shows that such is not the case. Through the neck, the Sphex reaches simply the ganglia of the thorax, or at any rate the first of them, which is more easily accessible through the thin skin of the neck than through the integuments of the chest.

And in a moment it is all over. Without the least shiver denoting pain, the Ephippiger becomes henceforth an inert mass. I remove the Sphex' patient for the second time and replace it by the other female at my disposal. The same proceedings are repeated, followed by the same result. The Sphex has performed her skilful surgery thrice over, almost in immediate succession, first with her own prey and then with my substitutes. Will she do so a fourth time with the male Ephippiger whom I still have left? I have my doubts, not because the Wasp is tired, but because the game does not suit her. I have never seen her with any prey but females, who, crammed with eggs, are the food which the larvæ appreciate above all others. My suspicion is well-founded; deprived of her capture, the Sphex stubbornly refuses the male whom I offer to her. She runs hither and thither, with hurried steps, in search of the vanished game; three or four times, she goes up to the Ephippiger, walks round him, casts a scornful glance at him; and at last she flies away. He is not what her larvæ want; experiment demonstrates this once again after an interval of twenty years.

The three females stabbed, two of them before my eyes, remain in my possession. In each case, all the legs are completely paralysed. Whether lying naturally, on its belly or on its back or side, the insect retains indefinitely whatever position we give it. A continued fluttering of the antennæ, a few intermittent pulsations of the belly and the play of the mouth-parts are the only signs of life. Movement is destroyed but not susceptibility; for, at the least prick administered to a thin-skinned spot, the whole body gives a slight shudder. Perhaps, some day, physiology will find in such victims the material for valuable work on the functions of the nervous system. The Wasp's sting, so incomparably skilful at striking a particular point and administering a wound which affects that point alone, will supplement, with immense advantage, the experimenter's brutal scalpel, which rips open where it ought to give merely a light touch. Meanwhile, here are the results which I have obtained from the three victims, but in another direction.

As only the movement of the legs has been destroyed, without any wound save that of the nerve-centres, which are the seat of that movement, the insect must die of inanition and not of its injuries. The experiment was conducted as follows: two sound and healthy Ephippigers, just as I picked them up in the fields, were imprisoned without food, one in the dark, the other in the light. The second died in four days, the first in five. This difference of a day is easily explained. In the light, the insect made greater exertions to recover its liberty; and, as every movement of the animal machine is accompanied by a corresponding expenditure of energy, a greater sum total of activity has involved a more rapid consumption of the reserve force of the organism. In the light, there is more restlessness and a shorter life; in the dark, less restlessness and a longer life, while no food at all was taken in either case.

One of my three stabbed Ephippigers was kept in the dark, fasting. In her case, there were not only the conditions of complete abstinence and darkness, but also the serious wounds inflicted by the Sphex; and nevertheless for seventeen days I saw her continually waving her antennæ. As long as this sort of pendulum keeps on swinging, the clock of life does not stop. On the eighteenth day, the creature ceased its antennary movements and died. The badly-wounded insect therefore lived, under the same conditions, four times as long as the insect that was untouched. What seemed as though it should be a cause of death was really a cause of life.

However paradoxical it may seem at first sight, this result is exceedingly simple. When untouched, the insect exerts itself and consequently uses up its reserve. When paralysed, it has merely the feeble, internal movements which are inseparable from any organism; and its substance is economized in proportion to the weakness of the action displayed. In the first case, the animal machine is at work and wears itself out; in the second, it is at rest and saves itself. There being no nourishment now to repair the waste, the moving insect spends its nutritive reserves in four days and dies; the motionless insect does not spend them and lives for eighteen days. Life is a continual dissolution, the physiologists tell us; and the Sphex' victims give us the neatest possible demonstration of the fact.

One remark more. Fresh food is absolutely necessary for the Wasp's larvæ. If the prey were warehoused in the burrow intact, in four or five days it would be a corpse abandoned to corruption; and the scarce-hatched grub would find nothing to live upon but a putrid mass. Pricked with the sting, however, it can keep alive for two or three weeks, a period more than long enough to allow the egg to hatch and the larva to grow. The paralysing of the victim therefore has a twofold result: first, the living dish remains motionless and the safety of the delicate grub is not endangered; secondly, the meat keeps good a long time and thus ensures wholesome food for the larva. Man's logic, enlightened by science, could discover nothing better.

My two other Ephippigers stung by the Sphex were kept in the dark with food. To feed inert insects, hardly differing from corpses except by the perpetual waving of their long antennæ, seems at first an impossibility; still, the play of the mouth-parts gave me some hope and I tried. My success exceeded my anticipations. There was no question here, of course, of giving them a lettuce-leaf or any other piece of green stuff on which they might have browsed in their normal state; they were feeble valetudinarians, who needed spoon-feeding, so to speak, and supporting with liquid nourishment. I used sugar-and-water.

Laying the insect on its back, I place a drop of the sugary fluid on its mouth with a straw. The palpi at once begin to stir; the mandibles and jaws move. The drop is swallowed with evident satisfaction, especially after a somewhat prolonged fast. I repeat the dose until it is refused. The meal takes place once a day, sometimes twice, at irregular intervals, lest I should become too much of a slave to my patients. Well, one of the Ephippigers lived for twenty-one days on this meagre fare. It was not much, compared with the eighteen days of the one whom I had left to die of starvation. True, the insect had twice had a bad fall, having dropped from the experimenting-table to the floor owing to some piece of awkwardness on my part. The bruises which it received must have hastened its end. The other, which suffered no accidents, lived for forty days. As the nourishment employed, sugar-and-water, could not indefinitely take the place of the natural green food, it is very likely that the insect would have lived longer still if the usual diet had been possible. And so the point which I had in view is proved: the victims stung by the Digger-wasps die of starvation and not of their wounds.

VI

The Ignorance of Instinct

As was often the case with Fabre's major researches, the field-notes of many successive summers were combined to give the final picture of the wisdom and the ignorance of the instinctive acts of the Sphex. *The Bee-eating Philanthi, mentioned in this chapter are also hunting wasps. Several species are found in America, all of them preying on bees and in some instances becoming serious problems around apiaries. This section originally formed Chapter X of* THE HUNTING WASPS.

THE SPHEX HAS SHOWN US how infallibly and with what transcendental art she acts when guided by the unconscious inspiration of her instinct; she is now going to show us how poor she is in resource, how limited in intelligence, how illogical even, in circumstances outside of her regular routine. By a strange inconsistency, characteristic of the instinctive faculties, profound wisdom is accompanied by an ignorance no less profound. To instinct nothing is impossible, however great the difficulty may be. In building her hexagonal cells, with their floors consisting of three lozenges, the Bee solves with absolute precision the arduous problem of how to achieve the maximum result at a minimum cost, a problem whose solution by man would demand a powerful mathematical mind. The Wasps whose larvæ live on prey display in their murderous art methods hardly rivalled by those of a man versed in the intricacies of anatomy and physiology. Nothing is difficult to instinct, so long as the act is not outside the unvarying cycle of animal existence; on the other hand, nothing is easy to instinct, if the act is at all removed from the course usually pursued. The insect which astounds us, which terrifies us with its extraordinary intelligence, surprises us, the next moment, with its stupidity, when confronted with some simple fact that happens to lie outside its ordinary practice. The Sphex will supply us with a few instances.

Let us follow her dragging her Ephippiger home. If fortune smile upon us, we may witness some such little scene as that which I will now describe. When entering her shelter under the rock, where she has made her burrow, the Sphex finds, perched on a blade of grass, a Praying Mantis, a carnivorous insect which hides cannibal habits under a pious appearance. The danger threatened by this robber ambushed on her path must be known to the Sphex, for she lets go her game and pluckily rushes upon the Mantis, to inflict some heavy blows and dislodge her, or at all events to frighten her and inspire her with respect. The robber does not move, but closes her lethal machinery, the two terrible saws of the arm and fore-arm. The Sphex goes back to her capture, harnesses herself to the antennæ and boldly passes under the blade of grass whereon the other sits perched. By the direction of her head we can see that she is on her guard and that she holds the enemy rooted, motionless, under the menace of her eyes. Her courage meets with the reward which it deserves: the prey is stored away without further mishap.

A word more on the Praying Mantis, or, as they say in Provence, *lou Prégo Diéou*, the Pray-to-God. Her long, pale-green wings, like spreading veils, her head raised heavenwards, her folded arms, crossed upon her breast, are in fact a sort of travesty of a nun in ecstasy. And yet she is a ferocious creature, loving carnage. Though not her favourite spots, the work-yards of the various Digger-wasps receive her visits pretty frequently. Posted near the burrows, on some bramble or other, she waits for chance to bring within her reach some of the arrivals, forming a double capture for her, as she seizes both the huntress and her prey. Her patience is long put to the test: the Wasp suspects something and is on her guard; still, from time to time, a rash one gets caught. With a sudden rustle of wings half-unfurled as by the violent release of a clutch, the Mantis terrifies the newcomer, who hesitates for a moment, in her fright. Then, with the sharpness of a spring, the toothed fore-arm folds back on the toothed upper arm; and the insect is caught between the blades of the doublesaw. It is as though the jaws of a Wolf-trap were closing on the animal that had nibbled at its bait. Thereupon, without unloosing the cruel machine, the

Mantis gnaws her victim by small mouthfuls. Such are the ecstasies, the prayers, the meditations of the *Prégo Diéou*.

Of the scenes of carnage which the Praying Mantis has left in my memory, let me relate one. The thing happens in front of a work-yard of Bee-eating Philanthi. These diggers feed their larvæ on Hive-bees, whom they catch on the flowers while gathering pollen and honey. If the Philanthus who has made a capture feels that her Bee is swollen with honey, she never fails, before storing her, to squeeze her crop, either on the way or at the entrance of the dwelling, so as to make her disgorge the delicious syrup, which she drinks by licking the tongue which her unfortunate victim, in her death-agony, sticks out of her mouth at full length. This profanation of a dying creature, whose enemy squeezes its belly to empty it and feast on the contents, has something so hideous about it that I should denounce the Philanthus as a brutal murderess, if animals were capable of wrongdoing. At the moment of some such horrible banquet, I have seen the Wasp, with her prey, seized by the Mantis: the bandit was rifled by another bandit. And here is an awful detail: while the Mantis held her transfixed under the points of the double saw and was already munching her belly, the Wasp continued to lick the honey of her Bee, unable to relinquish the delicious food even amid the terrors of death. Let us hasten to cast a veil over these horrors.

We will return to the Sphex, with whose burrow we must make ourselves acquainted before we go further. This burrow is a hole made in fine sand, or rather in a sort of dust at the bottom of a natural shelter. Its entrance-passage is very short, merely an inch or two, without a bend, and leads to a single, roomy, oval chamber. The whole thing is a rough den, hastily dug out, rather than a leisurely and artistically excavated dwelling. I have explained that the reason for this simplicity is that the game is captured first and set down for a moment on the hunting-field while the Wasp hurriedly makes a burrow in the vicinity, a method of procedure which allows of but one chamber or cell to each retreat. For who can tell whither the chances of the day will lead the huntress for her second capture? The prisoner is heavy and the burrow must therefore be near; so today's home, which is too far away for the next Ephippiger to be conveyed to it, cannot be utilized tomorrow. Thus, as each prey is caught, there is a fresh excavation, a fresh burrow, with its single chamber, now here, now there. Having said this, we will try a few experiments to see how the insect behaves when we create circumstances new to it.

Experiment I

A Sphex, dragging her prey along, is a few inches from the burrow. Without disturbing her, I cut with a pair of scissors the Ephippiger's antennæ, which the Wasp, as we know, uses for harness-ropes. On recovering from the surprise caused by the sudden lightening of her load, the Sphex goes back to her victim and, without hesitation, now seizes the root of the antenna, the short stump left by the scissors. It is very short indeed, hardly a millimetre; no matter: it is enough for the Sphex, who grips this fag-end of a rope and resumes her hauling. With the greatest precaution, so as not to injure the Wasp, I now cut the two antennary stumps level with the skull. Finding nothing left to catch hold of at the familiar points, the insect seizes, close by, one of the victim's long palpi and continues its hauling-work, without appearing at all perturbed by this change in the harness. I leave it alone. The prey is brought home and placed so that its head faces the entrance to the burrow; and the Wasp goes in by herself, to make a brief inspection of the inside of the cell before proceeding to warehouse the provisions. Her behaviour reminds us of that of the Yellow-winged Sphex in similar circumstances. I take advantage of this short moment to seize the abandoned prey, remove all its palpi and place it a little farther off, about half a yard from the burrow. The Sphex reappears and goes straight to her captive, whom she has seen from her threshold. She looks at the top of the head, she looks underneath, on either side and finds nothing to take hold of. A desperate attempt is made: the Wasp, opening wide her mandibles, tries to grab the Ephippiger by the head; but the pincers have not a sufficient compass to take in so large a bulk and they slip off the round, polished skull. She makes several fresh endeavours, each time without result. She is at length convinced of the uselessness of her efforts. She draws back a little to one side and appears to be renouncing further attempts. One would say that she was discouraged; at least, she smoothes her wings with her hind-legs, while with her front tarsi, which she first puts into her mouth, she washes her eyes. This, so it has always seemed to me, is a sign in Hymenoptera of giving up a job.

Nevertheless there is no lack of parts by which the Ephippiger might be seized and dragged along as easily as by the antennæ and the palpi. There are the six legs, there is the ovipositor: all organs slender enough to be gripped boldly and to serve as hauling-ropes. I agree that the easiest way to effect the storing is to introduce the prey head first, drawn down by the antennæ; but it would enter almost as readily if drawn by a leg, especially one of the front legs, for the orifice is wide and the passage short or sometimes even non-existent. Then how is it that the Sphex did not once try to seize one of the six tarsi or the tip of ovipositor, whereas she attempted the impossible, the absurd, in striving to grip, with her much too short mandibles, the huge skull of her prey? Can it be that the idea did not occur to her? We will suggest it.

I offer her, right under her mandibles, first a leg, next the end of the abdominal rapier. The insect obstinately refuses to bite; my repeated blandishments lead to nothing. A singular huntress, to be embarrassed by her game, not knowing how to seize it by a leg when she is not able to take it by the horns! Perhaps my prolonged presence and the unusual events that have just occurred have disturbed her faculties. Then let us leave the Sphex to herself, between her Ephippiger and her burrow; let us give her time to collect herself and, in the calm of solitude, to think out some way of managing her business. I leave her therefore and continue my walk; and, two hours later, I return to the same place. The Sphex is gone, the burrow is still open and the Ephippiger is lying just where I placed her. Conclusion: the Wasp has tried nothing; she went away, abandoning everything, her home and her game, when, to utilize them both, all that she had to do was to take her prey by one leg. And so this rival of Flourens, who but now was startling us with her cleverness as she dexterously squeezed her victim's brain to produce lethargy, becomes incredibly helpless in the simplest case outside her usual habits. She, who so well knows how to attack a victim's thoracic ganglia with her sting and its cervical ganglia with her mandibles; she, who makes such a judicious difference between a poisoned prick annihilating the vital influence of the nerves forever and a pressure causing only momentary torpor, cannot grip her prey by this part when it is made impossible for her to grip it by any other. To understand that she can take a leg instead of an antenna is utterly beyond her powers. She must have the antenna, or some other string attached to the head, such as one of the palpi. If these cords did not exist, her race would perish, for lack of the capacity to solve this trivial problem.

Experiment II

The Wasp is engaged in closing her burrow, where the prey has been stored and the egg laid upon it. With her front tarsi, she brushes her doorstep, working backwards and sweeping into the entrance a stream of dust which passes under her belly and spurts behind in a parabolic spray as continuous as a liquid spray, so nimble is the sweeper in her actions. From time to time, the Sphex picks out with her mandibles a few grains of sand, so many solid blocks which she inserts one by one into the mass of dust, causing it all to cake together by beating and compressing it with her forehead and mandibles. Walled up by this masonry, the entrance-door soon disappears from sight.

I intervene in the middle of the work. Pushing the Sphex aside, I carefully clear the short gallery with the blade of a knife, take away the materials that close it and restore full communication between the cell and the outside. Then, with my forceps, without damaging the edifice, I take the Ephippiger from the cell, where she lies with her head at the back and her ovipositor towards the entrance. The Wasp's egg is on the victim's breast, at the usual place, the root of one of the hinder thighs: a proof that the Sphex was finishing the burrow, with the intention of never returning.

Having done this and put the stolen prey safely away in a box, I yield my place to the Sphex, who has been on the watch beside me while I was rifling her home. Finding the door open, she goes in and stays for a few moments. Then she comes out and resumes her work where I interrupted it; that is to say, she starts conscientiously stopping the entrance to the cell by sweeping dust backwards and carrying grains of sand, which she continues to heap up with scrupulous care, as though she were doing useful work. When the door is once again thoroughly walled up, the insect brushes itself, seems to give a glance of satisfaction at the task accomplished and finally flies away.

The Sphex must have known that the burrow contained nothing, because she went inside and even stayed there for some time; and yet, after this inspection of the pillaged abode, she once more proceeds to close up the cell with the same care as though nothing out of the way had happened. Can she be proposing to use this burrow later, to return to it with a fresh victim and lay a new egg there? If so, her work of closing would be intended to prevent the access of intruders to the dwelling during her absence; it would be a measure of prudence against the attempts of other diggers who might covet the ready-made chamber; it might also be a wise precaution against internal dilapidations. And, as a matter of fact, some Hunting Wasps do take care to protect the entrance to the burrow by closing it temporarily, when the work has to be suspended for a time. Thus I have seen certain Ammophilæ, whose burrow is a perpendicular shaft, block the entrance to the home with a small flat stone when the insect goes off hunting or ceases its mining-operations at sunset, the hour for striking work. But this is a slight affair, a mere slab laid over the mouth of the shaft. When the insect comes, it only takes a moment to remove the little flat stone; and the entrance is free.

On the other hand, the obstruction which we have just seen built by the Sphex is a solid barrier, a stout piece of masonry, where dust and gravel form alternate layers all the way down the passage. It is a definite performance and not a provisional defence, as is proved by the care with which it is constructed. Besides, as I think I have shown pretty clearly, it is very doubtful, considering the way in which she acts, whether the Sphex will ever return to make use of the home which she has prepared. The next Ephippiger will be caught elsewhere; and the warehouse destined to receive her will be dug elsewhere too. But these, after all, are only arguments: let us rather have recourse to experiment, which is more conclusive here than logic.

I allowed nearly a week to elapse, in order to give the Sphex time to return to the burrow which she had so methodically closed and to make use of it for her next laying if such were her intention. Events corresponded with the logical inferences: the burrow was in the condition wherein I left it, still firmly closed, but without provisions, egg or larva. The proof was decisive: the Wasp had not been back.

So the plundered Sphex enters her house, makes a leisurely

inspection of the empty chamber and, a moment afterwards, behaves as though she had not perceived the disappearance of the bulky prey which but now filled the cell. Did she, in fact, fail to notice the absence of the provisions and the egg? Is she, who is so clear-sighted in her murderous proceedings, dense enough not to realize that the cell is empty? I dare not accuse her of such stupidity. She is aware of it. But then why that other piece of stupidity which makes her close— and very conscientiously close—an empty burrow, one which she does not purpose to victual later? Here the work of closing is useless, is supremely absurd; no matter: the insect performs it with the same ardour as though the larva's future depended on it. The insect's various instinctive actions are then fatally linked together. Because one thing has been done, a second thing must inevitably be done to complete the first or to prepare the way for its completion; and the two acts depend so closely upon each other that the performing of the first entails that of the second, even when, owing to casual circumstances, the second has become not only inopportune but sometimes actually opposed to the insect's interests. What object can the Sphex have in blocking up a burrow which has become useless, now that it no longer contains the victim and the egg, and which will always remain useless, since the insect will not return to it? The only way to explain this inconsequent action is to look upon it as the inevitable complement of the actions that went before. In the normal order of things, the Sphex hunts down her prey, lays an egg and closes her burrow. The hunting has been done; the game, it is true, has been withdrawn by me from the cell; never mind: the hunting has been done, the egg has been laid; and now comes the business of closing up the home. This is what the insect does, without another thought, without in the least suspecting the futility of her present labours.

Experiment III

To know everything and to know nothing, according as it acts under normal or exceptional conditions: that is the strange antithesis presented by the insect race. Other examples, also drawn from the Sphex tribe, will confirm this conclusion. The White-edged Sphex (*S. albisecta*) attacks medium-sized Locusts, whereof the different species to be found in the neighbourhood of the burrow all furnish her with their tribute of victims. Because of the abundance of these Acridians, there is no need to go hunting far afield. When the burrow, which takes the form of a perpendicular shaft, is ready, the Sphex merely explores the purlieus of her lair, within a small radius, and is not long in finding some Locust browsing in the sunshine. To pounce upon her and sting her, despite her kicking, is to the Sphex the matter of a moment. After some fluttering of its wings, which unfurl their carmine or azure fan, after some drowsy stretching of its legs, the victim ceases to move. It has now to be brought home, on foot. For this laborious operation, the Sphex employs the same method as her kinswomen, that is to say, she drags her prize along between her legs, holding one of its antennæ in her mandibles. If she encounters some grassy jungle, she goes hopping and flitting from blade to blade, without ever letting slip her prey. When at last she comes within a few feet of her dwelling, she performs a manœuvre which is also practised by the Languedocian Sphex; but she does not attach as much importance to it, for she frequently neglects it. Leaving her captive on the road, the Wasp hurries home, though no apparent danger threatens her abode, and puts her head through the entrance several times, even going part of the way down the burrow. She next returns to the Locust and, after bringing her nearer the goal, leaves her a second time to revisit the burrow. This performance is repeated over and over again, always with the same haste.

These visits are sometimes followed by grievous accidents. The victim, rashly abandoned on hilly ground, rolls to the bottom of the slope; and the Sphex on her return, no longer finding it where she left it, is obliged to seek for it, sometimes fruitlessly. If she finds it, she must renew a toilsome climb, which does not prevent her from once more abandoning her booty on the same unlucky declivity. Of these repeated visits to the mouth of the shaft, the first can be very logically explained. The Wasp, before arriving with her heavy burden, enquires whether the entrance to the home be really clear, whether nothing will hinder her from bringing in her game. But, once this first reconnaissance is made, what can be the use of the rest, following one after the other, at close intervals? Is the Sphex so volatile in her ideas that she forgets the visit which she has just paid and runs afresh to the burrow a moment later, only to forget this new inspection also and to start doing the same thing over and over again? That would be a memory with very fleeting recollections, whence the impression vanished almost as soon as it was produced. Let us not linger too long on this obscure point.

At last the game is brought to the brink of the shaft, with its antennæ hanging down the hole. We now again see, faithfully imitated, the method employed in the like case by the Yellow-winged Sphex and also, but under less striking conditions, by the Languedocian Sphex. The Wasp enters alone, inspects the interior, reappears at the entrance, lays hold of the antennæ and drags the Locust down. While the Locust-huntress was making her examination of the home, I have pushed her prize a little farther back; and I obtained results similar in all respects to those which the Cricket-huntress gave me. Each Sphex displays the same obstinacy in diving down her burrow before dragging in the prey. Let us recall here that the Yellow-winged Sphex does not always allow herself to be caught by this trick of pulling away her Cricket. There are picked tribes, strong-minded families which, after a few disappointments, see through the experimenter's wiles and know how to baffle them. But these revolutionaries, fit subjects for progress, are the minority; the remainder, mulish conservatives clinging to the old manners and customs, are the majority, the crowd. I am unable to say whether the Locust-huntress also varies in ingenuity according to the district which she hails from.

But here is something more remarkable; and it is this with which I wanted to conclude the present experiment. After repeatedly withdrawing the White-edged Sphex' prize from the mouth of the pit and compelling her to come and fetch it again, I take advantage of her descent to the bottom of the shaft to seize the prey and put it in a place of safety where she cannot find it. The Sphex comes up, looks about for a long time and, when she is convinced that the prey is really lost, goes down into her home again. A few moments after, she reappears. Is it with the intention of resuming the chase? Not the least in the world: the Sphex begins to stop up the burrow. And what we see is not a temporary closing, effected with a small flat stone, a slab covering the mouth of the well; it is a final closing, carefully done with dust and gravel swept into the passage until it is filled up. The White-edged Sphex makes only one cell at the bottom of her shaft and puts one head of game into this cell. That single Locust has been caught and dragged to the edge of the hole. If she was not stored away, it was not the huntress' fault, but mine. The Wasp performed her task according to the inflexible rule; and, also according to the inflexible rule, she completes her work by stopping up the dwelling, empty though it be. We have here an exact repetition of the useless exertions made by the Languedocian Sphex whose home has just been plundered.

Experiment IV

It is almost impossible to make certain whether the Yellow-winged Sphex, who constructs several cells at the end of the same passage and stacks several Crickets in each, is equally illogical when accidentally disturbed in her proceedings. A cell can be closed though empty or imperfectly victualled and the Wasp will none the less continue to come to the same burrow in order to work at the others. Nevertheless, I have reason to believe that this Sphex is subject to the same aberrations as her two kinswomen. My conviction is based on the following facts: the number of Crickets found in the cells, when all the work is done, is usually four to each cell, although it is not uncommon to find only three, or even two. Four appears to me to be the normal number, first, because it is the most frequent and, secondly, because, when rearing young larvæ dug up while they were still engaged on their first joint, I found that all of them, those actually provided with only two or three pieces of game as well as those which had four, easily managed the various Crickets wherewith I served them one by one, up to and including the fourth, but that after this they refused all nourishment, or barely touched the fifth ration. If four Crickets are necessary to the larva to acquire the full development called for by its organization, why are sometimes only three, sometimes only two provided for it? Why this enormous difference in the quantity of the victuals, some larvæ having twice as much as the others? It cannot be because of any difference in the size of the dishes provided to satisfy the grub's appetite, for all have very much the same dimensions; and it can therefore be due only to the wastage of game on the way. We find, in fact, at the foot of the banks whose upper stages are occupied by the Sphex-wasps, Crickets that have been paralysed but lost, owing to the slope of the ground, down which they have slipped when the huntresses have momentarily left them, for some reason or other. These Crickets fall a prey to the Ants and Flies; and the Sphex-wasps who come across them take good care not to pick them up, for, if they did, they would themselves be admitting enemies into the house.

These facts seem to me to prove that, while the Yellow-winged Sphex' arithmetical powers enable her to calculate exactly how many victims to capture, she cannot achieve a census of those which have safely reached their destination. It is as though the insect had no mathematical guide beyond an irresistible impulse that prompts her to hunt for game a definite number of times. When the Sphex has made the requisite number of journeys, when she has done her utmost to store the captures that result from these, her work is ended; and she closes the cell whether completely or incompletely provisioned. Nature has endowed her with only those faculties called for in ordinary circumstances by the interests of her larvæ; and, as these blind faculties, which cannot be modified by experience, are sufficient for the preservation of the race, the insect is unable to go beyond them.

I conclude therefore as I began: instinct knows everything, in the undeviating paths marked out of it; it knows nothing, outside those paths. The sublime inspirations of science and the astounding inconsistencies of stupidity are both its portion, according as the insect acts under normal or accidental conditions.

The Great Peacock Moth

Printed first in English in THE LIFE OF THE CATERPILLAR, *this account of the assembling of the male moths is one of the best known of Fabre's experiments. It has even been mentioned in a Hollywood movie. However, before it got on the screen, it was given a super-colossal twist. According to the dialogue: "This scientist, Fabre, was in the heart of Africa. He caught a female moth. When he returned home, a male followed him all the way from Africa to Paris!" In several of his experiments, including this one, Fabre tended to underrate the importance of smell. The smelling equipment of many insects is highly specialized; it is concentrated on detecting one or a very few odors; it is like a radio permanently set to a certain wave length. In laboratory tests, since Fabre's time, scientists have removed the scent-producing organs from female moths and have found that the males fly direct to this fragment of the moth's body, ignoring the female entirely. Phil Rau, an amateur experimenter near St. Louis, Missouri, found that a number of American moths tend to arrive at certain hours of the night; the males of one moth, for instance, are more likely to appear before midnight, those of another moth after midnight.*

IT WAS A MEMORABLE EVENING. I shall call it the Great Peacock evening. Who does not know the magnificent Moth, the largest in Europe, clad in maroon velvet with a necktie of white fur? The wings, with their sprinkling of grey and brown, crossed by a faint zig-zag and edged with smoky white, have in the centre a round patch, a great eye with a black pupil and a variegated iris containing successive black, white, chestnut and purple arcs.

Well, on the morning of the 6th of May, a female emerges from her cocoon in my presence, on the table of my insect-laboratory. I forthwith cloister her, still damp with the humours of the hatching, under a wire-gauze bell-jar. For the rest, I cherish no particular plans. I incarcerate her from mere habit, the habit of the observer always on the look-out for what may happen.

It was a lucky thought. At nine o'clock in the evening, just as the household is going to bed, there is a great stir in the room next to mine. Little Paul, half-undressed, is rushing about, jumping and stamping, knocking the chairs over like a mad thing. I hear him call me:

"Come quick!" he screams. "Come and see these Moths, big as birds! The room is full of them!"

I hurry in. There is enough to justify the child's enthusiastic and hyperbolical exclamations, an invasion as yet unprecedented in our house, a raid of giant Moths. Four are already caught and lodged in a bird-cage. Others, more numerous, are fluttering on the ceiling.

At this sight, the prisoner of the morning is recalled to my mind.

"Put on your things, laddie," I say to my son. "Leave your cage and come with me. We shall see something interesting."

We run downstairs to go to my study, which occupies the right wing of the house. In the kitchen I find the servant, who is also bewildered by what is happening and stands flicking her apron at great Moths whom she took at first for Bats.

The Great Peacock, it would seem, has taken possession of pretty well every part of the house. What will it be around my prisoner, the cause of this incursion? Luckily, one of the two windows of the study had been left open. The approach is not blocked.

We enter the room, candle in hand. What we see is unforgettable. With a soft flick-flack the great Moths fly around the bell-jar, alight, set off again, come back, fly up to the ceiling and down. They rush at the candle, putting it out with a stroke of their wings; they descend on our shoulders, clinging to our clothes, grazing our faces. The scene suggests a wizard's cave, with its whirl of Bats. Little Paul holds my hand tighter than usual, to keep up his courage.

How many of them are there? About a score. Add to these the number that have strayed into the kitchen, the nursery and the other rooms of the house; and the total of those who have arrived from the outside cannot fall far short of forty. As I said, it was a memorable evening, this

Great Peacock evening. Coming from every direction and apprised I know not how, here are forty lovers eager to pay their respects to the marriageable bride born that morning amid the mysteries of my study.

For the moment let us disturb the swarm of wooers no further. The flame of the candle is a danger to the visitors, who fling themselves into it madly and singe their wings. We will resume the observation tomorrow with an experimental interrogatory thought out beforehand.

But first let us clear the ground and speak of what happens every night during the week that my observation lasts. Each time it is pitch dark, between eight and ten o'clock, when the Moths arrive one by one. It is stormy weather, the sky is very much overcast and the darkness is so profound that even in the open air, in the garden, far from the shadow of the trees, it is hardly possible to see one's hand before one's face.

In addition to this darkness there is the difficulty of access. The house is hidden by tall plane-trees; it is approached by a walk thickly bordered with lilac- and rose-trees, forming a sort of outer vestibule; it is protected against the mistral by clumps of pines and screens of cypresses. Clusters of bushy shrubs make a rampart a few steps away from the door. It is through this tangle of branches, in complete darkness, that the Great Peacock has to tack about to reach the object of his pilgrimage.

Under such conditions, the Brown Owl would not dare leave the hole in his olive-tree. The Moth, better-endowed with his faceted optical organs than the night-bird with its great eyes, goes forward without hesitating and passes through without knocking against things. He directs his tortuous flight so skilfully that, despite the obstacles overcome, he arrives in a state of perfect freshness, with his big wings intact, with not a scratch upon him. The darkness is light enough for him.

Even if we grant that it perceives certain rays unknown to common retinæ, this extraordinary power of sight cannot be what warns the Moth from afar and brings him hurrying to the spot. The distance and the screens interposed make this quite impossible.

Besides, apart from deceptive refractions, of which there is no question in this case, the indications provided by light are so precise that we go straight to the thing seen. Now the Moth sometimes blunders, not as to the general direction which he is to take, but as to the exact spot where the interesting events are happening. I have said that the children's nursery, which is at the side of the house opposite my study, the real goal of my visitors at the present moment, was occupied by the Moths before I went there with a light in my hand. These certainly were ill-informed. There was the same throng of hesitating visitors in the kitchen; but here the light of a lamp, that irresistible lure to nocturnal insects, may have beguiled the eager ones.

Let us consider only the places that were in the dark. In these there are several stray Moths. I find them more or less everywhere around the actual spot aimed at. For instance, when the captive is in my study, the visitors do not all enter by the open window, the safe and direct road, only two or three yards away from the caged prisoner. Several of them come in downstairs, wander about the hall and at most reach the staircase, a blind alley barred at the top by a closed door.

These data tell us that the guests at this nuptial feast do not make straight for their object, as they would if they derived their information from some kind of luminous radiation, whether known or unknown to our physical science. It is something else that apprises them from afar, leads them to the proximity of the exact spot and then leaves the final discovery to the airy uncertainty of random searching. It is very much like the way in which we ourselves are informed by hearing and smell, guides which are far from accurate when we want to decide the precise point of origin of the sound or the smell.

What are the organs of information that direct the rutting Moth on his nightly pilgrimage? One suspects the antennæ, which, in the males, do in fact seem to be questioning space with their spreading tufts of feathers. Are those glorious plumes mere ornaments, or do they at the same time play a part in the perception of the effluvia that guide the enamoured swain? A conclusive experiment seems to present no difficulty. Let us try it.

On the day after the invasion, I find in the study eight of my visitors of the day before. They are perched motionless on the transoms of the second window, which is kept closed. The others, when their dance was over, about ten o'clock in the evening, went out as they came in, that is to say, through the first window, which is left open day and night. Those eight persevering ones are just what I want for my schemes.

With a sharp pair of scissors, without otherwise touching the Moths, I cut off their antennæ, near the base. The patients take hardly any notice of the operation. Not one moves; there is scarcely a flutter of the wings. These are excellent conditions: the wound does not seem at all serious. Undistraught by pain, the Moths bereft of their horns will adapt themselves all the better to my plans. The rest of the day is spent in placid immobility on the cross-bars of the window.

There are still a few arrangements to be made. It is important in particular to shift the scene of operations and not to leave the female before the eyes of the maimed ones at the moment when they resume their nocturnal flight, else the merit of their quest would disappear. I therefore move the bell-jar with its captive and place it under a porch at the other end of the house, some fifty yards from my study.

When night comes, I go to make a last inspection of my eight victims. Six have flown out through the open window; two remain behind, but these have dropped to the floor and no longer have the strength to turn over if I lay them on their backs. They are exhausted, dying. Pray do not blame my surgical work. This quick decrepitude occurs invariably, even without the intervention of my scissors.

Six, in better condition, have gone off. Will they return to the bait that attracted them yesterday? Though deprived of their antennæ, will they be able to find the cage, now put in another place, at a considerable distance from its original position?

The cage is standing in the dark, almost in the open air. From time to time, I go out with a lantern and a Butterfly-net. Each visitor is captured, examined, catalogued and forthwith let loose in an adjoining room, of which I close the door. This gradual elimination will enable me to tell the exact number, with no risk of counting the same Moth more than once. Moreover, the temporary gaol, which is spacious and bare, will in no way endanger the prisoners, who will find a quiet retreat there and plenty of room. I shall take similar precautions during my subsequent investigations.

At half past ten no more arrive. The sitting is over. In

all, twenty-five males have been caught, of whom only one was without antennæ. Therefore, of the six on whom I operated yesterday and who were hale enough to leave my study and go back to the fields, one alone has returned to the bell-jar. It is a poor result, on which I dare not rely when it comes to asserting or denying that the antennæ play a guiding part. We must begin all over again, on a larger scale.

Next morning I pay a visit to the prisoners of the day before. What I see is not encouraging. Many are spread out on the floor, almost lifeless. Several of them give hardly a sign of life when I take them in my fingers. What can I hope from these cripples? Still, let us try. Perhaps they will recover their vigour when the time comes to dance the lovers' round.

The twenty-four new ones undergo amputation of the antennæ. The old, hornless one is left out of count, as dying or close to it. Lastly, the prison-door is left open for the remainder of the day. He who will may leave the room, he who can shall join in the evening festival. In order to put such as go out to the test of searching for the bride, the cage, which they would be sure to notice on the threshold, is once more removed. I shift it to a room in the opposite wing, on the ground-floor. The access to this room is of course left free.

Of the twenty-four deprived of their antennæ, only sixteen go outside. Eight remain, powerless to move. They will soon die where they are. Out of the sixteen who have left, how many are there that return to the cage in the evening? Not one! I sit up to capture just seven, all newcomers, all sporting feathers. This result would seem to show that the amputation of the antennæ is a rather serious matter. Let us not draw conclusions yet: a doubt remains and an important one.

"A nice state I'm in!" said Mouflard, the Bull-pup, when his pitiless breeder has docked his ears. "How dare I show my face before the other Dogs?"

Can it be that my Moths entertain Master Mouflard's apprehensions? Once deprived of their fine plumes, dare they no longer appear amidst their rivals and a-wooing go? Is it bashfulness on their part or lack of guidance? Or might it not rather be exhaustion after a wait that exceeds the duration of an ephemeral flame? Experiment shall tell us.

On the fourth evening, I take fourteen Moths, all new ones, and imprison them, as they arrive, in a room where I intend them to pass the night. Next morning, taking advantage of their daytime immobility, I remove a little of the fur from the center of their corselet. The silky fleece comes off so easily that this slight tonsure does not inconvenience the insects at all; it deprives them of no organ which may be necessary to them later, when the time comes to find the cage. It means nothing to the shorn ones; to me it means the unmistakable sign that the callers have repeated their visit.

This time there are no weaklings incapable of flight. At night, the fourteen shaven Moths escape into the open. Of course the place of the cage is once more changed. In two hours, I capture twenty Moths, including two tonsured ones, no more. Of those who lost their antennæ two days ago, not one puts in an appearance. Their nuptial time is over for good and all.

Only two return out of the fourteen marked with a bald patch. Why do the twelve others hang back, although supplied with what we have assumed to be their guides, their antennary plumes? Why again that formidable list of defaulters, which we find nearly always after a night of sequestration? I perceive but one reply: the Great Peacock is quickly worn out by the ardours of pairing-time.

With a view to his wedding, the one and only object of his life, the Moth is gifted with a wonderful prerogative. He is able to discover the object of his desire in spite of distance, obstacles and darkness. For two or three evenings, he is allowed a few hours wherein to indulge his search and his amorous exploits. If he cannot avail himself of them, all is over: the most exact of compasses fails, the brightest of lamps expires. What is the use of living after that? Stoically we withdraw into a corner and sleep our last sleep, which is the end of our illusions and of our woes alike.

The Great Peacock becomes a Moth only in order to perpetuate his species. He knows nothing of eating. While so many others, jolly companions one and all, flit from flower to flower, unrolling the spiral of their proboscis and dipping it into the honeyed cups, he, the incomparable faster, wholly freed from the bondage of the belly, has no thought of refreshment. His mouth-parts are mere rudiments, vain simulacra, not real organs capable of performing their functions.

Not a sup enters his stomach: a glorious privilege, save that it involves a brief existence. The lamp needs its drop of oil, if it is not to be extinguished. The Great Peacock renounces that drop, but at the same time he renounces long life. Two or three evenings, just time enough to allow the couple to meet, and that is all: the big Moth has lived.

Then what is the meaning of the staying away of those who have lost their antennæ? Does it show that the absence of these organs has made them incapable of finding the wire bell in which the prisoner awaits them? Not at all. Like the shorn ones, whose operation has left them uninjured, they prove only that their time is up. Whether maimed or intact, they are unfit for duty because of their age; and their non-return is valueless as evidence. For lack of the time necessary for experimenting, the part played by the antennæ escapes us. Doubtful it was and doubtful it remains.

My caged prisoner lives for eight days. Every evening she draws for my benefit a swarm of visitors, in varying numbers, now to one part of the house, now to another, as I please. I catch them, as they come, with the net and transfer them, the moment they are captured, to a closed room, in which they spend the night. Next morning, I mark them with a tonsure on the thorax.

The aggregate of the visitors during those eight evenings amounts to a hundred and fifty, an astounding number when I consider how hard I had to seek during the following two years to collect the materials necessary for continuing these observations. Though not impossible to find in my near neighbourhood, the cocoons of the Great Peacock are at least very rare, for old almond-trees, on which the caterpillars live, are scarce in these parts. For two winters I visited every one of those decayed trees at the lower part of the trunk, under the tangle of hard grasses in which they are clad, and time after time I returned empty-handed. Therefore my hundred and fifty Moths came from afar, from very far, within a radius of perhaps a mile and a half or more. How did they know of what was happening in my study?

The perceptive faculties can receive information from a distance by means of three agents: light, sound and smell. Is it permissible to speak of vision in this instance? I will readily admit that sight guides the visitors once they have passed through the open window. But before that, in the mystery out of doors! It would not be enough to grant them the fabulous eye of the Lynx, which was supposed to see through walls; we should have to admit a keenness of sight which could be exercised miles away. It is useless to discuss anything so outrageous; let us pass on.

Sound is likewise out of the question. The great fat Moth, capable of sending a summons to such a distance, is mute even to the most acute hearing. It is just possible that she possesses delicate vibrations, passionate quivers, which might perhaps be perceptible with the aid of an extremely sensitive microphone; but remember that the visitors have to be informed at considerable distances, thousands of yards away. Under these conditions, we cannot waste time thinking of acoustics. That would be to set silence the task of waking the surrounding air.

There remains the sense of smell. In the domain of our senses, scent, better than anything else, would more or less explain the onrush of the Moths, even though they do not find the bait that allures them until after a certain amount of hesitation. Are there, in point of fact, effluvia similar to what we call odour, effluvia of extreme subtlety, absolutely imperceptible to ourselves and yet capable of impressing a sense of smell better-endowed than ours? There is a very simple experiment to be made. It is a question of masking those effluvia, of stifling them under a powerful and persistent odour, which masters the olfactory sense entirely. The too-strong scent will neutralize the very faint one.

I began by sprinkling naphthaline in the room where the males will be received this evening. Also, in the bell-jar, beside the female, I lay a big capsule full of the same stuff. When the visiting-hour comes, I have only to stand in the doorway of the room to get a distinct smell of gasworks. My artifice fails. The Moths arrive as usual, they enter the room, pass through its tarry atmosphere and make for the cage with as much certainty of direction as though in unscented surroundings.

My confidence in the olfactory explanation is shaken. Besides, I am now unable to go on. Worn out by her sterile wait, my prisoner dies on the ninth day, after laying her unfertilized eggs on the wirework of the cage. In the absence of a subject of experiment, there is no more to be done until next year.

This time I shall take my precautions, I shall lay in a stock so as to be able to repeat as often as I wish the experiments which I have already tried and those which I am contemplating. To work, then; and that without delay.

In the summer, I proclaim myself a buyer of caterpillars at a sou apiece. The offer appeals to some urchins in the neighbourhood, my usual purveyors. On Thursdays, emaciated from the horrors of parsing, they scour the fields, find the fat caterpillar from time to time and bring him to me clinging to the end of a stick. They dare not touch him, poor mites; they are staggered at my audacity when I take him in my fingers as they might take the familiar Silk-worm.

Reared on almond-tree branches, my menagerie in a few days supplies me with magnificent cocoons. In the winter, assiduous searches at the foot of the fostering tree complete my collection. Friends interested in my enquiries come to my assistance. In short, by dint of trouble, much running about, commercial bargains and not a few scratches from brambles, I am the possessor of an assortment of cocoons, of which twelve, bulkier and heavier than the others, tell me that they belong to females.

A disappointment awaits me, for May arrives, a fickle month which brings to naught my preparations, the cause of so much anxiety. We have winter back again. The mistral howls, tears the budding leaves from the plane-trees and strews the ground with them. It is as cold as in December. We have to light the fires again at night and resume the thick clothes which we were beginning to leave off.

My Moths are sorely tried. They hatch late and are torpid. Around my wire cages, in which the females wait, one today, another tomorrow, according to the order of their birth, few males or none come from the outside. And yet there are some close at hand, for the plumed gallants resulting from my harvest were placed out in the garden as soon as they were hatched and recognized. Whether near neighbours or strangers from afar, very few arrive; and these are only half-hearted. They enter for a moment, then disappear and do not return. The lovers have grown cold.

It is also possible that the low temperature is unfavourable to the tell-tale effluvia, which might well be enhanced by the warmth and decreased by the cold, as happens with scents. My year is lost. Oh, what laborious work is this experimenting at the mercy of the sudden changes and deceptions of a short season!

I begin all over again, for the third time. I rear caterpillars, I scour the country in search of cocoons. When May returns, I am suitably provided. The weather is fine and responds to my hopes. I once more see the incursions which had struck me so powerfully at the beginning, at the time of the historic invasion which first led to my researches.

Nightly the visitors turn up, in squads of twelve, twenty or more. The female, a lusty, big-bellied matron, clings firmly to the trellis-work of the cage. She makes no movement, gives not so much as a flutter of the wings, seems indifferent to what is going on. Nor is there any odour, so far as the most sensitive nostrils in the household can judge, nor any rustle perceptible to the most delicate hearing among my family, all of whom are called in to bear evidence. In motionless contemplation she waits.

The others, in twos or threes or more, flop down upon the dome of the cage, run about it briskly in every direction, lash it with the tips of their wings in continual movement. There are no affrays between rivals. With not a sign of jealousy in regard to the others suitors, each does his utmost to enter the enclosure. Tiring of their vain attempts, they fly away and join the whirling throng of dancers. Some, giving up all hope, escape through the open window; fresh arrivals take their places; and, on the top of the cage, until ten o'clock in the evening, attempts to approach are incessantly renewed, soon to be abandoned and as soon resumed.

Every evening the cage is moved to a different place. I put it on the north side and the south, on the ground-floor and the first floor, in the right wing and fifty yards away in the left, in the open air or hidden in a distant room. All these sudden displacements, contrived if possible to put the seekers off the scent, do not trouble the Moths in the least. I waste my time and ingenuity in trying to deceive them.

Recollection of places plays no part here. Yesterday, for instance, the female was installed in a certain room. The feathered males came fluttering thither for a couple of hours; several even spent the night there. Next day, at sunset, when I move the cage, all are out of doors. Ephemeral though they be, the newest comers are ready to repeat their nocturnal expeditions a second time and a third. Where will they go first, these veterans of a day?

They know all about the meeting-place of yesterday. One is inclined to think that they will go back to it, guided by memory, and that, finding nothing left, they will proceed elsewhither to continue their investigations. But no: contrary to my expectations, they do nothing of the sort. Not one reappears in the place which was so thickly crowded last night; not one pays even a short visit. The room is recognized as deserted, without the preliminary enquiry which recollection would seem to demand. A more positive guide than memory summons them elsewhere.

Until now the female has been left exposed, under the meshes of a wire gauze. The visitors, whose eyes are used to piercing the blackest gloom, can see her by the vague light of what to us is darkness. What will happen if I imprison her under an opaque cover? According to its nature, will not this cover either set free or arrest the tell-tale effluvia?

Physical science is to-day preparing to give us wireless telegraphy, by means of the Hertzian waves. Can the Great Peacock have anticipated our efforts in this direction? In order to set the surrounding air in motion and to inform pretenders miles away, can the newly-hatched bride have at her disposal electric or magnetic waves, which one sort of screen would arrest and another let through? In a word, does she, in her own manner, employ a kind of wireless telegraphy? I see nothing impossible in this: insects are accustomed to invent things quite as wonderful.

I therefore lodge the female in boxes of various characters. Some are made of tin, some of cardboard, some of wood. All are hermetically closed, are even sealed with stout putty. I also use a glass bell-jar standing on the insulating support of a pane of glass.

Well, under these conditions of strict closing, never a male arrives, not one, however favourable the mildness and quiet of the evening. No matter its nature, whether of metal or glass, of wood or cardboard, the closed receptable forms an insuperable obstacle to the effluvia that betray the captive's whereabouts.

A layer of cotton two fingers thick gives the same result. I place the female in a large jar, tying a sheet of wadding over the mouth by way of a lid. This is enough to keep the neighbourhood in ignorance of the secrets of my laboratory. No male puts in an appearance.

On the other hand, make use of ill-closed, cracked boxes,

or even hide them in a drawer, in a cupboard; and, notwithstanding this added mystery, the Moths will arrive in numbers as great as when they come thronging to the trellised case standing in full view on a table. I have retained a vivid recollection of an evening when the recluse was waiting in a hat-box at the bottom of a closed wall-cupboard. The Moths arrived, went to the door, struck it with their wings, knocked at it to express their wish to enter. Passing wayfarers, coming no one knows whence across the fields, they well knew what was inside there, behind those boards.

We must therefore reject the idea of any means of information similar to that of wireless telegraphy, for the first screen set up, whether a good conductor or a bad, stops the female's signals completely. To give these a free passage and carry them to a distance, one condition is indispensable: the receptacle in which the female is contained must be imperfectly closed, so as to establish a communication between the inner and the outer air. This brings us back to the probability of an odour, though that was contradicted by my experiment with naphthaline.

My stock of cocoons is exhausted and the problem is still obscure. Shall I try again another year, the fourth? I abandon the thought for the following reasons: Moths that mate at night are difficult to observe if I want to watch their intimate actions. The gallant certainly needs no illuminant to attain his ends; but my feeble human powers of vision cannot dispense with one at night. I must have at least a candle, which is often extinguished by the whirling swarm. A lantern saved us from these sudden eclipses; but its dim light, streaked with broad shadows, does not suit a conscientious observer like myself, who wants to see and to see clearly.

Nor is this all. The light of a lamp diverts the Moths from their object, distracts them from their business and, if persistent, gravely compromises the success of the evening. The visitors no sooner enter the room than they make a wild rush for the flame, singe their fluff in it and henceforth, frightened by the scorching received, cease to be trustworthy witnesses. When they are not burnt, when they are kept at a distance by a glass chimney, they perch as closely as they can to the light and there stay, hypnotized.

One evening, the female was in the dining-room, on a table facing the open window. A lighted paraffin-lamp, with a large white-enamel shade, was hanging from the ceiling.

Two of the arrivals alighted on the dome of the cage and fussed around the prisoner; seven others, after greeting her as they passed, made for the lamp, circled about it a little and then, fascinated by the radiant glory of the opal cone, perched on it, motionless, under the shade. Already the children's hands were raised to seize them.

"Don't," I said. "Leave them alone. Let us be hospitable and not disturb these pilgrims to the tabernacle of light."

All that evening, not one of the seven budged. Next morning, they were still there. The intoxication of light had made them forget the intoxication of love.

With creatures so madly enamoured of the radiant flame, precise and prolonged experiment becomes unfeasible the moment the observer requires an artificial illuminant. I give up the Great Peacock and his nocturnal nuptials. I want a Moth with different habits, equally skilled in keeping conjugal appointments, but performing in the daytime.

Before continuing with a subject that fulfils these conditions, let us drop chronological order for a moment and say a few words about a late-comer who arrived after I had completed my enquiries, I mean the Lesser Peacock (*Attacus pavonia minor*, LIN.). Somebody brought me, I don't know where from, a magnificent cocoon loosely wrapped in an ample white-silk envelope. Out of this covering, with its thick, irregular folds, it was easy to extract a case similar in shape to the Great Peacock's, but a good deal smaller. The fore-end, worked into the fashion of an eel-trap by means of free and converging fibres, which prevent access to the dwelling while permitting egress without a breach of the walls, indicated a kinswoman of the big nocturnal Moth; the silk bore the spinner's mark.

And, in point of fact, towards the end of March, on the morning of Palm Sunday, the cocoon with the eel-trap formation provides me with a female of the Lesser Peacock, whom I at once seclude under a wire-gauze bell in my study. I open the window to allow the event to be made known all over the district; I want the visitors, if any come, to find free entrance. The captive grips the wires and does not move for a week.

A gorgeous creature is my prisoner, in her brown velvet streaked with wavy lines. She has white fur around her neck; a speck of carmine at the tip of the upper wings; and four large, eye-shaped spots, in which black, white, red and yellow-ochre are grouped in concentric crescents. The dress is very like that of the Great Peacock, but less dark in colouring. I have seen this Moth, so remarkable for size and costume, three or four times in my life. It was only the other day that I first saw the cocoon. The male I have never seen. I only know that, according to the books, he is half the size of the female and of a brighter and more florid colour, with orange-yellow on the lower wings.

Will he come, the unknown spark, the plume-wearer on whom I have never set eyes, so rare does he appear to be in my part of the country? In his distant hedges will he receive news of the bride that awaits him on my study table? I venture to feel sure of it; and I am right. Here he comes, even sooner than I expected.

On the stroke of noon, as we were sitting down to table, little Paul who is late owing to his eager interest in what is likely to happen, suddenly runs up to us, his cheeks aglow. In his fingers flutters a pretty Moth, a Moth caught that moment hovering in front of my study. Paul shows me his prize; his eyes ask an unspoken question.

"Hullo!" I say. "This is the very pilgrim we were expecting. Let's fold up our napkins and go and see what's happening. We can dine later."

Dinner is forgotten in the presence of the wonders that are taking place. With inconceivable punctuality, the plume-wearers hasten to answer the captive's magic call. They arrive one by one, with a tortuous flight. All of them come from the north. This detail has its significance. As a matter of fact, during the past week we have experienced a fierce return of winter. The north wind has been blowing a gale, killing the imprudent almond-blossoms. It was one of those ferocious storms which, as a rule, usher in the spring in our part of the world. Today the temperature has suddenly grown milder, but the wind is still blowing from the north.

Now at this first visit all the Moths hurrying to the prisoner enter the enclosure from the north; they follow the movement of the air; not one beats against it. If their compass were a sense of smell similar to our own, if they were guided by odoriferous particles dissolved in the air, they ought to arrive from the opposite direction. If they came from the south, we might believe them to be informed by effluvia carried by the wind; coming as they do from the north, through the mistral, that mighty sweeper of the atmosphere, how can we suppose them to have perceived, at a great distance, what we call a smell? This reflux of scented atoms in a direction contrary to the aerial current seems to me inadmissible.

For a couple of hours, in radiant sunshine, the visitors come and go outside the front of the study. Most of them search for a long while, exploring the wall, flitting along the ground. To see their hesitation, one would think that they were at a loss to discover the exact place of the bait that attracts them. Though they have come from very far without a mistake, they seem uncertain of their bearings once they are on the spot. Nevertheless, sooner or later they enter the room and pay their respects to the captive, without much importunity. At two o'clock all is over. Ten Moths came.

All through the week, each time at noon-day, when the light is at its brightest, Moths arrive, but in decreasing numbers. The total is nearly forty. I see no reason to repeat experiments which could add nothing to what I already know; and I confine myself to stating two facts. In the first place, the Lesser Peacock is a day insect, that is to say, he celebrates his wedding in the brilliant light of the middle of the day. He needs radiant sunshine. The Great Peacock, on the contrary, whom he so closely resembles in his adult form and in the work which he does as a caterpillar, requires the dusk of the early hours of the night. Let him who can explain this strange contrast of habits.

VIII

The Song of the Cicada

As anyone knows who has listened to the shrill din of the summer cicadas, these insects are lovers of heat. The hotter the day, the more vehement their music becomes. Thus, Fabre's sun-baked Provence village was to the liking of the insect musicians. His amusing efforts to outdo the din of the sap-drinking cicadas, related here, is taken from THE LIFE OF THE GRASSHOPPER.

MY NEIGHBOURS the peasants say that, at harvest-time, the Cicada sings, "*Sego, sego, sego!* Reap, reap, reap!" to encourage them to work. Whether harvesters of wheat or harvesters of thought, we follow the same occupation, one for the bread of the stomach, the other for the bread of the mind. I can understand their explanation, therefore; and I accept it as an instance of charming simplicity.

Science asks for something better; but she finds in the insect a world that is closed to us. There is no possibility of divining or even suspecting the impression produced by the clash of the cymbals upon those who inspire it. All that I can say is that their impassive exterior seems to denote complete indifference. Let us not insist too much: the private feelings of animals are an unfathomable mystery.

Another reason for doubt is this: those who are sensitive to music always have delicate hearing; and this hearing, a watchful sentinel, should give warning of any danger at the least sound. The birds, those skilled songsters, have an exquisitely fine sense of hearing. Should a leaf stir in the branches, should two wayfarers exchange a word, they will be suddenly silent, anxious, on their guard. How far the Cicada is from such sensibility!

He has very clear sight. His large faceted eyes inform him of what happens on the right and what happens on the left; his three stemmata, like little ruby telescopes, explore the expanse above his head. The moment he sees us coming, he is silent and flies away. But place yourself behind the branch on which he is singing, arrange so that you are not within reach of the five visual organs; and then talk, whistle, clap your hands, knock two stones together. For much less than this, a bird, though it would not see you, would interrupt its singing and fly away terrified. The imperturbable Cicada goes on rattling as though nothing were afoot.

Of my experiments in this matter, I will mention only one, the most memorable. I borrow the municipal artillery, that is to say, the mortars which are made to thunder forth on the feast of the patron-saint. The gunner is delighted to load them for the benefit of the Cicadæ and to come and fire them off at my place. There are two of them, crammed as though for the most solemn rejoicings. No politician making the circuit of his constituency in search of reelection was ever honoured with so much powder. We are careful to leave the windows open, to save the panes from breaking. The two thundering engines are set at the foot of the plane-trees in front of my door. No precautions are taken to mask them: the Cicadæ singing in the branches overhead cannot see what is happening below.

We are an audience of six. We wait for a moment of comparative quiet. The number of singers is checked by each of us, as are the depths and rhythm of the song. We are now ready, with ears pricked up to hear what will happen in the aerial orchestra. The mortar is let off, with a noise like a genuine thunder-clap.

There is no excitement whatever up above. The number of executants is the same, the rhythm is the same, the volume of sound the same. The six witnesses are unanimous: the mighty explosion has in no way affected the song of the Cicadæ. And the second mortar gives an exactly similiar result.

What conclusion are we to draw from this persistence of the orchestra, which is not at all surprised or put out by the firing of a gun? Am I to infer from it that the Cicada is deaf? I will certainly not venture so far as that; but, if any one else, more daring than I, were to make the assertion, I should really not know what arguments to employ in contradicting him. I should be obliged at least to concede that the Cicada is extremely hard of hearing and that we may apply to him the familiar saying, to bawl like a deaf man.

When the Blue-winged Locust takes his luxurious fill of sunshine on a gravelly path and with his great hind-shanks rubs the rough edge of his wing-cases; when the Green Tree-frog, suffering from as chronic a cold as the *Cacan*, swells his throat among the leaves and distends it into a resounding bladder at the approach of a storm, are they both calling to their absent mates? By no means. The bow-strokes of the first produce hardly a perceptible stridulation; the throaty ex-uberance of the second is no more effective: the object of their desire does not come.

Does the insect need these sonorous outbursts, these lo-quacious avowals, to declare its flame? Consult the vast majority, whom the meeting of the two sexes leaves silent. I see in the Grasshopper's fiddle, the Tree-frog's bagpipes and the cymbals of the *Cacan* but so many methods of express-ing the joy of living, the universal joy which every animal species celebrates after its kind.

If any one were to tell me that the Cicadæ strum on their noisy instruments without giving a thought to the sound produced and for the sheer pleasure of feeling themselves alive, just as we rub our hands in a moment of satisfaction, I should not be greatly shocked. That there may be also a secondary object in their concert, an object in which the dumb sex is interested, is quite possible, quite natural, though this has not yet been proved.

IX

The Praying Mantis

The European mantis of which Fabre writes, Mantis religiosa,
*is now a naturalized insect citizen of the United States. About
the time of the Spanish-American War, a nurseryman at
Rochester, N. Y., noticed these striking creatures among his
trees. They had come from the south of France in the form
of egg-cases attached to packing material around nursery
stock. Since then, the Rochester colony has spread north-
ward until the insects are now found across the Canadian
line. At almost the same time the European mantis was
found at Rochester, an Oriental mantis,* Tenodera sinensis
*was discovered by another nurseryman outside of Phila-
delphia, Pa. It, too, had crossed the ocean in the form of an
egg-case attached to packing material. This mantis has now
spread into New England and west along the Great Lakes. A
native species,* Stagmomantis carolina, *is indigenous to the
South. It is found as far north as southern New Jersey. Men-
tion is made in this selection, from* THE LIFE OF THE
GRASSHOPPER, *of the big Grey Locust,* Pachytylus cinerescens
(FAB). *It should be noted that the "Fab"—the abbreviation
of the name of the namer of the insect—does not stand for
Fabre but for Johan Christian Fabricius (1745-1808) the
Danish entomologist and friend of Linnaeus who contributed
so many scientific names to the lists of entomology.*

ANOTHER CREATURE of the south is at least as interesting
as the Cicada, but much less famous, because it makes no
noise. Had Heaven granted it a pair of cymbals, the one
thing needed, its renown would eclipse the great musician's,
for it is most unusual in both shape and habits. Folk here-
abouts call it *lou Prègo-Diéou,* the animal that prays to
God. Its official name is the Praying Mantis (*M. religiosa,*
LIN.).

The language of science and the peasant's artless vocabulary agree in this case and represent the queer creature as a pythoness delivering her oracles or an ascetic rapt in pious ecstasy. The comparison dates a long way back. Even in the time of the Greeks the insect was called Μάντις, the divine, the prophet. The tiller of the soil is not particular about analogies: where points of resemblance are not too clear, he will make up for their deficiencies. He saw on the sunscorched herbage an insect of imposing appearance, drawn up majestically in a half-erect posture. He noticed its gossamer wings, broad and green, trailing like long veils of finest lawn; he saw its forelegs, its arms so to speak, raised to the sky in a gesture of invocation. That was enough; popular imagination did the rest; and behold the bushes from ancient times stocked with Delphic priestesses, with nuns in orison.

Good people, with your childish simplicity, how great was your mistake! Those sanctimonious airs are a mask for Satanic habits; those arms folded in prayer are cut-throat weapons: they tell no beads, they slay whatever passes within range. Forming an exception which one would never have suspected in the herbivorous order of the Orthoptera, the Mantis feeds exclusively on living prey. She is the tigress of the peaceable entomological tribes, the ogress in ambush who levies a tribute of fresh meat. Picture her with sufficient strength; and her carnivorous appetites, combined with her traps of horrible perfection, would make her the terror of the country-side. The *Prègo-Diéou* would become a devilish vampire.

Apart from her lethal implement, the Mantis has nothing to inspire dread. She is not without a certain beauty, in fact, with her slender figure, her elegant bust, her pale-green colouring and her long gauze wings. No ferocious mandibles, opening like shears; on the contrary, a dainty pointed muzzle that seems made for billing and cooing. Thanks to a flexible neck, quite independent of the thorax, the head is able to move freely, to turn to right or left, to bend, to lift itself. Alone among insects, the Mantis directs her gaze; she inspects and examines; she almost has a physiognomy.

Great indeed is the contrast between the body as a whole, with its very pacific aspect, and the murderous mechanism of the forelegs, which are correctly described as raptorial. The haunch is uncommonly long and powerful. Its function is to throw forward the rat-trap, which does not await its victim but goes in search of it. The snare is decked out with some show of finery. The base of the haunch is adorned on the inner surface with a pretty, black mark, having a white spot in the middle; and a few rows of bead-like dots complete the ornamentation.

The thigh, longer still, a sort of flattened spindle, carries on the front half of its lower surface two rows of sharp spikes. In the inner row there are a dozen, alternately black and green, the green being shorter than the black. This alternation of unequal lengths increases the number of cogs and improves the effectiveness of the weapon. The outer row is simpler and has only four teeth. Lastly, three spurs, the longest of all, stand out behind the two rows. In short, the thigh is a saw with two parallel blades, separated by a groove in which the leg lies when folded back.

The leg, which moves very easily on its joint with the thigh, is likewise a double-edged saw. The teeth are smaller, more numerous and closer together than those on the thigh. It ends in a strong hook whose point vies with the finest needle for sharpness, a hook fluted underneath and having a double blade like a curved pruning-knife.

This hook, a most perfect instrument for piercing and tearing, has left me many a painful memory. How often, when Mantis-hunting, clawed by the insect which I had just caught and not having both hands at liberty, have I been obliged to ask somebody else to release me from my tenacious captive! To try to free yourself by force, without first disengaging the claws implanted in your flesh, would expose you to scratches similar to those produced by the thorns of a rose-tree. None of our insects is so troublesome to handle. The Mantis claws you with her pruning-hooks, pricks you with her spikes, seizes you in her vise and makes self-defence almost impossible if, wishing to keep your prize alive, you refrain from giving the pinch of the thumb that would put an end to the struggle by crushing the creature.

When at rest, the trap is folded and pressed back against the chest and looks quite harmless. There you have the insect praying. But, should a victim pass, the attitude of prayer is dropped abruptly. Suddenly unfolded, the three long sections of the machine throw to a distance their terminal grapnel, which harpoons the prey and, in returning, draws it back between the two saws. The vice closes with a movement like that of the fore-arm and the upper arm; and all is over: Locusts, Grasshoppers and others even more powerful, once

caught in the mechanism with its four rows of teeth, are ir-
retrievably lost. Neither their desperate fluttering nor their
kicking will make the terrible engine release its hold.

An uninterrupted study of the Mantis' habits is not practicable in the open fields; we must rear her at home. There
is no difficulty about this; she does not mind being interned
under glass, on condition that she be well fed. Offer her
choice viands, served up fresh daily, and she will hardly
feel her absence from the bushes.

As cages for my captives I have some ten large wire-gauze
dish-covers, the same that are used to protect meat from
the Flies. Each stands in a pan filled with sand. A dry tuft
of thyme and a flat stone on which the laying may be done
later constitute all the furniture. These huts are placed in a
row on the large table in my insect laboratory, where the
sun shines on them for the best part of the day. I install
my captives in them, some singly, some in groups.

It is in the second fortnight of August that I begin to
come upon the adult Mantis in the withered grass and on
the brambles by the roadside. The females, already notably
corpulent, are more frequent from day to day. Their slender
companions, on the other hand, are rather scarce; and I
sometimes have a good deal of difficulty in making up my
couples, for there is an appalling consumption of these
dwarfs in the cages. Let us keep these atrocities for later
and speak first of the females.

They are great eaters, whose maintenance, when it has to
last for some months, is none too easy. The provisions,
which are nibbled at disdainfully and nearly all wasted, have
to be renewed almost every day. I trust that the Mantis is
more economical on her native bushes. When game is not
plentiful, no doubt she devours every atom of her catch; in
my cages she is extravagant, often dropping and abandoning
the rich morsel after a few mouthfuls, without deriving any
further benefit from it. This appears to be her particular
method of beguiling the tedium of captivity.

To cope with these extravagant ways I have to employ
assistants. Two or three small local idlers, bribed by the
promise of a slice of melon or bread-and-butter, go morning
and evening to the grass-plots in the neighbourhood and fill
their game-bags—cases made of reed-stumps—with live Locusts and Grasshoppers. I on my side, net in hand, make a

daily circuit of my enclosure, in the hope of obtaining some choice morsel for my boarders.

These tit-bits are intended to show me to what lengths the Mantis' strength and daring can go. They include the big Grey Locust (*Pachytylus cinerescens*, FAB.), who is larger than the insect that will consume him; the White-faced Decticus, armed with a vigorous pair of mandibles whereof our fingers would do well to fight shy; the quaint Tryxalis, who wears a pyramid-shaped mitre on her head; the Vine Ephippiger, who clashes cymbals and sports a sword at the bottom of her pot-belly. To this assortment of game that is not any too easy to tackle, let us add two monsters, two of the largest Spiders of the district: the Silky Epeira, whose flat, festooned abdomen is the size of a franc piece; and the Cross Spider, or Diadem Epeira, who is hideously hairy and obese.

I cannot doubt that the Mantis attacks such adversaries in the open, when I see her, under my covers, boldly giving battle to whatever comes in sight. Lying in wait among the bushes, she must profit by the fat prizes offered by chance even as, in the wire cage, she profits by the treasures due to my generosity. Those big hunts, full of danger, are no new thing; they form part of her normal existence. Nevertheless they appear to be rare, for want of opportunity, perhaps to the Mantis' deep regret.

Locusts of all kinds, Butterflies, Dragonflies, large Flies, Bees and other moderate-sized captures are what we usually find in the lethal limbs. Still the fact remains that, in my cages, the daring huntress recoils before nothing. Sooner or later, Grey Locust and Decticus, Epeira and Tryxalis are harpooned, held tight between the saws and crunched with gusto. The facts are worth describing.

At the sight of the Grey Locust who has heedlessly approached along the trelliswork of the cover, the Mantis gives a convulsive shiver and suddenly adopts a terrifying posture. An electric shock would not produce a more rapid effect. The transition is so abrupt, the attitude so threatening that the observer beholding it for the first time at once hesitates and draws back his fingers, apprehensive of some unknown danger. Old hand as I am, I cannot even now help being startled, should I happen to be thinking of something else.

You see before you, most unexpectedly, a sort of bogeyman or Jack-in-the-box. The wing-covers open and are turned back on either side, slantingly; the wings spread to their full extent and stand erect like parallel sails or like a huge heraldic crest towering over the back; the tip of the abdomen curls upwards like a crosier, rises and falls, relaxing with short jerks and a sort of sough, a "Whoof! Whoof!" like that of a Turkey-cock spreading his tail. It reminds one of the puffing of a startled Adder.

Planted defiantly on its four hind-legs, the insect holds its long bust almost upright. The murderous legs, originally folded and pressed together upon the chest, open wide, forming a cross with the body and revealing the arm-pits decorated with rows of beads and a black spot with a white dot in the centre. These two faint imitations of the eyes in a Peacock's tail, together with the dainty ivory beads, are warlike ornaments kept hidden at ordinary times. They are taken from the jewel-case only at the moment when we have to make ourselves brave and terrible for battle.

Motionless in her strange posture, the Mantis watches the Locust, with her eyes fixed in his direction and her head turning as on a pivot whenever the other changes his place. The object of this attitudinizing is evident: the Mantis wants to strike terror into her dangerous quarry, to paralyse it with fright, for, unless demoralized by fear, it would prove too formidable.

Does she succeed in this? Under the shiny head of the Decticus, behind the long face of the Locust, who can tell what passes? No sign of excitement betrays itself to our eyes on those impassive masks. Nevertheless it is certain that the threatened one is aware of the danger. He sees standing before him a spectre, with uplifted claws, ready to fall upon him; he feels that he is face to face with death; and he fails to escape while there is yet time. He who excels in leaping and could so easily hop out of reach of those talons, he, the big-thighed jumper, remains stupidly where he is, or even draws nearer with a leisurely step.

They say that little birds, paralysed with terror before the open jaws of the Snake, spell-bound by the reptile gaze, lose their power of flight and allow themselves to be snapped up. The Locust often behaves in much the same way. See him within reach of the enchantress. The two grapnels fall, the claws strike, the double saws close and clutch. In vain the poor wretch protests: he chews space with his mandibles and, kicking desperately, strikes nothing but the air. His fate is sealed. The Mantis furls her wings, her battle-standard; she resumes her normal posture; and the meal begins.

In a fit of hunger, after a fast of some days' duration, the Praying Mantis will gobble up a Grey Locust whole, except for the wings, which are too dry; and yet the victim of her voracity is as big as herself, or even bigger. Two hours are enough for consuming this monstrous head of game. An orgy of the sort is rare. I have witnessed it once or twice and have always wondered how the gluttonous creature found room for so much food and how it reversed in its favour the axiom that the cask must be greater than its contents. I can but admire the lofty privileges of a stomach through which matter merely passes, being at once digested, dissolved and done away with.

The usual bill of fare in my cages consists of Locusts of greatly varied species and sizes. It is interesting to watch the Mantis nibbling her Acridian, firmly held in the grip of her two murderous forelegs. Notwithstanding the fine, pointed muzzle, which seems scarcely made for this gorging, the whole dish disappears, with the exception of the wings, of which only the slightly fleshy base is consumed. The legs, the tough skin, everything goes down. Sometimes the Mantis seizes one of the big hinder thighs by the knuckle-end, lifts it to her mouth, tastes it and crunches it with a little air of satisfaction. The Locust's fat and juicy thigh may well be a choice morsel for her, even as a leg of mutton is for us.

The prey is first attacked in the neck. While one of the two lethal legs holds the victim transfixed through the middle of the body, the other presses the head and makes the neck open upwards. The Mantis' muzzle roots and nibbles at this weak point in the armour with some persistency. A large wound appears in the head. The Locust gradually ceases kicking and becomes a lifeless corpse; and, from this moment, freer in its movements, the carnivorous insect picks and chooses its morsel.

The Mantis naturally wants to devour the victuals in peace, without being troubled by the plunges of a victim who absolutely refuses to be devoured. A meal liable to interruptions lacks savour. Now the principal means of defence in this case are the hind-legs, those vigorous levers which can kick out so brutally and which moreover are armed with toothed saws that would rip open the Mantis' bulky paunch if by ill-luck they happen to graze it. What shall we do to reduce them to helplessness, together with the others, which are not dangerous but troublesome all the same, with their desperate gesticulations?

Strictly speaking, it would be practicable to cut them off one by one. But that is a long process and attended with a certain risk. The Mantis has hit upon something better. She has an intimate knowledge of the anatomy of the spine. By first attacking her prize at the back of the half-opened neck and munching the cervical ganglia, she destroys the muscular energy at its main seat; and inertia supervenes, not suddenly and completely, for the clumsily-constructed Locust has not the Bee's exquisite and frail vitality, but still sufficiently, after the first mouthfuls. Soon the kicking and the gesticulating die down, all movement ceases and the game, however big it be, is consumed in perfect quiet.

X

Mating of the Mantis

In regions where the mantis is found, museums and zoos are flooded with telephone calls each autumn when the insects reach full size. Few other species arouse more general interest than these large, striking appearing members of the Orthoptera order. I have given several chapters relating to the Praying Mantis, partly because of the unusual interest in the insect and partly because Fabre is at his best in describing the strange habits of the creature. His outlook on the insects was sympathetic but not sentimental. He recorded facts. The following selection is from the seventh chapter of THE LIFE OF THE GRASSHOPPER.

THE LITTLE THAT WE HAVE SEEN of the Mantis' habits hardly tallies with what we might have expected from her popular name. To judge by the term *Prègo-Diéou*, we should look to see a placid insect, deep in pious contemplation; and we find ourselves in the presence of a cannibal, of a ferocious spectre munching the brain of a panic-stricken victim. Nor is even this the most tragic part. The Mantis has in store for us, in her relations with her own kith and kin, manners even more atrocious than those prevailing among the Spiders, who have an evil reputation in this respect.

To reduce the number of cages on my big table and give myself a little more space while still retaining a fair-sized menagerie, I install several females, sometimes as many as a dozen, under one cover. So far as accommodation is concerned, no fault can be found with the common lodging. There is room and to spare for the evolutions of my captives, who naturally do not want to move about much with their unwieldy bellies. Hanging to the trelliswork of the dome, motionless, they digest their food or else await an

110

unwary passer-by. Even so do they act when at liberty in the thickets.

Cohabitation has its dangers. I know that even Donkeys, those peace-loving animals, quarrel when hay is scarce in the manger. My boarders, who are less complaisant, might well, in a moment of dearth, become sour-tempered and fight among themselves. I guard against this by keeping the cages well supplied with Locusts, renewed twice a day. Should civil war break out, famine cannot be pleaded as the excuse.

At first, things go pretty well. The community lives in peace, each Mantis grabbing and eating whatever comes near her, without seeking strife with her neighbours. But this harmonious period does not last long. The bellies swell, the eggs are ripening in the ovaries, marriage and laying-time are at hand. Then a sort of jealous fury bursts out, though there is an entire absence of males who might be held responsible for feminine rivalry. The working of the ovaries seems to pervert the flock, inspiring its members with a mania for devouring one another. There are threats, personal encounters, cannibal feasts. Once more the spectral pose appears, the hissing of the wings, the fearsome gesture of the grapnels outstretched and uplifted in the air. No hostile demonstration in front of a Grey Locust or White-faced Decticus could be more menacing.

For no reason that I can gather, two neighbours suddenly assume their attitude of war. They turn their heads to right and left, provoking each other, exchanging insulting glances. The "Puff! Puff!" of the wings rubbed by the abdomen sounds the charge. When the duel is to be limited to the first scratch received, without more serious consequences, the lethal fore-arms, which are usually kept folded, open like the leaves of a book and fall back sideways, encircling the long bust. It is a superb pose, but less terrible than that adopted in a fight to the death.

Then one of the grapnels, with a sudden spring, shoots out to its full length and strikes the rival; it is no less abruptly withdrawn and resumes the defensive. The adversary hits back. The fencing is rather like that of two Cats boxing each other's ears. At the first blood drawn from her flabby paunch, or even before receiving the least wound, one of the duellists confesses herself beaten and retires. The other furls her battle-standard and goes off elsewhither to meditate the capture of a Locust, keeping apparently calm, but ever ready to repeat the quarrel.

Very often, events take a more tragic turn. At such times, the full posture of the duels to the death is assumed. The murderous fore-arms are unfolded and raised in the air. Woe to the vanquished! The other seizes her in her vise and then and there proceeds to eat her, beginning at the neck, of course. The loathsome feast takes place as calmly as though it were a matter of crunching up a Grasshopper. The diner enjoys her sister as she would a lawful dish; and those around do not protest, being quite willing to do as much on the first occasion.

Oh, what savagery! Why, even Wolves are said not to eat one another. The Mantis has no such scruples; she banquets off her fellows when there is plenty of her favourite game, the Locust, around her. She practises the equivalent of cannibalism, that hideous peculiarity of man.

These aberrations, these child-bed cravings can reach an even more revolting stage. Let us watch the pairing and, to avoid the disorder of a crowd, let us isolate the couples under different covers. Each pair shall have its own home, where none will come to disturb the wedding. And let us not forget the provisions, with which we will keep them well supplied, so that there may be no excuse of hunger.

It is near the end of August. The male, that slender swain, thinks the moment propitious. He makes eyes at his strapping companion; he turns his head in her direction; he bends his neck and throws out his chest. His little pointed face wears an almost impassioned expression. Motionless, in this posture, for a long time he contemplates the object of his desire. She does not stir, is as though indifferent. The lover, however, has caught a sign of acquiescence, a sign of which I do not know the secret. He goes nearer; suddenly he spreads his wings, which quiver with a convulsive tremor. That is his declaration. He rushes, small as he is, upon the back of his corpulent companion, clings on as best he can, steadies his hold. As a rule, the preliminaries last a long time. At last, coupling takes place and is also long drawn out, lasting sometimes for five or six hours.

Nothing worthy of attention happens between the two motionless partners. They end by separating, but only to unite again in a more intimate fashion. If the poor fellow is loved by his lady as the vivifier of her ovaries, he is also loved as a piece of highly-flavoured game. And, that same day, or at latest on the morrow, he is seized by his spouse, who first gnaws his neck, in accordance with precedent, and then eats him deliberately, by little mouthfuls, leaving only the wings. Here we have no longer a case of jealousy in the harem, but simply a depraved appetite.

I was curious to know what sort of reception a second male might expect from a recently fertilized female. The result of my enquiry was shocking. The Mantis, in many cases, is never sated with conjugal raptures and banquets. After a rest that varies in length, whether the eggs be laid or not, a second male is accepted and then devoured like the first. A third succeeds him, performs his function in life, is eaten and disappears. A fourth undergoes a like fate. In the course of two weeks I thus see one and the same Mantis use up seven males. She takes them all to her bosom and makes them all pay for the nuptial ecstasy with their lives.

Orgies such as this are frequent, in varying degrees, though there are exceptions. On very hot days, highly charged with electricity, they are almost the general rule. At such times the Mantes are in a very irritable mood. In the cages containing a large colony, the females devour one another more than ever; in the cages containing separate pairs, the males, after coupling, are more than ever treated as an ordinary prey.

I should like to be able to say, in mitigation of these conjugal atrocities, that the Mantis does not behave like this in a state of liberty; that the male, after doing his duty, has time to get out of the way, to make off, to escape from his terrible mistress, for in my cages he is given a respite, lasting sometimes until next day. What really occurs in the thickets I do not know, chance, a poor resource, having never instructed me concerning the love-affairs of the Mantis when at large. I can only go by what happens in the cages, where the captives, enjoying plenty of sunshine and food and spacious quarters, do not seem to suffer from home-sickness in any way. What they do here they must also do under normal conditions.

Well, what happens there utterly refutes the idea that the males are given time to escape. I find, by themselves, a horrible couple engaged as follows. The male, absorbed in the performance of his vital functions, holds the female in a tight embrace. But the wretch has no head; he has no neck; he has hardly a body. The other, with her muzzle turned over her shoulder continues very placidly to gnaw what remains of the gentle swain. And, all the time, that masculine stump, holding on firmly, goes on with the business!

Love is stronger than death, men say. Taken literally, the aphorism has never received a more brilliant confirmation. A headless creature, an insect amputated down to the middle of the chest, a very corpse persists in endeavouring to give life. It will not let go until the abdomen, the seat of the procreative organs, is attacked.

Eating the lover after consummation of marriage, making a meal of the exhausted dwarf, henceforth good for nothing, can be understood, to some extent, in the insect world, which has no great scruples in matters of sentiment; but gobbling him up during the act goes beyond the wildest dreams of the most horrible imagination. I have seen it done with my own eyes and have not yet recovered from my astonishment.

XI

The Hatching of the Mantis

Hardly larger than mosquitoes when they hatch from the hardened froth-mass that has been their insulated winter home, the young insects disappear among the grass and weeds. They are rarely noticed until late in summer when their large size makes them conspicuous and their newly-acquired wings enable them to travel about over greater distances. The chalcis parasites that prey upon the mantis are species of a widely distributed group. Some have the ability of laying eggs that multiply themselves, 2,000 or more individuals resulting from a single egg. This selection from THE LIFE OF THE GRASSHOPPER *originally appeared in the ninth chapter of that book.*

THE EGGS OF THE PRAYING MANTIS usually hatch in bright sunshine, at about ten o'clock on a mid-June morning. The median band or exit-zone is the only portion of the nest that affords an outlet to the youngsters.

From under each scale of that zone we see slowly appearing a blunt, transparent protuberance, followed by two large black specks, which are the eyes. Softly the new-born grub slips under the thin plate and half-releases itself. Is it the little Mantis in his larval form, so nearly allied to that of the adult? Not yet. It is a transition organism. The head is opalescent, blunt, swollen, with palpitations caused by the flow of the blood. The rest is tinted reddish-yellow. It is quite easy to distinguish, under a general overall, the large black eyes clouded by the veil that covers them, the mouth-parts flattened against the chest, the legs plastered to the body from front to back. Altogether, with the exception of the very obvious legs, the whole thing, with its big blunt head, its eyes, its delicate abdominal segmentation and its boatlike shape, reminds us somewhat of the first state of the Cicadæ on leaving the egg, a state which is pictured exactly by a tiny, finless fish.

Here then is a second instance of an organization of very brief duration having as its function to bring into the light of day, through narrow and difficult passes, a microscopic creature whose limbs, if free, would, because of their length, be an insurmountable impediment. To enable him to emerge from the exiguous tunnel of his twig, a tunnel bristling with woody fibres and blocked with shells already empty, the Cicada is born swathed in bands and endowed with a boat shape, which is eminently suited to slipping easily through an awkward passage. The young Mantis is exposed to similar difficulties. He has to emerge from the depths of the nest through narrow, winding ways, in which full-spread, slender limbs would not be able to find room. The high stilts, the murderous harpoons, the delicate antennæ, organs which will be most useful presently, in the brushwood, would now hinder the emergence, would make it very laborious, impossible. The creature therefore comes into existence swaddled and furthermore takes the shape of a boat.

The case of the Cicada and the Mantis opens up a new vein to us in the inexhaustible entomological mine. I extract from it a law which other and similar facts, picked up more or less everywhere, will certainly not fail to confirm. The true larva is not always the direct product of the egg. When the new-born grub is likely to experience special difficulties in effecting its deliverance, an accessory organism, which I shall continue to call the primary larva, precedes the genuine larval state and has as its function to bring to the light of day the tiny creature which is incapable of releasing itself.

To go on with our story, the primary larvæ show themselves under the thin plates of the exit-zone. A vigorous flow of humours occurs in the head, swelling it out and converting it into a diaphanous and ever-throbbing blister. In this way the splitting-apparatus is prepared. At the same time, the little creature, half-caught under its scale, sways, pushes forward, draws back. Each swaying is accompanied by an increase of the swelling in the head. At last the prothorax arches and the head is bent low towards the chest. The tunic bursts across the prothorax. The little animal tugs, wriggles, sways, bends and straightens itself again. The legs are drawn from their sheaths; the antennæ, two long parallel threads, are likewise released. The creature is now fastened to the nest only by a worn-out cord. A few shakes complete the deliverance.

We here have the insect in its genuine larval form. All that remains behind is a sort of irregular cord, a shapeless clout which the least breath blows about like a flimsy bit of fluff. It is the exit-tunic violently shed and reduced to a mere rag.

The hatching does not take place all over the nest at one time, but rather in sections, in successive swarms which may be separated by intervals of two days or more. The pointed end, containing the last eggs, usually begins. This inversion of chronological order, calling the last to the light of day before the first, may well be due to the shape of the nest. The thin end, which is more accessible to the stimulus of a fine day, wakes up before the blunt end, which is larger and does not so soon acquire the necessary amount of heat.

Sometimes, however, although still broken up in swarms, the hatching embraces the whole length of the exit-zone. A striking sight indeed is the sudden exodus of a hundred young Mantes. Hardly does the tiny creature show its black eyes under a scale before others appear instantly, in their numbers. It is as though a certain shock were being communicated from one to another, as though an awakening signal were transmitted, so swiftly does the hatching spread all round. Almost in a moment the median band is covered with young Mantes who run about feverishly, stripping themselves of their rent garments.

The nimble little creatures do not stay long on the nest. They let themselves drop off or else clamber into the nearest foliage. All is over in less than twenty minutes. The common cradle resumes its peaceful condition, prior to furnishing a new legion a few days later; and so on until all the eggs are finished.

I have witnessed this exodus as often as I wished to, either out of doors, in my enclosure, where I had deposited in sunny places the nests gathered more or less everywhere during my winter leisure, or else in the seclusion of a greenhouse, where I thought, in my simplicity, that I should be better able to protect the budding family. I have witnessed the hatching twenty times if I have once; and I have always beheld a scene of unforgettable carnage. The roundbellied Mantis may procreate germs by the thousands: she will never have enough to cope with the devourers who are destined to decimate the breed from the moment that it leaves the egg.

The Ants above all are zealous exterminators. Daily I surprise their ill-omened visits on my rows of nests. It is vain for me to intervene, however seriously; their assiduity never slackens. They seldom succeed in making a breach in the fortress: that is too difficult; but, greedy of the dainty flesh in course of formation inside, they await a favourable opportunity, they lie in wait for the exit.

Despite my daily watchfulness, they are there the moment that the young Mantes appear. They grab them by the abdomen, pull them out of their sheaths, cut them up. You see a piteous fray between tender babes gesticulating as their only means of defence and ferocious brigands carrying their *spolia opima* at the end of their mandibles. In less than no time the massacre of the innocents is consummated; and all that remains of the flourishing family is a few scattered survivors who have escaped by accident.

The future assassin, the scourge of the insect race, the terror of the Locust on the brushwood, the dread devourer of fresh meat, is herself devoured, from her birth, by one of the least of that race, the Ant. The ogress, prolific to excess, sees her family thinned by the dwarf. But the slaughter is not long continued. So soon as she has acquired a little firmness from the air and strengthened her legs, the Mantis ceases to be attacked. She trots about briskly among the Ants, who fall back as she passes, no longer daring to tackle her. With her grappling-legs brought close to her chest, like arms ready for self-defence, already she strikes awe into them by her proud bearing.

A second connoisseur in tender meats pays no heed to these threats. This is the little Grey Lizard, the lover of sunny walls. Appraised I know not how of the quarry, here he comes, picking up one by one, with the tip of his slender tongue, the stray insects that have escaped the Ants. They make a small mouthful but an exquisite one, so it seems, to judge by the blinking of the reptile's eye. For each little wretch gulped down, its lid half-closes, a sign of profound satisfaction. I drive away the bold Lizard who ventures to perpetrate his raid before my eyes. He comes back again and, this time, pays dearly for his rashness. If I let him have his way, I should have nothing left.

Is this all? Not yet. Another ravager, the smallest of all but not the least formidable, has anticipated the Lizard and the Ant. This is a very tiny Hymenopteron armed with a probe, a Chalcis, who establishes her eggs in the newly-built nest. The Mantis' brood shares the fate of the Cicada's: parasitic vermin attack the eggs and empty the shells. Out of all that I have collected I often obtain nothing or hardly anything. The Chalcis has been that way.

Let us gather up what the various exterminators, known or unknown, have left me. When newly hatched, the larva is of a pale hue, white faintly tinged with yellow. The swelling of its head soon diminishes and disappears. Its colour is not long in darkening and turns light-brown within twenty-four hours. The little Mantis very nimbly lifts up her grappling-legs, opens and closes them; she turns her head to right and left; she curls her abdomen. The fully-developed larva has no greater litheness and agility. For a few minutes the family stops where it is, swarming over the nest; then it scatters at random on the ground and the plants hard by.

XII

How I Met the Mason-bee

At the time of the events recorded here, Fabre had just obtained a diploma from the normal school at Avignon and began his teaching career as a schoolmaster at Carpentras. He was then nineteen years old. His salary, of which he spent his whole first month's income to purchase an illustrated book on insects, was $140 a year. THE MASON-BEES *is the source of the following selection.*

IT WAS WHEN I first began to teach, about 1843, that I made the Mason-bee's acquaintance. I had left the normal school at Vaucluse, some months before, with my diploma and all the simple enthusiasm of my eighteen years, and had been sent to Carpentras, there to manage the primary school attached to the college.

Among the subjects taught, one in particular appealed to both master and pupils. This was open-air geometry, practical surveying. The college had none of the necessary outfit; but, with my fat pay—seven hundred francs a year, if you please!—I could not hesitate over the expense. A surveyor's chain and stakes, arrows, level, square and compass were bought with my money. A microscopic graphometer, not much larger than the palm of one's hand and costing perhaps five francs, was provided by the establishment. There was no tripod to it; and I had one made. In short, my equipment was complete.

And so, when May came, once every week we left the gloomy schoolroom for the fields. It was a regular holiday. The boys disputed for the honour of carrying the stakes, divided into bundles of three; and more than one shoulder, as we walked through the town, felt the reflected glory of those erudite rods. I myself—why conceal the fact?—was not without a certain satisfaction as I piously carried that most delicate and precious apparatus, the historic five-franc graphometer. The scene of operations was an untilled, flinty plain, a *harmas*, as we call it in the district. Here, no curtain of green hedges or shrubs prevented me from keeping an eye upon my staff; here—an indispensable condition—I had not the irresistible temptation of the unripe apricots to fear for my scholars. The plain stretched far and wide, covered with nothing but flowering thyme and rounded pebbles. There was ample scope for every imaginable polygon; trapezes and triangles could be combined in all sorts of ways. The inaccessible distances had ample elbow-room; and there was even an old ruin, once a pigeon-house, that lent its perpendicular to the graphometer's performances.

Well, from the very first day, my attention was attracted by something suspicious. If I sent one of the boys to plant a stake, I would see him stop frequently on his way, bend down, stand up again, look about and stoop once more, neglecting his straight line and his signals. Another, who was told to pick up the arrows, would forget the iron pin and take up a pebble instead; and a third, deaf to the measurements of angles, would crumble a clod of earth between his fingers. Most of them were caught licking a bit of straw. The polygon came to a full stop, the diagonals suffered. What could the mystery be?

I enquired; and everything was explained. A born searcher and observer, the scholar had long known what the master had not yet heard of, namely, that there was a big black Bee who made clay nests on the pebbles in the *harmas*. These nests contained honey; and my surveyors used to open them and empty the cells with a straw. The honey, although rather strong-flavoured, was most acceptable. I acquired a taste for it myself and joined the nest-hunters, putting off the polygon till later. It was thus that I first saw Réaumur's Mason-bee, knowing nothing of her history and, for that matter, knowing nothing of her historian.

The magnificent Bee herself, with her dark-violet wings and black-velvet raiment, her rustic edifices on the sun-blistered pebbles amid the thyme, her honey, providing a diversion from the severities of the compass and the square, all made a great impression on my mind; and I wanted to know more than I had learned from the schoolboys, which was just how to rob the cells of their honey with a straw. As it happened, my bookseller had a gorgeous work on insects for sale. It was called *Histoire naturelle des animaux*

articulés, by de Castelnau, E. Blanchard and Lucas, and
boasted a multitude of most attractive illustrations; but the
price of it, the price of it! No matter; was not my splendid
income supposed to cover everything, food for the mind as
well as food for the body? Anything extra that I gave to
the one I could save upon the other: a method of balancing
painfully familiar to those who look to science for their live-
lihood. The purchase was effected. That day my professional
emoluments were severely strained: I devoted a month's
salary to the acquisition of the book. I had to resort to
miracles of economy for some time to come before making
up the enormous deficit.

The book was devoured; there is no other word for it. In
it, I learned the name of my black Bee; I read for the first
time various details of the habits of insects; I found, surrounded in my eyes with a sort of halo, the revered names of
Réaumur, Huber and Léon Dufour; and, while I turned
over the pages for the hundredth time, a voice within me
seemed to whisper:

"You also shall be of their company!"

XIII

Experiments with Mason-bees

"The best of witnesses," Fabre used to say, "are experiments." In this chapter, taken from THE MASON-BEES, *he is drawing from such witnesses one of the most amazing of all examples of the limitations of instinct, the story of an insect that bites its way through masonry and then dies a prisoner within a thin paper shell. One of Fabre's revered predecessors in the study of the insects was Réne Antoine Ferchault de Réaumur, French inventor and scientist. During his lifetime, from 1683 to 1757, Réaumur conducted many experiments, particularly with bees and ants. In several of his books, as in this chapter, Fabre pays homage to the pioneer work he accomplished.*

AS THE NESTS of the Mason-bee of the Walls are erected on small-sized pebbles, which can be easily carried wherever you like and moved about from one place to another, without disturbing either the work of the builder or the repose of the occupants of the cells, they lend themselves readily to practical experiment, the only method that can throw a little light on the nature of instinct. To study the insect's mental faculties to any purpose, it is not enough for the observer to be able to profit by some happy combination of circumstances: he must know how to produce other combinations, vary them as much as possible and to test them by substitution and interchange. Lastly, to provide science with a solid basis of facts, he must experiment. In this way, the evidence of formal records will one day dispel the fantastic legends with which our books are crowded: the Sacred Beetle calling on his comrades to lend a helping hand in dragging his pellet out of a rut; the Sphex cutting up her fly so as to be able to carry him despite the obstacle of the wind; and all the other fallacies which are the stock-in-trade of those who wish to see in the animal world what is not really there. In this way, again, materials will be prepared which will one day be worked up by the hand of a master and consign hasty and unfounded theories to oblivion.

Réaumur, as a rule, confines himself to stating facts as he sees them in the normal course of events and does not try to probe deeper into the insect's ingenuity by means of artificially produced conditions. In his time, everything had yet to be done; and the harvest was so great that the illustrious harvester went straight to what was most urgent, the gathering of the crop, and left his successors to examine the grain and the ear in detail. Nevertheless, in connection with the Chalicodoma of the Walls, he mentions an experiment made by his friend, Duhamel. He tells us how a Mason-bee's nest was enclosed in a glass funnel, the mouth of which was covered merely with a bit of gauze. From it there issued three males, who, after vanquishing mortar as hard as stone, either never thought of piercing the flimsy gauze or else deemed the work beyond their strength. The three Bees died under the funnel. Réaumur adds that insects generally know only how to do what they have to do in the ordinary course of nature.

The experiment does not satisfy me, for two reasons: first, to ask workers equipped with tools for cutting clay as hard as granite to cut a piece of gauze does not strike me as a happy inspiration; you cannot expect a navvy's pickaxe to do the same work as a dressmaker's scissors. Secondly, the transparent glass prison seems to me ill-chosen. As soon as the insect has made a passage through the thickness of its earthen dome, it finds itself in broad daylight; and to it daylight means the final deliverance, means liberty. It strikes against an invisible obstacle, the glass; and to it glass is nothing at all and yet an obstruction. On the far side, it sees free space, bathed in sunshine. It wears itself out in efforts to fly there, unable to understand the futile nature of its attempts against that strange barrier which it cannot see. It perishes, at last, of exhaustion, without, in its obstinacy, giving a glance at the gauze closing the conical chimney. I must devise a means of renewing the experiment under better conditions.

The obstacle which I select is ordinary brown paper, stout enough to keep the insect in the dark and thin enough not to offer serious resistance to the prisoner's efforts. As there is a great difference, in so far as the actual nature of the barrier is concerned, between a paper partition and a clay ceiling, let us begin by enquiring if the Mason-bee of the Walls knows how or rather is able to make her way through one of these partitions. The mandibles are pickaxes suitable for breaking through hard mortar: are they also scissors capable of cutting a thin membrane? This is the point to look into first of all.

In February, by which time the insect is in its perfect state, I take a certain number of cocoons, without damaging them, from their cells and insert them each in a separate stump of reed, closed at one end by the natural wall of the node and open at the other. These pieces of reed represent the cells of the nest. The cocoons are introduced with the insect's head turned toward the opening. Lastly, my artificial cells are closed in different ways. Some receive a stopper of kneaded clay, which, when dry, will correspond in thickness and consistency with the mortar ceiling of the natural nest. Others are plugged with a cylinder of sorghum, at least a centimetre thick; and the remainder with a disk of brown paper solidly fastened by the edge. All these bits of reed are placed side by side in a box, standing upright, with the roof of my making at the top. The insects, therefore, are in the exact position which they occupied in the nest. To open a passage, they must do what they would have done without my interference, they must break through the wall situated above their heads. I shelter the whole under a wide bell-glass and wait for the month of May, the period of the deliverance.

The results far exceed my anticipations. The clay stopper, the work of my fingers, is perforated with a round hole, differing in no wise from that which the Mason-bee contrives through her native mortar dome. The vegetable barrier, new to my prisoners, namely, the sorghum cylinder, also opens with a neat orifice, which might have been the work of a punch. Lastly, the brown-paper cover allows the Bee to make her exit not by bursting through, by making a violent rent, but once more by a clearly-defined round hole. My Bees therefore are capable of a task for which they were not born; to come out of their reed cells they do what probably none of their race did before them; they perforate the wall of sorghum-pith, they make a hole in the paper barrier, just as they would have pierced their natural clay ceiling. When the moment comes to free themselves, the nature of the impediment does not stop them, provided that it be not beyond their strength; and henceforth the argument of incapacity cannot be raised when a mere paper barrier is in question.

In addition to the cells made out of bits of reed, I put under the bell-glass, at the same time, two nests which are intact and still resting on their pebbles. To one of them I have attached a sheet of brown paper pressed close against the mortar dome. In order to come out, the insect will have to pierce first the dome and then the paper, which follows without any intervening space. Over the other, I have placed a little brown-paper cone, gummed to the pebble. There is here, therefore, as in the first case, a double wall—a clay partition and a paper partition—with this difference, that the two walls do not come immediately after each other, but are separated by an empty space of about a centimetre at the bottom, increasing as the cone rises.

The results of these two experiments are quite different. The Bees in the nest to which a sheet of paper was tightly stuck come out by piercing the two enclosures, of which the outer wall, the paper wrapper, is perforated with a very clean round hole, as we have already seen in the reed cells closed with a lid of the same material. We thus become aware, for the second time, that, when the Mason-bee is stopped by a paper barrier, the reason is not her incapacity to overcome the obstacle. On the other hand, the occupants of the nest covered with the cone, after making their way through the earthen dome, finding the sheet of paper at some distance, do not even try to perforate this obstacle, which they would have conquered so easily had it been fastened to the nest. They die under the cover without making any attempt to escape. Even so did Réaumur's Bees perish in the glass funnel, where their liberty depended only upon their cutting through a bit of gauze.

This fact strikes me as rich in inferences. What? Here are sturdy insects, to whom boring through granite is mere play, to whom a stopper of soft wood and a paper partition are walls quite easy to perforate despite the novelty of the material; and yet these vigorous housebreakers allow themselves to perish stupidly in the prison of a paper bag, which they could have torn open with one stroke of their mandibles? They are capable of tearing it, but they do not dream of doing so! There can be only one explanation of this suicidal inaction. The insect is well-endowed with tools and instinctive faculties for accomplishing the final act of its metamorphosis, namely, the act of emerging from the cocoon and from the cell. Its mandibles provide it with scissors, file, pick-axe and lever wherewith to cut, gnaw through and demolish either its cocoon and its mortar enclosure or any other not too obstinate barrier substituted for the natural covering of the nest. Moreover—and this is an important proviso, but for which the outfit would be useless—it has, I will not say the will to use those tools, but a secret stimulus inviting it to employ them. When the hour for the emergence arrives, this stimulus is aroused and the insect sets to work to bore a passage. It little cares in this case whether the material to be pierced be the natural mortar, sorghum-pith, or paper; the lid that holds it imprisoned does not resist for long. Nor even does it care if the obstacle be increased in thickness and a paper wall be added outside the wall of clay: the two barriers, with no interval between them, form but one to the Bee, who passes through them because the act of getting out is still one act and one only. With the paper cone, whose wall is a little way off, the conditions are changed, though the total thickness of wall is really the same. Once outside its earthen abode, the insect has done all that it was destined to do in order to release itself; to move freely on the mortar dome represents to it the end of the release, the end of the act of boring. Around the nest a new barrier appears, the wall made by the paper bag; but, in order to pierce this, the insect would have to repeat the act which it has just ac-complished, the act which it is not intended to perform more than once in its life; it would, in short, have to make into a double act that which by nature is a single one; and the insect cannot do this, for the sole reason that it has not the wish to. The Mason-bee perishes for lack of the smallest gleam of in-telligence.

XIV

Cricket Music

Wherever the active, omnivorous black field cricket is found its chirping music is well known. This study of the manner in which Fabre's field crickets produced their sounds is taken from Chapter XVI of THE LIFE OF THE GRASSHOPPER.

IN STEPS ANATOMY and says to the Cricket, bluntly: "Show us your musical-box."

Like all things of real value, it is very simple; it is based on the same principle as that of the Grasshoppers: a bow with a hook to it and a vibrating membrane. The right wing-case overlaps the left and covers it almost completely, except where it folds back sharply and encases the insect's side. It is the converse of what we see in the Green Grasshopper, the Decticus, the Ephippiger and their kinsmen. The Cricket is right-handed, the others left-handed.

I have never come across a Cricket that failed to conform with the general rule. All those whom I have examined—and they are many—without a single exception carried the right wing-case above the left.

Let us try to interfere and to bring about by artifice what natural conditions refuse to show us. Using my forceps, very gently, of course, and without straining the wing-cases, I make these overlap the opposite way. This result is easily obtained with a little dexterity and patience. The thing is done. Everything is in order. There is no dislocation at the shoulders; the membranes are without a crease. Things could not be better-arranged under normal conditions.

Was the Cricket going to sing, with his inverted instrument? I was almost expecting it, appearances were so much in its favour; but I was soon undeceived. The insect submits for a few moments; then, finding the inversion uncomfortable, it makes an effort and restores the instrument to its regular position. In vain I repeat the operation: the Cricket's

128

obstinacy triumphs over mine. The displaced wing-cases always resume their normal arrangement. There is nothing to be done in this direction.

Shall I be more successful if I make my attempt while the wing-cases are still immature? At the actual moment, they are stiff membranes, resisting any change. The fold is already there; it is at the outset that the material should be manipulated. What shall we learn from organs that are quite new and still plastic, if we invert them as soon as they appear? The thing is worth trying.

For this purpose I go to the larva and watch for the moment of its metamorphosis, a sort of second birth. The future wings and wing-cases form four tiny flaps which, by their shape and their scantiness, as well as by the way in which they stick out in different directions, remind me of the short jackets worn by the Auvergne cheese-makers. I am most assiduous in my attendance, lest I should miss the propitious moment, and at last have a chance to witness the moulting. In the early part of May, at about eleven in the morning, a larva casts off its rustic garments before my eyes. The transformed Cricket is now a reddish brown, all but the wings and wing-cases, which are beautifully white.

Both wings and wing-cases, which only issued from their sheaths quite recently, are no more than short, crinkly stumps. The former remain in this rudimentary state, or nearly so. The latter gradually develop bit by bit and open out; their inner edges, with a movement too slow to be perceived, meet one another, on the same plane and at the same level. There is no sign to tell us which of the two wing-cases will overlap the other. The two edges are now touching. A few moments longer and the right will be above the left. This is the time to intervene.

With a straw I gently change the position, bringing the left edge over the right. The insect protests a little and disturbs my manœuvring. I insist, while taking every possible care not to endanger these tender organs, which look as though they were cut out of wet tissue-paper. And I am quite successful: the left wing-case pushes forward above the right, but only very little, barely a twenty-fifth of an inch. We will leave it alone: things will now go of themselves.

They go as well as one could wish, in fact. Continuing to spread, the left wing-case ends by entirely covering the other. At three o'clock in the afternoon, the Cricket has changed from a reddish hue to black, but the wing-cases are still white. Two hours more and they also will possess the normal colouring.

It is over. The wing-cases have come to maturity under the artificial arrangement; they had opened out and moulded themselves according to my plans; they have taken breadth and consistency and have been born, so to speak, in an inverted position. As things now are, the Cricket is left-handed. Will he definitely remain so? It seems to me that he will; and my hopes rise higher on the morrow and the day after, for the wing-cases continue, without any trouble, in their unusual arrangement. I expect soon to see the artist wield that particular fiddle-stick which the members of his family never employ. I redouble my watchfulness, so as to witness his first attempt at playing the violin.

On the third day, the novice makes a start. A few brief grating sounds are heard, the noise of a machine out of gear shifting its parts back in their proper order. Then the song begins, with its accustomed tone and rhythm.

Veil your face, O foolish experimenter, overconfident in your mischievous straw! You thought that you had created a new type of instrumentalist; and you have obtained nothing at all. The Cricket has thwarted your schemes: he is scraping with his right fiddlestick and always will. With a painful effort, he has dislocated his shoulders, which were made to mature and harden the wrong way; and, in spite of a set that seemed definite, he has put back on top that which ought to be on top and underneath that which ought to be underneath. Your sorry science tried to make a left-handed player of him. He laughs at your devices and settles down to be right-handed for the rest of his life.

XV

Courtship of the Scorpion

*Like the Praying Mantis and numerous species of spiders,
the female scorpion devours her husband. Fabre's investigations of this phase of the life-story of the creature extended,
as his investigations often did, over a period of many years.
His step-by-step advance in understanding, as recorded in
his notes set down at the time, is given here. The source of
this selection is* THE LIFE OF THE SCORPION.

IN APRIL, when the Swallow returns to us and the Cuckoo
sounds his first note, a revolution takes place among my
hitherto peaceable Scorpions. Several whom I have established in the colony in the enclosure, leave their shelter at
nightfall, go wandering about and do not return to their
homes. A more serious business: often, under the same stone,
are two Scorpions of whom one is in the act of devouring the
other. Is this a case of brigandage among creatures of the
same order, who, falling into vagabond ways when the fine
weather sets in, thoughtlessly enter their neighbours' houses
and there meet with their undoing unless they be the stronger? One would almost think it, so quickly is the intruder
eaten up, for days at a time and in small mouthfuls, even as
the usual game would be.

Now here is something to give us a hint. The Scorpions
devoured are invariably of middling size. Their lighter colouring, their less protuberant bellies, mark them as males,
always males. The others, larger, more paunchy and a little
darker in shade, do not end in this unhappy fashion. So these
are probably not brawls between neighbours who, jealous of
their solitude, would soon settle the hash of any visitor and
eat him afterwards, a drastic method of putting a stop to
further indiscretions; they are rather nuptial rites, tragically
performed by the matron after pairing. To determine how

131

much ground there is for this suspicion is beyond my powers until next year: I am still too badly equipped.

Spring returns once more. I have prepared the large glass cage in advance and stocked it with twenty-five inhabitants, each with his bit of crockery. From mid-April onwards, every evening, when it grows dark, between seven and nine o'clock, great animation reigns in the crystal palace. That which seemed deserted by day now becomes a scene of festivity. As soon as supper is finished, the whole household runs out to look on. A lantern hung outside the panes allows us to follow events.

It is our distraction after the worries of the day; it is our play-house. In this theatre for simple folk, the performances are so highly interesting that, the moment the lantern is lighted, all of us, great and small alike, come and take our places in the stalls; all, down to Tom, the House-dog. Tom, it is true, indifferent to Scorpion affairs, like the true philosopher that he is, lies at our feet and dozes, but only with one eye, keeping the other always open on his friends the children.

Let me try to give the reader an idea of what happens. A numerous assembly soon gathers near the glass panes in the region discreetly lit by the lanterns. Every elsewhere, here, there, single Scorpions walk about and, attracted by the light, leave the shade and hasten to the illuminated festival. The very Moths betray no greater eagerness to flutter to the rays of our lamps. The newcomers mingle with the crowd, while others, tired of their pastimes, withdraw into the shade, snatch a few moments' rest and then impetuously return upon the scene.

These hideous devotees of gaiety provide a dance that is not wholly devoid of charm. Some come from afar: solemnly they emerge from the shadow; then, suddenly, with a rush as swift and easy as a slide, they join the crowd, in the light. Their agility reminds me of Mice scurrying along with their tiny steps. They seek one another and fly precipitately the moment they touch, as though they had mutually burnt their fingers. Others, after tumbling about a little with their play-fellows, make off hurriedly and wildly. They take fresh courage in the dark and return.

At times, there is a violent tumult: a confused mass of swarming legs, snapping claws, tails curving and clashing, threatening or fondling, it is hard to say which. In this af-fray, under favourable conditions, twin specks of light flare and shine like carbuncles. One would take them for eyes that emit flashing glances; in reality they are two polished, reflecting facets, which occupy the front of the head. All, large and small alike, take part in the brawl; it might be a battle to the death, a general massacre; and it is just a wanton frolic. Even so do kittens bemaul each other. Soon, the group disperses; all make off in all sorts of directions, without a scratch, without a sprain.

Behold the fugitives collecting once more beneath the lantern. They pass and pass again; they come and go, often meeting front to front. He who is in the greatest hurry walks over the back of the other, who lets him have his way without any protest but a movement of the body. It is no time for blows: at most, two Scorpions meeting will exchange a cuff, that is to say, a rap of the caudal staff. In their community, this friendly thump, in which the point of the sting plays no part, is a sort of a fisticuff in frequent use. There are better things than entangled legs and brandished tails; there are sometimes poses of the highest originality. Face to face, with claws drawn back, two wrestlers proceed to stand on their heads like acrobats, that is to say, resting only on the forequarters, they raise the whole hinder portion of the body, so much so that the chest displays the four little lung pockets uncovered. Then the tails, held vertically erect in a straight line, exchange mutual rubs, gliding one over the other, while their extremities are hooked together and repeatedly fastened and unfastened. Suddenly, the friendly pyramid falls to pieces and each runs off hurriedly, without ceremony.

What were these two wrestlers trying to do, in their eccentric posture? Was it a set-to between two rivals? It would seem not, so peaceful is the encounter. My subsequent observations were to tell me that this was the mutual teasing of a betrothed couple. To declare his flame, the Scorpion stands on his head.

To continue as I have begun and give a homogeneous picture of the thousand tiny particulars gathered day by day would have its advantages: the story would sooner be told; but, at the same time deprived of its details, which vary greatly between one observation and the next and are difficult to piece together, it would be less interesting. Nothing must be neglected in the relation of manners so strange and as yet so little known. At the risk of repeating one's self here and there, it is preferable to adhere to chronological order and to tell the story by fragments, as one's observations reveal fresh facts. Order will emerge from this disorder; for each of the more remarkable evenings supplies some feature that corroborates and completes those which go before. I will therefore continue my narration in the form of a diary.

25th April, 1904.—Hullo! What is this, something I have not yet seen? My eyes, ever on the watch, look upon the affair for the first time. Two Scorpions face each other, with claws outstretched and fingers clasped. It is a question of a friendly grasp of the hand and not the prelude to a battle, for the two partners are behaving to each other in the most peaceful way. There is one of either sex. One is paunchy and browner than the other: this is the female; the other is comparatively slim and pale: this is the male. With their tails prettily curled, the couple stroll with measured steps along the pane. The male is ahead and walks backwards, without jolt or jerk, without any resistance to overcome. The female follows obediently, clasped by her finger-tips and face to face with her leader.

The stroll is interrupted by halts that do not affect the method of conjunction; it is resumed, now here, now there, from end to end of the enclosure. Nothing shows the object which the strollers have in view. They loiter, they dawdle, they most certainly exchange ogling glances. Even so in my village, on Sundays, after vespers, do the youth of both sexes saunter along the hedges, every Jack with his Jill.

Often they tack about. It is always the male who decides which fresh direction the pair shall take. Without releasing her hands, he turns gracefully to the left or right about and places himself side by side with his companion. Then, for a moment, with tail laid flat, he strokes her spine. The other stands motionless, impassive.

For over an hour, without tiring, I watch these interminable comings and goings. A part of the household lends me its eyes in the presence of the strange sight which no one in the world has yet seen, at least with a vision capable of observing. In spite of the lateness of the hour, which upsets all our habits, our attention is concentrated and no essential thing escapes us.

At last, about ten o'clock, something happens. The male has hit upon a potsherd whose shelter seems to suit him. He releases his companion with one hand, with one alone, and continuing to hold her with the other, he scratches with his legs and sweeps with his tail. A grotto opens. He enters and, slowly, without violence, drags the patient Scorpioness after him. Soon both have disappeared. A plug of sand closes the dwelling. The couple are at home.

To disturb them would be a blunder: I should be interfering too soon, at an inopportune moment, if I tried at once to see what was happening below. The preliminary stages may last for the best part of the night; and it does not do for me, who have turned eighty, to sit up so late. I feel my legs giving way; and my eyes seem full of sand.

All night long I dream of Scorpions. They crawl under my bedclothes, they pass over my face; and I am not particularly excited, so many curious things do I see in my imagination. The next morning, at daybreak, I lift the stoneware. The female is alone. Of the male there is no trace, either in the home or in the neighbourhood. First disappointment, to be followed by many others.

10th May.—It is nearly seven o'clock in the evening; the sky is overcast with signs of an approaching shower. Under one of the potsherds is a motionless couple, face to face, with linked fingers. Cautiously I raise the potsherd and leave the occupants uncovered, so as to study the consequences of the interview at my ease. The darkness of the night falls and nothing, it seems to me, will disturb the calm of the home deprived of its roof. A sharp shower compels me to retire. They, under the lid of the cage, have no need to take shelter against the rain. What will they do, left to their business as they are but deprived of a canopy to their alcove?

An hour later, the rain ceases and I return to my Scorpions. They are gone. They have taken up their abode under a neighbouring tile. Still with their fingers linked, the female is outside and the male indoors, preparing the home. At intervals of ten minutes, the members of my family relieve one another, so as not to lose the exact moment of the pairing, which appears to be imminent. Wasted pains: at eight o'clock, it being now quite dark, the couple, dissatisfied with the spot, set out on a fresh ramble, hand in hand, and go prospecting elsewhere. The male, walking backwards, leads the way, chooses the dwelling as he pleases; the female follows with docility. It is an exact repetition of what I saw on the 25th of April.

At last a tile is found to suit them. The male goes in first but this time neither hand releases his companion for a moment. The nuptial chamber is prepared with a few sweeps of the tail. Gently drawn towards him, the Scorpioness enters in the wake of her guide.

I visit them a couple of hours later, thinking that I've given them time enough to finish their preparations. I lift the potsherd. They are there in the same posture, face to face and hand in hand. I shall see no more to-day.

The next day, nothing new either. Each sits confronting the other, meditatively. Without stirring a limb, the gossips, holding each other by the finger-tips, continue their endless interview under the tile. In the evening, at sunset, after sitting linked together for four-and-twenty hours, the couple separate. He goes away from the tile, she remains; and matters have not advanced by an inch.

This observation gives us two facts to remember. After the stroll to celebrate the betrothal, the couple need the mystery and quiet of a shelter. Never would the nuptials be consummated in the open air, amid the bustling crowd, in sight of all. Remove the roof of the house, by night or day, with all possible discretion; and the husband and wife, who seem absorbed in meditation, march off in search of another spot. Also, the sojourn under the cover of a stone is a long one: we have just seen it spun out to twenty-four hours and even then without a decisive result.

12th May.—What will this evening's sitting teach us? The weather is calm and hot, favourable to nocturnal pastimes. A couple has been formed: how things began I do not know. This time the male is greatly inferior to his corpulent mate. Nevertheless, the skinny wight performs his duty gallantly. Walking backwards, according to rule, with his tail rolled trumpetwise, he marches the fat Scorpioness around the glass ramparts. After one circuit follows another, sometimes in the same, sometimes in the opposite direction.

Pauses are frequent. Then the foreheads touch, bend a little to left and right, as if the two were whispering in each other's ears. The little forelegs flutter in feverish caresses. What are they saying to each other? How shall we translate their silent epithalamium into words?

The whole household turns out to see this curious team, which our presence in no way disturbs. The pair are pronounced to be "pretty"; and the expression is not exaggerated. Semitranslucent and shining in the light of the lantern, they seem carved out of a block of amber. Their arms outstretched, their tails rolled into graceful spirals, they wander on with a slow movement and with measured tread.

Nothing puts them out. Should some vagabond, taking the evening air and keeping to the wall like themselves, meet them on their way, he stands aside—for he understands these delicate matters—and leaves them a free passage. Lastly, the shelter of a tile receìves the strolling pair, the male entering first and backwards: that goes without saying. It is nine o'clock.

The idyll of the evening is followed, during the night, by a hideous tragedy. Next morning, we find the Scorpioness under the potsherd of the previous day. The little male is by her side, but slain, and more or less devoured. He lacks the head, a claw, a pair of legs. I place the corpse in the open, on the threshold of the home. All day long, the recluse does not touch it. When night returns, she goes out and, meeting the deceased on her passage, carries him off to a distance to give him a decent funeral, that is, to finish eating him.

This act of cannibalism agrees with what the open-air colony showed me last year. From time to time, I would find, under the stones, a pot-bellied female making a comfortable ritual meal off her companion of the night. I suspected that the male, if he did not break loose in time, once his functions were fulfilled, was devoured, wholly or partly, according to the matron's appetite. I now have the certain proof before my eyes. Yesterday, I saw the couple enter their home after their usual preliminary, the stroll; and, this morning, under the same tile, at the moment of my visit, the bride is consuming her mate.

XVI

The Cionus Weevil

Fabre devoted more of his pages to the beetles than to any other group of insects. Some of his researches, particularly those in connection with the Scarab, extended over a half a century. Among the beetles, the weevils are generally injurious to plants and seeds. The most famous member of the group in America, of course, is the destructive Boll Weevil of the South. This selection is taken from Chapter XV of THE LIFE OF THE WEEVIL.

AN INSECT, well known to every one, is often but a stupid creature, while another, of which nothing is known, is of real value. When endowed with talents worthy of attention, it passes unrecognized; when richly clad and of handsome appearance, it is familiar to us. We judge it by its coat and its size, as we judge our neighbour by the fineness of his clothing and the importance of the position which he fills. The rest does not count.

Of course, if it is to be honoured by the historian, it is best that the insect should enjoy popular renown. This saves the reader trouble, as he at once knows precisely what we are speaking of; furthermore, it shortens the story, which is not hampered by long and tedious descriptions. Moreover, if size facilitates observation, if elegance of shape and brilliance of costume captivate the eye, we should be wrong not to take this magnificence into our reckoning.

But far more important are the habits, the ingenious devices, which give a real charm to entomological study. Now it so happens that among the insects it is the largest, the most magnificent, that are generally the most inefficient: a freak of nature that recurs elsewhere. What can we expect of a Carabus, all shimmering with metallic gleams? Nothing but feasting amid the foam secreted by a murdered snail.

What can we expect of the Cetonia, who looks as though she had escaped from a jeweller's show-case? Nothing but drowsy slumbers in the heart of a rose. These magnificoes cannot do anything; they have no craft, no trade.

If, on the contrary, we wish to see original inventions, artistic masterpieces and ingenious contrivances, we must apply to the humble creatures that are oftener than not unknown to any one. And we must not allow ourselves to be disgusted by the spots frequented. Ordure has beautiful and curious things in store for us, the like of which we should never find on the rose. The Minotaur has edified us by his domestic habits. Long live the modest! Long live the little!

One of these little ones, smaller than a peppercorn, will set us a great problem, full of interest but probably insoluble. The official nomenclators call it *Cionus thapsus*, FAB. If you ask me what Cionus means, I shall reply frankly that I have not the least idea. Neither the writer of these lines nor the reader is any the worse off for that. In entomology a name is all the better for meaning nothing but the insect named.

If an amalgam of Greek or Latin has a meaning that alludes to the insect's manner of living, the reality is often inconsistent with the word, because the nomenclator, working in a necropolis, has preceded the observer, who is concerned with the living species. Moreover, rough guesses and even glaring mistakes too often disfigure the records of the insect world.

At the present moment, it is the word *thapsus* that deserves reproach, for the plant exploited by the Cionus is not the botanists' *Verbascum thapsus* at all, but quite another plant of wholly different character, *Verbascum sinuatum*. A lover of the wayside, having no fear of the ungrateful soil and the white dust, the scallop-leaved mullein is a southern plant which spreads over the ground a rosette of broad, fluffy leaves, the edges of which are gashed with deep, wavy incisions. Its flower-stalk is divided into a number of twigs bearing yellow blossoms whose staminal filaments are bearded with violet hairs.

At the end of May, let us open the umbrella, the collector's chief engine of the chase, underneath the plant. A few blows of a walking-stick on the chandelier ablaze with yellow flowers will bring down a sort of hail. This is our friend the Cionus, a roundish little creature huddled into a globule on its short legs. Its costume is not lacking in elegance and consists of a scaly jacket flecked with black specks on an ash-grey background. The insect is distinguished above all by two large tufts of black velvet, one on its back and the other on the lower extremity of the wing-case. No other Weevil of our countryside wears the like. The rostrum is fairly long, powerful and depressed towards the thorax.

For a long while this Weevil, with her decoration of black spots, has occupied my mind. I should like to know her larva, which, as everything seems to prove, must live in the capsules of the scallop-leaved mullein. The insect belongs to the series that nibble at seeds contained in a shell; it ought to share their botanical habits. But vainly, whatever the season, do I open the capsules of the exploited plant: never do I find the Cionus there, nor its larva, nor its nymph. This little mystery increases my curiosity. Perhaps the dwarf has interesting things to tell us. I propose to wrest her secret from her.

It so happens that a few scallop-leaved mulleins are spreading their rosettes amid the pebbles of my enclosure. They are not populated, but I can easily colonize them with specimens from the country round about, obtained by a few *battues* over the umbrella. No sooner said than done. From May onwards I have before my door, without fear of disturbance by passing Sheep, the means of following the Cionus' doings, in comfort, at any hour of the day.

My colonies flourish. The strangers, satisfied with their new camping-ground, settle down on the twigs on which I have placed them. They browse and gently tease one another with their legs: many of them pair off and gaily spend their lives revelling in the sunshine. Those coupled together, one on top of the other, are subject to sudden lurches from side to side, as though impelled by the release of a vibrating spring. Pauses follow, of varying length; then the lurches are repeated, cease and begin again.

Which of the two supplies the motive force of this little piece of machinery? It seems to me that it is the female, who is rather larger than the male. The jerking would then be a protest on her part, an attempt to free herself from the embraces of her companion, who holds on despite all this shaking. Or again, it may be a common manifestation, the pair joyfully exulting in a nuptial rolling from side to side.

Those who are not coupled plunge their rostrum into the

budding flowers and feast deliciously. Others bore little brown holes in the tiny twigs, whence oozes a drop of syrup which the Ants will come and lick up presently. And that, for the moment, is all. There is nothing to tell us where the eggs will be laid.

In July, certain capsules, still quite small, green and tender, have at their base a brown speck which might well be the work of the Cionus placing her eggs. I have my doubts: most of these punctured capsules contain nothing. The grubs then left their cell shortly after the hatching, the aperture, still open, allowing them to pass.

This emancipation of the new-born grubs, this premature exposure to the dangers of the outside world, is not consistent with the habits of the Weevils, who are great stay-at-homes while in the larval state. Legless, plump, fond of repose, the grub shrinks from change of place; it grows up on the spot where it was born.

Another circumstance increases my perplexity. Among the capsules which the Weevil seems to have perforated with her rostrum, some contain eggs of an orange yellow, grouped into a single heap of five or six or more. This multiplicity gives us food for reflection. When fully matured, the capsules of the scallop-leaved mullein are small, greatly inferior in size to those of other plants of the same genus. When still very young, green and tender, those containing the eggs are hardly as big as half a grain of wheat. There is not food for so many feasters in so tiny a morsel; there would not be enough for one.

All mothers are provident. The exploiter of the mullein cannot have endowed her six or more nurselings with such scanty possessions. For these various reasons, I doubt at first whether these are really the Cionus' eggs. What follows is not calculated to decrease my hesitation. The orange eggs hatch out, producing grubs which within twenty-four hours abandon their exiguous natal chamber. They emerge through the orifice which has been left open; they spread over the capsule, cropping its down, a pasture sufficient for their first mouthfuls. They descend to the thin little twigs, which they strip of their bark, and gradually move on to the small adjacent leaves, where the banquet is continued. Let us leave them to grow. Their final transformation will tell me that I really have the authentic larva of the Cionus before my eyes.

They are bare, legless grubs, of a uniform pale yellow, excepting the head, which is black, and the first segment of the thorax, which is adorned with two large black spots. They are varnished all over their bodies with a glutinous humour, so much so that they stick to the paint-brush used to collect them and are difficult to shake off. When teased, they emit from the end of their intestine a viscous fluid, apparently the origin of their varnish.

They wander idly over the young twigs, whose bark they gnaw down to the wood; they also browse on the leaves growing from the twigs, which are much smaller than those upon the ground. Having found a good grazing-place, they stay there without moving, curved into a bow and held in position by their glue. Their walk is an undulating crawl, based upon the support of their sticky behind. Helpless cripples, but coated with an adhesive varnish, they are firmly enough fixed to resist a shake of the bough that bears them without falling off. When you have no sort of grapnel to hold on by, the idea of clothing yourself in glue, so that you may shift your position without danger of falling, even in a gust of wind, is an original invention of which, as yet, I know no other instance.

Our grubs are easily reared. Placed in a glass jar, with a few tender twigs of the plant that feeds them, they go on browsing for some time and then make themselves a pretty ampulla in which the transformation will take place. To observe this performance and discover the method employed was the chief purpose of my inquiry. I succeeded, though not without a great expenditure of assiduity.

All its life long, the larva is smeared, on both its dorsal and its ventral surface, with a viscous, colourless, strongly adhesive fluid. Touch the creature lightly, anywhere, with the tip of a camel-hair pencil. The glutinous matter yields and draws out into a thread of a certain length. Repeat the touch in the hot sunshine, in very dry weather. The viscosity is not diminished. Our varnishes dry up; the grub's does not; and this is a property of the greatest value, enabling the feeble larva, without fear of being shrivelled by the wind or the rays of the sun, to adhere firmly to its food-plant, which loves the open air and warm, sunny places.

The laboratory producing this sticky varnish is easily discovered; we have only to make the creature move along a slip of glass. We see from time to time a sort of treacly dew oozing from the end of the intestine and lubricating the last segment. The glue is therefore supplied by the digestive canal. Is there a special glandular laboratory there, or is it the intestine itself that prepares the product? I will leave the question unanswered, for nowadays I no longer have the steady hand or the keen sight required for delicate dissection. The fact remains that the grub daubs itself with a glue of which the end of the intestine is at least the storehouse, if it is not the actual source.

How is the sticky emission distributed over the whole body, both above and below? The larva is a legless cripple; it moves about by obtaining a hold with its behind. Moreover, it is well segmented. The back, in particular, has a series of fairly protuberant cushions; the ventral surface, on the other hand, is puckered by knotty excrescences, which change their shape considerably in the act of crawling. When moving, with the flexible fore-part of the body groping to find its way, the grub consists of a series of waves that follow one another in perfect order.

Each wave starts from the hinder extremity and by swift degrees reaches the head. Straightway a second wave follows in the same direction, succeeded by a third, a fourth and so on, indefinitely. Each of these waves, proceeding from one end of the grub to the other, is a step. So long as the wave continues, the fulcrum, that is, the orifice of the intestine, remains in its place, at first a little before and then a little behind the movement as a whole. Hence the source of the sticky dew grazes first the tip of the abdomen and then the end of the back of the moving grub. In this way the tiny drop of gum is deposited above and below.

The glue has still to be distributed. This is done by crawling. Between the puckers, the cushions, which the locomotory wave brings together and then separates, alternately come into contact and open clefts into which the sticky fluid gradually makes its way by capillary action. The grub clothes itself in glue without exercising any special skill, merely by moving along. Each locomotory wave, each step, supplies its quota to the viscous doublet. This makes up for the losses which the larva cannot fail to suffer on the road as it roams from pasture to pasture; and, since the fresh material balances the wastage of the old, a suitable coat is obtained, neither too thin nor too thick.

The complete coating is rapidly effected. With the tip of a

camel-hair pencil, I wash a grub in a little water. The viscosity dissolves and disappears; and the water used for washing the larva, evaporated on a slip of glass, leaves a mark like that of a weak solution of gum arabic. I place the grub to dry on blotting-paper. When I now touch it with a straw, it no longer sticks to it; it has lost its coating of varnish.

How will it replace it? This is a very simple matter. I allow the grub to move about at will for a few minutes. No more is needed; the layer of gum is restored; the creature sticks to the straw that touches it. To sum up, the varnish with which the Cionus' larva is covered is a viscous fluid, soluble in water, quickly emitted and extremely slow to dry, even in an intensely hot sun and in the parching breath of the north wind.

Having obtained these data, let us see how the ampulla is constructed in which the transformation will take place. On the 8th of July, 1906, my son Paul, my zealous collaborator now that my once sturdy legs are failing me, brings me, on returning from his morning walk, a magnificent branching head of mullein peopled by the Cionus. It contains an abundance of larva. Two of them in particular delight me: while the others stand browsing, these two wander about restlessly, indifferent to their food. Beyond any doubt, they are looking for a spot favourable to the process of the nymphosis.

I place each of them singly in a small glass tube which will allow me to observe them easily. In case they might find the food-plant useful, I supply them with a sprig of mullein. And now, lens in hand, from morning to evening and then by night, as far as drowsiness and the doubtful light of a candle will permit, let us be on the alert; for very interesting things are about to happen. Let me describe them hour by hour.

8 A. M.—The larva is not making use of the twig with which I provided it. It is crawling along the glass, darting its pointed head now this way, now that. With a gentle creeping movement that causes an undulation of the back and belly, it is trying to settle itself comfortably. After two hours of this effort, which is certain to be accompanied by an emission of viscous fluid, it finds a position to its taste.

10 A. M.—Being now fixed to the glass, the larva has
shrunk into the semblance of a little barrel, or a grain of
wheat with rounded ends. At one end is a shining black
speck. This is the head, jammed into a fold of the first
segment. The grub's colour is unchanged: it is still a dirty
yellow.

1 P. M.—A copious emission of fine black granules, followed by semifluid dejecta. To avoid soiling its future
residence and to prepare the intestine for the delicate chemistry about to follow, the grub purges itself beforehand of
its impurities. It is now a uniform pale yellow, without the
cloudy markings that disfigured it at first. It is lying at full
length on its ventral surface.

3 P.M.—Under the skin, especially on the back, the lens
reveals subtle pulsations, slight tremors, like those of a liquid
surface on the point of boiling. The dorsal vessel itself is
dilating and contracting, throughout its length, more actively than usual. This means a fit of fever. Some internal
change must be preparing, which will affect the whole organism. Can it be the preparation for a moult?

5. P. M.—No, for the grub is no longer motionless. It
leaves its heap of dirt and begins to move along impetuously,
more restlessly than ever. What is happening that is in any
way unusual? I think I can obtain some idea of it by logic.

Remember that the sticky coat in which the grub is clad
does not dry up: this is a condition indispensable to liberty
of movement. If changed into a hard varnish, a dry film, it
would hamper, would indeed stop the crawling; but, so long
as it remains liquid, it is the drop of oil that lubricates the
locomotory machine. This moist coating will, however, constitute the material of the nymphosis-bladder: the fluid will
become goldbeater's-skin, the liquid will solidify.

This change of condition at first suggests oxidation. We
must abandon this idea. If the hardening were really the result of oxidation, the grub, being sticky from its birth and
always exposed to the air, would long ago have been clad not
in a delicate coat of adhesive, but in a stiff parchment sheath.
Desiccation obviously must take place at the last moment and
rapidly, when the grub is preparing to change its shape. Be-

fore then, this desiccation would be a danger; now, it is an excellent means of defence.

To "fix" oil-paintings our ingenuity employs siccatives, that is to say, ingredients that act upon the oil, giving it a resinous consistency. The Cionus likewise has its siccative, as the following facts prove. It may be that the grub was labouring to produce this desiccating substance, by some profound change in the process of its organic laboratory, at the time when its poor flesh was quivering with feverish tremors; it may be that it was proceeding to spread the siccative over the whole surface of its body by taking a long walk, the last of its larval life.

7. P. M.—The larva is once more motionless, lying flat on its belly. Is this the end of its preparations? Not yet. The globular structure must have a foundation, a base on which the grub can support itself in order to dilate its ampulla.

8 P. M.—Round the head and the fore-part of the thorax, which, like the rest of the body, are touching the slip of glass, a border of pure white now appears, as though snow had fallen at these points. This forms a sort of horse-shoe enclosing an area in which the snowy deposit is continued in a vague mist. From the base of this border some threads of the same white substance radiate in short tufts. This structure denotes work done with the mouth, a miniature wire-drawing. And in fact no such white substance is seen anywhere except around the head. Thus the creature's two ends take part in the building of the hut: the one in front provides the foundations, the one behind provides the edifice.

10 P.M.—The larva shrinks. With its support, that is to say, its head anchored to the snowy cushion, it brings its hinder end a little nearer; it coils up, hunches its back and gradually turns itself into a ball. Though not yet perceptible, the ampulla is being prepared. The siccative has taken effect; the original gumminess has been transformed into a sort of skin, flexible enough at this moment to be distended by the pressure of the back. When its capacity is large enough, the grub will become unglued, throw off its envelope and find itself at liberty in a spacious enclosure.

I should much like to see this peeling, but things happen so slowly as to drive one to despair. Let us go to bed. What

I have seen is enough to enable me to guess the little that remains to be seen.

Next day, when the pale dawn gives me sufficient light, I hasten to my two larva. The bladder is completed. It is a graceful ovoid of the finest gold-beater's-skin, adhering at no point to the insect inside. It has taken some twenty hours to manufacture. It has still to be strengthened with a lining. The transparency of the wall lets us follow the operation.

We see the grub's little black head rising and falling, swerving this way and that and from time to time gathering with its mandibles, at the door of the intestine, a particle of cement, which is instantly placed in position and meticulously smoothed. So the interior of the hut is plastered, point after point, by small touches. Lest I should not see clearly through the wall, I cut off the top of a bladder, partly uncovering the larva. The work is continued without much hesitation. The strange method is revealed as plainly as one could wish. The grub makes use of its behind as a store of consolidating cement; the end of the intestine serves as the equivalent of the hod from which the bricklayer takes his trowelful of mortar.

This original mode of procedure is familiar to me. At one time, a big Weevil, the Spotted Larinus, inhabiting the blue-headed globe-thistle (*Echinops Ritro*), enabled me to witness a similar method. The Larinus also expels its own cement. With the tips of its mandibles it gathers it from the evacuating orifice, applying it with strict economy. Moreover it has other materials at its disposal, the hairs and remnants of the florets of its thistle. Its cement is used only to plaster and glaze the work. The Cionus' larva, on the other hand, employs nothing but the oozings of its intestine; consequently the little hut resulting is of incomparable perfection.

Besides the Spotted Larinus, my notes mention other Weevils, for instance, the Garlic-Weevil (*Brachycerus algirus*), whose larvæ possess the art of coating their cells with a thin glaze provided by the rump. This intestinal artifice seems, therefore, to be pretty frequently employed by the Weevils that build little chambers in which the metamorphosis is to take place; but none of them excel in it as does the Cionus. Its task becomes yet more interesting when we consider that, in the same factory, after a very brief interval, three different products are compounded: first a liquid glue, a means of adhesion to the swaying support of the mullein lashed by the winds; then a siccative fluid which transforms the sticky coating into gold-beater's-skin; and lastly a cement which strengthens the bladder separated from the larva by a sort of moult. What a laboratory; what exquisite chemistry in a scrap of intestine!

What use are these minute details, noted hour by hour? Why these puerilities? What matters to us the industry of a wretched grub, hardly known even to the experts?

Well, these puerilities involve the most weighty problems that we are privileged to discuss. Is the world a harmonious creation, governed by a primordial force, a *causa causarum?* Or is it a chaos of blind conflicting forces, whose reciprocal thrusts produce a chance equilibrium, for better or for worse? Minute entomological details examined with some thoroughness, may serve us better than syllogisms, in the scientific investigation of these trifles and others like them. The humble Cionus, for its part, tells us of a primordial force, the motive power of the smallest as of the greatest things.

A day is not too long to give the bladder a good lining. Next day the larva moults and passes into the nymphal state. Let us complete its story with the data gleaned in the fields. The cocoons are often found on the grass near the food-plant, on the stalks and dead blades of the Gramineæ. Generally, however, they occupy the little twigs of the mullein, stripped of their bark and withered. The adult insect emerges sooner or later in September. The gold-beater's-skin capsule is not torn irregularly, at random; it is neatly divided into two equal parts, like the two halves of a soap-box.

Has the enclosed insect gnawed the casing with its patient tooth and made a fissure along the equator? No, for the edges of either hemisphere are perfectly clean-cut. There must, therefore, have been a circular line ready to facilitate the opening. All that the insect had to do was to hunch its back and give a slight push, in order to unfasten the roof of its cabin all in one piece and set itself free.

I can just see this line of easy rupture on certain intact capsules. It is a faint line ringing the equator. What does the insect do beforehand to contrive that its cell shall open in this way? A humble plant, flowering early in the spring, the blue or scarlet pimpernel, has also its soap-box, its pyxidium, which splits easily into two hemispheres when the time comes for the seed to be scattered. In either case it is the work of an unconscious ingenuity. The grub does not plan its methods any more than the pimpernel: it has hit upon its ingenious scheme of joining the halves of its capsule by the inspiration of instinct alone.

More numerous than the capsules which burst accurately are others which are clumsily torn by a shapeless breach. Through this some parasite must have emerged, some ruthless creature which, unacquainted with the secret of the delicate joint, has released itself by tearing the gold-beater's-skin. I find its larva in cells which are not yet perforated. It is a small, white grub, fixed to a discoloured tit-bit which is all that remains of the Cionus' nymph. The intruder is sucking dry the rightful occupant, whose budding flesh is still quite tender. I think I can identify the murderess as a bandit of the Chalcid tribe, which is addicted to such massacres.

Her appearance and her gluttonous ways have not misled me. My rearing-jars provide me with abundant supplies of a small bronze-coloured Chalcid with a large head and a round, tapering body, but with no visible boring-tool. To enquire her name of the experts will not help me much. I do not ask the insect, "what are you called?" but "what are you able to do?"

The anonymous parasite hatched in my jars has no implement similar to that of the Leucospis, the chief of the Chalcididæ; it has no probe which is able to penetrate a wall and place the egg, at some distance, on the food-ration. Her germ, therefore, was laid in the very flanks of the Cionus' larva, before the latter had built its shell.

The methods of these tiny brigands appointed to the task of thinning out the too numerous are extremely varied. Each guild has its own method, which is always horribly effective. How should so small a creature as the Cionus cumber the earth? No matter: it has to be massacred, to perish in its cradle, a victim of the Chalcid. Like other creatures, the peaceful dwarf must furnish its share of organizable matter, which will be further and further refined as it passes from stomach to stomach.

Let us recapitulate the habits of the Cionus, very strange habits in an insect of the Weevil series. The mother entrusts her eggs to the swelling capsules of the scallop-leaved mullein. So far, everything is according to rule. Other Weevils, as a matter of fact, prefer, when setting their children up in life, the pods of some other mullein, or those of the figwort or of the snapdragon, two plants belonging to one and the same botanical family. But now we are suddenly confronted with the strange and exceptional. The mother Cionus chooses the mullein with the smallest capsules, whereas in the neighbourhood and at the same season there are others loaded with fruit whose dimensions would provide spacious lodgings and abundance of food. She prefers dearth to plenty and narrow to spacious quarters.

Worse still. Indifferent to leaving provision for her brood, she nibbles the tender seeds, destroys them, extirpates them, in order to obtain a cavity in the heart of the tiny globule. Into this she slips more or less half a dozen eggs. With the edible substance left, were the whole cell to be consumed, there would not be enough to feed a single grub.

When the bread-pan is empty, the house is deserted. The young abandon their famine-stricken dwelling on the day when they are hatched. They are bold innovators and practice a method which is held in detestation among the Weevils, who are all preeminently stay-at-homes: they dare the dangers of the outer world: they travel, passing from one leaf to another in search of food. This strange exodus, unprecedented in a Weevil, is not a mere caprice but a necessity imposed on them by hunger; they migrate because their mother has not provided them with anything to eat.

If traveling has its pleasures, enough to make the insect forget the delights of the cell in which it digests at peace, it also has its drawbacks. The legless grub can progress only by a sort of creeping gait. It has no instrument of adherence which will enable it to remain fixed to the twig, whence the least breath of wind may make it fall. Necessity is the mother of invention. To guard against the danger of falling, the wanderer smears itself with a viscous fluid, which varnishes it and makes it adhere to the trail which it is following.

But this is not all. When the ticklish moment of the nymphosis arrives, a retreat in which the grub can undergo its transformation in peace becomes indispensable. The vagabond has nothing of the sort. It is homeless, it sleeps in the open air; yet it is able, when the time comes, to make itself a tent, a capsule, the materials for which are supplied by its intestine. No other insect of its order can build a home like this. Let us hope that the hateful Chalcid, the murderer of nymphs, will not visit it in its pretty little tent.

The grub that lives on the scallop-leaved mullein has shown an utter revolution in the habits of the Weevil clan. The better to judge of this, let us consult a cognate species, placed not far from the Cionus by the classifiers; let us compare the two kinds of life, on the one hand the exception and on the other the rule. The comparison will be all the more useful inasmuch as the new witness also exploits a mullein. It is known as *Gymnetron thapsicola*, GERM.

Dressed in russet homespun, with a plump round body and about the size of the Cionus: there you have the creature. Note the qualifying *thapsicola*, meaning an inhabitant of the thapsus. On this occasion, I am glad to see, the term could not possibly be happier: it enables the novice to identify the insect exactly, without other data than the name of the plant on which it lives.

The botanist gives the name of *Verbascum thapsus* to the common mullein, or shepherd's club, a lover of the tilled fields in both the north and the south. Its bloom, instead of branching out like that of the scallop-leaved mullein, consists of one thick cone of yellow flowers. These flowers are followed by close-packed capsules about as big as a fair-sized olive. Here we no longer have the niggardly pods in which the grub of the Cionus would die of starvation if it did not abandon them as soon as it is hatched; these caskets contain plenty of victuals for one larva and even for two. A partition divides them into two equal compartments, both of them crammed with seeds.

The fancy took me to estimate roughly the mullein's wealth of seeds. I have counted as many as 321 in a single shell. Now a spike of ordinary size contains 150 capsules. The total number of seeds is therefore 48,000. What can the plant want with such abundance? Allowing for the small number of seeds required to maintain the species in a thriving state, it is evident that the mullein is a hoarder of nutritive atoms; it creates foodstuffs; it summons guests to its opulent banquet.

Knowing these facts, the Gymnetron, from May onwards, visits the luxuriant flower-spike and there installs her grubs. The inhabited capsules may be recognized by the brown speck at their base. This is the hole bored by the mother's rostrum, the aperture needed for inserting the eggs. Usually there are two, corresponding with the two cells of the fruit. Soon the oozings from the cell set hard and dry and obstruct the tiny window; and the capsule is closed again, without any communication with the outer world.

In June and July, let us open the shells marked with brown specks. Nearly always we find two grubs, looking fat as butter, with their fore-parts swollen and their hinder parts shrunken and curved like a comma. Not a vestige of legs, which members would be very useless in such a lodging. Lying at its ease, the grub has plenty of food ready to its mouth: first the tender, sugary seeds; then the placenta, their common support, which is likewise fleshy and highly flavoured. It is pleasant to live under such conditions, motionless and devoting one's self entirely to the joys of the stomach.

It would take a cataclysm to upset the smug hermit. This cataclysm I bring about by opening the cell. Then and there, the grub begins to twist and wriggle desperately, hating any exposure to the air and light. It takes more than an hour to recover from its excitement. Here assuredly is a grub that will never be tempted to leave its home and go wandering about like the Cionus' larva. It is most highly domestic by inheritance and domestic it will remain.

It refused even to go next door. In the same capsule, on the other side of the partition, a neighbour is nibbling away. Never does it pay the neighbour a visit, though it could easily do so by perforating the partition, which at this moment is an actual sort of cake, no less tender than the seeds and the placenta. Each holds the other's share of the capsule inviolable. On the one hand is one grub; on the other hand is another; and never do the two hold the least communication through the little skylight. A grub's home is its castle.

The Gymnetron is so happy in her cell that she stays there for a long time after assuming her adult form. For ten months out of the twelve she does not leave it. In April, when the buds of the new twigs are swelling, she pierces the natal capsule, now a mighty donjon; she comes out and revels in the sun on the recent flower-spikes, which grow daily longer and thicker; she frisks in couples and, in May, establishes her family, which will obstinately repeat the sedentary habits of the elders.

With these data before us, let us philosophize awhile. Every Weevil spends its larval life on the spot where the egg was laid. Various larvæ, it is true, when the time of metamorphosis approaches, migrate and make their way underground. The Brachycerus abandons its clove of garlic, the Balaninus its nut or acorn, the Rhynchites its vine-leaf or poplar-leaf cigar, the Ceuthorhynchus its cabbage stalk. But these instances of desertion on the part of grubs which have attained their full growth do not in any way invalidate the rule: all Weevil-larvæ grow up in the actual place where they are born.

Now here, by a most unexpected change of tactics, the Cionus-grub, while still quite young, quits its natal cell, the capsule of the mullein; it longs for the outer world, that it may browse in the open air on the bark of a twig; and this entails upon it two inventions elsewhere unknown: the sticky coat, which gives it a firm hold when it moves from place to place, and the gold-beater's-skin ampulla, which serves to house the nymph.

What is the cause of this aberration? Two theories are suggested, one based on decadence, the other on progress. Of old, we tell ourselves, the mother Cionus, far back in the ages, used to obey the conventions of her tribe. Like the other Weevils that munch unripe seeds, she favoured large capsules, enough to feed a sedentary family. Later, by inadvertence or flightiness or for some other reason, she turned her attention to the stingy scallop-leaved mullein. Faithful to ancient custom, she rightly chose for her domain a plant of the same family as that which she first exploited; but it unfortunately happens that the mullein adopted is incapable of feeding a single grub in its fruit, which is too small for the purpose. The mother's ineptitude has led to decadence; the perils of a wandering life have taken the place of a peaceful, sedentary existence. The species is on the high road to extinction.

Again, we might argue as follows at the outset, the Cionus had the scallop-leaved mullein as her portion; but, since the grubs do not thrive when thus installed, the mother is searching for a better means of setting them up in life. Gradual experiment will one day show her the way. From time to time, indeed, I find her on *Vervascum maiale* or *Verbascum thapsus*, both of which have large capsules; only she is there by accident, in the course of a trip, thinking of obtaining a good drink and not of laying her eggs. Sooner or later, the future will establish her there for the sake of her family. The species is in process of improvement.

By dressing up the matter in uncouth phrases, calculated to

conceal the vagueness of the thought behind them, we might represent the Cionus as a magnificent example of the changes which the centuries bring about in the habits of insects. This would sound extremely learned, but would it be very intelligible? I doubt it. When my eyes fall upon a page bristling with barbarous and so-called scientific locution, I say to myself:

"Take care! The author has not quite grasped what he is saying, or he would have found, in the vocabulary hammered out by so many brilliant minds, words that would express his thought more plainly."

Boileau, who has been denied poetic inspiration, but who certainly possessed common sense and plenty of it, tells us:

"That which is well conceived is also clearly stated."

Just so, Nicolas! Yes, clearness, clearness always! He calls a spade a spade. Let us do as he does, let us qualify as gibberish any over-learned prose that reminds us of Voltaire's witty sally:

"When the listener does not understand and the speaker does not himself know what he is saying, then they are talking metaphysics."

"And advanced science," let us add.

We will confine ourselves to stating the problem of the Cionus, without much hope that some day it will be clearly solved. For that matter, if the truth be told, it may be that there is no problem at all. The grub of the Cionus was a vagabond in the beginning and a vagabond it will remain, among the other Weevil-grubs, which are all essentially stay-at-home larvæ. Let us leave it at that: it is the simplest and most lucid explanation.

XVII

The Burying-beetle

*One of the remarkable features of Fabre's writing is his
ability to make the repulsive interesting. This study of the
activity of those sanitary workers of the fields, the Burying-
Beetles—selected from* THE GLOW-WORM AND OTHER BEETLES
*—is a case in point. Various species of Necrophorus bury-
ing beetles are found in the United States; also those of
Silpha, the carrion beetle. The Dermestes beetles are minute
insects that feed upon dried animal matter, often riddling
the pinned specimens of neglected insect-collections. The
Saprini are carnivorous beetles of small size. More than
3,000 kinds of Staphylinus, or Rove Beetles, have been described from the United States.*

BESIDE THE FOOTPATH in April lies the Mole, disembow-
elled by the peasant's spade; at the foot of the hedge the pitiless urchin has stoned to death the Lizard, who was about to
don his green, pearl-embellished costume. The passer-by
has thought it a meritorious deed to crush beneath his heel
the chance-met Adder; and a gust of wind has thrown a
tiny unfledged bird from its nest. What will become of these
little bodies and so many other pitiful remnants of life?
They will not long offend our sense of sight and smell. The
sanitary officers of the fields are legion.

An eager freebooter, ready for any task, the Ant is the
first to come hastening and begin, particle by particle, to
dissect the corpse. Soon the odour attracts the Fly, the geni-
trix of the odious maggot. At the same time, the flattened
Silpha, the glistening, slow-trotting Cellar-beetle, the Dermestes powdered with snow upon the abdomen, and the slender Staphylinus, all, whence coming no one knows, hurry
hither in squads, with never-wearied zeal, investigating, probing and draining the infection.

What a spectacle, in the spring, beneath a dead Mole!

The horror of this laboratory is a beautiful sight for one who is able to observe and to meditate. Let us overcome our disgust; let us turn over the unclean refuse with our foot. What a swarming there is beneath it, what a tumult of busy workers! The Silphæ, with wing-cases wide and dark, as though in mourning, flee distraught, hiding in the cracks in the soil; the Saprini, of polished ebony which mirrors the sunlight, jog hastily off, deserting their workshop; the Dermestes, of whom one wears a fawn-coloured tippet flecked with white, seek to fly away, but, tipsy with the putrid nectar, tumble over and reveal the immaculate whiteness of their bellies, which forms a violent contrast with the gloom of the rest of their attire.

What were they doing there, all these feverish workers? They were making a clearance of death on behalf of life. Transcendent alchemists, they were transforming that horrible putrescence into a living and inoffensive product. They were draining the dangerous corpse to the point of rendering it as dry and sonorous as the remains of an old slipper hardened on the refuse-heap by the frosts of winter and the heats of summer. They were working their hardest to render the carrion innocuous.

Others will soon put in their appearance, smaller creatures and more patient, who will take over the relic and exploit it ligament by ligament, bone by bone, hair by hair, until the whole has been restored to the treasury of life. All honour to these purifiers! Let us put back the Mole and go our way.

Some other victim of the agricultural labours of spring, a Shrew-mouse, Field-mouse, Mole, Frog, Adder, or Lizard, will provide us with the most vigorous and famous of these expurgators of the soil. This is the Burying-beetle, the Necrophorus, so different from the cadaveric mob in dress and habits. In honour of his exalted functions he exhales an odour of musk; he bears a red tuft at the tip of his antennæ; his breast is covered with nankeen; and across his wing-cases he wears a double, scalloped scarf of vermillion. An elegant, almost sumptuous costume, very superior to that of the others, but yet lugubrious, as befits your undertaker's man.

He is no anatomical dissector, cutting his subject open, carving its flesh with the scalpel of his mandibles; he is literally a grave-digger, a sexton. While the others—Silphæ, Dermestes, Cellar-beetle—gorge themselves with the exploited flesh, without, of course, forgetting the interests of the family, he, a frugal eater, hardly touches his find on his own account. He buries it entire, on the spot, in a cellar where the thing, duly ripened, will form the diet of his larvæ. He buries it in order to establish his progeny.

This hoarder of dead bodies, with his stiff and almost heavy movements, is astonishingly quick at storing away wreckage. In a shift of a few hours, a comparatively enormous animal, a Mole, for instance, disappears, engulfed by the earth. The others leave the dried, emptied carcass to the air, the sport of the winds for months on end; he, treating it as a whole, makes a clean job of things at once. No visible trace of his work remains but a tiny hillock, a burial-mound, a tumulus.

With his expeditious method, the Necrophorus is the first of the little purifiers of the fields. He is also one of the most celebrated of insects in respect of his psychical capacities. This undertaker is endowed, they say, with intellectual faculties approaching to reason, such as are not possessed by the most gifted of the Bees and Wasps, the collectors of honey or game. He is honoured by the two following anecdotes, which I quote from Lacordaire's *Introduction a l'entomologie,* the only general treatise at my disposal:

"Clairville," says the author, "reports that he saw a *Necrophorus vespillo,* who, wishing to bury a dead Mouse and finding the soil on which the body lay too hard, went to dig a hole at some distance, in soil more easily displaced. This operation completed, he attempted to bury the Mouse in the cavity, but, not succeeding, he flew away and returned a few moments later, accompanied by four of his fellows, who assisted him to move the Mouse and bury it."

In such actions, Lacordaire adds, we cannot refuse to admit the intervention of reason.

"The following case," he continues, "recorded by Gleditsch, has also every indication of the intervention of reason. One of his friends, wishing to desiccate a Frog, placed it on the top of a stick thrust into the ground, in order to make sure that the Necrophori should not come and carry it off. But this precaution was of no effect; the insects, being unable to reach the Frog, dug under the stick and, having caused it to fall, buried it as well as the body."

To grant, in the intellect of the insect, a lucid understanding of the relations between cause and effect, between the end and the means, is to make a statement of serious import. I know of scarcely any more suited to the philosophical brutalities of my time. But are these two anecdotes really true? Do they involve the consequences deduced from them? Are not those who accept them as sound evidence just a little too simple?

To be sure, simplicity is needed in entomology. Without a good dose of this quality, a mental defect in the eyes of practical folk, who would busy himself with the lesser creatures? Yes, let us be simple, without being childishly credulous. Before making insects reason, let us reason a little ourselves; let us, above all, consult the experimental test. A fact gathered at random, without criticism, cannot establish a law.

I do not propose, O valiant grave-diggers, to depreciate your merits; such is far from being my intention. I have that in my notes, on the other hand, which will do you more honour than the story of the gibbet and the Frog; I have gleaned, for your benefit, examples of prowess which will shed a new lustre upon your reputation.

No, my intention is not to belittle your renown. Besides, it is not the business of impartial history to maintain a given thesis; it follows facts. I wish simply to question you upon the power of logic attributed to you. Do you or do you not enjoy gleams of reason? Have you within you the humble germ of human thought? That is the problem before us.

To solve it we will not rely upon the accidents which good fortune may now and again procure for us. We must employ the breeding-cage, which will permit of assiduous visits, continuous enquiry and a variety of artifices. But how to stock the cage? The land of the olive-tree is not rich in Necrophori. To my knowledge it possesses only a single species, *N. vestigator*, HERSCH.; and even this rival of the grave-diggers of the north is pretty scarce. The discovery of three or four in the spring was as much as my hunting-expeditions yielded in the old days. This time, if I do not resort to the ruses of the trapper, I shall obtain no more than that, whereas I stand in need of at least a dozen.

These ruses are very simple. To go in search of the sexton, who exists only here and there in the country-side, would be nearly always a waste of time; the favourable month, April, would be past before my cage was suitably stocked.

To run after him is to trust too much to accident; so we will make him come to us by scattering in the orchard an abundant collection of dead Moles. To this carrion, ripened by the sun, the insect will not fail to hasten from the various points of the horizon, so accomplished is he in detecting such a delicacy.

I make an arrangement with a gardener in the neighbour-hood, who, two or three times a week, makes up for the penury of my two acres of stony ground by providing me with vegetables raised in a better soil. I explain to him my urgent need of Moles in unlimited numbers. Battling daily with trap and spade against the importunate excavator who uproots his crops, he is in a better position than any one to procure for me what I regard for the moment as more precious than his bunches of asparagus or his white-heart cabbages.

The worthy man at first laughs at my request, being greatly surprised by the importance which I attribute to the abhor-rent animal, the *Darboun;* but at last he consents, not with-out suspicion at the back of his mind that I am going to make myself a gorgeous winter waist-coat with the soft, velvety skins of the Moles. A thing like that must be good for pains in the back. Very well. We settle the matter. The essential thing is that the *Darbouns* reach me.

They reach me punctually, by twos, by threes, by fours, packed in a few cabbage-leaves, at the bottom of the gar-dener's basket. The excellent fellow who lent himself with such good grace to my strange wishes will never guess how much comparative psychology will owe him! In a few days I was the possessor of thirty Moles, which were scattered here and there, as they reached me, in bare spots of the orchard, among the rosemary-bushes, the strawberry-trees and the lavender-beds.

Now it only remained to wait and to examine, several times a day, the under-side of my little corpses, a disgust-ing task which any one would avoid whose veins were not filled with the sacred fire of enthusiasm. Only little Paul, of all the household, lent me the aid of his nimble hand to seize the fugitives. I have already said that the entomologist needs simplicity of mind. In this important business of the Necrophori, my assistants were a small boy and an illiterate.

Little Paul's visits alternating with mine, we had not long to wait. The four winds of heaven bore forth in all directions the odours of the carrion; and the undertakers hurried up, so that the experiments, begun with four subjects, were continued with fourteen, a number not attained during the whole of my previous searches, which were unpremeditated and in which no bait was used as decoy. My trapper's ruse was completely successful.

Before I report the results obtained in the cage, let us stop for a moment to consider the normal conditions of the labours that fall to the lot of the Necrophori. The Beetle does not select his head of game, choosing one in proportion to his strength, as do the Hunting Wasps; he accepts what chance offers. Among his finds some are small, such as the Shrew-mouse; some medium-sized, such as the Field-mouse; some enormous, such as the Mole, the Sewer-rat and the Snake, any of which exceeds the digging-powers of a single sexton. In the majority of cases, transportation is impossible, so greatly disproportioned is the burden to the motive-power. A slight displacement, caused by the effort of the insects' backs, is all that can possibly be effected.

Ammophila and Cerceris, Sphex and Pompilus excavate their burrows wherever they please; they carry their prey on the wing, or, if too heavy, drag it afoot. The Necrophorus knows no such facilities in his task. Incapable of carting the monstrous corpse, no matter where encountered, he is forced to dig the grave where the body lies.

This obligatory place of sepulture may be in stony soil or in shifting sands; it may occupy this or that bare spot, or some other where the grass, especially the couch-grass, plunges into the ground its inextricable network of little cords. There is a great probability, too, that a bristle of stunted brambles may be supporting the body at some inches above the soil. Slung by the labourer's spade, which has just broken his back, the Mole falls here, there, anywhere, at random; and where the body falls, no matter what the obstacles, provided that they be not insurmountable, there the undertaker must utilize it.

The difficulties of inhumation are capable of such variety as causes us already to foresee that the Necrophorus cannot employ fixed methods in performing his task. Exposed to fortuitous hazards, he must be able to modify his tactics within the limits of his modest discernment. To saw, to break, to disentangle, to lift, to shake, to displace: these are so many means which are indispensable to the grave-

digger in a predicament. Deprived of these resources, reduced to uniformity of procedure, the insect would be incapable of pursuing its calling.

We see at once how imprudent it would be to draw conclusions from an isolated case in which rational co-ordina-
tion or premeditated intention might appear to play its part.
Every instinctive action no doubt has its motive; but does
the animal in the first place judge whether the action is
opportune? Let us begin by a careful consideration of the
creature's labours; let us support each piece of evidence by
others; and then we shall perhaps be able to answer the
question.

First of all, a word as to diet. A general scavenger, the
Burying-beetle refuses no sort of cadaveric putrescence. All
is good to his senses, feathered game or furry, provided
that the burden do not exceed his strength. He exploits the
batrachian or the reptile with no less animation. He accepts
without hesitation extraordinary finds, probably unknown to
his race, as witness a certain Goldfish, a red Chinese Carp,
whose body, placed in one of my cages, was forthwith considered an excellent tit-bit and buried according to the rules.
Nor is butcher's meat despised. A mutton-cutlet, a strip of
beef-steak, in the right stage of maturity, disappeared beneath the soil, receiving the same attentions as those lavished
on the Mole or the Mouse. In short, the Necrophorus has
no exclusive preferences; anything putrid he conveys underground.

The maintenance of his industry, therefore, presents no
sort of difficulty. If one kind of game be lacking, some
other, the first to hand, will very well replace it. Nor is
there much trouble in fixing the site of his industry. A
capacious wire-gauze cover, resting on an earthen pan filled
to the brim with fresh, heaped sand, is sufficient. To obviate
criminal attempts on the part of the Cats, whom the game
would not fail to tempt, the cage is installed in a closed
glass-house, which in winter shelters the plants and in summer serves as an entomological laboratory.

Now to work. The Mole lies in the centre of the enclosure. The soil, easily shifted and homogeneous, realizes
the best conditions for comfortable work. Four Necrophori,
three males and a female, are there with the body. They
remain invisible, hidden beneath the carcase, which from
time to time seems to return to life, shaken from end to

end by the backs of the workers. An observer not in the secret would be somewhat astonished to see the dead creature move. From time to time, one of the sextons, almost always a male, comes out and walks round the animal, which he explores, probing its velvet coat. He hurriedly returns, appears again, once more investigates and creeps back under the corpse.

The tremors become more pronounced; the carcase oscillates, while a cushion of sand, pushed out from below grows up all around it. The Mole, by reason of his own weight and the efforts of the grave-diggers, who are labouring at their task underneath, gradually sinks, for lack of support, into the undermined soil.

Presently the sand which has been pushed out quivers under the thrust of the invisible miners, slips into the pit and covers the interred Mole. It is a clandestine burial. The body seems to disappear of itself, as though engulfed by a fluid medium. For a long time yet, until the depth is regarded as sufficient, the body will continue to descend.

It is, on the whole, a very simple operation. As the diggers below deepen the cavity into which the corpse, shaken and tugged above, sinks without the direct intervention of the sextons, the grave fills of itself by the mere slipping of the soil. Stout shovels at the tips of their claws, powerful backs, capable of creating a little earthquake: the diggers need nothing more for the practice of their profession. Let us add—for this is an essential point—the art of continually jerking the body, so as to pack it into a lesser volume and make it glide through difficult passages. We shall soon see that this art plays a leading part in the industry of the Necrophori.

Although he has disappeared, the Mole is still far from having reached his destination. Let us leave the undertakers to finish their job. What they are now doing below ground is a continuation of what they did on the surface and would teach us nothing new. We will wait for two or three days.

The moment has come. Let us inform ourselves of what is happening down there. Let us visit the place of corruption. I shall never invite anybody to the exhumation. Of those about me, only little Paul has the courage to assist me.

The Mole is a Mole no longer, but a greenish horror, putrid, hairless, shrunk into a sort of fat, greasy rasher. The thing must have undergone careful manipulation to be thus condensed into a small volume, like a fowl in the hands of the cook, and, above all, to be so completely deprived of its furry coat. Is this culinary procedure undertaken in respect of the larvæ, which might be incommoded by the fur? Or is it just a casual result, a mere loss of hair due to putridity? I am not certain. But it is always the case that these exhumations, from first to last, have revealed the furry game furless and the feathered game featherless, except for the pinion- and tail-feathers. Reptiles and fish, on the other hand, retain their scales.

Let us return to the unrecognizable thing that was once a Mole. The tit-bit lies in a spacious crypt, with firm walls, a regular workshop, worthy of being the bake-house of a Copris. Except for the fur, which lies scattered about in flocks, it is intact. The grave-diggers have not eaten into it: it is the patrimony of the sons, not the provision of the parents, who, to sustain themselves, levy at most a few mouthfuls of the ooze of putrid humours.

Beside the dish which they are kneading and protecting are two Necrophori; a couple, no more. Four collaborated in the burial. What has become of the other two, both males? I find them hidden in the soil, at a distance, almost on the surface.

This observation is not an isolated one. Whenever I am present at a funeral undertaken by a squad in which the males, zealous one and all, predominate, I find presently, when the burial is completed, only one couple in the mortuary cellar. After lending their assistance, the rest have discreetly retired.

XVIII

Experiments with Burying-beetles

Also from THE GLOW-WORM AND OTHER BEETLES, *this account of Fabre's researches with the long-suffering beetles of his harmas is one of his most celebrated chapters. Like a scientific detective story, it unfolds engrossingly and logically, step by step, link by link. The Copres, Sisyphi and Gymnopleuri, mentioned by Fabre, are all dung beetles. Audubon is, of course, John James Audubon (1780–1851), the great American bird-painter and ornithologist. Fabre admired Audubon greatly and once said he found in him the man most nearly akin to himself in mind and temperament.*

LET US COME to the feats of reason which have earned for the Necrophorus the best part of his fame and, to begin with, submit the case related by Clairville, that of the too hard soil and the call for assistance, to the test of experiment.

With this object I pave the centre of the space beneath the cover, flush with the soil, with a brick, which I sprinkle with a thin layer of sand. This will be the soil that cannot be dug. All around it, for some distance and on the same level, lies the loose soil, which is easy to delve.

In order to approach the conditions of the anecdote, I must have a Mouse; with a Mole, a heavy mass, the removal would perhaps present too much difficulty. To obtain one, I place my friends and neighbours under requisition; they laugh at my whim but none the less proffer their traps. Yet, the moment a very common thing is needed, it becomes rare. Defying decency in his speech, after the manner of his ancestors' Latin, the Provençal says, but even more crudely than in my translation:

"If you look for dung, the Donkeys become constipated!"

At last I possess the Mouse of my dreams! She comes to me from that refuge, furnished with a truss of straw, in which official charity grants a day's hospitality to the pauper wandering over the face of the fertile earth, from that municipal hostel whence one inevitably issues covered with Lice. O Réaumur, who used to invite marchionesses to see your caterpillars change their skins, what would you have said of a future disciple conversant with such squalor as this? Perhaps it is well that we should not be ignorant of it, so that we may have compassion with that of the beast.

The Mouse so greatly desired is mine. I place her upon the centre of the brick. The grave-diggers under the wire cover are now seven in number, including three females. All have gone to earth; some are inactive, close to the surface; the rest are busy in their crypts. The presence of the fresh corpse is soon perceived. About seven o'clock in the morning, three Necrophori come hurrying up, two males and a female. They slip under the Mouse, who moves in jerks, a sign of the efforts of the burying party. An attempt is made to dig into the layer of sand which hides the brick, so that a bank of rubbish accumulates round the body.

For a couple of hours the jerks continue without results. I profit by the circumstance to learn the manner in which the work is performed. The bare brick allows me to see what the excavated soil would conceal from me. When it is necessary to move the body, the Beetle turns over; with his six claws he grips the hair of the dead animal, props himself upon his back and pushes, using his forehead and the tip of his abdomen as a lever. When he wants to dig, he resumes the normal position. So, turn and turn about, the sexton strives, now with his legs in the air, when it is a question of shifting the body or dragging it lower down; now with his feet on the ground, when it is necessary to enlarge the grave.

The point at which the Mouse lies is finally recognized as unassailable. A male appears in the open. He explores the corpse, goes round it, scratches a little at random. He goes back; and immediately the dead body rocks. Is he advising his collaborators of what he has discovered? Is he arranging the work with a view to their establishing themselves, elsewhere on propitious soil?

The facts are far from confirming this idea. When he shakes the body, the others imitate him and push, but without combining their efforts in a given direction, for, after advancing a little towards the edge of the brick, the burden goes back again, returning to the point of departure. In the absence of a concerted understanding, their efforts of leverage are wasted. Nearly three hours are occupied by oscillations which mutually annul one another. The Mouse does not cross the little sand-hill heaped about her by the rakes of the workers.

For the second time, a male appears and makes a round of exploration. A boring is effected in loose earth, close beside the brick. This is a trial excavation, to learn the nature of the soil, a narrow well, of no great depth, into which the insect plunges to half its length. The well-sinker returns to the other workers, who arch their backs, and the load progresses a finger's breadth towards the point recognized as favourable. Have we done the trick this time? No, for after a while the Mouse recoils. There is no progress towards a solution of the difficulty.

Now two males come out in search of information, each of his own accord. Instead of stopping at the point already sounded, a point most judiciously chosen, it seemed, on account of its proximity, which would save laborious carting, they precipitately scour the whole area of the cage, trying the soil on this side and on that and ploughing superficial furrows in it. They get as far from the brick as the limits of the enclosure permit.

They dig, by preference, against the base of the cover; here they make several borings, without any reason, so far as I can see, the bed of soil being everywhere equally assailable away from the brick; the first point sounded is abandoned for a second, which is rejected in its turn. A third and fourth are tried; then another. At this sixth point the choice is made. In all these cases the excavation is by no means a grave destined to receive the Mouse, but a mere trial boring, of inconsiderable depth and of the diameter of the digger's body.

Back again to the Mouse, who suddenly shakes, swings, advances, recoils, first in one direction, then in another, until in the end the hillock of sand is crossed. Now we are free of the brick and on excellent soil. Little by little the load advances. This is no cartage by a team hauling in the opening, but a jerky removal, the work of invisible levers. The body seems to shift of its own accord.

This time, after all those hesitations, the efforts are concerted; at least, the load reaches the region sounded far more rapidly than I expected. Then begins the burial, according to the usual method. It is one o'clock. It has taken the Necrophori half-way round the clock to ascertain the condition of the locality and to displace the dead Mouse.

In this experiment it appears, in the first place, that the males play a major part in the affairs of the household. Better-equipped, perhaps, than their mates, they make investigations when a difficulty occurs; they inspect the soil, recognize whence the check arises and choose the spot at which the grave shall be dug. In the lengthy experiment of the brick, the two males alone explored the surroundings and set to work to solve the difficulty. Trusting her assistants, the female, motionless beneath the Mouse, awaited the result of their enquiries. The tests which are to follow will confirm the merits of these valiant auxiliaries.

In the second place, the points where the Mouse lies being recognized as presenting an insurmountable resistance, there is no grave dug in advance, a little farther off, in the loose soil. All the attempts are limited, I repeat, to shallow soundings, which inform the insect of the possibility of inhumation.

It is absolute nonsense to speak of their first preparing the grave to which the body will afterwards be carted. In order to excavate the soil, our sextons have to feel the weight of their dead upon their backs. They work only when stimulated by the contact of its fur. Never, never in this world, do they venture to dig a grave unless the body to be buried already occupies the site of the cavity. This is absolutely confirmed by my two months and more of daily observations.

The rest of Clairville's anecdote bears examination no better. We are told that the Necrophorus in difficulties goes in search of assistance and returns with companions who assist him to bury the Mouse. This, in another form, is the edifying story of the Sacred Beetle whose pellet has rolled into a rut. Powerless to withdraw his booty from the abyss, the wily Dung-beetle summons three or four of his neighbours, who kindly pull out the pellet and return to their labours when the work of salvage is done.

The ill-interpreted exploit of the thieving pill-roller sets me on my guard against that of the undertaker. Shall I be too particular if I ask what precautions the observer took to recognize the owner of the Mouse on his return, when he reappears, as we are told, with four assistants? What sign denotes that one of the five who was able, in so rational a manner, to call for help? Can we even be sure that the one to disappear returns and forms one of the band? There is nothing to tell us so; and this was the essential point which a sterling observer was bound not to neglect. Were they not rather five chance Necrophori who, guided by the smell, without any previous understanding, hastened to the abandoned Mouse to exploit her on their own account? I incline to this opinion, the likeliest of all in the absence of exact information.

Probability becomes certainty if we check the fact by experiment. The test with the brick already tells us something. For six hours my three specimens exhausted themselves in efforts before they succeeded in removing their booty and placing it on practicable soil. In this long and heavy job, helpful neighbours would have been most welcome. Four other Necrophori, buried here and there under a little sand, comrades and acquaintances, fellow-workers of the day before, were occupying the same cage; and not one of the busy ones thought of calling on them to assist. Despite their extreme embarrassment, the owners of the Mouse accomplished their task to the end, without the least help, though this could have been so easily requisitioned.

Being three, one might say, they deemed themselves strong enough; they needed no one else to lend them a hand. The objection does not hold good. On many occasions and under conditions even more difficult than those presented by a hard soil, I have again and again seen isolated Necrophori wearing themselves out against my artifices; yet not once did they leave their workshop to recruit helpers. Collaborators, it is true, often arrive but they are summoned by their sense of smell, not by the first occupant. They are fortuitous helpers; they are never called in. They are received without strife but also without gratitude. They are not summoned; they are tolerated.

In the glazed shelter where I keep the cage I happened to catch one of these chance assistants in the act. Passing that way in the night and scenting dead flesh, he had entered where none of his kind had yet penetrated of his own accord. I surprised him on the dome of the cover. If the wire had not prevented him, he would have set to work incontinently, in company with the rest. Had my captives invited this one? Assuredly not. Heedless of others' efforts, he hastened up, attracted by the odour of the Mole. So it

was with those whose obliging assistance is extolled. I repeat, in respect of their imaginary prowess, what I have said
elsewhere of the Sacred Beetle's: it is a child's story, worthy
to rank with any fairy-tale for the amusement of the simple.

A hard soil, necessitating the removal of the body, is not
the only difficulty with which the Necrophori are acquainted.
Frequently, perhaps more often than not, the ground is covered with grass, above all with couch-grass, whose tenacious
rootlets form an inextricable network below the surface. To
dig in the interstices is possible, but to drag the dead animal
through them is another matter: the meshes of the net are
too close to give it passage. Will the grave-digger find himself helpless against such an obstacle, which must be an extremely common one? That could not be.

Exposed to this or that habitual impediment in the exercise
of its calling, the animal is always equipped accordingly;
otherwise its profession would be impracticable. No end is
attained without the necessary means and aptitudes. Besides
that of the excavator, the Necrophorus certainly possesses
another art: the art of breaking the cables, the roots, the
stolons, the slender rhizomes which check the body's descent
into the grave. To the work of the shovel and the pick
must be added that of the shears. All this is perfectly logical
and may be clearly foreseen. Nevertheless let us call in
experiment, the best of witnesses.

I borrow from the kitchen-range an iron trivet whose legs
will supply a solid foundation for the engine which I am
devising. This is a coarse network made of strips of raffia,
a fairly accurate imitation of that of the couch-grass. The
very irregular meshes are nowhere wide enough to admit
of the passage of the creature to be buried, which this time
is a Mole. The machine is planted by its three feet in the
soil of the cage, level with the surface. A little sand conceals
the ropes. The Mole is placed in the centre; and my bands
of sextons are let loose upon the body.

The burial is performed without a hitch in the course of
an afternoon. The raffia hammock, almost the equivalent of
the natural network of the couch-grass, scarcely disturbs the
burying-process. Matters do not proceed quite so quickly;
and that is all. No attempt is made to shift the Mole, who sinks
into the ground where he lies. When the operation is finished, I remove the trivet. The network is broken at the
spot where the corpse was lying. A few strips have been

gnawed through; a small number, only as many as were strictly necessary to permit the passage of the body.

Well done, my undertakers! I expected no less of your skill and tact. You foiled the experimenter's wiles by employing the resources which you use against natural obstacles. With mandibles for shears, you patiently cut my strings as you would have gnawed the threads of the grass-roots. This is meritorious, if not deserving of exceptional glorification. The shallowest of the insects that work in earth would have done as much if subjected to similar conditions.

Let us ascend a stage in the series of difficulties. The Mole is now fixed by a strap of raffia fore and aft to a light horizontal cross-bar resting on two firmly-planted forks. It is like a joint of venison on the spit, eccentrically fastened. The dead animal touches the ground throughout the length of its body.

The Necrophori disappear under the corpse and, feeling the contact of its fur, begin to dig. The grave grows deeper and an empty space appears; but the coveted object does not descend, retained as it is by the cross-bar which the two forks keep in place. The digging slackens, the hesitations become prolonged.

However, one of the grave-diggers climbs to the surface, wanders over the Mole, inspects him and ends by perceiving the strap at the back. He gnaws and ravels it tenaciously. I hear the click of the shears that completes the rupture. Crack! The thing is done. Dragged down by his own weight, the Mole sinks into the grave, but slantwise, with his head still outside, kept in place by the second strap.

The Beetles proceed with the burial of the hinder part of the Mole; they twitch and jerk it now in this direction, now in that. Nothing comes of it; the thing refuses to give. A fresh sortie is made by one of them, to find out what is happening overhead. The second strap is perceived, is severed in turn; and henceforth the work goes on as well as could be wished.

My compliments, perspicacious cable-cutters! But I must not exaggerate. The Mole's straps were for you the little cords with which you are so familiar in turfy soil. You broke them, as well as the hammock of the previous experiment, just as you sever with the blades of your shears any natural thread stretching across your catacombs. It is an indispensable trick of your trade. If you had had to learn it by experience, to think it out before practising it, your race would have disappeared, killed by the hesitation of its apprenticeship, for the spots prolific of Moles, Frogs, Lizards and other viands to your taste are usually covered with grass.

You are capable of much better things still; but before setting forth these, let us examine the case when the ground bristles with slender brushwood, which holds the corpse at a short distance from the ground. Will the find thus hanging where it chances to fall remain unemployed? Will the Necrophori pass on, indifferent to the superb morsel which they see and smell a few inches above their heads, or will they make it drop from its gibbet?

Game does not abound to such a point that it can be despised if a few efforts will obtain it. Before I see the thing happen, I am persuaded that it will fall, that the Necrophori, often confronted with the difficulties of a body not lying on the soil, must possess the instinct to shake it to the ground. The fortuitous support of a few bits of stubble, of a few interlaced twigs, so common in the fields, cannot put them off. The drop of the suspended body, if placed too high, must certainly form part of their instinctive methods. For the rest, let us watch them at work.

I plant in the sand of the cage a meagre tuft of thyme. The shrub is at most some four inches in height. In the branches I place a Mouse, entangling the tail, the paws and the neck among the twigs to increase the difficulty. The population of the cage now consists of fourteen Necrophori and will remain the same until the close of my investigations. Of course they do not all take part simultaneously in the day's work: the majority remain underground, dozing or occupied in setting their cellars in order. Sometimes only one, often two, three or four, rarely more, busy themselves with the corpse which I offer them. Today, two hasten to the Mouse, who is soon perceived overhead on the tuft of thyme.

They gain the top of the plant by way of the trelliswork of the cage. Here are repeated, with increased hesitation, due to the inconvenient nature of the support, the tactics employed to remove the body when the soil is unfavourable. Th insect props itself against a branch, thrusting alternately with back and claws, jerking and shaking vigorously until the point whereat it is working is freed from its fetters. In one brief shift, by dint of heaving their backs, the two collaborators extricate the body from the tangle. Yet another shake; and the Mouse is down. The burial follows.

There is nothing new in this experiment: the find has been treated just as though it lay on soil unsuitable for burial. The fall is the result of an attempt to transport the load.

The time has come to set up the Frog's gibbet made famous by Gleditsch. The batrachian is not indispensable; a Mole will serve as well or even better. With a ligament of raffia I fix him, by his hind-leg, to a twig which I plant vertically in the ground, inserting it to no great depth. The creature hangs plump against the gibbet, its head and shoulders making ample contact with the soil.

The grave-diggers set to work beneath the part which lies along the ground, at the very foot of the stake; they dig a funnel into which the Mole's muzzle, head and neck sink little by little. The gibbet becomes uprooted as they descend and ends by falling, dragged over by the weight of its heavy burden. I am assisting at the spectacle of the overturned stake, one of the most astonishing feats of reason with which the insect has ever been credited.

This, for one who is considering the problem of instinct, is an exciting moment. But let us beware of forming conclusions just yet; we might be in too great a hurry. Let us first ask ourselves whether the fall of the stake was intentional or accidental. Did the Necrophori lay it bare with the express purpose of making it fall? Or did they, on the contrary, dig at its base solely in order to bury that part of the Mole which lay on the ground? That is the question, which, for the rest, is very easy to answer.

The experiment is repeated; but this time the gibbet is slanting and the Mole, hanging in a vertical position, touches the ground at a couple of inches from the base of the apparatus. Under these conditions, absolutely no attempt is made to overthrow it. Not the least scrape of a claw is delivered at the foot of the gibbet. The entire work of excavation is performed at a distance, under the body, whose shoulders are lying on the ground. Here and here only a hole is dug to receive the front of the body, the part accessible to the sextons.

A difference of an inch in the position of the suspended animal destroys the famous legend. Even so, many a time, the most elementary sieve, handled with a little logic, is enough to winnow a confused mass of statements and to release the good grain of truth.

Yet another shake of this sieve. The gibbet is slanting or perpendicular no matter which; but the Mole, fixed by his hind-legs to the top of the twig, does not touch the soil; he hangs a few fingers'-breadths from the ground, out of the sextons' reach.

What will they do now? Will they scrape at the foot of the gibbet in order to overturn it? By no means; and the ingenuous observer who looked for such tactics would be greatly disappointed. No attention is paid to the base of the support. It is not vouchsafed even a stroke of the rake. Nothing is done to overturn it, nothing, absolutely nothing! It is by other methods that the Burying-beetles obtain the Mole.

These decisive experiments, repeated under many different forms, prove that never, never in this world, do the Necrophori dig, or even give a superficial scrape, at the foot of the gallows, unless the hanging body touch the ground at that point. And, in the latter case, if the twig should happen to fall, this is in no way an intentional result, but a mere fortuitous effect of the burial already commenced.

What, then, did the man with the Frog, of whom Gleditsch tells us, really see? If his stick was overturned, the body placed to dry beyond the assaults of the Necrophori must certainly have touched the soil: a strange precaution against robbers and damp! We may well attribute more foresight to the preparer of dried Frogs and allow him to hang his animal a few inches off the ground. In that case, as all my experiments emphatically declare, the fall of the stake undermined by the sextons is a pure matter of imagination.

Yet another of the fine arguments in favour of the reasoning-power of insects flies from the light of investigation and founders in the slough of error! I wonder at your simple faith, O masters who take seriously the statements of chance-met observers, richer in imagination than in veracity; I wonder at your credulous zeal, when, without criticism, you build up your theories on such absurdities!

Let us continue. The stake is henceforth planted perpendicularly, but the body hanging on it does not reach the base: a condition enough to ensure that there will never be any digging at this point. I make use of a Mouse, who, by reason of her light weight, will lend herself better to the insect's manœuvres. The dead animal is fixed by the hind-legs to the top of the apparatus with a raffia strap. It hangs plumb, touching the stick.

Soon two Necrophori have discovered the morsel. They climb the greased pole; they explore the prize, poking their foreheads into its fur. It is recognized as an excellent find. To work, therefore. Here we have again, but under more difficult conditions, the tactics employed when it was necessary to displace the unfavourably situated body: the two collaborators slip between the Mouse and the stake and, taking a grip of the twig and exerting a leverage with their backs, they jerk and shake the corpse, which sways, twirls about, swings away from the stake and swings back again. All the morning is passed in vain attempts, interrupted by explorations on the animal's body.

In the afternoon, the cause of the check is at last recognized; not very clearly, for the two obstinate gallow-robbers first attack the Mouse's hind-legs, a little way below the strap. They strip them bare, flay them and cut away the flesh about the foot. They have reached the bone, when one of them finds the string of raffia beneath his mandibles. This, to him, is a familiar thing, representing the grass-thread so frequent in burials in turfy soil. Tenaciously the shears gnaw at the band; the fibrous fetter is broken; and the Mouse falls, to be buried soon after.

If it stood alone, this breaking of the suspending tie would be a magnificent performance; but considered in connection with the sum of the Beetle's customary labours it loses any far-reaching significance. Before attacking the strap, which was not concealed in any way, the insect exerted itself for a whole morning in shaking the body, its usual method. In the end, finding the cord, it broke it, as it would have broken a thread of couch-grass encountered underground.

Under the conditions devised for the Beetle, the use of the shears is the indispensable complement of the use of the shovel; and the modicum of discernment at his disposal is enough to inform him when it will be well to employ the clippers. He cuts what embarrasses him, with no more exercise of reason than he displays when lowering his dead Mouse underground. So little does he grasp the relation of cause and effect that he tries to break the bone of the leg before biting the raffia which is knotted close beside him. The difficult task is attempted before the extremely easy one.

Difficult, yes, but not impossible, provided that the Mouse

be young. I begin over again with the strip of iron wire, on which the insect's shears cannot get a grip, and a tender Mousekin, half the size of an adult. This time a tibia is gnawed through, sawed in two by the Beetle's mandibles, near the spring of the heel. The detached leg leaves plenty of space for the other, which readily slips from the metal band; and the little corpse falls to the ground.

But, if the bone be too hard, if the prize suspended be a Mole, an adult Mouse or a Sparrow, the wire ligament opposes an insurmountable obstacle to the attempts of the Necrophori, who, for nearly a week, work at the hanging body, partly stripping it of fur or feather and dishevelling it until it forms a lamentable object, and at last abandon it when desiccation sets in. And yet a last recourse remained, one as rational as infallible: to overthrow the stake. Of course, not one dreams of doing so.

For the last time let us change our artifices. The top of the gibbet consists of a little fork, with the prongs widely opened and measuring barely two-fifths of an inch in length. With a thread of hemp, less easily attacked than a strip of raffia, I bind the hind-legs of an adult Mouse together, a little above the heels; and I slip one of the prongs in between. To bring the thing down one has only to slide it a little way upwards; it is like a young Rabbit hanging in the window of a poulterer's shop.

Five Necrophori come to inspect what I have prepared. After much futile shaking, the tibiæ are attacked. This, it seems, is the method usually employed when the corpse is caught by one of its limbs in some narrow fork of a low-growing plant. While trying to saw through the bone—a heavy job this time—one of the workers slips between the shackled legs; in this position, he feels the furry touch of the Mouse against his chin. No more is needed to arouse his propensity to thrust with his back. With a few heaves of the lever the thing is done: the Mouse rises a little, slides over the supporting peg and falls to the ground.

Is this manœuvre really thought out? Has the insect indeed perceived, by the light of a flash of reason, that to make the morsel fall it was necessary to unhook it by sliding it along the peg? Has it actually perceived the mechanism of the hanging? I know some persons—indeed, I know many —who, in the presence of this magnificent result, would be satisfied without further investigation.

More difficult to convince, I modify the experiment before drawing a conclusion. I suspect that the Necrophorus, without in any way foreseeing the consequences of his action, heaved his back merely because he felt the animal's legs above him. With the system of suspension adopted, the push of the back, employed in all cases of difficulty, was brought to bear first upon the point of support; and the fall resulted from this happy coincidence. That point, which has to be slipped along the peg in order to unhook the object, ought really to be placed at a short distance from the Mouse, so that the Necrophori may no longer feel her directly on their backs when they push.

A wire binds together now the claws of a Sparrow, now the heels of a Mouse and is bent, three-quarters of an inch farther away, into a little ring, which slips very loosely over one of the prongs of the fork, a short, almost horizontal prong. The least push of this ring is enough to bring the hanging body to the ground; and because it stands out it lends itself excellently to the insect's methods. In short, the arrangement is the same as just now, with this difference, that the point of support is at a short distance from the animal hung up.

My trick, simple though it be, is quite successful. For a long time the body is repeatedly shaken, but in vain; the tibiæ, the hard claws, refuse to yield to the patient saw. Sparrows and Mice grow dry and shrivel, unused, upon the gallows. My Necrophori, some sooner, some later, abandon the insoluble mechanical problem: to push, ever so little, the movable support and so to unhook the coveted carcase.

Curious reasoners, in faith! If, just now, they had a lucid idea of the mutual relations between the tied legs and the suspending peg; if they made the Mouse fall by a reasoned manœuvre, whence comes it that the present artifice, no less simple than the first, is to them an insurmountable obstacle? For days and days they work on the body, examining it from head to foot, without noticing the movable support, the cause of their mishap. In vain I prolong my watch; I never see a single one of them push the support with his foot or butt it with his head.

Their defeat is not due to lack of strength. Like the Geotrupes, they are vigorous excavators. When you grasp them firmly in your hand, they slip into the interstices of the fingers and plough up your skin so as to make you quickly loosen your hold. With his head, a powerful ploughshare, the Beetle might very easily push the ring off its short support. He is not able to do so, because he does not think of it; he does not think of it, because he is devoid of the faculty attributed to him, in order to support their theories, by the dangerous generosity of the evolutionists.

Divine reason, sun of the intellect, what a clumsy slap in thy august countenance, when the glorifiers of the animal degrade thee with such denseness!

Let us now examine the mental obscurity of the Necrophori under another aspect. My captives are not so satisfied with their sumptuous lodging that they do not seek to escape, especially when there is a dearth of labour, that sovran consoler of the afflicted, man or beast. Interment within the wire cover palls upon them. So when the Mole is buried and everything in order in the cellar, they stray uneasily over the trellised dome; they clamber up, come down, go up again and take to flight, a flight which instantly becomes a fall, owing to collision with the wire grating. They pick themselves up and begin all over again. The sky is splendid; the weather is hot, calm and propitious for those in search of the Lizard crushed beside the footpath. Perhaps the effluvia of the gamy tit-bit have reached them from afar, imperceptible to any other sense than that of the grave-diggers. My Necrophori therefore would be glad to get away.

Can they? Nothing would be easier, if a glimmer of reason were to aid them. Through the trelliswork, over which they have so often strayed, they have seen, outside the free soil, the promised land which they want to reach. A hundred times if once have they dug at the foot of the rampart. There, in vertical wells, they take up their station, drowsing whole days on end while unemployed. If I give them a fresh Mole, they emerge from their retreat by the entrance-corridor and come to hide themselves beneath the belly of the beast. The burial over, they return, one here, one there, to the confines of the enclosure and disappear underground.

Well, in two and a half months of captivity, despite long stays at the base of the trellis, at a depth of three-quarters of an inch beneath the surface, it is rare indeed for a Necrophorus to succeed in circumventing the obstacle, in prolonging his excavation beneath the barrier, in digging an elbow and bringing it out on the other side, a trifling task for these vigorous creatures. Of fourteen only one succeeds in escaping.

A chance deliverance and not premeditated; for, if the happy event had been the result of a mental combination, the other prisoners, practically his equals in powers of perception, would all, from first to last, have discovered by rational means the elbowed path leading to the outer world; and the cage would promptly be deserted. The failure of the great majority proves that the single fugitive was simply digging at random. Circumstances favoured him; and that is all. We must not put it to his credit that he succeeded where all the others failed.

We must also beware of attributing to the Necrophori a duller understanding than is usual in insect psychology. I find the ineptness of the undertaker in all the Beetles reared under the wire cover, on the bed of sand into which the rim of the dome sinks a little way. With very rare exceptions, fortuitous accidents, not one thinks of circumventing the barrier by way of the base; not one manages to get outside by means of a slanting tunnel, not even though he be a miner by profession, as are the Dung-beetles *par excellence*. Captives under the wire dome and anxious to escape, Sacred Beetles, Geotrupes, Copres, Gymnopleuri, Sisyphi, all see about them the free space, the joys of the open sunlight; and not one thinks of going round under the rampart, which would present no difficulty to their pickaxes.

Even in the higher ranks of animality, examples of similar mental obfuscation are not lacking. Audubon tells us how, in his days, wild Turkeys were caught in North America. In a clearing known to be frequented by these birds, a great cage was constructed with stakes driven into the ground. In the centre of the enclosure opened a short tunnel, which dipped under the palisade and returned to the surface outside the cage by a gentle slope, which was opened to the sky. The central opening, wide enough to give a bird free passage, occupied only a portion of the enclosure, leaving around it, against the circle of stakes, a wide unbroken zone. A few handfuls of maize were scattered in the interior of the trap, as well as round about it, and in particular along the sloping path, which passed under a sort of bridge and led to the centre of the contrivance. In short, the Turkey-trap presented an ever-open door. The bird found it in order to enter, but did not think of looking for it in order to go out.

According to the famous American ornithologist, the Turkeys, lured by the grains of maize, descended the insidious slope, entered the short underground passage and beheld, at the end of it, plunder and the light. A few steps farther and the gluttons emerged, one by one, from beneath the bridge. They distributed themselves about the enclosure. The maize was abundant; and the Turkeys' crops grew swollen.

When all was gathered, the band wished to retreat, but not one of the prisoners paid any attention to the central hole by which he had arrived. Gobbling uneasily, they passed again and again across the bridge whose arch was yawning beside them; they circled round against the palisade, treading a hundred times in their own footprints; they thrust their necks, with their crimson wattles, through the bars; and there, with their beaks in the open air, they fought and struggled until they were exhausted.

Remember, O inept one, what happened but a little while ago; think of the tunnel that led you hither! If that poor brain of yours contains an atom of ability, put two ideas together and remind yourself that the passage by which you entered is there and open for your escape! You will do nothing of the kind. The light, an irresistible attraction, holds you subjugated against the palisade; and the shadow of the yawning pit, which has but lately permitted you to enter and will quite as readily permit you to go out, leaves you indifferent. To recognize the use of this opening you would have to reflect a little, to recall the past; but this tiny retrospective calculation is beyond your powers. So the trapper, returning a few days later, will find a rich booty, the entire flock imprisoned!

Of poor intellectual repute, does the Turkey deserve his name for stupidity? He does not appear to be more limited than another. Audubon depicts him as endowed with certain useful ruses, in particular when he has to baffle the attacks of his nocturnal enemy, the Virginian Owl. As for his behavior in the snare with the underground passage, any other bird, impassioned of the light, would do the same.

Under rather more difficult conditions, the Necrophorus repeats the ineptness of the Turkey. When he wishes to return to the daylight, after resting in a short burrow against the rim of the cover, the Beetle, seeing a little light filtering through the loose soil, reascends the entrance-well, incapable of telling himself that he has only to prolong the tunnel as far in the opposite direction to reach the outer world beyond the wall and gain his freedom. Here again is one in whom we shall seek in vain for any sign of reflection. Like the rest, in spite of his legendary renown, he has no guide but the unconscious promptings of instinct.

XIX

The Oil-beetle's Journey

The Sunken Road near Carpentras, that site of so many of Fabre's early observations, is again celebrated in this account of the oil-beetle and its fantastic piggy-back ride through the air to its future home. The material originally appeared in Chapter Four of THE GLOW-WORM AND OTHER BEETLES. *There are a number of species of Meloe beetles in the United States. Their common name of oil-beetles arises from their habit of giving off a disagreeable oily fluid when disturbed. As many as 10,000 eggs are laid by the females of some species.*

A VERTICAL BANK on the road from Carpentras to Bédoin is this time the scene of my observations. This bank, baked by the sun, is exploited by numerous swarms of Anthophoræ, who, more industrious than their congeners, are in the habit of building, at the entrance to their corridors, with serpentine fillets of earth, a vestibule, a defensive bastion in the form of an arched cylinder. In a word, they are swarms of *A. parietina*. A sparse carpet of turf extends from the edge of the road to the foot of the bank. The more comfortably to follow the work of the Bees, in the hope of wresting some secret from them, I had been lying for a few moments upon this turf, in the very heart of the inoffensive swarm, when my clothes were invaded by legions of little yellow lice, running with desperate eagerness through the hairy thickets of the nap of the cloth. In these tiny creatures, with which I was powdered here and there as with yellow dust, I soon recognized an old acquaintance, the young Oil-beetles, whom I now saw for the first time elsewhere than in the Bees' fur or the interior of their cells. I could not lose so excellent an opportunity of learning how these larvæ manage to establish themselves upon the bodies of their foster-parents.

In the grass where, after lying down for a moment, I had caught these lice were a few plants in blossom, of which the most abundant were three composites: *Hedypnois polymorpha, Senecio gallicus* and *Anthemis arvensis*. Now it was on a composite, a dandelion, that Newport seemed to remember seeing some young Oil-beetles; and my attention therefore was first of all directed to the plants which I have named. To my great satisfaction, nearly all the flowers of these three plants, especially those of the camomile (*Anthemis*) were occupied by young Oil-beetles in greater or lesser numbers. On one head of camomile I counted forty of these tiny insects, cowering motionless in the centre of the forests. On the other hand, I could not discover any on the flowers of the poppy or of a wild rocket (*Diplotaxis muralis*) which grew promiscuously among the plants aforesaid. It seems to me, therefore, that it is only on the composite flowers that the Meloe-larvæ await the Bees' arrival.

In addition to this population encamped upon the heads of the composites and remaining motionless, as though it had achieved its object for the moment, I soon discovered yet another, far more numerous, whose anxious activity betrayed a fruitless search. On the ground, in the grass, numberless little larvæ were running in a great flutter, recalling in some respects the tumultuous disorder of an overturned Ant-hill; others were hurriedly climbing to the tip of a blade of grass and descending with the same haste; others again were plunging into the downy fluff of the withered everlastings, remaining there a moment and quickly reappearing to continue their search. Lastly, with a little attention, I was able to convince myself that within an area of a dozen square yards there was perhaps not a single blade of grass which was not explored by several of these larvæ.

I was evidently witnessing the recent emergence of the young Oil-beetles from their maternal lairs. Part of them had already settled on the groundsel- and camomile-flowers to await the arrival of the Bees; but the majority were still wandering in search of this provisional refuge. It was by this wandering population that I had been invaded when I lay down at the foot of the bank. It was impossible that all these larvæ, the tale of whose alarming thousands I would not venture to define, should form one family and recognize a common mother; despite what Newport has told us of the Oil-beetles' astonishing fecundity, I could not believe this, so great was their multitude.

Though the green carpet was continued for a considerable distance along the side of the road, I could not detect a single Meloe-larva elsewhere than in the few square yards lying in front of the bank inhabited by the Mason-bee. These larvæ therefore could not have come far; to find themselves near the Anthophoræ they had had no long pilgrimage to make, for there was not a sign of the inevitable stragglers and laggards that follow in the wake of a travelling caravan. The burrows in which the eggs were hatched were therefore in that turf opposite the Bees' abode. Thus the Oil-beetles, far from laying their eggs at random, as their wandering life might lead one to suppose, and leaving their young to the task of approaching their future home, are able to recognize the spots haunted by the Anthophoræ and lay their eggs in the near neighbourhood of those spots.

With such a multitude of parasites occupying the composite flowers in close proximity to the Anthophora's nests, it is impossible that the majority of the swarm should not become infested sooner or later. At the time of my observations, a comparatively tiny proportion of the starving legion was waiting on the flowers; the others were still wandering on the ground, where the Anthophoræ very rarely alight; and yet I detected the presence of several Meloe-larvæ in the thoracic down of nearly all the Anthophoræ which I caught and examined.

I have also found them on the bodies of the Melecta- and Cœlioxys-bees, who are parasitic on the Anthophoræ. Suspending their audacious patrolling before the galleries under construction, these spoilers of the victualled cells alight for an instant on a camomile-flower and lo, the thief is robbed! A tiny, imperceptible louse has slipped into the thick of the downy fur and, at the moment when the parasite, after destroying the Anthophora's egg, is laying her own upon the stolen honey, will creep upon this egg, destroy it in its turn and remain sole mistress of the provisions. The mess of honey amassed by the Anthophora will thus pass through the hands of three owners and remain finally the property of the weakest of the three.

Let us now turn our attention to the young Meloes waiting expectant upon the camomile-flowers. There they are, ten, fifteen or more, lodged half-way down the florets of a single blossom or in their interstices; it therefore needs a certain degree of scrutiny to perceive them, their hiding-place being the more effectual in that the amber colour of their bodies merges in the yellow hue of the florets. So long as nothing unusual happens upon the flower, so long as no sudden shock announces the arrival of a strange visitor, the Meloes remain absolutely motionless and give no sign of life. To see them dipping vertically, head downwards, into the florets, one might suppose that they were seeking some sweet liquid, their food; but in that case they ought to pass more frequently from one floret to another, which they do not, except when, after a false alarm, they regain their hiding-places and choose the spot which seems to them the most favourable. This immobility means that the florets of the camomile serve them only as a place of ambush, even as later the Anthophora's body will serve them solely as a vehicle to convey them to the Bee's cell. They take no nourishment, either on the flowers or on the Bees; and, as with the Sitares, their first meal will consist of the Anthophora's egg, which the hooks of their mandibles are intended to rip open.

Their immobility is, as we have said, complete; but nothing is easier than to arouse their suspended activity. Shake a camomile-blossom lightly with a bit of straw: instantly the Meloes leave their hiding-places, come up and scatter in all directions on the white petals of the circumference, running over them from one end to the other with all the speed which the smallness of their size permits. On reaching the extreme end of the petals, they fasten to it either with their caudal appendages, or perhaps with a sticky substance similar to that furnished by the anal button of the Sitares; and, with their bodies hanging outside and their six legs free, they bend about in every direction and stretch as far out as they can, as though striving to touch an object out of their reach. If nothing offers for them to seize upon, after a few vain attempts they regain the centre of the flower and soon resume their immobility.

But, if we place near them any object whatever, they do not fail to catch on to it with surprising agility. A blade of grass, a bit of straw, the handle of my tweezers which I hold out to them: they accept anything in their eagerness to quit the provisional shelter of the flower. It is true that, after finding themselves on these inanimate objects, they soon recognize that they have gone astray, as we see by their bustling movements to and fro and their tendency to go back to the flower if there still be time. Those which have thus giddily flung themselves upon a bit of straw and are allowed to return to their flower do not readily fall a second time into the same trap. There is therefore, in these animated specks, a memory, an experience of things.

After these experiments I tried others with hairy materials imitating more or less closely the down of the Bees, with little pieces of cloth or velvet cut from my clothes, with plugs of cotton wool, with pellets of flock gathered from the everlastings. Upon all these objects, offered with the tweezers, the Meloes flung themselves without any difficulty; but, instead of keeping quiet, as they do on the bodies of the Bees, they soon convinced me, by their restless behaviour, that they found themselves as much out of their element on these furry materials as on the smooth surface of a bit of straw. I ought to have expected this: had I not just seen them wandering without pause upon the everlastings enveloped with cottony flock? If reaching the shelter of a downy surface were enough to make them believe themselves safe in harbour, nearly all would perish, without further attempts, in the down of the plants.

Let us now offer them live insects and, first of all, Anthophoræ. If the Bee, after we have rid her of the parasites which she may be carrying, be taken by the wings and held for a moment in contact with the flower, we invariably find her, after this rapid contact, overrun by Meloes clinging to her hairs. The larvæ nimbly take up their position on the thorax, usually on the shoulders or sides, and once there they remain motionless: the second stage of their strange journey is compassed.

After the Anthophoræ, I tried the first live insects that I was able to procure at once: Drone-flies, Bluebottles, Hivebees, small Butterflies. All were alike overrun by the Meloes, without hesitation. What is more, there was no attempt made to return to the flowers. As I could not find any Beetles at the moment, I was unable to experiment with them. Newport, experimenting, it is true, under conditions very different from mine, since his observations related to young Meloes held captive in a glass jar, while mine were made in the normal circumstances, Newport, I was saying, saw Meloes fasten to the body of a Malachius and stay there without moving,

which inclines me to believe that with Beetles I should have
obtained the same results as, for instance, with a Drone-fly.
And I did, in fact, at a later date, find some Meloe-larvæ on
the body of a big Beetle, the Golden Rose-chafer (*Cetonia
aurata*), an assiduous visitor of the flowers.

After exhausting the insect class, I put within their reach
my last resource, a large black Spider. Without hesitation
they passed from the flower to the arachnid, made for places
near the joints of the legs and settled there without moving.
Everything therefore seems to suit their plans for leaving the
provisional abode where they are waiting; without distinction of species, genus, or class, they fasten to the first living
creature that chance brings within their reach. We now understand how it is that these young larvæ have been observed
upon a host of different insects and especially upon the
early Flies and Bees pillaging the flowers; we can also understand the need for that prodigious number of eggs laid by a
single Oil-beetle, since the vast majority of the larvæ
which come out of them will infallibly go astray and will not
succeed in reaching the cells of the Anthophoræ. Instinct is
at fault here; and fecundity makes up for it.

But instinct recovers its infallibility in another case. The
Meloes, as we have seen, pass without difficulty from the
flower to the objects within their reach, whatever these may
be, smooth or hairy, living or inanimate. This done, they
behave very differently, according as they have chanced to
invade the body of an insect or some other object. In the
first case, on a downy Fly or Butterfly, on a smooth-skinned
Spider or Beetle, the larvæ remain motionless after reaching
the point which suits them. Their instinctive desire is therefore satisfied. In the second case, in the midst of the nap of
cloth or velvet, or the filaments of cotton, or the flock of the
everlasting, or, lastly, on the smooth surface of a leaf or a
straw, they betray the knowledge of their mistake by their
continual coming and going, by their efforts to return to the
flower imprudently abandoned.

How then do they recognize the nature of the object to
which they have just moved? How is it that this object, whatever the quality of its surface, will sometimes suit them and
sometimes not? Do they judge their new lodging by sight?
But then no mistake would be possible; the sense of sight
would tell them at the outset whether the object within reach
was suitable or not; and emigration would or would not take

place according to its decision. And then how can we suppose that, buried in the dense thicket of a pellet of cotton-wool or in the fleece of an Anthophora, the imperceptible larva can recognize, by sight, the enormous mass which it is perambulating?

Is it by touch, by some sensation due to the inner vibrations of living flesh? Not so, for the Meloes remain motionless on insect corpses that have dried up completely, on dead Anthophoræ taken from cells at least a year old. I have seen them keep absolutely quiet on fragments of an Anthophora on a thorax long since nibbled and emptied by the Mites. By what sense then can they distinguish the thorax of an Anthophora from a velvety pellet, when sight and touch are out of the question? The sense of smell remains. But in that case what exquisite subtlety must we not take for granted? Moreover, what similarity of smell can we admit between all the insects which, dead or alive, whole or in pieces, fresh or dried, suit the Meloes, while anything else does not suit them? A wretched louse, a living speck, leaves us mightily perplexed as to the sensibility which directs it. Here is yet one more riddle added to all the others.

After the observations which I have described, it remained for me to search the earthen surface inhabited by the Anthophoræ: I should then have followed the Meloe-larva in its transformations. It was certainly *cicatricosus* whose larvæ I had been studying; it was certainly this insect which ravaged the cells of the Mason-bee, for I found it dead in the old galleries which it had been unable to leave. This opportunity, which did not occur again, promised me an ample harvest. I had to give it all up. My Thursday was drawing to a close; I had to return to Avignon, to resume my lessons on the electrophorus and the Toricellian tube. O happy Thursdays! What glorious opportunities I lost because you were too short!

We will go back a year to continue this history. I collected, under far less favourable conditions, it is true, enough notes to map out the biography of the tiny creature which we have just seen migrating from the camomile-flowers to the Anthophora's back. From what I have said of the Sitaris-larvæ, it is plain that the Meloe-larvæ perched, like the former, on the back of a Bee, have but one aim: to get themselves conveyed by this Bee to the victualled cells. Their object is not to live for a time on the body that carries them.

Were it necessary to prove this, it would be enough to say that we never see these larvæ attempt to pierce the skin of the Bee, or else to nibble at a hair or two, nor do we see them increase in size so long as they are on the Bee's body. To the Meloes, as to the Sitares, the Anthophora serves merely as a vehicle which conveys them to their goal, the victualled cell.

It remains for us to learn how the Meloe leaves the down of the Bee which has carried it, in order to enter the cell. With larvæ collected from the bodies of different Bees, before I was fully acquainted with the tactics of the Sitares, I undertook, as Newport had done before me, certain investigations intended to throw light on this leading point in the Oil-beetle's history. My attempts, based upon those which I made with the Sitares, resulted in the same failure. The tiny creatures, when brought into contact with Anthophora-larvæ or -nymphs, paid no attention whatever to their prey; others, placed near cells which were open and full of honey, did not enter them, or at most ventured to the edge of the orifice; others, lastly, put inside the cell, on the dry wall or on the surface of the honey, came out again immediately or else got stuck and died. The touch of the honey is as fatal to them as to the young Sitares.

Searches made at various periods in the nests of the Hairy-footed Anthophora had taught me some years earlier that *Meloe cicatricosus,* like the Sitares, is a parasite of that Bee; indeed I had at different times discovered adult Meloes, dead and shrivelled, in the Bee's cells. On the other hand, I knew from Léon Dufour that the little yellow animal, the Louse found in the Bee's down, had been recognized, thanks to Newport's investigations, as the larva of the Oil-beetle. With these data, rendered still more striking by what I was learning daily on the subject of the Sitares, I went to Carpentras, on the 21st of May, to inspect the nests of the Anthophoræ, then building, as I have described. Though I was almost certain of succeeding, sooner or later, with the Sitares, who were excessively abundant, I had very little hope of the Meloes, which on the contrary are very scarce in the same nests. Circumstances, however, favoured me more than I dared hope and, after six hours' labour, in which the pick played a great part, I became the possessor, by the sweat of my brow, of a considerable number of cells occupied by Sitares and two other cells appropriated by Meloes.

While my enthusiasm had not had time to cool at the sight, momentarily repeated, of a young Sitaris perched upon an Anthophora's egg floating in the center of the little pool of honey, it might well have burst all restraints on beholding the contents of one of these cells. On the black, liquid honey a wrinkled pellicle is floating; and on this pellicle, motionless, is a yellow louse. The pellicle is the empty envelope of the Anthophora's egg; the louse is a Meloe-larva.

The story of this larva becomes self-evident. The young Meloe leaves the down of the Bee at the moment when the egg is laid; and, since contact with the honey would be fatal to the grub, it must, in order to save itself, adopt the tactics followed by the Sitaris, that is to say, it must allow itself to drop on the surface of the honey with the egg which is in the act of being laid. There, its first task is to devour the egg which serves it for a raft, as is attested by the empty envelope on which it still remains; and it is after this meal, the only one that it takes so long as it retains its present form, that it must commence its long series of transformations and feed upon the honey amassed by the Anthophora.

XX

The Edge of the Unknown

"The more I observe and experiment," Fabre once wrote, "the more clearly I see rising out of the black mists of possibility an enormous note of interrogation." To a friend, he said on another occasion: "Because I have shifted a few grains of sand upon the shore, am I in a position to understand the abysmal depths of the ocean? Life has unfathomable secrets. Human knowledge will be erased from the world's archives before we possess the last word that a gnat has to say to us." His philosophy, his outlook on the insects—maintained through a lifetime of labor—his essential humility of mind, are reflected in this last selection. It is taken from the fifth chapter of THE MASON-WASPS.

IS IT REALLY WORTH WHILE to spend our time, the time which escapes us so swiftly, this stuff of life, as Montaigne calls it, in gleaning facts of indifferent moment and of highly contestable utility? Is it not childish to enquire so minutely into an insect's actions? Too many interests of a graver kind hold us in their grasp to leave leisure for these amusements. That is how the harsh experience of age impels us to speak: that is how I should conclude, as I bring my investigations to a close, if I did not perceive, amid the chaos of my observations, a few gleams of light touching the loftiest problems which we are privileged to discuss.

What is life? Will it ever be possible for us to trace it to its sources? Shall we ever be permitted to excite, in a drop of albumen, the uncertain quiverings which are the preludes of organization? What is human intelligence? What is instinct? Are these two mental aptitudes irreducible, or can they both be traced back to a common factor? Are the species connected with one another, are they related by evolution? Or are they, as it were, so many unchanging medals, each struck from a separate die upon which the tooth of time has no effect, except to destroy it sooner or later? These questions are and always will be the despair of every cultivated mind, even though the insanity of our efforts to solve them urges us to cast them into the limbo of the unknowable. The theorists, proudly daring, have an answer nowadays for every question; but as a thousand theoretical views are not worth a single fact, thinkers untrammelled by preconceived ideas are far from becoming convinced. Problems such as these, whether their scientific solution be possible or not, require an enormous mass of well-established data, to which entomology, despite its humble province, can contribute a quota of some value. And that is why I am an observer, why, above all, I am an experimenter.

It is something to observe; but it is not enough: we must experiment, that is to say, we must ourselves intervene and create artificial conditions which oblige the animal to reveal to us what it would not tell if left to the normal course of events. Its actions, marvellously contrived to attain the end pursued, are capable of deceiving us as to their real meaning and of making us accept, in their linked sequence, that which our own logic dictates to us. It is not the animal that we are now consulting upon the nature of its aptitudes, upon the primary motives of its activity, but our own opinions, which always yield a reply in favor of our cherished notions. As I have already repeatedly shown, observation in itself is often a snare: we interpret its data according to the exigencies of our theories. To bring out the truth, we must needs resort to experiment, which alone is able to some extent to fathom the obscure problem of animal intelligence. It has sometimes been denied that zoology is an experimental science. The accusation would be well-founded if zoology confined itself to describing and classifying; but this is the least important part of its function: it has higher aims than that; and, when it consults the animal upon some problem of life, its method of questioning lies in experiment. In my own modest sphere, I should be depriving myself of the most potent method of study if I were to neglect experiment. Observation sets the problem; experiment solves it, always presuming that it can be solved; or at least, if powerless to yield the full light of truth, it sheds a certain gleam over the edges of the impenetrable cloud.